Criminal Justice
A Brief Introduction
Thirteenth Edition

Frank Schmalleger, Ph.D.
Distinguished Professor Emeritus
The University of North Carolina at Pembroke

 Pearson

For Ava, Malia, Michelle, and Nicole

Brief Contents

Contents

CHAPTER 3 Criminal Law 61

PART 3 *Adjudication*

CHAPTER 7 **The Courts** 212

PART 4   *Corrections*

CHAPTER 10 Probation, Parole, and Reentry 314

Preface

Criminal justice is a dynamic field of study. Consider these challenges for instructors and students trying to keep pace with a field that is undergoing continual modification: the ever-evolving nature of crime, our changing understanding of justice, police-community relations in an age of social media, budgetary constraints, ongoing threats to our nation's security, newly enacted statutes, innovations in enforcement and justice-system technology, precedent-setting U.S. Supreme Court decisions, a changing American society, and rapidly emerging innovations in correctional practice.

As accelerated change engulfs the American criminal justice system today, it is appropriate that streamlined and up-to-date learning materials should be in the hands of students. Quick and easy access to accurate and current information has become a vital part of contemporary life. *Criminal Justice: A Brief Introduction* provides such access through its printed pages and interactive website with videos, point-counterpoint exercises, and numerous other features.

The first edition of *Criminal Justice: A Brief Introduction*, which was published before the Internet had become the ubiquitous tool that it is today, resulted from the realization that justice students need to have current information presented in a concise and affordable source. With each new edition, the availability of up-to-date crime- and justice-related information has increased. Like many of its predecessors, the thirteenth edition draws upon the wealth of Internet resources that serve the needs of criminal justice students and practitioners. It ties those important resources to central ideas in the text, expanding learning opportunities far beyond what was possible in the mere 400 pages of the first edition. In particular, URLs printed in the book point the way to criminal justice agencies and organizations on the Internet, as well as to full-text documentation of many critical contemporary issues.

True to its origins, the thirteenth edition, which is available in a variety of print and electronic formats, focuses on the crime picture in America and the three traditional elements of the criminal justice system: police, courts, and corrections. Real-life stories, career information, up-to-date examples and issues, engaging graphics, and interactive media all contribute to this timely and user-friendly introduction to criminal justice. Key features include:

Freedom or Safety? You Decide boxes in each chapter highlight the book's ever-evolving theme of individual rights versus public order, a hallmark feature of this text since the first edition. In each chapter of the text, Freedom or Safety boxes build on this theme by illustrating some of the personal rights issues that challenge policymakers today. Each box includes critical-thinking questions that ask readers to ponder whether and how the criminal justice system balances individual rights and public safety.

Evidence-Based Justice Reinvestment boxes, which are found in many chapters, emphasize the possibilities made available through contemporary strategies, including effective evidence-based practices that use criminal justice resources wisely.

Evidence-based practices are introduced in early chapters and are stressed throughout the text, including in the book's sections on policing, the courts, and corrections.

CJ News boxes in each chapter present case stories from the media to bring a true-to-life dimension to the study of criminal justice and allow insight into the everyday workings of the justice system.

CJ Issues boxes that provide the information students need to participate in a discussion of critical issues facing the justice system, such as excessive use of force by the police, the use of mass imprisonment as a tool of social engineering, and coming changes in the juvenile justice process.

CJ Careers boxes outline the characteristics of a variety of criminal justice careers in a Q&A format, to introduce today's pragmatic students to an assortment of potential career options and assist them in making appropriate career choices.

Multiculturalism and Diversity boxes present aspects of criminal justice that are related to the diverse nature of American society and emphasize the need for justice-system personnel capable of working with culturally diverse groups.

Ethics and Professionalism boxes present ethical codes that criminal justice practitioners are asked to uphold, highlighting the vital role of moral and ethical standards and behavior in their daily lives and to the high social expectations inherent in justice–related careers. Included are the ethical codes of the American Correctional Association, the American Probation and Parole Association, the International Association of Chiefs of Police, the American Bar Association, and the American Jail Association.

Graphics including full-color diagrams, illustrations, timelines, and photographs reinforce key concepts for easier understanding and make the chapter topics both understandable and interesting. In recognition of the visual orientation of today's learners, we have worked to achieve a comprehensive integration of graphic art with the concepts and ideas of criminal justice. Consequently, the layout and design of both the printed and the Revel versions of this text are highly visual, inviting readers to explore its pages while powerfully illustrating the critical concepts that are central to the field of criminal justice.

As the author of numerous books on criminal justice, I have often been amazed at how the end result of the justice process is sometimes barely recognizable as "justice" in any practical sense of the word. It is my sincere hope that the technological and publishing revolutions that have contributed to the creation and development of this book will combine with a growing social awareness to facilitate needed changes in our system and will help replace self-serving, system-perpetuated injustices with new standards of equity, compassion, understanding, fairness, and heartfelt justice for all.

New to the Thirteenth Edition

Chapter 1   What Is Criminal Justice?

- The term *procedural justice* is introduced as a new key term, taking its place in Chapter 1 alongside of *procedural fairness*.
- The resurgence in public support for the police is discussed within the context of public polling.
- The discussion about white-collar and corporate crime has been updated with coverage of Volkswagen's emissions scandal.
- Cybercrimes are discussed in more detail, especially as they impact our understanding of the criminal landscape in America.

Chapter 2   The Crime Picture

- Visually stimulating graphics have been introduced into the chapter, reflecting the interactivity of the Revel version of the printed book.
- Discussion of the FBI's NIBRS program has been clarified and enhanced.
- The new National Crime-Statistics Exchange (NCS-X) is now described.
- Crime statistics have been updated throughout the chapter.
- The Equifax data breech is discussed, and its consequences for the justice system explained.
- The information on mass shootings has been revised and updated.
- The national opioid crisis and its significance for the justice system is now discussed.
- The discussion of computer crimes has been enhanced.

Chapter 3   Criminal Law

- Updates on terrorism cases discussed in the chapter have been added.
- The discussion of the insanity defense has been updated and simplified.

Chapter 4   Policing: Purpose and Organization

- An Evidence-Based Justice Reinvestment box has been added to the chapter.
- New information is provided about fusion centers, and the fusion center discussion has been simplified.
- The notion of procedural fairness is now discussed in the chapter.
- "Overpolicing" and the unnecessary use of force by the police is discussed.
- The discussion of police body-worn cameras has been updated.
- Changes in COPS Office funding is now discussed.

Chapter 5   Policing: Legal Aspects

- Discussion of the Freddy Gray case has been updated.
- The discussion of both warrantless and protective searches have been updated.
- A new Careers Box has been added to this chapter.
- Investigative detention is now discussed, and it has been added as a key term.

Chapter 6   Policing: Issues and Challenges

- The discussion of police subculture has been updated with information from new studies.
- Police corruption in the city of Baltimore is discussed.
- The 2018 federal Law Enforcement Mental Health and Wellness Act is described.
- The discussion of police stress and the impact of stress on health has been expanded.
- An online gateway for use by law enforcement agencies (LEEP) is described.
- The change in name for the Smart Policing Initiative (now known as Strategies for Policing Innovation) is included.
- The U.S. Supreme Court case of *Los Angeles v. Mendez,* including its ramifications for qualified immunity by police, is discussed.
- The 2017 Supreme Court case of *White v. Pauly,* which focused on qualified immunity is discussed.
- The new National Consensus Policy on Use of Force, developed by eleven influential U.S. law enforcement organizations is explained.
- The Death in Custody Reporting Act (DCRA) is described, and it's implications for law enforcement demonstrated.
- *Accreditation* (of police agencies) is now a key term in the chapter.

Chapter 7   The Courts

- The results of a new study of community courts are introduced.
- Problem-solving, mental health, and youth specialty courts are now discussed.
- The addition of Neil Gorsuch and Brett Kavanaugh to the list of active Supreme Court justices is mentioned.

Chapter 8   The Courtroom Work Group and the Criminal Trial

- A discussion of the factors that are commonly used to determine client indigence in state-run indigent defense systems have been added in the form of a graph.

Chapter 9   Sentencing

- New Jersey's new racial impact law is discussed.
- The discussion of indeterminate sentencing has been clarified.
- The discussion of state sentencing guidelines has been brought up to date.
- New charts and graphs replace ones that were previously used.
- The discussion of the impact of California's strategy of prisoner realignment has been updated.
- The activities of the California Victim Compensation Board (CalVCB) are now discussed.
- The state and local practice of charging inmates for jail stays is explained.
- California's Proposition 66 is discussed in the context of capital punishment. The proposition speeds up the appeals process in capital cases.
- A new key term, *wrongful conviction*, has been added to the chapter, and its discussion has been enhanced.

Chapter 10   Probation, Parole, and Community Corrections

- Discussion has been added of Washington, D.C.'s Youth Rehabilitation Act (YRA), which gives offenders under the age of 22 a second chance by permitting judges to dramatically reduce sentences for young offenders.
- Data on probation and parole have been updated throughout the chapter.
- A discussion of the case of Philadelphia-based rapper Meek Mill has been added to the chapter.
- The 2017 parole board hearing for O.J. Simpson has been included, along with a video link to the recorded proceedings.
- The discussion involving the use of ankle bracelets to facilitate GPS monitoring of defendants sentenced to home confinement has been expanded and now includes the Bill Cosby case as an example.
- The results of two new studies focused on reentry courts are now included.

Chapter 11   Prisons and Jails

- The chapter now shows how savings that result from reduced prison populations can be used to expand probation and parole programs, to fund jail operations, and to enhance rehabilitation programs generally.
- The feature showing the annual costs to incarcerate an inmate in prison in California has been considerably refined and updated.
- A new section on prison overcrowding has been built into the chapter.
- The discussion on private prisons has been modified.
- The figure showing federal prison populations by offense has been updated and modified.

Chapter 12   Prison Life

- The list of prison argot has been updated and expanded.
- Information on prison riots has been updated.
- New information on prison libraries is included.
- The section describing the impact of aging on inmate populations has been expanded.
- The discussion of the mentally ill in prisons has been expanded, while a previous discussion of HIV/AIDS among inmate populations has been eliminated.

- A new diagram showing inmates with and without serious mental illness has been added.
- The discussion of prisons as breeding grounds for terrorism has been expanded.

Chapter 13   Juvenile Justice

- Added discussion of the 2018 U.S. Supreme Court case of *Bostic v. Pash,* in which the court allowed a 241-year sentence for crimes committed by a juvenile to stand.
- Added discussion of Pennsylvania's Juvenile Justice System Enhancement Strategy (JJSES), which is a statewide commitment to employ evidence-based practices in the juvenile justice system.
- The term *justice-involved* youth is introduced and defined.
- A new graphic showing the locations of juvenile detention facilities around the country is now included in the chapter.
- The definition of the term *abused child* has been clarified, to include the consequences of California's 2016 Proposition 57, which ended the ability of prosecutors to "direct file" criminal cases against juveniles.
- The discussion of direct file laws has been enhanced and clarified.
- Changing state laws that define the age of criminal responsibility are discussed, with specific mention of New York and North Carolina.
- *Detention hearing* has been added as a new key term, including its definition.

Instructor Supplements

▶ **Instructor's Manual with Test Bank.** Includes content outlines for classroom discussion, teaching suggestions, and answers to selected end-of-chapter questions from the text. This also contains a Word document version of the test bank.

▶ **TestGen.** This computerized test generation system gives you maximum flexibility in creating and administering tests on paper, electronically, or online. It provides state-of-the-art features for viewing and editing test bank questions, dragging a selected question into a test you are creating, and printing sleek, formatted tests in a variety of layouts. Select test items from test banks included with TestGen for quick test creation, or write your own questions from scratch. TestGen's random generator provides the option to display different text or calculated number values each time questions are used.

▶ **PowerPoint Presentations.** Our presentations offer clear, straightforward outlines. Photos, illustrations, charts, and tables from the book are included in the presentations when applicable.

▶ **Annotated Instructors Edition (AIE).** The AIE contains notes in the top margins identifying key topics with suggestions for stimulating and guiding class discussion.

To access supplementary materials online, instructors need to request an instructor access code. Go to **www.pearsonhighered.com/irc**, where you can register for an instructor access code. Within 48 hours after registering, you will receive a confirming email, including an instructor access code. Once you have received your code, go to the site and log on for full instructions on downloading the materials you wish to use.

Alternate Versions

► **eBooks.** This text is also available in multiple eBook formats. These are an exciting new choice for students looking to save money. As an alternative to purchasing the printed textbook, students can purchase an electronic version of the same content. With an eTextbook, students can search the text, make notes online, print out reading assignments that incorporate lecture notes, and bookmark important passages for later review. For more information, visit your favorite online eBook reseller or visit **www.mypearsonstore.com**.

► **REVEL™** is Pearson's newest way of delivering our respected content. Fully digital and highly engaging, REVEL replaces the textbook and gives students everything they need for the course. Seamlessly blending text narrative, media, and assessment, REVEL enables students to read, practice, and study in one continuous experience— for less than the cost of a traditional textbook. Learn more at **www.pearsonhighered .com/revel**.

REVEL for *Criminal Justice: A Brief Introduction,* *13e* by Schmalleger

Designed for how you want to teach–and how your students want to learn

Revel is an interactive learning environment that engages students and helps them prepare for your class. Reimagining their content, our authors integrate media and assessment throughout the narrative so students can read, explore, and practice, all at the same time. Thanks to this dynamic reading experience, students come to class prepared to discuss, apply, and learn about criminal justice—from you and from each other.

Revel seamlessly combines the full content of Pearson's bestselling criminal justice titles with multimedia learning tools. You assign the topics your students cover. Author Explanatory Videos, application exercises, survey questions, interactive CJ data maps, and short quizzes engage students and enhance their understanding of core topics as they progress through the content. Through its engaging learning experience, Revel helps students better understand course material while preparing them to meaningfully participate in class.

Author Explanatory Videos

Short 2–3 minute Author Explanatory Videos, embedded in the narrative, provide students with a verbal explanation of an important topic or concept and illuminating the concept with additional examples.

Point/CounterPoint Videos

Instead of simply reading about criminal justice, students are empowered to think critically about key topics through Point/Counterpoint videos that explore different views on controversial issues such as the effectiveness of the fourth amendment, privacy, search and seizure, Miranda, prisoner rights, death penalty and many other topics.

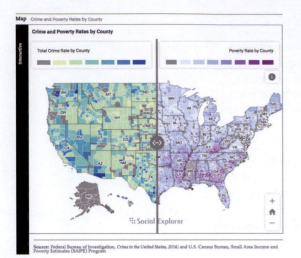

New Social Explorer Criminal Justice Data Maps

Social Explorer Maps integrated into the narrative ask students to examine crime and corrections data correlated with socio-economic and other criminal justice data. Maps also show differences in state statutes on major issues such as marijuana legalization, the death penalty, and the distribution of hate organizations across the US.

New Student Survey Questions

Student Survey Questions appear within the narrative asking students to respond to questions about controversial topics and important concepts. Students then see their response versus the responses of all other students who have answered the question in the form of a bar chart. We provide the instructor with a PowerPoint deck with links to each survey and map, making it easy to pull these items up in class for discussion.

Criminal Justice Simulations

In our introduction to Criminal Justice Revel etexts, there are 13 simulations that ask the student to evaluate scenarios and make decisions regarding CJ issues or procedures. Examples of topics dealt with include recognizing crime elements, determining policing styles, search and seizure procedures, warrants and arrest documentation sentencing options, determining conditions for parole.

Track time-on-task throughout the course

The Performance Dashboard allows you to see how much time the class or individual students have spent reading a section or doing an assignment, as well as points earned per assignment. This data helps correlate study time with performance and provides a window into where students may be having difficulty with the material.

Learning Management System Integration

Pearson provides Blackboard Learn™, Canvas™, Brightspace by D2L, and Moodle integration, giving institutions, instructors, and students easy access to Revel. Our Revel integration delivers streamlined access to everything your students need for the course in these learning management system (LMS) environments.

The Revel App

The Revel mobile app lets students read, practice, and study—anywhere, anytime, on any device. Content is available both online and offline, and the app syncs work across all registered devices automatically, giving students great flexibility to toggle between phone, tablet, and laptop as they move through their day. The app also lets students set assignment notifications to stay on top of all due dates. Available for download from the App Store or Google Play. Visit **www.pearsonhighered.com/revel/** to learn more.

Acknowledgments

Many thanks go to all who assisted in many different ways in the development of this text-book. I am grateful to the manuscript reviewers for their helpful comments and valuable insights:

Clare Armstrong-Seward, Morrisville State College

Chris Carmean, Houston Community College

Addrain Conyders, Marist College

Anthony LaRose, University of Tampa

Michael Raymond, New Hampshire Technical Institute

James Blair, South Texas College

Addrain Conyers, Marist College

Tracy Hearn, Tarrant County College

Carly Hillinski-Rosick, Grand Valley State University

Frank Leonard, Tallahassee Community College

Patricia Nunally, Southwest Tennessee Community College

Lisa Pitts, Washburn University

Gina Robertiello, Felician College

I also appreciate the many valuable comments made by Kevin Barret, E. Elaine Bartgis, Bruce Bayley, John M. Boal, Jack Brady, Michelle Brown, Jeffrey B. Bumgarner, Michael Eskey, Joan Luxenburg, Rick Michaelson, Carl E. Russell, Dave Seip, Jim Smith, Kevin M. Thompson, and Richard A. Wilson.

I'd also like to thank the editorial and production team Andrew Gilfillan, VP, Courseware Portfolio Management; Gary Bauer, Executive Portfolio Manager; Heather Taylor, Product Marketing Manager; Bob Nisbet, Field Marketing Manager; Neha Sharma, Content Producer; Holly Shufeldt, Content Producer; Jennifer Sargunar; Manager Producer; Cynthia Zonneveld, Managing Producer; Maura Snow, Content Producer; Lynda Cramer, Portfolio Management Assistant; Indu Sambantham, Senior Project Manager, Integra Software Services; Philip Alexander, Senior Project Manager, Integra Software Services.

Thanks also to my wife, Willow Szirandi Schmalleger, whose unfailing help and constant support have made this book detailed, accurate, and enjoyable.

About the Author

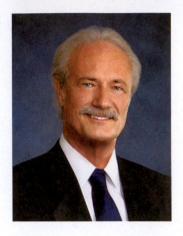

Frank Schmalleger, Ph.D., is Distinguished Professor Emeritus at the University of North Carolina at Pembroke, where he taught criminal justice courses for 20 years and chaired the university's Department of Sociology, Social Work, and Criminal Justice for 16 of those years. In 1991 the university awarded him the title of Distinguished Professor, and the university named him Professor Emeritus in 2001.

Dr. Schmalleger holds degrees from the University of Notre Dame and Ohio State University, having earned both a master's (1970) and a doctorate in sociology (1974) with a special emphasis in criminology from Ohio State University.

As an adjunct professor with Webster University in St. Louis, Missouri, Schmalleger helped develop the university's graduate program in security administration and loss prevention. He taught courses in that curriculum for more than a decade. Schmalleger has also taught in the online graduate program of the New School for Social Research, helping to build the world's first electronic classrooms. Schmalleger is the creator of a number of award-winning websites, including one that supports this textbook.

Frank Schmalleger is the author of numerous articles and many books, including the widely used *Criminal Justice Today* (Pearson, 2019), *Criminology Today* (Pearson, 2019); *Criminal Law Today* (Pearson, 2016), and *The Definitive Guide to Criminal Justice and Criminology on the World Wide Web* (Pearson, 2009).

Schmalleger is also founding editor of the journal *Criminal Justice Studies*. He has served as editor for the Pearson series *Criminal Justice in the Twenty-First Century* and as imprint adviser for Greenwood Publishing Group's criminal justice reference series.

Schmalleger's philosophy of both teaching and writing can be summed up in these words: "In order to communicate knowledge, we must first catch, then hold, a person's interest—be it student, colleague, or policymaker. Our writing, our speaking, and our teaching must be relevant to the problems facing people today, and they must in some way help solve those problems."

"Justice is truth in action!"
—Benjamin Disraeli

"Injustice anywhere is a threat
to justice everywhere."
—Martin Luther King, Jr.

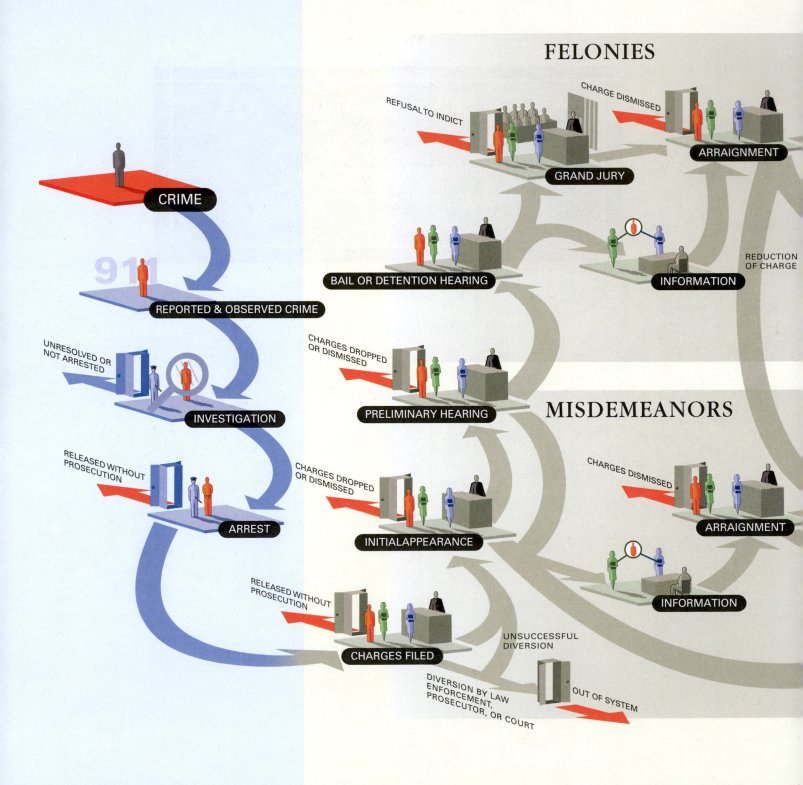

FELONIES

REFUSAL TO INDICT

CHARGE DISMISSED

CRIME

GRAND JURY

ARRAIGNMENT

911

BAIL OR DETENTION HEARING

INFORMATION

REDUCTION OF CHARGE

REPORTED & OBSERVED CRIME

UNRESOLVED OR NOT ARRESTED

CHARGES DROPPED OR DISMISSED

INVESTIGATION

PRELIMINARY HEARING

MISDEMEANORS

RELEASED WITHOUT PROSECUTION

CHARGES DROPPED OR DISMISSED

CHARGES DISMISSED

ARREST

INITIAL APPEARANCE

ARRAIGNMENT

RELEASED WITHOUT PROSECUTION

INFORMATION

UNSUCCESSFUL DIVERSION

CHARGES FILED

DIVERSION BY LAW ENFORCEMENT, PROSECUTOR, OR COURT

OUT OF SYSTEM

JUSTICE SYSTEM

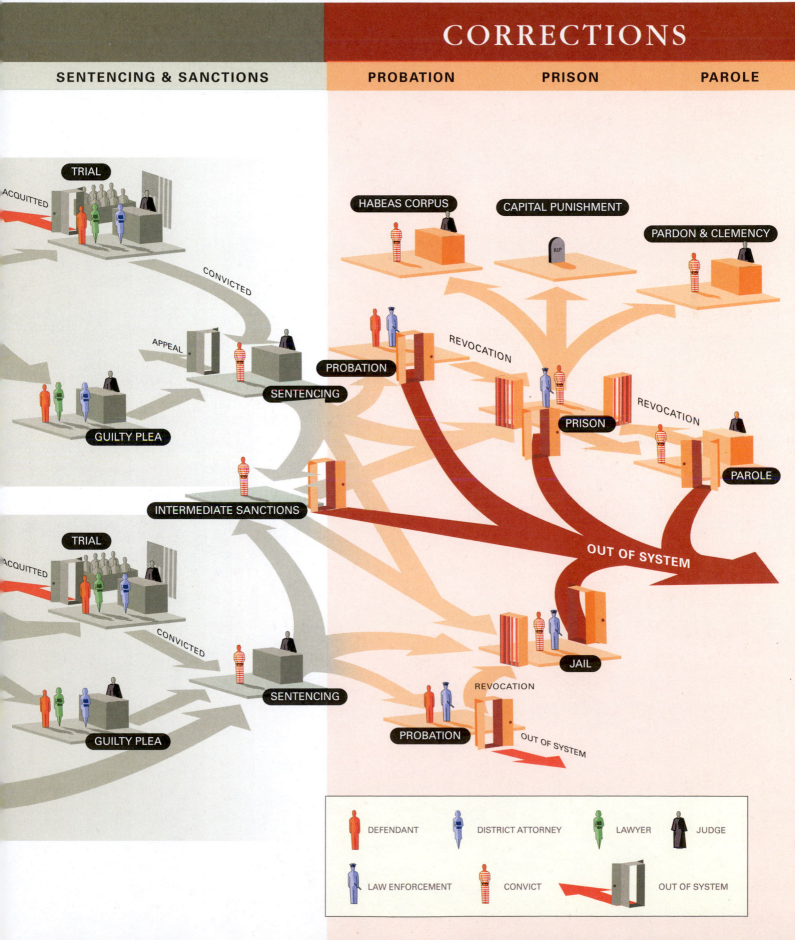

CORRECTIONS

SENTENCING & SANCTIONS | PROBATION | PRISON | PAROLE

TRIAL
ACQUITTED

CONVICTED

HABEAS CORPUS

CAPITAL PUNISHMENT

PARDON & CLEMENCY

RIP

APPEAL

SENTENCING

GUILTY PLEA

PROBATION

REVOCATION

REVOCATION

PRISON

PAROLE

INTERMEDIATE SANCTIONS

OUT OF SYSTEM

TRIAL
ACQUITTED

JAIL

CONVICTED

REVOCATION

SENTENCING

PROBATION

OUT OF SYSTEM

GUILTY PLEA

DEFENDANT   DISTRICT ATTORNEY   LAWYER   JUDGE

LAW ENFORCEMENT   CONVICT   OUT OF SYSTEM

What Is Criminal Justice?

> *People expect both safety and justice and do not want to sacrifice one for the other.*
>
> —Christopher Stone, President,
> Open Society Foundations

CHAPTER

1

ELAINE THOMPSON/AP Image

Learning Objectives

After reading this chapter, you should be able to:

1. Summarize the history of crime in America and corresponding changes in the American criminal justice system. **3**

2. Describe the public-order (crime-control) and individual-rights (due-process) perspectives of criminal justice, concluding with how the criminal justice system balances the two perspectives. **6**

3. Explain the relationship of criminal justice to general concepts of equity and fairness. **8**

4. Describe the American criminal justice system in terms of its three major components and their respective functions. **10**

5. Describe the process of American criminal justice, including the stages of criminal case processing. **12**

6. Define due process of law, including where the American legal system guarantees due process. **13**

7. Describe the role of evidence-based practice in contemporary criminal justice. **15**

8. Explain how multiculturalism and social diversity present challenges to and opportunities for the American system of criminal justice. **16**

Introduction

Ask anyone who has come into contact with it, and you will hear that the American criminal justice system wields a lot of power. Agencies of the justice system have the authority to arrest (the police), to convict (the courts), and to imprison (corrections). In the most serious cases, the system even has control over who lives and who dies (capital punishment). For those who commit **crimes**, the "full weight and power" of the system comes crashing down on them, beginning with arrest. Yet, for all of its power, the American system of justice is a consensual system that relies upon both public acceptance and public cooperation for it to function effectively. Were citizens to lose faith in the justice process and question its legitimacy, then the day-to-day work of law enforcement officers, court personnel, and corrections officers would become insurmountably difficult—and their jobs would be impossible to perform.

Today, the criminal justice system in this country may be teetering on the edge of just such a crisis. It's a crisis that arose quickly and spontaneously, fed by social media, following grand jury refusals in Missouri and New York to indict police officers in the death of two black suspects in separate incidents. The first involved Michael Brown, an 18-year-old unarmed African-American man who died in hail of bullets fired by a Ferguson, Missouri, police officer after an initial confrontation between the two turned violent.[1] The second involved Eric Garner, another unarmed black man who died after an NYPD officer placed him in a chokehold while they struggled—apparently preventing him from being able to breathe.[2] Garner, a father of six, had been arrested numerous times before the fatal encounter for illegally selling cigarettes on city streets—a minor offense.

Protests followed both grand jury decisions, with demonstrators in Ferguson rioting, looting, and burning down stores over a period of days. New York City protestors emblazoned the slogan "No Justice, No Peace" on placards they carried, and Missouri protestors chanted "Hands up, don't shoot!" in the belief that Brown was surrendering to police when he was shot (the grand jury, however, concluded otherwise).

Confrontations between police and demonstrators remained largely peaceful, but led to an especially surprising result. Police officers in Ferguson made no arrests during the first few nights of looting and rioting, even though arsonists and thieves were in plain sight; and NYPD officers stopped making "quality-of-life arrests"—or arrests for minor crimes. By the start of 2015, arrests in New York City for minor crimes, such as traffic violations, and public drinking and urination, had plummeted 94% from the year before.[3] Arrests for other crimes nosedived by 66% from only a week earlier. Police in New York City were reported to be making arrests "only when they have to."[4] In Seattle, police chief Kathleen O'Toole made the rounds of her department's stations telling officers that it was OK to arrest people. "If you get agitators who threaten the police or the public, you have to arrest them," she said.[5] It was as though police officers in Ferguson, New York City, and elsewhere—perhaps wary of stoking more public unrest—had become afraid to enforce the law.

Matters became even uglier when assaults on police officers rose significantly following the protests. On December 20, 2014, two uniformed NYPD police officers were shot dead as they sat in their marked police cruiser on a Brooklyn street corner.[6] The assassination-style attack was carried out by 28-year-old Ismaaiyl Brinsley, who soon shot and killed himself on a nearby subway platform. Prior to the killings, Brinsley had posted anti-police threats on his Instagram page, referencing the "unjust" killings of Garner and Brown. "I'm putting wings on pigs today," he wrote, "They take 1 of ours ... Let's take 2 of Theirs." Soon, police officers around the country were doubling up on patrol, and bracing for further attacks.

crime

Conduct in violation of the criminal laws of a state, the federal government, or a local jurisdiction, for which there is no legally acceptable justification or excuse.[i]

🐦 Follow the author's tweets about the latest crime and justice news @schmalleger

▲ Retiring Dallas, Texas, police chief David Brown speaks during a funeral service for one of five officers killed in an ambush-style attack in 2016. The killings led to debates over the fairness of the American criminal justice system. How would you assess that system's fairness?

Danny Hurley/Polaris/Newscom

> American society is built upon a delicate balance between the demand for *personal freedoms* and the need for *public safety*.

Attacks on the police have continued. On July 7, 2016, five police officers were killed in an ambush in Dallas, Texas, while nine other officers were wounded. The shootings happened at the end of what had been a peaceful protest against killings by police.[7] Ten days later, three law enforcement officers were killed, and another three wounded in Baton Rouge, Louisiana, by a man who went on a shooting rampage that targeted officers on his 29th birthday. Later, a San Antonio 20-year police veteran was shot and killed at a traffic stop in Austin, Texas, and another two officers were killed in an ambush near Des Moines, Iowa.[8]

Although the anti-police movement was embraced by only a relatively small portion of the American population, it not only signified distrust of the police, but also reflected a fundamental sense of injustice about how suspects—especially African Americans—were being treated by the entire justice system. Some saw the protests as releasing pent-up frustration that resulted from a decades-long war on drugs, during which a hugely disproportionate number of young blacks were arrested, and a get-tough-on-crime era that resulted in dramatically overcrowded prisons throughout the country. Whatever the cause, it soon became clear that public acceptance of the justice system's authority is based significantly on the perception of fair and equitable treatment by all of its component agencies.[9] One of the lessons learned from the events of recent years was that fairness has a wider meaning than ensuring just outcomes and upholding due process (issues that we will later discuss).

As we shall see throughout this text, **procedural fairness**, which is the process by which decisions that *feel* fair are made, is a vital component of our American justice system. When the concept of procedural fairness is applied to the criminal justice system, it is known as **procedural justice**. Procedural justice is crucial to effective criminal justice practices, and helps to ensure the legitimacy of justice organizations and their acceptance by the people they serve.

Finally, it is worth noting that a recent Gallup poll found that Americans' respect for local police had jumped to its highest level since 1967. In that poll, 76% of those interviewed said that they have a "great deal" of respect for police—an increase of 12 percentage points from the year before.[10] Experts attributed the rise to a nationwide "reflection on what the role of police should be and the complex challenges they face."[11]

A Brief History of Crime in America

What we call *criminal activity* has undoubtedly been with us since the dawn of history, and crime control has long been a primary concern of politicians and government leaders worldwide. Still, the American experience with crime during the last half century has been especially influential in shaping the criminal justice system of today (Figure 1–1). In this country, crime waves have come and gone, including an 1850–1880 crime epidemic that was apparently related to social upheaval caused by large-scale immigration and the Civil War.[12] A spurt of widespread organized criminal activity was associated with the Prohibition years of the early twentieth century. Following World War II, however, American crime rates remained relatively stable until the 1960s.

> **1** Summarize the history of crime in America and corresponding changes in the American criminal justice system.

The 1960s and 1970s saw a burgeoning concern for the rights of ethnic and racial minorities, women, people with physical and mental challenges, and many other groups. The civil rights movement of the period emphasized equality of opportunity and respect for individuals, regardless of race, color, creed, gender, or personal attributes. As new laws were passed and suits filed, court involvement in the movement grew. Soon a plethora of hard-won individual rights and prerogatives, based on the U.S. Constitution, the Bill of Rights, and new federal and state legislation, were recognized and guaranteed. By the 1980s, the civil rights movement had profoundly affected all areas of social life—from education and employment to the activities of the criminal justice system.

---

procedural fairness
The process by which procedures that feel fair to those involved are made.

procedural justice
The implementation of fair and equitable procedures in the administration of justice.

individual rights
The rights guaranteed to all members of American society by the U.S. Constitution (especially those rights found in the first ten amendments to the Constitution, known as the *Bill of Rights*). These rights are particularly important to criminal defendants facing formal processing by the criminal justice system.

FIGURE 1–1
Milestones in Crime History

1850–1880 A crime epidemic spurred by social upheaval brought on by large-scale immigration and the Civil War.

1920–1933 Prohibition spurs the growth of organized crime.

Following World War II, American crime rates remained relatively stable until the 1960s.

1960–1970 The civil rights movement of the period emphasized equality of opportunity and respect for individuals regardless of race, color, creed, gender, or personal attributes. This period also saw a dramatic increase in reported criminal activity.

1970s Reports of crimes such as murder, rape, and assault increased considerably.

1980s By the mid-1980s, the dramatic increase in sale and use of illicit drugs led to increased crime. Large cities became havens for drug gangs and cities experienced dramatic declines in property values and quality of life. President Reagan declared a "war on drugs."

1992 The videotaped beating of Rodney King, an African American, by Los Angeles–area police officers was seen as an example of the abuse of police power.

By the late **1990s,** the public perception was that crime rates were growing and that many offenders went unpunished. This led to a growing emphasis on responsibility and punishment and the development of a "get-tough-on-crime" era.

2001 A series of terrorist attacks on New York City, Washington, D.C., and elsewhere changed the focus of law enforcement to a proactive and more global approach.

2001 **USA PATRIOT Act** dramatically increases the investigatory authority of federal, state, and local police agencies.

The incidence of personal crime declined throughout the 1990s.

2009 Bernard Madoff pleads guilty to the largest Ponzi scheme in history. The crimes of Madoff, and widespread suspicions about the activities of Wall Street financiers, led to a number of white-collar crime investigations. White-collar crime came into focus as a serious threat to the American way of life.

2011 FBI most-wanted terrorist Osama Bin Laden was killed by U.S. special operations forces in Pakistan, leading to fears of a renewed terrorist onslaught on American targets throughout the world.

2012–2018 Epidemic of mass shootings and random violence sweeps public venues across the United States.

2019–present Cybercrimes become commonplace and threaten both national security, and corporate and personal financial integrity.

social disorganization
A condition said to exist when a group is faced with social change, uneven development of culture, maladaptiveness, disharmony, conflict, and lack of consensus.

This emphasis on **individual rights** was accompanied by a dramatic increase in reported criminal activity. Although some researchers doubted the accuracy of official accounts, reports by the FBI of "traditional" crimes such as murder, rape, and assault increased considerably during the 1970s and into the 1980s. Many theories were advanced to explain this leap in observed criminality. Some analysts of American culture, for example, suggested that the combination of newfound freedoms and long-pent-up hostilities of the socially and economically deprived worked to produce **social disorganization**, which in turn increased criminality.

By the mid-1980s, the dramatic increase in the sale and use of illicit drugs threatened the foundation of American society. Cocaine, and later laboratory-processed "crack," spread to every corner of America. Large cities became havens for drug gangs, and many inner-city areas were all but abandoned to highly armed and well-financed drug racketeers. Cities experienced dramatic declines in property values, and residents wrestled with an eroding quality of life.

By the close of the 1980s, neighborhoods and towns were fighting for their communal lives. Huge rents had been torn in the national social fabric, and the American way of life, long taken for granted, was under the gun. Traditional values appeared in danger of going up in smoke along with the "crack" being consumed openly in some parks and resorts. Looking for a way to stem the tide of increased criminality, many took up the call for "law and order." In response, President Ronald Reagan created a cabinet-level "drug czar" position to coordinate the "war on drugs." Careful thought was given at the highest levels to using the military to patrol the sea-lanes and air corridors through which many of the illegal drugs entered the country. President George H. W. Bush, who followed Reagan into office, quickly embraced and expanded the government's antidrug efforts.

A decade later, a few spectacular crimes that received widespread coverage in the news media fostered a sense among the American public that crime in the United States was out of hand and that strict new measures were needed to combat it. One such crime was the 1995 bombing of the Alfred P. Murrah Federal Building in Oklahoma City by anti-government extremists. Another was the 1999 Columbine High School massacre in Colorado that left 12 students and 1 teacher dead.[13]

The public's perception that crime rates were growing, coupled with a belief that offenders frequently went unpunished or received only a judicial slap on the wrist, led to a burgeoning emphasis on responsibility and punishment. By the late 1990s, a newfound emphasis on individual accountability began to blossom among an American public fed up with crime and fearful of its own victimization. Growing calls for enhanced responsibility quickly began to replace the previous emphasis on individual rights. As a juggernaut of conservative opinion made itself felt on the political scene, Senator Phil Gramm of Texas observed that the public wants to "grab violent criminals by the throat, put them in prison [and] stop building prisons like Holiday Inns."[14]

Then, in an event that changed the course of our society, public tragedy became forever joined with private victimization in our collective consciousness after a series of highly destructive and well-coordinated terrorist attacks on New York City and Washington, D.C., on September 11, 2001. Those attacks resulted in the collapse and total destruction of the twin 110-story towers of the World Trade Center and a devastating explosion at the Pentagon. Thousands of people perished, and many were injured. Although law enforcement and security agencies were unable to prevent the September 11 attacks, many have since moved from a reactive to a proactive posture in the fight against terrorism—a change that is discussed in more detail in Chapter 6.

> By the late 1990s, a newfound emphasis on individual accountability began to blossom among an American public fed up with crime and fearful of its own victimization.

The September 11 attacks also made clear that adequate law enforcement involves a global effort at controlling crime and reducing the risk of injury and loss to law-abiding people both at home and abroad. The attacks showed that criminal incidents that take place on the other side of the globe can impact those of us living in the United States, and they illustrated how the acquisition of skills needed to understand diverse cultures can help in the fight against crime and terrorism. As Chapter 2 points out, terrorism is a criminal act, and preventing terrorism and investigating terrorist incidents after they occur are highly important roles for local, state, and federal law enforcement agencies.

A different kind of offending, corporate and white-collar crime, took center stage in 2002 and 2003 as Congress stiffened penalties for unscrupulous business executives who knowingly falsify their company's financial reports.[15] The changes came amidst declining stock market values, shaken investor confidence, and threats to the viability of employee pension plans in the wake of a corporate crime wave involving criminal activities that had been planned and undertaken by executives at a number of leading corporations. In an effort to restore order to American financial markets, President George W. Bush signed the Sarbanes—Oxley Act on July 30, 2002.[16] The law, which has been called "the single most important piece of legislation affecting corporate governance, financial disclosure and the practice of public accounting since the US securities laws of the early 1930s,"[17] is intended to deter corporate fraud and to hold business executives accountable for their actions.

Today, white-collar crime continues to be a focus of federal prosecutors. In 2017, for example, Volkswagen AG pled guilty to three criminal felony counts and agreed to pay $4.3 billion in criminal and civil penalties. The company had used software in some of its cars that was designed to improve exhaust emissions tests. VW executives were accused of perpetrating a massive fraud, and the U.S. Justice Department filed a civil lawsuit asking for as much as $18 billion in compensation from the company. In addition, a federal grand jury returned an indictment charging six VW executives and employees for their roles in the nearly 10-year-long conspiracy.[18]

Also, in a 2009 story that many readers will remember, investment fund manager Bernard Madoff pleaded guilty to operating a Ponzi scheme that defrauded investors out of as much as $50 billion.[19] Madoff pleaded guilty to 11 felony counts, including securities fraud, mail fraud, wire fraud, money laundering, and perjury. Following the plea, he was sentenced to serve 150 years in federal prison—three times as long as federal probation officers had recommended.[20] White-collar crime is discussed in more detail in Chapter 2.

The current era is characterized by low and declining rates of "traditional" crimes, such as rape, robbery, and burglary (see Chapter 2 for more details), but the specter of random mass shootings, a high number of inner-city murders, and novel forms of criminal activity complicates today's crime picture. In 2018, for example, many American cities reported more murders than at any time in their history. Similarly, as Chapter 2 explains in greater detail, many other types of crimes today are Internet-based or involve other forms of high technology.

▲ Freedom Tower at the World Trade Center site in New York City. The tower opened in 2014. It stands 1,776 feet tall and will be surrounded by several other buildings. It is a memorial to the nearly 3,000 people who were killed in the terrorist attacks that demolished the Twin Towers in 2001. How did those attacks change the American justice system?

Life In Pixels/Shutterstock

🐦 Follow the author's tweets about the latest crime and justice news @schmalleger

◄ A scene from a computer game. Crimes today have undergone a significant change, with computer-related and high-technology offenses impacting more Americans than ever before. Is the justice system ready for these new challenges?

Game Shots/Alamy Stock Photo

Criminal perpetrators who illegally gain access to digital information (and money, including Bitcoins and other virtual currencies) through social media or Internet-based transaction are responsible for a significant level of criminal activity in the virtual world. Such crimes can have very significant impact on real people. Moreover, crimes committed through the medium of cyberspace frequently remain undiscovered, or are found out only with the passage of time. If we were to examine all forms of crime, we would find that crimes today have undergone a significant shift away from historical forms of offending to more innovative schemes involving computers and other digital devices. A 2018 article in the *New York Times* summarizes the situation well, saying, "the Internet's virtual superhighways have supplanted brick-and-mortar streets as the scenes for muggings, prostitution rings or commercial burglaries… A surge in the evolving crimes of the digital era, and the fact that they are not fully captured in law enforcement's reporting systems" leads to a misperception of today's true crime picture.[21]

2 Describe the public-order (crime-control) and individual-rights (due-process) perspectives of criminal justice, concluding with how the criminal justice system balances the two perspectives.

The Theme of This Book

This book examines the American system of criminal justice and the agencies and processes that constitute it. It builds on a theme that is especially valuable for studying criminal justice today: *individual rights versus public order.* This theme draws on historical developments that have shaped our legal system and our understandings of crime and justice. It is one of the primary determinants of the nature of contemporary criminal justice—including criminal law, police practice, sentencing, and corrections.

A strong emphasis on individual rights rose to the forefront of American social thought during the 1960s and 1970s, a period known as the *civil rights era.* The civil rights era led to the recognition of fundamental personal rights that had previously been denied illegally to many people on the basis of race, ethnicity, gender, sexual preference, or disability. The civil rights movement soon expanded to include the rights of many other groups, including criminal suspects, parolees and probationers, trial participants, prison and jail inmates, and victims. As the emphasis on civil rights grew, new laws and court decisions broadened the rights available to many.

The treatment of criminal suspects was afforded special attention by those who argued that the purpose of any civilized society should be to secure rights and freedoms for each of its citizens—including those suspected and convicted of crimes. Rights advocates feared unnecessarily restrictive government action and viewed it as an assault on basic human dignity and individual liberty. They believed that at times it was necessary to sacrifice some degree of public safety and predictability to guarantee basic freedoms. Hence, criminal rights activists demanded a justice system that limits police powers and that holds justice agencies accountable to the highest procedural standards.

During the 1960s and 1970s, the dominant philosophy in American criminal justice focused on guaranteeing the rights of criminal defendants while seeking to understand the root causes of crime and violence. The past 30 years, however, have witnessed increased interest in an ordered society, in public safety, and in the rights of crime victims. This change in attitudes was likely brought about by national frustration with the perceived inability of our society and its justice system to prevent crimes and to consistently hold offenders to heartfelt standards of right and wrong. Increased conservatism in the public-policy arena was given new life by the September 11, 2001, terrorist attacks and by widely publicized instances of sexual offenses targeting children. It continues to be sustained by the many stories of violent victimization, such as random mass shootings, that seem to be the current mainstay of the American media.

> By the start of the twenty-first century, public opinion had shifted away from seeing the criminal as an unfortunate victim of poor social and personal circumstances who is inherently protected by fundamental human and constitutional rights to seeing him or her as a dangerous social predator who usurps the rights and privileges of law-abiding citizens.

By the start of the twenty-first century, public opinion had shifted away from seeing the criminal as an unfortunate victim of poor social and personal circumstances who is inherently protected by fundamental human and constitutional rights to seeing him or her as a dangerous social predator who usurps the rights and privileges of law-abiding citizens. Reflecting the "get-tough-on-crime" attitudes of recent times, many Americans demand to know how offenders can better be held accountable for violating the criminal law. In late 2010, for example,

In 2009, U.S. Supreme Court Justice Clarence Thomas spoke to a group of high school essay contest winners in a Washington, D.C., hotel ballroom. Thomas used the occasion, which was dedicated to our nation's Bill of Rights, to point out the importance of obligations as well as rights. "Today there is much focus on our rights," said Thomas. "Indeed, I think there is a proliferation of rights." But then he went on to say, "I am often surprised by the virtual nobility that seems to be accorded those with grievances. Shouldn't there at least be equal time for our Bill of Obligations and our Bill of Responsibilities?"

The challenge for the criminal justice system today, it seems, is to balance individual rights and personal freedoms with social control and respect for legitimate authority. Years ago, during the height of what was then a powerful movement to win back control of our nation's cities and to rein in skyrocketing crime rates, the *New York Post* sponsored a conference on crime and civil rights. The keynote speaker at that conference was the mayor of New York, Rudolph W. Giuliani. In his speech, Giuliani, who sought the Republican nomination as a presidential candidate in 2008, identified the tension between personal freedoms and individual responsibilities as the crux of the crime problem then facing his city and the nation. We mistakenly look to government and elected officials, Giuliani said, to assume responsibility for solving the problem of crime when, instead, each individual citizen must become accountable for fixing what is wrong with our society. "We only see the oppressive side of authority. . . . What we don't see is that freedom is not a concept in which people can do anything they want, be anything they can be. Freedom is about authority. Freedom is about the willingness of every single human being to cede to lawful authority a great deal of discretion about what you do."

YOU DECIDE

How can we, as suggested by Justice Thomas, achieve a balance of rights and obligations in American society? What did Giuliani mean when he said, "What we don't see is that freedom is not a concept in which people can do anything they want, be anything they can be"? Is it possible to balance individual rights and personal freedoms with social control and respect for legitimate authority?

References: Adam Liptak, "Reticent Justice Opens up to a Group of Students," *New York Times*, April 13, 2009, http://www.nytimes.com/2009/04/14/us/14bar.html (accessed June 2, 2018); and Philip Taylor, "Civil Libertarians: Giuliani's Efforts Threaten First Amendment," Freedom Forum Online, http://www.freedomforum.org.

California state senators unanimously passed Chelsea's Law, a bill intended to increase prison sentences and extend parole terms for offenders who commit sex crimes against minors. The bill, named after 17-year-old Chelsea King, who was raped and murdered by a convicted sex offender earlier in 2010, was signed into law by the state's governor soon after it passed the legislature.[22] Even in an era of difficult budgetary challenges, a number of states are continuing to extend prison sentences for sex offenders, restrict where released sex offenders can live, and improve public notification of their whereabouts.[23]

Although today's financial constraints, soaring imprisonment rates, and social concerns like those identified in the story that opens this chapter have tempered the zeal of legislators to expand criminal punishments, the tension between individual rights and social responsibility still forms the basis for most policymaking activity in the criminal justice arena. Those who fight for individual rights continue to carry the banner of civil and criminal rights for the accused and the convicted, while public-order activists proclaim the rights of the victimized and call for an increased emphasis on social responsibility and criminal punishment for convicted criminals. In keeping with these realizations, the theme of this book can be stated as follows:

> There is widespread recognition in contemporary society of the need to balance (1) the freedoms and privileges of our nation's citizens and the respect accorded the rights of individuals faced with criminal prosecution against (2) the valid interests that society has in preventing future crimes, in maintaining public safety, and in reducing the harm caused by criminal activity. While the personal freedoms guaranteed to law-abiding citizens as well as to criminal suspects by the Constitution, as interpreted by the U.S. Supreme Court, must be closely guarded, the urgent social needs of communities for controlling unacceptable behavior and protecting law-abiding citizens from harm must be recognized. Still to be adequately addressed are the needs and interests of victims and the fear of crime and personal victimization often prevalent in the minds of many law-abiding citizens. It is important to recognize, however, that the drama between individual rights and public safety advocates now plays out in a tenuous economic environment characterized by financial constraints and a concern with effective public policy.

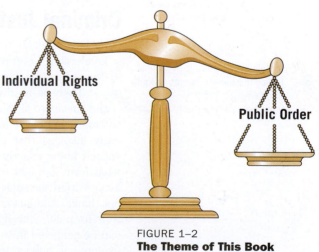

FIGURE 1–2
The Theme of This Book
Note: Balancing the concern for individual rights with the need for public order through the administration of criminal justice is the theme of this book.

Figure 1–2 represents our theme and shows that most people today who intelligently consider the criminal justice system assume one of two viewpoints. We will refer to those

▲ Demonstrators protest a 2017 executive order by President Donald Trump that banned refugees from certain Middle Eastern countries from entering the United States for 90 days. The White House argued that the order was necessary to ensure national security; protestors claimed that it violated the spirit of a free America. How can the balance between individual rights and public safety be guaranteed?

Albin Lohr-Jones/Pacific Press/Alamy Stock Photo

individual-rights advocate
One who seeks to protect personal freedoms within the process of criminal justice.

social order
The condition of a society characterized by social integration, consensus, smooth functioning, and lack of interpersonal and institutional conflict. Also, a lack of social disorganization.

public-order advocate
One who believes that under certain circumstances involving a criminal threat to public safety, the interests of society should take precedence over individual rights.

3 Explain the relationship of criminal justice to general concepts of equity and fairness.

who seek to protect personal freedoms and civil rights within society, and especially within the criminal justice process, as **individual-rights advocates**. Those who suggest that, under certain circumstances involving criminal threats to public safety, the interests of society (especially crime control and **social order**) should take precedence over individual rights will be called **public-order advocates**. Recently, retired U.S. Supreme Court Justice Sandra Day O'Connor summed up the differences between these two perspectives by asking, "At what point does the cost to civil liberties from legislation designed to prevent terrorism [and crime] outweigh the added security that the legislation provides?"[24] We seek to look at ways in which the individual-rights and public-order perspectives can be balanced to serve both sets of needs. Hence, you will find our theme discussed throughout this text and within "Freedom or Safety?" boxes.

Criminal Justice and Basic Fairness

In a 1967 speech that Martin Luther King, Jr., made before the Southern Christian Leadership Conference, he said, "The arc of the moral universe is long; but it bends toward justice."[25]

There is no denying that the word *justice* is powerful, and speaks to all Americans. The reality, however, is that *justice* is an elusive term. Although most listeners came away inspired that night, few who heard the 1967 speech knew exactly what justice might mean and what form it might eventually take. Even to those living within the same society, *justice* means different things. And just as *justice* can be an ambiguous term for politicians, it is not always clear how justice can be achieved in the criminal justice system. For example, is "justice for all" a reasonable expectation of today's—or tomorrow's—system of criminal justice? The answer is unclear because individual interests and social needs often diverge. From the perspective of a society

The arc of the moral universe is long, but it bends towards justice.

—Martin Luther King, Jr. (1929–1968)

or an entire nation, justice can look very different than it does from the perspective of an individual or a small group of people. Because of this dilemma, we now turn our attention to the nature of justice.

British philosopher and statesman Benjamin Disraeli (1804–1881) defined **justice** as "truth in action," and noted that it also encompasses the principle of moral rightness. A popular dictionary defines it as "conformity to truth, fact, or reason."[26] **Social justice** is a concept that embraces all aspects of civilized life. It is linked to notions of fairness and to cultural beliefs about right and wrong. Questions of social justice can arise about relationships between individuals, between parties (such as corporations and agencies of government), between the rich and the poor, between the sexes, between ethnic groups and minorities—between social connections of all sorts. In the abstract, the concept of social justice embodies the highest personal and cultural ideals.

Civil justice, one component of social justice, concerns itself with fairness in relationships between citizens, government agencies, and businesses in private matters, such as those involving contractual obligations, business dealings, hiring, and equality of treatment. **Criminal justice**, on the other hand, refers to the aspects of social justice that concern violations of the criminal law. As mentioned earlier, community interests in the criminal justice sphere demand the apprehension and punishment of law violators. At the same time, criminal justice ideals extend to the protection of the innocent, the fair treatment of offenders, and fair play by the agencies of law enforcement, including courts and correctional institutions.

Criminal justice, ideally speaking, is "truth in action" within the process that we call the **administration of justice**. It is therefore vital to remember that justice, in the truest and most satisfying sense of the word, is the ultimate goal of criminal justice—and of the day-to-day practices and challenges that characterize the American criminal justice system. Reality, unfortunately, typically falls short of the ideal and is severely complicated by the fact that justice seems to wear different guises when viewed from diverse vantage points. To some people, the criminal justice system and criminal justice agencies often seem biased in favor of the powerful. The laws they enforce seem to emanate more from well-financed, organized, and vocal interest groups than they do from any idealized sense of social justice. As a consequence, disenfranchised groups, those who do not feel as though they share in the political and economic power of society, are often wary of the agencies of justice, seeing them more as enemies than as benefactors.

On the other hand, justice practitioners, including police officers, prosecutors, judges, and corrections officials, frequently complain that their efforts to uphold the law garner unfair public criticism. The realities of law enforcement and of "doing justice," they say, are often overlooked by critics of the system who have little experience in dealing with offenders and victims. We must recognize, practitioners often tell us, that those accused of violating the criminal law face an elaborate process built around numerous legislative, administrative, and organizational concerns. Viewed realistically, although the criminal justice process can be fine-tuned to take into consideration the interests of ever-larger numbers of people, it rarely pleases everyone. The outcome of the criminal justice process in any particular case is a social product, and like any product that is the result of group effort, it must inevitably be a patchwork quilt of human emotions, reasoning, and concerns.

Whichever side we choose in the ongoing debate over the nature and quality of criminal justice in America, it is vital that we recognize the plethora of pragmatic issues involved in the administration of justice while also keeping a clear focus on the justice ideal.[27] Was justice done, for example, in the 2005 criminal trial of pop music superstar Michael Jackson on charges of child molestation, or after Jackson's death in the 2011 trial of his personal physician, Conrad Murray? Was justice served in the case of Casey Anthony, who authorities say killed her young daughter; or in the case of Jody Arias or George Zimmerman? Similarly, we might ask whether justice was done in the 2014 trial (and 2017 resentencing) of Oscar Pistorius, the South African Paralympic athlete known as the "Blade Runner," who was convicted of the shooting death of his model girlfriend, Reeva Steenkamp.[28] While answers to such questions may reveal a great deal about the American criminal justice system, they also have much to say about the perspectives of those who provide them.

justice
The principle of fairness; the ideal of moral equity.

social justice
An ideal that embraces all aspects of civilized life and that is linked to fundamental notions of fairness and to cultural beliefs about right and wrong.

civil justice
The civil law, the law of civil procedure, and the array of procedures and activities having to do with private rights and remedies sought by civil action. Civil justice cannot be separated from social justice because the justice enacted in our nation's civil courts reflects basic American understandings of right and wrong.

criminal justice
In the strictest sense, the criminal (penal) law, the law of criminal procedure, and the array of procedures and activities having to do with the enforcement of this body of law. Criminal justice cannot be separated from social justice because the justice enacted in our nation's criminal courts reflects basic American understandings of right and wrong.

administration of justice
The performance of any of the following activities: detection, apprehension, detention, pretrial release, post-trial release, prosecution, adjudication, correctional supervision, or rehabilitation of accused persons or criminal offenders.[ii]

Follow the author's tweets about the latest crime and justice news @schmalleger

American Criminal Justice: System and Functions

The Consensus Model

criminal justice system

The aggregate of all operating and administrative or technical support agencies that perform criminal justice functions. The basic divisions of the operational aspects of criminal justice are law enforcement, courts, and corrections.

consensus model

A criminal justice perspective that assumes that the system's components work together harmoniously to achieve the social product we call *justice*.

We have been discussing a **criminal justice system**[29] consisting of the component agencies of police, courts, and corrections. Each of these components can, in turn, be described in terms of its functions and purpose (Figure 1–3).

> **4** Describe the American criminal justice system in terms of its three major components and their respective functions.

The systems perspective on criminal justice is characterized primarily by its assumption that the various parts of the justice system work together by design to achieve the wider purpose we have been calling *justice*. Hence, the systems perspective on criminal justice generally encompasses a point of view called the **consensus model**. The consensus model assumes that each of the component parts of the criminal justice system strives toward a common goal and that the movement of cases and people through the system is smooth because of cooperation between the various components of the system.

The systems model of criminal justice is more an analytic tool than a reality, however. An analytic model, whether in the hard sciences or in the social sciences, is simply a convention chosen for its explanatory power. By explaining the actions of criminal justice officials—such as arrest, prosecution, and sentencing—as though they were systematically related, we are able to envision a fairly smooth and predictable process.

The systems model has been criticized for implying a greater level of organization and cooperation among the various agencies of justice than actually exists. The word *system* calls to mind a near-perfect form of social organization. People today associate the idea of a system with machine-like precision in which the problems of wasted effort, redundancy, and

FIGURE 1–3

The Core Components of the American Criminal Justice System and Their Functions

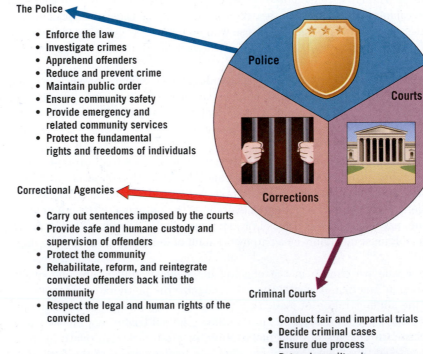

The Police

- Enforce the law
- Investigate crimes
- Apprehend offenders
- Reduce and prevent crime
- Maintain public order
- Ensure community safety
- Provide emergency and related community services
- Protect the fundamental rights and freedoms of individuals

Correctional Agencies

- Carry out sentences imposed by the courts
- Provide safe and humane custody and supervision of offenders
- Protect the community
- Rehabilitate, reform, and reintegrate convicted offenders back into the community
- Respect the legal and human rights of the convicted

Criminal Courts

- Conduct fair and impartial trials
- Decide criminal cases
- Ensure due process
- Determine guilt or innocence
- Impose sentences on the guilty
- Uphold the law
- Require fairness throughout the justice process
- Protect the rights and freedoms of anyone facing processing by the justice system
- Provide a check on the exercise of power by other justice system agencies*

*Fairness, professionalism, integrity, and impartiality are expected of all criminal justice personnel at every stage of criminal case processing, and it is a special duty of the courts to ensure that these expectations are met.

conflicting actions are quickly corrected. In practice, the justice system has nowhere near this level of perfection, and the systems model is admittedly an oversimplification. Conflicts among and within agencies are rife; individual actors within the system often do not share immediate goals; and the system may move in different directions depending on political currents, informal arrangements, and personal discretion.

🐦 Follow the author's tweets about the latest crime and justice news @schmalleger

---

CJ News
Surveillance Technology Has Been Blanketing the Nation since 9/11

▲ A Chicago Police Department surveillance camera system and microphone unit positioned high above the street. This surveillance system includes a camera, high-bandwidth wireless communication, a strobe light, and a gunshot-recognition system, all in a bulletproof enclosure. The city is installing the surveillance system to spot crimes and terrorist activity. Do such units infringe on the personal freedoms of Chicago residents?

Charles Rex Arbogast/AP Images

In the book *1984*, written more than 60 years ago, George Orwell envisioned a totalitarian regime that created an extensive surveillance network to monitor people's every move. Today, in the wake of the terrorist attacks of September 11, 2001, America has built a surveillance network that rivals that of *1984*, but without a totalitarian regime involved.

A decade after 9/11, there were an estimated 30 million surveillance cameras in the United States, says IMS Research. U.S. law enforcement is also implementing facial recognition technology, license plate readers, and gunfire alert systems. These developments prompted Jay Stanley of the American Civil Liberties Union to warn that the nation is heading toward "a total surveillance society in which your every move, your every transaction, is duly registered and recorded by some computer."

Most Americans, however, are not alarmed and actually welcome the trend. An ABC News/*Washington Post* poll showed that 71% of respondents favored increased video surveillance. In addition, courts have indicated that surveillance cameras, placed in plain view in public spaces, do not violate the Fourth Amendment, which bars governments from conducting unreasonable searches or seizures.

Technology has come a long way since surveillance cameras took small, grainy photos of two 9/11 hijackers boarding their plane at Boston's Logan Airport. Today's cameras collect and store images with many more pixels of information, making it possible to enlarge photographs and capture previously undetected details.

In 2003, the city of Chicago began building what has become one of the most extensive surveillance systems in the United States, with 2,000 cameras operated by the police department and central monitoring over additional cameras operated by the transit system, school system, and private entities.

A recent study by the Urban Institute examining the use of surveillance cameras in three Chicago neighborhoods found they reduced crime in two of the neighborhoods. In the Humboldt Park neighborhood, for example, drug-related offenses and robberies fell by nearly 33% and violent crime declined by 20%.

Chicago has spent more than $60 million on its video surveillance network. Although that cost was supplemented by federal Homeland Security grants, such systems have high maintenance costs and compete for scarce tax dollars with other law enforcement activities, such as patrolling. The Urban Institute, however, found that Chicago saved $4.30 for every dollar spent on cameras in Humboldt Park.

Chicago uses wireless cameras mounted on poles with a "pan-tilt-zoom" technology that allows operators to follow subjects and focus in on them. Officers can do this manually, but as images proliferate, law enforcement has been increasingly turning to video analytic software that can sort through thousands of pictures to look for a specific image. This involves use of sophisticated software that recognizes faces or specific shapes and colors. The same technology is also used for scanners that read license plates and automatically check the number through a direct feed with state car license databases.

Police departments across the country are also implementing new sound-wave technology to monitor gunshots. This type of system, the best known of which is Shotspotter™, requires installing sensors throughout the city that can triangulate sound waves and identify the location of the gunshot within 5 yards. The Boston Police Department spent about $1.5 million to install gunshot detection systems and spends $150,000 to $175,000 in annual maintenance fees. The city of Chicago, following the recent increase in street shootings there, is expanding its existing Shotspotter program to cover 14 square miles (up from 3 square miles), and will match information from gunshot sensors to real-time camera feeds, 9-1-1 transcripts, and arrest records. Soon, the system will be able to brighten street lights immediately after gunfire is detected.

The effectiveness of gunfire alert systems has not been independently studied. According to the manufacturer, about one-third of reports are false alarms involving backfiring cars, construction, and other urban noises. But one definite advantage is that gunshot reports arrive in 1 to 2 minutes faster than 9-1-1 calls, bringing officers to the scene more quickly. And sometimes the systems pick up gunshots that were never called in.

REFERENCES

Ann Givens, "The Chicago PD's Top Tech Officer Is Betting on Sensors and Smartphones to Help Curb Shootings," *The Trace*, January 25, 2017, https://www.thetrace.org/2017/01/chicago-homicide-rate-shotspotter-curb-shootings (accessed March 20, 2017).

Delores Handy, "Surveillance Technology Helps Boston Police Find Location of Gunfire," *WBUR*, December 23, 2011, http://www.wbur.org/2011/12/23/shotspotter.

"Surveillance Cameras Cost-Effective Tools for Cutting Crime, 3-Year Study Concludes," Urban Institute, September 19, 2011, http://www.urban.org/publications/901450.html.

FIGURE 1–4
The American Criminal
Justice Process

Investigation ▶	Warrant ▶	Arrest ▶	Booking ▶
After a crime has been discovered, evidence is gathered and follow-up investigations attempt to reconstruct the sequence of activities leading up to and including the criminal event. Efforts to identify suspects are initiated.	An arrest warrant issued by a judge provides the legal basis for an apprehension of suspects by police.	In an arrest, a person is taken into custody, limiting the arrestee's freedom. Arrest is a serious step in the process of justice. During arrest and before questioning, defendants are usually advised of their constitutional rights, or Miranda rights.	Following arrest, suspects are booked. Booking is an administrative procedure where pictures, fingerprints, and personal information are obtained. A record of the events leading up to and including the arrest is created. In some jurisdictions, DNA evidence may be collected from arrestees.

conflict model
A criminal justice perspective that assumes that the system's components function primarily to serve their own interests. According to this theoretical framework, justice is more a product of conflicts among agencies within the system than it is the result of cooperation among component agencies.

The Conflict Model

The **conflict model** provides another approach to the study of American criminal justice. The conflict model says that the interests of criminal justice agencies tend to make actors within the system self-serving. According to this model, the goals of individual agencies often conflict, and pressures for success, promotion, pay increases, and general accountability fragment the efforts of the system as a whole, leading to a criminal justice *non*system.[30]

A classic study of clearance rates by criminologist Jerome H. Skolnick provides support for the idea of a criminal justice nonsystem.[31] Clearance rates are a measure of crimes solved by the police. The more crimes the police can show they have solved, the better they look to the public they serve. Skolnick discovered an instance in which a burglar was caught red-handed during the commission of a burglary. After his arrest, the police suggested that he confess to many unsolved burglaries that they knew he had not committed. In effect they said, "Help us out, and we will try to help you out." The burglar did confess—to more than 400 other burglaries. Following the confession, the police were satisfied because they could say they had "solved" many burglaries, and the suspect was pleased as well because the police and the prosecutor agreed to speak on his behalf before the judge.

Both models have something to tell us. Agencies of justice with a diversity of functions (police, courts, and corrections) and at all levels (federal, state, and local) are linked closely enough for the term *system* to be meaningfully applied to them. On the other hand, the very size of the criminal justice undertaking makes effective cooperation between component agencies difficult. The police, for example, have an interest in seeing offenders put behind bars. Prison officials, on the other hand, are often working with extremely overcrowded facilities. They may favor early release programs for certain categories of offenders, such as those judged to be nonviolent. Who wins out in the long run might just be a matter of internal politics and quasi-official wrangling. Everyone should be concerned, however, when the goal of justice is affected, and sometimes even sacrificed, because of conflicts within the system.

American Criminal Justice: The Process

Whether part of a system or a nonsystem, the agencies of criminal justice must process the cases that come before them. An analysis of criminal justice case processing provides both a useful guide to this book and a "road map" to the criminal justice system itself. Figure 1–4 illustrates the processing of a criminal case through the federal justice system, beginning with the investigation of reported crimes. The process in most state systems is similar. Learn more about the criminal justice process at **https://www.justicestudies .com/pubs/perspectives.pdf**.

5 Describe the process of American criminal justice, including the stages of criminal case processing.

The stages illustrated in Figure 1–4 are discussed in detail at various places throughout this book. Chapter 5, "Policing: Legal Aspects," discusses investigation and arrest. All aspects of the first appearance and arraignment, including bail bonds and possible pretrial release, are discussed in Chapter 7, "The Courts." The criminal trial and its participants are described fully in Chapter 8, "The Courtroom Work Group and the Criminal Trial."

First Appearance ▶	**Preliminary Hearing** ▶	**Information or Indictment** ▶	**Arraignment** ▶
Within hours of arrest, suspects must be brought before a magistrate (a judicial officer) for a first (or initial) appearance. The judge will tell them of the charges against them, will advise them of their rights, and may provide the opportunity for bail.	The purpose of a preliminary hearing is to establish whether sufficient evidence exists against a person to continue the justice process. At the preliminary hearing, the hearing judge will seek to determine whether there is probable cause. The process provides the prosecutor with an opportunity to test the strength of the evidence.	In some states, the prosecutor may seek to continue the case against a defendant by filing an "information" with the court. Other states require an indictment be returned by a grand jury. The grand jury hears evidence presented by the prosecutor and decides whether the case should go to trial.	At arraignment, the accused stands before a judge and hears the information or indictment against him or her. Defendants are again notified of their rights and asked to enter a plea. Please include not guilty, guilty, and no contest. No contest may result in a conviction but cannot be used in trial as an admission of guilt.

FIGURE 1–4
The American Criminal Justice Process *(continued)*

Chapter 9, "Sentencing," outlines modern sentencing practices and describes the many modern alternatives to imprisonment. Chapter 10, "Probation, Parole, and Community Corrections," deals with the practice of probation and parole and with the issues surrounding it. Chapter 11, "Prisons and Jails," discusses the philosophy behind imprisonment, and Chapter 12, "Prison Life," portrays life on the inside and delineates the social structures that develop in response to the pains of imprisonment. For a critical look at the justice system, visit **http://www.360degrees.org.**

Due Process and Individual Rights

The U.S. Constitution requires that criminal justice case processing be conducted with fairness and equity; this requirement is referred to as **due process**, which, simply put, means procedural fairness.[32] It recognizes the individual rights of criminal defendants facing prosecution by a state or the federal government. Under the due-process standard, rights violations may become the basis for the dismissal of evidence or of criminal charges, especially at the appellate level. Table 1–1 outlines the basic rights to which defendants in criminal proceedings are generally entitled.

> **6** Define due process of law, including where the American legal system guarantees due process.

Due process underlies the first ten amendments to the Constitution, which are collectively known as the *Bill of Rights*. It is specifically guaranteed by the Fourth, Fifth, Sixth, and Fourteenth Amendments and is succinctly stated in the Fifth, which reads, "No person shall be . . . deprived of life, liberty, or property, without due process of law." The Fourteenth Amendment makes due process binding on the states; that is, it requires individual states to respect the due-process rights of U.S. citizens who come under their jurisdiction.

The courts, and specifically the U.S. Supreme Court, have interpreted and clarified the guarantees of the Bill of Rights. The due-process standard was set in the 1960s by the Warren Court (1953–1969), following a number of far-reaching Supreme Court decisions that affected criminal procedure. Led by Chief Justice Earl Warren, the Warren Court is remembered for its concern with protecting the innocent against the massive power of the state in criminal proceedings.[33] As a result of its tireless efforts to institutionalize the Bill of Rights, the daily practice of modern American criminal justice is now set squarely upon the due-process standard.

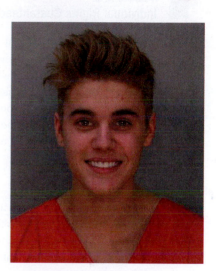

▲ Canadian singer Justin Bieber's mug shot. Bieber, 19, was arrested in Miami Beach, Florida, on January 23, 2014, and charged with speeding in a yellow Lamborghini, driving with an expired license, and driving under the influence of alcohol, marijuana, and prescription drugs. The justice system comprises three major subcomponents: police, courts, and corrections. The justice process starts when a crime has been committed and a perpetrator arrested.
David Bro/ZUMA Press, Inc./Alamy Stock Photo

The Role of the Courts in Defining Rights

Although the Constitution deals with many issues, what we have been calling *rights* are open to interpretation. Many modern rights, although written into the Constitution, would not exist in practice were it not for the fact that the U.S. Supreme Court decided, at some point in history, to recognize them in cases brought before it. In the well-known case of *Gideon* v. *Wainwright* (1963),[34] for example, the Supreme Court embraced the Sixth Amendment guarantee of a

Adjudication ►	Sentencing ►	Corrections ►	Reentry
A criminal trial may be held, or the defendant may decide to enter a guilty plea. A criminal trial involves an adversarial process that pits the prosecution against the defense. In most trials, a jury hears the evidence and decides issues of guilt or innocence, while the judge ensures the fairness of the proceedings.	After the person has been convicted, it is up to the judge to determine the punishment. Prior to sentencing, a sentencing hearing is sometimes held in which attorneys for both sides can present information to influence the judge's decision.	The corrections period begins following sentencing. Corrections involves a variety of sentences that can be imposed on a defendant.	Not everyone who has been convicted of a crime goes to prison. Probation imposes requirements or restrictions upon offenders. Offenders are required to check in with a probation officer on a regular basis.

Similarly, after a defendant has served a portion of his or her prison term he or she may be freed on parole. Like probation, parole may come with obligations and requires the offender to check in with a parole officer. |

Photo sources *(from top): Dave King/Dorling Kindersley, Ltd.; Gibsons/Shutterstock; Marc Dietrich/Shutterstock*

FIGURE 1–4
The American Criminal Justice Process (continued)

TABLE 1-1
Individual Rights Guaranteed by the Bill of Rights[a]

A right to be assumed innocent until proven guilty

A right against unreasonable searches of person and place of residence

A right against arrest without probable cause

A right against unreasonable seizure of personal property

A right against self-incrimination

A right to fair questioning by the police

A right to protection from physical harm throughout the justice process

A right to an attorney

A right to trial by jury

A right to know the charges

A right to cross-examine prosecution witnesses

A right to speak and present witnesses

A right not to be tried twice for the same crime

A right against cruel or unusual punishment

A right to due process

A right to a speedy trial

A right to assistance of counsel in criminal proceedings

A right against excessive bail

A right against excessive fines

A right to be treated the same as others, regardless of race, sex, religious preference, and other personal attributes

[a]Know Your Rights, A guide to the United States Constitution, as interpreted by the U.S. Supreme Court.

due process
A right guaranteed by the Fourth, Fifth, Sixth, and Fourteenth Amendments of the U.S. Constitution and generally understood, in legal contexts, to mean the due course of legal proceedings according to the rules and forms established for the protection of individual rights. In criminal proceedings, due process of law is generally understood to include the following basic elements: a law creating and defining the offense, an impartial tribunal having jurisdictional authority over the case, accusation in proper form, notice and opportunity to defend, trial according to established procedure, and discharge from all restraints or obligations unless convicted.

crime-control model
A criminal justice perspective that emphasizes the efficient arrest and conviction of criminal offenders.

right to a lawyer for all criminal defendants and mandated that states provide lawyers for defendants who are unable to pay for them. Before *Gideon*, court-appointed attorneys for defendants unable to afford their own counsel were practically unknown, except in capital cases and in some federal courts. After the *Gideon* decision, court-appointed counsel became commonplace, and measures were instituted in jurisdictions across the nation to select attorneys fairly for indigent defendants. It is important to note, however, that although the Sixth Amendment specifically says, among other things, that "in all criminal prosecutions, the accused shall enjoy the right . . . to have the Assistance of Counsel for his defence," it does not say, in so many words, that the state is *required* to provide counsel. It is the U.S. Supreme Court interpreting the Constitution that has said that.

The U.S. Supreme Court is very powerful, and its decisions often have far-reaching consequences. The decisions rendered by the justices in cases like *Gideon* become, in effect, the law of the land. For all practical purposes, such decisions often carry as much weight as legislative action. For this reason, we speak of "judge-made law" (rather than legislated law) in describing judicial precedents that affect the process of justice.

Rights that have been recognized by court decisions are subject to continual refinement, and although the process of change is usually very slow, new interpretations may broaden or narrow the scope of applicability accorded to constitutional guarantees.

The Ultimate Goal: Crime Control through Due Process

Two primary goals were identified in our discussion of this book's theme: (1) the need to enforce the law and to maintain public order and (2) the need to protect individuals from injustice, especially at the hands of the criminal justice system. The first of these principles values the efficient arrest and conviction of criminal offenders. It is often referred to as the **crime-control model** of justice. The crime-control model was first brought to the attention of the academic community in Stanford University law professor Herbert Packer's cogent analysis of the state of criminal justice in the late 1960s.[35] For that reason, it is sometimes referred to as *Packer's crime-control model*.

The second principle is called the **due-process model** because of its emphasis on individual rights. Due process is intended to ensure that innocent people are not convicted

CJ Exhibit
Sentinel Events

The National Institute of Justice (NIJ), an arm of the U.S. Department of Justice, recently unveiled a new framework for improving the criminal justice system, and for keeping it true to the ideal of justice that underpins it. That framework is built around the concept of a **sentinel event**, or problematic justice system outcomes, whose study could benefit from an evidence-based (or scientific) approach. The evidence-based approach to criminal justice is discussed in this chapter. NIJ defines sentinel event as "a bad outcome that no one wants repeated and that signals the existence of underlying weaknesses in the system." Sentinel events are especially significant because they can lead to the public's loss of confidence in the system, and because of the perceived injustices that they create.

Read the entire report on sentinel event reviews at **https://justicestudies.com/pubs/sentinel.pdf**.

Source: Mending Justice: Sentinel Event Reviews (Washington, D.C.: National Institute of Justice, 2014).

of crimes; it is a fundamental part of American criminal justice. It requires a careful and informed consideration of the facts of each individual case. Under the due-process model, police are required to recognize the rights of suspects during arrest, questioning, and handling. Similarly, prosecutors and judges must recognize constitutional and other guarantees during trial and the presentation of evidence.

The dual goals of crime control and due process are often assumed to be opposing goals. Indeed, some critics of American criminal justice argue that the practice of justice is too often concerned with crime control at the expense of due process. Other analysts of the American scene maintain that our type of justice coddles offenders and does too little to protect the innocent. Although it is impossible to avoid ideological conflicts like these, we can think of the American system of justice as representative of *crime control through due process*—that is, as a system of **social control** that is fair to those whom it processes. This model of *law enforcement infused with the recognition of individual rights* provides a workable conceptual framework for understanding the American system of criminal justice.

For intriguing in-depth coverage of crime and justice in America today, as seen through the eyes of victims, offenders, and professional justice system participants, see **https://www.newyorker.com/news/news-desk/we-are-witnesses-portrait-of-crime-and-punishment-in-america-today.** The same videos can also be accessed at **https://www.themarshallproject.org/witnesses.**

Evidence-Based Practice in Criminal Justice

In 2011, John H. Laub, then director of the National Institute of Justice (NIJ), called for the creation of a "culture of science and research within the institute."[36] What that means, said Laub, "is embracing empirical data, embracing transparency and also embracing a critical perspective."

Science, Laub continued, challenges conventional wisdom and has the ability to evaluate programs and strategies to show what works in the area of criminal justice. The NIJ, said Laub, should be thought of "as a science agency." You can view Laub's comments online at **https://tinyurl.com/ydxuzlyw**.

Describe the role of evidence-based practice in contemporary criminal justice.

As the word is used here, *evidence* does not refer to evidence of a crime but means, instead, findings that are supported by studies. Hence, **evidence-based practice** refers to crime-fighting strategies that have been scientifically tested and are based on social science research. Scientific research has become a major element in the increasing professionalization of criminal justice, both as a career field and as a field of study. As Laub recognized, there is a strong call today within criminal justice policymaking circles for the application of evidence-based practice throughout the justice field.

Based on experts' assessment of the evidence and studies, programs included on CrimeSolutions.gov are rated as either "effective," "promising," or "no effects." As Chapter 4 of this text points out, evidence-based practices can be expected to play an expanded role in policymaking and in the administration of criminal justice in the years to come. For additional insight into some of the issues facing criminal justice policymakers today, read the U.S. Department of Justice's "Smart on Crime" report at **https://www.justicestudies.com/pubs/smartoncrime.pdf**.

due-process model
A criminal justice perspective that emphasizes individual rights at all stages of justice-system processing.

sentinel event
A bad outcome that no one wants repeated and that signals the existence of underlying weaknesses in the system.

social control
The use of sanctions and rewards within a group to influence and shape the behavior of individual members of that group. Social control is a primary concern of social groups and communities, and it is their interest in the exercise of social control that leads to the creation of both criminal and civil statutes.

Follow the author's tweets about the latest crime and justice news @schmalleger

evidence-based practice
Crime-fighting strategies that have been scientifically tested and are based on social science research.

The Start of Academic Criminal Justice

The study of criminal justice as an academic discipline began in this country in the late 1920s, when August Vollmer (1876–1955), then chief of police in Berkeley, California, persuaded the University of California to offer courses on the subject.[37] Vollmer was joined by his former student Orlando W. Wilson (1900–1972) and by William H. Parker (who later served as chief of the LAPD from 1950 to 1966) in calling for increased professionalism in police work through better training.[38] Largely as a result of Vollmer's influence, early criminal justice education was practice oriented; it was a kind of extension of on-the-job training for working practitioners. Hence, in the early days of the discipline, criminal justice students were primarily focused on the application of general management principles to the administration of police agencies. Criminal justice came to be seen as a practical field of study concerned largely with issues of organizational effectiveness.

By the 1960s, however, police training came to be augmented by criminal justice education[39] as students of criminal justice began to apply the techniques of social scientific research—many of them borrowed from sister disciplines, such as **criminology**, sociology, psychology, and political science—to the study of all aspects of the justice system. Scientific research into the operation of the criminal justice system was encouraged by the 1967 President's Commission on Law Enforcement and Administration of Justice, which influenced passage of the Safe Streets and Crime Control Act of 1968. The Safe Streets Act led to the creation of the National Institute of Law Enforcement and Criminal Justice, which later became the National Institute of Justice (NIJ). As a central part of its mission, the NIJ continues to support research in the criminal justice field through substantial funding for scientific explorations into all aspects of the discipline, and it funnels much of the $3 billion spent annually by the U.S. Department of Justice to local communities to help fight crime. Now, almost 100 years after its beginning as a field of study, criminal justice is being revitalized by an evidence-based approach to its subject matter (described earlier). Former Assistant Attorney General Robinson put it this way: "Justice professionals have been collecting, analyzing, and using evidence for centuries—in laboratories and courtrooms. As financial realities demand more innovative approaches, social science research is forming the basis for new programs in areas ranging from reentry to victim services. Evidence has found a new home: in the field."[40]

Multiculturalism and Social Diversity in Criminal Justice

Multiculturalism describes a society that is home to a multitude of different cultures, each with its own set of norms, values, and routine behaviors. Although American society today is truly multicultural, composed of a wide variety of racial and ethnic heritages, diverse religions, incongruous values, disparate traditions, and distinct languages, multiculturalism in America is not new. For thousands of years before Europeans arrived in the Western Hemisphere, tribal nations of Native Americans each spoke their own language, were bound to customs that differed significantly from one another, and practiced a wide range of religions. European immigration, which began in earnest in the seventeenth century, led to greater **social diversity** still. Successive waves of immigrants, along with the slave trade of the early and mid-nineteenth century,[41] brought a diversity of values, beliefs, and patterns of behavior to American shores that frequently conflicted with those of prevailing cultures. Differences in languages and traditions fed the American melting pot of the late nineteenth and early twentieth centuries and made effective communication between groups difficult.

The face of multiculturalism in America today is quite different than it was in the past, largely because of relatively high birth rates among some minority populations and the huge but relatively recent immigration of Spanish-speaking people from Mexico, Cuba, Central America, and South America. Part of that influx consists of substantial numbers of undocumented immigrants who have entered the country illegally and who, because of experiences in their home countries, may have a special fear of police authority and a general distrust of the law. Such fears make members of this group hesitant to report being victimized, and their

---

Follow the author's tweets about the latest crime and justice news @schmalleger

criminology
The scientific study of the causes and prevention of crime and the rehabilitation and punishment of offenders.

multiculturalism
The existence within one society of diverse groups that maintain unique cultural identities while frequently accepting and participating in the larger society's legal and political systems.[iii] *Multiculturalism* is often used in conjunction with the term *diversity* to identify many distinctions of social significance.

social diversity
Differences between individuals and groups in the same society, including differences based on culture, race, religion, ethnicity, age, gender identity, and disabilities.

justice reinvestment
A data-driven approach to criminal justice reform that examines and addresses justice system expenditures and population drivers in order to generate cost savings that are then reinvested in high-performing public safety strategies.

sustainable justice
Criminal laws and criminal justice institutions, policies, and practices that achieve justice in the present without compromising the ability of future generations to have the benefits of a just society.

Evidence-based practices can be expected to play an ever-increasing role in policymaking and in the administration of criminal justice in the years to come.

8 Explain how multiculturalism and social diversity present challenges to and opportunities for the American system of criminal justice.

EVIDENCE-BASED JUSTICE REINVESTMENT
Data-Driven, Cost-Efficient Criminal Justice

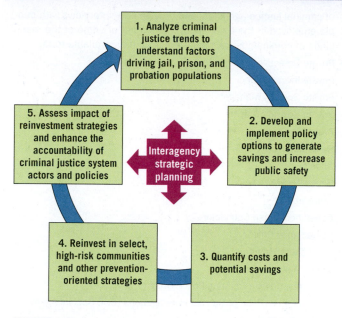

1. Analyze criminal justice trends to understand factors driving jail, prison, and probation populations

2. Develop and implement policy options to generate savings and increase public safety

3. Quantify costs and potential savings

4. Reinvest in select, high-risk communities and other prevention-oriented strategies

5. Assess impact of reinvestment strategies and enhance the accountability of criminal justice system actors and policies

Interagency strategic planning

FIGURE 1–5
**The Justice Reinvestment Decision-Making Process.
What Is Justice Reinvestment?**

Source: Bureau of Justice Assistance.

Two of the most recent and promising practices to have emerged in criminal justice in recent years are (1) justice reinvestment strategies and (2) evidence-based practices. Increased budgetary restraints over the past few years have forced state and local governments to make some hard choices about expenditures. As government revenues declined as a result of a drop in taxable income, less consumer spending, lower property values, and fewer licensing fees, officials in many locales have been forced to reduce expenditures and to curb services. Criminal justice agencies were not immune to the impact of budget cuts, and many found themselves looking for ways to offer quality services at a lower cost. It was out of that environment that the Justice Reinvestment Initiative (JRI) was born. **Justice reinvestment** is a data-driven approach to criminal justice reform that examines and addresses justice system expenditures and population drivers in order to generate cost savings that are then reinvested in high-performing public safety strategies. The JRI found important support at the federal level when the Bureau of Justice Assistance announced a JRI initiative under which state governments could apply for seed money to be used to explore reinvestment strategies, and gauge the probability of their success, while providing accountability and transparency in their operations.

The second answer to today's justice system challenges can be found in evidence-based practices – meaning programs and procedures that have proven their effectiveness through the

application of rigorous social scientific analysis. The phrase "evidence-based" is now commonly used in the justice arena, where new and existing programs are being analyzed to see what works, and which are the most cost-effective. Both evidence-based criminal justice and justice reinvestment will be discussed (and defined) in greater detail later in this chapter.

Today, the federal JRI provides participating states with a means for all state government branches and other stakeholders to work together to identify and implement results-oriented, evidence-based justice systems reform. In other words, federal funding allows states to examine their unique law enforcement needs, their sentencing and correctional systems, and their courts, in order to make better-informed and cost-effective decisions about treatment, programs, and justice system resources. Savings from these reforms are then reinvested in high-performing public safety strategies. To date, 30 states have used federal JRI funding to take a comprehensive look at their criminal justice systems. The JRI cycle is illustrated in Figure 1–5.

Both evidence-based and justice reinvestment efforts are facilitated by U.S. Department of Justice website located at **http://crimesolutions.gov**. The site, run by the Washington, D.C.–based National Institute of Justice (NIJ), has been described by federal officials as a "single, credible, online resource to inform practitioners and policymakers about what works in criminal justice, juvenile justice, and crime victim services."

Once criminal justice programs have been selected for review, experts working with the NIJ analyze available research documenting the program's effectiveness and cost-efficiency. Programs are then scored on **CrimeSolutions.gov** according to established criteria and identified as either (1) effective, (2) promising, or (3) no effect. Where evidence on a program is insufficient or inconsistent, it receives no ranking. As of this writing, 33% of programs reviewed have been scored as "effective," whereas another 57% were identified as "promising."

Finally, the concept of **sustainable justice** was advanced by Melissa Hickman Barlow, in her 2012 presidential address to the Academy of Criminal Justice Sciences. Sustainable justice, said Barlow, can be defined as "criminal laws and criminal justice institutions, policies, and practices that achieve justice in the present without compromising the ability of future generations to have the benefits of a just society." Sustainable justice, in other words, refers to criminal justice practices and institutions that are affordable now, and into the future. Visit the topics page of **CrimeSolutions.gov** at **http://www.crimesolutions.gov/topics .aspx** to learn more about the programs being evaluated.

References: CrimeSolutions.gov; Melissa Hickman Barlow, "Sustainable Justice: 2012 Presidential Address to the Academy of Criminal Justice Sciences," *Justice Quarterly*, Vol. 30, No. 1 (2013), pp. 1–17; USDOJ press release, "Justice Department Announces $17.5 Million in Grants to Support Correctional Reform, Enhance Public Safety," September 13, 2016 (accessed February 10, 2017); and Georgia Department of Corrections, "Justice Reinvestment in Public Safety," http://www.dcor.state.ga.us/sites/default/files/Justice_Reinvestment.pdf (accessed March 5, 2017).

undocumented status makes them easy prey for illegal scams involving extortion, blackmail, and documentation crimes. Learn more about immigration and crime via **http://www.npr.org/2013/03/08/173642807/does-crime-drop-when-immigrants-move-in**.

Diversity characterizes both immigrant and U.S.-born individuals. Census Bureau statistics show that people identifying themselves as white account for 71% of the U.S. population—a percentage that has been dropping steadily for at least the past 40 years. People of Hispanic origin constitute approximately 12% of the population and are the fastest-growing group in the country. Individuals identifying themselves as African American make up another 12% of the population, and people of Asian and Pacific Island origin make up almost 4% of the total. Native Americans, including American Indians, Eskimos, and Aleuts, account for slightly less

CJ Careers
Careers in Criminal Justice

Throughout this book, you will find a number of "Career Profile" boxes showcasing individuals currently working in the justice field. These boxes highlight job opportunities within various kinds of criminal justice agencies, and provide brief interviews with people employed in the field. Following is a list of some of the many kinds of criminal justice career opportunities available today:

Arson/Fire Investigator

Bailiff

Bounty Hunter

Computer Forensic Technician

Correctional Officer

Correctional Treatment Specialist

Court Clerk

Court Reporter

Crime Laboratory Analyst

Crime Prevention Specialist

Crime Scene Investigator

Crime Scene Technician

Criminal Investigator

Criminalist

Criminologist

Criminology Researcher/Research Associate

Deputy Sheriff

Electronic Crime Scene Investigator

Federal Bureau of Investigation (FBI) Forensic Accountant

Federal Bureau of Investigation (FBI) Special Agent

Federal Protective Service (FPS) Officer

Fish and Game Warden

Forensic Nurse

Forensic Psychologist

Forensic Science Technician

Fraud Investigator

Gaming Surveillance Officer

Highway Patrol Officer

Homeland Security Investigator

Information Security Manager

Judge

Juvenile Probation Officer

K-9 Officer

Lawyer/Attorney

Legal Clerk

Loss Prevention Specialist (retail)

Magistrate

Motorcycle Officer

National Security Agency (NSA) Police

Native American Tribal Police Officer

Nuclear Security Officer

Paralegal

Park Ranger

Parole Officer

Penologist

Police Detective

Police Dispatcher

Police Officer

Police Sniper

Private Detective

Private Investigator

Private Security Manager

Private Security Officer

Probation Officer

Railroad Police

Sheriff

Social Worker

State Trooper

Substance Abuse Counselor

Surveillance Officer

SWAT Team Member

Transit Authority Police

University/College Campus Police Officer

U.S. Air Force Office of Special Investigations (OSI) Special Agent

U.S. Air Marshal

U.S. Army Criminal Investigator (CID)

U.S. Army Military Police Officer

U.S. Bureau of Alcohol, Tobacco, Firearms and Explosives (ATF) Special Agent

U.S. Bureau of Indian Affairs (BIA) Corrections Officer

U.S. Bureau of Indian Affairs (BIA) Drug Enforcement Special Agent

U.S. Bureau of Indian Affairs (BIA) Investigator

U.S. Bureau of Indian Affairs (BIA) Police Officer

U.S. Bureau of Reclamation Security, Safety, and Law Enforcement Officer

U.S. Coast Guard (USCG) Compliance Officer

U.S. Coast Guard (USCG) Sea Marshal

U.S. Customs and Border Protection (CBP) Special Agent

U.S. Department of Agriculture (USDA) Compliance Officer

U.S. Department of Agriculture (USDA) Criminal Investigator

U.S. Department of Agriculture (USDA) Investigative Attorney

U.S. Department of Homeland Security Investigator

U.S. Department of State Civilian Response Corps Team Member

U.S. Department of State Diplomatic Security Officer

U.S. Department of Veterans Affairs (VA) Police

U.S. Drug Enforcement Agency (DEA) Special Agent

U.S. Fish and Wildlife Service Division of Refuge Law Enforcement Officer

U.S. Immigration and Customs Enforcement (ICE) Special Agent

U.S. Internal Revenue Service (IRS) Special Agent

U.S. Marine Corps Criminal Investigator

U.S. Marine Corps Military Police Officer

U.S. Marshal

U.S. Navy Criminal Investigator (NCIS)

U.S. Navy Law Enforcement Officer

U.S. Navy Security Officer

U.S. Park Police

U.S. Secret Service Special Agent

U.S. Secret Service Uniformed Division Officer

U.S. Transportation Security Administration (TSA) Screener

than 1% of all Americans.[42] Statistics like these, however, are only estimates, and their interpretation is complicated by the fact that surveyed individuals may be of mixed race. Nonetheless, it is clear that American society today is ethnically and racially quite diverse.

Race and ethnicity are only buzzwords that people use when they talk about multiculturalism. After all, neither race nor ethnicity determines a person's values, attitudes, or behavior. Just as there is no uniquely identifiable "white culture" in American society, it is a mistake to think that all African Americans share the same values or that everyone of Hispanic descent honors the same traditions or even speaks Spanish.

Multiculturalism, as the term is used today, is but one form of diversity. Taken together, these two concepts—multiculturalism and diversity—encompass many distinctions of social significance. The broad brush of contemporary multiculturalism and social diversity draws attention to variety along racial, ethnic, subcultural, generational, faith, economic, and gender lines. Lifestyle diversity is also important. The fact that influential elements of the wider society are less accepting of some lifestyles than others doesn't mean that such lifestyles aren't recognized from the viewpoint of multiculturalism. It simply means that, at least for now, some lifestyles are accorded less official acceptability than others. As a result, certain lifestyle choices, even within a multicultural society that generally respects and encourages diversity, may still be criminalized, as in the case of polygamy.

Multiculturalism and social diversity will be discussed in various chapters throughout this textbook, along with the related areas of international and comparative criminal justice. For now, it is sufficient to recognize that the diverse values, perspectives, and behaviors characteristic of various groups within society have a significant impact on the justice system and that anyone who works in that system should be expected to have a significant level of **cultural competence**. Whether it is the confusion that arises from a police officer's commands to a non-English-speaking suspect, the need for interpreters in the courtroom, a deep-seated distrust of the police in some minority communities, a lack of willingness among some immigrants to report crime, the underrepresentation of women in criminal justice agencies, or some people's irrational suspicions of Arab-Americans, social diversity and multiculturalism present special challenges to the everyday practice of criminal justice in America. Finally, as we shall see, the demands and expectations placed on justice agencies in multicultural societies involve a dilemma that is closely associated with the theme of this text: how to protect the rights of individuals to self-expression while ensuring social control and the safety and security of the public.

For an overview of cultural competence as it relates to the justice system, see **https://justicestudies.com/pubs/competence.pdf.**

> The demands and expectations placed on justice agencies in multicultural societies involve the dilemma of how to protect the rights of individuals to self-expression while ensuring social control and the safety and security of the public.

cultural competence
The ability to interact effectively with people of different cultures. Cultural competence helps to ensure that the needs of all community members are addressed.

◄ A group of immigrants who have just completed taking the pledge of allegiance during a naturalization ceremony in Washington, D.C. American society is multicultural, composed of a wide variety of racial and ethnic heritages, diverse religions, incongruous values, disparate traditions, and distinct languages. What impact does the multicultural nature of our society have on the justice system?
Jim Lo Scalzo/EPA/Shutterstock

Summary

WHAT IS CRIMINAL JUSTICE?

- The American experience with crime during the last half century has been especially influential in shaping the criminal justice system of today. Although crime waves have come and gone, some events during the past century stand out as especially significant, including a spurt of widespread organized criminal activity associated with the Prohibition years of the early twentieth century, the substantial increase in "traditional" crimes during the 1960s and 1970s, the threat to the American way of life represented by illicit drugs around the same time, the terrorist attacks of September 11, 2001, and the ongoing threat from radical Islam.

- The theme of this book is that of individual rights versus public order. As this chapter points out, the personal freedoms guaranteed to law-abiding citizens as well as to criminal suspects by the Constitution must be closely guarded. At the same time, the urgent social needs of communities for controlling unacceptable behavior and protecting law-abiding citizens from harm must be recognized. This theme is represented by two opposing groups: individual-rights advocates and public-order advocates. The fundamental challenge facing the practice of American criminal justice is in achieving efficient and cost-effective enforcement of the laws while simultaneously recognizing and supporting the legal rights of suspects and the legitimate personal differences and prerogatives of individuals.

- Even though justice may be an elusive concept, it is important to recognize that criminal justice is tied closely to notions of procedural fairness, which include personal and cultural beliefs about equity and fairness. Although community interests in the administration of criminal justice demand the apprehension and punishment of law violators, criminal justice ideals extend to the protection of the innocent, the fair treatment of offenders, and fair play by justice administration agencies. Procedural justice, a concept that is crucial to effective criminal justice practices, refers to the implementation of fair and equitable procedures in the administration of justice, and helps to ensure the legitimacy of justice organizations and their acceptance by the people they serve.

- In this chapter, we described the process of American criminal justice as a system with three major components—police, courts, and corrections—all of which can be described as working together toward a common goal. We warned, however, that a systems viewpoint is useful primarily for the simplification that it provides. A more realistic approach to understanding criminal justice may be the nonsystem approach. As a nonsystem, the criminal justice process is depicted as a fragmented activity in which individuals and agencies within the process have interests and goals that at times coincide but often conflict.

- The stages of criminal case processing include investigation, the issuance of a warrant, arrest, booking, first appearance in court, defendant's preliminary hearing, return of an indictment by the grand jury or filing of an information by the prosecutor, arraignment of the defendant before the court, adjudication or trial, sentencing, and corrections. As a field of study, corrections includes jails, probation, imprisonment, and parole.

- The principle of due process, which underlies the first ten amendments to the U.S. Constitution, is central to American criminal justice. Due process (also called *due process of law*) means procedural fairness and requires that criminal case processing be conducted with fairness and equity. The ultimate goal of the criminal justice system in America is achieving crime control through due process.

- The study of criminal justice as an academic discipline began in this country in the late 1920s and is well established today. Scientific research has become a major element in the increasing professionalization of criminal justice, and there is a strong call today for the application of evidence-based practices in the justice field. Evidence-based practices are crime-fighting strategies that have been scientifically tested and that are based on social science research.

- American society today is a multicultural society, composed of a wide variety of racial and ethnic heritages, diverse religions, incongruous values, disparate traditions, and distinct languages. Multiculturalism complicates the practice of American criminal justice because there is rarely universal agreement in our society about what is right or wrong or about what constitutes "justice." As such, multiculturalism presents both challenges and opportunities for today's justice practitioners.

QUESTIONS FOR REVIEW

1. Describe the American experience with crime during the last half century. What noteworthy criminal incidents or activities occurred during that time, and what social and economic conditions might have produced them?

2. What is the theme of this book? According to that theme, what are the differences between the individual-rights perspective and the public-order perspective?

3. What is justice? What aspects of justice does this chapter discuss? How does criminal justice relate to other, wider notions of equity and fairness?

4. What are the main components of the criminal justice system? How do they interrelate? How might they conflict?

5. List the stages of case processing that characterize the American system of criminal justice, and describe each stage.

6. What is meant by due process of law? Where in the American legal system are guarantees of due process found?

7. What is the role of research in criminal justice? What is evidence-based practice? How can research influence crime control policy?

8. What is multiculturalism? What is social diversity? What impact do multiculturalism and diversity have on the practice of criminal justice in contemporary American society?

The Crime Picture

> *No one way of describing crime describes it well enough.*
>
> —President's Commission on Law Enforcement and Administration of Justice

Learning Objectives

After reading this chapter, you should be able to:

Ralph/PacificCoastNews/Newscom

Introduction

A few years ago, officials with the Dickson (Tennessee) County Sheriff's Office reported that the department had been extorted into paying a fee to unknown cybercriminals after ransomware had locked detectives and deputies out of more than 72,000 files stored on the agency's computers. Ransomware is malicious software that takes over personal computers and forces their users to pay a fee in order to regain control. After consulting with the FBI and military security experts, the department was forced to pay $500 in Bitcoins to recover the data. Jeff McCliss, the agency's Information Technology director, told *Police Magazine*, "It's a very bad feeling to be the victim instead of the investigator."[1] A video describing the event was posted on the Web at **http://www.policemag.com/channel/technology/news/2014/11/13/video-tennessee-sheriff-s-office-pays-ransom-for-case-files.aspx**.

As this story shows, a wide range of new forms of crime are victimizing all areas of contemporary society—and they are not always easy to solve, or even to discover!

This chapter has a dual purpose. First, it provides a statistical overview of crime in contemporary America by examining information on reported and discovered crimes. Second, it identifies special categories of crime that are of particular interest today, including crime against women, crime against the elderly, hate crime, corporate and white-collar crime, organized crime, gun crime, drug crime, cybercrime, and terrorism.

Although we will look at many crime statistics in this chapter, it is important to remember that statistical aggregates of reported crime, whatever their source, do not reveal the lost lives, human suffering, lessened productivity, and reduced quality of life that crime causes. Unlike the fictional characters on TV crime shows, real-life crime victims as well as real-life offenders lead intricate lives—they have families, hold jobs, and dream dreams. As we examine the crime statistics, we must not lose sight of the people behind the numbers.

Crime Data and Social Policy

Crime statistics provide an overview of criminal activity. If used properly, a statistical picture of crime can serve as a powerful tool for creating social policy. Decision makers at all levels, including legislators, other elected officials, and administrators throughout the criminal justice system, rely on crime data to analyze and evaluate existing programs, to fashion and design new crime-control initiatives, to develop funding requests, and to plan new laws and crime-control legislation. Many "get-tough" policies, such as the three-strikes movement that swept the country during the 1990s, were based in large part on the measured ineffectiveness of existing programs to reduce the incidence of repeat offending.

However, some people question just how comprehensive and objective—and therefore how useful—crime statistics are. Social events, including crime, are complex and difficult to quantify. Even the decision of which crimes should be included and which excluded in statistical reports is itself a judgment reflecting the interests and biases of policymakers. Moreover, definitions of particular crimes used by data-gathering strategies are generally not the same as statutory descriptions. Finally, as mentioned in Chapter 1, the number of Internet-based offenses and crimes making use of other forms of high technology is constantly increasing, and statistical reporting programs that were designed years ago may not fully count such crimes. As famed criminologist Herbert Packer once observed, "We can have as much or as little crime as we please, depending on what we choose to count as criminal."[2]

We should also note that public opinion about crime is not always realistic. As well-known criminologist Norval Morris points out, the news media do more to influence public perceptions of crime than any official data do.[3] During the 4-year period (in the mid-1990s) covered by Morris's study, for example, the frequency of crime stories reported in the national media increased fourfold. During the same time period, crime was at the top of the list in subject matter

Public safety personnel in Sacramento, California, work on laptops. This chapter opens with a story about a sheriff's office that was victimized by ransomware. What other new forms of crime can you think of that were not known a generation ago?
Rich Pedroncelli/AP Images

> A wide range of new forms of crime are victimizing all areas of contemporary society—and they are not always easy to solve, or even to uncover!

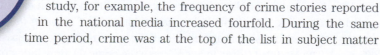
Follow the author's tweets about the latest crime and justice news @schmalleger

> How much crime we have depends on what we count as criminal.

covered in news stories at both the local and national levels. The irony, says Morris, is that "the grossly increasing preoccupation with crime stories came at a time of steadily declining crime and violence." However, as Morris adds, "aided and abetted by this flood of misinformation, the politicians, federal and state and local, fostered the view that the public demands our present 'get-tough' policies."[4]

The Collection of Crime Data

Nationally, crime statistics come from two major sources: (1) the FBI's **Uniform Crime Reporting Program** (also known today as the UCR/NIBRS Program), which produces an annual overview of major crime titled *Crime in the United States*; and (2) the **National Crime Victimization Survey (NCVS)** of the **Bureau of Justice Statistics (BJS)**. The most widely quoted numbers purporting to describe crime in America today probably come from the UCR/NIBRS Program, although the statistics it produces are based largely on *reports* to the police by victims of crime.

A third source of crime data is offender self-reports based on surveys that ask respondents to reveal any illegal activity in which they have been involved. Offender self-reports are not discussed in detail in this chapter because surveys utilizing them are not national in scope and are not undertaken regularly. Moreover, offenders are often reluctant to accurately report ongoing or recent criminal involvement, making information derived from these surveys somewhat unreliable and less than current. However, the available information from offender self-reports reveals that serious criminal activity is considerably more widespread than most "official" surveys show (Figure 2–1).

Other data sources also contribute to our knowledge of crime patterns throughout the nation. One important source is the *Sourcebook of Criminal Justice Statistics*—an compilation of national information on crime and on the criminal justice system. *Sourcebook* data were produced by the BJS, and made available on the Web through the auspices of the State University of New York at Albany. The National Institute of Justice (NIJ), the primary research arm of the U.S. Department of Justice; the Office of Juvenile Justice and Delinquency Prevention (OJJDP); the Federal Justice Statistics Resource Center; and the National Victims Resource Center provide still more information on crime patterns. The *Sourcebook* is available online at **http://www.albany.edu/sourcebook**.

The UCR/NIBRS Program
Development of the UCR Program

1 Describe the FBI's UCR/NIBRS Program, including its purpose, its history, and what it tells us about crime in the United States today.

In 1930, Congress authorized the U.S. attorney general to survey crime in America, and the Federal Bureau of Investigation (FBI) was designated to implement the program. In short order, the bureau built on earlier efforts by the International Association of Chiefs of Police (IACP) to create a national system of uniform crime statistics. As a practical measure, the IACP had recommended the use of readily available information, and so it was that citizens' crime reports to the police became the basis of the FBI's plan.[5]

During its first year of operation, the FBI's UCR Program received reports from 400 cities in 43 states; 20 million people were covered by that first comprehensive survey. Today, approximately 18,000 law enforcement agencies provide crime information for the program, with data coming from city, county, university and college, tribal, and state departments. To ensure uniformity in reporting, the FBI has developed standardized definitions of offenses and terminologies used in the program. Numerous publications, including the *Uniform Crime Reporting Handbook* and the *Manual of Law Enforcement Records*, are supplied to participating agencies, and training for effective reporting is available through FBI-sponsored seminars and instructional literature.

Following the IACP recommendations, the original UCR Program was designed to permit comparisons over time through construction of a **Crime Index**. As originally constituted, the index summed the occurrences of seven major offenses—murder, forcible rape, robbery, aggravated assault, burglary, larceny-theft, and motor vehicle theft—and expressed the result as a crime rate based on population. In 1979, by congressional mandate, an eighth offense—arson—was added to the index. The Crime Index, first published in *Crime in the United States* in 1960, was the title used for a simple aggregation of the seven main offense classifications (called Part I offenses). The Modified Crime Index refers to the original Crime Index offenses plus arson.

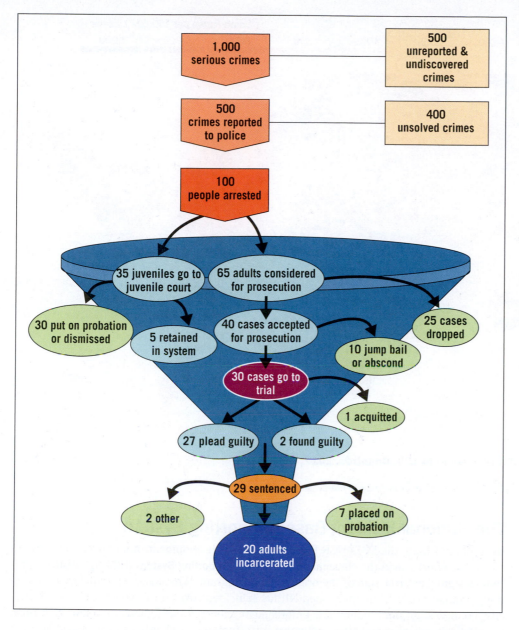

FIGURE 2–1
The Criminal Justice Funnel
Source: Adapted from Brian A. Reaves, *Felony Defendants in Large Urban Counties* (U.S. Department of Justice).

Over the years, however, concern grew that the Crime Index did not provide a clear picture of criminality because it was skewed by the offense with the highest number of reports—typically larceny-theft. The sheer volume of larceny-theft offenses overshadowed more serious but less frequently committed offenses, skewing perceptions of crime rates for jurisdictions with high numbers of larceny-thefts but low numbers of serious crimes such as murder and rape. In 2004, the FBI's Criminal Justice Information Services (CJIS) Advisory Policy Board officially discontinued the use of the Crime Index in the UCR/NIBRS Program and in its publications and directed the FBI to instead publish simple violent crime totals and property crime totals until a more viable index could be developed.[6]

Although work to develop such an index is still ongoing, UCR/NIBRS Program crime categories continue to provide useful comparisons of specific reported crimes over time and between jurisdictions (Figure 2–2). It is important to recognize, as you read through the next few pages, that today's UCR/NIBRS Program categories tend to parallel statutory definitions of criminal behavior, but they are not legal classifications—only conveniences created for statistical reporting purposes. Because many of the offense definitions used in this textbook are derived from official UCR/NIBRS Program terminology, you should remember that these definitions may differ from statutory definitions of crime.

Follow the author's tweets about the latest crime and justice news @schmalleger

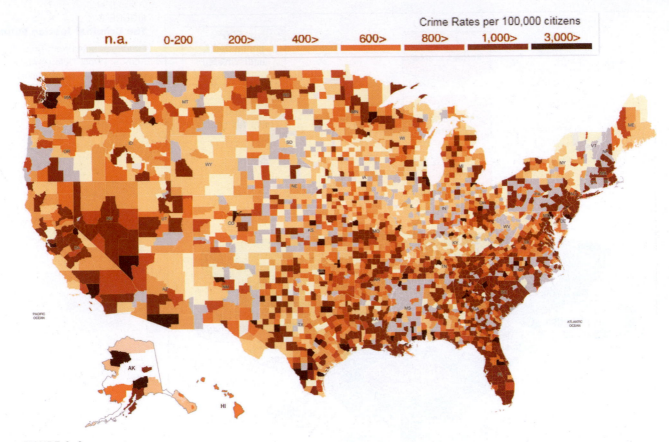

Crime Rates per 100,000 citizens

n.a.   0-200   200>   400>   600>   800>   1,000>   3,000>

FIGURE 2–2
Reported Crimes per 100,000 People by U.S. Counties, 2017.
Source: Pearson Education.
Note: Grey areas indicate areas for which complete crime data is not available.

National Incident-Based Reporting System (NIBRS)
An incident-based reporting system that collects detailed data on every single crime occurrence. NIBRS data are replacing the kinds of summary data that have traditionally been provided by the FBI's Uniform Crime Reporting Program.

The National Incident-Based Reporting System

Beginning in 1988, the FBI's UCR Program initiated development of a new national crime-collection effort called the **National Incident-Based Reporting System** (**NIBRS**). NIBRS represents a significant redesign of the original UCR Program. Whereas the original UCR system was "summary based," the enhanced NIBRS is incident driven (Table 2-1). Under NIBRS, city, county, state, and federal law enforcement agencies throughout the country furnish detailed data on crime and arrest activities at the incident level either to the individual state incident-based reporting programs or directly to the federal NIBRS Program.

NIBRS can be thought of as a significant new methodology underlying the contemporary UCR system—hence our use of the term *UCR/NIBRS* in describing today's Uniform Crime Reporting Program. Whereas the old UCR system depended on statistical tabulations of crime data, which were often little more than frequency counts, the new UCR/NIBRS system gathers many details about each criminal incident. Included among them is information on place of occurrence, weapon used, type and value of property damaged or stolen, personal characteristics of the offender and the victim, nature of any relationship between the two, and disposition of the complaint.

Under UCR/NIBRS, the traditional distinctions between Part I and Part II offenses are being replaced with 24 general offense categories made up of 52 specific crimes called Group A offenses. They are: animal cruelty, arson, assault, bribery, burglary, counterfeiting, destruction/vandalism of property, drug/narcotics offenses, embezzlement, extortion, fraud, gambling, homicide, human trafficking, kidnapping, larceny, motor vehicle theft, pornography, prostitution, receiving stolen property, robbery, sex offenses (forcible), sex offenses (nonforcible), and weapons law violations. In addition, there are 10 Group B offense categories for which only arrest data are reported. They include bad checks, vagrancy, disorderly conduct, driving under the influence, drunkenness, nonviolent family offenses, liquor-law violations, Peeping

TABLE 2-1

Differences between Traditional UCR and Enhanced UCR/NIBRS Reporting

Traditional UCR	Enhanced UCR/NIBRS
Consists of monthly aggregate crime counts	Consists of 24 "Group A" offense categories with details on offense, victim, offender, and property involved
Records one offense per incident, as determined by the hierarchy rule, which suppresses counts of lesser offenses in multiple-offense incidents	Records each offense occurring in an incident (no hierarchy rule)
Does not distinguish between attempted and completed crimes	Distinguishes between attempted and completed crimes
Collects assault information in five categories	Restructures definition of assault to include intimidation
Collects weapon information for murder, robbery, and aggravated assault	Collects weapon information for all violent offenses
Provides counts on arrests for the eight major crimes and 21 other offenses	Also provides details on 10 "Group B" offense categories
Distinguishes between personal (violent) and property crimes	General categories of crime consist of crimes against persons, property, and society
Sees robbery as a personal crime	Classifies robbery as a property crime

Source: Federal Bureau of Investigation, National Incident-Based Reporting System: Crimes against Persons, Property, and Society, https://ucr.fbi.gov/nibrs-in-brief (accessed July 30, 2018).

Tom activity, trespass, and a general category of all "other" criminal law violations. UCR/NIBRS also collects data on an expanded array of attributes involved in the commission of offenses, including whether the offender is suspected of using alcohol, drugs, or narcotics or may have used a computer in the commission of the offense.

The FBI began accepting crime data in the NIBRS format in January 1989. Although the bureau intended to have NIBRS fully in place by 1999, delays have been routine, and the NIBRS format has not yet been fully adopted.[7] Plans call for the UCR Program to transition to a NIBRS-only data format by January 1, 2021. In anticipation of the transition, BJS recently established the **National Crime Statistics Exchange (NCS-X)**, which is designed to supplement existing NIBRS data by a close sampling of 400 carefully chosen law enforcement agencies. Data from those 400 agencies will be combined with data from more than 6,000 other law enforcement agencies that currently report NIBRS data in order to produce national estimates of crime that can be analyzed in many different ways.

The goals of the innovations introduced under NIBRS are to enhance the quantity, quality, and timeliness of crime-data collection by law enforcement agencies and to improve the methodology used for compiling, analyzing, auditing, and publishing the collected data. A major advantage of UCR/NIBRS, beyond the sheer increase in the volume of data collected, is the ability that NIBRS provides to break down and combine crime offense data into specific information.[8] The latest edition of *Crime in the United States* can be viewed at **http://www.fbi.gov/stats-services/crimestats**. You can also access the UCR table-building tool at **http://ucrdatatool.gov** to create a view of crime statistics that are of special interest to you.

One other important crime data source was created with passage of the 1990 Crime Awareness and Campus Security Act, which requires colleges to publish annual security reports.[9] Most campuses share crime data with the FBI, increasing the reported national incidence of a variety of offenses. The U.S. Department of Education reported that 28 murders and 7,970 rapes occurred on U.S. college campuses in 2015. Also reported were 1,049 robberies, 2,254 aggravated assaults, 12,298 burglaries, and 3,251 motor vehicle thefts.[10] Although these numbers may seem high, it is important to realize that except for the crimes of rape and sexual assault, college students experience violence at average annual rates that are lower than those for nonstudents in the same age group.[11] Rates of rape and sexual assault do not differ statistically between students and nonstudents. For the latest campus crime information, see **https://ope.ed.gov/campussafety**.

🐦 Follow the author's tweets about the latest crime and justice news @schmalleger

National Crime Statistics Exchange (NCS-X)
A BJS-sponsored program designed to generate nationally-representative incident-based data on crimes reported to law enforcement agencies.

FIGURE 2–3
American Crime Rates:
Historical Trends

1933–1959 ▶

From 1933 to 1941, the crime rate declined from 770 to 508 offenses per every 100,000 Americans.

In 1941, crime decreased sharply based on the large numbers of young men entering the military during World War II.

Young men make up the most crime-prone segment of the population, and their removal to European and Pacific theaters of war reduced the incidence of offending throughout the country.

1960–1989 ▶

From 1960 to 1989, crime rates rose from 1,887 to 5,741 offenses per every 100,000 Americans.

Starting around 1960, crime rates began to increase based on several factors.

The end of the war brought many young men home to the U.S., and birth rates skyrocketed in the years between 1945 and 1955.

By 1960, these baby boomers had become teenagers and had entered a crime-prone age.

Also, reporting procedures were simplified and publicity surrounding crime increased the number of reports. Police agencies were becoming more professional, resulting in increased data and more accurate data collection.

Moreover, the 1960s were tumultuous years. The Vietnam War, civil rights struggles, and an influx of drugs combined to create an imbalance in society that led to an increase in crime.

| 1933 | 1937 | 1941 | 1945 | 1949 | 1953 | 1959 | 1960 | 1963 | 1967 | 1975 | 1979 | 1983 | 1989 |

Historical Trends

🐦 Follow the author's tweets about the latest crime and justice news @schmalleger

Most UCR/NIBRS information is reported as a rate of crime. Rates are computed as the number of crimes per some unit of population. National reports generally make use of large units of population, such as 100,000 people. Hence, the rate of rape reported by the UCR/NIBRS Program for 2017 was 30.7 rapes per every 100,000 inhabitants of the United States.[12] Rates allow for a meaningful comparison over areas and across time. The rate of reported rape for 1960, for example, was only about 10 per 100,000. We expect the number of crimes to increase as population grows, but rate increases are cause for concern because they indicate that reports of crime are increasing faster than the population is growing. Rates, however, require interpretation. Although there is a tendency to judge an individual's risk of victimization based on rates, such judgments tend to be inaccurate because they are based purely on averages and do not take into consideration individual life circumstances, such as place of residence, wealth, and educational level. Although rates may tell us about aggregate conditions and trends, we must be very careful when applying them to individual cases.

Since the FBI's UCR Program began, there have been three major shifts in crime rates—and we now seem to be witnessing the beginning of a fourth (Figure 2–3). The first occurred during the early 1940s, when crime decreased sharply due to the large number of young men who entered military service during World War II. Young males make up the most crime-prone segment of the population, and their deployment overseas did much to lower crime rates at home. From 1933 to 1941, the Crime Index declined from 770 to 508 offenses per every 100,000 members of the American population.[13]

The second noteworthy shift in offense statistics was a dramatic increase in most forms of crime between 1960 and the early 1990s. Several factors contributed to the increase in reported crime during this period. One was also linked to World War II. With the end of the war and the return of millions of young men to civilian life, birth rates skyrocketed between 1945 and 1955, creating a postwar baby boom. By 1960, the first baby boomers were teenagers—and had entered a crime-prone age. This disproportionate number of young people produced a dramatic increase in most major crimes.

Other factors contributed to the increase in reported crime during the same period. Modified reporting requirements made it less stressful for victims to file police reports, and the publicity associated with the rise in crime sensitized victims to the importance of reporting. Crimes that might have gone undetected in the past began to figure more prominently in official statistics. Similarly, the growing professionalization of some police departments

1990–2017 ▶ 2018–present

From 1990 to 2017, crime rates dropped from 5,897 to 2,758 offenses per every 100,000 Americans.

Strict laws, an expanded justice system, and increased police funding for personnel and for crime-fighting technologies are cited as reasons for the drop in crime. Other changes beyond the control of the police may have played a role as well and include economic expansion and an aging population. During the 1990s, unemployment decreased by 36% and likely contributed to the decline in crime rates.

Some cities have recently experienced increases in traditional forms of crime, but online criminal activity is difficult to assess using existing measures.

A fourth shift in rates of traditional crime may be about to begin, and online forms of crime may soon overshadow even those numbers. Economic uncertainty, a growing number of ex-convicts back on the streets as well as an increase in teen populations and gang activity may soon lead to sustained increases in traditional crime.

1990   1994   1997   2001   2005   2009   2017   2018   2019   2020

Source: Frank Schmalleger, Criminal Justice: A Brief Introduction, 12e, © 2018. Pearson Education, Inc., New York, NY. Photo sources (from left to right); Everett Collection/SuperStock; Everett Collection/SuperStock; Micheal Matthews/Police Images/Alamy Stock Photo; Jim West/Alamy Stock Photo

resulted in greater and more accurate data collection, making some of the most progressive departments appear to be associated with the largest crime increases.[14]

The 1960s were tumultuous years. The Vietnam War, a vibrant civil rights struggle, the heady growth of secularism, a dramatic increase in the divorce rate, diverse forms of "liberation," and the influx of psychedelic and other drugs all combined to fragment existing institutions. Social norms were blurred, and group control over individual behavior declined substantially. The "normless" quality of American society in the 1960s contributed greatly to the rise in crime.

From 1960 to 1989, crime rates rose from 1,887 to 5,741 offenses per every 100,000 U.S. residents. In the early 1980s, when postwar boomers began to age out of the crime-prone years and American society emerged from the cultural drift that had characterized the previous 20 years, crime rates leveled out briefly. Soon, however, an increase in drug-related criminal activity led crime rates—especially violent crime rates—to soar once again.

A third major shift came with a significant decline in the rates of most major crimes being reported between 1990 and 2017. During those years, the rate of reported crime dropped from 5,897 to 2,758 offenses per every 100,000 residents—sending it down to levels not seen since 1975. The U.S. Department of Justice suggests various reasons for the decline:[15]

- A coordinated, collaborative, and well-funded national effort to combat crime, beginning with the Safe Streets Act of 1968 and continuing through the USA PATRIOT Act of 2001
- Stronger, better-prepared criminal justice agencies, resulting from increased spending by federal and state governments on crime-control programs
- The growth in popularity of innovative police programs, such as community policing (see Chapter 4)
- A strong victims' movement and enactment of the 1984 federal Victims of Crime Act (see Chapter 9) and the 1994 Violence against Women Act (discussed later in this chapter), which established the Office for Victims of Crime in the U.S. Department of Justice
- Sentencing reform, including various "get-tough-on-crime" initiatives (see Chapter 9)
- A substantial growth in the use of incarceration (see Chapter 11) due to changes in sentencing law practice (see Chapter 9)
- Advances in forensic science and enforcement technology, including video surveillance, the increased use of real-time communications, the growth of the Internet, and the advent of DNA evidence (see Chapter 9)

> A fourth shift in crime trends may be on the horizon and could lead to sustained increases in crime.

Follow the author's tweets about the latest crime and justice news @schmalleger

More important than new strict laws, an expanded justice system and police funding, and changes in crime-fighting technologies, however, may have been influential economic and demographic factors that were largely beyond the control of policymakers but that combined to produce substantial decreases in rates of crime—including economic expansion and the increased use of security cameras and surveillance equipment, along with a significant shift in demographics caused by the aging of the population. During the 1990s, unemployment decreased by 36% in the United States while the number of people ages 20 to 34 declined by 18%. Hence, it may have been the ready availability of jobs combined with demographic shifts in the population—not the official efforts of policymakers—that produced most of the decrease in crime during the 1990s and 2000s.

> Shifts in crime patterns away from more "traditional" crimes, and toward innovative forms of law violation using high technology, may mask the true face of crime in America.

Confounding matters even more, the digital age has brought with it a plethora of new criminal opportunities—many of which were inconceivable only a decade or two ago. Shifts in crime patterns away from more "traditional" crimes (like those measured by the UCR and NCVS), and toward innovative forms of law violation using high technology, may mask the true face of crime in America—leading to a mistaken sense that the total number of criminal offenses in our society is lower than it actually is. Bank robbery, for example, is a "traditional" crime and is scored by the FBI as one form of "robbery" in the crime statistics that it reports; but while bank robberies have fallen in number over the years, illicit computer attempts to access and misappropriate funds held by banks have risen significantly. Many such attempted computer heists, however, are not reportable under historical crime categories.[16]

It's important to recognize that today's law enforcement administrators often feel judged by their success in lowering crime rates. Consequently, police departments may put pressure on officers to artificially reduce crime rates through techniques such as downgrading crimes to lesser offenses when completing official paperwork. In fact, a recent study of nearly 2,000 retired NYPD officers found that the manipulation of crime reports has become a part of police culture in the NYPD.[17] Indications are that the underreporting of crime statistics by the police may be a nationwide phenomenon. Recent criticisms of police practices, however, have resulted in calls for new measures of policing effectiveness, including (1) the number of crimes averted (not arrests made) and (2) citizens' views of the police and their tactics.[18]

A fourth shift in crime trends may be on the horizon. Some think that recent economic uncertainty, a lack of well-paying jobs for unskilled workers, the growing number of ex-convicts who are back on the streets, the recent growth in the teenage population in this country, the increasing influence of gangs, copycat crimes, and the lingering social disorganization brought on by natural disasters such as Hurricane Maria and Hurricane Irma in 2017 may lead to sustained increases in crime.[19] "We're probably done seeing declines in crime rates for some time to come," says Jack Riley, director of the Public Safety and Justice Program at RAND Corporation in Santa Monica, California. "The question," says Riley, "is how strong and how fast will those rates [rise], and what tools do we have at our disposal to get ahead of the curve."[20]

The specter of frequent but random mass shootings, and a high number of inner-city murders, is also changing the face of crime in America. One recent study, for example, showed that while rates of traditional crimes have been falling, some cities are experiencing dramatically higher rates of murder. In 2015, for example, murder rates in Milwaukee increased by 76%; in

▼ Los Angeles emergency personnel working at the scene of an apparent gang-related shooting at Sunset Boulevard and Pacific Coast Highway. Some experts fear that violent crime may be starting to rise in big cities after three decades of decline. What would be the consequences for American cities if crime were to increase?

Andrew McKenzie/AP Images

St. Louis, Missouri, the rate grew by 60% while murder rates in Baltimore rose by 56%; and Houston experienced a nearly 50% increase.[21]

Finally, it is important to realize that while official U.S. crime rates may be close to multi-year lows, a number of other countries are experiencing high levels of criminal activity. Mexico, for example, where an ongoing war between the government and drug cartels has led to the deaths of more than 70,000 people and the disappearance of 27,000 more in the past 8 years, is caught up in a rapid rate of violent crime escalation.[22] Violent crime, much of it associated with tribal and political conflicts, now extends across borders in Africa, the Middle East, and parts of Europe, leading one writer to recently comment that "crime has become a global anxiety, alongside climate change, banking crises, and outbreaks of disease."[23]

UCR/NIBRS in Transition

Reports of U.S. crime data available through the UCR/NIBRS Program are going through a transitional phase as the FBI integrates more NIBRS data into its official summaries. The transition to NIBRS reporting is complicated by the fact that not only does NIBRS gather more kinds of data than the older summary UCR Program did, but the definitions used for certain kinds of criminal activity under NIBRS are different than they were under the traditional UCR Program. The standard reference publication that the FBI designates for use by police departments in scoring and reporting crimes that occur within their jurisdiction is the *Uniform Crime Reporting Handbook*, and it is the most recent edition of that handbook that guides and informs the discussion of crime statistics that you will find in the next few pages. You can access the entire 164-page *Uniform Crime Reporting Handbook* at **https://www.justicestudies.com/pubs/ucrhandbook.pdf**. A thorough review of that document shows that much of the traditional UCR summary data-reporting terminology and structure remains in place.

Figure 2–4 shows the FBI crime clock, which has long been calculated annually as a shorthand way of diagramming crime frequency in the United States. It should not be taken to imply regularity in the commission of crime.[24] Also, although the crime clock is a useful diagrammatic tool, it is not a rate-based measure of criminal activity and does not allow easy comparisons over time. Seven major crimes are included in the figure: murder, rape, robbery, aggravated assault, motor vehicle theft, burglary, and larceny-theft.

The crime clock distinguishes between two categories of offenses: violent crimes and property crimes. **Violent crimes** (also called *personal crimes*) include murder, rape, robbery, and aggravated assault. It is worth noting that in California and in some other states, almost all violent crimes are referred to as "strikable," as two- and three-strikes laws in those states can result in long prison terms for anyone who commits two or more such crimes. **Property crimes** are motor vehicle theft, burglary, arson (which is not shown in the crime clock), and larceny-theft. Other than the use of this simple dichotomy, UCR/NIBRS data do not provide a clear measure of the severity of the crimes they cover.

Like most UCR/NIBRS statistics, crime clock data are based on crimes reported to (or discovered by) the police. For a few offenses, the numbers reported are probably close to the numbers that actually occur. Murder, for example, is a crime that is difficult to conceal because of its seriousness. Even when the crime is not immediately discovered, the victim is

violent crime
A UCR/NIBRS summary offense category that includes murder, rape, robbery, and aggravated assault.

property crime
A UCR/NIBRS summary offense category that includes burglary, larceny-theft, motor vehicle theft, and arson.

clearance rate
A measure of investigative effectiveness that compares the number of crimes reported or discovered to the number of crimes solved through arrest or other means (such as the death of the suspect).

2017 CRIME CLOCK STATISTICS	
A Violent Crime occurred every	**24.6 seconds**
One Murder every	30.5 minutes
One Rape every	3.9 minutes
One Robbery every	1.7 minutes
One Aggravated Assault every	39.0 seconds
A Property Crime occurred every	**4.1 seconds**
One Burglary every	22.6 seconds
One Larceny-theft every	5.7 seconds
One Motor Vehicle Theft every	40.9 seconds

FIGURE 2–4
The FBI Crime Clock, Which Shows the Frequency of the Commission of Major Crimes in 2017
Source: 2017 Crime in United States Federal Bureau of Investigations. Retrieved from https://ucr.fbi.gov/crime-in-the-u.s/2017/crime-in-the-u.s.-2017/topic-pages/crime-clock.

often quickly missed by family members, friends, and associates, and someone files a "missing persons" report with the police. Auto theft is another crime that is reported in numbers similar to its actual rate of occurrence, probably because insurance companies require that the victim file a police report before they will pay the claim.

A commonly used term in today's UCR/NIBRS reports is **clearance rate**, which refers to the proportion of reported crimes that have been "solved." Clearances are judged primarily on the basis of arrests and do not involve judicial disposition. Once an arrest has been made, a crime is regarded as having been "cleared" for reporting purposes. Exceptional clearances (sometimes called *clearances by exceptional means*) can result when law enforcement authorities believe they know who committed a crime but cannot make an arrest. The perpetrator may, for example, have fled the country or died.

Table 2-2 summarizes UCR/NIBRS program statistics for 2017.

Part I Offenses

Murder

murder
The unlawful killing of a human being. *Murder* is a generic term that in common usage may include first- and second-degree murder, manslaughter, involuntary manslaughter, and other similar offenses.

Murder is the unlawful killing of one human being by another.[25] UCR/NIBRS statistics on murder describe the yearly incidence of all willful and unlawful homicides within the United States. Included in the count are all cases of nonnegligent manslaughter that have been reported to or discovered by the police. Not included in the count are suicides, justifiable homicides (i.e., those committed in self-defense), deaths caused by negligence or accident, and murder attempts. In 2017, some 14,249 murders came to the attention of police departments across the United States. First-degree murder is a criminal homicide that is

Follow the author's tweets about the latest crime and justice news @schmalleger

---

Freedom or Safety? You Decide
A Dress Code for Bank Customers?

Hoodies, or hooded sweatshirts, made the national news following the fatal shooting of Trayvon Martin in Florida in 2012. Martin, a black 17-year-old, was wearing a hoodie when he apparently confronted George Zimmerman, a Hispanic community-watch volunteer working in a gated community. Following the shooting, hooded sweatshirts became a symbol of racial profiling, and inspired protests, including one by U.S. Representative Bobby Rush (D-Ill.), who wore sunglasses and a hoodie on the House floor.

Even before the Martin shooting, however, dark glasses, hooded sweatshirts, and hats had been banned by some banks—which called them the "uniform of choice" for bank robbers. In an effort to thwart an increase in robberies, many banks post requests for customers to remove hats, hoods, and sunglasses before entering financial establishments. In 2009, for example, Houston-area banks began putting up signs requiring that customers remove even their cowboy hats—a request that some saw as going too far. Since Sterling Bank, with 60 branches across Texas, asked customers to follow such rules, none of its branches has been robbed. Graham Painter, a Sterling Bank spokesman, said, "We don't want our regular customers thinking that we're telling them how they ought to dress. But . . . it seems reasonable and not too much to ask to give us an advantage over the robber."

Not all banks, however, are following the trend. "I think what you have to weigh is convenience to customers versus the added benefits in terms of identifying suspects with a measure like this," said Melodie Jackson, spokeswoman for Citizens Bank of Massachusetts. "We're taking a very close look at things."

Nonetheless, dress code signs are becoming commonplace at banks throughout the country, and it is likely that this request will soon become the *de facto* standard at banking and other financial venues.

YOU DECIDE

Are bank "dress codes" asking too much of customers? How would you feel about doing business with a bank that posts requests like those described here? Would you discriminate against certain members of the public if they dressed in ways that you considered suspicious? If so, what type of clothing would arouse your suspicions?

▲ Many banks and some retail establishments require customers to remove hats, hoodies, and sunglasses before entering their place of business. Do you see such requests as limitations on personal rights and freedoms, or as reasonable and necessary precautions?
David Kilpatrick/Alamy Stock Photo

References: Cindy Horswell, "Some Banks Strike Hats, Sunglasses from Dress Code," *Houston Chronicle*, April 23, 2009; Michael S. Rosenwald and Emily Ramshaw, "Banks Post Dress Code to Deter Robbers," *Boston Globe*, July 13, 2002; and "Missouri Banks Attempt Unmasking Robbers," *Police Magazine* Online, October 25, 2002, http://www.policemag.com/t_newspick .cfm?rank571952 (accessed August 8, 2018).

TABLE 2-2
Major Crimes Known to the Police, 2017

Offense	Number	Rate per 100,000	Clearance Rate (%)
Personal/Violent Crimes			
Murder	17,284	5.3	61.6
Rape	99,856	30.7	34.5
Robbery	319,356	98.0	29.7
Aggravated assault	810,825	248.9	53.3
Property Crimes			
Burglary	1,401,840	430.4	13.5
Larceny-theft	5,519,107	1,694.4	19.2
Motor vehicle theft	773,139	237.4	13.7
Arson[a]	36,660	13.2	21.7
U.S. Total	**8,978,067**	**2,758.3**	

[a] Arson can be classified as either a property crime or a violent crime, depending on whether personal injury or loss of life results from its commission. It is generally classified as a property crime, however. Arson statistics are incomplete for 2017, and are not included in other annual crime rate calculations in this chapter.

Source: Data from Federal Bureau of Investigation, Crime in the United States, 2017 (Washington, D.C.: U.S. Department of Justice, 2018).

Part I offenses
A traditional UCR/NIBRS offense group used to report murder, rape, robbery, aggravated assault, burglary, larceny-theft, motor vehicle theft, and arson, as defined under the FBI's UCR/NIBRS Program.

planned; second-degree murder is an intentional and unlawful killing but one that is generally unplanned and that happens "in the heat of the moment."

Murder is the smallest numerical category in the **Part I offenses**. The 2017 murder rate was 5.3 homicides for every 100,000 residents of the United States. Generally, murder rates peak in the warmest months; in 2017, the greatest number of murders occurred in August. Geographically, murder is most common in the southern states. However, because those states are also the most populous, a meaningful comparison across regions of the country is difficult.

Age is no barrier to murder. Statistics for 2017 reveal that 167 infants (children under the age of one) were victims of homicide, as were 266 people age 75 and over.[26] Young adults between ages 25 and 29 were the most likely to be murdered. Murder perpetrators were also most common in the 20–24 year old age group.

Firearms are the weapon used most often to commit murder. In 2017, guns were used in 72.6% of all killings. Handguns outnumbered shotguns almost 18 to 1 in the murder statistics, with rifles used almost as often as shotguns. Knives were used in approximately 10.5% of all murders. Other weapons included explosives, poison, narcotics overdose, blunt objects like clubs, and hands, feet, and fists.

Only 9.7% of all murders in 2017 were perpetrated by offenders classified as "strangers." In 49.95% of all killings, the relationship between the parties had not yet been determined. The largest category of killers was officially listed as "acquaintances," which probably includes a large number of former friends. Arguments cause most murders, but murders also occur during the commission of other crimes, such as robbery, rape, and burglary. Homicides that follow from other crimes are more likely to be impulsive rather than planned.

Murders may occur in sprees, which "involve killings at two or more locations with almost no time break between murders."[27] One spree killer, John Allen Muhammad, 41, part of the "sniper team" that terrorized the Washington, D.C., area in 2002, was arrested along with 17-year-old Jamaican immigrant Lee Boyd Malvo in the random shootings of 13 people in Maryland, Virginia, and Washington, D.C., over a three-week period. Ten of the victims died.[28] In 2003, Muhammad and Malvo were convicted of capital murder; Muhammad was sentenced to die, and Malvo was given a second sentence of life without the possibility of parole in 2006 after he struck a deal with prosecutors in an effort to avoid the death penalty.[29]

In contrast to spree killing, mass murder entails "the killing of four or more victims at one location, within one event."[30] Recent mass murderers have included Nikolas Cruz (who killed 17 high school students in an attack on a high school in Parkland, Florida in 2018); Stephen Paddock (who killed 58 people and injured 851 more on the Las Vegas Strip in 2017);

> The public is properly obsessed with safety. Of industrialized countries, the United States has the highest rate of violent crime.
>
> —Bob Moffitt, Heritage Foundation

▲ A memorial to the victims of the October 1, 2017, Las Vegas mass shooting, which claimed the lives of 58 people, and injured 851 others. The shooter, 64-year-old Stephen Paddock, fired thousands of rounds from the 32nd floor of the Mandalay Bay Resort and Casino into a nearby music festival crowd of over 30,000.

Gene Bievens/Zuma Press/Alamy Stock

rape (UCR/NIBRS)
Unlawful sexual intercourse achieved through force and without consent. More specifically, penetration, no matter how slight, of the vagina or anus with any body part or object, or oral penetration by a sex organ of another person, without the consent of the victim. *Statutory rape* differs from other types of rape in that it generally involves nonforcible sexual intercourse with a minor. Broadly speaking, the term *rape* has been applied to a wide variety of sexual attacks and may include same-sex rape and the rape of a male by a female. Some jurisdictions refer to same-sex rape as sexual battery.

sexual battery
The intentional and wrongful physical contact with a person, without his or her consent, that entails a sexual component or purpose.

Omar Mateen (who killed 49 at an Orlando nightclub, and wounded more than 50 others in 2016); Newtown, Connecticut, shooter Adam Lanza (who killed 20 first-graders and six adults at Sandy Hook Elementary School); Aurora, Colorado, movie theater shooter, James Eagan Holmes (who killed 12 people and injured 58 others); Seung-Hui Cho, who killed 33 people and wounded 20 on the campus of Virginia Polytechnic Institute and State University in Blacksburg, Virginia, in 2007; Timothy McVeigh, who was the antigovernment Oklahoma City bomber; Mohammed Atta and the terrorists he led, who carried out the September 11, 2001 attacks.

Yet another kind of murder, serial murder, happens over time and officially "involves the killing of several victims in three or more separate events."[31] In cases of serial murder, days, months, or even years may elapse between killings.[32] Some of the more infamous serial killers of recent years are the confessed 43-year-old Gary, Indiana, sex-killer, Darren Vann; Wichita BTK murderer, Dennis Rader;[33] Jeffrey Dahmer, who received 936 years in prison for the murders of 15 young men (and who was himself later murdered in prison); Ted Bundy, who killed many college-age women; Henry Lee Lucas, now in a Texas prison, who confessed to 600 murders but later recanted (yet was convicted of 11 murders and linked to at least 140 others);[34] Ottis Toole, who was Lucas's partner in crime; cult leader Charles Manson, who is still serving time for ordering followers to kill seven Californians, including famed actress Sharon Tate; Andrei Chikatilo, the Russian "Hannibal Lecter," who killed 52 people, mostly schoolchildren;[35] David Berkowitz, also known as the "Son of Sam," who killed six people on lovers' lanes around New York City; Theodore Kaczynski, the Unabomber, who perpetrated a series of bomb attacks on "establishment" figures; and Seattle's Green River killer, Gary Leon Ridgway, a 54-year-old painter who in 2003 confessed to killing 48 women in the 1980s. Learn more about serial murder from the FBI at **https://justicestudies.com/pubs/serial.pdf**; and read the FBI's 2018 study of the pre-attack behaviors of active shooters at **https://www.justicestudies.com/pubs/active.pdf**.

Federal homicide laws changed in 2004 when President George Bush signed the Unborn Victims of Violence Act.[36] The act, which passed the Senate by only one vote, made it a separate federal crime to "kill or attempt to kill" a fetus "at any stage of development" during an assault on a pregnant woman. The fetal homicide statute, better known as Laci and Conner's Law, after homicide victims Laci Peterson and her unborn son (whom she had planned to name Conner), specifically prohibits the prosecution of "any person for conduct relating to an abortion for which the consent of the pregnant woman, or a person authorized by law to act on her behalf, has been obtained."

Because murder is such a serious crime, it consumes substantial police resources. Consequently, over the years, the offense has shown the highest clearance rate of any major crime. More than 61.6% of all homicides were cleared in 2017. Learn more about murder trends in the United States from the Bureau of Justice Statistics at **https://justicestudies.com/pubs/murdertrends.pdf**.

Rape

The terms **rape** and forcible rape are often applied to a wide variety of sexual attacks, including same-sex rape and the rape of a male by a female. Under the FBI's UCR program, the term *forcible rape* historically meant the carnal knowledge of a female forcibly and against her will.[37] Today rape is described in gender-neutral fashion by the UCR program as "penetration, no matter how slight, of the vagina or anus with any body part or object, or oral penetration by a sex organ of another person, without the consent of the victim."[38] The FBI began using that terminology in 2012, after it abandoned an earlier definition of a phrase that allowed only for rape of a female. Previously, violent sexual crimes committed against men were termed **sexual battery**, sexual assault, or something similar under the FBI's reporting program. Statutory rape, where no force is involved but the victim is younger than the age of consent, is not included in rape statistics, but attempts to commit rape by force or the threat of force are.

Rape is the least reported of all violent crimes. Estimates are that only one out of every four rapes is reported to the police. An even lower figure was reported by a

1992 government-sponsored study, which found that only 16% of rapes were reported.[39] The victim's fear of embarrassment was the most commonly cited reason for the failure to report. In the past, many states routinely permitted a person's past sexual history to be revealed in detail in the courtroom if a trial ensued. But the past few decades have seen many changes that have facilitated the accurate reporting of rape and other sex offenses. Trained female detectives often interview female victims, physicians have become better educated in handling the psychological needs of victims, and sexual histories are no longer regarded as relevant in most trials.

UCR/NIBRS statistics show 99,856 reported rapes for 2017, an increase over the number of offenses reported for the previous year. Rape reports, however, have generally risen, even in years when reports of other violent crimes have been on the decline. The offense of rape follows homicide in its seasonal variation. The greatest numbers of rapes in 2017 were reported in the hot summer months, whereas the lowest numbers were recorded in January, February, November, and December.

Rape is frequently committed by a person known to the victim, as in the case of **date rape**. Victims may be held captive and subjected to repeated assaults.[40] In the crime of heterosexual rape, any female—regardless of age, appearance, or occupation—is a potential victim. Through personal violation, humiliation, and physical battering, rapists seek a sense of personal aggrandizement and dominance. Victims of rape often experience a lessened sense of personal worth; feelings of despair, helplessness, and vulnerability; a misplaced sense of guilt; and a lack of control over their personal lives.

Contemporary wisdom holds that rape is often a planned violent crime that serves the offender's need for power rather than sexual gratification.[41] The "power thesis" has its origins in the writings of feminist Susan Brownmiller, who argued in 1975 that the primary motivation leading to heterosexual rape is the rapist's desire to "keep women in their place" and to preserve gender inequality through violence.[42] Although many writers on the subject of heterosexual rape have generally accepted the power thesis, at least one study has caused some to rethink it. In a classic survey of imprisoned serial rapists, for example, Dennis Stevens found that "lust" was reported most often (41%) as "the primary motive for predatory rape."[43]

Statistically speaking, most rapes are committed by acquaintances of the victims and often betray a trust or friendship. Date rape, which falls into this category, appears to be far more common than previously believed. Two decades ago, the growing number of rapes perpetrated with the use of the "date rape drug" Rohypnol alarmed law enforcement personnel. Rohypnol is an illegal pharmaceutical substance that is virtually tasteless. Available on the black market, it dissolves easily in drinks and can leave anyone who consumes it unconscious for hours, making them vulnerable to sexual assault.

Rape within marriage, which has not always been recognized as a crime, is now an area of concern in American criminal justice, and many laws have been enacted during the past few decades to deter it. Similarly, even though some state laws on rape continue to encompass only the rape or attempted rape of a female by a male, they also criminalize the sexual abuse of a male by a female. When it occurs, this offense is typically charged as statutory rape, or falls under some other state statute.

date rape
The unlawful forced sexual intercourse with a person, without his or her consent, that occurs within the context of a dating relationship. Date rape, or acquaintance rape, is a subcategory of rape that is of special concern today.

Follow the author's tweets about the latest crime and justice news @schmalleger

Robbery

Robbery is a personal crime involving a face-to-face confrontation between victim and perpetrator. It is often confused with burglary, which is primarily a property crime. (We'll examine burglary later.) Weapons may be used in robbery, or strong-arm robbery may occur through intimidation. Purse snatching and pocket picking are not classified as robbery by the UCR/NIBRS Program but are included under the category of larceny-theft.

In 2017, as Figure 2–5 shows, individuals were the most common target of robbers (shown under the category of "street/highway" robbery). Banks, gas stations, convenience stores, and other businesses were the second most common target, with residential robberies accounting for only 16.0% of the total. In 2017, 319,356 robberies were reported to the police. Of that number, 37.2% were street or highway robberies, meaning that the crime occurred outdoors, most commonly as the victim was walking in a public place. Strong-arm robberies, in which the victim was intimidated but no weapon was used, accounted for 41.5%

robbery (UCR/NIBRS)
The unlawful taking or attempted taking of property that is in the immediate possession of another by force or violence and/or by putting the victim in fear. Armed robbery differs from unarmed, or strong-arm, robbery in that it involves a weapon. Contrary to popular conceptions, highway robbery does not necessarily occur on a street—and rarely in a vehicle. The term *highway robbery* applies to any form of robbery that occurs outdoors in a public place.

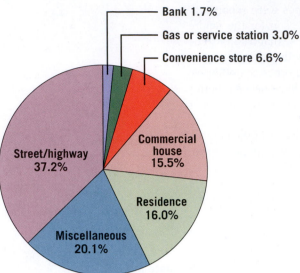

FIGURE 2–5
Robbery Types, 2017

Source: FBI, *Crime in the United States, 2017* (Washington, D.C.: U.S. Department of Justice, 2018).

🐦 Follow the author's tweets about the latest crime and justice news @schmalleger

assault (UCR/NIBRS)
An unlawful attack by one person upon another. Historically, *assault* meant only the attempt to inflict injury on another person; a completed act constituted the separate offense of *battery*. Under modern statistical usage, however, attempted and completed acts are grouped together under the generic term *assault*.

of the total robberies reported. Guns were used in 40.6% of all robberies, and knives were used in 8.1%. Armed robbers are dangerous; guns are actually discharged in 20% of all robberies.[44] The FBI considers bank robbery to be a special category of robbery. The locations of recent bank robberies in the United States are shown in Figure 2–6. Visit the FBI's bank robbery page at **https://bankrobbers.fbi .gov** to find the clickable map, which expands to describe each recorded instance.

When a robbery occurs, the UCR Program would score the event as one robbery, even when a number of victims were robbed during the event. With the move toward incident-driven reporting, however, the revised UCR/NIBRS Program now makes data available on the number of individuals robbed in each incident. UCR statistics on crime follow what's known as the *hierarchy rule* and show only the most serious offense that occurred during a particular episode. Hence, robberies are often hidden when they occur in conjunction with more serious crimes. For example, 3% of robbery victims are also raped, and a large number of homicide victims are robbed.[45]

Robbery is primarily an urban offense, and most arrestees are young male minorities. The robbery rate in cities in 2017 was 261.3 per every 100,000 inhabitants, whereas it was much lower in rural areas. Of those arrested for robbery in 2017, 44% were white, 54% were black, and 2% were other minorities.[46]

Aggravated Assault

In April 2006, Arthur J. McClure, 22, of Fort Myers, Florida, was arrested when he allegedly took the head off of an Easter Bunny costume that he was wearing and punched Erin Johansson of Cape Coral, Florida, after the young mother apparently became upset that a mall photo set was closing 10 minutes early.[47] The incident was witnessed by dozens of people, including many children who had gathered to have their pictures taken with the rabbit. McClure, who denied he struck Johansson, was fired after the incident.

Assaults are of two types: simple (misdemeanor) and aggravated (felonious). For statistical reporting purposes, simple assaults typically involve pushing and shoving.

FIGURE 2–6
Bank Robberies in the United States—Recent Locations
Source: Wanted bank robbers, Federal Bureau of Investigations. Retrieved from https://bankrobbers.fbi.gov/.

CJ | News
"Flash Robs"—A Social Media Phenomenon

`3/11/2012 20:03:28`

Richard Sennott/Newscom

▲ The immediate aftermath of a flash robbery showing young people streaming out of a store that they just attacked. How has social media changed the nature of criminal activity in this country?

"Flash mobs," where coordination over social media brings together large groups of people for spontaneous events, have irked police because they may be disruptive. Now, however, police are facing a more serious problem: "flash robs" and "flash fights" where posts on social media direct people—often teenagers—to go to shopping malls to steal and brawl. During the 2016 Christmas season, for example, hundreds of teenagers, their actions coordinated through Snapchat, took public transportation to the Philadelphia Mills Mall, forced their way inside, and began fighting. Security guards were overwhelmed, and Philadelphia police officers were called to the scene. At least four teenagers were arrested, including two who attacked an officer. Another four teenagers were arrested the next night when the mob returned and fights again broke out in the same mall. Similar events took place at dozens of malls across the country before the chaos ended.

Flash robberies take place when social media channels are used to bring people together for the purpose of looting or stealing merchandise. Some flash rob videos have been posted to YouTube showing scores of jubilant teenagers overwhelming stores and security personnel. When the mob leaves, the shelves are bare, and store displays destroyed.

This is "mob behavior but it has some premeditation, which is a new thing," said Read Hayes, a University of Florida research scientist, in an interview with the *Wall Street Journal*.

According to a recent poll by the National Retail Federation, 10% of storeowners reported they were victims of flash robs in the past 12 months, and half of them said they experienced two to five incidents in that period. Social media or texting was involved in at least 42% of cases where suspects were apprehended, and 83% of incidents involved juveniles.

Because flash robs involve many people, store employees can do little to stop them and may even suffer injury. Participants have been known to punch an employee on the way out. In addition to the loss of merchandise, retailers are concerned about losing customers. "A frenzied group of teens snatching merchandise and running through store aisles creates panic and potential safety issues for customers and store employees," according to a white paper by the National Retail Federation.

One flash robbery at a retail store can involve thousands of dollars worth of goods, and the toll can be even greater at high-end retailers. About 20 flash robbers stole $20,000 worth of merchandise from a Washington, D.C., clothing store in April 2011.

Swarms of young people assembled through social media may also commit acts of violence or vandalism, without stealing. In Philadelphia, for example, teens knocked down passers-by and assaulted shoppers in an upscale department store. Such incidents prompted Mayor Michael A. Nutter to intensify police patrols and move a curfew for teens to 9 p.m.

In many cases, flash robbers are recorded by surveillance cameras, making it easier to arrest and convict them. They may also be identified on social media or be apprehended leaving the scene. Police simply have to look for large groups of young people who have items from the store but no receipts (although the legal issues involved in stopping and searching people can pose problems for law enforcers).

Even though the total value of stolen goods can be high, the value of what each person stole is often quite low, making it difficult to charge the participants with a serious crime. Guns are not used and criminal conspiracy charges don't apply when participants don't even know each other.

After several flash mobs occurred in Chicago, Illinois Governor Pat Quinn signed legislation that could land participants in violent mobs in prison for up to 6 years. Taking a different tack, the city of Cleveland considered making it a criminal offense to summon any kind of flash mob through social media, but the proposal was withdrawn.

Resources: "Police Arrest 4 Teens after Flash Mob Fight in Philadelphia Mills Mall: Cops," NBC TV 10, December 28, 2016, http://www.nbcphiladelphia.com/news/local/Philadelphia-Mills-Mall-Possible-Flash-Mob-Fight-Northeast-Philadelphia—408448935.html (accessed January 1, 2017); "Flash Robs" Vex Retailers, *Wall Street Journal*, October 21, 2011, http://online.wsj.com/article/SB10001424052970203752604576643422390552158.html; and "Multiple Offender Crimes," *National Retail Federation White Paper*, August 2011, http://www.nrf.com/modules.php?name=News&op=viewlive&sp_id=1167.

Although simple assault may also at times include fistfights, the correct legal term to describe such incidents is *battery*. **Aggravated assaults** are distinguished from simple assaults in that either a weapon is used or the assault victim requires medical assistance. When a deadly weapon is employed, an aggravated assault may be charged as attempted murder even if no injury results.[48] In some cases, the UCR/NIBRS Program scores these attempted assaults as aggravated assaults because of the potential for serious consequences.

In 2017, 810,825 cases of aggravated assault were reported to law enforcement agencies in the United States. Like reports of rape, assault reports were most frequent in the summer months and least frequent in January, February, November, and December. Most aggravated assaults were committed with blunt objects or objects near at hand; hands, feet, and

aggravated assault
The unlawful, intentional inflicting, or attempted or threatened inflicting, of serious injury upon the person of another. Although *aggravated assault* and *simple assault* are standard terms for reporting purposes, most state penal codes use labels like *first-degree* and *second-degree* to make such distinctions.

fists were also commonly used (25%). Also used were knives (17%) and firearms (26%). Because those who commit assaults are often known to their victims, aggravated assaults are relatively easy to solve. About 53% of all aggravated assaults reported to the police in 2017 were cleared by arrest.

Burglary

Although it may involve personal and even violent confrontation, **burglary** is primarily a property crime. Burglars are interested in financial gain and usually fence (i.e., illegally sell) stolen items, recovering a fraction of their cash value. About 1.4 million burglaries were reported to the police in 2017. Dollar losses to burglary victims totaled $3.4 billion, with an average loss per offense of $2,416.

The UCR/NIBRS Program employs three classifications of burglary: (1) forcible entry, (2) unlawful entry where no force is used, and (3) attempted forcible entry. In most jurisdictions, force need not be employed for a crime to be classified as burglary. Unlocked doors and open windows are invitations to burglars, and the legal essence of burglary consists not so much of a forcible entry as it does of the intent to trespass and steal. In 2017, 57.5% of all burglaries were forcible entries, 36.2% were unlawful entries, and 6.3% were attempted forcible entries.[49] The most dangerous burglaries were those in which a household member was home (about 10% of all burglaries).[50] Residents who were home during a burglary suffered a greater than 30% chance of becoming the victim of a violent crime.[51] However, although burglary may evoke images of dark-clothed strangers breaking into houses in which families lie sleeping, burglaries more often are of unoccupied homes and take place during daylight hours.

The clearance rate for burglary, as for other property crimes that we'll look at later, is generally low. In 2017, the clearance rate for burglary was only 13.5%. Burglars usually do not know their victims, and in cases where they do, burglars conceal their identity by committing their crime when the victim is not present.

Larceny-Theft

A few years ago, a pair of women in the United Kingdom were caught on a surveillance camera stealing an entire front lawn of newly placed sod.[52] The theft occurred in Skelmersdale, England, and the homeowner posted the recording on YouTube.

Larceny is another name for theft, and, as is true in this example, almost anything of value can be stolen. The UCR/NIBRS Program uses the term **larceny-theft** to describe theft offenses of all kinds. Some states distinguish between simple larceny and grand larceny, categorizing the crime based on the dollar value of what is stolen. Larceny-theft, as defined by the UCR/NIBRS Program, includes the theft of valuables of any dollar amount. The reports specifically list the following offenses as types of larceny (listed here in order of declining frequency):

- Thefts from motor vehicles
- Shoplifting
- Thefts from buildings
- Thefts of motor vehicle parts and accessories
- Bicycle thefts
- Thefts from coin-operated machines
- Purse snatching
- Pocket picking

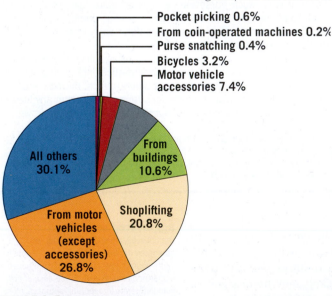

Pocket picking 0.6%
From coin-operated machines 0.2%
Purse snatching 0.4%
Bicycles 3.2%
Motor vehicle accessories 7.4%
From buildings 10.6%
All others 30.1%
Shoplifting 20.8%
From motor vehicles (except accessories) 26.8%

FIGURE 2–7
Larceny-Theft Distribution, 2017

Source: Larceny-Theft, Federal Bureau of Investigations, Retrieved from https://ucr.fbi.gov/crime-in-the-u.s/2017/crime-in-the-u.s.-2017/topic-pages/larceny-theft.

From a statistical standpoint, the most common form of larceny in recent years has been theft of motor vehicle parts, accessories, and contents. Tires, wheels, dash video cameras, radar detectors, satellite radios, and cellular phones account for many of the items reported stolen (Figure 2–7).

CJ | Issues
Race and the Criminal Justice System

▲ Protestors in Ferguson, Missouri, following the shooting of 18-year-old Michael Brown in 2014. Brown was black and unarmed; the officer who shot him was white, leading to claims of racial injustice—especially after a grand jury called to investigate the incident declined to indict the officer. The Brown case was among the first of similar incidents to be widely circulated on social media. Is the American criminal justice system equitable? Explain your answer.

Ed Endicott/Alamy Stock Photo

Recently, Gallup Poll researchers reported that black Americans saw race relations and unemployment as the most important problems facing the United States. More significant, however, was the disparity between perceptions of blacks and whites about the state of race relations in this country. Only 4% of whites identified race relations as the number one issue, and the percentage-point gap between blacks' and whites' perception of race relations as the top U.S. problem was significantly wider than it was in the years preceding the Gallup Poll.

Sensitivity to race relations in the United States escalated quickly among African Americans after a series of police shootings of unarmed young black men by white officers that were widely circulated on social media beginning in 2014. Many of the killings happened over seemingly minor offenses. Initially, few of the officers involved in the shootings were charged with the use of excessive force, causing protestors to take to the streets. Riots broke out in a number of cities, police property was destroyed by angry mobs, and intense media coverage of disaffected black leaders stoked a sense of injustice that had long festered in minority areas. The social upheaval that followed led some to compare it to the civil rights era of the 1960s.

In June 2015, members of Harvard University's Executive Session on Policing and Public Safety found that "concern about race seemed to become stalled in discussion rather than advancing to action." They recognized that American criminal justice personnel "confront issues of race daily in almost everything they do." That confrontation can be found in the geographic distribution of criminality and in the fear of crime found especially in the inner city, as well as "in assumptions about what criminals look like." The police, they said, "confront race in the suspicion and hostility of many young African-American men they encounter on the street." And, they found, charges of racial profiling and unequal justice are often intertwined with hiring practices of justice agencies, including the promotion and assignment of personnel.

One of the most difficult problems to address is the fact that the highest rates of violent crime are in minority neighborhoods. This, said the Harvard writers, "creates the impression that race or ethnicity is implicated in criminality and that serious crime in America is particularly a 'black problem.'" Such reasoning, they argued, "gets the causality backward." Race is not a causal factor in criminality; instead, "the circumstances that create compacted disadvantage for minority groups also create criminality." Due to a long history of exclusion from important economic and social opportunities, residents of disadvantaged urban neighborhoods are primarily minorities and often black. Lost in all of this, said the report, is the fact that minorities are more likely than the majority of white people to be victims of crime—and hence most in need of help from the justice system. Those who say that "black-on-black" crime is the major problem that needs to be addressed may be statistically correct, but according to a second paper by Harvard researchers, "To the vast majority of urban black residents who are not involved in violence or criminal behavior, the term invokes visions of indiscriminate and aggressive police enforcement responses applied to a broad range of black people."

While it will not be easy to address today's concerns over race, one solution might see justice system agencies begin to focus more on procedural fairness than on objective statistics like the number of crimes solved.

References: Alyssa Brown, "Views of Race Relations as Top Problem Still Differ by Race," *Gallup*, June 16, 2015, http://www.gallup.com/poll/183572/race-divides-views-race-relations-top-problem.aspx; David H. Bayley, Michael A. Davis, and Ronald L. Davis, *Race and Policing: An Agenda for Action* (Washington, D.C.: National Institute of Justice, June 2015); and Anthony A. Braga and Rod K. Brunson, *The Police and Public Discourse on 'Black-on-Black' Violence* (Washington, D.C.: National Institute of Justice, May 2015).

Thefts of farm animals (known as *rustling*) and thefts of most types of farm machinery also fall into the larceny category. In fact, larceny is such a broad category that it serves as a kind of catchall in the UCR/NIBRS Program. In 1995, for example, Yale University officials filed larceny charges against 25-year-old student Lon Grammer, claiming that he had fraudulently obtained university funds.[53] The university maintained that Grammer had stolen his education by forging college and high school transcripts and concocting letters of recommendation prior to admission. Grammer's alleged misdeeds, which Yale University officials said misled them into thinking that Grammer, a poor student before attending Yale, had

🐦 Follow the author's tweets about the latest crime and justice news @schmalleger

an exceptional scholastic record, permitted him to receive $61,475 in grants and loans during the time he attended the school. Grammer was expelled.

Reported thefts vary widely, in terms of both the objects stolen and their value. Stolen items range from pocket change to a $100 million aircraft. For reporting purposes, crimes entailing embezzlement, con games, forgery, and worthless checks are specifically excluded from the count of larceny. Because larceny has traditionally been considered a crime that requires physical possession of the item appropriated, some computer crimes, including thefts engineered through online access or thefts of software and information, have not been scored as larcenies unless computer equipment, electronic circuitry, or computer media were actually stolen.

Reports to the police in 2017 showed 5,519,107 larcenies nationwide, with the total value of property stolen placed at $5.6 billion. Larceny-theft is the most frequently reported major crime, according to the UCR/NIBRS Program. It may also be the program's most underreported crime category because small thefts rarely come to the attention of the police. The average value of items reported stolen in 2017 was about $1,007.

> Larceny-theft is the most frequently reported major crime, according to the UCR/NIBRS Program. It may also be the program's most underreported crime category because small thefts rarely come to the attention of the police.

Identity Theft: A New Kind of Larceny

In 2017, Equifax, one of the world's largest credit monitoring agencies, reported that hackers had gained access to sensitive information on 143 million Americans. The hackers were able to access drivers' license numbers, birth dates, and Social Security numbers. Credit card numbers for hundreds of thousands of people were also taken. Much of the stolen information was quickly made available for sale on the Dark Web—and identity thieves were able to use it to make purchases worldwide.[54] *Identity theft* is the unauthorized access to personal information.

Identity fraud, which involves obtaining credit, merchandise, or services by fraudulent personal representation, is a special kind of larceny. According to a 2018 survey, 16.7 million Americans were victims of identity fraud in that year. Although most did not report the crime, the total amount of money lost to identity fraud was $16.8 billion.[55] Information from the Bureau of Justice Statistics shows that 7.0% of all households in the United States had at least one member who had their identity stolen in 2014.[56] The BJS also says that identity theft is the fastest-growing type of crime in America.[57]

identity fraud
A crime in which an imposter obtains key pieces of information, such as Social Security and driver's license numbers, to obtain credit, merchandise, and services in the name of the victim. The victim is often left with a ruined credit history and the time-consuming and complicated task of repairing the financial damage.[i]

Identity fraud became a federal crime in 1998 with the passage of the Identity Theft and Assumption Deterrence Act.[58] The law makes it a crime whenever anyone "knowingly transfers or uses, without lawful authority, a means of identification of another person with the intent to commit, or to aid or abet, any unlawful activity that constitutes a violation of federal law, or that constitutes a felony under any applicable state or local law."

The 2004 Identity Theft Penalty Enhancement Act[59] added 2 years to federal prison sentences for criminals convicted of using stolen credit card numbers and other personal data to commit crimes. It also prescribed prison sentences for those who use identity theft to commit other crimes, including terrorism, and it increased penalties for defendants who exceed or abuse the authority of their position in unlawfully obtaining or misusing means of personal identification.

According to the National White Collar Crime Center, identity thieves use several common techniques. Some engage in "Dumpster diving," going through trash bags, cans, or dumpsters to get copies of checks, credit card and bank statements, credit card applications, or other records that typically bear identifying information. Others use a technique called "shoulder surfing," which involves looking over the victim's shoulder as he or she

▲ Equifax headquartered in Atlanta, Georgia. In 2017, hackers stole personal information on 143 million people that was stored in the company's computers. Why is identity fraud so prevalent today? How can it be stopped?
Kristoffer Tripplaar/Alamy Stock Photo

enters personal information into a computer or on a written form. Eavesdropping is another simple, yet effective, technique that identity thieves often use. Eavesdropping can occur when the victim is using an ATM, giving credit card or other personal information over the phone, or dialing the number for a telephone calling card. Criminals can also obtain personal identifying information from potential victims through the Internet. Some Internet users, for example, reply to "spam" (unsolicited e-mail) that promises them all sorts of attractive benefits while requesting identifying data, such as checking account or credit card numbers and expiration dates, along with their name and address.[60] Identity theft perpetrated through the use of high technology depends on the fact that a person's legal and economic identity in contemporary society is largely "virtual" and supported by technology. Read the National Strategy to Combat Identity Theft at **https://www.justicestudies.com/pubs/natlstrategy.pdf**.

Motor Vehicle Theft

For record-keeping purposes, the UCR/NIBRS Program defines *motor vehicles* as self-propelled vehicles that run on the ground and not on rails. Included in the definition are automobiles, motorcycles, motor scooters, trucks, buses, and snowmobiles. Excluded are trains, airplanes, bulldozers, most farm and construction machinery, ships, boats, and spacecraft; the theft of these would be scored as larceny-theft.[61] Vehicles that are temporarily taken by individuals who have lawful access to them are not thefts. Hence, spouses who jointly own all property may drive the family car, even though one spouse may think of the vehicle as his or her exclusive personal property.

As we said earlier, because most insurance companies require police reports before they will reimburse car owners for their losses, most occurrences of **motor vehicle theft** are reported to law enforcement agencies. Some reports of motor vehicle thefts, however, may be false. People who have damaged their own vehicles in solitary crashes or who have been unable to sell them may try to force insurance companies to "buy" them through reports of theft.

In 2017, 773,139 motor vehicles were reported stolen. The average value per stolen vehicle was $7,708, making motor vehicle theft a $6 billion crime. The clearance rate for motor vehicle theft was only 13.7% in 2017. Large city agencies reported the lowest rates of clearance, whereas rural counties had the highest rate. Many stolen vehicles are quickly disassembled and the parts resold, as auto parts are much more difficult to identify and trace than are intact vehicles. In some parts of the country, chop shops—which take stolen vehicles apart and sell their components—operate like big businesses, and one shop may strip a dozen or more cars per day.

Motor vehicle theft can turn violent, as in cases of carjacking—a crime in which offenders usually force the car's occupants onto the street before stealing the vehicle. The BJS estimates that around 34,000 carjackings occur annually and account for slightly more than 1% of all motor vehicle thefts.[62] Arrest reports for motor vehicle theft show that the typical offender is a young male: 42.9% of all arrestees in 2017 were under the age of 25, and 77.7% were male.

Arson

The UCR/NIBRS Program received crime reports from more than 15,000 law enforcement agencies in 2017.[63] Of these, only 14,854 submitted data on **arson** (the intentional burning of property). Even fewer agencies provided complete data as to the type of property burned, the estimated monetary value of the property, the ownership, and so on. Arson data include only the fires that are determined through investigation to have been willfully or maliciously set. Fires of unknown or suspicious origin are excluded from arson statistics.[64]

The intentional and unlawful burning of structures (houses, storage buildings, manufacturing facilities, and so on) was the type of arson reported most often in 2017 (16,477 instances). The arson of vehicles was the second most common category, with 8,883 such burnings reported. The average dollar loss per instance of arson in 2017 was $15,573, and total nationwide property damage was placed at close to $1 billion.[65] As with most property crimes, the clearance rate for arson was low—21.7% nationally. The crime of arson exists in a kind of statistical limbo. In 1979, Congress ordered that it be added as an eighth Part I offense. Today, however, many law enforcement agencies still have not begun making regular reports to the FBI on arson offenses in their jurisdictions.

Some of these difficulties have been resolved through the Special Arson Program, authorized by Congress in 1982. In conjunction with the National Fire Data Center, the FBI now operates a Special Arson Reporting System which focuses on fire departments across the nation. The reporting system is designed to provide data to supplement yearly UCR arson tabulations.[66]

Follow the author's tweets about the latest crime and justice news @schmalleger

motor vehicle theft (UCR/NIBRS)
The theft or attempted theft of a motor vehicle. *Motor vehicle* is defined as a self-propelled road vehicle that runs on land surface and not on rails. The stealing of trains, planes, boats, construction equipment, and most farm machinery is classified as larceny under the UCR/NIBRS Program, not as motor vehicle theft.

arson (UCR/NIBRS)
Any willful or malicious burning or attempt to burn, with or without intent to defraud, a dwelling house, public building, motor vehicle or aircraft, personal property of another, and so on. Some instances of arson result from malicious mischief, some involve attempts to claim insurance money, and some are committed in an effort to disguise other crimes, such as murder, burglary, or larceny.

TABLE 2-3
UCR/NIBRS Part II Offenses, 2017

Offense Category	Number of Arrests
Simple assaults	1,062,370
Forgery and counterfeiting	55,604
Fraud	124,232
Embezzlement	15,967
Stolen property (e.g., receiving)	98,660
Vandalism	188,350
Weapons (e.g., carrying)	164,984
Prostitution and related offenses	36,248
Sex offenses (e.g., statutory rape)	48,525
Drug-abuse violations	1,632,921
Gambling	3,237
Offenses against the family (e.g., nonsupport)	94,062
Driving under the influence	990,678
Liquor-law violations	207,332
Public drunkenness	366,824
Disorderly conduct	353,151
Vagrancy	23,321
Curfew violations/loitering	30,131

Source: Federal Bureau of Investigation, Crime in the United States, 2017 (Washington, D.C.: U.S. Department of Justice, 2018).

🐦 Follow the author's tweets about the latest crime and justice news @schmalleger

Part II Offenses

Part II offenses
A traditional UCR/NIBRS offense group used to report arrests for less serious offenses. Agencies are limited to reporting only arrest information for Part II offenses, with the exception of simple assault.

The UCR Program also includes information on what the FBI calls **Part II offenses**. Part II offenses, which are generally less serious than those that make up the Part I offenses category, include a number of social-order, or so-called victimless, crimes. The statistics on Part II offenses are for *recorded arrests*, not for crimes reported to the police. The logic inherent in this form of scoring is that most Part II offenses would never come to the attention of the police were it not for arrests. Part II offenses are shown in Table 2-3, with the number of estimated arrests made in each category for 2017. You can access the BJS data analysis tool at **http://www.bjs.gov/index.cfm?ty=datool&surl=/arrests/index.cfm** to view customized national and local arrest data by age, sex, and race for many different offenses.

A Part II offense is counted each time a person is taken into custody. As a result, the statistics in Table 2–3 do not report the number of suspects arrested but rather the number of arrests made. Some suspects were arrested more than once.

The National Crime Victimization Survey

dark figure of crime
Crime that is not reported to the police and that remains unknown to officials.

A second major source of statistical data about crime in the United States is the National Crime Victimization Survey (NCVS), which is based on victim self-reports rather than on police reports. The NCVS is designed to estimate the occurrence of all crimes, whether reported or not.[67] The NCVS was first conducted in 1972. It built on efforts in the

2 Describe the National Crime Victimization Survey Program, including its purpose, its history, and what it tells us about crime in the United States today.

late 1960s by both the National Opinion Research Center and the President's Commission on Law Enforcement and the Administration of Justice to uncover what some had been calling the **dark figure of crime**. This term refers to those crimes that are not reported to the police and that remain unknown to officials. Before the development of the NCVS, little was known about such unreported and undiscovered offenses.

Freedom or Safety? You Decide
Can Citizens Have Too Much Privacy?

In 2018 Apple, maker of the iPhone, iPad, iMac, and similar devices, announced that it would implement a software feature designed to block iPhone and iPad unlocking tools. Those tools, many of which use the Lightning port on Apple devices, are commonly employed by police to gain access to content on handheld devices, and figure prominently in many criminal investigations. In blocking their future use, Apple executives noted their potential for misuse and assured consumers that the privacy of their users was paramount.

Apple's actions were presaged by a talk at Fordham University that then-FBI director James B. Comey gave about the "cyber threat" challenging the American justice system. Comey's main concern was about new encryption technologies that put many types of information (including text messages, e-mail, and other forms of Internet-based communication) beyond the reach of investigators—even when enforcement officials are armed with a warrant. What follows is excerpted from his talk.

Let me start by telling you what you know, which is that everything has changed in ways that are so fundamental that it's difficult to describe what it means when we say the world is changing because of cyber. . . .

I always look for ways to describe just how fundamental the transformation we're standing in the middle of is.

. . . . Cisco provided some stats that I saw recently that I just wanted to mention as I start. In 2003 there were 6.3 billion human beings on the earth and 500 million devices connected to the Internet. In 2010 there were 6.8 billion people on the earth and 12.5 billion devices connected to the Internet. One-point-eight-four per person.

Cisco projects that in 2020, there will be seven billion people on the earth and 50 billion devices connected to the Internet. Six-and-a-half devices on average per person. . . .

There is no doubt that everything has changed because we've connected our entire lives to the Internet. That is why, because all of life is there, that all of the parts of life that the FBI is responsible for trying to protect—whether it is criminal, counterintelligence, counterterrorism, protecting children, fighting fraud—it all happens there because that's where life is.

. . . . I actually try to describe to people in very simple ways what we're talking about today because I don't see cyber as a thing, I see it as a way. As a vector. Because my children play on the Internet. Because that's where I bank. Because that's where my health care is. Because that's—I don't have a social life, but if I had one, that's where I'm sure it would be. That's where our nation's critical infrastructure is, that's where our government's secrets are and that's—because life is there, that's where bad people come who want to hurt children, who want to steal money, who want to take identities, who want to steal secrets, who want to damage dams and critical infrastructure in the United States. It's the way they come at us because that's where life is.

. . . Dillinger or Bonnie and Clyde could not do a thousand robberies in all 50 states in the same day from their pajamas from Belarus. That's the challenge we face today. The traditional notions of space and time and venue and border and my jurisdiction and your jurisdiction are blown away by a threat that moves not at 40 miles an hour or 50 downhill, but at 186,000 miles per second. The speed of light.

Traditional notions, frameworks, are destroyed by that kind of threat. That requires every part of the FBI, those who are spending their days protecting kids, fighting fraud, fighting spies, fighting terrorism, protecting intellectual property, all of those things; it requires those people to be digitally literate. It requires me to have the right kind of people, the right kind of equipment and deploy them in a way that deals with a vector change that is mind boggling compared to the Dillinger era.

. . . We need to equip our state and local partners to be able to be digitally literate and to conduct their investigations in responding to the same threats coming through the vector that is cyber. And so one of the things we're trying to do is work with the Secret Service to offer training to the 17,000 state and local law enforcement organizations in this country to equip their people to be digitally literate. A ton of work going on there. Lots more needs to be done.

Before I leave you though I want to mention something . . . the problem of what we call Going Dark.

This is very, very important to us in law enforcement. . . . We are drifting to a place in this country without serious public discussion that I don't think a democracy should drift to without discussion.

. . . . We're making it increasingly difficult for us with lawful authority, especially in our criminal work, to be able to intercept the communications of drug dealers, organized criminals, of bad people of all sorts with court approval.

But there's another dimension to it that made it blink even more brightly—directly in front of me . . . Increasingly what we're finding ourselves up against is data . . . that is sitting in a place or in a device that, even with a search warrant, we can't get access to. And this is everywhere in law enforcement.

This . . . is about us drifting to a place where there will be zones beyond the reach of the law in the United States. The Fourth Amendment is one of the most important parts of this entire democracy because the government may not search and seize the people's papers and effects without a warrant. But now we're drifting to a place that, even with a warrant, there will be papers and effects, even with court authority, that are beyond the reach of the law. Maybe we want to go there. Maybe that's where we want to end up as a democracy. Maybe people decide that privacy is that important. But I don't think we're talking about it enough. I don't think we're thinking about, "So what are the trade-offs involved there?"

My job, I don't believe, is to tell people what to do. I mean, in a democracy, the people should decide what to do. My job, I think, is simply to say there are significant public safety implications here and let's talk about it before we get to the place . . . Where people look at us with tears in their eyes and say, "What do you mean you can't? What do you mean you can't? This little girl has disappeared. What do you mean you can't tell me who she was texting with before she disappeared? You've got the phone. You've got a court order." Before we get to "what do you mean you can't," I think we've got to talk about it as a people.

YOU DECIDE

1. **What does Director Comey mean when he asks "So, what are the trade-offs involved there?" Can you identify any of those "trade-offs"? How comfortable are you with them?**

2. **In 2016, the FBI and Apple fought over privacy rights when the agency requested that the computer company provide backdoor access to a cell phone used by one of the San Bernardino terrorists in a December 2015 attack that killed 14 people and injured 22 others. Apple declined the FBI's request for access, saying that it would jeopardize the security of all of its customers. Whose side are you on? Is there a middle ground?**

Reference: Ed Hardy, "Apple Commits to Blocking iPhone Unlockers Used by Police," June 14, 2018, Techristic, https://www.techristic.com/apple-commits-to-blocking-iphone-unlockers-used-by-police (accessed July 8, 2018); James B. Comey, remarks made before the International Conference on Cyber Security, Fordham University, New York, January 7, 2015, http://www.fbi.gov/news/speeches/addressing-the-cyber-security-threat?utm_campaign=email-Immediate&utm_medium=email&utm_source=executive-speeches&utm_content=391299 (accessed March 7, 2016).

Early data from the NCVS changed the way criminologists thought about crime in the United States. The use of victim self-reports led to the discovery that crimes of all types were more prevalent than UCR statistics indicated. Many cities were shown to have victimization rates that were more than twice the rate of reported offenses. Others, like St. Louis, Missouri, and Newark, New Jersey, were found to have rates of victimization that very nearly approximated those of reported crime. New York, often thought of as a high-crime city, was discovered to have one of the lowest rates of self-reported victimization. The NCVS shows that approximately 54% of all violent victimizations, and 63% of thefts, are not reported to the police.[68]

NCVS data are gathered by the BJS through a cooperative arrangement with the U.S. Census Bureau.[69] Twice each year, Census Bureau personnel interview household members in a nationally representative sample of approximately 90,000 households (about 160,000 people). Only individuals age 12 or older are interviewed. Households stay in the sample for 3 years, and new households rotate into the sample regularly.

The NCVS collects information on crimes suffered by individuals and households, whether or not those crimes were reported to law enforcement. It estimates the proportion of each crime type reported to law enforcement, and it summarizes the reasons that victims give for reporting or not reporting. BJS statistics are published in annual reports made available on the Internet.

Using definitions similar to those employed by the UCR/NIBRS Program, the NCVS includes data on the national incidence of rape, sexual assault, robbery, assault, burglary, personal and household larceny, and motor vehicle theft. Not included are murder, kidnapping, and victimless crimes (crimes that, by their nature, tend to involve willing participants). Commercial robbery and the burglary of businesses were dropped from NCVS reports in 1977. The NCVS employs a hierarchical counting system similar to that of the pre-NIBRS system: It counts only the most "serious" incident in any series of criminal events perpetrated against the same individual. Both completed and attempted offenses are counted, although only people 12 years of age and older are included in household surveys.

NCVS statistics for recent years reveal the following:

- Approximately 9% of American households are touched by crime every year.

- About 21 million victimizations occur each year.

- City residents are almost twice as likely as rural residents to be victims of crime.

- About half of all violent crimes, and slightly more than one-third of all property crimes, are reported to police.[70]

- Victims of crime are more often men than women.

- Younger people are more likely than the elderly to be victims of crime.

- Blacks are more likely than members of other racial groups to be victims of violent crimes.

- Violent victimization rates are highest among people in lower-income families.

Since 1993, the rate of violent crime reported by the NCVS has declined from 79.8 to 23.2 victimizations per 1,000 persons age 12 or older.[71] Since 1993, the rate of property crime has declined from 351.8 to 131.4 victimizations per 1,000 households. The decline in theft accounted for the majority of the decrease in property crime. UCR statistics, however, which go back almost 100 years, show that today's crime rate is still many times what it was in the early and middle years of the twentieth century.[72] Like the UCR, however, NCVS major data categories do not fully encompass the shifting nature of criminal activity in the United States. Nonetheless, some researchers trust NCVS data more than UCR/NIBRS data because they believe that victim self-reports provide a more accurate gauge of criminal incidents than do police reports in which victims had to initiate the reporting process. A comparison of UCR/NIBRS and NCVS data can be found in Table 2-4.

Explore the NCVS Victimization Analysis Tool at **http://www.bjs.gov//index .cfm?ty=nvat**. The tool, which became available in 2012, analyzes data on victims, households,

🐦 Follow the author's tweets about the latest crime and justice news @schmalleger

TABLE 2-4
Comparison of UCR/NIBRS and NCVS Data

Offense	UCR/NIBRS	NCVS[a]
Personal/Violent Crimes		
Homicide	17,284	—
Rape[b]	99,856	323,450
Robbery	319,356	500,680
Aggravated assault	810,825	1,084,340
Property Crimes		
Burglary[c]	1,401,840	3,291,490
Larceny	5,519,107	12,040,440
Motor vehicle theft	773,139	585,500
Arson[d]	36,660	—
Total Crimes	8,978,067	21,666,760[e]

[a] NCVS data on property crimes cover "households touched by crime," not absolute numbers of crime occurrences. More than one victimization may occur per household, but only the number of households in which victimizations occur enters the tabulations.
[b] NCVS statistics include both rape and sexual assault.
[c] NCVS statistics include household burglaries and attempted burglaries.
[d] Arson data are incomplete in the UCR/NIBRS and are not reported by the NCVS.
[e] Includes NCVS crimes not shown in the table, including 3.8 million simple assaults.

Source: Federal Bureau of Investigation, *Crime in the United States, 2017* (Washington, D.C.: U.S. Department of Justice, 2018); Bureau of Justice Statistics, *Criminal Victimization, 2016* (Washington, D.C.: BJS, 2017).

and incidents, and can instantly generate tables with national estimates of the numbers, rates, and percentages of both violent and property victimization from 1993 to the most recent year that NCVS data are available.

Comparisons of the UCR and the NCVS

3 Compare and contrast the UCR and the NCVS data-collection and reporting programs.

As mentioned earlier in this chapter, crime statistics from the UCR/NIBRS and the NCVS reveal crime patterns that are often the bases for social policies created to deter or reduce crime. These policies also build on explanations for criminal behavior found in more elaborate interpretations of the statistical information. Unfortunately, however, researchers too often forget that statistics, which are merely descriptive, can be weak in explanatory power. For example, NCVS data show that "household crime rates" are highest for households (1) headed by blacks, (2) headed by younger people, (3) with six or more members, (4) headed by renters, and (5) located in central cities.[73] Such findings, combined with statistics that show that most crime occurs among members of the same race, have led some researchers to conclude that values among certain black subcultural group members both propel them into crime and make them targets of criminal victimization. The truth may be, however, that crime is more a function of inner-city location than of culture. From simple descriptive statistics, it is difficult to know which is the case.

Like most statistical data-gathering programs in the social sciences, the UCR/NIBRS and the NCVS programs are not without problems. Because UCR/NIBRS data are based primarily on citizens' crime reports to the police, there are several inherent difficulties. First, not all people report when they are victimized. Some victims are afraid to contact the police whereas others may not believe that the police can do anything about the offense. Second, certain kinds of crimes are reported rarely, if at all. These include victimless crimes, also known as *social-order offenses*, such as drug use, prostitution, and gambling. Similarly, white-collar offenses, such as embezzlement—because they often go undiscovered, or because they are difficult to score in terms of traditional UCR

> Like most statistical data-gathering programs in the social sciences, the UCR/NIBRS and the NCVS programs are not without problems.

categories—probably enter the official statistics only rarely. The FBI acknowledges such shortcomings by saying that "it is well documented that the major limitation of the traditional Summary Reporting System is its failure to keep up with the changing face of crime and criminal activity. The inability to grasp the extent of white-collar crime is a specific example of that larger limitation."[74] Third, high-technology and computer crime, like white-collar crime, don't always "fit" well with traditional reporting categories, leading to their possible underrepresentation in today's crime statistics.[75] Fourth, victims' memories may be faulty, victims may feel the need to impress or please the police, or they may be under pressure from others to misrepresent the facts. Fifth, all reports are filtered through a number of bureaucratic levels, which increases the likelihood that inaccuracies will enter the data. As noted methodologist Frank Hagan points out, "The government is very keen on amassing statistics. They collect them, add to them, raise them to the nth power, take the cube root, and prepare wonderful diagrams. But what you must never forget is that every one of these figures comes in the first instance from the *chowty dar* [village watchman], who puts down what he damn pleases."[76]

In contrast to the UCR/NIBRS dependence on crimes reported by victims who seek out the police, the NCVS relies on door-to-door surveys and personal interviews (some conducted by phone) for its data. Survey results, however, may be skewed for several reasons. First, no matter how objective survey questions may appear to be, survey respondents inevitably provide their personal interpretations and descriptions of what may or may not have been a criminal event. Second, by its very nature, the survey includes information from those people who are most willing to talk to surveyors; more reclusive people are less likely to respond regardless of the level of victimization they may have suffered. Also, some victims are afraid to report crimes even to nonpolice interviewers, whereas others may invent victimizations for an interviewer's sake. As the first page of the NCVS report admits, "Details about the crimes come directly from the victims, and no attempt is made to validate the information against police records or any other source."[77]

Finally, because both the UCR/NIBRS and the NCVS are human artifacts, they contain only data that their creators think appropriate. UCR/NIBRS statistics for 2001, for example, do not include a tally of those who perished in the September 11, 2001, terrorist attacks because FBI officials concluded that the events were too "unusual" to count. Although the FBI's 2001 *Crime in the United States* acknowledges "the 2,830 homicides reported as a result of the events of September 11, 2001," it goes on to say that "these figures have been removed" from the reported data.[78] Crimes resulting from an anomalous event but excluded from reported data highlight the arbitrary nature of the data collection process itself.

Special Categories of Crime

4   Describe how any three of the special categories of crime discussed in this chapter are significant today.

crime typology
A classification of crimes along a particular dimension, such as legal category, offender motivation, victim behavior, or characteristics of individual offenders.

A **crime typology** is a classification scheme used in the study and description of criminal behavior. There are many typologies, all of which have an underlying logic. The system of classification that derives from any particular typology may be based on legal criteria, offender motivation, victim behavior, characteristics of individual offenders, or the like. Criminologists Terance D. Miethe and Richard C. McCorkle note that crime typologies "are designed primarily to simplify social reality by identifying homogeneous groups of crime behaviors that are different from other clusters of crime behaviors."[79] Hence, one common but simple typology contains only two categories of crime: violent and property. In fact, many crime typologies contain overlapping or nonexclusive categories—just as violent crimes may involve property offenses, and property offenses may lead to violent crimes. Thus, no one typology is likely to capture all of the nuances of criminal offending.

Social relevance is a central distinguishing feature of any meaningful typology, and it is with that in mind that the remaining sections of this chapter briefly highlight crimes of special importance today. They are crime against women, crime against the elderly, hate crime, corporate and white-collar crime, organized crime, gun crime, drug crime, high-technology and computer crime, and terrorism.

Crime against Women

The victimization of women is a special area of concern, and both the UCR/NIBRS and the NCVS contain data on gender as it relates to victimization. Statistics show that women are victimized less frequently than men in every major personal crime category other than rape.[80] The overall U.S. rate of violent victimization is about 9.4 per 1,000 males age 12 or older, and 6.6 per 1,000 females.[81] When women become victims of violent crime, however, they are more likely than men to be injured (29% versus 22%, respectively).[82] Moreover, a larger proportion of women than men make modifications in the way they live because of the threat of crime.[83] Women, especially those living in cities, have become increasingly careful about where they travel and the time of day they leave their homes—particularly if they are unaccompanied—and in many settings are often wary of unfamiliar males.

Date rape, familial incest, intimate partner violence, **stalking**, and the exploitation of women through social-order offenses, such as prostitution and pornography, are major issues facing American society today. Testimony before Congress tagged domestic violence as the largest cause of injury to American women.[84] Former Surgeon General C. Everett Koop once identified violence against women by their partners as the number one health problem facing women in America.[85] Findings from the National Violence against Women Survey (NVAWS) and the National Intimate Partner and Sexual Violence Survey[86] reveal the following:

- Physical assault is widespread among American women. Fifty-two percent of surveyed women said that they had been physically assaulted as a child or as an adult.

- Approximately 1.9 million women are physically assaulted in the United States each year.

- Eighteen percent of women experienced a completed or attempted rape at some time in their lives.

- Of those reporting rape, 22% were under 12 years old, and 32% were between 12 and 17 years old, when they were first raped.

- Native American and Alaska Native women were most likely to report rape and physical assault whereas Asian/Pacific Islander women were least likely to report such victimization. Hispanic women were less likely to report rape than non-Hispanic women.

- Women report significantly more partner violence than men. Twenty-five percent of surveyed women and only 8% of surveyed men said they had been raped or physically assaulted by a current or former spouse, cohabiting partner, or date.

- Violence against women is primarily partner violence. Seventy-six percent of the women who had been raped or physically assaulted since age 18 were assaulted by a current or former husband, cohabiting partner, or date, compared with 18% of the men.

- Women are significantly more likely than men to be injured during an assault. Thirty-two percent of the women and 16% of the men who had been raped since age 18 were injured during their most recent rape.

- Eight percent of surveyed women and 2% of surveyed men said they had been stalked at some time in their lives. According to survey estimates, approximately one million women and 371,000 men are stalked annually in the United States.

- Twenty-seven percent of women and 12% of men report significant short- or long-term impact from sexual or physical violence or from stalking by an intimate partner.

The Violence against Women Act

Survey findings like these show that more must be done to alleviate the social conditions that result in the victimization of women. Suggestions already under consideration call for expansion in the number of federal and state laws designed to control domestic violence, broadening of the federal Family Violence Prevention and Services Act, federal help in setting up state advocacy offices for battered women, increased funding for battered women's shelters, and additional funds for prosecutors and courts to develop spousal abuse units.

stalking
Repeated harassing and threatening behavior by one individual against another, aspects of which may be planned or carried out in secret. Stalking might involve following a person, appearing at a person's home or place of business, making harassing phone calls, leaving written messages or objects, or vandalizing a person's property. Most stalking laws require that the perpetrator make a credible threat of violence against the victim or members of the victim's immediate family.

Follow the author's tweets about the latest crime and justice news @schmalleger

▲ President Obama signing Violence against Women Act (VAWA) reauthorization legislation in 2013. Intimate partner violence is a problem of special concern to the criminal justice system, and violence against women is an area that is receiving legislative attention, as evidenced by the federal VAWA. How might laws designed to protect women be improved?

HHS Photos/Alamy Stock Photo

cyberstalking
The use of the Internet, e-mail, and other electronic communication technologies to stalk another person.[ii]

The Violent Crime Control and Law Enforcement Act of 1994 included significant provisions intended to enhance gender equality throughout the criminal justice system. Title IV of the Violent Crime Control and Law Enforcement Act, known as the Violence against Women Act (VAWA) of 1994, contains the Safe Streets for Women Act. This act increased federal penalties for repeat sex offenders and requires mandatory restitution for sex crimes, including costs related to medical services (including physical, psychiatric, and psychological care); physical and occupational therapy or rehabilitation; necessary transportation, temporary housing, and child-care expenses; lost income; attorneys' fees, including any costs incurred in obtaining a civil protection order; and any other losses suffered by the victim as a result of the offense. The act also requires that compliance with a restitution order be made a condition of probation or supervised release (if such a sentence is imposed by the court) and provides that violation of the order will result in the offender's imprisonment.

Chapter 2 of VAWA provided funds for grants to combat violent crimes against women. The purpose of funding was to assist states and local governments to "develop and strengthen effective law enforcement and prosecution strategies to combat violent crimes against women, and to develop and strengthen victim services in cases involving violent crimes against women."

The act also created the crime of crossing state lines in violation of a protection order and the crime of crossing state lines to commit assault on a domestic partner. It established federal penalties for the latter offense of up to life in prison in cases where death results.

Chapter 5 of VAWA funded the creation of hot lines, educational seminars, informational materials, and training programs for professionals who provide assistance to victims of sexual assault. Another portion of the law, titled the Safe Homes for Women Act, increased grants for battered women's shelters, encouraged arrest in cases of domestic violence, and provided for the creation of a national domestic violence hot line to provide counseling, information, and assistance to victims of domestic violence. The act also mandates that any protection order issued by a state court must be recognized by the other states and by the federal government and must be enforced "as if it were the order of the enforcing state."

VAWA was reauthorized by Congress in 2000, in 2005, and again in 2013.[87] The 2005 VAWA reauthorization included a new statute known as the International Marriage Broker Regulation Act (IMBRA). IMBRA provides potential life-saving protections to prospective foreign brides who may immigrate to the United States. Finally, the 2013 reauthorization made $659 million available each year for 5 years for programs that strengthen the justice system's response to crimes against women and some men, including protections for gay, lesbian, bisexual, and transgender Americans.

Finally, the passage of antistalking legislation by all 50 states and the District of Columbia provides some measure of additional protection to women, who make up 80% of all stalking victims.[88] On the federal level, the seriousness of stalking was addressed when Congress passed the interstate stalking law in 1996.[89] The law[90] also addresses **cyberstalking**, or the use of the Internet by perpetrators seeking to exercise power and control over their victims by threatening them directly or by posting misleading and harassing information about them. Cyberstalking can be especially insidious because it does not require that the perpetrator and the victim be in the same geographic area. Similarly, electronic communication technologies lower the barriers to harassment and threats; a cyberstalker does not need to confront the victim physically.[91]

Crime against the Elderly

Relative to other age groups, older victims rarely appear in the crime statistics. Criminal victimization seems to decline with age, suggesting that older people are only infrequently targeted by violent and property criminals. Moreover, older people are more likely than younger individuals to live in secure areas and to have the financial means to provide for their own personal security.

Victimization data pertaining to older people come mostly from the NCVS, which, for such purposes, looks at people age 65 and older. The elderly generally experience the lowest rate of victimization of any age group in both violent and property crime categories.[92] Some aspects of crime against older people are worth noting, however. In general, elderly crime victims are more likely than younger victims to

- be victims of property crime (nine out of ten crimes committed against the elderly are property crimes, compared to fewer than four in ten crimes against people between ages 12 and 24)

- face offenders who are armed with guns

- be victimized by strangers

- be victimized in or near their homes during daylight hours

- report their victimization to the police, especially when they fall victim to violent crime

- be physically injured

In addition, elderly people are less likely to attempt to protect themselves when they are victims of violent crime.

The elderly face special kinds of victimization that only rarely affect younger adults, such as abuse and neglect at the hands of caregivers. This falls into two categories: domestic and institutional. Domestic abuse usually occurs in the victim's own home and often involves caregivers who are related to their victims; institutional abuse occurs in residential settings, such as assisted living facilities, nursing homes, and hospitals. Both forms may involve physical abuse, sexual victimization, financial exploitation, and neglect.

The elderly are also more often targeted by con artists. Confidence schemes center on commercial and financial fraud (including telemarketing fraud), charitable donation fraud, funeral and cemetery fraud, real estate fraud, caretaker fraud, automobile and home repair fraud, living trust fraud, health-care fraud (e.g., promises of "miracle cures"), and health-care-provider fraud (overbilling and unjustified repeat billing by otherwise legitimate health-care providers). False "friends" may intentionally isolate elderly targets from others in the hopes of misappropriating money through short-term secret loans or outright theft. Similarly, a younger person may feign romantic involvement with an elderly victim or pretend to be devoted to the senior in order to solicit money or receive an inappropriate gift or inheritance.

Finally, crime against the elderly will likely undergo a significant increase as baby boomers enter their retirement years—a process that is now happening. Not only will the elderly make up an increasingly larger segment of the population as boomers age, but it is anticipated that they will be wealthier than any preceding generation of retirees, making them attractive targets for scam artists and property criminals.[93] The National Center for Elder Abuse, which provides additional information for researchers and justice system participants, can be reached at **https://ncea.acl.gov**. Likewise, the U.S. Department of Justice's new Elder Justice website can be visited at **http://www.justice.gov/elderjustice**.

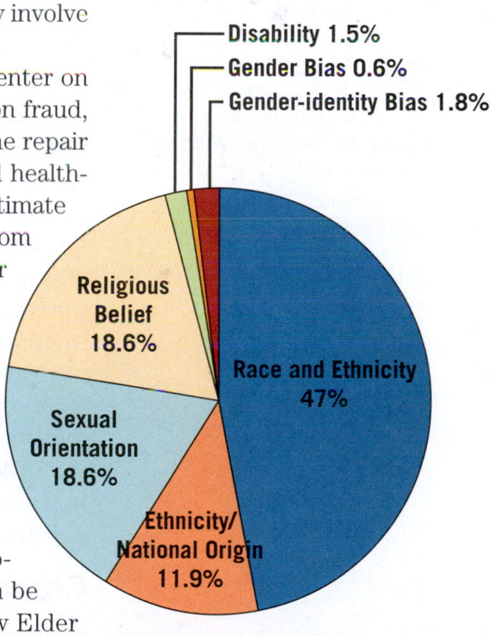

Hate Crime

A significant change in crime-reporting practices resulted from the Hate Crime Statistics Act,[94] signed into law by President George H. W. Bush in 1990. The act mandates a statistical tally of **hate crimes**; data collection under the law began in 1991. Congress defined *hate crime* as an offense "in which the defendant's conduct was motivated by hatred, bias, or prejudice, based on the actual or perceived race, color, religion, national origin, ethnicity, gender, or sexual orientation of another individual or group of individuals."[95] In 2017, police agencies reported a total of 5,479 hate-crime incidents, including four murders, across the country. As Figure 2–8 shows, 18.6% of the incidents were motivated by religious bias, 47.0% were caused by racial hatred, and 11.9% were driven by prejudice against ethnicity or national origin. Another 18.6% of all hate crimes were based on sexual orientation, most committed against males believed by their victimizers to be homosexuals.[96] A relatively small number of hate crimes targeted people with physical or mental disabilities.

FIGURE 2–8
Motivation of Hate-Crime Offenders, 2017

Note: Total does not equal 100% due to rounding.
Source: Federal Bureau of Investigation.

hate crime (UCR/NIBRS)
A criminal offense committed against a person, property, or society that is motivated, in whole or in part, by the offender's bias against a race, religion, disability, sexual orientation, or ethnicity/national origin.

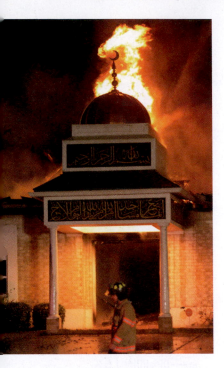

The Islamic Center of Victoria (Texas) burns in 2017. Investigators said the cause of the blaze was arson and labeled it a "bias fire." What are hate crimes?

Barclay Fernandez/The Victoria Advocate/AP Images

Following the terrorist attacks of September 11, 2001, authorities in some jurisdictions reported a dramatic shift in the nature of hate crime, with race-motivated crimes declining and crimes motivated by religion or ethnicity increasing sharply.[97] Islamic individuals, in particular, became the target of many such crimes.

Most hate crimes consist of intimidation, although vandalism, simple assault, and aggravated assault also account for a number of hate-crime offenses. A few robberies and rapes were also classified as hate crimes in 2017.

Although hate crimes are popularly conceived of as crimes motivated by racial enmity, the Violent Crime Control and Law Enforcement Act of 1994 created a new category of "crimes of violence motivated by gender." Congress defined this crime as "a crime of violence committed because of gender or on the basis of gender, and due, at least in part, to an animus based on the victim's gender." The 1994 act did not establish separate penalties for gender-motivated crimes, anticipating that they would be prosecuted as felonies under existing laws. The 1994 act also mandated that crimes motivated by biases against people with disabilities be considered hate crimes.

In 2010, President Obama signed the Matthew Shepard and James Byrd, Jr., Hate Crimes Prevention Act into law. The act expanded the definition of federal hate crimes to include crimes based on gender identity, or disability. The law also amended the Hate Crimes Statistics Act to include crimes motivated by gender identity, as well as hate crimes committed by and against juveniles.

Hate crimes are sometimes called *bias crimes*. One form of bias crime that bears special mention is *homophobic homicide*, a term that refers to the murder of a homosexual by those opposed to that lifestyle. The Southern Poverty Law Center, which tracks hate groups, identified 939 such groups operating in the United States.[98] The center, which is based in Montgomery, Alabama, says that the number of hate groups has jumped 66% since 2000, mostly because of the formation of new anti-immigrant organizations and antigovernment "patriot" organizations. So-called patriot groups are "sovereign citizen" extremists who don't recognize government authority, including its power to tax and to enforce laws. According to the center, California has the most hate groups (77). Nationwide, the center identified 170 neo-Nazi, 136 white nationalist, 136 racist skinhead, 36 anti-Muslim, 26 Christian identity, 149 black separatist, 42 neoconfederate, and 221 Ku Klux Klan groups. Another 122 general hate groups—or those that "espouse a variety of hateful doctrines"— were also identified.

It is worth noting that hate crime statistics vary dramatically between data sources, and that the NCVS reports much larger numbers of hate crimes than does the UCR.[99] Unlike the UCR, however, the NCVS collects data on hate crimes both reported and not reported to police, and permits the victim to decide whether a hate crime has occurred. Learn more about combatting hate crimes at **https://www.justice.gov/hatecrimes**.

Corporate and White-Collar Crime

White-collar crime was mentioned in Chapter 1, where the fraudulent activities of Volkswagen AG in manufacturing cars designed to bypass strict American emissions tests were described.

The most infamous financial crime of recent years involved investment fund manager Bernard ("Bernie") Madoff, who pled guilty in 2009 to operating what some called "Wall Street's biggest fraud"—a Ponzi scheme that defrauded investors out of as much as $50 billion.[100] Madoff, a former chairman of the NASDAQ stock market, pleaded guilty to 11 felony counts, including securities fraud, mail fraud, wire fraud, money laundering, and perjury. He was sentenced to 150 years in prison.[101]

The recent economic downturn, combined with the collapse of the housing market around 2006 and the loss of jobs in many sectors of the economy, sparked a rapid growth in mortgage fraud scams. Mortgage fraud, which is a federal crime, can involve making false or misleading statements about one's identity, personal income, assets, or debts during the mortgage application process. It also includes efforts to knowingly overvalue land or property to defraud purchasers and lenders.

A study by the Mortgage Asset Research Institute concluded that mortgage fraud was more prevalent in 2009 than it had been at the height of the nation's building boom just a few years earlier.[102] Federal agencies say they're still inundated with

> The recent economic downturn, combined with the collapse of the housing market and a loss of jobs in many sectors of the economy, sparked a rapid growth in mortgage fraud scams.

mortgage fraud cases but are also starting to look into a new breed of scams perpetrated by those who offer to refinance homes or save them from foreclosure. In one of the new scams, criminals offer to help people who are about to lose their homes, collecting several thousand dollars up front before disappearing.[103] Recently, the Federal Trade Commission announced a wave of law enforcement actions against businesses using deceptive tactics to market mortgage modification and home foreclosure relief services, including firms that gave the false impression they were affiliated with the federal government.[104]

Under the American system of criminal justice, corporations can be treated as separate legal entities and can be convicted of violations of the criminal law under a legal principle known as the *identification doctrine.* In 2002, for example, a federal jury convicted global accounting firm Arthur Andersen of obstruction of justice after its employees shredded documents related to Enron's bankruptcy in an effort to impede an investigation by securities regulators. The conviction, which was overturned by a unanimous U.S. Supreme Court in 2005,[105] capped the firm's demise, and it ended U.S. operations in August 2002.[106]

Although corporations may be convicted of a crime, the human perpetrators of **corporate crime** are business executives known as *white-collar criminals.* **White-collar crime** was first defined in 1939 by Edwin H. Sutherland in his presidential address to the American Sociological Society.[107] Sutherland described white-collar crime as "Violations of the criminal law committed by a person of respectability and high social status in the course of his or her occupation." He proposed that "crime in the suites" (a reference to corporate offices) rivaled the importance of street crime in its potential impact on American society.

In July 2002, President George W. Bush created a Corporate Fraud Task Force within the federal government and proposed a new law providing criminal penalties for corporate fraud. A few months later, the president signed into law the Sarbanes–Oxley Act.[108] The new law created tough provisions designed to deter and punish corporate and accounting fraud and corruption and to protect the interests of workers and shareholders. Under the Sarbanes–Oxley Act, corporate officials (chief executive officers and chief financial officers) must personally vouch for the truth and accuracy of their companies' financial statements. The act also substantially increased federal penalties for obstructing justice and, specifically, for shredding or destroying documents that might aid in a criminal investigation of business practices. Learn more about corporate and white-collar crime at the National White Collar Crime Center (NW3C) via **http://www.nw3c.org**. Established in 1992, the NW3C provides a national support system for the prevention, investigation, and prosecution of multijurisdictional economic crimes.

▲ A Volkswagen production line in South Carolina. In 2017, the company admitted installing software in some of its vehicles that produced misleading emissions readings and agreed to pay $4.3 billion in criminal and civil penalties. How is white-collar crime different from other crimes? How is it similar?
Heriberto Rodriguez/REUTERS/Alamy Stock Photo

Follow the author's tweets about the latest crime and justice news @schmalleger

Organized Crime

For many people, the term **organized crime** conjures up images of the Mafia (also called the *Cosa Nostra*) or the hit HBO TV series *The Sopranos* and *Boardwalk Empire*. Although organized criminal activity is decidedly a group phenomenon, the groups involved in such activity in the United States today display a great deal of variation. During the past few decades in the United States, the preeminence of traditional Sicilian American criminal organizations has fallen to such diverse criminal associations as the Black Mafia, the Cuban Mafia, the Haitian Mafia, the Colombian cartels, and Asian criminal groups like the Chinese Tongs, Japanese yakuza, and Vietnamese gangs. Included here as well might be inner-city gangs, the best known of which are probably the Los Angeles Crips and Bloods and the Chicago Vice Lords, international drug rings, outlaw motorcycle gangs like the Hell's Angels and the Pagans, and other looser associations of small-time thugs, prison gangs, and drug dealers. Noteworthy among these groups—especially for their involvement in the lucrative drug trade—are the Latino organized bands, including the Dominican, Colombian, Mexican, and Cuban importers of cocaine, heroin, opiates, and other controlled substances.

The unlawful activities of organized groups that operate across national boundaries are especially significant. Such activity is referred to as **transnational organized crime**. Transnational criminal associations worthy of special mention are the Hong Kong-based Triads, the South American cocaine cartels, the Italian Mafia, the Japanese yakuza, the

corporate crime
A violation of a criminal statute by a corporate entity or by its executives, employees, or agents acting on behalf of and for the benefit of the corporation, partnership, or other form of business entity.[iii]

white-collar crime
Financially motivated nonviolent crime committed by business and government professionals.

organized crime
The unlawful activities of the members of a highly organized, disciplined association engaged in supplying illegal goods or services, including gambling, prostitution, loan-sharking, narcotics, and labor racketeering, and in other unlawful activities.[iv]

transnational organized crime
Unlawful activity undertaken and supported by organized criminal groups operating across national boundaries.

Russian *Mafiya*, and the West African crime groups—each of which extends its reach well beyond its home country. In some parts of the world, close links between organized crime and terrorist groups involve money laundering, which provides cash to finance the activities of terrorist cells and to finance paramilitary efforts to overthrow established governments.

Former Central Intelligence Agency (CIA) Director R. James Woolsey points out that "while organized crime is not a new phenomenon today, some governments find their authority besieged at home and their foreign policy interests imperiled abroad. Drug trafficking, links between drug traffickers and terrorists, smuggling of illegal aliens, massive financial and bank fraud, arms smuggling, potential involvement in the theft and sale of nuclear material, political intimidation, and corruption all constitute a poisonous brew—a mixture potentially as deadly as what we faced during the cold war."[109] The challenge for today's criminal justice student is to recognize that crime does not respect national boundaries. Crime is global, and what happens in one part of the world could affect us all.[110]

Gun Crime

Guns and gun crime seem to pervade American culture. In 2018, a 19-year-old armed with an AR-15 assault rifle opened fire in a Parkland, Florida, high school, killing 17 people and seriously wounding 15 more. Less than one year earlier, a shooter fired over 1,000 rounds from a Las Vegas hotel room window into a crowd of concert-goers, killing more than 50 people and injuring over 800. Not long before the Las Vegas attack, 49 people were killed and 58 others injured in a nightclub shooting in Orlando, Florida; and in 2015 the Emanuel AME Church shooting in Charleston, South Carolina, took nine lives.

Constitutional guarantees of the right to bear arms have combined with historical circumstances to make ours a well-armed society. Guns are used in many types of crimes. Each year, approximately one million serious crimes—including homicide, rape, robbery, and assault—involve the use of a handgun. In a typical year, approximately 9,800 murders are committed in the United States with firearms. A report by the BJS found that 18% of state prison inmates and 15% of federal inmates were armed at the time they committed the crime for which they were imprisoned,[111] and 9% of those in state prisons said they fired a gun while committing the offense for which they were serving time.[112] In some parts of the country, people are so well armed that those who aren't worry about their safety. In 2016, for example, Chicago police superintendent Eddie Johnson said that jail inmates with whom he spoke told him that their greatest fear is being caught on the street without a gun. "It's not that they'll get caught with a gun, and then they gotta go to prison," he said. "It's that they'll be caught out there without a gun and they'll be the next dead person."[113]

Ten years ago, however, the U.S. Supreme Court came down heavily in support of the individual's right to bear arms. The Second Amendment to the U.S. Constitution reads, "A well regulated Militia, being necessary to the security of a free State, the right of the people to keep and bear Arms, shall not be infringed." In the 2008 case of *District of Columbia* v. *Heller*,[114] the U.S. Supreme Court struck down a District of Columbia gun-control regulation and ruled that "the Second Amendment protects an individual's right to possess firearms and that the city's total ban on handguns, as well as its requirement that firearms in the home be kept nonfunctional even when necessary for self-defense, violated that right." The Court's holding in *Heller* was sweeping and unambiguous. The decision clearly declared the Second Amendment protection of "an individual right to possess a firearm unconnected with service in a militia, and to use that arm for traditionally lawful purposes, such as self-defense within the home."

Following *Heller*, some questioned whether the Court's ruling might be limited to federal enclaves, like the District of Columbia, or whether it was applicable to other jurisdictions. In 2010, in the case of *McDonald* v. *City of Chicago*,[115] the U.S. Supreme Court answered that question when it struck down gun-banning ordinances in Chicago and the city of Oak Park, Illinois. The Justices found that "the right to keep and bear arms must be regarded as a substantive guarantee" inherent in the U.S. Constitution. In *McDonald*, the Court established an individual's right to keep a gun for self-defense in the home as

> Guns and gun crime seem to pervade American culture.

a "fundamental" constitutional right. Any right that the Court declares to be fundamental cannot be contravened by laws at any level unless the government can demonstrate a compelling need to do so and only if limits imposed take the narrowest possible approach to addressing the issue. Consequently, in the wake of *McDonald,* states and local jurisdictions may still place restrictions on gun ownership, such as registration requirements or prohibiting the possession of handguns by convicted felons, but those restrictions must be reasonable and cannot be extreme.

One of the most significant laws enacted prior to *Heller* was the 1993 Brady Handgun Violence Prevention Act,[116] which mandated a 5-day waiting period before the purchase of a handgun, and it established a national instant criminal background check system that firearms dealers must use before selling a handgun.[117] The 5-day waiting period was discontinued in 1998 when the instant computerized background checking system became operational.

Another important piece of legislation relating to gun ownerships was the 1994 Violent Crime Control and Law Enforcement Act,[118] which regulated the sale of firearms within the United States and originally banned the manufacture of 19 military-style assault weapons, including those with specific combat features, such as high-capacity ammunition clips capable of holding more than ten rounds. The ban on assault weapons ended in 2004, however, when it was not renewed by Congress. The 1994 law also prohibited the sale or transfer of a gun to a juvenile, as well as the possession of a gun by a juvenile, and it prohibits gun sales to, and possession by, people subject to family violence restraining orders.

The 1996 Domestic Violence Offender Gun Ban[119] prohibits individuals convicted of misdemeanor domestic violence offenses from owning or using firearms. Soon after the law was passed, however, it became embroiled in controversy when hundreds of police officers across the country who had been convicted of domestic-violence offenses were found to be in violation of the ban. A number of officers lost their jobs, while others were placed in positions that did not require them to carry firearms.[120]

Following the 1999 Columbine High School shooting, a number of states moved to tighten controls over handguns and assault weapons. The California legislature, for example, restricted gun purchases to one per month and tightened a 10-year-old ban on assault weapons. Similarly, Illinois passed a law requiring that gun owners lock their weapons away from anyone under age 14.

In 2004, at the urging of major police organizations, the U.S. Senate scuttled plans for a gun-industry protection bill. However, the bill was revived in 2005 and passed both houses of Congress before being signed into law by President George W. Bush on October 31. Known as the Protection of Lawful Commerce in Firearms Act, the law grants gunmakers and most gun dealers immunity from lawsuits brought by victims of gun crimes and their survivors. The law removes negligence as viable grounds for a civil suit against a gun dealer who carelessly sells a gun to someone who is at risk for using it in a crime; the law states that the dealer can be sued only if he or she knew of the gun buyer's criminal intent before the purchase. Gunmakers were made similarly immune from suits alleging product liability for having manufactured potentially lethal items.

Recently, however, the need for greater gun-control measures were highlighted by a series of random mass shootings that shocked the nation (which were described earlier). Consequently, President Obama signed 23 executive orders on gun safety and called upon Congress to address the problem of gun violence in America.[121]

Although federal law limits retail purchases of handguns by felons, a BJS study found that most offenders obtain weapons from friends or family members or "on the street" rather than attempt to purchase them at retail establishments.[122] One recent study, for example, found no evidence that stringent gun-control laws have an impact on crime.[123] The study, which used data from all 50 states, found that gun-control laws do not have an impact on the crime rate or on the occurrence of any specific type of serious crime. Such laws are ineffective in reducing crime, the study authors said, because they do not substantially reduce the availability of firearms to criminal offenders.

▲ A visitor to a technology fair views a fully functional plastic handgun created using a 3-D printing process. The weapon is undetectable by standard metal detectors. What's your position on gun ownership and gun control? *Oli Scarff/Getty Images News/Getty Images*

🐦 Follow the author's tweets about the latest crime and justice news @schmalleger

A few years ago, Congress renewed a 10-year ban on the manufacture of undetectable plastic handguns.[124] Such weapons can be produced on readily available 3-D printers which are guided by digital blueprints. Debate continues about whether to require gun manufacturers to create and retain "ballistic fingerprints" (the marks left on a bullet by the barrel of the gun from which it was fired) of each weapon they produce. Although a national ballistics fingerprinting requirement may still be years away, a number of jurisdictions are already considering new gun tracking technologies such as microstamping.[125] Microstamping uses laser engraving to encode a weapon's serial number on each cartridge that it fires, and California authorities believe that the technology will allow handguns to be traced to their manufacturer and then to the first purchaser using only spent cartridges left at crime scenes.

For the latest information on gun violence and gun laws, visit the Brady Campaign to Prevent Gun Violence via **http://www.bradycampaign.org/about-brady**. The National Rifle Association site at **http://home.nra.org** provides support for responsible access to firearms.

Drug Crime

FBI statistics show that drug-related crimes continued to rise during the early part of this century even while rates of many other crimes have been decreasing. In fact, the number of arrests for drug crimes grew almost fivefold in the United States between 1973 and 2006, an increase that was unrelenting even while arrests for violent and property crimes started dropping in the mid-1990s—a decrease that continues today. Drug arrests finally began to abate around 2006, but the significant increase in drug violations prior to that time led to substantial growth in America's prison populations. Today, the total number of drug arrests in the United States exceeds the annual number of arrests for any other crime (including driving under the influence) and helps explain why *arrest* rates in this country are not declining with anywhere near the speed of declines in official crime rates (which do not count drug crime in the summary information that they provide).

The White House Office of National Drug Control Policy (ONDCP) estimates annual illicit major drug sales in the United States of around $100 billion, while the United Nations says that illegal drug revenue in the United States, Canada, and Mexico totals around $142 billion yearly.[126] The national opioid crisis, which began in the 2010s, involves the use of prescription pain relievers, heroin, and synthetic opioid products such as fentanyl and carfentanil. In 2018, the National Institute on Drug Abuse put the number of Americans dying daily after overdosing on opioids at 115.[127] In a recent analysis, the White House estimated that the total cost of U.S. opioid abuse totals more than $500 billion annually—mostly in health-care costs, criminal justice spending, and lost productivity.[128] In 2017, President Trump declared opioid abuse a national public health emergency.

Alone, drug-law violations are themselves criminal, but more and more studies are linking drug abuse to other serious crimes. One survey by RAND found that most of the "violent predators" among prisoners had extensive histories of heroin abuse, often in combination with alcohol and other drugs.[129] Some cities reported that a large percentage of their homicides were drug related.[130] More recent studies also link drug abuse to other serious crimes. Community leaders perceive, and data analyses confirm, that heroin, synthetic opioid, and cocaine use profoundly affects violent crime, with homicide rates closely tracking levels of use of those drugs among adult male arrestees.[131] Prisoner survey data show that 19% of state inmates and 16% of federal prisoners reported committing their most recent offense to obtain money for drugs.[132] One study found that 13.3% of convicted jail inmates said that they had committed their offense to get money for drugs.[133]

Enforcement of drug laws has another side, and that is the conviction and imprisonment of many nonviolent offenders whose only interest is in recreational use of "soft" drugs, such as marijuana. Consequently, within the past few years some states (notably Washington, Oregon, California, Nevada, Maine, Massachusetts, Vermont, Alaska, and Colorado) have modified their laws to allow for personal nonpublic use of recreational marijuana. Whether other states will follow those that have already legalized recreational use of marijuana remains to be seen. Even so, it is apparent that public attitudes toward at least some drugs are changing. That change is likely to break part of the relationship between drug use and

Follow the author's tweets about the latest crime and justice news @schmalleger

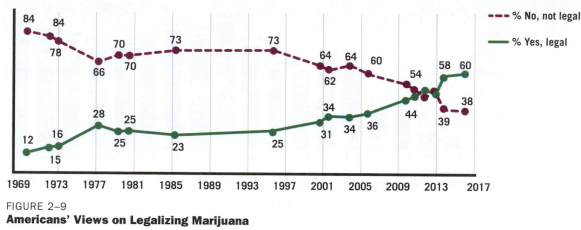

FIGURE 2–9
Americans' Views on Legalizing Marijuana
Source: Pearson Education, Inc.

continued criminal involvement that in part may be due to exclusion from the workforce and the virtual nonemployability that so often results from a drug conviction of any kind.

Twenty-two other states and the District of Columbia have legalized marijuana for medical use and more are considering it.[134] Driving under the influence, however, remains illegal, and marijuana intoxication cannot be offered as a defense to other crimes committed while high. Marijuana cultivation, sale, and use still remain federal crimes, although federal enforcement efforts are focused more on combating the importation of controlled substances by drug cartels and on preventing the sale of such substances to minors. Figure 2–9 shows Americans' changing views on marijuana. Learn more about drug crime and efforts being made to combat it from the White House's Office of National Drug Control Strategy at **http://www.whitehouse.gov/ondcp**.

Cybercrime

In 2018, Taylor Huddleston, 27, of Hot Springs, Arkansas, was sentenced by a U.S. District Court judge to 33 months in prison followed by 2 years of supervised release for developing and distributing two types of computer malware.[135] The first, called NanoCore RAT, is used to steal sensitive information from victims' computers, including passwords, e-mails, and instant messages. NanoCore RAT can also be used to turn on computer-connected cameras and to spy on people using infected computers. Huddleston's other product, Net Seal, was used to distribute malware for co-conspirators for a fee. **Computer crimes**, also called *cybercrimes or information technology crimes*, use computers and computer technology as tools in crime commission. Thefts of computer equipment, although sometimes spectacular, are not computer crimes but are instead classified as larcenies. "True" computer criminals go beyond the theft of hardware, focusing instead on the information stored in computer systems and manipulating it in a way that violates the law. The incidence of cybercrime is shown graphically in Figure 2–10, which displays the number of complaints filed with the Internet Crime Complaint Center (IC3) from 2000 to 2017.

Many crimes committed via the Internet, such as prostitution, drug sales, theft, and fraud, are not new forms of offending. Rather, they are traditional offenses that use technology in their commission or that build on the possibilities for criminal activity that new technologies make possible. Recently, for example, an international operation led by U.S. Immigration and Customs Enforcement agents led to arrest of 245 suspected child pornographers who communicated through the Internet.[136] Of those arrested, 213 were from the United States, and 23 from other countries. The enforcement effort, known as Operation Sunflower, led to the identification of 123 victims of child exploitation and the removal of 44 children from the control of alleged abusers. Five of the rescued children were 3 years old, and nine were between the ages of 4 and 6.

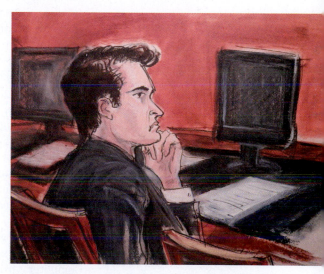

▲ Ross Ulbricht, aka Dread Pirate Roberts. Ulbricht was sentenced to life in prison in 2015 for creating and operating the dark website Silk Road. Silk Road offered drugs, weapons, sex, and even murder to users who paid in untraceable Bitcoins. What is cybercrime, and why is it a threat?
Elizabeth Williams/AP Images

computer crime
Any crime perpetrated through the use of computer technology. Also, any violation of a federal or state computer-crime statute. Also called *cybercrime.*

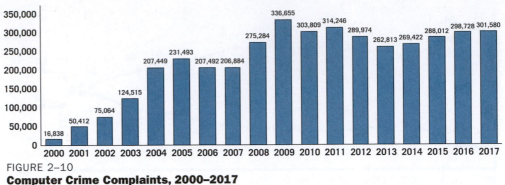

FIGURE 2–10
Computer Crime Complaints, 2000–2017
Source: Based on data from the Internet Crime Complaint Center.

malware
Malicious computer programs such as viruses, worms, and Trojan horses.

computer virus
A computer program designed to secretly invade systems and either modify the way in which they operate or alter the information they store. Viruses are destructive software programs that may effectively vandalize computers of all types and sizes.

spam
Unsolicited commercial bulk e-mail whose primary purpose is the advertisement or promotion of a commercial product or service.

Cybercrime, sometimes called computer crime or information-technology crime, uses computers and computer technology as tools in crime commission.

Peter Grabosky of the Australian Institute of Criminology suggests that most computer-related crimes fall into one of the following broad categories:[137] (1) theft of services, such as telephone or long-distance access; (2) communications in furtherance of criminal conspiracies—for example, the e-mail communications said to have taken place between members of Osama bin Laden's al-Qaeda terrorist network;[138] (3) information piracy and forgery—that is, the stealing of trade secrets or copyrighted information; (4) dissemination of offensive materials, such as child pornography, and extortion threats, such as those made against financial institutions by hackers claiming the ability to destroy the institutions' electronic records; (5) electronic money laundering and tax evasion through electronic funds transfers that conceal the origin of financial proceeds; (6) electronic vandalism and terrorism, including **malware** such as computer viruses, worms, Trojan horses, and cyberterrorism—that is, cyberattacks on critical components of a nation's infrastructure, such as its banking system; (7) telemarketing fraud, including investment frauds and illegitimate electronic auctions; (8) illegal interception of telecommunications—that is, illegal eavesdropping; and (9) electronic funds transfer fraud—specifically, the illegal interception and diversion of legitimate transactions.

Computer viruses have become a special concern of the general computer user during the past several years, especially as more people have connected to the Internet. Computer viruses were brought to public attention in 1988 when the Pakistani virus (or Pakistani brain virus) became widespread in personal and office computers across the United States.[139] The Pakistani virus was created by Amjad Farooq Alvi and his brother Basit Farooq Alvi, two cut-rate computer software dealers in Lahore, Pakistan. The Alvi brothers made copies of costly software products and sold them at low prices to mostly Western shoppers looking for a bargain. Motivated by convoluted logic, the brothers hid a virus on each disk they sold to punish buyers for seeking to evade copyright laws. Since then, many other virus attacks have made headlines, including the infamous Michelangelo virus in 1992; the intentional distribution of infected software on an AIDS-related research CD-ROM distributed about the same time; the Kournikova virus in 2000; and the Sircam, Nimda, W32, NastyBrew, Berbew, Mydoom, and Code Red worms, all of which made their appearance or were substantially modified by their creators between 2001 and 2006.

In 2003, federal legislators acted to criminalize the sending of unsolicited commercial e-mail, or **spam**. The federal CAN-SPAM Act (Controlling the Assault of Nonsolicited Pornography and Marketing), which took effect on January 1, 2004, regulates the sending of "commercial electronic mail messages."[140] The law, which applies equally to mass mailings and to individual e-mail messages, defines *commercial electronic mail messages* as electronic mail whose *primary purpose* is the "commercial advertisement or promotion of a commercial product or service." The CAN-SPAM law requires that a commercial e-mail message include the following three features: (1) a clear and conspicuous identification that the message is an advertisement or solicitation, (2) an opt-out feature allowing recipients to opt out of future mailings, and (3) a valid physical address identifying the sender. Some experts estimate that 80% of all e-mail today is spam,[141] and a number of states have enacted their own antispam laws.

Computer-related crimes can also involve copyright infringement. In 2005, for example, the U.S. Supreme Court agreed to hear an appeal from the music industry, and in the landmark case of *MGM* v. *Grokster*,[142] the Court found that online file-sharing services may be held liable for copyright infringement if they promote their services explicitly as a way for users to download copyrighted music and other content.

One form of cybercrime that relies primarily on social engineering to succeed is *phishing* (pronounced *fishing*). Phishing is a relatively new form of high-technology fraud that uses official-looking e-mail messages to elicit responses from victims, directing them to phony websites. Microsoft Corporation says that phishing is "the fastest-growing form of online fraud in the world today."[143] Phishing e-mails typically instruct recipients to validate or update account information before their accounts are canceled. Phishing schemes, which have targeted most major banks, the Federal Deposit Insurance Corporation, IBM, eBay, PayPal, and some major health-care providers, are designed to steal valuable information such as credit card numbers, Social Security numbers, user IDs, and passwords.

Some researchers have determined that some of the most serious corporate computer security threats come from employees, including 70% of all incidents involving unauthorized access to information systems and 95% of all network intrusions that result in significant financial loss.[144]

In 2005, the federal government published its National Computer Security Survey (NCSS). The NCSS was sponsored by the U.S. Department of Justice, Bureau of Justice Statistics and the U.S. Department of Homeland Security, National Cyber Security Division. This data-collection effort was part of the president's 2003 National Strategy to Secure Cyberspace. You may access the latest NCSS at **https://www.bjs.gov/index. cfm?ty=dcdetail&iid=260**. Learn more about federal laws designed to enhance computer security in Chapter 7.

▲ The FBI's 2017 National Cyber Security Awareness Month poster. How can you be sure you are safe online?

From Federal Bureau of Investigation.

Terrorism

Terrorism as a criminal activity and the prevention of further acts of terrorism became primary concerns of American justice system officials following the September 11, 2001, attacks on the World Trade Center and the Pentagon. Long before the September 11 attacks, however, terrorism was far from unknown. In 2001, for example, international terrorist attacks totaled 864 worldwide—down from the 1,106 reported a year earlier.[145]

There is no single definition of terrorism that is applicable to all places and all circumstances. Some definitions are statutory in nature whereas others were created for such practical purposes as gauging success in the fight against terrorism. The FBI, for example, defines **terrorism** as "a violent act or an act dangerous to human life in violation of the criminal laws of the United States or of any state to intimidate or coerce a government, the civilian population, or any segment thereof, in furtherance of political or social objectives."[146] One of the most comprehensive and widely used definitions of terrorist activity can be found in the federal Immigration and Nationality Act, an excerpt of which appears in CJ Exhibit 2-1.

Types of Terrorism

It is important to distinguish between two major forms of terrorism: domestic and international. Such distinctions are generally made in terms of the origin, base of operations, and objectives of a terrorist organization. **Domestic terrorism** refers to the unlawful use of force or violence by a group or an individual who is based and operates entirely within the United States and its territories without foreign direction and whose acts are directed against elements of the U.S. government or population.[147] **International terrorism**, in contrast, is the unlawful use of force or violence by a group or an individual who has some connection to a foreign power or whose activities transcend national boundaries against people or property to intimidate or coerce a government, the civilian population, or any segment thereof in furtherance of political or social objectives.[148] International terrorism is

terrorism
A violent act or an act dangerous to human life in violation of the criminal laws of the United States or of any state, committed to intimidate or coerce a government, the civilian population, or any segment thereof in furtherance of political or social objectives.[v]

domestic terrorism
The unlawful use of force or violence by a group or an individual who is based and operates entirely within the United States and its territories without foreign direction and whose acts are directed at elements of the U.S. government or population.[vi]

international terrorism
The unlawful use of force or violence by a group or an individual who has some connection to a foreign power or whose activities transcend national boundaries against people or property in order to intimidate or coerce a government, the civilian population, or any segment thereof in furtherance of political or social objectives.[vii]

CJ Exhibit 2-1
What Is Terrorist Activity?

Federal law enforcement efforts directed against agents of foreign terrorist organizations derive their primary authority from the Immigration and Nationality Act, found in Chapter 12 of the U.S. Code. The act defines *terrorist activity* as follows:

(ii)   "Terrorist activity" defined

As used in this chapter, the term "terrorist activity" means any activity which is unlawful under the laws of the place where it is committed (or which, if committed in the United States, would be unlawful under the laws of the United States or any State) and which involves any of the following:

I.   The hijacking or sabotage of any conveyance (including an aircraft, vessel, or vehicle).

II.   The seizing or detaining, and threatening to kill, injure, or continue to detain, another individual in order to compel a third person (including a governmental organization) to do or abstain from doing any act as an explicit or implicit condition for the release of the individual seized or detained.

III.   A violent attack upon an internationally protected person (as defined in section 1116(b)(4) of title 18) or upon the liberty of such a person.

IV.   An assassination.

V.   The use of any—

a.   biological agent, chemical agent, or nuclear weapon or device, or

b.   explosive or firearm (other than for mere personal monetary gain), with intent to endanger, directly or

indirectly, the safety of one or more individuals or to cause substantial damage to property.

VI.   A threat, attempt, or conspiracy to do any of the foregoing.

(iii)   "Engage in terrorist activity" defined

As used in this chapter, the term "engage in terrorist activity" means to commit, in an individual capacity or as a member of an organization, an act of terrorist activity or an act which the actor knows, or reasonably should know, affords material support to any individual, organization, or government in conducting a terrorist activity at any time, including any of the following acts:

I.   The preparation or planning of a terrorist activity.

II.   The gathering of information on potential targets for terrorist activity.

III.   The providing of any type of material support, including a safe house, transportation, communications, funds, false documentation or identification, weapons, explosives, or training, to any individual the actor knows or has reason to believe has committed or plans to commit a terrorist activity.

IV.   The soliciting of funds or other things of value for terrorist activity or for any terrorist organization.

V.   The solicitation of any individual for membership in a terrorist organization, terrorist government, or to engage in a terrorist activity.

---

cyberterrorism
A form of terrorism that makes use of high technology, especially computers and the Internet, in the planning and carrying out of terrorist attacks.

▲ A commuter being helped away from the Edgware Road Station following terrorist bombings in London's subway system in 2005. How might future acts of terrorism be prevented?

Jane Mingay/AP Images

sometimes mistakenly called *foreign terrorism*, a term that, strictly speaking, refers only to acts of terrorism that occur outside the United States.

Another kind of terrorism, called **cyberterrorism**, is lurking on the horizon. Cyberterrorism makes use of high technology, especially computers and the Internet, in the planning and carrying out of terrorist attacks. The term was coined in the 1980s by Barry Collin, a senior research fellow at the Institute for Security and Intelligence in California, who used it to refer to the convergence of cyberspace and terrorism.[149] It was later popularized by a 1996 RAND report that warned of an emerging "new terrorism" distinguished by how terrorist groups organize and by how they use technology. The report warned of a coming "netwar" or "infowar" consisting of coordinated cyberattacks on our nation's economic, business, and military infrastructure.[150] A year later, FBI Agent Mark M. Pollitt offered a working definition of *cyberterrorism*, saying that it is "the premeditated, politically motivated attack against information, computer systems, computer programs, and data which results in violence against noncombatant targets by subnational groups or clandestine agents."[151]

Scenarios describing cyberterrorism possibilities are imaginative and diverse. Some have suggested that a successful cyberterrorist attack on the nation's air traffic control system might cause airplanes to collide in mid-air or that an attack on food- and cereal-processing plants that drastically altered the levels of certain nutritional supplements might sicken or kill a large number of our nation's young children. Other such attacks might cause the country's power grid to collapse or might muddle the records and transactions of banks and stock exchanges. Possible targets in such attacks are almost endless. A 2005 national survey of computer security experts found that almost half were expecting a "digital Pearl Harbor," in which American society would be plunged into chaos by malicious hackers, to occur within the next few years.[152]

Organization and Scope of Terrorist Groups

Prior to his retirement in 2013, FBI Director Robert S. Mueller III identified three organizational levels that characterize violent extremists seeking to damage the United States and its interests.[153] The top tier, Mueller said, are groups like ISIS and al-Qaeda, which have established new sanctuaries in the ungoverned spaces, tribal areas, and frontier provinces of Pakistan. The middle tier Mueller called the most complex. "We are finding," he said, "small groups who have some ties to an established terrorist organization but are largely self-directed. Think of them as al-Qaeda franchises—hybrids of homegrown radicals and more sophisticated operatives." The bottom tier, Mueller noted, "is made up of homegrown extremists. They are self-radicalizing, self-financing, and self-executing. They meet up on the Internet instead of in foreign training camps. They have no formal 'affiliation with al-Qaeda or ISIS,' but they are inspired by its message of violence."

Terrorist groups are active throughout the world, and the United States is not their only target. Terrorist organizations operate in South America, Africa, the Middle East, Latin America, the Philippines, Japan, India, Ireland, England, Nepal, and some of the now independent states of the former Soviet Union. The Central Intelligence Agency (CIA) reports that "terrorist tactics will become increasingly sophisticated and designed to achieve mass casualties."[154] The CIA also notes that nations "with poor governance; ethnic, cultural, or religious tensions; weak economies; and porous borders will be prime breeding grounds for terrorism."[155]

Initial efforts to develop a comprehensive plan of protection for the nation's critical infrastructure began in 2001 when President George W. Bush created the Office of Homeland Security, making its director a cabinet member. It became a department of the federal government in 2002. Visit the Department of Homeland Security via **https://www.dhs.gov**. You can track national and international terror incidents as they occur through the National Counterterrorism Center's Worldwide Incidents Tracking Center, which is available at **https://www.dni.gov/index.php/nctc-home**.

Follow the author's tweets about the latest crime and justice news @schmalleger

Crime in International Context

Although space does not permit an in-depth discussion of cross-national crimes in this text, it is worthwhile to note that criminal activity has become big business around the globe and that many criminal organizations are linked together in the commission of **transnational offenses**. Included here are drug running, human trafficking and smuggling, cybercrime, money laundering, and other more "traditional" forms of crime. Recently, for example, the United Nations reported that crime is one of the largest "businesses" in the world, and calculated that it generates $2.1 trillion in global annual proceeds—or approximately 3.6% of the world's gross domestic product.[156]

transnational offenses
Unlawful activity that occurs across national boundaries.

The UN Survey on Crime Trends and Operations of Criminal Justice Systems (UN-CTS) which reports official crime statistics from nearly 100 countries, provide a global portrait of criminal activity. Seen historically, the surveys have shown that crimes against property are most characteristic of nations with developed economies (where they constitute approximately 82% of all reported crime) whereas crimes against the person occur much more frequently in developing countries (where they account for 43% of all crime).[157] Complementing the official statistics of the UN-CTS are data from the European Crime and Safety Survey (EU-ICS), which is conducted by the Gallup Organization Europe and collaborating agencies.

Additional information about the justice systems of many countries can be found in the *World Factbook of Criminal Justice Systems*, available at **https://www.bjs.gov/content/pub/html/wfcj.cfm**.

Summary

THE CRIME PICTURE

- The FBI's Uniform Crime Reporting (UCR) Program began in the 1930s when Congress authorized the U.S. attorney general to survey crime in America. Today's UCR/NIBRS Program provides annual data on the number of reported Part I offenses, or major crimes, as well as information about arrests that have been made for less serious Part II offenses. The Part I offenses are murder, rape, robbery, aggravated assault, burglary, larceny-theft, motor vehicle theft, and arson. The Part II offenses category covers many more crimes, including drug offenses, driving under the influence, and simple assault. Modifications to the UCR Program, which has traditionally provided only summary crime data, occurred with the implementation of the National Incident-Based Reporting System (NIBRS). It represents a significant redesign of the original UCR Program and gathers many details about each criminal incident, such as place of occurrence, weapon used, type and value of property damaged or stolen, personal characteristics of the offender and the victim, nature of any relationship between the two, and disposition of the complaint.

- The National Crime Victimization Survey (NCVS) is the second major source of statistical data about crime in the United States. The NCVS, which was first conducted in 1972, is based on victim self-reports rather than on police reports. The NCVS originally built on efforts by both the National Opinion Research Center and the 1967 President's Commission on Law Enforcement and the Administration of Justice to uncover what some had been calling the *dark figure of crime*—that is, those crimes that are not reported to the police and that are relatively hidden from justice system officials. An analysis of victim self-report data led to the realization that crimes of all types were more prevalent than UCR statistics had previously indicated.

- The UCR/NIBRS and NCVS differ in a number of significant ways. First, whereas the UCR/NIBRS Program makes use of data gleaned from citizens' reports of crime made to enforcement agencies, the NCVS utilizes survey data in compiling its reports. Second, because both the UCR/NIBRS and the NCVS are human creations, they contain only data that their creators think appropriate, and the reports they generate are structured differently.

- This chapter introduces a number of special categories of crime, including crime against women, crime against the elderly, hate crime, corporate and white-collar crime, organized crime, gun crime, drug crime, high-technology and computer crime, and terrorism. Each of these categories is of special concern in contemporary society.

QUESTIONS FOR REVIEW

1. Describe the historical development of the FBI's Uniform Crime Reporting Program, and list the crimes on which it reports. How is the ongoing implementation of the National Incident-Based Reporting System changing the UCR Program? How do data reported under the new UCR/NIBRS differ from the crime statistics reported under the traditional UCR Program?
2. Describe the history of the National Crime Victimization Survey. What do data from the NCVS tell us about crime in the United States today?
3. How does the NCVS differ from the UCR/NIBRS? Which program would you regard as more reliable? Why?
4. What are the special categories of crime discussed in this chapter? Why are they important?

Criminal Law

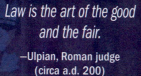

Law is the art of the good and the fair.

—Ulpian, Roman judge (circa a.d. 200)

Every law is an infraction of liberty.

—Jeremy Bentham (1748–1832)

Learning Objectives

After reading this chapter, you should be able to:

1. Summarize the purpose, primary sources, and development of law. **62**

2. Define the rule of law, including its importance in Western democratic societies. **63**

3. Summarize the various types of law, including the purpose of each. **64**

4. Describe six categories of crimes and their characteristics. **66**

5. Describe the eight general features of crime. **69**

6. Explain what is meant by the elements of a specific criminal offense. **74**

7. Compare and contrast the four general categories of accepted criminal defense. **76**

Photogl/Fotolia

▲ Dr. Hsiu-Ying "Lisa" Tseng, a Los Angeles-area physician who was convicted of second-degree murder in 2016 for over-prescribing painkillers that resulted in the deaths of three of her patients. Might she have been ignorant of relevant law?

Luis Sinco/Los Angeles Times/Getty Images

law

A rule of conduct, generally found enacted in the form of a statute, that proscribes or mandates certain forms of behavior.

Introduction

In 2016, Dr. Hsiu-Ying "Lisa" Tseng, a Los Angeles-area physician, was convicted of second-degree murder for over-prescribing painkillers that resulted in the deaths of three of her patients. Tseng routinely provided powerful painkillers, such as Percocet (oxycodone) and Vicodin (hydrocodone), to people who were addicted to them, and ignored pleas from patient's family members to stop.[1] She was sentenced to 30 years to life in prison by Los Angeles County Superior Court Judge George Lomell who said that Tseng continued to write reckless prescriptions even after learning that her patients were dying.

Laws govern many aspects of our lives, and we are expected to know what the law *says* as it applies to our daily lives and to *follow* it. As this chapter will show, laws provide for predictability because people can study the law and know exactly what is required of them. In the case of Dr. Tseng, however, her defenders argued that she was naïve and never realized that patients were using her to support their drug habits.[2]

The Nature and Purpose of Law

Imagine a society without laws. A **law** mandates or proscribes a certain behavior and can be a product of rule creation, a guide for people's behavior, or both. Without civil law, people would not know what to expect from one another nor would they be able to plan for the future with any degree of certainty. Without criminal law, people wouldn't feel safe because the more powerful could take what they wanted from the less powerful. Without constitutional law, people could not exercise the basic rights that are available to them as citizens of a free nation. A society needs laws to uphold fairness and to prevent the victimization of innocents.

> **1** Summarize the purpose, primary sources, and development of law.

Practically speaking, laws regulate relationships between people and also between parties, such as government agencies and individuals. They channel and simultaneously constrain human behavior, and they empower individuals while contributing to public order. Laws also serve other purposes. They ensure that the philosophical, moral, and economic perspectives of their creators are protected and made credible. They maintain values and uphold established patterns of social privilege. They sustain existing power relationships; finally, they support a system for the punishment and rehabilitation of offenders (Table 3-1). Modifications of the law, when gradually induced, promote orderly change in the rest of society.

Our laws are found in statutory provisions and constitutional enactments,[3] as well as in hundreds of years of rulings by courts at all levels. According to the authoritative *Black's Law Dictionary*, the word *law* "generally contemplates both statutory and case law."[4] **Statutory law** is "the law on the books." It results from legislative action and is often thought of as "the law of the land." Written laws exist in both criminal and civil areas and are called *codes*. Once laws have been written down in organized fashion, they are said to be *codified*. Federal statutes are compiled in the United States Code (U.S.C.) which is available online in its entirety at **http://www.law.cornell.edu/uscode**. State codes and municipal ordinances are also readily available in written, or statutory, form. The written form of the criminal law is called the **penal code**. **Case law**, which we will discuss in detail a bit later, is the law that results from judicial decisions.

statutory law

The written or codified law; "the law on the books," as enacted by a government body or agency having the power to make laws.

But the laws of our country are not unambiguous. If all of "the law" could be found in written legal codes, it would be plain to nearly everyone, and we would need far fewer lawyers than are practicing today. But some laws—the precedents established by courts—do not exist "on the books," and even those that do are open to interpretation. This is where common law comes into play. **Common law** is the traditional body of unwritten historical precedents created from everyday social customs, rules, and practices, many of which were supported by judicial decisions during early times. Common law principles are still used to interpret many legal issues in quite a few states. Hence, it is not uncommon to hear of jurisdictions within the United States referred to as "common law jurisdictions" or "common law states."

The Rule of Law

2 Define the rule of law, including its importance in Western democratic societies.

The social, economic, and political stability of any society depends largely on the development and institutionalization of a predictable system of laws. Western democratic societies adhere to the **rule of law**, which is sometimes also referred to as the *supremacy of law*. The rule of law centers on the belief that an orderly society must be governed by established principles and known codes that are applied uniformly and fairly to all of its members. Under this tenet, no one is above the law, and those who make or enforce the law must also abide by it. The principle was well illustrated when, in 2012, former Democratic Mayor Kwame Kilpatrick of Detroit was convicted by a federal jury of 24 crimes, including using his position as mayor and as a Michigan State House Representative to execute a wide-ranging racketeering conspiracy.[5] In 2013, Kilpatrick was sentenced to 28 years in prison.[6]

The rule of law has been called the greatest political achievement of our culture. Without it, few other human achievements—especially those that require the coordinated efforts of a large number of people—would be possible. President John F. Kennedy eloquently explained the rule of law, saying, "Americans are free to disagree with the law, but not to disobey it; for [in] a government of laws and not of men, no man, however prominent and powerful, no mob, however unruly or boisterous, is entitled to defy a court of law."[7]

The rule of law has also been called "the foundation of liberties in the Western world,"[8] for it means that due process (which was discussed in Chapter 1) has to be followed in any criminal prosecution, and it is due process that serves as a check on arbitrary state power.

The American Bar Association notes that the rule of law includes these elements:[9]

- Freedom from private lawlessness provided by the legal system of a politically organized society

- A relatively high degree of objectivity in the formulation of legal norms and a like degree of evenhandedness in their application

- Legal ideas and juristic devices for the attainment of individual and group objectives within the bounds of ordered liberty

- Substantive and procedural limitations on governmental power in the interest of the individual for the enforcement of which there are appropriate legal institutions and machinery

Jurisprudence is the philosophy of law or the science and study of the law, including the rule of law. To learn more about the rule of law, including its historical development, visit **http://www.lexisnexis.com/about-us/rule-of-law**.

TABLE 3-1
What Do Laws Do?

- Laws maintain order in society.
- Laws regulate human interaction.
- Laws enforce moral beliefs.
- Laws define the economic environment.
- Laws enhance predictability.
- Laws support the powerful.
- Laws promote orderly social change.
- Laws sustain individual rights.
- Laws redress wrongs.
- Laws identify wrongdoers.
- Laws mandate punishment and retribution.

penal code
The written, organized, and compiled form of the criminal laws of a jurisdiction.

case law
The body of judicial precedent, historically built on legal reasoning and past interpretations of statutory laws, that serves as a guide to decision making, especially in the courts.

common law
The body of law originating from usage and custom rather than from written statutes. The term refers to an unwritten body of judicial opinion, originally developed by English courts, that is based on nonstatutory customs, traditions, and precedents that help guide judicial decision making.

rule of law
The maxim that an orderly society must be governed by established principles and known codes that are applied uniformly and fairly to all of its members.

jurisprudence
The philosophy of law. Also, the science and study of the law.

The law isn't justice. It's a very imperfect mechanism. If you press exactly the right buttons and are also lucky, justice may show up in the answer.

—Raymond Chandler (1888–1959)

▲ Former Detroit Mayor Kwame Kilpatrick (left), former New Orleans Mayor Ray Nagin (second from left), former U.S. Representative William Jefferson (second from right), and J. Dennis Hastert (right). As their cases demonstrate, the rule of law means that no one is above the law—not even those who create it. Kilpatrick, charged with ten felony counts, pleaded guilty to reduced charges and served 99 days in jail before being released in February 2009; he reentered prison in 2010 for violating probation, and was again found guilty in 2013 of using his office as mayor to execute a wide-ranging racketeering conspiracy. Nagin was convicted in 2014 and sentenced to 10 years in federal prison for participation in a half-million dollar bribery and conspiracy scheme that ran through most of his time in office. Jefferson served nine terms in the U.S. House of Representatives prior to being sentenced in 2009 to 13 years in prison for using his office to solicit bribes. Hastert was sentenced to 15 months in prison for illegally structuring bank transactions to cover up the sexual abuse of young boys. How would you explain the rule of law to someone who is unfamiliar with it?

Bill Pugliano/Getty Images; Danita Delimont/Alamy Stock Photo; Kevin Wolf/AP Images; Joshua Lott/Stringer/Getty Images

Types of Law

Criminal and civil laws are the best-known types of modern law. However, scholars and philosophers have drawn numerous distinctions between categories of law that rest on the source, intent, and application of the law (Figure 3–1).

Criminal Law

Criminal law, also called *penal law*, refers to the body of rules and regulations that define and specify the nature of and punishments for offenses of a public nature or for wrongs committed against the state or society. Public order is compromised whenever a criminal act occurs, and those found guilty of violating the criminal law are punished. Punishment for crime is philosophically justified by the fact that the offender *intended* the harm and is responsible for it. Criminal law, which is built on constitutional principles and which operates within an established set of procedures applicable to the criminal justice system, is composed of both statutory (written law) and case law.

> **3** Summarize the various types of law, including the purpose of each.

🐦 Follow the author's tweets about the latest crime and justice news @schmalleger

Statutory Law

Written law is of two types: substantive and procedural. **Substantive criminal law** describes what constitutes particular crimes, such as murder, rape, robbery, and assault, and specifies the appropriate punishment for each particular offense. **Procedural law** is a body of rules that determines the proceedings by which legal rights are enforced. The law of criminal procedure, for example, regulates the gathering of evidence and the processing of offenders by the criminal justice system. General rules of evidence, search and seizure, procedures to be followed in an arrest, trial procedures, and other specified processes by which the justice system operates are all contained in procedural law. Each state has its own set of criminal procedure laws, as does the federal government. Laws of criminal procedure balance a suspect's rights against the state's interests in the speedy and efficient processing of criminal defendants. View the Federal Rules of Criminal Procedure at **http://www.law.cornell.edu/rules/frcrmp** and the Federal Rules of Evidence at **http://www.law.cornell.edu/rules/fre**.

criminal law
The body of rules and regulations that define and specify the nature of and punishments for offenses of a public nature or for wrongs committed against the state or society. Also called *penal law*.

substantive criminal law
The part of the law that defines crimes and specifies punishments.

procedural law
The part of the law that specifies the methods to be used in enforcing substantive law.

CRIMINAL LAW

Criminal law is defined as the body of rules and regulations that define and specify the nature of and punishments for offenses of a public nature or for wrongs committed against the state or society. Fundamental to the concept of criminal law is the assumption that criminal acts injure not just individuals but society as a whole. Criminal law is also called *penal law*.

These crimes not only offend their victims but also disrupt the peaceful order of society. It is for this reason that the state begins the official process of bringing the offender to justice. The state will be the plaintiff in the criminal proceeding. Those found guilty of violating a criminal law are punished.

EXAMPLES: Murder, rape, robbery, and assault are examples of criminal offenses against which there are laws.

ADMINISTRATIVE LAW

Administrative law is the body of regulations that governments create to control the activities of industries, businesses, and individuals. For the most part, a breach of administrative law is not a crime.

Administrative agencies will sometimes arrange settlements that fall short of court action but that are considered binding on individuals or groups that have not followed the rules of administrative law.

EXAMPLES: Tax laws, health codes, restrictions on pollution and waste disposal, vehicle regulation laws, and building codes are examples of administrative laws.

STATUTORY LAW

Refers to the law on the books; written, codified laws.

EXAMPLE: The acts of legislatures.

Substantive criminal law is a form of statutory law that describes what constitutes particular crimes and specifies the appropriate punishment for the offense.

Procedural law is a type of statutory law. It is a body of rules that determines the proceedings by which legal rights are enforced. These laws regulate the gathering of evidence and the processing of offenders by the criminal justice system.

CIVIL LAW

Civil law governs relationships between and among people, businesses and other organizations, and agencies of government. In contrast to the criminal law, whose violation is against the state or the nation, civil law governs relationships between parties.

Typically civil suits seek compensation (usually in the form of property or money). A violation of the civil law is not a crime. It may be a contract violation or a tort. A tort is a wrongful act, damage, or injury not involving a breach of contract. Because a tort is a personal wrong and not a crime, it is left to the aggrieved individual to bring the case to court. Civil law is more concerned with assessing liability than it is with intent. Civil suits can also be brought against a crime where the intent is clear. His or her victim may decide to seek monetary compensation.

EXAMPLES: Includes things such as rules for contracts, divorces, child support and custody, the creation of wills, property transfers, libel, and many other contractual and social obligations.

CASE LAW

Case law comes from judicial decisions and is also referred to as the law of precedent. It represents the accumulated wisdom of trial and appellate courts. Once a court decision is rendered, it is written down. At the appellate level, the reasoning behind the decision is recorded as well.

The Supreme Court is the highest-level appellate court. *Stare decisis* refers to the principle of recognizing previous decisions as precedents for guiding future deliberations.

A vertical rule requires that decisions made by a higher court be taken into consideration by lower courts.

The horizontal dimension refers to cases handled by the same court that should be decided in a similar way.

EXAMPLES: Under the law of precedent, the reasonings of previous courts should be taken into consideration by other courts in settling similar future cases.

COMMON LAW

Common law is that body of law originating from usage and custom rather than from written statutes.

EXAMPLE: English common law is the basis for much American criminal law, although most states have codified common law principles in their written statutes.

FIGURE 3-1
Types of Law

Civil Law

Civil law, in contrast to criminal law, governs relationships between and among people, businesses and other organizations, and agencies of government. It contains rules for contracts, divorces, child support and custody, the creation of wills, property transfers, negligence, libel, unfair practices in hiring, the manufacture and sale of consumer goods with hidden hazards for the user, and many other contractual and social obligations. When the civil law is violated, a civil suit may follow. Typically, civil suits seek compensation (usually in the form of property or monetary damages), not punishment. A violation of the civil law is not a crime. It may be a contract violation or a **tort**—which is a wrongful act, damage, or injury not involving a breach of contract. Because a tort is a personal wrong and not a crime, it is left to the aggrieved individual to set the machinery of the court in motion—that is, to bring a suit. The parties to a civil suit are referred to as the *plaintiff*, who seeks relief, and the

civil law
The branch of modern law that governs relationships between parties.

tort
A wrongful act, damage, or injury not involving a breach of contract. Also, a private or civil wrong or injury.

defendant, against whom relief is sought. Civil suits are also sometimes brought by crime victims against those whose criminal intent is clear. Once the perpetrator of a crime has been convicted, the victim may decide to seek monetary compensation from him or her through our system of civil laws.

Administrative Law

Still another kind of law, *administrative law,* is the body of regulations that governments create to control the activities of industries, businesses, and individuals. Tax laws, health codes, restrictions on pollution and waste disposal, vehicle registration laws, and building codes are examples of administrative laws. Other administrative laws cover practices in the areas of customs (imports and exports), immigration, agriculture, product safety, and most areas of manufacturing. For the most part, a breach of administrative law is not a crime. However, criminal law and administrative regulations may overlap. For instance, organized criminal activity is prevalent in the area of toxic waste disposal—an area covered by many administrative regulations—which has led to criminal prosecutions in several states.

Case Law

precedent
A legal principle that ensures that previous judicial decisions are authoritatively considered and incorporated into future cases.

Legal experts also talk about case law, or the law of **precedent**. Case law comes from judicial decisions and represents the accumulated wisdom of trial and appellate courts (those that hear appeals) in criminal, civil, and administrative law cases over the years. Once a court decision is rendered, it is written down. At the appellate level, the reasoning behind the decision is recorded as well. Under the law of precedent, this reasoning is then taken into consideration by other courts in settling similar future cases. The principle of recognizing previous decisions as precedents to guide future deliberations, called **stare decisis**, forms the basis for our modern law of precedent. *Stare decisis* makes for predictability in the law. The court with the greatest influence, of course, is the U.S. Supreme Court, and the precedents it establishes are used as guidelines in the process of legal reasoning by which lower courts reach conclusions.

stare decisis
A legal principle that requires that in subsequent cases on similar issues of law and fact, courts are bound by their own earlier decisions and by those of higher courts having jurisdiction over them. The term literally means "standing by decided matters."

Learn more about the evolution of American criminal law at **https://justicestudies.com/pubs/evolution.pdf**. Some online criminal law journals may be accessed at **https://www.law.berkeley.edu/students/student-journals**.

General Categories of Crime

4 Describe six categories of crimes and their characteristics.

Violations of the *criminal* law can be of many different types and can vary in severity. Six general categories of criminal law violations can be identified: (1) felonies, (2) misdemeanors, (3) infractions, (4) treason, (5) espionage, and (6) inchoate offenses (Figure 3–2).

Felonies

felony
A criminal offense punishable by death or by incarceration in a prison facility for at least one year.

Felonies are serious crimes; they include murder, rape, aggravated assault, robbery, burglary, and arson. Today, many felons receive prison sentences, although the range of potential penalties includes everything from probation and a fine to capital punishment. Under common law (which was discussed earlier in this chapter), felons could be sentenced to death, could have their property confiscated, or both. Following common law tradition, people who are convicted of felonies today usually lose certain privileges. Some states, for example, make a felony conviction and incarceration grounds for uncontested divorce. Others prohibit offenders from voting, running for public office, or owning a firearm and exclude them from some professions, such as medicine, law, and police work.

Misdemeanors

misdemeanor
An offense punishable by incarceration, usually in a local confinement facility, for a period whose upper limit is prescribed by statute in a given jurisdiction, typically one year or less.

Misdemeanors are relatively minor crimes, consisting of offenses such as petty theft, which is stealing items of little worth; simple assault, in which the victim suffers no serious injury and in which none was intended; breaking and entering; possessing burglary tools; being

FELONY

A criminal offense punishable by death or by incarceration in a prison facility for at least one year.

INCHOATE OFFENSE

An offense not yet completed. Also, an offense that consists of an action or conduct that is a step toward the intended commission of another offense.

INFRACTION

A minor offense, such as jaywalking, that is sometimes described as *ticketable*.

MISDEMEANOR

An offense punishable by incarceration, usually in a local confinement facility, for a period whose upper limit is prescribed by statute in a given jurisdiction, typically one year or less.

TREASON

A U.S. citizen's actions to help a foreign government overthrow, make war against, or seriously injure the United States. Also, the attempt to overthrow the government of the society of which one is a member.

ESPIONAGE

The "gathering, transmitting, or losing" of information related to the national defense in such a manner that the information becomes available to enemies of the United States and may be used to their advantage.

FIGURE 3–2
General Categories of Crime

disorderly in public; disturbing the peace; filing a false crime report; and writing bad checks, although the amount for which the check is written may determine the classification of this offense. In general, misdemeanors are any crime punishable by a year or less in prison. In fact, most misdemeanants receive suspended sentences involving a fine and supervised probation.

Infractions

The term **infraction** is used specifically to refer to minor violations of the law that are less serious than misdemeanors. Infractions typically include such things as jaywalking, spitting on the sidewalk, littering, and committing certain traffic violations, including the failure to wear a seat belt. People committing infractions are typically ticketed and released, usually on a promise to appear later in court. Court appearances may often be waived through payment of a small fine that can be mailed to the court.

Treason

Felonies, misdemeanors, infractions, and the people who commit them constitute the daily work of the justice system. However, special categories of crime do exist and should be recognized. They include treason and espionage, two crimes that are often regarded as the most serious of felonies. **Treason** can be defined as "a U.S. citizen's actions to help a foreign government overthrow, make war against, or seriously injure the United States."[10]

Espionage

Espionage, an offense akin to treason but which can be committed by noncitizens, is the "gathering, transmitting, or losing" of information related to the national defense in such a manner that the information becomes available to enemies of the United States and may be used to their advantage.[11] In 2014, for example, 40-year-old Robert Patrick Hoffman, II, of Virginia Beach, Virginia, was sentenced to 30 years in prison for attempting to commit espionage against the United States.[12] While serving in the U.S. Navy, Hoffman held a cryptologic technician position, which gave him access to various forms of sensitive information. After Hoffman initiated efforts to sell information to representatives of the Russian Federation, FBI agents posed as Russian operatives and contacted him. The undercover agents arranged with Hoffman to fill a drop site with encrypted thumb drives containing answers to questions posed to him by people he believed to be Russian agents. In his answers, Hoffman supplied classified national defense information.

🐦 Follow the author's tweets about the latest crime and justice news @schmalleger

infraction
A minor violation of state statute or local ordinance punishable by a fine or other penalty or by a specified, usually limited, term of incarceration.

treason
A U.S. citizen's actions to help a foreign government overthrow, make war against, or seriously injure the United States.[i] Also, the attempt to overthrow the government of the society of which one is a member.

espionage
The "gathering, transmitting, or losing"[ii] of information related to the national defense in such a manner that the information becomes available to enemies of the United States and may be used to their advantage.

Freedom or Safety? You Decide
Should Violent Speech Be Free Speech?

In 2005, a Virginia jury convicted 42-year-old Muslim scholar Ali al-Timimi for a number of offenses, including the crime of incitement, conspiring to carry firearms and explosives, and soliciting others to make war against the United States. The U.S. born Islamic spiritual adviser had spoken frequently at the Center for Islamic Information and Education—also known as the Dar al Arqam Islamic Center—in Falls Church, Virginia. Prosecutors told jurors that al-Timimi had verbally encouraged his followers to train with terrorist organizations and to engage in violent Jihad, or holy war, against America and its allies. Al-Timimi lived much of his life in the Washington, D.C., area and had earned a doctorate in computational biology from George Mason University. As a teenager, he spent 2 years in Saudi Arabia with his family, where he became interested in Islam.

Following conviction, al-Timimi was sentenced to life in prison without the possibility of parole, plus 70 years—a sentence meant to guarantee that he would never leave prison.

The al-Timimi case raises a number of interesting issues, among them the question of when violent speech crosses the line from free expression into criminal advocacy. The First Amendment to the U.S. Constitution guarantees the right to free speech. It is a fundamental guarantee of our democratic way of life. So, for example, the speech of those who advocate a new form of government in the United States is protected, even though their ideas may appear anti-American and ill considered. In the 1957 case of *Roth* v. *United States*, the U.S. Supreme Court held that "the protection given speech and press was fashioned to assure unfettered interchange of ideas for the bringing about of political and social changes desired by the people."

It is important to remember, however, that constitutional rights are not without limit—that is, they have varying applicability under differing conditions. Some forms of speech are too dangerous to be allowed, even under our liberal rules.

Freedom of speech does not mean, for example, that you have a protected right to stand up in a crowded theater and yell "Fire!" That's because the panic that would follow such an exclamation would likely cause injuries and would put members of the public at risk of harm. Hence, the courts have held that although freedom of speech is guaranteed by the Constitution, there are limits to it. (Shouting "Fire!" in a public park would likely not be considered an actionable offense.)

Similarly, saying, "The president deserves to die," horrific as it may sound, may be merely a matter of personal opinion. Anyone who says "I'm going to kill the president," however, can wind up in jail because threatening the life of the president is a crime—as is the act of communicating threats of imminent violence in most jurisdictions.

Al-Timimi's mistake may have been the timing of his remarks, which were made to a public gathering in Virginia 5 days after the September 11, 2001, attacks. In his speech, al-Timimi called for a "holy war" and "violent Jihad" against the West. He was later quoted by converts with whom he met as referring to American forces in Afghanistan as "legitimate targets."

Critics of al-Timimi's conviction point to a seeming double standard under which people can be arrested for unpopular speech, but not for popular speech—regardless of the degree of violence it implies. They note, for example, that conservative columnist Ann Coulter has suggested in writing that "we should invade (Muslim) countries, kill their leaders and convert them to Christianity," but she was never arrested for what she wrote.

In 2010, in an effort to distinguish what would otherwise be protected free speech from speech that constitutes criminal support of terrorist organization, the U.S. Supreme Court decided the case of *Holder* v. *Humanitarian Law Project*. In that case, Chief Justice John G. Roberts, Jr., wrote that for speech to constitute criminal support of terrorist organizations, "it has to take the form of training, expert advice or assistance conveyed in coordination with or under the direction of a foreign terrorist organization."

Finally, in 2015, the United States Court of Appeals for the Fourth Circuit remanded the Al-Timimi case back to a lower court for rehearing. The court found that the FBI had withheld evidence in the original trial. That rehearing has yet to take place.

YOU DECIDE

Should al-Timimi's advocacy of violence be unlawful? Why or why not? Do you think that al-Timimi's rhetoric rises to the level of criminal support of terrorist organizations according to the standard set in Holder v. Humanitarian Law Project? *Might we have more to fear from the suppression of speech (even speech like al-Timimi's) than from its free expression? If so, how?*

References: "Virginia Man Convicted of Urging War on U.S.," *USA Today*, April 27, 2005; Jonathan Turley, "When Is Violent Speech Still Free Speech?" *USA Today*, May 3, 2005; Pamela K. Browne and Catherine Herridge, "Circuit Court Remands Terrorism Case on Grounds FBI Withheld info of al-Awlaki Investigation," Fox News, Sept. 26, 2015 *Holder* v. *Humanitarian Law Project*, U.S. Supreme Court, No. 08-1498 (decided June 21, 2010).

> Justice is incidental to law and order.
>
> —J. Edgar Hoover (1895–1972)

inchoate offense
An offense not yet completed. Also, an offense that consists of an action or conduct that is a step toward the intended commission of another offense.

Inchoate Offenses

Another special category of crime is called *inchoate*. The word *inchoate* means "incomplete or partial," and **inchoate offenses** are those that have not been fully carried out. Conspiracies are an example. When a person conspires to commit a crime, any action undertaken in furtherance of the conspiracy is generally regarded as a sufficient basis for arrest and prosecution. For instance, a woman who intends to kill her husband may make a phone call or conduct an Internet search to find a hit man to carry out her plan. The call and search are themselves evidence of her intent and can result in her imprisonment for conspiracy to commit murder. Another type of inchoate offense is the attempt to commit a crime, which occurs when an offender is unable to complete the intended crime. For example, homeowners may arrive just as a burglar is beginning to enter their residence, causing the burglar to drop his tools and run. In most jurisdictions, this frustrated burglar can be arrested and charged with attempted burglary.

General Features of Crime

5 Describe the eight general features of crime.

From the perspective of Western jurisprudence, all crimes can be said to share certain features (Figure 3–3), and the notion of crime itself can be said to rest on such general principles. Taken together, these features, which are described in this section, make up the legal essence of the concept of crime. Conventional legal wisdom holds that the essence of crime consists of three conjoined elements: (1) the criminal act, which in legal parlance is termed the *actus reus*; (2) a culpable mental state, or *mens rea*; and (3) a concurrence of the two. Hence, as we shall see in the following paragraphs, the essence of criminal conduct consists of a concurrence of a criminal act with a culpable mental state.

▲ Former navy submariner, Robert Patrick Hoffman, II. Hoffman was sentenced to 30 years in prison for attempting to sell classified information to the Russians. What's the difference between espionage and treason?
Steve Earley/The Virginian-Pilot/ AP Images

actus reus
An act in violation of the law. Also, a guilty act.

The Criminal Act (*Actus Reus*)

A necessary first feature of any crime is some act in violation of the law. Such an act is termed the **actus reus** of a crime. The term means "guilty act." Generally, a person must commit some voluntary act before he or she is subject to criminal sanctions. To *be something* is not a crime; to *do something* may be. For example, someone who is caught using drugs can be arrested, while someone who simply admits that he or she is a drug user (perhaps on a TV talk show or on a website) cannot be arrested on that basis. Police who hear the drug user's admission might begin gathering evidence to prove some specific law violation in that person's past, or perhaps they might watch that individual for future behavior in violation of the law. A subsequent arrest would then be based on a specific action in violation of the law pertaining to controlled substances.

Vagrancy laws, popular in the early part of the twentieth century, have generally been invalidated by the courts because they did not specify what act violated the law. In fact, the less a person did, the more vagrant he or she was. An omission to act, however, may be criminal where the person in question is required by law to do something. Child-neglect laws, for example, focus on parents and guardians who do not live up to their responsibility to care for their children.

Threatening to act can be a criminal offense. For example, threatening to kill someone can result in an arrest for the offense of communicating threats. Such threats against the president of the United States are taken seriously by the Secret Service, and individuals are arrested for boasting about planned violence directed at the president. Attempted criminal activity is also illegal. An attempt to murder or rape, for example, is a serious crime, even when the planned act is not accomplished.

Conspiracies (mentioned earlier in this chapter) are another criminal act. When a conspiracy unfolds, the ultimate act that it aims to bring about does not have to occur for the parties to the conspiracy to be arrested. When people plan to bomb a public building, for example, they can be legally stopped before the bombing. As soon as they take steps to "further" their plan, they have met the requirement for an act. Buying explosives, telephoning one another, and drawing plans of the building may all be actions in "furtherance of the conspiracy." But not all conspiracy statutes require actions in furtherance of the "target crime" before an arrest can be made. Technically speaking, crimes of conspiracy can be seen as entirely distinct from the target crimes that the conspirators are contemplating. For example, in 1994 the U.S. Supreme Court upheld the drug-related conviction of Reshat Shabani when it ruled that in the case of certain antidrug laws,[13] "it is presumed that Congress intended to adopt the common law definition of conspiracy, which does not make the doing of any act other than the act of conspiring a condition of liability."[14] Hence, according to the Court, "the criminal agreement itself," even in the absence of actions directed toward realizing the target crime, can be grounds for arrest and prosecution.

🐦 Follow the author's tweets about the latest crime and justice news @schmalleger

By definition, a crime requires *actus reus*, *mens rea*, and the concurrence of the two:

Actus Reus

A necessary feature of any crime is some act in violation of the law. This violation is called the *actus reus* (guilty act). Generally, a person must commit the act voluntarily for it to be considered a crime.

Mens Rea

A second component of crime is *mens rea*, or guilty mind. This refers to the person's state of mind when they commit the act. There are four types of *mens rea*:

Concurrence

Concurrence requires that the act and the mental state occur together in order for a crime to have taken place.

Purposeful (intentional) is an act that is undertaken to achieve some goal.

Knowing behavior is undertaken with awareness. A person who acts purposefully always acts knowingly, but a person may act in a knowing way, but without criminal intent.

Reckless behavior is activity that increases the risk of harm. In this activity, the person may not have intended harm but should know that his behavior could endanger others.

Negligent behavior refers to a situation where the person should have known better and her act, or failure to act, endangers others.

Motive is not the same as *mens rea*. A motive refers to a person's reason for committing a crime. Motive is not an essential feature of a crime.

Special Categories of Crime

Strict liability (or absolute liability) is a special category of crime that requires no culpable mental state and presents a significant exception to the principle that all crimes require *actus reus* and *mens rea*. These offenses make it a crime to simply do something without the intention of violating the law. Routine traffic offenses are considered an example of strict liability.

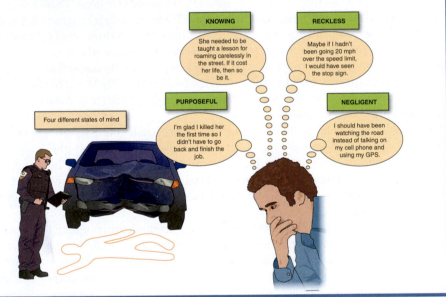

FIGURE 3–3
Features of a Crime

Source: Pearson Education.

A Guilty Mind (*Mens Rea*)

mens rea

The state of mind that accompanies a criminal act. Also, a guilty mind.

Mens rea, the second general component of crime, is a term that literally means "guilty mind," referring to the defendant's specific mental state at the time the behavior in question occurred. The importance of *mens rea* as a component of crime cannot be overemphasized. It can be seen in the fact that some courts have held that "[a]ll crime exists primarily in the mind."[15] The extent to which a person can be held criminally responsible for his or her actions generally depends on the nature of the mental state under which he or she was laboring at the time of the offense.

Four levels, or types, of *mens rea* can be distinguished: (1) purposeful (or intentional), (2) knowing, (3) reckless, and (4) negligent. Purposeful or intentional action is that which is undertaken to achieve some goal. Sometimes the harm that results from intentional action may be unintended; however, this does not reduce criminal liability. The doctrine of *transferred intent*, for example, which operates in all U.S. jurisdictions, holds a person guilty of murder if he or she took aim and shot at an intended victim but missed, killing another person instead. The philosophical notion behind the concept of transferred intent is that the killer's intent to kill, which existed at the time of the crime, transferred from the intended victim to the person who was struck by the bullet and died.

Knowing behavior is action undertaken with awareness. A person who acts purposefully always acts knowingly, but a person may act in a knowingly criminal way but for a purpose other than criminal intent. For example, an airline captain who allows a flight attendant to transport cocaine aboard an airplane may do so to gain sexual favors from the attendant, but without the purpose of drug smuggling. Knowing behavior involves near-certainty. In this scenario, if the airline captain allows the flight attendant to carry cocaine aboard the plane, it *will* be transported, and the pilot knows it. In another example, if an HIV-infected individual knowingly has unprotected sexual intercourse with another person, the partner *will* be exposed to the virus.

Reckless Behavior and Criminal Negligence

Reckless behavior is an activity that increases the risk of harm. In contrast to knowing behavior, knowledge may be part of recklessness, but it exists more in the form of probability than certainty. As a practical example, reckless driving is a frequent charge in many jurisdictions; it is generally brought when a driver engages in risky activity that endangers others.

Nevertheless, *mens rea* is said to be present when a person should have known better, even if the person did not directly intend the consequences of his or her action. A person who acts negligently and thereby endangers others may be found guilty of **criminal negligence** when harm occurs, even though no negative consequences were intended. For example, a parent who leaves a 12-month-old child alone in the tub can be prosecuted for negligent homicide if the child drowns.[16] It should be emphasized, however, that negligence in and of itself is not a crime. Negligent conduct can be evidence of crime only when it falls below some acceptable standard of care. That standard is applied today in criminal courts through the fictional creation of a *reasonable person*. The question to be asked in a given case is whether a reasonable person, in the same situation, would have known better and acted differently from the defendant. The reasonable person criterion provides a yardstick for juries faced with thorny issues of guilt or innocence.

It is important to note that *mens rea*, even in the sense of intent, is not the same thing as motive. A **motive** refers to a person's reason for committing a crime. While evidence of motive may be admissible during a criminal trial to help prove a crime, motive itself is not an essential element of a crime. As a result, we cannot say that a bad or immoral motive makes an act a crime.

Mens rea is a tricky concept. Not only is it philosophically and legally complex, but a person's state of mind during the commission of an offense can rarely be known directly unless the person confesses. Hence, *mens rea* must generally be inferred from a person's actions and from all the circumstances surrounding those actions. Pure accident, however, which involves no recklessness or negligence, cannot serve as the basis for either criminal or civil liability. "Even a dog," the famous Supreme Court Justice Oliver Wendell Holmes once wrote, "distinguishes between being stumbled over and being kicked."[17]

Strict Liability

A special category of crimes called **strict liability** requires no culpable mental state and pre-sents a significant exception to the principle that all crimes require a concurrence of *actus reus* and *mens rea*. Strict liability offenses, also called *absolute liability offenses*, make it a crime simply to *do* something, even if the offender has no intention of violating the law. Strict liability is philosophically based on the presumption that causing harm is in itself blameworthy, regardless of the actor's intent.

Routine traffic offenses are generally considered strict liability offenses. Driving 65 mph in a 55-mph zone is a violation of the law, even though the driver may be listening to music, thinking, or simply going with the flow of traffic, entirely unaware that his or her vehicle is

reckless behavior
An activity that increases the risk of harm.

criminal negligence
A behavior in which a person fails to reasonably perceive substantial and unjustifiable risks of dangerous consequences.

motive
A person's reason for committing a crime.

strict liability
A liability without fault or intention. Strict liability offenses do not require *mens rea*.

exceeding the posted speed limit. Statutory rape is another example of strict liability.[18] This crime generally occurs between two consenting individuals; it requires only that the offender have sexual intercourse with a person under the age of legal consent. Statutes describing the crime routinely avoid any mention of a culpable mental state. In many jurisdictions, it matters little whether the "perpetrator" knew the exact age of the "victim" or whether the "victim" lied about his or her age or had given consent, since statutory rape laws are "an attempt to prevent the sexual exploitation of persons deemed legally incapable of giving consent."[19]

Concurrence

concurrence
The coexistence of (1) an act in violation of the law and (2) a culpable mental state.

The concurrence of an unlawful act and a culpable mental state provides the third basic component of crime. **Concurrence** requires that the act and the mental state occur together in order for a crime to take place. If one precedes the other, the requirements of the criminal law have not been met. A person may intend to kill a rival, for example. He drives to the intended victim's house with his gun, fantasizing about how he will commit the murder. Just as he nears the victim's home, the victim crosses the street on the way to the grocery store. If the two accidentally collide and the intended victim dies, there has been no concurrence of act and intent.

Other Features of Crime

Some scholars contend that the three features of crime that we have just outlined—*actus reus, mens rea,* and concurrence—are sufficient to constitute the essence of the legal concept of *crime.* Other scholars, however, see modern Western law as more complex. They argue that recognition of five additional principles is necessary to fully appreciate contemporary understandings of crime: (1) causation, (2) resulting harm, (3) the principle of legality, (4) the principle of punishment, and (5) necessary attendant circumstances. We will now discuss each of these additional features in turn.

Causation

Causation refers to the fact that the concurrence of a guilty mind and a criminal act may cause harm. While some statutes criminalize only conduct, others require that the offender *cause* a particular result before criminal liability can be incurred. Sometimes, however, a causal link is unclear. For example, let's consider a case of assault with a deadly weapon with intent to kill. A person shoots another, and the victim is seriously injured but is not immediately killed. The victim, who remains in the hospital, survives for more than a year. The victim's death occurs due to a blood clot that forms from lack of activity. In such a case, it is likely that defense attorneys will argue that the defendant did not cause the death; rather, the death occurred because of disease. If a jury agrees with the defense's claim, the shooter may go free or be found guilty of a lesser charge, such as assault.

legal cause
A legally recognizable cause. A legal cause must be demonstrated in court in order to hold an individual criminally liable for causing harm.

To clarify the issue of causation, the American Law Institute suggests use of the term **legal cause** to emphasize the notion of a legally recognizable cause and to preclude any assumption that such a cause must be close in time and space to the result it produces. Legal causes can be distinguished from those causes that may have produced the result in question but do not provide the basis for a criminal prosecution because they are too complex, too indistinguishable from other causes, not knowable, or not provable in a court of law.

Harm

A harm occurs in any crime, although not all harms are crimes. When a person is murdered or raped, harm can be clearly identified. Some crimes, however, can be said to be *victimless.* Perpetrators (and their attorneys) maintain that in committing such crimes, they harm no one but themselves; rather, they say, the crime may actually be pleasurable for those involved. Prostitution, illegal gambling, and drug use are commonly classified as "victimless." What these offenders fail to recognize, say legal theorists, is the social harm caused by their behavior. In areas afflicted with chronic prostitution, illegal gambling, and drug use, property values fall; family life disintegrates; other, more traditional crimes increase as money is sought to support the "victimless" activities; and law-abiding citizens abandon the area.

In a criminal prosecution, however, it is rarely necessary to prove harm as a separate element of a crime since it is subsumed under the notion of a guilty act. In the crime of murder, for example, the "killing of a human being" brings about a harm but is, properly speaking, an act. When committed with the requisite *mens rea*, it becomes a crime. A similar type of reasoning applies to the criminalization of *attempts* that cause no harm. A scenario commonly raised to illustrate this dilemma is one in which attackers throw rocks at a blind man, but because of bad aim, the rocks hit no one and the intended target remains unaware that anyone is trying to harm him. In such a case, should throwing rocks provide a basis for criminal liability? As one authority on the subject observes, "Criticism of the principle of harm has . . . been based on the view that the harm actually caused may be a matter of sheer accident and that the rational thing to do is to base the punishment on the *mens rea*, and the action, disregarding any actual harm or lack of harm or its degree."[20] This observation also shows why we have said that the essence of crime consists only of three things: (1) *actus reus*, (2) *mens rea*, and (3) concurrence of an illegal act and a culpable mental state.

> The greatest happiness of the greatest number is the foundation of morals and legislation.
>
> —Jeremy Bentham (1748–1832)

Legality

The principle of legality highlights the fact that a behavior cannot be criminal if no law exists that defines it as such. For example, as long as you are of drinking age, it is all right to drink beer because there is no statute on the books prohibiting it. During Prohibition, of course, the situation was quite different. (In fact, some parts of the United States are still "dry," and the purchase or public consumption of alcohol can be a law violation regardless of age.) The principle of legality also includes the notion that **ex post facto** laws are not binding, which means that a law cannot be created tomorrow that will hold a person legally responsible for something he or she does today—laws are binding only from the date of their creation or from some future date at which they are specified as taking effect.[21]

ex post facto
Latin for "after the fact." The Constitution prohibits the enactment of *ex post facto* laws, which make acts committed before the laws in question were passed punishable as crimes.

Punishment

The principle of punishment holds that no crime can be said to occur where punishment has not been specified in the law. Larceny, for example, would not be a crime if the law simply said, "It is illegal to steal." Punishment for the crime must be specified so that if a person is found guilty of violating the law, sanctions can be lawfully imposed.

🐦 Follow the author's tweets about the latest crime and justice news @schmalleger

Necessary Attendant Circumstances

Finally, statutes defining some crimes specify that certain additional elements must be present for a conviction to be obtained. Generally speaking, these **attendant circumstances** are the "facts surrounding an event";[22] they include such things as time and place. Attendant circumstances that are specified by law as necessary elements of an offense are sometimes called *necessary attendant circumstances*, indicating that the existence of such circumstances is necessary, along with the other elements included in the relevant statute, for a crime to have been committed. Florida law, for example, makes it a crime to "[k]nowingly commit any lewd or lascivious act in the presence of any child under the age of 16 years."[23] In this case, the behavior in question might not be a crime if committed in the presence of someone who is older than 16 years. Sometimes attendant circumstances increase the degree, or level of seriousness, of an offense.

attendant circumstances
The facts surrounding an event.

Circumstances surrounding a crime can also be classified as aggravating or mitigating and may, by law, increase or lessen the penalty that can be imposed on a convicted offender. Aggravating and mitigating circumstances are not elements of an offense, however, since they are primarily relevant at the sentencing stage of a criminal prosecution. They are discussed in Chapter 9.

Elements of a Specific Criminal Offense

Now that we have identified the principles that constitute the *general* notion of crime, we can examine individual statutes to see what particular statutory **elements (of a crime)** constitute a *specific* crime. Written laws specify exactly what conditions are necessary for a

element (of a crime)
In a specific crime, one of the essential features of that crime, as specified by law or statute.

6 Explain what is meant by the elements of a specific criminal offense.

🐦 Follow the author's tweets about the latest crime and justice news @schmalleger

person to be charged in a given instance of criminal activity, and they do so for every offense. Hence, elements of a crime are specific legal aspects of a criminal offense that the prosecution must prove to obtain a conviction. In almost every jurisdiction in the United States, for example, the crime of first-degree murder involves four quite distinct elements:

1. An unlawful killing
2. Of a human being
3. Intentionally
4. With planning (or "malice aforethought")

The elements of any specific crime are the statutory minimum without which that crime cannot be said to have occurred. Since statutes differ between jurisdictions, the specific elements of a particular crime may vary. To convict a defendant of a particular crime, prosecutors must prove to a judge or jury that all of the required statutory elements are present[24] and that the accused was responsible for producing them. If even one element of an offense cannot be established beyond a reasonable doubt, criminal liability will not have been demonstrated, and the defendant will be found not guilty.

The Example of Murder

Every statutory element of a crime serves a purpose. As mentioned, the crime of first-degree murder includes an *unlawful killing* as one of its required elements. Not all killings are unlawful. In war, for instance, human beings are killed. These killings are committed with planning and sometimes with "malice" and are certainly intentional, yet killing in war is not unlawful as long as the belligerents wage war according to international conventions.

The second element of first-degree murder specifies that the killing must be *of a human being.* People kill all the time. They kill animals for meat, they hunt, and they practice euthanasia on aged and injured pets. Even if the killing of an animal is planned and involves malice (perhaps a vendetta against a neighborhood dog that overturns trash cans), it does not constitute first-degree murder. Such a killing, however, may violate statutes pertaining to cruelty to animals.

The third element of first-degree murder, *intentionality,* is the basis for the defense of accident. An unintentional or nonpurposeful killing is not first-degree murder, although it may violate some other statute.

Finally, murder has not been committed unless *malice* is involved. There are different kinds of malice. Second-degree murder involves malice in the sense of hatred or spite. A more extreme form of malice is necessary for a finding of first-degree murder; sometimes the phrase used to describe this requirement is *malice aforethought.* This extreme kind of malice can be demonstrated by showing that planning was involved in the commission of the murder. Often, first-degree murder is described as "lying in wait," a practice that shows that thought and planning went into the illegal killing.

A charge of second-degree murder in most jurisdictions would necessitate proving that a voluntary (or intentional) killing of a human being had taken place—although without the degree of malice necessary for it to be classified as first-degree murder. A crime of passion is an example of second-degree murder. In a crime of passion, the malice felt by the perpetrator is hatred or spite, which is considered less severe than malice aforethought. Manslaughter, or third-degree murder, another type of homicide, can be defined simply as the unlawful killing of a human being. Not only is malice lacking in third-degree murder cases, but so is intention; in fact, the killer may not have intended that *any* harm come to the victim.

Manslaughter charges are often brought when a defendant acted in a negligent or reckless manner. The 2001 sentencing of 21-year-old Nathan Hall to 90 days in jail on charges of criminally negligent homicide following a fatal collision with another ski racer on Vail Mountain near Eagle, Colorado, provides such an example.[25] Hall had been tried on a more serious charge of reckless manslaughter, which carries a sentence of up to 16 years under Colorado law, but the jury convicted him of the lesser charge.

Manslaughter statutes, however, frequently necessitate some degree of negligence on the part of the killer. When a wanton disregard for human life is present—legally defined as "gross negligence"—some jurisdictions permit the offender to be charged with a more serious count of murder.

The *Corpus Delicti* of a Crime

The term **corpus delicti** literally means "the body of the crime." One way to understand the concept of *corpus delicti* is to realize that a person cannot be tried for a crime unless it can first be shown that the offense has, in fact, occurred. In other words, to establish the *corpus delicti* of a crime, the state has to demonstrate that a criminal law has been violated and that someone violated it (Figure 3–4). This term is often confused with the statutory elements of a crime, and sometimes it is mistakenly thought to refer to the body of a murder victim or some other physical result of criminal activity. It actually means something quite different.

There are two aspects to the *corpus delicti* of an offense: (1) that a certain result has been produced, and (2) that a person is criminally responsible for its production. For

corpus delicti
The facts that show that a crime has occurred. The term literally means "the body of the crime."

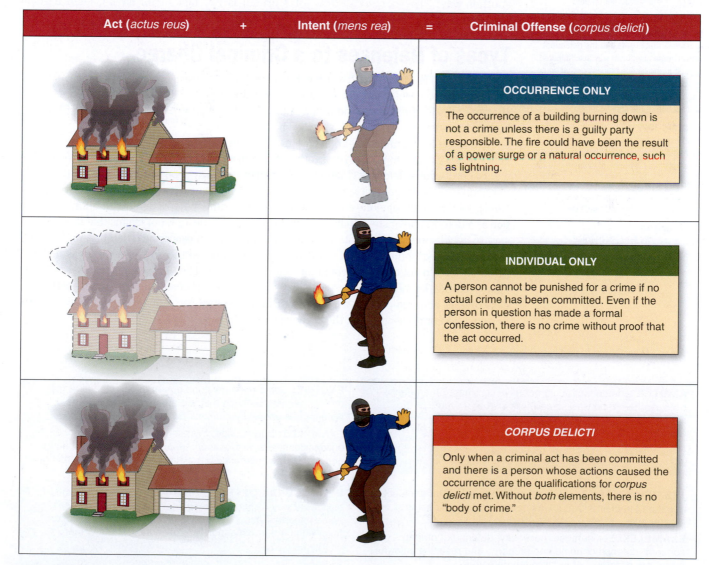

| Act (*actus reus*) | + | Intent (*mens rea*) | = | Criminal Offense (*corpus delicti*) |

OCCURRENCE ONLY

The occurrence of a building burning down is not a crime unless there is a guilty party responsible. The fire could have been the result of a power surge or a natural occurrence, such as lightning.

INDIVIDUAL ONLY

A person cannot be punished for a crime if no actual crime has been committed. Even if the person in question has made a formal confession, there is no crime without proof that the act occurred.

CORPUS DELICTI

Only when a criminal act has been committed and there is a person whose actions caused the occurrence are the qualifications for *corpus delicti* met. Without *both* elements, there is no "body of crime."

FIGURE 3–4
Body of Crime

Source: Pearson Education.

defense (to a criminal charge)
The evidence and arguments offered by a defendant and his or her attorney to show why the defendant should not be held liable for a criminal charge.

alibi
A statement or contention by an individual charged with a crime that he or she was so distant when the crime was committed, or so engaged in other provable activities, that his or her participation in the commission of that crime was impossible.

justification
A legal defense in which the defendant admits to committing the act in question but claims it was necessary in order to avoid some greater evil.

excuse
A legal defense in which the defendant claims that some personal condition or circumstance at the time of the act was such that he or she should not be held accountable under the criminal law.

procedural defense
A defense that claims that the defendant was in some significant way discriminated against in the justice process or that some important aspect of official procedure was not properly followed in the investigation or prosecution of the crime charged.

Islamic law
A system of laws, operative in some Arab countries, based on the Muslim religion and especially the holy book of Islam, the Koran.

Hudud crime
A serious violation of Islamic law that is regarded as an offense against God.

Tazir crime
A minor violation of Islamic law that is regarded as an offense against society, not God.

example, the crime of larceny requires proof that the property of another has been stolen—that is, unlawfully taken by someone whose intent it was to permanently deprive the owner of its possession.[26] Hence, evidence offered to prove the *corpus delicti* in a trial for larceny is insufficient if it fails to prove that any property was stolen or if property found in a defendant's possession cannot be identified as having been stolen. "In an arson case, the *corpus delicti* consists of (1) a burned building or other property, and (2) some criminal agency which caused the burning. . . . In other words, the *corpus delicti* includes not only the fact of burning, but it must also appear that the burning was by the willful act of some person, and not as a result of a natural or accidental cause."[27]

We should note that the identity of the perpetrator is not an element of the *corpus delicti* of an offense. Hence, the fact that a crime has occurred can be established without having any idea who committed it or even why it was committed. This principle was clearly enunciated in a Montana case when that state's supreme court held that "the identity of the perpetrator is not an element of the *corpus delicti*." In *State* v. *Kindle* (1924),[28] the court said, "We stated that '[i]n a prosecution for murder, proof of the *corpus delicti* does not necessarily carry with it the identity of the slain nor of the slayer.' . . . The essential elements of the *corpus delicti* are . . . establishing the death and the fact that the death was caused by a criminal agency, nothing more." *Black's Law Dictionary* puts it another way: "The *corpus delicti* [of a crime] is the fact of its having been actually committed."[29]

Types of Defenses to a Criminal Charge

When a person is charged with a crime, he or she typically offers some defense. A **defense (to a criminal charge)** consists of evidence and arguments offered by the defendant to show why he or she should not be held liable for a criminal charge. Our legal system generally recognizes four broad categories of defenses: (1) alibi, (2) justifications, (3) excuses, and (4) procedural defenses (Figure 3–5). An **alibi**, if shown to be valid, means that the defendant could not have committed the crime in question because he or she was somewhere else (and generally with someone else) at the time of the crime. When a defendant offers a **justification** as a defense, he or she admits committing the act in question but claims that it was necessary to avoid some greater evil. A defendant who offers an **excuse** as a defense, on the other hand, claims that some personal condition or circumstance at the time of the act was such that he or she should not be held accountable under the criminal law. **Procedural defenses** make the claim that the defendant was in some significant way discriminated against in the justice process or that some important aspect of official procedure was not properly followed in the investigation or prosecution of the crime charged.

> **7**   Compare and contrast the four general categories of accepted criminal defense.

ALIBI: The defendant could not have committed the offense because he or she was somewhere else at the time of the crime.

EXCUSE: Some personal condition or circumstance at the time of the act was such that the actor should not be held accountable under the criminal law.

EXAMPLES: Duress, age, mistake, involuntary intoxication, unconsciousness, provocation, insanity, diminished capacity, and mental incompetence are examples of excuse defenses.

JUSTIFICATION: The defendant admits committing the act in question but claims that it was necessary to avoid some greater evil.

EXAMPLES: Self-defense, necessity, defense of others, consent, defense of home and property, and resisting unlawful arrest are examples of justification defenses.

PROCEDURAL DEFENSE: The defendant was in some significant way discriminated against in the justice process, or some important aspect of official procedure was not properly followed in the investigation or prosecution of the crime charged.

EXAMPLES: Entrapment, denial of a speedy trial, double jeopardy, prosecutorial misconduct, *collateral estoppel*, police fraud, and selective prosecution are examples of procedural defenses.

FIGURE 3–5
Types of Defenses to a Criminal Charge
Source: Pearson Education.

Multiculturalism and Diversity
Islamic Law

▲ An Iraqi man holding a picture of top Shiite cleric Ayatollah Ali Sistani during a protest in support of an Islamic constitution. The traditions and legal systems of many Middle Eastern countries are strongly influenced by Islamic law, which is based on the teachings of the Koran and the sayings of the prophet Muhammad. How does Islamic law differ from the laws of most Western nations?

Karim Kadim/AP Images

In 2012, Amina bint Abdul Halim bin Salem Nasser, a woman in her 60s, was beheaded in the Kingdom of Saudi Arabia for practicing witchcraft and sorcery.[1] Even though the Kingdom does not specify capital punishment for witchcraft, the execution was carried out by local authorities in the northwest province of Jawf after powerful conservative clerics urged the strongest possible punishment for fortune tellers and faith healers.

Like many Arabian countries, Saudi Arabia follows **Islamic law** (or *Shari'ah* in Arabic, which means "path of God"). Islamic law has been of much interest in the United States since the September 11, 2001, terrorist attacks on the United States, the resulting destruction of the Taliban regime in Afghanistan, and the war in Iraq. It is important for American students of criminal justice to recognize that Islamic law refers to legal ideas based on the teachings of Islam and that it bears no intrinsic relationship to acts of terrorism committed by misguided zealots with Islamic backgrounds. Similarly, Islamic law is by no means the same thing as Jihad (Muslim holy war) or Islamic fundamentalism.

Various interpretations of Islam form the basis of laws in many countries, and the entire legal systems of some nations are based on Islamic principles. For example, Article 2 of Chapter 1 (titled "Basic Principles") of the Iraqi Constitution declares that "Islam is the official religion of the state and is a basic source of legislation." Subsection (a) reads: "No law can be passed that contradicts the undisputed rules of Islam." The Iraqi Constitution was approved by a wide margin in a 2005 national referendum. Islamic law also holds considerable sway in many other countries, including Syria, Iran, Pakistan, Saudi Arabia, Kuwait, the United Arab Emirates, Bahrain, Algeria, Jordan, Lebanon, Libya, Ethiopia, Tajikistan, Uzbekistan, and Turkey (which practices official separation of church and state).

Islamic law is based on four historical sources. In order of importance, these sources are (1) the Koran (also spelled *Quran* and *Qur'an*), or Holy Book of Islam, which Muslims believe is the word of God, or Allah; (2) the teachings of the prophet Muhammad; (3) a consensus of the clergy in cases where neither the Koran nor the prophet directly addresses an issue; and (4) reason or logic, which should be used when no solution can be found in the other three sources.[2]

The prophet Muhammad, whom the *Cambridge Encyclopedia of Islam* describes as a "prophet-lawyer,"[3] rose to fame in the city of Mecca (in what is now Saudi Arabia) as a religious reformer. Later, however, he traveled to Medina, where he became the ruler and lawgiver of a newly formed religious society. In his role as lawgiver, Muhammad enacted legislation whose aim was to teach people what to do and how to behave to achieve salvation. As a consequence, Islamic law today is a system of duties and rituals founded on legal and moral obligations, all of which are ultimately sanctioned by the authority of a religious leader (or leaders) who may issue commands (known as fatwas) that the faithful are bound to obey.

Contemporary Islamic law recognizes seven **Hudud crimes**— or crimes based on religious strictures. *Hudud* (sometimes spelled *Hodood* or *Huddud*) crimes are essentially violations of "natural law" as interpreted by Arab culture. These crimes are often described as crimes against God. Four *Hudud* crimes for which punishments are specified in the Koran are (1) war against Allah and His messengers, (2) theft, (3) adultery or fornication, and (4) false accusation of fornication or adultery. Three other *Hudud* offenses are mentioned by the Koran for which no punishment is specified: (1) "corruption on earth," (2) drinking of alcohol, and (3) highway robbery. The punishments for these crimes are determined by tradition.[4] "Corruption on earth" is a general category of religious offense, not well understood in the West, which includes activities such as embezzlement, revolution against lawful authority, fraud, and "weakening the society of God."

All crimes other than *Hudud* crimes fall into an offense category called *tazirat*. **Tazir crimes** are regarded as any actions not considered acceptable in a spiritual society. They include crimes against society and against individuals, but not against God. *Tazir* crimes may call for *quesas* (retribution) or *diya* (compensation or fines). Crimes requiring *quesas* are based on the Arabic principle of "an eye for an eye, a nose for a nose, a tooth for a tooth" and generally require physical punishments up to and including death. *Quesas* offenses may include murder, manslaughter, assault, and maiming.

Unlike statutory law in the West, Islamic law is not codified, meaning that judges are empowered to interpret the law based on their readings of the holy texts, precedent, and their own personal judgment. In some countries governed by Sharia law, however, the law of criminal procedure can be found in written form, similar to its counterpart in the West.

---

[1] "Saudi Woman Executed for 'Witchcraft and Sorcery,'" *BBC News Middle East,* December 12, 2011, http://www.bbc.co.uk/news/world-middle-east-16150381 (accessed May 15, 2012).

[2] Parviz Saney, "Iran," in Elmer H. Johnson, ed., *International Handbook of Contemporary Developments in Criminology* (Westport, CT: Greenwood, 1983), p. 359.

[3] J. Schact, "Law and Justice," *Cambridge Encyclopaedia of Islam,* 2nd ed., Vol. 2, p. 539, from which most of the information in this paragraph comes.

[4] This paragraph owes much to Matthew Lippman, "Iran: A Question of Justice?" *Criminal Justice International* (1987), pp. 6–7.

▲ George Zimmerman is shown wearing restraints as he is escorted by a sheriff's deputy to his chair in the Seminole County courthouse in Orlando, Florida. Zimmerman was acquitted in 2013 on charges of second-degree murder and man-slaughter in the Florida shooting death of 17-year-old Trayvon Martin. If you were on the jury, would you have found Zimmerman guilty?

Gary Green/UPI/Newscom

Alibi

A reference book for criminal trial lawyers says, "Alibi is different from all of the other defenses . . . because . . . it is based upon the premise that the defendant is truly innocent."[30] The defense of alibi denies that the defendant committed the act in question. All of the other defenses we are about to discuss grant that the defendant committed the act but deny that he or she should be held criminally responsible. While justifications and excuses may produce findings of "not guilty," the defense of alibi claims outright innocence.

Alibi is best supported by witnesses and documentation. A person charged with a crime can use the defense of alibi to show that he or she was not present at the scene when the crime was alleged to have occurred. Hotel receipts, eyewitness identifications, and participation in social events have all been used to prove alibis.

Justifications

As defenses, justifications claim a kind of moral high ground. Justifications may be offered by people who find themselves forced to choose between "two evils." Generally speaking, conduct that a person believes is necessary to avoid harm to him or herself or to another is justifiable if the harm he or she is trying to avoid is greater than the harm his or her conduct may cause. For example, a firefighter might set a controlled fire to create a firebreak to head off a conflagration threatening a community; while intentionally setting a fire might constitute arson, destroying property to save a town by creating a firebreak may be justifiable behavior in the eyes of the community and in the eyes of the law. Included under the broad category of justifications are: (1) self-defense, (2) defense of others, (3) defense of home and property, (4) necessity, (5) consent, and (6) resisting unlawful arrest.

Self-Defense

self-defense
The protection of oneself or of one's property from unlawful injury or from the immediate risk of unlawful injury. Also, the justification that the person who committed an act that would otherwise constitute an offense reasonably believed that the act was necessary to protect self or property from immediate danger.

Self-defense is probably the best known of the justifications. This defense strategy makes the claim that it was necessary for someone to inflict harm on another to ensure his or her own safety in the face of near-certain injury or death. A person who harms an attacker can generally use this defense. However, the courts have generally held that where a "path of retreat" exists for a person being attacked, it should be taken. In other words, the safest use of self-defense, legally speaking, is only when cornered, with no path of escape. Some states, such as Florida, have enacted "stand your ground" laws, which remove the retreat requirement, and allow for the use of force without the need for a victim to evade his or her attacker or to give ground. By 2013, close to 30 states had passed such laws,[31] although the statutes came under close scrutiny after the acquittal on murder charges of Florida neighborhood watchman George Zimmerman, who shot and killed 17-year-old Trayvon Martin during a physical confrontation. Ironically, Zimmerman's defense did not invoke any stand your ground claims, but relied instead on a traditional self-defense strategy.

The amount of defensive force used must be proportional to the amount of force or the perceived degree of threat that one is seeking to defend against. **Reasonable force** is the degree of force that is appropriate in a given situation and that is not excessive. Reasonable force can also be thought of as the minimum degree of force necessary to protect oneself, one's property, a third party, or the property of another in the face of a substantial threat. Deadly force, the highest degree of force, is considered reasonable only when used to counter an immediate threat of great bodily harm or death. Deadly force cannot be used against nondeadly force.

reasonable force
A degree of force that is appropriate in a given situation and is not excessive. Also, the minimum degree of force necessary to protect oneself, one's property, a third party, or the property of another in the face of a substantial threat.

Force, as the term is used within the context of self-defense, means physical force and does not extend to emotional, psychological, economic, psychic, or other forms of coercion. A person who turns the tables on a robber and assaults him during a robbery attempt, for example, may be able to claim self-defense, but a businessperson who physically assaults a financial rival to prevent a hostile takeover of her company will have no such recourse.

Self-defense has sometimes been claimed in killings of abusive spouses. A jury is likely to accept as justified a killing that occurs while the physical abuse is in progress, especially where a history of such abuse can be shown. On the other hand, wives who suffer repeated abuse but coldly plan the killing of their husbands have not fared well in court.

Defense of Others

The use of force to defend oneself has generally been extended to permit the use of reasonable force to defend others who are or who appear to be in imminent danger. The defense of others, sometimes called *defense of a third person*, is circumscribed in some jurisdictions by the **alter ego rule**. This rule holds that a person can only defend a third party under circumstances and only to the degree that the third party could act. In other words, a person who aids another whom he sees being attacked may become criminally liable if that person initiated the attack or if the assault is a lawful one—for example, an assault made by a law enforcement officer conducting a lawful arrest of a person who is resisting. A few jurisdictions, however, do not recognize the alter ego rule and allow a person to act in defense of another if the actor reasonably believes that his or her intervention is immediately necessary to protect the third person.

Defense of others cannot be claimed by an individual who joins an illegal fight merely to assist a friend or family member. Likewise, one who intentionally aids an offender in an assault, even though the tables have turned and the offender is losing the battle, cannot claim defense of others. Under the law, defense of a third person always requires that the defender be free from fault and that he or she act to aid an innocent person who is in the process of being victimized. The same restrictions that apply to self-defense also apply to the defense of a third party. Hence, a defender may act only in the face of an immediate threat to another person, cannot use deadly force against nondeadly force, and must act only to the extent and use only the degree of force needed to repel the attack.

Defense of Home and Property

In most jurisdictions, the owner of property can justifiably use reasonable *nondeadly* force to prevent others from unlawfully taking or damaging it. As a general rule, the preservation of human life outweighs the protection of property, and the use of deadly force to protect property is not justified unless the perpetrator of the illegal act may intend to commit, or is in the act of committing, a violent act against another human being. A person who shoots and kills an unarmed trespasser, for example, could not claim "defense of property" to avoid criminal liability.[32] However, a person who shoots and kills an armed robber while being robbed can make such a claim.

The use of mechanical devices to protect property is a special area of law. Because deadly force is usually not permitted in defense of property, the setting of booby traps, such as spring-loaded shotguns, electrified gates, and explosive devices, is generally not permitted to protect property that is unattended and unoccupied. If an individual is injured as a result of a mechanical device intended to cause injury or death in the protection of property, criminal charges may be brought against the person who set the device.

On the other hand, acts that would otherwise be criminal may carry no criminal liability if undertaken to protect one's home. For purposes of the law, one's "home" is one's dwelling, whether owned, rented, or merely borrowed. Hotel rooms, rooms aboard vessels, and rented rooms in houses belonging to others are all considered, for purposes of the law, one's home. The retreat rule referred to earlier, which requires a person under attack to retreat when possible before resorting to deadly force, is subject to what some call the *castle exception*. The castle exception can be traced to the writings of the sixteenth-century English jurist Sir Edward Coke, who said, "A man's house is his castle—for where shall a man be safe if it be not in his house?"[33] The castle exception generally recognizes that a person has a fundamental right to be in his or her home and that the home is a final and inviolable place of retreat. That is, the home offers a place of retreat from which a person can be expected to retreat no farther. Hence, it is not necessary for one to retreat from one's home in the face of an immediate threat, even where such retreat is possible, before resorting to deadly force in protection of the home. A number of court decisions have extended the castle exception to include one's place of business, such as a store or an office.

alter ego rule
In some jurisdictions, a rule of law that holds that a person can only defend a third party under circumstances and only to the degree that the third party could legally act on his or her own behalf.

🐦 Follow the author's tweets about the latest crime and justice news @schmalleger

> No
> State shall . . .
> deprive any person of life,
> liberty, or property, without
> due process of law.
> —Fourteenth Amendment to the
> U.S. Constitution

Necessity

Necessity, or the claim that some illegal action was needed to prevent an even greater harm, is a useful defense in cases that do not involve serious bodily harm. A famous but unsuccessful use of this defense occurred in *The Crown* v. *Dudley & Stephens* in the late nineteenth century.[34] This British case involved a shipwreck in which three sailors and a cabin boy were set adrift in a lifeboat. After a number of days at sea without food, two of the sailors decided to kill and eat the cabin boy. At their trial, they argued that it was necessary to do so, or none of them would have survived. The court, however, reasoned that the cabin boy was not a direct threat to the survival of the men and rejected this defense. Convicted of murder, they were sentenced to death, although they were spared the gallows by royal intervention. Although cannibalism may be against the law, courts have sometimes recognized the necessity of consuming human flesh where survival was at issue. Those cases, however, involved only "victims" who had already died of natural causes.

Consent

The defense of consent claims that whatever harm was done occurred only after the injured person gave his or her permission for the behavior in question. In the "Condom Rapist Case," for example, Joel Valdez was found guilty of rape in 1993 after a jury in Austin, Texas, rejected his claim that the act became consensual once he complied with his victim's request to use a condom. Valdez, who was drunk and armed with a knife at the time of the offense, claimed that his victim's request was a consent to sex. After that, he said, "we were making love."[35]

Resisting Unlawful Arrest

All jurisdictions make resisting arrest a crime. Resistance is rarely warranted or wise—although it may be justifiable in rare cases, especially if the arresting officer uses excessive force. Some states have statutory provisions detailing the limits imposed on such resistance and the conditions under which it can be used. Such laws generally say that a person may use a reasonable amount of force, other than deadly force, to resist arrest or an unlawful search by a law enforcement officer if the officer uses or attempts to use greater force than necessary to make the arrest or search. The rationale underlying such laws is that officers are no longer engaged in the performance of their duties under the law once they exceed the legal authority afforded to them under the law. Under California law, for example, an officer is not lawfully performing his or her duties when he or she "detains an individual without reasonable suspicion or arrests an individual without probable cause."[36] Resisting unlawful arrest as a defense is inapplicable in cases where the defendant is the first to resort to force. Deadly force to resist arrest is never justified unless the law enforcement officer resorts to the illegal use of deadly force.

Excuses

In contrast to a justification, an excuse does not claim that the conduct in question is justified by the situation or that it is moral. An excuse claims, rather, that the actor who engaged in the unlawful behavior was, at the time, not legally responsible for his or her actions and should not be held accountable under the law. For example, a person who assaults a police officer, thinking that the officer is really a disguised space alien who has come to abduct him, may be found "not guilty" of the charge of assault and battery by reason of insanity. Actions for which excuses are offered do not morally outweigh the wrong committed, but criminal liability may still be negated on the basis of some personal disability that the actor has or because of some special circumstances that characterize the situation. Excuses recognized by the law include (1) duress, (2) age, (3) mistake, (4) involuntary intoxication, (5) unconsciousness, (6) provocation, (7) insanity, (8) diminished capacity, and (9) mental incompetence.

Duress

The defense of duress depends on an understanding of the situation. *Duress* has been defined as "any unlawful threat or coercion used by a person to induce another to act (or to refrain from acting) in a manner he or she otherwise would not (or would)."[37] A person may act under duress if, for example, he or she steals an employer's payroll to meet a ransom demand for kidnappers holding the person's children. Should the person later be arrested for larceny or embezzlement, the person can claim that he or she felt compelled to commit the crime to help ensure the safety of the children. Duress is generally not a useful defense when the crime committed involves serious physical harm, since the harm committed may outweigh the coercive influence in the minds of jurors and judges. Duress is sometimes also called *coercion*.

Age

Age offers another kind of excuse to a criminal charge. The defense of "infancy"—as it is sometimes known in legal jargon—has its roots in the ancient belief that children cannot reason logically until around the age of seven. Early doctrine in the Christian church sanctioned that belief by declaring that rationality develops around that age. As a consequence, only older children could be held responsible for their crimes.

The defense of infancy today has been expanded to include young people well beyond the age of seven. Many states set 16 as the age at which a person becomes an adult for purposes of criminal prosecution; others use the age of 17, and still others 18. When a person younger than the age required for adult prosecution commits a "crime," it is termed a *juvenile offense* (see Chapter 13). He or she is not guilty of a criminal violation of the law by virtue of youth. In most jurisdictions, children below the age of seven cannot be charged even with juvenile offenses, no matter how serious their actions may appear to others.

Mistake

Two types of mistakes can serve as a defense. One is mistake of law, and the other is mistake of fact. Rarely is mistake of law held to be an acceptable defense. Most people realize that it is their responsibility to know the law as it applies to them. "Ignorance of the law is no excuse" is an old dictum still heard today. On occasion, however, cases do arise in which such a defense is accepted by authorities. For example, an elderly woman raised marijuana plants because they could be used to make a tea that relieved her arthritis pain. When her garden was discovered, she was not arrested but was advised as to how the law applied to her.

Mistake of fact is a much more useful form of the mistake defense. In 2000, for example, the statutory rape conviction of 39-year-old Charles Ballinger of Bradley County, Tennessee, was reversed by Tennessee's Court of Criminal Appeals at Knoxville on a mistake-of-fact claim.[38] Ballinger admitted that he had sex with his 15-year-old neighbor, who was under the age of legal consent at the time of the act. In his defense, however, Ballinger claimed that he had good reason to mistake the girl's age.

Involuntary Intoxication

The claim of involuntary intoxication may form the basis for another excuse defense. Both drugs and alcohol may produce intoxication. Voluntary intoxication is rarely a defense to a criminal charge because it is a self-induced condition. It is widely recognized in our legal tradition that an altered mental condition that is the product of voluntary activity cannot be used to exonerate guilty actions that follow from it. Some state statutes formalize this general principle of law and specifically state that voluntary intoxication cannot be offered as a defense against a charge of criminal behavior.[39]

Involuntary intoxication, however, is another matter. A person might be tricked into consuming an intoxicating substance. Secretly "spiked" punch, popular aphrodisiacs, or drug-laced desserts might be ingested unknowingly. Because the effects and taste of alcohol are so widely known in our society, the defense of involuntary intoxication due to alcohol consumption can be difficult to demonstrate.

Unconsciousness

A very rarely used excuse is that of unconsciousness. An individual cannot be held responsible for anything he or she does while unconscious. Because unconscious people rarely do anything at all, this defense is almost never seen in the courts. However, cases of sleepwalking, epileptic seizure, and neurological dysfunction may result in injurious, although unintentional, actions by people so afflicted. Under such circumstances, a defense of unconsciousness might be argued with success.

Follow the author's tweets about the latest crime and justice news @schmalleger

▲ Saiqa Akhter, the Texas woman who was found not guilty by reason of insanity after admitting to the murder of her two young children by strangulation. Akhter, who had been charged with two counts of capital murder, claimed the children were autistic, and told first responders, "I want normal kids." What is the M'Naghten rule? Might it apply to Akhter?

Courtney Perry/MCT/Newscom

insanity defense
A legal defense based on claims of mental illness or mental incapacity.

🐦 Follow the author's tweets about the latest crime and justice news @schmalleger

Provocation

Provocation recognizes that a person can be emotionally enraged by another who intends to elicit just such a reaction. Should the person then strike out at the tormentor, some courts have held, he or she may not be guilty of criminality or may be guilty of a lesser degree of criminality than might otherwise be the case. The defense of provocation is commonly used in cases arising from barroom brawls in which a person's parentage was called into question, although most states don't look favorably on verbal provocation alone. This defense has also been used in some spectacular cases where wives have killed their husbands, or children their fathers, citing years of verbal and physical abuse. In these latter instances, perhaps because the degree of physical harm inflicted—the death of the husband or father—appears to be out of proportion to the abuse suffered by the wife or child, the courts have not readily accepted the defense of provocation. As a rule, the defense of provocation is generally more acceptable in minor offenses than in serious violations of the law.

Insanity

In 2013, 55-year-old Michael Selleneit of Centerville, Utah, pleaded guilty but mentally ill and was sentenced to prison for shooting his 41-year-old neighbor, Tony Pierce, 3 years earlier.[40] Selleneit claimed that Pierce had raped his wife telepathically, although he admitted that the neighbor had never touched the woman physically. Court documents showed that Selleneit had been diagnosed with organic brain disorder years earlier, perhaps as a result of a car crash in which he had injured his head.

From the point of view of the criminal law, *insanity* is a legal concept, not a medical one. The legal definition of insanity often has very little to do with psychological or psychiatric understandings of mental illness; rather, it is a concept developed to enable the judicial system to assign guilt or innocence to particular defendants. As a consequence, medical conceptions of mental illness do not always fit well into the legal categories of mental illness created by courts and legislatures. The differences between psychiatric and legal conceptualizations of insanity often lead to disagreements among expert witnesses who, in criminal court, may provide conflicting testimony as to the sanity of a defendant.

The **insanity defense** is given a lot of play in the entertainment industry; movies and television shows regularly employ it because it makes for good drama. In practice, however, the defense of insanity is rarely raised. According to an eight-state study funded by the National Institute of Mental Health, the insanity defense was used in less than 1% of the cases that came before county-level courts.[41] The study showed that only 26% of all insanity pleas were argued successfully and that 90% of those who employed the defense had been previously diagnosed with a mental illness. As the American Bar Association says, "The best evidence suggests that the mental nonresponsibility defense is raised in less than one percent of all felony cases in the United States and is successful in about a fourth of these."[42] Even so, there are several rules that guide the legal definition of insanity.

The M'Naghten Rule

The insanity defense, as we know it today, was nonexistent prior to the nineteenth century. Until then, insane people who committed crimes were punished in the same way as other law violators. It was Daniel M'Naghten (sometimes spelled McNaughten or M'Naughten), a woodworker from Glasgow, Scotland, who became the first person to be found not guilty of a crime by reason of insanity in 1844. M'Naghten had tried to assassinate Sir Robert Peel, the British prime minister. He mistook Edward Drummond, Peel's secretary, for Peel himself and killed Drummond instead. At his trial, defense attorneys argued that M'Naghten suffered from vague delusions centered on the idea that the Tories, a British political party, were persecuting him. Medical testimony at the trial supported the defense's assertion that he didn't know what he was doing at the time of the shooting. The jury accepted M'Naghten's claims, and the insanity defense was born. Later, the House of Lords defined the criteria necessary for a

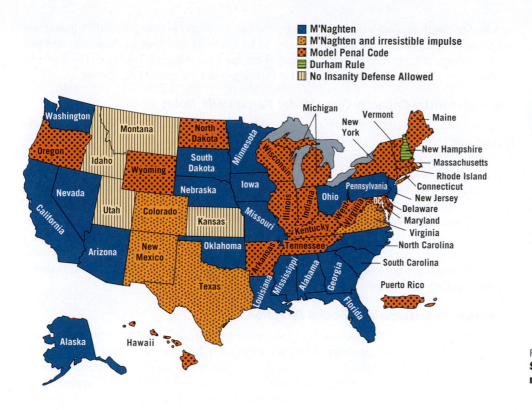

M'Naghten
M'Naghten and irresistible impulse
Model Penal Code
Durham Rule
No Insanity Defense Allowed

FIGURE 3–6
Standards for Insanity Determinations by Jurisdictions

finding of insanity. The **M'Naghten rule**, as it is called today, holds that a person is not guilty of a crime if, at the time of the crime, the person either didn't know what he or she was doing or didn't know that it was wrong. The inability to distinguish right from wrong must be the result of some mental defect or disability.

The M'Naghten rule, or a derivation of it, is followed in many U.S. jurisdictions (Figure 3–6) today. In those states, the burden of proving insanity falls on the defendant. Just as defendants are assumed to be innocent, they are also assumed to be sane at the outset of any criminal trial. Learn more about the M'Naghten rule at **http://tinyurl.com/6yfbybh**.

Irresistible Impulse

The M'Naghten rule worked well for a time. Eventually, however, some cases arose in which defendants clearly knew what they were doing, and they knew it was wrong. Even so, they argued in their defense that they couldn't stop doing what they knew was wrong. Such people are said to suffer from an *irresistible impulse*, and in a number of states today, they may be found not guilty by reason of that particular brand of insanity. Some states that do not use the irresistible-impulse test in determining insanity may still allow the successful demonstration of such an impulse to be considered in sentencing decisions.

The irresistible-impulse test has been criticized on a number of grounds. Primary among them is the belief that all of us suffer from compulsions. Most of us, however, learn to control them. If we give in to a compulsion, the critique goes, then why not just say it was unavoidable so as to escape any legal consequences?

The Durham Rule

Another rule for gauging insanity is called the *Durham rule*. Originally created in 1871 by a New Hampshire court, it was later adopted by Judge David Bazelon in 1954 as he decided the case of *Durham* v. *U.S.* for the court of appeals in the District of Columbia.[43] The Durham rule states that a person is not criminally responsible for his or her behavior if the person's illegal actions were the result of some mental disease or defect.

Courts that follow the Durham rule, while few in number, typically hear from an array of psychiatric specialists as to the mental state of the defendant. Their testimony is inevitably clouded by the need to address the question of cause. A successful defense under the Durham rule necessitates that jurors be able to see the criminal activity in question as the

M'Naghten rule
A rule for determining insanity that asks whether the defendant knew what he or she was doing or whether the defendant knew that what he or she was doing was wrong.

product of the defendant's mental deficiencies. And yet many people who suffer from mental diseases or defects never commit crimes. In fact, low IQ, intellectual disability, and lack of general mental capacity are not allowable excuses for criminal behavior. Because the Durham rule is especially vague, it provides fertile ground for conflicting claims.

The Substantial-Capacity Test (Model Penal Code Rule)

Many states follow another guideline—the substantial-capacity test—as found in the Model Penal Code (MPC) of the American Law Institute (ALI).[44] Also called the *ALI rule* or the *MPC rule*, it suggests that insanity should be defined as the lack of a substantial capacity to control one's behavior. This test requires a judgment to the effect that the defendant suffered from a mental disease or defect that resulted in the individual lacking the "substantial capacity either to appreciate the criminality of his conduct or to conform his conduct to the requirements of the law."[45] The substantial-capacity test is a blending of the M'Naghten rule and the irresistible-impulse standard. "Substantial capacity" does not require total mental incompetence nor does the rule require the behavior in question to live up to the criterion of total irresistibility. However, the problem of establishing just what constitutes "substantial mental capacity" has plagued this rule from its conception.

The Insanity Defense and Social Reaction

The insanity defense originated as a way to recognize the social reality of mental disease. However, the history of this defense has been rife with difficulty and contradiction. First, psychiatric testimony is expensive, and expert witnesses are often at odds with one another. Another difficulty with this defense is society's acceptance of it. When "not guilty due to insanity" findings have been made, the public has not always been satisfied that justice has been served. Dissatisfaction with the jumble of rules defining legal insanity peaked in 1982 when John Hinckley was acquitted of trying to assassinate then-President Ronald Reagan. At his trial, Hinckley's lawyers claimed that a series of delusions brought about by a history of schizophrenia left him unable to control his behavior. Government prosecutors were unable to counter defense contentions of insanity. The resulting acquittal shocked the nation and resulted in calls for a review of the insanity defense.

One response has been to ban the insanity defense from use at trial. A ruling by the U.S. Supreme Court in support of a Montana law allows states to prohibit defendants from claiming that they were insane at the time they committed their crimes. In 1994, without comment, the high court let stand a Montana Supreme Court ruling that held that eliminating the insanity defense does not violate the U.S. Constitution. Currently, only four states—Kansas, Montana, Idaho, and Utah—bar use of the insanity defense.[46]

The Guilty But Mentally Ill Verdict

guilty but mentally ill (GBMI)
A verdict, equivalent to a finding of "guilty," that establishes that the defendant, although mentally ill, was in sufficient possession of his or her faculties to be morally blameworthy for his or her acts.

Another response to public frustration with the insanity and responsibility issue is the **guilty but mentally ill (GBMI)** verdict, now possible in at least 11 states. (In a few states, the finding is "guilty but insane.") A GBMI verdict means that a person can be held responsible for a specific criminal act even though a degree of mental incompetence may be present in his or her personality. In most GBMI jurisdictions, a jury must return a finding of "guilty but mentally ill" if (1) every element necessary for a conviction has been proved beyond a reasonable doubt, (2) the defendant is found to have been *mentally ill* at the time the crime was committed, and (3) the defendant was *not* found to have been *legally insane* at the time the crime was committed. The difference between mental illness and legal insanity is a crucial one, since a defendant can be mentally ill by standards of the medical profession but sane for purposes of the law.

Upon return of a GBMI verdict, a judge may impose any sentence possible under the law for the crime in question. Mandated psychiatric treatment, however, is often part of the commitment order. Once cured, the offender is usually placed in the general prison population to serve any remaining sentence.

As some authors have observed, the GBMI finding has three purposes: "first, to protect society; second, to hold some offenders who were mentally ill accountable for their criminal acts; [and] third, to make treatment available to convicted offenders suffering from some form of mental illness."[47] The U.S. Supreme Court case of *Ford* v. *Wainwright* recognized an issue of a different sort.[48] The 1986 decision specified that prisoners who become insane while incarcerated cannot be executed. Hence, although insanity may not always be a successful defense to criminal prosecution, it can later become a block to the ultimate punishment.

Temporary Insanity

Temporary insanity is another possible defense against a criminal charge. Widely used in the 1940s and 1950s, temporary insanity means that the offender claims to have been insane only at the time of the commission of the offense. If a jury agrees, the defendant goes free. The defendant is not guilty of the criminal action by virtue of having been insane at the time, yet he or she cannot be ordered to undergo psychiatric counseling or treatment because the insanity is no longer present. This type of plea has become less popular as legislatures have regulated the circumstances under which it can be made.

The Insanity Defense under Federal Law

Yet another response to the public's concern with the insanity defense and responsibility issue is the federal Insanity Defense Reform Act (IDRA). In 1984, Congress passed this act, which created major revisions in the federal insanity defense. Insanity under the law is now defined as a condition in which the defendant can be shown to have been suffering under a "severe mental disease or defect" and, as a result, "was unable to appreciate the nature and quality or the wrongfulness of his acts."[49] This definition of insanity comes close to that set forth in the old M'Naghten rule.

The act also places the burden of proving the insanity defense squarely on the defendant—a provision that has been challenged a number of times since the act was passed. The Supreme Court supported a similar requirement prior to the act's passage. In 1983, in the case of *Jones* v. *U.S.*,[50] the Court ruled that defendants can be required to prove their insanity when it becomes an issue in their defense. Shortly after the act became law, the Court held in *Ake* v. *Oklahoma* (1985)[51] that the government must ensure access to a competent psychiatrist whenever a defendant indicates that insanity will be an issue at trial.

The Consequences of an Insanity Ruling

The insanity defense today is not an easy way out of criminal prosecution, as some people assume. Once a verdict of "not guilty by reason of insanity" is returned, the judge may order the defendant to undergo psychiatric treatment until cured. Because psychiatrists are reluctant to declare any potential criminal "cured," such a sentence may result in more time spent in a psychiatric institution than would have been spent in a prison. In *Foucha* v. *Louisiana* (1992),[52] however, the U.S. Supreme Court held that a defendant found not guilty by reason of insanity in a criminal trial could not thereafter be institutionalized indefinitely without a showing that he or she was either dangerous or mentally ill.

Diminished Capacity

Diminished capacity, or *diminished responsibility*, is a defense available in some jurisdictions. In 2003, the U.S. Sentencing Commission issued a policy statement saying that diminished capacity may mean that "the defendant, although convicted, *has a significantly impaired ability* to (A) understand the wrongfulness of the behavior comprising the offense or to exercise the power of reason; or (B) control behavior that the defendant knows is wrongful."[53] Still, "the terms 'diminished responsibility' and 'diminished capacity' do not have a clearly accepted meaning in [many] courts."[54] Some defendants who offer diminished-capacity defenses do so in recognition of the fact that such claims may be based on a mental condition that would not qualify as mental disease or mental defect or be sufficient to support the defense of insanity but that might still lower criminal culpability. According to Peter Arenella, professor of law at UCLA, "the defense [of diminished capacity] was first recognized by Scottish common law courts to reduce the punishment of the 'partially insane' from murder to culpable homicide, a non-capital offense."[55]

Follow the author's tweets about the latest crime and justice news @schmalleger

diminished capacity
A defense based on claims of a mental condition that may be insufficient to exonerate the defendant of guilt but that may be relevant to specific mental elements of certain crimes or degrees of crime.

The diminished-capacity defense is similar to the defense of insanity in that it depends on a showing that the defendant's mental state was impaired at the time of the crime. As a defense, diminished capacity is most useful when it can be shown that because of some defect of reason or mental shortcoming, the defendant's capacity to form the *mens rea* required by a specific crime was impaired. Unlike an insanity defense, however, which can result in a finding of "not guilty," a diminished-capacity defense is built on the recognition that "[m]ental condition, though insufficient to exonerate, may be relevant to specific mental elements of certain crimes or degrees of crime."[56] For example, a defendant might present evidence of mental abnormality in an effort to reduce first-degree murder to second-degree murder, or second-degree murder to manslaughter, when a killing occurs under extreme emotional disturbance. Similarly, in some jurisdictions, very low intelligence will, if proved, serve to reduce first-degree murder to manslaughter.[57]

As is the case with the insanity defense, some jurisdictions have entirely eliminated the diminished-capacity defense. The California Penal Code, for example, abolished the defense,[58] stating that "[a]s a matter of public policy there shall be no defense of diminished capacity, diminished responsibility, or irresistible impulse in a criminal action or juvenile adjudication hearing."[59]

Mental Incompetence

In most states, the defendant must be capable of understanding the nature of the proceedings and must be able to assist in his or her own legal defense before being deemed competent to stand trial. Whereas insanity refers to an assessment of the offender's mental condition at the time the crime was committed, mental incompetence refers to his or her condition immediately before prosecution. Mental illness short of being found **incompetent to stand trial** can bar a defendant from self-representation. In 2008, in the case of *Indiana* v. *Edwards*, the U.S. Supreme Court held that even defendants found competent to stand trial can be prohibited from representing themselves before the court if they are too mentally disturbed to conduct trial proceedings by themselves.[60]

Procedural Defenses

Procedural defenses make the claim that the defendant was in some manner discriminated against in the justice process or that some important aspect of official procedure was not properly followed. As a result, those offering this defense say, the defendant should be released from any criminal liability. The procedural defenses we will discuss here are (1) entrapment, (2) double jeopardy, (3) *collateral estoppel*, (4) selective prosecution, (5) denial of a speedy trial, (6) prosecutorial misconduct, and (7) police fraud.

Entrapment

Entrapment is an improper or illegal inducement to crime by enforcement agents. Entrapment defenses argue that enforcement agents effectively created a crime where there would otherwise have been none. For entrapment to occur, the idea for the criminal activity must originate with official agents of the criminal justice system. Entrapment can also result when overzealous undercover police officers convince a defendant that the contemplated law-violating behavior is not a crime. To avoid claims of entrapment, officers must not engage in activity that would cause a person to commit a crime that he or she would not otherwise commit. Merely providing an opportunity for a willing offender to commit a crime, however, is not entrapment.

Double Jeopardy

The Fifth Amendment to the U.S. Constitution makes it clear that no person may be tried twice for the same offense, which is known as **double jeopardy**. In other words, people who have been acquitted or found innocent may not again be "put in jeopardy of life or limb" for the same crime. The same is true of those who have been convicted: They cannot be tried

incompetent to stand trial
In criminal proceedings, a finding by a court that as a result of mental illness, defect, or disability, a defendant is incapable of understanding the nature of the charges and proceedings against him or her, of consulting with an attorney, and of aiding in his or her own defense.

entrapment
An improper or illegal inducement to crime by agents of law enforcement. Also, a defense that may be raised when such inducements have occurred.

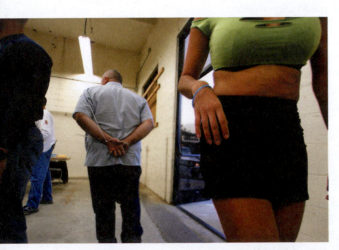

▲ A handcuffed man in police custody walks away from the female police officer who arrested him while posing as a prostitute in Pomona, California. How might entrapment be a defense in a case like this? How can police avoid claims of entrapment?

David McNew/Getty Images

again for the same offense. Cases that are dismissed for a lack of evidence also come under the double jeopardy rule and cannot result in a new trial. The U.S. Supreme Court has ruled that "the Double Jeopardy Clause protects against three distinct abuses: a second prosecution for the same offense after acquittal; a second prosecution for the same offense after conviction; and multiple punishments for the same offense."[61]

Double jeopardy does not apply in cases of trial error. A defendant whose conviction was set aside because of some error in proceedings at a lower court level (for example, inappropriate instructions to the jury by the trial court judge) can be retried on the same charges. Similarly, when a defendant's motion for a mistrial is successful or when members of the jury cannot agree on a verdict (resulting in a hung jury), a second trial may be held. Defendants, however, may be tried in both federal and state courts without necessarily violating the principle of double jeopardy.

Generally, because civil and criminal laws differ as to purpose, it is possible to try someone in civil court to collect damages for a possible violation of civil law, even if they were found "not guilty" in criminal court, without violating the principle of double jeopardy. For example, the 2005 civil trial of actor Robert Blake, following his acquittal at a criminal trial for murdering his wife, resulted in Blake's being ordered to pay $30 million to his wife's children.[62] In cases where civil penalties are "so punitive in form and effect as to render them criminal,"[63] however, a person sanctioned by a court in a civil case may not be tried in criminal court.

Collateral Estoppel

Collateral estoppel is similar to double jeopardy, but it applies to facts that have been determined by a "valid and final judgment."[64] Such facts cannot become the object of new litigation. For example, if a defendant has been acquitted of a murder charge by virtue of an alibi, it would not be permissible to try that person again for the murder of a second person killed along with the first.

Selective Prosecution

The procedural defense of selective prosecution is based on the Fourteenth Amendment's guarantee of "equal protection of the laws." This defense may be available where two or more individuals are suspected of criminal involvement but not all are actively prosecuted. Selective prosecution based fairly on the strength of available evidence is not the object of this defense. However, when prosecution proceeds unfairly on the basis of some arbitrary and discriminatory attribute, such as race, sex, friendship, age, or religious preference, this defense may offer protection. In 1996, in a case that reaffirmed reasonable limits on claims of selective prosecution, the U.S. Supreme Court ruled that for a defendant to successfully "claim that he was singled out for prosecution on the basis of his race, he must make a . . . showing that the Government declined to prosecute similarly situated suspects of other races."[65]

Denial of a Speedy Trial

The Sixth Amendment to the Constitution guarantees a right to a speedy trial. The purpose of the guarantee is to prevent unconvicted and potentially innocent people from languishing in jail. The federal government[66] and most states have laws (generally referred to as *speedy trial acts*) that define the time limit necessary for a trial to be "speedy." They generally set a reasonable period, such as 90 or 120 days following arrest. Excluded from the total number of days are delays that result from requests by the defense to prepare the defendant's case. If the limit set by law is exceeded, the defendant must be set free, and no trial can occur.

Speedy trial claims became an issue in New Orleans after it was ravaged by Hurricane Katrina in August 2005. Nine months after the storm battered the city, Chief District Judge Calvin Johnson told reporters that his staff was continuing to find people who shouldn't be in jail and who were doing "Katrina time."[67] Most pre-Katrina arrestees discovered by Johnson's staff had been taken into custody for misdemeanors before the storm hit. The judge said that he released them when they were found. "We can't have people in jail indeterminately," he said. Speedy trial laws are discussed in more detail in Chapter 8.

> No person shall be . . . twice put in jeopardy of life or limb.
> —Fifth Amendment to the U.S. Constitution

double jeopardy
A common law and constitutional prohibition against a second trial for the same offense.

Follow the author's tweets about the latest crime and justice news @schmalleger

🐦 Follow the author's tweets about the latest crime and justice news @schmalleger

Prosecutorial Misconduct

Another procedural defense is prosecutorial misconduct. Generally speaking, legal scholars use the term *prosecutorial misconduct* to describe actions undertaken by prosecutors that give the government an unfair advantage or that prejudice the rights of a defendant or a witness. Prosecutors are expected to uphold the highest ethical standards in the performance of their roles. When they knowingly permit false testimony, when they hide information that would clearly help the defense, or when they make unduly biased statements to the jury in closing arguments, the defense of prosecutorial misconduct may be available to the defendant.

Police Fraud

The defense of police fraud is available to defendants victimized by the police through planted evidence, the fabrication of "facts" uncovered during police investigations, and false arrests. In 2011, for example, Stephen Anderson, a former NYPD narcotics detective, testified in court that the practice of "flaking," or the planting of drugs on innocent people was common practice in the NYPD's narcotics division. Flaking, said Anderson, was a quick and easy way to boost arrest numbers and to impress supervisors.[68]

Similarly, during the 1995 double-murder trial of O. J. Simpson, defense attorneys suggested that evidence against Simpson had been concocted and planted by police officers with a personal dislike of the defendant.

Not all claims of police fraud are supportable, however, and some defendants will claim fraud as a defense even when they know that they are guilty. As one observer put it, the defense of police fraud builds on extreme paranoia about the government and police agencies. This type of defense, says political economist Francis Fukuyama, carries "to extremes a distrust of government and the belief that public authorities are in a vast conspiracy to violate the rights of individuals."[69] As a defense strategy the claim of police fraud, when it is not warranted, can subject otherwise well-meaning public servants to intense public scrutiny, effectively shifting attention away from criminal defendants and onto the police officers—sometimes with disastrous personal results.

Summary

CRIMINAL LAW

- Laws are rules of conduct, usually found enacted in the form of statutes, that regulate relationships between people and also between parties. One of the primary functions of the law is to maintain public order. Laws also serve to regulate human interaction, enforce moral beliefs, define the economic environment of a society, enhance predictability, promote orderly social change, sustain individual rights, identify wrongdoers and redress wrongs, and mandate punishment and retribution. Because laws are made by those in power and are influenced by those with access to power brokers, they tend to reflect and support the interests of society's most powerful members.

- The rule of law, which is sometimes referred to as the *supremacy of law*, encompasses the principle that an orderly society must be governed by established principles and known codes that are applied uniformly and fairly to all of its members. It means that no one is above the law, and it mandates that even those who make or enforce the law must also abide by it. The rule of law is regarded as a vital underpinning in Western democracies, for without it disorder and chaos might prevail.

- This chapter identified various types of law, including criminal law, civil law, administrative law, case law, and procedural law. This chapter is concerned primarily with criminal law, which is that form of the law that defines and specifies punishments for offenses of a public nature or for wrongs committed against the state or against society.

- Violations of the criminal law can be of many different types and can vary in severity. Six categories of violations were discussed in this chapter: (1) felonies, (2) misdemeanors, (3) infractions, (4) treason (5) espionage, and (6) inchoate offenses.

- From the perspective of Western jurisprudence, all crimes can be said to share certain features. Taken together, these features make up the legal essence of the concept of crime. The essence of crime consists of three conjoined elements: (1) the criminal act, which in legal parlance is termed the *actus reus;* (2) a culpable mental state, or *mens rea;* and (3) a concurrence of the two. Hence, the essence of criminal conduct consists of a concurrence of a criminal act with a culpable mental state. Five additional principles, added to these three, allow us to fully appreciate contemporary understandings of crime: (1) causation, (2) resulting harm, (3) legality, (4) punishment, and (5) necessary attendant circumstances.

- Written laws specify exactly what conditions are required for a person to be charged in a given instance of criminal activity. The elements of a crime are specific legal aspects of the criminal offense that the prosecution must prove in order to obtain a conviction. Guilt can be demonstrated, and criminal offenders convicted, only if all of the statutory elements of the particular crime can be proved in court.

- Our legal system recognizes four broad categories of defenses to a criminal charge: (1) alibi, (2) justifications, (3) excuses, and (4) procedural defenses. An alibi, if shown to be valid, means that the defendant could not have committed the crime in question because he or she was not present at the time of the crime. When a defendant offers a justification as a defense, he or she admits committing the act in question but claims that it was necessary to avoid some greater evil. A defendant who offers an excuse as a defense claims that some personal condition or circumstance at the time of the act was such that he or she should not be held accountable under the criminal law. Procedural defenses make the claim that the defendant was in some significant way discriminated against in the justice process or that some important aspect of official procedure was not properly followed in the investigation or prosecution of the crime charged.

QUESTIONS FOR REVIEW

1. What is the purpose of law? What would a society without laws be like?
2. What is the rule of law? What is its importance in Western democracies? What does it mean to say that "nobody is above the law"?
3. What types of law does this chapter discuss? What purpose does each serve?
4. What are the six categories of criminal law violations? Describe each, and rank the categories in terms of seriousness.
5. List and describe the eight general features of crime. What are the "three conjoined elements" that make up the legal essence of the concept of crime?
6. Explain what is meant by the *elements* of a specific criminal offense.
7. What four broad categories of criminal defenses does our legal system recognize? Under what circumstances might each be employed?

Policing: Purpose and Organization

CHAPTER

4

> The police in the United States are not separate from the people. They draw their authority from the will and consent of the people, and they recruit their officers from them. The police are the instrument of the people to achieve and maintain order; their efforts are founded on principles of public service and ultimate responsibility to the public.
>
> —National Advisory Commission on Criminal Justice Standards and Goals

Learning Objectives

After reading this chapter, you should be able to:

1. Explain the police mission in democratic societies. **91**

2. Describe the three major levels of policing in the United States today. **96**

3. Describe private protective services in the United States and their possible future roles. **104**

4. Summarize the typical organizational structure of a police department. **107**

5. Summarize the historical development of policing in America, along with the characteristics of each stage. **109**

6. Explain how community policing differs from traditional forms of policing. **112**

7. Discuss the impact of evidence-based policing in the area of police management. **117**

8. Explain how police discretion affects contemporary law enforcement. **121**

Introduction

In 2014, 18-year-old Michael Brown was shot and killed by 28-year-old Ferguson, Missouri, police officer Darren Wilson, sparking days of racially charged protests. Brown, who was shot multiple times, had been unarmed at the time he died. Witnesses at the scene provided conflicting stories, with some saying that the 6 foot 4 inch, 292 lb. Brown had been raising his arms in surrender, while others said that he lunged at the officer. Tensions increased as police released video of a store robbery in which Brown was said to have participated immediately before the shooting, and detailed serious facial injuries that Wilson suffered during the encounter. A grand jury refused to indict Wilson in the shooting.

▲ Police in Ferguson, Missouri, arrest a looter during a night of rioting following the shooting death of an unarmed black teenager by a white police officer in 2014. What aspects of the police mission can you identify?

Scott Olson/Getty Images

The death of Michael Brown revealed a deep distrust of the police by minorities—something that national opinion polls continue to document. Combined Gallup Poll data from 2011 to 2014, for example, show that 59% of whites have a "great deal" or "quite a lot" of confidence in the police, compared with only 37% of blacks.[1] The police department in Ferguson, a suburb of St. Louis, was more than 90% white at the time of Brown's shooting while the town's population was nearly 70% African American.

A post-Brown analysis by *The New York Times* of nearly 400 police departments nationwide found that, in general, the "share of white officers was greater than the share of white residents by more than 50 percentage points."[2] Critics point out, however, that "it's very, very, very difficult" to hire qualified minorities for police work, and that "there is little hard evidence that diversity correlates with better performance…"[3] Consequently, while the police mission may seem relatively straightforward, it is complicated by the many calls for individual and civil rights that surround police work.

The Police Mission

1	Explain the police mission in democratic societies.

The basic purposes of policing in democratic societies are to (1) enforce the laws of the society of which the police are a part, (2) apprehend offenders who participate in crime, (3) prevent crime, (4) preserve domestic peace and tranquility, and (5) provide the community with needed enforcement-related services (Figure 4–1). Simply put, as Sir Robert Peel, founder of the British system of policing, explained in 1822, "The basic mission for which the police exist is to reduce crime and disorder."[4] In the paragraphs that follow, we turn our attention to these five basic elements of the police mission.

> Most police officers spend the majority of their time answering nonemergency public-service calls.

Enforcing the Law

The police operate under an official public mandate that requires them to enforce the law. Collectively speaking, police agencies are the primary enforcers of federal, state, and local criminal laws. Not surprisingly, police officers see themselves as crime fighters, a view shared by the public and promoted by the popular media.

Although it is the job of the police to enforce the law, it is not their *only* job. Practically speaking, most officers spend the majority of their time answering nonemergency public-service calls,[5] controlling traffic, or writing tickets. Most are not involved in intensive, ongoing crime-fighting activities. Research shows that only about 10% to 20% of all calls to the police involve situations that actually require a law enforcement response (i.e., situations that might lead to arrest and eventual prosecution), a fact that is described in more detail later in this chapter.[6]

Even when the police are busy enforcing laws, they can't enforce them all. Police resources, including labor, vehicles, and investigative assets, are limited, causing officers to focus more on

FIGURE 4–1
The Basic Purposes of Policing in Democratic Societies
Source: Pearson Education, Inc.

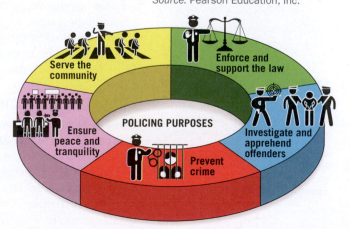

POLICING PURPOSES

Serve the community

Enforce and support the law

Ensure peace and tranquility

Investigate and apprehend offenders

Prevent crime

An NYPD station in Times Square. As the story that opens this chapter shows, order maintenance is an important part of the police mission. What other aspects of the police mission can you identify?

Justice Research Association

🐦 Follow the author's tweets about the latest crime and justice news @schmalleger

criminal investigation
The process of discovering, collecting, preparing, identifying, and presenting evidence to determine what happened and who is responsible when a crime occurs.[i]

crime prevention
The anticipation, recognition, and appraisal of a crime risk and the initiation of action to eliminate or reduce it.

certain types of law violation than on others. Old laws prohibiting minor offenses that today hold little social significance, such as spitting on the sidewalk or scaring horses with a noisy automobile, are typically relegated to the dustbin of statutory history. Even though they are still "on the books," few (if any) officers even think about enforcing such laws. A number of writers have observed that the police tend to tailor their enforcement efforts to meet the contemporary concerns of the populace they serve.[7] For example, if the local community is upset about "massage parlors" operating in certain neighborhoods, it is likely that the local police department will bring enforcement efforts to bear that might eventually lead to the relocation or closing of such businesses. Although the enforcement practices of police agencies are significantly influenced by community interests, individual officers take their cue on enforcement priorities from their departments, their peers, and their supervisors.

The police are expected not only to enforce the law but also to support it. This means that the personal actions of law enforcement personnel should be exemplary and should inspire others to respect and obey the law. Off-duty officers who are seen speeding down the highway or smoking marijuana at a party, for example, do a disservice to the police profession and engender disrespect for all agents of enforcement and for the law itself. Hence, in an important sense, we can say that respect for the law begins with the personal and public behavior of law enforcement officers.

Apprehending Offenders

Some offenders are apprehended during the investigation of a crime or even during its commission or immediately afterward. Fleeing Oklahoma City bomber Timothy McVeigh, for example, was stopped by an Oklahoma Highway Patrol officer on routine patrol only 90 minutes after the destruction of the Alfred P. Murrah Federal Building[8] for driving a car with no license plate. When the officer questioned McVeigh about a bulge in his jacket, McVeigh admitted that it was a gun. The officer then took McVeigh into custody for carrying a concealed weapon. Typically, McVeigh would then have made an immediate appearance before a judge and have been released on bail. As fate would have it, however, the judge assigned to see McVeigh was involved in a protracted divorce case. The longer jail stay proved to be McVeigh's undoing. As the investigation into the bombing progressed, profiler Clinton R. Van Zandt of the Federal Bureau of Investigation (FBI) Behavioral Science Unit concluded that the bomber was likely a native-born white male in his 20s who had been in the military and was probably a member of a fringe militia group—all of which were true of McVeigh.[9] Working together, the FBI and the Oklahoma State Police realized that McVeigh was a likely suspect and questioned him.

While McVeigh's capture was the result of a bit of good luck, many offenders are only caught as the result of extensive police work involving a painstaking investigation, which may begin when a complaint is filed, or with the analysis of a crime scene (Figure 4–2). A **criminal investigation** is "the process of discovering, collecting, preparing, identifying, and presenting evidence to determine what happened and who is responsible"[10] when a crime occurs. Criminal investigators are often referred to as *detectives*, and many work in hand with other police resources, including those provided by *crime scene investigators* or other forensic analysts.

Preventing Crime

Crime prevention is a proactive approach to the problem of crime; it is "the anticipation, recognition and appraisal of a crime risk and initiation of action to remove or reduce it."[11] In preventing crime, police agencies act before a crime happens, thus preventing victimization from occurring. Although the term *crime prevention* is relatively new, the idea is probably as old as human society. Securing valuables, limiting access to sensitive areas, and monitoring the activities of suspicious people are techniques that were in use long before the establishment of Western police forces in the 1800s.

Note: This diagram pertains to crime scene analysis, although a wider investigation will include identifying the victim, interviews with significant others in her life, and an examination of her background, recent activities and lifestyle. The area surrounding the swimming pool, to include the house and the electronic devices it contains, will also be searched for possible evidence, as will the victim's vehicle if she has one. The crime scene will be photographed and video recordings will be made.

Computer forensic experts will examine the laptop found at the scene for possible digital evidence—including texts or e-mail communications, especially those involving recent conversations. Ownership of the laptop will be established, and any GPS information will be collected showing where the computer might have been recently used. A record of Internet connections will be logged, and social media applications and other communications software will be evaluated for possible recent use.

A medical examination by a pathologist or medical examiner will be ordered to determine the cause of death and to identify any injuries to (or marks on) the body. The pathologist will analyze the person's blood for the presence of prescription drugs, illegal substances, and alcohol. Evidence of any possible sexual activity will be recorded. Should the death be ruled a homicide, the evidence gathered in the other steps shown in this box will become relevant.

Persons living nearby or who were in the area at the time of the incident will be contacted and asked if they heard or saw anything of relevance to the investigation.

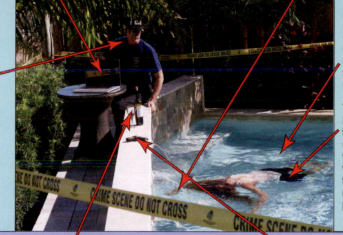

Pool water and pool equipment will be examined to see if they might have contributed to death (i.e., electrical shock, hair caught in drain, etc.).

The victim's clothing will be examined for possible trace evidence. Pocket contents, rents, and tears will be noted. Fingernails will be examined for any forensic DNA evidence resulting from a possible physical struggle.

The body of a young woman was found floating in a home swimming pool by neighbors who called 911; they also reported hearing screams and calls for help. First responders determined that the woman was dead, and crime scene investigators were called to examine and collect evidence to determine whether the death was an accident, a suicide, or a homicide. Although foul play was suspected, the investigators noted the absence of blood in the pool, and they considered that the woman could have been killed elsewhere and her body later dumped into the swimming pool.

The wine bottle and wine glass will be examined for fingerprints and for DNA traces—whether that of the victim or any possible perpetrators. Remnants of any toxic or other substances that might have been added to the wine will be identified.

The handgun found at the scene will be examined by ballistics experts to determine whether it has been fired recently, and the area will be searched for spent shell casings. Fingerprints might also be found on the weapon, and ownership of the pistol will be established.

FIGURE 4–2
The Crime Scene Investigation Process

Source: Data from Justice Research Association.

Techniques and Programs

Modern crime-prevention efforts aim not only to reduce crime and criminal opportunities and lower the potential rewards of criminal activity but also to lessen the public's fear of crime.[12] Law enforcement–led crime-prevention efforts include both techniques and programs. Crime-prevention *techniques* include access control (including barriers to entry and exit), surveillance (such as video surveillance), theft-deterrence devices (i.e., locks, alarms, and tethers), security lighting, and visibility landscaping. *Crime prevention through environmental design* (CPTED) is a tool that can be used by crime-prevention specialists,

hot-spot policing
A contemporary policing strategy in which law enforcement agencies focus their resources on known areas of criminal activity.

Follow the author's tweets about the latest crime and justice news @schmalleger

CompStat
A crime-analysis and police-management process built on crime mapping that was developed by the New York City Police Department in the mid-1990s.

predictive policing
A contemporary policing strategy that uses statistical techniques to analyze data in order to anticipate or predict the likelihood of crime occurrence in locations of interest.

Although desirable, public order has its own costs.

including architects and public-safety consultants. Another technique is **hot-spot policing**, which focuses police resources on geographic areas showing significant criminal activity. *Predictive policing*, also known as crime forecasting, is a third technique in which quantitative techniques are applied to crime data in an effort to identify likely targets for police intervention in an effort to thwart criminal activity.[13]

In contrast to techniques, crime-prevention *programs* are individualized organized efforts that focus resources on reducing a specific form of criminal threat. The Philadelphia Police Department's Operation Identification, for example, is designed to discourage theft and to help recover stolen property.[14] The program seeks to educate citizens on the importance of identifying, marking, and listing their valuables to deter theft and to aid in their recovery. Through Operation Identification, the police department provides engraving pens, suggests ways of photographing and engraving valuables, and provides window decals and car bumper stickers that identify citizens as participants in the program. Other crime-prevention programs typically target school-based crime, gang activity, drug abuse, violence, domestic abuse, identity theft, vehicle theft, or neighborhood crimes such as burglary.

Today's crime-prevention programs depend on community involvement, an open flow of information, and public education about risks and possible preventive measures. For example, Neighborhood Watch programs build on active observation by homeowners and businesspeople on the lookout for anything unusual. Crime Stoppers International and Crime Stoppers USA are examples of privately sponsored programs that accept tips about criminal activity that they pass on to the appropriate law enforcement organization. Crime Stoppers International can be accessed via **https://csiworld.org** and the National Crime Prevention Council can be found at **http://www.ncpc.org**.

Predicting Crime

Law enforcement's ability to prevent crimes relies in part on the ability of police planners to predict when and where crimes will occur. Effective prediction means that limited police resources can be correctly assigned to the areas with the greatest need, often referred to as "hot spots." One technique for predicting criminal activity is **CompStat**.[15] Although CompStat may sound like a software program, it is actually a process of crime analysis and police management developed by the New York City Police Department in the mid-1990s to help police managers better assess their performance and foresee the potential for crime.[16] The CompStat process involves first collecting and analyzing the information received from 9-1-1 calls and officer reports.[17] This detailed and timely information is then mapped using special software developed for the purpose. The resulting map sequences, generated over time, reveal the time and place of crime patterns and identify hot spots of ongoing criminal activity. The maps also show the number of patrol officers active in an area, ongoing investigations, arrests made, and so on, thus helping commanders see which anticrime strategies are working.

CrimeStat, a Windows-based spatial statistics analysis software program for analyzing crime-incident locations, is a second technique for predicting criminal activity. It produces results similar to CompStat's.[18] Developed by Ned Levine and Associates with grants from the National Institute of Justice (NIJ), CrimeStat provides statistical tools for crime mapping and analysis—including identification of crime hot spots, spatial distribution of incidents, and distance analysis—that help crime analysts target offenses that might be related to one another. A link to overlays of crime statistics on maps of Chicago, is available at **http://chicago.everyblock.com/crime**.

CompStat is a form of **predictive policing**, and was mentioned earlier. Predictive policing can be defined as "the application of analytical techniques—particularly quantitative techniques—to identify likely targets for police intervention and prevent crime or solve past crimes by making statistical predictions."[19] Predictive methods can be divided into four categories: (1) methods for predicting crimes, (2) methods for predicting offenders (i.e., individuals at risk of future offending), (3) methods for predicting perpetrators' identities (i.e., creating profiles that likely match offenders with crimes under investigation), and (4) methods for predicting victims of crime, whether they be groups or individuals. Some argue, however, that CompStat is primarily concerned only with the first of these categories, and that true predictive policing includes the other three goals mentioned here.

Preserving the Peace

Enforcing the law, investigating crime and apprehending offenders, and preventing crime are all daunting tasks requiring the full attention of police departments. There are, after all, many laws and numerous offenders. Still, crimes are clearly defined by statute and are therefore limited in number. Peacekeeping, however, is a virtually limitless police activity involving not only activities that violate the law (and hence the community's peace) but many other activities as well. Law enforcement officers who supervise parades, public demonstrations, and picketing strikers, for example, typically attempt to ensure that the behavior of everyone involved remains civil so that it does not disrupt community life.

Robert H. Langworthy, who has written extensively about the police, says that keeping the peace is often left to individual officers.[20] Basically, he says, departments depend on patrol officers "to define the peace and decide how to support it." An officer is doing a good job when his or her beat is quiet, "meaning there are no complaints about loiterers or traffic flow, and commerce is supported."

Many police departments focus on quality-of-life offenses as a crime-reduction and peacekeeping strategy. **Quality-of-life offenses** are minor law violations (sometimes called *petty crimes*) that demoralize residents and businesspeople by creating disorder (for example, excessive noise, graffiti, abandoned cars, and vandalism) or by reflecting social decay (panhandling and aggressive begging, public urination, prostitution, roaming youth gangs, public consumption of alcohol, and street-level substance abuse).[21] Homelessness, although not necessarily a violation of the law (unless it involves some form of trespass),[22] is also typically addressed under quality-of-life programs through police interviews with the homeless, many of whom are relocated to shelters or hospitals or are arrested for some other offense. Many claim that reducing the number of quality-of-life offenses in a community can restore a sense of order, reduce the fear of crime, and lessen the number of serious crimes that occur. However, quality-of-life programs have been criticized by those who say that the police should not be taking a law enforcement approach to social and economic problems.[23]

A similar approach to keeping the peace can be found in the **broken windows** theory of policing.[24] This idea is based on the notion that physical decay, such as litter and abandoned buildings, can breed disorder in a community and can lead to crime by signaling that laws are not being enforced.[25] Such decay, the theory postulates, pushes law-abiding citizens to withdraw from the streets, which sends a signal that lawbreakers can operate freely.[26] The broken windows theory suggests that by encouraging the repair of rundown buildings and controlling disorderly behavior in public spaces, police agencies can create an environment in which serious crime cannot easily flourish.[27]

While desirable, public order has its own costs. Noted police author Charles R. Swanson says, "The degree to which any society achieves some amount of public order through police action depends in part upon the price that society is willing to pay to obtain it."[28] Swanson goes on to describe the price to be paid in terms of (1) police resources paid for by tax dollars and (2) "a reduction in the number, kinds, and extent of liberties" that are available to members of the public.

Providing Services

Writers for the NIJ observe that "any citizen from any city, suburb, or town across the United States can mobilize police resources by simply picking up the phone and placing a direct call to the police."[29] "Calling the cops" has been described as the cornerstone of policing in a democratic society. About 70% of the millions of daily calls to 9-1-1 systems across the country are directed to the police, although callers can also request emergency medical and fire services.

Calls received by 9-1-1 operators are prioritized and then relayed to patrol officers, specialized field units, or other emergency personnel. An online service, **http://crimereports.com**, provides a map overlaid with crime-related incidents and calls to 9-1-1 dispatchers. You can use it to view incidents in your neighborhood. Some cities have also adopted nonemergency

quality-of-life offense

A minor violation of the law (sometimes called a *petty crime*) that demoralizes community residents and businesspeople. Quality-of-life offenses involve acts that create physical disorder (for example, excessive noise and vandalism) or that reflect social decay (for example, panhandling and prostitution).

broken windows

A model of policing based on the notion that physical decay, such as litter and abandoned buildings, can breed disorder in a community and can lead to crime by signaling that laws are not being enforced. The broken windows theory suggests that by encouraging the repair of rundown buildings and controlling disorderly behavior in public spaces, police agencies can create an environment in which serious crime cannot easily flourish.

▲ Chief Deputy Paula Townsend of the Watauga County (North Carolina) Sheriff's Department carrying 11-month-old Breanna Chambers to safety in 2005 after the capture of the child's parents. The parents, who were already wanted on charges related to methamphetamine manufacture, were charged with additional counts of child abduction, felonious restraint, and assault with a gun after they abducted Breanna and her two-year-old brother, James Paul Chambers, from a foster home. Today's police officers are expected to enforce the law while meeting the needs of the community. Do those goals conflict? If so, how?
Marie Freeman/Watauga Democrat/ AP Images

"Citizen Service System" call numbers in addition to 9-1-1. Dozens of metropolitan areas, including Baltimore, Dallas, Detroit, Las Vegas, New York, and San Jose, now staff 3-1-1 non-emergency systems around the clock and many have moved to online customer relationship management (CRM) systems to address citizens' needs. Plans are afoot in some states to adopt 3-1-1 and CRM systems statewide. Learn more about a career in policing at **http://discoverpolicing.org**.

American Policing Today: From the Federal to the Local Level

2 Describe the three major levels of policing in the United States today.

The organization of American law enforcement has been called the most complex in the world. Three major legislative and judicial jurisdictions exist in the United States—federal, state, and local—and each has created a variety of police agencies to enforce its laws. Unfortunately, little uniformity is seen among jurisdictions regarding the naming, function, or authority of enforcement agencies. The matter is complicated still more by the rapid growth of private security firms, which operate on a for-profit basis and provide services that have traditionally been regarded as law enforcement activities.

Federal Agencies

The majority of police patrol activity is interactive because officers on patrol commonly interact with the public.

Dozens of federal law enforcement agencies are distributed among 14 U.S. government departments and 28 nondepartmental entities (Table 4-1). In addition to the enforcement agencies listed in the table, many other federal government offices are involved in enforcement through inspection, regulation, and control activities. The Government Accounting Office (GAO) reports that nonmilitary federal agencies employ a total of 137,929 law enforcement officers, which it defines as individuals authorized to perform any of four specific functions: (1) conduct criminal investigations, (2) execute search warrants, (3) make arrests, or (4) carry firearms.[30] The FBI, one of the best-known federal law enforcement agencies, is described in the paragraphs that follow.

Visit the home pages of many federal law enforcement agencies at **https://www.justicestudies.com/federal.html**.

The FBI

The FBI may be the most famous law enforcement agency in the country and in the world. The FBI has traditionally been held in high regard by many Americans, who think of it as an example of what a law enforcement organization should be and who believe that FBI agents are exemplary police officers. William Webster, former director of the FBI, reflected this sentiment when he said, "Over the years the American people have come to expect the most professional law enforcement from the FBI. Although we use the most modern forms of management and technology in the fight against crime, our strength is in our people—in the character of the men and women of the FBI. For that reason we seek only those who have demonstrated that they can perform as professional people who can, and will, carry on our tradition of fidelity, bravery, and integrity."[31]

The history of the FBI spans more than 100 years. It began in 1908 as the Bureau of Investigation. It was designed to serve as the investigative arm of the U.S. Department of Justice. The creation of the bureau was motivated, at least in part, by the inability of other agencies to stem the rising tide of American political and business corruption.[32] Learn about the history of the FBI at **http://www.fbi.gov/about-us/history/brief-history**.

The official purpose of today's FBI is succinctly stated in the agency's mission statement: "The Mission of the FBI is to protect and defend the United States against terrorist and foreign intelligence threats, to uphold and enforce the criminal laws of the United States, and to provide leadership and criminal justice services to federal, state, municipal, and international agencies and partners."[33]

FBI headquarters are located in the J. Edgar Hoover Building on Pennsylvania Avenue in Washington, D.C. Special agents and support personnel who work at the agency's headquarters organize and coordinate FBI activities throughout the country and around the world.

TABLE 4-1
American Policing: Federal Law Enforcement Agencies

Department of Agriculture
U.S. Forest Service

Department of Commerce
Bureau of Export Enforcement
National Marine Fisheries Administration

Department of Defense
Air Force Office of Special Investigations
Army Criminal Investigation Division
Defense Criminal Investigative Service
Naval Investigative Service

Department of Energy
National Nuclear Safety Administration
Office of Mission Operations
Office of Secure Transportation

Department of Health and Human Services
Food and Drug Administration (FDA), Office of Criminal Investigations

Department of Homeland Security (DHS)
Federal Law Enforcement Training Center (FLETC)
Federal Protective Service
Transportation Security Administration
U.S. Coast Guard
U.S. Customs and Border Protection (CBP), including U.S. Border Patrol
U.S. Immigration and Customs Enforcement (ICE)
U.S. Secret Service (SS)

Department of the Interior
Bureau of Indian Affairs
Bureau of Land Management
Fish and Wildlife Service
National Park Service
U.S. Park Police

Department of Justice
Bureau of Alcohol, Tobacco, Firearms and Explosives (ATF)
Bureau of Prisons (BOP)
Drug Enforcement Administration (DEA)
Federal Bureau of Investigation (FBI)
U.S. Marshals Service

Department of Labor
Office of Labor Racketeering

Department of State
Diplomatic Security Service

Department of Transportation
Federal Air Marshals Program

Department of the Treasury
Internal Revenue Service (IRS), Criminal Investigation Division
Treasury Inspector General for Tax Enforcement

Department of Veterans Affairs (VA)
Office of Security and Law Enforcement

U.S. Postal Service
Postal Inspection Service

Other Offices with Enforcement Personnel
Amtrak Police
Bureau of Engraving and Printing Police
Environmental Protection Agency (EPA), Criminal Investigations Division
Federal Reserve Board
Tennessee Valley Authority (TVA)
U.S. Capitol Police
U.S. Mint
U.S. Supreme Court Police
Washington, D.C., Metropolitan Police Department

Note: Virtually every cabinet-level federal agency has its own Office of Inspector General, which has enforcement authority—not all of which are listed here.

Headquarters staffers determine investigative priorities, oversee major cases, and manage the organization's resources, technology, and personnel.

The daily work of the FBI is done by approximately 13,500 special agents and 20,100 civilian employees assigned to 56 field offices and 400 satellite offices (known as *resident agencies*). A special agent in charge oversees each field office, except for the three largest field offices in Washington, D.C., Los Angeles, and New York City, each of which is headed by an assistant director. Women account for more than 2,600 of the FBI's agents (nearly 20%), and 11 of the FBI's field offices have female special agents in charge.[34]

The FBI also operates legal attaché offices (called *Legats*) in a number of major cities around the world, including London and Paris. Such offices permit the international coordination of enforcement activities and facilitate the flow of law enforcement-related information between the FBI and police agencies in host countries. In 1995, a few years after the end of the cold war, the FBI opened a legal attaché office in Moscow. The Moscow office assists Russian police agencies in the growing battle against organized crime

Follow the author's tweets about the latest crime and justice news @schmalleger

▲ The author visiting the International Law Enforcement Academy in Budapest, Hungary. The ILEA is run by the FBI and the Hungarian government and serves as a global training ground for police executives and criminal justice leaders from across Eastern Europe and much of Asia. Why is it important to build bridges in international policing?

Frank Schmalleger

🐦 Follow the author's tweets about the latest crime and justice news @schmalleger

in that country and helps American officials track suspected Russian criminals operating in the United States. Also in 1995, an Eastern European version of the FBI Academy, known as the International Law Enforcement Academy (ILEA), opened in Budapest, Hungary. Its purpose is to train police administrators from all of Eastern Europe in the latest crime-fighting techniques.[35] Ten years later, in 2005, the FBI's then-director Robert S. Mueller III spoke at the Budapest ILEA, telling gathered government ministers and diplomats that in times past, "Good fences make good neighbors." He added that, "seen from the perspective of the 21st-century global law enforcement community, dividing walls mean less security, not more. . . . Today, good bridges make good neighbors" —an assertion that some challenge in today's world of international terrorism.[36]

The FBI also operates the Combined DNA Index System (CODIS), a computerized forensic database of DNA profiles of offenders convicted of serious crimes (such as rape, other sexual assaults, murder, and certain crimes against children), as well as DNA profiles from unknown offenders.[37] CODIS, now a part of the National DNA Index System (NDIS), was formally authorized by the federal DNA Identification Act of 1994.[38] It is being enhanced daily through the work of federal, state, and local law enforcement agencies that take DNA samples from biological evidence gathered at crime scenes and from offenders themselves. CODIS can rapidly identify a perpetrator when it finds a match between an evidence sample and a stored profile. By 1998, every state had enacted legislation establishing a CODIS database and requiring that DNA from offenders convicted of certain serious crimes be entered into the system. By late-2018, the CODIS database contained more than 13.5 million DNA profiles.[39] Learn more about CODIS at **https://www.fbi.gov/about-us/lab/biometric-analysis/codis/ndis-statistics**.

The FBI Laboratory Division, located in Quantico, Virginia, operates one of the largest and most comprehensive crime laboratories in the world. It provides services related to the scientific solution and prosecution of crimes throughout the country. It is also the only full-service federal forensic laboratory in the United States. Laboratory activities include crime scene searches, special surveillance photography, latent-fingerprint examinations, forensic examinations of evidence (including DNA testing), court testimony by laboratory personnel, and other scientific and technical services. The FBI offers laboratory services, free of charge, to all law enforcement agencies in the United States.

The FBI also runs a National Academy Program, which is part of its Training Division. The program offered its first class in 1935 and had 23 students. It was then known as the FBI National Police Training School. In 1940, the school moved from Washington, D.C., to the U.S. Marine Amphibious Base at Quantico, Virginia. In 1972, the facility expanded to 334 acres, and the FBI Academy, as we know it today, officially opened.[40] By mid-year

> Much of what is wrong with the police is the result of the absurd, fragmented, unworkable nonsystem of more than 17,000 local [police] departments.
>
> —Patrick V. Murphy, former New York City police commissioner

Ethics and Professionalism
The FBI Oath

On their first day at the FBI Academy, new-agent trainees raise their right hands and take this oath as they are sworn in:

> I [name] do solemnly swear (or affirm) that I will support and defend the Constitution of the United States against all enemies, foreign and domestic; that I will bear true faith and allegiance to the same; that I take this obligation freely, without any mental reservation or purpose of evasion; and that I will well and faithfully discharge the duties of the office on which I am about to enter. So help me God.

Similar ceremonies are conducted periodically in every state by every law enforcement agency for officers across the country, usually upon completion of their training. Although the wording of the oaths may vary, each officer promises to do one important thing—support and defend the Constitution of the United States.

THINKING ABOUT ETHICS

1. *How is the FBI oath similar to the Law Enforcement Code of Ethics presented in Chapter 6? How does it differ?*

2. *What do the words "I will well and faithfully discharge the duties of the office" mean?*

Source: "Our Oath of Office," *The FBI Law Enforcement Bulletin*, September, 2009.

2017, the academy program had produced over 50,000 graduates from 176 foreign countries as well as graduates from U.S. territories and possessions. More than 200 sessions have been offered since inception of the training program. The FBI offers support personnel a variety of training opportunities throughout their careers, including classroom training, distance learning via satellite, and courses offered through the "Virtual Academy" on the FBI's intranet.

The FBI and Counterterrorism

Soon after the attacks of September 11, 2001, the FBI reshaped its priorities to focus on preventing future terrorist attacks. To combat terrorism, the FBI's Counterterrorism Division collects, analyzes, and shares information and critical intelligence with various federal agencies and departments—including the Central Intelligence Agency (CIA), the National Security Agency (NSA), and the Department of Homeland Security (DHS)—

▲ Former FBI Director Robert S. Mueller III, explaining his agency's shift in priorities following the 2001 terrorist attacks on the World Trade Center and the Pentagon. In 2013, Mueller retired as director, and 52-year-old James Comey became the head of the FBI. How has the FBI's mission changed since the events of September 11, 2001? How have criminal threats evolved since that time?
Stefan Zaklin/epa european press-photo agency b.v./Alamy Stock Photo

and with law enforcement agencies throughout the country. This effort is managed by the Counterterrorism Division at FBI headquarters and is emphasized at every field office, resident agency, and Legat. Headquarters administers a national threat warning system that allows the FBI to instantly distribute important terrorism-related bulletins to law enforcement agencies and public-safety departments throughout the country. "Flying Squads" provide specialized counterterrorism knowledge and experience, language capabilities, and analytic support as needed to FBI field offices and Legats. One essential weapon in the FBI's battle against terrorism is the Joint Terrorism Task Force (JTTF). JTTFs are discussed in more detail in Chapter 6.

In 2009, following crises in the nation's economic sector, mortgage and financial fraud investigations began to once again consume a significant amount of investigative effort. About that time the FBI created a National Mortgage Fraud Team at FBI headquarters, and "increased its agent and analyst manpower working mortgage fraud investigations."[41] One new tool used by the agency is a property-flipping analytical computer application that searches property transaction records to identify persons and companies that purchase properties and artificially inflate their value through fake appraisals before putting them back on the market.

EVIDENCE-BASED JUSTICE REINVESTMENT
Policing in an Economic Downturn

In 2013, the Police Executive Research Forum (PERF) released a report entitled *Policing and the Economic Downturn*. The subtitle of the publication was "Striving for Efficiency Is the New Normal." The 50-page document was based on a series of four surveys that PERF began sending to police administrators across the nation in 2008 asking about their department's economic situation. In the words of the report, "The first three surveys produced findings that could be summarized as 'grim', meaning that almost all agencies reported facing budget cutbacks and were making plans to reduce services or layoff officers."

PERF found that during the depths of the economic crisis around 2008, 32% of agencies had eliminated recruitment of new officers, while 72% reported a reduction in the amount of money being spent on training. Similarly, 67% of agencies had eliminated pay raises, and 58% of departments were implementing plans to decrease services. Thirty-one percent of agencies that responded to the survey also said that response time to citizens' request for services had increased, or would likely increase due to budget cuts. While not all agencies reported laying off officers, 45% reported hiring freezes. Finally, slightly more than half of all agencies responding to the early PERF surveys reported eliminating plans to acquire new technology.

Police departments have also been restructured in the face of budget cutbacks. Almost half of all departments reported discontinuing or significantly reducing specialty units such as bike patrols, and 22% said that they had consolidated some services with other departments. Many law enforcement agencies also said that they had shifted more officers into the field by staffing some internal positions, such as dispatch, crime analysis, and desk work, with civilian employees and volunteers. Finally, 34% of agencies said that patrol levels, meaning the number of officers assigned to an area at any given time, or the number of hours that an area was patrolled, had been lowered.

Since those initial surveys, however, trends in police funding have improved, with some departments reporting stable or increased monetary inflows. Today, only half as many agencies have cut back on recruiting efforts compared with those who responded to earlier surveys, and agencies today are making fewer cuts to training. Almost half are instituting pay increases for their officers.

Many departments now report paying their officers overtime, rather than expanding the number of full-time officers on their payrolls. Funding overtime hours can be less expensive in the long run than hiring more full-time officers whose employment benefits, including health insurance and retirement expenses, can add substantially to an agency's costs.

One good thing that appears to have resulted from police budget cuts over the past six or more years has been increased efficiency in many areas of law enforcement. Some have used the term **smart policing** to describe the shift in attitude that came about as a result of the economic squeeze that law enforcement administrators have been facing.

The goal of smart policing is to "develop tactics and strategies that are effective, efficient and economical—as measured by reduced crime and high case closure rates."

One form of smart policing is being used in Sunnyvale, California, a city of around 140,000. There, police officers and firefighters are cross-trained so that, in a pinch, they can fill in for one another. A few years ago, for example, the city was able to call

▲ First responders. In some cities, public-safety officers are cross-trained as police officers, firefighters, and in emergency medical services. What advantages accrue to communities who cross-train their first responders?
Tom Grill/corbis/Getty Images

upon firefighters who were finishing their shifts to switch into police uniforms and help canvas an area of the city looking for a man who had killed three people in a workplace shooting. Studies show that, because of cross-training, Sunnyvale is able to spend less on public safety than do surrounding communities—$519 per capita, versus $950 in Palo Alto, and $683 in Mountain View (California).

Another form of smart policing was initiated in Los Angeles, where computer models alert officers to crimes that are likely to happen, and tell dispatchers to send officers to likely crime scenes. The program, called "predictive policing" by the LAPD, identifies potential "hot spots" of crime (sometimes as small as a 500-square-foot "zone") and makes predictions about the likelihood of future crime occurrences in those locations. Officers who are on patrol are then directed to "go in the box."

Unless municipalities can implement effective smart policing strategies, however, saving money on policing might not be such a good idea. In 2012, researchers at the University of California at Berkeley who studied crime in medium-sized to large U.S. cities between 1960 and 2010 found that "each dollar spent on police is associated with approximately $1.60 in reduced victimization costs, suggesting that U.S. cities employ too few police."

References: Police Executive Research Forum, *Policing and the Economic Downturn: Striving for Efficiency Is the New Normal* (Washington, D.C.: PERF, February 2013); Aaron Chalfin and Justin McCrary, "The Effect of Police on Crime: New Evidence from U.S. Cities, 1960–2010," unpublished manuscript (University of California at Berkeley, November 8, 2012); Greg Risling, "Sci-Fi Policing: Predicting Crime before It Occurs," *Associated Press*, July 2, 2012, http://news.yahoo.com/sci-fi-policing-predicting-crime-occurs-150157831.html (accessed July 1, 2017); Lee Romney, "Cross-Training of Public Safety Workers Attracting More Interest," *The Los Angeles Times*, January 1, 2013, http://articles.latimes.com/2013/jan/01/local/la-me-sunnyvale-20130101 (accessed August 1, 2017).

smart policing
A law enforcement initiative that makes use of techniques shown to work at both reducing costs and solving crimes.

State Agencies

Most state police agencies were created in the late nineteenth or early twentieth century to meet specific needs. The Texas Rangers, created in 1835 before Texas attained statehood, functioned as a military organization responsible for patrolling the republic's borders. The apprehension of Mexican cattle rustlers was one of its main concerns.[42] Massachusetts, targeting vice control, was the second state to create a law enforcement agency. Today, a wide diversity of state policing agencies exists. Table 4-2 provides a list of typical state-sponsored law enforcement agencies.

State law enforcement agencies are usually organized after one of two models. In the first, a centralized model, the tasks of major criminal investigations are combined with the patrol of state highways. Centralized state police agencies generally do the following:

- Assist local law enforcement departments in criminal investigations when asked to do so
- Operate a centralized identification bureau
- Maintain a centralized criminal records repository
- Patrol the state's highways
- Provide select training for municipal and county officers

The Pennsylvania Constabulary, known today as the Pennsylvania State Police, was the first modern force to combine these duties and has been called the "first modern state police agency."[43] Michigan, New Jersey, New York, Vermont, and Delaware are a few of the states that patterned their state-level enforcement activities after the Pennsylvania model.

The second state model, the decentralized model of police organization, characterizes operations in the southern United States but is found as well in the Midwest and in some western states. The model draws a clear distinction between traffic enforcement on state highways and other state-level law enforcement functions by creating at least two separate agencies. North Carolina, South Carolina, and Georgia are a few of the many states that employ both a highway patrol and a state bureau of investigation. The names of the respective agencies may vary, however, even though their functions are largely the same. In North Carolina, for example, the two major state-level law enforcement agencies are the North Carolina Highway Patrol and the State Bureau of Investigation. Georgia fields a highway patrol and the Georgia Bureau of Investigation, and South Carolina operates a highway patrol and the South Carolina Law Enforcement Division.

States that use the decentralized model usually have a number of other adjunct state-level law enforcement agencies. North Carolina, for example, has created a State Wildlife Commission with enforcement powers, a Board of Alcohol Beverage Control with additional agents, and a separate Enforcement and Theft Bureau for enforcement of certain motor vehicle and theft laws. Like government agencies everywhere, state police agencies have seen their budgets impacted by the recent recession.

Local Agencies

Local law enforcement agencies, including city and county agencies, represent a third level of police activity in the United States. The term *local police* encompasses a wide variety of agencies. Municipal departments, rural sheriff's departments, and specialized groups like campus police and transit police can all be grouped under the "local" rubric. Large municipal departments are highly visible because of their vast size, huge budgets, and innovative programs. The nation's largest law enforcement agency, the New York City Police Department (NYPD), for example, has about 45,000 full-time employees, including about 34,500 full-time **sworn officers**.[44] Learn more about the NYPD via "Inside the Department" podcasts available at **http://www.nyc.gov/html/nypd/html/pr/podcasts.shtml**.

TABLE 4-2
American Policing: State Law Enforcement Agencies

Alcohol law enforcement agencies	Port authorities	State police
Fish and wildlife agencies	State bureaus of investigation	State university police
Highway patrol	State park services	Weigh station operations

▲ The Los Angeles Police Department's, $437 million headquarters building, which opened in 2009. The 500,000-square-foot headquarters building is home to over 9,000 LAPD officers and over 2,700 civilian employees. How do the roles of federal, state, and municipal law enforcement agencies differ?

Per Andersen/Alamy Stock Photo

Most state police agencies were created in the late nineteenth or early twentieth century to meet specific needs.

sworn officer
A law enforcement officer who is trained and empowered to perform full police duties, such as making arrests, conducting investigations, and carrying firearms.

municipal police department
A city- or town-based law enforcement agency.

Far greater in number, however, are small-town and county sheriff's departments. There are approximately 12,000 **municipal police departments** and over 3,000 sheriff's departments in the United States.[45] Local police and sheriff's offices employ more than one million people, of which approximately 636,000 are sworn law enforcement officers.[46]

Every incorporated municipality in the country has the authority to create its own police force. Some very small communities hire only one officer, who fills the roles of chief, investigator, and night watch—as well as everything in between. About half of all local agencies employ fewer than ten full-time officers, and about 3,220 employ fewer than five full-time officers. These smaller agencies include 2,125 (or 12%) with just one full-time officer and 1,100 (or 6%) with only part-time officers.[47] A few communities contract with private security firms for police services, and still others have no active police force at all, depending instead on local sheriff's departments to deal with law violators.

City police chiefs are typically appointed by the mayor or selected by the city council. Their departments' jurisdictions are limited by convention to the geographic boundaries of their communities. **Sheriffs**, on the other hand, are elected public officials whose agencies are responsible for law enforcement throughout the counties in which they function. Sheriff's deputies mostly patrol the unincorporated areas of the county, or those that lie between municipalities. They do, however, have jurisdiction throughout the county, and in some areas they routinely work alongside municipal police to enforce laws within towns and cities.

sheriff
The elected chief officer of a county law enforcement agency. The sheriff is usually responsible for law enforcement in unincorporated areas and for the operation of the county jail.

Sheriff's departments are generally responsible for serving court papers, including civil summonses, and for maintaining security within state courtrooms. Sheriffs also run county jails and are responsible for more detainees awaiting trial than any other type of law enforcement department in the country. For example, the Los Angeles County Jail System, operated by the Custody Operations Division of the L.A. County Sheriff's Department (LASD), is the largest in the world.[48] In 2018, with seven separate facilities, the Custody Operations Division of the LASD had an average daily population of approximately 18,000 inmates—considerably larger than the number of inmates held in many state prison systems.[49] More than 9,437 sworn officers and 2,927 civilian employees work in the Custody Division of the LASD. That division alone operates with a yearly budget in excess of $3 billion.[50] Overall, the LASD has more than 10,000 sworn and 8,000 civilian personnel, plus more than 830 reserve deputies and over 4,000 civilian volunteers.[51]

Sheriff's departments remain strong across most of the country, although in parts of New England, deputies mostly function as court agents with limited law enforcement duties. One report found that most sheriff's departments are small, with more than half of them employing fewer than 25 sworn officers.[52] Only 18 departments employ more than 1,000 officers. Even so, southern and western sheriffs are still considered the chief law enforcement officers in their counties.

A list of conventional police agencies found at the local level is shown in Table 4-3.

Follow the author's tweets about the latest crime and justice news @schmalleger

TABLE 4-3
American Policing: Local Law Enforcement Agencies

Campus police	Housing authority agencies	Sheriff's departments
City/county agencies	Marine patrol agencies	Transit police
Constables	Municipal police departments	Tribal police
Coroners or medical examiners		

Fusion Centers

In 2017, U.S. Attorney General Jeff Sessions spoke to the National Fusion Center Association at its tenth annual conference in Alexandria, Virginia. He had a simple message, "Law enforcement cooperation is what fusion centers are all about."[53]. **Fusion centers**, a relatively new concept in policing, "fuse" intelligence from participating agencies to create a comprehensive threat picture, locally and nationally (Table 4-4). They don't just collect information; they integrate new data into existing information, evaluate it to determine its worth, analyze it for links and trends, and disseminate their findings to the agency in the best position to act on the intelligence they generate. The Department of Homeland Security says that the national network of fusion centers "contribute[s] to the Information Sharing Environment (ISE) through their role in receiving threat information; analyzing that information in the context of their local environment; disseminating that information to local agencies; and gathering tips, leads, and suspicious activity reporting (SAR) from local agencies and the public."[54]

fusion center
A multiagency law enforcement facility designed to enhance cooperative efforts through a coordinated process for collecting, sharing, and analyzing information in order to develop actionable intelligence.

More than 70 fusion centers currently operate in 49 states (there are another 20 regional centers).[55] These centers are largely an outgrowth of one of the 9/11 Commission's criticisms that law enforcement agencies do not communicate with one another as they should.

Guidelines for the development and operation of fusion centers were created by a collaborative effort involving the U.S. Department of Justice (DOJ) and the U.S. Department of Homeland Security (DHS). According to those guidelines, a *fusion center* can be defined as a "collaborative effort of two or more agencies that provide resources, expertise, and information to the center with the goal of maximizing their ability to detect, prevent, investigate, and respond to criminal and terrorist activity."[56]

Fusion centers vary greatly in size and in the equipment and personnel available to them. Some are small, consisting of little more than limited conference room-type facilities, and have only a few participants. Others are large, high-technology offices that make use of the latest information and computer technologies and that house representatives from many different organizations. Some fusion centers are physically located within the offices of other agencies. The Kentucky Fusion Center, for example, is housed within the state's Department of Transportation building in the state's capitol. Others operate out of stand-alone facilities that are physically separated from parent agencies.

Similarly, although information sharing is their central purpose, the activities of fusion centers are not uniform. Some centers perform investigations, some make arrests, and some exist only to share information. Some fusion centers, such as the National Counterterrorism Center and the National Gang Intelligence Center, focus on clearly defined issues. Most of today's fusion centers do more than target terrorists, however. They work to collect information on a wide variety of offenders, gangs, immigrant smuggling operations, and other threats. Michael Mines, the FBI's deputy assistant director of intelligence, recognizes that actionable intelligence can come from seemingly unrelated areas. He notes that the nation's network of fusion

▲ Former Texas governor Rick Perry speaking to a group of Texas Rangers in Austin, Texas. The Texas Rangers have long been held in high regard among state police agencies. How many levels of policing are there in the United States?

Harry Cabluck/AP Images

▊ TABLE 4-4
Fusion Centers versus Joint Terrorist Task Forces (JTTFs)

Fusion Centers	Joint Terrorism Task Forces
Run by state and local authorities	Sponsored by the FBI
Are state and locally focused	Are regionally and nationally focused
Deal with terrorism, criminal, and public-safety matters	Deal exclusively with terrorism matters
Produce actionable intelligence for dissemination to appropriate law enforcement agencies but do not generally conduct investigations	Conduct investigations

Source: FBI.

▲ Inside the Miami-Dade Police Department's Fusion Center, which serves much of South Florida. The center's combined technologies enhance the power of instant collaboration and information sharing among analysts and investigators from various law enforcement agencies. Why did fusion centers develop?

Ed Andrieski/AP Images

> As the private security field grows, its relationship to public law enforcement continues to evolve.

private protective services
The independent or proprietary commercial organizations that provide protective services to employers on a contractual basis.

centers is intended to "maximize the ability to detect, prevent, investigate, and respond to criminal and terrorist activity."[57]

Fusion centers face some continuing problems. Obtaining the needed security clearances for employees of local law enforcement agencies who want to view intelligence gathered by other agencies, for example, has sometimes been difficult or time consuming. Even representatives of federal agencies such as the DHS and the FBI sometimes refuse to accept one another's security clearances. Learn more about fusion centers from a DHS factsheet at **https://justicestudies.com/pubs/fusionhandout.pdf**, and read the *2014–2017 National Strategy for the National Network of Fusion Centers* at **http://tinyurl.com/p9smlju**.

Private Protective Services

Private protective services constitute a fourth level of enforcement activity in the United States today. Whereas public police are employed by the government and enforce public laws, private security personnel work for corporate employers and secure private interests.

3 Describe private protective services in the United States and their possible future roles.

Private security has been defined as "those self-employed individuals and privately funded business entities and organizations providing security-related services to specific clientele for a fee, for the individual or entity that retains or employs them, or for themselves, in order to protect their persons, private property, or interests from various hazards."[58]

The growth in the size of private security in recent years has been phenomenal. In 2004, for example, official estimates put the total amount spent to secure the Olympic Games in Athens at $1.5 billion—or $283 per paid ticket.[59] Given Greece's geopolitical situation and its proximity to the Balkans and the Middle East, officials in Athens wanted to be sure they could prevent terrorist attacks. Eight years later, in 2012, England spent around $13.8 billion to host the Thirtieth Olympiad, of which $870 million was spent on security (more than twice what had been originally budgeted).[60] The London games involved 23,700 security personnel securing more than 100 venues—supplemented by British troops and police, adding another $65 million in expenses.[61] The 2014 Winter Olympics in Sochi, Russia, were estimated to involve security expenditures of over $3 billion.[62]

Major reasons for the quick growth of the American proprietary security sector include (1) an increase in crimes in the workplace; (2) an increase in fear (real or perceived) of crime and terrorism; (3) the fiscal crises of the states, which have limited public protection; and (4) an increased public and business awareness and use of more cost-effective private security products and services.[63]

ASIS International, with more than 33,000 members, is the preeminent international organization for private security professionals.[64] ASIS International members include corporate security managers and directors, as well as architects, attorneys, and federal, state, and local law enforcement personnel. Founded in 1955, ASIS International, formerly known as the American Society for Industrial Security, is dedicated to increasing the effectiveness and productivity of security professionals by developing educational and certification programs and training materials that address the needs of the security profession.

A report released by the NIJ, titled *The New Structure of Policing*, found that "policing is being transformed and restructured in the modern world" in ways that were unanticipated only a few decades ago.[65] Much of the change is due to the development of private protective services as an important adjunct to public law enforcement activities in the United States and throughout much of the rest of the world. The NIJ report says that "the key to understanding the transformation is that policing, meaning the activity of making societies safe, is no longer carried out exclusively by governments" and that the distinction between private and public police has begun to blur. According to the NIJ, "gradually, almost imperceptibly, policing has been 'multilateralized,'" meaning that "a host of nongovernmental agencies have undertaken to provide security services." As a result, the NIJ report says, "policing has entered a new era, an era characterized by a transformation in the governance of security."

Table 4-5 lists some of the largest private security agencies in business today and a few of the services they offer.

Some analysts of the current scene suggest that the drop in crime rates that our country has experienced may be due just as much to the expansion of private security as to efforts by public law enforcement agencies to control crime and to protect property. A recent RAND study, for example, found that private security patrols were a significant factor in lowering theft and other crimes in business districts.[66]

As the private security field grows, its relationship to public law enforcement continues to evolve. Some argue that "today, a distinction between public and private policing is increasingly meaningless."[67] As a result, the focus has largely shifted from an analysis of competition between the sectors to the recognition that each form of policing can help the other. One especially important policy area involves building private security–public policing partnerships to prevent terrorism and to respond to threats of terrorism.

▲ A security guard at a political gathering. Why has the privatization of policing become a major issue facing governments and public justice agencies everywhere?

Hill Street Studios LLC/DigitalVision/ Getty Images

International Police Agencies

Every country has its own police organizations; whereas some are highly centralized (like the Russian national police, or *politsiya*), others are not (like policing in the United States). Two important agencies, Interpol and Europol, function to coordinate the activities of police agencies throughout the world, and each will be briefly discussed.

🐦 Follow the author's tweets about the latest crime and justice news @schmalleger

Interpol

The **International Criminal Police Organization (Interpol)**, headquartered in Lyons, France, traces its origins back to the first International Criminal Police Congress of 1914, which met in Monaco.[68] The theme of that meeting was international cooperation in the investigation of crimes and the apprehension of fugitives. Interpol, however, did not officially begin operations until 1946, when the end of World War II brought about a new spirit of international harmony.

International Criminal Police Organization (Interpol)

An international law enforcement support organization that began operations in 1946 and today has 192 member nations.

TABLE 4-5
Private Security Agencies

Largest Private Security Agencies in the United States

Allied Universal	Globe Security	Securitas Security Services
American Protective Services Andrews International (AI)	Guardsmark, Inc.	Security Bureau, Inc.
Barton Protective Services Brinks	Initial Security	
Burns International Security Services	Johnson Security Bureau, Inc.	
G4S	Pinkerton's, Inc.	

Private Security Services Sectors

Airline security	Critical infrastructure security	Nuclear facility security
Automated teller machine (ATM) services	Executive protection	Railroad detectives
Bank guards	Hospital security	School security
Company guards	Loss prevention	Store/mall security
Computer/information security		Data Center Security

Today, 192 nations belong to Interpol.[69] The U.S. Interpol unit is called the U.S. National Central Bureau (USNCB) and is a separate agency within the U.S. Department of Justice. The USNCB is staffed with personnel from 12 federal agencies, including the Drug Enforcement Administration, the Secret Service, and the FBI. Through USNCB, Interpol is linked to all major U.S. computerized criminal records repositories, including the FBI's National Crime Information Index, the State Department's Advanced Visa Lookout System, and the Department of Homeland Security's Master Index.

Interpol's primary purpose is to act as a clearinghouse for information on offenses and suspects who are believed to operate across national boundaries. The organization is committed to promoting "the widest possible mutual assistance between all criminal police authorities within the limits of laws existing in . . . different countries and in the spirit of the Universal Declaration of Human Rights."[70] Historically, Interpol pledged itself not to intervene in religious, political, military, or racial disagreements in participant nations. As a consequence, numerous bombings and hostage situations that were related to these types of disagreements were not officially investigated until 1984, when Interpol officially entered the fight against international terrorism.

At Interpol's Eighty-Seventh General Assembly, held at Dubai's World Trade Center in 2018, senior law enforcement officials from around the world discussed critical challenges facing police agencies in responding to current and developing criminal phenomena, and shared best practices based on national and international experience. Today, Interpol continues to expand its activities. It is in the process of developing a centralized international forensic DNA database and is creating an international framework for disaster victim identification.[71]

Interpol does not have its own field investigators. The agency has no powers of arrest or of search and seizure in member countries. Instead, Interpol's purpose is to facilitate, coordinate, and encourage police cooperation as a means of combating international crime. It draws on the willingness of local and national police forces to lend support to its activities. The headquarters staff of Interpol consists of about 250 individuals, many with prior police experience, who direct data-gathering efforts around the world and who serve to alert law enforcement organizations to the movement of suspected offenders within their jurisdiction.

European Police Office (Europol)
The integrated police intelligence-gathering and information-dissemination arm of the member nations of the European Union.

human smuggling
Illegal immigration in which an agent is paid to help a person cross a border clandestinely.

Europol

The members of the European Union (EU) agreed to the establishment of the **European Police Office (Europol)** in the Maastricht Treaty of February 7, 1992. Based in The Hague, the Netherlands, Europol started limited operations in 1994 in the form of the Europol Drugs Unit. Over time, other important law enforcement activities were added to the Europol agenda. The Europol Convention was ratified by all member states in 1998, and Europol commenced full operations the next year.

Europol's mission is to improve the effectiveness and cooperation of law enforcement agencies within the member states of the EU, with the ultimate goal of preventing and combating terrorism, illegal drug trafficking, illicit trafficking in radioactive and nuclear substances, illegal money laundering, trafficking in human beings, and other serious forms of international organized crime. Europol is sometimes described as the "European Union police clearing house."[72] Following the July 2005 London underground and bus bombings, in which more than 50 people died and hundreds were injured, German Interior Minister Otto Schilly asked his EU counterparts meeting in Brussels to give Europol executive powers to conduct EU-wide investigations.[73]

Europol and Interpol work together to develop information on international terrorism, drug trafficking, and trafficking in human beings including sex trafficking.[74] According to the United Nations,[75] trafficking in persons and **human smuggling** are some of the fastest-growing areas of international criminal activity today. There are important distinctions that must be made between these two forms of crime.

▲ The entrance hall of Interpol headquarters in Lyon, France. What does Interpol do?

Laurent Cipriani/AP Images

Following federal law, the U.S. State Department defines human smuggling as "the facilitation, transportation, attempted transportation or illegal entry of a person(s) across an international border, in violation of one or more country's laws, either clandestinely or through deception, such as the use of fraudulent documents." In other words, human smuggling refers to illegal immigration in which an agent is paid to help a person cross a border clandestinely.[76] Human smuggling generally occurs with the consent of those being smuggled, and they often pay a smuggler for his or her services.

In contrast to smuggling, **trafficking in persons (TIP)** can be compared to a modern-day form of slavery, prompting former Secretary of State Condoleezza Rice to say that "defeating human trafficking is a great moral calling of our day."[77] Trafficking involves the exploitation of unwilling or unwitting people through force, coercion, threat, or deception and includes human rights abuses such as debt bondage, deprivation of liberty, or lack of control over freedom and labor. Trafficking is often undertaken for purposes of sexual or labor exploitation.[78] A recent study released by the NIJ found that the majority of human trafficking cases in the United States involve sex trafficking (85%), whereas a much smaller percentage of all investigated cases involve labor trafficking (11%).[79] The key components that generally distinguish trafficking from smuggling are the elements of fraud, force, or coercion. However, under U.S. law, if the person is under 18 and induced to perform a commercial sex act, then it is considered trafficking, regardless of whether fraud, force, or coercion is involved.

Visit Europol on the Web at **http://www.europol.europa.eu**. Interpol headquarters can be viewed via **http://www.interpol.int**.

trafficking in persons (TIP)
The exploitation of unwilling or unwitting people through force, coercion, threat, or deception.

Follow the author's tweets about the latest crime and justice news @schmalleger

Police Administration

4 Summarize the typical organizational structure of a police department.

Police management entails administrative activities that control, direct, and coordinate police personnel, resources, and activities in the service of crime prevention, the apprehension of criminals, the recovery of stolen property, and the performance of a variety of regulatory and helping services.[80] Police managers include sworn law enforcement personnel with administrative authority, from the rank of sergeant to captain, chief, or sheriff, and civilian personnel, such as police commissioners, attorneys general, state secretaries of crime control, and public-safety directors.

police management
The administrative activities of controlling, directing, and coordinating police personnel, resources, and activities in the service of crime prevention, the apprehension of criminals, the recovery of stolen property, and the performance of a variety of regulatory and helping services.

Police Organization and Structure

Almost all American law enforcement organizations are formally structured among divisions and along lines of authority. Roles within police agencies generally fall into one of two categories: line and staff. **Line operations** are field or supervisory activities directly related to daily police work; **staff operations** include support roles such as administration. In organizations that have line operations only, authority flows from the top down in a clear, unbroken line,[81] and no supporting elements (media relations, training, fiscal management divisions, and so on) exist. All line operations are directly involved in providing field services. Because almost all police agencies need support, only the smallest departments have only line operations.

Most police organizations include both line and staff operations. In such organizations, line managers are largely unencumbered with staff operations, such as budgets, training, scientific analysis of evidence, legal advice, shift assignments, and personnel management. Support personnel handle these activities, freeing line personnel to focus on the day-to-day requirements of providing field services.

In a line and staff agency, divisions are likely to exist within both line operations and staff operations. For example, field services, a line operation, may be broken down into enforcement and investigation. Administrative services, a staff operation, may be divided into human resources management, training and education, materials supply, financial

line operations
In police organizations, the field activities or supervisory activities directly related to day-to-day police work.

staff operations
In police organizations, activities (such as administration and training) that provide support for line operations.

CJ Careers
Security Professional

Name: Suzette Baker

Position: Assistant Supervisor, G4S Security Solutions, Charlotte, North Carolina

Colleges attended: Kaplan University

Majors: Criminal Justice/Juvenile Justice

Year hired: 2013

Please give a brief description of your job: As an assistant supervisor for a large private security company, I assist with the professional operation, administration, profitability, and quality assurance of uniformed services for a single shift at a client's site. In addition, I assist with staffing, scheduling, and training of security officers assigned to my shift, ensure that contract-required training elements for security officers are met, ensure quality of service by inspecting the uniforms and security license/first aid/CPR cards of security officers on my shift, review and maintain incident reports, assist in preparation of post orders, and make recommendations for positive and negative personnel actions for officers on my shift. Customer service is a very important aspect of the security industry, so I also respond to client requests.

What appealed to you most about the position when you applied for it? The security industry has greatly evolved from the days of the night watchman who drank coffee and watched TV or read the newspaper to pass the time. The industry has applied new technology to expand the services we offer to include CCTV cameras, computer programs, Secure Trax devices, and in-depth training in areas such as terrorism, fire and life safety, and access control to our sites. Because many security companies are going global, there are many fields of security that are now open to security officers both domestically and internationally. Some of these include special police forces, assisting with disaster relief, airports, and homeland security.

How would you describe the interview process? The interview process is a multi-step process that begins once an online application is reviewed and the applicant is scheduled for an interview with a site manager at the local office. During the interview, the applicant will be asked why he or she wants to work in the security field and what strengths and/or skills they have to offer. The site manager will review the application and any questions he or she may have with the applicant, and if all criteria are met an offer of employment will be made. Once the offer of employment is accepted, the applicant is referred to office personnel to be scheduled for classes to obtain a PPSB (Private Protective Services Bureau) license. On completion of this class, the applicant will a take CPR/First Aid class and any other class(es) required by the company.

▲ Suzette Baker
Suzette Baker

Classes (orientation) can last anywhere from 3 to 7 days and vary between security companies. Upon successful completion of all classes, the applicant will be considered an employee and assigned to the site of the manager who interviewed them.

What is a typical day like? A typical day varies depending on which shift is worked. Security officers on all shifts patrol designated areas inside and outside of buildings, ensuring that only authorized personnel gain access to certain areas of a site. The designated areas to be patrolled depend on the post the officer is working. For example, one officer may be assigned to parking decks and parking lots while another will check in vendors and contractors. Yet another officer will control access to the buildings and others will be responsible for interior and exterior patrols. Another officer will be responsible for checking in visitors and alerting key company personnel of their arrival. It is worth noting that some smaller sites only have one security officer per shift who is responsible for all of these job functions. Every security officer is responsible for reporting any fire or life safety issues to their supervisor.

What qualities/characteristics are most helpful for this job? Security officers encounter people from all walks of life, so it is vital that the officer remain unbiased and have the ability to keep personal opinions private. The ability to walk, stand, or sit for long periods of time; be flexible in working different posts, listen and respond to visitors and the customer's employees; accurately follow written and oral directions; patience; honesty; and attention to detail are important characteristics of security officers.

What is a typical starting salary? Starting salary varies between companies and locations. The salary for a security officer ranges from $17,000 to $34,000. This is accompanied by medical and retirement benefits.

What is the salary potential as you move up into higher-level jobs? The salary potential varies depending on the company and location. Experience does not significantly affect salaries for this career. Moving into management positions does provide a small increase in salary ranging from $31,000 to $37,000 annually.

What career advice would you give someone in college beginning studies in criminal justice? If you are thinking about a career in the security industry, a bachelor's degree in criminal justice or other helping field is more valuable than an associate's degree. Adding a human resources component to your degree will allow for easier transition into administrative positions within a security company.

Source: Copyright © by Suzette Baker. Used with permission.

management, and facilities management. The line and staff structure easily accommodates functional areas of responsibility within line and staff divisions. A typical organizational chart of a local police department is shown in Figure 4–3.[82]

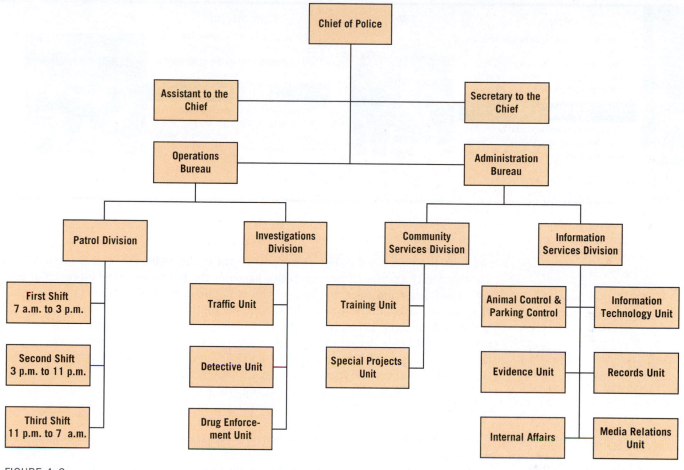

FIGURE 4–3
Typical Organizational Chart of a Local Police Department

Chain of Command

The organizational chart of any police agency shows a hierarchical **chain of command**, or the order of authority within the department. The chain of command clarifies who reports to whom. Usually, the chief of police or sheriff is at the top of the command chain (although his or her boss may be a police commissioner, city council, or mayor), followed by the subordinate leaders of each division.

Because law enforcement agencies employ a quasi-military chain-of-command structure, the titles assigned to personnel (captain, lieutenant, sergeant) are similar to those used by the military. It is important for individual personnel to know who is in charge; hence unity of command is an important principle that must be firmly established within the department. When unity of command exists, every individual has only one supervisor to whom he or she answers and from whom, under normal circumstances, he or she takes orders. **Span of control** refers to the number of police personnel or the number of units supervised by a particular commander. For example, one sergeant may be in charge of five or six officers; they represent the sergeant's span of control.

chain of command
The unbroken line of authority that extends through all levels of an organization, from the highest to the lowest.

Follow the author's tweets about the latest crime and justice news @schmalleger

span of control
The number of police personnel or the number of units supervised by a particular officer.

Policing Epochs and Styles

Policing Epochs

The history of American policing can be divided into four time periods,[83] each distinguishable by the relative dominance of a particular approach to police operations (Figure 4–4). The first period, the political era, was characterized by close

5 Summarize the historical development of policing in America, along with the characteristics of each stage.

FIGURE 4–4 Historical Eras in American Policing

Political Era

- Close ties between the police and political officials
- Police were organized in paramilitary style, focused on serving the politically powerful
- Politicians appointed/hired the police

1840s–1930

- Came about because of a need for social order and security in a dynamic and rapidly changing society

Reform Era

- Police gained pride in their profession
- Law enforcement focused on "traditional" crime fighting and the capture of criminals
- Crackdown on organized crime

1930–1970s

- Progressive policing policy led by August Vollmer and O. W. Wilson
- Came about because citizens called for reform and the removal of politics from policing

ties between police and public officials. It began in the 1840s and ended around 1930. Throughout the period, American police agencies tended to serve the interests of powerful politicians and their cronies, providing public-order and order-maintenance services almost as an afterthought. The second period, the reform era, began around 1930 and lasted until the 1970s. It was characterized by pride in professional crime fighting. Police departments during this period focused most of their resources on solving "traditional" crimes, such as murder, rape, and burglary, and on capturing offenders. The third period, and the one that continues to characterize much of contemporary policing in America today, is the community policing era. This approach to policing stresses the service role of police officers and envisions a partnership between police agencies and their communities.

A fourth period, which we call the *new era*, has made its appearance only recently and is still evolving. Some say that the primary feature of this new law enforcement era is policing to secure the homeland, and they have dubbed it the *homeland security era*.[84] From their perspective, the homeland security era has grown out of national concerns with terrorism prevention born of the terrorist attacks of September 11, 2001. As police scholar Gene Stephens explains it, "The twenty-first century has put policing into a whole new milieu—one in which the causes of crime and disorder often lie outside the immediate community, demanding new and innovative approaches."[85] A decline in street crime, says Stephens, has been replaced by concern with new and more insidious types of offending, including terrorism and Internet-assisted crimes. These new kinds of crimes, while they threaten the integrity of local communities, often involve offenders thousands of miles away.

Others, however, see the new era as underpinned by an emphasis on intelligence-led policing (ILP), and they refer to it as the *ILP era*. (ILP is discussed in detail in Chapter 6.) Michael Downing, commander of the Counter-terrorism/Criminal Intelligence Bureau of the Los Angeles Police Department, says that ILP represents the next evolutionary stage in how police and sheriff's officers should approach their work. "The necessity to successfully shift into a [new] era, the intelligence-led policing era, with seamless precision has never been more important considering the great threat we face as a nation," says Downing.[86] Still others see evidence-based practices as the highlight of the new era, and emphasize the need for cost-effective policies and practices in an economy that remains challenging. They refer to it as *the evidence-based era* (evidence-based policing is discussed later in this chapter). The new era, whatever we choose to call it, is still emerging, but it clearly involves the need to develop cost-effective efforts to deal with threats to the homeland and to inform those efforts with situational awareness and shared intelligence.

The influence of the first three historical phases survives today in what noted social commentator and Presidential Medal of Freedom recipient James Q. Wilson[87] calls "policing styles."[88] A style of policing describes how a particular agency sees its purpose and chooses the methods it uses to fulfill that purpose. Wilson's three

Follow the author's tweets about the latest crime and justice news @schmalleger

Crime is a community problem and stands today as one of the most serious challenges of our generation. Our citizens must . . . recognize their responsibilities in its suppression.

—O. W. Wilson (1900–1972)

Community Era ▶	The New Era
• Police departments work to identify and serve the needs of their communities • Envisions a partnership between the police and the community	• Policing to secure the homeland; emphasis on terrorism prevention, intelligence-led policing, and evidence-based policing • Emphasis on procedural fairness, increased concern with citizen satisfaction, and evidence-based practices
1970s–Today	**2001–Today**
• Police focus on quality-of-life offenses • Broken windows model of policing • Came about because of a realization that effective community partnerships can help prevent and solve crimes	• Creation of counterterrorism divisions and offices within police departments and the development of actionable intelligence • Came about because of the terrorist attacks of September 11, 2001, combined with recent claims of "overpolicing" and unnecessary use of force by the police

Sources: (from left) World History Archive/SuperStock; Shutterstock; Steve Debenport/E+/Getty Images; Department of Homeland Security, ho/AP Images.

FIGURE 4–4
Historical Eras in American Policing (continued)

policing styles—which he does not link to any particular historical era—are (1) the watchman (which is characteristic of the political era), (2) the legalistic (which is akin to the professional crime fighting of the reform era), and (3) the service (which is common today). These three styles characterize nearly all municipal law enforcement agencies now operating in the United States, although some departments are a mixture of two or more styles.

The Watchman Style of Policing

Police departments marked by the **watchman style** of policing are primarily concerned with achieving a goal that Wilson called "order maintenance." They see their job as controlling illegal and disruptive behaviors. The watchman style makes considerable use of discretion compared to the legalistic style. Order in watchman-style communities may be arrived at by using informal police intervention, including persuasion and threats, or even by "roughing up" a few disruptive people from time to time. Some authors have condemned this style of policing, suggesting that it is unfairly found in lower-class or lower-middle-class communities, especially where interpersonal relations include a fair amount of violence or physical abuse.

The watchman style was typified by the Los Angeles police officers who took part in the infamous beating of Rodney King in 1992. After the ensuing riots, the Independent Commission on the Los Angeles Police Department (the Christopher Commission) determined that the Los Angeles police "placed greater emphasis on crime control over crime prevention, a policy that distanced cops from the people they serve."[89]

watchman style
A style of policing marked by a concern for order maintenance. Watchman policing is characteristic of lower-class communities where informal police intervention into the lives of residents is employed in the service of keeping the peace.

Freedom or Safety? You Decide
Liberty Is a Double-Edged Sword

This chapter builds on the following theme: For police action to be "just," it must recognize the rights of individuals while holding them accountable to the social obligations defined by law. It is important to realize that many democratically inspired legal restraints on the police stem from the Bill of Rights, which comprises the first ten amendments to the U.S. Constitution. Such restraints help ensure individual freedoms in our society and prevent the development of a "police state" in America.

In police work and elsewhere, the principles of individual liberty and social justice are cornerstones on which the American way of life rests. Ideally, the work of police agencies, as well as the American system of criminal justice, is to ensure justice while guarding liberty. The liberty-justice issue is the dual thread that holds together the tapestry of the justice system, from the simplest daily activities of police officers on the beat to the often complex and lengthy renderings of the U.S. Supreme Court.

For the criminal justice system as a whole, the question becomes this: How can individual liberties be maintained in the face of the need for official action, including arrest, interrogation, incarceration, and the like? The answer is far from simple, but it begins with the recognition that liberty is a double-edged sword, entailing obligations as well as rights.

YOU DECIDE

What does it mean to say "For police action to be 'just,' it must recognize the rights of individuals while holding them accountable to the social obligations defined by law"? How can police agencies accomplish this? What can individual officers do to help their agencies in this regard?

The Legalistic Style of Policing

Departments operating under the **legalistic style** of policing enforce the letter of the law. For example, an officer who tickets a person going 71 mph in a 70-mph zone is likely a member of a department that adheres to the legalistic style of policing. Conversely, legalistic departments routinely avoid community disputes arising from violations of social norms that do not break the law. Police expert Gary Sykes calls this enforcement style "laissez-faire policing" in recognition of its hands-off approach to behaviors that are simply bothersome or inconsiderate of community principles.[90]

The Service Style of Policing

In police departments using the **service style**, which strives to meet the needs of the community and serve its members, the police see themselves more as helpers than as soldiers in a "war on crime," and they work with social services and other agencies to provide counseling for minor offenders and to assist community groups in preventing crimes and solving problems. Prosecutors may support the service style of policing by agreeing not to prosecute law violators who seek psychiatric help or who voluntarily participate in programs such as Alcoholics Anonymous, family counseling, or drug treatment. The service style is supported in part by citizens who seek to avoid the embarrassment that might result from a public airing of personal problems, thereby reducing the number of criminal complaints filed, especially in minor disputes. Although the service style of policing may seem more appropriate to wealthy communities or small towns, it can also exist in cities whose police departments actively seek citizen involvement in identifying issues that the police can help address.

Police–Community Relations

6   Explain how community policing differs from traditional forms of policing.

The 1960s were fraught with riots, unrest, and student activism as the war in Vietnam, civil rights concerns, and other social movements produced large demonstrations and marches. The police, generally inexperienced in crowd control, were all too often embroiled in tumultuous encounters—even pitched battles—with citizen groups that viewed the police as agents of "the establishment." To manage these new challenges, the legalistic style of policing, so common in America until then, began to yield to the newer service-oriented style of policing.

As social disorganization increased, police departments across the nation, seeking to understand and better cope with the problems they faced, created **police–community relations (PCR)** programs. PCR programs represented a movement away from an exclusive police emphasis on the apprehension of law violators and meant increasing the level of positive police–citizen interaction. At the height of the PCR movement, city police departments across the country opened storefront centers where citizens could air complaints and interact easily with police representatives. As police scholar Egon Bittner recognized in 1976, PCR programs need to reach to "the grassroots of discontent," where citizen dissatisfaction with the police exists,[91] if they are to be truly effective.

In many contemporary PCR programs, public-relations officers are appointed to provide an array of services, such as Neighborhood Watch programs, drug-awareness workshops, identification projects (using police equipment and expertise to mark valuables for identification in the event of theft), and victims' assistance programs. Modern PCR programs, however, often fail to achieve their goal of increased community satisfaction with police services because they focus on servicing groups already well satisfied with the police. PCR initiatives that do reach disaffected community groups are difficult to manage and may even alienate participating officers from the communities they are assigned to serve. Thus, as Bittner noted, "while the first approach fails because it leaves out those groups to which the program is primarily directed, the second fails because it leaves out the police department."

---

legalistic style
A style of policing marked by a strict concern with enforcing the precise letter of the law. Legalistic departments may take a hands-off approach to disruptive or problematic behavior that does not violate the criminal law.

service style
A style of policing marked by a concern with helping rather than strict enforcement. Service-oriented police agencies are more likely to refer citizens to community resources, such as drug-treatment programs, than are other types of agencies.

police–community relations (PCR)
An area of police activity that recognizes the need for the community and the police to work together effectively and is based on the notion that the police derive their legitimacy from the community they serve. Many police agencies began to explore PCR in the 1960s and 1970s.

Every society gets the kind of criminal it deserves. What is equally true is that every community gets the kind of law enforcement it insists on.

—Robert Kennedy, former U.S. attorney general[ii]

Freedom or Safety? You Decide
Police Body-Worn Cameras: The Good and the Bad

In 2018, New York City Mayor Bill de Blasio sped up plans to equip all of the city's police officers below the rank of sergeant with body cameras. The officers, he announced, would all be wearing body cameras by the end of 2018—instead of 2019, which had been the original target date. The mayor's announcement was in compliance with a 2013 federal court order which held that the NYPD had unfairly discriminated against minority residents through overpolicing. The Mayor's initial announcement came two years and two months after the White House asked Congress for $263 million to provide up to 50,000 body cameras for police across the country.

Most law enforcement officials agree that body cameras are an important next step in recording technology—supplementing the thousands of patrol car-mounted video cameras currently in use.

Patrol cars equipped with video cameras have been on the nation's highways since the late 1980s, and the footage they've produced has been a staple of real-life police TV shows for years. In 2014, in what many see as a next step, Denver Police Chief Robert White called for equipping all of the city's 800 officers with body cameras, saying that "only bad cops fear wearing body cams." After cameras were introduced in the department in 2012, public complaints against Denver officers fell 88% compared to previous years, and officers' use of force fell by 60%. A few years later, the NYPD announced the start of an "Omnipresence" initiative under which cameras and officers were deployed to high-crime areas throughout the city. Today, the LAPD is in the midst of deploying more than 7,000 body-worn cameras to all of its field officers, and many other jurisdictions are moving in that direction.

Some people believe that equipping both cars and personnel with continuous recording devices will lead to a reduction in police abuses, while serving to capture evidence of illegal behavior by suspects. Video footage can also be used for identification purposes and might be coupled with software that provides facial and license tag recognition, allowing officers to quickly identify stolen cars and wanted individuals.

Others, however, fear that the combination of video images and recognition software will lead to the creation of a suspect database that will inevitably include many otherwise innocent people and that might be improperly shared with other agencies or the media. At the same time, police officials worry that too many cameras may make citizens wary of interacting with officers. Chuck Wexler, executive director of the Police Executive Research Forum, warns that "Body-worn cameras can increase accountability, but police agencies must also find a way to preserve the informal and unique relationships between police officers and community members."

One study, however, by the International Association of Chiefs of Police surveyed 47 state law enforcement agencies that received federal grants to buy in-car cameras and concluded that

▲ A Rialto Police Department (California) officer wears a body camera while he confers with another officer. Why do most departments favor the use of such equipment?
Jonathan Alcorn/ZUMA Press, Inc./Alamy Stock Photo

such cameras substantially improved public trust in the police and protected officers against unfounded lawsuits.

The National Institute of Justice offers a body-worn camera page, which is available at **http://www.nij.gov/topics/law-enforcement/technology/Pages/body-worn-cameras.aspx**.

YOU DECIDE

Do you think that equipping all of the nation's patrol officers with body cameras is a good idea? What negative impact, if any, might such an initiative have on personal freedoms in our society? How might it affect policing?

References: "Atlantic City Becomes Latest N.J. City to Outfit Officers with Body Cameras," *Associated Press*, August 24, 2014; International Association of Chiefs of Police, *The Impact of Video Evidence on Modern Policing* (Alexandria, VA: IACP, 2005); Mara Gay, "De Blasio Steps Up Plan to Equip NYPD Officers with Body Cameras, *The Wall Street Journal*, January 30, 2018 (accessed March 4, 2018). Kevin Johnson, "Police Body Cameras Offer Benefits, Require Training," *USA Today*, September 12, 2014; Mark Landler, "Obama Offers New Standards on Police Gear," *The New York Times*, December 1, 2014, www.nytimes.com/2014/12/02/us/politics/obama-to-toughen-standards-on-police-use-of-military-gear.html (accessed January 30, 2015); and Sarah Breitenbach, "States Impose Wildly Different Policies in Releasing Police Videos," The Pew Charatiable Trusts, October 11, 2016, http://www.pewtrusts.org/en/research-and-analysis/blogs/stateline/2016/10/11/states-impose-wildly-different-policies-in-releasing-police-videos (accessed June 3, 2018).

Team Policing

During the 1960s and 1970s, a number of communities experimented with the concept of **team policing**, which rapidly became an extension of the PCR movement. With team policing, officers were assigned semipermanently to particular neighborhoods, where they were expected to become familiar with the inhabitants and with their problems and concerns. Patrol officers were given considerable authority in processing complaints, from receipt through resolution. Crimes were investigated and solved at the local level, with specialists called in only if the resources needed to continue an investigation were not available locally. Some authors called team policing a "technique to deliver total police services to a neighborhood."[92] Others, however, dismissed it as "little more than an attempt to return to the style of policing that was prevalent in the United States over a century ago."[93]

team policing
The reorganization of conventional patrol strategies into "an integrated and versatile police team assigned to a fixed district."[iii]

🐦 Follow the author's tweets about the latest crime and justice news @schmalleger

▲ Charleston police officers comfort mourners gathered outside the Fieldings Funeral home in Charleston, South Carolina, in 2015. Scenes like this help foster the community policing ideal through which law enforcement officers and members of the public become partners in controlling crime and keeping communities safe.
How does such a partnership help the police? The community?
Richard Ellis/Alamy Stock Photo

strategic policing
A type of policing that retains the traditional police goal of professional crime fighting but enlarges the enforcement target to include nontraditional kinds of criminals, such as serial offenders, gangs and criminal associations, drug-distribution networks, and sophisticated white-collar and computer criminals. Strategic policing generally makes use of innovative enforcement techniques, including intelligence operations, undercover stings, electronic surveillance, and sophisticated forensic methods.

problem-solving policing
A type of policing that assumes that many crimes are caused by existing social conditions within the community and that crimes can be controlled by uncovering and effectively addressing underlying social problems. Problem-solving policing makes use of community resources, such as counseling centers, welfare programs, and job-training facilities. It also attempts to involve citizens in crime prevention through education, negotiation, and conflict management.

community policing
"A philosophy that promotes organizational strategies, which support the systematic use of partnerships and problem-solving techniques, to proactively address the immediate conditions that give rise to public-safety issues such as crime, social disorder, and fear of crime."[iv]

Community Policing

Over the past quarter century, the role of the police in PCR has changed considerably. Originally, the PCR model was based on the fact that many police administrators saw police officers as enforcers of the law who were isolated from, and often in opposition to, the communities they policed. As a result, PCR programs were often a shallowly disguised effort to overcome public suspicion and community hostility.

Today, increasing numbers of law enforcement administrators embrace the role of service provider. Modern departments frequently help citizens solve a vast array of personal problems, many of which involve no lawbreaking activity. For example, officers regularly aid sick or distraught people, organize community crime-prevention efforts, resolve minor domestic disputes, regulate traffic, and educate children and teens about drug abuse. Because service calls far exceed calls directly related to law violations, most officers more often make referrals for interpersonal problems to agencies such as Alcoholics Anonymous, domestic-violence centers, and drug-rehabilitation programs rather than make arrests.

In contemporary America, some say, police departments function a lot like business corporations. According to Harvard University's Executive Session on Policing, three generic kinds of "corporate strategies" guide American policing: (1) strategic policing, (2) problem-solving policing, and (3) community policing.[94]

Strategic policing, which is something of a holdover from the reform era, "emphasizes an increased capacity to deal with crimes that are not well controlled by traditional methods."[95] Strategic policing retains the traditional police goal of professional crime fighting but enlarges the enforcement target to include nontraditional kinds of criminals, such as serial offenders, gangs and criminal associations, drug-distribution networks, and sophisticated white-collar and computer criminals. To meet its goals, strategic policing generally makes use of innovative enforcement techniques, including intelligence operations, undercover sting operations, electronic surveillance, and sophisticated forensic methods.

The other two strategies give greater recognition to Wilson's service style. **Problem-solving policing** (or problem-oriented policing) takes the view that many crimes are caused by existing social conditions in the communities. To control crime, problem-oriented police managers attempt to uncover and effectively address these underlying social problems. Problem-solving policing makes thorough use of community resources, such as counseling centers, welfare programs, and job-training facilities. It also attempts to involve citizens in crime prevention through education, negotiation, and conflict management. For example, police may ask residents of poorly maintained housing areas to clean up litter, install better lighting, and provide security devices for their houses and apartments in the belief that clean, well-lighted, secure areas are a deterrent to criminal activity.

The third and newest strategy, **community policing** (sometimes called community-oriented policing), goes a step beyond the other two. It has been described as a partnership between the police and the community, so that they can work together on solving problems of crime and disorder.[96] A more formal definition, offered by the Office of Community Oriented Policing Services (COPS) office, says that community policing "is a philosophy that promotes organizational strategies, which support the systematic use of partnerships and problem-solving techniques, to proactively address the immediate conditions that give rise to public-safety issues such as crime, social disorder, and fear of crime."[97]

The community policing concept evolved from the early works of police researchers George Kelling and Robert Trojanowicz. Their studies of foot-patrol programs in Newark, New Jersey,[98] and Flint, Michigan,[99] showed that "police could develop more positive attitudes toward community members and could promote positive attitudes toward police if they spent time on foot in their neighborhoods."[100] Trojanowicz's *Community Policing*, published in 1990,[101] may be the definitive work on this topic.

Follow the author's tweets about the latest crime and justice news @schmalleger

Community policing seeks to actively involve the community in the task of crime control by creating an effective working partnership between the community and the police.[102] Under the community policing ideal, community members and the police are expected to share responsibility for establishing and maintaining peaceful neighborhoods.[103] As a result, community policing permits members of the community to participate more fully than ever before in defining the police role. Police expert Jerome H. Skolnick says community policing is "grounded on the notion that, together, police and public are more effective and more humane coproducers of safety and public order than are the police alone."[104] According to Skolnick, community policing involves at least one of four elements: (1) community-based crime prevention, (2) reorientation of patrol activities to emphasize the importance of nonemergency services, (3) increased police accountability to the public, and (4) decentralization of command, including a greater use of civilians at all levels of police decision making.[105] As one writer explains it, "Community policing seeks to integrate what was traditionally seen as the different law enforcement, order maintenance and social service roles of the police. Central to the integration of these roles is a working partnership with the community in determining what neighborhood problems are to be addressed, and how."[106]

Community policing is a two-way street. It requires not only police awareness of community needs but also both involvement and crime-fighting action on the part of citizens themselves. As Detective Tracie Harrison of the Denver Police Department explains, "When the neighborhood takes stock in their community and they're serious they don't want crime, then you start to see crime go down. . . . They're basically fed up and know the police can't do it alone."[107]

Although community policing efforts began in metropolitan areas, the community engagement and problem-solving spirit of these programs has spread to rural regions. Sheriff's departments operating community policing programs sometimes refer to them as *neighborhood-oriented policing* in recognition of the decentralized nature of rural communities. A Bureau of Justice Assistance (BJA) report on neighborhood-oriented policing notes that "the stereotypical view is that police officers in rural areas naturally work more closely with the public than do officers in metropolitan areas."[108] This view, warns the BJA, may not be entirely accurate, and rural departments would do well "to recognize that considerable diversity exists among rural communities and rural law enforcement agencies." As in metropolitan areas, effective community policing requires the involvement of all members of the community in identifying and solving problems.

In continuing a long tradition of federal support for community policing, in 2017 the U.S. Department of Justice announced nearly $100 million in grant funding through the federal Office of Community-Oriented Policing Services (COPS).[109] The money, which went to 179 law enforcement agencies across the nation, allowed for the hiring of an additional 802 full-time law enforcement officers.

Community Policing and Antiterrorism

Noted police scholar David L. Carter says that "a common concern expressed by police executives is that the shift toward increased counterterrorism responsibilities may require a shift of resources away from community policing."[110] That concern, he says, is misdirected because community policing provides a natural conduit for information gathering and the development of counterterrorism intelligence. Information gathered by state and local police departments can be funneled to federal agencies, especially the FBI, that have been charged with developing national security intelligence. Carter notes that the "increased social tension" resulting from the current concern with terrorism has led to a greater need "to maintain a close, interactive dialogue between law enforcement and the community."

Citizens are coproducers of justice.

—Bureau of Justice Statistics, Princeton Project

🐦 Follow the author's tweets about the latest crime and justice news @schmalleger

Critique of Community Policing

As some authors have noted, "Community policing has become the dominant theme of contemporary police reform in America."[111] Yet problems have plagued the movement since its inception.[112] For one thing, the range, complexity, and evolving nature of community policing programs make their effectiveness difficult to measure.[113] Moreover, citizen satisfaction with police performance can be difficult to conceptualize and quantify.

Those who study community policing have often been stymied by ambiguity surrounding the concept of community.[114] Sociologists, who sometimes define the word *community* as "any area in which members of a common culture share common interests,"[115] tend to deny that a community needs to be limited geographically. Police departments, on the other hand, tend to define communities "within jurisdictional, district or precinct lines, or within the confines of public or private housing developments."[116] Robert Trojanowicz cautioned police planners that "the impact of mass transit, mass communications and mass media [has] widened the rift between a sense of community based on geography and one [based] on interest."[117]

Researchers who follow the police definition of *community* recognize that there may be little consensus within and between members of a local community about community problems and appropriate solutions. Robert Bohm and colleagues at the University of Central Florida have found, for example, that while there may be some "consensus about social problems and their solutions . . . the consensus may not be community-wide." It may, in fact, exist only among "a relatively small group of 'active' stakeholders who differ significantly about the seriousness of most of the problems and the utility of some solutions."[118]

Finally, there is continuing evidence that not all police officers or managers are willing to accept nontraditional images of police work. One reason is that the goals of community policing often conflict with standard police performance criteria (such as arrests), leading to a perception among officers that community policing is inefficient at best and, at worst, a waste of time.[119] Similarly, many officers are loathe to take on new responsibilities as service providers whose role is more defined by community needs and less by strict interpretation of the law.

Some authors have cautioned that police subculture is so committed to a traditional view of police work, which is focused almost exclusively on crime fighting, that efforts to promote community policing can demoralize an entire department, rendering it ineffective at its basic tasks.[120] Others says that only when the formal values espoused by today's innovative police administrators begin to match those of rank-and-file officers can any police agency begin to perform well in terms of the goals espoused by community policing reformers.[121]

▲ Police officers dispersing souvenirs during a visit to a grade-school classroom, as part of a community policing effort. How important is community policing today?

Marla Brose/Albuquerque Journal/ ZUMA Press Inc/Alamy Stock Photo

CJ Exhibit 4–1
The President's Task Force on 21st Century Policing

In 2015, the President's Task Force on 21st Century Policing released its final report, which was intended to provide "a road map for the future of policing." The task force had been appointed by President Obama some months earlier following a number of serious incidents between law enforcement and some American communities. Consequently, members also wanted to provide "clear direction on how to build trust with the public." Over the course of three months, the task force held seven hearings and interviewed 140 witnesses. It also reviewed volumes of written testimony submitted, much of it submitted online. In its final report, the task force generated 59 recommendations built around six themes, or "pillars." The six pillars, along with abbreviated commentary from the Task Force, are:

PILLAR ONE: BUILDING TRUST AND LEGITIMACY

Building trust and nurturing legitimacy on both sides of the police/citizen divide is the foundational principle underlying the nature of relations between law enforcement agencies and the communities they serve.... [P]eople are more likely to obey the law when they believe that those who are enforcing it have authority ... perceived as legitimate by those subject to [it]. The public confers legitimacy only on those whom they believe are acting in procedurally just ways.... [L]aw enforcement cannot build community trust if it is seen as an occupying force.... Law enforcement culture should embrace a guardian—rather than a warrior—mindset to build trust and legitimacy both within agencies and with the public. Toward that end, law enforcement agencies should adopt procedural justice as [their] guiding principle...

PILLAR TWO: POLICY AND OVERSIGHT

[I]f police are to carry out their responsibilities according to established policies, those policies must reflect community values. Law enforcement agencies should collaborate with community members, especially in communities and neighborhoods disproportionately affected by crime, to develop policies and strategies for deploying resources that aim to reduce crime by improving relationships, increasing community engagement, and fostering cooperation...

PILLAR THREE: TECHNOLOGY & SOCIAL MEDIA

The use of technology can improve policing practices and build community trust and legitimacy, but its implementation must be built on a defined policy framework with its purposes and goals clearly delineated. Implementing new technologies can give police departments an opportunity to fully engage and educate communities in a dialogue about their expectations for transparency, accountability, and privacy....

PILLAR FOUR: COMMUNITY POLICING & CRIME REDUCTION

... Law enforcement agencies should... work with community residents to identify problems and collaborate on implementing solutions that produce meaningful results for the community....Law enforcement agencies should also engage in multidisciplinary, community team approaches for planning, implementing, and responding to crisis situations with complex causal factors....

PILLAR FIVE: TRAINING & EDUCATION

As our nation becomes more pluralistic and the scope of law enforcement's responsibilities expands, the need for expanded and more effective training has become critical. Today's line officers and leaders must be trained and capable to address a wide variety of challenges including international terrorism, evolving technologies, rising immigration, changing laws, new cultural mores, and a growing mental health crisis....

PILLAR SIX: OFFICER WELLNESS & SAFETY

Pillar six emphasizes the support and proper implementation of officer wellness and safety as a multi-partner effort.... Two specific strategies [are] recommended: (1) encouraging and assisting departments in the implementation of scientifically supported shift lengths by law enforcement and (2) expanding efforts to collect and analyze data not only on officer deaths but also on injuries and "near misses."

Read the entire report at: **http://www.americanbarfoundation.org/uploads/cms/documents/executive_summary_policing_task_force.pdf**.

Source: President's Task Force on 21st Century Policing, *Final Report of the President's Task Force on 21st Century Policing* (Washington, D.C.: Office of Community Oriented Policing Services, 2015).

Evidence-Based Policing

In 1968, with the passage of the Omnibus Crime Control and Safe Streets Act, the U.S. Congress created the **Law Enforcement Assistance Administration (LEAA)**. LEAA was charged with combating crime through the expenditure of huge amounts of money in support of crime-prevention and crime-reduction programs. Some have compared the philosophy establishing LEAA to that which supported the American space program's goal of landing people on the moon: Put enough money into any problem, and it will be solved! Unfortunately, the crime problem was more difficult to address than the challenge of a moon landing; even after the expenditure of nearly $8 billion, LEAA had not come close to its goal. In 1982, LEAA expired when Congress refused it further funding.

7 Discuss the impact of evidence-based policing in the area of police management.

Law Enforcement Assistance Administration (LEAA)
A now-defunct federal agency established under Title I of the Omnibus Crime Control and Safe Streets Act of 1969 to funnel federal funding to state and local law enforcement agencies.

scientific police management
The application of social sciences techniques to the study of police administration for the purpose of increasing effectiveness, reducing the frequency of citizen complaints, and enhancing the efficient use of available resources.

The legacy of LEAA is an important one for police managers, however. The research-rich years of 1969 to 1982, supported largely through LEAA funding, have left a plethora of scientific findings relevant to police administration and, more important, have established a tradition of program evaluation within police-management circles. This tradition, which is known as **scientific police management**, is a natural outgrowth of the LEAA's insistence that every funded program contain a plan for its evaluation. *Scientific police management* refers to the application of social science techniques to the study of police administration for the purpose of increasing effectiveness, reducing the frequency of citizen complaints, and enhancing the efficient use of available resources. The heyday of scientific police management occurred in the 1970s, when federal monies were far more readily available to support such studies than they are today.

LEAA was not alone in funding police research during the 1970s. On July 1, 1970, the Ford Foundation announced the establishment of a Police Development Fund totaling $30 million, to be spent over the next 5 years to support major crime-fighting strategies of police departments. This funding led to the establishment of the Police Foundation, which continues to exist today with the mission of "foster[ing] improvement and innovation in American policing."[122] Police Foundation-sponsored studies during the past 30 years have added to the growing body of scientific knowledge about policing.

Today, federal support for criminal justice research and evaluation continues under the NIJ and the BJS, both part of the Office of Justice Programs (OJP). The OJP, created by Congress in 1984, provides federal leadership in developing the nation's capacity to prevent and control crime. The National Criminal Justice Reference Service (NCJRS), a part of the NIJ, assists researchers nationwide in locating information applicable to their research projects. "Custom searches" of the NCJRS computer database can be done online and can yield abundant information in most criminal justice subject areas. The NIJ also publishes a series of informative periodic reports, such as the *NIJ Journal* and *NIJ Research in Review*, which serve to keep criminal justice practitioners and researchers informed about recent findings. Search all NIJ online publications at **http://www.nij.gov/publications**.

Kansas City experiment
The first large-scale scientific study of law enforcement practices. Sponsored by the Police Foundation, it focused on the practice of preventive patrol.

▲ Kansas City, Missouri, police crime scene technicians unload equipment as officers and agents prepare to search the woods in an effort to find 11-month-old Lisa Irwin in 2011. The girl was not found. Scientific police management was first supported by studies of preventive patrol undertaken in Kansas City in 1974. How does today's evidence-based policing build on that tradition?

Shane Keyser/The Kansas City Star/ MCT/Newscom

The Kansas City Experiment

History

The most famous application of social research principles to police management was the **Kansas City experiment** regarding preventive patrol.[123] The results of the yearlong experiment were published in 1974. The study, sponsored by the Police Foundation, divided the southern part of Kansas City, Missouri, into 15 areas. Five of these "beats" were patrolled in the usual fashion. In another group of five beats, patrol activities were doubled. The final third of the beats received a novel treatment indeed: No patrols were assigned to them, and no uniformed officers entered that part of the city unless they were called. The program was kept secret, and citizens were unaware of the difference between the patrolled and unpatrolled parts of the city.

The results of the Kansas City experiment were surprising. Records of "preventable crimes" (those toward which the activities of patrol were oriented), such as burglary, robbery, auto theft, larceny, and vandalism, showed no significant differences in rate of occurrence among the three experimental beats. Similarly, citizens didn't seem to notice the change in patrol patterns in the two areas where patrol frequency was changed. Surveys conducted at the conclusion of the experiment showed no difference in citizens' fear of crime before and after the study. The 1974 study can be summed up in the words of the author of the final report: "The whole idea of riding around in cars to create a feeling of omnipresence just hasn't worked. . . . Good people with good intentions tried something that logically should have worked, but didn't."[124] This study has been credited with beginning the now-established tradition of scientific studies of policing.

A second Kansas City study focused on "response time."[125] It found that even consistently fast police response to citizen reports of crime had little effect either on citizen satisfaction with the police or on the arrest of suspects. The study uncovered the fact that most reports made to the police came only after a considerable amount of time had passed. Hence, the police were initially handicapped by the timing of the report, and even the fastest police response was not especially effective.

Effects

The Kansas City studies greatly affected managerial assumptions about the role of preventive patrol and traditional strategies for responding to citizen calls for assistance. As Joseph Lewis, then director of evaluation at the Police Foundation, said, "I think that now almost everyone would agree that almost anything you do is better than random patrol."[126]

Although the Kansas City studies called into question some basic assumptions about patrol, it remains the backbone of police work. New patrol strategies for the effective utilization of human resources have led to various activities of **directed patrol**. One form of directed patrol varies the number of officers involved in patrolling according to the time of day or the frequency of reported crimes within an area. The idea is to put the most officers on the street where and when crime is most prevalent. Wilmington, Delaware, was one of the first cities to make use of split-force patrol, in which only a part of the patrol force performs routine patrol.[127] The remaining officers respond to calls for service, take reports, and conduct investigations.

In response to the Kansas City study on response time, some cities have prioritized calls for service,[128] ordering a quick police response only when crimes are in progress or when serious crimes have occurred. Less significant offenses, such as minor larcenies and certain citizen complaints, are handled by using the mail or by having citizens come to the police station to make a report.

Early policing studies, such as the Kansas City patrol experiment, were designed to identify and probe some of the basic assumptions that guided police work. The initial response to many such studies was "Why should we study that? Everybody knows the answer already!" As in the case of the Kansas City experiment, however, it soon became obvious that conventional wisdom was not always correct.

Evidence-Based Policing Today

At the close of the twentieth century, noted police researcher Lawrence W. Sherman addressed an audience of criminal justice policymakers, scholars, and practitioners at the Police Foundation in Washington, D.C., and called for a new approach to American policing that would use research to guide and evaluate practice. "Police practices should be based on scientific evidence about what works best," Sherman told his audience. Sherman's lecture, titled "Evidence-Based Policing: Policing Based on Science, Not Anecdote,"[129] popularized the term **evidence-based policing (EBP)**. EBP, says Sherman, "is the use of best available research on the outcomes of police work to implement guidelines and evaluate agencies, units, and officers."[130] In other words, EBP uses research into everyday police procedures to evaluate current practices and to guide officers and police executives in future decision making. In any discussion of EBP, it is important to remember that the word *evidence* refers to scientific evidence, not criminal evidence.

"The basic premise of evidence-based practice," says Sherman, "is that we are all entitled to our own opinions, but not to our own facts."[131] Our own facts, or our beliefs about the way things should be done, often turn out to be wrong. During the civil rights movement of the 1960s and 1970s, for example, police executives in many areas took a heavy-handed approach in their attempts to control demonstrators. Images of tear gas filling the streets,

directed patrol
A police-management strategy designed to increase the productivity of patrol officers through the scientific analysis and evaluation of patrol techniques.

evidence-based policing (EBP)
The use of the best available research on the outcomes of police work to implement guidelines and evaluate agencies, units, and officers.[v]

high-pressure fire hoses being aimed at marchers, and police dogs biting demonstrators symbolize that era for many people. This heavy-handed approach had unintended consequences and served to inflame protesters. Situations that might have otherwise been contained with simple crowd-control tactics and the use of physical barriers became largely uncontrollable. Sherman reminds us that "the mythic power of subjective and unstructured wisdom holds back every field and keeps it from systematically discovering and implementing what works best in repeated tasks."

Today's EBP model has been called the single "most powerful force for change" in policing today.[132] Leading the EBP movement are such organizations as the FBI's Futures Working Group and the Campbell Crime and Justice Group, and the Center for Evidence-Based Crime Policy at George Mason University. FBI Supervisory Special Agent Carl J. Jensen III, a member of the Futures Working Group, notes that in the future "successful law enforcement executives will have to be consumers and appliers of research." They won't need to be researchers themselves, Jensen notes, "but they must use research in their everyday work."[133] The Campbell Collaboration Crime and Justice Group, which emphasizes the use of experimental studies in crime and justice policy-making, can be accessed via **https://www.campbellcollaboration.org**.

A program of the Center for Evidence-Based Crime Policy (CEBCP) at George Mason University, the Evidence-Based Policing Hall of Fame, recognizes innovative law enforcement practitioners who have been central to the implementation of a high-quality research program in their respective agencies. Membership in the Hall of Fame highlights excellence in using and conducting policing research. An informative CEBCP YouTube channel is available at **https://www.youtube.com/user/clsMason**.

The Institute of Criminology at Cambridge University identified the following questions as goals to be answered by evidence-based studies:[134]

- How can policing produce greater public safety without eroding civil liberties?
- How can more value for money be returned from investments in policing to cut the costs of crime?
- Can crime be better forecast for preventive policing by time and place?
- Can unsuccessful police methods be distinguished from cost-effective ones?
- Can better policing reduce the high costs of a growing prison population?
- Can evaluation tools used in evidence-based medicine be adopted by police?
- What are the possibilities for a police service based on cost-effectiveness?
- What are the prospects for developing the knowledge base for such evidence?

Visit the Center for Evidence-Based Crime Policy at **http://cebcp.org**, and explore the Evidence-Based Policing Hall of Fame at **http://cebcp.org/hall-of-fame**. Read about the evidence-based paradigm in police science at Harvard's Kennedy School of Government at **http://tinyurl.com/gr8rajs**. Also, an EBP matrix is available at **http://cebcp.org/evidence-based-policing/the-matrix**. The matrix, provided by the CEBCP, is a research-to-practice translation tool that visually organizes strong EBP studies. Finally, Strategies for Policing Innovation (SPI), a project of the federal BJA, "supports law enforcement agencies in building evidence-based, data-driven law enforcement tactics and strategies that are effective, efficient, and economical."[135] SPI, which can be reached on the Web at **http://www.strategiesforpolicinginnovation.com/**, and which is further discussed in a box in this chapter, "brings more 'science' into police operations by leveraging innovative applications of analysis, technology, and evidence-based practices."

> Today's evidence-based policing model has been called the single "most powerful force for change" in policing today.

Follow the author's tweets about the latest crime and justice news @schmalleger

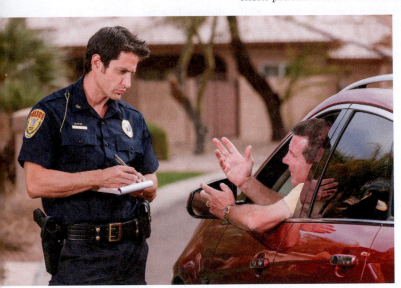

▲ An officer writing a traffic ticket. Police officers wield a wide degree of discretion, and an individual officer's decision to enforce a particular law or to effect an arrest varies not just with the law's applicability to a particular set of circumstances but with the officer's subjective judgments about the nature of appropriate enforcement activity. What other factors influence police discretion?

Avid_creative/E+/Getty Images

Discretion and the Individual Officer

8 Explain how police discretion affects contemporary law enforcement.

Even as law enforcement agencies struggle to adapt to the threats posed by international terrorism, individual officers continue to retain considerable discretion in terms of their actions. **Police discretion** refers to the exercise of choice by law enforcement officers in the decision to investigate or apprehend, the disposition of suspects, the carrying out of official duties, and the application of sanctions. As one author has observed, "Police authority can be, at once, highly specific and exceedingly vague."[136] Decisions to stop and question someone, arrest a suspect, and perform many other police tasks are made solely by individual officers and must often be made quickly and in the absence of any close supervision. Kenneth Culp Davis, who pioneered the study of police discretion, says, "The police make policy about what law to enforce, how much to enforce it, against whom, and on what occasions."[137] To those who have contact with the police, the discretionary authority exercised by individual officers is of greater significance than all the department manuals and official policy statements combined.

Patrolling officers often decide against a strict enforcement of the law, preferring instead to handle situations informally. Infractions where minor law violations are committed, crimes committed out of the officer's presence where the victim refuses to file a complaint, and certain violations of criminal law where the officer suspects that sufficient evidence to guarantee a conviction is lacking may all lead to discretionary action short of arrest. The widest exercise of discretion is more likely in routine situations involving relatively less serious violations of the law, but serious and clear-cut criminal behavior may occasionally result in discretionary decisions not to make an arrest. Underage drinking, possession of controlled substances, and assault are but a few examples of crimes in which on-the-scene officers may decide warnings or referrals are more appropriate than arrest. Figure 4–5 illustrates a number of factors that studies of police discretion have found to influence the discretionary decisions of individual officers.

police discretion
The opportunity of law enforcement officers to exercise choice in their daily activities.

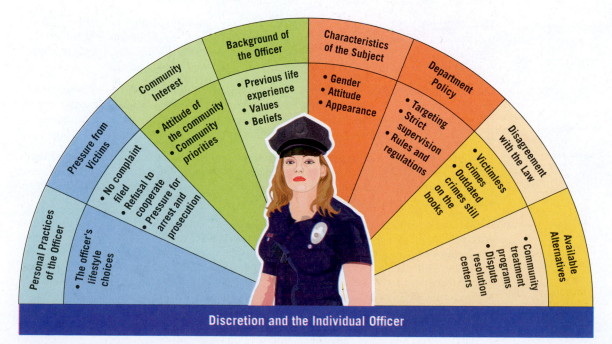

FIGURE 4–5
Discretion and the Individual Officer

Summary

POLICING: PURPOSE AND ORGANIZATION

- The fundamental police mission in democratic societies includes five components: (1) enforcing the law (especially the criminal law), (2) apprehending offenders, (3) preventing crime, (4) preserving the peace, and (5) providing the community with needed enforcement-related services.

- Contemporary American policing presents a complex picture that is structured along federal, state, and local lines. Each federal agency empowered by Congress to enforce specific statutes has its own enforcement arm. In addition, tasks deemed especially significant by state legislatures, such as patrol of the highways, have resulted in the creation of specialized law enforcement agencies under state jurisdiction. For many of today's local law enforcement agencies, created under county and municipal authority, patrol retains a central role—with investigation, interrogation, and numerous support roles rounding out an increasingly specialized profession.

- Private policing, represented by the recent tremendous growth of for-hire security agencies, adds another important dimension to American policing. Whereas public police are employed by the government and enforce public laws, private security personnel work for corporate or private employers and secure private interests. Private security personnel outnumber public law enforcement officers in the United States, and private agencies provide tailored protective services funded by the guarded organization rather than by taxpayers. Recognizing the important services that private security personnel provide, many municipal police departments have begun concerted efforts to involve security organizations in their crime-detection and crime-prevention efforts.

- Police administration involves the activities of managing, controlling, directing, and coordinating police personnel, resources, and activities in the service of preventing crime, apprehending criminals, recovering stolen property, and performing regulatory and helping services. Virtually all American law enforcement organizations are formally structured among divisions and along lines of authority. Roles within police agencies usually fall into one of two categories: line and staff. Line operations are field or supervisory activities directly related to daily police work; staff operations include support roles such as administration.

- Four historical policing epochs are identified in this chapter: (1) the political era, (2) the reform era, (3) the community policing era, and (4) the new era. Some say that the primary feature of the new law enforcement era is policing to secure the homeland. Others see the new era as being underpinned by an emphasis on intelligence-led policing.

- Police–community relations programs represent a movement away from an exclusive police emphasis on the apprehension of law violators and signify an increasing level of positive police–citizen interaction. Community policing is built on the principle that police departments and the communities they serve should work together as partners in the fight against crime.

- Evidence-based policing consists of the use of best available research on the outcomes of police work to implement guidelines and evaluate agencies, units, and officers. EBP uses research into everyday police procedures to evaluate current practices and to guide officers and police executives in future decision making.

- *Police discretion* refers to the opportunity for police officers to exercise choice in their enforcement activities. Put another way, discretion is the exercise of choice by law enforcement officers in the decision to investigate or apprehend, the disposition of suspects, the carrying out of official duties, and the application of sanctions. The widest exercise of discretion can be found in routine situations involving relatively less serious violations of the law, but serious criminal behavior may also result in discretionary decisions not to make an arrest.

QUESTIONS FOR REVIEW

1. What are the basic purposes of policing in democratic societies? How are they consistent with one another? In what ways might they be inconsistent?

2. What are the three major levels of public law enforcement described in this chapter? Why do we have so many different types of enforcement agencies in the United States? What problems, if any, do you think are created by such a diversity of agencies?

3. What are the nature and extent of private protective services in the United States today? What role do you think private protective services will play in the future? How can the quality of these services be ensured?

4. What are the various features of police administration described in this chapter? What is a chain of command?

5. What were the stages of historical development in American policing? How did policing styles differ by historical era?

6. What is community policing? How does it differ from traditional policing? Does community policing offer a real opportunity to improve policing services in the United States? Why or why not?

7. What is evidence-based policing? What potential does it hold for managing police organizations in the future?

8. What is police discretion? How does the practice of discretion by today's officers affect their departments and the policing profession as a whole?

Policing: Legal Aspects

> *No one is compelled to choose the profession of a police officer, but having chosen it, everyone is obliged to live up to the standard of its requirements.*
>
> —Calvin Coolidge[1]

Learning Objectives

After reading this chapter, you should be able to:

1. Describe legal restraints on police action and instances of police abuse of power. **125**

2. Explain how the Bill of Rights and democratically inspired legal restraints help protect our personal freedoms. **127**

3. Describe the circumstances under which police officers may conduct searches or seize property legally. **128**

4. Describe arrest and types of searches. **139**

5. Describe the intelligence function, including the roles of police interrogation and the *Miranda* warning. **152**

John G. Mabanglo/EPA/Newscom

Introduction

In 2015, six Baltimore, Maryland, police officers were indicted in the death of 25-year-old Freddie Gray.[2] Gray, who was black and unarmed, died a week after he was arrested and transported in a police van, apparently without proper safety restraints. Gray had reportedly asked for medical assistance a number of times while he was in the van, but prosecutors claimed that his pleas were ignored. Gray's death led to a series of protests, some of which turned violent, resulting in the looting and burning of local businesses and the injury of 15 police officers. The Maryland National Guard was deployed throughout portions of the city and a night curfew was imposed. In September 2015, a $6.4 million settlement was reached between Gray family members and the city of Baltimore.[3] None of the six officers who were indicted in the Gray case, however, were convicted of a crime, although the killing resulted in a U.S. Department of Justice investigation of the Baltimore Police Department.[4]

▲ In 2015, Freddie Gray, an unarmed black man was arrested by Baltimore, MD, police officers and died as a result of serious injuries that he suffered while being transported in a police van. In a later settlement, the city agreed to pay $6.4 million to Gray's survivors. Shown here is Gray's stepfather, Richard Shipley (center), surrounded by Gray's mother and family lawyer at a press conference. Some say that there are two sides to stories like this. What might those sides be?
SHAWN THEW/EPA/Newscom

🐦 Follow the author's tweets about the latest crime and justice news @schmalleger

The Abuse of Police Power

Another 2015 incident—the shooting of 50-year-old Walter Scott—led to continued media attention.[5] Scott, who was black and unarmed, was shot in the back eight times by Michael Slager, a 33-year-old Charleston, South Carolina, police officer as he ran away following a traffic stop. Much of the incident was captured on cell phone video by a bystander. The video evidence showed Slager dropping his Taser by Scott's lifeless body after the shooting. Slager told his supervisors that Scott had attempted to gain control over the Taser before running away. In 2016, Slager's state trial for murder resulted in a hung jury, but in 2017 he pled guilty to federal charges of violating Scott's civil rights by using excessive force. He was sentenced to 20 years in federal prison.

1 Describe legal restraints on police action and instances of police abuse of power.

One year earlier, a 400-pound asthmatic Staten Island man who was selling untaxed cigarettes on a sidewalk died after NYPD officers slammed his head against the sidewalk and held him in a chokehold—a dangerous restraint tactic that was against department policy.[6] Like Scott, the man who died, Eric Garner, 43, was black and unarmed—and the incident was also recorded on cell phone video by others at the scene. Although a local grand jury refused to indict any of the officers involved, the city of New York paid a $5.9 million settlement to Garner's survivors.

Organized public reaction to the police killing of unarmed black men culminated in the development of the "Black Lives Matter" movement—a social justice initiative that had its roots in the 2014 shooting death of unarmed 18-year-old Michael Brown by a white Ferguson, Missouri, police officer.[7] The incident, which is described in more detail in Chapter 4, occurred after Brown stole cigars from a nearby convenience store and later got into a scuffle with the officer. Although details of the shooting were in dispute, a grand jury later refused to indict the officer.

Prior to the incidents described here, the most widely discussed abuse of police power was the 1991 videotaped beating of motorist Rodney King by LAPD officers. King, an unemployed 25-year-old black man, was stopped by LAPD officers for an alleged violation of motor vehicle laws.[8] Police said King had been speeding and had refused to stop for a pursuing patrol car. Eventually King did stop, but then officers of the LAPD appeared to attack him, shocking him twice with stun guns and striking him with nightsticks and fists. Kicked in the stomach, face, and back, King was left with 11 skull fractures, missing teeth, a crushed cheekbone, and a broken ankle. A witness told reporters that she heard King begging officers to stop the beating but that they "were all laughing, like they just had a party." In 1994, King settled a civil suit against the city of Los Angeles for a reported $3.8 million. King's 1991 beating served for many years as a rallying point for individual-rights activists who wanted to ensure that citizens remain protected from the abuse of police power.

This chapter shows how no one is above the law—even the police. It describes the legal environment surrounding police activities, from search and seizure through arrest and the interrogation of suspects. As we shall see throughout, democratically inspired legal restraints on the police help ensure individual freedoms in our society and prevent the development of a police state in America. Like anything else, however, the rules by which the police are expected to operate are in constant flux, and their continuing development forms the meat of this chapter. For a police perspective on these issues, visit **http://www.policedefense.org**.

Bill of Rights
The popular name given to the first ten amendments to the U.S. Constitution, which are considered especially important in the processing of criminal defendants.

> There is more law at the end of the policeman's nightstick than in all the decisions of the Supreme Court.
>
> —Alexander "Clubber" Williams, late-nineteenth-century New York police officer

A Changing Legal Climate

The Constitution of the United States is designed—especially in the **Bill of Rights**— to protect citizens against abuses of police power (Table 5-1). However, the legal environment surrounding the police in modern America is much more complex than it was just 45 years ago. Up until that time, the Bill of Rights was largely given only lip service in criminal justice proceedings around the country. In practice, law enforcement, especially on the state and local levels, revolved around tried-and-true methods of search, arrest, and interrogation that sometimes left little room for recognition of individual rights. Police operations during that period were often far more informal than they are today, and investigating officers frequently assumed that they could come and go as they pleased, even to the extent of invading someone's home without a search warrant. Interrogations could quickly turn violent, and the infamous "rubber hose," which was reputed to leave few marks on the body, was probably more widely used

TABLE 5-1
Constitutional Amendments of Special Significance to the American System of Justice

This Right Is Guaranteed	By This Amendment
The right against unreasonable searches and seizures	Fourth
The right against arrest without probable cause	Fourth
The right against self-incrimination	Fifth
The right against "double jeopardy"	Fifth
The right to due process of law	Fifth, Sixth, and Fourteenth
The right to a speedy trial	Sixth
The right to a jury trial	Sixth
The right to know the charges	Sixth
The right to cross-examine witnesses	Sixth
The right to a lawyer	Sixth
The right to compel witnesses on one's behalf	Sixth
The right to reasonable bail	Eighth
The right against excessive fines	Eighth
The right against cruel and unusual punishments	Eighth
The applicability of constitutional rights to all citizens, regardless of state law or procedure	Fourteenth

Note: The Fourteenth Amendment is not a part of the Bill of Rights.

during the questioning of suspects than many would like to believe. Similarly, "doing things by the book" could mean the use of thick telephone books for beating suspects, since the books spread out the force of blows and left few visible bruises. Although such abuses were not necessarily day-to-day practices in all police agencies and although they probably did not characterize more than a relatively small proportion of all officers, such conduct pointed to the need for greater control over police activities so that even the potential for abuse might be curtailed.

In the 1960s the U.S. Supreme Court, under the direction of Chief Justice Earl Warren (1891–1974), accelerated the process of guaranteeing individual rights in the face of criminal prosecution. Warren Court rulings bound the police to strict procedural requirements in the areas of investigation, arrest, and interrogation. Later rulings scrutinized trial court procedures and enforced humanitarian standards in sentencing and punishment. The Warren Court also seized on the Fourteenth Amendment and made it a basis for judicial mandates requiring that both state and federal criminal justice agencies adhere to the Court's interpretation of the Constitution. The apex of the individual-rights emphasis in Supreme Court decisions was reached in the 1966 case of *Miranda* v. *Arizona*,[9] which established the famous requirement of a police "rights advisement" of suspects. In wielding its brand of idealism, the Warren Court (which held sway from 1953 until 1969) accepted the fact that a few guilty people would go free so that the rights of the majority of Americans would be protected.

In the decades since the Warren Court, a new conservative Court philosophy has resulted in Supreme Court decisions that have brought about what some call a reversal of Warren-era advances in the area of individual rights. By creating exceptions to some of the Warren Court's rules and restraints and by allowing for the emergency questioning of suspects before they are read their rights, a changed Supreme Court has recognized the realities attending day-to-day police work and the need to ensure public safety. The changing judicial philosophy of the U.S. Supreme Court will be discussed later in this chapter.

🐦 Follow the author's tweets about the latest crime and justice news @schmalleger

Individual Rights

Checks and Balances

The Constitution of the United States provides for a system of checks and balances among the legislative, judicial, and executive (presidential) branches of government. One branch of government is always held accountable to the other branches. The system is designed to ensure that no one individual or agency can become powerful enough to usurp the rights and freedoms guaranteed under the Constitution. Without accountability, it is possible to imagine a police state in which the power of law enforcement is absolute and is related more to political considerations and personal vendettas than to objective considerations of guilt or innocence.

2 Explain how the Bill of Rights and democratically inspired legal restraints help protect our personal freedoms.

Under our system of government, courts become the arena for dispute resolution, not just between individuals but between citizens and the agencies of government. After handling by the justice system, people who feel they have not received the respect and dignity due to them under the law can appeal to the courts for redress. Such appeals are usually based on procedural issues and are independent of more narrow considerations of guilt or innocence.

In this chapter, we focus on cases that are important for having clarified constitutional guarantees concerning individual liberties within the criminal justice arena. They involve issues that most of us have come to call *rights*. Rights are concerned with procedure, that is, with how police and other actors in the criminal justice system handle each part of the process of dealing with suspects. Rights violations have often become the basis for the dismissal of charges, the acquittal of defendants, or the release of convicted offenders after an appeal to a higher court.

> [The police] are not perfect; we don't sign them up on some far-off planet and bring them into police service. They are products of society.
> —Daryl Gates, former Los Angeles police chief

Due-Process Requirements

As you may recall from Chapter 1, the Fourth, Fifth, Sixth, and Fourteenth Amendments to the U.S. Constitution require due process, which mandates that justice system officials respect the rights of accused individuals throughout the criminal justice process. Most due-process requirements of relevance to the police pertain to three major areas: (1) evidence and investigation (often called *search* and *seizure*), (2) detention and arrest, and (3) interrogation. Each of these areas has been addressed by a plethora of landmark U.S. Supreme Court decisions. **Landmark cases** produce substantial changes both in the understanding of the requirements of due process and in the practical day-to-day operations of the justice system. Another way to think of landmark cases is that they help significantly in clarifying the "rules of the game"—the procedural guidelines that the police and the rest of the justice system must follow.

The three areas we will discuss have been well defined by decades of court precedent. Keep in mind, however, that judicial interpretations of the constitutional requirement of due process are constantly evolving. As new decisions are rendered and as the composition of the Court itself changes, major changes and additional refinements may occur.

Search and Seizure

The Fourth Amendment to the U.S. Constitution declares that people must be secure in their homes and in their persons against unreasonable searches and seizures. This amendment reads, "The right of the people to be secure in their persons, houses, papers, and effects, against unreasonable searches and seizures, shall not be violated, and no Warrants shall issue, but upon probable cause, supported by Oath or affirmation, and particularly describing the place to be searched, and the persons or things to be seized." The Fourth Amendment, a part of the Bill of Rights, was adopted by Congress and became effective on December 15, 1791.

3 Describe the circumstances under which police officers may conduct searches or seize property legally.

The language of the Fourth Amendment is familiar to all of us. "**Warrant**," "probable cause," and other phrases from the amendment are frequently cited in editorials, TV news shows, and daily conversations about **illegally seized evidence**. It is the interpretation of these phrases over time by the U.S. Supreme Court, however, that has given them the impact they have on the justice system today.

The Exclusionary Rule

The first landmark case concerning search and seizure was that of *Weeks* v. *U.S.* (1914).[10] Freemont Weeks was suspected of using the U.S. mail to sell lottery tickets, a federal crime. Weeks was arrested, and federal agents went to his home to conduct a search. They had no search warrant, because at the time investigators did not routinely use warrants. They confiscated many incriminating items of evidence, as well as some of the suspect's personal possessions, including clothes, papers, books, and even candy.

Prior to trial, Weeks's attorney asked that the personal items be returned, claiming that they had been illegally seized under Fourth Amendment guarantees. A judge agreed and ordered the materials returned. On the basis of the evidence that was retained, however, Weeks was convicted in federal court and was sentenced to prison. He appealed his conviction through other courts, and his case eventually reached the U.S. Supreme Court. There, his lawyer reasoned that if some of his client's belongings had been illegally seized, then the remainder of them were also taken improperly. The Court agreed and overturned Weeks's earlier conviction.

The *Weeks* case forms the basis of what is now called the **exclusionary rule**, which holds that evidence illegally seized by the police cannot be used in a trial. The rule acts as a control over police behavior and specifically focuses on the failure of officers to obtain warrants authorizing them either to conduct searches or to effect arrests, especially where arrest may lead to the acquisition of incriminating statements or to the seizure of physical evidence.

The decision of the Supreme Court in the *Weeks* case was binding, at the time, only on federal officers because only federal agents were involved in the illegal seizure. Learn more

THE FOURTH AMENDMENT TO THE U.S. CONSTITUTION

The right of the people to be secure in their persons, houses, papers, and effects, against unreasonable searches and seizures, shall not be violated, and no Warrants shall issue, but upon probable cause, supported by Oath or affirmation, and particularly describing the place to be searched, and the persons or things to be seized.

Based upon the Fourth Amendment, **the Exclusionary Rule** holds that evidence of an offense that is collected or obtained by law enforcement officers in violation of a defendant's constitutional rights is inadmissible for use in a criminal prosecution in a court of law.

SIGNIFICANT CASES

Weeks v. U.S. (1914)

Established the exclusionary rule at the federal level, holding that evidence that is illegally obtained cannot be used in a criminal trial; and that federal officers must have a valid warrant before conducting searches or seizing evidence. Prior to *Weeks*, common practice generally allowed all relevant evidence, no matter how it was obtained, to be used in court.

Silverthorne Lumber Co. v. U.S. (1920)

Set forth the **Fruit of the Poisonous Tree Doctrine**, which says that just as illegally seized evidence cannot be used in a trial, neither can evidence that *derives* from an illegal search or seizure. Under this doctrine, complex cases developed after years of police investigative effort may be ruined if defense attorneys are able to demonstrate that the prosecution's case was originally based on a search or seizure that, at the time it occurred, violated due process.

Mapp v. Ohio (1961)

Applied the exclusionary rule to criminal prosecutions at the state level. The Court held that the due process clause of the Fourteenth Amendment to the U.S. Constitution makes Fourth Amendment provisions applicable to state proceedings.

SUBSTANTIAL SOCIAL COSTS

U.S. v. Leon (1984) and **Hudson v. Michigan (2006)**
Recognized that the exclusionary rule generates "substantial social costs," which may include letting the guilty go free and setting the dangerous at large.

EXCEPTIONS TO THE EXCLUSIONARY RULE

THE GOOD-FAITH EXCEPTION

U.S. v. Leon (1984)
Allowed evidence that officers had seized in "reasonable good faith" to be used in court, even though the search was later ruled illegal.

Illinois v. Krull (1987)
The *good-faith exception* applied to a warrantless search supported by state law even though the state statute was later found to violate the Fourth Amendment.

Maryland v. Garrison (1987)
The use of evidence obtained by officers with a search warrant that was inaccurate in its specifics was allowed.

THE PLAIN-VIEW DOCTRINE

Harris v. U.S. (1968)
Police officers have the opportunity to begin investigations or to confiscate evidence, without a warrant, based on what they find in plain view and open to public inspection.

CLERICAL ERRORS EXCEPTION

Arizona v. Evans (1995)
A traffic stop that led to the seizure of marijuana was legal even though officers conducted the stop based on an arrest warrant that should have been deleted from the computer database to which they had access.

Herring v. U.S. (2009)
When police mistakes leading to an unlawful search are the result of isolated negligence rather than systemic error or reckless disregard of constitutional requirements, the exclusionary rule does not apply.

EMERGENCY SEARCHES OF PROPERTY/EMERGENCY ENTRY

Brigham City v. Stuart (2006)
Certain emergencies may justify a police officer's decision to search or enter premises without a warrant.

FIGURE 5–1
The Exclusionary Rule

about *Weeks* v. *U.S.* at **http://tinyurl.com/59rsve**. See Figure 5–1 for more about the exclusionary rule and its development since *Weeks*.

Problems with Precedent

The *Weeks* case demonstrates the Supreme Court's power in enforcing what we have called the "rules of the game." It also lays bare the much more significant role that the Court plays in rule creation. Until the *Weeks* case was decided, federal law enforcement officers had little reason to think they were acting in violation of due process. Common practice had not required that they obtain a warrant before conducting searches. The rule that resulted from *Weeks* was new, and it would forever alter the enforcement activities of federal officers.

🐦 Follow the author's tweets about the latest crime and justice news @schmalleger

The *Weeks* case reveals that the present appeals system, focusing as it does on the "rules of the game," presents a ready-made channel for the guilty to go free. There is little doubt that Freemont Weeks had violated federal law; a jury had convicted him. Yet he escaped punishment because of the illegal behavior of the police—behavior that, until the Court ruled, had been widely regarded as legitimate. Even if the police knowingly violate the principles of due process, which they sometimes do, our sense of justice is compromised when the guilty go free. Famed Supreme Court Justice Benjamin Cardozo (1870–1938) once complained, "The criminal is to go free because the constable has blundered."

One solution to the problem would be to allow the Supreme Court to address theoretical questions involving issues of due process. Concerned supervisors and officials could ask how the Court would rule "if. . . ." As things now work, however, the Court can only address real cases and does so on a **writ of *certiorari***, in which the Court orders the record of a lower court case to be prepared for review.

The Fruit of the Poisonous Tree Doctrine

The Court continued to build on the rules concerning evidence with its decision in *Silverthorne Lumber Co.* v. *U.S.* (1920).[11] The case against the Silverthornes, owners of a lumberyard, was built on evidence that was illegally seized. Although the tainted evidence was itself not used in court, its "fruits" (later evidence that derived from the illegal seizure) were and the Silverthornes were convicted. The Supreme Court overturned the decision, holding that any evidence that derives from a seizure that was in itself illegal cannot be used at trial.

> The public safety exception [to the exclusionary rule] was intended to protect the police, as well as the public, from danger.
> —*U.S.* v. *Brady* (1987)

The *Silverthorne* case articulated a new principle of due process that today we call the **fruit of the poisonous tree doctrine**. This doctrine is potentially far reaching. Complex cases developed after years of police investigative effort may be ruined if defense attorneys are able to demonstrate that the prosecution's case was originally based on a search or seizure that violated due process. In such cases, it is likely that all evidence will be declared "tainted" and will become useless.

▼ A female officer patting down a suspect. The legal environment surrounding the police helps ensure proper official conduct. In a stop like this, inappropriate behavior on the part of the officer can later become the basis for civil or criminal action against the officer and the police department. What might constitute inappropriate behavior?

Hill Street Studios/Glow Images

Protective Searches

Practically speaking, most police searches are conducted without a warrant and are referred to as warrantless searches. One especially important Warren-era case, that of *Chimel* v. *California* (1969),[12] involved both arrest and a **warrantless search** by local law enforcement officers. Ted Chimel was convicted of the burglary of a coin shop based on evidence gathered at his home, where he was arrested. Officers, armed with an arrest warrant but not a search warrant, took Chimel into custody when they arrived at his residence and then searched his entire three-bedroom house, including the attic, a small workshop, and the garage. Although officers realized that the search might be challenged in court, they justified it by claiming that it was conducted not so much to uncover evidence but as part of the arrest process. Searches that are conducted incident to arrest, they argued, are necessary for the officers' protection and should not require a search warrant. Coins taken from the burglarized coin shop were found in various places in Chimel's residence, including the garage, and were presented as evidence against him at trial.

Chimel's appeal eventually reached the U.S. Supreme Court, which ruled that the search of Chimel's residence, although incident to arrest, became invalid when it went beyond the person arrested and the area subject to that person's "immediate

TABLE 5-2
Implications of *Chimel* v. *California* (1969)

What Arresting Officers May Search
The defendant
The physical area within easy reach of the defendant

Valid Reasons for Conducting a Search
To protect the arresting officers
To prevent evidence from being destroyed
To keep the defendant from escaping

When a Search Becomes Illegal
When it goes beyond the defendant and the area within the defendant's immediate control
When it is conducted for other than a valid reason

control." The thrust of the Court's decision was that searches during arrest can be made to protect arresting officers but that without a search warrant, their scope must be strongly circumscribed. In other words, a search that is incidental to arrest is extremely limited in scope and only applies to a search of the suspect and the immediate vicinity. During such a search, officers may not move the suspect around to widen the geographic scope of the search (e.g., a suspect arrested in the kitchen can't be walked around his house as a pretext to search each room). The legal implications of *Chimel* v. *California* are summarized in Table 5-2.

Since the early days of the exclusionary rule, other court decisions have highlighted the fact that "the Fourth Amendment protects people, not places."[13] In other words, although the commonly heard claim that "a person's home is his or her castle" has a great deal of validity within the context of constitutional law, people can have a reasonable expectation to privacy in "homes" of many descriptions. Apartments, duplex dwellings, motel rooms—even the cardboard boxes or makeshift tents of the homeless— can all become protected places under the Fourth Amendment. In *Minnesota* v. *Olson* (1990),[14] for example, the U.S. Supreme Court extended the protection against warrantless searches to overnight guests residing in the home of another. The capacity to claim the protection of the Fourth Amendment, said the Court, depends on whether the *person* who makes that claim has a legitimate expectation of privacy in the place searched.

In 1998, in the case of *Minnesota* v. *Carter*,[15] the Court held that for a defendant to be entitled to Fourth Amendment protection, "he must demonstrate that he personally has an expectation of privacy in the place searched, and that his expectation is reasonable." The Court noted that "the extent to which the Amendment protects people may depend upon where those people are. While an overnight guest may have a legitimate expectation of privacy in someone else's home . . . one who is merely present with the consent of the householder may not." Hence, an appliance repair person visiting a residence is unlikely to be accorded privacy protection while on the job.

In 2006, in the case of *Georgia* v. *Randolph*,[16] the Court ruled that police officers may not enter a home to conduct a warrantless search if one resident gives permission but another refuses. The *Randolph* ruling was a narrow one and centered on the stated refusal by a physically present co-occupant to permit warrantless entry in the absence of evidence of physical abuse or other circumstances that might otherwise justify an immediate police entry.[17] In 2014, in the case of *Fernandez* v. *California*, the Court clarified it's ruling in *Randolph* by finding that consent to search may be given by a remaining resident after another has been removed.[18]

Finally, in 2013, in the case of *Bailey* v. *U.S.*, the Court limited the power of police to detain people who are away from their homes when police conduct a search of their residence, unless they have probable cause for an arrest.[19] One expert commenting on *Bailey* noted that "if you allow this, then whenever you do a search, people associated with that home could be arrested, no matter where they are, and that just goes too far."[20]

fruit of the poisonous tree doctrine
A legal principle that excludes from introduction at trial any evidence later developed as a result of an illegal search or seizure.

warrantless search
An examination by police of a person, place, or thing without a written judicial order authorizing that activity.

Follow the author's tweets about the latest crime and justice news @schmalleger

► Police officers examining suspected controlled substances after a raid. The exclusionary rule means that illegally gathered evidence cannot be used later in court, requiring that police officers pay close attention to how they gather and handle evidence. How did the exclusionary rule come into being?

Chris O'Meara/AP Images

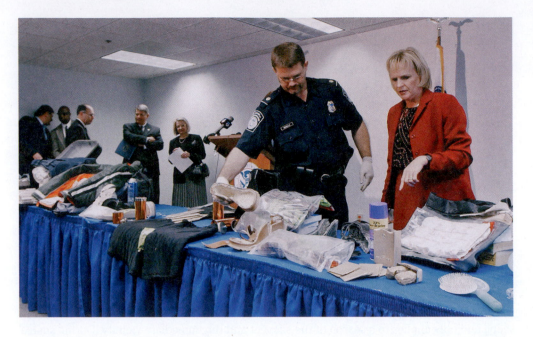

🐦 Follow the author's tweets about the latest crime and justice news @schmalleger

Judicial Philosophy and the U.S. Supreme Court

As you read through this chapter, you will encounter descriptions of numerous U.S. Supreme Court opinions. It is important to realize that our theme of individual rights versus the need for public safety and security has manifested itself over time in important decision made by the Court. Sometimes, for example, the Court has generally been on the side of public safety needs, while at other times, a concern for individual rights has been its guiding principle. The philosophy of the Court is often associated with the historical era during which decisions were rendered. For convenience, we can identify these eras using the names of Chief Justices, and the time periods during which they led the Court.

The Warren Court (1953–1969)

Before the 1960s, the U.S. Supreme Court intruded only infrequently on the overall operation of the criminal justice system at the state and local levels. As one author has observed, however, the 1960s were a time of youthful idealism, and "without the distraction of a depression or world war, individual liberties were examined at all levels of society."[21]

Although the exclusionary rule became an overriding consideration in federal law enforcement from the time that it was first defined by the Supreme Court in the *Weeks* case in 1914, it was not until 1961 that the Court, under Chief Justice Earl Warren, decided a case that was to change the face of American law enforcement forever. That case, *Mapp* v. *Ohio* (1961),[22] made the exclusionary rule applicable to criminal prosecutions at the state level. Beginning with the now-famous *Mapp* case, the Warren Court (led by Chief Justice Earl Warren) charted a course that would guarantee nationwide recognition of individual rights, as it understood them, by agencies at all levels of the criminal justice system. Because of the decisions it rendered, the Warren Court became known as a liberal court (today, some would say it was "progressive"). Learn more about the case of *Mapp* v. *Ohio* at **http://tinyurl.com/66yotaz**.

The Burger Court (1969–1986)

Throughout the late 1970s and the early 1980s, the U.S. Supreme Court mirrored the nation's conservative tenor by distancing itself from some earlier decisions of the Warren Court. While the Warren Court embodied the individual-rights heyday in Court jurisprudence, Court decisions beginning in the 1970s were generally supportive of a "greater good era"—one in which the justices increasingly acknowledged the importance of social order and communal safety.

Under Chief Justice Warren E. Burger, the new Court adhered to the principle that criminal defendants who claimed violations of their due-process rights needed to bear most of the responsibility of showing that police went beyond the law in the performance of their duties.

The Rehnquist Court (1986–2005)

During the 1980s and 1990s, the United States underwent a strong swing toward conservatism, giving rise to a renewed concern with protecting the interests—financial and otherwise—of those who live within the law. The Reagan–Bush years, and the popularity of the two presidents who many thought embodied "old-fashioned" values, reflected the tenor of a nation seeking a return to "simpler," less volatile times.

During William Rehnquist's tenure as chief justice, the Court invoked a characteristically conservative approach to many important criminal justice issues—from limiting the exclusionary rule[23] and generally broadening police powers, to sharply limiting the opportunities for state prisoners to bring appeals in federal courts.[24] Preventive detention, "no-knock" police searches,[25] the death penalty,[26] and habitual offender statutes[27] (often known as three-strikes laws), all found decisive support under Chief Justice Rehnquist.[28] The particular cases in which the Court addressed these issues are discussed elsewhere in this text.

The Roberts Court (2005–Today)

Following Rehnquist's death in 2005, John G. Roberts, Jr., became the nation's 17th chief justice. Roberts had previously served as a judge on the U.S. Court of Appeals for the District of Columbia Circuit. The Roberts Court is known for its conservative nature, although many of the opinions it issues are closely divided, often by a 5–4 vote. Because the "swing vote"—especially in deciding issues of criminal procedure—is often cast by Associate Justice Anthony Kennedy, some commentators ruefully refer to today's court as "the Kennedy Court." The Court today is generally conservative in the area of crime and justice, but there have been some striking exceptions to that rule. Court observers have noted that "precedent and *stare decisis* are given little weight by the Roberts Court; it is a Court quite willing to change the law. . ."[29]

The Roberts Court's erosion of the exclusionary rule is especially important. In 2009, in a 5-to-4 decision, for example, the Court significantly modified the exclusionary rule. The case, *Herring* v. *U.S.*, has been called "the most important change in the exclusionary rule since *Mapp* v. *Ohio* applied it to the states in 1961."[30]

In *Herring*, the issue was whether the exclusionary rule applies when police officers commit an illegal search based on good-faith reliance on erroneous information from another jurisdiction. The Court held that the exclusionary rule did not apply when officers acted in good faith, and added that the rule should be used only as a "last resort" and is to be applied only in those instances where it will have significant additional deterrent effect on police misconduct. In effect, the Court held that the exclusionary rule may be used only if there is an intentional or reckless violation of Fourth Amendment rights, or if there are systemic police department violations with regard to searches and seizures.

Good-Faith Exceptions to the Exclusionary Rule

The Burger Court, which held sway from 1969 until 1986, "chipped away" at the strict application of the exclusionary rule originally set forth in the *Weeks* and *Silverthorne* cases. In the 1984 case of *U.S.* v. *Leon*,[31] the Court recognized what has come to be called the **good-faith exception** to the exclusionary rule. In this case, the Court modified the exclusionary rule to allow evidence that officers had seized in "reasonable good faith" to be used in court, even though the search was later ruled illegal. The suspect, Alberto Leon, was placed under surveillance for drug trafficking following a tip from a confidential informant. Burbank (California) Police Department investigators applied for a search warrant based on information gleaned from the surveillance, believing they were in compliance with the Fourth Amendment requirement that "no Warrants shall issue, but upon probable cause."

Probable cause is a tricky but important concept. Its legal criteria are based on facts and circumstances that would cause a reasonable person to believe that a particular other person has committed a specific crime. Before a warrant can be issued, police officers must satisfactorily demonstrate probable cause in a written affidavit to a magistrate[32]—a low-level judge who ensures that the police establish the probable cause needed for warrants to be obtained. Upon a demonstration of probable cause, the magistrate will issue a warrant authorizing law enforcement officers to effect an arrest or conduct a search.

In *U.S.* v. *Leon*, a warrant was issued, and a search of Leon's three residences yielded a large amount of drugs and other evidence. Although Leon was convicted of drug trafficking,

good-faith exception
An exception to the exclusionary rule. Law enforcement officers who conduct a search or who seize evidence on the basis of good faith (i.e., when they believe they are operating according to the dictates of the law) and who later discover that a mistake was made (perhaps in the format of the application for a search warrant) may still use the seized evidence in court.

probable cause
A set of facts and circumstances that would induce a reasonably intelligent and prudent person to believe that a particular other person has committed a specific crime. Also, reasonable grounds to make or believe an accusation. Probable cause refers to the necessary level of belief that would allow for police seizures (arrests) of individuals and full searches of dwellings, vehicles, and possessions.

Before a warrant can be issued, police officers must demonstrate probable cause.

a later ruling in a federal district court resulted in the suppression of evidence against him on the basis that the original affidavit prepared by the police had not, in the opinion of the reviewing court, been sufficient to establish probable cause.

The federal government petitioned the U.S. Supreme Court to consider whether evidence gathered by officers acting in good faith as to the validity of a warrant should fairly be excluded at trial. The good-faith exception was presaged in the first paragraph of the Court's written decision: "When law enforcement officers have acted in objective good faith or their transgressions have been minor, the magnitude of the benefit conferred on . . . guilty defendants offends basic concepts of the criminal justice system." Reflecting the renewed conservatism of the Burger Court, the justices found for the government and reinstated Leon's conviction.

In that same year, the Supreme Court case of *Massachusetts* v. *Sheppard* (1984)[33] further reinforced the concept of good faith. In the *Sheppard* case, officers executed a search warrant that failed to describe accurately the property to be seized. Although they were aware of the error, a magistrate had assured them that the warrant was valid. After the seizure was complete and a conviction had been obtained, the Massachusetts Supreme Judicial Court reversed the finding of the trial court. Upon appeal, the U.S. Supreme Court reiterated the good-faith exception and reinstated the original conviction.

The cases of *Leon* and *Sheppard* represented a clear reversal of the Warren Court's philosophy, and the trend continued with the 1987 case of *Illinois* v. *Krull.*[34] In *Krull*, the Court, now under the leadership of Chief Justice William H. Rehnquist, held that the good-faith exception applied to a warrantless search supported by state law even though the state statute was later found to violate the Fourth Amendment. Similarly, another 1987 Supreme Court case, *Maryland* v. *Garrison,*[35] supported the use of evidence obtained with a search warrant that was inaccurate in its specifics. In *Garrison*, officers had procured a warrant to search an apartment, believing it was the only dwelling on the building's third floor. After searching the entire floor, they discovered that it housed more than one apartment. Even so, evidence acquired in the search was held to be admissible based on the reasonable mistake of the officers.

The 1990 case of *Illinois* v. *Rodriguez*[36] further diminished the scope of the exclusionary rule. In *Rodriguez*, a badly beaten woman named Gail Fischer complained to police that she had been assaulted in a Chicago apartment. Fischer led police to the apartment—which she indicated she shared with the defendant—produced a key, and opened the door to the dwelling. Inside, investigators found the defendant, Edward Rodriguez, asleep on a bed, with drug paraphernalia and cocaine spread around him. Rodriguez was arrested and charged with assault and possession of a controlled substance.

> The touchstone of the Fourth Amendment is reasonableness. The Fourth Amendment does not proscribe all state-initiated searches and seizures. It merely proscribes those which are unreasonable.
>
> —*Florida* v. *Jimeno* (1991)

Upon appeal, Rodriguez demonstrated that Fischer had not lived with him for at least a month and argued that she could no longer be said to have legal control over the apartment. Hence, the defense claimed, Fischer had no authority to provide investigators with access to the dwelling. According to arguments made by the defense, the evidence, which had been obtained without a warrant, had not been properly seized. The Supreme Court disagreed, ruling that "even if Fischer did not possess common authority over the premises, there was no Fourth Amendment violation if the police *reasonably believed* at the time of their entry that Fischer possessed the authority to consent."

In 1995, in the case of *Arizona* v. *Evans,*[37] the U.S. Supreme Court created a "computer errors exception" to the exclusionary rule, holding that a traffic stop that led to the seizure of marijuana was legal even though officers conducted the stop based on an arrest warrant that should have been deleted from the computer database to which they had access. The arrest warrant reported to the officers by their computer had actually been quashed a few weeks earlier but, through the oversight of a court employee, had never been removed from the database.

In reaching its decision, the High Court reasoned that police officers could not be held responsible for a clerical error made by a court worker and concluded that the arresting officers had acted in good faith based on the information available to them at the time of the arrest. In addition, the majority opinion said that "the rule excluding evidence obtained without a warrant was intended to deter police misconduct, not mistakes by court employees." In 2009, in the previously mentioned case of *Herring* v. *U.S.,*[38] the Court reinforced its ruling in *Evans*, holding that "when police mistakes leading to an unlawful search are the result of isolated negligence . . . rather than systemic error or reckless disregard of constitutional requirements, the exclusionary rule does not apply." A general listing of established exceptions to the exclusionary rule, along with other investigative powers created by court precedent, is provided in Table 5-3.

TABLE 5-3
Selected Investigatory Activities Supported by Court Precedent

This Police Action	Is Supported By
An anonymous and uncorroborated tip can provide a sufficient basis for an officer's reasonable suspicion to make an investigative stop.	*Prado Navarette* v. *California* (2014)
Where multiple occupants are involved, the search of a dwelling is permissible without a warrant if one person living there consents after officers have removed another resident who objects.	*Fernandez* v. *California* (2014)
Arrest based on isolated clerical error	*Herring* v. *U.S.* (2009) *Arizona* v. *Evans* (1995)
Authority to enter and/or search an "open field" without a warrant	*U.S.* v. *Dunn* (1987) *Oliver* v. *U.S.* (1984) *Hester* v. *U.S.* (1924)
Authority to search incident to arrest and/or to conduct a protective sweep in conjunction with an in-home arrest	*Maryland* v. *Buie* (1990) *U.S.* v. *Edwards* (1974) *Chimel* v. *California* (1969)
Gathering of incriminating evidence during interrogation in noncustodial circumstances	*Yarborough* v. *Alvarado* (2004) *Thompson* v. *Keohane* (1996) *Stansbury* v. *California* (1994) *U.S.* v. *Mendenhall* (1980) *Beckwith* v. *U.S.* (1976)
Gathering of incriminating evidence during *Miranda*-less custodial interrogation	*Montejo* v. *Louisiana* (2009) *U.S.* v. *Patane* (2004)
Inevitable discovery of evidence	*Nix* v. *Williams* (1984)
"No-knock" searches or quick entry	*Brigham City* v. *Stuart* (2006) *Hudson* v. *Michigan* (2006) *U.S.* v. *Barnes* (2003) *Richards* v. *Wisconsin* (1997) *Wilson* v. *Arkansas* (1995)
Prompt action in the face of threat to public or personal safety or destruction of evidence	*U.S.* v. *Banks* (2003) *Borchardt* v. *U.S.* (1987) *New York* v. *Quarles* (1984) *Warden* v. *Hayden* (1967)
Seizure of evidence in good faith, even in the face of some exclusionary rule violations	*Illinois* v. *Krull* (1987) *U.S.* v. *Leon* (1984)
Seizure of evidence in plain view	*Horton* v. *California* (1990) *Coolidge* v. *New Hampshire* (1971) *Harris* v. *U.S.* (1968)
Stop and frisk/request personal identification	*Arizona* v. *Johnson* (2009) *Hiibel* v. *Sixth Judicial District Court of Nevada* (2004) *Terry* v. *Ohio* (1968)
Use of police informants in jail cells	*Arizona* v. *Fulminante* (1991) *Illinois* v. *Perkins* (1990) *Kuhlmann* v. *Wilson* (1986)
Warrantless naked-eye aerial observation of open areas and/or greenhouses	*Florida* v. *Riley* (1989) *California* v. *Ciraolo* (1986)
Warrantless search incident to a lawful arrest	*U.S.* v. *Rabinowitz* (1950)
Warrantless seizure of abandoned materials and refuse	*California* v. *Greenwood* (1988)
Warrantless vehicle search where probable cause exists to believe that the vehicle contains contraband and/or that the occupants have been lawfully arrested	*Thornton* v. *U.S.* (2004) *Ornelas* v. *U.S.* (1996) *California* v. *Acevedo* (1991) *California* v. *Carney* (1985) *U.S.* v. *Ross* (1982) *New York* v. *Belton* (1981) *Carroll* v. *U.S.* (1925)

Source: Pearson-Education, Inc.

The Plain-View Doctrine

Police officers have the opportunity to begin investigations or to confiscate evidence, without a warrant, based on what they find in **plain view** and open to public inspection. The plain-view doctrine was succinctly stated in the U.S. Supreme Court case of *Harris* v. *U.S.* (1968),[39] in which a police officer inventorying an impounded vehicle discovered evidence of a robbery.[40] In the *Harris* case, the Court ruled that "objects falling in the plain view of an officer who has a right to be in the position to have that view are subject to seizure and may be introduced in evidence."[41]

The plain-view doctrine is applicable in common situations, such as crimes in progress, fires, accidents, and other emergencies. A police officer responding to a call for assistance, for example, might enter a residence intending to provide aid to an injured person and find drugs or other contraband in plain view. If so, the officer would be within his or her legitimate authority to confiscate the materials and to effect an arrest if the owner can be identified.

However, the plain-view doctrine applies only to sightings by the police under legal circumstances—that is, in places where the police have a legitimate right to be and, typically, only if the sighting was coincidental. Similarly, the incriminating nature of the evidence seized must have been "immediately apparent" to the officers making the seizure.[42] If officers conspired to avoid the necessity for a search warrant by helping to create a plain-view situation through surveillance, duplicity, or other means, the doctrine likely would not apply.

The plain-view doctrine was restricted by later federal court decisions. In the 1982 case of *U.S.* v. *Irizarry*,[43] the First Circuit Court of Appeals held that officers could not move objects to gain a view of evidence otherwise hidden from view. In the Supreme Court case of *Arizona* v. *Hicks* (1987),[44] the requirement that evidence be in plain view, without requiring officers (who did not have a warrant but who had been invited into a residence) to move or dislodge objects, was reiterated.

Most evidence seized under the plain-view doctrine is discovered "inadvertently"—that is, by accident.[45] However, in 1990, the U.S. Supreme Court ruled in the case of *Horton* v. *California*[46] that "even though inadvertence *is* a characteristic of most legitimate 'plain view' seizures, it is not a necessary condition."[47] In the *Horton* case, a warrant was issued authorizing the search of Terry Brice Horton's home for stolen jewelry. The affidavit, completed by the officer who requested the warrant, alluded to an Uzi submachine gun and a stun gun—weapons purportedly used in the jewelry robbery. It did not request that those weapons be listed on the search warrant. Officers searched the defendant's home but did not find the stolen jewelry. They did, however, seize a number of weapons, among them an Uzi, two stun guns, and a .38-caliber revolver. Horton was convicted of robbery in a trial in which the seized weapons were introduced into evidence. He appealed his conviction, claiming that officers had reason to believe that the weapons were in his home at the time of the search, so they were not seized inadvertently. His appeal was rejected by the Court. As a result of the *Horton* case, inadvertence is no longer considered a condition necessary to ensure the legitimacy of a seizure that results when evidence other than that listed in a search warrant is discovered. See CJ Exhibit 5–1 for more on evidence and the plain-view doctrine.

Plain-view searches present a special problem in the area of electronic evidence (which is discussed in more detail later in this chapter). If, let's say, a police officer obtains a warrant to seize and search a computer that he suspects was used to commit a particular crime, he then has easy access to other documents and information stored on that computer. An officer conducting a fraud investigation, for example, might obtain a warrant to seize a personal computer, but then will need to examine individual files on it in order to determine

plain view
A legal term describing the ready visibility of objects that might be seized as evidence during a search by police in the absence of a search warrant specifying the seizure of those objects. To lawfully seize evidence in plain view, officers must have a legal right to be in the viewing area and must have cause to believe that the evidence is somehow associated with criminal activity.

Emergencies may justify a police officer's decision to search or enter premises without a warrant.

Follow the author's tweets about the latest crime and justice news @schmalleger

---

CJ Exhibit 5–1
Plain-View Requirements

Following the opinion of the U.S. Supreme Court in the case of *Horton* v. *California* (1990), items seized under the plain-view doctrine may be admissible as evidence in a court of law if *both* of the following conditions are met:

1. The officer who seized the evidence was in the viewing area lawfully.
2. The officer had probable cause to believe that the evidence was somehow associated with criminal activity.

which ones (if any) are related to the investigation. If, however, he discovers pirated videos stored on the machine, he can then generally charge the owner of the computer with illegally copying the digital media because it is protected by copyright law. Consequently, some legal experts have called for limiting the range of potential types of prosecution available in such cases—and confining them to the offense specified in the original warrant.[48] That no such limitations are currently in place has prompted some commentators to propose "statutory solutions eliminating plain view for computer searches."[49]

Emergency Searches of Property and Emergency Entry

Certain emergencies may justify a police officer's decision to search or enter premises without a warrant. In 2006, for example, in the case of *Brigham City* v. *Stuart*,[50] the Court recognized the need for emergency warrantless entries under certain circumstances when it ruled that police officers "may enter a home without a warrant when they have an objectively reasonable basis for believing that an occupant is seriously injured or imminently threatened with such injury." The case involved police entry into a private home to break up a fight.

According to the Legal Counsel Division of the Federal Bureau of Investigation (FBI), there are three threats that "provide justification for emergency warrantless action."[51] They are clear dangers (1) to life, (2) of escape, and (3) of the removal or destruction of evidence. Any one of these situations may create an exception to the Fourth Amendment's requirement of a search warrant.

Emergency searches, or those conducted without a warrant when special needs arise, are legally termed *exigent circumstances searches*. When emergencies necessitate a quick search of premises, however, law enforcement officers are responsible for demonstrating that a dire situation existed that justified their actions. Failure to do so successfully in court will, of course, taint any seized evidence and make it unusable.

The U.S. Supreme Court first recognized the need for emergency searches in 1967 in the case of *Warden* v. *Hayden*.[52] In that case, the Court approved the warrantless search of a residence following reports that an armed robber had fled into the building, saying that "the Fourth Amendment does not require police officers to delay in the course of an investigation if to do so would gravely endanger their lives or the lives of others."[53]

A 1990 decision, rendered in the case of *Maryland* v. *Buie*,[54] extended the authority of police to search locations in a house where a potentially dangerous person could hide while an arrest warrant is being served. The *Buie* decision was meant primarily to protect investigators from potential danger and can apply even when officers lack a warrant, probable cause, or even reasonable suspicion.

emergency search
A search conducted by the police without a warrant, which is justified on the basis of some immediate and overriding need, such as public safety, the likely escape of a dangerous suspect, or the removal or destruction of evidence.

◀ Tarpon Springs, Florida, sheriff's deputies talk to a person inside a home. How might the plain-view doctrine apply to this situation? How would you explain the concept of plain view?
Jim Damaske/ZUMA Press/Newscom

In 1995, in the case of *Wilson* v. *Arkansas*,[55] the U.S. Supreme Court ruled that police officers generally must knock and announce their identity before entering a dwelling or other premises, even when armed with a search warrant. Under certain emergency circumstances, however, exceptions may be made, and officers may not need to knock or to identify themselves before entering.[56] In *Wilson*, the Court added that the Fourth Amendment requirement that searches be reasonable "should not be read to mandate a rigid rule of announcement that ignores countervailing law enforcement interests." Officers need not announce themselves, the Court said, when suspects may be in the process of destroying evidence, officers are pursuing a recently escaped arrestee, or officers' lives may be endangered by such an announcement. Because the *Wilson* case involved an appeal from a drug dealer who was apprehended by police officers who entered her unlocked house while she was flushing marijuana down a toilet, some said that it establishes a "drug-law exception" to the knock-and-announce requirement.

In 1997, in *Richards* v. *Wisconsin*,[57] the Supreme Court clarified its position on "no-knock" exceptions, saying that individual courts have the duty in each case to "determine whether the facts and circumstances of the particular entry justified dispensing with the requirement." The Court went on to say that "[a] 'no knock' entry is justified when the police have a reasonable suspicion that knocking and announcing their presence, under the particular circumstances, would be dangerous or futile, or that it would inhibit the effective investigation of the crime." The Court noted, "This standard strikes the appropriate balance between the legitimate law enforcement concerns at issue in the execution of search warrants and the individual privacy interests affected by no knock entries."

In 2001, in the case of *Illinois* v. *McArthur*,[58] the U.S. Supreme Court ruled that police officers with probable cause to believe that a home contains contraband or evidence of criminal activity may reasonably prevent a suspect found outside the home from reentering it while they apply for a search warrant. In 2003, in a case involving drug possession, the Court held that a 15- to 20-second wait after officers knocked, announced themselves, and requested entry was sufficient to satisfy the Fourth Amendment requirements.[59]

In the 2006 case of *Hudson* v. *Michigan*,[60] the Court surprised many when it ruled that evidence found by police officers who enter a home to execute a warrant without first following the knock-and-announce requirement can be used at trial despite that constitutional violation. In the words of the Court, "The interests protected by the knock-and-announce rule include human life and limb (because an unannounced entry may provoke violence from a surprised resident), property (because citizens presumably would open the door upon an announcement, whereas a forcible entry may destroy it), and privacy and dignity of the sort that can be offended by a sudden entrance." But, said the Court, "the rule has never protected one's interest in preventing the government from seeing or taking evidence described in a warrant." The justices reasoned that the social costs of strictly adhering to the knock-and-announce rule are considerable and may include "the grave adverse consequence that excluding relevant incriminating evidence always entails—the risk of releasing dangerous criminals." In a ruling that some said signaled a new era of lessened restraints on the police, the Court's majority opinion said that because the interests violated by ignoring the knock-and-announce rule "have nothing to do with the seizure of the evidence, the exclusionary rule is inapplicable."

In 2011, in the case of *Kentucky* v. *King*, the U.S. Supreme Court overruled a Kentucky Supreme Court decision and found that Lexington, Kentucky, police officers had legally entered a suspected drug dealer's apartment without a warrant when they smelled marijuana outside the residence.[61] After knocking loudly and announcing their presence, the officers heard noises coming from inside the apartment that they believed indicated the destruction of evidence. They then kicked in the door and saw evidence of drug use in plain view. Writing for the majority, Justice Samuel Alito said, "Occupants who choose not to stand on their constitutional rights but instead elect to attempt to destroy evidence have only themselves to blame for the warrantless exigent-circumstances search that may ensue." Learn more about another type of exception to the exclusionary rule via **https://www. justicestudies.com/pubs/emergency.pdf**.

CJ Careers
School Resource Officer (SRO)

Name: Jessica L. Rezak

Position: School Resource Officer, Firearms Instructor

College attended: Colorado Christian University (BS)

Major: Criminal Justice

Year hired: 2009

Please give a brief description of your job: I am responsible for being present in my assigned schools along with handling criminal offenses and other issues arising within the schools. Being present in the school has been a great way of building rapports with students and parents.

What appealed to you most about the position when you applied for it? I had been a patrol officer for approximately 6 years prior to applying for the School Resource Officer position. I was looking for a change and although hesitant I applied for the position. Dealing and interacting with school staff, students and parents on a positive note was what appealed to me the most. The schedule was also appealing as I worked swing shifts and weekends for years prior.

How would you describe the interview process? The interview process was minimal. I completed a letter of interest and met with the Chief of Police for an interview. This may seem unconventional; however, my department is small so the Chief interviewed me, then I met with the rest of the command staff to discuss my interest.

▲ Jessica L. Rezak, SRO

What is a typical day like? I start my day by working traffic and being present during the time students are arriving at school. I alternate which schools I am at daily unless there is a specific concern at a certain school. I then begin my rounds to each of my schools. I will show my presence during passing periods, meet with school staff, and take care of any criminal complaints presented to me at that time. I visit and help in Special Education classes on a daily basis. I am also responsible for helping the district with lockdown and shelter in place drills and pointing out any safety concerns that can be addressed.

What qualities/characteristics are most helpful for this job? A successful school resource officer needs to know how to communicate with juveniles and parents. A SRO also needs to know district and department policies when it comes to dealing with juveniles.

What is a typical starting salary? Between $38,000 and $48,000.

What career advice would you give someone in college beginning studies in criminal justice? Classroom instruction will provide insight into the career of a police officer, and some basic understanding. I would highly recommend that students interested in becoming a police officer do ride-alongs with police agencies to gain insight into their chosen career.

Anticipatory Warrants

Anticipatory warrants are search warrants issued on the basis of probable cause to believe that evidence of a crime, while not currently at the place described, will likely be there when the warrant is executed. Such warrants anticipate the presence of contraband or other evidence of criminal culpability but do not claim that the evidence is present at the time that the warrant is requested or issued.

Anticipatory warrants are no different in principle from ordinary search warrants. They require an issuing magistrate to determine that it is probable that contraband, evidence of a crime, or a fugitive will be on the described premises when the warrant is executed.

The constitutionality of anticipatory warrants was affirmed in 2006, in the U.S. Supreme Court case of *U.S.* v. *Grubbs*. In *Grubbs*,[62] an anticipatory search warrant had been issued for Grubbs's house based on a federal officer's affidavit stating that the warrant would not be executed until a parcel containing a videotape of child pornography—which Grubbs had ordered from an undercover postal inspector—was received at and physically taken into Grubbs's residence. After the package was delivered, the anticipatory search warrant was executed, the videotape seized, and Grubbs arrested.

anticipatory warrant
A search warrant issued on the basis of probable cause to believe that evidence of a crime, while not currently at the place described, will likely be there when the warrant is executed.

Detention and Arrest

Officers seize not only property but people as well, a process referred to as *arrest*. Most people think of arrest in terms of what they see on popular TV crime shows: The suspect is chased, subdued, and "cuffed" after committing some loathsome act in view of the camera. Some arrests do occur that way. In reality, however, most arrests are far more mundane.

4 Describe arrest and types of searches.

arrest
The act of taking an adult or juvenile into physical custody by authority of law for the purpose of charging the person with a criminal offense, a delinquent act, or a status offense, terminating with the recording of a specific offense.

> You can only protect your liberties in this world by protecting the other man's freedom.
>
> —Clarence Darrow
> (1857–1938)

investigative detention
A temporary seizure of an individual by a police officer for investigative purposes. Also, police custody, short of arrest, that is based on reasonable suspicion. Unlike arrest, the amount of time a person may be detained depends upon how long it would reasonably take to conduct an investigation of the facts at hand or to finish police business (i.e., to issue a traffic ticket).

In 1980, in the case of *U.S.* v. *Mendenhall*,[63] Justice Potter Stewart set forth the "free to leave" test, and wrote that an **arrest** occurs whenever a law enforcement officer restricts a person's freedom to leave. Under such a scenario, the officer may not yell, "You're under arrest!" No *Miranda* warnings may be offered, and in fact, the suspect may not even consider himself or herself to be in custody. As *Mendenhall* recognized, arrests, and the decisions to enforce them, evolve as the situations between officers and suspects develop. A situation usually begins with polite conversation and a request by the officer for information. Only when the suspect tries to leave and tests the limits of the police response may the suspect discover that he or she is really in custody. Stewart wrote, "A person has been 'seized' within the meaning of the Fourth Amendment only if in view of all the circumstances surrounding the incident, a reasonable person would have believed that he was not free to leave." The "free to leave" test has been repeatedly adopted by the Court as the test for a seizure. In 1994, in the case of *Stansbury* v. *California*,[64] the Court once again used such a test in determining the point at which an arrest had been made. In *Stansbury*, where the focus was on the interrogation of a suspected child molester and murderer, the Court ruled, "In determining whether an individual was in custody, a court must examine all of the circumstances surrounding the interrogation, but the ultimate inquiry is simply whether there [was] a formal arrest or restraint on freedom of movement of the degree associated with a formal arrest." More recently, in 2012, Justice Samuel A. Alito, Jr., in the case of *Howes* v. *Fields*, explained that "custody is a term of art that specifies circumstances that are thought generally to present a serious danger of coercion."[65]

Youth and inexperience do not automatically undermine a reasonable person's ability to assess when someone is free to leave. In the 2004 case of *Yarborough* v. *Alvarado*,[66] the U.S. Supreme Court found that a 17-year-old boy's 2-hour interrogation in a police station without a *Miranda* advisement was not custodial, even though the boy confessed to his involvement in a murder and was later arrested. The boy, said the Court, had not actually been in police custody even though he was in a building used by the police for questioning, because actions taken by the interviewing officer indicated that the juvenile had been free to leave. Whether a person is actually free to leave, said the Court, can only be determined by examining the totality of the circumstances surrounding the interrogation.[67]

The 2005 U.S. Supreme Court case of *Muehler* v. *Mena*[68] made clear that an officer's authority to detain occupants of a dwelling incident to the execution of a valid search warrant is absolute and unqualified and does not require any justification beyond the warrant itself—even when the occupants are not suspected of any wrongdoing. In other words, officers who are conducting a lawful search under the authority of a warrant may detain individuals found occupying the premises being searched in order to prevent flights in the event incriminating evidence is found, to minimize the risk of harm to the officers, and simply to facilitate the search itself.[69]

The distinction between *arrest* and *detention* is a very important one. In a refinement of the *Mendenhall* decision, the U.S. Supreme Court in the 2015 case of *Rodriguez* v. *U.S.* made clear that **investigative detention** is not the same as arrest. In *Rodriguez*, the Court held that police officers may detain an individual as long as it "reasonably takes police to conduct the investigation." For example, if a motorist has been stopped for speeding, then a police officer can detain him or her for the amount of time that it would take a reasonable officer to check your driver's license, insurance, call in to the dispatcher to validate your license plate number, write the ticket, and complete any associated administrative tasks. He might also detain you while he visually examines your vehicle to see if its lights are functioning properly. Unless he or she has probable cause to detain the driver any longer (such as smelling the odor of drugs wafting from the vehicle), then the detention must end and the driver will be free to go. During the time that the person has been detained, according to the Court, he was not under arrest.

Arrests that follow the questioning of a suspect are the most common type of arrest. When the decision to arrest is reached, the officer has come to the conclusion that a crime has been committed and that the suspect is probably the one who committed it. The presence of these elements constitutes the probable cause needed for an arrest. Probable cause is the minimum standard necessary for an arrest under any circumstances.

CJ News
Supreme Court Says Police Need Warrant for GPS Tracking

In 2014, NYPD officers tracked a pharmacy robber using a GPS device that they had hidden in a bottle of prescription painkillers that he had stolen. The robber, Scott Kato, 45, had a long criminal record and was soon cornered when his car was stopped in traffic. He was shot dead after he pointed a handgun at officers who surrounded the vehicle. Because the GPS device was hidden in a decoy bottle, its use as crime-fighting technology was legal. However, until recently, law enforcement officers did not need a warrant to attach a global positioning system (GPS) tracking device to a suspect's car and see where it went.

After all, the reasoning went, police don't need a warrant to get into their cars and follow suspects through the streets and, some argued, GPS systems are basically doing the same thing, only digitally.

The Supreme Court, however, in the 2012 case of *U.S.* v. *Jones,* decided that GPS devices are far more intrusive than just tailing a car. In *Jones,* the justices voted 9–0 that the FBI needed a warrant when attaching a GPS device to a suspected drug dealer's vehicle.

"GPS monitoring generates a precise, comprehensive record of a person's public movement that reflects a wealth of detail about her familial, political, religious and sexual associations," wrote Justice Sonia Sotomayor.

The *Jones* case was the first time the court dealt with the use of global positioning systems in law enforcement, which became a common police tool only in recent years.

In Jones, the Court's majority ruled that when FBI agents attached the GPS device, they were in effect trespassing. Their opinion held that a car cannot be touched, in the same way that a house cannot be entered, even when that car is on public streets.

But Justice Samuel Alito, speaking for the four-member minority, contended that the real violation was not touching the car, but was in violating the driver's expectation of privacy. This is part of a legal theory the Court has been applying for 45 years, which holds that the Fourth Amendment "protects people, not places," he wrote.

Alito explained there would be future cases when the majority's concept of trespassing would no longer apply to high-tech tracking. For instance, when a car comes with a GPS device already installed in it, the police do not even have to touch the car to gather information from the device. He added that more than 322 million cell phones in the nation have chips in them allowing phone companies to track customers' locations. Again, without touching the cell phone, police can simply obtain tracking data from the companies (see *Carpenter* v. *U.S.* later in this chapter).

Justice Sotomayor wrote that it could take a while for the courts to sort out all the implications of tracking technology. "In the course of carrying out mundane tasks," she wrote, Americans disclose which phone numbers they dial, which URLs they visit and "the books, groceries and medications they purchase."

▲ A Las Vegas police officer tracks a suspect vehicle using GPS tracking technology. What role did such devices play in the 2012 U.S. Supreme Court case of *U.S.* v. *Jones*? Following the justices' reasoning in that case, under what circumstances can the police use GPS devices to track suspects' vehicles?

Michael Matthews/Police Images/Alamy Stock Photo

Following *U.S.* v. *Jones,* the FBI was forced to turn off about 3,000 GPS tracking devices that it had in operation. In some cases, the agency had to get court orders to briefly turn the devices back on so they could be located and retrieved.

Police can still use GPS trackers if they get a search warrant; but Andrew Weissmann, the FBI's chief legal counsel, said that will be tricky. Officers now need to first justify their suspicions to a judge, showing "probable cause" and the need to use such a device.

REFERENCES
"Court Rules GPS Requires Warrant," *Associated Press,* November 4, 2013.

"FBI Still Struggling with Supreme Court's GPS Ruling," *NPR,* March 21, 2012, http://www.npr.org/2012/03/21/149011887/fbi-still-struggling-with-supreme-courts-gps-ruling; Joseph Goldstein and Michael Schwirtz, "Robbery Suspect Tracked by GPS and Killed," *The New York Times,* May 16, 2014, http://nyti.ms/S1ryFu (accessed January 5, 2015).

"Justices Rein in Police on GPS Trackers," *Wall Street Journal,* January 24, 2012, http://online.wsj.com/article/SB100014240529702038065045771788118008733358.html.

"Supreme Court: GPS Devices Equivalent of a Search, Police Must Get Warrant," *Fox News,* January 23, 2012, http://www.foxnews.com/politics/2012/01/23/supreme-court-gps-devices-equivalent-search-police-must-get-warrant-469182072/.

Arrests may also occur when an officer comes upon a crime in progress. Such situations often require apprehension of the offender to ensure the safety of the public. Most arrests made during crimes in progress, however, are for misdemeanors rather than felonies. In fact, many states do not allow arrest for a misdemeanor unless it is committed in the presence of an officer, since visible crimes in progress clearly provide the probable cause necessary for an arrest. In 2001, in a case that made headlines nationwide,[70] the U.S. Supreme Court upheld a warrantless arrest made by Lago Vista (Texas) Patrolman Bart Turek for a

🐦 Follow the author's tweets about the latest crime and justice news @schmalleger

Follow the author's tweets about the latest crime and justice news @schmalleger

seat-belt violation. In what many saw as an unreasonable exercise of discretion, Turek stopped and then arrested Gail Atwater, a young local woman whom he observed driving a pickup truck in which she and her two small children (ages three and five) were unbelted. Facts in the case showed that Turek verbally berated the woman after stopping her vehicle and that he handcuffed her, placed her in his squad car, and drove her to the local police station, where she was made to remove her shoes, jewelry, and eyeglasses and empty her pockets. Officers took her "mug shot" and placed her alone in a jail cell for about an hour, after which she was taken before a magistrate and released on $310 bond. Atwater was charged with a misdemeanor violation of Texas seat-belt law. She later pleaded no contest and paid a $50 fine. Soon afterward, she and her husband filed a Section 1983 lawsuit against the officer, his department, and the police chief, alleging that the actions of the officer violated Atwater's Fourth Amendment right to be free from unreasonable seizures. The Court, however, concluded that "the Fourth Amendment does not forbid a warrantless arrest for a minor criminal offense, such as a misdemeanor seatbelt violation punishable only by a fine."

Most jurisdictions allow arrest for a felony without a warrant when a crime is not in progress, as long as probable cause can be established; some, however, require a warrant. In those jurisdictions, arrest warrants are issued by magistrates when police officers can demonstrate probable cause. Magistrates will usually require that the officers seeking an arrest warrant submit a written affidavit outlining their reason for the arrest. In the case of *Payton* v. *New York* (1980),[71] the U.S. Supreme Court ruled that unless the suspect gives consent or an emergency exists, an arrest warrant is necessary if an arrest requires entry into a suspect's private residence.[72] In *Payton*, the justices held that "[a]bsent exigent circumstances," the "firm line at the entrance to the house . . . may not reasonably be crossed without a warrant." The Court reiterated its *Payton* holding in the 2002 case of *Kirk* v. *Louisiana*.[73] In *Kirk*, which involved an anonymous complaint about drug sales said to be taking place in the apartment of Kennedy Kirk, the justices reaffirmed their belief that "[t]he Fourth Amendment to the United States Constitution has drawn a firm line at the entrance to the home, and thus, the police need both probable cause to either arrest or search and exigent circumstances to justify a nonconsensual warrantless intrusion into private premises."

Searches Incident to Arrest

The U.S. Supreme Court has established a clear rule that police officers have the right to conduct a search of a person being arrested, regardless of gender, and to search the area under the arrestee's immediate control to protect themselves from attack.

This "rule of the game" regarding **search incident to an arrest** became firmly established in cases involving personal searches, such as the 1973 case of *U.S.* v. *Robinson*.[74] In *Robinson*, the Court upheld an officer's right to conduct a search without a warrant for purposes of personal protection and to use the fruits of the search when it turns up contraband. In the words of the Court, "A custodial arrest of a suspect based upon probable cause is a reasonable intrusion under the Fourth Amendment; that intrusion being lawful, a search incident to the arrest requires no additional jurisdiction."[75]

The Court's decision in *Robinson* reinforced an earlier ruling in *Terry* v. *Ohio* (1968)[76] involving a seasoned officer who conducted a pat-down search of two men whom he suspected were casing a store, about to commit a robbery. The arresting officer was a 39-year veteran of police work who testified that the men "did not look right." When he approached them, he suspected they might be armed. Fearing for his life, he quickly spun the men around, put them up against a wall, patted down their clothing, and found a gun on one of the men. The man, Terry, was later convicted in Ohio courts of carrying a concealed weapon.

Terry's appeal was based on the argument that the suspicious officer had no probable cause to arrest him and therefore no cause to search him. The search, he argued, was illegal, and the evidence obtained should not have been used against him. The Supreme Court disagreed, saying, "In view of these facts, we cannot blind ourselves to the need for law enforcement officers to protect themselves and other prospective victims of violence in situations where they may lack probable cause for an arrest."

The *Terry* case set the standard for a brief stop and frisk based on reasonable suspicion. Attorneys refer to such brief encounters as *Terry-type stops*. **Reasonable suspicion** can be

search incident to an arrest
A warrantless search of an arrested individual conducted to ensure the safety of the arresting officer. Because individuals placed under arrest may be in possession of weapons, courts have recognized the need for arresting officers to protect themselves by conducting an immediate search of arrestees without obtaining a warrant.

reasonable suspicion
The level of suspicion that would justify an officer in making further inquiry or in conducting further investigation. Reasonable suspicion may permit stopping a person for questioning or for a simple pat-down search. Also, a belief, based on a consideration of the facts at hand and on reasonable inferences drawn from those facts, that would induce an ordinarily prudent and cautious person under the same circumstances to conclude that criminal activity is taking place or that criminal activity has recently occurred. Reasonable suspicion is a *general* and reasonable belief that a crime is in progress or has occurred, whereas probable cause is a reasonable belief that a *particular* person has committed a *specific* crime.

defined as a belief, based on a consideration of the facts at hand and on reasonable inferences drawn from those facts, that would induce an ordinarily prudent and cautious person under the same circumstances to conclude that criminal activity is taking place or that criminal activity has recently occurred. It is the level of suspicion needed to justify an officer in making further inquiry or in conducting further investigation. Reasonable suspicion, which is a *general* and reasonable belief that a crime is in progress or has occurred, should be differentiated from probable cause.

Reasonable suspicion provides the basis for a brief investigative detention of a person, but is not enough for arrest. According to the courts, detention can last only for the amount of time that's reasonably sufficient for an officer to investigate the offense, question the person who was stopped, and conduct limited searches. Consequently, in 1991, 11 years after the *Mendenhall* decision, the Court accepted the common law definition of arrest, noting that "there must be either application of physical force (or the laying on of hands), or submission to the assertion of authority" for an arrest to have occurred. Probable cause, as noted earlier, is a reasonable belief that a *particular* person has committed a *specific* crime. It is important to note that the *Terry* case, for all the authority it conferred on officers, also made it clear that officers must have reasonable grounds for any stop and frisk that they conduct. Read more about the case of *Terry* v. *Ohio* at **http://tinyurl.com/yf2jhc2**.

In 1989, in the case of *U.S.* v. *Sokolow*,[77] the Supreme Court clarified the basis on which law enforcement officers, lacking probable cause to believe that a crime has occurred, may stop and briefly detain a person for investigative purposes. In *Sokolow*, the Court ruled that the legitimacy of such a stop must be evaluated according to a "totality of circumstances" criterion in which all aspects of the defendant's behavior, taken in concert, may provide the basis for a legitimate stop based on reasonable suspicion. In this case, the defendant, Andrew Sokolow, appeared suspicious to police because while traveling under an alias from Honolulu, he had paid $2,100 in $20 bills (from a large roll of money) for two airplane tickets after spending a surprisingly small amount of time in Miami. In addition, the defendant was obviously nervous and checked no luggage. A warrantless airport investigation by Drug Enforcement Administration (DEA) agents uncovered more than 1,000 grams of cocaine in the defendant's belongings. In upholding Sokolow's conviction, the Court ruled that although no single type of behavior was proof of illegal activity, all his actions together created circumstances under which suspicion of illegal activity was justified.

In 2002, the Court reinforced the *Sokolow* decision in *U.S.* v. *Arvizu* when it ruled that the "balance between the public interest and the individual's right to personal security"[78] "tilts in favor of a standard less than probable cause in brief investigatory stops of persons

◄ Plain-clothes police detectives searching drug suspects in Harlem, New York City. The courts have generally held that to protect themselves and the public, officers have the authority to search suspects being arrested. What are the limits of such searches?

Michael Matthews/Police Images/ Alamy Stock Photo

or vehicles . . . if the officer's action is supported by reasonable suspicion to believe that criminal activity may be afoot."[79] In the words of the Court, "This process allows officers to draw on their own experiences and specialized training to make inferences from and deductions about the cumulative information available."[80]

In 1993, in the case of *Minnesota* v. *Dickerson*,[81] the U.S. Supreme Court placed new limits on an officer's ability to seize evidence discovered during a pat-down search conducted for protective reasons when the search itself was based merely on suspicion and failed to immediately reveal the presence of a weapon. In this case, the high court ruled that "if an officer lawfully pats down a suspect's outer clothing and feels an object whose contour or mass makes its identity immediately apparent, there has been no invasion of the suspect's privacy beyond that already authorized by the officer's search for weapons." However, in *Dickerson*, the justices ruled that "the officer never thought that the lump was a weapon, but did not immediately recognize it as cocaine." The lump was determined to be cocaine only after the officer "squeezed, slid, and otherwise manipulated the pocket's contents." Hence, the Court held, the officer's actions in this case did not qualify under what might be called a "plain-feel" exception. In any case, said the Court, the search in *Dickerson* went far beyond what is permissible under *Terry*, where officer safety was the crucial issue. The Court summed up its ruling in *Dickerson* this way: "While *Terry* entitled [the officer] to place his hands on respondent's jacket and to feel the lump in the pocket, his continued exploration of the pocket after he concluded that it contained no weapon was unrelated to the sole justification for the search under *Terry*" and was therefore illegal.

Just as arrest must be based on probable cause, officers may not stop and question an unwilling citizen whom they have no reason to suspect of a crime. In the case of *Brown* v. *Texas* (1979),[82] two Texas law enforcement officers stopped the defendant and asked for identification. Ed Brown, they later testified, had not been acting suspiciously, nor did they think he might have a weapon. The stop was made simply because officers wanted to know who he was. Brown was arrested under a Texas statute that required a person to identify himself properly and accurately when asked to do so by peace officers. Eventually, his appeal reached the U.S. Supreme Court, which ruled that under the circumstances of the *Brown* case, a person "may not be punished for refusing to identify himself."

In the 2004 case of *Hiibel* v. *Sixth Judicial District Court of Nevada*,[83] however, the Court upheld Nevada's "stop-and-identify" law that requires a person to identify himself or herself to police if they encounter the person under circumstances that reasonably indicate that he or she "has committed, is committing or is about to commit a crime." The *Hiibel* case was an extension of the reasonable suspicion doctrine set forth earlier in *Terry*.

In *Smith* v. *Ohio* (1990),[84] the Court held that an individual has the right to protect his or her belongings from unwarranted police inspection. In *Smith*, the defendant was approached by two officers in plain clothes who observed that he was carrying a brown paper bag. The officers asked him to "come here a minute" and, when he kept walking, identified themselves as police officers. The defendant threw the bag onto the hood of his car and attempted to protect it from the officers' intrusion. Marijuana was found inside the bag, and the defendant was arrested. Because there was little reason to stop the suspect in this case and because control over the bag was not thought necessary for the officers' protection, the Court found that the Fourth Amendment protects both "the traveler who carries a toothbrush and a few articles of clothing in a paper bag" and "the sophisticated executive with the locked attaché case."

The following year, however, in what some Court observers saw as a turnabout, the Court ruled in *California* v. *Hodari D.* (1991)[85] mentioned earlier, that suspects who flee from the police and throw away evidence as they retreat may later be arrested based on the incriminating nature of the abandoned evidence. The significance of *Hodari* for future police action was highlighted by California prosecutors who pointed out that cases like *Hodari* occur "almost every day in this nation's urban areas."[86]

In 2000, the Court decided the case of William Wardlow.[87] Wardlow had fled upon seeing a caravan of police vehicles converge on an area of Chicago known for narcotics trafficking. Officers caught him, however, and conducted a pat-down search of his clothing for weapons, revealing a handgun. The officers arrested Wardlow on weapons charges, but his lawyer argued that police had acted illegally in stopping him because they did not have reasonable suspicion that he had committed an offense. The Illinois Supreme Court agreed with

Police work is the only profession that gives you the test first, then the lesson.

—Anonymous

CJ News
Supreme Court Says Police Need Warrants before Searching Cell Phones

In 2014, in the case of *Riley* v. *California*, the U.S. Supreme Court ruled that under most circumstances police officers are required to obtain a warrant before accessing and searching the data stored on a suspect's cell phone. In the words of the Court:

> . . . . Riley was stopped for a traffic violation, which eventually led to his arrest on weapons charges. An officer searching Riley incident to the arrest seized a cell phone from Riley's pants pocket. The officer accessed information on the phone and noticed the repeated use of a term associated with a street gang. At the police station two hours later, a detective specializing in gangs further examined the phone's digital contents. Based in part on photographs and videos that the detective found, the State charged Riley in connection with a shooting that had occurred a few weeks earlier and sought an enhanced sentence based on Riley's gang membership. Riley moved to suppress all evidence that the police had obtained from his cell phone. The trial court denied the motion, and Riley was convicted. The California Court of Appeal affirmed.

The Supreme Court held, however, that the police generally may not, without a warrant, search digital information on a cell phone seized from an individual who has been arrested.

Here's how the Court reasoned:

> Cell phones differ in both a quantitative and a qualitative sense from other objects that might be carried on an arrestee's person. Notably, modern cell phones have an immense storage capacity. Before cell phones, a search of a person was limited by physical realities and generally constituted only a narrow intrusion on privacy. But cell phones can store millions of pages of text, thousands of pictures, or hundreds of videos. This has several interrelated privacy consequences. First, a cell phone collects in one place many distinct types of information that reveal much more in combination than any isolated record. Second, the phone's capacity allows even just one type of information to convey far more than previously

possible. Third, data on the phone can date back for years. In addition, an element of pervasiveness characterizes cell phones but not physical records. A decade ago officers might have occasionally stumbled across a highly personal item such as a diary, but today many of the more than 90% of American adults who own cell phones keep on their person a digital record of nearly every aspect of their lives.

Four years later, in the 2018 case of *Carpenter* v. *U.S.*, the Supreme Court decided one of the most important cases in today's era of personal digital communications. In *Carpenter*, the FBI identified the cell phone numbers of several robbery suspects, and prosecutors were granted court orders to obtain the suspects' cell phone records. A lower court issued those orders based on a federal law pertaining to cellular providers, so the actions undertaken by the police in procuring Carpenters' phone records were technically not considered a Fourth Amendment Search (i.e., one based on probable cause). The records obtained by the police for Carpenter's phone allowed them to track his past movements over a 127 day period. Significantly, his phone was found to have been near four robbery locations at the time those robberies occurred, and he was soon convicted of the crime of robbery. Carpenter's attorneys, however, argued that the seizure of his phone records had been unlawful, as the court orders on which they were based had not been supported by probable cause. The Supreme Court agreed, and ruled that the seizure violated the Fourth Amendment of the United States Constitution. In the words of the Court, "The Government's acquisition of Carpenter's cell-site records was a Fourth Amendment search. The Fourth Amendment protects not only property interests but certain expectations of privacy as well. Thus, when an individual 'seeks to preserve something as private,' and his expectation of privacy is 'one that society is prepared to recognize as reasonable,' official intrusion into that sphere generally qualifies as a search and requires a warrant supported by probable cause."

References: Riley v. *California*, U.S. Supreme Court (decided June 25, 2014); and U.S. Supreme Court, *Carpenter* v. *U.S.* (decided June 22, 2018).

Wardlow's attorney, holding that "sudden flight in a high crime area does not create a reasonable suspicion justifying a *Terry* stop because flight may simply be an exercise of the right to 'go on one's way.'"[88] The case eventually reached the U.S. Supreme Court, which overturned the Illinois court, finding instead that the officers' actions did not violate the Fourth Amendment. In the words of the Court, "This case, involving a brief encounter between a citizen and a police officer on a public street, is governed by *Terry*, under which an officer who has a reasonable, articulable suspicion that criminal activity is afoot may conduct a brief, investigatory stop. While 'reasonable suspicion' is a less demanding standard than probable cause, there must be at least a minimal level of objective justification for the stop. An individual's presence in a 'high-crime area,' standing alone, is not enough to support a reasonable, particularized suspicion of criminal activity, but a location's characteristics are relevant in determining whether the circumstances are sufficiently suspicious to warrant further investigation. . . . In this case, moreover, it was also Wardlow's unprovoked flight that aroused the officers' suspicions. Nervous, evasive behavior is another pertinent factor in determining reasonable suspicion . . . and headlong flight is the consummate act of evasion."[89]

Emergency Searches of Persons

It is easy to imagine emergency situations in which officers may have to search people based on quick decisions: a person who matches the description of an armed robber, a woman who is found unconscious on the floor, a man who has what appears to be blood on his shoes. Such

🐦 Follow the author's tweets about the latest crime and justice news @schmalleger

searches can save lives by disarming fleeing felons or by uncovering a medical reason for an emergency situation. They may also prevent criminals from escaping or destroying evidence.

Emergency searches of persons, like those of premises, fall under the exigent circumstances exception to the warrant requirement of the Fourth Amendment. In the 1979 case of *Arkansas* v. *Sanders*,[90] the Supreme Court recognized the need for such searches "where the societal costs of obtaining a warrant, such as danger to law officers or the risk of loss or destruction of evidence, outweigh the reasons for prior recourse to a neutral magistrate."[91]

The 1987 case of *U.S.* v. *Borchardt*,[92] decided by the Fifth Circuit Court of Appeals, held that Ira Eugene Borchardt could be prosecuted for heroin uncovered during medical treatment, even though the defendant had objected to the treatment.

The Legal Counsel Division of the FBI provides the following guidelines for conducting emergency warrantless searches of individuals when the possible destruction of evidence is at issue.[93] (Keep in mind that there may be no probable cause to *arrest* the individual being searched.) All four conditions must apply:

1. There was probable cause at the time of the search to believe that there was evidence concealed on the person searched.
2. There was probable cause to believe an emergency threat of destruction of evidence existed at the time of the search.
3. The officer had no prior opportunity to obtain a warrant authorizing the search.
4. The action was no greater than necessary to eliminate the threat of destruction of evidence.

Vehicle Searches

Vehicles present a special law enforcement problem. They are highly mobile, and when a driver or an occupant is arrested, the need to search the vehicle may be immediate.

The first significant Supreme Court case involving an automobile was that of *Carroll* v. *U.S.*[94] in 1925. In the *Carroll* case, a divided Court ruled that a warrantless search of an automobile or other vehicle is valid if it is based on a reasonable belief that contraband is present. In 1964, however, in the case of *Preston* v. *U.S.*,[95] the limits of warrantless vehicle searches were defined. Preston was arrested for vagrancy and taken to jail. His vehicle was impounded, towed to the police garage, and later searched. Two revolvers were uncovered in the glove compartment, and more incriminating evidence was found in the trunk. Preston was convicted on weapons possession and other charges and eventually appealed to the U.S. Supreme Court. The Court held that the warrantless search of Preston's vehicle had occurred while the automobile was in secure custody and had therefore been illegal. Time and circumstances would have permitted acquisition of a warrant to conduct the search, the Court reasoned. Similarly, in 2009, the Court, in the case of *Arizona* v. *Gant*,[96] found that vehicle searches "incident to a recent occupant's arrest" cannot be authorized without a warrant if there is "no possibility the arrestee could gain access to the vehicle at the time of the search."

When the search of a vehicle occurs after it has been impounded, however, that search may be legitimate if it is undertaken for routine and reasonable purposes. In the case of *South Dakota* v. *Opperman* (1976),[97] for example, the Court held that a warrantless search undertaken for purposes of inventorying and safekeeping the personal possessions of the car's owner was not illegal. The intent of the search, which had turned up marijuana, had not been to discover contraband but to secure the owner's belongings from possible theft. Again, in *Colorado* v. *Bertine* (1987),[98] the Court reinforced the idea that officers may open closed containers found in a vehicle while conducting a routine search for inventorying purposes. In the words of the Court, such searches are "now a well-defined exception in the warrant requirement." In 1990, however, in the precedent-setting case of *Florida* v. *Wells*,[99] the Court agreed with a lower court's suppression of marijuana evidence discovered in a locked suitcase in the trunk of a defendant's impounded vehicle. In *Wells*, the Court held that standardized criteria authorizing the search of a vehicle for inventorying purposes were necessary before such a discovery could be legitimate. Standardized criteria, said the Court, might take the form of department policies, written general orders, or established routines.

Generally speaking, where vehicles are concerned, an investigatory stop is permissible under the Fourth Amendment if supported by reasonable suspicion,[100] and a warrantless search of a stopped car is valid if it is based on probable cause.[101] Reasonable suspicion can expand into probable cause when the facts in a given situation so warrant. In the 1996 case of *Ornelas* v. *U.S.*,[102] for example, two experienced Milwaukee police officers stopped a car with California license plates that had been spotted in a motel parking lot known for drug trafficking after the Narcotics and Dangerous Drugs Information System (NADDIS) identified the car's owner as a known or suspected drug trafficker. One of the officers noticed a loose panel above an armrest in the vehicle's backseat and then searched the car. A package of cocaine was found beneath the panel, and the driver and a passenger were arrested. Following conviction, the defendants appealed to the U.S. Supreme Court, claiming that no probable cause to search the car existed at the time of the stop. The majority opinion, however, noted that in the view of the court that originally heard the case, "the model, age, and source-State origin of the car, and the fact that two men traveling together checked into a motel at 4 o'clock in the morning without reservations, formed a drug-courier profile and . . . this profile together with the [computer] reports gave rise to a reasonable suspicion of drug-trafficking activity. . . . [I]n the court's view, reasonable suspicion became probable cause when [the deputy] found the loose panel."[103] Probable cause permits a warrantless search of a vehicle because it is able to quickly leave a jurisdiction. This exception to the exclusionary rule is called the **fleeting-targets exception**.[104]

Warrantless vehicle searches can extend to any area of the vehicle and may include sealed containers, the trunk, and the glove compartment if officers have probable cause to conduct a purposeful search or if officers have been given permission to search the vehicle. In the 1991 case of *Florida* v. *Jimeno*,[105] arresting officers stopped a motorist, who gave them permission to search his car. The defendant was later convicted on a drug charge when a bag on the floor of the car was found to contain cocaine. Upon appeal to the U.S. Supreme Court, however, he argued that the permission given to search his car did not extend to bags and other items within the car. In a decision that may have implications beyond vehicle searches, the Court held that "[a] criminal suspect's Fourth Amendment right to be free from unreasonable searches is not violated when, after he gives police permission to search his car, they open a closed container found within the car that might reasonably hold the object of the search. The amendment is satisfied when, under the circumstances, it is objectively reasonable for the police to believe that the scope of the suspect's consent permitted them to open the particular container."[106]

In *U.S.* v. *Ross* (1982),[107] the Court found that officers had not exceeded their authority in opening a bag in the defendant's trunk that was found to contain heroin. The search was held to be justifiable on the basis of information developed from a search of the passenger compartment. The Court said, "If probable cause justifies the search of a lawfully stopped vehicle, it justifies the search of every part of the vehicle and its contents that may conceal the object of the search."[108] Moreover, according to the 1996 U.S. Supreme Court decision in *Whren* v. *U.S.*,[109] officers may stop a vehicle being driven suspiciously and then search it once probable cause has developed, even if their primary assignment centers on duties other than traffic enforcement or "if a reasonable officer would not have stopped the motorist absent some additional law enforcement objective" (which in the case of *Whren* was drug enforcement).

Motorists[110] and their passengers may be ordered out of stopped vehicles in the interest of officer safety, and any evidence developed as a result of such a procedure may be used in court. In 1997, for example, in the case of *Maryland* v. *Wilson*,[111] the U.S. Supreme Court overturned a decision by a Maryland court that held that crack cocaine found during a traffic stop was seized illegally when it fell from the lap of a passenger ordered out of a stopped vehicle by a Maryland state trooper. The Maryland court reasoned that the police should not have authority to order seemingly innocent passengers out of vehicles—even vehicles that have been stopped for legitimate reasons. The Supreme Court cited concerns for officer safety in overturning the Maryland court's ruling and held that the activities of passengers are subject to police control. Similarly, in 2007, in the case of *Brendlin* v. *California*,[112] the Court ruled that passengers in stopped vehicles are necessarily detained as a result of the stop and that they should expect that, for safety reasons, officers will exercise "unquestioned police command" over them for the duration of the stop. However, any passenger in a stopped automobile may use his or her Fourth Amendment rights to challenge the stop's legality.

In 1998, however, the U.S. Supreme Court placed clear limits on warrantless vehicle searches. In the case of *Knowles* v. *Iowa*,[113] an Iowa policeman stopped Patrick Knowles for

fleeting-targets exception (also known as the automobile exception)
An exception to the exclusionary rule that permits law enforcement officers to search a motor vehicle based on probable cause but without a warrant. The fleeting-targets exception is predicated on the fact that vehicles can quickly leave the jurisdiction of a law enforcement agency.

Follow the author's tweets about the latest crime and justice news @schmalleger

Freedom or Safety? You Decide
Religion and Public Safety

In 2014, 20-year-old Cassandra Belin was convicted by a French court and fined 150 Euros for wearing a full-face Islamic veil (or niqab) in public in violation of a 2011 French law. The French government initiated a ban on the wearing of veils, or Islamic burkas, following a number of terrorist incidents. French police can impose fines on women who wear veils in public, although recent reports reveal that few women have actually been ticketed.

▲ A woman wearing a burqa. Can religious values, like those requiring the wearing of a burqa, be reconciled with public interests in safety and security?

Chrisstockphoto/Alamy Stock Photo

The French ban was preceded by an incident in Florida in 2003, when state Judge Janet Thorpe ruled that a Muslim woman could not wear a veil while being photographed for a state driver's license. The woman, Sultaana Freeman, claimed that her religious rights were violated when the state department of motor vehicles required that she reveal her face for the photograph. She offered to show her eyes, but not the rest of her face, to the camera.

Judge Thorpe said, however, that a "compelling interest in protecting the public from criminal activities and security threats" did not place an undue burden on Freeman's ability to practice her religion.

After the hearing, Freeman's husband, Abdul-Maalik Freeman, told reporters, "This is a religious principle; this is a principle that's imbedded in us as believers. So, she's not going to do that." Howard Marks, the Freemans' attorney, supported by the ACLU, filed an appeal claiming that the ruling was counter to guarantees of religious freedom inherent in the U.S. Constitution. Two years later, however, a Florida court of appeals denied further hearings in the case.

YOU DECIDE

Do the demands of public safety justify the kinds of restrictions on religious practice described here? If so, would you go so far as the French practice of banning the wearing of veils in public? As an alternative, should photo IDs, such as driver's licenses, be replaced with other forms of identification (such as an individual's stored DNA profile) in order to accommodate the beliefs of individuals like the Freemans?

References: "French Court Upholds Controversial Burqa Ban," *Al Arabiya News*, http://english.alarabiya.net/en/News/world/2014/01/08/French-court-upholds-controversial-burqa-ban-.html (January 8, 2014); "Judge: No Veil in Driver's License Photo," *Associated Press*, June 6, 2003; "FL Appeals Court Upholds Ban of Veil in Driver's License Photo," *Associated Press*, September 7, 2005, http://www.newsday.com/news/nationworld/nation/orl-bk-free-man090705,0,2758466.story?coll=ny-leadnationalnews-headlines (accessed April 17, 2012); Andrew Chung, "French Ban on Islamic Veil Turns out to Be Toothless," *Toronto Star*, March 31, 2012, http://www.thestar.com/news/world/article/1154781-french-ban-on-islamic-veil-turns-out-to-be-toothless (accessed May 20, 2012).

speeding, issued him a citation, but did not make a custodial arrest. The officer then conducted a full search of his car without Knowles's consent and without probable cause. Marijuana was found, and Knowles was arrested. At the time, Iowa state law gave officers authority to conduct full-blown automobile searches when issuing only a citation. The Supreme Court found, however, that while concern for officer safety during a routine traffic stop may justify the minimal intrusion of ordering a driver and passengers out of a car, it does not by itself justify what it called "the considerably greater intrusion attending a full field-type search." While a search incident to arrest may be justifiable in the eyes of the Court, a search incident to citation clearly is not.

In the 1999 case of *Wyoming* v. *Houghton*,[114] the Court ruled that police officers with probable cause to search a car may inspect passengers' belongings found in the car that are capable of concealing the object of the search. *Thornton* v. *U.S.* (2004) established the authority of arresting officers to search a car without a warrant even if the driver had previously exited the vehicle.[115]

In 2005, in the case of *Illinois* v. *Caballes*,[116] the Court held that the use of a drug-sniffing dog during a routine and lawful traffic stop is permissible and may not even be a search within the meaning of the Fourth Amendment. In writing for the majority, Justice John Paul Stevens said that "the use of a well-trained narcotics-detection dog—one that

◀ A Mississippi state trooper searches a car. Warrantless vehicle searches, where the driver is suspected of a crime, have generally been justified by the fact that vehicles are highly mobile and can quickly leave police jurisdiction. Can passengers in the vehicle also be searched?

Matt Bush/The Hattiesburg American/ AP Images

does not expose noncontraband items that otherwise would remain hidden from public view—during a lawful traffic stop generally does not implicate legitimate privacy interests."

In 2011, the Court created a good-faith exception to the exclusionary rule applicable to a search that was authorized by precedent at the time of the search but which was a type of search that was subsequently ruled unconstitutional. In that case, *Davis*. v. *U.S.*, Willie Gene Davis was a passenger in a car stopped for a traffic violation in 2007.[117] He subsequently gave officers a false name, and was arrested for giving false information to a police officer. The vehicle in which he was riding was searched, and officers discovered a handgun in Davis's jacket, which he had left on the seat. Davis was charged and convicted for possession of an illegal weapon. Later, however, the U.S. Court of Appeals for the Eleventh Circuit found that the search was illegal, based on a previous Supreme Court ruling in the 2009 case of *Arizona* v. *Gant*.[118] Nonetheless, the lower court upheld Davis's conviction because the *Gant* ruling came after Davis's arrest. The Supreme Court agreed, saying, "Searches conducted in objectively reasonable reliance on binding appellate precedent are not subject to the exclusionary rule."

Finally, in 2018, the U.S. Supreme Court ruled that the automobile exception to the exclusionary rule did not apply in the case of a police officer who discovered photographs on Facebook of what appeared to be a stolen orange and black motorcycle parked in the driveway of a house and partially covered by a white tarp. After arriving at the house seen in the photo, the officer walked onto the driveway, removed the tarp, and confirmed that the motorcycle was, in fact, stolen. When the owner of the house returned he was arrested and charged with receiving stolen property. The high court held that "the automobile exception does not permit the warrantless entry of a home or its curtilage in order to search a vehicle therein."[119]

Roadblocks and Motor Vehicle Checkpoints

The Fourth and Fourteenth Amendments to the U.S. Constitution guarantee liberty and personal security to all people residing within the United States. Courts have generally held that police officers have no legitimate authority to detain or arrest people who are going about their business in a peaceful manner, unless there is probable cause to believe that a crime has been committed. In a number of instances, however, the U.S. Supreme Court has decided that community interests may necessitate a temporary suspension of personal liberty, even when probable cause is lacking. One such case is that of *Michigan Dept. of State Police* v. *Sitz* (1990),[120] which involved the legality of highway sobriety checkpoints, including those at which nonsuspicious drivers are subjected to scrutiny. In *Sitz*, the Court ruled that such stops are reasonable insofar as they are essential to the welfare of the community as a whole.

In a second case, *U.S.* v. *Martinez-Fuerte* (1976),[121] the Court upheld brief suspicionless seizures at a fixed international checkpoint designed to intercept illegal aliens. The Court noted that "to require that such stops always be based on reasonable suspicion would be impractical because the flow of traffic tends to be too heavy to allow the particularized

🐦 Follow the author's tweets about the latest crime and justice news @schmalleger

study of a given car necessary to identify it as a possible carrier of illegal aliens. Such a requirement also would largely eliminate any deterrent to the conduct of well-disguised smuggling operations, even though smugglers are known to use these highways regularly."[122]

In fact, in 2004, in the case of *Illinois* v. *Lidster*,[123] the Court held that information-seeking highway roadblocks are permissible. The stop in *Lidster*, said the Court, was permissible because its intent was merely to solicit motorists' help in solving a crime. "The law," said the Court, "ordinarily permits police to seek the public's voluntary cooperation in a criminal investigation."

Watercraft and Motor Homes

The 1983 case of *U.S.* v. *Villamonte-Marquez*[124] widened the *Carroll* decision (discussed earlier) to include watercraft. In this case, the Court reasoned that a vehicle on the water can easily leave the jurisdiction of enforcement officials, just as a car or truck can.

In *California* v. *Carney* (1985),[125] the Court extended police authority to conduct warrantless searches of vehicles to include motor homes. Earlier arguments had been advanced that a motor home, because it is more like a permanent residence, should not be considered a vehicle for purposes of search and seizure. In a 6–3 decision, the Court rejected those arguments, reasoning that a vehicle's appointments and size do not alter its basic function of providing transportation.

Houseboats were brought under the automobile exception to the Fourth Amendment warrant requirement in the 1988 Tenth Circuit Court case of *U.S.* v. *Hill*.[126] Learn more about vehicle pursuits and the Fourth Amendment at **https://www.justicestudies.com/ pubs/veh_pursuits.pdf**.

Suspicionless Searches

In two 1989 decisions, the U.S. Supreme Court ruled for the first time in its history that there may be instances when the need to ensure public safety provides a **compelling interest** that negates the rights of any individual to privacy, permitting **suspicionless searches**— those that occur when a person is not suspected of a crime. In the case of *National Treasury Employees Union* v. *Von Raab* (1989),[127] the Court, by a 5–4 vote, upheld a program of the U.S. Customs Service that required mandatory drug testing for all workers seeking promotions or job transfers involving drug interdiction and the carrying of firearms. The Court's majority opinion read, "We think the government's need to conduct the suspicionless searches required by the Customs program outweighs the privacy interest of employees engaged directly in drug interdiction, and of those who otherwise are required to carry firearms."

The second case, *Skinner* v. *Railway Labor Executives' Association* (1989),[128] was decided on the same day. In *Skinner*, the justices voted 7–2 to permit the mandatory testing of railway crews for the presence of drugs or alcohol following serious train accidents. The *Skinner* case involved evidence of drugs in a 1987 train wreck outside of Baltimore, Maryland, in which 16 people were killed and hundreds were injured.

The 1991 Supreme Court case of *Florida* v. *Bostick*,[129] which permitted warrantless "sweeps" of intercity buses, moved the Court deeply into conservative territory. The *Bostick* case came to the attention of the Court as a result of the Broward County (Florida) Sheriff's Department's routine practice of boarding buses at scheduled stops and asking passengers for permission to search their bags. Terrance Bostick, a passenger on one of the buses, gave police permission to search his luggage, which was found to contain cocaine. Bostick was arrested and eventually pleaded guilty to charges of drug trafficking. The Florida Supreme Court, however, found merit in Bostick's appeal, which was based on a Fourth Amendment claim that the search of his luggage had been unreasonable. The Florida court held that "a reasonable passenger in [Bostick's] situation would not have felt free to leave the bus to avoid questioning by the police," and it overturned the conviction.

The state appealed to the U.S. Supreme Court, which held that the Florida Supreme Court had erred in interpreting Bostick's *feelings* that he was not free to leave the bus. In the words of the Court, "Bostick was a passenger on a bus that was scheduled to depart. He would not have felt free to leave the bus even if the police had not been present. Bostick's movements were 'confined' in a sense, but this was the natural result of his decision to take the bus." In other words, Bostick was constrained not so much by police action as by his own

The reasonable person test presumes an innocent person.

feelings that he might miss the bus were he to get off. Following this line of reasoning, the Court concluded that warrantless, suspicionless "sweeps" of buses, "trains, planes, and city streets" are permissible as long as officers (1) ask individual passengers for permission before searching their possessions, (2) do not coerce passengers to consent to a search, and (3) do not convey the message that citizen compliance with the search request is mandatory. Passenger compliance with police searches must be voluntary for the searches to be legal.

In contrast to the tone of Court decisions more than two decades earlier, the justices did not require officers to inform passengers that they were free to leave or that they had the right to deny officers the opportunity to search (although Bostick himself was so advised by Florida officers). Any reasonable person, the Court ruled, should feel free to deny the police request. In the words of the Court, "The appropriate test is whether, taking into account all of the circumstances surrounding the encounter, a reasonable passenger would feel free to decline the officers' requests or otherwise terminate the encounter." The Court continued, "Rejected, however, is Bostick's argument that he must have been seized because no reasonable person would freely consent to a search of luggage containing drugs, since the 'reasonable person' test presumes an innocent person."

Critics of the decision saw it as creating new "gestapo-like" police powers in the face of which citizens on public transportation will feel compelled to comply with police searches. Dissenting Justices Harry Blackmun, John Paul Stevens, and Thurgood Marshall held that "the bus sweep at issue in this case violates the core values of the Fourth Amendment." The Court's majority, however, defended its ruling by writing, "[T]he Fourth Amendment proscribes unreasonable searches and seizures; it does not proscribe voluntary cooperation." In 2000, however, in the case of *Bond* v. *U.S.*,[130] the Court ruled that physical manipulation of a carry-on bag in the possession of a bus passenger without the owner's consent does violate the Fourth Amendment's proscription against unreasonable searches.

In the case of *U.S.* v. *Drayton* (2002),[131] the U.S. Supreme Court reiterated its position that police officers are not required to advise bus passengers of their right to refuse to cooperate with officers conducting searches or to refuse to be searched.

In 2004, the U.S. Supreme Court made it clear that suspicionless searches of vehicles at our nation's borders are permitted, even when the searches are extensive. In the case of *U.S.* v. *Flores-Montano*,[132] customs officials disassembled the gas tank of a car belonging to a man entering the country from Mexico and found that it contained 37 kilograms of marijuana. Although the officers admitted that their actions were not motivated by any particular belief that the search would reveal contraband, the Court held that Congress has always granted "plenary authority to conduct routine searches and seizures at the border without probable cause or a warrant." The Court stated that "the Government's authority to conduct suspicionless inspections at the border includes the authority to remove, disassemble, and reassemble a vehicle's fuel tank." Learn more about public-safety exceptions to *Miranda* at **https://www.justicestudies.com/pubs/psafety.pdf**.

High-Technology Searches

The burgeoning use of high technology to investigate crime and to uncover violations of the criminal law is forcing courts throughout the nation to evaluate the applicability of constitutional guarantees in light of high-tech searches and seizures. In 1996, the California appellate court decision in *People* v. *Deutsch*[133] presaged the kinds of issues that are being encountered as American law enforcement expands its use of cutting-edge technology. In *Deutsch*, judges faced the question of whether a warrantless scan of a private dwelling with a thermal-imaging device constitutes an unreasonable search within the meaning of the Fourth Amendment. Such devices (also called *forward-looking infrared [FLIR] systems*) measure radiant energy in the radiant heat portion of the electromagnetic spectrum[134] and display their readings as thermographs. The "heat picture" that a thermal imager produces can be used, as it was in the case of Dorian Deutsch, to reveal unusually warm areas or rooms that might be associated with the cultivation of drug-bearing plants, such as marijuana. Two hundred cannabis plants, which were being grown hydroponically under high-wattage lights in two walled-off portions of Deutsch's home, were seized following an exterior thermal scan of her home by a police officer who drove by at 1:30 in the morning. Because no entry of the house was anticipated during the search, the officer had acted

Follow the author's tweets about the latest crime and justice news @schmalleger

without a search warrant. The California court ruled that the scan was an illegal search because "society accepts a reasonable expectation of privacy" surrounding "nondisclosed activities within the home."[135]

In the similar case of *Kyllo* v. *U.S.* (2001),[136] the U.S. Supreme Court reached much the same conclusion. Based on the results of a warrantless search conducted by officers using a thermal-imaging device, investigators applied for a search warrant of Kyllo's home. The subsequent search uncovered more than 100 marijuana plants that were being grown under bright lights. In overturning Kyllo's conviction on drug-manufacturing charges, the Court held (with regard to the original warrantless search with the thermal-imaging device), "Where, as here, the Government uses a device that is not in general public use, to explore details of a private home that would previously have been unknowable without physical intrusion, the surveillance is a Fourth Amendment 'search,' and is presumptively unreasonable without a warrant."[137] Learn more about the issues surrounding search and seizure at **https://constitution.findlaw.com/amendment4.html**.

The Intelligence Function

The need for information leads police investigators to question both suspects and informants and, even more often, potentially knowledgeable citizens who may have been witnesses or victims. Data gathering is a crucial form of intelligence; without it, enforcement agencies would be virtually powerless to plan and effect arrests.

5 Describe the intelligence function, including the roles of police interrogation and the *Miranda* warning.

The importance of gathering information in police work cannot be overstressed. Studies have found that the one factor most likely to lead to arrest in serious crimes is the presence of a witness who can provide information to the police. Undercover operations, Neighborhood Watch programs, Crime Stoppers groups, and organized detective work all contribute this vital information.

Informants

Information gathering is a complex process, and many ethical questions have been raised about the techniques police use to gather information. The use of paid informants, for example, is an area of concern to ethicists who believe that informants are often paid to get away with crimes. The police practice (endorsed by some prosecutors) of agreeing not to charge one offender out of a group if he or she will talk and testify against others is another concern.

The right of the people to be secure in their persons, houses, papers, and effects, against unreasonable searches and seizures, shall not be violated, and no Warrants shall issue, but upon probable cause, supported by Oath or affirmation, and particularly describing the place to be searched, and the persons or things to be seized.

—Fourth Amendment to the U.S. Constitution

As we have seen, probable cause is an important aspect of both police searches and legal arrests. The Fourth Amendment specifies that "no Warrants shall issue, but upon probable cause." As a consequence, the successful use of informants in supporting requests for a warrant depends on the demonstrable reliability of their information. The case of *Aguilar* v. *Texas* (1964)[138] clarified the use of informants and established a two-pronged test. The U.S. Supreme Court ruled that informant information could establish probable cause if both of the following criteria are met:

1. The source of the informant's information is made clear.
2. The police officer has a reasonable belief that the informant is reliable.

The two-pronged test of *Aguilar* v. *Texas* was intended to prevent the issuance of warrants on the basis of false or fabricated information. The case of *U.S.* v. *Harris* (1971)[139] provided an exception to the two-pronged *Aguilar* test. The *Harris* Court recognized the fact that when an informant provides information that is damaging to him or her, it is probably true. In *Harris*, an informant told police that he had purchased non-tax-paid whiskey from another person. Because the information also implicated the informant in a crime, it was held to be accurate, even though it could not meet the second prong of the *Aguilar* test. "Admissions of crime," said the Court, "carry their own indicia of credibility—sufficient at least to support a finding of probable cause to search."[140]

In 1983, in the case of *Illinois* v. *Gates*,[141] the Court adopted a totality-of-circumstances approach, which held that sufficient probable cause for issuing a warrant exists where an informant can be reasonably believed on the basis of everything that the police know. The *Gates* case involved an anonymous informant who provided incriminating information about another person through a letter to the police. Although the source of the information was not stated and the police were unable to say whether the informant was reliable, the overall sense of things, given what was already known to police, was that the information supplied was probably valid. In *Gates*, the Court held that probable cause exists when "there is a fair probability that contraband or evidence of a crime will be found in a particular place."

In the 1990 case of *Alabama* v. *White*,[142] the Supreme Court ruled that an anonymous tip, even in the absence of other corroborating information about a suspect, could form the basis for an investigatory stop if the informant accurately predicted the *future* behavior of the suspect. The Court reasoned that the ability to predict a suspect's behavior demonstrates a significant degree of familiarity with the suspect's affairs. In the words of the Court, "Because only a small number of people are generally privy to an individual's itinerary, it is reasonable for the police to believe that a person with access to such information is likely to also have access to reliable information about that individual's illegal activities."[143]

In 2000, in the case of *Florida* v. *J.L.*,[144] the Court held that an anonymous tip that a person is carrying a gun does not, without more, justify a police officer's stop and frisk of that person. Ruling that such a search is invalid under the Fourth Amendment, the Court rejected the suggestion of a firearm exception to the general stop-and-frisk rule.

The identity of informants may be kept secret only if sources have been explicitly assured of confidentiality by investigating officers or if a reasonably implied assurance of confidentiality has been made. In *U.S. Dept. of Justice* v. *Landano* (1993),[145] the U.S. Supreme Court required that an informant's identity be revealed through a request made under the federal Freedom of Information Act. In that case, the FBI had not specifically assured the informant of confidentiality, and the Court ruled that "the government is not entitled to a presumption that all sources supplying information to the FBI in the course of a criminal investigation are confidential sources."

Police Interrogation

In 2003, Illinois became the first state in the nation to require the electronic recording of police interrogations and confessions in homicide cases.[146] State lawmakers hoped that the use of recordings would reduce the incidence of false confessions as well as the likelihood of convictions based on such confessions. Under the law, police interrogators must create video- or audiotape recordings of any questioning involving suspects. The law prohibits the introduction in court of statements and confessions that have not been taped. Proponents of the law say that it will prevent police intimidation of murder suspects and will put an end to coerced confessions.

Some argue that the mandatory recording of police interrogations offers overwhelming benefits at minimal cost. "By creating an objective and reviewable record," says University of San Francisco Law School's Richard A. Leo, "electronic recording promotes truth-finding in the criminal process, relegates 'swearing contests' to the past, and saves scarce resources at multiple levels of the criminal justice system."[147] According to Leo, requiring that all interrogations be recorded will benefit police and prosecutors by increasing the accuracy of confessions and convictions and "will also reduce the number of police-induced false confessions and the wrongful convictions they cause."

The U.S. Supreme Court has defined **interrogation** as any behaviors by the police "that the police should know are reasonably likely to elicit an incriminating response from the suspect."[148] Interrogation may involve activities that go well beyond mere verbal questioning, and the Court has held that interrogation may include "staged lineups, reverse lineups, positing guilt, minimizing the moral seriousness of crime, and casting blame on the victim or society." It is noteworthy that the Court has also held that "police words or actions normally attendant to arrest and custody do not constitute interrogation" unless they involve pointed

The mandatory recording of police interrogations offers overwhelming benefits at minimal cost.

interrogation
The information-gathering activity of police officers that involves the direct questioning of suspects.

or directed questions. An arresting officer may instruct a suspect on what to do and may chitchat with him or her without engaging in interrogation within the meaning of the law. Once police officers make inquiries intended to elicit information about the crime in question, however, interrogation has begun. The interrogation of suspects, like other areas of police activity, is subject to constitutional limits as interpreted by the courts. A series of landmark decisions by the U.S. Supreme Court has focused on police interrogation (Figure 5–2).

Physical Abuse

The first in a series of significant cases was that of *Brown* v. *Mississippi*,[149] decided in 1936. The *Brown* case began with the robbery of a white store owner in Mississippi in 1934. During the robbery, the victim was killed. A posse formed and went to the home of a local African-American man rumored to have been one of the perpetrators. They dragged the suspect from his home, put a rope around his neck, and hoisted him into a tree. They repeated this process a number of times, hoping to get a confession from the man but failing to do so. The posse was headed by a deputy sheriff who then arrested other suspects in the case and laid them over chairs in the local jail and whipped them with belts and buckles until they "confessed." These confessions were used in the trial that followed, and all three defendants were convicted of murder. Their convictions were upheld by the Mississippi Supreme Court. In 1936, however, the case was reviewed by the U.S. Supreme Court, which overturned all of the convictions, saying that it was difficult to imagine techniques of interrogation more "revolting" to the sense of justice than those used in this case.

inherent coercion
The tactics used by police interviewers that fall short of physical abuse but that nonetheless pressure suspects to divulge information.

Inherent Coercion

Interrogation need not involve physical abuse for it to be contrary to constitutional principles. In the case of *Ashcraft* v. *Tennessee* (1944),[150] the U.S. Supreme Court found that interrogation involving **inherent coercion** was not acceptable. Ashcraft had been charged

INTERROGATION

The U.S. Supreme Court has defined interrogation as any behaviors by the police "that the police should know are reasonably likely to elicit an incriminating response from the suspect." The Court also noted that "police words or actions normally attendant to arrest and custody do not constitute interrogation" unless they involve pointed or directed questions. The interrogation of suspects, like other areas of police activity, is subject to constitutional limits as interpreted by the courts, and a series of landmark decisions by the U.S. Supreme Court has focused on police interrogations.

Physical Abuse:
The first in a series of significant cases was **Brown v. Mississippi**. In 1936, the court determined that physical abuse cannot be used to obtain a confession or elicit information from a suspect.

Inherent Coercion:
In the case of **Ashcraft v. Tennessee** (1944), the U.S. Supreme Court found that interrogation involving inherent coercion was not acceptable. Inherent coercion refers to any form of non-physical coercion, hostility, or pressure to try to force a confession from a suspect.

Psychological Manipulation:
Interrogation should not involve sophisticated trickery or manipulation. In the case of **Arizona v. Fulminante** (1991), the U.S. Supreme Court determined that it was not legal to allow an FBI informant posing as a fellow inmate to trick the suspect into a confession. Interrogators do not have to be scrupulously honest in confronting suspects, but there must be limits to the lengths that can be pursued in questioning a suspect.

Right to Lawyer at Interrogation:
Escobedo v. Illinois (1964) and *Minnick v. Mississippi* (1990).

FIGURE 5–2
Police Interrogation

with the murder of his wife, Zelma. He was arrested on a Saturday night and interrogated by relays of skilled interrogators until Monday morning, when he purportedly made a statement implicating himself in the murder. During questioning, he had faced a blinding light but was not physically mistreated. Investigators later testified that when the suspect requested cigarettes, food, or water, they "kindly" provided them. The Court's ruling, which reversed Ashcraft's conviction, made it plain that the Fifth Amendment guarantee against self-incrimination prohibits any form of official coercion or pressure during interrogation.

A similar case, *Chambers* v. *Florida*, was decided in 1940.[151] In that case, four black men were arrested without warrants as suspects in the robbery and murder of an elderly white man. After several days of questioning in a hostile atmosphere, the men confessed to the murder. The confessions were used as the primary evidence against them at their trial, and all four were sentenced to die. Upon appeal, the U.S. Supreme Court held that "the very circumstances surrounding their confinement and their questioning, without any formal charges having been brought, were such as to fill petitioners with terror and frightful misgivings."[152] Learn more about the case of *Chambers* v. *Florida* at **http://tinyurl.com/4uy3c2w**.

Psychological Manipulation

Not only must interrogation be free of coercion and hostility, but it also cannot involve sophisticated trickery designed to ferret out a confession. Interrogators do not necessarily have to be scrupulously honest in confronting suspects, and the expert opinions of medical and psychiatric practitioners may be sought in investigations. However, the use of professionals skilled in **psychological manipulation** to gain confessions was banned by the Court in the case of *Leyra* v. *Denno*[153] in 1954, during the heyday of psychiatric perspectives on criminal behavior.

In 1991, in the case of *Arizona* v. *Fulminante*,[154] the U.S. Supreme Court threw an even more dampening blanket of uncertainty over the use of sophisticated techniques to gain a confession. Oreste Fulminante was an inmate in a federal prison when he was approached secretly by a fellow inmate who was an FBI informant. The informant told Fulminante that other inmates were plotting to kill him because of a rumor that he had killed a child. He offered to protect Fulminante if he was told the details of the crime. Fulminante then described his role in the murder of his 11-year-old stepdaughter. Fulminante was arrested for that murder, tried, and convicted.

On appeal to the U.S. Supreme Court, Fulminante's lawyers argued that his confession had been coerced because of the threat of violence communicated by the informant. The Court agreed that the confession had been coerced and ordered a new trial at which the confession could not be admitted into evidence. Simultaneously, however, the Court found that the admission of a coerced confession should be considered a harmless "trial error" that need not necessarily result in reversal of a conviction if other evidence still proves guilt. The decision was especially significant because it partially reversed the Court's earlier ruling, in *Chapman* v. *California* (1967),[155] where it was held that forced confessions were such a basic form of constitutional error that they automatically invalidated any conviction to which they related. At a second trial, where his confession was not entered into evidence, Fulminante was convicted again and sentenced to die. The Arizona Supreme Court overturned his conviction, however, ruling that testimony describing statements the victim had made about fearing for her life prior to her murder, and which had been entered into evidence, were hearsay and had prejudiced the jury.[156] Finally, the area of eyewitness identification bears discussion. In 2011, in the case of *State* v. *Henderson*,[157] the New Jersey Supreme Court held that the current legal standard for assessing eyewitness identifications must be revised because it did not offer adequate measures for reliability; did not sufficiently deter inappropriate police conduct; and overstated the jury's ability to evaluate identification evidence.

In 2012, in the case of *Perry* v. *New Hampshire*,[158] the U.S. Supreme Court recognized problems with eyewitness identification, especially when such identification is obtained by skilled law enforcement interrogators. Still, the court denied that the Due Process Clause of the U.S. Constitution requires a preliminary judicial inquiry into the reliability of an eyewitness identification when the identification was not procured under unnecessarily suggestive circumstances arranged by law enforcement. Learn more about detecting deception from the FBI at **https://www.justicestudies.com/pdf/truth_deception.pdf**.

psychological manipulation
The manipulative actions by police interviewers, designed to pressure suspects to divulge information, that are based on subtle forms of intimidation and control.

Follow the author's tweets about the latest crime and justice news @schmalleger

▲ Ernesto Miranda, shown here after a jury convicted him for a second time. Miranda was convicted on rape and kidnapping charges. Arresting officers did not advise him of his rights. His case led to the now-famous *Miranda* warnings. How do the *Miranda* warnings read?

AP Images

Miranda warnings
The advisement of rights due criminal suspects by the police before questioning begins. *Miranda* warnings were first set forth by the U.S. Supreme Court in the 1966 case of *Miranda* v. *Arizona*.

🐦 Follow the author's tweets about the latest crime and justice news @schmalleger

The Right to a Lawyer at Interrogation

In 1964, in the case of *Escobedo* v. *Illinois*,[159] the right to have legal counsel present during police interrogation was formally recognized. In 1981, the case of *Edwards* v. *Arizona*[160] established a "bright-line rule" (i.e., it specified a criterion that cannot be violated) for investigators to use in interpreting a suspect's right to counsel. In *Edwards*, the U.S. Supreme Court reiterated its *Miranda* concern that once a suspect who is in custody and is being questioned has requested the assistance of counsel, all questioning must cease until an attorney is present.

The 1986 case of *Michigan* v. *Jackson*[161] provided further support for *Edwards*. In *Jackson*, the Court forbade police from initiating the interrogation of criminal defendants who had invoked their right to counsel at an arraignment or similar proceeding. In 1990, the Court refined the rule in *Minnick* v. *Mississippi*,[162] when it held that after the suspect has had an opportunity to consult his or her lawyer, interrogation may *not* resume unless the lawyer is present. Similarly, according to *Arizona* v. *Roberson* (1988),[163] the police may not avoid the suspect's request for a lawyer by beginning a new line of questioning, even if it is about an unrelated offense.

In 1994, in the case of *Davis* v. *U.S.*,[164] the Court "put the burden on custodial suspects to make unequivocal invocations of the right to counsel." In the *Davis* case, a man being interrogated in the death of a sailor waived his *Miranda* rights but later said, "Maybe I should talk to a lawyer." Investigators asked the suspect clarifying questions, and he responded, "No, I don't want a lawyer." Upon conviction he appealed, claiming that interrogation should have ceased when he mentioned a lawyer. The Court, in affirming the conviction, stated that "it will often be good police practice for the interviewing officers to clarify whether or not [the suspect] actually wants an attorney."

In 2009, in something of an about-face, the U.S. Supreme Court held that "*Michigan* v. *Jackson* should be and now is overruled." In the case of *Montejo* v. *Louisiana*,[165] the Court found that strict interpretations of *Jackson* could lead to practical problems. Montejo had been charged with first-degree murder, and appointment of counsel was ordered at his arraignment. He did not, however, ask to see his attorney. Later that same day, the police read Montejo his *Miranda* rights, and he agreed to accompany them on a trip to locate the murder weapon. During the trip, he wrote an incriminating letter of apology to the victim's widow. Upon returning, he met with his court-appointed attorney for the first time. At trial, his letter was admitted over defense objection, and he was convicted and sentenced to death. In the words of the Court, "Both *Edwards* and *Jackson* are meant to prevent police from badgering defendants into changing their minds about the right to counsel once they have invoked it, but a defendant who never asked for counsel has not yet made up his mind." In effect, although an attorney had been appointed to represent Montejo, he had never actually invoked his right to counsel.

Finally, in 2010, in the case of *Maryland* v. *Shatzer*,[166] the Court held that police could reopen the interrogation of a suspect who has invoked his right to counsel following a 14-day or longer break in questioning. Even though the defendant (Shatzer) had been in state prison during the break, the justices said, he had been free "from the coercive power of an interrogator" during that time.

Suspect Rights: The *Miranda* Decision

In the area of suspect rights, no case is as famous as that of *Miranda* v. *Arizona* (1966),[167] which established the well-known **Miranda** warnings. Many people regard *Miranda* as the centerpiece of the Warren Court due-process rulings.

The case involved Ernesto Miranda, who was arrested in Phoenix, Arizona, and was accused of having kidnapped and raped a young woman. At police headquarters, he was identified by the victim. After being interrogated for 2 hours, Miranda signed a confession that formed the basis of his later conviction on the charges.

On appeal, the U.S. Supreme Court rendered what some regard as the most far-reaching opinion to have affected criminal justice in the last half century. The Court ruled that Miranda's conviction was unconstitutional because "[t]he entire aura and atmosphere of police interrogation without notification of rights and an offer of assistance of counsel [tend] to subjugate the individual to the will of his examiner."

CJ Exhibit 5–2
The *Miranda* Warnings

ADULT RIGHTS WARNING

Suspects 18 years old or older who are in custody must be advised of the following rights before any questioning begins:

1. You have the right to remain silent.
2. Anything you say can be used against you in a court of law.
3. You have the right to talk to a lawyer and to have a lawyer present while you are being questioned.
4. If you want a lawyer before or during questioning but cannot afford to hire a lawyer, one will be appointed to represent you at no cost before any questioning.
5. If you answer questions now without a lawyer here, you still have the right to stop answering questions at any time.

WAIVER OF RIGHTS

After reading and explaining the rights of a person in custody, an officer must also ask for a waiver of those rights before any questioning. The following waiver questions must be answered affirmatively, either by express answer or by clear implication. Silence alone is not a waiver.

1. Do you understand each of these rights I have explained to you? (Answer must be YES.)
2. Having these rights in mind, do you now wish to answer questions? (Answer must be YES.)
3. Do you now wish to answer questions without a lawyer present? (Answer must be YES.)

The following question must be asked of juveniles under the age of 18:

1. Do you now wish to answer questions without your parents, guardians, or custodians present? (Answer must be YES.)

The Court continued, saying that the suspect "must be warned prior to any questioning that he has the right to remain silent, that anything he says can be used against him in a court of law, that he has the right to the presence of an attorney, and that if he cannot afford an attorney one will be appointed for him prior to any questioning if he so desires. Opportunity to exercise these rights must be afforded to him throughout the interrogation. After such warnings have been given, and such opportunity afforded him, the individual may knowingly and intelligently waive these rights and agree to answer the questions or make a statement. But unless and until such warnings and waiver are demonstrated by the prosecution at the trial, no evidence obtained as a result of interrogation can be used against him."

To ensure that proper advice is given to suspects at the time of their arrest, the now-famous *Miranda* rights are read before any questioning begins. These rights, as they appear on a *Miranda* warning card commonly used by police agencies, are shown in CJ Exhibit 5–2.

Once suspects have been advised of their *Miranda* rights, they are commonly asked to sign a paper that lists each right in order to confirm that they were advised of their rights and that they understand each right. Questioning may then begin, but only if suspects waive the right not to talk or to have a lawyer present during interrogation.

In 1992, *Miranda* rights were effectively extended to illegal immigrants living in the United States. In a settlement of a class-action lawsuit reached in Los Angeles with the Immigration and Naturalization Service, U.S. District Court Judge William Byrne, Jr., approved the printing of millions of notices in several languages to be given to arrestees. The approximately 1.5 million illegal aliens arrested each year must be told they may (1) talk with a lawyer, (2) make a phone call, (3) request a list of available legal services, (4) seek a hearing before an immigration judge, (5) possibly obtain release on bond, and (6) contact a diplomatic officer representing their country. Notice of this type was "long overdue," said Roberto Martinez of the American Friends Service Committee's Mexico—U.S. border program. "Up to now, we've had total mistreatment of civil rights of undocumented people."[168]

When the *Miranda* decision was originally handed down, some hailed it as ensuring the protection of individual rights guaranteed under the Constitution. To guarantee those rights, they suggested, no better agency is available than the police themselves, as the police are present at the initial stages of the criminal justice process. Critics of *Miranda*, however, argued that the decision put police agencies in the uncomfortable and contradictory position not only of enforcing the law but also of having to offer defendants advice on how they might circumvent conviction and punishment. Under *Miranda*, the police partially assume the role of legal adviser to the accused.

In 1999, however, in the case of *U.S.* v. *Dickerson*,[169] the Fourth Circuit U.S. Court of Appeals upheld an almost-forgotten law that Congress had passed in 1968 with the intention of overturning *Miranda*. That law, Section 3501 of Chapter 223, Part II of Title 18 of the U.S.

Code, says that "a confession . . . shall be admissible in evidence if it is voluntarily given." Upon appeal in 2000, the U.S. Supreme Court upheld its original *Miranda* ruling by a 7–2 vote and found that *Miranda* is a constitutional rule (i.e., a fundamental right inherent in the U.S. Constitution) that cannot be dismissed by an act of Congress. "*Miranda* and its progeny," the majority wrote in *Dickerson* v. *U.S.*, will continue to "govern the admissibility of statements made during custodial interrogation in both state and federal courts."[170]

In 2004, in the case of *U.S.* v. *Patane*,[171] the U.S. Supreme Court continued to refine its original 1966 *Miranda* ruling. *Patane* surprised some Court watchers because in it the Court held that "a mere failure to give *Miranda* warnings does not, by itself, violate a suspect's constitutional rights or even the *Miranda* rule."

The *Patane* case began with the arrest of a convicted felon after a federal agent told officers that the man owned a handgun illegally. At the time of arrest, the officers tried to advise the defendant of his rights, but he interrupted them, saying that he already knew his rights. The officers then asked him about the pistol, and he told them where it was. After the weapon was recovered, the defendant was charged with illegal possession of a firearm by a convicted felon.

At first glance, *Patane* appears to contradict the fruit of the poisonous tree doctrine that the Court established in the 1920 case of *Silverthorne Lumber Co.* v. *U.S.*[172] and that *Wong Sun* v. *U.S.* (1963)[173] made applicable to verbal evidence derived immediately from an illegal search and seizure. An understanding of *Patane*, however, requires recognition of the fact that the *Miranda* rule is based on the self-incrimination clause of the Fifth Amendment to the U.S. Constitution. According to the Court in *Patane*, "that Clause's core protection is a prohibition on compelling a criminal defendant to testify against himself at trial." It cannot be violated, the Court said, "by the introduction of nontestimonial evidence obtained as a result of voluntary statements." In other words, according to the Court, only (1) coerced statements and (2) those voluntary statements made by a defendant that might directly incriminate him or her at a later trial are precluded by a failure to read a suspect his or her *Miranda* rights. Such voluntary statements would, of course, include such things as an outright confession.

Significantly, however, oral statements must be distinguished, the Court said, from the "physical fruits of the suspect's unwarned but voluntary statements." In other words, if an unwarned suspect is questioned by police officers and tells the officers where they can find an illegal weapon or a weapon that has been used in a crime, the weapon can be recovered and later introduced as evidence at the suspect's trial. If the same unwarned suspect, however, tells police that he committed a murder, then his confession will not be allowed into evidence at trial. The line drawn by the Court is against the admissibility of *oral statements* made by an unwarned defendant, not the *nontestimonial physical evidence* resulting from continued police investigation of such statements. Under *Patane*, the oral statements themselves cannot be admitted, but the physical evidence derived from them can be. "Thus," wrote the justices in *Patane*, "admission of nontestimonial physical fruits (the pistol here) does not run the risk of admitting into trial an accused's coerced incriminating statements against himself."

Waiver of *Miranda* Rights by Suspects

Suspects in police custody may legally waive their *Miranda* rights through a voluntary "knowing and intelligent" waiver. A knowing waiver can only be made if a suspect has been advised of his or her rights and was in a condition to understand the advisement. A rights advisement made in English to a Spanish-speaking suspect, for example, cannot produce a knowing waiver. Likewise, an intelligent waiver of rights requires that the defendant be able to understand the consequences of not invoking the *Miranda* rights. In the case of *Moran* v. *Burbine* (1986),[174] the U.S. Supreme Court defined an intelligent and knowing waiver as one "made with a full awareness both of the nature of the right being abandoned and the consequences of the decision to abandon it." In *Colorado* v. *Spring* (1987),[175] the Court held that an intelligent and knowing waiver can be made even though a suspect has not been informed of all the alleged offenses about which he or she is about to be questioned.

Inevitable-Discovery Exception to *Miranda*

The case of Robert Anthony Williams provides a good example of the change in the U.S. Supreme Court philosophy, alluded to earlier in this chapter, from an individual-rights

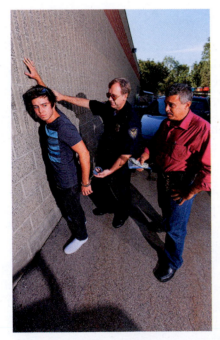

▲ A suspect being read his *Miranda* rights immediately after arrest. Officers often read *Miranda* rights from a card or digital device to preclude the possibility of making a mistake. What might the consequences of a mistake be?

Terry J Alcorn/E+/Getty Images

perspective toward a public-order perspective. The case epitomizes what some have called a "nibbling away" at the advances in defendant rights, which reached their apex in *Miranda*. The case began in 1969, at the close of the Warren Court era, when Williams was convicted of murdering a 10-year-old girl, Pamela Powers, around Christmastime. Although Williams had been advised of his rights, detectives searching for the girl's body were riding in a car with the defendant when one of them made what has since come to be known as the "Christian burial speech." The detective told Williams that since Christmas was almost upon them, it would be "the Christian thing to do" to see to it that Pamela could have a decent burial rather than having to lay in a field somewhere. Williams relented and led detectives to the body. However, because Williams had not been reminded of his right to have a lawyer present during his conversation with the detective, the Supreme Court in *Brewer* v. *Williams* (1977)[176] overturned Williams's conviction, saying that the detective's remarks were "a deliberate eliciting of incriminating evidence from an accused in the absence of his lawyer."

In 1977, Williams was retried for the murder, but his remarks in leading detectives to the body were not entered into evidence. The discovery of the body was itself used, however, prompting another appeal to the Supreme Court based on the argument that the body should not have been used as evidence because it was discovered as a result of the illegally gathered statements. This time, in *Nix* v. *Williams* (1984),[177] the Supreme Court affirmed Williams's second conviction, holding that the body would have been found anyway, as detectives were searching in the direction where it lay when Williams revealed its location. That ruling came during the heyday of the Burger Court and clearly demonstrates a tilt by the Court away from suspects' rights and an accommodation with the imperfect world of police procedure. The *Williams* case, as it was finally resolved, is said to have created the *inevitable-discovery exception* to the *Miranda* requirements. The inevitable-discovery exception means that evidence, even if it was otherwise gathered inappropriately, can be used in a court of law if it would have invariably turned up in the normal course of events.

Public-Safety Exception to *Miranda*

In 2013, U.S. officials announced that they would question 19-year-old Dzhokhar Tsarnaev, the surviving Boston Marathon bomber, before reading him his *Miranda* rights. Tsarnaev had been wounded and was captured after his brother had been killed in a police shootout. Law enforcement officials said that they would question the hospitalized Tsarnaev under the well-established *public-safety exception* to the *Miranda* rule. The public-safety exception was created in 1984, when the U.S. Supreme Court decided the case of *New York* v. *Quarles*[178] centered on a rape in which the victim told police her assailant had fled, with a gun, into a nearby A&P supermarket. Two police officers entered the store and apprehended the suspect. One officer immediately noticed that the man was wearing an empty shoulder holster and, apparently fearing that a child might find the discarded weapon, quickly asked, "Where's the gun?" Quarles was convicted of rape but appealed his conviction, requesting that the weapon be suppressed as evidence because officers had not advised him of his *Miranda* rights before asking him about it. The Supreme Court disagreed, stating that considerations of public safety were overriding and negated the need for rights advisement before limited questioning that focused on the need to prevent further harm.

The U.S. Supreme Court has also held that in cases when the police issue *Miranda* warnings, a later demonstration that a person may have been suffering from mental problems does not necessarily negate a confession. *Colorado* v. *Connelly* (1986)[179] involved a man who approached a Denver police officer and said he wanted to confess to the murder of a young girl. The officer immediately informed him of his *Miranda* rights, but the man waived them and continued to talk. When a detective arrived, the man was again advised of his rights and again waived them. After being taken to the local jail, the man began to hear "voices" and later claimed that it was these voices that had made him confess. At the trial, the defense moved to have the earlier confession negated on the basis that it was not voluntarily or freely given because of the defendant's mental condition. Upon appeal, the U.S. Supreme Court disagreed, saying that "no coercive government conduct occurred in this case." Hence, "self-coercion," be it through the agency of a guilty conscience or faulty thought processes, does not appear to bar prosecution based on information revealed willingly by a suspect.

Suspects may legally waive their *Miranda* rights through a voluntary "knowing and intelligent" waiver.

Follow the author's tweets about the latest crime and justice news @schmalleger

▲ The aftermath of a terrorist explosion at the finish line of the 2013 Boston Marathon. Dzhokhar Tsarnaev, one of two brothers who planted the explosive devices among the crowd, survived a citywide manhunt, but authorities invoked the public-safety exception to the *Miranda* requirement in not advising him of his rights for a couple of days following his arrest. Why did they do that, and what information were they hoping to uncover by questioning Tsarnaev?

Kelvin Ma/ZUMA Press, Inc./Alamy Stock Photo

In-court references to a defendant's silence following *Miranda* warnings are unconstitutional.

Miranda triggers
The dual principles of custody and interrogation, both of which are necessary before an advisement of rights is required.

In another refinement of *Miranda*, the lawful ability of a police informant placed in a jail cell along with a defendant to gather information for later use at trial was upheld in the 1986 case of *Kuhlmann* v. *Wilson*.[180] The passive gathering of information was judged to be acceptable, provided that the informant did not make attempts to elicit information.

In the case of *Illinois* v. *Perkins* (1990),[181] the Court expanded its position to say that under appropriate circumstances, even the active questioning of a suspect by an undercover officer posing as a fellow inmate does not require *Miranda* warnings. In *Perkins*, the Court found that, lacking other forms of coercion, the fact that the suspect was not aware of the questioner's identity as a law enforcement officer ensured that his statements were freely given. In the words of the Court, "The essential ingredients of a 'police-dominated atmosphere' and compulsion are not present when an incarcerated person speaks freely to someone that he believes to be a fellow inmate."

Miranda and the Meaning of Interrogation

Modern interpretations of the applicability of *Miranda* warnings turn on an understanding of interrogation. The *Miranda* decision, as originally rendered, specifically recognized the need for police investigators to make inquiries at crime scenes to determine facts or to establish identities. As long as the individual questioned is not yet in custody and as long as probable cause is lacking in the investigator's mind, such questioning can proceed without *Miranda* warnings. In such cases, interrogation, within the meaning of *Miranda*, has not yet begun.

The case of *Rock* v. *Zimmerman* (1982)[182] provides a different sort of example—one in which a suspect willingly made statements to the police before interrogation began. The suspect had burned his own house and shot and killed a neighbor. When the fire department arrived, he began shooting again and killed the fire chief. Cornered later in a field, the defendant, gun in hand, spontaneously shouted at police, "How many people did I kill? How many people are dead?"[183] These spontaneous questions were held to be admissible evidence at the suspect's trial.

It is also important to recognize that the Supreme Court, in the *Miranda* decision, required that officers provide warnings only in those situations involving *both* arrest and custodial interrogation—what some call the **Miranda triggers**. In other words, it is generally permissible for officers to take a suspect into custody and listen without asking questions while he or she tells a story. Similarly, they may ask questions without providing a *Miranda* warning, even within the confines of a police station house, as long as the person questioned is not a suspect and is not under arrest.[184] Warnings are required only when officers begin to actively and deliberately elicit responses from a suspect who they know has been indicted or who is in custody.

A third-party conversation recorded by the police after a suspect has invoked the *Miranda* right to remain silent may be used as evidence, according to a 1987 ruling in *Arizona* v. *Mauro*.[185] In *Mauro*, a man who willingly conversed with his wife in the presence of a police tape recorder, even after invoking his right to keep silent, was held to have effectively abandoned that right.

When a waiver is not made, however, in-court references to a defendant's silence following the issuing of *Miranda* warnings are unconstitutional. In the 1976 case of *Doyle* v. *Ohio*,[186] the U.S. Supreme Court definitively ruled that "a suspect's [post-*Miranda*] silence will not be used against him." Even so, according to the Court in *Brecht* v. *Abrahamson* (1993),[187] prosecution efforts to use such silence against a defendant may not invalidate a finding of guilt by a jury unless the "error had substantial and injurious effect or influence in determining the jury's verdict."[188]

The 2004 case of *Missouri* v. *Seibert*[189] addressed the legality of a two-step police interrogation technique in which suspects were questioned and—if they made incriminating statements—were then advised of their *Miranda* rights and questioned again. The justices found that such a technique could not meet constitutional muster, writing, "When the [*Miranda*] warnings are inserted in the midst of coordinated and continuing interrogation, they are likely to mislead and deprive a defendant of knowledge essential to his ability to understand the nature of his rights and the consequences of abandoning them. . . . And it would be unrealistic to treat two spates of integrated and proximately conducted questioning as independent interrogations . . . simply because *Miranda* warnings formally punctuate them in the middle."

In the 2010 case of *Florida* v. *Powell*, the U.S. Supreme Court held that although *Miranda* warnings are generally required prior to police interrogation, the wording of those warnings is not set in stone. The Court ruled that "in determining whether police warnings were satisfactory, reviewing courts are not required to examine them as if construing a will or defining the terms of an easement. The inquiry is simply whether the warnings reasonably convey to a suspect his rights as required by *Miranda*."[190]

Also, in 2010, in the case of *Berghuis* v. *Thompkins*, the Court held that a Michigan suspect did not invoke his right to remain silent by simply not answering questions that interrogators put to him.[191] Instead, the justices ruled, a suspect must unambiguously assert his right to remain silent before the police are required to end their questioning. In this case, the defendant, Van Chester Thompkins, was properly advised of his rights prior to questioning, and, although he was largely silent during a 3-hour interrogation, he never said that he wanted to remain silent, that he did not want to talk with the police, or that he wanted an attorney. Near the end of the interrogation, however, he answered "yes" when asked whether he prayed to God to forgive him for the shooting death of a murder victim.

Finally, in 2013, in the case of *Salinas* v. *Texas*, the Supreme Court found that an offender must expressly invoke his *Miranda* privileges, and that failure to do so can later result in use at trial of the offender's silence as evidence of his guilt.[192] According to the Court, "A defendant normally does not invoke the privilege (against self-incrimination) by remaining silent."

Gathering of Special Kinds of Nontestimonial Evidence

The role of law enforcement is complicated by the fact that suspects are often privy to special evidence of a nontestimonial sort. Nontestimonial evidence is generally physical evidence, and most physical evidence is subject to normal procedures of search and seizure. A special category of nontestimonial evidence, however, includes very personal items that may be within or part of a person's body, such as ingested drugs, blood cells, foreign objects, medical implants, and human DNA. Also included in this category might be fingerprints and other kinds of biological residue. The gathering of such special kinds of nontestimonial evidence is a complex area rich in precedent. The Fourth Amendment guarantees that people be secure in their homes and in their persons has generally been interpreted by the courts to mean that the improper seizure of physical evidence of any kind is illegal and will result in exclusion of that evidence at trial. When very personal kinds of nontestimonial evidence are considered, however, the issue becomes more complicated.

The Right to Privacy

Two 1985 cases, *Hayes* v. *Florida*[193] and *Winston* v. *Lee*,[194] are examples of limits the courts have placed on the seizure of very personal forms of nontestimonial evidence. The *Hayes* case established the right of suspects to refuse to be fingerprinted when probable cause necessary to effect an arrest does not exist. *Winston* demonstrated the inviolability of the body against surgical and other substantially invasive techniques that might be ordered by authorities against a suspect's will.

In the *Winston* case, Rudolph Lee, Jr., was found a few blocks from the scene of a robbery with a gunshot wound in his chest. The robbery had involved an exchange of gunshots by a store owner and the robber, with the owner noting that the robber had apparently been hit by a bullet. At the hospital, the store owner identified Lee as the robber. The prosecution sought to have Lee submit to surgery to remove the bullet in his chest, arguing that the bullet would provide physical evidence linking him to the crime. Lee refused the surgery, and in *Winston* v. *Lee*, the U.S. Supreme Court ruled that Lee could not be ordered to undergo surgery because such a magnitude of intrusion into his body was unacceptable under the right to privacy guaranteed by the Fourth Amendment. The *Winston* case was based on precedent established in *Schmerber* v. *California* (1966).[195] The *Schmerber* case

In October of 2015, then-FBI director, James B. Comey, spoke at the University of Chicago Law School and addressed what some have called "depolicing" (aka the "Ferguson effect"). Comey noted that depolicing, or the less aggressive enforcement of the law following widespread unfavorable media reports about the police, may embolden criminals and contribute to increased crime. National media coverage of the police was intense following a number of police shootings of unarmed black men across the country in 2014 and 2015. Civil protests against the unnecessary use of deadly force by law enforcement officers took place in many American cities, and frequent news reports condemned the actions of officers who were involved in the incidents.

Comey noted that violent crime rates were trending up in major cities across the country. He offered various reasons as to why that's happening, but then he added: "Nobody says it on the record, nobody says it in public, but police and elected officials are quietly saying it to themselves. And they're saying it to me, and I'm going to say it to you. And it is the one explanation that does explain the calendar and the map and that makes the most sense to me. Maybe something in policing has changed."

Comey went on to ask: "In today's YouTube world, are officers reluctant to get out of their cars and do the work that controls violent crime? Are officers answering 911 calls but avoiding the informal contact that keeps bad guys from standing around, especially with guns?" He continued, "I spoke to officers privately in one big city precinct who described being surrounded by young people with mobile phone cameras held high, taunting them the moment they get out of their cars. They told me, 'We feel like we're under siege and we don't feel much like getting out of our cars.'"

The question, Comey said, "is whether these kinds of things are changing police behavior all over the country." His answer? "I do have a strong sense that . . . a chill wind that has blown through American law enforcement . . ."

We need to be careful, the FBI director said, that good policing "doesn't drift away from us in the age of viral videos, or there will be profound consequences."

YOU DECIDE

Some say that close scrutiny of law enforcement activities are a positive force for change, and that they will produce better enforcement efforts—ones that are in close keeping with the civil rights of all citizens. Do you agree?

Reference: James B. Comey, "Remarks Delivered at the University of Chicago Law School, Chicago, IL, October 23, 2015," FBI press release, https://www.fbi.gov/news/speeches/law-enforcement-and-the-communities-we-serve-bending-the-lines-toward-safety-and-justice (accessed March 3, 2016).

turned on the extraction against the defendant's will of a blood sample to be measured for alcohol content. In *Schmerber*, the Court ruled that warrants must be obtained for bodily intrusions unless fast action is necessary to prevent the destruction of evidence by natural physiological processes.

Body-Cavity Searches

In early 2005, officers of the Suffolk County (New York) Police Department arrested 36-year-old Terrance Haynes and charged him with marijuana possession.[196] After placing him in the back of a patrol car, Haynes appeared to choke and had difficulty breathing. Soon his breathing stopped, prompting officers to use the Heimlich maneuver, which dislodged a plastic bag from Haynes's windpipe. The bag contained 11 packets of cocaine. Although Haynes survived the ordeal, he faced up to 25 years in prison.

Some suspects might literally "cough up" evidence, some are more successful at hiding it *in* their bodies. Body-cavity searches are among the most problematic types of searches for police today. "Strip" searches of convicts in prison, including the search of body cavities, have generally been held to be permissible.

The 1985 Supreme Court case of *U.S.* v. *Montoya de Hernandez*[197] focused on the issue of "alimentary canal smuggling," in which the offender typically swallows condoms filled with cocaine or heroin and waits for nature to take its course to recover the substance. In the *Montoya* case, a woman known to be a "balloon swallower" arrived in the United States on a flight from Colombia. She was detained by customs officials and given a pat-down search by a female agent. The agent reported that the woman's abdomen was firm and suggested that X-rays be taken. The suspect refused and was given the choice of submitting to further tests or taking the next flight back to Colombia. No flight was immediately available, however, and the suspect was placed in a room for 16 hours, where she refused all food and drink. Finally, a court order for an X-ray was obtained. The procedure revealed "balloons," and the woman was detained another 4 days, during which time she passed numerous cocaine-filled plastic condoms. The Court ruled that the woman's confinement was not unreasonable, based as it was on the supportable suspicion that she was "body-packing" cocaine. Any discomfort she experienced, the Court ruled, "resulted solely from the method that she chose to smuggle illicit drugs."[198]

🐦 Follow the author's tweets about the latest crime and justice news @schmalleger

Electronic Eavesdropping

Modern technology makes possible increasingly complex forms of communication. One of the first and best known of the U.S. Supreme Court decisions involving electronic communications was the 1928 case of *Olmstead* v. *U.S.*[199] In *Olmstead*, bootleggers used their home telephones to discuss and transact business. Agents tapped the lines and based their investigation and ensuing arrests on conversations they overheard. The defendants were convicted and eventually appealed to the high court, arguing that the agents had in effect seized information illegally without a search warrant in violation of the defendants' Fourth Amendment right to be secure in their homes. The Court ruled, however, that telephone lines were not an extension of the defendants' home and therefore were not protected by the constitutional guarantee of security. Subsequent federal statutes (discussed shortly) have substantially modified the significance of *Olmstead*.

Recording devices carried on the body of an undercover agent or an informant were ruled to produce admissible evidence in *On Lee* v. *U.S.* (1952)[200] and *Lopez* v. *U.S.* (1963).[201] The 1967 case of *Berger* v. *New York*[202] permitted wiretaps and "bugs" in instances where state law provided for the use of such devices and where officers obtained a warrant based on probable cause.

The Court appeared to undertake a significant change of direction in the area of electronic eavesdropping when it decided the case of *Katz* v. *U.S.* in 1967.[203] Federal agents had monitored a number of Katz's telephone calls from a public phone using a device separate from the phone lines and attached to the glass of the phone booth. The Court, in this case, stated that what a person makes an effort to keep private, even in a public place, requires a judicial decision, in the form of a warrant issued upon probable cause, to unveil. In the words of the Court, "The government's activities in electronically listening to and recording the petitioner's words violated the privacy upon which he justifiably relied while using the telephone booth and thus constituted a 'search and seizure' within the meaning of the Fourth Amendment."

In 1968, with the case of *Lee* v. *Florida*,[204] the Court applied the Federal Communications Act[205] to telephone conversations that may be the object of police investigation and held that evidence obtained without a warrant could not be used in state proceedings if it resulted from a wiretap. The only person who has the authority to permit eavesdropping, according to that act, is the sender of the message.

The Federal Communications Act, originally passed in 1934, does not specifically mention the potential interest of law enforcement agencies in monitoring communications. Title III of the Omnibus Crime Control and Safe Streets Act of 1968, however, mostly prohibits wiretaps but does allow officers to listen to electronic communications when (1) an officer is one of the parties involved in the communication, (2) one of the parties is not the officer but willingly decides to share the communication with the officer, or (3) officers obtain a warrant based on probable cause. In the 1971 case of *U.S.* v. *White*,[206] the Court held that law enforcement officers may intercept electronic information when one of the parties involved in the communication gives his or her consent, even without a warrant.

In 1984, the Supreme Court decided the case of *U.S.* v. *Karo*,[207] in which Drug Enforcement Agency (DEA) agents had arrested James Karo for cocaine importation. Officers had placed a radio transmitter inside a 50-gallon drum of ether purchased by Karo for use in processing the cocaine. The transmitter was placed inside the drum with the consent of the seller of the ether but without a search warrant. The shipment of ether was followed to the Karo house, and Karo was arrested and convicted of cocaine-trafficking charges. Karo appealed to the U.S. Supreme Court, claiming that the radio beeper had violated his reasonable expectation of privacy inside his premises and that, without a warrant, the evidence it produced was tainted. The Court agreed and overturned his conviction.

Minimization Requirement for Electronic Surveillance

The Supreme Court established a minimization requirement pertinent to electronic surveillance in the 1978 case of *U.S.* v. *Scott*.[208] *Minimization* means that officers must make every reasonable effort to monitor only those conversations, through the use of phone taps, body bugs, and the like, that are specifically related to the criminal activity under investigation. As soon as it becomes obvious that a conversation is innocent, then the monitoring personnel

> Recording devices carried on the body of an undercover agent produce admissible evidence.

are required to cease their invasion of privacy. Problems arise if the conversation occurs in a foreign language, if it is "coded," or if it is ambiguous. It has been suggested that investigators involved in electronic surveillance maintain logbooks of their activities that specifically show monitored conversations, as well as efforts made at minimization.[209]

The Electronic Communications Privacy Act of 1986

Passed by Congress in 1986, the **Electronic Communications Privacy Act (ECPA)**[210] brought major changes in the requirements law enforcement officers must meet to intercept wire communications (those involving the human voice). The ECPA deals specifically with three areas of communication: (1) wiretaps and bugs, (2) pen registers that record the numbers dialed from a telephone, and (3) tracing devices that determine the number from which a call emanates. The act also addresses the procedures to be followed by officers in obtaining records relating to communications services, and it establishes requirements for gaining access to stored electronic communications and records of those communications. The ECPA basically requires that investigating officers must obtain wiretap-type court orders to eavesdrop on *ongoing communications.* The use of pen registers and recording devices, however, is specifically excluded by the law from court order requirements.[211]

A related measure, the Communications Assistance for Law Enforcement Act of 1994,[212] appropriated $500 million to modify the U.S. phone system to allow for continued wiretapping by law enforcement agencies. The law also specifies a standard-setting process for the redesign of existing equipment that would permit effective wiretapping in the face of coming technological advances. In the words of the FBI's Telecommunications Industry Liaison Unit, "This law requires telecommunications carriers, as defined in the Act, to ensure law enforcement's ability, pursuant to court order or other lawful authorization, to intercept communications notwithstanding advanced telecommunications technologies."[213] In 2016, 3,168 wiretap requests were approved by federal and state judges, and approximately 5 million conversations were intercepted by law enforcement agencies throughout the country (Figure 5–3).[214]

The Telecommunications Act of 1996

Title V of the Telecommunications Act of 1996[215] made it a federal offense for anyone engaged in interstate or international communications to knowingly use a telecommunications device "to create, solicit, or initiate the transmission of any comment, request, suggestion, proposal, image, or other communication which is obscene, lewd, lascivious, filthy, or indecent, with intent to annoy, abuse, threaten, or harass another person." The law also provided special penalties for anyone who "makes a telephone call . . . without disclosing his identity and with intent to annoy, abuse, threaten, or harass any person at the called number or who receives the communication" or who "makes or causes the telephone of another repeatedly or continuously to ring, with intent to harass any person at the called number; or makes repeated telephone calls" for the purpose of harassing a person at the called number.

A section of the law, known as the Communications Decency Act (CDA),[216] criminalized the transmission to minors of "patently offensive" obscene materials over the Internet or other computer telecommunications services. Portions of the CDA, however, were invalidated by the U.S. Supreme Court in the case of *Reno* v. *ACLU* (1997).[217]

The USA PATRIOT Act of 2001

The **USA PATRIOT Act** of 2001, which is also discussed in CJ Exhibit 5–3, made it easier for police investigators to intercept many forms of electronic communications. Under previous federal law, for example, investigators could not obtain a wiretap order to intercept *wire* communications for violations of the Computer Fraud and Abuse Act.[218] In several well-known investigations, however, hackers had stolen teleconferencing services from telephone companies and then used those services to plan and execute hacking attacks.

The act[219] added felony violations of the Computer Fraud and Abuse Act to Section 2516(1) of Title 18 of the U.S. Code—the portion of federal law that lists specific types of crimes for which investigators may obtain a wiretap order for wire communications.

Electronic Communications Privacy Act (ECPA)
A law passed by Congress in 1986 establishing the due-process requirements that law enforcement officers must meet in order to legally intercept wire communications.

USA PATRIOT Act
A federal law (Public Law 107–56) enacted in response to terrorist attacks on the World Trade Center and the Pentagon on September 11, 2001. The law, officially titled the Uniting and Strengthening America by Providing Appropriate Tools Required to Intercept and Obstruct Terrorism Act, substantially broadened the investigative authority of law enforcement agencies throughout America and is applicable to many crimes other than terrorism. The law has recently been revised and reauthorized by Congress.

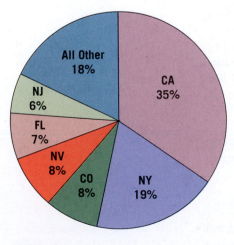

FIGURE 5–3
State Wiretap Authorizations, 2016
Source: Office of the United States Courts, *Wiretap Report 2016.*

The USA PATRIOT Act also modified that portion of the ECPA that governs law enforcement access to stored electronic communications (such as e-mail) to include stored wire communications (such as voice mail). Before the modification, law enforcement officers needed to obtain a wiretap order (rather than a search warrant) to obtain unopened voice communications. Because today's e-mail messages may contain digitized voice "attachments," investigators were sometimes required to obtain both a search warrant and a wiretap order to learn the contents of a specific message. Under the act, the same rules now apply to both stored wire communications and stored electronic communications. Wiretap orders, which are often much more difficult to obtain than search warrants, are now only required to intercept real-time telephone conversations.

> The PATRIOT Act has not diminished our liberty. It has defended our liberty and made America more secure.
>
> —George W. Bush, 43rd president of the United States

Before passage of the USA PATRIOT Act, federal law allowed investigators to use an administrative subpoena (i.e., a subpoena authorized by a federal or state statute or by a federal or state grand jury or trial court) to compel Internet service providers to provide a limited class of information, such as a customer's name, address, length of service, and means of payment. Also, under previous law, investigators could not subpoena certain records, including credit card numbers or details about other forms of payment for Internet service. Such information, however, can be highly relevant in determining a suspect's true identity because, in many cases, users register with Internet service providers using false names.

Previous federal law[220] was also technology specific, relating primarily to telephone communications. Local and long-distance telephone billing records, for example, could be subpoenaed but not billing information for Internet communications or records of Internet session times and durations. Similarly, previous law allowed the government to use a subpoena to obtain the customer's "telephone number or other subscriber number or identity" but did not define what that phrase meant in the context of Internet communications.

The USA PATRIOT Act amended portions of this federal law[221] to update and expand the types of records that law enforcement authorities may obtain with a subpoena. "Records of session times and durations," as well as "any temporarily assigned network address," may now be gathered. Such changes should make the process of identifying computer criminals and tracing their Internet communications faster and easier.

Finally, the USA PATRIOT Act facilitates the use of roving, or multipoint, wiretaps. Roving wiretaps, issued with court approval, target a specific individual and not a particular telephone number or communications device. Hence, law enforcement agents armed with an order for a multipoint wiretap can follow the flow of communications engaged in by a person as he or she switches from one cellular phone to another or to a wired telephone.

In 2006, President George W. Bush signed the USA PATRIOT Improvement and Reauthorization Act of 2005[222] into law. The act, also referred to as PATRIOT II, made permanent 14 provisions of the original 2001 legislation that had been slated to expire and extended others for another 4 years (including the roving wiretap provision and a provision that allows authorities to seize business records). It also addressed some of the concerns of civil libertarians who had criticized the earlier law as too restrictive. Finally, the new law provided additional protections for mass transportation systems and seaports, closed some legal loopholes in laws aimed at preventing terrorist financing, and included a subsection called the Combat Methamphetamine Epidemic Act (CMEA). The CMEA contains significant provisions intended to strengthen federal, state, and local efforts designed at curtailing the spread of methamphetamine use.

In May 2011, President Barack Obama signed into law legislation extending a number of provisions of the USA PATRIOT Act that would have otherwise expired. The president's signature gave new life to the roving wiretap and business records provisions of the act, as well as some others.[223]

Cybersecurity Information Sharing Act (CISA)

In 2015, President Obama signed the Cybersecurity Information Sharing Act (CISA) into law.[224] That law, which was passed as part of the U.S. government's annual omnibus spending bill, is designed to improve cybersecurity in the United States by facilitating the sharing of information about cybersecurity threats. It allows for the easy sharing of Internet traffic information between the U.S. government and technology and manufacturing companies.

Follow the author's tweets about the latest crime and justice news @schmalleger

CJ Exhibit 5–3
The USA PATRIOT Act of 2001 and the USA Freedom Act of 2015

On October 26, 2001, President George W. Bush signed into law the USA PATRIOT Act, also known as the Uniting and Strengthening America by Providing Appropriate Tools Required to Intercept and Obstruct Terrorism Act. The law, which was drafted in response to the September 11, 2001, terrorist attacks on American targets, substantially increased the investigatory authority of federal, state, and local police agencies.

The act permits longer jail terms for certain suspects arrested without a warrant, broadens authority for **"sneak and peek" searches** (searches conducted without prior notice and in the absence of the suspect), and enhances the power of prosecutors. The law also increases the ability of federal authorities to tap phones (including wireless devices), share intelligence information, track Internet usage, crack down on money laundering, and protect U.S. borders. Many of the crime-fighting powers created under the legislation are not limited to acts of terrorism but apply to many different kinds of criminal offenses.

The 2001 law led individual-rights advocates to question whether the government unfairly expanded police powers at the expense of civil liberties. Although many aspects of the USA PATRIOT Act have been criticized as potentially unconstitutional, Section 213, which authorizes delayed notice of the execution of a warrant, may be most vulnerable to court challenge. The American Civil Liberties Union (ACLU) maintains that under this section, law enforcement agents could enter a house, apartment, or office with a search warrant while the occupant is away, search through his or her property, and take photographs without having to tell the suspect about the search until later.[a] The ACLU also believes that this provision is illegal because

the Fourth Amendment to the Constitution protects against unreasonable searches and seizures and requires the government to obtain a warrant and to give notice to the person whose property will be searched before conducting the search. The notice requirement enables the suspect to assert his or her Fourth Amendment rights.

In 2005, the U.S. Congress reauthorized most provisions of the USA PATRIOT Act, and in May, 2011, President Barack Obama signed legislation providing for an extension of several terrorist surveillance provisions included in the USA PATRIOT Act and in the Intelligence Reform and Terrorism Prevention Act of 2004. Finally, in 2015, the USA Freedom Act became law. It continued the use of roving wiretaps and limited bulk collection of telecommunications data on U.S. citizens by the National Security Agency.

Read the original USA PATRIOT Act of 2001 in its entirety at **https://www.justicestudies.com/pubs/patriot.pdf**. Title 18 of the U.S. Code is available at **http://uscode.house.gov/browse/prelim@title18&edition**.

---

[a] Much of the information in this paragraph is taken from American Civil Liberties Union, "How the Anti-Terrorism Bill Expands Law Enforcement 'Sneak and Peek' Warrants," http://www.aclu.org/congress/1102301b.html (accessed February 12, 2010).

References: USA PATRIOT Improvement and Reauthorization Act of 2005 (Public Law 109–177); U.S. Department of Justice, *Field Guidance on Authorities (Redacted) Enacted in the 2001 Anti-Terrorism Legislation* (Washington, D.C.: U.S. Dept. of Justice, no date), http://www.epic.org/terrorism/DOJguidance.pdf (accessed August 28, 2018); USA PATRIOT Act, 2001 (Public Law 107–56).

"sneak and peek" search
A search that occurs in the suspect's absence and without his or her prior knowledge. Also known as a *delayed-notification search*.

The purpose of the law is to make it easier for private companies to quickly and directly share personal information with the government, especially in cases involving specific cybersecurity threats. Easier information sharing facilitates faster law enforcement and security responses than were possible under previous law.

The law also creates a portal for a variety of federal agencies including the FBI and the National Security Agency, to receive threat information directly from private companies, without the need for the involvement of the Department of Homeland Security. Critics of the legislation say that it facilitates mass surveillance of private communications via the sharing of information between companies and the government, most notably the National Security Agency.

Electronic and Latent Evidence

The Internet, computer networks, and automated data systems present many new opportunities for committing criminal activity.[225] Computers and other electronic devices are increasingly being used to commit, enable, or support crimes perpetrated against people, organizations, and property. Whether the crime involves attacks against computer systems or the information they contain or more traditional offenses such as murder, money laundering, trafficking, or fraud, the proper seizure of **electronic evidence** that is specifically described in a valid search warrant has become increasingly important.

electronic evidence
Information and data of investigative value that are stored in or transmitted by an electronic device.[i]

Electronic evidence is "information and data of investigative value that are stored in or transmitted by an electronic device."[226] Such evidence is often acquired when physical items, such as computers, external disk drives, CDs, DVDs, SSDs, flash drives, smart phones, SIM cards, iPads, iPods, Blackberrys, and other electronic devices, are collected from a crime scene or are obtained from a suspect.

latent evidence
Evidence of relevance to a criminal investigation that is not readily seen by the unaided eye.

Electronic evidence has special characteristics: (1) It is latent; (2) it can be sent across national and state borders quickly and easily; (3) it is fragile and can easily be altered, damaged, compromised, or destroyed by improper handling or improper examination; (4) it may be time sensitive. Like DNA or fingerprints, electronic evidence is **latent evidence** because it is not readily visible to the human eye under normal conditions. Special equipment and software are required to "see" and evaluate electronic evidence. In the courtroom, expert testimony may be needed to explain the acquisition of electronic evidence and the examination process used to interpret it.

In 2002, in recognition of the special challenges posed by electronic evidence, the Computer Crime and Intellectual Property Section (CCIPS) of the Criminal Division of the U.S. Department of Justice released a how-to manual for law enforcement officers called *Searching and Seizing Computers and Obtaining Electronic Evidence in Criminal Investigations.*[227] The manual, which is a how-to in **digital criminal forensics**, can be accessed via **https://www.justicestudies.com/pubs/electronic.pdf**.

digital criminal forensics
The lawful seizure, acquisition, analysis, reporting, and safeguarding of data from digital devices that may contain information of evidentiary value to the trier of fact in criminal events.[ii]

About the same time, the Technical Working Group for Electronic Crime Scene Investigation (TWGECSI) released a much more detailed guide for law enforcement officers to use in gathering electronic evidence. The manual, *Electronic Crime Scene Investigation: A Guide for First Responders,*[228] grew out of a partnership formed in 1998 between the National Cybercrime Training Partnership, the Office of Law Enforcement Standards, and the National Institute of Justice. The working group was asked to identify, define, and establish basic criteria to assist federal and state agencies in handling electronic investigations and related prosecutions.

TWGECSI guidelines say that law enforcement must take special precautions when documenting, collecting, and preserving electronic evidence to maintain its integrity. The guidelines also note that the first law enforcement officer on the scene (commonly called the *first responder*) should take steps to ensure the safety of everyone at the scene and to protect the integrity of all evidence, both traditional and electronic. The entire TWGECSI guide, which includes many practical instructions for investigators working with electronic evidence, is available at **https://www.justicestudies.com/pubs/ecsi.pdf**.

Once digital evidence has been gathered, it must be analyzed. Consequently, a few years ago, the government-sponsored Technical Working Group for the Examination of Digital Evidence (TWGEDE) published *Forensic Examination of Digital Evidence: A Guide for Law Enforcement.*[229] Among the guide's recommendations are that digital evidence should be acquired in a manner that protects and preserves the integrity of the original evidence and that examination should only be conducted on a *copy* of the original evidence. The entire guide, which is nearly 100 pages long, can be accessed via **https://www.justicestudies.com/pubs/forensicexam.pdf**. A more recent and even more detailed guide, titled *Investigations Involving the Internet and Computer Networks*, published by the National Institute of Justice, is available at **https://www.justicestudies.com/pubs/internetinvest.pdf**.

Follow the author's tweets about the latest crime and justice news @schmalleger

Recently, the National Institute of Justice established the Electronic Crime Technology Center of Excellence (ECTCoE) to assist in building the electronic crime prevention and investigation and digital evidence collection and examination capacity of state and local law enforcement. The Center works to identify electronic crime and digital evidence tools, technologies and training gaps. Many of the Center's publications are available through the federal Justice Technology Information Center (JTIC), which is part of the National Law Enforcement and Corrections Technology Center (NLECTC). Visit the JTIC website at **http://www.justnet.org**.

Warrantless searches bear special mention in any discussion of electronic evidence. In the 1999 case of *U.S.* v. *Carey,*[230] a federal appellate court held that the consent a defendant had given to police for his apartment to be searched did not extend to the search of his computer once it was taken to a police station. Similarly, in *U.S.* v. *Turner* (1999),[231] the First Circuit Court of Appeals held that the warrantless police search of a defendant's personal computer while in his apartment exceeded the scope of the defendant's consent. Finally, in 2014, the U.S. Supreme Court found that "the police generally may not, without a warrant, search digital information on a cell phone seized from an individual who has been arrested."[232] The case, *Riley* v. *California*, involved a defendant who had been stopped for a traffic violation, which led to his arrest on weapons charges. Officers confiscated the defendant's cell phone and accessed the information on it, learning that he was associated with a street gang. Eventually, he was charged in connection with a shooting, and prosecutors sought an enhanced sentence based on the evidence of gang activity found on the cell phone. The Court concluded that the search of a cell phone "implicates substantially greater individual privacy interests than a brief physical search." Learn more about gathering digital evidence from the FBI at **https://www.justicestudies.com/digital_evidence.pdf**.

Summary

POLICING: LEGAL ASPECTS

- Legal restraints on police action stem primarily from the U.S. Constitution's Bill of Rights, especially the Fourth, Fifth, and Sixth Amendments, which (along with the Fourteenth Amendment) require due process of law. Most due-process requirements of relevance to police work concern three major areas: (1) evidence and investigation (often called *search* and *seizure*), (2) arrest, and (3) interrogation. Each of these areas has been addressed by a number of important U.S. Supreme Court decisions, and this chapter discusses those decisions and their significance for police work.

- The Bill of Rights was designed to protect citizens against abuses of police power. It does so by guaranteeing due process of law for everyone suspected of having committed a crime and by ensuring the availability of constitutional rights to all citizens, regardless of state or local law or procedure. Within the context of criminal case processing, due-process requirements mandate that all justice system officials, not only the police, respect the rights of accused individuals throughout the criminal justice process.

- The Fourth Amendment to the Constitution declares that people must be secure in their homes and in their persons against unreasonable searches and seizures. Consequently, law enforcement officers are often required to demonstrate probable cause in order to obtain a search warrant from a judge if they are to conduct searches and seize the property of criminal suspects legally. Not all searches require a warrant. Many searches conducted by law enforcement officers fall into the category of warrantless searches, or searches for which a warrant has not been issued by legitimate judicial authority. While most warrantless searches are permissible, some searches require the issuance of a warrant prior to the conduct of the search. The Supreme Court has also established that police officers, in order to protect themselves from attack, have the right to search a person being arrested and to search the area under the arrestee's immediate control.

- Technically, arrest takes place whenever a law enforcement officer restricts a person's freedom to leave. Arrests may occur when an officer comes upon a crime in progress, but most jurisdictions also allow warrantless arrests for felonies when a crime is not in progress, as long as probable cause can later be demonstrated. Reasonable suspicion, which requires a lesser degree of certainty than probable cause, permits the limited detention of persons of interest in an investigation. Consequently, an investigative detention is defined as a temporary seizure of an individual by a police officer for investigative purposes.

- Information that is useful for law enforcement purposes is called *intelligence*, and as this chapter has shown, intelligence gathering is vital to police work. The need for useful information often leads police investigators to question suspects, informants, and potentially knowledgeable citizens. When suspects who are in custody become subject to interrogation, they must be advised of their *Miranda* rights before questioning begins. The *Miranda* warnings, which were mandated by the Supreme Court in the 1966 case of *Miranda* v. *Arizona*, are listed in this chapter. They ensure that suspects know their rights—including the right to remain silent—in the face of police interrogation.

QUESTIONS FOR REVIEW

1. Name some of the legal restraints on police action, and list some types of behavior that might be considered abuse of police authority.
2. Explain how the idea of due process and democratically inspired legal restraints on the police help to protect our personal freedoms.
3. Describe the legal standards for assessing searches and seizures conducted by law enforcement agents.
4. What is arrest, and when does it occur? How do legal understandings of the term differ from popular depictions of the arrest process?
5. What is the role of interrogation in intelligence gathering? List each of the *Miranda* warnings. Which recent U.S. Supreme Court cases have affected *Miranda* warning requirements?

Policing: Issues and Challenges

The continuous threat of terrorism has thrust domestic preparedness obligations to the very top of the law enforcement agenda.

—Colonel Joel Leson, director, IACP Center for Police Leadership[1]

Learning Objectives

After reading this chapter, you should be able to:

1. Describe the police working personality, relating it to police subculture. **170**

2. Describe different types of police corruption and possible methods for building police integrity. **173**

3. Describe the dangers, conflicts, challenges, and sources of stress that police officers face in their work. **178**

4. Describe the changed role of American police in the post-9/11 environment. **184**

5. Describe civil liability issues associated with policing, including common sources of civil suits against the police. **188**

6. Describe racial profiling and biased policing, including why they have become significant issues in policing. **193**

7. Summarize the guidelines for using force and for determining when excessive force has been used. **197**

8. Demonstrate why professionalism and ethics are important in policing today. **203**

9. Identify some of the issues related to ethnic and gender diversity in policing, and suggest ways of addressing them. **206**

Darron Cummings/AP Images

▲ NYPD officer Larry DePrimo. DePrimo made headlines in 2012 when he was photographed by a tourist giving shoes and socks to a homeless man on a cold winter night, and the photo went viral on Facebook. Is DePrimo a typical police officer?

Doug Meszler/Splash News/Alamy Stock Photo

Introduction

On a cold evening in late November 2012, a young NYPD officer was caught on a tourist's cell phone camera giving clean socks and shoes to a homeless man sitting on a sidewalk in Times Square. The photo was posted to Facebook and soon went viral, causing an outpouring of well wishes for the officer, Larry DePrimo. What DePrimo did that night was not part of his job, but a personal act of kindness that demonstrated the human side of police work. Interviewed later by *People Magazine*, DePrimo said, "Honestly, I feel undeserving of so much thanks. I just love to help people. That's why I became a cop."[2]

Today's police officers and administrators face many complex issues, and not all of the stories involving police work end well. Some concerns, such as corruption, on-the-job dangers, and the use of deadly force, derive from the very nature of policing. Others, like racial profiling and exposure to civil liability, have arisen from common practices, characteristic police values, public expectations, legislative action, and ongoing societal change. One of the most significant challenges facing American law enforcement today is policing a multicultural society. All of these issues are discussed in the pages that follow. We begin, however, with the police recruit socialization process. It is vital to understand this process because the values and expectations learned through it not only contribute to the nature of many important police issues but also determine how the police view and respond to those issues.

Police Personality and Culture

New police officers learn what is considered appropriate police behavior by working with seasoned veterans. Through conversations with other officers

> **1** Describe the police working personality, relating it to police subculture.

in the locker room, in a squad car, or over a cup of coffee, a new recruit is introduced to the value-laden subculture of police work. **Police subculture** can be understood as "the set of informal values which characterize the police force as a distinct community with a common identity."[3] This process of informal socialization plays a much bigger role than formal police academy training in determining how rookies come to see police work. Through it, new officers gain a shared view of the world that can best be described as

► Police cadets in St. Paul, Minnesota, celebrate their graduation from the police academy. The police working personality has been characterized as authoritarian, suspicious, and conservative. How does the police working personality develop?

Marlin Levison/Minneapolis Star Tribune/ZUMA Press Inc/Alamy Stock Photo

■ **TABLE 6-1**
Characteristics of the Police Personality

Authoritarian			
Honorable	Cynical	Secret	Efficient
Insecure	Loyal	Individualistic	Dogmatic
Suspicious	Hostile	Conservative	Prejudiced

"streetwise." Streetwise cops know what official department policy is, but they also know the most efficient way to get a job done. By the time rookie officers become streetwise, they know which of the various informal means of accomplishing the job are acceptable to other officers. The police subculture creates few real mavericks, but it also produces few officers who view their jobs exclusively in terms of public mandates and official dictums.

In the 1960s, renowned criminologist Jerome Skolnick described what he called the **police working personality**.[4] Skolnick's description of the police personality was consistent with William Westley's classic study of the Gary (Indiana) Police Department, in which he found a police subculture with its own "customs, laws, and morality,"[5] and with Arthur Niederhoffer's observation that cynicism was pervasive among officers in New York City.[6] More recent authors have claimed that the "big curtain of secrecy" surrounding much of police work shields knowledge of the nature of the police personality from outsiders.[7] Taken in concert, these writers offer the picture of the police working personality shown in Table 6-1.

> The police subculture creates few real mavericks, but it also produces few officers who view their jobs exclusively in terms of public mandates and official dictums.

Some characteristics of the police working personality are essential for survival and effectiveness. For example, because officers are often exposed to highly emotional and potentially threatening confrontations with belligerent people, they must develop efficient authoritarian strategies for gaining control over others. Similarly, a suspicious nature makes for a good police officer, especially during interrogations and investigations.

However, other characteristics of the police working personality are not as advantageous. For example, many officers are cynical, and some can be hostile toward members of the public who do not share their conservative values. These traits result from regular interaction with suspects, most of whom deny any wrongdoing even when they are clearly guilty in the eyes of the police. Eventually, personal traits that result from typical police work become firmly ingrained, setting the cornerstone of the police working personality.

There are at least two sources of the police personality. On the one hand, it may be that components of the police personality already exist in some individuals and draw them toward police work.[8] Supporting this view are studies indicating that police officers who come from conservative backgrounds view themselves as defenders of middle-class morality.[9] On the other hand, some aspects of the police personality can be attributed to the socialization into the police subculture that rookie officers experience when they are inducted into police ranks.

Researchers have reported similar elements in police subculture throughout the United States.[10] They have concluded that, like all cultures, police subculture is a relatively stable collection of beliefs and values that is unlikely to change from within. However, an important study published in 2017, found that police subculture can be influenced significantly by strong and effective leadership; and that support among supervisors for procedural justice (see Chapter 1) can change the attitudes and behavior of officers in the field.[11] Similarly, police subculture may be changed through external pressures, such as new hiring practices, investigations into police corruption or misuse of authority, and commission reports that create pressure for police reform. Learn more about police subculture and police behavior at **http://clontz.mc-companies.com/additional_readings/subculture.htm**.

police subculture
A particular set of values, beliefs, and acceptable forms of behavior characteristic of American police with which the police profession strives to imbue new recruits. Socialization into the police subculture commences with recruit training and continues thereafter.

police working personality
All aspects of the traditional values and patterns of behavior evidenced by police officers who have been effectively socialized into the police subculture. Characteristics of the police personality often extend to the personal lives of law enforcement personnel.

🐦 Follow the author's tweets about the latest crime and justice news @schmalleger

CJ | Issues
Rightful Policing

In the wake of a heated national debate about racially biased police practices, the Program in Criminal Justice Policy and Management at Harvard University's Kennedy School released a report on what it called "rightful policing." The report's author, Tracey L. Meares, noted that success in police work has traditionally been measured in two ways: (1) the extent to which the police are successful at fighting crime; and (2) the degree to which police agencies and their officers adhere to the law.

Effectiveness at crime fighting has long been used to judge the success of police activities at all levels. Around the turn of the twenty-first century, for example, police administrators—along with politicians—took credit for declining crime rates, and "success stories" featuring city and local police departments were frequently heard.

The second criteria by which the police have often been judged, fidelity to the law, rests on the notion that law enforcement officers must respect legal strictures as much as anyone else. It means that authorities should be held accountable when they violate the rights guaranteed to suspects under the Constitution and by law—including statutes that authorize police action and the internal administrative rules and regulations that agencies develop to help ensure the lawful treatment of anyone who comes into contact with the police.

As the Harvard study notes, these two traditional criteria of police effectiveness can be objectively evaluated. Measures of declining crime rates, for example, would appear to indicate the success of police work. Likewise, the relative lack of civil lawsuits brought against departments, and success at making arrests that "stick" are common indicators of effective police work.

Nonetheless, recent widespread dissatisfaction with a number of grand jury decisions to exonerate police officers involved in the death of unarmed black suspects in a number of jurisdictions serve to show that a third way of assessing police effectiveness may be more important today than any other. Cases such as those in Ferguson, Missouri, Charleston, South Carolina, and Staten Island, New York, outraged many people who thought that the lives of the suspects could have been spared had the officers chosen to act differently. The fact that the officers who were involved in two of those incidents were not indicted meant that their actions had met strict legal requirements, but the lack of indictments brought about nationwide protests over what was seen as the unwarranted use of lethal force. Soon traditional and social media were inundated with debates over the quality of American policing, with discussions focused on claimed racial discrimination. The slogan "Black lives matter" quickly became a rallying cry for protestors.

On the heels of those events, the Harvard study examined how ordinary people assess their treatment by authorities. It concluded that "there is a third way, in addition to lawfulness and effectiveness, to evaluate policing—*rightful policing*." The concept of rightful policing does not depend on the lawfulness of police conduct, nor does it look to statistics demonstrating efficiency at crime fighting. "Rather," as the Harvard study says, "it depends primarily on . . . procedural justice or fairness of . . . conduct." In other words, rightful policing is about how to achieve fairness in policing and about how to engender trust in police. The Harvard study says:

> People typically care much more about how law enforcement agents treat them than about the outcome of the contact. Even when people receive a negative outcome in an encounter,

▲ Demonstrators protesting grand jury decisions in Missouri and New York that exonerated police officers in the deaths of unarmed black men. What is "rightful policing"?

Guy Corbishley/Alamy Stock Photo

such as a speeding ticket, they feel better about that incident than about an incident in which they do not receive a ticket but are treated poorly. In addition to being treated with dignity and respect, research demonstrates that people look for behavioral signals that allow them to assess whether a police officer's decision to stop or arrest them was made fairly—that is, accurately and without bias. These two factors—quality of treatment and indications of high-quality decision-making—matter much more to people than the outcome of the encounter.

The study also notes that people report higher levels of satisfaction with police encounters if they feel that they had the opportunity to explain their situation than if they did not; and people say that they want to believe that authorities are acting in a benevolent way—that is, in a way that is meant to protect and help them, rather than to harass and control them.

The study concludes that "all four of these factors—quality of treatment, decision-making fairness, voice, and expectation of benevolent treatment—constitute *procedural justice* in the minds of citizens who interact with the police; and that positive perceptions of procedural justice matter more to most people than do other criteria of assessing law enforcement success."

Study authors suggest that "a focus on the procedural justice of encounters can help policing agencies identify behavior, tactics, and strategies that many members of minority communities find problematic and that lead to disaffection, even though they may be lawful and, considered in isolation, appear effective."

References: Tracey L. Meares, *Rightful Policing.* New Perspectives in Policing Bulletin (Washington, DC: U.S. Department of Justice, National Institute of Justice, 2015); Tom R. Tyler and Jeffrey Fagan, "Legitimacy and Cooperation: Why Do People Help the Police Fight Crime in Their Communities?," *Ohio State Journal of Criminal Law,* Vol. 6 (2008), pp. 231 and 262; and Tom R. Tyler and Cheryl Wakslak, "Profiling and Police Legitimacy: Procedural Justice, Attributions of Motive, and Acceptance of Police Authority," *Criminology,* Vol. 42 (2004), pp. 253 and 255.

Corruption and Integrity

In 2018, all but one of the Baltimore Police Department's Gun Trace Task Force (GTTF) either plead guilty to, or were convicted in federal court of abusing their official police power to steal money, drugs, and guns from the city's citizens.[12] From its start, the GTTF was expected to be an elite squad of highly trained officers who would use their special skills and training to combat the city's gun problem, and help bring violent crime under control. Instead, the group went rogue, confiscating illegal guns and drugs, and reselling them for personal profit. Members of the group even committed masked home invasion robberies, stole from houses where they served search warrants, and planted drugs on people they arrested. Sometimes they helped drug dealers they knew evade arrest.

Police corruption has been a problem in American society since the early days of policing. It is probably an ancient and natural tendency of human beings to attempt to placate or win over those in positions of authority over them, and some people with authority will always be tempted to abuse it. These tendencies become even more complicated in today's materialistic society by greed and by the personal and financial benefits to be derived from evading the law. The temptations toward illegality offered to police range from a free cup of coffee from a restaurant owner to huge monetary bribes arranged by drug dealers to guarantee that the police will look the other way as an important shipment of contraband arrives. As noted criminologist Carl B. Klockars says, policing, by its very nature, "is an occupation that is rife with opportunities for misconduct. Policing is a highly discretionary, coercive activity that routinely takes place in private settings, out of the sight of supervisors, and in the presence of witnesses who are often regarded as unreliable."[13]

The effects of police corruption can be far reaching. As Michael Palmiotto of Wichita State University notes, "Not only does misconduct committed by an officer personally affect that officer, it also affects the community, the police department that employs the officer and every police department and police officer in America. Frequently, negative police actions caused by inappropriate police behavior reach every corner of the nation, and at times, the world."[14]

Exactly what constitutes corruption is not always clear. Ethicists say that police corruption ranges from minor offenses to serious violations of the law. In recognition of what some have called corruption's "slippery slope,"[15] most police departments now explicitly prohibit even the acceptance of minor gratuities, such as a free cup of coffee. The slippery slope perspective holds that even a small thank-you accepted from a member of the public can lead to a more ready acceptance of larger bribes. An officer who begins to accept, and then expect, gratuities may soon find that his or her practice of policing becomes influenced by such gifts and that larger ones soon follow. At that point, the officer may easily slide to the bottom of the moral slope, which was made slippery by previous small concessions.

Thomas Barker and David Carter, who have studied police corruption in depth, make the distinction between "occupational deviance," which is motivated by the desire for personal benefit, and "abuse of authority, which occurs most often to further the organizational goals of law enforcement, including arrest, ticketing, and the successful conviction of suspects."[16]

FBI Special Agent Frank Perry, former chief of the bureau's ethics unit, distinguishes between police deviance and police corruption. Police deviance, according to Perry, consists of "unprofessional on- and off-duty misconduct, isolated instances of misuse of position, improper relationships with informants or criminals, sexual harassment, disparaging racial or sexual comments, embellished/falsified reporting, time and attendance abuse, insubordination, nepotism, cronyism, and noncriminal unauthorized disclosure of information."[17] Deviance, says Perry, is a precursor to individual and organizational corruption. It may eventually lead to outright corruption unless police supervisors and internal affairs units are alert to the warning signs and actively intervene to prevent corruption from developing.

Figure 6–1 sorts examples of police corruption by their level of seriousness, though not everyone would agree with this ranking. In fact, a survey of 6,982 New York City police officers found that 65% did not classify excessive force, which we define later in this chapter, as a corrupt behavior.[18] Likewise, 71% of responding officers said that accepting a free meal is not a corrupt practice, and another 15% said that the personal use of illegal drugs by law enforcement officers should not be considered corruption.

2 Describe different types of police corruption and possible methods for building police integrity.

Follow the author's tweets about the latest crime and justice news @schmalleger

police corruption
The abuse of police authority for personal or organizational gain.[i]

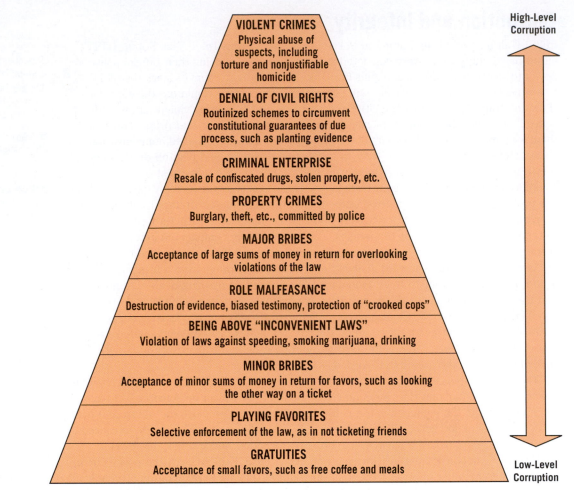

FIGURE 6–1
Types and Examples of Police Corruption

In the early 1970s, Frank Serpico made headlines as he testified before the **Knapp Commission** on police corruption in New York City.[19] Serpico, an undercover operative within the police department, revealed a complex web of corruption in which money and services routinely changed hands in "protection rackets" created by unethical officers. The authors of the Knapp Commission report distinguished between two types of corrupt officers, which they termed "grass eaters" and "meat eaters."[20] "Grass eating," the most common form of police corruption, was described as illegitimate activity that occurs from time to time in the normal course of police work. It involves mostly small bribes or relatively minor services offered by citizens seeking to avoid arrest and prosecution. "Meat eating" is a much more serious form of corruption, involving the active seeking of illicit moneymaking opportunities by officers. Meat eaters solicit bribes through threat or intimidation, whereas grass eaters make the simpler mistake of not refusing bribes that are offered.

In 1993, during 11 days of corruption hearings reminiscent of the Knapp Commission era, a parade of crooked New York police officers testified before a commission headed by Milton Mollen, a former judge and deputy mayor of New York. Among the many revelations, officers spoke of dealing drugs, stealing confiscated drug funds, stifling investigations, and beating innocent people. Officer Michael Dowd, for example, told the commission that he had run a cocaine ring out of his station house in Brooklyn and had bought three homes on Long Island and a Corvette with the money he made. Most shocking of all, however, were allegations that high-level police officials attempted to hide embarrassing incidents in a "phantom file" and that many officials may have condoned unprofessional and even criminal practices by the officers under their command. Honest officers, including internal affairs investigators,

> As long as there is a market for illegal drugs, the financial as well as societal pressures on the police to profit from the drug trade will remain substantial.

◄ A Riviera Beach, Florida, police sergeant receives an award naming him officer of the year. The appropriate and timely recognition of outstanding and professional police activity can go a long way toward building police integrity and offsetting possible temptations for individual officers to engage in inappropriate behavior. What kinds of activities should be rewarded?

Gary Coronado/The Palm Beach Post/ ZUMA Press Inc/Alamy Stock Photo

described how their efforts to end corruption among their fellows had been defused and resisted by higher authorities.

Repercussions from the Mollen Commission hearings continue to be felt. In 2004, for example, a New York State judge ruled that the city of New York must pay special disability benefits to former police detective Jeffrey W. Baird, who served as an informer for the commission. Baird helped uncover corruption while working as an internal affairs officer but suffered from post-traumatic stress disorder after fellow officers threatened him, vandalized his work area, and sent obscene materials to his home.[21]

Money—The Root of Police Evil?

Years ago, criminologist Edwin Sutherland applied the concept of *differential association* to the study of deviant behavior.[22] Sutherland suggested that the frequent, continued association of one person with another makes the associates similar. Of course, Sutherland was talking about criminals, not police officers. Consider, however, the dilemma of average officers: Their job entails issuing traffic citations to citizens who try to talk their way out of a ticket, dealing with prostitutes who feel hassled by police, and arresting drug users who think it should be their right to do what they want as long as "it doesn't hurt anyone." Officers regularly encounter personal hostility and experience consistent and often quite vocal rejection of society's formalized norms. And they receive relatively low pay, which indicates to them that their work is not really valued. By looking at the combination of these factors, it is easy to understand how officers often develop a jaded attitude toward the society they are sworn to protect.

Police officers' low pay may be a critical ingredient of the corruption mix. Salaries paid to police officers in this country have been notoriously low when compared to those of other professions involving personal dedication, extensive training, high stress, and risk of bodily harm. As police professionalism increases, many police administrators hope that salaries will rise. No matter how much police pay grows, however, it will never be able to compete with the staggering amounts of money to be made through dealing in contraband.

Working hand in hand with monetary pressures toward corruption is the moral dilemma produced by unenforceable laws that provide the basis for criminal profit. During the Prohibition era, the Wickersham Commission warned of the potential for official corruption inherent in the legislative taboos on alcohol. The immense demand for drink called into question the wisdom of the law while simultaneously providing vast resources designed to circumvent it. Today's drug scene bears some similarities to the Prohibition era. As long as many people are willing to make large financial and other sacrifices to feed the drug trade, the pressures on the police to embrace corruption will remain substantial.

🐦 Follow the author's tweets about the latest crime and justice news @schmalleger

Building Police Integrity

The difficulties of controlling corruption can be traced to several factors, including the reluctance of police officers to report corrupt activities by their fellow officers, the reluctance of police administrators to acknowledge the existence of corruption in their agencies, the benefits of corrupt transactions to the parties involved, and the lack of victims willing to report corruption. High moral standards, however, embedded in the principles of the police profession and effectively communicated to individual officers through formal training and peer-group socialization, can raise the level of integrity in any department. There are, of course, many officers of great personal integrity who hold to the highest of professional ideals. There is evidence that law enforcement training programs are becoming increasingly concerned with instruction designed to reinforce the high ideals many recruits bring to police work. As one Federal Bureau of Investigation (FBI) article explains it, "Ethics training must become an integral part of academy and in-service training for new and experienced officers alike."[23]

> High moral standards embedded in the principles of the police profession and effectively communicated to individual officers through formal training and peer-group socialization can raise the level of integrity in any department.

Ethics training is part of a "reframing" strategy that emphasizes integrity to target police corruption. In 2001, the Department of Justice (DOJ) published a document titled *Principles for Promoting Police Integrity*.[24] The foreword to that document states, "For community policing to be successful, and crime reduction efforts to be effective, citizens must have trust in the police. All of us must work together to address the problems of excessive use of force and racial profiling, and—equally important—the perceptions of many minority residents that law enforcement treats them unfairly, if we are to build the confidence in law enforcement necessary for continued progress. Our goal must be professional law enforcement that gives all citizens of our country the feeling that they are being treated fairly, equally and with respect." The report covered such topics as the use of force; complaints and misconduct investigations; accountability and effective management; training; nondiscriminatory policing; and recruitment, hiring, and retention. Read the full report, which provides examples of promising police practices and policies in support of increased integrity, at **https://www.justicestudies.com/pubs/integrity.pdf**.

In 2000, the International Association of Chiefs of Police (IACP), in an effort to reinforce the importance of ethical standards in policing, adopted the Law Enforcement Oath of Honor, shown in an "Ethics and Professionalism" box in this chapter. The IACP suggests that the Law Enforcement Oath of Honor should be seen by individual officers as a statement of commitment to ethical behavior. It is meant to reinforce the principles embodied in the Law Enforcement Code of Ethics, which is printed in another "Ethics and Professionalism" box in this chapter.

In December 2005, the National Institute of Justice weighed in on the issue of police integrity with a Research for Practice report titled *Enhancing Police Integrity*.[25] The report noted that "an agency's culture of integrity, as defined by clearly understood and implemented policies and rules, may be more important in shaping the ethics of police officers than hiring the 'right' people."[26] Report authors also noted that officers tend to evaluate the seriousness of various types of misconduct by observing and assessing their department's response in detecting and disciplining it. If unwritten policies conflict with written policies, the authors observed, then the resulting confusion undermines an agency's overall integrity-enhancing efforts. *Enhancing Police Integrity* is available online at **https://www.justicestudies.com/pubs/epi.pdf**. An FBI-sponsored article on police corruption and ethics can be accessed at **https://www.justicestudies.com/pubs/policecorrup.pdf**.

internal affairs
The branch of a police organization tasked with investigating charges of wrongdoing involving members of the department.

Most large law enforcement agencies have their own division of **internal affairs**, which is empowered to investigate charges of wrongdoing made against officers. Where necessary, state police agencies may be called on to examine reported incidents. Federal agencies, including the FBI and the Drug Enforcement Administration (DEA), involve themselves when corruption goes far enough to violate federal statutes. The DOJ, through various investigative offices, has the authority to examine possible violations of civil rights that may result from the misuse of police authority. The DOJ is often supported in these endeavors by the American Civil Liberties Union (ACLU), the National Association for the Advancement of Colored People (NAACP), and other watchdog groups.

Ethics and Professionalism
The Law Enforcement Oath of Honor

On my honor, I will never

Betray my badge, my integrity,

My character or the public trust.

I will always have the courage to hold

Myself and others accountable

for our actions.

I will always uphold the Constitution,

My community, and the agency I serve.

Honor means that one's word is given as a guarantee.

Betray is defined as breaking faith with the public trust.

Badge is the symbol of your office.

Integrity is being the same person in both private and public life.

Character means the qualities that distinguish an individual.

Public trust is a charge of duty imposed in faith toward those you serve.

Courage is having the strength to withstand unethical pressure, fear, or danger.

Accountability means that you are answerable and responsible to your oath of office.

Community is the jurisdiction and citizens served.

THINKING ABOUT ETHICS

1. **How is the Law Enforcement Oath of Honor similar to the Law Enforcement Code of Ethics, which is also found in this chapter? How does it differ?**

2. **How do the two support one another?**

Source: Adopted at the 107th International Association of Chiefs of Police Annual Conference, November 15, 2000. Reprinted with permission.

Officers suspected of law violations may invoke their *Garrity rights*—which are protections that officers have against self-incrimination in the face of questioning. Like the *Miranda* rights guaranteed to civilian criminal suspects who face questioning by police officers, Garrity rights protect officers themselves when being questioned by representatives of their department's internal affairs division or by their superior officers.

Follow the author's tweets about the latest crime and justice news @schmalleger

Drug Testing of Police Employees

The widespread potential for police corruption created by illicit drugs has led to focused efforts to combat drug use by officers. Drug-testing programs in local police departments are an example of such efforts. The IACP has developed a Model Drug Testing Policy for police managers. The policy, designed to meet the needs of local departments, suggests routinely testing all applicants and recruits as well as all employees who are assigned to special "high-risk" areas, such as narcotics and vice.[27]

Today, many police departments require all officers to submit to routine drug testing, and in 2008, the New York Police Department (NYPD) began randomly testing its officers for anabolic steroid abuse. The department began the testing after several police officers were linked to the investigation of a Brooklyn pharmacy suspected of illegally selling millions of dollars of steroids and human growth hormone.[28]

The courts have supported drug testing based on a reasonable suspicion that drug abuse has been or is occurring,[29] although random testing of officers was banned by a 1986 New York State supreme court.[30] Citing overriding public interests, a 1989 decision by the U.S. Supreme Court upheld the testing of U.S. Customs personnel applying for transfer into positions involving drug-law enforcement or requiring a firearm.[31] Many legal issues surrounding employee drug testing remain to be resolved in court, however.

Complicating this issue is the fact that drug and alcohol addictions are "handicaps" protected by the Federal Rehabilitation Act of 1973. As such, federal law enforcement employees, as well as those working for agencies with federal contracts, are entitled to counseling and treatment before action can be taken toward termination.

Employee drug testing in police departments, as in many other agencies, is a sensitive subject. Some claim that existing tests for drug use are inaccurate, yielding a significant number of "false positives." Repeated testing and high threshold levels for narcotic substances in the blood may eliminate many of these concerns. Less easy to address, however, is the belief that drug testing intrudes on the personal rights and professional dignity of individual employees.

Internal affairs divisions are empowered to investigate charges of wrongdoing made against officers.

▲ NYPD officer James Smith makes a rubbing of his wife Moira Smith's freshly engraved name at the National Law Enforcement Officers Memorial in Washington, D.C. Inscribed on the walls of the memorial are the names of the more than 18,000 police officers who gave their lives in the line of duty. Tour the memorial online by visiting **http://www.nleomf.com.**
Roger L. Wollenberg/UPI Photo Service/Newscom

The Dangers of Police Work

In 2018, President Trump signed the Law Enforcement Mental Health and Wellness Act into law. Among other things, the law provides for the development of additional mental health resources needed by law enforcement officers and acknowledges the stressful nature of police work.[32]

> **3** Describe the dangers, conflicts, challenges, and sources of stress that police officers face in their work.

Police work is, by its very nature, dangerous. Although many officers never once fire their weapons at a suspect, we also know that some officers are injured or die while performing their jobs. A 2018 article published in the *American Journal of Preventive Medicine* found that members of the police profession are more likely to sustain nonfatal work-related injuries than members of any other occupation.[33] Stress, training accidents, assorted injuries, and vehicle crashes impact at least some officers during the course of their careers. However, it is violent death at the hands of criminal offenders that police officers and their families fear most.

Violence in the Line of Duty

When officers are shot and killed, it is most often by a lone suspect armed with a single weapon. In 2017, 135 American law enforcement officers were killed in the line of duty.[34] Figure 6–2 shows the number of officers killed in different types of incidents in 2017. In 2001, the attacks on the World Trade Center resulted in the greatest ever single-incident loss of life of on-duty law enforcement officers when 72 police officers perished.[35]

A study by the FBI found that, generally, slain officers appeared to be good-natured and conservative in the use of physical force, "as compared to other law enforcement officers in similar situations. They were also perceived as being well liked by the community and the department, friendly to everyone, laid back, and easy going."[36] Finally, the study, which was published before the September 11, 2001, terrorist attacks, also found that most officers who were killed failed to wear protective vests.

For statistics on police killings to have meaning beyond the personal tragedy they entail, it is necessary to place them within a larger framework. There are approximately 732,000 state and local police employees in this country[37] and another 105,000 federal agents.[38] Such numbers demonstrate that the rate of violent death among law enforcement officers—although tragic—is relatively small.

FIGURE 6–2
U.S. Law Enforcement Officers Killed in the Line of Duty, 2017
Source: Based on data from the Officer Down Memorial Page website, http://www.odmp.org (accessed July 8, 2018).

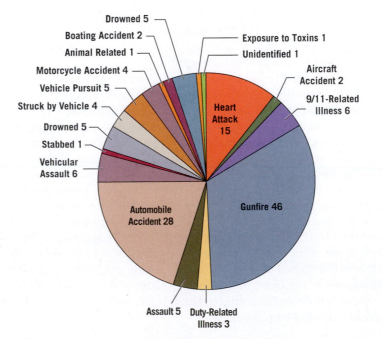

For two decades, Francisco Acevedo managed to elude detection for three killings committed outside New York City from 1989 through 1996.

He slipped past dedicated investigators because he did not fit the profile of a serial killer: a middle-aged white man with a high IQ. But when he submitted a DNA sample as part of a drunken-driving arrest, it inextricably linked him to DNA found at the crime scenes. He was convicted of homicide in January 2012, essentially on the strength of the DNA alone.

DNA seems to have become the premier crime evidence of the twenty-first century, even supplanting fingerprints. It can easily be collected from potential suspects by swabbing the inside of the mouth. And as long as the sample from the crime scenes is not damaged, chances of identifying the wrong person are thought to be one in 1.1 million.

The effectiveness of DNA evidence was further enhanced when the FBI created the Combined DNA Index System in 1998. Through CODIS, federal, state, and local law enforcement officials can share DNA profiles and evidence. The FBI says the database contains more than ten million DNA samples and has been used in 171,800 matches.

Encouraged by added convictions using DNA evidence, Congress and the states have been progressively widening the kinds of people who are required to undergo DNA collection. In the 1990s, collection mandates covered only convicted sex offenders. Then they were expanded to include people convicted of violent crimes and then people convicted of felonies. More recently, the federal government and more than half the states have added anyone who is arrested, without waiting for them to be convicted.

As a result, the number of profiles added to CODIS each year grew 15-fold from 75,000 in 2008 to an estimated 1.2 million in 2012, according to the Justice Department. Such a huge expansion in volume has often overwhelmed crime labs, which have to convert each DNA sample into a numeric sequence for the database. Backlogs have built up, slowing the pace of court cases, and pressures to get samples processed has led some labs to erroneously identify DNA sequences, prompting faulty convictions that were discovered later. This happened in Houston, Las Vegas, and Tulsa, according to a report by the American Constitution Society for Law and Policy.

To alleviate the backlogs, the federal government gave $785 million in grants to state and local DNA labs from 2006 to 2012, and the FBI announced in September 2011 that it had effectively eliminated its own backlog. But in April 2012, the Alabama Department of

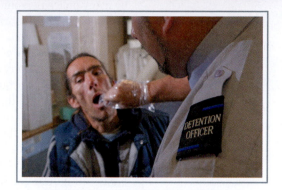

▲ A detained criminal suspect provides a DNA swab for analysis. The story in this box describes Francisco Acevdeo, 43, who was sentenced to 75 years in prison in 2012 for the cold-case murders of three women in New York more than 20 years ago. He was arrested after a DNA sample that he voluntarily provided following an arrest for driving under the influence (DUI) matched genetic material found at the crime scenes. Should everyone who is arrested be required to provide DNA samples?
Mark Harvey/Alamy Stock Photo

Forensics reported that budget cuts required the elimination of 15 % of its workforce, resulting in a backlog of 1,000 DNA cases.

Learn more about the forensic use of DNA and mandatory genetic testing of arrestees in Chapter 9.

REFERENCES

Maryland v. *King*, U.S. Supreme Court, No. 12-207 (decided June 3, 2013).

"Federal Court: If You're Arrested, Officials Can Take a DNA Sample," *Christian Science Monitor*, July 25, 2011, http://news.yahoo.com/federal-court-youre-arrested-officials-dna-sample-235110510.html.

"A New Era of DNA Collections: At What Cost to Civil Liberties?" American Constitution Society for Law and Policy, September 2007, http://www.councilforresponsiblegenetics.org/pageDocuments/PG6T8WPI4A.pdf.

"Suspect in Yonkers Serial Killings Flew under the Radar," *The Journal News*, December 19, 2010, http://murderpedia.org/male.A/a/acevedo-francisco.htm.

Finally, we must recognize that over the past few years premeditated attacks on law enforcement officers have escalated—especially by alienated members of society. Nonetheless, as Montel Williams commented following the 2016 attack on Dallas police, "No civilized society can tolerate shooting at cops."[39] In other words, while mistakes are made by those who wear the badge, American society without effective law enforcement would be unthinkable, leading to anarchy and destroying the rule of law on which our shared traditions are based.

🐦 Follow the author's tweets about the latest crime and justice news @schmalleger

Risk of Disease and Infected Evidence

Dangers other than violence also threaten enforcement officers. The increase in serious diseases that can be transmitted by blood and other body fluids, the possible planned release of active **biological weapons** such as anthrax or smallpox, and the fact that crime and accident scenes are inherently dangerous combine to make *caution* a necessary watchword among investigators and first responders. Routine criminal and accident investigations hold the potential for infection through minor cuts and abrasions resulting from contact with

biological weapon
A biological agent used to threaten human life (for example, anthrax, smallpox, or any infectious disease).[ii]

the broken glass and torn metal of a wrecked vehicle, the sharp edges of knives found at the scene of an assault or murder, or drug implements such as razor blades and hypodermic needles secreted in vehicles, homes, and pockets. Such minor injuries, previously shrugged off by many police personnel, have become a focal point for warnings about the dangers of AIDS, Ebola, hepatitis B, tuberculosis, and other diseases spread through contact with bodily fluids.

Infection can also occur from the use of instruments that measure breath alcohol on infected persons, the handling of evidence of all types, seemingly innocuous implements such as staples, the emergency delivery of babies in squad cars, and attacks (especially bites) by infected individuals who are being questioned or who are in custody. Understandably, officers are concerned about how to handle the threat of AIDS and other diseases, such as Ebola. However, as a publication of the NYPD reminds its officers, "Police officers have a professional responsibility to render assistance to those who are in need of our services. We cannot refuse to help. Persons with infectious diseases must be treated with the care and dignity we show all citizens."[40]

Of equal concern is the threat of biological agents. Although crime scenes and sites known to harbor (or that are suspected of harboring) dangerous active biological agents require a response by teams equipped with special protective equipment, all law enforcement officers should take reasonable precautions against exposure to the wide variety of infectious agents known to exist at even routine crime scenes. Emergency management agencies generally recommend a number of precautions to defend against exposure to infectious substances, as shown in Table 6-2.

To better combat the threat of infectious diseases among public-safety employees and health-care professionals, the federal Bloodborne Pathogens Act of 1991[41] requires that police officers receive proper training in how to prevent contamination by blood-borne infectious agents. The act also requires that police officers undergo an annual refresher course on the topic.

Police departments will face an increasing number of legal challenges in the years to come in cases involving infectious diseases and in cases involving the release of biological

TABLE 6-2
Biological Incident Law Enforcement Concerns

Concern	Precaution and Response
Suspicious material	Responding officers should not handle or come in close physical contact with suspicious material. If it is necessary to handle the material to evaluate it, officers should wear surgical gloves and masks and wash their hands thoroughly with soap and water after handling it.
Human bites	The biter usually receives the victim's blood. Viral transmission through saliva is highly unlikely. If bitten by anyone, milk the wound to make it bleed, wash the area thoroughly, and seek medical attention.
Spitting	Viral transmission through saliva is possible in cases of Ebola, but highly unlikely with HIV.
Urine/feces	Unprotected contact with urine, feces, or vomit should be avoided.
Cuts/puncture wounds	Use caution when handling sharp objects and searching areas hidden from view. Needle-stick studies show risk of infection by the AIDS virus is very low.
CPR/first aid	To eliminate the risk associated with CPR, always use masks/airways.
	Avoid blood-to-blood contact by keeping open wounds covered and wearing gloves when in contact with bleeding wounds.
Body removal	Observe crime scene rules; do not touch anything. Those who must come in contact with blood or other body fluids should wear gloves.
Casual contact	No cases of AIDS or AIDS virus infection have been attributed to casual contact, although CDC guidelines acknowledge that the Ebola virus can be spread through direct casual contact (i.e., touching saliva).
Any contact with blood or body fluids	Wear gloves if contact with blood or body fluids is considered likely. If contact occurs, wash thoroughly with soap and water; clean up spills with one part water to nine parts household bleach.
Post-incident response	Notify health officials if you have had direct contact with blood or body fluids, such as but not limited to, feces, saliva, urine, vomit, and semen of a person who is sick with AIDS or Ebola. The Ebola virus can enter the body through broken skin or unprotected mucous membranes in the eyes, nose, or mouth.

References: Michigan Department of Community Health, "Anthrax (Bacillus anthracis) Information for Health Care Providers," http://www.michigan.gov/documents/Healthcare_provider_FAQ-anthrax_08-2004_104327_7.pdf (accessed June 12, 2014); Massachusetts Administrative Office of the Trial Court, Personnel Policies and Procedures Manual, Section 24.000 ("Statement of Policy and Procedures on AIDS"), http://www.state.ma.us/courts/admin/hr/section24.html (accessed January 25, 2014); Centers for Disease Control and Prevention, "Ebola Virus Disease," http://www.cdc.gov/vhf/ebola/prevention (accessed October 10, 2014); and "Collecting and Handling Evidence Infected with Human Disease-Causing Organisms," FBI Law Enforcement Bulletin, July 1987.

agents. Predictable areas of concern include (1) the need to educate officers and other police employees about AIDS, anthrax, Ebola, and other infectious diseases; (2) the responsibility of police departments to prevent the spread of infectious diseases in police lockups; and (3) the necessity of effective and nondiscriminatory enforcement activities and lifesaving measures by police officers in environments contaminated with active biological agents. With regard to nondiscriminatory activities, the National Institute of Justice (NIJ) has suggested that legal claims in support of an officer's refusal to render assistance to people with AIDS would probably not be effective in court.[42] The reason is twofold: The officer has a basic duty to render assistance to individuals in need of it, and the possibility of AIDS transmission by casual contact has been scientifically established as extremely remote. Viral infections that the CDC acknowledges can be spread by direct casual contact (i.e., touching saliva), such as Ebola, however, may fall into a different category.

A final issue of growing concern involves activities by police officers infected with the AIDS virus. Few statistics are currently available on the number of officers with AIDS, but public reaction to those officers may become a problem that police managers will need to address.

> Police departments will face an increasing number of legal challenges in the years to come in cases of infectious diseases like AIDS and in cases involving the release of biological agents.

Stress and Fatigue among Police Officers

In the week after Hurricane Katrina, two New Orleans police officers used their service weapons to take their own lives. One was Sergeant Paul Accardo, the department's spokesperson; the other was patrolman Lawrence Celestine, an officer described by Deputy Police Chief W. J. Riley as "an outstanding cop."[43] Feelings of powerlessness, personal loss, and an inability to help those in need all seriously heightened the level of stress felt by officers in New Orleans following the 2005 hurricane. "The most stressing part is seeing the citizens we serve every day being treated like refugees," said Riley. "There were cops walking through the crowd at the convention center and people were coming up to beg for food. Not being able to help is a difficult thing. People were calling our names because we knew them and to not be able to help, man, that's stressful."[44]

Traumatic events, such as hurricanes, terrorist attacks, and violent confrontations, are instantly stressful, but long-term stress, the debilitating effects of which accumulate over years, may be the most insidious and least visible of all threats facing law enforcement personnel today. Although some degree of stress can be a positive motivator, serious stress over long periods of time is generally regarded as destructive, even life-threatening.

Stress is a natural component of police work (Figure 6–3).[45] The American Institute of Stress, based in Yonkers, New York, ranks policing among the top ten stress-producing jobs in the country.[46] Danger, frustration, paperwork, the daily demands of the job, and a lack of understanding from family members and friends contribute to the negative stress that officers experience. The Bureau of Justice Statistics points out the following:

> Exposure to violence, suffering, and death is inherent to the profession of the law enforcement officer. There are other sources of stress as well. Officers who deal with offenders on a daily basis may perceive the public's opinion of police performance to be unfavorable; they often are required to work mandatory, rotating shifts; and they may not have enough time to spend with their families. Police officers also face unusual, often highly disturbing, situations, such as dealing with a child homicide victim or the survivors of vehicle crashes.[47]

Some stressors in police work are particularly destructive. One is frustration brought on by the inability to be effective, regardless of the amount of personal effort expended. The crux of police work involves making arrests based on thorough investigations that lead to convictions and the removal of individuals who are damaging to the social fabric of the community—all under the umbrella of criminal law. Unfortunately, reality is often far from the ideal: Arrests may not lead to convictions; evidence available to the officer may not be allowed in court; the sentences imposed may seem too light to the arresting officer. The feelings of powerlessness and frustration that come from seeing repeat offenders back on the streets and from witnessing numerous injustices worked on seemingly innocent victims may greatly stress police officers

Follow the author's tweets about the latest crime and justice news @schmalleger

FIGURE 6–3
Stress and Fatigue among Police Officers

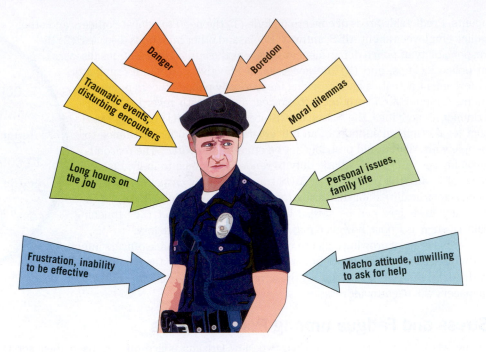

and cause them to question the purpose of their professional lives. It may also lead to desperate attempts to find relief. As one researcher observes, "The suicide rate of police officers is more than twice that of the general population."[48]

Stress is not unique to the police profession, but because of the "macho" attitude that has traditionally been associated with police work, denial of the stress is more prevalent among police officers than in other occupational groups. Certain types of individuals are probably more susceptible to the negative effects of stress than are others. The type A personality, defined through research 30 years ago, is more likely to perceive life in terms of pressure and performance, whereas type B people are more laid back and less likely to suffer from the negative effects of stress. Police ranks, drawn as they are from the general population, are filled with both stress-sensitive and stress-resistant personalities.

Stress Reduction

Follow the author's tweets about the latest crime and justice news @schmalleger

It is natural to want to reduce stress.[49] Humor helps, even if it's somewhat cynical. Healthcare professionals, for example, are noted for their ability to joke even though they are caring for patients who are seriously ill or even dying. At times, police officers use humor similarly to defuse their reactions to dark or threatening situations. Keeping an emotional distance from stressful events is another way of coping with them, although such distance is not always easy to maintain. Police officers who have had to deal with serious cases of child abuse often report that they experienced emotional turmoil as a consequence.

Exercise, meditation, deep breathing, biofeedback, self-hypnosis, guided imaging, induced relaxation, subliminal conditioning, music, prayer, and diet have all been cited as useful techniques for stress reduction. Devices to measure stress levels are available in the form of handheld heart-rate monitors, blood pressure devices, "biodots" (which change color according to the amount of blood flow in the extremities), and psychological inventories.

One theory regarding stress among police officers holds that the amount of stress an officer experiences is directly related to his or her reactions to potentially stressful situations.[50] Officers who can filter out extraneous stimuli and who can distinguish between truly threatening situations and those that are benign are much less likely to report job-related stressors than officers lacking these abilities. Because stress-filtering abilities are often closely linked to innate personality characteristics, some researchers suggest careful psychological screening of police applicants to better identify those who have a natural ability to cope with situations that others might perceive as stressful.[51]

A police officer's family members often report feelings of stress that are directly related to the officer's work. As a result, some departments have developed innovative programs to

CJ Careers
Police Officer

Name: Narcotics Agent Christian Tomas

Position: QRT Agent (Quick Response Team/Narcotics) City of West Palm Beach, Florida

Colleges attended: Palm Beach State College

Majors: Psychology

Year hired: 2007

Please give a brief description of your job: As a narcotics agent, my co-workers and I target street-level drug dealers and other quality-of-life issues, to include prostitution as well as other illegal business practices. We use our own initiative to begin investigations throughout the city. We buy narcotics in an undercover capacity and work with the S.W.A.T. team by writing search warrants for them to execute.

What is a typical day like? Typical day involves doing research and identifying a target. Once an investigation is complete, we move on to another. Some days are spent primarily on surveillance, while on others we are directly involved with drug dealers.

What qualities/characteristics are most helpful for this job? Common sense, honesty, integrity, confidence, self-discipline, dedication, humility, composure, physical and mental toughness, tactical awareness and the ability to work with minimal, to no, supervision.

▲ Christian Tomas
Justice Research Association

What is a typical starting salary? The West Palm Beach Police Department starting salary is $45,324 annually, with excellent benefits.

What is the salary potential as you move up into higher-level jobs? An officer reaching PFC (Patrolman First Class) and MPO (Master Patrol Officer) will receive a 22% raise for each level attained. Promotion in rank produces significant raises over time.

What advice would you give someone in college beginning studies in criminal justice? This isn't a job for someone expecting to win all of the battles. You try as hard as you can, but you have to be prepared for some disappointments when a case doesn't go the way you wanted it to. Get your degree, as it will help you get promoted. When choosing a department, make sure that it's the kind of department that you are looking for. I came to West Palm Beach for the experience and to be busy; I wanted to be challenged and to do as much as I possibly could. Policing is a very rewarding career if you have the motivation and determination to succeed.

---

allay family stress. The Collier County (Florida) Spousal Academy, for example, is a family support program that offers training to spouses and other domestic partners of deputies and recruits who are enrolled in the department's training academy. The 10-hour program deals directly with issues that are likely to produce stress and informs participants of department and community resources that are available to help them. Peer-support programs for spouses and life partners and for the adolescent children of officers are also beginning to operate nationwide. One organization, Badge of Life, promotes mental health services for police officers. The organization has created an Emotional Self-Care Training (ESC) initiative that asks officers to perform a periodic mental health check by visiting a licensed therapist at least once a year. Badge of Life can be reached on the Web at **http://www.badgeoflife.com**.

Officer Fatigue

Like stress, fatigue can affect a police officer's performance. As criminologist Bryan Vila points out, "Tired, urban street cops are a national icon. Weary from overtime assignments, shift work, night school, endless hours spent waiting to testify, and the emotional and physical demands of the job, not to mention trying to patch together a family and social life during irregular islands of off-duty time, they fend off fatigue with coffee and hard-bitten humor."[52] Vila found levels of police officer fatigue to be six times as high as those of shift workers in industrial and mining jobs.[53] As Vila notes, few departments set work-hour standards, and fatigue associated with the pattern and length of work hours may be expected to contribute to police accidents, injuries, and misconduct.

To address the problem, Vila recommends that police departments "review the policies, procedures, and practices that affect shift scheduling and rotation, overtime moonlighting, the number of consecutive work hours allowed, and the way in which the department deals with overly tired employees."[54] Vila also suggests controlling the work hours of police officers, "just as we control the working hours of many other occupational groups."[55]

CJ News
NYPD Permits Wearing of Turban, Beards, by Sikh Officers

▲ An NYPD officer wearing a Sikh turban and beard. In 2016 the NYPD changed its uniform policies in recognition of Sikh religious requirements. Should it do the same for other groups?

Leonard Zhukovsky/Shutterstock

inspirational stories, O'Neil told the new officers that the NYPD was making changes in its hiring practices "to make sure that we allow everybody in New York City that wants to apply and have the opportunity to work for the greatest police department in the nation." O'Neil, who was flanked by NYPD officers wearing blue turbans with badges on them, said that Sikh officers will be permitted to wear turbans instead of traditional police headgear and would be permitted to grow beards up to half an inch long in keeping with their religious practices. The turbans, he said, would have to be an appropriate color and would need to be worn with police shields attached to them.

In making the announcement, O'Neil embraced the growing Sikh community in the city, eliminating the requirement that Sikh officers had to conform to a long-standing dress code. O'Neil also spoke of police shortages throughout the city's precincts, and added that "[h]opefully, with this change in policy, we're going to be able to get more people to apply."

Following O'Neil's graduation address, NYC Sikh Coalition's legal director told Fox News that "[i]f the NYPD's new policy indeed allows for Sikhs to maintain unshorn beards and turbans, that sends a powerful message to the rest of America that Sikhs are an important part of our nation's fabric."

Sikhism is a religion that originated in the fifteenth century in the Punjab region of India and Pakistan. It requires its male adherents to wear beards and to cover their heads with turbans.

Following his speech, O'Neill told reporters: "We want to make the NYPD as diverse as possible and I think this is going to go a long way to help us with that."

Not everyone agreed. As O'Neil spoke, a Muslim officer, Masood Syed, who had been suspended a few months earlier for wearing a beard longer than NYPD protocol allows and was reinstated through a temporary restraining order issued by a Manhattan federal judge, spoke with members of the press. It seems unfair to change standards for one group, but not for others, he said. "We have Sikh officers, we have Jewish officers, we have Israelite officers," and they all have their own sets of religious requirements concerning how to dress.

As the last NYPD police academy graduates of 2016 took their seats at Madison Square Garden, NYPD Commissioner James O'Neil stood at the podium. In addition to the usual congratulatory words and

Resources: Andrew O'Reilly, "NYPD to Allow Sikh Officers to Wear Turbans and Beards While on Duty," *FoxNews.com*, December 29, 2016, http://www.foxnews.com/us/2016/12/29/nypd-to-allow-sikh-officers-to-wear-turbans-and-beards-while-on-duty.html (accessed March 4, 2017); and David Shortell, "NYPD Changes Policy, Will Allow Officers to Wear Turbans," *CNN*, December 29, 2016, http://www.cnn.com/2016/12/29/homepage2/nypd-sikh-officers-turbans-policy-change/index.html (accessed March 3, 2017).

Terrorism's Impact on Policing

4 Describe the changed role of American police in the post-9/11 environment.

The terrorist attacks of September 11, 2001, had a significant impact on policing in the United States. Although the core mission of American police departments has not changed, law enforcement agencies at all levels now devote an increased amount of time and other resources to preparing for possible terrorist attacks and to gathering the intelligence necessary to thwart them.

In today's post-9/11 world, local police departments play an especially important role in responding to the challenges of terrorism. They must help prevent attacks and respond when attacks occur—offering critical evacuation, emergency medical, and security functions to help stabilize communities following an incident. A survey of 250 police chiefs by the Police Executive Research Forum (PERF) found that the chiefs strongly believe that their departments can make valuable contributions to terrorism prevention by using community policing networks to exchange information with citizens and to gather intelligence.[56]

◀ A harbor patrol boat makes its way down the Hudson River on the city's West side. How has the threat of terrorism altered the police role in America?

Justice Research Association

The Council on Foreign Relations, headquartered in New York City and Washington, D.C., agrees with PERF that American police departments can no longer assume that federal counterterrorism efforts alone will be sufficient to protect the communities they serve. Consequently, says the council, many police departments have responded to the terrorist threat by strengthening liaisons with federal, state, and local agencies (including fire departments and other police departments); by refining their training and emergency response plans; by creating antiterrorism divisions; and in a number of other ways.[57]

The extent of local departments' engagement in preventive activities depends substantially on budgetary considerations and is strongly influenced by the assessed likelihood of attack. For example, the NYPD, which has firsthand experience in responding to terrorist attacks (23 of its officers were killed when the World Trade Center towers collapsed), has created a special bureau headed by a deputy police commissioner responsible for counterterrorism training, prevention, and investigation.[58] About 1,000 officers have been reassigned to antiterrorism duties, and the department has trained its entire 36,000-member force in how to respond to biological, radiological, and chemical attacks.[59] The NYPD has assigned detectives to work abroad with law enforcement agencies in Canada, Israel, Southeast Asia, and the Middle East to track terrorists who might target New York City,[60] and it now employs officers with a command of the Pashto, Farsi, and Urdu languages of the Middle East to monitor foreign television, radio, and Internet communications. The department has also invested heavily in new hazardous materials protective suits, gas masks, and portable radiation detectors.

> In today's post-9/11 world, local police departments play an especially important role in responding to the challenges of terrorism.

The FBI's Joint Terrorism Task Forces

Workable antiterrorism programs at the local level require effective sharing of critical information between agencies. FBI-sponsored Joint Terrorism Task Forces (JTTFs) facilitate this by bringing together federal and local law enforcement personnel to focus on specific threats. The FBI currently has established or authorized JTTFs in each of its 56 field offices. In addition to the JTTFs, the FBI has created Regional Terrorism Task Forces (RTTFs)

🐦 Follow the author's tweets about the latest crime and justice news @schmalleger

to share information with local enforcement agencies. Through the RTTFs, FBI special agents assigned to terrorism prevention and investigation meet twice a year with their federal, state, and local counterparts for common training, discussion of investigations, and intelligence sharing. The FBI says that "the design of this non-traditional terrorism task force provides the necessary mechanism and structure to direct counterterrorism resources toward localized terrorism problems within the United States."[61] Six RTTFs are currently in operation: Inland Northwest, South Central, Southeastern, Northeast Border, Deep South, and Southwest.

Given the changes that have taken place in American law enforcement since the terrorist attacks of September 11, 2001, some say that traditional distinctions between crime, terrorism, and war are fading and that, at least in some instances, military action and civil law enforcement are becoming integrated. The critical question for law enforcement administrators in the near future may be one of discerning the role that law enforcement is to play in the emerging global context.

> Workable antiterrorism programs at the local level require effective sharing of critical information between agencies.

▲ A Joint Terrorism Task Force (JTFF) member arrives at a crime scene. What are JTTFs?

Mark Ralston/AFP/Getty Images

Intelligence-Led Policing and Antiterrorism

Fifteen years ago, the DOJ embraced the concept of **intelligence-led policing (ILP)** as an important technique to be employed by American law enforcement agencies in the battle against terrorism.[62] Intelligence is information that has been analyzed and integrated into a useful perspective. The information used in the development of effective intelligence is typically gathered from many sources, such as newspapers, surveillance, covert operations, financial records, electronic eavesdropping, interviews, the Internet, and interrogations. Law enforcement intelligence, or **criminal intelligence**, is the result of a "process that evaluates information collected from diverse sources, integrates the relevant information into a cohesive package, and produces a conclusion or estimate about a criminal phenomenon by using the scientific approach to problem solving."[63] Although criminal investigation is typically part of the intelligence-gathering process, the intelligence function of a police department is more exploratory and more broadly focused than a single criminal investigation.[64]

ILP (also known as *intelligence-driven policing*) is the use of criminal intelligence to guide policing. A detailed description of ILP and its applicability to American law enforcement agencies is provided in the FBI publication *The Law Enforcement Intelligence Function* by David L. Carter of Michigan State University's School of Criminal Justice. The document is available at **https://www.justicestudies.com/pubs/intelligence function.pdf**.

According to Carter, criminal intelligence "is a synergistic product intended to provide meaningful and trustworthy direction to law enforcement decision makers about complex criminality, criminal enterprises, criminal extremists, and terrorists."[65] Carter goes on to point out that law enforcement intelligence consists of two types: tactical and strategic. Tactical intelligence "includes gaining or developing information related to threats of terrorism or crime and using this information to apprehend offenders, harden targets, and use strategies that will eliminate or mitigate the threat." Strategic intelligence, in contrast, provides information to decision makers about the changing nature of threats for the purpose of "developing response strategies and reallocating resources" to accomplish effective prevention.

Not every agency (especially small ones) has the staff or resources needed to create a dedicated intelligence unit. Even without an intelligence unit, however, a law enforcement organization should have the ability to effectively utilize the information and intelligence products that are developed and disseminated by organizations at all levels of government. In other words, even though a police agency may not have the resources necessary to analyze all of the information it acquires, it should still be able to mount an effective response to credible threat information that it receives. Learn more about the law enforcement intelligence function and intelligence-led policing at **https://www.justicestudies.com/pubs/intelled.pdf**.

intelligence-led policing (ILP)
The collection and analysis of information to produce an intelligence end product designed to inform police decision making at both the tactical and strategic levels.[iii]

criminal intelligence
The information compiled, analyzed, and/or disseminated in an effort to anticipate, prevent, or monitor criminal activity.[iv]

Information Sharing and Antiterrorism

The need to effectively share criminal intelligence across jurisdictions and between law enforcement agencies nationwide became apparent with the tragic events of September 11, 2001. Consequently, governments at all levels have been working toward the creation of a fully integrated criminal justice information system. According to a recent task force report, a fully integrated system would be "a network of public safety, justice and homeland security computer systems which provides to each agency the information it needs, at the time it is needed, in the form that it is needed, regardless of the source and regardless of the physical location at which it is stored."[66] The information that is provided would be complete, accurate, and formatted in whatever way is most useful for the agency's tasks. In a fully integrated criminal justice information system, information would be made available at the practitioner's workstation, whether that workstation is a patrol car, desk, laptop, or judge's bench. Within such a system, each agency would share information not only with other agencies in its own jurisdiction but with multiple justice agencies at the federal, state, and local levels. In such an idealized justice information system, accurate information would also be available to nonjustice agencies with statutory authority and a legal obligation to check criminal histories before licensure, employment, weapons purchase, and so on.

Some widely used online information-sharing systems include the Law Enforcement Enterprise Portal (LEEP), which is maintained by the FBI, and Law Enforcement Online (LEO). LEEP is an online gateway providing law enforcement agencies, intelligence-gathering and analysis groups, and criminal justice entities access to a wealth of beneficial resources. Users can strengthen case development with the collaborative investigative tools available, and securely share sensitive documents. LEEP facilitates global cybercrime tracking data and counterterrorism threat tracking and enables virtual command centers. LEO, an intranet intended exclusively for use by the law enforcement community, is a national interactive computer communications system and information service. Like LEEP, it can be accessed by any approved employee of a duly constituted local, state, or federal law enforcement agency or by an approved member of an authorized law enforcement special-interest group. LEO provides a state-of-the-art communications mechanism to link all levels of law enforcement throughout the United States. The system includes password-accessed e-mail, Internet chat rooms, an electronic library, an online calendar, special-interest topical focus areas, and self-paced distance-learning modules.[67]

Another important law enforcement information-sharing resource is the International Justice and Public Safety Network, which uses the acronym **NLETS**. NLETS members include all 50 states, most federal agencies and territories, and the Royal Canadian Mounted Police (RCMP). NLETS, which has been in operation for nearly 40 years, was formerly called the National Law Enforcement Telecommunications System. It has recently been enhanced to facilitate a variety of encrypted digital communications. It now links 30,000 agencies and more than half a million access devices in the United States and Canada, and it facilitates nearly 41 million transmissions each month. Information available through NLETS includes state criminal histories, homeland alert messages, immigration databases, driver's records and vehicle registrations, aircraft registrations, AMBER Alerts, weather advisories, and hazardous materials (HAZMAT) notifications and regulations. You can reach NLETS on the Web via **http://www.nlets.org**.

The National Criminal Intelligence Sharing Plan

Although information-sharing efforts continue to evolve, most experts agree that a fully integrated, nationwide criminal justice information system does not yet exist.[68] Efforts to create one began with the 2003 National Criminal Intelligence Sharing Plan (NCISP). The NCISP was developed under the auspices of the DOJ's Global Justice Information Sharing Initiative and was authored by its Global Intelligence Working Group (GIWG).[69] Federal, local, state, and tribal law enforcement representatives all had a voice in the development of the plan. The NCISP provides specific steps that law enforcement agencies can take to participate in the sharing of critical law enforcement and terrorism-prevention information.

Follow the author's tweets about the latest crime and justice news @schmalleger

NLETS
An acronym referring to the International Justice and Public Safety Information Sharing Network, an important law enforcement information-sharing resource.

EVIDENCE-BASED JUSTICE REINVESTMENT
Cost-Efficient Policing

A few years ago, Camden (New Jersey) city officials disbanded their police department and turned policing services over to a newly formed Camden County Police Department (CCPD). The CCPD began as a cost-sharing effort between Camden and other municipalities in Camden County. Officials believed that substantial costs would be saved as smaller agencies were absorbed into the larger unified force.

Although today's combined department represent one approach to cost savings, others include prioritizing activities, reducing, and modifying service delivery; reorganizing and rightsizing agencies; partnering with other agencies and organizations; using proactive policing methods instead of reactive ones; adopting preventive and problem-solving service models; increasing efficiency; outsourcing services; and implementing force multipliers.

Force multipliers, the last of the options listed here, refer to using technologies that permit a few personnel to do the work of many. Cameras placed in crime-prone areas, for example, and monitored by police employees can sometimes reduce the need for active police patrols, thereby savings huge expenditures on personnel, vehicles, communications, and administrative expenses.

Finally, another initiative, smart policing (also discussed in Chapter 4), makes use of techniques shown to work at both reducing costs and solving crimes. Hot-spot policing, in which agencies focus their resources on known areas of criminal activity, is one such technique; whereas predictive policing, which provides the ability to anticipate or predict crime through the use of statistical techniques, helps guide enforcement operations, and is an increasingly important concept in policing today.

Two programs that support effective policing are Strategies for Policing Innovation (SPI)—formerly known as the Smart Policing Initiative—and the National Law Enforcement and Corrections Technology Center (NLECTC). NLECTC works to identify emerging technologies, as well as to assess their efficiency; whereas SPI, a collaborative consortium composed of the Bureau of Justice Assistance, the CNA's Center for Naval Analyses, and over 30 local law enforcement agencies, works to build evidence-based law enforcement strategies that are effective, efficient, and economical. Visit SPI on the Web at **http://www.strategiesforpolicinginnovation.com**. The National Law Enforcement and Corrections Technology Center (NLECTC) can be accessed at **http://www.justnet.org**.

References: "Strategies for Policing Innovation," http://www.strategiesfor policinginnovation.com (accessed August 10, 2018); Joe Cordero, Reducing the Costs of Quality Policing: Making Community Safety Cost Effective and Sustainable (The Cordero Group), **http://www.njlmef.org/policy-papers/FoLG_v_3_1. pdf** (accessed May 29, 2017); Charlie Beck, "Predictive Policing: What Can We Learn from Wal-Mart and Amazon about Fighting Crime in a Recession?" *The Police Chief*, April 2012, **http://www.policechiefmagazine.org/magazine/ index.cfm?fuseaction=display_arch&article_id=1942&issue_id=112009** (accessed May 25, 2017); JustNet, "About NLECTC," **https://www.justnet.org/About_ NLECTC.html** (accessed May 29, 2018); James R. Coldren, Jr., Alissa Huntoon, and Michael Medaris, "Introducing Smart Policing: Foundations, Principles, and Practice," *Police Quarterly*, Vol. 16, No. 3 (2013), pp. 275–286.

🐦 Follow the author's tweets about the latest crime and justice news @schmalleger

Authors of the plan note that not every agency has the staff or resources needed to create a formal intelligence unit. Even without a dedicated intelligence unit, however, the plan says that every law enforcement organization must have the ability to effectively consume the intelligence available from a wide range of organizations at all levels of government.[70] The NCISP is available in its entirety at **https://www.justicestudies.com/ pubs/ncisp.pdf**.

Police Civil Liability

> **5** Describe civil liability issues associated with policing, including common sources of civil suits against the police.

In 2013, officials with the city of Chicago, Illinois, agreed to pay $22.5 million to settle a lawsuit brought against the city's police department.[71] The award, paid to Christina Eilman, members of her family, and her attorneys, was thought to be the largest amount of money ever offered to a single victim of police misconduct. The civil suit against the city stemmed from the arrest and relatively quick release of Eilman after she had spent less than 24 hours in police custody. Eilman, who was a 21-year-old diminutive white woman at the time of her arrest, had been taken into custody at Chicago's Midway airport in May 2006 after airport officials alerted police officers to her erratic and aggressive behavior. She was taken to a police station where officers learned that she was suffering from bipolar disorder. Released the next day around sundown, she was offered no assistance as she stepped onto the streets of a gang-infested African-American neighborhood. Soon after she wandered away from the police station, and was lured into a high-crime housing project, where a number of young men threatened to attack her sexually. In what appears to have been an effort to escape, Eilman flung herself out of a seven-story window and suffered serious injury—including a shattered pelvis, many broken bones, and serious brain injury. Although she survived, she lives today in a permanent childlike mental state. Faulting the police department, Chief Judge Frank Easterbrook of the Seventh U.S. Circuit Court of Appeals wrote that officers "might as well have released her into the lion's den at the Brookfield Zoo."

Suits of **civil liability** brought against law enforcement personnel are of two types: state and federal. Suits brought in state courts have generally been the more common form of civil litigation involving police officers. In recent years, however, increasing numbers of suits have been brought in federal courts on the claim that the civil rights of the plaintiff, as guaranteed by federal law, were denied.

Common Sources of Civil Suits

Police officers may become involved in a variety of situations that could result in civil suits against the officers, their superiors, and their departments. One of the earliest lawsuits (*Thurman* v. *City of Torrington*) was brought against the city of Torrington, Connecticut, police department by a woman who sued after she had been attacked, stabbed, and nearly killed by her husband. The woman claimed that police had ignored restraining orders that had been issued against her husband, telling him to stay away from his wife. The woman who brought the suit was awarded $2.3 million.

Major sources of police civil liability are listed in Table 6-3. Charles R. Swanson, an expert in police procedure, says that the most common sources of lawsuits against the police are "assault, battery, false imprisonment, and malicious prosecution."[72]

Of all complaints brought against the police, assault charges are the best known, being subject to high media visibility. Less visible (but not uncommon) are civil suits charging the police with false arrest or false imprisonment. In the 1986 case of *Malley* v. *Briggs*,[73] the U.S. Supreme Court held that a police officer who effects an arrest or conducts a search on the basis of an improperly issued warrant may be liable for monetary damages when a reasonably well-trained officer, under the same circumstances, "would have known that his affidavit failed to establish probable cause and that he should not have applied for the warrant." Significantly, the Court ruled that an officer "cannot excuse his own default by pointing to the greater incompetence of the magistrate."[74] The officer, rather than the judge who issued the warrant, is ultimately responsible for establishing the basis for pursuing the arrest or search.

When an officer makes an arrest without just cause or simply impedes an individual's right to leave the scene without good reason, he or she may be liable for the charge of false arrest. Officers who "throw their weight around" are especially subject to this type of suit, grounded as it is in the abuse of police authority. Because employers may be sued for the negligent or malicious actions of their employees, many police departments are being named as codefendants in lawsuits today.

Civil suits are also brought against officers whose actions are deemed negligent. High-speed vehicle pursuits are especially dangerous because of the potential for injury to innocent bystanders. In the case of *Biscoe* v. *Arlington County* (1984),[75] for example, Alvin Biscoe was awarded $5 million after he lost both legs as a consequence of a high-speed chase while he was waiting to cross the street. Biscoe, an innocent bystander, was struck by a police car that went out of control. The officer driving the car had violated department policies prohibiting high-speed chases, and the court found that he had not been properly trained.

Departments may protect themselves from lawsuits to a significant degree by providing proper and adequate training to their personnel, and by creating regulations limiting the authority of employees. The 2011 Justice Department's civil rights investigation into the New Orleans Police Department, for example, found that "the Department's failure to provide sufficient guidance, training, and support to its officers," along with "its failure to implement systems to ensure officers are wielding their authority effectively and safely," could be addressed by implementing policies and practices to "properly recruit, train, and

civil liability
The potential responsibility for payment of damages or other court-ordered enforcement as a result of a ruling in a lawsuit. Civil liability is not the same as criminal liability, which means "open to punishment for a crime."[v]

■ **TABLE 6-3**
Major Sources of Police Civil Liability

Failure to protect property in police custody

Negligence in the care of suspects in police custody

Failure to render proper emergency medical assistance

Failure to prevent a foreseeable crime

Failure to aid private citizens

Lack of due regard for the safety of others

False arrest

False imprisonment

Inappropriate use of deadly force

Unnecessary assault or battery

Malicious prosecution

Violation of constitutional rights

Pattern of unfair and inequitable treatment

Racial profiling

supervise officers."[76] "This understanding," the report's authors pointed out, "serves as the foundation upon which to build sustainable reform that will reduce . . . and prevent crime more effectively, police all parts of the New Orleans community fairly, respect the rights of all New Orleans residents and visitors, and prepare and protect officers."

The FBI states that "a traffic accident constitutes the most common terminating event in an urban pursuit."[77] Some cities are actively replacing high-speed vehicle pursuits with surveillance technologies employing unmanned aerial vehicles (UAVs). Although helicopters have long been used in this capacity, the advent of UAV technology promises to make the tracking of fleeing suspects much quicker and far safer for all involved.

Law enforcement supervisors may be the object of lawsuits by virtue of the fact that they are responsible for the actions of their officers. If it can be shown that supervisors were negligent in hiring (as when someone with a history of alcoholism, mental problems, sexual deviance, or drug abuse is employed) or if supervisors failed in their responsibility to properly train officers before arming and deploying them, they may be found liable for damages.

In the 1989 case of the *City of Canton, Ohio* v. *Harris*,[78] the U.S. Supreme Court ruled that a "failure to train" can become the basis for legal liability on the part of a municipality where the "failure to train amounts to deliberate indifference to the rights of persons with whom the police come in contact."[79] In that case, Geraldine Harris was arrested and taken to the Canton, Ohio, police station. While at the station, she slumped to the floor several times. Officers left her on the floor and did not call for medical assistance. Upon release, Harris's family took her to a local hospital, where she was found to be suffering from several emotional ailments. Harris was hospitalized for a week and received follow-up outpatient treatment for the next year.

In the 1997 case of *Board of the County Commissioners of Bryan County, Oklahoma* v. *Brown*, however, the Supreme Court ruled that to establish liability, plaintiffs must show that "the municipal action in question was not simply negligent, but was taken with 'deliberate indifference' as to its known or obvious consequences."[80] Learn more about vehicle pursuits and the Fourth Amendment at **https://www.justicestudies.com/pubs/pursuits.pdf**.

Federal Lawsuits

The 2017 U.S. Supreme Court case of *Los Angeles* v. *Mendez* had its start when The Los Angeles County Sheriff's Department (LASD) received word from a confidential informant that a potentially armed and dangerous parolee-at-large had been seen at a named residence.[81] While other officers searched the main house, deputies Conley and Pederson searched the back of the property, where, unknown to the deputies, two other people, Mendez and Garcia, were napping inside a shack. Without a search warrant and without announcing their presence, the deputies opened the door of the shack. Mendez rose from the bed, holding a BB gun that he used to kill pests. One of the deputies yelled, "Gun!" and both officers immediately opened fire, shooting Mendez and Garcia multiple times. Officers did not find the parolee in the shack or anywhere else on the property. Mendez and Garcia both survived the shooting and sued deputies Conley and Pederson and Los Angeles County under 42 U. S. C. §1983 for use of excessive force.

1983 lawsuit
A civil suit brought under Title 42, Section 1983, of the U.S. Code against anyone who denies others their constitutional right to life, liberty, or property without due process of law.

Civil suits alleging police misconduct that are filed in federal courts are often called **1983 lawsuits** because they are based on Section 1983 of Title 42 of the U.S. Code—an Act passed by Congress in 1871 to ensure the civil rights of men and women of all races. That Act requires due process of law before any person can be deprived of life, liberty, or property and specifically provides redress for the denial of these constitutional rights by officials acting under color of state law. It reads as follows:

> Every person who, under color of any statute, ordinance, regulation, custom, or usage, of any State or Territory, subjects, or causes to be subjected, any citizen of the United States or other person within the jurisdiction thereof to the deprivation of any rights, privileges, or immunities secured by the Constitution and laws, shall be liable to the party injured in an action at law, suit in equity, or other proper proceeding for redress.[82]

A 1983 suit may be brought, for example, against officers who shoot suspects under questionable circumstances, thereby denying them, without due process, their right to life. Similarly, an officer who makes an arrest based on accusations that he or she knows to be untrue may be subject to a 1983 lawsuit. In the case with which this section opened, the

1983 suit brought by Mendez and Garcia was dismissed by the Supreme Court, which ruled that "when an officer carries out a seizure that is reasonable, taking into account all relevant circumstances, there is no valid excessive force claim."

Another type of liability action, this one directed specifically at federal officials or enforcement agents, is called a **Bivens** action. The case of *Bivens* v. *Six Unknown Federal Agents* (1971)[83] established a path for legal action against agents enforcing federal laws, which is similar to that found in a 1983 suit. *Bivens* actions may be addressed against individuals but not against the United States or its agencies.[84] Federal officers have generally been granted a court-created qualified immunity and have been protected from suits where they were found to have acted in the belief that their action was consistent with federal law.[85]

In the past, the doctrine of sovereign immunity barred legal actions against state and local governments. Sovereign immunity was a legal theory that held that a governing body could not be sued because it made the law and therefore could not be bound by it. Immunity is a much more complex issue today. Some states have officially abandoned any pretext of immunity through legislative action. New York State, for example, has declared that public agencies are equally as liable as private agencies for violations of constitutional rights. Other states, such as California, have enacted statutory provisions that define and limit governmental liability.[86]

Numerous state immunity statutes have been struck down by court decisions. In general, states are moving in the direction of setting dollar limits on liability and adopting federal immunity principles to protect individual officers, including "good-faith" and "reasonable-belief" rules.

At the federal level, the concept of sovereign immunity is embodied in the Federal Tort Claims Act (FTCA),[87] which grants broad immunity to federal government agencies engaged in discretionary activities. When a federal employee is sued for a wrongful or negligent act, the Federal Employees Liability Reform and Tort Compensation Act of 1988, commonly known as the Westfall Act, empowers the attorney general to certify that the employee was acting within the scope of his or her office or employment at the time of the incident. Upon certification, the employee is dismissed from the action, and the United States is substituted as defendant; the case then falls under the governance of the FTCA.

The U.S. Supreme Court has supported a type of "qualified immunity" for individual officers (as opposed to the agencies for which they work) that "shields law enforcement officers from constitutional lawsuits if reasonable officers believe their actions to be lawful in light of clearly established law and the information the officers possess." The Supreme Court has also described qualified immunity as a defense "which shields public officials from actions for damages unless their conduct was unreasonable in light of clearly established law."[88] The Court said that "the qualified immunity doctrine's central objective is to protect public officials from undue interference with their duties and from potentially disabling threats of liability."[89] In the context of a warrantless arrest, the Court said in *Hunter* v. *Bryant* (1991),[90] "even law enforcement officials who reasonably but mistakenly conclude that probable cause is present are entitled to immunity."[91]

The doctrine of qualified immunity, as it exists today, rests largely on the 2001 U.S. Supreme Court decision of *Saucier* v. *Katz*,[92] in which the Court established a two-pronged test for assessing constitutional violations by government agents.[93] First, the court hearing the case must decide whether the facts, taken in the light most favorable to the party asserting the injury, show that the defendant's conduct violated a constitutional right. Second, the court must then decide whether that right was clearly established. For a right to be clearly established, the Court ruled, "it would be clear to a reasonable [defendant] that his conduct was unlawful in the situation he confronted." In summary, qualified immunity protects law enforcement agents from being sued for damages unless they violate clearly established law that a reasonable official in the agents' position would have known.

The *Saucier* decision has recently faced substantial legal challenges, leading the Court to rule in 2009 that "the rigid *Saucier* procedure" has serious shortcomings. The Court noted that "*stare decisis* does not prevent this Court from determining whether the *Saucier* procedure should be modified or abandoned."

In 2007, in the case of *Scott* v. *Harris*, the Supreme Court sided with an officer who had rammed a speeding car driven by a teenager, sending it down an embankment and leaving

Bivens action
A civil suit, based on the case of *Bivens* v. *Six Unknown Federal Agents*, brought against federal government officials for denying the constitutional rights of others.

CJ News
Is the Video Recording of Police Activity in a Public Place Legal?

Simon Glik was walking in the Boston Common in 2007 when he saw police officers putting a suspected drug offender into a chokehold and heard someone yell, "You are hurting him, stop."

Glik pulled out his cell phone camera and began recording the scene, but the officers arrested him for filming them and confiscated the device. Taking him to jail, they charged him under a state law that bars secret recordings, even though the officers could plainly see the cell phone.

The charges against Glik were quickly dismissed in municipal court, but Boston Police continued over the next 4 years to seek qualified immunity for their actions. In August 2011, however, a federal appeals court once and for all denied any qualified immunity claims and confirmed that filming an on-duty police officer is protected by the First Amendment, which also guarantees freedom of speech. An internal investigation by the Boston Police Department in January 2012 concluded the officers had shown poor judgment, and the city agreed 2 months later to pay Glik $170,000 to settle his civil rights lawsuit against the city.

Today, 10 years after the original incident, just about every cell phone in America has a camera in it, and arrests like Glik's are occurring quite regularly. In May 2011, for example, a police officer in Rochester, New York, arrested a woman standing in her own yard, taking pictures of him searching a man's car.

Before arresting her, the officer said, "I don't feel safe with you standing behind me." She was not holding a gun, but the video camera in her hands was, in some ways, even more potent. Clearly, some officers are not comfortable being filmed, even when doing nothing wrong. They perhaps recall that when camera phones didn't exist some 20 years ago, a bystander's film of Los Angeles police beating Rodney King literally caused a riot in South Central Los Angeles, with $1 billion in damages. Two of the officers caught on videotape were sentenced to 30 months in prison.

In the Glik decision, the appeals court welcomed citizens filming the police. "Ensuring the public's right to gather information about their officials," the court declared, "not only aids in the uncovering of abuses but also may have a salutary effect on the functioning of government more generally." In any case, officers who make such arrests end up suffering public scorn and internal investigation. The Rochester woman was acquitted and, after her video went viral on the Internet, Rochester police made an apology and initiated training programs about the right of people to record police activity that takes place in public. Similarly in mid-2012, the Metropolitan Police Department of the District of Columbia issued a general order stating that "the Metropolitan Police Department (MPD) recognizes that members of the general public have a First Amendment right to video record, photograph, and/or audio record MPD members while MPD members are conducting official business or while acting in an official capacity in any public space, unless such recordings interfere with police activity."

Training programs and policy statements may not be enough, however. Philadelphia police were trained on the use of cameras by members of the public, but in March 2012, they arrested a college student for taking photos of officers conducting a traffic stop in front of his house. He was charged with obstruction of justice, resisting arrest, and disorderly conduct.

▲ New York City police officers arrest a demonstrator while a bevy of news photographers record the scene. Courts have held that the photographic recording of police activities that occur in public is permissible unless the recording interferes with or hinders those activities.
Stan Honda/AFP/Getty Images

The law on making recordings is not that easy to follow. For example, unlike photography and video, there is no general right to make audio recordings, the ACLU says. As Michael Allison found out in the tiny town of Bridgeport, Illinois, secret audio recordings are definitely out-of-bounds in many jurisdictions.

Told that there would be no court reporter provided for his legal hearing in late 2011, Allison taped it on a small digital recorder in his pocket, without telling the judge. When he was found out, Allison was arrested and charged with felony eavesdropping. Four more counts were added when other secret recordings were detected on his device, meaning he faced a possible 75-year prison sentence. The charges were thrown out, but the Illinois attorney general appealed the ruling to get them reinstated.

REFERENCES

"Police Reverse Stance on Taping of Officers' Actions," *The Boston Globe*, January 10, 2012, http://www.bostonglobe.com/metro/2012/01/10/police-reverse-stance-taping-officers-actions/va6glfwq9L1mUElv6a33HK/story.html.

"Chief Sheppard, the RPD, and Emily Good," *Rochester City Newspaper*, September 2, 2011, http://www.rochestercitynewspaper.com/news/blog/2011/09/Chief-Sheppard-the-RPD-and-Emily-Good/.

"Eavesdropping Case in Tiny Illinois Town Makes Big Waves," *Chicago Tribune*, January 2, 2012, http://articles.chicagotribune.com/2012-01-02/news/ct-met-eavesdropping-law-sidebar-20120102_1_eavesdropping-case-tiny-illinois-town-big-waves.

Metropolitan Police Department (Washington, D.C.), General Order 3-4-19, July 19, 2012, http://legaltimes.typepad.com/files/go_304_19.pdf.

the driver a quadriplegic.[94] The justices reasoned that the driver "intentionally placed himself and the public in danger by unlawfully engaging in reckless, high-speed flight" and noted that those who might have been harmed had the officer not forced him off the road "were entirely innocent." The Court concluded that it was reasonable for the officer, Deputy Timothy Scott, to take the action that he did and rejected the "argument that safety could have been assured if the police simply ceased their pursuit." In essence, the Court found that "a police officer's attempt to terminate a dangerous high-speed car chase that threatens the lives of innocent bystanders does not violate the Fourth Amendment, even when it places the fleeing motorist at risk of serious injury or death." In 2015, however, the U.S. Supreme Court, in *Mullenix* v. *Luna*, held that the doctrine of qualified immunity shields police officers from civil liability so long as their conduct "does not violate clearly established statutory or constitutional rights of which a reasonable person would have known." A clearly established right is one that is "sufficiently clear that every reasonable official would have understood that what he is doing violates that right."[95] That standard was again reiterated in the 2017 Supreme Court case of *White* v. *Pauly*, in which the Court wrote: "Qualified immunity attaches when an official's conduct does not violate clearly established statutory or constitutional rights of which a reasonable person would have known."[96] The Court added that "reasonableness is judged against the backdrop of the law at the time of the conduct."

Criminal charges can be brought against officers who overstep legal boundaries or who act in violation of set standards. In 2001, for example, in the case of *Idaho* v. *Horiuchi*,[97] the Ninth U.S. Circuit Court of Appeals ruled that federal law enforcement officers are not immune from state prosecution where their actions violate state law "either through malice or excessive zeal." The case involved FBI sharpshooter Lon Horiuchi, who was charged with negligent manslaughter by prosecutors in Boundary County, Idaho, following the 1992 incident at Ruby Ridge.

According to a report by the Police Executive Research Forum (PERF), the issues that most often result in civil suits against police departments and follow-up justice department investigations are (1) police use of inappropriate force, (2) early intervention systems which flag officers who may be engaging in inappropriate behavior, (3) the inadequate management and supervision of officers, (4) biased policing and unlawful stops, searches, and arrests, (5) gender bias in the handling of sexual assaults, and (6). police interactions with persons with mental illness.[98]

Today, most police departments at both state and federal levels carry liability insurance to protect themselves against the severe financial damage that can result from the loss of a large civil suit. Some officers also acquire private policies that provide coverage in the event they are named as individuals in a civil suit. Both types of insurance policies generally cover legal fees up to a certain amount, regardless of the outcome of the case. Police departments that face civil prosecution because of the actions of an officer may find that legal and financial liability extends to supervisors, city managers, and the community itself. Where insurance coverage does not exist or is inadequate, city coffers may be nearly drained to meet the damages awarded.[99]

One study of a large sample of police chiefs throughout Texas found that most believed that lawsuits or the threat of civil litigation against the police makes it harder for individual officers to do their jobs. Most of the chiefs espoused the idea that adequate training, better screening of applicants, close supervision of officers, and "treating people fairly" all reduced the likelihood of lawsuits.[100] PERF suggests three strategies to "help avoid a federal investigation and consent decree": (1) adopting strong policies on key issues such as use of force, (2) ensuring that officers are trained and managed so that policies will be followed, and (3) developing strong management and supervision measures to help ensure that police managers are aware of and can quickly respond to problems as they develop.[101]

▲ Major Juanita Walker-Kirkland of the Miami Police Department (left) listening to Manjit Singh (right), chairman of Sikh Mediawatch and Task Force, during a Building Cultural Competency training program. The training program was sponsored by the U.S. Department of Justice in hopes of improving community relations between law enforcement officials and diverse cultural and religious groups. Why are such programs important?

Yesikka Vivancos/AP Images

🐦 Follow the author's tweets about the latest crime and justice news @schmalleger

Racial Profiling and Biased Policing

Racial Profiling

In December 2014, the U.S. Department of Justice released a 12-page document intended to provide guidance for federal law enforcement officers regarding the use of personal characteristics in routine investigations. The document, which followed in the wake of two highly controversial deaths of black men at the hands of local police officers in Ferguson, Missouri, and New York City, stated that "Even-handed

6 Describe racial profiling and biased policing, including why they have become significant issues in policing.

▲ An elderly woman showing her displeasure with Transportation Security Administration requirements. Some people fear that the use of profiling techniques could lead to unfair discrimination against members of certain racial and ethnic groups. Others suggest that the careful use of profiling can provide an important advantage in an age of scarce resources. Which perspective appeals to you?

Henny Ray Abrams/AP Images

racial profiling

Any police-initiated action that relies on the race, ethnicity, national origin, sexual orientation, gender or religion, rather than (1) the behavior of an individual, or (2) information that leads the police to a particular individual who has been identified as being, or having been, engaged in criminal activity.

law enforcement is . . . central to the integrity, legitimacy, and efficacy of all Federal law enforcement activities."[102] It set forth two standards that were intended to "guide use by Federal law enforcement officers of race, ethnicity, gender, national origin, religion, sexual orientation, or gender identity in law enforcement or intelligence activities." Those standards read:

1. In making routine or spontaneous law enforcement decisions, such as ordinary traffic stops, Federal law enforcement officers may not use race, ethnicity, gender, national origin, religion, sexual orientation, or gender identity to any degree, except that officers may rely on the listed characteristics in a specific suspect description. This prohibition applies even where the use of a listed characteristic might otherwise be lawful.

2. In conducting all activities other than routine or spontaneous law enforcement activities, Federal law enforcement officers may consider race, ethnicity, gender, national origin, religion, sexual orientation, or gender identity only to the extent that there is trustworthy information, relevant to the locality or time frame, that links persons possessing a particular listed characteristic to an identified criminal incident, scheme, or organization, a threat to national or homeland security, a violation of Federal immigration law, or an authorized intelligence activity. In order to rely on a listed characteristic, law enforcement officers must also reasonably believe that the law enforcement, security, or intelligence activity to be undertaken is merited under the totality of the circumstances, such as any temporal exigency and the nature of any potential harm to be averted. This standard applies even where the use of a listed characteristic might otherwise be lawful.[103]

The document, which is available at **https://justicestudies.com/pubs/racialprofiling_ feds.pdf**, includes a number of useful examples to guide law enforcement officers in their daily activities. While it applies only to federal agencies, the principles set forth in the document were meant to guide policing at all levels throughout the United States.

Racial profiling has been defined as any police action initiated on the basis of the race, ethnicity, or national origin of a suspect rather than on the behavior of that individual or on information that identifies the individual as being, or having been, engaged in criminal activity.[104]

Profiling was originally intended to help catch drug couriers attempting to enter the country. The U.S. Customs Service and the DEA developed a number of "personal indicators" that seemed, from the agency's day-to-day enforcement experiences, to be associated with increased likelihood of law violation. Among the indicators were these: speaking Spanish, entering the United States on flights originating in particular Central and South American countries, being an 18- to 32-year-old male, having purchased tickets with cash, and having a short planned stay (often of only a day or two) in the United States. Federal agents frequently used these criteria in deciding which airline passengers to search and which bags to inspect.

Racial profiling is different because it uses an individual's personal characteristics as the sole or predominate factor in determining criminal intent or culpability.[105] The alleged use by police of racial profiling may take a number of forms. Minority accounts of disparate treatment at the hands of police officers include being stopped for being "in the wrong car" (for example, driving an expensive, late-model BMW); being stopped and questioned for being in the wrong neighborhood (i.e., driving through a traditionally white residential neighborhood); and being harassed at the hands of police officers for petty traffic violations (such as having underinflated tires, or having an illegible license plate).[106]

Racial profiling has been derisively referred to as "driving while black" or "driving while brown," although it may also apply to situations other than those involving traffic violations. Racial profiling came to the attention of the public in the late 1990s when police in New Jersey and Maryland were accused of unfair treatment of African-American motorists and admitted that race was a factor in traffic stops. (For a more recent BJS report on traffic stops and race, see **https://justicestudies.com/policebehavior.pdf**.)

In 2003, in response to widespread public outcry over the use of racial profiling, the DOJ banned its practice in all federal law enforcement agencies except in cases that involve the possible identification of terrorist suspects.[107] At the time, the DOJ said, "The guidance provides that in making routine law enforcement decisions—such as deciding which motorists to stop for traffic infractions—consideration of the driver's race or ethnicity is absolutely forbidden."[108] In contrast to the 2014 Department of Justice policy discussed at the start of this section, the 2003 ban was limited to race and ethnicity—and did not extend to religion, national origin, or sexual orientation.

Even those who say that race or ethnicity can be useful descriptors readily admit that neither inherently causes crime (or that they somehow cause poverty or increase the risk of victimization). If anything, personal characteristics may simply display a significant correlation with certain types of crime, as they do with certain kinds of victimization. Hence, although the *real* causes of criminality may be socialization into criminal subcultures, economically deprived neighborhoods, lack of salable job skills, and intergenerational poverty, and not race per se, to some law enforcement agencies race provides one more indicator of the likelihood of criminality. David Cole, a professor at Georgetown University's Law Center, for example, notes that in the minds of many police officials, "racial and ethnic disparities reflect not discrimination [or bigotry] but higher rates of offenses among minorities."[109] "Nationwide," says Cole, "blacks are 13 times more likely to be sent to state prisons for drug convictions than are whites, so it would seem rational for police to assume that all other things being equal, a black driver is more likely than a white driver to be carrying drugs." Similarly, a study published in 2014 showed that officer-initiated traffic stops were most likely to be influenced by criminal history, and not by the race of the driver—with black drivers being "1.8 times more likely to possess a criminal history relative to white citizens."[110] Such observations led esteemed sociologist Amitai Etzioni following the turn of the century to declare that racial profiling, even though repugnant to most, is not necessarily racist.[111] Moreover, warned Etzioni, an end to racial profiling "would penalize those African-American communities with high incidences of violent crime" because they would lose the levels of policing that they need to remain relatively secure.

> **Racial profiling uses a person's race as the sole or predominate factor in determining criminal intent or culpability.**

Freedom or Safety? You Decide
Was the NYPD's Monitoring of Muslim Groups a Form of Religious Profiling?

In 2013, civil rights lawyers filed suit in federal court asking for the appointment of an independent commission to review the New York Police Department's monitoring of Muslim groups. Officials with the NYPD admitted to having conducted surveillance of Islamic mosques and Muslim groups in and around New York City over the past few years. At times, the surveillance involved planting undercover officers in Islamic groups and the monitoring of Muslim student groups at 16 colleges in the city and surrounding areas. The department was seeking to identify radical Islamists and Al-Qaida sympathizers who might represent a danger to the city's inhabitants.

Once news of the program became public, it drew quick criticism from many corners. Islamic leaders felt that it was a thinly disguised form of racial and religious profiling and that it was aimed unfairly at them and at members of their communities. New York City Comptroller John Liu also questioned the monitoring program, saying, "We should not as a matter of policy profile people based on religion or race—it goes against everything this city stands for." Robert Jackson, the sole Muslim on the New York City council, added, "When you step on one religious group, Muslims, then you're stepping on every religious group."

Even some law enforcement officials questioned the program. Michael Ward, director of the FBI's Newark office, told reporters that his agency had spent years building up trust in Muslim neighborhoods. "What we have now," he said, "is . . . that they're [Muslim communities] not sure they trust law enforcement in general, they're fearing being watched, they're starting to withdraw their activities." "The impact of that sinking tide of cooperation," said Ward, "means that we don't have our finger on the pulse of what's going on in the community, as well—we're less knowledgeable, we have blind spots, and there's more risk."

At the time, New York Police Commissioner Raymond Kelly made no apologies for the intelligence program and said that he and Mayor Michael Bloomberg are committed to doing whatever is needed to lawfully protect the city. "It is not as if would-be terrorists aren't trying," Kelly told city council members. "To the contrary, they've attempted to kill New Yorkers in 14 different plots." In mid-2014, however, after William Bratton took over as police commissioner, the monitoring program was discontinued and the unit's officers were assigned to other duties. One NYPD official, who chose to remain unnamed, told reporters, "It sends the message that the NYPD is going to back down on its counterterrorism effort in the name of political correctness."

YOU DECIDE

Was the NYPD's monitoring program really a form of religious and ethnic profiling? Should such profiling be permitted in order to safeguard the city? Why or why not?

References: Joseph Goldstein, "Lawyers Say Surveillance of Muslims Flouts Accord," *The New York Times*, http://www.nytimes.com/2013/02/04/nyregion/police-department-flouts-surveillance-guidelines-lawyers-say.html (accessed February 4, 2013); Adam Peck, "FBI Officials: News of NYPD Muslim Surveillance Program Is 'Starting to Have a Negative Impact,'" *ThinkProgress*, March 8, 2012, http://thinkprogress.org/security/2012/03/08/440780/fbi-official-nypd-muslim-surveillance/?mobile=nc (accessed May 1, 2012); Michael Howard Saul, "Speaker Quinn Voices Support for NYPD Monitoring of Muslims," *The Wall Street Journal*, February 27, 2012, http://blogs.wsj.com/metropolis/2012/02/27/speaker-quinn-voices-support-for-nypd-monitoring-of-muslims (accessed May 1, 2012); "NYPD Police Commissioner Ray Kelly Not Sorry about NJ Muslim Surveillance," *The Huffington Post*, February 27, 2012, http://www.huffingtonpost.com/2012/02/27/nypd-police-commissioner-_n_1304710.html (accessed May 1, 2012); "New York Police End Muslim Surveillance Program," *USA Today*, April 15, 2014, http://www.usatoday.com/story/news/nation/2014/04/15/nypd-muslim-surveillance/7758229 (accessed February 5, 2015).

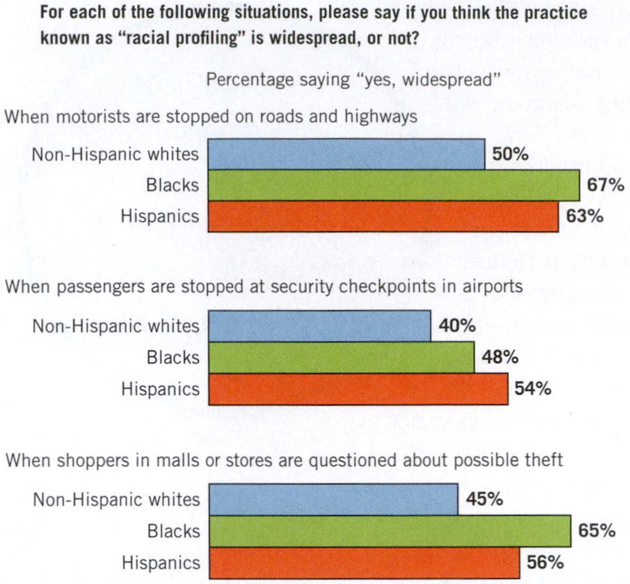

For each of the following situations, please say if you think the practice known as "racial profiling" is widespread, or not?
Percentage saying "yes, widespread"
When motorists are stopped on roads and highways
Non-Hispanic whites
50%
Blacks
67%
Hispanics
63%
When passengers are stopped at security checkpoints in airports
Non-Hispanic whites
40%
Blacks
48%
Hispanics
54%
When shoppers in malls or stores are questioned about possible theft
Non-Hispanic whites
45%
Blacks
65%
Hispanics
56%

FIGURE 6–4
Racial Profiling and Biased Policing, Perceptions by Race
Source: Copyright © Gallup Inc. All Rights Reserved. The content is used with permission; however, Gallup retains all rights of republication.

Regardless of arguments offered in support of racial profiling as an enforcement tool, the practice has been widely condemned as being contrary to basic ethical principles. National public opinion polls conducted by the Gallup Poll Organization show that more than 80% of respondents are morally opposed to the practice of racial profiling by the police, although beliefs about the use of racial profiling vary widely by race (Figure 6–4).[112] From a more pragmatic viewpoint, however, racial profiling is unacceptable because it weakens the public's confidence in the police, thereby decreasing police–citizen trust and cooperation.[113] Numerous states have enacted legislation banning the use of racial profiling by justice agencies (Figure 6–5).

It should be noted that racial profiling is significantly different from the practice of *behavioral profiling*, which makes use of a person's demeanor, actions, bearing, and manner to identify an offender before he can act.[114] As such, behavioral profiling can be both a useful predictive and proactive tool. Behavioral profiling has been successfully used, for example, by Israeli security forces to prevent acts of terrorism. In that country, potential offenders have been identified by their simple actions like wearing loose clothing (to conceal bombs or weapons), smoking on the Sabbath (something that Orthodox Jews would not do), or simply fidgeting and avoiding eye contact while standing in line.

Racially Biased Policing

A decade ago, PERF released a detailed report titled *Racially Biased Policing: A Principled Response*.[115] PERF researchers surveyed more than 1,000 police executives, analyzed material from over 250 law enforcement agencies, and sought input from law enforcement agency personnel, community activists, and civil rights leaders about racial bias in policing. Researchers concluded that "the vast majority of law enforcement officers—of all ranks, nationwide—are dedicated men and women committed to serving all citizens with fairness and dignity."[116] Most police officers, said the report, share an intolerance for racially biased policing. The report's authors noted that some police behaviors may be misinterpreted as biased when, in fact, the officers are just doing their job. "The good officer continually scans the environment for anomalies to normalcy—for conditions, people and behavior that are unusual for that environment," they said. "In learning and practicing their craft, officers quickly develop a sense for what is normal and expected, and conversely, for what is not."[117] Hence, for officers of any race to take special notice of unknown young white males who unexpectedly appear in a traditionally African-American neighborhood, for example, might be nothing other than routine police procedure. Such an observation, however, is not in itself sufficient for an investigatory stop but might be used in conjunction with other trustworthy

AK
WA
OR
CA
ID
NV
MT
WY
UT
AZ
CO
NM
ND
SD
NE
KS
OK
TX
MN
IA
MO
AR
LA
WI
IL
MI
IN
OH
KY
TN
MS
AL
GA
FL
SC
NC
VA
WV
PA
NY
VT
NH
ME
MA
RI
CT
NJ
DE
MD
DC
HI
State with racial profiling laws

FIGURE 6–5
States with Racial Profiling Laws
Source: From *Trends in Juvenile Justice State Legislation 2011-2015*. Copyright © 2015 by National Conference of State Legislatures. Used by permission of National Conference of State Legislatures.

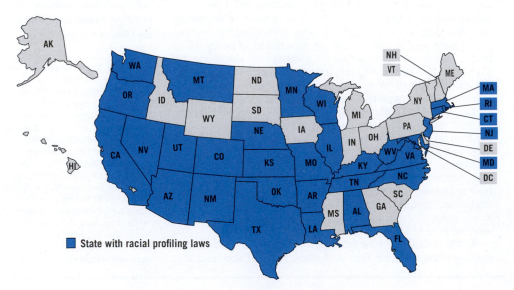

and relevant information already in the officers' possession—such as the officers' prior knowledge that young white men have been routinely visiting a particular apartment complex in the neighborhood to purchase drugs—to justify such a stop.

The PERF report provides many specific recommendations to help police departments be free of bias. One recommendation, for example, says that "supervisors should monitor activity reports for evidence of improper practices and patterns. They should conduct spot-checks and regular sampling of in-car videotapes, radio transmissions, and in-car computer and central communications records to determine if both formal and informal communications are professional and free from racial bias and other disrespect."[118] Read the entire PERF report at **https://www.justicestudies.com/pubs/rbiasp.pdf**.

Police Use of Force

In 2016, the Civil Rights Division of the U.S. Department of Justice released the results of its investigation into the day-to-day practices of the Baltimore, Maryland, police department (BPD).[119] DOJ investigators were looking for systemic constitutional violations committed by the department's officers. One of the most important questions raised was whether the department had engaged in patterned discrimination against minorities. The investigation followed the death of Freddie Gray, a 25-year-old black man who died while in police custody. Report authors concluded that "there is reasonable cause to believe that BPD engages in a pattern or practice of conduct that violates the Constitution or federal law."

Police use of force can be defined as the use of physical restraint by a police officer when dealing with a member of the public.[120] Decisions to use force, including how much force to use, are within the discretion of individual police officers. However, as law enforcement officers are authorized to use only the amount of force that is reasonable and necessary given the circumstances facing them. Most officers are trained in the use of force and typically encounter numerous situations during their careers when the use of force is appropriate—for example, when making some arrests, restraining unruly combatants, or controlling a disruptive demonstration. Force may involve hitting; holding or restraining; pushing; choking; threatening with a flashlight, baton, or chemical or pepper spray; restraining with a police dog; or threatening with a gun. Some definitions of police use of force also include handcuffing. It is important to note that some police departments no longer use the phrase "use of force," preferring instead to talk about "response to resistance."

In 2017, eleven of the most influential U.S. law enforcement leadership organizations developed the National Consensus Policy on Use of Force.[121] The policy emphasized de-escalation techniques and asked officers to de-escalate situations wherever possible before resorting to force. According to the policy, "Use of deadly force is justified when one or both of the following apply: (a) to protect the officer or others from what is reasonably believed to be an immediate threat of death or serious bodily injury, and (b) to prevent the escape of a fleeing subject when the officer has probable cause to believe that the person has committed, or intends to commit a felony involving serious bodily injury or death, and the officer reasonably believes that there is an imminent risk of serious bodily injury or death to the officer or another if the subject is not immediately apprehended." The policy continued, saying that an officer is authorized to use deadly force only "when it is objectively reasonable under the totality of the circumstances."[122]

Studies show that police use force in fewer than 20% of adult custodial arrests. Even in instances where force is used, the police primarily use weaponless tactics. Female officers have been found less likely to use physical force and firearms and are more likely to use chemical weapons (mostly pepper spray) than their male counterparts. Figure 6–6 shows the types of encounters in which the use of force is most likely to be employed.

A more complex issue is the use of excessive force. The IACP defines **excessive force** as "the application of an amount and/or frequency of force greater than that required to compel compliance from a willing or unwilling subject."[123] When excessive force is employed,

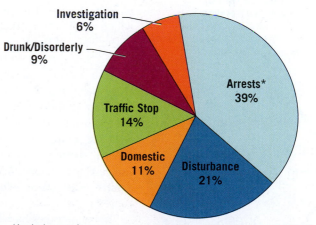

*Includes serving arrest warrants, making field arrests, and effecting other arrests.

FIGURE 6–6
Police Use of Force by Type of Encounter
Source: From Police Use of Force in America. Copyright © 2001 by International Association of Chiefs of Police. Used with permission of the International Association of Chiefs of Police, Alexandria, VA. Further reproduction without express permission from IACP is strictly prohibited.

🐦 Follow the author's tweets about the latest crime and justice news @schmalleger

7 Summarize the guidelines for using force and for determining when excessive force has been used.

police use of force
The use of physical restraint by a police officer when dealing with a member of the public.[vi]

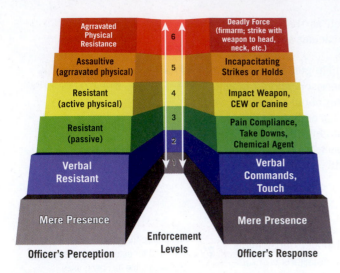

FIGURE 6–7
Police Use-of-Force Continuum

Source: From Less Lethal Weapon Effectiveness, Use of Force, and Suspect & Officer Injuries: A FiveYear Analysis. Published by National Institute of Justice.

excessive force

The application of an amount or frequency of force greater than that required to compel compliance from a willing or unwilling subject.[vii]

problem police officer

A law enforcement officer who exhibits problem behavior, as indicated by high rates of citizen complaints and use-of-force incidents and by other evidence.[viii]

> Studies show that police use force in fewer than 20% of adult custodial arrests.

🐦 Follow the author's tweets about the latest crime and justice news @schmalleger

the activities of the police often come under public scrutiny and receive attention from the media and legislators. Police officers' use of excessive force can also result in lawsuits by members of the public who feel that they have been treated unfairly. Whether the use of excessive force is aberrant behavior on the part of an individual officer or is a practice of an entire law enforcement agency, both the law and public opinion generally condemn it.

Kenneth Adams, an expert in the use of force by police, notes that there is an important difference between the terms *excessive force*, such as shoving or pushing when simply grabbing a suspect would be adequate, and the *excessive use of force*, which refers to the phenomenon of force being used unacceptably, often on a department-wide basis. The second term, says Adams, "deals with relative comparisons among police agencies, and there are no established criteria for judgment."[124] *Use of excessive force* and the *excessive use of force* may be distinguished from the *illegal use of force*, which refers to situations in which the use of force by police violates a law or statute.[125]

In one study, Geoffrey Alpert and Roger Dunham found that the "force factor"—the level of force used by the police relative to the suspect's level of resistance—is a key element to consider in attempting to reduce injuries to both the police and suspects.[126] The force factor is calculated by measuring both the suspect's level of resistance and the officer's level of force on an equivalent scale and by then subtracting the level of resistance from the level of police force used. Results from the study indicate that, on average, the level of force that officers use is closely related to the type of training that their departments emphasize. Figure 6–7 shows a use-of-force continuum containing six levels of force, starting with the potential for force implied by the mere physical presence of a police officer and ranging to deadly force. The figure conceptualizes of force not as a static concept but rather as a continuum of responses, ranging from the minor use of force such as verbal commands to deadly force, the maximum amount of force possible.[127]

Excessive force can also be symptomatic of **problem police officers**. Problem police officers are those who exhibit problem behavior, as indicated by high rates of citizen complaints and use-of-force incidents and by other evidence.[128] The Christopher Commission, which studied the structure and operation of the Los Angeles police Department (LAPD) in the wake of the Rodney King beating, found a number of repeat offenders on the LAPD force.[129] According to the commission, approximately 1,800 LAPD officers were alleged to have used excessive force or improper tactics between 1986 and 1990. Of these officers, more than 1,400 had only one or two allegations against them, another 183 officers had four or more allegations, 44 had six or more, 16 had eight or more, and one had 16 such allegations. The commission also found that, generally speaking, the 44 officers with six complaints or more had received positive performance evaluations that failed to record "sustained" complaints or to discuss their significance. In 2014, the New York City Police Commissioner William J. Bratton told police commanders that the agency's "gains against crime were being undercut by its most troublesome officers," and they had to be rooted out.[130]

Recent studies have found that problem police officers do not differ significantly in race or ethnicity from other officers, although they tend to be male and have disciplinary records that are more serious than those of other officers. Some departments are developing early-warning systems to allow police managers to identify potentially problematic officers and to reduce problem police officer behavior.

In 2014 the U.S. Congress enacted the Death in Custody Reporting Act (DCRA), which requires state and federal law enforcement agencies to submit data to the U.S. Department of Justice about civilians who died during interactions with law enforcement officers or while in their custody—whether resulting from use or force or some other manner of death, such as suicide or natural causes. Finally, in 2015, the FBI began work on a National Use of Force Data Collection, an online portal to collect use-of-force data from law enforcement agencies across the country.[131] Learn more about the police use of force, as well as force used against the police, from **https://www.justicestudies.com/pubs/measureforce.pdf**. An FBI article on excessive force is available at **https://www.justicestudies.com/pubs/excessiveforce.pdf**.

Deadly Force

Generally speaking, **deadly force** is likely to cause death or great bodily harm. The FBI defines *deadly force* as "the intentional use of a firearm or other instrument resulting in a high probability of death."[132]

The use of deadly force by law enforcement officers, especially when it is *not* considered justifiable (as in the *Horiuchi* case mentioned earlier in this chapter), is one area of potential civil liability that has received considerable attention in recent years. Historically, the fleeing-felon rule applied to most U.S. jurisdictions. It held that officers could use deadly force to prevent the escape of a suspected felon even when that person represented no immediate threat to the officer or to the public.

deadly force
The force likely to cause death or great bodily harm. Also, "the intentional use of a firearm or other instrument resulting in a high probability of death."[ix]

CJ Exhibit 6-1
Taking Policing to a Higher Standard

In 2016, the Police Executive Research Forum, responding to a number of highly-publicized use-of-force incidents around the country, released a report entitled "Use of Force: Taking Policing to a Higher Standard." The report contained 30 "guiding principles," or recommendations. Some of the most significant are provided here:

1. **The sanctity of human life should be at the heart of everything a police agency does.** Agency mission statements, policies, and training curricula should emphasize the sanctity of all human life—the general public, police officers, and criminal suspects—and the importance of treating all persons with dignity and respect.

2. **Police departments should adopt policies that hold themselves to a higher standard than the legal requirements of *Graham v. Connor*.** Agency use-of-force policies should go beyond the legal standard of "objective reasonableness" outlined in the 1989 U.S. Supreme Court decision *Graham v Connor*. This landmark decision should be seen as "necessary but not sufficient," because it does not provide police with sufficient guidance on use of force. As a result, prosecutors and grand juries often find that a fatal shooting by an officer is not a crime, even though they may not consider the use of force proportional or necessary. Agencies should adopt policies and training to hold themselves to a higher standard, based on sound tactics, consideration of whether the use of force was proportional to the threat, and the sanctity of human life.

3. **Police use of force must meet the test of proportionality.** In assessing whether a response is proportional, officers must ask themselves, "How would the general public view the action we took? Would they think it was appropriate to the entire situation and to the severity of the threat posed to me or to the public?"

4. **Police departments must adopt de-escalation as formal agency policy.** Agencies should adopt General Orders and/or policy statements making it clear that de-escalation is the preferred, tactically sound approach in many critical incidents. Officers should receive training on key de-escalation principles.

5. **Officers need to prevent other officers from using excessive force.** Officers should be obligated to intervene when they believe another officer is about to use excessive or unnecessary force, or when they witness colleagues using excessive or unnecessary force, or engaging in other misconduct. Agencies should also train officers to detect warning signs that another officer might be moving toward excessive or unnecessary force and to intervene *before* the situation escalates.

6. **Police departments must prohibit the use of deadly force against individuals who pose a danger only to themselves.** Agencies should prohibit the use of deadly force, and carefully consider the use of many less-lethal options, against individuals who pose a danger only to themselves and not to other members of the public or to officers. Officers should be prepared to exercise considerable discretion to wait as long as necessary so that the situation can be resolved peacefully.

7. **De-escalation should be a core theme of an agency's training program.** Police agencies should train their officers on a comprehensive program of de-escalation strategies and tactics. De-escalation can be used in a range of situations, especially when confronting subjects who are combative and/or suffering a crisis because of mental illness, substance abuse, developmental disabilities, or other conditions that can cause them to behave erratically and dangerously.

8. **Police departments must implement a comprehensive agency training program on dealing with people with mental health issues.** Officers must be trained in how to recognize people with mental health issues and deal with them in a safe and humane manner. At a minimum, agencies should seek to provide all officers with awareness and recognition of mental health and substance abuse issues, as well as basic techniques for communicating with people with these problems.

9. **Police agencies need to be transparent in providing information following use-of-force incidents.** Agencies that experience an officer-involved shooting or other serious use-of-force incident should release as much information as possible to the public, as quickly as possible, acknowledging that the information is preliminary and may change as more details unfold.

Source: From Guiding Principles on Use of Force. Used by permission of Police Executive Research Forum.

The 1985 U.S. Supreme Court case of *Tennessee* v. *Garner*[133] specified the conditions under which deadly force could be used in the apprehension of suspected felons. Edward Garner, a 15-year-old suspected burglar, was shot to death by Memphis police after he refused their order to halt and attempted to climb over a chain-link fence. In an action initiated by Garner's father, who claimed that his son's constitutional rights had been violated, the Court held that the use of deadly force by the police to prevent the escape of a fleeing felon could be justified only where the suspect could reasonably be thought to represent a significant threat of serious injury or death to the public or to the officer and where deadly force is necessary to effect the arrest. In reaching its decision, the Court declared that "[t]he use of deadly force to prevent the escape of all felony suspects, whatever the circumstances, is constitutionally unreasonable."

In 1989, in the case of *Graham* v. *Connor*,[134] the Court established the standard of "objective reasonableness" under which an officer's use of deadly force could be assessed in terms of "reasonableness at the moment." In other words, whether deadly force has been used appropriately should be judged, the Court said, from the perspective of a reasonable officer on the scene and not with the benefit of "20/20 hindsight." The justices wrote, "The calculus of reasonableness must embody allowance for the fact that police officers are often forced to make split-second judgments—in circumstances that are tense, uncertain, and rapidly evolving—about the amount of force that is necessary in a particular situation." The Graham decision was later reiterated by the Court in the 2018 case of *Kisela* v. *Hughes*.[135]

In 1995, following investigations into the actions of federal agents at the deadly siege of the Branch Davidian compound at Waco, Texas, and the tragic deaths associated with a 1992 FBI assault on antigovernment separatists in Ruby Ridge, Idaho, the federal government announced that it was adopting an "imminent danger" standard for the use of deadly force by federal agents. The imminent-danger standard restricts the use of deadly force to those situations in which the lives of agents or others are in danger. As the new standard was announced, federal agencies were criticized for having taken so long to adopt it. The federal deadly force policy, as adopted by the FBI, contains the following elements:[136]

- *Defense of life.* Agents may use deadly force only when necessary, that is, only when they have probable cause to believe that the subject poses an imminent danger of serious physical injury or death to the agents or to others.

- *Fleeing subject.* Deadly force may be used to prevent the escape of a fleeing subject if there is probable cause to believe that the subject has committed a felony involving the infliction or threatened infliction of serious physical injury or death and that the subject's escape would pose an imminent danger of serious physical injury or death to the agents or to others.

- *Verbal warning.* If feasible, and if doing so would not increase the danger to the agents or to others, a verbal warning to submit to the authority of the agents should be given before the use of deadly force.

- *Warning shot.* Agents may not fire warning shots.

- *Vehicle.* Agents may not fire weapons solely to disable moving vehicles. Weapons may be fired at the driver or other occupant of a moving motor vehicle only when the agents have probable cause to believe that the subject poses an imminent danger of serious physical injury or death to the agents or to others and when the use of deadly force does not create a danger to the public that outweighs the likely benefits of its use.

🐦 Follow the author's tweets about the latest crime and justice news @schmalleger

Studies of killings by the police have often focused on claims of discrimination—that black and minority suspects are more likely to be shot than whites—but research has not provided solid support for such claims. Although individuals shot by police are more likely to be minorities, an early study by James Fyfe found that police officers will generally respond with deadly force when mortally threatened and that minorities are considerably more likely to use weapons in assaults on officers than are whites.[137] Complicating the picture further, Fyfe's study showed that minority officers are involved in the shootings of suspects more often than other officers, a finding that may be due to the assignment of minority officers to inner-city and ghetto areas. However, a later study by Fyfe, which analyzed police shootings in Memphis, Tennessee, found that black property offenders were twice as likely as whites to be shot by police.[138]

Although relatively few police officers ever fire their weapons at suspects during the course of their careers, those who do may find themselves embroiled in a web of social, legal, and personal complications. It is estimated that in an average year, 600 suspects are killed by public police in America, while another 1,200 are shot and wounded, and 1,800 are shot at and missed.[139] The personal side of police shootings is well summarized in the title of an article that appeared in *Police Magazine*. The article, "I've Killed That Man Ten Thousand Times," demonstrates how police officers who have to use their weapons may be haunted by years of depression and despair.[140] Not long ago, according to author Anne Cohen, all departments did to help an officer who had shot someone was to "give him enough bullets to reload his gun." The stress and trauma that result from police shootings are only now being realized, and many departments have yet to develop mechanisms for adequately dealing with them.[141]

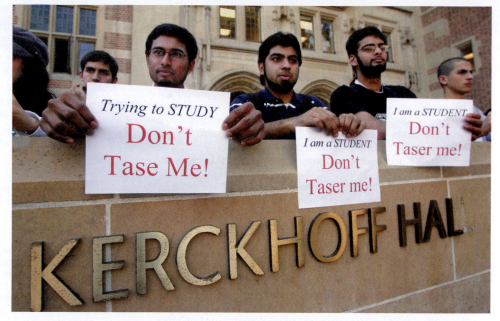

▲ UCLA students protesting the police use of Tasers. This less-lethal weapon, manufactured by Taser International, incapacitates potential attackers by delivering an electrical shock to the person's nervous system. The technology is intended to reduce injury rates to both suspects and officers. Why do some people oppose its use?

Reed Saxon/AP Images

Police officers have particular difficulty dealing with instances of "suicide by cop," in which individuals bent on dying engage in behavior that causes responding officers to resort to deadly force. On March 10, 2005, for example, John T. Garczynski, Jr., a father of two preteen boys, died in a hail of 26 bullets fired by police officers who had surrounded his vehicle in a Boca Raton, Florida, condominium parking lot.[142] Garczynski, a Florida Power and Light Company employee, had been separated from his wife months earlier and appeared to have been despondent over financial problems and the breakup of his marriage. The night before his death, Garczynski met his wife at a bowling alley and handed her a packet containing a suicide note, a typed obituary, and a eulogy to be read at his funeral. After he left, Garczynski's wife called police, and officers used the help of a cell phone company to access the GPS capability of his cell phone in order to locate Garczynski. As deputies surrounded Garczynski's 2003 Ford Explorer, he attempted to start the vehicle. One of the officers yelled "Freeze!" and then shouted "Let me see your hands!" It was at that point, deputies said, that Garczynski pointed a gun at them and they fired.

Rebecca Stincelli, author of the book *Suicide by Cop: Victims from Both Sides of the Badge*,[143] says an incident like that involving Garczynski can be devastating for police officers. "In the past, people have used rope, a gun, gas, jumped off a building. A police officer is just another method," said Stincelli. "They say it's nothing personal. [But] they are wrong. It's very personal" for the officers involved.[144] The FBI says, "Suicide-by-cop incidents are painful and damaging experiences for the surviving families, the communities, and all law enforcement professionals."[145]

A study of fatal shootings by Los Angeles police officers found that an astonishingly large number—over 10%—could be classified as "suicide by cop."[146] Recently, researchers have identified three main "suicide-by-cop" categories: direct confrontations, in which suicidal subjects instigate attacks on police officers for the purpose of dying; disturbed interventions, in which potentially suicidal subjects take advantage of police intervention in their suicide attempt in order to die; and criminal interventions, in which criminal suspects prefer death to capture and arrest.[147]

The imminent-danger standard restricts the use of deadly force to those situations in which the lives of agents or others are in danger.

CJ | Issues
California's Proposed Lethal Force Standard

In 2018, several California state legislators proposed a law that would restrict the use of lethal force by police officers by requiring that it be "necessary" before being employed. The current legal standard throughout the United States holds that such force must be "reasonable." Under the proposed law, California officers would only be allowed to use deadly force if no other reasonable alternatives were available. In short, the proposed legislation would shift the current "reasonable force" rule to a "necessary force" standard.

The goal of the legislation is to reduce the use of deadly force, and to encourage officers to consider less-than lethal techniques before resorting to tactics likely to result in the death of a suspect. The new standard, if passed into law, might require that officers call for backup before engaging a suspect, or it might require them to give explicit verbal warnings that the suspect will be killed unless he or she submits to police authority.

After learning of the proposed legislation, many California police chiefs voiced their opposition to it. "We find ourselves dumbfounded that legislation of this magnitude was introduced without consulting law enforcement stakeholders," said California Police Chiefs Association President David Swing. One chief said that changing the use of deadly force standard to "necessary" was "unreasonable."

1. What is the difference between "necessary" and "reasonable"? Could they mean the same thing?
2. Do you agree with the California legislators who proposed the necessary standard for the use of deadly force? Why or why not?

References: Don Thompson, "California Eyes Lethal Force Law after Shootings by Police," *The Seattle Times*, April 2, 2018, https://www.seattletimes.com/nation-world/california-eyes-lethal-force-law-after-shootings-by-police (accessed September 18, 2018); California Legislators Want to Require Police Shootings to Be "Necessary," Not "Reasonable," *Police Magazine*, April 3, 2018, http://www.policemag.com/channel/patrol/news/2018/04/03/california-legislators-want-to-require-police-shootings-to-be-necessary-not-reasonable.aspx (accessed June 1, 2018); "California Chiefs Rail against Proposed Use of Force Bill," *Police Magazine*, April 11, 2018, http://www.policemag.com/channel/patrol/news/2018/04/11/california-chiefs-rail-against-proposed-use-of-force-bill.aspx?utm_source=email&utm_medium=enewsletter&utm_campaign=20180411-NL-POL-OnTarget-BOBCD180405010&omdt=NL-POL-OnTarget&omid=1004322806 (accessed September 20, 2018).

Less-Lethal Weapons

Follow the author's tweets about the latest crime and justice news @schmalleger

Recent media reports tell of weapons being developed for the military that incapacitate rather than kill. Among them are flash guns (more formally known as optical systems incapacitators), which use powerful strobe lights to trigger "flicker illness"; sonic weapons, which employ intense inaudible sounds to cause pain; and focused microwave beams, which can produce extreme physical pain at close range. Such weapons, which employ less-lethal technologies, are being contemplated for use by military planners seeking to separate enemy fighters from civilian populations.[148] They might also be used by civilian law enforcement agencies in border enforcement or during riots or in other crowd-control situations where physical force is needed but where permanent injury must be avoided.

less-lethal weapon
A weapon that is designed to disable, capture, or immobilize—but not kill—a suspect. Occasional deaths do result from the use of such weapons, however.

Less-lethal weapons also offer what may be a problem-specific solution to potential incidents of "suicide by cop," as well as a generic solution to at least some charges of use of excessive force. **Less-lethal weapons** are those that are designed to disable, capture, or immobilize a suspect rather than kill him or her. Efforts to provide law enforcement officers with less-lethal weapons began in 1987.[149] Stun guns, Tasers (also known as conducted energy devices), rubber bullets, beanbag projectiles, and pepper spray are examples of such weapons that are currently in use. More exotic types of less-lethal weapons, however, are on the horizon. These include snare nets that are fired from shotguns, disabling sticky foam that can be sprayed from a distance, microwave beams that heat the tissue of people exposed to them until they desist in their illegal or threatening behavior or lose consciousness, and high-tech guns that fire bolts of electromagnetic energy at a target, causing painful sensory overload and violent muscle spasms. The NIJ states, "The goal is to give line officers effective and safe alternatives to lethal force."[150]

As their name implies, however, less-lethal weapons are not always safe. On October 21, 2004, for example, 21-year-old Emerson College student Victoria Snelgrove died hours after being hit in the eye with a plastic pepper spray-filled projectile that police officers fired at a rowdy crowd celebrating a Red Sox victory. Witnesses said that officers fired the projectile into the crowd after a reveler near Fenway Park threw a bottle at a mounted Boston police officer.[151] Learn more about less-lethal weapons from the FBI at **https://www.justicestudies.com/pubs/lesslethal.pdf**.

Professionalism and Ethics

Police administrators have responded in a variety of ways to issues of corruption, danger, and liability. Among the most significant responses have been calls for increased **police professionalism** at all levels of policing. A profession is an organized undertaking characterized by a body of specialized knowledge acquired through extensive education,[152] and by a well-considered set of internal standards and ethical guidelines that hold members of the profession accountable to one another and to society. Associations of like-minded practitioners generally serve to create and disseminate standards for the profession as a whole.

Contemporary policing has many of the attributes of a profession. Specialized knowledge in policing includes a close familiarity with criminal law, laws of procedure, constitutional guarantees, and relevant Supreme Court decisions; a working knowledge of weapons and hand-to-hand tactics, driving skills, and vehicle maintenance; a knowledge of radio communications; report-writing abilities; interviewing and interrogation techniques; and media and human relations skills. Other specialized knowledge may include equipment operation (such as vehicular radar, the Breathalyzer, and the polygraph), special weapons skills, conflict resolution, and hostage negotiation. Supervisory personnel require an even wider range of skills, including general and personnel administrative skills, management techniques, and strategies for optimum utilization of human and physical resources.

Police work is guided by an ethical code that was originally developed in 1956 by the Peace Officer's Research Association of California (PORAC) in conjunction with Dr. Douglas M. Kelley of Berkeley's School of Criminology.[153] The current version of the Law Enforcement Code of Ethics is reproduced in an "Ethics and Professionalism" box in this chapter. Ethics training has been integrated into most basic law enforcement training programs, and calls for expanded training in **police ethics** are being heard from many corners. A comprehensive resource for enhancing awareness of law enforcement ethics, called the "Ethics Toolkit," is available from the IACP and the federal office of Community Oriented Policing Services (COPS) at **http://www.theiacp.org/ethics**.

Many professional associations support police work. One such organization, the Arlington, Virginia-based IACP, has done much to raise professional standards in policing and continually strives for improvements in law enforcement nationwide. In like manner, the

8 Demonstrate why professionalism and ethics are important in policing today.

police professionalism
The increasing formalization of police work and the accompanying rise in public acceptance of the police.

police ethics
The special responsibility to adhere to moral duty and obligation that is inherent in police work.

Ethics and Professionalism
The Law Enforcement Code of Ethics

As a Law Enforcement Officer, my fundamental duty is to serve mankind; to safeguard lives and property; to protect the innocent against deception, the weak against oppression or intimidation, and the peaceful against violence or disorder; and to respect the Constitutional rights of all men to liberty, equality, and justice.

I will keep my private life unsullied as an example to all; maintain courageous calm in the face of danger, scorn, or ridicule; develop self-restraint; and be constantly mindful of the welfare of others. Honest in thought and deed in both my personal and official life, I will be exemplary in obeying the laws of the land and the regulations of my department. Whatever I see or hear of a confidential nature or that is confided to me in my official capacity will be kept secret unless revelation is necessary in the performance of my duty.

I will never act officiously or permit personal feelings, prejudices, animosities, or friendships to influence my decisions. With no compromise for crime and with relentless prosecution of criminals, I will enforce the law courteously and appropriately without fear or favor, malice or ill will, never employing unnecessary force or violence, and never accepting gratuities.

I recognize the badge of my office as a symbol of public faith, and I accept it as a public trust to be held so long as I am true to the ethics of the police service. I will constantly strive to achieve these objectives and ideals, dedicating myself before God to my chosen profession . . . law enforcement.

THINKING ABOUT ETHICS

1. **Why does the Law Enforcement Code of Ethics ask law enforcement officers "to respect the Constitutional rights of all men to liberty, equality, and justice"? Does such respect further the goals of law enforcement? Why or why not?**

2. **Why is it important for law enforcement officers to keep their private lives "unsullied as an example to all"? What are the potential consequences of not doing so?**

Source: International Association of Chiefs of Police. Reprinted with permission.

Fraternal Order of Police (FOP) is one of the best-known organizations of public-service workers in the United States. The FOP is the world's largest organization of sworn law enforcement officers, with more than 318,000 members in more than 2,100 lodges.

Accreditation is another avenue toward police professionalism. The Commission on Accreditation for Law Enforcement Agencies (CALEA) was formed in 1979. Police departments seeking accreditation through the commission must meet hundreds of standards in areas as diverse as day-to-day operations, administration, review of incidents involving the use of a weapon by officers, and evaluation and promotion of personnel. As of March 1, 2017, more than 800 (nearly 4%) of the nation's 17,784 law enforcement agencies were accredited,[154] and numerous others were undergoing the accreditation process. However, many accredited agencies are among the nation's largest; as a result, 25% of full-time law enforcement officers in the United States at the state and local levels are members of CALEA-accredited programs.[155] Although accreditation makes possible the identification of high-quality police departments, it is often not valued by agency leaders because it offers few incentives. Accreditation does not guarantee a department any rewards beyond that of peer recognition. Visit CALEA online at **http://www.calea.org**.

Education and Training

Basic law enforcement training requirements were begun in the 1950s by the state of New York and through a voluntary **Peace Officer Standards and Training (POST) program** in California. Today, every jurisdiction mandates POST-like requirements, although they vary considerably from region to region. Modern police education generally involves training in subject areas as diverse as self-defense, human relations, firearms and weapons, communications, legal aspects of policing, patrol, criminal investigations, administration, report writing, ethics, computers and information systems, and cultural diversity. According to a 2016 Bureau of Justice Statistics report, the median number of hours of training required of new officers is 840. It was 1,029 in county departments, 883 in municipal agencies, and 706 in sheriff's departments.[156]

Federal law enforcement agents receive schooling at the Federal Law Enforcement Training Center (FLETC) in Glynco, Georgia. The center provides training for about 60 federal law enforcement agencies, excluding the FBI and the DEA, which have their own training academies in Quantico, Virginia. The center also offers advanced training to state and local police organizations through the National Center for State and Local Law Enforcement Training, located on the FLETC campus. Specialized schools, such as Northwestern University's Traffic Institute, have also been credited with raising the level of police practice from purely operational concerns to a more professional level.

In 1987, in a move to further professionalize police training, the American Society for Law Enforcement Trainers was formed at the Ohio Peace Officer Training Academy. Today, the organization is known as the American Society for Law Enforcement Training (ASLET). Based in Frederick, Maryland, ASLET works to ensure quality in peace officer training and confers the title Certified Law Enforcement Trainer (CLET) on police training professionals who meet its high standards. ASLET also works with the Police Training Network to provide an ongoing and comprehensive calendar of law enforcement training activities nationwide.

A more recent innovation in law enforcement training is the Police Training Officer (PTO) program, whose development was funded by the COPS office starting in 1999.[157] The PTO program was designed by the Reno (Nevada) Police Department, in conjunction with PERF, as an alternative model for police field training. At its start, it represented the first new postacademy field training program for law enforcement agencies in more than 30 years. PTO uses contemporary methods of adult education and a version of problem-based learning specifically adapted to the police environment. It incorporates community policing and problem-solving principles and, according to the COPS office, fosters "the foundation for life-long learning that prepares new officers for the complexities of policing today and in the future."[158]

As the concern for quality policing builds, increasing emphasis is being placed on the formal education of police officers. As early as 1931, the National Commission on Law Observance and Enforcement (the Wickersham Commission) highlighted the importance of a well-educated police force by calling for "educationally sound" officers.[159] In 1967, the President's Commission on Law Enforcement and Administration of

---

Accreditation
A credentialing process which, if successful, provides recognized professional status for an organization—especially those engaged in law enforcement, public safety communications, public safety training, and the provision of campus security services.

Peace Officer Standards and Training (POST) program
The official program of a state or legislative jurisdiction that sets standards for the training of law enforcement officers. All states set such standards, although not all use the term *POST*.

As the concern for quality policing builds, increasing emphasis is also being placed on the formal education of police officers.

Justice voiced the belief that "the ultimate aim of all police departments should be that all personnel with general enforcement powers have baccalaureate degrees."[160] At the time, the average educational level of police officers in the United States was 12.4 years—slightly beyond a high school degree. In 1973, the National Advisory Commission on Criminal Justice Standards and Goals made the following specific recommendation: "Every police agency should, no later than 1982, require as a condition of initial employment the completion of at least four years of education ... at an accredited college or university."[161]

However, recommendations do not always translate into practice. One report found that one in three state agencies has a college requirement for new officers, with 12% requiring a 2-year degree and 2% requiring a 4-year degree. About one in four municipal and county police departments has a college requirement, with about one in ten requiring a degree.[162] One in seven sheriff's offices have a college requirement, including 6% that require a minimum of a 2-year degree for new hires.[163] A 2002 report on police departments in large cities found that the percentage of departments requiring new officers to have at least some college rose from 19% in 1990 to 37% in 2000, and the percentage requiring a 2- or 4-year degree grew from 6% to 14% over the same period.[164] A Dallas Police Department policy requiring a minimum of 45 semester hours of successful college-level study for new recruits[165] was upheld in 1985 by the Fifth U.S. Circuit Court of Appeals in the case of *Davis* v. *Dallas*.[166]

An early survey of police departments by PERF stressed the need for educated police officers, citing the following benefits that accrue to police agencies from the hiring of educated officers:[167] (1) better written reports, (2) enhanced communications with the public, (3) more effective job performance, (4) fewer citizen complaints, (5) greater initiative, (6) wiser use of discretion, (7) heightened sensitivity to racial and ethnic issues, and (8) fewer disciplinary problems. However, there are drawbacks to having more educated police forces: Educated officers are more likely to leave police work and to question orders, and they request reassignment more frequently than other officers.

Police training standards continue to change. In 2016, for example, the Chicago Police Department announced that it would begin retraining its officers in "force mitigation," or de-escalation tactics. The two-day training session was intended to help officers understand when lethal force is needed and when it can be avoided.[168]

Today, most federal agencies require college degrees for entry-level positions. Among them are the FBI; the DEA; the Bureau of Alcohol, Tobacco, Firearms and Explosives(ATF); the Secret Service; the Bureau of Customs and Border Protection(CBP); and the Bureau of Immigration and Customs Enforcement(ICE).

Recruitment and Selection

All professions need informed, dedicated, and competent personnel. When the National Advisory Commission on Criminal Justice Standards and Goals issued its 1973 report on the police, it bemoaned the fact that "many college students are unaware of the varied, interesting, and challenging assignments and career opportunities that exist within the police service."[169] Today, police organizations actively recruit new officers from 2- and 4-year colleges and universities, technical institutions, and professional organizations. The national commission report stressed the setting of high standards for police recruits and recommended a strong emphasis on minority recruitment, an elimination of residence requirements (which required officers to live in the area they were hired to serve) for new officers, a decentralized application and testing procedure, and various recruiting incentives.

A recent Bureau of Justice Statistics study found that local police departments use a variety of applicant-screening methods.[170] Nearly all use personal interviews, and a large majority use basic skills tests, physical agility measurements, medical exams, drug tests, psychological evaluations, and background investigations into the personal character of applicants. Among departments serving 25,000 or more residents, about eight in ten use physical agility tests and written aptitude tests, more than half check credit records, and about half use personality inventories and polygraph exams. After training, successful applicants are typically placed on probation for one year. The probationary period in police work has been called the "first true job-related test . . . in the selection procedure,"[171] providing the opportunity for supervisors to gauge the new officer's response to real-life situations.

Follow the author's tweets about the latest crime and justice news @schmalleger

▲ Former D.C. Metropolitan Police Chief Cathy Lanier. She headed the agency for 9 years before stepping down to become the head of security for the National Football League. How do communities benefit from police agencies that are socially and culturally diverse?

Pete Marovich/ZUMA Press, Inc/Alamy Stock Photo

Effective policing, however, may depend more on innate personal qualities than on educational attainment or credit history. One of the first people to attempt to describe the personal attributes necessary in a successful police officer, famed 1930's police administrator August Vollmer, said that the public expects police officers to have "the wisdom of Solomon, the courage of David, the strength of Samson, the patience of Job, the leadership of Moses, the kindness of the Good Samaritan, the strategic training of Alexander, the faith of Daniel, the diplomacy of Lincoln, the tolerance of the Carpenter of Nazareth, and finally, an intimate knowledge of every branch of the natural, biological, and social sciences."[172] More practically, O. W. Wilson, the well-known police administrator of the 1940s and 1950s, once enumerated some "desirable personal qualities of patrol officers":[173] (1) initiative; (2) responsibility; (3) the ability to deal alone with emergencies; (4) the capacity to communicate effectively with people from diverse social, cultural, and ethnic backgrounds; (5) the ability to learn a variety of tasks quickly; (6) the attitude and ability necessary to adapt to technological changes; (7) the desire to help people in need; (8) an understanding of others; (9) emotional maturity; and (10) sufficient physical strength and endurance.

High-quality police recruits, an emphasis on training with an eye toward ethical aspects of police performance, and higher levels of education are beginning to raise police pay, which has traditionally been low. The acceptance of police work as a true profession should contribute to significantly higher rates of pay in coming years.

Ethnic and Gender Diversity in Policing

9 Identify some of the issues related to ethnic and gender diversity in policing, and suggest ways of addressing them.

In 2003, Annetta W. Nunn took the reins of the Birmingham (Alabama) Police Department. For many, Nunn, a 44-year-old African-American mother and Baptist choir singer, symbolized the changes that had taken place in American policing during the past few decades. The new chief sat in a chair once occupied by Eugene "Bull" Connor, the arch segregationist and a national symbol of the South's fight against integration who jailed thousands of civil rights demonstrators during the 1960s. A 23-year veteran of the department, Nunn headed a force of 838 men and women. She left the department in 2008 to become an advocate for a domestic-violence education program in municipal courts.

More than 30 years before Nunn assumed the job of chief, a 1968 survey of police supervisors by the National Advisory Commission on Civil Disorders[174] found a marked disparity between the number of black and white officers in leadership positions. One of every 26 black police officers had been promoted to the rank of sergeant, whereas the ratio among whites was 1 in 12. Only 1 of every 114 black officers had become a lieutenant, whereas among whites the ratio was 1 in 26. At the level of captain, the disparity was even greater: 1 out of every 235 black officers had achieved the rank of captain, whereas 1 of every 53 whites had climbed to that rank.

▼ African-American and Hispanic police officers in Los Angeles. Ethnic minorities, although still underrepresented in the criminal justice field, have many opportunities for employment throughout the system. Can the same be said for women?

David R. Frazier/Science Source

Today, many departments, through dedicated recruitment efforts, have increased their complement of officers from underrepresented groups. The Metropolitan Detroit Police Department, for example, now has a force that is more than 30% black. Nationwide, racial and ethnic minorities comprised 27.2% of full-time sworn police personnel in local agencies—up from 17.0% in 1990[175]—and getting closer to the percentage of racial and ethnic minorities in our nation's population, which the U.S. Census Bureau reports is approximately 32%.[176]

Although ethnic minorities are now employed in policing in significant numbers, women are still significantly underrepresented. A 2016 report found that only 14% of full-time sworn officers were female, and only 12% of first-line supervisors were female.[177] A Status of Women in Policing Survey conducted by the National Center for Women and Policing (NCWP) notes that women account for 46.5% of employed people over the age of 16 nationwide, meaning that they are "strikingly under-represented within the field of sworn law enforcement."[178] A 2010 Bureau of Justice Statistics (BJS) study of women in law enforcement found the following:[179]

- Of 62 federal law enforcement agencies responding to the study, there were about 90,000 sworn officers, of whom approximately 18,200 (20%) were women.

- Women accounted for approximately 18% of total sworn law enforcement officers in large local police departments—those with 2,000 or more personnel. Women, however, held only 6% of full-time sworn positions in small local police departments—those with between one and ten full-time sworn officers.

- Female officers comprised about 13% of total sworn officers in large sheriff's departments; but they held only 4% of sworn positions in small sheriff's offices.

It is unclear just how many women actually *want* to work in policing. Nonetheless, many police departments continue to make substantial efforts to recruit and retain women because they understand the benefits of having more women among the ranks of sworn officers. Benefits stem from the fact that female police officers tend to use less physical force than male officers and are less likely to be accused of using excessive force; female officers are better at defusing and de-escalating potentially violent confrontations with citizens; female officers often possess better communication skills than their male counterparts; and they are better able to facilitate the cooperation and trust required to implement a community policing model. Moreover, the NCWP says that "female officers often respond more effectively to incidents of violence against women—crimes that represent one of the largest categories of calls to police departments. Increasing the representation of women on the force is also likely to address another costly problem for police administrators—the pervasive problem of sex discrimination and sexual harassment—by changing the climate of modern law enforcement agencies."[180] Finally, "because women frequently have different life experiences than men, they approach policing with a different perspective, and the very presence of women in the field will often bring about changes in policies and procedures that benefit both male and female officers."[181]

> Today, many departments, through dedicated recruitment efforts, have dramatically increased their complement of officers from underrepresented groups.

Women as Effective Police Officers

A recent review of the status of women in policing found that "women police officers are no longer viewed as a unique presence in law enforcement and their ability to perform the job is less likely to be measured against traditional standards, though indoctrination in law enforcement continues to stress masculinity over ability."[182] One research report on female police officers in Massachusetts found that female officers (1) are "extremely devoted to their work," (2) "see themselves as women first, and then police officers," and (3) are more satisfied when working in nonuniformed capacities.[183] The researcher identified two groups of female officers: (1) those who felt themselves to be well integrated into their departments and were confident in their jobs and (2) those who experienced strain and on-the-job isolation. The officers' children were cited as a significant influence on what their self-perceptions were and on the way in which they viewed their jobs. The demands that attend child rearing in contemporary society were found to be a major factor contributing to the resignation of female officers. The study also found that the longer female officers stayed on the job, the greater the stress and frustration they tended to experience, primarily as a consequence of the uncooperative attitudes of male officers. Some of the female officers interviewed identified networking as a potential solution to the stresses encountered by female officers but also said that when women get together to solve problems, they are seen as "crybabies" rather than professionals. Said one of the women in the study, "We've lost a lot of good women who never should have left the job. If we had helped each other, maybe they wouldn't have left."[184] For more information on working in policing, visit **http://discoverpolicing.org**.

🐦 Follow the author's tweets about the latest crime and justice news @schmalleger

Some studies have found that female officers are often underutilized and that many departments are hesitant to assign women to patrol and to other potentially dangerous field activities.[185] As a consequence, some women in police work experience frustration and a lack of satisfaction with their jobs. An analysis of the genderization of the criminal justice workplace by Susan Ehrlich Martin and Nancy C. Jurik, for example, points out that gender inequality is part of a historical pattern of entrenched forms of gender interaction relating to the division of labor, power, and culture.[186] According to Martin and Jurik, women working in the justice system are viewed in terms of such historically developed filters, causing them to be judged and treated according to normative standards developed for men rather than for women. As a consequence, formal and informal social controls continue to disenfranchise women who wish to work in the system and make it difficult to recognize the specific contributions that they make as women.

CJ | Issues
Trust and Diversity in Law Enforcement

Today, our nation is in the midst of an unprecedented national conversation on community-police relations. All across our country—from small suburban hamlets to large, urban centers—tragic events have brought to national consciousness pressing issues about the ways in which law enforcement agencies engage with the communities that they are sworn to protect and serve. In 2015, the President's Task Force on Twenty-First Century Policing (described in Chapter 4) tried to pinpoint "the best means to provide an effective partnership between law enforcement and local communities that reduces crime and increases trust." Among its recommendations, the Task Force identified increasing the diversity of the nation's law enforcement agencies as an important aspect in developing that trust. At the time, an analysis of data collected by the federal government found that "[i]n hundreds of police departments across the country, the proportion of whites on the force is more than 30% higher than in the communities they serve" (Figure 6–8).

In 2016, the U.S. Department of Justice's Civil Rights Division, the U.S. Equal Employment Opportunity Commission (EEOC), and the Center for Policing Equity (CPE) joined together

to launch a research initiative intended to help law enforcement agencies recruit, hire, retain, and promote officers in a way that reflects the diversity of the communities they serve. The resulting publication, *Advancing Diversity in Law Enforcement*, contained a number of observations, research results, and recommendations intended to meet that goal.

The publication noted that "[a]lthough the spotlight on these issues may seem new to some, for many—including law enforcement personnel, government officials, and community leaders—this is only one part of a decades-long conversation about how law enforcement and the communities they serve can best work together. Many law enforcement agencies, as well as organizations that work with law enforcement, have devoted considerable time, energy, and attention in their efforts to recruit and retain workforces that reflect the diversity within their jurisdictions. For many years, the federal government has also worked to address challenges and barriers to diversity in law enforcement."

The challenge of recruiting, hiring, and retaining a diverse workforce is certainly not limited to law enforcement. Throughout the country, in nearly every sector of society, people and organizations

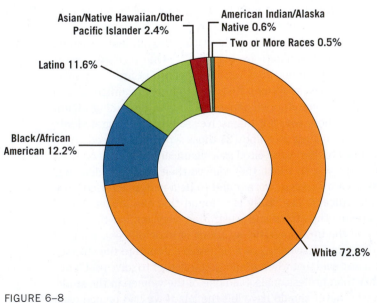

FIGURE 6–8
The Racial Composition of Local Police Departments

have been grappling with this issue. Employers in a variety of industries have engaged in proactive efforts to bolster diversity. Yet this challenge remains particularly urgent in the field of law enforcement. Law enforcement agencies fulfill a fundamental role in our society, and in many communities, individual police officers are often the public face of local government. Hence, *Advancing Diversity* noted that it is critical that our nation's law enforcement agencies broadly reflect the diversity of the communities they serve.

Diversity within law enforcement agencies can be seen not only in terms of race and gender, but also in terms of other characteristics including religion, sexual orientation, gender identity, language ability, background, and experience.

Advancing Diversity found that decades of research confirms that "when members of the public believe their law enforcement organizations represent them, understand them, and respond to them—and when communities perceive authorities as fair, legitimate, and accountable—it deepens trust in law enforcement, instills public confidence in government, and supports the integrity of democracy." Trust, said the report, is essential to defusing tension, to solving crimes, and to creating a system in which residents view law enforcement as fair and just. Victims and witnesses of crime may not approach or engage with law enforcement if they do not perceive such authorities to be responsive to their experiences and concerns. This trust—and the cooperation it facilitates—also enables officers to more effectively and safely perform their jobs.

The report said that "research further suggests that increased diversity also can make law enforcement agencies more open to reform, more willing to initiate cultural and systemic changes, and more responsive to the residents they serve. Some have pointed to increased diversity as a catalyst for reform, enabling officers and law enforcement leaders alike to become more introspective and reflective about problems with their departments."

Advancing Diversity highlighted promising practices that law enforcement agencies have found to be particularly effective at increasing their diversity. It pointed out that successful diversity-building efforts by law enforcement agencies share several common themes, including:

1. Ensuring that the agency's organizational culture is guided by community policing (a strategy of policing that focuses on police building ties and working closely with community members); procedural justice (the principle of fairness in processes that resolve disputes), and cultural inclusivity (welcoming and including all people).

2. Engaging stakeholders—both from within and outside the law enforcement agency—to help create a workforce that reflects the diversity of the community.

3. Being willing to re-evaluate employment criteria, standards, and benchmarks to ensure that they are tailored to the skills needed to perform job functions, and consequently attract, select, and retain the most qualified and desirable sworn officers.

Achieving diversity is not an easy task, and the report noted that "law enforcement agencies that are committed to increasing the diversity of their workforces and ensuring that the demographic makeup of their sworn officers reflect the diversity of the communities they serve face a plethora of challenges." These challenges manifest themselves at every stage of the recruitment, selection, and retention processes, and may appear daunting; but, said the report, they are far from insurmountable. In fact, agencies that have undertaken this effort have found that increased diversity brings a range of benefits that can be seen both within their workforces as well as in their relations with the communities they serve.

Advancing Diversity in Law Enforcement highlights promising practices that help agencies better reflect the diversity of the communities they serve. It is available for download at **https://www. justicestudies.com/pubs/diversity.pdf.**

Source: U.S. Department of Justice, *Advancing Diversity in Law Enforcement* (Washington, DC: USDOJ, 2016), p. 12.

Summary

POLICING: ISSUES AND CHALLENGES

- The police personality is created through informal pressures on officers by a powerful police subculture that communicates values that support law enforcement interests. This chapter described the police personality as (among other things) authoritarian, conservative, honorable, loyal, cynical, dogmatic, hostile, prejudiced, secret, and suspicious.

- Various types of police corruption were described in this chapter. One type, "grass eating," includes officers who accept small bribes and free services by those wishing to avoid legal problems. "Meat eating" includes much more serious forms of corruption, such as officers who actively seek illegal moneymaking opportunities through the exercise of their law enforcement duties. Ethics training was mentioned as part of a reframing strategy that emphasizes integrity in an effort to target police corruption. Also discussed was an NIJ report that focused on enhancing policing integrity. The report noted that a police department's "culture of integrity" might be more important "in shaping the ethics of police officers than hiring the 'right' people."

- The dangers of police work are many and varied. They consist of violent victimization, disease, exposure to biological or chemical toxins, stressful encounters with suspects and victims, and on-the-job fatigue. Stress-management programs, combined with department policies designed to reduce exposure to dangerous situations and agency practices that support officers' needs, can help combat the dangers and difficulties that police officers face in their day-to-day work.

- Policing in America was forever changed by the events of September 11, 2001. Local law enforcement agencies, many of which previously saw community protection and peacekeeping as their primary roles, are being called upon to protect against potential terrorist threats with international roots. The contemporary emphasis on terrorism prevention, alongside the need for a rapid response to threats of terrorism, has led to what some see as a new era of policing to secure the homeland. Homeland security policing builds upon the established framework of community policing for the purpose of gathering intelligence to prevent terrorism. Consequently, the notion of intelligence-led policing has become significant and provides a glimpse at one of the features that may characterize American policing in the future.

- Civil liability issues are very important in policing. They arise because officers and their agencies sometimes inappropriately use power to curtail the civil and due-process rights of criminal suspects. Both police departments and individual police officers can be targeted by civil lawsuits. Federal suits based on claims that officers acted with disregard for an individual's right to due process are called *1983 lawsuits* because they are based on Section 1983 of Title 42 of the U.S. Code. Another type of civil suit that can be brought specifically against federal agents is a *Bivens* action. Although the doctrine of sovereign immunity barred legal action against state and local governments in the past, recent court cases and legislative activity have restricted the opportunity for law enforcement agencies and their officers to exercise claims of immunity.

- Racial profiling, or racially biased policing, is any police action initiated on the basis of the race, ethnicity, or national origin of a suspect rather than on the behavior of that individual or on information that identifies the individual as being or having been engaged in criminal activity. Racial profiling is a bigoted practice unworthy of the law enforcement professional. It has been widely condemned as being contrary to basic ethical principles, and it weakens the public's confidence in the police, thereby decreasing police–citizen trust and cooperation. This chapter pointed out, however, that racial or ethnic indicators associated with particular suspects or suspect groups may have a place in legitimate law enforcement strategies if they accurately relate to suspects who are being sought for criminal law violations.

- Law enforcement officers are authorized to use the amount of force that is reasonable and necessary in a particular situation. Many officers have encounters where the use of force is appropriate. Nonetheless, studies show that the police use force in fewer than 20% of adult custodial arrests. Even in instances where force is used, police officers primarily use weaponless tactics. Excessive force is the application of an amount or frequency of force greater than that required to compel compliance from a willing or unwilling subject.

- Police professionalism requires that today's law enforcement officers adhere to ethical codes and standards established by the profession. Police professionalism places important limits on the discretionary activities of individual enforcement personnel and helps officers and the departments they work for gain the respect and regard of the public they police.

- This chapter points out that ethnic minorities are now employed in policing in numbers that approach their representation in the general population. Women, however, are still significantly underrepresented. Questions can be raised about the degree of minority participation in the command structure of law enforcement agencies, about the desire of significant numbers of women to work in policing, and about the respect accorded to women and members of other underrepresented groups in law enforcement by their fellow officers.

QUESTIONS FOR REVIEW

1. What is the police working personality? What are its central features? How does it develop? How does it relate to police subculture?

2. What are the different types of police corruption? What themes run through the findings of the Knapp Commission and the Wickersham Commission? What innovative steps might police departments take to reduce or eliminate corruption among their officers?

3. What are the dangers of police work? What can be done to reduce those dangers?

4. How has the threat of terrorist attack affected American policing today? Are American police agencies prepared to prevent and respond to terrorism? Explain.

5. What are some of the civil liability issues associated with policing? How can civil liability be reduced?

6. What is racial profiling? Why has it become a significant issue in policing today?

7. In what kinds of situations are police officers most likely to use force? When has too much force been used?

8. Is police work a profession? Explain. What are the advantages of viewing policing as a profession? How can police professionalism be enhanced?

9. What ethnic and gender differences characterize policing today? What is the social significance of this diversity?

The Courts

The criminal court is the central, crucial institution in the criminal justice system. It is the part of the system that is the most venerable, the most formally organized, and the most elaborately circumscribed by law and tradition. It is the institution around which the rest of the system has developed.

—The President's Commission on Law Enforcement and Administration of Justice[1]

Learning Objectives

After reading this chapter, you should be able to:

R-o-x-o-r/Fotolia

Introduction

A few years ago, former TSA employee Dennis Marx of Cummings, Georgia, walked into the Forysth County Courthouse and opened fire, injuring a deputy sheriff.[2] The 48-year-old Marx, who was armed with an assault rifle and a number of improvised explosive devices, was known to locals as a self-proclaimed "sovereign citizen." Officials said that he planned to "take the courthouse hostage." Marx had been due to appear in court on drug and gun charges. The local SWAT team, which was rushing to answer another call, arrived on the scene within 37 seconds of Marx's attack, and shot him dead before he could inflict further damage.[3]

Incidents like the Georgia courthouse attack highlight the critical role that our nation's courts and the personnel who staff them play in the American system of justice. Without courts to decide guilt or innocence and to impose sentence on those convicted of crimes, the activities of law enforcement officials would become meaningless.

There are many different kinds of courts in the United States, but courts at all levels dispense justice daily and work to ensure that all official actors in the justice system carry out their duties in recognition of the rule of law. At many points in this textbook and in three specific chapters (Chapters 5, 10, and 11), we take a close look at court precedents that have defined the legality of enforcement efforts and correctional action. In Chapter 3, we explored the law-making function of courts. To provide a picture of how courts work, this chapter will describe the American court system at both the state and federal levels. Then in Chapter 8, we will look at the roles of courtroom actors—from attorneys to victims and from jurors to judges—and we will examine each of the steps in a criminal trial.

▲ The Forsyth County Courthouse in Cummings, Georgia. In 2014, the courthouse became the target of an attack by a "sovereign citizen" who had planned to take it over. What role do the courts play in the American criminal justice system?
Tami Chappell/Reuters

Follow the author's tweets about the latest crime and justice news @schmalleger

History and Structure of the American Court System

Two types of courts function within the American criminal justice system: state courts and federal courts. Figure 7–1 outlines the structure of today's **federal court system**, and Figure 7–2 diagrams show variation among **state court systems**. This dual-court system is the result of general agreement among the nation's founders about the need for individual states to retain significant legislative authority and judicial autonomy separate from federal control. Under this concept, the United States developed as a relatively loose federation of semi-independent provinces. New states joining the union were assured of limited federal intervention into local affairs. State legislatures were free to create laws, and state court systems were needed to hear cases alleging violations of those laws.

In the last 200 years, states' rights have gradually waned relative to the power of the federal government, but the dual-court system still exists. Even today, state courts do not hear cases involving alleged violations of federal law, nor do federal courts get involved in deciding issues of state law unless there is a conflict between local or state statutes and federal constitutional guarantees. When such conflicts arise, claimed violations of federal due-process guarantees—especially those found in the Bill of Rights—can provide the basis for appeals made to federal courts by offenders convicted in state court systems. Learn more about the dual-court system in America at **http://public.findlaw.com/abaflg/flg-2-2a-1.html**.

This chapter describes both state and federal court systems in terms of their historical development, **jurisdiction**, and current structure. Because it is within state courts that the majority of criminal cases originate, we turn our attention first to them.

federal court system
The three-tiered structure of federal courts, comprising U.S. district courts, U.S. courts of appeals, and the U.S. Supreme Court.

state court system
A state judicial structure; most states generally have at least three court levels: trial courts, appellate courts, and a state supreme court.

1 Summarize the development of American courts, including the concept of the dual-court system.

jurisdiction
The territory, subject matter, or people over which a court or other justice agency may exercise lawful authority, as determined by statute or constitution.

FIGURE 7–1
The Structure of the Federal Courts

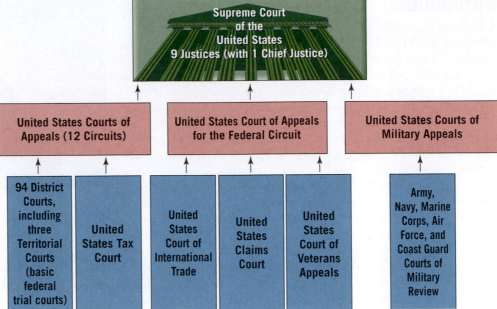

FIGURE 7–1
The Structure of the Federal Courts

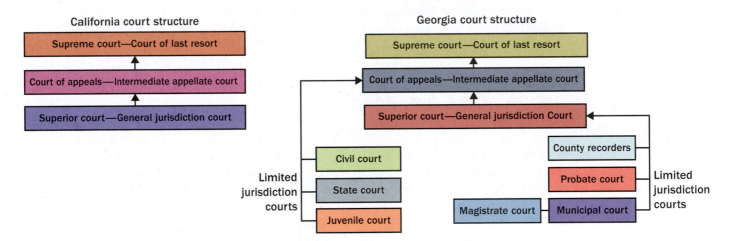

FIGURE 7–2
Different Structures of Trial and Appellate State Court Organization
Source: State Court Organization, 2011, Bureau of Justice Statistics, U.S. Department of Justice.

The State Court System

The Development of State Courts

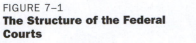

2 Describe a typical state court system, including some of the differences between the state and federal court systems.

original jurisdiction
The lawful authority of a court to hear or to act on a case from its beginning and to pass judgment on the law and the facts. The authority may be over a specific geographic area or over particular types of cases.

Each of the original American colonies had its own court system for resolving disputes, both civil and criminal. In 1629, the Massachusetts Bay Colony created a General Court, composed of the governor, his deputy, 18 assistants, and 118 elected officials. The General Court was a combined legislature and court that made laws, held trials, and imposed sentences.[4] By 1776, all of the American colonies had established fully functioning court systems.

Following the American Revolution, state court systems were anything but uniform. Initially, most states made no distinction between **original jurisdiction** (the lawful authority of a court to hear cases that arise within a specified geographic area or that involve particular kinds of law violations) and **appellate jurisdiction** (the lawful authority of a court to review a decision made by a lower court). Many, in fact, had no provisions for appeal;

Delaware, for example, did not allow appeals in criminal cases until 1897. States that did permit appeals often lacked any established appellate courts and sometimes used state legislatures for that purpose.

By the late nineteenth century, a dramatic increase in population, growing urbanization, the settlement of the West, and other far-reaching changes in the American way of life led to a tremendous increase in civil litigation and criminal arrests. Legislatures tried to keep pace with the rising tide of cases. They created a multiplicity of courts at the trial, appellate, and supreme court levels, calling them by a diversity of names and assigning them functions that sometimes bore little resemblance to those of similarly named courts in neighboring states. City courts, which were limited in their jurisdiction by community boundaries, arose to handle the special problems of urban life, such as disorderly conduct, property disputes, and enforcement of restrictive and regulatory ordinances. Other tribunals, such as juvenile courts, developed to handle special kinds of problems or special clients. Some, such as magistrate's or small-claims courts, handled only minor law violations and petty disputes; still others, such as traffic courts, were very narrow in focus. The result was a patchwork quilt of hearing bodies, some only vaguely resembling modern notions of a trial court.

State court systems developed by following one of several models. One was the New York State Field Code of 1848, which was eventually copied by most other states. The Field Code clarified jurisdictional claims and specified matters of court procedure, but it was later amended so extensively that its usefulness as a model dissolved. Another court system model was provided by the federal Judiciary Act of 1789 and later by the federal Reorganization Act of 1801. States that followed the federal model developed a three-tiered structure of (1) trial courts of limited jurisdiction, (2) trial courts of general jurisdiction, and (3) appellate courts.

State Court Systems Today

The three-tiered federal model was far from perfect, however. Within the structure it provided, many local and specialized courts proliferated. Traffic courts, magistrate's courts, municipal courts, recorder's courts, probate courts, and courts held by justices of the peace were but a few that functioned at the lower levels. A movement toward simplification of state court structures, led primarily by the American Bar Association and the American Judicature Society, began in the early twentieth century. Proponents of state court reform sought to unify redundant courts that held overlapping jurisdictions. Most reformers suggested a uniform model for states everywhere that would build on (1) a centralized court structure composed of a clear hierarchy of trial and appellate courts, (2) the consolidation of numerous lower-level courts with overlapping jurisdictions, and (3) a centralized state court authority that would be responsible for budgeting, financing, and managing all courts within a state.

The court reform movement continues today. Although reformers have made substantial progress in many states, there are still many differences between and among state court systems (as Figure 7–2 shows). Reform states, like California, which early on embraced the reform movement, are now characterized by streamlined judicial systems consisting of precisely conceived trial courts of limited and general jurisdiction, supplemented by one or two appellate court levels. Nonreform, or traditional, states, like Georgia, retain judicial systems that are a conglomeration of multilevel and sometimes redundant courts with poorly defined jurisdictions. Even in nonreform states, however, most criminal courts can be classified within the three-tiered structure of two trial court echelons and an appellate tier.

State Trial Courts

Trial courts are where criminal cases begin. The trial court conducts arraignments, sets bail, takes pleas, and conducts trials. (We will discuss these separate functions in more depth later in this chapter and in the next.) If the defendant is found guilty (or pleads guilty), the trial court imposes sentence. Trial courts of limited (or special) jurisdiction are also called *lower courts*. Lower courts are authorized

appellate jurisdiction
The lawful authority of a court to review a decision made by a lower court.

Follow the author's tweets about the latest crime and justice news @schmalleger

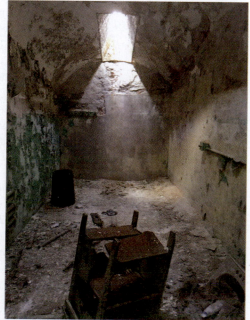

▼ An abandoned prison cell in the old Eastern State Penitentiary in Philadelphia, Pennsylvania. Just as criminal punishments have changed throughout the centuries, so too have criminal courts, which today provide a civilized forum for exploring conflicting claims about guilt and innocence. How might our courts continue to evolve?
Courtesy of the Justice Research Association.

courts of limited jurisdiction
Courts of law that have jurisdiction on a restricted range of cases, primarily lesser criminal and civil matters, including misdemeanors, small claims, traffic, parking, and civil infractions. Such courts are also called inferior courts or lower courts. They can also handle the preliminary stages of felony cases in some states.

courts of general jurisdiction
Courts of law with primary jurisdiction on all issues not delegated to lower courts. Most often called major trial courts, they most often hear serious criminal or civil cases. Cases are also designated to courts of general jurisdiction based on the severity of the punishment or allegation or on the dollar value of the case.

trial *de novo*
Literally, "new trial." The term is applied to cases that are retried on appeal, as opposed to those that are simply reviewed on the record.

court of last resort
The court authorized by law to hear the final appeal on a matter.

appeal
The request that a court with appellate jurisdiction review the judgment, decision, or order of a lower court and set it aside (reverse it) or modify it.

to hear only less serious criminal cases, usually involving misdemeanors, or to hear special types of cases such as traffic violations, family disputes, and small claims. **Courts of limited jurisdiction**, which are depicted in TV shows such as *Judge Judy* and *The People's Court*, rarely hold jury trials, depending instead on the hearing judge to make determinations of both fact and law. At the lower court level, a detailed record of the proceedings is not maintained, and case files only include information on the charge, the plea, the finding of the court, and the sentence. All but six of the states make use of trial courts of limited jurisdiction.[5] These lower courts are much less formal than **courts of general jurisdiction**.

Trial courts of general jurisdiction—variously called *high courts*, *circuit courts*, or *superior courts*—are authorized to hear any criminal case. In many states, they also provide the first appellate level for courts of limited jurisdiction. In most cases, superior courts offer defendants whose cases originated in lower courts the chance for a new trial instead of a review of the record of the earlier hearing. When a new trial is held, it is referred to as a **trial *de novo***.

Trial courts of general jurisdiction operate within a fact-finding framework called the *adversarial process.* That process pits the interests of the state, represented by prosecutors, against the professional skills and abilities of defense attorneys. The adversarial process is not a free-for-all; rather, it is constrained by procedural rules specified in law and sustained through tradition.

State Appellate Courts

Most states today have an appellate division, consisting of an intermediate appellate court (often called the *court of appeals*) and a high-level appellate court (generally termed the *state supreme court*). High-level appellate courts are referred to as **courts of last resort**, indicating that no other appellate route remains to a defendant within the state court system once the high court rules on a case. All states have supreme courts, although only 39 have intermediate appellate courts.[6]

An **appeal** by a convicted defendant asks that a higher court review the actions of a lower court. Once they accept an appeal, courts within the appellate division do not conduct a new trial; instead, they review the case on the record. In other words, appellate courts examine the written transcript of lower court hearings to ensure that those proceedings were carried out in a fair manner and in accordance with proper procedure and state law. They may also allow attorneys for both sides to make brief oral arguments and will generally consider other briefs or information filed by the appellant (the party initiating the appeal) or the appellee (the side opposed to the appeal). State statutes generally require that sentences of life imprisonment or death be automatically reviewed by the state supreme court.

Most convictions are affirmed on appeal. Occasionally, however, an appellate court will determine that the trial court erred in allowing certain kinds of evidence to be heard, that it failed to interpret properly the significance of a relevant statute, or that some other impropriety occurred. When that happens, the verdict of the trial court will be reversed, and the case may be sent back for a new trial, or *remanded.* When a conviction is overturned by an appellate court because of constitutional issues or when a statute is determined to be invalid, the state usually has recourse to the state supreme court; when an issue of federal law is involved, as when a state court has ruled a federal law unconstitutional, it goes to the U.S. Supreme Court.

Defendants who are not satisfied with the resolution of their case within the state court system may attempt an appeal to the U.S. Supreme Court. For such an appeal to have any chance of being heard, it must be based on claimed violations of the defendant's rights, as guaranteed under federal law or the U.S. Constitution. Under certain circumstances, federal district courts may also provide a path of relief for state defendants who can show that their federal constitutional rights were violated. However, in the 1992 case of *Keeney* v. *Tamayo-Reyes*,[7] the U.S. Supreme Court ruled that a "respondent is entitled to a federal evidentiary hearing [only] if he can show cause for his failure to develop the facts in the state-court proceedings and actual prejudice resulting from that failure, or if he can show that a fundamental miscarriage of justice would result from failure to hold such a hearing." Justice Byron White, writing for the Court, said, "It is hardly a good use of scarce judicial resources to duplicate fact-finding in federal court merely because a petitioner has negligently failed to take advantage of opportunities in state court proceedings."

Likewise, in *Herrera* v. *Collins* (1993),[8] the Court ruled that new evidence of innocence is no reason for a federal court to order a new state trial if constitutional grounds are lacking. The *Keeney* and *Herrera* decisions have severely limited access by state defendants to federal courts.

State Court Administration

To function efficiently, courts require uninterrupted funding, adequate staffing, trained support personnel, well-managed case flow, and coordination between levels and among jurisdictions. To oversee these and other aspects of judicial management, every state today has its own mechanism for court administration. Most make use of **state court administrators** who manage these operational functions.

State court administrators can receive assistance from the National Center for State Courts (NCSC) in Williamsburg, Virginia. The NCSC, founded in 1971 at the behest of Chief Justice Warren E. Burger, is an independent, nonprofit organization dedicated to the improvement of the American court system. You can visit the NCSC at **http://www.ncsc.org**.

At the federal level, the court system is administered by the Administrative Office of the United States Courts (AOUSC), located in Washington, D.C. The AOUSC, created by Congress in 1939, prepares the budget and legislative agenda for federal courts. It also performs audits of court accounts, manages funds for the operation of federal courts, compiles and publishes statistics on the volume and type of business conducted by the courts, and recommends plans and strategies to efficiently manage court business. You can visit the AOUSC at **http://www.uscourts.gov**.

state court administrator
A coordinator who assists with case-flow management, operating funds budgeting, and court docket administration.

dispute-resolution center
An informal hearing place designed to mediate interpersonal disputes without resorting to the more formal arrangements of a criminal trial court.

Dispute-Resolution Centers and Specialized Courts

Often, it is possible to resolve minor disputes (in which minor criminal offenses might otherwise be charged) without a formal court hearing. Some communities have **dispute-resolution centers** that hear victims' claims of minor wrongs they have suffered, such as being subject to the passing of bad checks, trespassing, shoplifting, or petty theft. Such centers function today in more than 200 locations throughout the country.[9] Frequently staffed by volunteer mediators, such programs work to resolve disagreements without assigning blame. Dispute-resolution programs began in the early 1970s, with the earliest being the Community Assistance Project in Chester, Pennsylvania; the Columbus, Ohio, Night Prosecutor Program; and the Arbitration as an Alternative Program in Rochester, New York. Following the lead of these programs, the U.S. Department of Justice helped promote the development of three experimental Neighborhood Justice Centers in Los Angeles, Kansas City, and Atlanta. Each center accepted both minor civil and criminal cases.

▲ A small claims court mediation session in progress. Staffed largely by volunteers, dispute-resolution centers facilitate cooperative solutions to relatively low-level disputes in which minor criminal offenses might otherwise be charged. How do dispute-resolution centers help relieve some of the pressure facing our criminal courts?
Larry Fisher/Quad-City Times/ZUMA Press Inc/Alamy Stock Photo

Mediation centers are often closely integrated with the formal criminal justice process and may substantially reduce the caseload of lower-level courts. Some centers are, in fact, run by the courts and work only with court-ordered referrals; others are semiautonomous but may be dependent on courts for endorsement of their decisions; and still others function with complete autonomy. Rarely, however, do dispute-resolution programs entirely supplant the formal criminal justice mechanism, and defendants who appear before a community mediator may later be charged with a crime. Community mediation programs have become a central feature of today's restorative-justice movement (discussed in more detail in Chapter 9).

community court
A low-level court that focuses on quality-of-life crimes that erode a neighborhood's morale, that emphasizes problem solving rather than punishment, and that builds on restorative principles such as community service and restitution.

Unlike dispute-resolution centers, **community courts** are always *official* components of the formal justice system and can hand down sentences, including fines and jail time, without the need for further judicial review. Community courts began as grassroots movements undertaken by community residents and local organizations seeking to build confidence in the way offenders are handled for less serious offenses. A 2016 federal study of community courts put their number at around 3,050 throughout the United States.[10]

A distinguishing feature of community courts is their focus on quality-of-life crimes that erode a neighborhood's morale. Like dispute-resolution centers they emphasize problem solving rather than punishment, and build on restorative principles such as community service and restitution. Other authors note that "The basic premise behind the problem-solving court model is the idea that instead of merely adjudicating legal questions or punishing criminal behavior after the fact, courts should seek to prevent crime by directly addressing its underlying causes."[11]

Community courts typically *divert* offenders from criminal prosecution, incarceration, or other typical criminal justice outcomes. They frequently sentence convicted offenders to work within the community, "where neighbors can see what they are doing."[12] A recent study of the Red Hook Community Justice Center in Red Hook, New York, found that defendants considered the community court to be more fair than traditional courts.[13] According to the study, perceptions of fairness were primarily related to the more personal role played by community court judges, who dispense with much of the formality of traditional courts and who often offer support and praise to defendants who work within the parameters set by the court. Finally, a 2013 National Center for State Courts' study found the Red Hook center to be effective in reducing recidivism, noting that "RHCJC defendants were significantly less likely than downtown defendants to be re-arrested."[14]

problem-solving courts
Low-level specialized courts that focus on relatively minor offenses and handle special populations or address special issues. Problem-solving courts are often a form of community courts.

Problem-solving courts generally handle special populations or address special issues. Some hear only cases involving veterans; others focus on the needs of the mentally ill or the homeless. Still others handle only sex offenders charged with lessor offenses. The Brooklyn Treatment Court provides an example of a problem-solving court that, in its own words, "seeks to craft a meaningful response to the problems posed by defendants with mental illness in the criminal justice system."[15] The Brooklyn court attempts to address both the needs of defendants with mental illness and public-safety concerns. It uses the authority of the court to provide counseling and treatment for defendants with identified serious and persistent mental illnesses in lieu of jail or prison time. The court employs on-site clinical teams to assess the degree of mental illness from which a defendant suffers, and to gauge the risk that the defendant represents to the community were he or she to be released into a community-based supervision program.

Follow the author's tweets about the latest crime and justice news @schmalleger

Problem-solving courts that deal with specific offenses include gun courts, domestic violence courts, mental health courts, driving while intoxicated (DWI) or driving under the influence (DUI) courts, youth specialty courts, and drug courts. Other specialized courts, called reentry courts, utilize the drug-court model to facilitate the reintegration of drug-involved offenders paroled into the community after being released from prison. Using the authority of the court to apply graduated sanctions and positive reinforcement, reentry courts marshal resources to support positive reintegration by the returning offender. Reentry courts are discussed in more detail in Chapter 10.

The judicial Power of the United States shall be vested in one supreme Court, and in such inferior Courts as the Congress may from time to time ordain and establish.
—Article III of the U.S. Constitution

Most specialized court programs are motivated by two sets of goals: (1) case management, in which the court works to expedite case processing and reduce caseloads, as well as to reduce time to disposition (thus increasing trial capacity for more serious crimes); and (2) therapeutic jurisprudence, in which the court works to reduce criminal offending through therapeutic and interdisciplinary approaches that address addiction and other underlying issues without jeopardizing public safety and due process.[16]

Specialized courts can be distinguished from other criminal courts by the fact that they operate according to a problem-solving model, rather than a retributive one—meaning that they seek to address the root causes of law violation, whether they lie within the individual, the community, or the larger culture.[17] Their purpose is not only to make justice more efficient, but more effective as well.

The Federal Court System

Whereas state courts evolved from early colonial arrangements, federal courts were created by the U.S. Constitution. Article III, Section 1, of the Constitution provides for the establishment of "one supreme Court, and . . . such inferior Courts as the Congress may from time to time ordain and establish." Article III, Section 2, specifies that such courts are to have jurisdiction over cases arising under the Constitution, federal laws, and treaties. Federal courts are also to settle disputes between states and to have jurisdiction in cases where one of the parties is a state.

3 Describe the structure of the federal court system, including the various types of federal courts.

Today's federal court system represents the culmination of a series of congressional mandates that have expanded the federal judicial infrastructure so that it can continue to carry out the duties envisioned by the Constitution. Notable federal statutes that have contributed to the present structure of the federal court system include the Judiciary Act of 1789, the Judiciary Act of 1925, and the Magistrate's Act of 1968.

As a result of constitutional mandates, congressional action, and other historical developments, today's federal judiciary consists of three levels: (1) U.S. district courts, (2) U.S. courts of appeal, and (3) the U.S. Supreme Court. Each is described in turn in the following sections.

U.S. District Courts

The U.S. district courts are the trial courts of the federal court system.[18] Within limits set by Congress and the Constitution, the district courts have jurisdiction to hear nearly all categories of federal cases, including both civil and criminal matters. There are 94 federal judicial districts, including at least one district in each state (some states, like New York and California, have as many as four), the District of Columbia, and Puerto Rico. Each district includes a U.S. bankruptcy court as a unit of the district court. Three territories of the United States—the Virgin Islands, Guam, and the Northern Mariana Islands—have district courts that hear federal cases, including bankruptcy cases. There are two special trial courts that have nationwide jurisdiction over certain types of cases. The Court of International Trade addresses cases involving international trade and customs issues. The U.S. Court of Federal Claims has jurisdiction over most claims for money damages against the United States, disputes over federal contracts, unlawful "takings" of private property by the federal government, and a variety of other claims against the United States.

Federal district courts have original jurisdiction over all cases involving alleged violations of federal statutes. A district may itself be divided into divisions and may have several places where the court hears cases. District courts were first authorized by Congress through the Judiciary Act of 1789, which allocated one federal court to each state. Because of population increases over the years, new courts have been added in a number of states.

Nearly 650 district court judges staff federal district courts. Because some courts are much busier than others, the number of district court judges varies from a low of 2 in some jurisdictions to a high of 27 in others. District court judges are appointed by the president and confirmed by the Senate, and they serve for life. An additional 369 full-time and 110 part-time magistrate judges (referred to as *U.S. magistrates* before 1990) serve the district

▲ Demonstrators in support of a 2012 ruling by the Ninth Circuit Court of Appeals affirming a decision by U.S. District Court Judge Vaughn R. Walker that overturned California's ban on gay marriages. The Ninth Circuit Court held that the fact that Walker is gay was immaterial. Do judges' personal perspectives influence their decisions? Should they?

Funcrunch Photo/Alamy Stock Photo

court system and assist the federal judges. Magistrate judges have the power to conduct arraignments and may set bail, issue warrants, and try minor offenders.

U.S. district courts handle tens of thousands of cases per year. During 2017, for example, 75,861 criminal cases[19] and 292,076 civil cases[20] were filed in U.S. district courts. Drug prosecutions and the prosecution of illegal immigrants, especially in federal courts located close to the U.S.–Mexico border, have led to considerable growth in the number of cases filed. During the last 20 years, the number of cases handled by the entire federal district court system has grown exponentially. The hiring of new judges and the creation of new courtroom facilities have not kept pace with the increase in caseload, and questions persist as to the quality of justice that overworked judges can deliver.

Another pressing issue facing district court judges is the fact that their pay, which at $208,000 in mid-2018[21] placed them in the top 1% of income-earning Americans, is small compared to what most could earn in private practice. U.S. Supreme Court Justice, John Roberts, once noted that because of relatively low pay, "judges effectively serve for a term dictated by their financial position rather than for life."[22] Learn more about the federal courts at **https://www.justicestudies.com/pubs/fedcourts.pdf**.

U.S. Courts of Appeal

There are 13 U.S. courts of appeals, although only 11 are officially numbered.[23] A court of appeals hears appeals from the district courts located within its circuit, as well as appeals from decisions of federal administrative agencies.

The U.S. Court of Appeals for the Federal Circuit, plus the District of Columbia Circuit, and the remaining 11 regional courts of appeal are referred to as *circuit courts*. Early in the nation's history, the judges of the first courts of appeal visited each of the courts in one region in a particular sequence, traveling by horseback and riding the "circuit." Today, the regional courts of appeal review matters from the district courts of their geographic regions, from the U.S. Tax Court, and from certain federal administrative agencies. A disappointed party in a district court often has the opportunity to have the case reviewed in the court of appeals for the circuit. Each of the First through Eleventh Circuits includes three or more states, as illustrated in Figure 7–3.

FIGURE 7–3
Geographic Boundaries of the U.S. Courts of Appeal and U.S. District Courts
Source: Administrative Office of the United States Courts. Retrieved from https://www.fjc.gov/sites/default/files/2012/IJR00007.pdf.

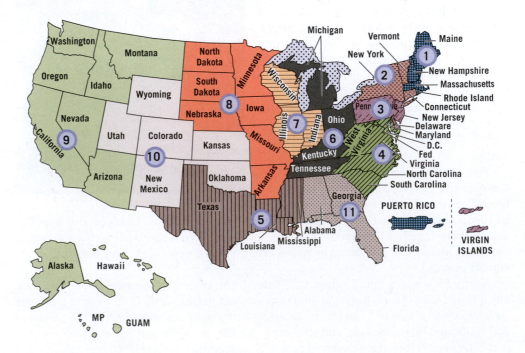

Each court of appeals consists of six or more judges, depending on the caseload of the court. Circuit court judges are appointed for life by the president (with the advice and consent of the Senate). The judge who has served on the court the longest and who is under 65 years of age is designated as the chief judge. The chief judge performs administrative duties in addition to hearing cases and serves for a maximum term of 7 years. There are 167 judges on the 12 regional courts of appeal.

The U.S. Court of Appeals for the District of Columbia, which is often called the Twelfth Circuit, hears cases arising in the District of Columbia and has appellate jurisdiction assigned by Congress in legislation concerning many departments of the federal government. The U.S. Court of Appeals for the Federal Circuit (in effect, the Thirteenth Circuit) was created in 1982 by the merging of the U.S. Court of Claims and the U.S. Court of Customs and Patent Appeals. The court hears appeals in cases from the U.S. Court of Federal Claims, the U.S. Court of International Trade, the U.S. Court of Veterans Appeals, the International Trade Commission, the Board of Contract Appeals, the Patent and Trademark Office, and the Merit Systems Protection Board. The court also hears appeals from certain decisions involving the secretaries of the Department of Agriculture and the Department of Commerce and cases from district courts involving patents and minor claims against the federal government.

Almost all appeals from federal district courts go to the court of appeals serving the circuit in which the case was first heard. Federal appellate courts have appellate jurisdiction over the decisions of district courts within their circuits. Criminal appeals from federal district courts are usually heard by panels of three judges sitting on a court of appeals rather than by all the judges of each circuit. A defendant's request for appeal, when granted, has been interpreted to mean the opportunity for one appeal; hence, the U.S. Supreme Court need not necessarily hear the appeals of defendants who are dissatisfied with the decision of a federal appeals court.

Federal appellate courts operate under the Federal Rules of Appellate Procedure, although each has also created its own separate Local Rules. Local Rules may mean that one circuit, such as the Second, will depend heavily on oral arguments, whereas others may prefer written summary depositions. Appeals generally fall into one of three categories: (1) frivolous appeals, which have little substance, raise no significant new issues, and are generally disposed of quickly; (2) ritualistic appeals, which are brought primarily because of the demands of litigants, even though the probability of reversal is negligible; and (3) nonconsensual appeals, which entail major questions of law and policy and on which there is considerable professional disagreement among the courts and within the legal profession.[24] The probability of reversal is, of course, highest in the case of nonconsensual appeals.

The U.S. Supreme Court

At the apex of the federal court system stands the U.S. Supreme Court. The Supreme Court is located in Washington, D.C., across the street from the U.S. Capitol. The Court consists of nine justices. Eight are associate justices, and the ninth presides over the Court as the chief justice of the United States (Table 7-1). Supreme Court justices are nominated by the president, are confirmed by the Senate, and serve for life. Lengthy terms of service are a tradition among justices. One of the earliest chief justices, John Marshall, served the Court for 34 years, from 1801 to 1835. The same was true of Justice Stephen J. Field, who sat on the bench between 1863 and 1897. Justice Hugo Black passed the 34-year milestone, serving an additional month before retiring in 1971. Justice William O. Douglas set a record for longevity on the bench, retiring in 1975 after 36 years and 6 months of service. You can view the biographies of today's Supreme Court justices via **http://www.supremecourt.gov/about/ biographies.aspx**.

The Supreme Court of the United States wields immense power. The Court's greatest authority lies in its capacity for **judicial review** of lower court decisions and state and federal statutes. By exercising its power of judicial review, the Court decides what laws and lower court decisions are in keeping with the intent of the U.S. Constitution. The power of judicial review is not explicit in the Constitution but was anticipated by its framers. In the *Federalist Papers*, which urged adoption of the Constitution, Alexander Hamilton

> Circuit court judges are appointed for life by the president with the advice and consent of the Senate.

judicial review
The power of a court to review actions and decisions made by other agencies of government.

TABLE 7-1
Justices of the U.S. Supreme Court (as of November 2018)

Justice	Start of Duty	Views
Chief Justice		
John G. Roberts, Jr.	September 2005	Conservative
Associate Justices		
Clarence Thomas	October 1991	Conservative
Ruth Bader Ginsburg	August 1993	Moderate to liberal
Stephen G. Breyer	August 1994	Moderate
Samuel A. Alito, Jr.	January 2006	Conservative
Sonia M. Sotomayor	August 2009	Moderate to liberal
Elena Kagan	August 2010	Liberal
Neil M. Gorsuch	April 2017	Conservative
Brett Kavanaugh	October 2018	Conservative

wrote that through the practice of judicial review, the Court would ensure that "the will of the whole people," as grounded in the Constitution, would be supreme over the "will of the legislature," which might be subject to temporary whims.[25] It was not until 1803, however, that the Court forcefully asserted its power of judicial review. In an opinion written for *Marbury* v. *Madison* (1803),[26] Chief Justice John Marshall established the Court's authority as final interpreter of the U.S. Constitution, declaring, "It is emphatically the province of the judicial department to say what the law is."

▲ U.S. Supreme Court Justice Neil Gorsuch, following his 2017 nomination by President Trump to join the Court. How does the U.S. Supreme Court decide which cases it will review?

MediaPunch Inc/Alamy Stock Photo

The Supreme Court Today

The Supreme Court reviews the decisions of lower courts and may accept cases both from U.S. courts of appeal and from state supreme courts. It has limited original jurisdiction and does not conduct trials except for disputes between states and for some cases of attorney disbarment. For a case to be heard, at least four justices must vote in favor of a hearing. When the Court agrees to hear a case, it will issue a writ of *certiorari* to a lower court, ordering it to send the records of the case forward for review. Once having granted *certiorari*, the justices can revoke the decision. In such cases, a writ is dismissed by ruling it improvidently granted.

The U.S. Supreme Court may review any decision appealed to it that it decides is worthy of review. In fact, however, the Court elects to review only cases that involve a substantial federal question. Of approximately 5,000 requests for review received by the Court yearly, only about 200 are actually heard.

A term of the Supreme Court begins, by statute, on the first Monday in October and lasts until early July. The term is divided among sittings, when cases will be heard, and periods of time for the writing and delivering of opinions. Between 22 and 24 cases are heard at each sitting, with each side allotted 30 minutes for arguments before the justices. Intervening recesses allow justices time to study arguments and supporting documentation and to work on their opinions.

Decisions rendered by the Supreme Court are rarely unanimous. Instead, the opinion that a majority of the Court's justices agree on becomes the judgment of the Court. Justices who

Evidence-Based Justice Reinvestment
Cost-Efficient Courts

It might seem strange to spend money in order to save it. Yet, that's just what the Washington, D.C.–based Justice Policy Institute recommended with publication of its recent report *System Overload*. The Institute pointed out that nearly four out of five people charged with a crime in the United States are eligible for assistance from court-appointed counsel; yet the funding allocated to public defender's offices has historically been so poor in many areas that they have been in a state of "chronic crisis" for decades. It's only by upping the quality of America's public defense system, the Institute says, that innocent people can be prevented from being convicted and going to prison—which would ultimately cost taxpayers far more than funding quality public defender programs.

Special-purpose courts, which divert nonviolent offenders from prison, can also serve taxpayers effectively. In Champaign County, Illinois, for example, felony drug offenders are routinely adjudicated in the area's special drug court. If found guilty, most offenders are placed on probation and ordered to undergo treatment at county expense, especially when judged not to be a danger to themselves or to the community. Some of the money spent on treatment can be recouped when offenders are also ordered to participate in mandatory community service programs and to pay restitution. Experts estimate that imprisonment in Illinois costs the state $21,500 per year for every offender kept behind bars. In contrast, probation, combined with drug treatment, costs approximately $4,000.

Drug courts, like many other special-purpose courts, effectively divert nonviolent defendants not only from prison, but from the more elaborate, and far more expensive, formal processing of trial courts.

Treatment courts, which serve mentally ill populations, are another recent innovation, designed to divert offenders with mental issues from prison and place them into treatment programs. The state of Michigan runs eight mental health courts, serving nearly 700 people per year. Typical defendants seen by Michigan's treatment court have gotten into trouble with the law for relatively minor offenses, but because of their frequently lengthy arrest records, they might have ended up in jail or prison when handled by traditional criminal courts. Instead, Michigan's treatment courts

work with community-based nonprofit organizations, such as the Detroit Central City Community Mental Health agency, and order psychotherapy, medication, and even residential treatment for the most serious cases. The cost savings are obvious: In Detroit, community treatment costs about $10,000 per year, versus around $35,000 for incarceration.

Moreover, special-purpose courts hold the promise of breaking the revolving door of imprisonment. Many drug-involved and mentally ill offenders are bound to a vicious cycle of crime commission and, without the treatment options offered by these special courts, would keep the revolving door of prison spinning.

Special-purpose courts are not the only way that money can be saved in the court system. Recently, the National Center for State Courts (NCSC) performed an analysis on the use of e-filings versus paper documents in selected courthouses. The NCSC found that effective e-filing systems could cut the costs of document intake and storage to as little as 11 cents per page compared with 69 cents per page for costs of paper intake and storage. Moreover, said the Center, "courthouses are incredibly expensive storage spaces." A small file room measuring 20 by 60 feet, said the Center, "would cost $360,000 to construct and at 5% per year, cost $18,000 per year to heat/cool and maintain." A typical computer hard drive, which could contain all of that digitized data in that room, might be purchased for as little as $300, although backup and associated computer costs would raise the costs somewhat. Learn more about using technology to achieve greater efficiency in courtroom operation from the NCSC at **http://www.ncsc.org**.

References: Champaign County Drug Court, "General Information," http://www.co.champaign.il.us/circt/DrugCourt/Info.htm (accessed August 1, 2012); Jeff Gerritt, "Salvaging Lives, Saving Money: Eight Pilot Courts That Divert Mentally Ill Offenders from Prison," *Detroit Free Press*, March 4, 2012, http://www.freep.com/article/20120304 (accessed August 1, 2012); James E. McMillan, Carole D. Pettijohn, and Jennifer K. Berg, "Calculating an E-Court Return on Investment (ROI)," *Court Technology Bulletin*, February 16, 2012, http://courttechbulletin.blogspot.com/2012/02/calculating-e-court-return-on.html (accessed August 2, 2013).

---

agree with the Court's judgment write concurring opinions if they agree for a different reason than the majority opinion or if they feel that they have some new light to shed on a legal issue involved in the case. Justices who do not agree with the decision of the Court write dissenting opinions, and those dissenting opinions may offer new possibilities for successful appeals at a later date. Visit the U.S. Supreme Court via **http://www.supremecourt.gov**.

Pretrial Activities

The next chapter discusses the steps in a criminal trial and describes the many roles assumed by courtroom participants, including judges, prosecutors, defense attorneys, victims, and defendants. Numerous court-related activities, however, routinely take place *before* trial can begin (Figure 7–4). Although these activities (as well as the names given to them) vary among jurisdictions, they are described generally in the pages that follow.

The First Appearance

Following arrest, most defendants do not come into contact with an officer of the court until their **first appearance** before a magistrate or a lower court judge.[27] A first appearance, sometimes called an *initial appearance* or *magistrate's review*, occurs when defendants are brought before a judge (1) to be given formal notice of the charges against them, (2) to be

🐦 Follow the author's tweets about the latest crime and justice news @schmalleger

4 Describe the pretrial steps and activities.

first appearance
An appearance before a magistrate during which the legality of the defendant's arrest is initially assessed and the defendant is informed of the charges on which he or she is being held. At this stage in the criminal justice process, bail may be set or pretrial release arranged. Also called *initial appearance*.

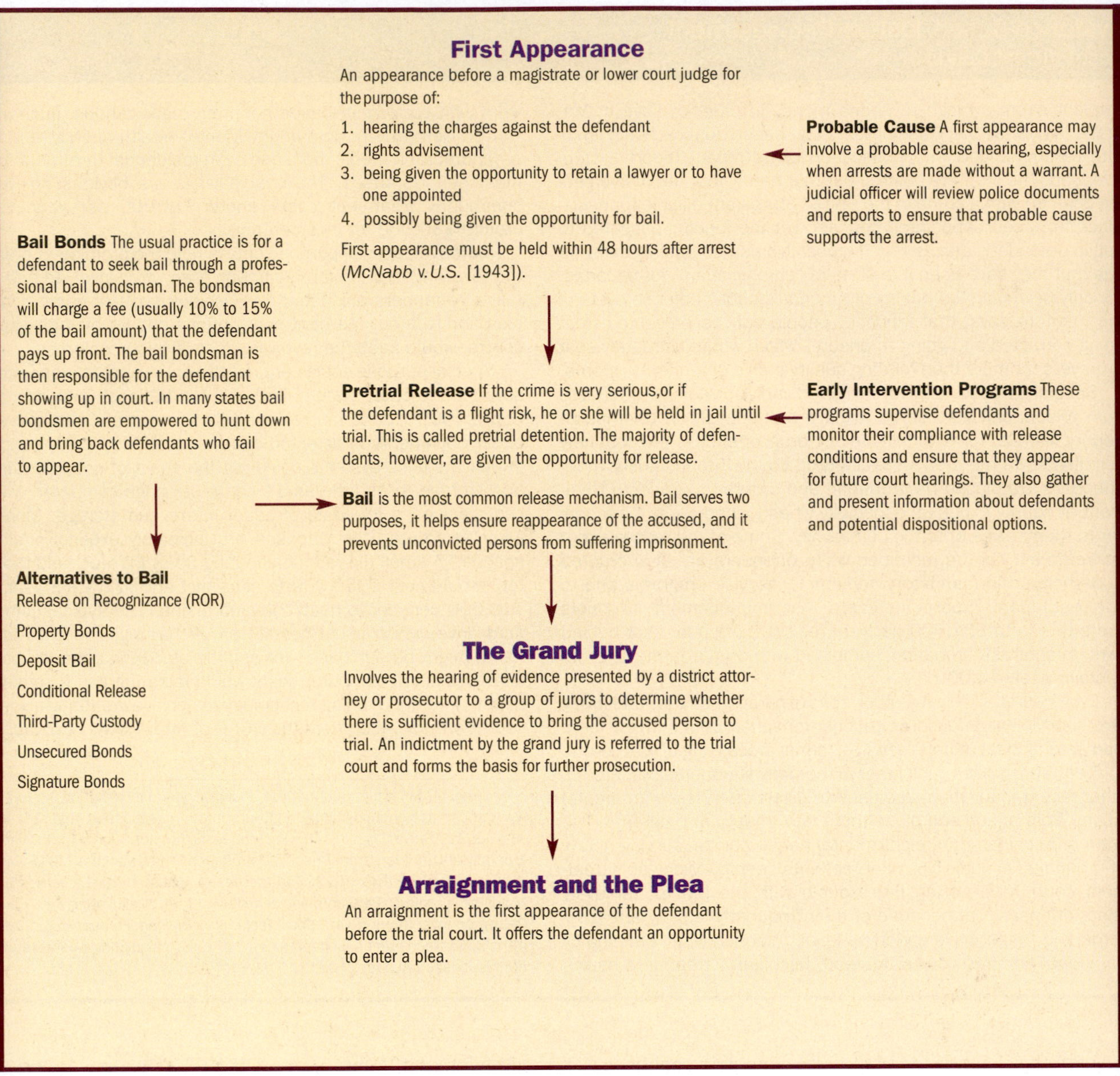

Frank Schmalleger, Criminal Justice: A Brief Introduction, 12e, © 2018. Pearson Education, Inc., New York, NY.

FIGURE 7-4 Pretrial Activities

First Appearance

An appearance before a magistrate or lower court judge for the purpose of:

1. hearing the charges against the defendant
2. rights advisement
3. being given the opportunity to retain a lawyer or to have one appointed
4. possibly being given the opportunity for bail.

First appearance must be held within 48 hours after arrest (*McNabb* v. *U.S.* [1943]).

Probable Cause A first appearance may involve a probable cause hearing, especially when arrests are made without a warrant. A judicial officer will review police documents and reports to ensure that probable cause supports the arrest.

Bail Bonds The usual practice is for a defendant to seek bail through a professional bail bondsman. The bondsman will charge a fee (usually 10% to 15% of the bail amount) that the defendant pays up front. The bail bondsman is then responsible for the defendant showing up in court. In many states bail bondsmen are empowered to hunt down and bring back defendants who fail to appear.

Pretrial Release If the crime is very serious, or if the defendant is a flight risk, he or she will be held in jail until trial. This is called pretrial detention. The majority of defendants, however, are given the opportunity for release.

Early Intervention Programs These programs supervise defendants and monitor their compliance with release conditions and ensure that they appear for future court hearings. They also gather and present information about defendants and potential dispositional options.

Bail is the most common release mechanism. Bail serves two purposes, it helps ensure reappearance of the accused, and it prevents unconvicted persons from suffering imprisonment.

Alternatives to Bail

Release on Recognizance (ROR)

Property Bonds

Deposit Bail

Conditional Release

Third-Party Custody

Unsecured Bonds

Signature Bonds

The Grand Jury

Involves the hearing of evidence presented by a district attorney or prosecutor to a group of jurors to determine whether there is sufficient evidence to bring the accused person to trial. An indictment by the grand jury is referred to the trial court and forms the basis for further prosecution.

Arraignment and the Plea

An arraignment is the first appearance of the defendant before the trial court. It offers the defendant an opportunity to enter a plea.

---

bail

The money or property pledged to the court or actually deposited with the court to effect the release of a person from legal custody.

advised of their rights, (3) to be given the opportunity to retain a lawyer or to have one appointed to represent them, and (4) to possibly be afforded the opportunity for **bail**.

According to the procedural rules of all jurisdictions, defendants who have been taken into custody must be offered an in-court appearance before a magistrate "without unnecessary delay." The 1943 U.S. Supreme Court case of *McNabb* v. *U.S.*[28] established that any unreasonable delay in an initial court appearance would make confessions inadmissible if interrogating officers obtained them during the delay. Based on the *McNabb* decision, 48 hours following arrest became the standard maximum time by which a first appearance should be held.

The first appearance may also involve a probable cause hearing, although such hearings may be held separately because they do not require the defendant's presence. (In some jurisdictions, the probable cause hearing may be combined with the preliminary hearing.) Probable cause hearings are necessary when arrests are made without a warrant because such arrests do not require a prior judicial determination of probable cause. During a probable cause hearing, also called a *probable cause determination*, a judicial officer will review police documents and reports to ensure that probable cause supported the arrest. The review of the arrest proceeds in a relatively informal fashion, with the judge seeking to

🐦 Follow the author's tweets about the latest crime and justice news @schmalleger

CJ Careers
Surety Agent

Name: Anya Pulai

Position: Bail Bond Agent / Bail Enforcement Agent, Good To Go Bail Bonds, Denver, Colorado

Colleges attended: Associate of Arts in Criminal Justice from University of Phoenix (2007); currently attending Regis University pursuing a bachelor's degree in criminology.

Year hired: 2008 to present, Bail Enforcement Agent; 2009 to present, Surety Agent, Sun Surety Insurance Company

Please give a brief description of your job: Bail bond amounts are set by a judge or magistrate during the intake process or a bail hearing. The judge will consider a variety of factors, including the severity of the crime, previous convictions, the defendant's ties to the community, family, and whether or not the defendant has steady employment. Typically, a family member or associate or the defendant will contact a surety agent or bond agent to arrange for release. These calls are accepted 24/7/365 by the surety office, which then begins a risk assessment process. In Colorado, a surety agent may charge no more than 15% of the bond amount. Once terms are agreed upon, and all the various collateral documentation including indemnity agreements, statements of collateral taken, rate deviation forms, and applications are completed, the bail bond is posted at the detention facility holding the defendant. In the event the defendant fails to appear (FTA) at a scheduled appearance date or time, warrants and mug shots must be obtained and efforts to apprehend the defendant and bring him or her into custody begin.

What appealed most about the position when you applied for it? This is not a "desk job." This career involves elements of customer service, sales, computer skills, area travel, and being physically fit. Understanding various criminal behavior models as well as supporting every citizen's right to defend himself without detention appealed to me.

How would you describe the interview process? Demonstrating the physical presence and ability to apprehend a suspected fugitive was critical. During my interview process, a female defendant was to be remanded back into custody for violations of the terms and conditions of her bond. The defendant fled the site and I was required to pursue. A two-block sprint and apprehension ensued. Shortly thereafter, I obtained certification as a surety agent and began writing bail bonds as well.

What is a typical day like? We receive calls on a wide spectrum of bail bond needs. After verifying the detention facility, the amount of the bond, and the ability of the indemnitor to cosign for the bond, we will meet to complete the required documentation. I must then travel to the detaining facility to post the bond. Using various computer-based tools, I monitor my clients, court schedules. If a failure to appear is identified, the bail enforcement process begins in a passive mode. This includes contacting the cosigner, family, employer, and associates of the defendant. Based on the specific scenario, several activities may be required, including rescheduling an appearance date or time, locating the defendant, motioning the court, or apprehension of the defendant, all the while accepting new clients.

▲ Anya Pulai
Courtesy: Anya Pulai

What qualities/characteristics are most helpful for this job? Computer skills are required for database management and various tool sets used in locating fugitive defendants. Knowledge of area demographics greatly assists both the determination of risk management and the bail enforcement efforts. Understanding the educational background and emotional state of the client(s) is helpful. Having a basic understanding of the court and law enforcement process and ongoing physical conditioning are all helpful, as well.

What is a typical starting salary? New agents tend to work for established bail bond companies, and they are usually paid based on commission, or a percentage of the amount of bail written. About $25,000 to $40,000 year.

What is the salary potential as you move up into higher-level jobs? More experienced bail bond agent can make between $45,000 and $150,000 per year.

What career advice would you give someone in college beginning studies in criminal justice? There are many career opportunities in the criminal justice system, so career paths are not always clear for students entering college. My advice would be to research various career areas. Be wise. Ask questions. Study what you would like to pursue and don't settle for a job that you are not passionate about.

Source: CJ Careers Surety Agent, Courtesy of Anya Pulai. Used by permission of Anya Pulai.

---

decide whether, at the time of apprehension, the arresting officer had reason to believe both (1) that a crime had been or was being committed and (2) that the defendant was the person who committed it. Most of the evidence presented to the judge comes either from the arresting officer or from the victim. If probable cause is not found to exist, the suspect is released. As with a first appearance, a probable cause hearing should take place within 48 hours.

In 1991, in a class-action suit entitled *County of Riverside* v. *McLaughlin*,[29] the U.S. Supreme Court imposed a promptness requirement on probable cause determinations for in-custody arrestees. The Court held that "a jurisdiction that provides judicial determinations of probable cause within 48 hours of arrest will, as a general matter, comply with the promptness requirement." The Court specified, however, that weekends and holidays could not be excluded from the 48-hour requirement (as they had been in Riverside County, California) and that, depending on the specifics of the case, delays of fewer than 2 days may still be unreasonable.

During a first appearance, the suspect is not given an opportunity to present evidence, although the U.S. Supreme Court has held that defendants are entitled to representation by counsel at their first appearance,[30] and that an indigent person is entitled to have an attorney appointed for him or her at the initial appearance.[31] Following a reading of the charges and advisement of rights, counsel may be appointed to represent indigent defendants and proceedings may be adjourned until counsel can be obtained. In cases where a suspect is unruly, intoxicated, or uncooperative, a judicial review may occur without the suspect being present.

Some states waive a first appearance and proceed directly to arraignment (discussed later), especially when the defendant has been arrested on a warrant. In states that move directly to arraignment, the procedures undertaken to obtain a warrant are regarded as sufficient to demonstrate a basis for detention before arraignment.

Pretrial Release

pretrial release
The release of an accused person from custody, for all or part of the time before or during prosecution, upon his or her promise to appear in court when required.

A significant aspect of the first appearance hearing is the consideration of **pretrial release**. Defendants charged with very serious crimes, as well as those thought likely to escape or to injure others, are usually held in jail until trial. Such a practice is called *pretrial detention*. Most defendants, however, are afforded the opportunity for release. Many jurisdictions make use of pretrial services programs, which may also be called *early intervention programs.*[32] Such programs, which are typically funded by the states or by individual counties, perform two critical functions: (1) They gather and present information about newly arrested defendants and about available release options for use by judicial officers in deciding what (if any) conditions are to be set for defendants' release before trial, and (2) they supervise defendants released from custody during the pretrial period by monitoring their compliance with release conditions and by helping to ensure that they appear for scheduled court events. Learn more about pretrial services at **https://www.justicestudies.com/pubs/pretrial.pdf**.

The initial pretrial release/detention decision is usually made by a judicial officer or by a specially appointed hearing officer after considering the background information provided by the pretrial services program, along with the representations made by the prosecutor and the defense attorney. In making this decision, judicial officers are concerned about two types of risk: (1) the risk of flight or nonappearance for scheduled court appearances and (2) the risk to public safety.

Bail

Bail is the most common release/detention decision-making mechanism in American courts. Bail serves two purposes: (1) It helps ensure reappearance of the accused, and (2) it prevents unconvicted persons from suffering imprisonment unnecessarily.

bail bond
A document guaranteeing the appearance of a defendant in court as required and recording the pledge of money or property to be paid to the court if he or she does not appear. The bail bond is signed by the person to be released and by anyone else acting on his or her behalf.

Bail generally involves the posting of a bond as a pledge that the accused will return for further hearings. **Bail bonds** usually involve cash deposits but may be based on property or other valuables. A fully secured bond requires the defendant to post the full amount of bail set by the court. The usual practice, however, is for a defendant to seek privately secured bail through the services of a professional bail bond agent. The bond agent will assess a percentage (usually 10% to 15%) of the required bond as a fee, which the defendant will have to pay up front. Those who "skip bail" by hiding or fleeing will sometimes find that the court has ordered them to forfeit their bail. Forfeiture hearings must be held before a bond can be taken, and most courts will not order bail forfeited unless it appears that the defendant intends to avoid prosecution permanently. Bail forfeiture will often be reversed if the defendant later appears willingly to stand trial.

In many states, bail bond agents are empowered to hunt down and bring back defendants who have fled.

🐦 Follow the author's tweets about the latest crime and justice news @schmalleger

Multiculturalism and Diversity
The International Criminal Court

On April 12, 2000, the International Criminal Court (ICC) was created under the auspices of the United Nations. The ICC is a permanent criminal court for trying individuals (not countries) who commit the most serious crimes of concern to the international community, such as genocide, war crimes, and crimes against humanity (including the wholesale murder of civilians, torture, and mass rape). The goal of the ICC is to be a global judicial institution with international jurisdiction complementing national legal systems around the world. Support for the ICC was developed through the United Nations (UN). More than 70 countries approved the court's creation by ratifying the Rome Statute of the International Criminal Court. The ICC's first prosecutor, Luis Moreno Ocampo of Argentina, was elected in April 2003, and served in that capacity until the end of his term in 2013.[a]

The ICC initiative began after World War II with unsuccessful efforts to establish an international tribunal to try individuals accused of war crimes.[b] In lieu of such a court, military tribunals were held in Nuremberg, Germany, and Tokyo, Japan, to try defendants accused of war crimes. Although the 1948 Genocide Convention called for an international criminal court, efforts to establish a permanent court were delayed for decades by the cold war and by the refusal of some national governments to accept the court's proposed international legal jurisdiction.

In December 1948, the UN General Assembly adopted the Universal Declaration of Human Rights and the Convention on the Prevention and Punishment of the Crime of Genocide. It also called for criminals to be tried "by such international penal tribunals as may have jurisdiction." A number of member states soon asked the United Nations International Law Commission (ILC) to study the possibility of establishing an international criminal court.

Development of the ICC was delayed by the cold war that took place between the world's superpowers, which were not willing to subject their military personnel or commanders to international criminal jurisdiction in the event of a "hot" war. In 1981, however, the UN General Assembly asked the ILC to consider creating an international Code of Crimes.

The 1992 war in Bosnia-Herzegovina, which involved clear violations of the Genocide and Geneva Conventions, heightened world interest in the establishment of a permanent ICC. A few years later, 160 countries participated in a UN conference, held in Rome, to establish a criminal court.[c] At the end of that conference, member

▲ The International Criminal Court (ICC) in the Hague, Netherlands. What is the jurisdiction of the ICC?

Iain Masterton/Alamy Stock Photo

states voted overwhelmingly in favor of the Rome Statute calling for the establishment of the ICC.

In 2012, in the first verdict ever reached by the ICC, judges found Thomas Lubanga, a rebel leader in eastern Congo, guilty of conscripting child soldiers.[d] Learn more about this case and other activities of the ICC by visiting the Coalition for the International Criminal Court at **http://www.iccnow.org**.

[a] See the Coalition for an International Criminal Court, "Building the Court," http://www.iccnow.org/buildingthecourt.html (accessed July 10, 2010).

[b] Much of the information and some of the wording in this box are adapted from "The International Criminal Court Home Page," http://www.icc-cpi.int/menus/icc (accessed October 1, 2010); and the ICC "Timeline," http://www.iccnow.org/html/timeline.htm (accessed April 12, 2010).

[c] The conference was officially known as the Conference of Plenipotentiaries on the Establishment of an International Criminal Court. *Plenipotentiary* is another word for "diplomat."

[d] Roy Gutman, "Is International Criminal Court the Best Way to Stop War Crimes?" McClatchy Newspapers, April 27, 2012, http://www.kentucky.com/2012/04/26/2164351/is-international-criminal-court.html (accessed August 12, 2012).

In many states, bail bond agents are empowered to hunt down and bring back defendants who have fled. In some jurisdictions, bond agents hold virtually unlimited powers and have been permitted by courts to pursue, arrest, and forcibly extradite their charges from foreign jurisdictions without concern for the due-process considerations or statutory limitations that apply to law enforcement officers.[33] Recently, however, numerous states have enacted laws that eliminate for-profit bail bond businesses, replacing them instead with state-operated pretrial services agencies. Visit the Professional Bail Agents of the United States at **http://www.pbus.com** to learn more about the job of bail bond agent and to view the group's code of ethics.

Alternatives to Bail

The Eighth Amendment to the U.S. Constitution does not guarantee the opportunity for bail but does state that "[e]xcessive bail shall not be required." Some studies, however, have found that many defendants who are offered the opportunity for bail are unable to raise the money. Years ago, a report by the National Advisory Commission on Criminal Justice Standards and Goals found that as many as 93% of felony defendants in some jurisdictions were unable to make bail.[34]

▲ A typical bail bond office. Bail bond offices like this one are usually found near courthouses where criminal trials are held. Should all criminal suspects be afforded bail? Why or why not?

Spencer Grant/PhotoEdit, Inc.

release on recognizance (ROR)
The pretrial release of a criminal defendant on his or her written promise to appear in court as required. No cash or property bond is required.

property bond
The setting of bail in the form of land, houses, stocks, or other tangible property. In the event that the defendant absconds before trial, the bond becomes the property of the court.

To extend the opportunity for pretrial release to a greater proportion of nondangerous arrestees, a number of states and the federal government now make available various alternatives to the cash bond system. Alternatives include (1) release on recognizance, (2) property bond, (3) deposit bail, (4) conditional release, (5) third-party custody, (6) unsecured bond, and (7) signature bond.

Release on Recognizance

Release on recognizance (ROR) involves no cash bond, requiring as a guarantee only that the defendant agree in writing to return for further hearings as specified by the court. As an alternative to a cash bond, ROR was tested during the 1960s in a social experiment called the Manhattan Bail Project.[35] In the experiment, not all defendants were eligible for release on their own recognizance; those arrested for serious crimes, including murder, rape, and robbery, and defendants with extensive prior criminal records were excluded from participating in the project. The rest of the defendants were scored and categorized according to a number of "ideal" criteria used as indicators of both dangerousness and likelihood of pretrial flight. Criteria included (1) no previous convictions, (2) residential stability, and (3) good employment record. Those likely to flee were not released.

Studies of the bail project revealed that it released four times as many defendants before trial as had been freed under the traditional cash bond system.[36] Even more surprising was the finding that only 1% of those released fled from prosecution—the same percentage as for those set free on cash bonds.[37] Later studies, however, were unclear as to the effectiveness of ROR, with some finding a no-show rate as high as 12%.[38]

Property Bonds

Property bonds substitute other items of value in place of cash. Land, houses, automobiles, stocks, and so on may be consigned to the court as collateral against pretrial flight.

Deposit Bail

Deposit bail, an alternative form of cash bond available in some jurisdictions, places the court in the role of the bond agent, allowing the defendant to post a percentage of the full bail with the court. Unlike private bail bond agents, court-run deposit bail programs usually return the amount of the deposit except for a small administrative fee (perhaps 1%). If the defendant fails to appear for court, the entire amount of court-ordered bail is forfeited.

Conditional Release

Conditional release imposes a set of requirements on the defendant that might include participation in a drug-treatment program; staying away from specified others, such as potential witnesses; and attendance at a regular job. *Release under supervision* is similar to conditional release but adds the stipulation that defendants report to an officer of the court or to a police officer at designated times.

See CJ Exhibit 7-1 for a discussion of the different people and systems involved in making pretrial release decisions.

Third-Party Custody

Third-party custody is a bail bond alternative that assigns custody of the defendant to an individual or agency that promises to ensure his or her later appearance in court.[39] Some pretrial release programs allow attorneys to assume responsibility for their clients in this fashion. If a defendant fails to appear, the attorney's privilege to participate in the program may be ended.

CJ Exhibit 7-1
Nonjudicial Pretrial Release Decisions

In most American jurisdictions, judicial officers decide whether an arrested person will be detained or released. Some jurisdictions, however, allow others to make that decision. Some observers argue that the critical issue is not whether the decision maker is a judge but whether there are clear and appropriate criteria for making the decision, whether the decision maker has adequate information, and whether he or she has been well trained in pretrial release/detention decision making. Nonjudicial decision makers and release/detention mechanisms include the following:

- **Police officers and desk appearance tickets.** Desk appearance tickets, or citations, are summonses given to defendants at the police station, usually for petty offenses or misdemeanor charges. The tickets can greatly reduce the use of pretrial detention and can save the court system a great deal of time by avoiding initial pretrial release or bail hearings in minor cases. However, because they are typically based only on the current charge (and sometimes on a computer search to check for outstanding warrants), high-risk defendants could be released without supervision or monitoring. As computerized access to more criminal history information becomes available, enabling rapid identification of individuals with prior records who pose a risk to the community, desk appearance tickets may be more widely used.

- **Jail administrators.** In many jurisdictions, jail officials have the authority to release (or to refuse to book into jail) arrestees who meet certain criteria. In some localities, jail officials exercise this authority pursuant to a court order that specifies priorities with respect to the categories of defendants who can be admitted to the jail and those who are to be released when the jail population exceeds a court-imposed ceiling. The "automatic release" approach helps minimize jail crowding, but it does so at the risk of releasing some defendants who pose a high risk of becoming fugitives or committing criminal acts. To help minimize these risks, some sheriffs and jail administrators have developed their own pretrial services or "release on recognizance" units with staff who conduct risk assessments based on interviews with arrestees, information from references, and criminal history checks.

- **Bail schedules.** These predetermined schedules set levels of bail (from release on recognizance to amounts of surety bond) based solely on the offense charged. Depending on local practices, release pursuant to a bail schedule may take place at a police station, at the local jail, or at court. This practice saves time for judicial officers and allows the rapid release of defendants who can afford to post the bail amount. However, release determinations based solely on the current charge are of dubious value because there is no proven relationship between a particular charge and the risk of flight or subsequent crime. Release pursuant to a bail schedule depends simply on the defendant's ability to post the amount of the bond; moreover, when a defendant is released by posting bond, there is generally no procedure for supervision to minimize the risks of nonappearance and subsequent crime.

- **Bail bond agents.** When a judicial officer sets the amount of bond that a defendant must produce to be released or when bond is set mechanically on the basis of a bail schedule, the real decision makers are often the surety bail bond agents. If no bond agent will offer bond, the defendant without other sources of money remains in jail. The defendant's ability to pay a bond agent the 10% fee (and sometimes to post collateral) bears no relationship to his or her risk of flight or danger to the community.

- **Pretrial services agencies.** In some jurisdictions, pretrial services agencies have authority to release certain categories of defendants. The authority is usually limited to relatively minor cases, although agencies in a few jurisdictions can release some categories of felony defendants. Because the pretrial services agency can obtain information about the defendant's prior record, community ties, and other pending charges, its decision to release or detain is based on more extensive information and criteria than when the decision is based on a bail schedule. However, because these programs lack the independence of judicial officers, they can be targets of political and public pressure.

Source: From Barry Mahoney et al., *Pretrial Services Programs: Responsibilities and Potential* (National Institute of Justice, 2001).

Unsecured and Signature Bonds

Unsecured bonds are based on a court-determined dollar amount of bail. Like a credit contract, this bail alternative requires no monetary deposit with the court. The defendant agrees in writing that failure to appear will result in forfeiture of the entire amount of the bond, which might then be taken in seizures of land, personal property, bank accounts, and so on.

Bail Reform

A growing bail reform movement today focuses on the elimination of cash bonds, replacing them with risk management techniques for pretrial defendants. The movement is predicated on the belief that money bail is unfair because it discriminates against those who do not have the funds needed for release.

In 2018, California, a leader in the bail reform movement, scrapped cash bail, replacing it with computer-based risk assessment tools, and other states are poised to follow.

Pretrial Release and Public Safety

Pretrial release is common practice. Approximately 57% of all state-level felony defendants[40] and 36% of all federal defendants[41] are released before trial. At the state level, 43% of all defendants are detained until the court disposes of their case. Murder defendants (88%) are the most likely to be detained. A majority of state-level defendants charged with motor vehicle theft (61%), robbery (58%), or burglary (54%) are also detained until case disposition. At the federal level 88% of defendants in immigration cases were detained, while only 30% of violent offenders were held until trial.[42]

A growing movement, arguing that defendants released before trial may be dangerous to themselves or to others, seeks to reduce the number of defendants released under any conditions. Advocates of this conservative policy cite a number of studies documenting crimes committed by defendants released on bond. One study found that 16% of defendants released before trial were rearrested, and of those, 30% were arrested more than once.[43] Another study determined that as many as 41% of those released before trial for serious crimes, such as rape and robbery, were rearrested before their trial date.[44] A 2018 study, which followed nearly 68,000 state prisoners who had been released in 2005, found that 83% of the former prisoners were arrested at least once during the 9 years following release. About 44% of the former prisoners were arrested at least once during their first year outside of prison. Not surprisingly, such studies generally find that the longer the time spent between release and trial, the greater the likelihood of misconduct.[45]

In response to findings like these, some states have enacted **danger laws**, which limit the right to bail to certain kinds of offenders.[46] Other states, including Arizona, California, Colorado, Florida, and Illinois, have approved constitutional amendments restricting the use of bail.[47] Most such provisions exclude defendants charged with certain crimes from being eligible for bail and mandate that other defendants being considered for bail meet stringent conditions. Some states combine these strictures with tough release conditions designed to keep close control over defendants before trial.

The 1984 federal Bail Reform Act[48] allows federal judges to assess the danger of an accused to the community and to deny bail to defendants who are thought to be dangerous. In the words of the Act, a suspect held in pretrial custody on federal criminal charges must be detained if "after a hearing . . . he is found to pose a risk of flight and a danger to others or the community and if no condition of release can give reasonable assurances against these contingencies."[49] Defendants seeking bail must demonstrate a high likelihood of later court appearance. The Act also requires that a defendant have a speedy first appearance and that a detention hearing be held in conjunction with the initial appearance if he or she is to be detained. Learn more about pretrial release at the federal level at **https://www.justicestudies.com/fedpretrial.pdf**.

In the 1990 case of *U.S.* v. *Montalvo-Murillo*,[50] however, a defendant who was not provided with a detention hearing at the time of his first appearance and was subsequently released by an appeals court was found to have no "right" to freedom because of this "minor" statutory violation. The Supreme Court held that "unless it has a substantial influence on the outcome of the proceedings . . . failure to comply with the Act's prompt hearing provision does not require release of a person who should otherwise be detained" because "[a]utomatic release contravenes the statutory purpose of providing fair bail procedures while protecting the public's safety and assuring a defendant's appearance at trial."[51]

Court challenges to the constitutionality of pretrial detention legislation have not met with much success. The U.S. Supreme Court case of *U.S.* v. *Hazzard* (1984),[52] decided only a few months after enactment of federal bail reform, held that Congress was justified in providing for denial of bail to offenders who represent a danger to the community. Later cases have supported the presumption of flight, which federal law presupposes for certain types of defendants.[53]

danger law
A law intended to prevent the pretrial release of criminal defendants judged to represent a danger to others in the community.

I have tried to minimize what I feel is one of the less desirable aspects of the job . . . that judges can become isolated from the people whose lives their decisions affect.

—Stephen Breyer,
U.S. Supreme Court justice

The Grand Jury

The federal government and about half of the states use grand juries as part of the pretrial process. **Grand juries** comprise private citizens (ranging in number from 5 to 23, depending on the state and the grand jury's purpose) who hear evidence presented by the prosecution. Grand juries serve primarily as filters to eliminate from further processing any cases for which there is not sufficient evidence.

In early times, grand juries served a far different purpose. The grand jury system began in England in 1166 as a way of identifying law violators. Lacking a law enforcement agency with investigative authority, the government looked to the grand jury as a source of information on criminal activity in the community. Even today, grand juries in most jurisdictions may initiate prosecution independently of the prosecutor, although they rarely do.

Grand jury hearings are held in secret, and the defendant is generally not afforded the opportunity to appear before the grand jury.[54] Similarly, the defense has no opportunity to cross-examine prosecution witnesses. Grand juries have the power to subpoena witnesses and to mandate a review of books, records, and other documents crucial to their investigation.

After hearing the evidence, the grand jury votes on the **indictment** (a formal listing of proposed charges) presented to it by the prosecution. If the majority of grand jury members agree to forward the indictment to the trial court, it becomes a "true bill" on which further prosecution will turn.

The United States is one of only a few countries in which grand juries are still used. In 2014, a grand jury in St. Louis County, Missouri, grabbed the nation's attention when it refused to indict Ferguson police officer Darren Wilson. Wilson shot and killed 18-year-old Michael Brown during a street-stop that turned violent. The grand jury's decision led to nights of protest in cities across the nation by those who felt that the killing of the young black man was unjustified.

The Preliminary Hearing

States that do not use grand juries rely instead on a **preliminary hearing** "for charging defendants in a fashion that is less cumbersome and arguably more protective of the innocent."[55] In these jurisdictions, the prosecutor files an accusatory document called an **information**, or complaint, against the accused. A preliminary hearing is then held to determine whether there is probable cause to hold the defendant for trial. A few states, notably Georgia and Tennessee, use both the grand jury mechanism and a preliminary hearing as a "double check against the possibility of unwarranted prosecution."[56]

Although the preliminary hearing is not nearly as elaborate as a criminal trial, it has many of the same characteristics. The defendant is taken before a lower court judge, who summarizes the charges and reviews the rights to which all criminal defendants are entitled. The prosecution may present witnesses and offers evidence in support of the complaint. The defendant is afforded the right to testify and may also call witnesses.

The primary purpose of the preliminary hearing is to give the defendant an opportunity to challenge the legal basis for his or her detention. At this point, defendants who appear to be or claim to be mentally incompetent may be ordered to undergo further evaluation to determine whether they are **competent to stand trial**, which was briefly discussed in Chapter 3, may become an issue when a defendant appears to be incapable of understanding the proceedings or is unable to assist in his or her own defense due to mental disease or defect.

In 2003, the U.S. Supreme Court placed strict limits on the government's power to

grand jury
A group of jurors who have been selected according to law and have been sworn to hear the evidence and to determine whether there is sufficient evidence to bring the accused person to trial, to investigate criminal activity generally, or to investigate the conduct of a public agency or official.

indictment
A formal written accusation submitted to the court by a grand jury, alleging that a specified person has committed a specified offense, usually a felony.

preliminary hearing
A proceeding before a judicial officer in which three matters must be decided: (1) whether a crime was committed, (2) whether the crime occurred within the territorial jurisdiction of the court, and (3) whether there are reasonable grounds to believe that the defendant committed the crime.

information
A formal written accusation submitted to a court by a prosecutor, alleging that a specified person has committed a specified offense.

competent to stand trial
A finding by a court, when the defendant's sanity at the time of trial is at issue, that the defendant has sufficient present ability to consult with his or her attorney with a reasonable degree of rational understanding and that the defendant has a rational as well as factual understanding of the proceedings against him or her.

▼ A grand jury in action. Grand jury proceedings are generally very informal, as this picture shows. What is the grand jury's job?
Archives du 7eme Art/Photos 12/ Alamy Stock Photo

forcibly medicate some mentally ill defendants to make them competent to stand trial.[57] In the case of *Sell v. U.S.*,[58] the Court ruled that the use of antipsychotic drugs on a nonviolent offender who does not represent a danger while institutionalized must be in the defendant's best medical interest and be "substantially unlikely" to cause side effects that might compromise the fairness of the trial.

Barring a finding of mental incompetence, all that is required for the wheels of justice to grind forward is a demonstration "sufficient to justify a prudent man's belief that the suspect has committed or was committing an offense" within the jurisdiction of the court.[59] If the magistrate finds enough evidence to justify a trial, the defendant is bound over to the grand jury. In states that do not require grand jury review, the defendant is sent directly to the trial court. If the complaint against the defendant cannot be substantiated during the preliminary hearing, he or she is released. A release is not a bar to further prosecution, however, and the defendant may be rearrested if further evidence comes to light.

Arraignment and the Plea

arraignment
Strictly, the hearing before a court having jurisdiction in a criminal case in which the identity of the defendant is established, the defendant is informed of the charge and of his or her rights, and the defendant is required to enter a plea. Also, in some usages, any appearance in criminal court before trial.

plea
In criminal proceedings, the defendant's formal answer in court to the charge contained in a complaint, information, or indictment that he or she is guilty of the offense charged, is not guilty of the offense charged, or does not contest the charge.

nolo contendere
A plea of "no contest." A no-contest plea is used when the defendant does not wish to contest conviction. Because the plea does not admit guilt, however, it cannot provide the basis for later civil suits that might follow a criminal conviction.

Once an indictment has been returned or an information has been filed, the accused will be formally arraigned. **Arraignment** is "the first appearance of the defendant before the court that has the authority to conduct a trial."[60] Arraignment is generally a brief process with two purposes: (1) to once again inform the defendant of the specific charges against him or her and (2) to allow the defendant to enter a **plea**. The Federal Rules of Criminal Procedure allow for one of three types of pleas to be entered: guilty, not guilty, and *nolo contendere*. A *nolo contendere* (no-contest) plea is much the same as a guilty plea. A defendant who pleads "no contest" is immediately convicted and may be sentenced just as though he or she had pleaded guilty. A no-contest plea, however, is not an admission of guilt and provides one major advantage to defendants: It may not be used later as a basis for civil proceedings that seek monetary or other damages against the defendant.

Some defendants refuse to enter any plea and are said to "stand mute." Standing mute is a defense strategy that is rarely employed. Defendants who choose this alternative simply do not answer the request for a plea; however, for procedural purposes, a defendant who stands mute is considered to have entered a plea of not guilty.

Plea Bargaining

plea bargaining
The process of negotiating an agreement among the defendant, the prosecutor, and the court as to an appropriate plea and associated sentence in a given case. Plea bargaining circumvents the trial process and dramatically reduces the time required for the resolution of a criminal case.

In 2012, 53-year-old Kenneth Kassab, of Marquette, Michigan, was on the verge of pleading guilty to federal charges of illegally transporting thousands of pounds of explosives, but changed his mind at the last minute and decided to go to trial.[61] Kassab, who always maintained his innocence, was arrested after his employer had ordered him to use a truck to move a large number of 50-pound bags of fertilizer similar to those that had been used in the 1995 bombing of the Alfred P. Murrah federal building in Oklahoma City, Oklahoma. Kassab had thought of accepting a plea deal offered by prosecutors in order to avoid what might have been a lengthy prison sentence—which a judge could have imposed had he been convicted at trial. Instead, a week after deciding to reject the plea arrangement, a federal jury found him not guilty and he was set free. Kassab's case is unusual because 97% of all federal criminal defendants agree to plead guilty rather than going to trial—a significant increase from the 84% who made that choice in 1990.[62]

Guilty pleas often are not as straightforward as they might seem and are typically arrived at only after complex negotiations. **Plea bargaining** is a process of negotiation that usually involves the defendant, the prosecutor, and the defense counsel and is founded on the mutual interests of all involved. Defense attorneys and their clients will agree to a plea of guilty when they are unsure of their ability to win acquittal at trial. Prosecutors may be willing to bargain because the evidence they have against the defendant is weaker than they would like it to be. Plea bargaining offers prosecutors the additional advantage of a quick conviction without the need to commit the time and resources necessary for trial. Benefits to the accused include the possibility of reduced or combined charges, reduced defense costs, and a shorter sentence than might otherwise be anticipated.

The U.S. Supreme Court has held that a guilty plea constitutes conviction.[63] To validate the conviction, negotiated pleas require judicial consent. Judges often accept pleas that are the result of a bargaining process because such pleas reduce the court's workload. Although few judges are willing to guarantee a sentence before a plea is entered, most prosecutors and criminal trial lawyers know what sentences to expect from typical pleas.

Bargained pleas are commonplace in both federal and state courts. Some surveys have found that 94% of state criminal cases are eventually resolved through a negotiated plea.[64]

Some Supreme Court decisions, however, have enhanced the prosecutor's authority in the bargaining process by declaring that defendants cannot capriciously withdraw negotiated pleas.[65] Other rulings have supported discretionary actions by prosecutors in which sentencing recommendations were retracted even after bargains had been struck.[66] Some lower court cases have upheld the government's authority to withdraw from a negotiated plea when the defendant fails to live up to certain conditions.[67] Conditions may include requiring the defendant to provide information on other criminals, on criminal cartels, or on activities of smugglers.

In 2012, in two decisions that expanded the authority of judges in the plea-bargaining process, the U.S. Supreme Court held that the Sixth Amendment right to effective assistance of counsel applies to all critical states of criminal proceedings, including that of plea bargaining.[68] The Court also held that, "as a general rule, defense counsel has the duty to communicate formal prosecution offers to accept a plea on terms and conditions that may be favorable to the accused." Failure to communicate such offers to the defendant may be the basis for later appeal, but only where the defendant can demonstrate a reasonable probability that those offers would have been accepted and that the plea would have been entered without the prosecution's canceling it, or the trial court's refusing to accept it.

Although it is generally agreed that bargained pleas should relate in some way to the original charges, this is not always the case. Entered pleas may be chosen for the punishments likely to be associated with them rather than for their accuracy in describing the criminal offenses in which the defendants were involved.[69] This is especially true when the defendant wants to minimize the socially stigmatizing impact of the offense. For example, a charge of indecent liberties, in which the defendant is accused of sexual misconduct, may be pleaded out as assault. Such a plea, which takes advantage of the fact that indecent liberties can be considered a form of sexual assault, would effectively disguise the true nature of the offense.

Even though the Supreme Court has endorsed plea bargaining and protected suspects' rights during the process, the public sometimes views it suspiciously. Law-and-order advocates, who generally favor harsh punishments and long jail terms, claim that plea bargaining results in unjustifiably light sentences. As a consequence, prosecutors, almost all of whom regularly engage in the practice, rarely advertise it.

Plea bargaining can be a powerful prosecutorial tool, but this power carries with it the potential for misuse. Because they circumvent the trial process, plea bargains can be abused by prosecutors and defense attorneys who are more interested in the speedy resolution of cases than they are in seeing justice done. Carried to the extreme, plea bargaining may result in defendants being convicted of crimes they did not commit. Although it is rare, innocent defendants (especially those with prior criminal records) who think a jury will convict them—for whatever reason—may plead guilty to reduced charges to avoid a trial. In an effort to protect defendants against hastily arranged pleas, the Federal Rules of Criminal Procedure require judges to (1) inform the defendant of the various rights he or she is surrendering by pleading guilty, (2) determine that the plea is voluntary, (3) disclose any plea agreements, and (4) make sufficient inquiry to ensure there is a factual basis for the plea.[70]

> There is no such thing as justice—in or out of court.
> —Clarence Darrow (1857–1938)

Follow the author's tweets about the latest crime and justice news @schmalleger

Summary

THE COURTS

- In the United States, there are two judicial systems. One consists of state and local courts established under the authority of state and local governments. The other is the federal court system, created by Congress under the authority of the U.S. Constitution. This dual-court system historically results from general agreement among the nation's founders about the need for individual states to retain significant legislative authority and judicial autonomy separate from federal control.

- In most states, criminal courts can be classified within a three-tiered structure of two trial court echelons and an appellate level. There are many differences between and among state court systems, however. So-called reform states are characterized by relatively streamlined judicial systems consisting of trial courts of limited and general jurisdiction, supplemented by one or two appellate court levels. Nonreform, or traditional, states tend to retain judicial systems that are a conglomeration of multilevel and sometimes redundant courts with poorly defined jurisdictions. Regardless of their organizational style, state courts have virtually unlimited power to decide nearly every type of case, subject only to limitations imposed by the U.S. Constitution, their own state constitutions, and state law.

- Today's federal judiciary consists of three levels: (1) U.S. district courts, (2) U.S. courts of appeal, and (3) the U.S. Supreme Court. Federal courts, located principally in larger cities, decide only those cases over which the Constitution gives them authority. The highest federal court, the U.S. Supreme Court, is located in Washington, D.C., and hears cases only on appeal from lower courts.

- Pretrial activities involve the first appearance, the grand jury hearing (in some states), the preliminary hearing, the arraignment, and the plea, all of which are described in this chapter. Before trial, one of the most important decisions facing the courts is that of pretrial release. In considering whether a criminal defendant should be released prior to trial, courts must balance the rights of the unconvicted defendant against the potential for future harm that person may represent.

QUESTIONS FOR REVIEW

1. How did the American court system develop? What are some of the unique features of American court history? What is the dual-court system? Why do we have a dual-court system in America?
2. How is a typical state court system structured? What different types of courts might exist at the state level, and what kinds of jurisdiction might they have?
3. What are the three levels characteristic of the federal judiciary? What are some of the differences between the state and federal court systems in America?
4. What steps are typically taken before the start of a criminal trial?

The Courtroom Work Group and the Criminal Trial

CHAPTER

8

Learning Objectives

After reading this chapter, you should be able to:

1. Explain the roles of courtroom work group members. **236**

2. Describe the roles of outsiders, or nonprofessional courtroom participants. **249**

3. State the procedure, nature, and purpose of the criminal trial. **253**

4. Describe the criminal trial process. **255**

Introduction

In 2016, Jodi Arias, who was convicted of the brutal killing of her boyfriend Travis Alexander in 2013, was found guilty of a disciplinary violation at the Perryville Prison in Arizona where she is serving a life sentence.[2] Arias, a former waitress, entered the prison in April 2015 and had been approved to have contact visits. After the violation, which involved calling a prison staffer by a vulgar name, the privilege was revoked and Arias was advised that she could earn it back after 180 days of good behavior. At trial, Arias had admitted shooting and stabbing her 30-year-old lover at his home in 2008, and claimed that she had been trying to defend herself from emotional, physical, and sexual abuse. Arias appeared as a petite and demure woman during her trial, and dressed like a schoolgirl while on the stand. Although her appearance might have been unremarkable, Arias's trial captured the attention of the nation and the world as it wound through 5 months of testimony, cross-examination, and jury debate. *USA Today* described it this way, "the Jodi Arias trial, which would ordinarily be a run-of-the-mill domestic murder case," drew a media circus that fed a large following of TV viewers who watched the trial unfold.[3] They were captivated by its intimate details of "love, lies, sex, and dirty secrets." At one point, an audio recording was played during the trial in which Alexander said that he wanted to tie Arias to a tree and commit deviant sex acts on her.

Alexander's body had been found in the shower of his Mesa, Arizona, home. He had been shot in the face, stabbed 30 times, and his throat had been cut from ear-to-ear. Court testimony revealed that Arias was a jilted lover who turned into a stalker, even though Alexander continued to invite her to his house and have sex with her while he saw other women.

▲ Jodi Arias, convicted of the brutal murder of her boyfriend, Travis Alexander. Arias escaped the death penalty when the judge declared a mistrial in the sentencing phase of her trial in 2015. Why did her televised trial draw such a large audience?

Rob Schumacher/UPI/Newscom

🐦 Follow the author's tweets about the latest crime and justice news @schmalleger

> The American criminal justice system is theater to the world.
>
> —Alan Dershowitz, Harvard University

The Courtroom Work Group: Professional Courtroom Actors

1 Explain the roles of courtroom work group members.

To the public eye, criminal trials frequently appear to be well-managed events even though they may entail quite a bit of drama. Like plays on a stage, trials involve many participants, each of whom has a different role to fill. Unlike such plays, however, they are real-life events, and the impact that a trial's outcome has on people's lives can be far reaching.

Participants in a criminal **trial** can be divided into two categories: professionals and outsiders (Figure 8–1). The professionals are the official courtroom actors. They are well versed in criminal trial practice and set the stage for and conduct the business of the court. Judges, prosecuting attorneys, defense attorneys, public defenders, and others who earn a living serving the court fall into this category. Professional courtroom actors are also called the **courtroom work group**. Some writers have pointed out that aside from statutory requirements and ethical considerations, courtroom interaction among professionals involves an implicit recognition of informal rules of civility, cooperation, and shared goals.[4] Hence, even within the adversarial framework of a criminal trial, the courtroom work group is dedicated to bringing the procedure to a successful close.[5]

In contrast, outsiders—those trial participants who are only temporarily involved with the court—are generally unfamiliar with courtroom organization and trial procedure. Jurors and witnesses are outsiders; defendants and victims are also outsiders, even though they may have a greater personal investment in the outcome of the trial than anyone else.

This chapter examines trial court activities, building on the pretrial process described in Chapter 7. To place the trial process within its human context, however, the various roles of the many participants in a criminal trial are discussed first.

trial
In criminal proceedings, the examination in court of the issues of fact and relevant law in a case for the purpose of convicting or acquitting the defendant.

courtroom work group
The professional courtroom actors, including judges, prosecuting attorneys, defense attorneys, public defenders, and others who earn a living serving the court.

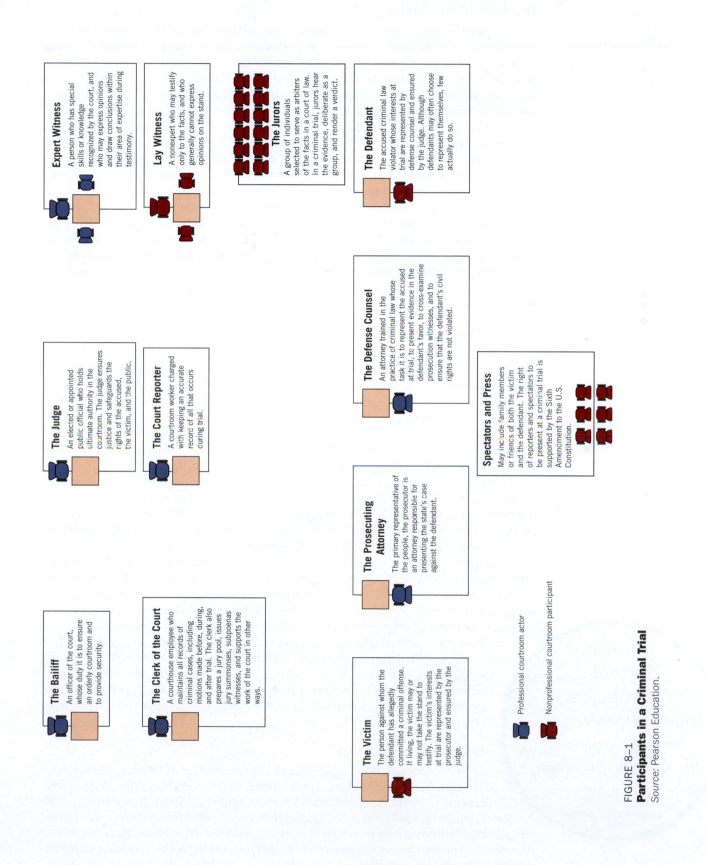

Expert Witness
A person who has special skills or knowledge recognized by the court, and who may express opinions and draw conclusions within their area of expertise during testimony.

Lay Witness
A nonexpert who may testify only to the facts, and who generally cannot express opinions on the stand.

The Jurors
A group of individuals selected to serve as arbiters of the facts in a court of law. In a criminal trial, jurors hear the evidence, deliberate as a group, and render a verdict.

The Defendant
The accused criminal law violator whose interests at trial are represented by defense counsel and ensured by the judge. Although defendants may often choose to represent themselves, few actually do so.

The Judge
An elected or appointed public official who holds ultimate authority in the courtroom. The judge ensures justice and safeguards the rights of the accused, the victim, and the public.

The Court Reporter
A courtroom worker charged with keeping an accurate record of all that occurs during trial.

The Defense Counsel
An attorney trained in the practice of criminal law whose task it is to represent the accused at trial, to present evidence in the defendant's favor, to cross-examine prosecution witnesses, and to ensure that the defendant's civil rights are not violated.

Spectators and Press
May include family members or friends of both the victim and the defendant. The right of reporters and spectators to be present at a criminal trial is supported by the Sixth Amendment to the U.S. Constitution.

The Bailiff
An officer of the court, whose duty it is to ensure an orderly courtroom and to provide security.

The Clerk of the Court
A courthouse employee who maintains all records of criminal cases, including motions made before, during, and after trial. The clerk also prepares a jury pool, issues jury summonses, subpoenas witnesses, and supports the work of the court in other ways.

The Prosecuting Attorney
The primary representative of the people, the prosecutor is an attorney responsible for presenting the state's case against the defendant.

The Victim
The person against whom the defendant has allegedly committed a criminal offense. If living, the victim may or may not take the stand to testify. The victim's interests at trial are represented by the prosecutor and ensured by the judge.

Professional courtroom actor

Nonprofessional courtroom participant

FIGURE 8–1
Participants in a Criminal Trial
Source: Pearson Education.

The Judge

The Role of the Judge

judge
An elected or appointed public official who presides over a court of law and who is authorized to hear and sometimes to decide cases and to conduct trials.

The trial **judge** has the primary duty of ensuring justice. The American Bar Association (ABA) *Standards for Criminal Justice* describes the duties of the trial judge as follows: "The trial judge has the responsibility for safeguarding both the rights of the accused and the interests of the public in the administration of criminal justice. . . . The purpose of a criminal trial is to determine whether the prosecution has established the guilt of the accused as required by law, and the trial judge should not allow the proceedings to be used for any other purpose."[6]

In the courtroom, the judge holds ultimate authority, ruling on matters of law, weighing objections from both sides, deciding on the admissibility of evidence, and disciplining anyone who challenges the order of the court. In most jurisdictions, judges also sentence offenders after a verdict has been returned; in some states, judges decide guilt or innocence for defendants who waive a jury trial.

Most state jurisdictions have a chief judge who, besides serving on the bench as a trial judge, must also manage the court system. Management includes hiring staff, scheduling sessions of court, ensuring the adequate training of subordinate judges, and coordinating activities with other courtroom actors. Chief judges usually assume their position by virtue of seniority and rarely have any formal training in management. Hence, the managerial effectiveness of a chief judge is often a matter of personality and dedication more than anything else.

Judicial Selection

As we discussed in Chapter 7, judges at the federal level are nominated by the president of the United States and take their place on the bench only after confirmation by the Senate. At the state level, things work somewhat differently. Depending on the jurisdiction, state judgeships are won through either popular election or political (usually gubernatorial) appointment. The processes involved in judicial selection at the state level are set by law.

Both judicial election and appointment have been criticized because each system allows politics to enter the judicial arena—although in somewhat different ways. Under the election system, judicial candidates must receive the endorsement of their parties, generate contributions, and manage an effective campaign. Under the appointment system, judicial hopefuls must be in favor with incumbent politicians to receive appointments. Because partisan politics plays a role in both systems, critics have claimed that sitting judges can rarely be as neutral as they should be. They carry to the bench with them campaign promises, personal indebtedness, and possible political agendas.

To counter some of these problems, numerous states have adopted the Missouri Plan (or the Missouri Bar Plan) for judicial selection,[7] which combines elements of both election and appointment. It requires candidates for judicial vacancies to undergo screening by a nonpartisan state judicial nominating committee. Candidates selected by the committee are reviewed by an arm of the governor's office, which selects a final list of names for appointment. Incumbent judges must face the electorate after a specified term in office. They then run unopposed in nonpartisan elections in which only their records may be considered. Voters have the choice of allowing a judge to continue in office or asking that another be appointed to take his or her place. Because the Missouri Plan provides for periodic public review of judicial performance, it is also called the *merit plan of judicial selection*.

Judicial Qualifications

A few decades ago, many states did not require any special training, education, or other qualifications for judges. Anyone (even someone without a law degree) who won election or was appointed could assume a judgeship. Today, however, almost all states require that judges in general jurisdiction and appellate courts hold a law degree, be a licensed attorney, and be a member of their state bar association. Many states also require newly elected judges to attend state-sponsored training sessions dealing with such subjects as courtroom procedure, evidence, dispute resolution, judicial writing, administrative record keeping, and ethics.

To hear patiently, to weigh deliberately and dispassionately, and to decide impartially; these are the chief duties of a judge.
—Albert Pike (1809–1891)

Follow the author's tweets about the latest crime and justice news @schmalleger

Although most states provide instruction to meet the needs of trial judges, other organizations also provide specialized training. The National Judicial College (NJC), located on the campus of the University of Nevada at Reno, is one such institution. The NJC was established in 1963 by the Joint Committee for the Effective Administration of Justice, chaired by Justice Tom C. Clark of the U.S. Supreme Court.[8] More than 3,000 judges enroll annually in courses offered by the NJC, and many courses are offered online. The NJC, in collaboration with the National Council of Juvenile and Family Court Judges and the University of Nevada at Reno, offers the nation's only advanced judicial degree programs, leading to a master's degree and a doctorate in judicial studies.[9] Visit the NJC at **http://www.judges.org**.

In some parts of the United States, lower court judges, such as justices of the peace, local magistrates, and "district" court judges, may still be elected without educational and other professional requirements. Today, in 43 states, some 1,300 nonlawyer judges are serving in mostly rural courts of limited jurisdiction.[10] In New York, for example, of the 3,150 judges in the state's unified court system, approximately 1,886 are part-time town or village justices, and approximately 63% of town and village justices are not lawyers.[11] The majority of cases that come before New York lay judges involve alleged traffic violations, although the cases may also include misdemeanors, small-claims actions, and some civil cases of up to $3,000.

Even though some have defended lay judges as being closer to the citizenry in their understanding of justice,[12] in most jurisdictions the number of lay judges is declining. States that continue to use lay judges in lower courts do require that candidates for judgeships not have criminal records, and most states require that they attend special training sessions if elected. Learn more about state courts and state court judges at **https://www.justicestudies.com/pubs/statecourts.pdf**.

Follow the author's tweets about the latest crime and justice news @schmalleger

The Prosecuting Attorney

The **prosecutor**—also called the *solicitor, district attorney, state's attorney, county attorney,* or *commonwealth attorney*—is responsible for presenting the state's case against the defendant. Technically speaking, the prosecuting attorney is the primary representative of the people by virtue of the belief that violations of the criminal law are an affront to the public. Except for federal prosecutors (called *U.S. attorneys*) and solicitors in five states, prosecutors are elected and generally serve 4-year terms, with the possibility of continuing reelection.[13] Widespread criminal conspiracies, whether they involve government officials or private citizens, may require the services of a special prosecutor whose office can spend the time and resources needed for efficient prosecution.[14]

Because the job of prosecutor entails too many duties for one person to handle, most prosecutors supervise a staff of assistant district attorneys who do most in-court work. Assistants are trained attorneys, licensed to practice law in the state where they work. They are usually hired directly by the chief prosecutor. Approximately 2,300 chief prosecutors, assisted by 24,000 deputy attorneys, serve the nation's counties and cities.[15]

Another prosecutorial role has traditionally been that of quasi-legal adviser to local police departments. Because prosecutors are sensitive to the kinds of information needed for conviction, they may help guide police investigations and will exhort detectives to identify credible witnesses, uncover additional evidence, and the like. This role is limited, however. Police departments are independent of the administrative authority of the prosecutor, and cooperation between them, although based on the common goal of conviction, is purely voluntary.

Once a trial begins, the job of the prosecutor is to vigorously present the state's case against the defendant. Prosecutors introduce evidence against the accused, steer the testimony of witnesses "for the people," and argue in favor of conviction. Because defendants are presumed innocent until proven guilty, the burden of demonstrating guilt beyond a reasonable doubt rests with the prosecutor.

Prosecutorial Discretion

American prosecutors occupy a unique position in the nation's criminal justice system by virtue of the considerable **prosecutorial discretion** they exercise. As U.S. Supreme Court Justice Robert H. Jackson noted in 1940, "The prosecutor has more control over life, liberty, and reputation than any other person in America."[16] Before a case comes to trial, the

prosecutor
An attorney whose official duty is to conduct criminal proceedings on behalf of the state or the people against those accused of having committed criminal offenses.

prosecutorial discretion
The decision-making power of prosecutors, based on the wide range of choices available to them, in the handling of criminal defendants, the scheduling of cases for trial, the acceptance of negotiated pleas, and so on. The most important form of prosecutorial discretion lies in the power to charge, or not to charge, a person with an offense.

CJ Careers
Assistant District Attorney

Name: Robert S. Jaegers

Position: Assistant State Attorney, Palm Beach County, Florida

Colleges attended: Ohio Northern University Pettit College of Law, Ada, Ohio; Pennsylvania State University

Majors: English and law

Year hired: Joined the State Attorney's Office in Palm Beach County, Florida, in 1988

Please give a brief description of your job: Currently Felony Division Trial Prosecutor with over 200 cases pending trial. Caseload includes aggravated batteries, drug trafficking, burglaries, robberies, economic crimes.

What appealed to you most about the position when you applied for it? Immediately following law school, I was commissioned as Captain, Judge Advocate General's Department, U.S. Air Force in 1977. In 1982, I left active duty and moved to Florida to become an associate at a law firm that had a general law practice, including criminal defense and appeals. After working for 3 years as a Criminal Appellate Attorney for the Florida Attorney General's Office (1984–1988), I again wanted to argue cases before juries.

How would you describe the interview process? The current state attorney interview process involves an interview with three experienced prosecutors, then an interview with two of the three chief assistants, then an interview with the elected state attorney. The process has varied over the years, depending upon the wishes of the elected state attorney, from a single interview with the state attorney to the current process but without an interview with the state attorney. Law school internship experience is a plus, as is any prior experience as an attorney or legal support person.

What is a typical day like? A "typical" day begins at 8:30 a.m. with a morning-long session of short hearings (around 120 cases with sometimes as many different defendants), with four regularly assigned division prosecutors and as many as six specialty division prosecutors, and four public defender attorneys regularly assigned to the division, plus varying numbers of privately retained attorneys. All discuss arraignments, plea offers, demands for discovery from both sides, scheduling of trials, scheduling of motion hearings, scheduling plea conferences, conducting plea conferences, demands by defendants to represent themselves, restitution hearings, requests to enter appearances by private

▲ Robert S. Jaegers
Heidi Jaegers

attorneys, requests to withdraw from representation by private attorneys, requests to continue, demands for speedy trial, and so on. In short, we conduct all the proceedings necessary to move cases to conclusion, either by plea or by trial. If this is all concluded by 10 or 11 a.m., the judge may call for a jury pool and commence a trial. Following a lunch break there are trials, or motions to suppress or dismiss with evidentiary hearings, or more lengthy hearings specially set by the parties and the judge.

What qualities/characteristics are most helpful for this job? The ability to be flexible in preparation, articulate in English, and able to read opposing motions and conduct research on legal opinions is paramount. Next is an ability to speak to groups of people from all backgrounds and abilities, and select a group of fair and impartial jurors to be your fact-finders. You must be able to communicate your arguments, and help your witnesses convey the evidence they have to present to the fact-finders in a readily understandable manner. Preparation is key. You must be able to work with and cooperate with your support staff of secretaries, investigators, information managers, judges' secretaries, clerks, and opposing counsel's secretaries, and do this even with opposing counsel. You must also be willing to devote the time to prepare for each trial and each hearing, even while knowing that the opposing side may decide at the last moment to concede and enter a plea. If you aren't prepared, the defense will sense that, and use it against you.

What is a typical starting salary? Starting salary as of 2012 is $40,000 per year. This is accompanied by medical benefits, retirement benefits, travel reimbursements, and continuing legal education opportunities.

What is the salary potential as you move up into higher-level jobs? The statutory maximum salary of the state attorney is $150,000 per year. Assistants are not usually compensated above this level.

What advice would you give someone in college beginning studies in criminal justice? If you are contemplating a career as a prosecuting attorney, take every opportunity to study creative writing, English literature, psychology, public speaking and debate, and dramatics, and make sure to keep yourself physically fit. You may find yourself in many stressful situations, some physical and some mental, and a sound mind in a sound body gives you an advantage.

Source: Courtesy of Heidi Jaegers. Reprinted with permission of Robert S. Jaegers.

---

prosecutor may decide to accept a plea bargain, divert the suspect to a public or private social services agency, ask the suspect to seek counseling, or dismiss the case entirely for lack of evidence or for a variety of other reasons. Studies have found that the prosecution dismisses from one-third to one-half of all felony cases before trial or before a plea bargain is made.[17] Prosecutors also play a significant role before grand juries because states that use the grand jury system depend on prosecutors to bring evidence before the grand jury and to be effective in seeing indictments returned against suspects.

In preparation for trial, the prosecutor decides what charges are to be brought against the defendant, examines the strength of the incriminating evidence, and decides which witnesses to call. Two important U.S. Supreme Court decisions have held that it is the duty of prosecutors to, in effect, assist the defense in building its case by making available any evidence in their possession. In the first case, *Brady* v. *Maryland* (1963),[18] the Court held that the prosecution is required to disclose to the defense evidence that directly relates to claims of either guilt or innocence. The second and more recent case is that of *U.S.* v. *Bagley*,[19] decided in 1985. In *Bagley*, the Court ruled that the prosecution must disclose any evidence that the defense requests. The Court reasoned that to withhold evidence, even when it does not relate directly to issues of guilt or innocence, may mislead the defense into thinking that such evidence does not exist.

In 2004, in a decision predicated upon *Brady*, the U.S. Supreme Court intervened to stop the execution of 45-year-old Texan Delma Banks 10 minutes before it was scheduled to begin. The Court found that prosecutors had withheld vital **exculpatory evidence**, or information that might have cleared Banks of blame, during his trial for the 1980 shooting death of a 16-year-old boy. The Court said that "a rule declaring 'prosecutor may hide, defendant must seek,' is not tenable in a system constitutionally bound to accord defendants due process."[20] Banks had spent 24 years on death row.

One special decision that the prosecutor makes concerns the filing of separate or multiple charges. The decision to try a defendant simultaneously on multiple charges allows for the presentation of a considerable amount of evidence and permits an in-court demonstration of a complete sequence of criminal events. This strategy has an additional practical advantage: It saves time and money by substituting one trial for what might otherwise be a number of trials if each charge were to be brought separately before the court. From the prosecutor's point of view, however, trying the charges one at a time carries the advantage of allowing for another trial on a new charge if a "not-guilty" verdict is returned.

The activities of the prosecutor do not end with a finding of guilt or innocence. Following conviction, prosecutors are usually allowed to make sentencing recommendations to the judge. They can be expected to argue that aggravating factors (discussed in Chapter 9), prior criminal record, or especially heinous qualities of the offense in question call for strict punishment. When a convicted defendant appeals, prosecutors may need to defend their own actions and to argue, in briefs filed with appellate courts, that the conviction was properly obtained. Most jurisdictions also allow prosecutors to make recommendations when defendants they have convicted are being considered for parole or for early release from prison.

Until relatively recently, it had generally been held that prosecutors enjoyed much the same kind of immunity against liability in the exercise of their official duties that judges do. The 1976 U.S. Supreme Court case of *Imbler* v. *Pachtman*[21] provided the basis for such thinking with its ruling that "state prosecutors are absolutely immune from liability . . . for their conduct in initiating a prosecution and in presenting the State's case." However, in the 1991 case of *Burns* v. *Reed*,[22] the Court held that "[a] state prosecuting attorney is absolutely immune from liability for damages . . . for participating in a probable cause hearing, but not for giving legal advice to the police." The *Burns* case involved Cathy Burns of Muncie, Indiana, who allegedly shot her sleeping sons while laboring under a multiple personality disorder. To explore the possibility of multiple personality further, the police asked the prosecuting attorney if it would be appropriate for them to hypnotize the defendant. The prosecutor agreed that hypnosis would be a permissible avenue for investigation, and the suspect confessed to the murders while hypnotized. She later alleged in her complaint to the Supreme Court "that [the prosecuting attorney] knew or should have known that hypnotically induced testimony was inadmissible" at trial.[23]

Finally, in 2009, in the case of *Van de Kamp* v. *Goldstein*,[24] the U.S. Supreme Court clarified its holding in *Imbler* and found that a prosecutor's absolute immunity from Section 1983 claims (discussed in a previous chapter) extends to: (1) a failure properly to train prosecutors, (2) a failure to properly supervise prosecutors, and (3) a failure to establish an information system containing potential impeachment material about informants. In the words of the justices, a prosecutor is absolutely immune from liability in civil suits when his or her actions are "intimately associated with the judicial phase of the criminal process" and he or she is serving as "an officer of the court."

Follow the author's tweets about the latest crime and justice news @schmalleger

exculpatory evidence
Any information having a tendency to clear a person of guilt or blame.

Until relatively recently, prosecutors generally enjoyed much of the same kind of immunity against liability in the exercise of their official duties that judges do.

The Abuse of Discretion

Because prosecutors have so much discretion in their decision making, there is considerable potential for abuse. Many types of discretionary decisions are always inappropriate: accepting guilty pleas to drastically reduced charges in exchange for personal considerations, deciding not to prosecute friends or political cronies, and overzealously prosecuting a case to seek heightened visibility to support political ambitions.

Administrative decisions such as case scheduling, which can wreak havoc with the personal lives of defendants and the professional lives of defense attorneys, can also be used by prosecutors to harass defendants into pleading guilty. Some forms of abuse may be unconscious. At least one study suggests that some prosecutors have an inherent tendency toward leniency where female defendants are concerned and tend to discriminate against minorities when deciding whether to prosecute.[25]

Although the electorate is the final authority to which prosecutors must answer, gross misconduct by prosecutors may be addressed by the state supreme court or by the state attorney general's office. Short of addressing *criminal* misconduct, however, most of the options available to the court and to the attorney general are limited.

In 2011, in an effort to deter prosecutorial misconduct at the federal level, the U.S. Department of Justice created a new internal watchdog office to oversee the actions of federal prosecutors. Called the Professional Misconduct Review Unit, the office is responsible for disciplining federal prosecutors who engage in intentional or reckless misconduct.[26]

The Prosecutor's Professional Responsibility

As members of the legal profession, prosecutors are expected to abide by various standards of professional responsibility, such as those found in the ABA *Model Rules of Professional Conduct*. Most state bar associations have adopted their own versions of the ABA rules and expect their members to respect those standards. Serious violations of the rules may result in a prosecutor's being disbarred from the practice of law. Official ABA commentary on Rule 3.8, Special Responsibilities of the Prosecutor, says that "a prosecutor has the responsibility of a minister of justice and not simply that of an advocate; the prosecutor's duty is to seek justice, not merely to convict. This responsibility carries with it specific obligations to see that the defendant is accorded procedural justice and that guilt is decided upon the basis of sufficient evidence."[27] Hence, prosecutors are barred by the standards of the legal profession from advocating any fact or position that they know is untrue.

Prosecutors have a voice in influencing public policy affecting the safety of America's communities through the National District Attorneys Association (NDAA). Visit the NDAA at **http://www.ndaa.org**.

The Defense Counsel

defense counsel
A licensed trial lawyer hired or appointed to conduct the legal defense of a person accused of a crime and to represent him or her before a court of law.

The **defense counsel** is a trained lawyer who may specialize in the practice of criminal law. The defense counsel's task is to represent the accused as soon as possible after arrest and to ensure that the defendant's civil rights are not violated during processing by the criminal justice system. Other duties of the defense counsel include testing the strength of the prosecution's case, taking part in plea negotiations, and preparing an adequate defense to be used at trial. In the preparation of a defense, criminal lawyers may enlist private detectives, experts, witnesses to the crime, and character witnesses. Some lawyers perform aspects of the role of private detective or investigator themselves. Defense attorneys also review relevant court precedents to identify the best defense strategy.

Defense preparation often entails conversations between lawyer and defendant. Such discussions are recognized as privileged communications protected under the umbrella of attorney–client confidentiality; in other words, lawyers cannot be compelled to reveal information that their clients have confided to them.[28]

If the defendant is found guilty, the defense attorney will be involved in arguments at sentencing, may be asked to file an appeal, and will probably counsel the defendant and the defendant's family about any civil matters (payment of debts, release from contractual obligations, and so on) that must be arranged after the sentence is imposed. Hence, the work of the defense attorney encompasses many roles, including attorney, negotiator, investigator, confidant, family and personal counselor, social worker, and even bill collector.

Three major categories of defense attorneys assist criminal defendants in the United States: (1) private attorneys, usually referred to as *criminal lawyers* or *retained counsel*; (2) court-appointed counsel; and (3) public defenders.

🐦 Follow the author's tweets about the latest crime and justice news @schmalleger

Private Attorneys

Private attorneys either have their own legal practices or work for law firms in which they are partners or employees. As those who have had to hire a defense attorney know, the fees of private attorneys can be high. Most privately retained criminal lawyers charge in the range of $100 to $200 per hour, and included in their bill is the time it takes to prepare for a case as well as time spent in the courtroom. High-powered criminal defense attorneys who have a reputation for successfully defending their clients can be far more expensive: Fees charged by famous criminal defense attorneys can run into the hundreds of thousands of dollars—and sometimes exceed $1 million—for handling just one case!

Few law students actually choose to specialize in criminal law, even though the job of a criminal lawyer may appear glamorous. Those who do specialize often begin their careers immediately following law school, whereas others seek to gain experience working as assistant district attorneys or assistant public defenders for a number of years before going into private practice. Visit the National Association of Criminal Defense Lawyers (NACDL) at **http://www.nacdl.org** to learn more about the practice of criminal law.

Court-Appointed Counsel

The Sixth Amendment to the U.S. Constitution guarantees criminal defendants the effective assistance of counsel. A series of U.S. Supreme Court decisions has established that defendants who are unable to pay for private criminal defense attorneys will receive adequate representation at all stages of criminal justice processing. In *Powell* v. *Alabama* (1932),[29] the Court held that the Fourteenth Amendment requires state courts to appoint counsel for defendants in capital cases who are unable to afford their own. In 1938, in *Johnson* v. *Zerbst*,[30] the Court overturned the conviction of an indigent federal inmate, holding that his Sixth Amendment due-process right to counsel had been violated. The Court declared, "If the accused . . . is not represented by counsel and has not competently and intelligently waived his constitutional right, the Sixth Amendment stands as a jurisdictional bar to a valid conviction and sentence depriving him of his life or his liberty." The decision established the right of indigent defendants to receive the assistance of appointed counsel in all criminal proceedings in federal courts. The 1963 case of *Gideon* v. *Wainwright*[31] extended the right to appointed counsel to all indigent defendants charged with a felony in state courts. In *Argersinger* v. *Hamlin* (1972),[32] the Court required adequate legal representation for anyone facing a potential sentence of imprisonment. Juveniles charged with delinquent acts were granted the right to appointed counsel in the case of *In re Gault* (1967).[33] In *Alabama* v. *Shelton* (2002),[34] a closely divided Court expanded the Sixth Amendment right to counsel, ruling that defendants in state courts who are facing relatively minor charges must be provided with an attorney at government expense even when they face only the slightest chance of incarceration.

States have responded to the federal mandate for indigent defense in a number of ways. Most now use one of three systems to deliver legal services to criminal defendants who are unable to afford their own: (1) assigned counsel, (2) public defenders, and (3) contractual arrangements. The three are also referred to as *court-appointed defense attorneys*. Most such systems are administered at the county level, although funding arrangements may involve state, county, and municipal monies, as well as federal grants and court fees.

Assigned Counsel

Assigned counsel are usually drawn from a roster of all practicing criminal attorneys within the jurisdiction of the trial court. Their fees are paid at a rate set by the state or local government. These fees are typically low, however, and may affect the amount of effort an assigned attorney puts into a case. In 2010, for example, New York's court-appointed attorneys were paid only $60 per hour for representing misdemeanants and $75 per hour for in-court representation of charged felons. Out-of-court preparation time was reimbursed at around $25 per hour—a rate of pay that is 10 to 20 times less than what attorneys normally earn.[35]

Public Defenders

public defender
An attorney employed by a government agency or subagency, or by a private organization under contract to a government body, for the purpose of providing defense services to indigents, or an attorney who has volunteered such service.

A **public defender** is a state-employed lawyer defending indigent defendants. A public defender program relies on full-time salaried staff, including defense attorneys, defense investigators, and office personnel. Defense investigators gather information in support of the defense effort and may interview friends, family members, and employers of the accused, with an eye toward effective defense.

A Bureau of Justice Statistics (BJS) report found that a public defender system is the primary method used to provide indigent counsel for criminal defendants in the United States.[36] According to BJS, approximately 1,000 public defender offices in 49 states and the District of Columbia received nearly 5.6 million cases and employed over 15,000 litigating attorneys. County-based public defender offices, a system used by 27 states and District of Columbia, received more than four million indigent defense cases per year, accounting for nearly three-quarters of the public defender cases received nationwide. Those offices employed about 10,700 litigating attorneys. Additionally, state-based public defender programs, used in the other 22 states, employed 4,300 litigating attorneys to handle the 1.5 million indigent defense cases that they received.

The BJS survey found that the majority of both state- and county-based public defender offices employed substantially fewer than the needed number of support staff, such as paralegals, investigators, indigency screeners, and clerical staff. Surveyors determined that the median entry-level salary for assistant public defenders ranged from $42,000 to $45,000 in county-based public defender offices and from $46,000 to $58,000 in state-based programs.

▲ Alix Tichelman, second from right, being arraigned on July 16, 2014 on manslaughter charges for the death of Google executive Forrest Hayes in Santa Cruz County Superior Court. To her left is California public defender Athena Reis. How might an effective public defender system be funded and run?

Shmuel Thaler/Santa Cruz Sentinel/ McClatchy-Tribune/Tribune Content Agency LLC/Alamy Stock Photo

Critics charge that public defenders, because they are government employees, are not sufficiently independent from prosecutors and judges. For the same reason, clients may be suspicious of public defenders, viewing them as state functionaries. Finally, the huge caseloads typical of public defenders' offices create pressure toward an excessive use of plea bargaining. Learn more about system overload in public defenders offices via **http://tinyurl.com/4yywlrt**.

Contractual Arrangements

Through a third type of indigent defense, contract attorney programs, county and state officials arrange with local criminal lawyers to provide for indigent defense on a contractual basis. Individual attorneys, local bar associations, and multipartner law firms may all be tapped to provide services. Contract defense programs are the least widely used form of indigent defense at present, although their popularity is growing.

Problems with Indigent Defense

Critics of the current system of indigent defense point out that the system is woefully underfunded. Findings from the most recent National Survey of Indigent Defense Systems were published in 2014.[37] Twenty years ago, however, a report by the National Symposium on Indigent Defense proclaimed, "Indigent defense today, in terms of funding, caseloads, and quality, is in a chronic state of crisis,"[38] an observation that is still true today. Some question the quality of services available through public defender systems due to the fact that entry-level public defenders are paid poorly in comparison to what new attorneys entering private law firms might earn.

> Critics charge that public defenders, because they are government employees, are not sufficiently independent from prosecutors and judges.

As a consequence of limited funding, many public defender offices employ what critics call a strategy of "plead 'em and speed 'em through," often involving a heavy use of plea bargaining and initial meetings with clients in courtrooms as trials are about to begin. Mary Broderick of the National Legal Aid and Defender Association says, "We aren't being given the same weapons. . . . It's like trying to deal with smart bombs when all you've got is a couple of cap pistols."[39] Proposed enhancements to indigent defense systems are offered by the National Legal Aid and Defender Association (NLADA). You can visit the NLADA at **http://www.nlada.org**. A 200-page report by the National Symposium on Indigent Defense, showing what individual states spend on indigent defense, is available at **https://justicestudies.com/pubs/cjindig.pdf**. The factors that are commonly used to determine client indigence in state-run indigent defense systems are shown in Figure 8–2 (multiple factors may be used in any one state).

Although state indigent defense services are sometimes woefully underfunded, the same is not true of the federal system. The defense of indigent Oklahoma City bomber Timothy McVeigh, for example, cost taxpayers an estimated $13.8 million—which doesn't include the cost of his appeal or execution. McVeigh's expenses included $6.7 million for attorneys, $2 million for investigators, $3 million for expert witnesses, and approximately $1.4 million for office rent and secretarial assistance.[40]

Of course, defendants need not accept any assigned counsel. Defendants may waive their right to an attorney and undertake their own defense—a right held to be inherent in the Sixth Amendment to the U.S. Constitution by the U.S. Supreme Court in the 1975 case of *Faretta* v. *California*.[41] Self-representation is uncommon, however, and only 1% of federal inmates and 3% of state inmates report having represented themselves.[42] Some famous instances of self-representation can be found in the 1995 trial of Long Island Rail Road commuter train shooter Colin Ferguson, the 1999 trial of Dr. Jack Kevorkian, the 2002 federal competency hearings of Zacarias Moussaoui; and the 2017 death penalty hearing of Charleston church shooter Dylann Roof.

Defendants who are not pleased with the lawyer appointed to defend them are in a somewhat different situation. They may request, through the court, that a new lawyer be assigned to represent them, as Timothy McVeigh did following his conviction and death sentence in the Oklahoma City bombing case. However, unless there is clear reason for reassignment, such as an obvious personality conflict between defendant and attorney, few judges are likely to honor a request of this sort. Short of obvious difficulties, most judges will trust in the professionalism of appointed counsel.

State-supported indigent defense systems may also be called on to provide representation for clients upon appeal. An attorney who is appointed to represent an indigent defendant on appeal, however, may conclude that an appeal would be frivolous. If so, he or she may request that the appellate court allow him or her to withdraw from the case or that the

🐦 Follow the author's tweets about the latest crime and justice news @schmalleger

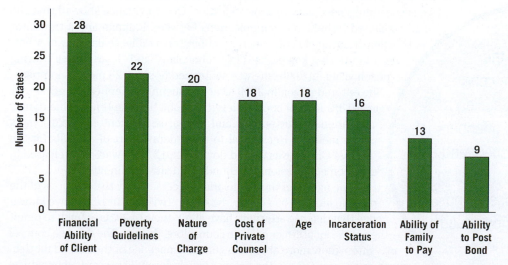

FIGURE 8–2
Factors Used to Determine Client Indigence in State Indigent Defense Systems
Source: Suzanne M. Strong, *State-Administered Indigent Defense Systems* (Washington, D.C.: BJS, 2016).

▲ Defense attorney Lynne Stewart, who was sentenced to prison in 2006 (and resentenced in 2010) for smuggling messages from her jailed client, the radical Egyptian sheik Omar Abdel-Rahman (also known as "the Blind Sheik"), to his terrorist followers outside prison. Our adversarial system requires that attorneys sometimes defend unpopular clients, but the defense role is carefully prescribed by ethical and procedural standards. How did Stewart's actions violate those standards?

Stephen Chernin/AP Images

court dispose of the case without requiring the attorney to file a brief arguing the merits of the appeal. In 1967, in the case of *Anders* v. *California*,[43] the U.S. Supreme Court found that to protect a defendant's constitutional right to appellate counsel, appellate courts must safeguard against the risk of accepting an attorney's negative assessment of a case where an appeal is not actually frivolous. The Court also found California's existing procedure for evaluating such requests to be inadequate, and the justices set forth an acceptable procedure. In 1979, in the case of *People* v. *Wende*,[44] the state of California adopted a new standardized procedure that, although not the same as that put forth in *Anders*, was designed to protect the right of a criminal defendant to appeal.

The *Wende* standard was put to the test in the 2000 case of *Smith* v. *Robbins*.[45] In that case, the U.S. Supreme Court held that the *Anders* procedure is only one method of satisfying the Constitution's requirements for indigent criminal appeals and that the states are free to adopt different procedures as long as those procedures adequately safeguard a defendant's right to appellate counsel.

Finally, in 2001, in the case of *Texas* v. *Cobb*,[46] the Court ruled that the Sixth Amendment right to counsel is "offense specific." It applies only to the offense with which a defendant is charged and not to other offenses, even if they are factually related to the charged offense.

The Ethics of Defense

The job of defense counsel, as we have already mentioned, is to prepare and offer a vigorous defense on behalf of the accused at trial and to appeal cases with merit. A proper defense at trial often involves the presentation of evidence and the examination of witnesses, both of which require careful thought and planning. Good attorneys may become emotionally committed to the outcomes of trials in which they are involved. Some lawyers, however, cross the line when they lose their professional objectivity and embrace the wider cause of their clients. That's what happened to Lynne Stewart, who was convicted in 2005 of smuggling messages from her jailed client, the radical Egyptian sheik Omar Abdel-Rahman ("the Blind Sheik"), to his terrorist followers outside prison.[47] Abdel-Rahman was serving life behind bars for his role in an unsuccessful 1993 plot to bomb New York City landmarks, prior to his death in 2017. Stewart, a 1960s-era radical, has often chosen to represent the most contemptible clients, believing that justice requires that everyone receive a vigorous defense. She was arrested, however, after she issued a public statement on behalf of the sheik expressing her client's withdrawal of support for a cease-fire involving his supporters in Egypt. Stewart had known in advance that making the statement violated an order to restrict the sheik's communications, but she later testified that she believed that violence is sometimes necessary to achieve justice. Other evidence showed that she had facilitated forbidden communications between Rahman and a translator by using prearranged cues, such as tapping on a table, shaking a water bottle, and uttering key phrases like "chocolate" and "heart attack" during prison visits. In 2006, she was sentenced to serve 28 months in prison. She entered prison in 2009 after exhausting the appeals process; but in 2010, a federal court ordered that she be resentenced due to new revelations about perjury and increased her sentence to 10 years and a month.[48] Her appeal to the federal Court of Appeals for the Second Circuit was turned down in 2012.[49] Stewart was released in 2014 on compassionate grounds, and she died in 2017.

The nature of the adversarial process, fed by the emotions of the participants combined with the often privileged and extensive knowledge that defense attorneys have about their cases, is enough to tempt the professional ethics of some counselors. Because the defense counsel may often know more about the guilt or innocence of the defendant than anyone else prior to trial, the defense role is carefully prescribed by ethical and procedural considerations. Attorneys violate both law and the standards of their profession if they knowingly misrepresent themselves or their clients.

> Society asks much of the criminal court. The court is expected to meet society's demand that serious offenders be convicted and punished, and at the same time it is expected to insure that the innocent and unfortunate are not oppressed.
>
> —President's Commission on Law Enforcement and Administration of Justice[i]

Ethics and Professionalism
The American Bar Association's *Model Rules of Professional Conduct*

To help attorneys understand what is expected of them, the ABA has provided significant guidance in the areas of legal ethics and professional responsibility. The ABA has developed professional standards intended to serve as models for state bar associations and to guide legislative bodies focused on ensuring ethical behavior among attorneys.

The ABA's first major foray into the area of ethical guidelines resulted in the adoption of its original *Canons of Professional Ethics* on August 27, 1908. In 1913, in an effort to keep the association informed about state and local bar activities concerning professional ethics, the ABA established its Standing Committee on Professional Ethics. The name of the group was changed to the Committee on Ethics and Professional Responsibility in 1971, and the committee continues to function under that name today.

In 1969, the ABA formally adopted the committee's *Model Code of Professional Responsibility*. Eventually, the majority of state and federal jurisdictions adopted their own versions of the Model Code.

In 1977, the ABA Commission on Evaluation of Professional Standards was created and charged with rethinking the ethical problems of the legal profession. During the next 6 years, the commission drafted the *Model Rules of Professional Conduct*, which the ABA adopted on August 2, 1983. The *Model Rules* effectively supplanted the *Model Code of Professional Responsibility*, and today most state and federal jurisdictions have adapted the *Model Rules* to their own particular circumstances.

The *Model Rules* have been periodically amended—most significantly in 2002—but continue to provide the touchstone ethical standards of the American legal profession today. Visit the American Bar Association on the Internet at **http://www.americanbar.org**, and learn about its Center for Professional Responsibility at **http://www.americanbar.org/groups/professional_responsibility.html**.

THINKING ABOUT ETHICS

1. *Should a defense attorney represent a client whom he or she knows to be guilty?*
2. *Would it be unethical for an attorney to refuse to represent such a client? Why or why not?*

Based on American Bar Association, Model Rules of Professional Conduct—Preface, http://www.abanet.org/cpr/mrpc/preface.html (accessed July 10, 2013).

As Michael Ratner, president of the Center for Constitutional Rights, put it when commenting on the Stewart case, "Lawyers need to be advocates, but they don't need to be accomplices."[50]

To help attorneys understand what is expected of them and what the appropriate limits of a vigorous defense might be, the ABA provides significant guidance in the areas of legal ethics and professional responsibility, as the Ethics and Professionalism box in this section explains. Even so, some attorney–client interactions remain especially tricky. Defense attorneys, for example, are under no obligation to reveal information obtained from a client without the client's permission. However, all states permit defense lawyers to violate a client's confidentiality without fear of reprisal if they reasonably believe that doing so could prevent serious injury or death to another person. In 2004, with passage of a new evidence law broadening the state's evidence code, California joined the other 49 states in freeing attorneys to violate client confidentiality in such cases. California law makes disclosure discretionary, not mandatory. Kevin Mohr, a professor at Western State University College of Law in Fullerton, California, noted that the new law provides the first exception to the attorney–client privilege in California in more than 130 years. "A lawyer can now take action and intervene and prevent [a] criminal act from occurring," said Mohr.[51]

Somewhat earlier, the 1986 U.S. Supreme Court case of *Nix* v. *Whiteside*[52] clarified the duty of lawyers to reveal known instances of client perjury. In that case, the Court held that a lawyer's duty to a client "is limited to legitimate, lawful conduct compatible with the very nature of a trial as a search for truth. . . . Counsel is precluded from taking steps or in any way assisting the client in presenting false evidence or otherwise violating the law."[53]

The Bailiff

The **bailiff**, another member of the professional courtroom work group, is usually an armed law enforcement officer. The job of the bailiff, also called a *court officer*, is to ensure order in the courtroom, to announce the judge's entry into the courtroom, to call witnesses, and to prevent the escape of the accused (if the accused has not been released on bond). The bailiff also supervises the jury when it is sequestered and controls public and media access to jury members. Bailiffs in federal courtrooms are deputy U.S. marshals.

bailiff
The court officer whose duties are to keep order in the courtroom, to secure witnesses, and to maintain physical custody of the jury.

Trial Court Administrators

Many states now employ trial court administrators whose job is to facilitate the smooth functioning of courts in particular judicial districts or areas. A major impetus toward the hiring

🐦 Follow the author's tweets about the latest crime and justice news @schmalleger

▲ An expert witness testifying in court. Expert witnesses may express opinions and draw conclusions in their area of expertise; they need not limit their testimony to facts alone. Why are expert witnesses permitted such leeway?

Guy Cali/Corbis/Getty Images

of local trial court administrators came from the 1967 President's Commission on Law Enforcement and Administration of Justice. Examining state courts, the report found "a system that treats defendants who are charged with minor offenses with less dignity and consideration than it treats those who are charged with serious crimes."[54] A few years later, the National Advisory Commission on Criminal Justice Standards and Goals recommended that all courts with five or more judges create the position of trial court administrator.[55]

Court administrators provide uniform court management, assuming many of the duties previously performed by chief judges, prosecutors, and court clerks. Where trial court administrators operate, the ultimate authority for running the court still rests with the chief judge. Administrators, however, are able to relieve the judge of many routine and repetitive tasks, such as record keeping, scheduling, case-flow analysis, personnel administration, space utilization, facilities planning, and budget management. They may also take the minutes at meetings of judges and their committees.

Juror management is another area in which trial court administrators are becoming increasingly involved. Juror utilization studies can identify problems such as the over selection of citizens for the jury pool and the reasons for excessive requests to be excused from jury service. They can also suggest ways to reduce the time jurors waste waiting to be called or impaneled.

Effective trial court administrators are able to track lengthy cases and identify bottlenecks in court processing. They then suggest strategies to make the administration of justice more efficient for courtroom professionals and more humane for lay participants.

The Court Reporter

The role of the court reporter (also called the *court stenographer* or *court recorder*) is to create a record of all that occurs during a trial. Accurate records are very important in criminal trial courts because appeals may be based entirely on what went on in the courtroom. Especially significant are all verbal comments made in the courtroom, including testimonies, objections, judge's rulings, judge's instructions to the jury, arguments made by lawyers, and results of conferences between the lawyers and the judge. Occasionally, the judge will rule that a statement should be "stricken from the record" because it is inappropriate or unfounded. The official trial record, often taken on a stenotype machine or an audio recorder, may later be transcribed in manuscript form and will become the basis for any appellate review of the trial.

Today's court reporters often employ computer-aided transcription (CAT) software, which translates typed stenographic shorthand into complete and readable transcripts. Court reporters may be members of the National Court Reporters Association, the United States Court Reporters Association, or the Association of Legal Administrators—all of which support the activities of these professionals. You can visit the National Court Reporters Association at **https://www.ncra.org**.

The Clerk of Court

The duties of the clerk of court (sometimes also known as the *county clerk*) extend beyond the courtroom. The clerk maintains all records of criminal cases, including all pleas and motions made both before and after the actual trial. The clerk also prepares a jury pool, issues jury summonses, and subpoenas witnesses for both the prosecution and the defense. During the trial, the clerk (or an assistant) marks physical evidence for identification as instructed by the judge and maintains custody of that evidence. The clerk also swears in witnesses and performs other functions as the judge directs. Some states allow the clerk limited judicial duties, such as the power to issue warrants, to handle certain matters relating to individuals declared mentally incompetent,[56] and to serve as a judge of probate to oversee wills and the administration of estates.

Expert Witnesses

Most of the courtroom "insiders" we've talked about so far either are employees of the state or have ongoing professional relationships with the court (as in the case of defense counsel). Expert witnesses, however, may not have that kind of status, although some do.

Expert witnesses are recognized as having specialized skills and knowledge in an established profession or technical area. They must demonstrate their expertise through education, work experience, publications, and awards. Their testimony at trial provides an effective way of introducing scientific evidence in such areas as medicine, psychology, ballistics, crime scene analysis, and photography. Unlike lay witnesses, they are allowed to express opinions and to draw conclusions, but only within their particular area of expertise. Expert witnesses, like the other courtroom actors described in this chapter, are generally paid professionals and (like all other witnesses) are subject to cross-examination.

In the 1993 civil case of *Daubert* v. *Merrell Dow Pharmaceuticals*,[57] the Supreme Court established that the test for the admissibility of scientific expert testimony is for the trial judge to decide "at the outset . . . whether the expert is proposing to testify to (1) scientific knowledge that (2) will assist the trier of fact to understand or determine a fact in issue." The Court concluded that the task of the trial judge is one of "ensuring that an expert's testimony both rests on a reliable foundation and is relevant to the task at hand. Pertinent evidence based on scientifically valid principles," said the Court, "will satisfy those demands."

In 2010, in the case of *Melendez-Diaz* v. *Massachusetts*,[58] the Court further defined the role of forensic analysts, deciding that they are "witnesses" and their reports are "testimonial"—meaning that, under the Constitution's confrontation clause, they must personally testify at trial unless the defendant waives his or her right to cross-examine them. Similarly, in the 2011 U.S. Supreme Court case of *Bullcoming* v. *New Mexico*,[59] the Court found that the confrontation clause does not permit the introduction into evidence during trial of a forensic laboratory report through the in-court testimony of an analyst who did not sign the document or personally observe the test it describes. In effect, the Court held that a forensic analyst who testifies at a criminal trial must be the one who performed or witnessed the lab tests being described.

One difficulty with expert testimony is that it can be confusing to the jury. Sometimes the trouble is due to the nature of the subject matter and sometimes to disagreements between the experts themselves. Often, however, it arises from the strict interpretation given to expert testimony by procedural requirements. The difference between medical and legal definitions of insanity, for example, points to a divergence in both history and purpose between the law and medical science. Courts that attempt to apply criteria like the M'Naghten rule (discussed in Chapter 3) in deciding claims of "insanity" are often faced with the testimony of psychiatric experts who refuse even to recognize the word. Such experts may prefer, instead, to speak in terms of *psychosis* and *neurosis*, words that have no place in legal jargon. Because of the uncertainties they create, legal requirements may pit experts against one another and may confound the jury.

Even so, most authorities agree that expert testimony is usually viewed by jurors as more trustworthy than other forms of evidence. In a study of scientific evidence, one prosecutor commented that if he had to choose between presenting a fingerprint or an eyewitness at trial, he would always go with the fingerprint.[60] As a consequence of the effectiveness of scientific evidence, the National Institute of Justice recommends that "prosecutors consider the potential utility of such information in all cases where such evidence is available."[61]

expert witness
A person who has special knowledge and skills recognized by the court as relevant to the determination of guilt or innocence. Unlike lay witnesses, expert witnesses may express opinions or draw conclusions in their testimony.

> One difficulty with expert testimony is that it can be confusing to the jury.

Outsiders: Nonprofessional Courtroom Participants

Defendants, victims, jurors, and most witnesses are usually unwilling or inadvertent participants in criminal trials. Although they are outsiders who lack the status of paid professional participants, these are precisely the people who provide the grist for the judicial mill. The press, a willing player in many criminal trials, makes up another group of outsiders. Let's look now at each of these courtroom actors.

2 Describe the roles of outsiders, or nonprofessional courtroom participants.

Lay Witnesses

Nonexpert witnesses, also known as **lay witnesses**, may be called to testify by either the prosecution or the defense. Lay witnesses may be eyewitnesses who saw the crime being committed or who came upon the crime scene shortly after the crime had occurred. Another type of lay witness is the character witness, who frequently provides information about the personality, family life, business acumen, and so on of the defendant in an effort to show that this is not the kind of person who would commit the crime with which he or she is charged.

lay witness
An eyewitness, character witness, or other person called on to testify who is not considered an expert. Lay witnesses must testify to facts only and may not draw conclusions or express opinions.

▲ A lay witness being sworn in before testifying in a criminal trial. Nonexpert witnesses must generally limit their testimony to facts about which they have direct knowledge. Why are such limits imposed?

Guy Cali/Corbis/Getty Images

subpoena
A written order issued by a judicial officer or grand jury requiring an individual to appear in court and to give testimony or to bring material to be used as evidence. Some subpoenas mandate that books, papers, and other items be surrendered to the court.

Of course, the victim may also be a witness, providing detailed and sometimes lengthy testimony about the defendant and the crime.

A written document called a **subpoena** officially notifies witnesses that they are to appear in court to testify. Subpoenas are generally served by an officer of the court or by a police officer, though they are sometimes mailed. Both sides in a criminal case may subpoena witnesses and might ask that individuals called to testify bring with them books, papers, photographs, recordings, or other forms of physical evidence. Witnesses who fail to appear when summoned may face contempt-of-court charges.

The job of a witness is to provide accurate testimony concerning only those things of which he or she has direct knowledge. Normally, witnesses are not allowed to repeat things that others have told them unless they must do so to account for certain actions of their own. Because few witnesses are familiar with courtroom procedure, the task of testifying is fraught with uncertainty and can be traumatizing.

Everyone who testifies in a criminal trial must do so under oath, in which some reference to God is made, or after affirmation,[62] which is a pledge to tell the truth used by those who find either a reference or swearing to God objectionable.

All witnesses are subject to cross-examination. Lay witnesses may be surprised to find that cross-examination can force them to defend their personal and moral integrity. A cross-examiner may question a witness about past vicious, criminal, or immoral acts, even when such matters have never been the subject of a criminal proceeding.[63] As long as the intent of such questions is to demonstrate to the jury that the witness is not credible, the judge will normally permit them.

Witnesses have traditionally been shortchanged by the judicial process. Subpoenaed to attend court, they have often suffered from frequent and unannounced changes in trial dates. A witness who promptly responds to a summons to appear may find that legal maneuvering has resulted in unanticipated delays. Strategic changes by either side may make the testimony of some witnesses entirely unnecessary, and people who have prepared themselves for the psychological rigors of testifying often experience an emotional letdown.

To compensate witnesses for their time and to make up for lost income, many states pay witnesses for each day that they spend in court. Payments range from $5 to $40 per day,[64] although some states pay nothing at all (federal courts pay $40 per day[65]). In a 2004 Chicago murder case in which Oprah Winfrey served as a juror, for example, all jurors, including Winfrey (a billionaire), were paid $17.20 a day for their services.[66] The 1991 U.S. Supreme Court case of *Demarest* v. *Manspeaker et al.*[67] held that federal prisoners subpoenaed to testify are entitled to witness fees just as other witnesses would be.

In an effort to make the job of witnesses less onerous, 39 states and the federal government have laws or guidelines requiring that witnesses be notified of scheduling changes and cancellations in criminal proceedings.[68] In 1982, Congress passed the Victim and Witness Protection Act, which required the U.S. attorney general to develop guidelines to assist victims and witnesses in meeting the demands placed on them by the justice system. A number of **victims' assistance programs** (also called *victim/witness assistance programs*) have also taken up a call for the rights of witnesses and are working to make the courtroom experience more manageable.

victims' assistance program
An organized program that offers services to victims of crime in the areas of crisis intervention and follow-up counseling and that helps victims secure their rights under the law.

Jurors

The Cook County (Chicago) jury on which television diva Oprah Winfrey served, convicted a man of first-degree murder in 2004. "It was an eye-opener for all of us," Winfrey said after the 3-day trial ended. "It was not an easy decision to make."[69]

Article III of the U.S. Constitution requires that "[t]he trial of all crimes . . . shall be by jury." **Jurors** are citizens selected for jury duty in a court of law. States have the authority to determine the number of jurors in criminal trial juries. Most states use juries composed of 12 people and one or two alternates designated to fill in for jurors who are unable to continue due to accident, illness, or personal emergency. Some states allow for juries smaller than 12 jurors, and juries with as few as six members have survived Supreme Court scrutiny.[70]

Jury duty is regarded as a responsibility of citizenship. Other than juveniles and people in certain occupations, such as police personnel, physicians, members of the armed services on active duty, and emergency services workers, those who are called for jury duty must serve unless they can convince a judge that they should be excused for overriding reasons. Noncitizens, convicted felons, and citizens who have served on a jury within the past 2 years are excluded from jury service in most jurisdictions.

The names of prospective jurors are often gathered from the tax register, motor vehicle records, or voter registration rolls of a county or municipality. Minimum qualifications for jury service include adulthood, basic command of spoken English, citizenship, "ordinary intelligence," and local residency. Jurors are also expected to possess their "natural faculties," meaning that they should be able to hear, speak, see, move, and so forth. Some jurisdictions have recently allowed people with physical disabilities to serve as jurors, although the nature of the evidence to be presented in a case may preclude people with certain kinds of disabilities from serving.

Ideally, the jury should be a microcosm of society, reflecting the values, rationality, and common sense of the average person. The U.S. Supreme Court has held that criminal defendants have a right to have their cases heard before a jury of their peers.[71] Peer juries are those composed of a representative cross section of the community in which the alleged crime occurred and where the trial is to be held. The idea of a peer jury stems from the Magna Carta's original guarantee of jury trials for "freemen." Freemen in England during the thirteenth century, however, were more likely to be of similar mind than is a cross section of Americans today. Hence, although the duty of the jury is to deliberate on the evidence and, ultimately, to determine guilt or innocence, social dynamics may play just as great a role in jury verdicts as do the facts of a case.

In a 1945 case, *Thiel v. Southern Pacific Co.*,[72] the Supreme Court clarified the concept of a "jury of one's peers" by noting that although it is not necessary for every jury to contain representatives of every conceivable racial, ethnic, religious, gender, and economic group in the community, court officials may not systematically and intentionally exclude any juror solely because of his or her social characteristics.

In 2005, the ABA released a set of 19 principles intended to guide jury reform.[73] Then-ABA President Robert J. Grey, Jr., said that the principles were aimed at improving the courts' treatment of jurors and to "move jury service into the 21st Century." Read the ABA's entire report, *Principles for Juries and Jury Trials*, at **https://www.americanbar.org/content/dam/aba/administrative/american_jury/principles.authcheckdam.pdf**.

juror
A member of a trial or grand jury who has been selected for jury duty and is required to serve as an arbiter of the facts in a court of law. Jurors are expected to render verdicts of "guilty" or "not guilty" as to the charges brought against the accused, although they may sometimes fail to do so (as in the case of a hung jury).

> The highest act of citizenship is jury service.
> —Abraham Lincoln, sixteenth president of the United States

The Victim

Not all crimes have clearly identifiable victims. Some, such as murder, do not have victims who survive. Where there is an identifiable surviving victim, however, he or she is often one of the most forgotten people in the courtroom. Although the victim may have been profoundly affected by the crime itself and is often emotionally committed to the proceedings and trial outcome, he or she may not even be permitted to participate directly in the trial process. Although a powerful movement to recognize the interests of victims is in full swing in this country, it is still not unusual for crime victims to be totally unaware of the final outcome of a case that intimately concerns them.[74]

Hundreds of years ago, the situation surrounding victims was far different. During the early Middle Ages in much of Europe, victims or their survivors routinely played a central role in trial proceedings and in sentencing decisions. They testified, examined witnesses, challenged defense contentions, and pleaded with the judge or jury for justice, honor, and often revenge. Sometimes they were even expected to carry out the sentence of the court,

🐦 Follow the author's tweets about the latest crime and justice news @schmalleger

by flogging the offender or by releasing the trapdoor used for hangings. This "golden age" of the victim ended with the consolidation of power into the hands of monarchs, who declared that vengeance was theirs alone.

Today, victims (like witnesses) experience many of the following hardships as they participate in the criminal court process:

- Uncertainty as to their role in the criminal justice process
- General lack of knowledge about the criminal justice system, courtroom procedure, and legal issues
- Trial delays resulting in frequent travel, missed work, and wasted time
- Fear of the defendant or of retaliation from the defendant's associates
- Trauma of testifying and of cross-examination

The trial process itself can make for a bitter experience. If victims take the stand, defense attorneys may test their memory, challenge their veracity, or even suggest that they were somehow responsible for their own victimization. After enduring cross-examination, some victims report feeling as though they—and not the offender—were portrayed as the criminal to the jury. The difficulties encountered by victims have been compared to a second victimization at the hands of the criminal justice system. Additional information on victims and victims' issues, including victims' assistance programs, is provided in Chapter 9.

The Defendant

Generally, defendants must be present at their trials. The Federal Rules of Criminal Procedure, like state rules, require a defendant's presence at every stage of a trial, except that a defendant who is initially present may be voluntarily absent after the trial has commenced.[75] In *Crosby* v. *U.S.* (1993),[76] the U.S. Supreme Court held that a defendant may not be tried in absentia, even if he or she was present at the beginning of a trial, if his or her absence is due to escape or failure to appear. In a related issue in *Zafiro* v. *U.S.* (1993),[77] the justices held that, at least in federal courts, defendants charged with similar or related offenses may be tried together, even when their defenses differ substantially.

The majority of criminal defendants are poor, uneducated, and often alienated from the philosophy that undergirds the American justice system. Many are relatively powerless and are at the mercy of judicial mechanisms. However, experienced defendants, notably those who are career offenders, may be well versed in courtroom demeanor. As we discussed earlier, defendants in criminal trials may even choose to represent themselves, though such a choice may not be in their best interests.

Even without self-representation, every defendant who chooses to do so can substantially influence events in the courtroom. Defendants exercise choice in (1) selecting and retaining counsel, (2) planning a defense strategy with their attorney, (3) deciding what information to provide to (or withhold from) the defense team, (4) deciding what plea to enter, (5) deciding whether to testify personally, and (6) determining whether to file an appeal if convicted.

Nevertheless, even the most active defendants suffer from a number of disadvantages. One is the tendency of others to assume that anyone on trial must be guilty. Although a person is "innocent until proven guilty," the very fact that he or she is accused of an offense casts a shadow of suspicion that may foster biases in the minds of jurors and other courtroom actors. Another disadvantage lies in the often-substantial social and cultural differences that separate the offender from the professional courtroom staff. Whereas lawyers and judges tend to identify with upper-middle-class values and lifestyles, few offenders do. The consequences of such a gap between defendant and courtroom staff may be insidious and far reaching.

Spectators and the Press

Spectators and the press are often overlooked because they do not have an official role in courtroom proceedings. Both spectators and media representatives may be present in large numbers at any trial. Spectators include members of the families of both the victim and the defendant, friends of either side, and curious onlookers—some of whom are avocational court watchers. Journalists, TV reporters, and other members of the press are apt to be present at spectacular trials (those involving an especially gruesome crime or a famous personality) and at those involving a great deal of community interest. The right of reporters and spectators to be present at a criminal trial is supported by the Sixth Amendment's requirement of a public trial.

Press reports at all stages of a criminal investigation and trial often create problems for the justice system. Significant pretrial publicity about a case may make it difficult to find jurors who have not already formed an opinion as to the guilt or innocence of the defendant. News reports from the courtroom may influence or confuse nonsequestered jurors who hear them, especially when the reports contain information brought to the bench but not heard by the jury.

In the 1976 case of *Nebraska Press Association* v. *Stuart*,[78] the U.S. Supreme Court ruled that trial court judges could not legitimately issue gag orders preventing the pretrial publication of information about a criminal case as long as the defendant's right to a fair trial and an impartial jury could be ensured by traditional means.[79] These means include (1) **change of venue**, whereby the trial is moved to another jurisdiction less likely to have been exposed to the publicity; (2) trial postponement, which would allow for memories to fade and emotions to cool; and (3) jury selection and screening to eliminate biased people from the jury pool. In 1986, the Court extended press access to preliminary hearings, which it said are "sufficiently like a trial to require public access."[80] In 1993, in the case of *Caribbean International News Corporation* v. *Puerto Rico*,[81] the Court effectively applied that requirement to territories under U.S. control. Today, members of the press and their video, television, and still cameras are allowed into most state courtrooms.

The U.S. Supreme Court has been far less favorably disposed to television coverage than have state courts. In 1981, a Florida defendant appealed his burglary conviction to the Supreme Court,[82] arguing that the presence of television cameras at his trial had turned the court into a circus for attorneys and made the proceedings more a sideshow than a trial. The Supreme Court, recognizing that television cameras have an untoward effect on many people, found in favor of the defendant. In the words of the Court, "Trial courts must be especially vigilant to guard against any impairment of the defendant's right to a verdict based solely upon the evidence and the relevant law."

Cameras of all kinds have been prohibited in all federal district criminal proceedings since 1946 by Rule 53 of the Federal Rules of Criminal Procedure.[83] In 1972, the Judicial Conference of the United States adopted a policy opposing broadcast of civil proceedings in district courts, and that policy was incorporated into the Code of Conduct for United States Judges. Nonetheless, some district courts have local rules that allow photographs and filming during selected proceedings.

A 3-year pilot project that allowed television cameras into six U.S. district courts and two appeals courts closed on December 31, 1994, when the Judicial Conference voted to end the project. Conference members expressed concerns that cameras were a distracting influence and were having a "negative impact on jurors [and] witnesses"[84] by exposing them to possible harm by revealing their identities. Today's new personal technologies, however, which include cellular telephones with digital camera capabilities, streaming Web-based video, and miniaturized recording devices, all threaten courtroom privacy. In fact, in 2014, members of an advocacy group smuggled a miniature camera into a session of the U.S. Supreme Court and recorded oral arguments in a case about campaign finance reform. The video was later posted to YouTube as part of a protest over the issue.[85]

> The majority of criminal defendants are poor, uneducated, and often alienated from the philosophy that undergirds the American justice system.

change of venue
The movement of a trial or lawsuit from one jurisdiction to another or from one location to another within the same jurisdiction. A change of venue may be made in a criminal case to ensure that the defendant receives a fair trial.

The Criminal Trial

From arrest through sentencing, the criminal justice process is carefully choreographed. Arresting officers must follow proper procedure in the gathering of evidence and in the arrest and questioning of suspects. Magistrates, prosecutors, jailers, and prison officials are all subject to their own strictures. Nowhere, however, is the criminal justice process more closely circumscribed than it is at the criminal trial.

3 State the procedure, nature, and purpose of the criminal trial.

Procedure

The procedure in a modern courtroom is highly formalized. **Rules of evidence**, which govern the admissibility of evidence, and other procedural guidelines determine the course of a criminal hearing and trial. Rules of evidence are partially based on tradition, but all U.S. jurisdictions have formalized rules of evidence in written form. Criminal trials at the federal level generally adhere to the requirements of the Federal Rules of Evidence.

Trials are also circumscribed by informal rules and professional expectations. An important component of law school education is the teaching of rules that structure and define appropriate courtroom demeanor. In addition to statutory rules, law students are thoroughly exposed to the ethical standards of their profession, as found in ABA standards and other writings.

Nature and Purpose of the Criminal Trial

In the remainder of this chapter, we will describe the chronology of a criminal trial and will comment on some of the widely accepted rules of criminal procedure. Before we begin the description, however, it is good to keep two points in mind. One is that the primary purpose of any criminal trial is the determination of the defendant's guilt or innocence. In this regard, it is important to recognize the crucial distinction that scholars make between factual guilt and legal guilt. The term *factual guilt* refers to the issue of whether the defendant is actually responsible for the crime of which he or she stands accused. If the defendant did it, then he or she is, in fact, guilty. *Legal guilt* is not as clear a term and is established only when the prosecutor presents evidence that is sufficient to convince the judge (when a jury trial has been waived and the judge determines the verdict) or the jury that the defendant is guilty as charged. The distinction between factual guilt and legal guilt is crucial because it points to the fact that the burden of proof rests with the prosecution. It indicates the possibility that guilty defendants may, nonetheless, be found "not guilty."

rules of evidence
The court rules that govern the admissibility of evidence at criminal hearings and trials.

▲ Oscar Pistorius, the South African Paralympic athlete, shown at his 2014 trial. Pistorius was convicted of the shooting death of his girlfriend and model, Reeva Steenkamp and sentenced to five years in prison. Following a 2016 appeal by prosecutors, six more years were added to his sentence. What is the primary purpose of a criminal trial?

Theana Breugem/epa european pressphoto agency b.v./Alamy Stock Photo

The second point to remember is that criminal trials under our system of justice are built around an **adversarial system** (prosecution versus defense) and that central to this system is the advocacy model. Participating in the adversarial system are advocates for the state (the prosecutor or the district attorney) and for the defendant (the defense counsel, the public defender, and so on). The philosophy behind the adversarial system is that the greatest number of just resolutions in criminal trials will occur when both sides are allowed to argue their cases effectively and vociferously before a fair and impartial jury. The system requires that advocates for both sides do their utmost, within the boundaries set by law and professional ethics, to protect and advance the interests of their clients (i.e., the defendant and the state). The advocacy model makes clear that it is not the job of the defense attorney or the prosecution to determine the guilt of any defendant. Even defense attorneys who are convinced that their client is guilty are still exhorted to offer the best possible defense and to counsel their client as effectively as possible.

The adversarial system has been criticized by some thinkers who point to fundamental differences between law and science in the way the search for truth is conducted.[86] Whereas proponents of traditional legal procedure accept the belief that truth can best be uncovered through an adversarial process, scientists adhere to a painstaking process of research and replication to acquire knowledge. Most of us would agree that scientific advances in recent years may have made factual issues less difficult to ascertain. For example, some of the new scientific techniques in evidence analysis, such as DNA fingerprinting, can now unequivocally link suspects to criminal activity or even show that offenders once thought guilty are actually innocent. Gary Dotson of Illinois became the first person convicted of a crime to be exonerated through the use of such evidence in 1989.[87] Since then, at least 328 convictions have been overturned using DNA evidence. According to Samuel R. Gross and colleagues at the University of Michigan Law School, who published a comprehensive study of exonerations in 2004, those 328 people "had spent more than 3,400 years in prison for crimes for which they should never have been convicted."[88] Exonerations tend to occur more frequently in cases where DNA evidence is relatively easy to acquire, such as rape and murder. False conviction rates for other crimes, such as robbery, are much more difficult to assess using DNA. Hence, says Gross, "the clearest and most important lesson from the recent spike in rape exonerations is that false convictions that come to light are the tip of an iceberg."

Whether scientific findings should continue to serve a subservient role to the adversarial process itself is a question now being raised. The ultimate answer will probably be determined by the results that the two processes are able to produce. If the adversarial model results in the acquittal of too many demonstrably guilty people because of legal "technicalities" or if the scientific approach identifies too many suspects inaccurately, either could be restricted.

adversarial system
The two-sided structure under which American criminal trial courts operate that pits the prosecution against the defense. In theory, justice is done when the more effective adversary is able to convince the judge or jury that his or her perspective on the case is the correct one.

Follow the author's tweets about the latest crime and justice news @schmalleger

> Whether scientific findings should continue to serve a subservient role to the adversarial process itself is a question now being raised.

Stages in a Criminal Trial

We turn now to a discussion of the steps in a criminal trial. As Figure 8–3 shows, trial chronology consists of eight stages:

4 Describe the criminal trial process.

1. Trial initiation
2. Jury selection
3. Opening statements
4. Presentation of evidence
5. Closing arguments
6. Judge's charge to the jury
7. Jury deliberations
8. Verdict

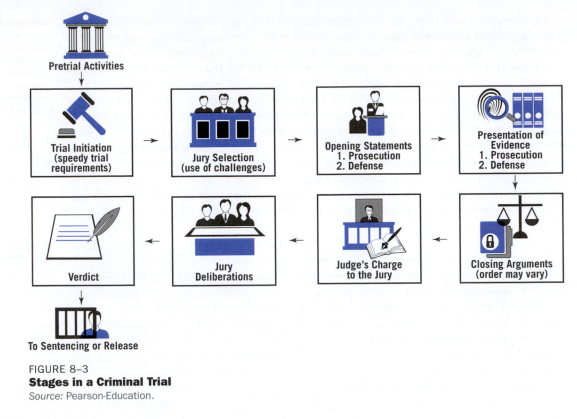

Pretrial Activities

Trial Initiation (speedy trial requirements) → Jury Selection (use of challenges) → Opening Statements 1. Prosecution 2. Defense → Presentation of Evidence 1. Prosecution 2. Defense

Verdict ← Jury Deliberations ← Judge's Charge to the Jury ← Closing Arguments (order may vary)

To Sentencing or Release

FIGURE 8–3
Stages in a Criminal Trial
Source: Pearson-Education.

▲ James Thomas, who was charged with murder in 1996 and freed in April 2005, after spending eight and a half years in a Louisiana jail waiting for his case to go to trial. A Louisiana state appeals court ruled that the state had taken too long to try him. Why does our system of justice require speedy trials?

Bill Feig/AP Images

🐦 Follow the author's tweets about the latest crime and justice news @schmalleger

Jury deliberations and the verdict are discussed jointly. If the defendant is found guilty, a sentence is imposed by the judge at the conclusion of the trial. Sentencing is discussed in the next chapter.

Trial Initiation

In 2005, a Louisiana state appeals court threw out murder charges against James Thomas and ordered him released. Thomas, an impoverished day laborer, had been arrested in 1996 and spent eight and a half years in jail waiting for a trial that never came. The ruling by the appeals court was widely seen as an indictment of Louisiana's understaffed and underfunded public defender system, members of which had simply been too busy to work on Thomas's case. A private attorney managed to get Thomas set free after his mother scraped together $500 to pay his fee.

The U.S. Constitution contains a speedy trial provision in its Sixth Amendment, which guarantees that "[i]n all criminal prosecutions, the accused shall enjoy the right to a speedy and public trial." Clogged court calendars, limited judicial resources, and general inefficiency, however, often combine to produce what appears to many to be unreasonable delays in trial initiation. The attention of the U.S. Supreme Court was brought to bear on trial delays in three precedent-setting cases: *Klopfer* v. *North Carolina* (1967),[89] *Barker* v. *Wingo* (1972),[90] and *Strunk* v. *U.S.* (1973).[91] The *Klopfer* case involved a Duke University professor and focused on civil disobedience in a protest against segregated facilities. In ruling on Klopfer's long-delayed trial, the Court asserted that the right to a speedy trial is a fundamental guarantee of the Constitution. In the *Barker* case, the Court held that Sixth Amendment guarantees to a quick trial could be illegally violated even in cases where the accused did not explicitly object to delays. In *Strunk*, it found that the denial of a speedy trial should result in the dismissal of all charges.

In 1974, against the advice of the Justice Department, the U.S. Congress passed the federal **Speedy Trial Act**.[92] The act allows for the dismissal of federal criminal charges in cases where the prosecution does not seek an indictment or information within 30 days of arrest (a 30-day extension is granted when the grand jury is not in session) or where a trial does not begin within 70 working days after indictment or initial appearance for defendants who plead not guilty. If a defendant is not available for trial or if witnesses cannot be called within the 70-day limit, the period may be extended up to 180 days. Delays brought about by the defendant, through requests for a continuance or because of escape, are not counted in the specified time periods.

In an important 1988 decision, *U.S.* v. *Taylor*,[93] the U.S. Supreme Court applied the requirements of the Speedy Trial Act to the case of a drug defendant who had escaped following arrest. The Court made it clear that trial delays that derive from the willful actions of the defendant do not apply to the 70-day period. The Court also held that trial delays, even when they result from government action, do not necessarily provide grounds for dismissal if they occur "without prejudice." Delays without prejudice are those that are due to circumstances beyond the control of criminal justice agencies.

In *Fex* v. *Michigan* (1993),[94] the U.S. Supreme Court ruled that "common sense compel[s] the conclusion that the 180-day period does not commence until the prisoner's disposition request has actually been delivered to the court and prosecutor of the jurisdiction that lodged the detainer against him." However, in a 1992 case, *Doggett* v. *U.S.*,[95] the Court held that a delay of eight and a half years violated speedy trial provisions because it resulted from government negligence.

In 2006, the Court refused to hear an appeal by suspected dirty bomb conspirator Jose Padilla, letting stand a lower court's decision that said the president could order a U.S. citizen who was arrested in this country for suspected terrorist ties to be held indefinitely without charges and without going to trial.[96]

The federal Speedy Trial Act is applicable only to federal courts. However, the *Klopfer* case effectively made constitutional guarantees of a speedy trial applicable to state courts. In keeping with the trend toward reduced delays, many states have since enacted their own speedy trial legislation. Most state legislation sets a limit of 90 or 120 days as a reasonable period of time for a trial to commence.

> In all criminal prosecutions, the accused shall enjoy the right to a speedy and public trial, by an impartial jury . . ., and to be informed of the nature and cause of the accusation; to be confronted with the witnesses against him; to have compulsory process for obtaining witnesses in his favor; and to have the Assistance of Counsel for his defence.
>
> —Sixth Amendment to the U.S. Constitution

Speedy Trial Act
A 1974 federal law requiring that proceedings against a defendant in a criminal case begin within a specified period of time, such as 70 working days after indictment. Some states also have speedy trial requirements.

Jury Selection

Challenges in Jury Selection

The Sixth Amendment guarantees the right to an impartial jury. An impartial jury is not necessarily an ignorant one. In other words, potential jurors will not always be excused from service on a jury if they have some knowledge of the case before them.[97] However, candidates who have already formed an opinion as to the guilt or innocence of the defendant are likely to be excused.

Some prospective jurors *try* to get excused, whereas others who would like to serve are excused because they are not judged to be suitable. Prosecution and defense attorneys use challenges to ensure the impartiality of the jury being impaneled. Three types of challenges are recognized in criminal courts: (1) challenges to the array, (2) challenges for cause, and (3) **peremptory challenges**.

Challenges to the array signify the belief, generally by the defense attorney, that the pool from which potential jurors are to be selected is not representative of the community or is biased in some significant way. A challenge to the array is argued before the hearing judge before jury selection begins.

During **jury selection**, both prosecution and defense attorneys question potential jurors in a process known as *voir dire* examination. Jurors are expected to be unbiased and free of preconceived notions of guilt or innocence. Challenges for cause, which may arise during *voir dire* examination, make the claim that an individual juror cannot be fair or impartial.

peremptory challenge
The right to challenge a potential juror without disclosing the reason for the challenge. Prosecutors and defense attorneys routinely use peremptory challenges to eliminate from juries individuals who, although they express no obvious bias, are thought to be capable of swaying the jury in an undesirable direction.

jury selection
The process whereby, according to law and precedent, members of a particular trial jury are chosen.

One special issue of juror objectivity has concerned the U.S. Supreme Court: whether jurors with philosophical opposition to the death penalty should be excluded from juries whose decisions might result in the imposition of capital punishment. In the case of *Witherspoon* v. *Illinois* (1968),[98] the Court ruled that a juror opposed to the death penalty could be excluded from such juries if it were shown that (1) the juror would automatically vote against conviction without regard to the evidence or (2) the juror's philosophical orientation would prevent an objective consideration of the evidence. The *Witherspoon* case left unresolved a number of issues, among them the concern that it is difficult to demonstrate how a juror would automatically vote, a fact that might not even be known to the juror before trial begins.

Another area of concern that the Supreme Court has addressed involves the possibility that jurors could be influenced by pretrial news stories. In 1991, for example, the Court decided the case of *Mu'Min* v. *Virginia*.[99] Dawud Majud Mu'Min was a Virginia inmate who was serving time for first-degree murder. While accompanying a work detail outside the prison, he committed another murder. At the ensuing trial, 8 of the 12 jurors who were seated admitted that they had heard or read something about the case, although none indicated that he or she had formed an opinion in advance as to Mu'Min's guilt or innocence. Following his conviction, Mu'Min appealed to the Supreme Court, claiming that his right to a fair trial had been denied due to pretrial publicity. The Court disagreed and upheld his conviction, citing the jurors' claims that they were not biased.

The third kind of challenge, the peremptory challenge, allows attorneys to remove potential jurors without having to give a reason. Peremptory challenges, used by both the prosecution and the defense, are limited in number: Federal courts allow each side up to 20 peremptory challenges in capital cases and as few as three in minor criminal cases.[100] States vary as to the number of peremptory challenges they permit.

A developing field that seeks to take advantage of peremptory challenges is **scientific jury selection**, which uses correlational techniques from the social sciences to gauge the likelihood that a potential juror will vote for conviction or acquittal. It makes predictions based on the economic, ethnic, and other personal and social characteristics of each member of the juror pool. Such techniques generally remove potential jurors who have any knowledge or opinions about the case to be tried. Also removed are people who have been trained in the law or in criminal justice. Anyone working for a criminal justice agency or anyone who has a family member working for such an agency or for a defense attorney will likely be dismissed through peremptory challenges on the chance that they may be biased in favor of one side or the other. Additionally, scientific jury selection techniques may result in the dismissal of highly educated or professionally successful individuals to eliminate the possibility of such individuals exercising undue control over jury deliberations.

Critics of the jury selection process charge that the end result is a jury composed of people who are uneducated, uninformed, and generally inexperienced at making any type of well-considered decision. Some jurors may not understand the charges against the defendant or comprehend what is required for a finding of guilt or innocence. Likewise, some may not even possess the attention span needed to hear all the testimony that will be offered in a case. As a consequence, critics say, decisions rendered by such a jury may be based more on emotion than on findings of fact.

Another emerging technique is the use of what is called a *shadow jury* to assess the impact of a defense attorney's arguments. Shadow jurors are hired court observers who sit in the courtroom and listen to what both sides in a criminal trial have to say. They hear evidence as it is presented and listen as witnesses are examined and cross-examined. Unlike professional legal experts, shadow jurors are laypeople who are expected to give defense attorneys a feel for what the "real" jurors are thinking and feeling as a case progresses, allowing for ongoing modifications in defense strategy.[101]

After the wrangling over jury selection has run its course, the jury is sworn in and alternate jurors are selected (alternates may be called to replace jurors taken ill or dismissed from the jury because they don't conform to the requirements of jury service once trial has begun). At this point, the judge will decide whether the jury is to be sequestered during the trial. Members of **sequestered juries** are not permitted to have contact with the public and are often housed in a motel or hotel until completion of the trial. Anyone who attempts to

scientific jury selection
The use of correlational techniques from the social sciences to gauge the likelihood that potential jurors will vote for conviction or for acquittal.

sequestered jury
A jury that is isolated from the public during the course of a trial and throughout the deliberation process.

contact a sequestered jury or to influence members of a nonsequestered jury may be held accountable for jury tampering. Following jury selection, the stage is set for opening arguments[102] to begin.

Jury Selection and Race

Race alone cannot provide the basis for jury selection, and juries may not be intentionally selected for racial imbalance. As long ago as 1880, the U.S. Supreme Court held that "a statute barring blacks from service on grand or petit juries denied equal protection of the laws to a black man convicted of murder by an all-white jury."[103] Even so, peremptory challenges continued to tend toward racial imbalance. In 1965, for example, a black defendant in Alabama was convicted of rape by an all-white jury (the local prosecutor had used his peremptory challenges to exclude blacks from the jury). The case eventually reached the Supreme Court, where the conviction was upheld.[104] At that time, the Court refused to limit the practice of peremptory challenges, reasoning that to do so would place them under the same judicial scrutiny as challenges for cause.

However, in the 1986 case of *Batson* v. *Kentucky*,[105] following what many claimed was widespread abuse of peremptory challenges by prosecution and defense alike, the Supreme Court was forced to overrule its earlier decision. Batson, an African-American man, had been convicted of second-degree burglary and other offenses by an all-white jury. The prosecutor had used his peremptory challenges to remove all African Americans from jury service at the trial. The Court agreed that the use of peremptory challenges for purposeful discrimination constitutes a violation of the defendant's right to an impartial jury.

The *Batson* decision laid out the requirements that defendants must prove when seeking to establish the discriminatory use of peremptory challenges. They include the need to prove that the defendant is a member of a recognized racial group that has been intentionally excluded from the jury and the need to raise a reasonable suspicion that the prosecutor used peremptory challenges in a discriminatory manner. Justice Thurgood Marshall, writing a concurring opinion in *Batson*, presaged what was to come: "The inherent potential of peremptory challenges to destroy the jury process," he wrote, "by permitting the exclusion of jurors on racial grounds should ideally lead the Court to ban them entirely from the criminal justice system."

A few years later, in *Ford* v. *Georgia* (1991),[106] the Court moved much closer to Justice Marshall's position when it remanded a case for a new trial because the prosecutor had misused peremptory challenges. The prosecutor had used nine of the ten peremptory challenges available under Georgia law to eliminate prospective black jurors. In *Ford*, the Court did not find that the right of the defendant to an impartial jury had been breached, but it did determine that the civil rights of the jurors themselves had been violated under the Fourteenth Amendment due to a pattern of discrimination based on race. In another 1991 case, *Powers* v. *Ohio*,[107] the Court found in favor of a white defendant who claimed that his constitutional rights had been violated by the intentional exclusion of blacks from his jury through the use of peremptory challenges.

In the 1992 case of *Georgia* v. *McCollum*,[108] the Court barred defendants and their attorneys from using peremptory challenges to exclude potential jurors on the basis of race. In *McCollum*, Justice Harry Blackmun, writing for the majority, said, "Be it at the hands of the state or defense, if a court allows jurors to be excluded because of group bias, it is a willing participant in a scheme that could only undermine the very foundation of our system of justice—our citizens' confidence in it."

Soon thereafter, peremptory challenges based on gender were similarly restricted (*J.E.B.* v. *Alabama*, 1994[109]), although at the time of this writing the Court has refused to ban peremptory challenges that exclude jurors because of religious or sexual orientation.[110] In the 1998 case of *Campbell* v. *Louisiana*,[111] the Court held that a white criminal defendant can raise equal protection and due-process objections to discrimination against blacks in the selection of grand jurors. The Supreme Court reasoned that "regardless of skin color, an accused suffers a significant 'injury in fact' when the grand jury's composition is tainted by racial discrimination." The Court also said, "The integrity of the body's decisions depends on the integrity of the process used to select the grand jurors."

> The jury is such a cornerstone of justice and the democratic process, [but] the jury process needs to be brought into the twenty-first century.
>
> —Robert Grey, president, American Bar Association[ii]

Finally, in the 2003 case of *Miller-El* v. *Cockrell*,[112] the Court found that a convicted capital defendant's constitutional rights had been violated by Dallas County (Texas) prosecutors who engaged in intentional efforts to remove eligible African Americans from the pool of potential jurors. Ten out of 11 eligible African Americans had been excluded through the use of peremptory strikes. The decision was reaffirmed in the 2005 U.S. Supreme Court case of *Miller-El* v. *Dretke*[113] and again in the 2008 case of *Snyder* v. *Louisiana*.[114] The Court's decision in *Snyder* v. *Louisiana*, which provides a good summary of its position on the use of peremptory strikes to eliminate black prospective jurors, is available at **http://tinyurl.com/3zgqtjf**.

Opening Statements

opening statement
The initial statement of the prosecution or the defense, made in a court of law to a judge, or to a judge and jury, describing the facts that he or she intends to present during trial to prove the case.

The presentation of information to the jury begins with **opening statements** made by the prosecution and the defense. The purposes of opening statements are to advise the jury of what the attorneys intend to prove and to describe how such proof will be offered. Evidence is not offered during opening statements. Eventually, however, the jury will have to weigh the evidence presented during the trial and decide which side made the more effective arguments. When a defendant has little evidence to present, the main job of the defense attorney will be to dispute the veracity of the prosecution's version of the facts. Under such circumstances, defense attorneys may choose not to present any evidence or testimony at all, focusing instead on the burden-of-proof requirement facing the prosecution. Such plans will generally be made clear during opening statements. At this time, the defense attorney is also likely to stress the human qualities of the defendant and to remind jurors of the awesome significance of their task.

Lawyers for both sides are bound by a good-faith ethical requirement in their opening statements. Attorneys may mention only the evidence that they believe actually can and will be presented as the trial progresses. Allusions to evidence that an attorney has no intention of offering are regarded as unprofessional and have been defined by the U.S. Supreme Court as "professional misconduct."[115] When material alluded to in an opening statement cannot, for whatever reason, later be presented in court, opposing counsel gains an opportunity to discredit the other side.

Presentation of Evidence

The crux of the criminal trial is the presentation of evidence. First, the state is given the opportunity to present evidence intended to prove the defendant's guilt. After prosecutors have rested their case, the defense is afforded the opportunity to provide evidence favorable to the defendant.

Types of Evidence

evidence
Anything useful to a judge or jury in deciding the facts of a case. Evidence may take the form of witness testimony, written documents, videotapes, magnetic media, photographs, physical objects, and so on.

direct evidence
The evidence that, if believed, directly proves a fact. Eyewitness testimony and videotaped documentation account for the majority of all direct evidence heard in the criminal courtroom.

circumstantial evidence
The evidence that requires interpretation or that requires a judge or jury to reach a conclusion based on what the evidence indicates. From the close proximity of the defendant to a smoking gun, for example, the jury might conclude that he or she pulled the trigger.

real evidence
Evidence that consists of physical material or traces of physical activity.

Evidence can be either direct or circumstantial. **Direct evidence**, if believed, proves a fact without requiring the judge or jury to draw inferences. For example, direct evidence may be the information contained in a photograph or videotape. It may be testimonial evidence provided by a witness on the stand. A straightforward statement by a witness—such as "I saw him do it!"—is a form of direct evidence.

Circumstantial evidence is indirect and requires the judge or jury to make inferences and to draw conclusions. At a murder trial, for example, a person who heard gunshots and moments later saw someone run by with a smoking gun in hand might testify to those facts. Even without an eyewitness to the actual homicide, the jury might later conclude that the person seen with the gun was the one who pulled the trigger and committed the crime. Contrary to popular belief, circumstantial evidence is sufficient to produce a verdict and conviction in a criminal trial. In fact, some prosecuting attorneys prefer to work entirely with circumstantial evidence, weaving a tapestry of the criminal act in their arguments to the jury.

Real evidence, which may be either direct or circumstantial, consists of physical material or traces of physical activity. Weapons, tire tracks, ransom notes, and fingerprints all fall into the category of real evidence. Real (or physical) evidence is introduced in the trial by means of *exhibits*, which are objects or displays that may be shown to members of the jury once they are formally accepted as evidence by the judge (see CJ Exhibit 8–1). Documentary evidence, which is one type of real evidence, includes writings such as business records, journals, written confessions, and letters. Documentary evidence can extend beyond paper and ink to include data on magnetic and optical storage devices used in computer operations and video and voice recordings.

Evaluation of Evidence

One of the most significant decisions a trial court judge makes is deciding which evidence can be presented to the jury. In making that decision, judges will examine the relevance of the evidence to the case at hand (relevant evidence has a bearing on the facts at issue). For example, a decade or two ago, it was not unusual for a woman's sexual history to be brought out in rape trials. Under what are called *rape shield statutes*, most states today will not allow this practice, recognizing that these details often have no bearing on the case. Rape shield statutes have been strengthened by U.S. Supreme Court decisions, including the 1991 case of *Michigan* v. *Lucas*.[116]

In evaluating evidence, judges must also weigh the **probative value** of an item of evidence (its usefulness and relevance) against its potential inflammatory or prejudicial qualities. Even useful evidence may unduly bias a jury if it is exceptionally gruesome or is presented in such a way as to imply guilt. For example, gory photographs, especially color photographs, may be withheld from the jury's eyes. In one recent case, a new trial was ordered when photos of the crime scene were projected on a wall over the head of the defendant as he sat in the courtroom, and an appellate court found that presentation to have prejudiced the jury.

Sometimes evidence is found to have only limited admissibility, which means that the evidence can be used for a specific purpose but that it might not be accurate in other details. Photographs, for example, may be admitted as evidence for the narrow purpose of showing spatial relationships between objects under discussion, even if the photographs were taken under conditions that did not exist when the offense was committed (such as daylight).

When judges allow the use of evidence that may have been illegally or unconstitutionally gathered, grounds may be created for a later appeal if the trial concludes with a "guilty" verdict. Even when evidence is improperly introduced at trial, however, numerous Supreme Court decisions[117] have held that there may be no grounds for an effective appeal unless such introduction "had substantial and injurious effect or influence in determining the jury's verdict."[118] Called the *harmless error rule*, this standard places the burden on the prosecution to show that the jury's decision would most likely have been the same even in the absence of the inappropriate evidence. The rule is not applicable when a defendant's constitutional guarantees are violated by "structural defects in the constitution of the trial mechanism" itself[119]—such as when a judge gives constitutionally improper instructions to a jury. (We'll discuss those instructions later in this chapter.)

probative value
The degree to which a particular item of evidence is useful in, and relevant to, proving something important in a trial.

Testimony of Witnesses

Testimony given by witnesses is generally the chief means by which evidence is introduced at trial. Witnesses may include victims, police officers, the defendant, specialists in recognized fields, and others with useful information to provide. Some of these witnesses may have been present during the commission of the offense, whereas most will have had only a later opportunity to investigate the situation or to analyze evidence.

Before a witness will be allowed to testify to any fact, the questioning attorney must establish the person's competence. Competence to testify requires that witnesses have personal knowledge of the information they will discuss and that they understand their duty to tell the truth.

One of the defense attorney's most critical decisions is whether to put the defendant on the stand. Defendants have a Fifth Amendment right to remain silent and to refuse to testify. In the precedent-setting case of *Griffin* v. *California* (1965),[120] the U.S. Supreme Court declared that if a defendant refuses to testify, prosecutors and judges are enjoined from even commenting on this fact, although a judge should instruct the jury that such a failure cannot be held to indicate guilt. In 2001, in the case of *Ohio* v. *Reiner*,[121] the U.S. Supreme Court extended Fifth Amendment protections to *witnesses* who deny any and all guilt in association with a crime for which another person is being prosecuted.

Direct examination of a witness takes place when a witness is first called to the stand. If the prosecutor calls the witness, the witness is referred to as a *witness for the prosecution*. When the direct examiner is a defense attorney, the witness is called a *witness for the defense*.

testimony
The oral evidence offered by a sworn witness on the witness stand during a criminal trial.

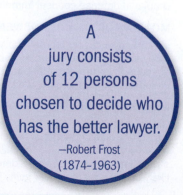

A jury consists of 12 persons chosen to decide who has the better lawyer.

—Robert Frost (1874–1963)

The direct examiner may ask questions that require a "yes" or "no" answer or may ask narrative questions that allow the witness to tell a story in his or her own words. During direct examination, courts generally prohibit the use of leading questions, that is, those that suggest answers to the witness.[122]

Cross-examination refers to the examination of a witness by someone other than the direct examiner. Anyone who offers testimony in a criminal court has the duty to submit to cross-examination.[123] The purpose of cross-examination is to test the credibility and the memory of the witness.

Most states and the federal government restrict the scope of cross-examination to material covered during direct examination. Questions about other matters, even though they may relate to the case before the court, are not allowed. A small number of states will allow the

---

CJ Exhibit 8–1
Pretrial and Post-Trial Motions

A *motion* is "an oral or written request made to a court at any time before, during, or after court proceedings, asking the court to make a specified finding, decision, or order."[a] Written motions are called *petitions*. This exhibit lists the most common motions made by both sides in a criminal case before and after trial.

MOTION FOR DISCOVERY

A motion for discovery, filed by the defense, asks the court to allow the defendant's lawyers to view the evidence that the prosecution intends to present at trial. Physical evidence, lists of witnesses, documents, photographs, and so on, which the prosecution plans to introduce in court, are usually made available to the defense as a result of a motion for discovery.

MOTION TO SUPPRESS EVIDENCE

The defense may file a motion to suppress evidence if it learns, in the preliminary hearing or through pretrial discovery, of evidence that it believes to have been unlawfully acquired.

MOTION TO DISMISS CHARGES

A variety of circumstances may result in the filing of a motion to dismiss charges. They include (1) an opinion, by defense counsel, that the indictment or information is not sound; (2) a violation of speedy trial legislation; (3) a plea bargain with the defendant, which may require testimony against codefendants; (4) the death of an important witness or the destruction or disappearance of necessary evidence; (5) the confession, by a supposed victim, that the facts in the case were fabricated; and (6) the success of a motion to suppress evidence that effectively eliminates the prosecution's case.

MOTION FOR CONTINUANCE

The motion for continuance seeks a delay in the start of the trial. Defense motions of this type are often based on an inability to locate important witnesses, the illness of the defendant, or a change in defense counsel immediately before trial.

MOTION FOR CHANGE OF VENUE

In well-known cases, pretrial publicity may lessen the opportunity for a case to be tried before an unbiased jury. A motion for change of venue asks that the trial be moved to some other area where prejudice against the defendant is less likely to exist.

MOTION FOR SEVERANCE OF OFFENSES

Defendants charged with a number of crimes may ask to be tried separately on all or some of the charges through use of a motion for severance of offenses. Although consolidating charges for trial saves time and money, some defendants believe that it is more likely to make them appear guilty.

MOTION FOR SEVERANCE OF DEFENDANTS

The motion for severance of defendants asks the court to try the accused separately from any codefendants. These motions are likely to be filed when the defendant believes that the jury may be prejudiced against him or her by evidence applicable only to other defendants.

MOTION TO DETERMINE PRESENT SANITY

A lack of "present sanity," even though it may be no defense against the criminal charge, can delay trial because a person cannot be tried, sentenced, or punished while insane. If a defendant is insane at the time a trial is to begin, a motion to determine present sanity may halt the proceedings until treatment can be arranged.

MOTION FOR A BILL OF PARTICULARS

The motion for a bill of particulars asks the court to order the prosecutor to provide detailed information about the charges that the defendant will be facing in court. Defendants charged with a number of offenses, or with a number of counts of the same offense, may make such a motion. They may, for example, seek to learn which alleged instances of an offense will become the basis for prosecution or which specific items of contraband allegedly found in their possession are held to violate the law.

MOTION FOR A MISTRIAL

A mistrial may be declared at any time, and a motion for a mistrial may be made by either side. Mistrials are likely to be declared in cases in which highly prejudicial comments are made by either attorney. Defense motions for a mistrial do not provide grounds for a later claim of double jeopardy.

MOTION FOR ARREST OF JUDGMENT

After the verdict of the jury has been announced but before the sentencing, the defendant may make a motion for arrest of judgment. With this motion, the defendant asserts that some legally acceptable reason exists as to why sentencing should not occur. Defendants who are seriously ill, who are hospitalized, or who have gone insane before judgment has been imposed may file such a motion.

MOTION FOR A NEW TRIAL

After a jury has returned a guilty verdict, the court may entertain a motion for a new trial from the defense. Acceptance of such a motion is usually based on the discovery of new evidence that is of significant benefit to the defense and that will set aside the conviction.

---

[a]U.S. Department of Justice, *Dictionary of Criminal Justice Data Terminology*, 2nd ed. (Washington, D.C.: U.S. Government Printing Office, 1982).

cross-examiner to raise any issue as long as the court deems it relevant. Leading questions, generally disallowed in direct examination, are regarded as the mainstay of cross-examination. Such questions allow for a concise restatement of testimony that has already been offered and serve to focus efficiently on potential problems that the cross-examiner seeks to address.

Some witnesses commit **perjury**—that is, they make statements that they know to be untrue. Reasons for perjured testimony vary, but most witnesses who lie on the stand probably do so in an effort to help friends accused of crimes. Witnesses who perjure themselves are subject to impeachment, in which either the defense or the prosecution demonstrates that a witness has intentionally offered false testimony. For example, previous statements made by the witness may be shown to be at odds with more recent declarations. When it can be demonstrated that a witness has offered inaccurate or false testimony, the witness has been effectively impeached. Perjury is a serious offense in its own right, and dishonest witnesses may face fines or jail time.

At the conclusion of the cross-examination, the direct examiner may again question the witness. This procedure is called *redirect examination* and may be followed by a recross-examination and so on, until both sides are satisfied that they have exhausted fruitful lines of questioning.

Children as Witnesses

An area of special concern involves the use of children as witnesses in a criminal trial, especially when the children are also victims. Currently, in an effort to avoid what may be traumatizing direct confrontations between child witnesses and the accused, 37 states allow the use of videotaped testimony in criminal courtrooms, and 32 permit the use of closed-circuit television, which allows the child to testify out of the presence of the defendant. In 1988, however, in the case of *Coy* v. *Iowa*,[124] the U.S. Supreme Court ruled that a courtroom screen, used to shield child witnesses from visual confrontation with a defendant in a child sex-abuse case, had violated the confrontation clause of the Constitution (found in the Sixth Amendment).

On the other hand, in the 1990 case of *Maryland* v. *Craig*,[125] the Court upheld the use of closed-circuit television to shield children who testify in criminal courts. The Court's decision was partially based on the realization that "a significant majority of States have enacted statutes to protect child witnesses from the trauma of giving testimony in child-abuse cases . . . [which] attests to the widespread belief in the importance of such a policy."

Although a face-to-face confrontation with a child victim may not be necessary in the courtroom, until 1992 the Supreme Court had been reluctant to allow into evidence descriptions of abuse and other statements made by children, even to child-care professionals, when those statements were made outside the courtroom. In *Idaho* v. *Wright* (1990),[126] the Court reasoned that such "statements [are] fraught with the dangers of unreliability which the Confrontation Clause is designed to highlight and obviate."

However, in *White* v. *Illinois* (1992),[127] the Court reversed its stance, ruling that in-court testimony given by a medical provider and the child's babysitter, which repeated what the child had said to them concerning White's sexually abusive behavior, was permissible.

The Hearsay Rule

Hearsay is anything not based on the personal knowledge of a witness. A witness may say, for example, "John told me that Fred did it!" Such a witness becomes a hearsay declarant, and following a likely objection by counsel, the trial judge will have to decide whether the witness's statement will be allowed to stand as evidence. In most cases, the judge will instruct the jury to disregard the witness's comment, thereby enforcing the **hearsay rule**, which prohibits the use of "secondhand evidence." The hearsay rule is based on the Sixth Amendment's confrontation clause, which gives a criminal defendant the right to confront his or her accusers. In today's courts, that generally means that the defendant has a right to cross-examine witnesses against him or her.

Exceptions to the hearsay rule have been established by both precedent and tradition. One exception is the dying declaration, which is a statement made by a person who is about to die. When heard by a second party, it may usually be repeated in court, provided that

🐦 Follow the author's tweets about the latest crime and justice news @schmalleger

perjury
The intentional making of a false statement as part of the testimony by a sworn witness in a judicial proceeding on a matter relevant to the case at hand.

hearsay
Something that is not based on the personal knowledge of a witness. Witnesses who testify about something they have heard, for example, are offering hearsay by repeating information about a matter of which they have no direct knowledge.

hearsay rule
The long-standing precedent that hearsay cannot be used in American courtrooms. Rather than accepting testimony based on hearsay, the court will ask that the person who was the original source of the hearsay information be brought in to be questioned and cross-examined. Exceptions to the hearsay rule may occur when the person with direct knowledge is dead or is otherwise unable to testify.

▲ An attorney making a closing argument to the jury. What other features of the adversarial system can you identify?
Fuse/Corbis/Getty Images

certain conditions have been met. A dying declaration is generally a valid exception to the hearsay rule when it is made by someone who knows that he or she is about to die and when the statement made relates to the cause and circumstances of the impending death.

Spontaneous statements, also called *excited utterances*, provide another exception to the hearsay rule. A statement is considered spontaneous when it is made in the heat of excitement before the person has had time to make it up. For example, a defendant who is just regaining consciousness following a crime may make an utterance that could later be repeated in court by those who heard it.

Out-of-court statements, especially if they were recorded during a time when a person was experiencing great excitement or while a person was under considerable stress, may also become exceptions to the hearsay rule. Many states, for example, permit juries to hear 9-1-1 tape recordings or to read police transcripts of victim interviews without requiring that the people who made them appear in court. In two cases, however, the U.S. Supreme Court barred admission of tape-recorded 9-1-1 calls when the people making them were alive and in good health but not available for cross-examination. In *Crawford* v. *Washington*,[128] a 2004 case, the Court disallowed a woman's tape-recorded eyewitness account of a fight in which her husband stabbed another man, holding that the Constitution bars admission of testimonial statements of a witness who did not appear at trial unless he or she was unable to testify and the defendant had a prior opportunity for cross-examination. In *Davis* v. *Washington*,[129] decided in 2006, the Court held that a 9-1-1 call made by a woman who said that her former boyfriend was beating her had been improperly introduced as testimonial evidence. The woman had been subpoenaed but failed to appear in court. The key word in both cases is *testimonial*, and the Court indicated that "statements are nontestimonial when made in the course of police interrogation under circumstances objectively indicating that the primary purpose of interrogation is to enable police assistance to meet an ongoing emergency."[130]

The use of other out-of-court statements, such as writings or routine video or audio recordings, usually requires the witness to testify that the statements or depictions were accurate at the time they were made. Witnesses who so testify may be subject to cross-examination by the defendant's attorney. Nonetheless, this "past recollection recorded" exception to the hearsay rule is especially useful in drawn-out court proceedings that occur long after the crime. Under such circumstances, witnesses may no longer remember the details of an event. Their earlier statements to authorities, however, can be introduced into evidence as past recollection recorded.

Closing Arguments

closing argument
An oral summation of a case presented to a judge, or to a judge and jury, by the prosecution or by the defense in a criminal trial.

At the conclusion of a criminal trial, both sides have the opportunity for a final narrative presentation to the jury in the form of a **closing argument**. This summation provides a review and analysis of the evidence. Its purpose is to persuade the jury to draw a conclusion favorable to the presenter. Testimony can be quoted, exhibits referred to, and attention drawn to inconsistencies in the evidence presented by the other side.

States vary as to the order of closing arguments. Nearly all allow the defense attorney to speak to the jury before the prosecution makes its final points. A few permit the prosecutor the first opportunity for summation. Some jurisdictions and the Federal Rules of Criminal

Procedure[131] authorize a defense rebuttal (a rebuttal is a response to the closing argument of the other side).

Some specific issues may need to be addressed during summation. If, for example, the defendant has not taken the stand during the trial, the defense attorney's closing argument will inevitably stress that this failure to testify cannot be regarded as indicating guilt. Where the prosecution's case rests entirely on circumstantial evidence, the defense can be expected to stress the lack of any direct proof, and the prosecutor is likely to argue that circumstantial evidence can be stronger than direct evidence, as it is not as easily affected by human error or false testimony.

Judge's Charge to the Jury

After closing arguments, the judge charges the jury to "retire and select one of your number as a foreman . . . and deliberate upon the evidence which has been presented until you have reached a verdict." The words of the charge vary somewhat between jurisdictions and among judges, but all judges will remind members of the jury of their duty to consider objectively only the evidence that has been presented and of the need for impartiality. Most judges also remind jury members of the statutory elements of the alleged offense, of the burden of proof that rests on the prosecution, and of the need for the prosecution to have proved the defendant's guilt beyond a **reasonable doubt** before the jury can return a guilty verdict. The **reasonable doubt standard** is the single most important criterion for determining the level of proof necessary for conviction in criminal trials. If the prosecutor fails to prove a defendant's guilt beyond a reasonable doubt, then the jury must return a not-guilty verdict.

In their charge, many judges also provide a summary of the evidence presented, usually from notes they have taken during the trial, as a means of refreshing the jurors' memories of events. About half of all the states allow judges the freedom to express their own views as to the credibility of witnesses and the significance of evidence. The other states only permit judges to summarize the evidence in an objective and impartial manner.

Recently, as the CJ News box in this section shows, the plethora of digital communications devices now available has made it difficult for courts to control jurors' access to out-of-court information. Read a set of jury instructions designed to alleviate this problem at **https://www.justicestudies.com/pubs/electronic_instructions.pdf**.

Following the charge, the jury is removed from the courtroom and is permitted to begin its deliberations. In the absence of the jury, defense attorneys may choose to challenge portions of the judge's charge. If they feel that some oversight has occurred in the original charge, they may ask the judge to provide the jury with additional instructions or information. Such objections, if denied by the judge, often become the basis for an appeal when a conviction is returned.

Jury Deliberations and the Verdict

Deliberations Process

In cases in which the evidence is either very clear or very weak, jury deliberations may be brief, lasting only a matter of hours or even minutes. Some juries, however, deliberate for days or sometimes weeks, carefully weighing all the nuances of the evidence they have seen and heard. Many jurisdictions require that juries reach a unanimous **verdict** (decision), although the U.S. Supreme Court has ruled that unanimous verdicts are not required in noncapital cases.[132] Even so, some juries are unable to agree on any verdict. When a jury is deadlocked, it is said to be a *hung jury*. When a unanimous decision is required, juries may be deadlocked by the strong opposition of only one member to a verdict agreed on by all the others.

In some states, judges are allowed to add a boost to nearly hung juries by recharging them under a set of instructions that the Supreme Court put forth in the 1896 case of *Allen v. U.S.*[133] The *Allen* charge, as it is known in those jurisdictions, urges the jury to vigorous deliberations and suggests to obstinate jurors that their objections may be ill-founded if they make no impression on the other jurors.

reasonable doubt
In legal proceedings, an actual and substantial doubt arising from the evidence, from the facts or circumstances shown by the evidence, or from the lack of evidence.[iii] Also, the state of a case such that, after the comparison and consideration of all the evidence, jurors cannot say they feel an abiding conviction of the truth of the charge.[iv]

reasonable doubt standard
The standard of proof necessary for conviction in criminal trials.

verdict
The decision of the jury in a jury trial or of a judicial officer in a nonjury trial.

Problems with the Jury System

Judge Harold J. Rothwax, a well-known critic of today's jury system, tells the tale of a rather startling case over which he presided in 1991. The case involved a murder defendant, a handsome young man who had been fired by a New York company that serviced automated teller machines (ATMs). After being fired, the defendant intentionally caused a machine in a remote area to malfunction. When two former colleagues arrived to fix it, he robbed them, stole the money inside the ATM, and shot both men repeatedly. One of the men survived long enough to identify his former coworker as the shooter. The man

---

CJ News
Social Media Pose New Threats during Criminal Trials

Growing use of the Internet and social media has made it much easier for jurors to violate age-old prohibitions against conversing with outsiders about a case, conducting outside research, and contacting plaintiffs or defendants.

The rise of Facebook, Twitter, and Wikipedia, combined with widespread use of smart phones, seems to have blurred the traditional line between jurors and the outside world. "This is a generational change, and I don't know if the legal system is ready for it," said Thaddeus Hoffmeister, a professor at the University of Dayton Law School, who specializes in jury issues.

Violations that once took some effort, such as going to a library to look up a term or just making a phone call to a friend, now can be done with a few keystrokes. Research suggests very few violators are caught. But when they are, the courts take the matter very seriously. They may throw out the verdict, cite jurors for contempt, and even jail them.

A recent study by Reuters Legal found that Internet-related juror misconduct had led to 21 overturned verdicts or new trials since January 2009. Because violations can occur away from the courthouse and jurors' online use is rarely monitored, courts have identified very few violators. A national survey of federal judges by the Federal Judicial Center, released in November 2011, found that just 6% were aware of social media used during deliberations, but 79% admitted they would have no way of knowing about violations.

Jurors' use of Facebook can be easy to spot. In a few high-profile cases, jurors have improperly "friended" plaintiffs, defendants, and even each other in the period before jurors can get together to deliberate. One juror who friended the plaintiff in an auto accident case was sentenced to 3 days in jail.

In a Twitter violation in Arkansas, a murder conviction was thrown out on appeal because the juror tweeted after being asked to stop, and one of his tweets revealed the verdict before it was announced. The court ordered a new trial, but it did not punish the juror.

Although jurors have never been allowed to conduct outside research, Internet-based research is so second-nature that it may not occur to jurors they are violating the rules. In 2014, a Florida juror, who happened to be a criminology student at a local college, was found in contempt of court and jailed after Web research he conducted revealed that he and fellow jurors were participating in a retrial that had been ordered after an earlier jury had been unable to decide on a verdict. In jailing the juror, the judge noted that implicit instructions had been given not to research the case on social media.

To prevent violations, experts say jury instructions should specify each kind of prohibited Internet use, explain the reasoning behind the ban, and show how the legal process could be damaged. For example, even when nothing is revealed on a juror's blog or a posting on Facebook, just reading the comments to the posts might improperly influence them.

Experts also recommend that candidates in the jury selection process be asked about their own online activities and

▲ A young man uses an iPad. Digital devices are commonplace today. How might jurors' unauthorized use of modern technology influence their deliberations?

Dandaman/Fotolia

whether they'd be comfortable stopping them for the duration of the trial. Some potential jurors who said they could not stop have withdrawn voluntarily. It has also been proposed that the courts ask jurors to name frequently used sites and to provide the passwords for them, so that they can be monitored during the trial.

In 2012, the federal Judicial Conference's Committee on Court Administration and Case Management (CACM) admonished federal judges to repeatedly warn jurors not to discuss cases that they are deliberating on social media or the Internet. The Committee's proposed model jury instructions can be accessed at **https://www.justicestudies.com/modelinst.pdf.**

REFERENCES

"Jurors' Use of Social Media during Trials Leading to Mistrials," Martindale-Hubble, March 22, 2012, http://blog.martindale.com/jurors-use-of-social-media-during-trials-leading-to-mistrials.

"Jurors' Use of Social Media during Trials and Deliberations," Federal Judicial Center, November 22, 2011, http://www.fjc.gov/public/pdf.nsf/lookup/dunnjuror.pdf/$file/dunnjuror.pdf.

"Friend or Foe? Social Media, the Jury and You," *The Jury Expert,* September 26, 2011, http://www.thejuryexpert.com/2011/09/friend-or-foe-social-media-the-jury-and-you/.

Terri Parker, "Jailed Goodman Juror Apologizes, Pleads Not Guilty to Contempt," WPBF TV, October 10, 2014, http://www.wpbf.com/news/jailed-goodman-juror-apologizes-pleads-not-guilty-to-contempt/29049970.

was arrested, and a trial ensued. After 3 weeks of hearing the case, the jury deadlocked. Judge Rothwax later learned that the jury had voted 11 to 1 to convict the defendant, but the one holdout just couldn't believe that "someone so good-looking could . . . commit such a crime."[134]

Many routine cases as well as some highly publicized cases—such as the murder trial of O. J. Simpson, which the whole world watched—have called into question the ability of the American jury system to do its job—that is, to sort through the evidence and to accurately determine the defendant's guilt or innocence. In a televised 1995 trial, Simpson was acquitted of the charge that he murdered his ex-wife, Nicole Brown, and her friend Ronald Goldman outside Brown's home in 1994. Many people believed that strong evidence tied Simpson to the crimes, and the criminal trial left many people feeling unsatisfied with the criminal justice system and with the criminal trial process. Later, a civil jury ordered Simpson to pay $33.5 million to the Goldman family and to Nicole Brown's estate.

Because jurors are drawn from all walks of life, many cannot be expected to understand modern legal complexities and to appreciate all the nuances of trial court practice. It is likely that even the best-intentioned jurors cannot understand and rarely observe some jury instructions.[135] In highly charged cases, emotions are often difficult to separate from fact,

Follow the author's tweets about the latest crime and justice news @schmalleger

Multiculturalism and Diversity
The Bilingual Courtroom

One of the central multicultural issues facing the criminal justice system today is the need for clear communication with recent immigrants and subcultural groups that have not been fully acculturated. Many such groups hold to traditions and values that differ from those held by the majority of Americans. Such differences influence the interpretation of things seen and heard. Even more basic, however, are language differences that might prevent effective communication with criminal justice system personnel.

Techniques that law enforcement officers can use in overcoming language differences were discussed in Chapter 6. This box focuses on the use of courtroom interpreters to facilitate effective and accurate communication. The role of the courtroom interpreter is to present neutral verbatim, or word-for-word, translations. Interpreters must provide true, accurate, and complete interpretations of the exact statements made by non-English-speaking defendants, victims, and witnesses—whether on the stand, in writing, or in court-related conferences. The Court Interpreters and Translators Association also requires, through its code of professional ethics, that translators remember their "absolute responsibility to keep all oral and written information gained completely confidential."

Although most court interpreters are actually present in the courtroom at the time of trial, telephone interpreting provides an alternative way for courts to reduce problems associated with the lack of access to qualified interpreters. Today, state court administrative offices in Florida, Idaho, New Jersey, and Washington State sponsor programs through which qualified interpreters in metropolitan counties are made available to courts in rural counties by telephone.

The federal Court Interpreters Act of 1978[a] specifically provides for the use of interpreters in federal courts if needed by a witness or defendant who speaks "only or primarily a language other than English" or suffers from a substantial hearing impairment. It applies to both criminal and civil trials and hearings. The act does not require that an interpreter be appointed when a person has a speech impairment that is not accompanied by a hearing impairment. A court is not prohibited, however, from providing assistance to that person if it will aid in the efficient administration of justice.

Because it is a federal law, the Court Interpreters Act does not apply to state courts. Nonetheless, most states have enacted similar legislation. A few states are starting to introduce high-standard testing for court interpreters, although most states currently conduct little or no interpreter screening. The federal government and states with high standards for court interpreters generally require interpreter certification. To become certified, an interpreter must pass an oral examination, such as the federal court interpreter's examination or an examination administered by a state court or by a recognized international agency such as the United Nations.

There is growing recognition among professional court interpreters of the need for standardized interstate testing and certification programs. To meet that need, the National Center for State Courts created the Consortium for State Court Interpreter Certification. The consortium works to pool state resources for developing and administering court interpreter testing and training programs. The consortium's founding states were Minnesota, New Jersey, Oregon, and Washington, although many other states have since joined.

Because certified interpreters are not always available, even by telephone, most states have created a special category of "language-skilled interpreters." To qualify as a language-skilled interpreter, a person must demonstrate to the court's satisfaction his or her ability to interpret court proceedings from English to a designated language and from that language to English. Many states require sign language interpreters to hold a Legal Specialist Certificate, or its equivalent, from the Registry of Interpreters for the Deaf, showing that they are certified in American Sign Language. Learn more about language interpretation in the courts from the National Association of Judiciary Interpreters and Translators via **http://www.najit.org**.

[a]28 U.S.C. Section 1827.

References: National Association of Judiciary Interpreters and Translators website, http://www.najit.org; Madelynn Herman and Anne Endress Skove, "State Court Rules for Language Interpreters," memorandum number IS 99.1242, National Center for State Courts, Knowledge Management Office, September 8, 1999; Madelynn Herman and Dot Bryant, "Language Interpreting in the Courts," National Center for State Courts, http://www.ncsc.dni.us/KMO/Projects/Trends/99-00/articles/CtInterpreters.htm; and National Crime Prevention Council, *Building and Crossing Bridges: Refugees and Law Enforcement Working Together* (Washington, D.C.: NCPC, 1994).

Follow the author's tweets about the latest crime and justice news @schmalleger

and during deliberations, some juries are dominated by one or two members with forceful personalities. Jurors may also suffer from inattention or may be unable to understand fully the testimony of expert witnesses or the significance of technical evidence.

Jurors may be less than effective in cases where they fear personal retaliation. In the state-level trial of the police officers accused in the infamous Rodney King beating, for example, jurors reported being afraid for their lives due to the riots in Los Angeles that broke out after their "not-guilty" verdict was announced. Some slept with weapons by their side, and others sent their children away to safe locations.[136] Because of the potential for harm that jurors faced in the 1993 federal trial of the same officers, U.S. District Judge John G. Davies ruled that the names of the jurors be forever kept secret. Members of the press called the secrecy order "an unprecedented infringement of the public's right of access to the justice system."[137] Similarly, in the 1993 trial of three black men charged with the beating of white truck driver Reginald Denny during the Los Angeles riots, the judge ordered that the identities of the jurors not be released.

Opponents of the jury system have argued that it should be replaced by a panel of judges who would both render a verdict and impose sentence. Regardless of how well considered such a suggestion may be, such a change could not occur without modification of the Constitution's Sixth Amendment right to trial by jury.

An alternative suggestion for improving the process of trial by jury has been the call for professional jurors. Professional jurors would be paid by the government—like judges, prosecutors, and public defenders—and would be expected to have the expertise to sit on any jury. Professional jurors would be trained to listen objectively and would be taught the kinds of decision-making skills necessary to function effectively within an adversarial context. They would hear one case after another, perhaps moving between jurisdictions in cases of highly publicized crimes.

> In Suits at common law . . . the right of trial by jury shall be preserved, and no fact tried by a jury, shall be otherwise re-examined in any Court of the United States, than according to the rules of the common law.
>
> —Seventh Amendment to the U.S. Constitution

Summary

THE COURTROOM WORK GROUP AND THE CRIMINAL TRIAL

- The courtroom work group comprises professional courtroom personnel, including the judge, the prosecuting attorney, the defense counsel, the bailiff, the trial court administrator, the court reporter, the clerk of court, and expert witnesses. The courtroom work group is guided by statutory requirements and ethical considerations, and its members are generally dedicated to bringing the criminal trial and other courtroom procedures to a successful close.

- Also present in the courtroom during a criminal trial are "outsiders"—nonprofessional courtroom participants such as lay witnesses, jurors, the victim, the defendant, and spectators and members of the press. Nonprofessional or nonjudicial courtroom personnel may be unwilling or inadvertent participants in a criminal trial.

- The criminal trial involves an adversarial process that pits the prosecution against the defense. Trials are peer-based fact-finding processes intended to protect the rights of the accused while disputed issues of guilt or innocence are resolved. The primary purpose of a criminal trial is to determine whether the defendant violated the criminal law of the jurisdiction in which the court has authority.

- A criminal trial has eight stages: trial initiation, jury selection, opening statements, presentation of evidence, closing arguments, judge's charge to the jury, jury deliberations, and verdict. Each is described in detail in this chapter. At least a few experts have suggested the training and use of a cadre of professional jurors, versed in the law and in trial practice, who could insulate themselves from media portrayals of famous defendants and who would resolve questions of guilt or innocence more on the basis of reason than emotion.

QUESTIONS FOR REVIEW

1. Who are the professional members of the courtroom work group, and what are their roles?
2. Who are the nonprofessional courtroom participants, and what are their roles?
3. What is the purpose of a criminal trial? What is the difference between factual guilt and legal guilt? What do we mean by the term *adversarial system*?
4. What are the various stages of a criminal trial? Describe each one.

Sentencing

> Excessive bail shall not be required, nor excessive fines imposed, nor cruel and unusual punishments inflicted.
>
> —Eighth Amendment to the U.S. Constitution

Learning Objectives

After reading this chapter, you should be able to:

Rubberball/Brand X Pictures/Getty Images

Introduction

On January 1, 2018, New Jersey's racial impact law went into effect.[1] Other states with similar laws are Connecticut, Oregon, Illinois, and Iowa. Racial impact laws require policymakers to conduct racial impact studies and to prepare racial impact statements for any proposed policy changes affecting criminal **sentencing**, probation, or parole. In 2013, however, North Carolina, which had been one of the first states to require racial impact studies, repealed its Racial Justice Act, noting that an unintended consequence of the legislation had been to effectively block executions in the state.[2]

Marc Mauer, head of the Washington, D.C.-based Sentencing Project, says, "The premise behind racial impact statements is that policies often have unintended consequences that would be best addressed prior to adoption of new initiatives."[3] One example Mauer gives is that of enhanced criminal penalties associated with drug sales near school grounds—a law more likely to be violated by minorities, he says, because they tend to live closer to schools. Studies of the racial impact of sentencing practices force us to examine twin problems in the justice system: (1) the need for policies and practices that can work effectively to promote public safety, and (2) the need to reduce disproportionate rates of minority incarceration when feasible. "These are not competing goals," says Mauer. "If we are successful in addressing crime in a proactive way, we will be able to reduce high imprisonment rates; conversely, by promoting racial justice we will increase confidence in the criminal justice system and thereby aid public-safety efforts."

Under an organized system of criminal justice, sentencing is the imposition of a penalty on a person convicted of a crime. Sentencing follows what is intended to be an impartial judicial proceeding during which criminal responsibility is ascertained. Most sentencing decisions are made by judges, although in some cases, especially where a death sentence is possible, juries may be involved in a special sentencing phase of courtroom proceedings. The sentencing decision is one of the most difficult made by any judge or jury. Not only does it affect the future of the defendant—and at times it is a decision about his or her life or death—but society looks to sentencing to achieve a diversity of goals, some of which are not fully compatible with others.

This chapter examines sentencing in terms of both philosophy and practice. We will describe the goals of sentencing as well as the historical development of various sentencing models in the United States. Consequences of various sentencing philosophies will be explained. This chapter also contains a detailed overview of victimization and victims' rights in general, especially as they relate to courtroom procedure and to sentencing practice. Federal sentencing guidelines and the significance of presentence investigations are also described. For an overview of sentencing issues, visit the Sentencing Project via **http://www.sentencingproject.org**.

sentencing
The imposition of a criminal sanction by a judicial authority.

Sentencing is the imposition of a penalty on a person convicted of a crime.

Follow the author's tweets about the latest crime and justice news @schmalleger

The Philosophy and Goals of Criminal Sentencing

Traditional sentencing options have included imprisonment, fines, probation, and (for very serious offenses) death. Limits on the range of options available to sentencing authorities are generally specified by law. Historically, those limits have shifted as the understanding of crime and the goals of sentencing have changed. Sentencing philosophies, or the justifications on which various sentencing strategies are based, are manifestly intertwined with issues of religion, morals, values, and emotions.[4] Philosophies that gained ascendancy at a particular point in history usually reflected more deeply held social values. Centuries ago, for example, it was thought that crime was due to sin and that suffering was the culprit's lot, and judges were expected to be harsh. Capital punishment, torture, and painful physical penalties served this view of criminal behavior.

An emphasis on equitable punishments became prevalent around the time of the American and French Revolutions, brought about (in part) by Enlightenment philosophies. Offenders came to be seen as highly rational beings who intentionally and somewhat carefully chose their course of action. Sentencing philosophies of the period stressed the need

1 Describe the five goals of contemporary criminal sentencing.

TABLE 9-1
Sentencing Goals and Purposes

Sentencing Goal	Purpose
Retribution	A just deserts perspective that emphasizes taking revenge on a criminal perpetrator or group of offenders
Incapacitation	The use of imprisonment or other means to reduce the likelihood that a particular offender will commit more crime
Deterrence	A sentencing rationale that seeks to inhibit criminal behavior through punishment or the fear of punishment
• General deterrence	Seeks to prevent future crimes like the one for which the sentence is being imposed
• Specific deterrence	Seeks to prevent a particular offender from engaging in repeat criminality
Rehabilitation	The attempt to reform a criminal offender
Restoration	A goal of sentencing that seeks to make the victim "whole again"

retribution

The act of taking revenge on a criminal perpetrator.

▲ A courtroom drawing showing Rosemary Dillard, whose husband was killed on September 11, 2001, speaking to Zacarias Moussaoui as family members of 9/11 victims listen during the sentencing hearing for the convicted al-Qaeda conspirator. In May 2006, Moussaoui was sentenced to life in prison with no possibility of release. Which of the sentencing goals discussed in this chapter likely played a role in the judge's sentencing decision?

Dana Verkouteren/AP Images

just deserts

A model of criminal sentencing that holds that criminal offenders deserve the punishment they receive at the hands of the law and that punishments should be appropriate to the type and severity of the crime committed.

for sanctions that outweighed the benefits to be derived from criminal activity. The severity of punishment became less important than quick and certain penalties.

Recent thinking has emphasized the need to limit offenders' potential for future harm by separating them from society. We also still believe that offenders deserve to be punished, and we have not entirely abandoned hope for their rehabilitation. Modern sentencing practices are influenced by five goals, which weave their way through widely disseminated professional and legal models, continued public calls for sentencing reform, and everyday sentencing practices. Each goal represents a quasi-independent sentencing philosophy, as each makes distinctive assumptions about human nature and holds implications for sentencing practice. The five general goals of contemporary sentencing are shown in Table 9-1.

Retribution

Retribution, the earliest-known rationale for punishment, is a call for punishment based on a perceived need for vengeance. Most early societies punished all offenders who were caught. Early punishments were immediate—often without the benefit of a hearing—and they were often extreme, with little thought given to whether the punishment fit the crime. Exile and death, for example, were commonly imposed, even for relatively minor offenses. The Old Testament dictum of "an eye for an eye, a tooth for a tooth"—often cited as an ancient justification for retribution—was actually intended to reduce the severity of punishment for relatively minor crimes.

Today, retribution corresponds to the model of sentencing called **just deserts**, which holds that offenders are responsible for their crimes. When they are convicted and punished, they are said to have gotten their "just deserts." Retribution sees punishment as deserved, justified, and even required by the offender's behavior.[5] The primary sentencing tool of the just deserts model is imprisonment, but in extreme cases capital punishment (i.e., death) becomes the ultimate retribution. Both in the public's view and in political policymaking, retribution is still a primary goal of criminal sentencing.

Incapacitation

Incapacitation, the second goal of criminal sentencing, seeks to protect innocent members of society from offenders who might harm them if not prevented from doing so. In ancient times, mutilation and amputation of the extremities were sometimes used to prevent offenders from repeating their crimes. Modern incapacitation strategies separate offenders from the community to reduce opportunities for further criminality. Incapacitation, sometimes called the "*lock 'em up*" *approach*, forms the basis for the modern movement toward prison "warehousing." Unlike retribution, incapacitation requires only restraint, not punishment.

Deterrence

Deterrence uses the example or threat of punishment to convince people that criminal activity is not worthwhile; its overall goal is crime prevention. **Specific deterrence** seeks to reduce the likelihood of **recidivism** (repeat offenses) by convicted offenders, whereas **general deterrence** strives to influence the future behavior of people who have not yet been arrested and who may be tempted to turn to crime. Deterrence is one of the more rational goals of sentencing because it is an easily articulated goal and because it is possible to investigate objectively the amount of punishment required to deter.

Deterrence is compatible with the goal of incapacitation, as at least specific deterrence can be achieved through incapacitating offenders. Tufts University Professor Hugo Adam Bedau, however, points to significant differences between retribution and deterrence.[6] Retribution is oriented toward the past, says Bedau. It seeks to redress wrongs already committed. Deterrence, in contrast, is a strategy for the future and aims to prevent new crimes.

> The ultimate goal of rehabilitation is a reduction in the number of criminal offenses.

Rehabilitation

Rehabilitation seeks to bring about fundamental changes in offenders and their behavior. As in the case of deterrence, the ultimate goal of rehabilitation is a reduction in the number of criminal offenses. Whereas deterrence depends on a fear of the consequences of violating the law, rehabilitation generally works through education and psychological treatment to reduce the likelihood of future criminality.

The term *rehabilitation*, however, is a misnomer for the kinds of changes that its supporters seek. Rehabilitation literally means to return a person to his or her previous condition. However, it is likely that in most cases restoring criminals to their previous state will result in nothing but a more youthful type of criminality.

In the late 1970s, the rehabilitative goal in sentencing fell victim to the nothing-works doctrine, which was based on studies of **recidivism rates** that consistently showed that rehabilitation was more an ideal than a reality.[7] With as many as 90% of former convicted offenders returning to lives of crime following release from prison-based treatment programs, public sentiments in favor of incapacitation grew. Although the rehabilitation ideal has clearly suffered in the public arena, emerging evidence has begun to suggest that effective treatment programs do exist and may be growing in number.[8]

Restoration

Victims of crime and their families are frequently traumatized by their experiences. Some victims are killed, and others receive lasting physical or emotional injuries. For many, the world is never the same. The victimized may live in constant fear, be reduced in personal vigor, and be unable to form trusting relationships. **Restoration** is a sentencing goal that seeks to address this damage by making the victim and the community "whole again."

incapacitation
The use of imprisonment or other means to reduce the likelihood that an offender will commit future offenses.

deterrence
A goal of criminal sentencing that seeks to inhibit criminal behavior through the fear of punishment.

specific deterrence
A goal of criminal sentencing that seeks to prevent a particular offender from engaging in repeat criminality.

recidivism
The act of relapsing into a problem or criminal behavior during or after receiving sanctions, or while undergoing an intervention due to a previous behavior or crime. In criminal justice settings, recidivism is often measured by criminal acts that result in rearrest, reconviction, or return to prison.

▼ Female inmates being trained to work with fiber optics at the Federal Correctional Institution in Danbury, Connecticut. Skills acquired through such prison programs might translate into productive, noncriminal careers for ex-convicts. Rehabilitation is an important, but infrequently voiced, goal of modern sentencing practices. What are some other sentencing goals identified in this chapter?
Drew Crawford/The Image Works

general deterrence
A goal of criminal sentencing that seeks to prevent others from committing crimes similar to the one for which a particular offender is being sentenced by making an example of the person sentenced.

A U.S. Department of Justice report explains restoration this way:

> Crime was once defined as a "violation of the State." This remains the case today, but we now recognize that crime is far more. It is—among other things—a violation of one person by another. While retributive justice may address the first type of violation adequately, restorative justice is required to effectively address the latter. . . . Thus [through restorative justice] we seek to attain a balance between the legitimate needs of the community, the . . . offender, and the victim.[9]

The "healing" of all parties has many aspects, ranging from victims' assistance initiatives to legislation supporting victims' compensation.

Restorative justice (RJ) is also referred to as *balanced and restorative justice.* Conceptually, balance is achieved by giving equal consideration to community safety and offender accountability. RJ focuses on "crime as harm, and justice as repairing the harm."[10] The community safety dimension of the RJ philosophy recognizes that the justice system has a responsibility to protect the public from crime and from offenders.[11] It also recognizes that the community can participate in ensuring its own safety. The accountability element defines criminal conduct in terms of obligations incurred by the offender, both to the victim and to the community.[12] RJ also has what some describe as a competency development element, which holds that offenders who enter the justice system should leave it more capable of participating successfully in the wider society than when they entered. In essence, RJ is community focused; its primary goal is improving the quality of life for all members of the community. See Table 9-2 for a comparison of retributive justice and restorative justice.

rehabilitation
The attempt to reform a criminal offender. Also, the state in which a reformed offender is said to be.

recidivism rate
A measure of the rate of reoffending (usually defined by arrest) for a given population of released prisoners, or for a group of criminally sanctioned offenders, over time. Rates of recidivism are generally calculated over a 3- or a 5-year time period.

Sentencing options that seek to restore the victim have focused primarily on restitution payments that offenders are ordered to make, either to their victims or to a general fund, which may then go to reimburse victims for lost wages, medical costs, and other out-of-pocket expenses. In support of these goals, the 1984 Federal Comprehensive Crime Control Act specifically states: "If sentenced to probation, the defendant must also be ordered to pay a fine, make restitution, and/or work in community service."[13]

Some advocates of the restoration philosophy of sentencing point out that restitution payments and work programs that benefit the victim can also have the added benefit of rehabilitating the offender. The hope is that such sentences will teach offenders personal responsibility through structured financial obligations, job requirements, and regularly scheduled payments. Learn more about RJ at **https://www.nij.gov/topics/courts/restorative-justice/pages/fundamental-concepts.aspx**.

restoration
A goal of criminal sentencing that attempts to make the victim "whole again."

TABLE 9-2
Differences between Retributive and Restorative Justice

Retributive Justice	Restorative Justice
Crime is an act against the state, a violation of a law, an abstract idea.	Crime is an act against another person or the community.
The criminal justice system controls crime. Offender accountability is defined as taking punishment.	Crime control lies primarily with the community. Offender accountability is defined as assuming responsibility and taking action to repair harm.
Crime is an individual act with individual responsibility.	Crime has both individual and social dimensions of responsibility.
Victims are peripheral to the process of resolving a crime.	Victims are central to the process of resolving a crime.
The offender is defined by deficits.	The offender is defined by the capacity to make reparation.
The emphasis is on adversarial relationships.	The emphasis is on dialogue and negotiation.
Pain is imposed to punish, deter, and prevent.	Restitution is a means of restoring both parties; the goal is reconciliation.
The community is on the sidelines, represented abstractly by the state.	The community is the facilitator in the restorative process.
The response is focused on the offender's past behavior.	The response is focused on harmful consequences of the offender's behavior; the emphasis is on the future and on reparation.
There is dependence on proxy professionals.	There is direct involvement by both the offender and the victim.

Source: From Gordon Bazemore and Mark S. Umbreit, *Balanced and Restorative Justice: Program Summary* (Washington, D.C.: Office of Juvenile Justice and Delinquency Prevention, 1994), p. 7.

Indeterminate Sentencing

2 Define *indeterminate sentencing*, including its purpose.

Although the *philosophy* of criminal sentencing is reflected in the goals of sentencing we have just discussed, different sentencing *practices* have been linked to each goal. During most of the twentieth century, for example, the rehabilitation goal was influential. Because rehabilitation requires that individual offenders' personal characteristics be closely considered in defining effective treatment strategies, judges were generally permitted wide discretion in choosing from among sentencing options. Many state criminal codes still allow judges to impose fines, probation, or widely varying prison terms, all for the same offense. These sentencing practices, characterized primarily by vast judicial choice, constitute a model of **indeterminate sentencing**.

Explanation of Indeterminate Sentencing

Indeterminate sentencing has both an historical and a philosophical basis in the belief that convicted offenders are more likely to participate in their own rehabilitation if participation will reduce the amount of time they have to spend in prison. Inmates exhibiting good behavior will be released early, whereas recalcitrant inmates will remain in prison until the end of their terms. For that reason, parole generally plays a significant role in states that employ the indeterminate sentencing model.

Indeterminate sentencing relies heavily on judges' discretion to choose among types of sanctions and to set upper and lower limits on the length of prison stays. Indeterminate sentences are typically imposed with wording like this: "The defendant shall serve not less than 5 and not more than 25 years in the state's prison, under the supervision of the state department of correction." Judicial discretion under the indeterminate model also extends to the imposition of concurrent or consecutive sentences when the offender is convicted on more than one charge. **Consecutive sentences** are served one after the other, whereas **concurrent sentences** are served simultaneously.

The indeterminate model was also created to take into consideration differences in degrees of guilt. Using this model, judges can weigh minute differences among cases, situations, and offenders. Under the indeterminate sentencing model, the inmate's behavior (while incarcerated) is the primary determinant of the amount of time served. State parole boards wield great discretion under this model, acting as the final arbiters of the actual sentence served.

A few states employ a partially indeterminate sentencing model. They allow judges to specify only the maximum amount of time to be served; some minimum is generally implied by law but is not under the control of the sentencing authority. General practice is to set 1 year as a minimum for all felonies, although a few jurisdictions assume no minimum time at all, making offenders eligible for immediate parole.

Critiques of Indeterminate Sentencing

Indeterminate sentencing is still the rule in many jurisdictions, including Georgia, Hawaii, Iowa, Kentucky, Massachusetts, Michigan, Nevada, New York, North Dakota, Oklahoma, Rhode Island, South Carolina, South Dakota, Texas, Utah, Vermont, West Virginia, and Wyoming.[14] Beginning in the 1970s, however, the model came under fire for contributing to inequality in sentencing. Critics claimed that the indeterminate model allows judges' personalities and personal philosophies to produce too wide a range of sentencing practices, from very lenient to very strict. The indeterminate model was also criticized for perpetuating a system under which offenders might be sentenced, at least by some judges, more on the basis of personal and social characteristics, such as race, gender, and social class, than on culpability.

Because of the personal nature of judicial decisions under the indeterminate model, offenders often depend on the advice and ploys of their attorneys to appear before a

restorative justice (RJ)
A sentencing model that builds on restitution and community participation in an attempt to make the victim "whole again."

indeterminate sentencing
A model of criminal punishment that encourages rehabilitation through the use of general and relatively unspecific sentences (such as a term of imprisonment of from 1 to 10 years).

consecutive sentence
One of two or more sentences imposed at the same time, after conviction for more than one offense, and served in sequence with the other sentence. Also, a new sentence for a new conviction, imposed upon a person already under sentence for a previous offense, which is added to the previous sentence, thus increasing the maximum time the offender may be confined or under supervision.

concurrent sentence
One of two or more sentences imposed at the same time, after conviction for more than one offense, and served at the same time. Also, a new sentence for a new conviction, imposed upon a person already under sentence for a previous offense, which is served at the same time as the previous sentence.

gain time
The amount of time deducted from time to be served in prison on a given sentence as a result of participation in special projects or programs.

good time
The amount of time deducted from time to be served in prison on a given sentence as a result of good behavior.

▶ Noise offenders in Fort Lupton, Colorado, were recently ordered to endure an hour of unpopular music. The music, selected by a judge who wanted to punish them for disturbing the tranquility of the community, included songs by Bing Crosby and Willie Nelson. Will alternative sentences like this deter others from committing similar offenses?

Leila Cutler/Alamy Stock Photo

judge who is thought to be a good sentencing risk. Requests for delays are a common defense strategy in indeterminate sentencing states, where they are used to try to manipulate the selection of the judge involved in the sentencing decision.

Another charge leveled against indeterminate sentencing is that it tends to produce "dishonesty" in sentencing. Because of sentence cutbacks for good behavior and involvement in work and study programs, time served in prison is generally far less than sentences would seem to indicate. An inmate sentenced to 5 to 10 years, for example, might actually be released in a couple of years after all **gain time** (time off in recognition of the inmate's project or program participation), **good time** (time off for good behavior), and other special allowances have been calculated. (Some of the same charges can be leveled against determinate sentencing schemes under which corrections officials can administratively reduce the time served by an inmate.) A survey by the Bureau of Justice Statistics found that even violent offenders released from state prisons during the study period served, on average, only 51% of the sentences they originally received.[15] Nonviolent offenders served even smaller portions of their sentences. Table 9-3 shows the percentage of an imposed sentence that an offender released from state prison had actually served.

To ensure long prison terms in indeterminate jurisdictions, some court officials have gone to extremes. In 1994, for example, in what may be a record, Oklahoma Judge Dan Owens, set a record that stands to this day when he sentenced convicted child molester Charles Scott Robinson to 30,000 years in prison.[16] Judge Owens, complying with the jury's efforts to ensure that Robinson would spend the rest of his life behind bars, sentenced him to serve six consecutive 5,000-year sentences (Robinson had 14 previous felony convictions).

proportionality
A sentencing principle that holds that the severity of sanctions should bear a direct relationship to the seriousness of the crime committed.

equity
A sentencing principle, based on concerns with social equality, that holds that similar crimes should be punished with the same degree of severity, regardless of the social or personal characteristics of the offenders.

Structured Sentencing

3 Describe the structured sentencing models that became popular during the late twentieth century, using the federal model as an example.

Until the 1970s, all 50 states used some form of indeterminate (or partially indeterminate) sentencing. Eventually, however, calls for equity and proportionality in sentencing, heightened by claims of racial disparity in the sentencing practices of some judges,[17] led many states to move toward greater control over their sentencing systems.

Critics of the indeterminate model called for the recognition of three fundamental sentencing principles: proportionality, equity, and social debt. **Proportionality** refers to the belief that the severity of sanctions should bear a direct relationship to the seriousness of the crime committed. **Equity** means that similar crimes should be punished with the same degree of severity, regardless of the social or personal characteristics of the offenders. According to the principle of equity, for example, two bank robbers in different parts of the country, who use the same techniques and weapons with the same degree of implied threat, should receive roughly the same sentence even though they are tried under separate circumstances and in different jurisdictions. The equity principle needs to be balanced, however, against

■ TABLE 9-3
Percentage of Sentence Served in State Prison by Offense and Race

Offense Type	Percentage of Sentence Served	
	White Inmates	Black Inmates
Violent	57.3	60.9
Property	37.0	41.5
Drug	31.7	36.1
Public-order	40.4	49.0
Average for all offenses	42.6	48.5

Source: National Corrections Reporting Program. Release Type, Sex, and Race.

the notion of **social debt**, meaning that an offender's criminal history should be considered in his or her sentencing. In the case of the bank robbers, the offender who has a prior criminal record can be said to have a higher level of social debt than the first-time robber, where all else is equal. Greater social debt, of course, suggests a more severe punishment or a greater need for treatment.

Beginning in the 1970s, a number of states addressed these concerns by developing a different model of sentencing, known as **structured sentencing**, which includes determinate, presumptive, and voluntary/advisory sentencing guidelines. One form of structured sentencing, called **determinate sentencing**, requires that a convicted offender be sentenced to a fixed term that may be reduced by good time or gain time. Determinate sentencing states eliminated the use of traditional parole and created explicit standards to specify the amount of punishment appropriate for a given offense. Determinate sentencing practices also specify an anticipated release date for each sentenced offender.

A report from the National Council on Crime and Delinquency (NCCD) that traced the historical development of determinate sentencing observed that "the term 'determinate sentencing' is generally used to refer to the sentencing reforms of the late 1970s. At that time, the legislatures of California, Illinois, Indiana, and Maine abolished the parole release decision and replaced indeterminate penalties with fixed (or flat) sentences that could be reduced by good-time provisions."[18]

In response to the then-growing determinate sentencing movement, a few states developed **voluntary/advisory sentencing guidelines** during the 1980s. These guidelines consisted of recommended sentencing policies that were not required by law, were usually based on past sentencing practices, but served as guides to judges. The guidelines may build on either determinate or indeterminate sentencing structures. Florida, Maryland, Massachusetts, Michigan, Rhode Island, Utah, and Wisconsin all experimented with voluntary/advisory guidelines during the 1980s. Voluntary/advisory guidelines constitute a second form of structured sentencing.

A third model of structured sentencing employs what the NCCD calls "commission-based presumptive sentencing guidelines." **Presumptive sentencing** became common in the 1980s as states began to experiment with sentencing guidelines developed by sentencing commissions. Guidelines for the model of presumptive sentencing differed from both determinate and voluntary/advisory guidelines in three respects: (1) They were not developed by the state legislature but by a sentencing commission that often represented a diverse array of criminal justice and sometimes private interests. (2) They were explicit and highly structured, typically relying on a quantitative scoring instrument to classify the offense for which a person was to be sentenced. (3) They were not voluntary/advisory in that judges had to adhere to the sentencing system or provide a written rationale for departing from it.

By 2006, the federal government and 16 states had established commission-created sentencing guidelines. Ten of the 16 states used presumptive sentencing guidelines; the remaining six relied on voluntary/advisory guidelines. As a consequence, sentencing guidelines authored by legislatively created sentencing commissions have become the most popular form of structured sentencing. By 2017, 20 states had enacted sentencing guidelines, although not all created sentencing commissions, depending instead on statutory guidelines enacted by their legislatures.[19]

Guideline jurisdictions, which specify a presumptive sentence for a given offense, generally allow for aggravating or mitigating circumstances—indicating a greater or lesser degree of culpability—which judges can take into consideration when imposing a sentence somewhat at variance with the presumptive term. **Aggravating circumstances** call for a tougher sentence and may include especially heinous behavior, cruelty, injury to more than one person, and so on.

Mitigating circumstances, which indicate that a lesser sentence is called for, are generally similar to legal defenses, although in this case they only reduce criminal responsibility, not eliminate it. Mitigating circumstances include such things as cooperation with the investigating authority, surrender, and good character. Common aggravating and mitigating circumstances are listed in CJ Exhibit 9–1.

---

social debt
A sentencing principle that holds that an offender's criminal history should objectively be taken into account in sentencing decisions.

structured sentencing
A model of criminal punishment that includes determinate and commission-created presumptive sentencing schemes, as well as voluntary/advisory sentencing guidelines.

determinate sentencing
A model of criminal punishment in which an offender is given a fixed term of imprisonment that may be reduced by good time or gain time. Under the model, for example, all offenders convicted of the same degree of burglary would be sentenced to the same length of time behind bars.

voluntary/advisory sentencing guidelines
Recommended sentencing policies that are not required by law.

presumptive sentencing
A model of criminal punishment that meets the following conditions: (1) The appropriate sentence for an offender convicted of a specific charge is presumed to fall within a range of sentences authorized by sentencing guidelines that are adopted by a legislatively created sentencing body, usually a sentencing commission. (2) Sentencing judges are expected to sentence within the range or to provide written justification for failing to do so. (3) There is a mechanism for review, usually appellate, of any departure from the guidelines.

aggravating circumstances
Circumstances relating to the commission of a crime that make it more grave than the average instance of that crime.

mitigating circumstances
Circumstances relating to the commission of a crime that may be considered to reduce the blameworthiness of the offender.

CJ Exhibit 9–1
Aggravating and Mitigating Circumstances

Listed here are typical aggravating and mitigating circumstances that judges may consider in arriving at sentencing decisions in presumptive sentencing jurisdictions.

AGGRAVATING CIRCUMSTANCES

- The defendant induced others to participate in the commission of the offense.
- The offense was especially heinous, atrocious, or cruel.
- The defendant was armed with or used a deadly weapon during the crime.
- The defendant committed the offense to avoid or prevent a lawful arrest or to escape from custody.
- The offense was committed for hire.
- The offense was committed against a current or former law enforcement or correctional officer while that person was engaged in the performance of official duties or because of the past exercise of official duties.
- The defendant took advantage of a position of trust or confidence to commit the offense.

MITIGATING CIRCUMSTANCES

- The defendant has no record of criminal convictions punishable by more than 60 days of imprisonment.
- The defendant has made substantial or full restitution.
- The defendant has been a person of good character or has a good reputation in the community.
- The defendant aided in the apprehension of another felon or testified truthfully on behalf of the prosecution.
- The defendant acted under strong provocation, or the victim was a voluntary participant in the criminal activity or otherwise consented to it.
- The offense was committed under duress, coercion, threat, or compulsion that was insufficient to constitute a defense but that significantly reduced the defendant's culpability.
- At the time of the offense, the defendant was suffering from a mental or physical condition that was insufficient to constitute a defense but that significantly reduced the defendant's culpability.

Note: Recent U.S. Supreme Court rulings have held that facts influencing sentencing enhancements, other than prior record or admissions made by a defendant, must be determined by a jury, not by a judge.

Federal Sentencing Guidelines

In 1984, with the passage of the Comprehensive Crime Control Act, the federal government adopted presumptive sentencing for nearly all federal offenders.[20] The act also addressed the issue of **truth in sentencing**, described as "a close correspondence between the sentence imposed upon those sent to prison and the time actually served prior to prison release."[21] Under the old federal system, on average, good-time credits and parole reduced time served to about one-third of the actual sentence.[22] At the time, the sentencing practices of most states reflected the federal model. Although sentence reductions may have benefited offenders, they often outraged victims, who felt betrayed by the sentencing process. The 1984 act nearly eliminated good-time credits[23] and began the process of both phasing out federal parole and eliminating the U.S. Parole Commission (read more about the commission in Chapter 10).[24] The emphasis on truth in sentencing created, in effect, a sentencing environment of "what you get is what you serve." Truth in sentencing has become an important policy focus of many state legislatures and the U.S. Congress. The Violent Crime Control and Law Enforcement Act of 1994 set aside $4 billion in federal prison construction funds (Truth in Sentencing Incentive Funds) for states that adopt truth-in-sentencing laws and are able to guarantee that certain violent offenders will serve 85% of their sentences.

Title II of the Comprehensive Crime Control Act, called the Sentencing Reform Act of 1984,[25] established the nine-member U.S. Sentencing Commission. The commission, which continues to function today, comprises presidential appointees, including three federal judges. The Sentencing Reform Act limited the discretion of federal judges by mandating the creation of federal sentencing guidelines, which federal judges were required to follow. The Sentencing Commission was given the task of developing structured sentencing guidelines to reduce disparity, promote consistency and uniformity, and increase fairness and equity in sentencing.

The guidelines established by the commission took effect in November 1987 but quickly became embroiled in a series of legal disputes, some of which challenged Congress's authority to form the U.S. Sentencing Commission. In January 1989, in the case of *Mistretta* v. *U.S.*,[26]

truth in sentencing
A close correspondence between the sentence imposed on an offender and the time actually served in prison.[i]

the U.S. Supreme Court held that Congress had acted appropriately in establishing the U.S. Sentencing Commission and that the guidelines developed by the commission could be applied in federal cases nationwide. The federal Sentencing Commission continues to meet at least once a year to review the effectiveness of the guidelines it created. Visit the U.S. Sentencing Commission via **http://www.ussc.gov**.

Federal Guideline Provisions

As originally established, federal sentencing guidelines specified a sentencing range from which judges had to choose, but if a particular case had atypical features, judges were allowed to depart from the guidelines. Departures were generally expected only in the presence of aggravating or mitigating circumstances, many of which are specified in the guidelines.[27] Aggravating circumstances may include the possession of a weapon during the commission of a crime, the degree of criminal involvement (whether the defendant was a leader or a follower in the criminal activity), and extreme psychological injury to the victim. Punishments also increase when a defendant violates a position of public or private trust, uses special skills to commit or conceal offenses, or has a criminal history. Defendants who express remorse, cooperate with authorities, or willingly make restitution may have their sentences reduced under the guidelines. Any departure from the guidelines may, however, become the basis for appellate review concerning the reasonableness of the sentence imposed, and judges who deviate from the guidelines were originally required to provide written reasons for doing so.

Federal sentencing guidelines are built around a table containing 43 rows, each corresponding to one offense level. The penalties associated with each level overlap those of the levels above and below to discourage unnecessary litigation. A person convicted of a crime involving $11,000, for example, and sentenced under the guidelines is unlikely to receive a penalty substantially greater than if the amount had been somewhat less than $10,000. A change of six levels roughly doubles the sentence imposed under the guidelines, regardless of the level at which one starts. Because of their matrix-like quality, federal sentencing provisions have been referred to as *structured*. The federal sentencing table is available at **https://www.justicestudies.com/pubs/sentable.pdf**.

The sentencing table also contains six rows corresponding to the criminal history category into which an offender falls, and these categories are determined on a point basis. Offenders earn points for previous convictions. For example, each prior sentence of imprisonment for more than 1 year and 1 month counts as three points, and two points are assigned for each prior prison sentence over 6 months or if the defendant committed the offense while on probation, parole, or work release. The system also assigns points for other types of previous convictions and for offenses committed less than 2 years after release from imprisonment. Points are added to determine the criminal history category into which an offender falls. Thirteen points or more are required for the highest category. At each offense level, sentences in the highest criminal history category are generally two to three times as severe as for the lowest category. The types of offenses for which federal offenders are sentenced, and how the proportion of those types have changed over time, can be seen in Figure 9–1.

Defendants may also move into the highest criminal history category by virtue of being designated a career offender. Under the sentencing guidelines, a defendant is a career offender if "(1) the defendant was at least 18 years old at the time of the . . . offense, (2) the . . . offense is a crime of violence or trafficking in a controlled substance, and (3) the defendant has at least two prior felony convictions of either a crime of violence or a controlled substance offense."[28]

According to the U.S. Supreme Court, an offender may be adjudged a career offender in a single hearing, even when previous convictions are lacking.[29]

Plea Bargaining under the Guidelines

Plea bargaining plays a major role in the federal judicial system. Approximately 90% of all federal sentences are the result of guilty pleas,[30] and the large majority of those stem from plea negotiations. In the words of former Sentencing Commission Chairman William W. Wilkins, Jr., "With respect to plea bargaining, the Commission has proceeded cautiously. . . . The Commission did not believe it wise to stand the federal criminal justice system on its head by making too drastic and too sudden a change in these practices."[31]

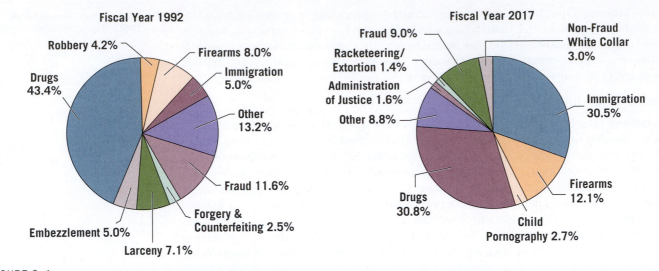

FIGURE 9–1
Distribution of Federal Offenders in Each Primary Offense Category, Fiscal Years 1992 and 2017
Source: U.S. Sentencing Commission, 2017 Datafile, and the 1992 Datafile, USSC FY12 and FY17.

Although the commission allowed plea bargaining to continue, it required that the agreement (1) be fully disclosed in the record of the court (unless there is an overriding and demonstrable reason why it should not be) and (2) detail the actual conduct of the offense. Under these requirements, defendants are unable to hide the actual nature of their offense behind a substitute plea, and information on the decision-making process itself is available to victims, the media, and the public.

In 1996, in the case of *Melendez* v. *U.S.*,[32] the U.S. Supreme Court held that a government motion requesting that a trial judge deviate from the federal sentencing guidelines as part of a cooperative plea agreement does not permit imposition of a sentence below a statutory minimum specified by law. In other words, under *Melendez*, although federal judges could depart from the guidelines, they could not accept plea bargains that would have resulted in sentences lower than the minimum required by law for a particular type of offense.

The Legal Environment of Structured Sentencing

A crucial critique of aggravating factors and their use in presumptive sentencing schemes was offered by the U.S. Supreme Court in 2000 in the case of *Apprendi* v. *New Jersey*.[33] In *Apprendi*, the Court questioned the fact-finding authority of judges in making sentencing decisions, ruling that other than the fact of a prior conviction, any fact that increases the penalty for a crime beyond the prescribed statutory maximum is, in effect, an element of the crime, which must be submitted to a jury and proved beyond a reasonable doubt. The case involved Charles Apprendi, a New Jersey defendant who pleaded guilty to unlawfully possessing a firearm—an offense that carried a prison term of 5 to 10 years under state law. Before sentence was imposed, however, the judge found that Apprendi had fired a number of shots into the home of an African-American family living in his neighborhood and concluded that he had done so to frighten the family and convince them to move. The judge held that statements made by Apprendi allowed the offense to be classified as a hate crime, which required a longer prison term under the sentencing enhancement provision of New Jersey's hate-crime statute than did the weapons offense to which Apprendi had confessed. The Supreme Court, in overturning the judge's finding and sentence, took issue with the fact that after Apprendi pleaded guilty, an enhanced sentence was imposed without the benefit of a jury-based fact-finding process. The high court ruled that "under the Due Process Clause of the Fifth Amendment and the notice and jury trial guarantees of the Sixth Amendment, any fact (other than prior conviction) that increases the maximum penalty for a crime must be charged in an indictment, submitted to a jury, and proven beyond a reasonable doubt."

The *Apprendi* case essentially says that requiring sentencing judges to consider facts not proven to a jury violates the federal Constitution. It raised the question of whether judges anywhere could legitimately deviate from established sentencing guidelines or apply sentence enhancements based solely on judicial determinations of aggravating factors—especially when such determinations involve findings of fact that might otherwise be made by a jury.[34]

In 2002, however, in the case of *Harris* v. *U.S.*, the Court concluded that "a fact increasing the mandatory *minimum* (but not extending the sentence beyond the statutory maximum), need not be alleged in the indictment, submitted to the jury, or proved beyond a reasonable doubt."[35] Under *Harris*, a judge is permitted to find aggravating factors by a preponderance of evidence, and to decide whether they should be used to increase a sentence beyond the minimum specified by law. As long as the judge does not exceed the maximum sentence specified, he or she does not need to treat those factors as elements of the crime that must be proved to a jury. In *Harris*, a majority of the justices reasoned that facts raising the sentencing floor are constitutionally different from facts raising the ceiling, or maximum sentence. To some, the *Harris* ruling seemed inconsistent with *Apprendi*, and is being questioned in cases currently before the Court.

Since *Apprendi*, the Court has expanded the number and types of facts that must be decided by a jury. In 2010, for example, in the case of *U.S.* v. *O'Brien*,[36] the Court held that a determination that a firearm was a machine gun, as described by relevant law, is an element to be proved to a jury beyond a reasonable doubt, not a sentencing factor to be proved to a sentencing judge. The finding affected a sentencing requirement that a 30-year minimum term of imprisonment be imposed for convictions involving the use of a fully automatic firearm during the commission of a crime.

The *O'Brien* case built upon the important 2004 case of *Blakely* v. *Washington*,[37] in which the U.S. Supreme Court effectively invalidated any state sentencing schema that allows judges rather than juries to determine any factor that increases a criminal sentence, except for prior convictions. The Court found that because the facts supporting Blakely's increased sentence were neither admitted by the defendant himself nor found by a jury, the sentence violated the Sixth Amendment right to trial by jury. The *Blakely* decision required that the sentencing laws of eight states be rewritten. Washington State legislators responded quickly and created a model law for other legislatures to emulate. The Washington law mandates that "the facts supporting aggravating circumstances shall be proved to a jury beyond a reasonable doubt," or "if a jury is waived, proof shall be to the court beyond a reasonable doubt."[38]

In 2007, in the case of *Cunningham* v. *California*,[39] the Supreme Court applied its reasoning in *Blakely* to California's determinate sentencing law, finding the law invalid because it placed sentence-elevating fact-finding within the judge's purview. As in *Blakely*, the California law was found to violate a defendant's Sixth Amendment right to trial by jury.

In 2005, in the combined cases of *U.S.* v. *Booker*[40] and *U.S.* v. *Fanfan*,[41] attention turned to the constitutionality of *federal* sentencing practices that relied on extra-verdict determinations of fact in the application of sentencing enhancements. In *Booker*, the U.S. Supreme Court issued what some have called an "extraordinary opinion,"[42] which actually encompasses two separate decisions. The combined cases brought a dual issue before the Court: (1) whether fact-finding done by judges under federal sentencing guidelines violates the Sixth Amendment right to trial by jury; and (2) if so, whether the guidelines are themselves unconstitutional. As in the preceding cases discussed in this section, the Court found that on the first question, defendant Freddie Booker's drug-trafficking sentence had been improperly enhanced under the guidelines on the basis of facts found solely by a judge. In the view of the Court, the Sixth Amendment right to trial by jury is violated where, under a mandatory guidelines system, a sentence is increased because of an enhancement based on facts found by the judge that were not found by a jury or admitted by the defendant.[43] Consequently, Booker's sentence was ruled unconstitutional and invalidated. On the second question, the Court reached a compromise and did not strike down the federal guidelines as many thought it would. Instead, the Court held that the guidelines could be *considered* by federal judges during sentencing but that they were no longer mandatory.

In effect, the decisions in *Booker* and *Fanfan* turned the federal sentencing guidelines on their head, making them merely advisory and giving federal judges wide latitude in imposing punishments. Although federal judges *must* still take the guidelines into consideration in reaching sentencing decisions, they do not have to follow them. In the words of the High Court, "[T]he federal sentencing statute, as modified by *Booker*, requires a court to give respectful consideration to the Guidelines but permits the court to tailor the sentence in light of other concerns as well."[44] Deviations from the guidelines must still be explained, and in the words of the justices, "a district judge must consider the extent of any departure from the Guidelines and must explain the appropriateness of an unusually lenient or harsh sentence with sufficient justifications."[45]

In 2007, in a continued clarification of *Booker*, the Supreme Court ruled that federal appeals courts that hear challenges from defendants about prison time may presume that federal criminal sentences are reasonable if they fall within federal sentencing guidelines.[46] In that case, *Rita* v. *U.S.*, the Court held that "even if the presumption increases the likelihood that the judge, not the jury, will find 'sentencing facts,' it does not violate the Sixth Amendment." The justices reasoned that "a nonbinding appellate reasonableness presumption for Guidelines sentences does not *require* the sentencing judge to impose a Guidelines sentence."

In another 2007 case, *Gall* v. *United States*, the Court clarified its position on appellate review of sentencing decisions by lower courts when it held that "because the Guidelines are now advisory, appellate review of sentencing decisions is limited to determining whether they are 'reasonable.'"

In 2013, in the case of *Alleyne* v. *U.S.*, the Court ruled that any fact that increases the mandatory minimum sentence is an "element" that must be submitted to the jury.[47] In this case, a federal judge had increased an offender's sentence after investigating his prior convictions and finding that he had been convicted of multiple crimes.[48] The *Alleyne* court held that "*Apprendi's* principle applies with equal force to facts increasing the mandatory minimum, for a fact triggering a mandatory minimum alters the prescribed range of sentences to which a criminal defendant is exposed." The justices also wrote, however, that: "This ruling does not mean that any fact that influences judicial discretion must be found by a jury." Nonetheless, the *Alleyne* decision makes it more difficult for the government to use the fact of a defendant's prior conviction to enhance a federal criminal sentence.

A recent report submitted to Congress by the U.S. Sentencing Commission found that "the sentencing guidelines remain the essential starting point for determining all federal sentences and continue to exert significant influence on federal sentencing trends over time." The commission found that "the rate at which courts impose sentences within the applicable guideline range [stood] at 53.9% during the most recent time period studied." In light of the Court's decisions, it is now up to Congress to reconsider federal sentencing law following *Booker*—a process that has been under way for the past few years. In 2011, the U.S. Sentencing Commission called upon Congress "to exercise its power to direct sentencing policy by enacting [new] mandatory minimum penalties" in modified format.[49] Read the commission's 2012 report about the impact of *U.S.* v. *Booker* on federal sentencing at **https://www.justicestudies.com/pubs/sentencing2012.pdf** and review a summary of important Supreme Court cases on sentencing issues at **https://www.justicestudies.com/pubs/sct_sentencing.pdf**.

Three-Strikes Laws

In the spring of 1994, California legislators passed the state's now-famous "three strikes and you're out" bill. Amid much fanfare, former Governor Pete Wilson signed the "three-strikes" measure into law, calling it "the toughest and most sweeping crime bill in California history."[50]

California's law, which is retroactive in that it counts offenses committed before the date the legislation was signed, requires a sentence of 25 years to life for three-time felons with convictions for two or more serious or violent prior offenses. Criminal offenders facing a "second strike" can receive up to double the normal sentence for their most recent offense. Parole consideration is not available until at least 80% of the sentence had been served.

Today, about half of the states have passed three-strikes legislation. At the federal level, the Violent Crime Control and Law Enforcement Act of 1994 contains a three-strikes provision that mandates life imprisonment for federal criminals convicted of three violent felonies or drug offenses.

Questions remain, however, about the effectiveness of three-strikes legislation, and many people are concerned about its impact on the justice system. A 2001 study of the original California legislation and its consequences concluded that three-strikes laws are overrated.[51] According to the study, which was conducted by the Washington, D.C.-based

> Three-strikes laws require mandatory sentences for offenders convicted of a third serious felony.

Sentencing Project, "California's three-strikes law has increased the number and severity of sentences for nonviolent offenders—and contributed to the aging of the prison population—but has had no significant effect on the state's decline in crime."

A 2012 review of three-strikes legislation found that 16 states had modified such laws in response to difficult economic conditions; meaning that the high cost of imprisonment is leading legislatures to rethink long prison terms. Modifications have included giving judges more discretion in sentencing and narrowing the types of crimes that count as a "strike."

Supporters of three-strikes laws argue that those convicted under them are career criminals who will be denied the opportunity to commit more violent crimes. "The real story here is the girl somewhere that did not get raped," said Mike Reynolds, a Fresno, California, photographer whose 18-year-old daughter was killed by a paroled felon. "The real story is the robbery that did not happen," he added.[52]

In 2003, in two separate cases, the U.S. Supreme Court upheld the three-strikes California convictions of Gary Ewing[53] and Leandro Andrade in California. Ewing, who had four prior felony convictions, had received a sentence of 25 years to life following his conviction for felony grand theft of three golf clubs. Andrade, who also had a long record, was sentenced to 50 years in prison for two petty theft convictions.[54] In writing for the Court in the *Ewing* case, Justice Sandra Day O'Connor noted that states should be able to decide when repeat offenders "must be isolated from society . . . to protect the public safety," even when nonserious crimes trigger the lengthy sentence. In deciding these two cases, both of which were based on Eighth Amendment claims, the Court found that it is *not* cruel and unusual punishment to impose a possible life term for a nonviolent felony when the defendant has a history of serious or violent convictions.

In November 2012, California voters overwhelmingly approved a change to their state's three-strikes law. The changes mean that now only two categories of offenders can be sentenced as three-strikers: (1) those who commit new "serious or violent" felonies as their third offense and (2) previously released murderers, rapists, or child molesters who are convicted of a new third-strike, even if it is not a "serious or violent" felony. Another California ballot initiative, Proposition 47, passed in 2014, changed many crime from felonies to misdemeanors. Consequently, most instances of drug possession and all property crimes involving amounts of less than $950 are no longer felonies in California. Both the 2012 and 2014 changes allow inmates who were sentenced under older laws to petition for release. By 2017, however, more than 13,500 low-level offenders who had been freed by changes in California law found themselves on the streets, with few opportunities for employment—causing critics to say that changes in the law had led to a cycle of homelessness, drug abuse, and petty crime.[55]

Mandatory Sentencing

Mandatory sentencing, another form of structured sentencing, deserves special mention.[56] **Mandatory sentencing** is just what its name implies: a structured sentencing scheme that mandates clearly enumerated punishments for specific offenses or for habitual offenders convicted of a series of crimes. Mandatory sentencing, because it is truly *mandatory*, differs from presumptive sentencing, which allows at least a limited amount of judicial discretion within ranges established by published guidelines. Some mandatory sentencing laws require only modest mandatory prison terms (e.g., 3 years for armed robbery), whereas others are much more far-reaching.

Typical of far-reaching mandatory sentencing schemes are the three-strikes laws just described. Three-strikes laws (and in some jurisdictions, two-strikes laws) require mandatory sentences (sometimes life in prison without the possibility of parole) for offenders convicted of a third (or second) serious felony. Such mandatory sentencing enhancements are aimed at deterring known and potentially violent offenders and are intended to incapacitate convicted criminals through long-term incarceration.

mandatory sentencing
A structured sentencing scheme that allows no leeway in the nature of the sentence imposed. Under mandatory sentencing, clearly enumerated punishments are mandated for specific offenses or for habitual offenders convicted of a series of crimes.

Rising incarceration rates have reached the point where they are imposing huge financial burdens on both state and federal governments.

Name: Leracia Blalock

Position: Medicolegal Death Investigator, Office of the Coroner for Adams and Broomfield Counties, Brighton, Colorado

Colleges attended: The Ohio State University

Major: Bachelor of Science in Forensic Biology

Year hired: 2014

Please give a brief description of your job: The term "medicolegal" pertains to medicine and the law. A medicolegal death investigator works in the combined field of medicine and law, and is commonly referred to as a "coroner investigator" or a "death investigator." As a death investigator, I am responsible for establishing a differential diagnosis of the cause and manner of death by conducting a competent and thorough investigation of the circumstances surrounding death; I also determine the decedent's identity and notify the next-of-kin that the death has occurred. In Adams and Broomfield Counties (Colorado), all deaths are reported to the Office of the Coroner. It is my responsibility to determine when the circumstances of a death require further investigation in accordance with Colorado Revised Statutes. A coroner's office is responsible for accurately determining the cause and manner of death. The cause of death refers to the injury or disease that brought about the death. The manner of death refers to the circumstances surrounding the cause of death. In Colorado, the manner of death is classified into one of five categories: natural, accident, homicide, suicide, and undetermined. Most deaths are natural and occur under the attendance of a physician, such as in a hospital. A death investigator will spend the majority of his/her time liaising with physicians to establish the manner and cause of death. If a death is unattended, such as a residential death, a death investigator will liaise with other law enforcement officials, crime scene investigators, families, and witnesses in order to conduct a competent investigation of the circumstances surrounding the death. It is imperative that the scene investigation is thorough so that the cause and manner of death can be accurately determined. Despite how media depicts scene investigations, a death investigator is responsible for completing a forensic examination of the scene and the deceased; documenting things such as trauma, injuries, identifying marks, postmortem changes, and indications of disease processes and exposure to toxins. After the scene investigation is complete, a death investigator will either release the body to a mortuary or transport the body to the coroner's office for further investigation, such as an autopsy. Other major job duties include collecting and inventorying the decedent's medications, securing the decedent's property, identifying and collecting evidence, reviewing medical records, assisting in autopsies, and testifying in court.

What appealed to you most about the position when you applied for it? I have always had an interest in a law enforcement career. However, my passion was for forensic death investigations. I wanted a career that had a primary emphasis on death investigations in addition to liaising with other law enforcement agencies. Once I obtained relative experience in the field of forensics and death investigation, I knew that this career path was meant for me.

How would you describe the interview process? The interview process, qualifications, and background investigation vary by counties and districts. At the location in which I was hired, the interview process started with a 10-hour job "shadow." During this time I observed

▲ Leracia Blalock

the shift of a death investigator employee and I was able to see what a typical work day is like for a death investigator. This helped to determine if the job was right for me. After the shadow experience, I underwent an interview with the Chief Coroner, Chief Deputy Coroner, Operations Manager, and a representative from Human Resources. Following this, I had to pass an extensive criminal background check including a polygraph test, a psychological evaluation, a medical examination, and a drug screening. Lastly, a written test was administered to determine my knowledge in death investigations. Typical candidates have a degree or prior experience in law enforcement, forensic science, pharmaceuticals, biology, chemistry, anthropology, or death investigations.

Prior to being hired, I was a volunteer in the Medicolegal Death Investigator Reserve Academy at the Office of the Coroner for Adams and Broomfield Counties. During this program I assisted death investigators by collecting and logging property and medications, photographing forensic evidence, and completing forensic external examinations.

What is a typical day like? Our office has a total of eight death investigators. We operate on a rotating schedule in order to provide 24/7 coverage; therefore, one investigator will be assigned per shift, with a 2-hour overlap period between shifts. The primary objective, when you arrive at work, is to brief with the previous shift and load up the van for any scenes you may need to attend to. You have to be prepared to leave for a scene at any minute during your shift. The morning shift typically consists of assisting other investigators with any follow-up, such as contacting a physician during normal business hours, whereas the night shift typically consists of logging medications and property, etc. In general, every investigator is responsible for assisting with any tasks that need to be completed, in addition to handling any calls, death reports, or scene responses in a timely manner and completing the paperwork. If law enforcement officials request a coroner's response to a scene, then you are responsible for documenting the scene with photographs and notes; interviewing family members, friends, and witnesses; completing a forensic examination on the decedent; and making death notifications to the next-of-kin.

What qualities/characteristics are most helpful for this job? Helpful characteristics include empathy, compassion, energy, and the ability to adapt. This job requires you to constantly keep an open mind and to think on your feet. In addition, you have be able to effectively work independently and with others.

What is a typical starting salary? In general, the average starting wage for a death investigator in the United States is approximately $20.00 per hour.

What is the salary potential as you move up into higher-level jobs? There are multiple career opportunities within the field of forensics. The increase in salary potential varies.

What advice would you give someone in college beginning studies in criminal justice? There are many career-oriented opportunities available for college students. Obtain career-oriented internships and classes to get your foot in the door, and network accordingly. Lastly, don't be afraid to take a risk—you never know what opportunities will result from it.

Source: Reprinted with permission of Leracia Blalock. Photo courtesy of Leracia Blalock.

Three-strikes laws impose longer prison terms than most earlier mandatory minimum sentencing laws. California's original three-strikes law, for example, required that offenders who are convicted of a violent crime and who had two prior convictions serve a minimum of 25 years in prison. It also doubled prison terms for offenders convicted of a second violent felony.[57] Three-strikes laws also vary in breadth. The laws of some jurisdictions stipulate that both of the prior convictions and the current one be for violent felonies; others require only that the prior convictions be for violent felonies. Some three-strikes laws count only prior adult convictions, whereas others permit consideration of juvenile offenses.

By passing mandatory sentencing laws, legislators conveyed the message that certain crimes are deemed especially grave and that people who commit them deserve, and should expect, harsh sanctions. These laws were often passed in response to public outcries following heinous or well-publicized crimes.

Research findings on the impact of mandatory sentencing laws on the criminal justice system have been summarized by British criminologist Michael Tonry.[58] Tonry found that under mandatory sentencing, officials tend to make earlier and more selective decisions involving arrest, charging, and **diversion** (suspension of criminal proceedings before sentencing and referral to a private agency). They also tend to bargain less and to bring more cases to trial.

In an analysis of federal sentencing guidelines, other researchers found that blacks receive longer sentences than whites, not because they received differential treatment by judges but because they constitute the large majority of those convicted of trafficking in crack cocaine (versus powdered cocaine)[59]—a crime that Congress had at one time singled out for especially harsh mandatory penalties. In 2006, for example, 82% of those sentenced under federal crack cocaine laws were black, and only 8.8% were white—even though more than two-thirds of people who used crack cocaine were white.[60] This seeming disparity led the U.S. Congress to eliminate the distinction between crack and regular cocaine for purposes of sentencing, and in 2010 President Barack Obama signed the federal Fair Sentencing Act (FSA)[61] into law. The act reduced a previous disparity in the amounts of powder cocaine and crack cocaine specified by the federal sentencing guidelines and eliminated what had been a mandatory minimum sentence under federal law for simple possession of crack cocaine. As a result of the FSA, a first conviction for simple possession of any amount of crack cocaine, such as simple possession of powder cocaine, is subject to a penalty range of 0 to 1 year of imprisonment, regardless of quantity. In 2016, the Federal Sentencing Commission announced that such changes in federal sentencing practices resulted in 26,000 convicted drug offenders serving less time over the previous 2 years than would have otherwise have been the case.[62]

Sentencing and Today's Prison Crisis

Over the past 30 years, mandatory sentencing, three-strikes laws, and other get-tough-on-crime and criminals policies have dramatically increased the use of incarceration as a sentencing option. Although crime rates began to fall throughout the nation beginning in the mid-1990s (see Chapter 2), more and more convicted offenders were sent to prison. Some people have argued that increasing rates of imprisonment produced lower crime rates, but it is noteworthy that many new prison admissions came from drug convictions, and were largely the result of the nation's "war on drugs"; not the consequence of violent or property crimes. As you'll recall from Chapter 2, drug crimes are excluded from the calculations used by the FBI and BJS in determining crime rates. Figure 9–2 contrasts combined rates of major violent and property crimes with the growth of incarceration between 1978 and 2017. As can be seen, while crime rates dipped by more than 30%, the number of persons sent to prison increased by almost 300%.

Rising incarceration rates, which are discussed in more detail in Chapter 10, have now reached the point where they are imposing huge financial burdens on both state and federal governments. In 2014, the Washington, D.C.-based Center on Budget and Policy Priorities found that sentencing policies, not crime rates are the biggest drivers of rising incarceration rates. The center also noted that:

- Seen historically, crime rates have risen and fallen independently of incarceration rates.
- The proportion of criminal offenders sent to prison has climbed dramatically over time.

diversion
The official suspension of criminal or juvenile proceedings against an alleged offender at any point after a recorded justice system intake, but before the entering of a judgment, and referral of that person to a treatment or care program administered by a nonjustice or private agency. Also, release without referral.

Follow the author's tweets about the latest crime and justice news @schmalleger

4 Tell how get-tough sentencing practices led to significant prison overcrowding in the United States.

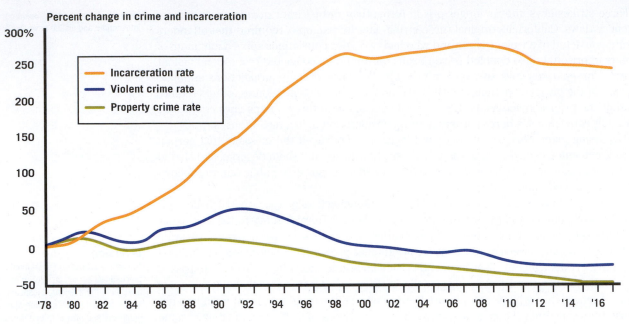

Percent change in crime and incarceration

FIGURE 9–2
Incarceration Rates versus Crime Rates in the United States, 1978–2017
Sources: U.S. Department of Justice, Bureau of Justice Statistics; FBI, Uniform Crime Reports; and Center on Budget and Policy Priorities.

- Lengths of prison stays have significantly increased for all types of crime.
- High levels of incarceration impose significant human economic costs without necessarily making society any safer.
- High incarceration rates present mounting financial challenges to governments at all levels.[63]

Innovations in Sentencing

In an ever-growing number of cases, innovative judges in certain jurisdictions are using discretionary sentencing to impose truly unique punishments. Faced with prison overcrowding, high incarceration costs, and continued public calls for retribution, some judges have used shaming strategies to deter wrongdoers. At least one Florida court ordered those convicted of drunk driving to put a "Convicted DUI" sticker on their license plates. Similarly, a few years ago Boston courts began ordering men convicted of sexual solicitation to spend time sweeping streets in Chinatown, an area known for prostitution, and the public was invited to watch men sentenced to the city's "John Sweep" program clean up streets and alleyways littered with used condoms and sexual paraphernalia. In still other examples, an Arkansas judge made shoplifters walk in front of the stores they stole from, carrying signs describing their crimes, and in California, a purse snatcher was ordered to wear noisy tap dancing shoes whenever he went out in public.[64]

There is considerable support in the criminal justice field for shaming as a crime-reduction strategy. Australian criminologist John Braithwaite, for example, found shaming to be a particularly effective strategy because, he said, it holds the potential to enhance moral awareness among offenders, thereby building conscience and increasing inner control.[65] Dan Kahan, a professor at the University of Chicago Law School, points out that "shame supplies the main motive why people obey the law, not so much because they're afraid of formal sanctions, but because they care what people think about them."[66]

5 Describe alternative sentences and their relationship to justice reinvestment strategies

Punishment, that is justice for the unjust.
—Saint Augustine (A.D. 354–430)

Whether public shaming will grow in popularity as an alternative sentencing strategy is unclear. What is clear, however, is that the American public and an ever-growing number of judicial officials are now looking for workable alternatives to traditional sentencing options.

Questions about Alternative Sanctions

Alternative sentencing includes the use of court-ordered community service, home detention, day reporting, drug treatment, psychological counseling, victim–offender mediation, or intensive supervision in lieu of other, more traditional sanctions, such as imprisonment and fines. Many of these strategies are discussed in more detail in the next chapter.

It is important to note here, however, that a new framework, known as justice reinvestment (see Chapter 1), is starting to make a significant impact on sentencing authorities. Justice reinvestment employs strategies that prioritizes the use of alternatives to incarceration for persons convicted of eligible nonviolent offenses, and reinvests savings from such initiatives into effective crime-prevention programs.[67] In general, justice reinvestment strategies included efforts to scale back harsh sentencing provisions and to reduce returns to prison for probation and parole violators.

As the term itself indicates, some recent legislative measures associated with the strategy also include statutory mechanisms for reinvesting savings that have been achieved through reducing prison populations into other aspects of the criminal justice system—including evidence-based in-prison treatment programs and local law enforcement efforts designed to deter crime.

A report by the Sentencing Project identified Georgia, Hawaii, Kansas, Missouri, Oklahoma, and Pennsylvania as leaders in the justice reinvestment movement.[68] Texas might be added to the list, as a recent study by the Council of State Governments determined, for example, that Texas saved almost $2 billion over 5 years by focusing on justice reinvestment efforts, including savings of $1.5 billion on prison constructions and more than $340 million in averted annual operations costs of confinement facilities.[69]

Some people and organizations have argued for broadening reinvestment opportunities to include paying for high-quality educational and developmental opportunities; creating living-wage jobs; expanding the availability of affordable housing; and broadening access to physical, mental, and behavioral health care.[70] A series of "Justice Reinvestment Boxes" in this text provides examples of states that are taking advantage of justice reinvestment opportunities.

As prison populations continue to rise, alternative sentencing strategies are likely to become increasingly attractive. A number of questions must be answered, however, before most alternative sanctions can be employed with confidence, including whether alternative sentencing programs increase the threat to public safety, whether alternative sanctions are cost-effective, and how program outcomes should be judged.[71] Learn more about the Justice Reinvestment Initiative, a project of the Council of State Governments and the Bureau of Justice Assistance, at **http://www.justicereinvestment.org**.

The Presentence Investigation

Before imposing sentence, a judge may request information on the background of a convicted defendant. This is especially true in indeterminate sentencing jurisdictions, where judges retain considerable discretion in selecting sanctions. One of the drivers behind many sentencing decisions today is offender risk and needs assessment (RNA). In one report, the National Center for State Courts identified certain factors that increase the likelihood of reoffending, and whose presence suggest that prison terms and removal from the community are better sentencing options than probation. High-risk factors include (1) antisocial personality patterns (impulsiveness, pleasure seeking, aggressive and irritable traits), (2) procriminal attitudes (negative attitudes toward the law), (3) social supports for crime (criminal friends), (4) substance abuse, (5) family and marital problems, (6) poor school or work performance, and (7) a lack of involvement in prosocial recreational and leisure activities.

alternative sentencing
The use of court-ordered community service, home detention, day reporting, drug treatment, psychological counseling, victim–offender programming, or intensive supervision in lieu of other, more traditional sanctions, such as imprisonment and fines.

🐦 Follow the author's tweets about the latest crime and justice news @schmalleger

Justice reinvestment prioritizes the use of alternatives to incarceration for persons convicted of eligible nonviolent offenses.

6 Explain the purpose of presentence investigations, presentence investigation reports, and presentencing hearings.

▲ Then-U.S. Attorney General Eric H. Holder, Jr., speaking at an Office for Victims of Crime Candlelight Ceremony. What more can the justice system do for crime victims? What more should it do?

S Craig Crawford/U.S. Department of Justice

presentence investigation (PSI)

The examination of a convicted offender's background prior to sentencing. Presentence examinations are generally conducted by probation or parole officers and are submitted to sentencing authorities.

Factors that are likely to increase the chances for rehabilitation, and which might indicate that probation or reduced prison terms are appropriate include a good job record, satisfactory educational attainment, strong family ties, church attendance, no prior arrests for violent offenses, and psychological stability.

Information about a defendant's background often comes to the judge in the form of a **presentence investigation (PSI)** report. The task of preparing PSI reports usually falls to the probation or parole office. The report takes one of three forms: (1) a detailed written report on the defendant's personal and criminal history, including an assessment of present conditions in the defendant's life (often called the *long form*); (2) an abbreviated written report summarizing the information most likely to be useful in a sentencing decision (the *short form*); and (3) a verbal report to the court made by the investigating officer based on field notes but structured according to established categories. A PSI report is much like a résumé, except that it focuses on what might be regarded as negative as well as positive life experiences.

The data on which a presentence report are based come from a variety of sources. The Federal Bureau of Investigation's National Crime Information Center (NCIC), begun in 1967, contains computerized information on people wanted for criminal offenses throughout the United States. Individual jurisdictions also maintain criminal records repositories that can provide comprehensive files on the criminal history of those who have been processed by the justice system.

Sometimes the defendant provides much of the information for the PSI. In this case, efforts must be made to corroborate the defendant's information. Unconfirmed data are generally marked on the report as "defendant-supplied data" or simply "unconfirmed."

In a PSI report, most third-party data are subject to ethical and legal considerations. The official records of almost all agencies and organizations, though often an ideal source of information, are protected by state and federal privacy requirements; in particular, the federal Privacy Act of 1974[72] may limit access to these records. Investigators must first check on the legal availability of all records before requesting them and must receive in writing the defendant's permission to access the records. Other public laws, among them the federal Freedom of Information Act,[73] may make the presentence report available to the defendant, although courts and court officers have generally been held to be exempt from the provision of such statutes.

The final section of a PSI report is usually devoted to the investigating officer's recommendations. A recommendation may be made in favor of probation, split sentencing, a term of imprisonment, or any other sentencing option available in the jurisdiction. Participation in community service programs or in drug- or substance-abuse programs may be recommended for probationers. Most judges are willing to accept the report writer's recommendation because they recognize the professionalism of the presentence investigator and because they know that the investigator may be assigned to supervise the defendant if he or she is sentenced to a community alternative.

Jurisdictions vary in their use of the information in a PSI. Federal law mandates PSI reports in federal criminal courts and specifies 15 topical areas that each report must cover. The 1984 federal Determinate Sentencing Act directs report writers to include the classification of the offense and of the defendant under the offense-level and criminal history categories established by the statute. Some states require presentence reports only in felony cases. Some require them in cases where the defendant faces the possibility of incarceration for 6 months or more. Other states have no requirement for PSI reports beyond those ordered by a judge.

Report writing, rarely anyone's favorite task, may seriously tax the limited resources of probation agencies. In September 2004, officers from the New York City Department of Probation wrote 2,414 reports for adult offenders and 461 reports for juvenile offenders, averaging about 10 reports per probation officer per month.[74]

The Victim—Forgotten No Longer
Victims' Rights

Thanks to a grassroots resurgence of concern for the plight of victims that began in this country in the early 1970s, the sentencing process now frequently includes consideration of the needs of victims and their survivors.[75] In times past, although victims might testify at trial, the criminal justice system frequently downplayed victims' experiences, including the psychological trauma engendered both by having been victims and by having to endure the criminal proceedings that bring a criminal to justice. That changed in 1982 when the President's Task Force on Victims of Crime gave focus to a burgeoning victims' rights movement and urged the widespread expansion of victims' assistance programs during what was then their formative period.[76] Victims' assistance programs today offer services in the areas of crisis intervention and follow-up counseling and help victims secure their rights under the law.[77] Following successful prosecution, some victims' assistance programs also advise victims on the filing of civil suits to recoup financial losses directly from the offender.

About the same time, voters in California approved Proposition 8, a resolution that called for changes in the state's constitution to reflect concern for victims. A continuing goal of victims' advocacy groups is an amendment to the U.S. Constitution, which such groups say is needed to provide the same kind of fairness to victims that is routinely accorded to defendants. In the past, for example, the National Victims' Constitutional Amendment Project (NVCAP) has sought to add a phrase to the Sixth Amendment—"likewise, the victim, in every criminal prosecution, shall have the right to be present and to be heard at all critical stages of judicial proceedings." The NVCAP now advocates the addition of a new amendment to the U.S. Constitution. Visit the NVCAP via **http://www.nvcap.org**.

In September 1996, a victims' rights constitutional amendment—Senate Joint Resolution 65—was proposed by a bipartisan committee in the U.S. Congress,[78] but problems of wording and terminology prevented its passage. A revised amendment was proposed in 1998,[79] but its wording was too restrictive for it to gain endorsement from victims' organizations.[80] In 1999, a new amendment was proposed by the Senate Judiciary Committee's Subcommittee on the Constitution, Federalism, and Property, but it did not make it to the Senate floor. The U.S. Department of Justice, which had previously supported the measure, reversed its position owing to a provision in the proposed amendment that gives crime victims the right to be notified of any state or federal grant of clemency. The U.S. attorney general apparently believed that the provision would impede the power of the president. The legislation also lacked the support of then-President Bill Clinton and was officially withdrawn by its sponsors in 2000. A revised Victim Rights Amendment was again proposed in Congress in 2012, but failed to pass. As introduced, the amendment would have added the following wording to the U.S. Constitution: "The rights of a crime victim to fairness, respect, and dignity, being capable of protection without denying the constitutional rights of the accused, shall not be denied or abridged by the United States or any State."

Although a victims' rights amendment to the federal Constitution may not yet be a reality, more than 30 states have passed their own victims' rights amendments.[81] According to the NVCAP, California Proposition 9, or the Victims' Rights and Protection Act of 2008 (also known as *Marsy's Law*), is the most comprehensive victims' bill of rights of any state in the nation.[82] Proposition 9, which appeared on the November 4, 2008, statewide ballot in California, passed with 53.8% of the vote. It amended the California Constitution by adding new provisions that provide victims in California with a number of specifically enforceable rights (CJ Exhibit 9–2).

At the federal level, the 1982 Victim and Witness Protection Act (VWPA) requires judges to consider victim-impact statements at federal sentencing hearings and places responsibility for their creation on federal probation officers. In 1984, the federal Victims of Crime Act (VOCA) was enacted with substantial bipartisan support. VOCA authorized federal funding to help states establish victims' assistance and victims' compensation programs. Under VOCA, the U.S. Department of Justice's Office for Victims of Crime provides a significant source of both funding and information for today's victims' assistance programs.

The rights of victims were further strengthened under the Violent Crime Control and Law Enforcement Act of 1994, which created a federal right of allocution, or right to speak,

7 Describe the history of victims' rights and services, including the growing role of the victim in criminal justice proceedings today.

Follow the author's tweets about the latest crime and justice news @schmalleger

A continuing goal of victims' advocacy groups is an amendment to the U.S. Constitution.

CJ Exhibit 9-2
Victims' Rights in California

In order to preserve and protect a victim's rights to justice and due process, a victim shall be entitled to the following rights:

1. To be treated with fairness and respect for his or her privacy and dignity, and to be free from intimidation, harassment, and abuse, throughout the criminal or juvenile justice process.

2. To be reasonably protected from the defendant and persons acting on behalf of the defendant.

3. To have the safety of the victim and the victim's family considered in fixing the amount of bail and release conditions for the defendant.

4. To prevent the disclosure of confidential information or records to the defendant, the defendant's attorney, or any other person acting on behalf of the defendant, which could be used to locate or harass the victim or the victim's family or which disclose confidential communications made in the course of medical or counseling treatment, or which are otherwise privileged or confidential by law.

5. To refuse an interview, deposition, or discovery request by the defendant, the defendant's attorney, or any other person acting on behalf of the defendant, and to set reasonable conditions on the conduct of any such interview to which the victim consents.

6. To reasonable notice of and to reasonably confer with the prosecuting agency, upon request, regarding the arrest of the defendant if known by the prosecutor, the charges filed, the determination whether to extradite the defendant, and, upon request, to be notified of and informed before any pretrial disposition of the case.

7. To reasonable notice of all public proceedings, including delinquency proceedings, upon request, at which the defendant and the prosecutor are entitled to be present and of all parole or other post-conviction release proceedings, and to be present at all such proceedings.

8. To be heard, upon request, at any proceeding, including any delinquency proceeding, involving a post-arrest release decision, plea, sentencing, post-conviction release decision, or any proceeding in which a right of the victim is at issue.

9. To a speedy trial and a prompt and final conclusion of the case and any related post-judgment proceedings.

10. To provide information to a probation department official conducting a pre-sentence investigation concerning the impact of the offense on the victim and the victim's family and any sentencing recommendations before the sentencing of the defendant.

11. To receive, upon request, the pre-sentence report when available to the defendant, except for those portions made confidential by law.

12. To be informed, upon request, of the conviction, sentence, place and time of incarceration, or other disposition of the defendant, the scheduled release date of the defendant, and the release of or the escape by the defendant from custody.

13. To restitution.

14. To the prompt return of property when no longer needed as evidence.

15. To be informed of all parole procedures, to participate in the parole process, to provide information to the parole authority to be considered before the parole of the offender, and to be notified, upon request, of the parole or other release of the offender.

16. To have the safety of the victim, the victim's family, and the general public considered before any parole or other post-judgment release decision is made.

17. To be informed of the rights enumerated in paragraphs (1) through (16).

Source: Section 28(e) of Article I of the California Constitution.

---

for victims of violent and sex crimes. This gave victims the right to speak at the sentencing of their assailants. The 1994 law also requires sex offenders and child molesters convicted under federal law to pay restitution to their victims and prohibits the diversion of federal victims' funds to other programs. Other provisions of the 1994 law provide civil rights remedies for victims of felonies motivated by gender bias and extend rape shield law protections to civil cases and to all criminal cases, prohibiting inquiries into a victim's sexual history. A significant feature of the 1994 law can be found in a subsection titled the Violence against Women Act (VAWA). VAWA, which has been reauthorized by Congress a number of times, provides financial support for police, prosecutors, and victims' services in cases involving sexual violence or domestic abuse. It is discussed in greater detail in Chapter 2.

Much of the philosophical basis of today's victims' movement can be found in the restorative-justice model, which was discussed briefly earlier in this chapter. RJ emphasizes offender accountability and victim reparation. It also provides the basis for victims' compensation programs, which are another means of recognizing the needs of crime victims. Today, all 50 states have passed legislation providing for monetary payments to victims of crime. Such payments are primarily designed to compensate victims for medical expenses and lost wages. All existing programs require that applicants meet certain eligibility criteria, and most set limits on the maximum amount of compensation that can be received. Generally disallowed are claims from victims who are significantly responsible for their own victimization, such as those who end up being the losers in fights they provoke. California, whose victims' rights amendment was discussed earlier, funds victim compensation through the California Victim Compensation Board (CalVCB). In the first half of 2016, the California legislature appropriated $448,452 for payouts to 210 victims whose claims were approved by CalVCB.[83]

Freedom or Safety? You Decide
To What Degree Should the Personal Values of Workers in the Criminal Justice System Influence Job Performance?

In 2007, a 21-year-old college student who was visiting Tampa, Florida, for the annual Gasparilla festival, a pirate-themed parade, called police to say that she was attacked and raped while walking back to her car. The woman's story took an interesting twist. Investigating officers first took her to a nearby rape crisis center, where she was physically examined and given the first dose of an emergency postcoital contraception pill, also known as a *morning-after pill*, to prevent unwanted pregnancy.

Officers then drove the victim through the area where the attack was said to have taken place in an effort to find the rapist and to pinpoint the scene of the crime. As they drove, officers entered the woman's identifying information into their car's computer system and discovered an outstanding juvenile warrant that had been issued against her in 2003 for unpaid restitution in a theft case. Once they discovered the warrant, they promptly arrested the woman. She remained behind bars for 2 days until her family could hire an attorney who arranged for her release.

While she was jailed, the victim said that a jail health-care worker refused to administer a second—and required—dose of the morning-after medication. The medicine's manufacturer specifies that two doses of the medication, administered 20 hours apart, are needed to prevent pregnancy. Some members of the local media, which accused the police department of insensitivity to the needs of crime victims, reported that the jail worker felt compelled to deny the woman the medication due to personal religious beliefs against use of the pill.

Some saw similarities between the Tampa case and the refusal by a Kentucky court clerk in 2015 to issue marriage licenses to same-sex couples, even though the U.S. Supreme Court had earlier found in favor of such unions. The clerk, Kim Davis, had argued that her Christian beliefs prevented her from recognizing same-sex unions. Unfortunately for Davis, the 2009 federal conscience-protection rule does not apply to state workers, and she was jailed for contempt of court.

YOU DECIDE

To what extent (if at all) should the values of workers within the criminal justice system be allowed to influence their performance of job-related tasks? Do you feel that the jail health-care worker was within her "rights" to deny a second dose of the morning-after pill to the victim of an alleged rape? What about the Kentucky court clerk?

References: Phil Davis, "Rape Victim Is Jailed on Old Warrant," *Associated Press*, January 31, 2007; and Steven Nelson, "Kentucky Clerk Kim Davis Jailed for Contempt," *U.S. News and World Report*, http://www.usnews.com/news/articles/2015/09/03/kentucky-clerk-kim-davis-jailed-for-contempt (accessed March 1, 2017).

In 2001, the USA PATRIOT Act amended the Victims of Crime Act of 1984 to make victims of terrorism and their families eligible for victims' compensation payments.[84] It also created an antiterrorism emergency reserve fund to help provide compensation to victims of terrorism. A year earlier, in November 2000, the federal Office for Victims of Crime (OVC) created the Terrorism and International Victims Unit (TIVU) to develop and manage programs and initiatives that help victims of domestic and international terrorism, mass violence, and crimes with transnational dimensions.[85]

On October 9, 2004, the U.S. Senate passed the Crime Victims' Rights Act,[86] as part of the Justice for All Act of 2004. Some saw the legislation as at least a partial statutory alternative to a constitutional crime victims' rights amendment. The Crime Victims' Rights Act establishes statutory rights for victims of federal crimes and gives them the necessary legal authority to assert those rights in federal court. The act grants the following rights to victims of federal crimes:[87]

1. The right to be reasonably protected from the accused

2. The right to reasonable, accurate, and timely notice of any public proceeding involving the crime or of any release or escape of the accused

3. The right to be included in any such public proceeding

4. The right to be reasonably heard at any public proceeding involving release, plea, or sentencing

5. The right to confer with the federal prosecutor handling the case

6. The right to full and timely restitution as provided by law

7. The right to proceedings free from unreasonable delay

8. The right to be treated with fairness and with respect for the victim's dignity and privacy

In addition to establishing these rights, the legislation expressly requires federal courts to ensure that they are afforded to victims. In like manner, federal law enforcement officials are required to make their "best efforts to see that crime victims are notified of, and accorded," these rights. To teach citizens about the rights of victims of crime, the federal government created a Website that you can access via **http://www.crimevictims.gov**. It includes an online directory of crime victims' services, which can be searched locally, nationally, and internationally. A user-friendly database of victims' rights laws can be found online at **http://www.victimlaw.info**.

Follow the author's tweets about the latest crime and justice news @schmalleger

Victim-Impact Statements

Another consequence of the national victims' rights movement has been a call for the use of a **victim-impact statement**—a written document describing the losses, suffering, and trauma experienced by the crime victim or by the victim's survivors—before sentencing. Judges are expected to consider such a statement in arriving at an appropriate sanction for the offender.

The drive to mandate inclusion of victim-impact statements in sentencing decisions, already required in federal courts by the 1982 VWPA, was substantially enhanced by the "right of allocution" provision of the Violent Crime Control and Law Enforcement Act of 1994. Victim-impact statements played a prominent role in the sentencing of Timothy McVeigh, who was convicted of the 1995 bombing of the Murrah Federal Building in Oklahoma City and was executed in 2001. Some states, however, have gone further than the federal government. In 1984, for example, California passed legislation giving victims a right to attend and participate in sentencing and parole hearings.[88] Approximately 20 states now have laws requiring citizen involvement in sentencing. All 50 states and the District of Columbia "allow for some form of submission of a victim-impact statement either at the time of sentencing or to be contained in the presentence investigation reports" made by court officers.[89] Where written victim-impact statements are not available, courts may invite the victim to testify directly at sentencing. An alternative to written statements and to the appearance of victims at sentencing hearings is the victim-impact video. Some contemporary victim-impact videos display photo montages of victims' lives and are set to music and narrated. In 2008, for example, the U.S. Supreme Court rejected an appeal from a death-row inmate wanting to exclude just such a digitized narrative set to music by Enya that had played to the jury during the sentencing phase of his trial.[90]

One study of the efficacy of victim-impact statements found that sentencing decisions are rarely affected by them. The authors concluded that victim-impact statements have little effect on courts because judges and other officials "have established ways of making decisions which do not call for explicit information about the impact of crime on victims."[91] Learn more about the rights of crime victims and the history of the victims' movement at **https://www.justicestudies.com/pubs/victimrights.pdf**. You can read the 2013 Office for Victims of Crime report, *Vision 21: Transforming Victim Services*, at **https://www.justice studies.com/pubs/vision21.pdf**. The thrust of the report is that victim services should be based on evidence of what works and what doesn't.

Traditional Sentencing Options

8 List the four traditional sentencing options.

> Today, all 50 states have passed legislation providing for monetary payments to victims of crime.

As the sun rose on a clear August day in 2017, 71-year-old photographer Edward French stood at the top of San Francisco's famed Twin Peaks to capture images of what he thought would be a glorious sunrise.[92] Before he could snap the first picture, however, he was attacked by Lamonte Mims, 19, and Fantasy Decuir, 20, who shot him to death with a handgun and stole his camera. Mims was on parole after serving 3 months in prison. Only a month before the shooting police had arrested him for gun possession and parole violations. Appearing before a judge only 5 days before the killing, Mims was released into the community by a judge who ordered that he be placed into an assertive case management program. The judge's decision was largely based on a public-safety assessment (PSA) score generated by a computer program that measures dangerousness. The software weighs nine risk factors, including things such as age, criminal history, and current and past criminal charges.

The decision to release Mims shows that sentencing is fundamentally a risk management strategy. If a judge makes a mistake and releases a dangerous person instead of sending them to prison (or back to prison, as would have been the case with Mims), then society pays the price. If, however, the judge errors on the side of caution, and imprisons someone who is not a danger to the community, then the offender is unnecessarily (and perhaps unfairly) punished, and society pays a different kind of price—the cost of keeping one more person behind bars.

Sentencing Rationales

Criminal sentencing is meant to protect the public while serving the ends of retribution, incapacitation, deterrence, rehabilitation, and restoration. Because the goals of sentencing are difficult to agree on, so too are sanctions. Lengthy prison terms do little for rehabilitation, whereas community release programs can hardly protect the innocent from offenders bent on continuing criminality.

Assorted sentencing philosophies continue to permeate state-level judicial systems. Each state has its own sentencing laws, and frequent revisions of those statutes are not uncommon. Because of huge variations from one state to another in the laws and procedures that control the imposition of criminal sanctions, sentencing has been called "the most diversified part of the Nation's criminal justice process."[93]

There is at least one commonality, however. It can be found in the four traditional sanctions that continue to dominate the thinking of most legislators and judges: fines, probation, imprisonment, and death (Figure 9–3). Fines and the death penalty are discussed in this chapter; probation is described in Chapter 10, and imprisonment is covered in Chapters 11 and 12.

In jurisdictions that employ indeterminate sentencing, fines, probation, and imprisonment are widely available to judges. The option selected generally depends on the severity of the offense and the judge's best guess as to the likelihood of the defendant's future criminal involvement. Sometimes two or more options are combined, such as when an offender is fined and sentenced to prison or placed on probation and fined in support of restitution payments.

Jurisdictions that operate under presumptive sentencing guidelines generally limit the judge's choice to only one option and often specify the extent to which that option can be applied. Dollar amounts of fines, for example, are rigidly set, and prison terms are specified for each type of offense. The death penalty remains an option in a fair number of jurisdictions, but only for a highly select group of offenders.

Sentencing Practices

State trial courts convict approximately 1,100,000 felons each year, and another 65,000 or so felony convictions occur each year in federal courts.[94] One recent report found that for felons convicted in state courts (Figure 9–4):

- About 41% were sentenced to active prison terms; another 28% received jail sentences involving less than 1 year's confinement.
- The average sentence length for those sent to state prisons has decreased since 1990 (from 6 to 4 years and 11 months).
- Felons sentenced today are likely to serve more of their sentence before release (50%) than those sentenced in 1990 (33%).
- Of the total, 27% were sentenced to probation with no jail or prison time to serve.
- The average probation sentence was 38 months.
- The largest offense category for which state felons were sent to prison was drug offenses.

Although the percentage of felons who receive active sentences may seem low, the number of criminal defendants receiving active prison time has increased dramatically. Figure 9–5 shows that the number of court-ordered prison commitments has increased nearly eightfold in the past 40 years. The number of *new* prison commitments peaked around 2010–2011, however, and has since shown a small decline. Much of the decline can be attributed to the use of alternative sanctions made necessary by skyrocketing imprisonment costs. Because non-violent property and drug offenders accounted for much of the growth in prison populations over the past 40 years, shorter prison stays and diversion from imprisonment for that group of offenders accounts for much of the recent decline in prison populations.

FIGURE 9–3
Four Traditional Sentencing Options
Source: Pearson Education, Inc., New York, NY.

Capital punishment

Fines

Imprisonment

Probation

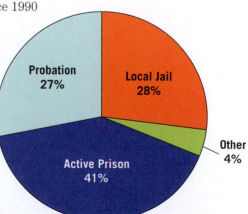

FIGURE 9–4
The Sentencing of Convicted Felons in State Courts, by Type of Sentence
Source: Data from Bureau of Justice Statistics.

FIGURE 9–5
Court-Ordered Prison Commitments, 1960–2016

Source: Data from Sean Rosenmerkel, Matthew Durose, and Donald Farole, Jr., *Felony Sentences in State Courts, 2006* (Washington, D.C.: Bureau of Justice Statistics, December 2009), and other years; and E. Ann Carson, *Prisoners in 2016* (Washington, D.C.: Bureau of Justice Statistics, 2018), p. 11, and other years.

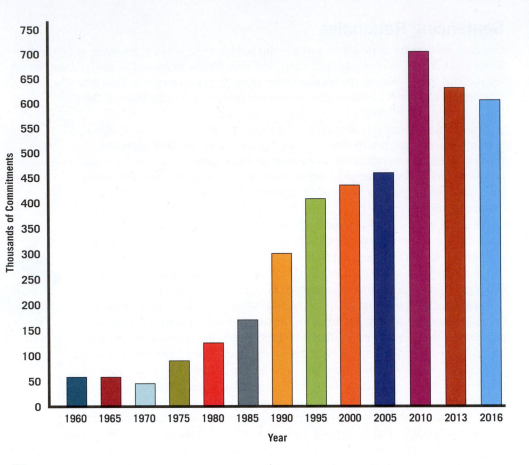

Fines

Although the fine is one of the oldest forms of punishment, the use of fines as a criminal sanction suffers from built-in inequities and a widespread failure to collect them. Inequities arise when offenders with vastly different financial resources are fined similar amounts. A fine of $100, for example, can place a painful economic burden on a poor defendant but is negligible when imposed on a wealthy offender.

Nonetheless, fines are once again receiving attention as a serious sentencing alternative. One reason for the renewed interest is the stress placed on state resources by burgeoning prison populations. The extensive imposition of fines not only results in less crowded prisons but can contribute to state and local coffers and can lower the tax burden of law-abiding citizens. There are other advantages:

- Fines can deprive offenders of the proceeds of criminal activity.
- Fines can promote rehabilitation by enforcing economic responsibility.
- Fines can be collected by existing criminal justice agencies and are relatively inexpensive to administer.
- Fines can be made proportionate to both the severity of the offense and the ability of the offender to pay.

A National Institute of Justice (NIJ) survey found that an average of 86% of convicted defendants in courts of limited jurisdiction receive fines as sentences, some in combination with another penalty.[95] Fines are also widely used in courts of general jurisdiction, where the NIJ study found judges imposing fines in 42% of all cases that came before them for sentencing. Some studies estimate that more than $1 billion in fines are collected nationwide each year.[96]

Fines are often imposed for relatively minor law violations, such as driving while intoxicated, reckless driving, disturbing the peace, disorderly conduct, public drunkenness, and vandalism. Judges in many courts, however, report the use of fines for relatively serious violations of the law, including assault, auto theft, embezzlement, fraud, and sale and pos-

Since the early 1970s, the use of incarceration as a criminal sentencing option had been growing steadily, primarily as a result of the enactment of "get-tough-on-crime" legislation, like two- and three-strikes laws, and the war on drugs, which accounted for a huge number of our nation's prisoners—especially at the federal level. Faced, however, with severe budget shortfalls, and rapidly rising prison populations, states were forced to find ways to save money and began looking at alternative sentencing practices and programs to lower the cost of handling convicted felons.

Four types of sentencing reforms, instituted in various ways by 28 states, have helped to lower justice systems costs by lowering prison populations in a number of jurisdictions over the past few years. They include (1) sentence modifications, (2) drug-law reform, (3) probation reforms, and (4) reforms in juvenile sentencing.

The first of these reforms, sentence modifications, effectively diverts many nonviolent offenders from prison, makes wider use of alternative sentencing options, and shifts inmates who would normally be incarcerated in state facilities to local jails or privately run facilities. The second, drug-law reform, makes wider use of drug courts and drug treatment as alternatives to imprisonment, and has also resulted in the reformation of drug statutes, shortening periods of confinement and making wider use of supervised early release into the community. The third strategy, probation reforms, works in two ways. First, some states allow selected probation violators to remain free in the community under more intense supervision, and require serious rule violation for probation revocation. Depending on the offense, some probation violators are now deemed ineligible for imprisonment through changes in the law, but face tougher lifestyle restrictions if they violate the conditions of their probation. The second way in which probation works is through early discharge from supervision, usually after probationers have met certain require-

ments. Finally, reforms in juvenile sentencing give judges greater leeway in the handling of delinquents and mean that fewer young people will spend time confined in state-run facilities.

The use of local jails to hold inmates who would otherwise be sent to state facilities, and contracts with private correctional services companies to house inmates needing confinement are other ways that states are attempting to lower the cost of confinement. In Tennessee, for example, the cost to house an inmate in a county jail averages around $62 per day, and moving that inmate to a state-run facility can cost much more. Private companies, which bid for state contracts, can often be more efficient than state-run departments of corrections, at least in dealing with certain types of inmates, resulting in significant cost savings. Some governments officials also claim that private prisons shelter states from at least some forms of civil liability that may arise from lawsuits brought by prisoners. Finally, one way of alleviating the high cost of incarceration, at least in jails, is charging inmates to pay for the costs of their incarceration. Anderson County, Tennessee, for example, charges jail inmates for just about everything they use. Toilet paper is sold in the jail commissary for 29 cents per roll, while prison-approved pants cost $9.15. Riverside County, California, charges jail inmates $142.42 for every night they spend locked up.

References: Steve Ahillen, "Explore Cost-Effective Alternatives to Prison," *Tennessee News Sentinel*, March 10, 2012, http://www.politifact.com/tennessee/promises/haslam-o-meter/promise/1072/explore-cost-effective-alternatives-to-prison (accessed May 30, 2013); The Sentencing Project, *The State of Sentencing, 2013: Developments in Policy and Practice* (Washington, D.C.: The Sentencing Project, 2014); and Lauren-Brooke Eisen, "Tennesse Inmates Must 'Pay-to-Stay'," Brennan Center for Justice, https://www.brennancenter.org/blog/tennessee-inmates-pay-stay (accessed March 31, 2018).

session of various controlled substances. Fines are most likely to be imposed where the offender has both a clean record and the ability to pay.[97]

Studies have found that courts of limited jurisdiction, which are the most likely to impose fines, are also the least likely to have adequate information on offenders' financial status.[98] Perhaps as a consequence, some judges are reluctant to impose fines. Two of the most widely cited objections by judges to the use of fines are that fines allow more affluent offenders to "buy their way out" and that poor offenders cannot pay fines.[99]

In 2010, for example, a Swiss court fined a multimillionaire $290,000 for driving his Ferrari 85 mph through a 35-mph speed limit zone.[100] The court calculated the fine based on the speeder's wealth (said to total $22.7 million) and his record of past offenses.

Follow the author's tweets about the latest crime and justice news @schmalleger

Death: The Ultimate Sanction

Some crimes are especially heinous and seem to cry out for severe punishment. In 2008, for example, a 28-year-old grocery store stock clerk named Kevin Ray Underwood was sentenced to death in the murder of a 10-year-old girl in what authorities said was an elaborate plan to cannibalize the girl's flesh.[101] Underwood had been the girl's neighbor in Purcell, Oklahoma, and her mutilated body, covered with deep saw marks, was discovered in his apartment. Investigators told reporters that Underwood had sexually assaulted the little girl and had planned to eat her corpse using the meat tenderizer and barbecue skewers that they confiscated from his kitchen. "In my 24 years as a prosecutor, this ranks as one of the most heinous and atrocious cases I've ever been involved with," said McClain County Prosecutor Tim Kuykendalls.

Many states today have statutory provisions that provide for a sentence of **capital punishment** (the death penalty) for especially repugnant crimes (known as **capital offenses**). Estimates are that more than 18,800 legal executions have been carried out in the United

9 State the arguments for and against capital punishment.

capital punishment
The death penalty. Capital punishment is the most extreme of all sentencing options.

capital offense
A criminal offense punishable by death.

▲ Kevin Ray Underwood, whom some have called the "poster boy" for capital punishment. Underwood, of Purcell, Oklahoma, was sentenced to death in 2008 in the atrocious murder of a 10-year-old girl in an elaborate plan to cannibalize her flesh. After sexually abusing and killing the girl, Underwood mutilated her body and planned to eat her corpse using meat tenderizer and barbecue skewers. What would be an appropriate sentence for Underwood?

Chris Landsberger/Pool/AP Images

States since 1608, when records began to be kept on capital punishment.[102] Although capital punishment was widely used throughout the eighteenth and nineteenth centuries, the mid-twentieth century offered a brief respite in the number of offenders legally executed in this country. Between 1930 and 1967, the year in which the U.S. Supreme Court ordered a nationwide stay of pending executions, nearly 3,800 people were put to death. The peak years were 1935 and 1936, with nearly 200 legal killings each year. Executions declined substantially every year thereafter. Between 1967 and 1977, a *de facto* moratorium existed, with no executions carried out in any U.S. jurisdiction. Following the lifting of the moratorium, executions resumed (Figure 9–6). In 1983, only 5 offenders were put to death, whereas 23 were executed nationwide in 2017.[103] A modern record for executions was set in 1999, with 98 executions—35 in Texas alone.

Today, the federal government and 31 of the 50 states[104] permit execution for first-degree murder, whereas treason, kidnapping, aggravated rape, murder of a police or correctional officer, and murder while under a life sentence are punishable by death in selected jurisdictions.

Illinois, which up until recently was among states with a death penalty, repealed its capital punishment statute in 2011, replacing it with a sentence of life in prison without possibility of parole. In 2012, Connecticut took capital punishment off its books, although the 11 men on death row at the time of repeal are still slated to be executed. The latest state to abolish the death penalty is Maryland, which repealed its death-penalty statute in 2013.

Not all states are moving away from the death penalty. In 2016, for example, California voters passed Proposition 66, an initiative that speeds up the appeals process in capital cases by establishing a 5-year deadline for appeals to be heard.[105] In that same year, Oklahoma voters passed a ballot initiative intended to make it more difficult for the legislature to change or repeal the state's death penalty law. Oklahomans were apparently reacting to a move by Nebraska's legislature only a year earlier to abolish the law in that state. Legislators in Nebraska had overridden their governor's veto and ended capital punishment in 2015—only to have their actions rescinded by popular vote in 2016. Similarly, in 2017, New Mexico Governor Susana Martinez called for reinstatement of the death penalty in that state.

The United States is not the only country to make use of capital punishment. In 2017, for example, the Kingdom of Saudi Arabia executed 130 people by beheading. Many of the condemned had been convicted of terrorism-related charges, but others were "common criminals."[106] Iran is reported to have one of the highest execution rates in the world, exceeded only by China. China, the world's most populous country, is reported to routinely execute more than 1,700 people annually—meaning that more people are executed in China than in

FIGURE 9–6
Court-Ordered Executions Carried Out in the United States since 1976

Note: Excludes executions ordered by military authority.
Source: Based on Death Penalty Information Center, "Executions by Year," http://www.deathpenaltyinfo.org/executionsyear (accessed October 26, 2018).

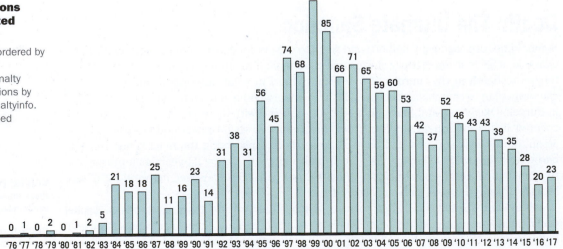

the rest of the world combined. According to Amnesty International, 993 executions were carried out in 23 countries in 2017.[107]

The list of crimes punishable by death under federal jurisdiction increased dramatically with passage of the Violent Crime Control and Law Enforcement Act of 1994 and was expanded still further by the 2001 USA PATRIOT Act, a federal law that focuses on fighting terrorism. The list now includes a total of about 60 offenses. State legislators have also worked to expand the types of crimes for which a death sentence can be imposed. In 1997, for example, the Louisiana Supreme Court upheld the state's year-old child rape statute, which allows for the imposition of a capital sentence when the victim is younger than 12 years of age. The case involved an AIDS-infected father who raped his three daughters, ages five, eight, and nine. In upholding the father's death sentence, the Louisiana court ruled that child rape is "like no other crime."[108] In 2008, however, in the case of *Kennedy* v. *Louisiana*,[109] the U.S. Supreme Court ruled that the Eighth Amendment bars Louisiana (and other states) from imposing the death penalty for the rape of a child where the crime did not result, and was not intended to result, in the victim's death.

A total of 2,743 criminal offenders are currently under sentence of death throughout the United States.[110] The latest statistics show that 98.2% of those on death row are male, approximately 42% are white, 13% are Hispanic, 42% are African American, and a small number are of other races (mostly Native American and Pacific Islander).[111]

Methods of imposing death vary by state. The majority of death-penalty states authorize execution through lethal injection. Electrocution is the second most common means of dispatch, and hanging, the gas chamber, and firing squads have survived, at least as options available to the condemned, in a few states.[112] For the most current statistical information on capital punishment, visit the Death Penalty Information Center via **http://www.deathpenaltyinfo.org**.

Habeas Corpus Review

The legal process through which a capital sentence is carried to conclusion is fraught with problems. One serious difficulty centers on the fact that automatic review of all death sentences by appellate courts and constant legal maneuvering by defense counsel often lead to a dramatic delay between the time the sentence is handed down and the time it is carried out. Today, an average of 15 years and 8 months passes between the imposition of a death penalty and execution.[113] Such lengthy delays, compounded by uncertainty over whether an execution will ever occur, directly contravene the generally accepted notion that punishment should be swift and certain. In one especially notable case, 71-year-old Edward Harold Schad, Jr., was executed in Arizona in October 2013 for a strangulation murder committed 35-years earlier.[114]

Even death-row inmates can undergo life-altering changes. When that happens, long-delayed executions can become highly questionable events. The case of Stanley "Tookie" Williams, who was executed at California's San Quentin Prison in 2005 at age 51, is illustrative.[115] Williams, self-described cofounder of the infamous Crips street gang in the early 1970s, was sentenced to die for the brutal shotgun murders of four people during a robbery 26 years earlier. In 1993, however, he experienced what he called a "reawakening" and began working from prison as an anti-gang crusader. Williams found a sympathetic publisher and wrote a series of children's books titled *Tookie Speaks Out against Gang Violence*. The series was intended to help urban youth reject the lure of gang membership and embrace traditional values. He also wrote *Life in Prison*, an autobiography describing the isolation and despair experienced by death-row inmates. In his final years, Williams worked with his editor, Barbara Cottman Becnel, to create the Internet Project for Street Peace, a demonstration project linking teens from the rough-and-tumble streets of Richmond, California, to peers in Switzerland in an effort to help them avoid street violence. In 2001, Williams was nominated for the Nobel Peace Prize by a member of the Swiss Parliament and for the Nobel Prize in Literature by a number of college professors. Pleas to spare his life, which came from Jesse Jackson, anti-death-penalty activist Sister Helen Prejean, the National Association for the Advancement of Colored People (NAACP), and others, were rejected by then-governor Arnold Schwarzenegger, who said that "there is no reason to second-guess the jury's decision of guilt or raise significant doubts or serious reservations about Williams' convictions and death sentence."[116]

In a speech before the American Bar Association (ABA) in 1989, then-Chief Justice William Rehnquist called for reforms of the federal *habeas corpus* system, which at the time allowed condemned prisoners virtually limitless opportunities for appeal. **Writs of *habeas corpus*** (Latin

writ of *habeas corpus*
A writ that directs the person detaining a prisoner to bring him or her before a judicial officer to determine the lawfulness of the imprisonment.

Follow the author's tweets about the latest crime and justice news @schmalleger

for "you have the body"), which require that a prisoner be brought into court to determine if he or she is being legally held, form the basis for many federal appeals made by prisoners on state death rows. In 1968, Chief Justice Earl Warren called the right to file *habeas* petitions, as guaranteed under the U.S. Constitution, the "symbol and guardian of individual liberty." Twenty years later, however, Rehnquist claimed that writs of *habeas corpus* were being used indiscriminately by death-row inmates seeking to delay executions even where grounds for delay did not exist. "The capital defendant does not need to prevail on the merits in order to accomplish his purpose," said Rehnquist. "He wins temporary victories by postponing a final adjudication."[117]

> I think this country would be much better off if we did not have capital punishment. . . . We cannot ignore the fact that in recent years a disturbing number of inmates on death row have been exonerated.
>
> —John Paul Stevens, U.S. Supreme Court justice[ii]

In a move to reduce delays in the carrying out of executions, the U.S. Supreme Court, in the case of *McCleskey* v. *Zant* (1991),[118] limited the number of appeals a condemned person may lodge with the courts. Saying that repeated filing for the sole purpose of delay promotes "disrespect for the finality of convictions" and "disparages the entire criminal justice system," the Court established a two-pronged criterion for future appeals. According to *McCleskey*, in any petition beyond the first filed with the federal court, a capital defendant must (1) demonstrate good cause why the claim now being made was not included in the first filing and (2) explain how the absence of that claim may have harmed the petitioner's ability to mount an effective defense. Two months later, the Court reinforced *McCleskey* when it ruled, in *Coleman* v. *Thompson* (1991),[119] that state prisoners could not cite "procedural default," such as a defense attorney's failure to meet a state's filing deadline for appeals, as the basis for an appeal to federal court.

In 1995, in the case of *Schlup* v. *Delo*,[120] the Court continued to define standards for further appeals from death-row inmates, ruling that before appeals based on claims of new evidence could be heard, "a petitioner must show that, in light of the new evidence, it is more likely than not that no reasonable juror would have found him guilty beyond a reasonable doubt." A "reasonable juror" was defined as one who "would consider fairly all of the evidence presented and would conscientiously obey the trial court's instructions requiring proof beyond a reasonable doubt."

Opportunities for federal appeals by death-row inmates were further limited by the Antiterrorism and Effective Death Penalty Act (AEDPA) of 1996,[121] which sets a one-year post-conviction deadline for state inmates filing federal *habeas corpus* appeals. The deadline is 6 months for state death-row inmates who were provided a lawyer for *habeas* appeals at the state level. The act also requires federal courts to presume that the factual findings of state courts are correct; does not permit the claim of state court misinterpretations of the U.S. Constitution as a basis for *habeas* relief unless those misinterpretations are "unreasonable"; and requires that all petitioners must show, prior to obtaining a hearing, facts sufficient to establish by clear and convincing evidence that but for constitutional error, no reasonable fact finder would have found the petitioner guilty. The act also requires approval by a three-judge panel before an inmate can file a second federal appeal raising newly discovered evidence of innocence. In 1996, in the case of *Felker* v. *Turpin*,[122] the U.S. Supreme Court ruled that limitations on the authority of federal courts to consider successive *habeas corpus* petitions imposed by the AEDPA are permissible because they do not deprive the U.S. Supreme Court of its original jurisdiction over such petitions.

Some recent statements by Supreme Court justices have indicated that long delays caused by the government in carrying out executions may render the punishment unconstitutionally cruel and unusual. One example comes from the 1998 case of *Elledge* v. *Florida*,[123] where the execution of William D. Elledge had been delayed for 23 years. Although the full Court refused to hear the case, Justice Stephen Breyer observed, "Twenty-three years under sentence of death is unusual—whether one takes as a measuring rod current practice or the practice in this country and in England at the time our Constitution was written." Moreover, wrote Breyer, execution after such a long delay could be considered cruel because Elledge "has experienced that delay because of the State's own faulty procedures and not because of frivolous appeals on his own part." Elledge died on death row at the Union Correctional Institution in Florida in 2008 while awaiting execution.[124] He had been under sentence of death for 34 years; at the time of his death from asthma, he was 57 years old.

Opposition to Capital Punishment

In 1969, David Magris, who was celebrating his twenty-first birthday with a crime spree, shot Dennis Tapp in the back during a holdup, leaving Tapp a paraplegic. Tapp had been working a late-night shift, tending his father's quick-serve gas station. Magris went on to commit more robberies that night, killing 20-year-old Steven Tompkins in a similar crime. Although Magris was sentenced to death by a California court, the U.S. Supreme Court overturned the state's death-penalty law in 1972, opening the door for Magris to be paroled in 1985. Long before Magris was freed from prison, however, Tapp had already forgiven him. A few minutes after the shooting happened, Tapp regained consciousness, dragged himself to a telephone, and called for help. The next thing he did was ask "God to forgive the man who did this to me."[125] Today, the men—both staunch death-penalty opponents—are friends, and Magris is president of the Northern California Coalition to Abolish the Death Penalty. "Don't get me wrong," says Tapp. "What [David] did was wrong . . . . He did something stupid and he paid for it."[126]

Because the death penalty is such an emotional issue for many, attempts have been made to abolish capital punishment since the founding of the United States. The first recorded effort to eliminate the death penalty occurred at the home of Benjamin Franklin in 1787.[127] At a meeting there on March 9 of that year, Dr. Benjamin Rush, a signer of the Declaration of Independence and a leading medical pioneer, read a paper against capital punishment to a small but influential audience. Although his immediate efforts came to naught, his arguments laid the groundwork for many debates that followed. Michigan, widely regarded as the first abolitionist state, joined the Union in 1837 without a death penalty. A number of other states, including Alaska, Hawaii, Illinois, Massachusetts, Minnesota, New York, New Jersey, New Mexico, West Virginia, and Wisconsin, have since spurned death as a possible sanction for criminal acts. As noted earlier, capital punishment remains a viable sentencing option in 31 of the states and in all federal jurisdictions, while arguments continue to rage over its value.

Today, six main rationales for abolishing capital punishment are heard, as shown in Table 9-4.

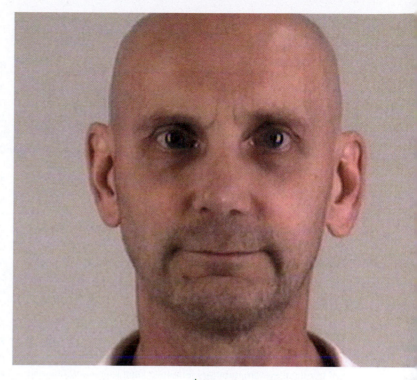

▲ Wrongful convictions undermine faith in the justice system. Shown here is Brian Franklin, a former Texas police officer who was exonerated in 2016, after spending 21 years in prison. He had been accused of raping a 13-year-old girl. A court later ruled that the girl made up the story. How can we guard against wrongful convictions?

Tarrant County Sheriff's Office/Fort Worth Star-Telegram/AP Images

The Death Penalty and Innocent People

In 2018, Richard Phillips gained an unwanted record after his first-degree murder conviction was vacated, and prosecutors dismissed the charges against him. Phillips had served 45 years and 2 months in prison—the longest time spent incarcerated after conviction by any wrongfully convicted defendant prior to exoneration.[128] Phillips, who had been previously convicted of manslaughter, was sent to prison in 1972 following a jury conviction for first-degree murder. His release came after another person admitted to the killing, and said that Phillips "had nothing to do with anything."

While **wrongful conviction** is a very serious miscarriage of justice, it does not always mean that an exonerated person is innocent of any crime. In some cases, defendants are released after serious doubts arise about their guilt, or it can be shown that they had inadequate legal representation. Except for the passage of time a retrial might be ordered, but 30 or 40 years is a long time, and evidence collected at the time of the crime is likely to have vanished, and witnesses might have died. The Death Penalty Information Center, however, claims that 163 people in 28 states were freed from death row between 1973 and late-2018 after it was determined that they were innocent of the capital crimes of which they had been convicted (Figure 9–7).[129] The Center also notes that the average time between being sentenced to death and exoneration for those who have been freed is 11.3 years.[130]

DNA testing can play a critical role in identifying wrongful convictions because, as Barry Scheck and Peter Neufeld (cofounders of the Innocence Project at the Benjamin N. Cardozo

wrongful conviction
An unfair criminal conviction, often made on the basis of inadequate representation by counsel, inaccurate forensics analysis, eyewitness misidentification, and improper behavior by prosecutors, law enforcement officers, or jury members.

🐦 Follow the author's tweets about the latest crime and justice news @schmalleger

TABLE 9-4
Capital Punishment: Abolitionist and Retentionist Rationales

Reasons to Abolish	Reasons to Keep
Innocent People Have Been Executed CLAIM. The death penalty can be and has been inflicted on innocent people. COUNTERCLAIM. Although it has been shown that some innocent people have been condemned to death, and although it can be assumed that a number of innocent people remain on death row, it has not been demonstrated that innocent people have actually been executed.	**Just Deserts** CLAIM. Some people deserve to die for what they have done. Anything less than death cannot suffice as a sanction for the most heinous crimes. COUNTERCLAIM. Capital punishment is a holdover from primitive times. Contemporary standards of human decency mandate alternatives, such as life imprisonment.
Lack of Proven Deterrence CLAIM. The death penalty is not an effective deterrent, as numerous studies have shown. COUNTERCLAIM. If capital punishment were imposed with both certainty and swiftness, then it would be effective as a deterrent. It is our system of appeals and lengthy delays that makes it ineffective.	**Revenge/Retribution** CLAIM. Capital punishment can be seen as revenge for the pain and suffering that the criminal inflicted on the victim. In Gregg v. Georgia, the U.S. Supreme Court wrote that "[t]he instinct for retribution is part of the nature of man." Hence, sentencing a capital offender to death can provide closure to a victim's family members. COUNTERCLAIM. Forgiveness and rehabilitation are higher goals than revenge and retribution.
Arbitrariness CLAIM. The imposition of the death penalty is, by the very nature of our legal system, arbitrary. Effective legal representation and access to the courts are not equally available to everyone. COUNTERCLAIM. Many safeguards exist at all levels of criminal justice processing to protect the innocent and to ensure that only the guilty are actually put to death.	**Protection** CLAIM. Executed offenders cannot commit further crimes, and execution serves as an example to other would-be wrongdoers of the fate that awaits them. Moreover, society has a duty to act in defense of others and to protect its innocent members. COUNTERCLAIM. Societal interests in protection can be met in other ways, such as incarceration.
Discrimination CLAIM. The death penalty discriminates against certain ethnic and racial groups. COUNTERCLAIM. Any examination of disproportionality must go beyond simple comparisons and must measure both frequency and seriousness of capital crimes between and within racial groups. The Supreme Court, in the 1987 case of McCleskey v. Kemp, held that a simple showing of racial discrepancies in the application of the death penalty does not constitute a constitutional violation. Members of underrepresented groups were more likely to be sentenced to death but only because they were more likely to be arrested on facts that could support a capital charge, not because the justice system acts in a discriminatory fashion.	
Expense CLAIM. Because of all the appeals involved in death-penalty cases, the cost to a state can run into the millions of dollars for each execution. COUNTERCLAIM. Although official costs associated with capital punishment are high, no cost is too high if it achieves justice.	
Human Life Is Sacred CLAIM. Killing at the hands of the state is not a righteous act but instead lowers all of us to the same moral level as the crimes committed by the condemned. COUNTERCLAIM. If life is sacred, then the taking of life demands revenge.	

Note: For additional perspectives, see The National Coalition to Abolish the Death Penalty, http://www.ncadp.org; Pro-Death Penalty.com, http://www.prodeathpenalty.com.

Source: Pearson Education, Inc., New York, NY.

FIGURE 9–7
Death Row Exonerations by State, 1973–2018
Source: Pearson Education, Data from Death Penalty Information Center.

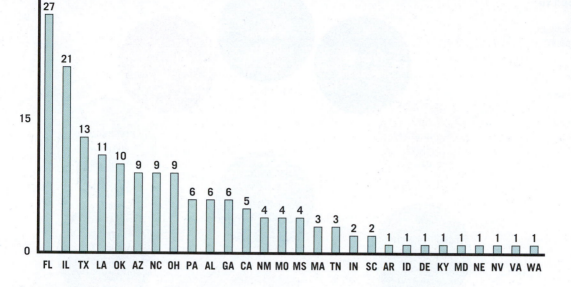

School of Law) point out, "Unlike witnesses who disappear or whose recollections fade over time, DNA in biological samples can be reliably extracted decades after the commission of the crime. The results of such testing have invariably been found to have a scientific certainty that easily outweighs the eyewitness identification testimony or other direct or circumstantial proof that led to the original conviction."[131] They go on to say, "Very simply, . . . DNA testing has demonstrated that far more wrongful convictions occur than even the most cynical and jaded scholars had suspected."[132] You can reach the Innocence Project at **http://www.innocenceproject.org**.

A study by Columbia Law School professors James S. Liebman, Jeffrey Fagan, and Valerie West examined 4,578 death-penalty cases that had been handled in state courts between 1973 and 1995.[133] The researchers found that appellate courts overturned the conviction or reduced the sentence in 68% of the cases examined. In 82% of the successful appeals, defendants were found to be deserving of a lesser sentence, and convictions were overturned in 7% of such appeals. According to the study's authors, "Our 23 years' worth of findings reveal a capital punishment system collapsing under the weight of its own mistakes." You can read the report in its entirety at **https://www.justicestudies.com/pubs/liebman.pdf**.

A recent NIJ-funded study found ten factors that can lead to a wrongful conviction of an innocent defendant instead of a dismal or acquittal.[134] Those factors are shown in Figure 9–8. The NIJ study also distinguished between cases in which erroneous convictions are returned and near misses, or cases in which innocent defendants came close to being convicted but were eventually acquitted. Cases that lead to erroneous convictions and those that lead to near misses were found to share many of the same characteristics, including false confession, official misconduct, eyewitness misidentification, or an incorrect tip to the police. Factors that lead to an erroneous conviction included a punitive state culture (a just deserts mind-set in which prosecutors seek convictions at all costs), forensic error (either incorrect or failed crime scene or crime laboratory analysis), weak facts still pressed by the prosecution, or a mistaken or lying eyewitness. Factors that led to a near miss included, but were not limited to, an older defendant with no criminal history, a strong defense, or prosecutorial disclosure of critical evidence.

Claims of innocence are being partially addressed today by recently passed state laws that mandate DNA testing of all death-row inmates in situations where DNA testing might help establish guilt or innocence (i.e., in cases where blood or semen from the perpetrator is available for testing).[135] In 2000, Illinois Governor George Ryan announced that he was suspending all executions in his state indefinitely, a proclamation that came after DNA testing showed that 13 Illinois death-row prisoners could not have committed the capital crimes of which they were convicted.[136] The state abolished the death penalty 11 years later. In 2006, the New Jersey legislature voted to suspend use of the death penalty until a state task force made its report on whether capital punishment is fairly imposed; and the state repealed its capital punishment statute a year later.[137]

FIGURE 9–8
Ten Factors That Can Lead to a Wrongful Conviction
Source: Data from Jon B. Gould, Julia Carrano, Richard Leo, and Joseph Young, "Predicting Erroneous Convictions: A Social Science Approach to Miscarriages of Justice—Final Report to the National Institute of Justice, February 2013," https://www.ncjrs.gov/pdffiles1/nij/grants/241389.pdf.

exoneration
The reversal of a criminal conviction by appropriate judicial authority.

In 2004, in recognition of the potential of DNA testing to exonerate the innocent, President George W. Bush signed the Innocence Protection Act[138] into law. The act provides federal funds to eliminate the backlog of unanalyzed DNA samples in the nation's crime laboratories.[139] It also sets aside money to improve the capacity of federal, state, and local crime laboratories to conduct DNA analyses.[140] In addition, the act facilitates access to post-conviction DNA testing for those serving time in state[141] or federal prisons or on death row, and it sets forth conditions under which a federal prisoner asserting innocence may obtain post-conviction DNA testing of specific evidence. Similarly, the legislation requires the preservation of biological evidence by federal law enforcement agencies for any defendant under a sentence of imprisonment or death. The Innocence Protection Act was reauthorized in 2016 with passage of the Justice for All Reauthorization Act.

In 2006, the North Carolina General Assembly established the North Carolina Innocence Inquiry Commission and charged it with investigating and evaluating post-conviction claims of factual innocence.[142] The commission, which was the first of its kind, comprises eight members selected by the chief justice of the North Carolina Supreme Court and the chief judge of the North Carolina Court of Appeals. It examines only new evidence that was not considered at trial and which may lead to **exoneration**. Today, 10 other states have established similar commissions, while privately funded innocence projects have been created in nearly all states. Most innocence projects are private initiatives based at law schools or universities.[143] One study estimated that around 4.1% of all death-row inmates are probably falsely convicted and could be exonerated, although only very few false convictions are actually ever discovered and overturned.[144]

Not all claims of innocence are supported by DNA tests or by other forms of inquiry, however. In 2006, for example, DNA test results confirmed the guilt of Roger Keith Coleman, a Virginia coal miner who had steadfastly maintained his innocence until he was executed in 1992. Coleman, executed for the 1981 rape and murder of his sister-in-law, Wanda McCoy, died declaring his innocence and proclaiming

There can be no doubt that the taking of the life of the President creates much more societal harm than the taking of the life of a homeless person.

—Charles Burson, Tennessee attorney general, arguing before the U.S. Supreme Court in *Payne* v. *Tennessee*[iii]

that he would one day be exonerated. His case became a cause célèbre for death-penalty opponents, who convinced Virginia Governor Mark Warner to order DNA tests on surviving evidence. Coleman's supporters claimed that the tests would provide the first scientific proof that an innocent man had been executed in the United States. Results from the tests, however, conclusively showed that blood and semen found at the crime scene had come from Coleman. Recent studies have confirmed the convictions of about 42% of inmates whose cases are selected for DNA testing through the Innocence Project.[145] About 43% are exonerated by the tests (the remaining 15% are classified as "inconclusive"). Because strong doubts about guilt already exist in cases where inmates are selected for testing, however, the percentage of confirmed convictions seems surprising.

Finally, in 2010, the U.S. Supreme Court ruled, in the case of *District Attorney's Office v. Osborne*,[146] that there is no fundamental constitutional right to access DNA-testable evidence long after a criminal conviction is final. Learn more about advancing justice through DNA technology at **https://www.justice.gov/archives/ag/advancing-justice-through-dna-technology-table-contents**.

Death Penalty and Deterrence

During the 1970s and 1980s, the deterrent effect of the death penalty became a favorite subject for debate in academic circles.[147] Studies of states that had eliminated the death penalty failed to show any increase in homicide rates.[148] Similar studies of neighboring states, in which jurisdictions retaining capital punishment were compared with those that had abandoned it, also failed to demonstrate any significant differences.[149] Although death-penalty advocates remain numerous, few still argue for the penalty based on its deterrent effects. One study that offers support for the deterrent effect of the death penalty was reported in 2001 by Hashem Dezhbakhsh and his colleagues at Emory University.[150] According to the researchers, "Our results suggest that capital punishment has a strong deterrent effect . . . . In particular, each execution results, on average, in 18 fewer murders."[151] They note that most other studies in the area not only have been methodologically flawed but have failed to consider the fact that a number of states sentence select offenders to death but do not carry out executions. They write, "If criminals know that the justice system issues many death sentences but the executions are not carried out, then they may not be deterred by an increase in probability of a death sentence."[152]

In 2012, however, in a succinct summary of studies on the deterrent effect of the death penalty, the Committee on Law and Justice of the National Academies of Sciences released *Deterrence and the Death Penalty*—a publication that included a detailed analysis of previous death-penalty research.

The Committee found that "research to date is not informative about whether capital punishment decreases, increases, or has no effect on homicide rates." It concluded that "claims that research demonstrates that capital punishment decreases or increases the homicide rate or has no effect on it should not influence policy judgments about capital punishment." Read the entire National Academy of Sciences report at **https://www.justicestudies.com/pdf/deathpenaltynas.pdf**.

Death Penalty and Discrimination

The claim that the death penalty is discriminatory is hard to investigate. Although past evidence suggests that blacks and other minorities in the United States have been disproportionately sentenced to death,[153] more recent evidence is not as clear. At first glance, disproportionality seems apparent: 45 of the 98 prisoners executed between January 1977 and May 1988 were black or Hispanic, and 84 of the 98 had been convicted of killing whites.[154] A 1996 study found that blacks accused of killing whites in Kentucky between 1976 and 1991 had a higher-than-average probability of being charged with a capital crime and of being sentenced to die than did homicide offenders of other races.[155] For an accurate appraisal to be made, however, any claims of disproportionality must go beyond simple comparisons with racial representation in the larger population and must somehow measure both frequency and seriousness of capital crimes between and within racial groups. Following that line of reasoning, the Supreme Court, in the 1987 case of *McCleskey v. Kemp*,[156] held that a simple showing of racial discrepancies in the application of the death

Follow the author's tweets about the latest crime and justice news @schmalleger

CJ News
Death-Row Exonerations Based on DNA Expose Flaws in Legal System

The Innocence Project, dedicated to freeing wrongly accused prisoners, says DNA testing has "opened a window into wrongful convictions so that we may study the causes and propose remedies that may minimize the chances that more innocent people are convicted."

Miscarriages of justice exposed by DNA testing include erroneous reports by witnesses, misidentification of evidence, biased jailhouse informants, and false confessions obtained by overzealous prosecutors.

Kirk Bloodsworth was the first death-row inmate exonerated by DNA. He was found guilty in 1985 of raping and strangling a 9-year-old girl in Rosedale, Maryland, based on the testimony of five eyewitnesses. After learning that DNA testing was used to convict a man for murder, Bloodsworth asked to use it to unconvict him. The $15,000 test, which his attorney financed out-of-pocket, ruled him out, and he was released in 1993.

Speaking in 2013, to an audience of anti-capital-punishment supporters, Bloodsworth said "I was accused of the most brutal murder in Maryland history . . . . It [only] took the jury two and a half hours to send me to the gas chamber."

In an even more serious miscarriage of justice, Claude Jones was executed in Texas in 2000 for murdering the owner of a Texas liquor store. Jones's conviction was largely based on a strand of hair at the crime scene that purportedly was his. But DNA tests 10 years after the execution showed that it actually belonged to the storeowner.

In another example of the power of DNA testing, Michael Blair had a sex crime conviction when he was picked up in 1993 for the murder of a 7-year-old girl in Plano, Texas. Three eyewitnesses said they saw him near the crime scene, even though the police had found him 17 miles away that day. Hairs in Blair's car were falsely linked to the victim. Blair was sentenced to death for the crime, but DNA testing 8 years later excluded him and identified two other men. He was released.

Although Juan Rivera was never sentenced to death, he was convicted three times for the 1992 rape and murder of an 11-year-old baby sitter in Waukegan, Illinois. On the night of the murder, he had been confined to his home by an electronic leg monitor for stealing a car stereo, but after many hours of interrogation he confessed to the crime. His confession allegedly contained details that only the killer would know, and three jailhouse informants also implicated him.

Before Rivera's third trial, tests showed his DNA did not match semen from the crime scene, but the prosecutor argued it could have come from an unidentified lover of the 11-year-old. "We don't quaver because somebody holds up three letters: DNA," he said. And Rivera was found guilty again. But in December 2011, an appeals court reversed the conviction and barred any more retrials, saying the evidence had been insufficient to convince any "rational trier of fact." Rivera was freed after spending nearly 20 years in prison.

The Innocence Project, founded in 1992 at the Cardozo School of Law of Yeshiva University in New York, receives 3,000 requests

▲ Kirk Bloodsworth, the first death-row inmate exonerated through the use of DNA evidence. Bloodsworth had been found guilty in 1985 of raping and strangling a 9-year-old Rosedale, Maryland, girl based on the testimony of five eyewitnesses. Later DNA testing absolved him of guilt, and he was released in 1993. Should wider use be made of DNA testing? If so, who should pay the costs?

Mladen Antonova/AFP/Getty Images/Newscom

for help every year and is evaluating 6,000 to 8,000 potential cases at any given time. It now has 61 chapters across the country.

A similar group, the Center on Wrongful Convictions at Northwestern University Law School in Chicago, has been instrumental in 48 exonerations, including cases pursued by its lawyers before the center was founded. Thirteen of those prisoners had been sentenced to death and 26 of the cases involved DNA testing.

In addition, the Death Penalty Information Center provides analysis and information on issues about capital punishment, including wrongful convictions.

REFERENCES

"230 Exonerated in U.S. by DNA Testing, 17 Were Sentenced to Die," The Innocence Project, http://www.dadychery.org/2012/02/01/230-exonerated-by-dna-17-were-sentenced-to-die/.

"1st Death Row Inmate Exonerated by DNA to Speak at UM," *The Missoulian*, October 11, 2011, http://missoulian.com/news/local/article_1c836748-f3b2-11e0-b14b-001cc4c002e0.html.

"'Never Think a Person in Prison Is Lost,' Juan Rivera Tells Law Students," *The Chicago Tribune*, April 4, 2012, http://www.chicagotribune.com/news/local/ct-met-juan-rivera-judge-20120404,0,1540689.story.

penalty does not constitute a constitutional violation. A 2001 study of racial and ethnic fairness in federal capital punishment sentences attempted to go beyond mere percentages in its analysis of the role played by race and ethnicity in capital punishment sentencing decisions.[157] Although the study, which closely reviewed 950 capital punishment cases, found that approximately 80% of federal death-row inmates are African American, researchers found "no intentional racial or ethnic bias in how capital punishment was administered in federal cases."[158] Underrepresented groups were more likely to be sentenced to death, "but only because they are more likely to be arrested on facts that could support a capital charge, not because the justice system acts in a discriminatory fashion," the report said.[159]

Another 2001 study, this one by New Jersey Supreme Court Special Master David Baime, found no evidence of bias against African-American defendants in capital cases in

New Jersey between August 1982 and May 2000. The study concluded, "Simply stated, we discern no sound basis from the statistical evidence to conclude that the race or ethnicity of the defendant is a factor in determining which cases advance to a penalty trial and which defendants are ultimately sentenced to death. The statistical evidence abounds the other way—it strongly suggests that there are no racial or ethnic disparities in capital murder prosecution and death sentencing rates."[160]

Evidence of socioeconomic discrimination in the imposition of the death penalty in Nebraska between 1973 and 1999 was found in a 2001 study of more than 700 homicide cases in that state. The study, which had been mandated by the state legislature, found that although race did not appear to influence death-penalty decisions, killers of victims with high-socioeconomic status received the death penalty four times as often as would otherwise be expected. According to the study, "The data document significant statewide disparities in charging and sentencing outcomes based on the socio-economic status of the victim."[161]

Follow the author's tweets about the latest crime and justice news @schmalleger

Justifications for Capital Punishment

On February 11, 2004, 47-year-old Edward Lewis Lagrone was executed by lethal injection in Huntsville, Texas, for the murder of three people in their home. Earlier, Lagrone had molested and impregnated one of the victims, a 10-year-old child, whom he shot in the head as she was trying to protect her 19-month-old sister.[162] Lagrone also killed two of the child's great-aunts who were in the house at the time of the attack. One of the women, 76-year-old Caola Lloyd, was deaf, blind, and bedridden with cancer. Prior to the killings, Lagrone had served 7 years of a 20-year prison sentence for another murder and was on parole. "He's a poster child to justify the death penalty," said David Montague, the Tarrant County assistant district attorney who prosecuted Lagrone.

Like many others today, Montague feels that "cold-blooded murder" justifies a sentence of death. Justifications for the death penalty are collectively referred to as the *retentionist position.* The three retentionist arguments are (1) just deserts, (2) revenge, and (3) protection.

The just deserts argument makes the simple and straightforward claim that some people deserve to die for what they have done. Death is justly deserved; anything less cannot suffice as a sanction for the most heinous crimes. As U.S. Supreme Court Justice Potter Stewart once wrote, "The decision that capital punishment may be the appropriate sanction in extreme cases is an expression of the community's belief that certain crimes are themselves so grievous an affront to humanity that the only adequate response may be the penalty of death."[163]

Those who justify capital punishment as revenge attempt to appeal to the idea that survivors, victims, and the state are entitled to closure. Only after execution of the criminal perpetrator, they say, can the psychological and social wounds engendered by the offense begin to heal.

The retentionist claim of protection asserts that offenders, once executed, can commit no further crimes. Clearly the least emotional of the retentionist claims, the protectionist argument may also be the weakest, as societal interests in protection can also be met in other ways, such as incarceration. In addition, various studies have shown that there is little likelihood of repeat offenses among people convicted of murder and later released.[164] (The heinous Lagrone case is the exception, not the rule.) One reason for such results, however, may be that murderers generally serve lengthy prison sentences prior to release and may have lost whatever youthful propensity for criminality they previously possessed. For an intriguing dialogue between two U.S. Supreme Court justices over the constitutionality of the death penalty, see **https://www.justicestudies.com/pubs/deathpenalty.pdf**.

The Courts and the Death Penalty

The U.S. Supreme Court has for some time served as a sounding board for issues surrounding the death penalty. One of the Court's earliest cases in this area was *Wilkerson* v. *Utah* (1878),[165] which questioned shooting as a method of execution and raised the Eighth Amendment claims that firing squads constituted a form of cruel and unusual punishment.

The Court disagreed, however, contrasting the relatively civilized nature of firing squads with the various forms of torture often associated with capital punishment around the time the Bill of Rights was written.

Similarly, the Court supported electrocution as a permissible form of execution in *In re Kemmler* (1890).[166] In *Kemmler*, the Court defined cruel and unusual methods of execution as follows: "Punishments are cruel when they involve torture or a lingering death; but the punishment of death is not cruel, within the meaning of that word as used in the Constitution. It implies there is something inhuman and barbarous, something more than the mere extinguishing of life."[167] Almost 60 years later, the Court ruled that a second attempt at the electrocution of a convicted person, when the first did not work, did not violate the Eighth Amendment.[168] The Court reasoned that the initial failure was the consequence of accident or unforeseen circumstances and not the result of an effort on the part of executioners to be intentionally cruel.

It was not until 1972, however, in the landmark case of *Furman* v. *Georgia*,[169] that the Court recognized "evolving standards of decency"[170] that might necessitate a reconsideration of Eighth Amendment guarantees. In a 5–4 ruling, the *Furman* decision invalidated Georgia's death-penalty statute on the basis that it allowed a jury unguided discretion in the imposition of a capital sentence. The majority of justices concluded that the Georgia statute, which permitted a jury to decide issues of guilt or innocence while it weighed sentencing options, allowed for an arbitrary and capricious application of the death penalty.

Many other states with statutes similar to Georgia's were affected by the *Furman* ruling but moved quickly to modify their procedures. What evolved was the two-step procedure used today in capital cases. In the first stage, guilt or innocence is decided. If the defendant is convicted of a crime for which execution is possible or if he or she pleads guilty to such an offense, a second (or penalty) phase ensues. The penalty phase, a kind of mini-trial, generally permits the introduction of new evidence that may have been irrelevant to the question of guilt but that may be relevant to punishment, such as drug use or childhood abuse. In most death-penalty jurisdictions, juries determine the punishment. However, in Arizona, Idaho, Montana, and Nebraska, the trial judge sets the sentence in the second phase of capital murder trials. Alabama, Delaware, Florida, and Indiana allow juries only to recommend a sentence to the judge. The Supreme Court formally approved the two-step trial procedure in *Gregg* v. *Georgia* (1976).[171] Post-*Gregg* decisions set limits on the use of death as a penalty for all but the most severe crimes. Other important U.S. Supreme Court decisions of relevance to the death penalty are shown in Table 9-5.

Following *Apprendi* v. *New Jersey* (discussed earlier in this chapter), attorneys for an Arizona death-row inmate successfully challenged that state's practice of allowing judges, sitting without a jury, to make factual determinations necessary for imposition of the death penalty. In *Ring* v. *Arizona* (2002),[172] a jury had found Timothy Stuart Ring guilty of felony murder occurring in the course of an armed robbery for the killing of an armored car driver in 1994 but deadlocked on the charge of premeditated murder. Under Arizona law, Ring could not be sentenced to death, the statutory maximum penalty for first-degree murder, unless a judge made further findings in a separate sentencing hearing. The death penalty could be imposed only if the judge found the existence of at least one aggravating circumstance specified by law that was not offset by mitigating circumstances. During such a hearing, the judge listened to an accomplice who said that Ring planned the robbery and shot the guard. The judge then determined that Ring was the actual killer and found that the killing was committed for financial gain (an aggravating factor). Following the hearing, Ring was sentenced to death. His attorneys appealed, claiming that by the standards set forth in *Apprendi*, Arizona's sentencing scheme violated the Sixth Amendment's guarantee of a jury trial because it entrusted a judge with fact-finding powers that allowed Ring's sentence to be raised above what would otherwise have been the statutory maximum. The U.S. Supreme Court agreed and overturned Ring's sentence, finding that "Arizona's enumerated aggravating factors operate as the functional equivalent of an element of a greater offense." *Ring* established that juries—not judges—must decide the facts that lead to a death sentence. The *Ring* ruling called into question at least

> A punishment is "cruel and unusual" . . . if it does not comport with human dignity.
>
> —William Brennan, former U.S. Supreme Court justice, concurring in *Furman* v. *Georgia*[iv]

CJ News
High Costs Lead to Reconsideration of Death Penalty

Judges, prosecutors, and legislators are reconsidering use of the death penalty, and the crippling cost of such convictions is a key factor.

"Death by execution is excessively expensive," wrote Florida Judge Charles M. Harris in a newspaper opinion column, "Most people who support the death penalty believe it is more cost-effective than life in prison. Perhaps at one time, when executions were swift and sure, this may have been the case. It is not now."

Countless studies support this argument. The state of Indiana, for example, found that the average death-penalty case cost 10 times more than life without parole. A recent Urban Institute study found the average capital case in Maryland cost almost $1 million more than a comparable non-death-penalty case.

In terms of absolute costs, a lone death-penalty conviction, not including later costs of appeals, can be over $10 million—as was the case with a federal trial in Philadelphia in 2013 where Kaboni Savage was sentenced to die. Savage was responsible for the deaths of at least 12 people, including four children and two women.

Much of the cost is racked up preparing for trial, but routine appeals add even more expense. The extra expenses can be traced back to a U.S. Supreme Court decision in 1976, 4 years after the High Court reinstated the death penalty, requiring additional precautions in death-penalty cases. Jury selection, for example, takes 3 to 4 weeks longer and costs $200,000 more than in life-without-parole cases, according to a California study.

In the sentencing phase of a death-penalty case, defendants have the right to present mitigating factors, requiring expensive expert testimony. After conviction, it can take years to exhaust appeals, which adds to incarceration costs. Death-row inmates require solitary cells and extra guards, costing California $100,663 more than regular confinement per inmate, according to a 2011 report.

County governments pick up the tab, resulting in tax increases or service cuts. The Peterson trial, for example, forced Stanislaus County to redistribute legal cases and cut its consumer fraud protection unit. Counties can't avoid this obligation. When commissioners of Lincoln County, Georgia, refused to allocate funds for a new trial ordered for death-row inmate Johnny Lee Jones, they were put in jail.

But despite punishing costs, the expensive legal rights of defendants facing death have not been rolled back—perhaps in part due to disturbing reports of wrongful convictions exposed by DNA evidence, recanted testimony, and other factors. "When innocent people are executed, those mistakes cannot be remedied," the American Civil Liberties Union (ACLU) observed.

Whatever the reason, Americans seem to be losing interest in execution. According to Gallup, support of the death penalty has fallen from a high of 80% in 1994 to 55% in 2017. The number of death sentences handed out nationwide declined from 284 in 1999 to only 39 in 2017, according to the Death Penalty Information Center.

For states struggling with crippling deficits, savings from abolishing capital punishment are very tempting. North Carolina put the savings at $11 million, Florida at $51 million a year, and

▲ A session of the California legislature. States such as California are considering the cost of capital punishment, along with public sentiment and moral aspects of court-ordered executions, in weighing the future of the death penalty in their states. What role, if any, should cost play in capital punishment decisions?

Max Whittaker/Getty Images News/Getty Images

a California study said the state could immediately save $1 billion by eliminating the death penalty.

Currently 19 states and the District of Columbia have no death penalty. Illinois joined the list in 2011, after the state imposed a 10-year moratorium in reaction to 13 mistaken death sentences; and in April 2012, the state of Connecticut officially ended the use of capital punishment. In 2013 Maryland abolished the death penalty, and the few remaining inmates had their sentences commuted to life in prison.

REFERENCES

John P. Martin, "Bill for Savage Trial Easily Tops $10 Million, *Philly News*," September 22, 2013, http://articles.philly.com/2013-09-23/news/42294616_1_kaboni-savage-savage-trial-savage-case (accessed February 8, 2014).

"Fight against Death Penalty Gains Momentum in States," *Los Angeles Times*, April 14, 2012, http://articles.latimes.com/2012/apr/14/nation/la-na-death-penalty-20120415.

"Just or Not, Cost of Death Penalty Is a Killer for State Budgets," Fox News, March 27, 2010, http://www.foxnews.com/us/2010/03/27/just-cost-death-penalty-killer-state-budgets/.

Gallup, "Death Penalty," http://www.gallup.com/poll/1606/Death-Penalty.aspx (accessed July 22, 2018); and Death Penalty Information Center, "Facts about the Death Penalty," http://www.deathpenaltyinfo.org/documents/FactSheet.pdf (accessed March 22, 2018).

150 judge-imposed death sentences[173] in at least five states (Arizona, Colorado, Idaho, Montana, and Nebraska).[174] In a similar 2016 decision, the U.S. Supreme court, in the case of *Hurst* v. *Florida*, invalidated Florida's death-penalty procedures because, like Arizona, the judge had independent authority to impose a death sentence which made the jury's function only advisory.[175]

Although questions may arise about sentencing practices, the majority of justices on today's High Court seem largely convinced of the fundamental constitutionality of a sentence

TABLE 9-5
U.S. Supreme Court Cases Relating to the Death Penalty

Year	U.S. Supreme Court Case	Ruling
2016	*Hurst* v. *Florida*	Florida's death penalty sentencing scheme was found to be unconstitutional under the Sixth Amendment because it allowed a judge to find and weigh aggravating circumstances independently of the jury.
2014	*Hall* v. *Florida*	States cannot rely solely on an IQ score of above 70 to bar an inmate from claiming mental disability in the face of execution. Doing so creates an "unacceptable risk" that inmates with intellectual disabilities might be executed in violation of the Constitution.
2008	*Kennedy* v. *Louisiana*	The Eighth Amendment bars states from imposing the death penalty for the rape of a child where the crime did not result, and was not intended to result, in the victim's death.
2008	*Baze* v. *Rees*	The capital punishment protocol of lethal injection involving a three-drug "cocktail" used by Kentucky does not violate the Eighth Amendment because it does not create a substantial risk of wanton and unnecessary infliction of pain, torture, or lingering death.
2005	*Deck* v. *Missouri*	The Constitution forbids the use of visible shackles during a capital trial's penalty phase, as it does during the guilt phase, unless that use is "justified by an essential state interest"—such as courtroom security—specific to the defendant on trial.
2005	*Roper* v. *Simmons*	The Eighth and Fourteenth Amendments forbid imposition of the death penalty on offenders who were under the age of 18 when their crimes were committed.
2004	*Schriro* v. *Summerlin*	The rule established in *Apprendi* and Ring cannot be applied retroactively to sentences already imposed because it is merely a new procedural rule and not a substantive change.
2002	*Atkins* v. *Virginia*	Executing mentally retarded people violates the Constitution's ban on cruel and unusual punishments.
2002	*Ring* v. *Arizona*	Juries—not judges—must decide the facts, including those relating to aggravating circumstances, that may lead to a death sentence.
1977	*Coker* v. *Georgia*	A Georgia law imposing the death penalty for the rape of an adult woman was struck down. The Court concluded that capital punishment under such circumstances is "grossly disproportionate" to the crime.
1976	*Gregg* v. *Georgia*	A new two-stage (bifurcated) procedural requirement of Georgia's revised capital punishment statute was upheld. The law requires guilt or innocence to be determined in the first stage of a bifurcated trial. Upon a guilty verdict, a presentence hearing is held where the judge or jury hears additional aggravating and mitigating evidence. At least one of ten specified aggravating circumstances must be found to exist beyond a reasonable doubt before a death sentence can be imposed.
1976	*Woodson* v. *North Carolina*	A state law requiring mandatory application of the death penalty for all first-degree murders was found to be unconstitutional.
1972	*Furman* v. *Georgia*	The Court recognized "evolving standards of decency" in invalidating Georgia's death-penalty statute because it allowed a jury unguided discretion in the imposition of a capital sentence. The Georgia statute, which permitted a jury to decide issues of guilt or innocence while simultaneously weighing sentencing options, was found to allow for an arbitrary and capricious application of the death penalty.

The just deserts argument makes the claim that some people deserve to die for what they have done.

of death. Open to debate, however, is the constitutionality of *methods* for execution. In a 1993 hearing, *Poyner* v. *Murray*,[176] the U.S. Supreme Court hinted at the possibility of revisiting questions first raised in *Kemmler*. The case challenged Virginia's use of the electric chair, calling it a form of cruel and unusual punishment. Syvasky Lafayette Poyner, who originally brought the case before the Court, lost his bid for a stay of execution and was electrocuted in March 1993. Nonetheless, in *Poyner*, Justices David H. Souter, Harry A. Blackmun, and John Paul Stevens wrote, "The Court has not spoken squarely on the underlying issue since *In re Kemmler* . . . and the holding of that case does not constitute a dispositive response to litigation of the issue in light of modern knowledge about the method of execution in question."

In a still more recent ruling, members of the Court questioned the constitutionality of hanging, suggesting that it too may be a form of cruel and unusual punishment. In that case,

Campbell v. *Wood* (1994),[177] the defendant, Charles Campbell, raped a woman, was released from prison at the completion of his sentence, and then went back and murdered her. His request for a stay of execution was denied because the law of Washington State, where the murder occurred, offered Campbell a choice of various methods of execution and, therefore, an alternative to hanging. Similarly, in 1996, the Court upheld California's death-penalty statute, which provides for lethal injection as the primary method of capital punishment in that state.[178] The constitutionality of the statute had been challenged by two death-row inmates who claimed that a provision in the law that permitted condemned prisoners the choice of lethal gas in lieu of injection brought the statute within the realm of allowing cruel and unusual punishments.

Questions about the constitutionality of electrocution as a means of execution again came to the fore in 1997, when flames shot from the head and the leather mask covering the face of Pedro Medina during his Florida execution. Similarly, in 1999, blood poured from behind the mask covering Allen Lee "Tiny" Davis's face as he was put to death in Florida's electric chair. State officials claimed that the 344-pound Davis suffered a nosebleed brought on by hypertension and the blood-thinning medication that he had been taking. Photographs of Davis taken during and immediately after the execution showed him grimacing while bleeding profusely onto his neck and chest. In 2001, the Georgia Supreme Court declared electrocution to be unconstitutional, ending its use in that state.[179] The Georgia court cited testimony from lower court records showing that electrocution may not result in a quick death or in an immediate cessation of consciousness. By the time of the court's decision, however, the Georgia legislature had already passed a law establishing lethal injection as the state's sole method of punishment for capital crimes.[180]

Lethal injections are certainly not a foolproof method of execution, however. In 2014, a burst vein in 38-year-old convicted murderer Clayton Lockett's groin led to a gruesome scene as witnesses watched him writhing and mumbling on a death chamber gurney. He died 43 minutes later of what authorities said was a massive heart attack.[181] A few years before Lockett's death, questions were raised about whether lethal injections constitute cruel and unusual punishment. Those questions originated with eyewitness accounts, postmortem blood testing, and execution logs that seemed to show that some of those executed remained conscious but paralyzed and experienced excruciating pain before dying.[182] Such claims focused on the composition of the chemical cocktail used in executions, which contains one drug (sodium thiopental, a short-acting barbiturate) to induce sleep, another (pancuronium bromide) to paralyze the muscles without causing unconsciousness, and a third (potassium chloride) to stop the heart. If the first chemical is improperly administered, the condemned person remains conscious, and the procedure can cause discomfort or even severe pain. Complicating matters is the fact that the ethical codes of most professional medical organizations forbid medical practitioners to take life—meaning that although the codes are not legally binding, medical professionals are largely excluded from taking part in executions, other than to verify the fact that death has occurred. To counter fears that lethal injections cause pain, some states have begun using medical monitoring devices that show brain activity and can ensure that sleep is occurring.[183]

Finally, in 2014, in the case of *Hall* v. *Florida*, the Supreme Court held that states cannot rely solely on an IQ score of above 70 to bar an inmate from claiming mental disability in the face of execution.[184] Doing so, the Court ruled, creates an "unacceptable risk" that inmates with intellectual disabilities might be executed, in violation of the Constitution.

In 2008, the U.S. Supreme Court took up this issue in the case of *Baze* v. *Rees*, which had been brought by prisoners on Kentucky's death row.[185] The Court held that the capital punishment protocol used by Kentucky does not violate the Eighth Amendment because it does not create a substantial risk of wanton and unnecessary infliction of pain, torture, or lingering death. "Because some risk of pain is inherent in even the most humane execution method," wrote the justices, "the Constitution does not demand the avoidance of all risk of pain."

▲ Timothy Ring, the Arizona death-row inmate who won a 2002 U.S. Supreme Court case that held the potential to invalidate the death sentences of many other prisoners. In that case, *Ring* v. *Arizona*, the Court held that criminal defendants have a Sixth Amendment right to have a jury, and not just a judge, determine the existence of aggravating factors justifying the death penalty. What other decisions, made by the Court since then, have further refined the *Ring* ruling?

Matt York/AP Images

🐦 Follow the author's tweets about the latest crime and justice news @schmalleger

Freedom or Safety? You Decide
What Are the Limits of Genetic Privacy?

By 2018, 30 states and the federal government had enacted arrestee DNA collection laws, which authorize the collection of suspect DNA following arrest or charging. All 50 states, however, require *post-conviction* DNA collection. A federal law, the DNA Fingerprint Act of 2005, requires that any adult arrested for a federal crime must provide a DNA sample. The law also mandates DNA collection from persons detained under the authority of the United States who are not U.S. citizens or are not lawfully in the country. Some states limit preconviction DNA collection to violent offenses or sex crimes, whereas other states include all felonies, and some extend the requirement to misdemeanors as well. Figure 9–9 shows states that have enacted arrestee DNA collection laws. In 2013, in the case of *Maryland* v. *King*, the U.S. Supreme Court upheld Maryland's practice of collecting and testing DNA from arrested felons without the use of a warrant. Writing for the majority in that case, Justice Kennedy said, "When officers make an arrest supported by probable cause to hold for a serious offense and bring the suspect to the station to be detained in custody, taking and analyzing a cheek swab of the arrestee's DNA is, like fingerprinting and photographing, a legitimate police booking procedure that is reasonable under the Fourth Amendment."

Forensic DNA can be a powerful tool in the hands of investigators. In 2005, for example, police in Truro, Massachusetts, charged Christopher M. McCowen, a garbage man with a long rap sheet, with the murder of 46-year-old Christa Worthington, a fashion writer who had been raped and stabbed to death in the kitchen of her isolated home in 2002. The case, which had baffled authorities for 3 years, drew national interest when Truro authorities asked the town's 790 male residents to voluntarily submit saliva-swab DNA samples for analysis. Investigators were hoping to use genetic testing to match semen recovered from the murder scene with the killer. "We're trying to find the person who has something to hide," said Sergeant David Perry of the Truro Police Department. Although McCowen voluntarily submitted a DNA sample from a cheek swab in early 2004, it took the state crime lab more than a year to analyze it.

DNA profiling has been used in criminal investigations for over 30 years. The first well-known DNA forensic analysis happened in 1986, when British police sought the help of Alec Jeffreys, a geneticist at the University of Leicester who is widely regarded as the "father of DNA fingerprinting." The police were trying to solve the vicious rape and murder of two young schoolgirls. At the center of their investigation was a young man who worked at a mental institution close to where the girls' bodies had been found. Soon after he was questioned, the man confessed to the crimes and was arrested, but police were uncertain of the suspect's state of mind and wanted to be sure that they had the right person.

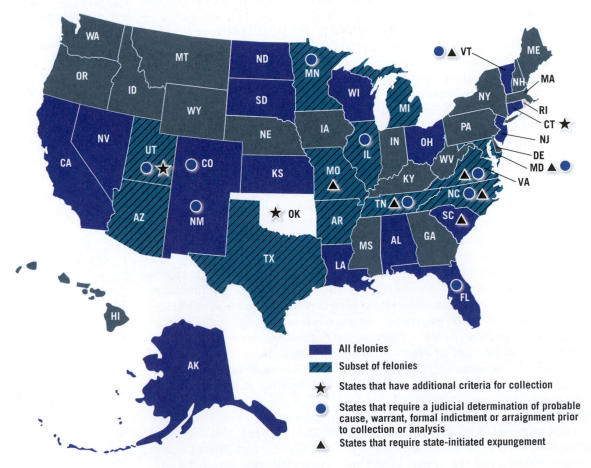

All felonies

Subset of felonies

★ **States that have additional criteria for collection**

● **States that require a judicial determination of probable cause, warrant, formal indictment or arraignment prior to collection or analysis**

▲ **States that require state-initiated expungement**

FIGURE 9–9
States That Have Enacted Arrestee DNA Collection Laws
Source: Collecting DNA From Arrestees: Implementation Lessons, National Institute of Justice Journal, June 2012, National Institute of Justice.

Jeffreys compared the suspect's DNA to DNA taken from semen samples found on the victims. The samples did not match, leading to a wider police investigation. Lacking any clear leads, the authorities requested that all males living in the area of the killings voluntarily submit to DNA testing so that they might be excluded as suspects. By the fall of 1987, the number of men tested had exceeded 4,500, but the murderer still hadn't been found. Then, however, investigators received an unexpected tip. They learned that a local baker named Colin Pitchfork had convinced another man to provide a DNA sample in his place. Pitchfork was picked up and questioned. He soon confessed, providing details about the crime that only the perpetrator could know. Pitchfork became the 4,583rd man to undergo DNA testing, and his DNA proved a perfect match with that of the killer.

In the past few decades, the use of DNA testing by police departments has come a long way. Today, the FBI's CODIS (Combined DNA Index System) database makes use of computerized records to match the DNA of individuals previously convicted of certain crimes with forensic samples gathered at crime scenes across the country. The federal 2017 Rapid DNA Act required the FBI to develop guidelines for allowing DNA evidence gathered by what are called "Rapid DNA instruments" to be included in CODIS. Rapid DNA describes the process of obtaining a simple DNA profile without human intervention via an automated instrument. At present, however, rapid DNA technology can only be used for identification purposes, not crime scene analysis.

Advocates of genetic privacy question whether anyone—even those convicted of crimes—should be sampled against their wishes and have their genetic profiles added to government databases. The Truro case, in which the American Civil Liberties Union (ACLU) sent letters to the town's police chief and Cape Code prosecutor calling for an end to the "DNA dragnet," highlights what many fear—especially when local police announced that they would pay close attention to those who refused to cooperate.

ACLU legislative director Shankar Narayan has said that "DNA [collection] goes far beyond mere identification. It's actually a catalog of an individual's most private biological information." One commentator, who agreed, noted that it is "a very old trap" to say that "if you have nothing to hide, then why not cooperate?" For additional information, read a Congressional Research Service report on compulsory DNA collection at **https://www .justicestudies.com/pubs/dnacollection.pdf**.

YOU DECIDE

What degree of "genetic privacy" should an individual be entitled to? Should the government require routine genetic testing of nonoffenders for identification purposes?

References: Maryland v. King, U.S. Supreme Court, No. 12-207 (decided June 3, 2013); Xiaochen Hu, Mai E. Naito and Rolando V. del Carmen, "Pre- and Post- Conviction DNA Collection Laws in the United States: An Analysis of Proposed Model Statutes," *Journal of Criminal Justice and Law*, Vol. 1, No. 1, pp. 23-42 (2016), https://www.uhd.edu/academics/public-service/jcjl/ Documents/2.%20Article.pdf (accessed March 30, 2018). "Man Charged with 2002 Murder of Cape Cod Writer," *USA Today*, April 15, 2005, http:// www.usatoday.com/news/nation/2005-04-15-cape-cod-murder_x.htm (accessed October 1, 2010); Forensic Technology Center of Excellence, "Rapid DNA Technology Forum: August 15-17, 2017," p. 2. and Howard C. Coleman and Eric D. Swenson, *DNA in the Courtroom: A Trial Watcher's Guide* (Seattle, WA:Genelex Corporation, web edition 2000), http://www.genelex .com/paternitytesting/paternitybook.html (accessed October 1, 2013).

The Future of the Death Penalty

Support for the death penalty varies considerably from state to state and from one region of the country to another. Short of renewed Supreme Court intervention, the future of capital punishment may depend more on popular opinion than on arguments pro or con.

A 2017 national poll of registered voters found that 55% were in favor of capital punishment for murder. Support for the death penalty has, for the most part, consistently declined since 1994 when 80% were in favor of the punishment. Support has increased, however, for death penalty alternatives, including life with no possibility of parole, or life with the possibility of parole.

Ultimately, public opinion about the death penalty may turn on the issue of whether innocent people have been executed. According to a number of recent studies, Americans from all walks of life are less likely to support capital punishment if they believe that innocent people have been put to death at the hands of the justice system or that the death penalty is being applied unfairly.[186]

Ring v. Arizona established that juries, not judges, must decide the facts that lead to a death sentence.

Summary

SENTENCING

- The goals of criminal sentencing include retribution, incapacitation, deterrence, rehabilitation, and restoration. Retribution corresponds to the just deserts model of sentencing, which holds that offenders are responsible for their crimes. Incapacitation seeks to protect innocent members of society from offenders who might harm them if not prevented from doing so. The goal of deterrence is to prevent future criminal activity through the example or threat of punishment. Rehabilitation seeks to bring about fundamental changes in offenders and their behavior to reduce the likelihood of future criminality, and restoration seeks to address the damage done by crime by making the victim and the community "whole again."

- The indeterminate sentencing model is characterized primarily by vast judicial choice. It builds on the belief that convicted offenders are more likely to participate in their own rehabilitation if such participation will reduce the amount of time that they have to spend in prison.

- Structured sentencing is largely a child of the just deserts philosophy that grew out of concerns with proportionality, equity, and social debt—all of which this chapter discusses. Numerous different types of structured sentencing models have been created, including determinate sentencing, which requires that a convicted offender be sentenced to a fixed term that may be reduced by good time or gain time, and voluntary/advisory sentencing, which consists of recommended sentencing guidelines that are not required by law, are usually based on past sentencing practices, and are meant to guide judges. Mandatory sentencing, another form of structured sentencing, requires clearly enumerated punishments for specific offenses or for habitual offenders convicted of a series of crimes. The applicability of structured sentencing guidelines has been called into question by recent U.S. Supreme Court decisions.

- Just deserts and get-tough-on-crime policies have increased prison populations to the point of overflowing, adding to budget crises that both the federal and state governments have been facing for the past couple of decades. Prison population in the United States have grown far faster than rates of serious violent and property crime, leading to calls for changes in some laws, and for the implementation of alternative forms of criminal sentencing.

- Alternative sentences include the use of court-ordered community service, home detention, day reporting, drug treatment, psychological counseling, victim–offender mediation, or intensive supervision in lieu of other, more traditional sentences such as imprisonment and fines. Alternative sentences are closely linked to the concept of justice reinvestment, whereby monies saved through alternative sentencing can be reinvested in other aspects of the justice system. Questions have been raised about alternative sentences, including questions about their impact on public safety, the cost-effectiveness of such sanctions, and the long-term effects of community sanctions on people assigned to alternative programs.

- Probation and parole officers routinely conduct presentence investigations to provide information that judges may use in deciding on the appropriate kind or length of sentence for convicted offenders.

- Historically, criminal courts have often allowed victims to testify at trial but have otherwise downplayed the experience of victimization and the suffering it causes. A new interest in the experience of victims, beginning in the 1970s in this country, has led to a greater legal recognition of victims' rights, including a right to allocution (the right to be heard during criminal proceedings). Many states have passed victims' rights amendments to their constitutions, although a federal victims' rights amendment has yet to be enacted. The Crime Victims' Rights Act of 2004 established statutory rights for victims of federal crimes and gives them the necessary legal authority to assert those rights in federal court.

- The four traditional sentencing options identified in this chapter are fines, probation, imprisonment, and—in cases of especially horrific offenses—death. Fines and the death penalty were discussed in this chapter, and the pros and cons of each were examined.

- Arguments for capital punishment identified in this chapter include revenge, just deserts, and protection of society. The revenge argument builds upon the need for personal and communal closure, whereas the just deserts argument makes the straightforward claim that some people deserve to die for what they have done. Societal protection is couched in terms of deterrence, as those who are executed cannot commit future crimes, and execution serves as an example to other would-be wrongdoers. Arguments against capital punishment are based on findings that a death sentence has been imposed on innocent people, that the death penalty has not been found to be an effective deterrent, that it is often arbitrarily imposed, that it tends to discriminate against powerless groups and individuals, and that it is very expensive because of the numerous court appeals involved. Opponents also argue that the state should recognize the sanctity of human life.

QUESTIONS FOR REVIEW

1. Describe the five goals of contemporary criminal sentencing. Which of these goals do you think ought to be the primary goal of sentencing? How might your choice vary with the type of offense? In what circumstances might your choice be less acceptable?

2. Describe the nature of indeterminate sentencing, and explain its positive aspects. What led some states to abandon indeterminate sentencing?

3. What is structured sentencing? What is the status of the federal structured sentencing model today?

4. How did get-tough sentencing policies lead to the overcrowding that we see in our prisons today?

5. What are alternative sanctions? Give some examples of alternative sanctions, and offer an assessment of how effective they might be.

6. What is a presentence investigation? How do PSIs contribute to the contents of presentence reports? How are presentence reports used?

7. Describe the history of victims' rights and services in this country. What role does the victim play in criminal justice proceedings today?

8. What are four modern sentencing options? Under what circumstances might each be appropriate?

9. Do you support or oppose the use of capital punishment? Outline the arguments on both sides of the issue.

Probation, Parole, and Reentry

> One of the first questions a police officer asks when arresting someone is "Are you on probation or parole?" and the answer generally expected is "yes."
>
> —Council of State Governments Justice Center (2013)[1]

Learning Objectives

After reading this chapter, you should be able to:

1. Describe the history, purpose, and characteristics of probation. **315**

2. Describe the history, purpose, and characteristics of parole. **319**

3. Compare the advantages and disadvantages of probation and parole. **322**

4. Identify significant court cases affecting probation and parole. **324**

5. Explain the work of probation officers and parole officers. **326**

6. Describe various intermediate sanctions. **329**

7. Describe the likely future of probation and parole. **334**

John Spink/Atlanta Journal Constitution/AP Images

Introduction

Not everyone convicted of a serious crime goes to prison. Washington, D.C.'s Youth Rehabilitation Act (YRA), for example, gives offenders under the age of 22 a second chance by permitting judges to dramatically reduce sentences for young offenders. Such sentencing practices can be effective, but have sometimes resulted in youthful offenders taking advantage of what was intended to be a chance at a new start—with some of them committing dozens (and even hundreds) of ever-more serious new crimes.[2] In the case of 24-year-old Will Smallwood, who was repeatedly granted leniency because of his age and released back into the community, early release gave him the opportunity to commit 100 new robberies to which he later admitted, and finally culminated in a murder conviction for which he is now serving time in federal prison. "It's just a slap on the wrist," Smallwood said of his court encounters. "And then you think you can get away with bigger crimes."[3]

While some see Smallwood as an example of the failure of early release, others acknowledge that many offenders turn the same opportunity into a positive experience.

This chapter takes a close look at the realities behind the practice of **community corrections** (also termed *community-based corrections*), which is a sentencing style that depends less on traditional confinement options and more on correctional resources available in the community. Its goal is to enhance desistance from crime, and to reduce the likelihood of recidivism.[4] Community corrections includes a wide assortment of activities, such as probation, parole, home confinement, remote location monitoring of offenders, and other new and developing programs—all of which are covered in this chapter. Approximately 1 in 55 adults in the United States were under community supervision at the start of 2017. Learn more about community corrections by visiting the International Community Corrections Association via **http://www.iccaweb.org**.

▲ The John A. Wilson building in Washington, D.C., home to the city council and mayor of the District of Columbia. It's where D.C.'s Youth Rehabilitation Act, which was intended to offer young offenders a second chance, was enacted. What's the difference between probation and parole?

B. Christopher/Alamy Stock Photo

community corrections
The use of a variety of officially ordered program-based sanctions that permit convicted offenders to remain in the community under conditional supervision as an alternative to an active prison sentence.

probation
A sentence of imprisonment that is suspended. Also, a court-ordered period of correctional supervision in the community, generally as an alternative to incarceration.

What Is Probation?

Probation, one aspect of community corrections, is "a sentence served while under supervision in the community."[5] Like other sentencing options, probation is a court-ordered sanction. Its goal is to retain some control over criminal offenders while using community programs to help rehabilitate them. Most of the alternative sanctions discussed later in this chapter are, in fact, predicated on probationary sentences in which the offender is ordered to abide by certain conditions—such as participation in a specified program—while remaining free in the community. Although the court in many jurisdictions can impose probation directly, most probationers are sentenced first to confinement but then immediately have their sentences suspended and are remanded into the custody of an officer of the court—the probation officer.

> **1** Describe the history, purpose, and characteristics of probation.

Probation has a long history. By the fourteenth century, English courts had established the practice of "binding over for good behavior,"[6] in which offenders could be entrusted into the custody of willing citizens. American John Augustus (1784–1859) is generally recognized as the world's first probation officer. Augustus, a Boston shoemaker, attended sessions of criminal court in the 1850s and offered to take carefully selected offenders into his home as an alternative to imprisonment.[7] At first, he supervised only drunkards, but by 1857 Augustus was accepting many kinds of offenders and was devoting all his time to the service of the court.[8]

Augustus died in 1859, having bailed out more than 2,000 convicts. In 1878, the Massachusetts legislature enacted a statute that authorized the city of Boston to hire a salaried probation officer. Missouri followed suit in 1897, along with Vermont (1898) and Rhode Island (1899).[9] Before the end of the nineteenth century, probation had become an accepted and widely used form of community-based supervision. By 1925, all 48 states had adopted probation legislation. In that same year, the federal government enacted legislation enabling federal district court judges to appoint paid probation officers and to impose probationary terms.[10]

🐦 Follow the author's tweets about the latest crime and justice news @schmalleger

The Extent of Probation

Today, probation is the most common form of criminal sentencing in the United States. Between 20% and 60% of those found guilty of crimes are sentenced to some form of probation. Figure 10–1 shows that 55% of all offenders under correctional supervision in the United States as of January 1, 2017, were on probation. The rest were either in jail, in prison, on parole, or under some other form of supervised or unsupervised release. The number of offenders under any type of correctional supervision increased dramatically between 1980 and 2017—from under two million to nearly seven million people. The annual *rate* of increase, however, has been declining steadily since 2007, and has finally turned negative. In terms of absolute numbers, persons supervised yearly on probation has increased from slightly more than 1 million in 1980 to around 3.7 million today—nearly a 400% increase.[11]

Even violent offenders stand about a one in five chance of receiving a probationary term. A Bureau of Justice Statistics study of felony sentences in state courts found that 3% of people convicted of homicide were placed on probation, as were 16% of convicted sex offenders.[12] Thirteen percent of convicted robbers and 25% of those committing aggravated assault were similarly sentenced to probation rather than active prison time. In one example, 47-year-old Carrie Mote of Vernon, Connecticut, was sentenced to probation for shooting her fiancé in the chest with a .38-caliber handgun after he called off their wedding.[13] Mote, who faced a maximum of 20 years in prison, claimed to be suffering from diminished psychological capacity at the time of the shooting because of the emotional stress brought on by the canceled wedding.[14]

At the beginning of 2017, a total of 3,673,120 adults were on probation throughout the nation.[15] Individual states, however, make greater or lesser use of probation. Wyoming authorities, with the smallest probationary population, supervise only 4,666 people, whereas Texas reports 374,285 offenders on probation. On a per capita basis, there are 1,466 people on probation for every 100,000 residents. About 51% of the 1.9 million adults discharged from probation successfully meet the conditions of their supervision. Approximately 15% of those discharged from supervision, however, are incarcerated because of a rule violation or because they committed a new offense, while another 7% abscond.[16]

Probation Conditions

Those sentenced to probation must agree to abide by court-mandated conditions of probation, with a violation of conditions possibly leading to **probation revocation**. Conditions are of two types: general and specific. General conditions apply to all probationers in a given jurisdiction and usually require that the probationer obey all laws, maintain employment, remain within the jurisdiction of the court, possess no firearms, allow the probation officer to visit at home or at work, and so forth. As a general condition of probation, many probationers are also required to pay a fine to the court, usually in a series of installments, that is designed to reimburse victims for damages and to pay lawyers' fees and other court costs.

Special conditions may be mandated by a judge who feels that the probationer is in need of particular guidance or control. Depending on the nature of the offense, a judge may require that the offender surrender his or her driver's license; submit at reasonable times to warrantless and unannounced searches by a probation officer; supply breath, urine, or blood samples as needed for drug or alcohol testing; complete a specified number of hours of community service; or pass the general equivalency diploma (GED) test within a specified time. The judge may also dictate special conditions tailored to the probationer's situation. Such

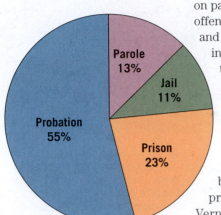

FIGURE 10–1

Offenders under Correctional Supervision in the United States, by Type of Supervision

Note: Numbers do not total 100 due to rounding.

Source: Danielle Kaeble, *Correctional Populations in the United States, 2016* (Washington, D.C.: Bureau of Justice Statistics, April 2018.

probation revocation

A court order taking away a convicted offender's probationary status and usually withdrawing the conditional freedom associated with that status in response to a violation of the conditions of probation.

> Even violent offenders stand about a one in five chance of receiving a probationary term.

individualized conditions may prohibit the offender from associating with named others (a codefendant, for example), they may require that the probationer be at home after dark, or they may demand that the offender complete a particular treatment program within a set time.

The Federal Probation System

The federal probation system, known as the United States Probation and Pretrial Services System, is nearly 100 years old.[17] In 1916, in the *Killets* case,[18] the U.S. Supreme Court ruled that federal judges did not have the authority to suspend sentences and to order probation. After a vigorous campaign by the National Probation Association, Congress passed the National Probation Act in 1925, authorizing the use of probation in federal courts. The bill came just in time to save a burgeoning federal prison system from serious overcrowding. The prostitution-fighting Mann Act, Prohibition legislation, and the growth of organized crime all led to increased arrests and a dramatic growth in the number of federal probationers in the early years of the system.

Although the 1925 act authorized one probation officer per federal judge, it allocated only $25,000 for officers' salaries. As a consequence, only eight officers were hired to serve 132 judges, and the system came to rely heavily on voluntary probation officers. Some sources indicate that as many as 40,000 probationers were under the supervision of volunteers at the peak of the system.[19] By 1930, however, Congress had provided adequate funding, and a corps of salaried professionals began to provide probation services to the U.S. courts. Today, approximately 7,750 federal probation officers (also known as *community corrections officers*), whose services are administered through the Administrative Office of the United States Courts, serve the 94 federal judicial districts in more than 500 locations across the country.[20] At any given time they supervise approximately 151,000 offenders—a number that has increased annually throughout the past decade.

Federal probation and pretrial services officers are federal law enforcement officers who have statutory authority to arrest or detain individuals suspected or convicted of federal offenses and to arrest probationers for violations of the conditions of probation. Under existing policy, however, they are encouraged to obtain an arrest warrant from a court, and the warrant is to be executed by the U.S. Marshals Service. Most federal probation officers may carry a firearm for defensive purposes while on duty. Before doing so, however, they must complete rigorous training and certification requirements, provide objective justification for doing so, and be approved to do so on an individual basis. Some federal districts do not allow any probation officers to carry firearms in the performance of their official duties. These include the eastern and western districts of Wisconsin, eastern Virginia, eastern Virgin Islands, central Tennessee, Massachusetts, Connecticut, and central California.[21]

Federal officials have implemented a results-based management and decision-making framework for the federal probation and pretrial services system. The Probation and Pretrial Services Automated Case Tracking System (PACTS) collects records from the electronic files of thousands of probation officers in all 94 federal districts and stores those records in a single data warehouse called the National PACTS Reporting (NPR) System.[22] The data are then fed into the federal Decision Support System (DSS), which combines data from NPR with data from other judiciary systems, the United States Sentencing Commission, the FBI, the Federal Bureau of Prisons, and the Bureau of the Census. Because of how it works, DSS provides a valuable evidence-based initiative at the federal level, and federal probation officials are using it to test underlying assumptions about the relationship between probation supervision practices and supervision outcomes.

▲ Meek Mill, born Robert Rihmeek Williams. The Philadelphia hip-hop recording artist became the focal point of a justice reform movement centered on reentry. Mill, who had been arrested in 2007 for drug possession and carrying a firearm without a license, served nine months behind bars before being paroled. While on parole, Mill was arrested a number of times for minor offenses and sent back to prison. Today he is back in his recording studio after the Pennsylvania Supreme Court ordered his release. The website **justice4meek.com** provides details about the case. Why would a judge send a promising artist like Mill back to prison for relatively minor parole violations?

Chelsea Lauren/Variety/Shutterstock

🐦 Follow the author's tweets about the latest crime and justice news @schmalleger

Multiculturalism and Diversity
Culturally Skilled Probation Officers

An article by Robert Shearer and Patricia Ann King in the journal *Federal Probation* describes the characteristics of "good therapeutic relationships" in probation work. The authors say that "one of the major impediments to building an effective relationship are found in cross-cultural barriers."

According to the article, probation officers who work with immigrants, or with those whose cultures differ substantially from that of mainstream America, must realize that a client's culture has to be taken into consideration. Doing so can make officers far more effective as both counselors and supervisors.

That's because differences in culture can lead to difficulties in developing the rapport that is necessary to build a helping relationship between an offender and a probation officer. Consequently, effective probation officers work to understand the values, norms, lifestyles, roles, and methods of communicating that characterize their clients.

Culturally skilled probation officers, Shearer and King say, are aware of and sensitive to their own cultural heritage, and they value and respect differences as long as they do not lead to continued law violation. Culturally skilled officers are also aware of their own preconceived notions, biases, prejudicial attitudes, feelings, and beliefs. They avoid stereotyping and labeling. Skilled officers are comfortable with the cultural differences that exist between themselves and their clients, and they are comfortable referring clients to someone who may be better qualified to help.

Developing multicultural awareness is the first step to becoming culturally skilled, the authors note. Developing awareness is an ongoing process—one that culminates in the ability to understand a client's worldview, or *cultural empathy*.

According to the article, developing cultural empathy involves six steps:

1. The counselor must understand and accept the context of family and community for clients from different cultural backgrounds (especially important in working with Hispanic clients, where relationships within the extended family are highly valued).
2. Counselors should incorporate indigenous healing practices from the client's culture whenever they can (as might be possible when working with Native Americans).
3. Counselors must become knowledgeable about the historical and sociopolitical backgrounds of clients (especially when clients have fled from repressive regimes in their home countries and might still fear authority figures).
4. They must become knowledgeable of the psychosocial adjustment that must be made by clients who have moved from one environment to another (including the sense of loneliness and separation that some immigrants feel on arrival in their adopted country).
5. They must be sensitive to the oppression, discrimination, and racism encountered by many people (for example, Kurdish people who suffered discrimination and experienced genocide under Saddam Hussein).
6. Counselors must facilitate empowerment for those clients who feel underprivileged and devalued (for example, immigrants who may feel forced to accept menial jobs even though they worked in prestigious occupations in their native countries).

Shearer and King conclude that developing cultural awareness provides the probation officer with an effective approach that actively draws the probationer into the therapeutic relationship and that increases the likelihood of a successful outcome.

Reference: Robert A. Shearer and Patricia Ann King, "Multicultural Competencies in Probation: Issues and Challenges," *Federal Probation*, Vol. 68, No. 1 (June 2004), pp. 3–9.

Freedom or Safety? You Decide
Probation Condition: Celibacy

In 2017, Idaho Judge Randy Stoker sentenced 19-year-old Cody Herrera to 5 to 15 years in prison, but suspended the sentence and ordered Herrera to attend a six month rehabilitation program while on probation. As a condition of Herrera's probation, Judge Stoker ordered him to remain celibate and to refrain from sexual activity until he was married. During the trial Herrera told the judge that he had had 34 sexual partners.

A similar story comes from Wisconsin, where Circuit Court Judge Tim Boyle ordered 44-year-old Corey Curtis to stop procreating until he could support the nine children whom he had fathered with six different women. The judge imposed the requirement on Curtis in 2012 as a condition of a 3-year probationary term, citing the fact that he owed more than $90,000 in back child support.

Critics of both the *Herrera* and *Curtis* cases point to the 1942 case of *Skinner* v. *Oklahoma*, which overturned Oklahoma's Habitual Criminal Sterilization Act and established procreation as a fundamental constitutional right.

YOU DECIDE

Did the judges in these cases go too far in setting special conditions of probation? Why or why not?

References: Skinner v. Oklahoma, 316 U.S. 535 (1942); Daniel Victor, "Idaho Judge Makes Celibacy Until Marriage a Condition of a Rapist's Probation," The New York Times, February 6, 2017 and "Wisconsin Judge Orders Deadbeat Dad of Nine (with Six Women) to Stop Procreating," The Smoking Gun, http://www.thesmokinggun.com/buster/wisconsin/judicial-procreation-ban-647901 (accessed October 25, 2018)

What Is Parole?

The Bureau of Justice Statistics defines **parole** as a period of conditional supervised release in the community following a prison term. It is a strategy of prisoner **reentry** into the community from prison that differs from probation in both purpose and implementation. Whereas probationers

> **2** Describe the history, purpose, and characteristics of parole.

generally avoid serving time in prison, parolees have already been incarcerated. Whereas probation is a sentencing option available to a judge who determines the form probation will take, parole results from an administrative decision by a legally designated paroling authority. Probation is a sentencing strategy; parole is a correctional strategy whose primary purpose is to return offenders gradually to productive lives. By making early release possible, parole can also act as a stimulus for positive behavioral change. Parole was a much-heralded tool of nineteenth-century corrections. Its advocates had been looking for a behavioral incentive to motivate youthful offenders to reform. Parole, through its promise of earned early release, seemed the ideal innovation. The use of parole in this country began with New York's Elmira Reformatory in 1876. Indeterminate sentences were then a key part of the rehabilitation philosophy, and they remain so today.

States differ as to the type of parole decision-making mechanism they use, as well as the level at which it operates. Two major models prevail: (1) **Parole boards** (state paroling authorities) grant parole based on the board members' judgment and assessment, and their release decisions are termed *discretionary parole*. (2) Statutory decrees produce mandatory release, with release dates usually set near the completion of the inmate's prison sentence, minus time off for good behavior and other special considerations. Sixteen states have entirely abolished **discretionary release** from prison by a parole board for all offenders. Another five states have abolished discretionary release for those who commit certain violent offenses or other crimes against a person. Some states, such as Alabama, have abandoned traditional parole but grant their parole boards the authority to revoke the postrelease supervision status of offenders who violate release conditions, ordering them to return to custody. As a result of the movement away from release by parole boards, statutory release, usually involving a brief mandatory period of postrelease supervision, has become the most common reentry model.[23]

One form of reentry that *is* on the increase, it should be noted, is medical parole. **Medical parole** is an early-release option available in some states under which an inmate who is deemed "low risk" due to a serious physical or mental health condition is released from prison earlier than he or she might have been under normal circumstances.[24]

States that do not utilize discretionary parole can still have substantial reentry populations, and everyone who is released from prison faces the challenges of reentering society. California, for example, one of the states that no longer uses parole boards for most release decisions, annually has one of the largest reentry populations in the country.[25] Although it does not have a parole board in the traditional sense, California does have a Board of Parole Hearings (BPH), which determines when the state's most serious offenders are ready for release from prison.

California's 2011 Public Safety Realignment Act[26] transferred jurisdiction and funding for managing lower-level criminal offenders from the state to the counties. In so doing, it shifted the postrelease supervision of most reentering inmates from state parole agents to county probation officers (or to other county-specified offices). Specifics of the change are described in the state's Postrelease Community Supervision (PRCS) Act of 2011,[27] which is available online at **https://www.justicestudies.com/pubs/pcsa2011.pdf**.

Under the law, BPH continues to hold release hearings for serious violent offenders, persons sentenced to life in prison, persons applying for medical parole, mentally disordered

▲ Kelly Sott, 33, girlfriend of Cameron Douglas (son of actor Michael Douglas) is photographed at federal court in Manhattan immediately after leaving a federal lockup, where she spent 7 months for attempting to smuggle heroin packed in an electric toothbrush to Cameron while he was under house arrest for drug dealing. How might court-ordered community supervision help Sott?

Steven Hirsch/Splash News/Newscom

parole
A period of conditional supervised release in the community following a prison term. The term applies to parolees released through discretionary or mandatory supervised release from prison, and to those released through other types of post-custody conditional supervision.

reentry
The managed return to the community of individuals released from prison. Also, the successful transitioning of a released inmate back into the community.

parole board
A state paroling authority. Many states have parole boards that decide when an incarcerated offender is ready for conditional release. Some boards also function as revocation hearing panels.

🐦 Follow the author's tweets about the latest crime and justice news @schmalleger

discretionary release
The release of an inmate from prison to supervision that is decided by a parole board or other authority.

medical parole
An early release option under which an inmate who is deemed "low risk" due to a serious physical or mental health condition is released from prison earlier than he or she might have been under normal circumstances.

offenders, and sexually violent predators held at the state level (also known as high-risk sex offenders, or HRSOs). Such inmates, when released, are supervised by the California Department of Corrections and Rehabilitation's Division of Adult Parole Operations (DAPO). All other inmates, sentenced after the realignment legislation went into effect, must be released on PRCS without any significant state-imposed restrictions or supervision and do not fall under DAPO supervision.

Persons released to PCRS must agree to a few general conditions of postrelease supervision (i.e., not to violate state law or to own or possess a firearm or ammunition), and are required to register with the county in which they live. They must also agree to submit to warrantless searches by law enforcement officers during the time they are on PCRS, but cannot be returned to prison for parole violations. Although it is up to the counties to establish appropriate supervisory procedures and conditions, California's Postrelease Community Supervision Act requires release from county supervision within 1 year for persons who demonstrate good behavior. County agencies may, however, elect to discharge persons from supervision even earlier.

Under California's Postrelease Community Supervision Act, an offender who violates a condition of postrelease supervision may be sent to jail for a period of 1 to 10 days. The program, known as "flash incarceration," is a tool which the law says can "punish an offender while preventing the disruption in a work or home establishment that typically arises from longer term revocations." A recent study of 1-year arrest and conviction rates of offenders under postrelease community supervision found that "the one-year return to prison rate was substantially less post-Realignment, since most offenders in this cohort were ineligible to return to prison on a parole violation."[28]

It is important to note that reentry strategies go by many names. Some states, like California, use the term "postrelease supervision"; others prefer "reentry," while many still use the word "parole" in describing what is essentially the same process. View a video of O. J. Simpson's entire 2017 hearing before the Nevada Board of Parole at **https://youtu.be/Rdq8BdlnM1Y**.

The Extent of Parole

Parolees make up one of the smallest of the correctional categories shown in Figure 10–1. While most states are working to lower their prison populations, the growing reluctance to use parole today seems to be due to the realization that correctional routines have generally been ineffective at producing any substantial reformation among many offenders before their release back into the community. The abandonment of the rehabilitation goal, combined with a return to determinate sentencing in many jurisdictions—including the federal judicial system—has substantially reduced the amount of time the average correctional client spends on supervised parole.

Although discretionary parole releases are far less common than they used to be, about 25% of inmates who are freed from prison are still paroled by a paroling authority such as a parole board.[29] States operating under determinate sentencing guidelines, however, often require that inmates serve a short period of time, such as 90 days, on *reentry parole*—a form of supervised **mandatory release**. Mandatory parole releases have increased 91% since 1990,[30] even though they typically involve either a very small amount of time on parole or no time under supervision. As a result, determinate sentencing schemes have changed the face of parole in America, resulting in a dramatic reduction in the average time spent under post-prison supervision. They have, however, had little or no impact on the actual number of offenders released from prison.

mandatory release
The release of an inmate from prison that is determined by statute or sentencing guidelines and is not decided by a parole board or other authority.

At the beginning of 2017, the number of people under parole supervision throughout the United States stood at 874,777.[31] As with probation, states vary considerably in the use they make of parole, influenced as they are by the legislative requirements of sentencing schemes. For example, on January 1, 2017, Maine (a state that is phasing out parole) reported only 21 people under parole supervision (the lowest of all the states). Delaware had only 387, whereas California had a parole population in excess of 93,500, and Texas officials were busy supervising more than 111,200 parolees.

🐦 Follow the author's tweets about the latest crime and justice news @schmalleger

Of those who exit parole, approximately 56% successfully complete parole. About 15% are returned to prison for **parole violation** (failure to meet parole conditions), another 7% go back to prison for new offenses during their parole period, and others may be transferred to new jurisdictions, abscond and not be caught, or may die.[32] (Those on probation who do not meet probation conditions commit **probation violations**.) An interesting parole decision-making tool is available on the Web at **http://www.insideprison.com/parole_decision_making.asp#.UWr9O6t4bYg**.

Parole Conditions

In those jurisdictions that retain discretionary parole, the **conditions of parole** remain very similar to the **conditions of probation** and usually include agreement not to leave the state as well as to obey extradition requests from other jurisdictions. Parolees must also periodically report to parole officers, and parole officers may visit parolees at their homes and places of business, often arriving unannounced.

The successful continued employment of parolees is one of the major concerns of parole boards and their officers, and studies have found that successful employment is a major factor in reducing the likelihood of repeat offenses.[33] Hence, the importance of continued employment is typically stressed on parole agreement forms, with the condition that failure to find employment within 30 days may result in **parole revocation** (loss of parole status and usually a return to prison). As with probationers, parolees who are working can be ordered to pay fines and penalties. A provision for making payments of **restitution** in the form of money or services to the victim is also frequently included as a condition of parole.

As with probation, special parole conditions may be added by the judge and might require the parolee to pay a "parole supervisory fee" (often around $15 to $20 per month). A relatively new innovation, the parole supervisory fee shifts some of the expense of community corrections to the offender.

Federal Parole

Federal offenders may be ordered to serve one of three distinct forms of community supervision, including (1) probation, (2) parole (i.e., mandatory release, military parole, and special parole), or (3) a term of supervised release after having served time in prison. Federal parole was planned to phase out under the Sentencing Reform Act of 1984, and offenders sentenced to federal prison after the act was passed are no longer eligible for parole. Instead, they are required to serve a term of supervised release (TSR) following discharge. Consequently, many federal offenders today who are under community supervision are serving a term of supervised release. TSR, which is similar to mandatory release, is ordered at the time of sentencing by a federal judge, and is served after discharge from a federal prison.

In 2008, the Bureau of Justice Statistics (BJS) added a new category to its Annual Parole Survey known as "term of **supervised release**." Under federal data-gathering programs, TSR is defined as "a fixed period of release to the community that follows a fixed period of incarceration based on a determinate sentencing statue; both are determined by a judge at the time of sentencing."[34] As BJS notes, this category was added to better classify the large majority of federal reentry offenders. Changed procedures in the federal system have resulted in a picture of postconviction supervision diagrammed in Figure 10–2.

The 1984 Comprehensive Crime Control Act (of which the Sentencing Reform Act of 1984 was a part) mandated federal fixed sentencing and abolished parole for most offenses committed after November 1, 1987. The act also called for a planned phaseout of the U.S. Parole Commission (USPC). Federal parole decisions continue to be made for federal inmates whose sentences were imposed before the act's deadline. They are made by the USPC located in Chevy Chase, Maryland. The USPC uses hearing examiners to visit federal prisons. Examiners typically ask parole-eligible inmates to describe why, in their opinion, they are ready for parole. The inmate's job readiness, home plans,

parole (probation) violation

An act or a failure to act by a parolee (or probationer) that does not conform to the conditions of his or her parole (or probation).

conditions of parole (probation)

The general and special limits imposed on an offender who is released on parole (or probation). General conditions tend to be fixed by state statute, whereas special conditions are mandated by the sentencing authority (court or board) and take into consideration the background of the offender and the circumstances of the offense.

parole revocation

The administrative action of a paroling authority removing a person from parole status in response to a violation of lawfully required conditions of parole, including the prohibition against committing a new offense, and usually resulting in a return to prison.

restitution

A court requirement that a convicted offender pay money or provide services to the victim of the crime.

supervised release

A form of reentry in the federal justice system consisting of a term of conditional community supervision, set by the court at the time of sentencing, to be served after release from prison.

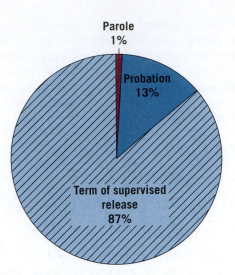

Parole
1%

Probation
13%

Term of supervised
release
87%

🐦 Follow the author's tweets about the
latest crime and justice news @schmalleger

past record, accomplishments while in prison, good behavior, and previous experiences on probation or parole form the basis for the examiners' report to the commission. Under the act, the commission was to be abolished by 1992, but various pieces of federal legislation have since extended the life of the commission. It continues to have jurisdiction over all federal offenders who committed their crimes before November 1, 1987; state probationers and parolees in the Federal Witness Protection Program; persons sentenced under the criminal code of the District of Columbia; and U.S. citizens convicted in foreign countries who have elected to serve their sentences in this country. The federal budget request for fiscal year 2019 included a total of $12.6 million, for 51 positions, including four attorneys, at the USPC.[35] Visit the commission's website via **http://www.justice.gov/uspc**.

Probation and Parole: The Pluses and Minuses

3 | Compare the advantages and disadvantages of probation and parole.

Probation is used to meet the needs of offenders who require some correctional supervision short of imprisonment while providing a reasonable degree of security to the community. Parole fulfills a similar purpose for offenders released from prison.

Advantages of Probation and Parole

Both probation and parole provide a number of advantages over imprisonment:

- *Lower cost.* Imprisonment is expensive. Incarcerating a single offender in Georgia, for example, costs approximately $54 per day, whereas the cost of parole is as little as $2.12 per day per parolee.[36] The expense of imprisonment in some other states may be more than three times as high as it is in Georgia.

- *Increased employment.* Few people in prison have the opportunity for productive employment. Work-release programs, correctional industries, and inmate labor programs operate in most states, but they usually provide only low-paying jobs and require few skills. At best, such programs include only a small portion of the inmates in any given facility. Probation and parole, on the other hand, make it possible for offenders under correctional supervision to work full time at jobs in the "free" economy. Offenders can contribute to their own and their families' support, stimulate the local economy by spending their wages, and support the government by paying taxes.

- *Restitution.* Offenders who are able to work are candidates for court-ordered restitution. Society's interest in restitution may be better served by a probationary sentence or parole than by imprisonment. Restitution payments to victims may help restore the victims' standard of living and personal confidence while teaching the offenders responsibility.

- *Community support.* The decision to sentence a convicted offender to probation is often partially based on considerations of family and other social ties. Such decisions are made in the belief that offenders will be more subject to control in the community if they participate in a web of positive social relationships. An advantage of both probation and parole is that they allow the offender to continue personal and social relationships. Probation avoids splitting up families, and parole may reunite family members separated from each other by a prison sentence.

- *Reduced risk of criminal socialization.* Criminal values permeate prisons. In fact, prison has been called a "school in crime." Probation insulates adjudicated offenders, at least to some degree, from these kinds of values. Parole, by virtue of the fact that it follows time served in prison, is less successful than probation in reducing the risk of criminal socialization.

- *Increased use of community services.* Probationers and parolees can take advantage of services offered through the community, including psychological therapy, substance-abuse counseling, financial services, support groups, church outreach programs, and social services. Although a few similar opportunities may be available in prison, the community environment itself can enhance the effectiveness of treatment programs by reducing the stigmatization of the offender and by allowing the offender to participate in a more "normal" environment.

- *Increased opportunity for rehabilitation.* Probation and parole can both be useful behavioral management tools: They reward cooperative offenders with freedom and allow for the opportunity to shape the behavior of offenders who may be difficult to reach through other programs.

Disadvantages of Probation and Parole

Any honest appraisal of probation and parole must recognize that they share a number of strategic drawbacks:

- *Relative lack of punishment.* The just deserts model of criminal sentencing insists that punishment should be a central theme of the justice process. Although rehabilitation and treatment are recognized as worthwhile goals, the model suggests that punishment serves both society's need for protection and victims' need for revenge. Many view probation, however, as practically no punishment at all. Parole is likewise accused of unhinging the scales of justice because (1) it releases some offenders early, even when they have been convicted of serious crimes, while some relatively minor offenders remain in prison; and (2) it is misleading to those harmed by crime because it does not require completion of the offender's entire sentence behind bars.

- *Increased risk to the community.* Probation and parole are strategies designed to deal with convicted criminal offenders. The release into the community of such offenders increases the risk that they will commit additional offenses. Community supervision can never be so complete as to eliminate such a possibility, and evaluations of parole have pointed out that an accurate assessment of offender dangerousness is beyond our present capability.[37]

- *Increased social costs.* Some offenders placed on probation and parole will effectively and responsibly discharge their obligations; others, however, will become social liabilities. In addition to the increased risk of new crimes, probation and parole increase the chance that added expenses will accrue to the community in the form of child support, welfare costs, housing expenses, legal aid, indigent health care, and the like.

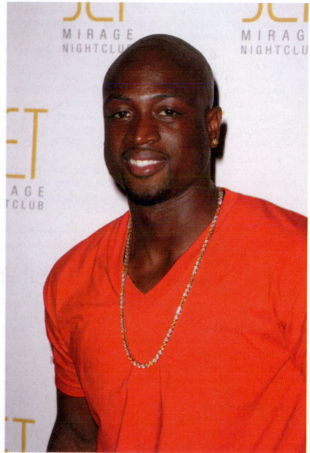

▲ NBA star Dwayne Wade. In 2016, Wade's 32-year-old cousin, Nykea Aldridge, died while pushing her young child in a stroller on a sidewalk in Chicago's south side. Aldridge had gotten caught in a cross fire between two paroled felons. One of the brothers had been out of prison for only two weeks before the shooting. Can the increased risk to the community represented by probation and parole be reduced? If so, how?

WENN Ltd/Alamy Stock Photo

Freedom or Safety? You Decide
Should DNA Links to Unsolved Cases Be Used to Deny Parole?

DNA testing has been called the "new fingerprinting in criminal investigations." It is a powerful tool that, when used correctly, leaves little doubt about the personal identity of a criminal suspect. The federal government has a huge DNA database, consisting of millions of records gathered from convicted offenders, members of the military, and federal employees in sensitive positions. Starting in 1990, states and the federal government began sharing their DNA records through the nation's Combined DNA Index System (CODIS).

Although most of the records in CODIS are those of convicted criminals, a number of states (including California, Kansas, Louisiana, Minnesota, New Mexico, Texas, and Virginia) and the federal government recently enacted legislation to allow the collection of DNA samples from all people who are arrested and charged with felonies. At least six other states are moving in the same direction.[a] In addition, federal authorities are contemplating adding the genetic records of terrorism suspects arrested overseas and of anyone detained for immigration law violations, including those caught illegally crossing the nation's borders (and often quickly returned to their country of origin). If advocates of preconviction genetic testing have their way, the number of records available through CODIS will soar.

Recently, the American Civil Liberties Union (ACLU) filed suit in federal court in San Francisco, challenging California's law that permits the genetic testing of unconvicted arrestees, saying that such testing amounts to an unconstitutional search. Complicating the picture is the fact that some parole authorities have begun hunting for DNA matches in CODIS for inmates who become eligible for early release and then using such matches to hold suspects longer. In Utah, for example, parole-eligible robber Rudy Romero had his release date pushed back 25 years after DNA linked him to five unsolved rapes—even though he has not been charged with any of them.[b] Authorities now think that Romero is the man who came to be known as the "Parkway Rapist" after an unsolved series of brutal attacks and rapes of ten teenage girls and three women near Salt Lake City's Jordan River Parkway between 1990 and 1993.

Although advocates of preconviction testing say that it helps secure justice, some of the matches that turn up involve crimes for which the statute of limitations has expired and that can never be prosecuted. Those opposed to the use of genetic testing to determine parole eligibility say that it is unfair because inmates seeking release do not have the opportunity to defend themselves and that the rules at parole hearings are not like those in criminal trials where defendants are allowed to be represented by attorneys.

YOU DECIDE

Should states inventory the DNA of all suspects who have been arrested for felonies? Of those convicted of felonies? Of those arrested for or convicted of misdemeanors? Should parole authorities be allowed to use apparent DNA links to unsolved crimes in denying the release of parole-eligible inmates?

---

[a]Although most state laws require the DNA records of anyone found not guilty to be expunged from their databases and for their DNA samples to be destroyed, records may still be available for a long time because there are delays in the justice process and because it takes time for the administrative process to conclude.

[b]It is unlikely that rape charges will ever be brought against Romero because Utah has a four-year statute of limitations that bars prosecution.

References: Kevin Johnson and Richard Willing, "New DNA Links Used to Deny Parole," *USA Today,* February 8–10, 2008; Richard Willing, "Many DNA Matches Aren't Acted On," *USA Today,* November 21, 2006; Richard Willing, "Officials Increase DNA Profiles," *USA Today,* May 1, 2006; Richard Willing, "Detainee DNA May Be Put in Database," *USA Today,* January 19–21, 2007; and Jennifer Dobner, "DNA May ID 1990s Rapist," *Desert Morning News* (Salt Lake City), September 3, 2004.

The Legal Environment

revocation hearing
A hearing held before a legally constituted hearing body (such as a parole board) to determine whether a parolee or probationer has violated the conditions and requirements of his or her parole or probation.

conditional release
The release of an inmate from prison to community supervision with a set of conditions for remaining on parole. If a condition is violated, the individual can be returned to prison or face another sanction in the community.[i]

Eleven especially significant U.S. Supreme Court decisions provide the legal framework for probation and parole supervision. Among those cases, that of *Griffin* v. *Wisconsin* (1987)[38] may be the most significant. In *Griffin*, the Supreme Court ruled that probation officers may conduct searches of a probationer's residence without either a search warrant or probable cause. According to the Court, "A probationer's home, like anyone else's, is protected by the Fourth Amendment's requirement that searches be 'reasonable.'" However, "[a] State's operation of a probation system . . . presents 'special needs' beyond normal law enforcement that may justify departures from the usual warrant and probable cause requirements." Probation, the Court concluded, is similar to imprisonment because it is a "form of criminal sanction imposed upon an offender after a determination of guilt."

Similarly, in the 1998 case of *Pennsylvania Board of Probation and Parole* v. *Scott,*[39] the Court declined to extend the exclusionary rule to apply to searches by parole officers, even where such searches yield evidence. Table 10-1 provides an overview of these and other significant cases in the field of probation and parole.

Other court cases focus on the conduct of probation or parole **revocation hearings**, which may result in an order that a probationer's suspended sentence be made "active" or that a parolee be returned to prison to complete his or her sentence in confinement. Revocation is a common procedure. Annually, about 16% of adults on parole throughout the United States have their **conditional release** (release into the community based on certain conditions) revoked.[40] The supervising officer may request that probation or parole be revoked if a client

4 Identify significant court cases affecting probation and parole.

Follow the author's tweets about the latest crime and justice news @schmalleger

TABLE 10-1
U.S. Supreme Court Decisions of Special Significance for Probation and Parole

In This Case	The Court Held That
Samson v. *California* (2006)	Police officers may conduct a warrantless search of a person who is subject to a parole search condition, even when there is no suspicion of criminal wrongdoing and even when the sole reason for the search is that the person is on parole.
U.S. v. *Knights* (2001)	The warrantless search authority normally reserved for probation and parole officers extends to police officers when supported by reasonable suspicion and authorized by the conditions of probation.
Pennsylvania Board of Probation and Parole v. *Scott* (1998)	The exclusionary rule does not apply to searches by parole officers, even when such searches yield evidence of parole violations.
Griffin v. *Wisconsin* (1987)	Probation officers may conduct searches of a probationer's residence without a search warrant or probable cause.
Minnesota v. *Murphy* (1984)	A probationer's incriminating statements to a probation officer may be used as evidence against him or her if the probationer does not specifically claim a right against self-incrimination.
Bearden v. *Georgia* (1983)	Probation cannot be revoked for failure to pay a fine and make restitution if it can't be shown that the defendant was responsible for the failure. Moreover, if a defendant lacks the capacity to pay a fine or make restitution, then the hearing authority must consider any viable alternatives to incarceration before imposing a prison sentence.
Greenholtz v. *Nebraska Penal Inmates* (1979)	Parole boards do not have to specify the evidence or reasoning used in deciding to deny parole.
Gagnon v. *Scarpelli* (1973)	The safeguards identified in *Morrissey* v. *Brewer* were extended to probationers.
Morrissey v. *Brewer* (1972)	Procedural safeguards are necessary in revocation hearings involving parolees. They include (a) written notice of the claimed violations of parole; (b) disclosure to the parolee of evidence against him or her; (c) opportunity to be heard in person and to present witnesses and documentary evidence; (d) the right to confront and cross-examine adverse witnesses (unless the hearing officer specifically finds good cause for not allowing confrontation); (e) a "neutral and detached" hearing body such as a traditional parole board, members of which need not be judicial officers or lawyers; and (f) a written statement.
Mempa v. *Rhay* (1967)	Both notice and a hearing are required before probation revocation, and the probationer should have the opportunity for representation by counsel before a deferred prison sentence is imposed.
Escoe v. *Zerbst* (1935)	Probation "comes as an act of grace to one convicted of a crime," and the revocation of probation without hearing or notice to the probationer is permissible. This decision has been greatly modified by later decisions.

has violated the conditions of community release or has committed a new crime. The most frequent violations for which revocation occurs are (1) failure to report as required to a probation or parole officer, (2) failure to participate in a stipulated treatment program, and (3) alcohol or drug abuse while under supervision.[41]

In 2010, a law went into effect in California authorizing the placement of parolees into nonrevocable parole (NRP).[42] Widely regarded as a correctional innovation, NRP is an effort to safely reduce state prison populations. NRP prohibits the California Department of Corrections and Rehabilitation (CDCR) from returning certain parolees to prison, placing a parole hold on those parolees, or reporting those parolees to the BPH for a violation of parole. Sex offenders, validated gang members, serious felons, and prisoners found guilty of serious disciplinary offenses are not eligible for NRP. Furthermore, only persons evaluated by the CDCR using a risk-assessment tool and not determined to pose a high risk of reoffending can be assigned to NRP. The parole period under NRP generally lasts for 1 year, during which time parolees are not required to report to a parole officer. They are, however, subject to being searched by any law enforcement officer at any time.

Another important legal issue surrounds the potential liability of probation officers and parole boards for the criminal actions of offenders they supervise or whom they have released. Some courts have held that officers are generally immune from suit because they are performing a judicial function on behalf of the state.[43] Other courts, however, have indicated that parole board members who do not carefully consider mandated criteria for judging parole eligibility could be liable for injurious actions committed by parolees.[44] In general,

▲ Georgia probation officers preparing to excavate a site at the Tri-State Crematory in Noble, Georgia, in 2002. Officials found the remains of hundreds of corpses on the crematory's 16-acre grounds. The crematory's operator, Ray Brent Marsh, was charged with 787 felony counts, including theft by deception, abuse of a corpse, and burial service fraud. He was also charged with 47 counts of making false statements to authorities. Convicted on many of the charges, he was sentenced to 12 years in prison in 2005. As this photo shows, a probation officer's job can involve a wide variety of duties. What are the typical duties of a probation officer?

Mark Humphrey/AP Images

however, most experts agree that parole board members cannot be successfully sued unless release decisions are made in a grossly negligent or wantonly reckless manner.[45] Discretionary decisions made by individual probation and parole officers that result in harm to members of the public, however, may be more actionable under civil law, especially where their decisions were not reviewed by a judicial authority.[46]

The Job of Probation and Parole Officers

Job Descriptions

The tasks performed by probation and parole officers are often quite similar, and some jurisdictions combine the roles of both into one job. This section describes the duties of probation and parole officers, whether performed by the same or different individuals. Probation or parole work consists primarily of four functions: (1) intake procedures, (2) presentence investigation, (3) diagnosis and needs assessment, and (4) client supervision.

5 Explain the work of probation officers and parole officers.

Where probation is a possibility, intake procedures may include a presentence investigation, which examines the offender's background to provide the sentencing judge with facts needed to make an informed sentencing decision. Intake procedures may also involve a dispute-settlement process during which the probation officer works with the defendant and the victim to resolve the complaint before sentencing. Intake duties tend to be more common for juvenile offenders than they are for adults, but all officers may eventually have to recommend to the judge the best sentencing alternative for a particular case.

Diagnosis, the psychological inventorying of the probation or parole client, may be done either formally with written tests administered by certified psychologists or through informal arrangements, which typically depend on the observational skills of the officer. Needs assessment, another area of officer responsibility, extends beyond the psychological needs of the client to a cataloging of the services necessary for a successful experience on probation or parole.

Supervision of sentenced probationers or released parolees is the most active stage of the probation or parole process. It might involve months (and sometimes years) of periodic meetings between the officer and the client and an ongoing assessment of the success of the probation or parole endeavor in each case.

All probation and parole officers must keep confidential the details of the presentence investigation, including psychological tests, needs assessment, and conversations between their clients and themselves. On the other hand, courts have generally held that communications between the officer and the client are not privileged, as they might be between a doctor and a patient or between a social worker and his or her client.[47] Hence, officers can share with the appropriate authorities any incriminating evidence that a client relates.

> Where probation is a possibility, intake procedures may include a presentence investigation, which examines the offender's background to provide the sentencing judge with facts needed to make an informed sentencing decision.

The Challenges of the Job

One of the biggest challenges that probation and parole officers face is the need to balance two conflicting sets of duties: to provide quasi–social work services and to handle custodial responsibilities. In effect, two inconsistent models of the officer's role coexist. The social

JUSTICE REINVESTMENT
Cost-Efficient Reentry Services

By 2018, the state of Georgia had closed most of its parole offices and changed the style of supervision used by its parole officers. Today, Georgia's parole consideration process is facilitated by CONS (the Clemency Online Navigation System)—which gathers all pertinent information on eligible correctional clients, making it quickly and easily available to the five-member State Board of Pardons and Paroles. The system then tallies votes on individual cases and automates the reentry process by sending release notifications to judges, wardens, prosecutors, and law enforcement agencies. All parolees in Georgia are tracked by "parole officer-friendly remote technology," providing a huge savings in leased office space statewide. "The day of the parolee reporting to a parole office is long gone," says Michael Nail, Commissioner of the Georgia Department of Community Supervision. Instead, two-person parole teams use vehicles as "virtual offices," to visit the communities where parolees live and work. "It's no longer parolees coming to where the parole officer works," says Nail.

Some of the new technologies used by Georgia's parole officers are facilitated through the Google Apps for government platform, and consist of a voice-recognition system teamed with GPS technologies that allow officers to verify a parolee's location at any time. Parolees deemed at higher risk of reoffending are supervised under an enhanced house arrest monitoring system, which uses cell phones and voice-recognition technology to track parolee's locations. The hardware used by the system is supported by a fee paid by the parolees themselves. That cost is substantially below the expenses associated with GPS bracelets and the monitoring systems they require.

The system allows offenders to use a cell phone to call a toll-free number and interact with an automated system through a series of questions and answers. Every contact is documented and offender identity is verified by voiceprint biometrics. The system conducts an automated interview for every caller and reports the results to the officer assigned to that parolee. GPS technology reveals the location of the caller. Officers are able to quickly review interview results through a computerized system that alerts them to problems that may require more direct intervention.

Typically, the states paroles around 10,500 persons every year, and spends about $53 million per year on parole supervision. The technological innovations mentioned here, however, have allowed the parole board to considerably reduce expenditures and have saved the state about $2 million per year in office-related expenses.

Georgia parole officers supervise around 23,000 parolees—a number which has not changed substantially since the electronic tracking system was implemented. Parolees assigned to the voice-recognition system show high rates of desistance, with only 1.7% of them returning to prison.

It is worth noting that in 2015 the Georgia General Assembly passed legislation creating a new department—the Department of Community Supervision (DCS). The legislation transferred responsibilities for the community supervision of parolees from the State Board of Pardons and Paroles, probationers from the Department of Corrections, and select Class A and B juveniles from the Department of Juvenile Justice to DCS. The bill also transferred the oversight responsibilities of misdemeanor probationers from the County and Municipal Probation Advisory Council to DCS. Recently, DCS created a new Prisoner Reentry Initiative (PRI). PRI mandates the creation of a reentry plan for each inmate from the time he or she enters prison. The purpose of the initiative is to enhance public safety by reducing crime through the implementation of a seamless plan of services and supervision developed with each returning citizen from the time of their entry to prison through their successful transition, reintegration, and aftercare in the community.

References: Georgia Department of Community Services, "About Us," https://dcs.georgia.gov/about-us (accessed July 5, 2018); Georgia State Board of Pardons and Paroles, *Annual Report*, 2017; https://pap.georgia.gov/sites/pap.georgia.gov/files/Annual_Reports/PAP_AnnualReport-Final_WEB.pdf, accessed September 18, 2018); "Georgia Prisoner Reentry Initiative," Georgia Department of Community Supervision, https://dcs.georgia.gov/georgia-prisoner-reentry-initiative (accessed March 9, 2018). "The Virtual Office," *Georgia State Board of Pardons and Paroles*, https://pap.georgia.gov/virtual-office (accessed March 15, 2018); Mike Klein, "End of an Era: Georgia Begins to Close Parole Offices," *Georgia Public Policy Foundation*, November 30, 2012, http://www.georgiapolicy.org/2012/11/end-of-an-era-georgia-begins-to-close-parole-offices/ (accessed March 19, 2018).

---

work model stresses an officer's service role and views probationers and parolees as clients. In this model, officers are caregivers whose goals are to accurately assess the needs of their clients and to match clients with community resources, such as job placement, indigent medical care, family therapy, and psychological and substance-abuse counseling. The social work model depicts probation or parole as a "helping profession" wherein officers assist their clients in meeting the conditions imposed on them by their sentence. The other model for officers is correctional. In this model, probation and parole clients are "wards" whom officers are expected to control. This model emphasizes community protection, which officers are supposed to achieve through careful and close supervision. Custodial supervision means that officers will periodically visit their charges at work and at home, often arriving unannounced. It also means that they must be willing to report clients for new offenses and for violations of the conditions of their release.

Most officers, by virtue of their personalities and experiences, probably identify more with one model than with the other. They think of themselves primarily either as caregivers or as correctional officers. Regardless of the emphasis that appeals more to individual officers, however, the demands of the job are bound to generate role conflict at one time or another.

A second challenge of probation and parole work is large **caseloads** (the number of clients assigned to probation or parole officers). Back in 1973, the President's Commission on Law Enforcement and Administration of Justice recommended that probation and parole caseloads average around 35 clients per officer.[48] However, caseloads of 250 clients are common in some

🐦 Follow the author's tweets about the latest crime and justice news @schmalleger

caseload
The number of probation or parole clients assigned to one probation or parole officer for supervision.

CJ Careers
Probation Officer

Name: Stephanie Drury

Position: Probation Officer, Pontiac, Michigan

College attended: Wayne State University

Major: Criminal Justice (BS and MS)

Year Hired: 2009

What criminal justice–related jobs have you held? Probation officer for the State of Michigan; probation officer for the Oakland County (Michigan) Adult Treatment Court

Please give a brief description of your job. I am a probation officer for approximately 110 men. The Adult Treatment Court is a specialty court for offenders with severe substance-abuse problems, and many of them also have a mental health diagnosis. My role there is to provide intensive supervision. I attend court with them every 2 weeks to inform the judge of their progress. Additionally, I see each of them at least once a week in order to ensure they are complying with all conditions of the program and maintaining their sobriety.

What appealed to you most about this job when you applied for it? I completed an internship with the federal probation department in Detroit and thoroughly enjoyed probation work, so I applied for the state probation job. The Adult Treatment Court position was appealing because I work directly with the judge and am able to provide intensive supervision to my probationers.

How would you describe the interview process? The interview consisted of a panel of three members of the Michigan Department of Corrections followed by a written test. Questions were based on my academic experience, along with any professional experience I had that would make me a perfect candidate. Also, real-

▲ Stephanie Drury
Stephanie Drury

life situations and scenarios were discussed in order to show the panel how I might deal with a particular situation.

What is a typical day like for you? I monitor the daily development of the females of the Adult Treatment Court, which includes probation supervision and making sure they are taking their medication, going to therapy, and attending programs such as Narcotics Anonymous. With the men on general supervision, I complete presentence investigations, fieldwork, jail visits, and court appearances.

What qualities or characteristics are most helpful for this job? You have to be strong and in control at all times. If you don't have a backbone, the offenders will walk all over you and not take you seriously. It is a demanding job, and you have to be very organized to successfully supervise so many individuals on your caseload. You can exercise a lot of discretion and be your own boss, yet you also have a supervisor who will assist you in times of need.

What is the typical starting salary for this position? $16.54 per hour with benefits

What is the salary potential as you move up into higher-level jobs? A probation officer with 6 years or more of experience will earn approximately $28.00 per hour or more, depending on his or her classification.

What career advice would you give someone in college beginning studies in criminal justice? Find internships to gain experience in specific areas in the field of criminal justice. Engage yourself in as much real-life experience as possible, and network with as many professionals as possible, as these two methods will set you apart from other job candidates.

Courtesy of Stephanie Drury. Used with permission.

jurisdictions today, and Internet-facilitated remote supervision (discussed in a CJ Issues box, Remote Reporting Probation, later in this chapter) can lead to higher case-loads still. Large caseloads, combined with limited training and the time constraints imposed by administrative demands, culminate in stopgap supervisory measures. "Postcard probation," in which clients mail in a letter or card once a month to report on their whereabouts and circumstances, is an example of one stopgap measure that harried agencies with large caseloads use to keep track of their wards. A comprehensive review of state parole practices in California found that 65% of the state's parolees saw their parole officer no more than twice every 3 months, and 23% saw their officers only once every 3 months. Parolees with the highest level of supervision, including high-risk sex offenders, averaged two face-to-face meetings with their parole officer each month.[49]

Another difficulty with probation and parole work is the frequent lack of opportunity for career mobility within the profession. Probation and parole officers are generally assigned to small agencies serving limited geographic areas, under the leadership of one or two chief probation officers. Unless retirement or death claims a supervisor, there is little chance for other officers to advance.

A recent report by the National Institute of Justice (NIJ) found that probation and parole officers experienced a lot of stress.[50] The major sources of stress for probation and parole officers were found to be high caseloads, extensive paperwork, and pressures associated with deadlines. Stress levels have also increased in recent years because

> The major sources of stress for probation and parole officers were found to be high caseloads, extensive paperwork, and pressures associated with deadlines.

offenders who are sentenced to probation and released on parole today have committed more serious crimes than in the past, and more offenders have serious drug-abuse histories and show less hesitation in using violence.[51] The NIJ study found that officers typically cope by requesting transfers, retiring early, or taking "mental health days" off from work. The report says, however, that "physical exercise is the method of choice for coping with the stress."[52]

Learn more about working as a probation or parole officer at the American Probation and Parole Association (APPA) website via **http://www.appa-net.org/eweb**.

Intermediate Sanctions

As noted in Chapter 9, significant new alternative sentencing options have become available to judges. These options are called **intermediate sanctions** because they employ sentencing alternatives that fall somewhere between outright imprisonment and simple probationary release back into the community. They are also sometimes termed *alternative sentencing strategies*. Michael J. Russell, former director of the NIJ, states:

> [I]ntermediate punishments are intended to provide prosecutors, judges, and corrections officials with sentencing options that permit them to apply appropriate punishments to convicted offenders while not being constrained by the traditional choice between prison and probation. Rather than substituting for prison or probation, however, these sanctions—which include intensive supervision, house arrest with electronic monitoring (also referred to as *remote location monitoring*), and shock incarceration (programs that stress a highly structured and regimented routine, considerable physical work and exercise, and at times intensive substance abuse treatment)—bridge the gap between those options and provide innovative ways to ensure swift and certain punishment.[53]

Numerous citizen groups and special-interest organizations are working to widen the use of sentencing alternatives. One organization of special note is the Sentencing Project. The Sentencing Project, based in Washington, D.C., is dedicated to promoting a greater use of alternatives to incarceration and provides technical assistance to public defenders, court officials, and other community organizations.

The Sentencing Project and other groups like it have contributed to the development of more than 100 locally based alternative sentencing programs. Most alternative sentencing programs work in conjunction with defense attorneys to develop written sentencing plans. Such plans are basically well-considered citizen suggestions as to appropriate sentencing in a given instance. They are often quite detailed and may include letters of support from employers, family members, the defendant, and even victims. Sentencing plans may be used in plea-bargaining sessions or may be presented to judges following trial and conviction. Some years ago, for example, lawyers for country western singer Willie Nelson successfully proposed an alternative option to tax court officials that allowed the singer to pay huge past tax liabilities by performing in concerts for that purpose. Lacking such an alternative, the tax court might have seized Nelson's property or even ordered the singer to be confined to a federal facility. About the same time, former NBA player DeShawn Stevenson was sentenced to 2 years of probation and ordered to perform 100 hours of community service for the statutory rape of a 14-year-old girl whom he had plied with brandy.[54] Stevenson, who played for the Utah Jazz at the time of the offense, fulfilled the terms of his sentence by delivering motivational speeches at Boys Clubs in California and New York.

The basic philosophy behind intermediate sanctions is this: When judges are offered well-planned alternatives to imprisonment for offenders who appear to represent little or no continuing threat to the community, the likelihood of a prison sentence is reduced. An analysis of alternative sentencing plans like those sponsored by the Sentencing Project shows that judges accept them in up to 80% of the cases in which they are recommended and that as many as two-thirds of offenders who receive intermediate sentences successfully complete them.[55]

Intermediate sanctions have three distinct advantages: (1) They are less expensive to operate per offender than imprisonment; (2) they are socially cost-effective because they keep the offender in the community, thus avoiding both the breakup of the family and the stigmatization of imprisonment; and (3) they provide flexibility in terms of resources, time of involvement, and place of service.[56] Some of these new sentencing options are described in the paragraphs that follow.

6 Describe various intermediate sanctions.

intermediate sanctions
The use of split sentencing, shock probation or parole, shock incarceration, mixed sentencing, community service, intensive probation supervision, or home confinement in lieu of other, more traditional sanctions, such as imprisonment and fines.

Follow the author's tweets about the latest crime and justice news @schmalleger

split sentence
A sentence explicitly requiring the convicted offender to serve a period of confinement in a local, state, or federal facility, followed by a period of probation.

shock probation
The practice of sentencing offenders to prison, allowing them to apply for probationary release, and enacting such release in surprise fashion. Offenders who receive shock probation may not be aware that they will be released on probation and may expect to spend a much longer time behind bars.

shock incarceration
A sentencing option that makes use of "boot camp"–type prisons to impress on convicted offenders the realities of prison life.

Split Sentencing

In jurisdictions where **split sentences** are an option, judges may impose a combination of a brief period of imprisonment and probation. Defendants who are given split sentences are often ordered to serve time in a local jail rather than in a long-term confinement facility. Ninety days in jail, together with 2 years of supervised probation, is a typical split sentence. Split sentences are frequently given to minor drug offenders. They serve notice that continued law violations may result in imprisonment for much longer periods.

Shock Probation and Shock Parole

Shock probation strongly resembles split sentencing because the offender serves a relatively short period of time in custody (usually in a prison rather than a jail) and is released on probation by court order, but the difference is that shock probation clients must *apply* for probationary release from confinement and cannot be certain of the judge's decision. In shock probation, the court in effect makes a resentencing decision. Probation is only a statutory possibility and often little more than a vague hope for the offender as imprisonment begins. If probationary release is ordered, it may well come as a "shock" to the offender, who, facing a sudden reprieve, may forswear future criminal involvement. Shock probation was begun in Ohio in 1965.[57] It is used today in about half of the states.[58] Shock probation lowers the cost of confinement, maintains community and family ties, and may be an effective rehabilitative tool.

Similar to shock probation is shock parole. Whereas shock probation is ordered by judicial authority, shock parole is an administrative decision made by a paroling authority. Parole boards or their representatives may order an inmate's early release, hoping that the brief exposure to prison has reoriented the offender's life in a positive direction.

Shock Incarceration

Shock incarceration, which became quite popular during the 1990s, utilized military-style "boot camp" prison settings to provide highly regimented environments involving strict discipline, physical training, and hard labor.[59] Shock incarceration programs were designed primarily for young first offenders and are of short duration, generally lasting for only 90 to 180 days. Offenders who successfully completed these programs were typically returned to the community under some form of supervision. Program "failures" were usually moved into the general prison population for longer terms of confinement.

Georgia established the first shock incarceration program in 1983.[60] Following Georgia's lead, more than 30 other states began their own programs.[61] About half of the states provided for voluntary entry into the program, and a few states allowed inmates to decide when and whether they want to quit. One of the most comprehensive studies of boot-camp prison programs focused on eight states: Florida, Georgia, Illinois, Louisiana, New York, Oklahoma, South Carolina, and Texas. The report found that boot camp programs have been popular because "they are . . . perceived as being tough on crime" and "have been enthusiastically embraced as a viable correctional option." The report concluded, however, that "the impact of boot camp programs on offender recidivism is at best negligible."[62]

▲ A boot camp staff member conducting a push-up drill with young offenders. Boot camps use military-style discipline in an attempt to reduce the chance for recidivism among young first-time offenders. Do you think that boot camps can reduce recidivism?

Vladimir Chaloupka/Las Cruces Sun-News/AP Images

In recent years, boot camp programs have fallen into disfavor and have largely been discontinued. In 2005, the federal Bureau of Prisons ended its boot camp programs (formerly known as "intensive confinement"), saving more than $1 million a year on programs that hadn't proven their worth;[63] and in 2006, Florida Governor Jeb Bush signed legislation ending state-run boot camps in that state following the death of a 14-year-old participant. Two of the last states to continue to operate boot camps are Wyoming and Nevada. Nevada runs a "program of regimental discipline" at its Three Lakes Valley facility. The facility has a capacity of 75 youthful detainees, and accepts only nonviolent offenders who have committed relatively

Ethics and Professionalism
American Probation and Parole Association Code of Ethics

- I will render professional service to the justice system and the community at large in effecting the social adjustment of the offender.
- I will uphold the law with dignity, displaying an awareness of my responsibility to offenders while recognizing the right of the public to be safeguarded from criminal activity.
- I will strive to be objective in the performance of my duties, recognizing the inalienable right of all persons, appreciating the inherent worth of the individual, and respecting those confidences which can be reposed in me.
- I will conduct my personal life with decorum, neither accepting nor granting favors in connection with my office.
- I will cooperate with my coworkers and related agencies and will continually strive to improve my professional competence through the seeking and sharing of knowledge and understanding.
- I will distinguish clearly, in public, between my statements and actions as an individual and as a representative of my profession.

- I will encourage policy, procedures, and personnel practices, which will enable others to conduct themselves in accordance with the values, goals, and objectives of the American Probation and Parole Association.
- I recognize my office as a symbol of public faith and I accept it as a public trust to be held as long as I am true to the ethics of the American Probation and Parole Association.
- I will constantly strive to achieve these objectives and ideals, dedicating myself to my chosen profession.

THINKING ABOUT ETHICS

1. *Which of the ethical principles enumerated here might also apply to correctional officers working in prisons and jails?*
2. *Which might apply to law enforcement officers?*
3. *Which might apply to prosecutors and criminal defense attorneys?*

Source: American Probation and Parole Association. Reprinted with permission.

---

minor crimes.[64] The Wyoming Boot Camp, which can house up to 56 inmates, is located in the Wyoming Honor Conservation Camp at Newcastle, Wyoming.[65] It accepts young offenders under the age of 25 who have been court-recommended, and runs for 180 days.

Mixed Sentencing and Community Service

Some **mixed sentences** require that offenders serve weekends in jail and receive probation supervision during the week. Other types of mixed sentencing require offenders to participate in treatment programs or **community service** (work administered by a community agency) while on probation. Community service programs began in Minnesota in 1972 with the Minnesota Restitution Program, which gave property offenders the opportunity to work and turn over part of their pay as restitution to their victims.[66] Courts throughout the nation quickly adopted the idea and began to build restitution orders into suspended-sentence agreements.

Community service is more an adjunct to rather than a type of correctional sentence and is compatible with most other forms of innovation in probation and parole. Even with home confinement (discussed later), offenders can be sentenced to community service activities that are performed in the home or at a job site during the hours they are permitted to be away from their homes. Washing police cars, cleaning school buses, refurbishing public facilities, and assisting in local government offices are typical forms of community service. Some authors have linked the development of community service sentences to the notion that work and service to others are good for the spirit.[67] Community service participants are usually minor criminals, drunk drivers, and youthful offenders.

One problem with community service sentences is that authorities rarely agree on what they are supposed to accomplish. Most people admit that offenders who work in the community are able to reduce the costs of their own supervision, but there is little agreement on whether such sentences reduce recidivism, act as a deterrent, or serve to rehabilitate offenders.

Intensive Supervision of Probationers and Parolees

Intensive probation/parole supervision (IPS)—described as the "strictest form of probation for adults in the United States"[68]—is designed to achieve control in a community setting over offenders who would otherwise go to prison. Some states have extended a type of IPS to parolees, allowing the early release of some who would otherwise serve longer prison terms.

Georgia was the first state to implement IPS, beginning its program in 1982. The Georgia program, which has since been replaced by other initiatives but was groundbreaking when it began, originally required a minimum of five face-to-face contacts between the probationer and the supervising officer per week, mandatory curfew, required employment,

mixed sentence
A sentence that requires that a convicted offender serve weekends (or other specified periods of time) in a confinement facility (usually a jail) while undergoing probationary supervision in the community.

community service
A sentencing alternative that requires offenders to spend at least part of their time working for a community agency.

🐦 Follow the author's tweets about the latest crime and justice news @schmalleger

intensive probation/parole supervision (IPS)
A form of probation or parole supervision involving frequent face-to-face contact between the correctional client and the probation/parole officer.

weekly check of local arrest records, routine and unannounced alcohol and drug testing, 132 hours of community service, and automatic notification of probation officers via the State Crime Information Network when an IPS client was arrested.[69] The caseloads of probation officers involved in IPS were found to be much lower than the national average.

Intensive supervision probation continues to be used in many states, although the names of programs may vary. Arizona, California, Connecticut, Illinois, and Nevada all operate IPS programs. The programs act as prison diversion channels for high risk offenders. Typically, IPS requires 12–18 months to complete.[70]

Other reentry services also make use of intensive supervision—particularly Intensive Parole Supervision. Names of the programs can vary. For example, Colorado currently offers Intensive Supervision Parole (ISP). The program was designed for inmates who present a high risk of continued criminal activity or who present a possible danger to the community. Many of the correctional clients in Colorado who are on ISP are mandatory parolees, who cannot be denied parole after their sentence has been served. Others are violent criminals, and many are sex offenders. ISP creates a highly structured environment in which electronic monitoring and global positioning technology are used in conjunction with daily check-ins with parole officers. The goal of the ISP program is to give parolees a positive and stable routine to rely on every day. Approximately 1,000 Colorado offenders are currently monitored by the program. Finally, the Texas Parole Division operates a Special Condition Super-Intensive Supervision Program (SISP) which supervises 2,900 high-risk offenders using GPS technology.[71]

One published study showed that IPS programs (whether in probation or parole) can be effective at reducing recidivism, especially if the programs are well planned and fully implemented.[72] The study, which examined programs in California's Contra Costa and Ventura Counties, found that such programs work because, among other things, they use team approaches in their supervision activities and have clear missions and goals.

Home Confinement and Remote Location Monitoring

home confinement
House arrest. Individuals ordered confined to their homes are sometimes monitored electronically to ensure they do not leave during the hours of confinement. Absence from the home during working hours is often permitted.

remote location monitoring
A supervision strategy that uses electronic technology to track offenders who are sentenced to house arrest or those who have been ordered to limit their movements while completing a sentence involving probation or parole.

Home confinement, also referred to as *house arrest*, can be defined as "a sentence imposed by the court in which offenders are legally ordered to remain confined in their own residences."[73] Home confinement usually makes use of a system of **remote location monitoring**, which is typically performed via a computerized system of electronic bracelets. Participants wear a waterproof, shock-resistant transmitting device around the ankle 24 hours a day. The transmitter continuously emits a radio-frequency signal that is detected by a receiving unit connected to the home telephone. Older systems use random telephone calls that require the offender to insert a computer chip worn in a wristband into a specially installed modem in the home, verifying his or her presence. Some use voice-recognition technology and require the offender to verify his or her presence in the home by answering computerized calls. Modern electronic monitoring systems alert the officer when a participant leaves a specific location or tampers with the electronic monitoring equipment. Some systems even make it possible to record the time a supervised person enters or leaves the home.

Much of the electronic monitoring equipment in use today only indicates when participants enter or leave the equipment's range, not where they have gone or how far they have traveled. Newer satellite-supported and cellular systems, however, are capable of continuously monitoring and tracking an offender as he or she moves from place to place (Figure 10–3). Such systems can alert officials when participants venture into geographically excluded locations or when they fail to present themselves at required locations at specific times.[74]

Most remotely monitored offenders on home confinement may leave home only to go to their jobs, attend to medical emergencies, or buy household essentials. Because of the strict limits it imposes on offender movements, house arrest has been cited as offering a valuable alternative to prison for offenders with special needs. Pregnant women, geriatric convicts, offenders with special handicaps, seriously or terminally ill offenders, and the intellectually disabled may all be better supervised through home confinement than traditional incarceration.

One of the best-known people to be placed under house arrest with a remote location monitoring system was comedian Bill Cosby in 2018. Cosby had been ordered confined to his home as he awaited sentencing following his conviction on sexual indecency charges.[75]

Intensive supervision involves frequent face-to-face contact between the correctional client and the probation/parole officer.

FIGURE 10–3
**Remote Location Monitoring—
How It Works**

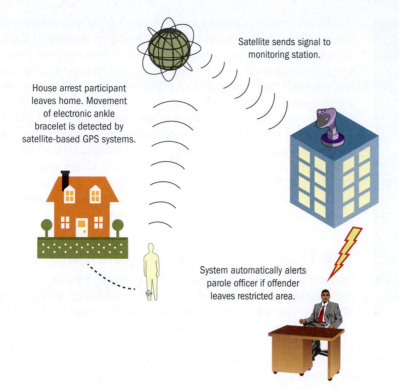

Satellite sends signal to monitoring station.

House arrest participant leaves home. Movement of electronic ankle bracelet is detected by satellite-based GPS systems.

System automatically alerts parole officer if offender leaves restricted area.

The electronic monitoring of offenders has steadily increased nationwide. A survey by the NIJ in 1987, as the use of electronic monitoring was just beginning, showed only 826 offenders being monitored electronically in the United States.[76] By 2000, however, more than 16,000 defendants and offenders under the supervision of U.S. pretrial services and probation officers were on home confinement, most under electronic monitoring programs.[77] Today, according to a survey conducted by the Pew Charitable Trusts, about 125,000 accused and convicted criminal offenders in the United States are monitored with ankle bracelets and other electronic tracking devices. All 50 states, the District of Columbia, and the federal government use electronic devices to monitor the movements and activities of pretrial defendants or convicted offenders on probation or parole.[78] Most offenders on electronic monitoring are tracked by GPS, which notify parole officers when the offender leaves a specified area.

The home confinement program in the federal court system has three components, or levels of restriction.[79] *Curfew* requires program participants to remain at home every day during certain times, usually in the evening. With *home detention*, the participant remains at home at all times except for preapproved and scheduled absences, such as for work, school, treatment, church, attorney's appointments, court appearances, and other court-ordered obligations. *Home incarceration*, the highest level of restriction, calls for 24-hour-a-day "lockdown" at home, except for medical appointments, court appearances, and other activities that the court specifically approves.

Many states and the federal government view house arrest as a cost-effective response to the high cost of imprisonment. Georgia, for example, estimates that home confinement costs approximately $1,130 per year per supervised probationer and $1,577 per supervised parolee.[80] Incarceration costs are much higher, running around $19,622 per year per Georgia inmate, with another $43,756 needed to build each new cell.[81] Advocates of house arrest argue that it is also socially cost-effective because it substantially decreases the opportunity for the kinds of negative socialization that occur in prison.[82] Opponents, however, have pointed out that house arrest may endanger the public and that it may provide little or no actual punishment. Critics of Bill Cosby's home confinement, for example, complained that he was able to enjoy all the amenities that his large and costly house in Pennsylvania provided—and that he should have been sent to prison instead.

A large NIJ-funded study of more than 5,000 Florida offenders placed on GPS monitoring found that electronic monitoring significantly reduced the likelihood of failure under community supervision.[83] The risk of failure was found to be about 31% less than that

Follow the author's tweets about the latest crime and justice news @schmalleger

of offenders placed on other forms of community supervision. Similarly, a recent NIJ study that compared a group of GPS-monitored California sex offenders over a 1-year period found "a clear pattern" success for those being monitored versus a control group who received traditional parole supervision.[84] Study authors noted that the chance for both parole revocation and any return-to-custody event was about 38% higher among the subjects who received traditional parole supervision. The NIJ study also examined costs and benefits associated with electronic monitoring, and concluded that "the GPS program costs roughly $35.96 per day per parolee, while the cost of traditional supervision is $27.45 per day per parolee—a difference of $8.51. However, the results favor the GPS group in terms of both noncompliance and recidivism. In other words, the GPS monitoring program is more expensive but more effective."

The Future of Probation and Parole

Parole was widely criticized during the 1980s and 1990s by citizen groups that claimed it unfairly reduces prison sentences imposed on serious offenders. Official attacks on parole came from some powerful corners. Senator Edward Kennedy called for the abolition of parole, as did former Attorney General Griffin Bell and former U.S. Bureau of Prisons Director Norman Carlson.[85] Academics chimed in, alleging that parole programs can provide no assurance that criminals will not commit further crimes. The media joined the fray, condemning parole for its inability to curb recidivism and highlighting the so-called revolving prison door as representative of the failure of parole.

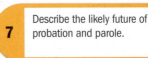

7 Describe the likely future of probation and parole.

These criticisms are not without warrant. Today, around 626,000 former prisoners—more than 1,700 per day—are released from state and federal prisons and returned to society each year, most of them on some form of supervised release.[86] Estimates are that over half of them will have been reincarcerated within 3 years (and some of them will have successfully completed parole prior to their return to prison).[87] Figure 10–4 shows recidivism rates within 3 years of release for prisoners in 15 states.

▲ Comedian Bill Cosby. Cosby was convicted in 2018 of three counts of aggravated indecent assault, and ordered to wear a GPS monitoring anklet while remaining at his house awaiting sentencing. Why is remote location monitoring becoming a popular alternative to jail, and even to imprisonment?

MediaPunch/Shutterstock

FIGURE 10–4
Three-Year Recidivism Rates of Prisoners Released from Prison in 15 States

Source: U.S. Department of Justice, Exploring the Role of the Police in Prisoner Reentry, New Perspectives in Policing Bulletin, 2012.

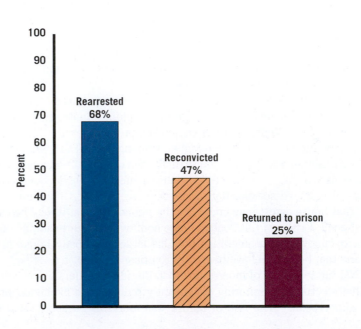

CJ News
How GPS Technology Keeps Track of Sex Offenders

In 2006, when 23 states had adopted global positioning systems (GPS) to monitor sex offenders, the approach was hailed as a promising control of habitual predators.

GPS monitors, strapped to the ankle, were seen as a less costly way to protect against offenders than prison or having a parole officer visit them every day. The monitor might even discourage recidivism, because offenders would be aware that someone was watching their every move.

Today, the number of participating states has reportedly not grown and authorities seem less enthusiastic. "GPS technology is far more limited than anticipated and should be viewed as a tool rather than depended upon as a control mechanism," said Gaylene Armstrong, a professor of criminal justice at Sam Houston State University.

In a 2-year study of GPS monitoring of sex offenders in Phoenix, published in the *Journal of Criminal Justice*, Dr. Armstrong discovered that a considerable number of alerts from the devices were due to harmless events such as equipment failure. Research on whether GPS monitors deter crimes has also been inconclusive, and many offenders have been cutting off the devices or trying to find other ways of fooling them.

Harmless events are a particular problem because they obscure actual trouble spots. The 274 parole officers working GPS caseloads in California, the largest user of GPS monitors for sex offenders, received almost a million alerts in 2009, according to a state report. Each alert is a dot on the computer screen. "We are just drowning in dots," said Robert Coombs, chair of the state's Sex Offender Management Board. "What happens is the more broadly we use it, the more difficult it becomes in identifying the meaningful data."

California's information overload has led to some colossal failures. One paroled sex offender in the state's GPS program was Phillip Garrido, who kidnapped 11-year-old Jaycee Lee Dugard and was keeping her in a shed behind his house for 18 years. After Garrido was arrested in 2009, a state inquiry determined officers failed to respond to hundreds of alerts from his monitor, and the state subsequently paid Dugard $20 million in a settlement. Garrido, who fathered two children with Dugard, is now serving a 431-year sentence.

Some states, however, are less overwhelmed. In Washington, D.C., each parole officer is assigned 20 to 30 offenders and tracks each offender's GPS movements several times a day. Michigan has created a central monitoring center to weed out false alarms, and Florida has hired a private company to sort through alerts.

But effective monitoring can be costly. The reported cost of monitoring one person ranges from $5 to as much as $33 per day, and California spent $60 million to track 6,500 parolees in 2010. Also, when parole officers devote a lot of time to GPS monitoring, it means less face-to-face and telephone time with parolees, considered to be more effective. Innovative jurisdictions have been experimenting with cost reductions. In 2015, a few areas were experimenting with using the GPS technology built into offenders' personal cell phones as a way to reduce cost while providing reliable monitoring. Probationers, who are called randomly at different

▲ An ankle bracelet with a built-in GPS. The bracelet can be placed on parolees and used by parole officers to monitor individuals under house arrest, or to follow the movements of those permitted by the court to move throughout the community while under supervision. What do you see as the advantages and disadvantages of this technology? How would individual-rights and public-safety advocates see GPS technology when used this way?

Paul Bersebach/Newscom

times of the day, are expected to answer calls from their supervising officers who can then use GPS to determine their client's whereabouts. Voice-recognition technology plays an important role in identifying probationers who receive such calls.

GPS may be useful in locating an offender when a child is missing, but many law enforcement officials now say the chief advantage of GPS tracking is not stopping a crime, but gathering evidence after a crime is committed. "Essentially, a GPS bracelet allows you to make a case after the fact," said Gerard Leone, a Massachusetts district attorney. "And that is why I stress it is not an appropriate substitution for incarceration."

Six states have authorized lifetime GPS tracking for sex offenders, extending beyond parole. Critics say such tracking is a violation of the Fourth Amendment ban on search and seizure and of the *ex post facto* clause prohibiting retroactively adding punishment to an offender's sentence. However, the North Carolina Supreme Court rejected the *ex post facto* argument in 2010.

REFERENCES

"GPS Monitoring of Sex Offenders Should Be Used as Tool, Not Control Mechanism, Researchers Find," *Science Daily*, August 8, 2011, http://www.sciencedaily.com/releases/2011/08/110808152417.htm.

"Calif. to Change Sex-Offender Tracking," *Associated Press*, May 26, 2011, http://abcnews.go.com/US/wireStory?id=13696574#.T5IkxRxvYzA.

"Tracking Sex Offenders Is No Easy Fix," *The Bay Citizen*, July 20, 2010, http://www.baycitizen.org/crime/story/gps-tracking-sex-offenders-imperfect; "Georgia Touts Technology Use to Cut Parole Revocations, Recidivism," *The Crime Report,* May 1, 2014, https://thecrimereport.org/2014/05/01/2014-05-technology-and-probation-parole (accessed March 29, 2018).

Parole violators account for more than half of prison admissions in many states, and 28% of parole violators sent to prison were arrested or were convicted of a new offense *while* on parole.[88] Many of these offenses involved drugs. A recent study by the Council of State Governments found that one in five arrests in four of California's largest cities involved individuals under probation or parole supervision at the time of their arrest.[89] The study also found that persons under supervision were involved in one in six arrests for

🐦 Follow the author's tweets about the latest crime and justice news @schmalleger

Today, around 626,000 former prisoners—almost 1,700 per day—are released from state and federal prisons and returned to society each year, most of them on some form of supervised release.

violent crime and one in three of all arrests for drug crime. Had the study also sought to identify persons arrested who had *previously* been on probation or parole, as well as those *currently* being supervised, the results would likely have been much higher.

Critics say that numbers like these are indicative of poor reintegration of prisoners into the community and are associated with wide-ranging social costs, including decreased public safety and weakened family and community ties.[90] Adequate reintegration efforts have also suffered in the face of today's budget shortfalls. In California, for example, the 2011 Realignment Legislation mentioned earlier in this chapter stipulated that any parolee (other than those originally sentenced to life in prison) whose parole is revoked will serve a term no longer than 180 days in the county jail. The bill also provides that parolees who do not incur any infractions will be released from parole supervision in 6 months. Under the law, California's BPH discontinued parole revocation hearings in mid-2013, and that responsibility was moved to local criminal court judges. Although thorough assessments of California's experiment with realignment have yet to be made, one report by a Los Angeles County advisory board found that responsibility for a large number of high-risk offenders, many with mental illness, has been shifted to counties that may be ill-prepared to deal with them adequately.[91]

Even some prisoners have challenged the fairness of parole, saying it is sometimes arbitrarily granted and creates an undue amount of uncertainty and frustration in the lives of inmates. Parolees have complained about the unpredictable nature of the parole experience, citing their powerlessness in the parole contract.

Against the pressure of attacks like these, parole advocates struggled to clarify and communicate the value of supervised release in the correctional process. As more and more states moved toward the elimination of parole, advocates called for moderation. A 1995 report by the APPA, for example, concluded that states that have eliminated parole "have jeopardized public safety and wasted tax dollars." The researchers wrote, "Getting rid of parole dismantles an accountable system of releasing prisoners back into the community and replaces it with a system that bases release decisions solely on whether a prison term has been completed."[92]

Changes in Reentry Policies

By the close of the twentieth century, criticisms of parole had begun to wane, and a number of recent reports have supported well-considered offender reentry and postrelease supervision programs that were able to demonstrate **desistance** from crime. In 2005, for example, the Reentry Policy Council, a bipartisan assembly of almost 100 leading elected officials, policymakers, corrections leaders, and practitioners from community-based organizations around the country, released a report on offender reentry titled *Charting the Safe and Successful Return of Prisoners to the Community*. The 500-page document pointed out that virtually every person incarcerated in a jail in this country, as well as 97% of those incarcerated in prisons, will eventually be released back into society—many of them without any form of postrelease supervision.[93]

As the report noted, almost two out of every three people released from prison are rearrested within 3 years of their release.[94] Report authors noted that although the number of people reentering society has increased fourfold in the past 20 years and spending on corrections has increased nearly sevenfold in the past two decades, the likelihood of a former prisoner succeeding in the community upon release has not improved.

A host of complex issues creates barriers to successful reentry. Three-quarters of those released from prison and jail, for example, have a history of substance abuse. Two-thirds have no high school diploma. Nearly half of those leaving jail earned less than $600 per month immediately prior to their incarceration, and they leave jail with significantly diminished opportunities for employment. Moreover, said the report, more than a third of jail inmates are saddled with a physical or mental disability, and the rate of serious mental illness among released inmates is at least three times higher than the rate of mental illness among the general population.[95]

🐦 Follow the author's tweets about the latest crime and justice news @schmalleger

desistance
The cessation of offending or other antisocial behavior.

According to the report, "the multi-faceted—and costly—needs of people returning to their families and communities require a reinventing of reentry akin to the reinvention of welfare in the 90s."[96] It requires, the report continued, "a multi-system, collaborative approach that takes into account all aspects of [the] problem." In other words, "the problems faced by reentering adults are not merely the problems of corrections or community corrections, but also of public health workers, housing providers, state legislators, workforce development staff, and others."

To guide states and local jurisdictions in the creation of successful offender reentry programs, the report provides 35 policy statements, each of which is supported by a series of research highlights. The report can be read in its entirety at **http://tinyurl.com/ hlhjxoj**.

In 2003, the U.S. Department of Justice, in conjunction with other federal agencies, initiated funding for 89 reentry sites across the country under the Serious Violent Offender Reentry Initiative (SVORI).[97] SVORI programs were geared toward serious and violent offenders, particularly adults released from prison and juveniles released from correctional facilities.[98] The goal of the SVORI initiative was to reduce the likelihood of reincarceration by providing tailored supervision and services to improve the odds for a successful transition to the community. SVORI services included employment assistance, education and skills training, substance-abuse counseling, and help with postrelease housing.

SVORI programs also tried to enhance desistance by closely monitoring participant noncompliance, reoffending, rearrest, reconviction, and reincarceration. The initiative's priorities included providing services both to those adults and juveniles who were most likely to pose a risk to the community upon release and to those who faced multiple challenges upon returning to the community. SVORI funding supported the creation of a three-phase continuum of services that (1) begins in prison, (2) moves to a structured reentry phase before and during the early months of release, and (3) continues for several years as released prisoners take on increasingly productive roles in the community.[99]

In 2012, after SVORI funding ended, the NIJ published a 560-page final report evaluating results of the SVORI program. The study found encouraging results for the effect of SVORI program participation on arrest and, to a lesser extent, incarceration outcomes. The effect of SVORI program participation was found to have been associated with longer times to arrest and with fewer arrests during follow-up periods. Results were weaker for the effects of SVORI on postrelease reincarceration, however. For adult males, SVORI program participation was associated with a longer time to reincarceration and also fewer reincarcerations. For the adult females, the results were mixed and not significant. The final SVORI report can be read in its entirety at **https://www.justicestudies.com/pubs/ final_svori.pdf**.

In response to high postrelease failure rates and the overwhelming needs of individuals returning from incarceration, many reentry-type programs designed to facilitate the transition from incarceration to the community have been implemented over the past several decades.[100] Not all of them fall under the SVORI model. Among the most significant alternatives are **reentry courts**, which combine intensive judicial oversight with rehabilitative services, arose as part of a broader national movement toward the development and implementation of specialized "problem-solving courts," such as drug, mental health, domestic violence, and community courts, as an approach for addressing specific problems among criminal justice populations.

Reentry courts are mostly based on the drug-court model, begun in Miami in 1989, which functions to rapidly place drug-affected defendants into appropriate treatment programs with close supervision by a single judge familiar with both the treatment and the offenders.[101] Similarly, under the reentry court concept, reentry court judges oversee an offender's supervised release into the community.[102] Hence, reentry courts address the critical needs of returning prisoners—particularly in the period immediately following release—through the combination of judicial oversight and a collaborative case management process. According to the Bureau of Justice Assistance, "the underlying goal of reentry courts is to establish a seamless system of offender accountability and support services throughout the reentry process."[103]

reentry courts
"Specialized courts that help reduce recidivism and improve public safety through the use of judicial oversight to apply graduated sanctions and positive reinforcement, to marshal resources to support the prisoner's reintegration, and to promote positive behavior by the returning prisoners."[ii]

The typical reentry court offers an array of reintegration services to which participants can be referred and provides continual oversight using a preestablished set of graduated sanctions and rewards. Throughout the reentry period, a reentry case-management team makes continual recommendations to the reentry court judge.

The National Reentry Resource Center—a joint effort by the Urban Institute, the APPA, the Center of Juvenile Justice Reform at Georgetown University, the Association of State Correctional Administrators, and the Council of State Governments' Justice Center—can be visited on the Web at **http://www.nationalreentryresourcecenter.org**.

In March 2008, in an effort to help the more than 600,000 people leaving prison each year, the U.S. Congress passed the Second Chance Act.[104] The bill was signed into law by President George W. Bush shortly afterward. The law's purpose is to reduce the number of people being returned to prison after parole release due to state-run "hair-trigger" parole systems that send large numbers of people back to prison not for new crimes, but for technical violations or other relatively minor reasons.

The act authorized the expenditure of approximately $400 million in federal funds to "break the cycle of criminal recidivism [by assisting] offenders reentering the community from incarceration to establish a self-sustaining and law-abiding life."[105] The legislation created the National Reentry Resource Center, a clearinghouse of information relating to prisoner reentry, and funded prison-to-community transition services and programs through grants to nonprofit organizations. Such services and programs include the following:

> The Second Chance Act was intended to break the cycle of criminal recidivism by assisting offenders reentering the community from incarceration to establish a self-sustaining and law-abiding life.

- Reentry courts
- Education and job training while in prison
- Mentoring programs for adults and juveniles leaving confinement
- Drug treatment (including family-based treatment) for incarcerated parents during and after incarceration
- Alternatives to incarceration for parents convicted of nonviolent drug offenses
- Supportive programming for children of incarcerated parents
- Early release for certain elderly prisoners convicted of nonviolent offenses
- Reentry research through research awards to study parole and postsupervision revocation and related community safety issues

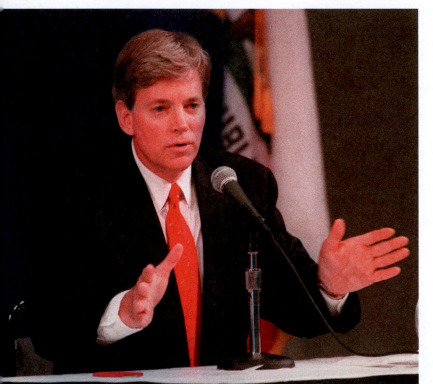

▲ David Duke, the former Ku Klux Klan leader whose case raised eyebrows when he was released on federal parole in 2004. Duke, who served a year in federal prison on fraud charges, was sent to a halfway house in Baton Rouge, Louisiana, and met the work requirements of his release by performing duties for the "white civil rights group" that he heads. Could a more suitable placement have been found for him?

Nick Ut/AP Images

In 2016 the U.S. Department of Justice announced reforms intended to strengthen reentry efforts made by the Federal Bureau of Prisons.[106] The reforms included the provision of an individualized reentry plan tailored to the needs of each inmate, along with the requirement that each inmate be provided with education, employment training, counseling, and like-skills training to help ensure their success upon release.

Finally, in 2018 two studies of reentry courts that had been funded by the Second Chance Act were published. One of the studies, which focused on 8 reentry courts across the country, found that only one of the courts it examined "had a clear positive impact" on recidivism.[107] The other study demonstrated "the importance of having team members who were committed to the success of clients and who believed in the reentry court model."[108]

The Reinvention of Probation and Evidence-Based Practices

Although probation has generally fared better than parole, it too has its critics. The primary purpose of probation has always been rehabilitation, and probation is a powerful rehabilitative tool because, at least in theory, it allows the resources of a community to be focused on the offender. Unfortunately, because it has been too frequently and inappropriately used with repeat or relatively serious offenders, the image of probation has been tarnished.

Consequently, today's reentry advocates have embraced the use of risk prediction tools to assess the likelihood of success for offenders who are being considered for community supervision. The Risk Prediction Index (RPI) is an eight-question prediction instrument used by federal probation officers to estimate the likelihood that an offender will be arrested or have supervision revoked during her or his term of supervision. RPI scores range from 0 to 9, with a low score representing a lower risk of reoffending and a high score a higher risk of reoffending. The average RPI score for those under federal supervised release in 2015 was 3.69.[109]

Of course, knowing what works in community supervision is important, too. Recently, the National Institute of Corrections published a report showing that, among programs studied, treatment-oriented intense supervision of offenders in the community had the largest impact on reducing recidivism.[110] That report, entitled *Evidence-Based Policy, Practice and Decisionmaking*, can be accessed at **https://www.justicestudies.com/pubs/ppdecisionmaking.pdf**.

In 2012, the NIJ funded studies of Hawaii's HOPE program, a highly touted probation initiative that addresses probation violations in a swift, certain, and proportionate manner. Early studies found that HOPE, which stands for Hawaii's Opportunity Probation with Enforcement, when compared with traditional probation programs results in (1) a 55% greater reduction in arrests for new crimes, (2) a 72% greater reduction in the likelihood of drug use, (3) a 61% greater reduction in skipped appointments with probation supervisors, and (4) a 53% greater reduction in probation revocation.[111] Later studies, were not so positive, with findings showing that replications of the program worked in only two (Hawaii and Washington state) out of seven states in which it was implemented.[112]

HOPE begins with a direct, formal warning delivered by a judge in court to offenders enrolled in the program. The warning explicitly states that any future probation violations will result in an immediate, brief jail stay. Probationers with drug issues are assigned a color code at the warning hearing and are required to call the HOPE hotline each weekday morning to find out which color has been chosen for that day. Probationers whose color is selected must appear at the probation office before 2 p.m. the same day for a drug test. Non-drug-involved offenders must comply with their conditions of probation and may be required to attend treatment.

When probationers violate the conditions of probation, they are arrested or an arrest warrant is issued. As soon as a probation officer detects a violation, he or she completes a "Motion to Modify Probation" form and sends it to the judge, who promptly holds a violation hearing. A probationer found to have violated the terms of probation is sentenced to a short jail stay. Upon release, the probationer reports to his or her probation officer and resumes participation in HOPE. Each successive violation is met with an escalated response (i.e., longer jail stays). Learn more about the HOPE program, including efforts to replicate it elsewhere, at **https://www.justicestudies.com/pubs/hope.pdf**.

Finally, an NIJ review of community corrections found that evidence-based practices are becoming firmly established in probation and parole.[113] The review describes innovations such as the development of a risk assessment model that categorizes new probationers using a variety of criteria to determine those most likely to reoffend. The model, developed through a collaboration between the Philadelphia Adult Probation and Parole Department and the University of Pennsylvania's Jerry Lee Center for Criminology, was found to provide highly accurate risk assessments. Using the tool, new probationers are assigned to one of three categories: low, moderate, or high. The lowest level of risk is assigned to those who are predicted not to commit any new offenses in the next 2 years.

CJ | ISSUES
Remote Reporting Probation

Recently, a number of Internet-based interactive probation services, such as Probation Check In (https://www.probationcheckin.com), have been adopted by states seeking to lower the costs of probation supervision. Probation Check In, along with similar other services, allows low-risk probationers to keep in touch with their probation officers through an Internet reporting service. These online services allow for easy communication between client and officers through e-mail, Web-based forms, and instant messaging. Probationers participating in Internet supervision can access the service from home, or through public computers such as those available at local libraries. Clients are generally assessed a monthly fee, typically in the range of $30 to $50, for participation in the program.

Remote reporting systems typically allow probation officers to send mass e-mailings to their entire caseload of clients, or to target individual probationers in their communications. Through the use of easy-to-complete online forms, clients are able to report changes in status (such as changes in jobs, hiring, or health issues) to the probation officer, and the system notifies officers of upcoming events, such as pending discharges from supervision. It can also flag probationers who report losing jobs, changing marital status, or changing place of residence. With links to law enforcement agencies and automated databases, Internet-based systems alerts probation officers of arrests, citations, and other law enforcement contacts with clients.

One major advantage of remote reporting programs is that they allow significantly increased caseloads. A Texas study, for example, showed that Internet reporting makes it possible for one probation officer to supervise up to 500 probationers—more than twice the normal number—without increasing the number of hours of work required over traditional supervision. This significant increase in supervisory capacity can be very important for jurisdictions seeking to make the most efficient use of limited resources.

Critics charge that high-tech supervision of probationers, whether online or through the use of kiosks, Internet services, or dial-in telephone numbers (often enhanced through the use of voice-recognition technologies), carries unacceptable risk. Without personal supervision, those critics say, probationers are more likely to reoffend—an assertion that is essentially untested. Other opponents say remote reporting services are far removed from meaningful "punishment," and that offenders deserve stricter treatment. Supporters, on the other hand, say that high-tech probation supervision will have to become commonplace as probation and parole budgets are strained.

References: "Probation Check In," https://www.probationcheckin.com (accessed March 19, 2018); and Marc A. Levin, "Salvation in Probation Automation?" https://www.texaspolicy.com/blog/detail/salvation-in-probation-automation (accessed March 20, 2018).

The moderate-risk level encompasses those who are likely to commit a crime, but not a serious crime. The high-risk level includes those who are most likely to commit a serious crime (defined as murder, attempted murder, aggravated assault, rape, or arson) within 2 years of probation. The style of community supervision is then determined based on the level of assessed risk, and probation and parole officers who are supervising high-risk individuals are given the smallest caseload.

Summary

PROBATION, PAROLE, AND REENTRY

- Probation, simply put, is a sentence of imprisonment that is suspended. Its goal is to retain some control over criminal offenders while using community programs to help rehabilitate them. Probation, a court-ordered sanction, is one form of community corrections, a sentencing style that depends less on traditional confinement options and more on correctional resources available in the community. In 1925, the federal government enacted legislation enabling federal district court judges to appoint paid probation officers and to impose probationary terms.

- Parole, the conditional early release of a convicted offender from prison, is a reentry strategy whose primary purpose is to return offenders gradually to productive lives. Parole differs from probation in that parolees, unlike probationers, have been incarcerated. Parole supports the concept of indeterminate sentencing, which allows a prisoner to earn early release through good behavior and self-improvement.

- Both probation and parole provide opportunities for the reintegration and reentry of offenders into the community through the use of resources not readily available in institutional settings. They are far less expensive than imprisonment, lead to increased employment among program participants, make possible restitution payments, and increase opportunities for rehabilitation. Unfortunately, however, increased freedom for criminal offenders also means some degree of increased risk for other members of society and increased social costs.

- Eleven especially significant U.S. Supreme Court decisions provide the legal framework for probation and parole supervision. The 1987 case of *Griffin* v. *Wisconsin* may be the most significant. In *Griffin*, the Supreme Court ruled that probation officers may conduct searches of a probationer's residence without either a search warrant or probable cause. Other important court decisions include the 1998 case of *Pennsylvania Board of Probation and Parole* v. *Scott*, in which the Court declined to extend the exclusionary rule to apply to searches by parole officers, and the 2001 case of *U.S.* v. *Knights*, which expanded the search authority normally reserved for probation and parole officers to police officers under certain circumstances.

- Probation or parole work consists primarily of four functions: (1) presentence investigations, (2) other intake procedures, (3) diagnosis and needs assessment, and (4) client supervision. The tasks performed by probation and parole officers are often quite similar, and some jurisdictions combine the roles of both into one job.

- Intermediate sanctions employ sentencing alternatives that fall somewhere between outright imprisonment and simple probationary release back into the community. These sanctions include shock incarceration, intensive probation supervision, and home confinement with remote location monitoring. Intermediate sanctions have three distinct advantages: (1) They are less expensive than imprisonment, (2) they are socially cost-effective because they keep the offender in the community, and (3) they provide flexibility in terms of resources, time of involvement, and place of service.

- In recent years, parole and sometimes probation have been criticized for increasing the risk of community victimization by known offenders. In response, many states eliminated or significantly curtailed parole opportunities. Now, however, as jurisdictions seek to reduce prison populations, reentry programs are once again seen as the best hope for successfully transitioning released inmates back into the community. The federal Second Chance Act of 2008 provides an example of new initiatives being undertaken in the reentry arena.

QUESTIONS FOR REVIEW

1. What is probation? What purpose does it serve?
2. What is reentry and how is it associated with parole? How do probation and parole differ? How are they alike?
3. List and explain the advantages and disadvantages of probation and parole.
4. Name and describe significant court cases that have had an impact on the practices of probation and parole.
5. What do probation and parole officers do? What role do probation officers play in the sentencing of convicted offenders?
6. What are intermediate sanctions? How do they differ from more traditional forms of sentencing? What advantages do they offer?
7. How are probation and parole changing? What does the future hold for each?

Prisons and Jails

Though the U.S. has only about 5% of the world's population, 25% of all prisoners are in American jails and prisons.

—American Bar Association[1]

Learning Objectives

After reading this chapter, you should be able to:

1. Describe the historical development of prisons. **343**

2. Describe today's prisons. **348**

3. Identify some of the issues facing prisons today. **353**

4. Provide an overview of the federal prison system. **357**

5. Identify the role jails currently play in American corrections and issues jail administrators face. **362**

6. Describe the current and likely future roles of private prisons. **368**

Farsh/Fotolia

Introduction

In 2010, a two-person panel of the California Board of Parole Hearings denied medical parole to 42-year-old Steven Martinez, a convicted rapist.[2] Martinez, a quadriplegic, was the first inmate to be considered for medical parole under a new law intended to save the state money by releasing inmates who are permanently incapacitated.

Paralyzed during a prison knife attack that severed his spinal cord, Martinez was serving a 157-year sentence for numerous felonies that he committed during the violent rape of a woman in 1998. The medical care he needs had been costing the state $625,000 per year.[3]

In deciding to deny Martinez's parole, parole commissioner John Peck stated, "This panel finds that he is a violent person who can use other people to carry out threats and would be a public safety threat to those attending to him outside prison walls." Even so, more than a year later, the U.S. Court of Appeals for the Fourth Circuit ordered that Martinez be released. His parents, who were still living, agreed to care for him in their San Diego home.[4]

Martinez's case illustrates the tension that exists today between the need to cut correctional costs and the concern over public safety. The fact that Martinez was denied parole seemed especially surprising to some observers because the denial came almost immediately after the U.S. Supreme Court found that California's prisons are dangerously overcrowded and upheld an earlier order by a three-judge federal panel that state officials must find a way to reduce the 143,335-inmate population by roughly 33,000. That order, originally issued in 2001, was based on a determination that overcrowding in California's prisons had led to conditions so egregious that they violated the Constitution's Eighth Amendment ban on cruel and unusual punishment.[5]

In 2011, in the case of *Brown* v. *Plata* (discussed later in this chapter), the High Court agreed that **prison** overcrowding left the state unable to deliver minimal care to prisoners with serious medical and mental health problems and produced "needless suffering and death."[6] The court gave California officials 2 years to comply with the order to reduce prison populations. In 2014, federal judges, finding that California had not met the original mandate for prison population reduction, ordered parole officials in that state to implement a plan by 2015 to free all nonviolent second-strike offenders (except sex offenders) on parole after serving half of their sentences.[7] California's booming prisons, which seriously undermined the state's financial situation, were the result of get-tough-on-crime policies that had permeated the national scene since the 1970s.

▲ The entrance to Folsom prison in Folsom, California. The institution was immortalized in a 1955 Johnny Cash song, "Folsom Prison Blues." In 2011, the U.S. Supreme Court held that California prisons were dangerously overcrowded. On what did the Court base its decision?
Dick Schmidt/Sacramento Bee/ZUMAPress/Newscom

prison
A state or federal confinement facility that has custodial authority over adults sentenced to confinement.

A Brief History of Prisons

The use of prisons as places where convicted offenders serve time as punishment for breaking the law is a relatively new development in the handling of offenders. In fact, the emphasis on time served as the essence of criminal punishment is scarcely 200 years old.

1 Describe the historical development of prisons.

Prior to the development of prisons, early punishments were often cruel and torturous. They included flogging, mutilation, branding, public humiliation (including the stocks and pillory), exile, and workhouses. Although fines were sometimes levied, convicted offenders were frequently subjected to physical punishment that often resulted in death.

Before the development of prisons, many British convicts were sent to the American colonies as well as to Australia. Russian prisoners were sent to Siberia, and French criminals were exiled to Devil's Island off the African Coast. In 1776, however, the American Revolution brought the practice of exile to America to an end, and British penology shifted to the use of aging ships, called hulks, as temporary prisons. Hulks were anchored in harbors throughout England and served as floating confinement facilities.

Workhouses, which vaguely resembled today's prisons, developed relatively late in the history of Western Europe and were primarily used to house debtors, the unemployed, and vagrants—most of whom had been left penniless by the advent of the Industrial Revolution. The economic shift that it engendered mechanized agriculture and virtually eliminated the need for a large agricultural workforce. Policymakers of the time failed to understand changing economic conditions, and attributed the large number of unemployed to a general spirit

workhouse
An early form of imprisonment whose purpose was to instill habits of industry in the idle.

▲ Warden T. M. Osborne and correctional officers stand in a cellblock at Sing Sing Prison at Ossining, New York, in 1915. How did imprisonment replace earlier forms of criminal punishment?

Picture History/Newscom

of laziness that had infested much of the population. The first workhouse in Europe opened in 1557 and taught work habits, but not specific skills. Inmates were made to fashion their own furniture, build additions to the facility, and raise gardens. When the number of inmates exceeded the need for useful work, make-work projects, including treadmills and hand cranks, were invented to keep inmates busy. Although workhouses were forerunners of our modern prisons, they did not incarcerate criminal offenders—only vagrants and the destitute. Nor were they designed to punish, but served instead to reinforce the value of hard work.

The identity of the world's first prison is unknown, but at some point, penalties for crime came to include incarceration. During the Middle Ages, "punitive imprisonment appears to have been introduced into Europe . . . by the Christian Church in the incarceration of certain offenders against canon law."[8] Similarly, debtors' prisons existed throughout Europe during the fifteenth and sixteenth centuries, although they housed inmates who had violated the civil law rather than criminals. John Howard, an early prison reformer, mentioned prisons housing criminal offenders in Hamburg, Germany; Bern, Switzerland; and Florence, Italy, in his 1777 book, *State of Prisons.*[9] Early efforts to imprison offenders led to the founding of the Hospice of San Michele, a papal prison that opened in 1704, and the Maison de Force, begun at Ghent, Belgium, in 1773. Both facilities became early alternatives to the use of physical and public punishments.

Near the end of the eighteenth century, the concept of using imprisonment as punishment for crime reached its clearest expression in the United States. Soon after they were opened, U.S. prisons came to serve as models for European reformers searching for ways to humanize criminal punishment. For that reason, and to better appreciate how today's prisons operate, it is important to understand the historical development of the prison movement in the United States.

As Figure 11–1 shows, imprisonment in the United States began with the *Penitentiary Era* in 1790. That era began with the conversion of Philadelphia's Walnut Street Jail into a penitentiary by the Quakers living in Pennsylvania. The Quakers viewed incarceration as an opportunity for penance and saw prisons as places where offenders might make amends with society and accept responsibility for their misdeeds. Since penance was the primary vehicle through which rehabilitation might be achieved, the word *penitentiary* came into use. Prisoners kept in the first penitentiary were strongly encouraged to study the Bible. Solitary confinement was the rule, and the penitentiary was architecturally designed to minimize contact between inmates and between inmates and staff. Fashioned after the Philadelphia model, the Western Penitentiary opened in Pittsburgh in 1826, and the Eastern Penitentiary opened in Cherry Hill, Pennsylvania, 3 years later. Solitary confinement and individual cells, supported by a massive physical structure with impenetrable walls, became synonymous with what soon came to be known as the Pennsylvania system of imprisonment.

The year 1825 is often cited as the beginning of the *mass prison era* in American corrections. Vermont, Massachusetts, Maryland, and New York all built institutions modeled after Pennsylvania's penitentiaries. As prison populations began to grow, however, solitary confinement became prohibitively expensive. One of the first large prisons to abandon the Pennsylvania model was the New York State Prison at Auburn. Auburn introduced a "congregate but silent" system, under which inmates lived, ate, and worked together in enforced silence. This style of imprisonment, which came to be known as the Auburn system, featured

Prison Era

	The Penitentiary Era	The Mass (Congregate) Prison Era	The Reformatory Era	The Industrial Era	The Punitive Era	The Treatment Era	The Community-Based (Decarceration) Era	The Warehousing Era	The Just Deserts Era	The Evidence-Based Era
Year	1790	1825	1876	1890	1935	1945	1967	1980	1995	2012
Philosophy	Rehabilitation, Deterrence	Incapacitation, Deterrence	Rehabilitation	Incapacitation, Restoration	Retribution	Rehabilitation	Restoration, Rehabilitation	Incapacitation	Retribution, Incapacitation, Deterrence	Cost-Effective Workable Solutions
Representative Institutions	Philadelphia Penitentiary; Eastern Penitentiary (Cherry Hill, PA); Western Penitentiary (Pittsburgh)	New York State Prison (Auburn, NY)	Elmira Reformatory (Elmira, NY)	Auburn (NY); Sing Sing (NY); Stateville (IL); San Quentin (CA); Attica (NY)	Alcatraz (CA)	Marion (IL)	Massachusetts Youth Services; Halfway Houses	Many State and Federal Prisons	Continues to Influence Many Prisons Today	A New and Growing Emphasis on "What Works" in an Era of Economic Retrenchment

FIGURE 11–1
Stages of Prison Development in the United States

group workshops rather than solitary handicrafts and reintroduced corporal punishments into the handling of offenders.

While isolation and enforced idleness were inherent punishments under the early Pennsylvania system, Auburn-style imprisonment depended on whipping and hard labor to maintain the rule of silence. The Auburn prison soon became the site of an experiment in solitary confinement. The experiment was a failure, and much of the rest of the country moved on to adopt the congregate system of imprisonment that had been developed at Auburn. One of the reasons for the Auburn system's success was likely the lower cost that resulted from the simpler facilities required by mass imprisonment and from group workshops that provided economies of scale unachievable under solitary confinement.

In the late 1800s, following practices that had been developed in other countries (see Chapter 9), the state of New York passed an indeterminate sentencing bill that made possible the early release of inmates for those who earned it. This led to a new period in corrections known as the *reformatory era*. The first reformatory opened in Elmira, New York, in 1876 and was known simply as the Elmira Reformatory. The correctional philosophy upon which it was built was earned early release. Inmates could earn release through good behavior, and did not necessarily have to complete their court-imposed sentence. Schooling was mandatory in the reformatory and trade training was available in telegraphy, tailoring, plumbing, carpentry, and other areas. Unfortunately, many inmates reentered lives of crime following their release, which called the success of the reformatory ideal into question. Some authors attributed the failure of the reformatory to an overemphasis on confinement and institutional security, rather than reformation, by the prison staff.[10] Even though the reformatory was not a success, the principles it established remain important today. Thus, indeterminate sentencing, parole, trade training, education, and the primacy of reformation over punishment all serve as a foundation for ongoing debates about the purpose of imprisonment.

With the failure of the reformatory style of prison, concerns over security and discipline became dominant in American prisons. Inmate populations rose, costs soared, and states began to study practical alternatives. An especially attractive option was found in the potential profitability of inmate labor, and the *industrial prison era* in American corrections was born. Industrial prisons, which began opening in the northern United States in 1890, were characterized by thick, high walls; stone or brick buildings; guard towers; and smokestacks rising from within the walls. These prisons smelted steel, manufactured cabinets, molded tires, and produced many other goods for the open market. Prisons in the South, which had been devastated by the Civil War, tended more toward farm labor and public-works projects. The South, with its labor-intensive agricultural practices, used inmates to replace slaves who had been freed during the war. Noteworthy prisons that were built or converted to industrialization included San Quentin in California, Sing Sing and Auburn in New York, and the Illinois State Penitentiary at Stateville. Many prison industries were quite profitable and contributed significantly to state treasuries.

With the arrival of the Great Depression of the 1930s, labor unions used their political might to put an end to prison industries—which they saw as unfair competition because of "free" inmate labor. The death blow to prison industries came in 1935 with passage of the Ashurst–Sumners Act that specifically prohibited the interstate transportation and sale of prison goods where state laws forbade them. Consequently, prison administrators were left with few alternatives, and seized on custody and institutional security as the long-lost central purposes of the correctional enterprise. This led to a *punitive era* in corrections. The punitive era was characterized by the belief that prisoners owed a debt to society that only a rigorous period of confinement could repay. Soon convicts were shunned and securely locked away from society. Large maximum-security institutions flourished, and the prisoner's daily routine became one of monotony and frustration. The punitive era was a lackluster time in American corrections. Innovations were rare, and a philosophy of "out of sight, out of mind" characterized American attitudes toward inmates. The term "stir-crazy" grew out of the experience of many prisoners with the punitive era's lack of educational, treatment, and work programs. In response, inmates created their own diversions, frequently attempting to escape or inciting riots. One especially secure and still notorious facility of the punitive era was the federal penitentiary on Alcatraz Island, which is described in some detail at **http://www.alcatrazhistory.com.**

In the late 1940s, the mood of the nation was euphoric. Memories of World War II were dimming, industries were productive beyond the best hopes of most economic forecasters, and America's position of world leadership was fundamentally unchallenged. Nothing seemed impossible. Amid the bounty of a postwar boom economy, politicians and the public accorded themselves the luxury of restructuring the nation's prisons. A new interest in "corrections" and reformation, combined with the latest in behavioral techniques, ushered in a new era— *the treatment era*. The treatment era was based on a medical model of corrections—one that implied that the offender was sick and that rehabilitation was only a matter of finding the right treatment. Inmates came to be seen more as "clients" or "patients" than as offenders, and terms like "resident" and "group member" replaced "inmate." Therapy during the period took a number of forms, many of which are still used today. Any honest evaluation of the treatment era would conclude that, in practice, treatment was more of an ideal than a reality. Many treatment programs existed, some of them quite intensive. Unfortunately, the correctional system that existed in America at the time was never capable of providing any consistent or widespread treatment because the majority of its guards and administrators were oriented primarily toward custody and were not trained to provide treatment. However, although we have identified 1967 as the end of the treatment era, many correctional rehabilitation programs survive to the present day, and new ones are continually being developed.

Beginning in the 1960s, the realities of prison overcrowding combined with a renewed faith in humanity and the treatment era's belief in the possibility of behavioral change to inspire the *era of community corrections*. That era was characterized by a movement away from institutionalized corrections and toward the creation of opportunities for reformation within local communities. The transition to community corrections (also called the deinstitutionalization movement) was based on the premise that rehabilitation could not occur in isolation from the free social world to which inmates would eventually return.[11] Advocates of community corrections portrayed prisons as dehumanizing, claiming that they further victimized offenders who had already been negatively labeled by society. Some states strongly embraced the movement toward decarceration. In 1972, for example, Massachusetts drew national attention when it closed all of its reform schools and replaced them with group homes.[12] During the community corrections era a variety of programs based on intermediate sanctions kept offenders in contact with the community and out of prison. Among them were halfway houses, work-release programs, and open institutions. By the late 1960s, conjugal visitation was under consideration in many other states, and the National Advisory Commission on Criminal Justice Standards and Goals recommended that correctional authorities should make "provisions for family visits in private surroundings conducive to maintaining and strengthening family ties."[13]

The mood of the nation changed when crime rates spiked in the 1980s, fueled in part by a drug epidemic that swept American cities. Concerns with community protection grew quickly to reach a near crescendo, and stiff drug laws and strict repeat offender statutes were enacted that put more and more people behind bars. Beginning around 1980, rates of imprisonment reached previously unheralded levels. About the same time, public disappointment in our nation's corrections system resulted at least partially from media reports of high recidivism,[14] coupled with descriptions of institutions where inmates lounged in relative luxury, enjoyed regular visits from spouses and lovers, and took frequent weekend passes—all of which created the image of "prison country clubs." In the history of criminal justice, the three decades from 1980 to 2010 will likely be remembered as a time of mass imprisonment. During that time, prisons served largely to warehouse prisoners, and the period is known as the *warehousing era* in corrections. It was based on a policy of **warehousing** serious offenders for the avowed purpose of protecting society.

In the 1990s, prison populations continued to grow because of a rise in the number of parole violators returned to prison; a drop in the annual release rates of inmates; a small number of inmates who would serve long terms or who would never be released; and enhanced punishments for drug offenders.[15] Average time served continued to increase. In 1990, for example, actual time served in prison for the crime of rape increased 27%, and drug offenders spent 35% more time behind bars.[16] American prison populations grew dramatically during the warehousing era. Between 1980 and 2012, state and federal prison populations more than quadrupled, from 329,000 inmates to around 1.6 million, and then began a slow decline.[17] Much of the rise that occurred in prison populations after 1980 can

Follow the author's tweets about the latest crime and justice news @schmalleger

warehousing
An imprisonment strategy that is based on the desire to prevent recurrent crime and that has abandoned all hope of rehabilitation.

be attributed directly to changes in sentencing laws aimed at taking drug offenders off the streets and to the resulting rapid growth in the number of incarcerated drug felons, and, more recently, immigration law violators. Warehousing also contributed to numerous administrative difficulties, many of which continue to affect prison systems throughout the nation today. To meet the housing needs of burgeoning prison populations during the 1980s and 1990s, some states constructed "temporary" tent cities within prison yards. Others moved more beds into already packed dormitories, often stacking prisoners three high in triple bunk beds. Most states shifted some of their correctional burden to local jails, and by 2000, 34 states, the District of Columbia, and the federal government were sending some prisoners to jails because of overcrowding at their own long-term institutions.[18]

🐦 Follow the author's tweets about the latest crime and justice news @schmalleger

Warehousing and prison overcrowding were primarily the result of both public and official frustration with rehabilitative efforts. In a sense, however, they were also consequences of a strategy without a clear-cut philosophy. Because rehabilitation didn't seem to work, early advocates of warehousing—not knowing what else to do—assumed a pragmatic stance and advocated separating criminals from society by keeping them locked up for as long as possible. Their avowed goal was the protection of law-abiding citizens. Consequently, by the early 2000s, prison populations approached the breaking point, requiring the construction of many new facilities. In the midst of a prison construction boom, a new philosophy became the operative principle underlying many correctional initiatives. The new philosophy was grounded squarely on the concept of just deserts, in which imprisonment is seen as a fully deserved and proper consequence of criminal and irresponsible behavior rather than just the end result of a bankrupt system unable to reform its charges. Unlike previous correctional eras, which layered other purposes on the correctional experience (the reformatory era, for example, was concerned with reformation, and the industrial era sought economic gain), the *era of just deserts* represented a kind of return to the root purpose of incarceration: punishment. "Get-tough" initiatives were reflected in a spike in drug-related arrests (which grew by more than 90% between 1980 and 2014[19]); and by the "three-strikes-and-you're-out" laws that swept through state legislatures in the late 1990s and early 2000s.[20] Three-strikes legislation, which is discussed in more detail in Chapter 9, generally mandates lengthy prison terms for criminal offenders convicted of a third violent crime or felony. Three-strikes laws have been enacted in almost 30 states and by the federal government.

Proponents of "get-tough" policies, although no doubt interested in personal safety, lower crime rates, and balanced state and federal budgets, were keenly focused on retribution. And where retribution fuels a correctional policy, deterrence, reformation, and economic considerations play only secondary roles. As more and more states enacted three-strikes and other "get-tough" legislation, prison populations across the nation continued to swell, eclipsing those of the warehousing era. The impact of the just deserts era remains with us today, leaving the United States with one of the highest rates of imprisonment in the world.[21]

Although the just deserts philosophy provided what became for many an acceptable rationale for continued prison expansion, it soon ran up against the very practical fiscal needs imposed by the Great Recession of the early twenty-first century. The recession made it necessary for states to save money and to cut their budgets, leading to an end of the just deserts era around 2012. In the grip of newfound motivation predicated upon forced financial austerity, many state legislatures began to question the wisdom of locking up nonviolent, elderly, and seriously ill offenders for long periods of time, and prison populations started to finally decline. The new era in corrections, the *evidence-based era*, is built around the need to employ cost-effective solutions to correctional issues. **Evidence-based corrections (EBC)** represents a rational science-based approach to corrections because it employs social scientific research in determining what practices to implement. Learn more about evidence-based practices in corrections in the "CJ Issues" box in this chapter.

evidence-based corrections (EBC)

The application of social scientific techniques to the study of everyday corrections procedures for the purpose of increasing effectiveness and enhancing the efficient use of available resources.

Prisons Today

2 | Describe today's prisons.

There are approximately 1,719 state prisons and 102 federal prisons in operation across the country today.[22] The growth of America's prison population has been slowing, and numbers in some states (most notably California) are starting to show a decrease as state budgetary concerns have led to fiscal conservatism (see Justice Reinvestment: California's Public Safety Realignment, on the following page).

On January 1, 2017, the nation's state and federal prisons held 1,506,800 inmates, of which 1,459,500 were serving sentences of a year or more.[23] Slightly more than 7% (or 105,683) of those imprisoned were women.[24] The incarceration rate for state and federal prisoners sentenced to more than a year stood at 450 prisoners for every 100,000 U.S. residents in 2016. In that year, males had an imprisonment rate (1,108 per 100,000 U.S. residents) that was almost 14 times higher than the rate for females (82 per 100,000).[25]

Figure 11–2 shows the rise in prison populations in the United States during the past 90 years. From a comparative perspective, the number of people behind bars in the United States is striking, and a recent report from the Public Safety Performance Project of the Pew Charitable Trusts notes that "the United States incarcerates more people than any country in the world, including the far more populous nation of China."[26]

High incarceration rates persist in the United States today even in the face of declining crime rates. As noted in Chapter 2, between 1991 and 2017 the official rate of crime in the United States dropped from 5,897 to 2,758 offenses per every 100,000 residents—a level that had not been seen since 1975.[27] Hence, a 44% *decrease* in the national crime rate over a 26-year period was accompanied by a 70% *increase* in the rate of imprisonment. Crime-control advocates, of course, would argue that increased rates of incarceration are at least partially responsible for reduced crime rates, as incarceration removes from the community those who are likely to reoffend.

The use of imprisonment varies considerably between states (Figure 11–3). While the average rate of imprisonment in the United States at the start of 2017 was 450 per every 100,000 people in the population,[28] some state rates were nearly double that.[29] Louisiana, for example, was holding 760 out of every 100,000 of its people in prison at the start of 2017, while Oklahoma was second with an incarceration rate of 673. Texas, a state with traditionally high rates of imprisonment, held 563 prisoners per every 100,000 people. Maine had the lowest rate of imprisonment of all the states (137), while other states with low rates include Minnesota (191), Rhode Island (192), and New Hampshire (211). As the CJ Issues box in this chapter shows, however, some states, particularly California, have found novel ways of reducing the official count of prisoners being held at the state level. In California's case, a strategy of realignment is used to shift selected nonviolent prisoners out of state-run prisons and into county lockups. Consequently, when comparing state incarceration rates and when examining national statistics on imprisonment, it may make more sense to talk about the number of criminal offenders sentenced to confinement, rather than merely counting those held in state prisons.

> High incarceration rates persist in the United States today even in the face of declining crime rates.

JUSTICE REINVESTMENT
California's Public Safety Realignment

This chapter began with the story of a paralyzed California inmate who had been denied release under the state's medical parole program. That story highlighted the high cost of confining prisoners who are in need of comprehensive medical care—in this case at a cost of $625,000 per year to the state's taxpayers.

In an effort to address budget shortfalls, however, some states have embraced cost-savings measures that have resulted in fewer people being confined to prison. One of the most significant of those measures, in terms of its impact on national prison statistics, is California's Public Safety Realignment (PSR) initiative, under which offenders convicted of less serious offenses are confined in local jails rather than in state prisons. The PSR program is discussed in a CJ Issues box in this chapter.

Another way to reduce costs and to achieve savings in corrections is to ensure that offenders receive only the degree of supervision that they need in order to protect society and to facilitate their rehabilitation. As a consequence, states today have begun using risk-measuring instruments (questionnaires or survey instruments completed by prison staff, probation officers, or specially designated evaluators) to assess the potential future risk posed to society by offenders facing sentencing, and by imprisoned offenders who might otherwise be released. In order to make the maximum use of such a strategy, many states are changing their sentencing standards in order to allow those convicted of minor offenses—especially those with no history of violence or sex crimes—to be placed on probation or to be confined under living arrangements that provide alternatives to imprisonment, such as home confinement or halfway houses. Savings that result from reduced prison populations can be used to expand probation and parole programs, to fund jail operations, and to enhance rehabilitation programs among those who are incarcerated. Learn more about California's public safety realignment at **http://www.cdcr.ca.gov/Blueprint-Update-2016/An-Update-to-the-Future-of-California-Corrections-January-2016.pdf**.

Resources: Barry Krisberg and Eleanor Taylor-Nicholson, *Criminal Justice Realignment: A Bold New Era in California Corrections* (Berkeley, CA: University of California, Berkeley Law School, 2011); and California Department of Corrections and Rehabilitation, "Funding of Realignment," http://www.cdcr.ca.gov/realignment/Funding-Realignment.html (accessed March 3, 2018).

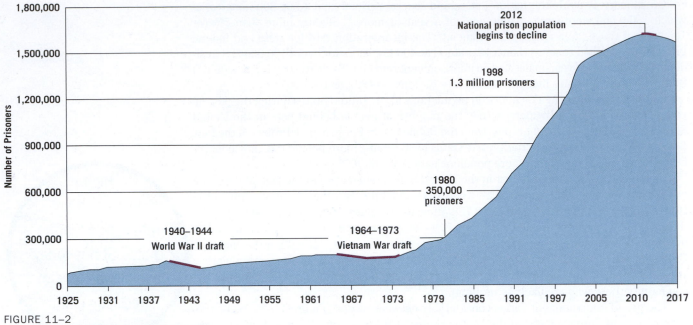

FIGURE 11–2
U.S. Prison Populations, 1925–2017

Note: Numbers include both state and federal prisoners, but may not reflect the actual number of persons sentenced to incarceration because some states, like California, have begun to house substantial numbers of inmates in local jails rather than in state prison facilities.
Source: Data from Bureau of Justice Statistics.

The size of prison facilities varies greatly. One out of every four state institutions is a large maximum-security prison, with a population approaching 1,000 inmates. A few exceed that figure, but the typical state prison is small, with an inmate population of less than 500. Community-based facilities average around 50 residents. The typical prison system in relatively populous states consists of:[30]

- One high-security prison for long-term high-risk offenders
- One or more medium-security institutions for non-high-risk offenders

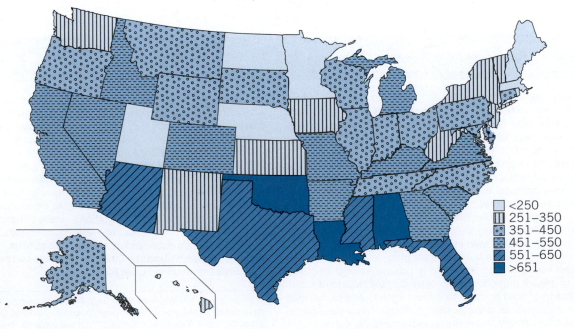

FIGURE 11–3
Rates of Imprisonment in the United States
Source: Data from Bureau of Justice Statistics.

- One (separate) institution for adult women
- One or two institutions for young adults (generally under age 25)
- One or two specialized mental hospital–type security prisons for mentally ill prisoners
- One or more open-type institutions for low-risk, nonviolent inmates

Incarceration costs average around $62 per inmate per day at the state level and $80.07 per day at the federal level when all types of adult correctional facilities are averaged together.[31] Imprisonment is especially costly in some states, such as California, where citizens pay over $190 per day to house each inmate (Table 11–1). According to a BJS report, the cost of running the nation's correctional programs exceeds $83 billion, of which more than half, or about $48 billion, goes to run state prisons.[32]

Follow the author's tweets about the latest crime and justice news @schmalleger

Approximate Annual Costs to Incarcerate an Inmate in Prison

Type of Expenditure	Per Inmate Costs
Security	**$ 32,019**
Inmate Health Care	**$ 21,582**
Medical care	$ 14,834
Psychiatric services	3,359
Pharmaceuticals	2,143
Dental care	1,246
Facility Operations and Records	**$ 7,025**
Facility operations (maintenance and utilities)	$ 4,334
Classification services	1,798
Maintenance of inmate records	723
Reception, testing, assignment	145
Transportation	24
Administration	**$ 4,171**
Inmate Food and Activities	**$ 3,484**
Food	$ 2,082
Inmate employment	823
Clothing	354
Inmate activities	102
Religious activities	123
Rehabilitation Programs	**$ 2,437**
Academic education	$ 1,237
Cognitive behavioral therapy	823
Vocational training	377
Miscellaneous	**$ 93**
Total	**$ 70,812**

TABLE 11–1

Annual Costs to Incarcerate an Inmate in Prison in California, 2016–2017

Source: The California Legislative Analyst's Office. Retrieved from https://lao.ca.gov/PolicyAreas/CJ/6_cj_inmatecost.

CJ | ISSUES
California's Public Safety Realignment (PSR) Program

In 2011, the California legislature passed the Public Safety Realignment Act and initiated the state's Public Safety Realignment (PSR) program (discussed in the last chapter). The program, which was implemented in response to a federal court order that required California to reduce overcrowding, places offenders convicted of less serious crime in local jails rather than in state prisons.

California's PSR legislation has been called the most significant change in the California Penal Code since the state's Determinate Sentencing Law was passed in 1977. The most important aspect of the law is that it shifts control over thousands of prisoners from the state to the county level. Specifically, the law does three things. First, it mandates that low-level felons sentenced to one to a few years in prison (who in the past would normally have served their time in state-run prisons) be sent to county jails instead. Second, the supervision of most persons released to supervision becomes the responsibility of county probation officials instead of state parole officers. Third, released offenders who violate a condition of postrelease supervision will serve time for violations in county jails instead of state prisons, and the amount of time they serve will generally be limited to 10 days.

PSR effectively divides the state's felon population into two categories: (1) those legally defined as violent, serious, and/or sex offenders (who continue to be sent to state prison and who are supervised by state parole officers upon release), and (2) lower-level offenders who may have been formerly housed in state prisons or managed by the state parole system, but who are now being managed by local justice system agencies and are housed in county jails or managed by county probation officers. The law also provides that offenders released to community supervision who do not incur any infractions must be released from supervision in 6 months or less.

California's realignment legislation shifts much of the burden of paying for correctional services from the state to the counties. Serious questions, however, remain about the adequacy of funding and local capacity to manage the changes mandated by the law. The realignment statute provided a one-time appropriation to cover costs associated with hiring and training new personnel and the costs of construction of needed facilities. A dedicated and permanent revenue stream flows to the counties through allocation of a portion of both state vehicle license fees and the state sales tax (which was raised in 2012 through a state-wide referendum). It is still too early to tell whether the shift of resources between state and county levels will be sufficient to sustain the dual goals of safety and rehabilitation in California corrections.

Consequently, while the imprisonment rate in states like California may appear to be falling when reported in national statistics, realignment strategies merely shift the responsibility for housing people who would formerly have been state prisoners to county governments, and tend to disguise the actual number of people being confined. Seventy percent of the recent nationwide decrease in prison populations reported by the Bureau of Justice Statistics, for example, has been due to California's Public Safety Realignment program.

Prisoners Today

Statistics tell us quite a bit about those in prison (Figure 11–4). Most people sentenced to state prisons were convicted of violent crimes (54%). Property crimes (18%) and drug crimes (15%) are the second and third most common type of offenses for which inmates were sentenced.[33] In contrast, prisoners sentenced for drug-law violations were the single largest group of federal inmates (54%), and the increase in the imprisonment of drug offenders accounts for more than three-quarters of the total growth in the number of federal inmates since 1980.[34] Immigration offenders now account for 10% of all federal prisoners, and their numbers are rising.[35]

An examination of imprisonment statistics by race highlights the huge disparity between blacks and whites in prison. While only an estimated 1,001 white men are imprisoned in the United States for every 100,000 white men in their late 20s, figures show an incarceration rate of 6,927 black men for every 100,000 black men of the same age—seven times greater than the figure for whites.[36] Almost 17% of adult black men in the United States have served time in prison—a rate over twice as high as that for adult Hispanic males (7.7%) and over six times as high as that for adult white males (2.6%).[37] According to the Bureau of Justice Statistics (BJS), a black male living in America today has a 32.3% lifetime chance of going to prison, and a black female has a 5.6% lifetime chance of imprisonment. That contrasts sharply with the lifetime chances of imprisonment for white males (5.9%) and white females (0.9%).[38]

> Prisoners sentenced for drug-law violations are the single largest group of federal inmates.

Prison Issues

Today's prison administrators are hamstrung by the substantial and continued increases in the American prison population that followed from the just deserts philosophy of the last century, and which continued to influence sentencing philosophies even as crime rates were

Follow the author's tweets about the latest crime and justice news @schmalleger

dropping. In 1990, for example, the U.S. rate of imprisonment stood at 292 prisoners per every 100,000 residents. By 1995, it had reached 399, and by 2016, it was 450. Beginning in 2011–2012 growth of prison populations finally began to decline.[39]

Overcrowding

Even though many new prisons were built throughout the nation to accommodate the growing number of inmates, and even though the use of imprisonment has begun to decline, prison overcrowding is still a reality in many

> **3** Identify some of the issues facing prisons today.

jurisdictions. Some of the most crowded prisons are those in the federal system, where the number of inmates, while high, is declining. The crowding rate in all federal prisons recently stood at 14% over capacity.[40] Prison overcrowding can be measured along a number of dimensions:

- Space available per inmate (such as square feet of floor space)
- Length of confinement of inmates in cells or housing units (versus time spent in recreation and other activities)
- Living arrangements (e.g., single versus double bunks)
- Type of housing (use of segregation facilities, tents, and so on in place of general housing)

Further complicating the picture is the fact that prison officials have developed three definitions of **prison capacity** (the size of a prison population that a facility can hold):[41]

1. **Rated capacity** refers to the size of the inmate population that a facility can handle according to the judgment of experts.
2. **Operational capacity** is the number of inmates that a facility can effectively accommodate based on an appraisal of the institution's staff, programs, and services.
3. **Design capacity** refers to the inmate population that the institution was originally built to handle.

Rated capacity estimates usually yield the largest inmate capacities, whereas design capacity (on which observations in this chapter are based) typically shows the highest amount of overcrowding.

Overcrowding by itself is not cruel and unusual punishment, according to the U.S. Supreme Court in *Rhodes* v. *Chapman* (1981),[42] which considered the issue of double bunking along with other alleged forms of "deprivation" at the Southern Ohio Correctional Facility. The Court, reasoning that overcrowding is not necessarily dangerous if other prison services are adequate, held that prison housing conditions may be "restrictive and even harsh," for they are part of the penalty that offenders pay for their crimes.

However, overcrowding combined with other negative conditions may lead to a finding against the prison system, as was the case with the 2011 U.S. Supreme Court case of *Brown* v. *Plata* (mentioned at the start of this chapter). The American Correctional Association (ACA) notes that such a totality-of-conditions approach has led courts to assess the overall quality of prison life while viewing overcrowded conditions in combination with other issues:

- The meeting of basic human needs
- The adequacy of the facility's staff
- The program opportunities available to inmates
- The quality and strength of the prison management

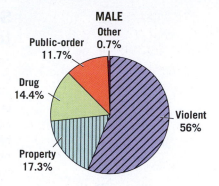

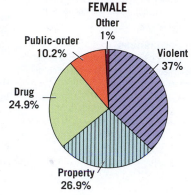

FIGURE 11–4
State Prisoners by Gender and Type of Crime, 2016

Note: Total may exceed 100% due to rounding.
Source: E. Ann Carson, *Prisoners in 2016* (Washington, D.C.: BJS, 2018).

prison capacity
The size of the correctional population an institution can effectively hold.[ii] There are three types of prison capacity: rated, operational, and design.

rated capacity
The number of inmates a prison can handle according to the judgment of experts.

operational capacity
The number of inmates a prison can effectively accommodate based on management considerations.

design capacity
The number of inmates a prison was intended to hold when it was built or modified.

Selective Incapacitation: A Contemporary Strategy to Reduce Prison Populations

Some authors have identified the central issue of imprisonment as one of selective versus collective incapacitation.[43] *Collective incapacitation*, a strategy that would imprison almost all serious offenders, is still found in jurisdictions that rely largely on predetermined, or fixed, sentences for given offenses or for a series of specified kinds of offenses (as in the case of some forms of three-strikes legislation). Collective incapacitation is, however, prohibitively expensive as well as unnecessary, in the opinion of many experts. Not all offenders need to be imprisoned because not all represent a continuing threat to society, but those who do are difficult to identify.[44]

selective incapacitation
A policy that seeks to protect society by incarcerating individuals deemed to be the most dangerous.

dangerousness
The likelihood that a given individual poses a significant risk of later harm to society or to others.

Selective incapacitation, which seeks to identify the most dangerous criminals with the goal of removing them from society, has become the rule. Consequently, the assessment of **dangerousness** is central to today's contemporary strategy of selective incapacitation. Repeat offenders with records of serious and violent crimes are the most likely candidates for imprisonment—as are child sex offenders given their especially negative status in the public eye.

In support of selective incapacitation, many states have enacted career offender statutes that attempt to identify potentially dangerous offenders out of known criminal populations. Selective incapacitation efforts, however, have been criticized for yielding a rate of "false positives" of over 60%,[45] and some authors have called selective incapacitation a "strategy of failure."[46] Nevertheless, in an analysis of recidivism studies, Canadians Paul Gendreau, Tracy Little, and Claire Goggin found that criminal history, a history of preadult antisocial behavior, and "criminogenic needs"—which were defined as measurable antisocial thoughts, values, and behaviors—were all dependable predictors of recidivism.[47]

Many states today, facing budgetary challenges, have had to scramble in an attempt to implement selective incarceration principles. A recent report by the Sentencing Project, for example, found that six states—California, Colorado, Florida, Illinois, Kentucky, and Louisiana—announced the closing of a combined number of 20 prisons, reducing prison capacity by over 14,100 beds.[48] The project also reported that 13 other states eliminated 15,500 additional prison beds. Savings due to the closing were estimated to total more than $337 million. The largest of the closures, the planned shuttering of the California Rehabilitation Center at Norco would eliminate 3,900 beds and would result in savings to the state of California of $125 million per year.[49]

▲ Inmates making collect phone calls at the Davidson County Prison in Tennessee. Approximately 1,325 state prisons and 84 federal prisons are in operation across the country today. Together, they hold around 1.56 million. The prison shown here is run by CoreCivic (formerly Corrections Corporation of America). Why is the number of inmates growing while the crime rate continues to fall?

A Ramey/PhotoEdit, Inc.

The state reductions came about by limiting the length of mandatory minimum sentences for drug offenses, diverting defendants with low-level convictions from incarceration, enhancing release programs, and reducing parole revocations. For example, Connecticut governor Dannel P. Malloy signed into law a hotly debated piece of legislation that gave inmates in that state sentence-reduction credits if they participate in various kinds of prison-run self-improvement programs. At the time, Connecticut House Majority Leader Brendan Sharkey explained the new law this way: "If this is about being soft on crime, I say 'baloney.' This is about being smart on crime."[50]

As state budget problems continue, the just deserts model has relinquished ground to selective incapacitation. As more and more states embrace the EBC model, it is likely that we will see the continued sentencing of violent criminals to lengthy prison stays with little possibility of release, combined with the early release of offenders deemed unlikely to reoffend, and the increased use of less expensive alternative sanctions and diversion for minor and nonviolent offenders.

Security Levels

Maximum-custody prisons tend to be massive old buildings with large inmate populations. However, some—like Central Prison in Raleigh, North Carolina—are much newer and incorporate advances in prison architecture to provide tight security without sacrificing building aesthetics. Such institutions provide a high level of security characterized by high fences, thick walls, secure cells, gun towers, and armed prison guards. Maximum-custody prisons tend to locate cells and other inmate living facilities at the center of the institution and place a variety of barriers between the living area and the institution's outer perimeter. Technological innovations, such as electric perimeters, laser motion detectors, electronic and pneumatic locking systems, metal detectors, X-ray machines, television surveillance, radio communications, and computer information systems, are frequently used today to reinforce the more traditional maximum-security strategies. These technologies have helped to lower the cost of new prison construction. However, some people argue that prisons may rely too heavily on electronic detection devices that have not yet been adequately tested.[51]

Death-row inmates are all maximum-security prisoners, although the level of security on death row exceeds even that experienced by most prisoners held in maximum custody. Prisoners on death row must spend much of the day in single cells. They are often permitted a brief shower only once a week under close supervision.

Most states today have one large, centrally located maximum-security institution. Some of these prisons combine more than one custody level and may be both maximum- and medium-security facilities. Medium security is a custody level that in many ways resembles maximum security. Medium-security prisoners, however, are generally permitted more freedom to associate with one another and can go to the prison yard, exercise room, library, and shower and bathroom facilities under less intense supervision than their maximum-security counterparts.

An important security tool in medium-security prisons is the count, which is literally a head count of inmates taken at regular intervals. Counts may be taken four times a day and usually require inmates to report to designated areas to be counted. Until the count has been "cleared," all other inmate activity must cease.

Medium-security prisons tend to be smaller than maximum-security institutions and often have barbed-wire-topped chain-link fences instead of the more secure stone or concrete block walls found in many of the older maximum-security facilities. Cells and living quarters tend to have more windows and are often located closer to the perimeter of the institution than is the case in maximum-security facilities. Dormitory-style housing, where

> As state budget problems continue, the just deserts model has relinquished ground to selective incapacitation.

🐦 Follow the author's tweets about the latest crime and justice news @schmalleger

---

CJ | ISSUES
Evidence-Based Corrections

The National Institute of Corrections (NIC) says that "in corrections, evidence-based practice is the breadth of research and knowledge around processes and tools which can improve correctional outcomes, such as reduced recidivism." The NIC has been promoting the use of evidence-based decision making (EBDM) for a number of years, and a little more than a decade ago, the NIC partnered with the Center for Effective Public Policy to build an EBDM framework that is intended to be relevant to the entire criminal justice system. The system-wide framework that the NIC developed focuses on justice system events from arrest through final disposition and discharge. The framework is intended to result in more collaborative evidence-based decision making throughout the criminal justice system nationwide. According to the NIC, the purpose of the EBDM decision-making initiative "is to equip criminal justice policymakers in local communities with the information, processes, and tools that will result in measurable reductions of pretrial misconduct and post-conviction reoffending."

There are five phases in the NIC initiative. Phase I produced the framework itself, which is outlined in the NIC publication *A Framework for Evidence-Based Decision Making in Local Criminal*

Justice Systems. That publication, available at the NIC website (**http://nicic.gov**), describes key criminal justice decision points and provides an overview of evidence-based knowledge about effective justice practices. It defines risk and harm reduction as key goals of the criminal justice system and lays out practical local-level strategies for applying these principles and techniques.

In the second phase of its initiative, the NIC selected seven seed sites from across the country that were interested in piloting principles included within the framework.

During Phase III, selected sites implemented the NIC framework and to participate in a long-term outcome evaluation to measure the impact of implementing the principles contained within the framework. Phase IV expanded the EBDM framework to the state level; and Phase V built EBDM capacity at a systemwide level.

References: National Institute of Corrections, *Evidence-Based Decision Making in Local Criminal Justice Systems,* https://nicic.gov/evidence-based-decision-making-local-criminal-justice-systems (accessed October 2, 2018); and National Institute of Corrections, "Evidence-Based Decision Making," http://nicic.gov/EBDM (accessed October 2, 2018).

prisoners live together in wardlike arrangements, may be employed in medium-security facilities, and there are generally more opportunities for inmates to participate in recreational and other prison programs than in maximum-custody facilities.

In minimum-security institutions, inmates are generally housed in dormitory-like settings and are free to walk the yard and to visit most of the prison facilities. Some newer prisons provide minimum-security inmates with private rooms, which they can decorate (within limits) according to their tastes. Inmates usually have free access to a canteen that sells items such as cigarettes, toothpaste, and candy bars. Minimum-security inmates often wear uniforms of a different color from those of inmates in higher custody levels. In some institutions, they may wear civilian clothes. They work under only general supervision and usually have access to recreational, educational, and skills-training programs on the prison grounds. Guards are unarmed, gun towers do not exist, and fences (if they are present at all) are usually low and sometimes even unlocked. Many minimum-security prisoners participate in some sort of work- or study-release program, and some have extensive visitation and furlough privileges. Counts may be taken, although most minimum-security institutions keep track of inmates through daily administrative work schedules. The primary "force" holding inmates in minimum-security institutions is their own restraint. Inmates live with the knowledge that minimum-security institutions are one step removed from close correctional supervision. If they fail to meet the expectations of administrators, they will be transferred into more secure institutions, which will probably delay their release. Inmates returning from assignments in the community may be frisked for contraband, but body-cavity searches are rare in minimum custody, being reserved primarily for inmates suspected of smuggling.

The typical American prison today is medium or minimum custody. Some states have as many as 80 or 90 small institutions, which may originally have been located in every county to serve the needs of public works and highway maintenance. Medium- and minimum-security institutions house the bulk of the country's prison population. They offer a number of programs and services designed to assist with the rehabilitation of offenders and to create the conditions necessary for a successful reentry of the inmates into society. Most prisons offer psychiatric services, academic education, vocational education, substance-abuse treatment, health care, counseling, recreation, library services, religious programs, and industrial and agricultural training.[52] To learn more about all aspects of contemporary prisons, visit the Corrections Connection via **http://www.corrections.com**.

classification system
A system used by prison administrators to assign inmates to custody levels based on offense history, assessed dangerousness, perceived risk of escape, and other factors.

Prison Classification Systems

Most states use a **classification system** to assign new prisoners to initial custody levels based on their type of offense, perceived dangerousness, and escape risk. A prisoner might be assigned to a minimum-, medium-, or maximum-custody institution. Inmates move through custody levels according to the progress they are judged to have made in self-control and demonstrated responsibility. Serious violent criminals who begin their prison careers with lengthy sentences in maximum custody have the opportunity in most states to work their way up to minimum security, although the process usually takes a number of years. Those prisoners who represent continual disciplinary problems are returned to closer custody levels. Minimum-security prisons, as a result, house inmates convicted of all types of criminal offenses.

Once an inmate has been assigned to a custody level, he or she may be reassessed for living and work assignments within the institution. Just as initial (or external) custody classification systems determine security levels, internal classification systems are designed to help determine appropriate housing plans and program interventions within a particular facility for inmates who share a common custody level. In short, initial classification determines the institution in which an inmate is placed, and internal classification determines placement and program assignment within that institution.[53]

▲ Inmates flashing gang signs for the camera. If you were a warden, what changes might you make to improve the management of a prison like this one?

Damian Dovarganes/AP Images

Objective prison classification systems were adopted by many states in the 1980s, but it wasn't until the late 1990s that such systems were refined and validated. Fueled by litigation and overcrowding, classification systems are now viewed as the principal management tool for allocating scarce prison resources efficiently and for minimizing the potential for violence or escape. Classification systems are also expected to provide greater accountability and to forecast future prison bed-space needs. A properly functioning classification system is the "brain" of prison management, governing and influencing many important decisions, including such fiscal matters as staffing levels, bed space, and programming.[54]

One of the best-known internal classification systems in use today is the adult internal management system (AIMS). AIMS was developed more than 20 years ago to reduce institutional predatory behavior by identifying potential predators and separating them from vulnerable inmates. AIMS assesses an inmate's predatory potential by quantifying aspects of his or her (1) record of misconduct, (2) ability to follow staff directions, and (3) level of aggression toward other inmates.

Before concluding this discussion of classification, it is important to recognize that the criteria used to classify prisoners must be relevant to the legitimate security needs of the institution. In the 2005 case of *Johnson* v. *California*,[55] for example, the U.S. Supreme Court invalidated the California Department of Corrections and Rehabilitation's (CDCR) unwritten policy of racially segregating prisoners in double cells for up to 60 days each time they entered a new correctional facility. The policy had been based on a claim that it prevented violence caused by racial gangs. The Court, however, held that the California policy was "immediately suspect" as an "express racial classification" and found that the CDCR was unable to demonstrate that the practice served a compelling state interest.

> Serious violent criminals who begin their prison careers with lengthy sentences in maximum custody have the opportunity in most states to work their way up to minimum security, although the process usually takes a number of years.

The Federal Prison System

The federal prison system consists of 122 institutions, 6 regional offices, the Central Office (headquarters), 2 staff-training centers, and 24 residential reentry management offices (which were previously known as community corrections offices). The regional offices and the Central Office provide administrative oversight and support to the institutions and to the community corrections offices, which oversee community corrections centers and home-confinement programs. The federal correctional workforce remains one of the fastest growing in the country, and at mid-2018, the Bureau of Prisons (BOP) employed close to 40,000 persons.[56]

4 Provide an overview of the federal prison system.

The BOP classifies its institutions according to five security levels (Figure 11–5): (1) administrative maximum (**ADMAX**), (2) high security, (3) medium security, (4) low security, and (5) minimum security. High-security facilities are called *U.S. penitentiaries* (USPs), medium- and low-security institutions are both called *federal correctional institutions* (FCIs), and minimum-security prisons are termed *federal prison camps* (FPCs).[57] Minimum-security facilities are essentially honor-type camps with barracks-type housing and no fencing. Low-security facilities in the federal prison system are surrounded by double chain-link fencing and employ vehicle patrols around their perimeters to enhance security. Medium-security facilities make use of similar fencing and patrols but supplement them with electronic monitoring of the grounds and perimeter areas. High-security facilities (USPs) are architecturally designed to prevent escapes and to contain disturbances, and they also make use of armed patrols and intense electronic surveillance. Combination facilities within the BOP, which include institutions with different missions and security levels, are called federal correctional complexes (FCCs).

ADMAX
An acronym for administrative maximum. This term is used by the federal government to denote ultra-high-security prisons.

A separate federal prison category is that of administrative facilities, consisting of institutions with special missions that are designed to house all types of inmates. Most administrative facilities are metropolitan detention centers (MDCs). MDCs, which are generally located in large cities close to federal courthouses, are the jails of the federal correctional system and hold defendants awaiting trial in federal court. Another five administrative facilities, medical centers for federal prisoners (MCFPs), function as hospitals.

► The Federal Bureau of Prisons ADMAX facility in Florence, Colorado, which opened in 1995. It is the only ultra-high-security institution in the federal system. What kinds of inmates are sent there?

Chris Mclean/Pueblo Chieftain/ AP Images

Federal correctional facilities exist either as single institutions or as federal correctional complexes, that is, sites consisting of more than one type of correctional institution. They are spread across the country, as Figure 11–6 shows. The federal correctional complex at Allenwood, Pennsylvania, for example, consists of a U.S. penitentiary, a federal prison camp, and two federal correctional institutions (one low and one medium security), each with its own warden. Federal institutions can be classified by type as follows: 55 are FPCs (holding 35% of all federal prisoners), 17 are low-security facilities (28%), 26 are medium-security facilities (23%), 8 are high-security prisons (13%), and 1 is an ADMAX facility (1%).

The federal system's only ADMAX unit, the $60 million ultra-high-security prison at Florence, Colorado, is a relatively recent addition to the federal system. Dubbed "the Alcatraz of the Rockies," the 575-bed facility was designed to be the most secure prison ever built by the government.[58] Opened in 1995, it holds mob bosses, spies, terrorists, murderers, and escape artists. Dangerous inmates are confined to their cells 23 hours per day and are not allowed to see or associate with other inmates. Electronically controlled doors throughout the institution channel inmates to individual exercise sessions. Educational courses, religious services, and administrative matters are conducted via closed-circuit television piped directly into the prisoners' cells. Remote-controlled heavy steel doors within the prison allow corrections staff to section off the institution in the event of rioting, and the system can be controlled from outside if the entire prison is compromised.

In an effort to combat rising expenses associated with a rapidly growing federal prison population, the U.S. Congress passed legislation in 1992 that imposes a "user fee" on federal inmates who are able to pay the costs associated with their incarceration.[59] Under the law, inmates may be assessed a dollar amount up to the cost of a year's incarceration—currently

🐦 Follow the author's tweets about the latest crime and justice news @schmalleger

Federal Bureau of Prisons: Institutional Security Levels and Terminology

The federal Bureau of Prisons (BOP) operates institutions at five different security levels (minimum, low, medium, high, and administrative). Security levels are distinguished based upon such features as the type of inmate housing within the institution; the presence of external patrols, towers, security barriers, or detection devices; internal security features; and staff-to-inmate ratio.

Minimum Security Federal Prison Camps (FPCs): Feature dormitory housing, limited or no perimeter fencing, and a relatively low staff-to-inmate ratio. Some are located next to military bases, making it possible for inmates to help serve the labor needs of the base. Many BOP facilities have a small, minimum-security camp adjacent to the main facility. These satellite prison camps provide inmate labor to the main institution and to off-site work programs.

Low Security Federal Correctional Institutions (FCIs): Feature double-fenced perimeters with electronic detection systems, mostly dormitory or cubicle housing, and a staff-to-inmate ratio that is somewhat higher than that of FPCs.

Medium Security Federal Correctional Institutions (FCIs): Have strengthened (double-fenced with electronic detection systems) perimeters, mostly cell-type housing, a higher staff-to-inmate ratio than low security FCIs, and greater internal controls.

High Security United States Penitentiaries (USPs): Have highly secured perimeters featuring walls or reinforced fences, multiple- and single-occupant cell housing, the highest staff-to-inmate ratio, and close control of inmate movement.

Administrative Facilities: Have special missions—for example, detaining pretrial offenders; treating inmates with serious or chronic medical problems; or containing extremely dangerous, violent, or escape-prone inmates. They include Metropolitan Correctional Centers (MCCs), Metropolitan Detention Centers (MDCs), Federal Detention Centers (FDCs), Federal Medical Centers (FMCs), the Medical Center for Federal Prisoners (MCFP), the Federal Transfer Center (FTC), and the Administrative-Maximum USP (ADX).

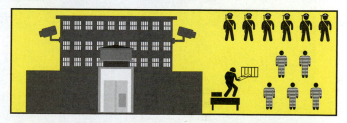

Federal Correctional Complexes (FCCs): Contain institutions with different missions and security levels located in close proximity, allowing them to gain cost efficiencies through shared services, enable staff to gain experience at various security levels, and enhance emergency preparedness by having additional resources readily available.

FIGURE 11–5
Federal Bureau of Prisons: Institutional Security Levels and Terminology
Source: Data from Federal Bureau of Prisons, *State of the Bureau 2010* (Washington, D.C.; U.S. Dept. of Justice, 2011), p. 2.

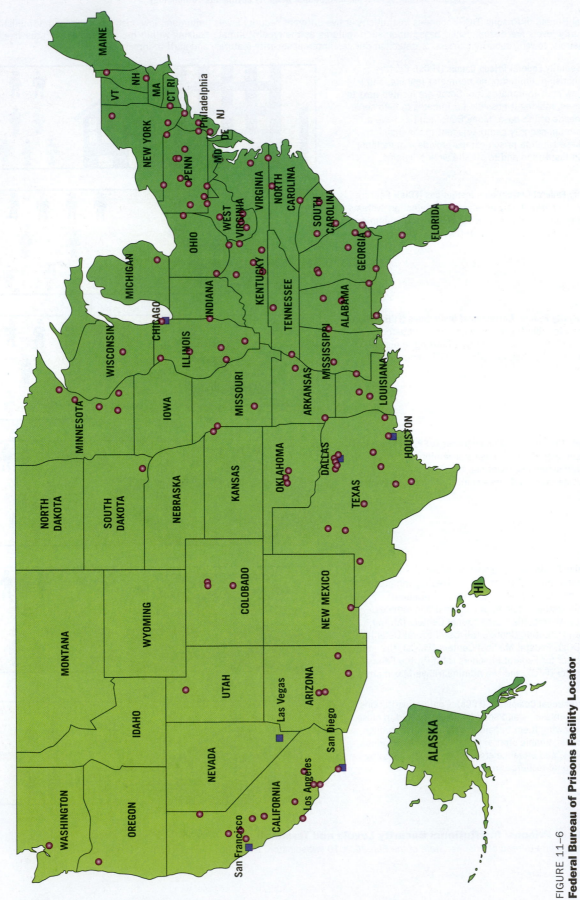

FIGURE 11-6
Federal Bureau of Prisons Facility Locator
Source: Federal Bureau of Prisons, https://www.bop.gov/locations/map.jsp.

around $29,226.[60] The statute, which was designed so as not to impose hardships on poor offenders or their dependents, directs that the collected funds (estimated to total $48 million per year) are to be used to improve alcohol- and drug-abuse programs within federal prisons. Visit the Federal Bureau of Prisons at **http://www.bop.gov**, and view the clickable map shown in Figure 11–6 at **https://www.bop.gov/locations/map.jsp**.

🐦 Follow the author's tweets about the latest crime and justice news @schmalleger

The Growth of Federal Prisons

From 1980 to 1989, the federal inmate population more than doubled, from just over 24,000 to almost 58,000. During the 1990s, the population more than doubled again, and it continued to grow throughout the early years of the twenty-first century, reaching 217,800 prisoners (or 40% over capacity).[61] Today, the number has dropped to around 184,000, although federal prisons are still overcrowded.[62] According to the Washington, D.C.–based Urban Institute, "the increase in expected time served by drug offenders was the single greatest contributor to growth in the federal prison population...." (Figure 11–7).[63]

Recent Improvements

In the midst of frequent lawsuits, court-ordered changes in prison administration, and large prison populations, outstanding prison facilities are being recognized through the ACA accreditation program. The ACA Commission on Accreditation has developed a set of standards that correctional institutions can use for conducting self-evaluations. Institutions that meet the standards can apply for accreditation under the program.

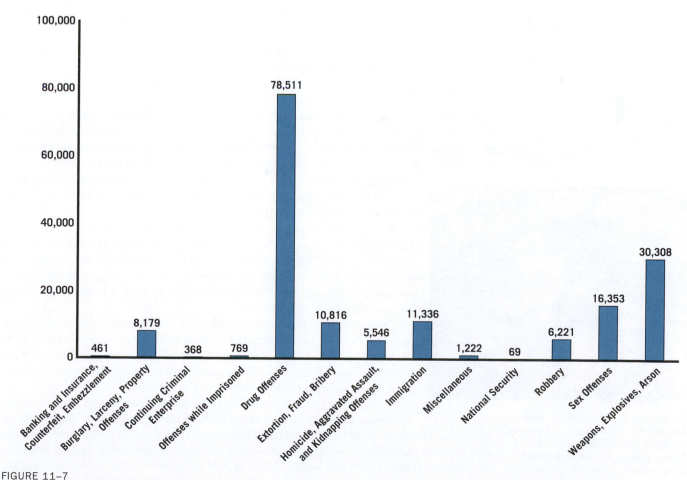

FIGURE 11–7
Federal Prison Population by Offense, 2018
Source: Federal Bureau of Prisons, Retrieved from https://www.bop.gov/about/statistics/statistics_inmate_offenses.jsp.

Another avenue toward improvement of the nation's prisons can be found in the National Academy of Corrections, the training arm of the National Institute of Corrections. The academy, located in Boulder, Colorado, offers seminars, videoconferencing, and training sessions for state and local corrections managers, trainers, personnel directors, sheriffs, and state legislators.[64] Issues covered include strategies to control overcrowding, community corrections program management, prison programs, gangs and disturbances, security, and public and media relations.[65]

Jails

jail

A confinement facility administered by an agency of local government, typically a law enforcement agency, intended for adults but sometimes also containing juveniles. Jails hold people who are being detained pending adjudication or who were committed after adjudication, usually those sentenced to a year or less.

Jails are locally operated short-term confinement facilities originally built to hold suspects following arrest and pending trial. Today's jails also serve other purposes:[66]

5 Identify the role jails currently play in American corrections and issues jail administrators face.

- Receiving individuals pending their arraignment, and holding them for trial, conviction, or sentencing
- Readmitting probation, parole, and bail bond violators and absconders
- Detaining juveniles, the mentally ill, and others temporarily, pending their transfer to appropriate facilities
- Holding individuals for the military, for protective custody, for contempt of court, and for the courts as witnesses
- Releasing convicted inmates to the community upon completion of their sentences
- Transferring inmates to federal, state, or other authorities
- Housing inmates for federal, state, or other authorities because of overcrowding in their facilities
- Operating community-based programs with day reporting, home detention, electronic monitoring, or other types of supervision
- Holding inmates sentenced to short terms (generally under 1 year)

A recent report by the BJS found that the nation's jails held 740,700 inmates, 14.5% of whom were women.[67] Juveniles held in local jails numbered 3,700. About 60% of jail inmates are pretrial detainees or are defendants involved in some stage of the trial process. Jail authorities also supervised an additional 54,200 men and women in the community under programs that included the following: electronic monitoring, home detention without electronic monitoring, day reporting, community service, and weekender programs.[68]

A total of 3,283 jails operate throughout the United States today, staffed by 226,300 jail employees—the equivalent of about one employee for every four jail inmates.[69] Overall, the nation's jail budget is huge, and facilities are overflowing. State and local governments spend $10 billion every year to operate the nation's jails,[70] and on average the annual housing of one jail inmate costs more than $14,500.[71]

Over 11 million people are admitted (or readmitted) to the nation's jails each year.[72] Some jail inmates stay for as little as 1 day, whereas others serve extended periods of time. Significantly, one of the fastest-growing sectors of today's jail population consists of sentenced offenders serving time in local jails because overcrowded prisons cannot accept them.

Most people processed through the country's jails are members of minority groups (52%), with 34% of jail inmates classifying themselves as African American, 14% as Hispanic, and 3% as other minorities. Less than 1% report being of more than one race, and 48% of jail inmates classify themselves as Caucasian. Slightly less than 86% are male, and 14.5% are female.[73] The typical jail inmate is an unmarried African-American male between 25 and 34 years of age who reports having had some high school education. Typical charges include drug trafficking (12.1%), assault (11.7%), drug possession (10.8%), and larceny (7%).[74]

▲ Los Angeles County's Twin Towers Jail. The $373-million jail, also known as the Twin Towers Correctional Facility, opened in 1997 and is one of the world's largest jails. What are the differences between a prison and a jail?

A Ramey/PhotoEdit, Inc.

The Charles Colson Task Force on Federal Corrections was established by congressional mandate in 2014 and charged with developing practical, data-driven recommendations to enhance public safety by creating a more just and efficient federal corrections system. The Task Force's recommendations were published in 2016, and are meant to provide strategies for reforms to the federal corrections system that are sensible, cost-effective, and which will work to reduce crime and restore lives. The six recommendations made by the Task Force are summarized below:

RECOMMENDATION 1: RESERVE PRISON FOR THOSE CONVICTED OF THE MOST SERIOUS FEDERAL CRIMES

Significant reform of the federal system cannot be achieved without addressing mandatory minimum drug penalties—the primary driver of BOP overcrowding and unsustainable growth. This policy should be revisited, with drug mandatory minimum sentences reserved for only the most serious offenses and judges empowered with greater discretion to consider the specific circumstances of each individual and case when determining a sentence.

RECOMMENDATION 2: PROMOTE A CULTURE OF SAFETY AND REHABILITATION IN FEDERAL FACILITIES

Federal prisons should be characterized by conditions of confinement that are safe, humane, and conducive to self-betterment. Staffing levels should be sufficient to ensure a safe environment and housing, treatment, and program offerings should be tailored to the specific needs of the many diverse populations in federal custody. Contact with relatives and other loved ones should be facilitated during incarceration as an important component of a rehabilitative environment. In support of such rehabilitation, a validated risk and needs assessment should be administered periodically to guide development of individualized case plans and delivery of the targeted services and programs necessary to support reintegration.

RECOMMENDATION 3: INCENTIVIZE PARTICIPATION IN RISK-REDUCTION PROGRAMMING

Public safety and rehabilitation are best achieved through meaningful incentives for participation in needed evidence-based programming. The most powerful incentive—earned time off one's sentence—should be used to encourage participation in addiction treatment, cognitive behavioral therapy, educational classes, faith-based programs, and other self-betterment activities prescribed in accordance with individualized case plans.

RECOMMENDATION 4: ENSURE SUCCESSFUL REINTEGRATION BY USING EVIDENCE-BASED PRACTICES IN SUPERVISION AND SUPPORT

Successful reintegration demands close coordination between correctional facilities and supervision agencies. All relevant federal criminal justice agencies should be encouraged to share case-level data in support of providing those leaving prison with the tools, services, supervision, and support necessary for successful reintegration.

RECOMMENDATION 5: ENHANCE SYSTEM PERFORMANCE AND ACCOUNTABILITY THROUGH BETTER COORDINATION ACROSS AGENCIES AND INCREASED TRANSPARENCY

To ensure success, federal agencies should operate collaboratively to carry out reforms in pursuit of the twin goals of minimizing incarceration and reducing recidivism. Performance measures and ongoing oversight are necessary to improve outcomes, hold agencies accountable for results, and enhance the effectiveness of the entire criminal justice system.

RECOMMENDATION 6: REINVEST SAVINGS TO SUPPORT THE EXPANSION OF NECESSARY PROGRAMS, SUPERVISION, AND TREATMENT

Up-front investments are critical to achieve successful implementation and desired public-safety outcomes. The BOP requires an initial funding infusion to carry out the practices and programs necessary to prepare individuals for release. Federal probation needs sufficient staffing and services to shoulder the projected increase in its caseload. The courts and federal oversight entities require resources to support new review, oversight, and coordination roles. And grant programs to courts and prosecutors' offices are necessary to incentivize problem-solving courts and front-end diversion programs. These expenditures will be recovered in savings realized through a reduced prison population.

Source: Urban Institute, Transforming Prisons, Restoring Lives", 2016.

According to the BJS, about 6% of jail facilities house almost half of all jail inmates in the nation.[75] So although most jails are small—many were built to house 50 or fewer inmates—most people who spend time in jail do so in larger institutions. Across the country, a handful of "megajails" house thousands of inmates each. The largest such facilities are in Los Angeles; New York City; Cook County, Illinois; Harris County, Texas; Philadelphia, Pennsylvania; and Maricopa County, Arizona. Los Angeles County's 4,000-bed Twin Towers Correctional Facility cost $373 million to build and opened in 1997.[76] The city of Los Angeles's 512-bed Metropolitan Detention Center, though not nearly as large, opened in 2011 and cost the city $84 million to build. The largest employer among the huge jails is Cook County Jail, with more than 1,200 personnel on its payroll.[77] The nation's 30 largest jail jurisdictions hold 20.4% of all jail inmates.[78] The two jurisdictions with the most jail inmates, Los Angeles County and New York City, together held approximately 31,085 inmates, or 4.2% of the national total.[79]

Women and Jail

Although women make up only around 14% of the country's jail population, they are the largest growth group in jails nationwide.[80] Jailed women face a number of special problems. Only 25.7% of the nation's jails report having a classification system specifically designed to evaluate female inmates.[81] Although many jurisdictions have plans "to build facilities geared to the female offender,"[82] not all jurisdictions today even provide separate housing areas for women. Educational levels are very low among jailed women, with fewer than half being high school graduates.[83] Drug abuse is another significant source of difficulty for jailed women: Over 30% of women who are admitted to jail have a substance-abuse problem at the time of admission, and in some parts of the country, that figure may be as high as 70%.[84]

Pregnancy is another problem. Nationally, 4% of female inmates are pregnant when they enter jail,[85] but in urban areas, as many as 10% of female inmates are reported to be pregnant on any given day.[86] As a consequence, a few hundred children are born in jails each year. However, substantive medical programs for female inmates, such as obstetrics and gynaecological care, are often lacking. Some writers have advised jail administrators to expect to see an increasingly common kind of inmate in the future: "an opiate-addicted female who is pregnant with no prior prenatal care having one or more sexually transmitted diseases, and fitting a high-risk category for AIDS (prostitution, IV drug use)."[87]

Not only are jailed mothers separated from their children, but they may have to pay for their support. About 12% of all jails in one study reported requiring employed female inmates to contribute to the support of their dependent children.

When we consider women and jails, female inmates are only half the story. Women who work in corrections are the other half. In one study, Linda Zupan, one of a new generation of jail scholars, found that women made up 22% of the correctional officer force in jails across the nation.[88] The deployment of female personnel, however, was disproportionately skewed toward jobs in the lower ranks: Although 60% of all support staff (secretaries, cooks, and janitors) were women, only one in every ten chief administrators was female. Zupan explains this pattern by pointing to the "token status" of female staff members in some of the nation's jails.[89] Even so, Zupan did find that female corrections employees were significantly committed to their careers and that the attitudes of male workers toward female coworkers in jails were generally positive. Zupan's study uncovered 626 jails in which over 50% of the corrections officer force consisted of women. On the opposite side of the coin, however, 954 of the nation's 3,316 jails operating at the time of the study had no female officers at all.[90] Zupan noted that "an obvious problem associated with the lack of female officers in jails housing females concerns the potential for abuse and exploitation of women inmates by male staff."[91]

Jails that do hire women generally accord them equal footing with male staffers. Although cross-gender privacy is a potential area of legal liability, few jails limit the supervisory areas that female officers working in male facilities may visit. In three-quarters of the jails studied by Zupan, female officers were assigned to supervise male housing areas, and only one in four jails that employed women restricted their access to unscreened shower and toilet facilities used by men or to other areas, such as sexual offender units.

The Growth of Jails

Jails have been called the "shame of the criminal justice system." Many are old, poorly funded, scantily staffed by underpaid and poorly trained employees, and given low priority in local budgets. By the end of the 1980s, many of our nation's jails had become seriously overcrowded, and court-ordered caps were sometimes placed on jail populations. One of the first such caps was imposed on the Harris County Jail in Houston (Texas) in 1990. In that year, the jail was forced to release 250 inmates after missing a deadline for reducing its resident population of 6,100 people.[92] A nationwide survey by the BJS, undertaken around this time, found that 46% of all jails had been built more than 25 years earlier, and of that percentage, over half were more than 50 years old.[93]

A 1983 national census revealed that jails were operating at 85% of their rated capacity (Table 11–2).[94] In 1990, however, the nation's jails were running at 104% of capacity, and

Approximately 11 million people are admitted (or readmitted) to the nation's jails each year.

TABLE 11–2
Jail Facts

	1983	1988	1993	2000	2005	2016
Number of jails	3,338	3,316	3,304	3,365	3,358	3,283
Number of jail inmates	223,551	343,569	459,804	621,149	747,529	740,700
Rated capacity of jails	261,556	339,949	475,224	677,787	789,001	915,400
Percentage of capacity occupied	85%	101%	97%	92%	95%	80%

Source: Zhen Zeng, Jail Inmates in 2016 (February 2018), Bureau of Justice Statistics.

new jails could be found on drawing boards and under construction across the country. By 2016, jail capacity had increased substantially, and overall jail occupancy was reported at 80% of rated capacity. Some individual facilities, however, were still desperately over-crowded.[95]

Although jail overcrowding is not the issue it was a decade ago, it is still a problem. Overcrowded prisons have taken a toll on jails, with thousands of inmates being held in local jails because of overcrowding in state and federal prisons. Today, approximately 83,700 inmates are being held in local jails because of overcrowding in state and federal prisons.[96] Also, the practice of giving jail sentences to offenders who are unable or unwilling to make restitution, alimony, or child-support payments has added to jail occupancy and has made the local lockup at least partially a debtors' prison. Symptomatic of problems brought on by huge jail populations, the BJS reported 314 suicides in jails across the nation during a recent year.[97] Jail deaths from all causes total about 980 annually.

Other factors conspire to keep jail populations high. These include the inability of jail inmates to make bond, delays between arrest and case disposition, an overburdened criminal justice system, and what some have called "unproductive statutes" requiring that speci-fied nonviolent offenders be jailed.[98]

Some innovative jurisdictions have successfully contained the growth of jail populations by diverting arrestees to community-based programs. San Diego, California, for example, uses a privately operated detoxification reception program to divert many inebriates from the "drunk tank."[99] Officials in Galveston County, Texas, routinely divert mentally ill arrest-ees directly to a mental health facility.[100] Other areas use pretrial services and magistrates' offices, which are open 24 hours a day, for setting bail, making release possible.

🐦 Follow the author's tweets about the latest crime and justice news @schmalleger

◀ Inmates playing cards at the Los Angeles North County Correctional Facility in Castaic, California. The Los Angeles County jail system is the largest in the world, housing more than 20,000 inmates on a given day. What kinds of inmates do jails hold?
Damian Dovarganes/AP Images

direct-supervision jail
A temporary confinement facility that eliminates many of the traditional barriers between inmates and corrections staff. Physical barriers in direct-supervision jails are far less common than in traditional jails, allowing staff members the opportunity for greater interaction with, and control over, residents.

Direct-Supervision Jails

Some suggest that the problems found in many jails stem from "mismanagement, lack of fiscal support, heterogeneous inmate populations, overuse and misuse of detention, overemphasis on custodial goals, and political and public apathy."[101] Others propose that environmental and organizational aspects of traditional jail architecture and staffing have led to many difficulties.[102] Traditional jails, say these observers, were built on the assumption that inmates are inherently violent and potentially destructive. They were constructed to give staff maximum control over inmates through the use of thick walls, bars, and other architectural barriers to the free movement of inmates. Such institutions, however, also limit the corrections staff's visibility and their access to confinement areas. As a consequence, they tend to encourage just the kinds of inmate behavior that jails were meant to control. Today, efficient hallway patrols and expensive video technology help in overcoming the limits that old jail architecture places on supervision.

In an effort to solve many of the problems that dogged jails in the past, a new jail management strategy emerged during the 1970s. Called the **direct-supervision jail**, or *podular/direct supervision (PDS) jail*, this approach joined "podular/unit architecture with a participative, proactive management philosophy."[103] Often built in a system of pods, or modular self-contained housing areas linked to one another, direct-supervision jails helped eliminate the old physical barriers that separated staff and inmates. Gone were the bars and the isolated, secure observation areas for officers, and they were replaced by an open environment in which inmates and corrections personnel could mingle with relative freedom. In a number of such "new-generation" jails, large reinforced Plexiglas panels supplanted walls and served to separate activity areas, such as classrooms and dining halls, from one another. Soft furniture is the rule throughout such institutions, and individual rooms take the place of cells, allowing inmates at least a modicum of personal privacy. In today's direct-supervision jails, 16 to 46 inmates typically live in one pod, with corrections staffers present among the inmate population around the clock.

Direct-supervision jails have been touted for their tendency to reduce inmate dissatisfaction and for their ability to deter rape and violence among the inmate population. By eliminating architectural barriers to staff–inmate interaction, direct-supervision facilities are said to place officers back in control of institutions. A number of studies have demonstrated the success of such jails at reducing the likelihood of inmate victimization. One such study, published in 1994, also found that staff morale in direct-supervision jails was far higher than in traditional institutions, that inmates reported reduced stress levels, and that fewer inmate-on-inmate and inmate-on-staff assaults occurred.[104] Similarly, sexual assault, jail rape, suicide, and escape have all been found to occur far less frequently in direct-supervision facilities than in traditional institutions.[105] Significantly, new-generation jails appear to be substantially less susceptible to lawsuits brought by inmates and to adverse court-ordered judgments against jail administrators.

Jails and the Future

In contrast to more visible issues confronting the justice system—such as the death penalty, gun control, terrorism, and big-city gangs—jails have received relatively little attention from the media and have generally escaped close public scrutiny.[106] National efforts are under way, however, to improve the quality of jail life. Some changes involve adding crucial programs for inmates. An American Jail Association (AJA) study of drug-treatment programs in jails, for example, found that "a small fraction (perhaps fewer than 10%) of inmates needing drug treatment actually receive these services."[107]

Jail industries are another growing programmatic area. The best of them serve the community while training inmates in marketable skills.[108] In an exemplary effort to humanize its megajails, for example, the Los Angeles County Sheriff's Department opened an inmate telephone-answering service.[109] Many callers contact the sheriff's department daily, requesting information about the county's 22,000 jail inmates. These requests for information were becoming increasingly difficult to handle due to the growing fiscal constraints facing local government. To handle the huge number of calls effectively without tying up sworn law enforcement personnel, the department began using inmates specially trained to handle

Ethics and Professionalism
American Jail Association Code of Ethics for Jail Officers

As an officer employed in a detention/correctional capacity, I swear (or affirm) to be a good citizen and a credit to my community, state, and nation at all times. I will abstain from all questionable behavior which might bring disrepute to the agency for which I work, my family, my community, and my associates. My lifestyle will be above and beyond reproach and I will constantly strive to set an example of a professional who performs his/her duties according to the laws of our country, state, and community and the policies, procedures, written and verbal orders, and regulations of the agency for which I work. On the job I promise to:

Keep the institution secure so as to safeguard my community and the lives of the staff, inmates, and visitors on the premises.

Work with each individual firmly and fairly without regard to rank, status, or condition.

Maintain a positive demeanor when confronted with stressful situations of scorn, ridicule, danger, and/or chaos.

Report either in writing or by word of mouth to the proper authorities those things which should be reported, and keep silent about matters which are to remain confidential according to the laws and rules of the agency and government.

Manage and supervise the inmates in an evenhanded and courteous manner.

Refrain at all times from becoming personally involved in the lives of the inmates and their families.

Treat all visitors to the jail with politeness and respect and do my utmost to ensure that they observe the jail regulations.

Take advantage of all education and training opportunities designed to assist me to become a more competent officer.

Communicate with people in or outside of the jail, whether by phone, written word, or word of mouth, in such a way so as not to reflect in a negative manner upon my agency.

Contribute to a jail environment which will keep the inmate involved in activities designed to improve his/her attitude and character.

Support all activities of a professional nature through membership and participation that will continue to elevate the status of those who operate our nation's jails.

Do my best through word and deed to present an image to the public at large of a jail professional, committed to progress for an improved and enlightened criminal justice system.

THINKING ABOUT ETHICS

1. Why does the AJA Code of Ethics require jail officers to "[t]ake advantage of all education and training opportunities designed to assist [them] to become a more competent officer"? What does education have to do with ethics?

2. Is there anything that you might add to this code? Is there anything that you might delete?

Source: American Jail Association, "Code of Ethics for Jail Officers".

---

incoming calls. Eighty inmates were assigned to the project, with groups of different sizes covering shifts throughout the day. Each inmate staffer went through a training program to learn how to use proper telephone procedures and how to run computer terminals containing routine data on the department's inmates. The new system now handles 4,000 telephone inquiries a day, and the time needed to answer a call and to provide information has dropped from 30 minutes under the old system to a remarkable 10 seconds today.

Capturing much recent attention are **regional jails**, that is, jails that are built and run using the combined resources of a variety of local jurisdictions. Regional jails have begun to replace smaller and often antiquated local jails in at least a few locations. One example of a regional jail is the Western Tidewater Regional Jail, serving the cities of Suffolk and Franklin and the county of Isle of Wright in Virginia.[110] Regional jails, which are just beginning to come into their own, may develop quickly in Virginia, where the state, recognizing the economies of consolidation, offers to reimburse localities up to 50% of the cost of building regional jails.

The emergence of state standards has become an increasingly important area in jail management. Thirty-two states have set standards for municipal and county jails,[111] and in 25 states, those standards are mandatory. The purpose of jail standards is to identify basic minimum conditions necessary for inmate health and safety. On the national level, the Commission on Accreditation for Corrections, operated jointly by the ACA and the federal government, has developed its own set of jail standards,[112] as has the National Sheriff's Association. Both sets of standards are designed to ensure a minimal level of comfort and safety in local lockups. Increased standards, though, are costly. Local jurisdictions, already hard-pressed to meet other budgetary demands, will probably be slow to upgrade their jails to meet such external guidelines unless forced to do so. In a study of 61 jails that was designed to test compliance with National Sheriff's Association guidelines, Ken Kerle discovered that in many standards areas—especially those of tool control, armory planning,

regional jail
A jail that is built and run using the combined resources of a variety of local jurisdictions.

> The emergence of state standards has become an increasingly important area in jail management.

community resources, release preparation, and riot planning—the majority of jails were badly out of compliance.[113] Lack of a written plan was the most commonly cited reason for failing to meet the standards.

One final element in the unfolding saga of jail development deserves special mention: the expansion of jails throughout California to accommodate inmates who have been reassigned under that state's realignment strategy (discussed earlier in this chapter). According to the California Board of State and Community Corrections, the state's jail population has been rising significantly as more and more inmates are sent to jail in lieu of state prison, and jail administrators are looking to increase jail capacity.[114] In Fresno County, for example, jail floors that had been closed have now been reopened, and the county is looking for additional places to house inmates.[115] Learn more about jails by visiting the AJA **http://www. aja.org**.

Private Prisons

6 Describe the current and likely future roles of private prisons.

privatization
The movement toward the wider use of private prisons.

private prison
A correctional institution operated by a private firm on behalf of a local or state government.

State-run prison systems have always contracted with private industries for food, psychological testing, training, and recreational and other services, and it is estimated that more than three dozen states today rely on private businesses to serve a variety of correctional needs. It follows, then, that states have now turned to private industry for the provision of prison space. The movement toward **privatization** (use of privately run rather than government-run prisons), which began in the early 1980s, was slow to catch on, but it has since grown at a rapid pace. In 1986, only 2,620 prisoners could be found in privately run confinement facilities,[116] but by 2016, privately operated correctional facilities serving as prisons and jails held 128,323 state and federal prisoners across 31 states and the District of Columbia.[117] **Private prisons** (prisons operated by private companies) held 7% of all state prisoners and 18% of federal prisoners at the start of 2017. New Mexico is the state that uses private prisons the most, with 43% of its inmates held there. One source says that the growth rate of the private prison industry has been around 35% annually,[118] which is comparable to the highest growth rates anywhere in the corporate sector.

Privately run prisons are operated by the GEO Group, Cornell Corrections, CoreCivic (formerly Corrections Corporation of America), Management and Training Corporation (MTC), Correctional Services Corporation (CSC), Wackenhut Corrections Corporation, and numerous other smaller companies. Most states that use private firms to supplement their prison resources contract with such companies to provide a full range of custodial and other correctional services. State corrections administrators use private companies to reduce overcrowding, lower operating expenses, and avoid lawsuits targeted at state officials and employees.[119] But some studies have shown that private prisons may not bring the kinds of cost savings that had been anticipated.[120] One 1996 study was done by the U.S. General Accounting Office.[121] It found, for example, "neither cost savings nor substantial differences in the quality of services" between private and publicly run prisons.[122] Similar findings emerged in a report by the Bureau of Justice Assistance. That report, titled *Emerging Issues on Privatized Prisons*, found that "private prisons offer only modest cost savings, which are basically a result of moderate reductions in staffing patterns, fringe benefits, and other labor-related costs."[123]

Many hurdles remain before the privatization movement can effectively provide large-scale custodial supervision. Among the most significant barriers to privatization are old state laws that prohibit private involvement in correctional management. Other practical hurdles exist as well. States that do contract with private firms may face the specter of strikes by correctional officers, who are not subject to state laws restricting the ability of public employees to strike. Moreover, because responsibility for the protection of inmate rights still lies with the states, their liability will not transfer to private corrections.[124] In today's legal climate, it appears that the courts are unlikely to allow states to shield themselves or their employees through private prison contracting. To limit their own liability, states will probably have to oversee private operations as well as set standards for training and custody. In 1997, in the case of *Richardson* v. *McKnight*,[125] the U.S. Supreme Court made it clear that correctional officers employed by a private firm are not entitled to qualified immunity from suits by prisoners charging a violation of Section 1983 of Title 42 of the

JUSTICE REINVESTMENT
Cost-Efficient Corrections and Sentencing

As this chapter notes, the total number of people in prison declined in 2011 for the first time in almost 30 years. Since the early 1970s, the use of incarceration had been growing steadily, primarily as a result of the enactment of "get-tough-on-crime" legislation, like two- and three-strikes laws, and the war on drugs, which accounted for a huge number of our nation's prisoners—especially at the federal level. Faced, however, with budget shortfalls, states were forced to find ways to save money and began looking at alternative sentencing practices and programs to lower the cost of handling convicted felons.

Four types of sentencing reforms, instituted in various ways by 28 states, have helped lower prison populations in a number of jurisdictions over the past few years: (1) sentence modifications, (2) drug-law reform, (3) probation revocation reforms, and (4) reforms in juvenile sentencing.

The first of these reforms, sentence modifications, effectively diverts many nonviolent offenders from prison, makes wider use of alternative sentencing options, and shifts inmates who would normally be incarcerated in state facilities to local jails or privately run facilities. The second, drug-law reform, makes wider use of drug courts and drug treatment as alternatives to imprisonment, and has also resulted in the reformation of drug statutes, shortening periods of confinement and making wider use of supervised early release into the community. The third strategy, probation revocation reforms, allows selected probation violators to remain free in the community under more intense supervision, and subsequently requires additional rule violation for probation revocation. Depending on the offense, some probation violators are now deemed ineligible for imprisonment through changes in

the law, but face tougher lifestyle restrictions if they violate the conditions of their probation. Finally, reforms in juvenile sentencing give judges greater leeway in the handling of delinquents and mean that fewer young people will spend time confined in state-run facilities.

The use of local jails to hold inmates who would otherwise be sent to state facilities and contracts with private correctional services companies to house inmates needing confinement are other ways that states are attempting to lower the cost of confinement. In Tennessee, for example, the cost to house an inmate in a county jail averages around $35 per day, and moving that inmate to a state-run facility ups the cost to almost $65 per day. Private companies, which bid for state contracts, can often be more efficient than state-run departments of corrections, at least in dealing with certain types of inmates, resulting in significant cost savings. Some governments officials also claim that private prisons shelter states from at least some forms of civil liability that may arise from lawsuits brought by prisoners. Finally, one way of alleviating the high cost of incarceration is being tried in Riverside, California, where county officials have begun charging jail inmates $142.42 for every night they spend locked up.

References: Steve Ahillen, "Explore Cost-Effective Alternatives to Prison," *Tennessee News Sentinel*, March 10, 2012, http://www.politifact.com/tennessee/promises/haslam-o-meter/promise/1072/explore-cost-effective-alternatives-to-prison (accessed May 30, 2012); Nicole D. Porter, *The State of Sentencing, 2011: Developments in Policy and Practice* (Washington, D.C.: The Sentencing Project, 2012); and Jennifer Medina, "In California, a Plan to Charge Inmates for Their Stay," *New York Times*, December 11, 2011.

U.S. Code. (See Chapter 6 for more information on Section 1983 lawsuits.) However, in the 2011 case of *Minneci* v. *Pollard*, the Court held that a *Bivens* action against employees of a privately run federal prison in California could not proceed because state tort law already "authorizes adequate alternative damages actions."[126] In 2001, however, in the case of *Correctional Services Corporation* v. *Malesko*,[127] the Court found that private corporations acting under color of federal law cannot be held responsible in a *Bivens* action because the purpose of *Bivens* (which was discussed in Chapter 6) "is to deter individual federal officers from committing Constitutional violations."[128]

🐦 Follow the author's tweets about the latest crime and justice news @schmalleger

◀ The 2,300-bed California City Correctional Center in the Mojave Desert town of California City. The facility, which opened in December 1999, was built by the Corrections Corporation of America (now CoreCivic) to provide medium-security correctional services under a contract with the Federal Bureau of Prisons. What are the advantages and disadvantages of private prisons?

Reed Saxon/AP Images

CJ Exhibit 11–1
Arguments for and against the Privatization of Prisons

REASONS TO PRIVATIZE

1. Private companies can provide construction financing options that allow the government to pay only for capacity as needed in lieu of assuming long-term debt.
2. Private companies offer modern state-of-the-art correctional facility designs that are more efficient to operate and built based upon value engineering specifications.
3. Private operators typically design and construct a new correctional facility in half the time of a comparable government project.
4. Private vendors provide government clients with the convenience and accountability of one entity for all compliance issues.
5. Private correctional companies are able to mobilize rapidly and specialize in unique facility missions.
6. Private companies provide economic development opportunities by hiring and, the extent possible, purchasing locally.
7. Government can reduce or share its liability exposure through effective contracts with private corrections companies.
8. Government can retain flexibility by limiting the contract duration and by specifying the facility's mission.
9. Adding other service providers injects competition among both public and private organizations.

REASONS NOT TO PRIVATIZE

1. There are certain responsibilities that only the government should undertake, such as public safety. The government has legal, political, and moral obligations to provide incarceration. Major constitutional competition among both public and private issues revolves around the deprivation of liberty, discipline, and preserving the constitutional rights of the detained.
2. Few private companies are available from which to choose.
3. Private operators may be inexperienced with key correctional and detention issues.
4. Private companies may become monopolies through political ingratiation, favoritism, etc.
5. Government may lose the ability to perform and properly oversee detention functions over time.
6. The profit motive will inhibit the proper performance of duties. Private companies have financial incentives to cut corners.
7. Procurement process is slow, inefficient, and open to risks.
8. Creating a good, clear contract with effective quality assurance mechanisms and accountability is a daunting task.
9. Lack of enforcement remedies in contracts along with the lack of willingness to utilize available remedies leaves only termination or lawsuits as recourse.

Source: Dennis Cunningham from presentation entitled "Public Strategies for Private Prisons," Department of Homeland Security Immigration and Customs Enforcement Detention Services Manager's Conference, August 10–12, 2012, Dallas, Texas. Used by permission of the author.

Follow the author's tweets about the latest crime and justice news @schmalleger

Perhaps the most serious legal issues confront states that contract to hold inmates outside their own jurisdiction. More than a decade ago, for example, two inmates escaped from a 240-man sex-offender unit run by CoreCivic under contract with the state of Oregon. Problems immediately arose because the CoreCivic unit was located near Houston, Texas—not in Oregon, where the men had originally been sentenced to confinement. Following the escape, Texas officials were unsure whether they even had arrest power over the former prisoners because the escapees had not committed any crimes in Texas. Although prison escape is a crime under Texas law, the law only applied to state-run facilities, not to private facilities where corrections personnel are not employed by the state or empowered in any official capacity by state law. Harris County (Texas) Prosecutor John Holmes explained the situation this way: "They have not committed the offense of escape under Texas law . . . and the only reason at all that they're subject to being arrested and were arrested was because during their leaving the facility, they assaulted a guard and took his motor vehicle. That we can charge them with and have."[129]

Opponents of the movement toward privatization cite many issues (see CJ Exhibit 11–1). They claim that, aside from legal concerns, cost reductions via the use of private facilities can only be achieved by lowering standards. They fear a return to the inhumane conditions of early jails as private firms seek to turn prisons into profit-making operations.

In 2016, the U.S. Department of Justice ordered the Bureau of Prisons to bring an end to the use of private prisons throughout the federal system. After coming to office, however, the Trump administration reversed the DOJ stance.

Summary

PRISONS AND JAILS

- Prisons in this country were originally built to rehabilitate criminal offenders and as an alternative to the corporal punishments that had been so common in earlier times. In the late twentieth century, however, the national attitude changed to a "lock-em-up" philosophy with emphasis on keeping offenders behind bars as long as possible. This, along with strict drug laws and new three-strikes legislation, combined to swell prison populations to the breaking point.

- Today's correctional environment is underpinned by both public and official frustration with rehabilitative efforts, but has been tempered by a growing clamor of calls claiming that the pendulum has swung too far in the direction of imprisonment. Pressure for change, and for a reduced reliance on incarceration, has come in the form of fiscal restraint, and recent requirements imposed by federal courts to provide more effective supervision and to improve confinement conditions.

- Today's prisons are classified according to security level, such as maximum, medium, and minimum security. Most contemporary American correctional facilities are medium or minimum security. Although the goals of recidivism and deterrence are once again growing in importance, today's prisons still tend to warehouse inmates awaiting release. Overcrowded facilities continue to be the norm in many jurisdictions. A nationwide effort is now under way to reduce the size of prison populations everywhere.

- Most states use a classification system to assign new prisoners to initial custody levels based on their type of offense, perceived dangerousness, and escape risk. Serious violent criminals who begin their prison careers with lengthy sentences in maximum custody often have the opportunity to work their way up to minimum security, while those prisoners who represent continual disciplinary problems are returned to closer custody levels.

- The federal prison system, officially operated by the Bureau of Prisons, consists of 122 institutions of various kinds spread across the country. It employs about 40,000 people, and holds around 220,000 inmates.

- In contrast to prisons, which are long-term confinement facilities designed to hold those who have been sentenced to serve time for committing crime, jails are short-term confinement facilities whose traditional purpose has been to hold those awaiting trial or sentencing. Inmates who have been tried and sentenced may also be held at jails until their transfer to a prison facility, and today's jails sometimes hold inmates serving short sentences of confinement. Recently, the emergence of direct-supervision jails seems to have reduced the incidence of jail violence and improved the conditions of jailed inmates in jurisdictions where such facilities operate. In direct-supervision jails, the traditional barriers between inmates and staff have been mostly eliminated.

- Until recently, the use of privately run correctional facilities, or private prisons, have grown in number as the movement toward the privatization of correctional facilities gained steam. Private prisons, operated by for-profit corporations, hold inmates on behalf of state governments or the federal government and provide for inmates' care and security. In 2016, the federal Bureau of Prisons moved to end the use of private correctional facilities in the federal system, saying that they were not meeting their goals. After taking office, however, the Trump administration reversed the BOP's initiative, and moved to support expanded use of private prisons.

QUESTIONS FOR REVIEW

1. How did American prisons develop? Through what stages did such development occur?
2. What are today's prisons like? What are some of the characteristics of today's inmates?
3. What are some of the issues facing prisons today?
4. What role do jails play in American corrections? What are some of the issues that jail administrators currently face?
5. What will be the likely state of private prisons two or three decades from now?

Prison Life

Prison walls do not form a barrier separating prison inmates from the protections of the Constitution.

—*Turner v. Safley*, 482 U.S. 78 (1987)

Learning Objectives

After reading this chapter, you should be able to:

1. Describe total institutions. **373**

2. Discuss the lives of male inmates, prison subcultures, prison lifestyles, and sexual behavior within prisons. **374**

3. Summarize the problems that female inmates face in prisons and the different ways of accommodating female prisoners. **379**

4. Describe prison life from a corrections officer's point of view. **387**

5. Describe the nature of security threat groups and describe riots in American prisons. **388**

6. Discuss the legal aspects of prisoners' rights, including the consequences of related, precedent-setting U.S. Supreme Court cases. **392**

7. Describe the major issues that prisons face today. **402**

Casey Christie/The Bakersfield Californian/ZUMA Press Inc/Alamy Stock Photo

Introduction

In 2012, 23-year-old Laura Kaeppeler, the newly crowned Miss America, dedicated the year of her reign to the theme "Circles of Support: Mentoring Children of Incarcerated Parents."[1] Kaeppeler said, "It's everyday life for millions of children, and it allows me to connect with people on a level they don't expect a pageant contestant to connect with them. This is a real problem people can relate to." Kaeppeler's father had been imprisoned when she was 17 for a white-collar crime.

For many years, prisons and prison life could be described by the phrase "out of sight, out of mind." Very few citizens cared about prison conditions, and those unfortunate enough to be locked away were regarded as lost to the world. By the mid-twentieth century, however, this attitude started to change. Concerned citizens began to offer their services to prison administrations, neighborhoods began accepting work-release prisoners and halfway houses, and social scientists initiated a serious study of prison life. Today, as shows like *Prison Break* make clear, prisons and prison life have entered the American mainstream. Part of the reason for this is that prisons today hold more people than ever before, and incarceration affects not only those imprisoned but also family members, friends, and victims on the outside.

This chapter describes the realities of prison life, including prisoner lifestyles, prison subcultures, sexuality in prison, prison violence, and prisoners' rights and grievance procedures. We discuss both the inmate world and the staff world. A separate section on women in prison details the social structure of women's prisons, daily life in those facilities, and the various types of female inmates. We begin with a brief overview of early research on prison life.

▲ Laura Kaeppeler, Miss America 2012. Kaeppeler dedicated the year of her reign to mentoring the children of incarcerated parents. What do most Americans think of prisons and prisoners?

James Atoa/Christopher Black/Everett Collection Inc/Alamy Stock Photo

Research on Prison Life: Total Institutions

In 1935, Hans Reimer, who was then chairman of the Department of Sociology at Indiana University, set the tone for studies of prison life when he voluntarily served 3 months in prison as an incognito participant-observer.[2] Reimer reported the results of his studies to the American Prison Association, stimulating many other, albeit less spectacular, efforts to examine prison life. Other early studies include Donald Clemmer's *The Prison Community* (1940),[3] Gresham M. Sykes's *The Society of Captives: A Study of a Maximum Security Prison* (1958),[4] Richard A. Cloward and Donald R. Cressey's *Theoretical Studies in Social Organization of the Prison* (1960),[5] and Cressey's edited volume, *The Prison: Studies in Institutional Organization and Change* (1961).[6]

1 Describe total institutions.

These studies and others focused primarily on maximum-security prisons for men. They treated correctional institutions as formal or complex organizations and employed the analytic techniques of organizational sociology, industrial psychology, and administrative science.[7] As modern writers on prisons have observed, "The prison was compared to a primitive society, isolated from the outside world, functionally integrated by a delicate system of mechanisms, which kept it precariously balanced between anarchy and accommodation."[8]

Another approach to the study of prison life was developed by Erving Goffman, who coined the term **total institutions** in a 1961 study of prisons and mental hospitals.[9] Goffman described total institutions as places where the same people work, recreate, worship, eat, and sleep together daily. Such places include prisons, concentration camps, mental hospitals, seminaries, and other facilities in which residents are cut off from the larger society either forcibly or willingly. Total institutions are small societies. They evolve their own distinctive values and styles of life and pressure residents to fulfill rigidly prescribed behavioral roles.

🐦 Follow the author's tweets about the latest crime and justice news @schmalleger

total institution

An enclosed facility separated from society both socially and physically, where the inhabitants share all aspects of their daily lives.

▶ A corrections officer escorts a prison inmate through a high-security area. What does the term *prisonization* mean?
Halfdark/Getty Images

Generally speaking, the work of prison researchers built on findings of other social scientists who discovered that any group with similar characteristics, confined in the same place at the same time, develops its own subculture with specific components that govern hierarchy, behavioral patterns, values, and so on. Prison subcultures, described in the next section, also provide the medium through which prison values are communicated and expectations are made known.

The Male Inmate's World

> **2** Discuss the lives of male inmates, prison subcultures, prison lifestyles, and sexual behavior within prisons.

Two social realities coexist in prison settings. One is the official structure of rules and procedures put in place by the wider society and enforced by prison staff. The other is the more informal but decidedly more powerful inmate world.[10] The inmate world, best described by how closely it touches the lives of inmates, is controlled by **prison subculture**, consisting of inmate values and behaviors. The realities of prison life—including a large and often densely packed inmate population that must look to the prison environment for all its needs—mean that prison subculture develops independently of the plans of prison administrators and is not easily subjected to the control of prison authorities.

Inmates entering prison discover a whole new social world in which they must participate or face consequences ranging from dangerous ostracism to physical violence and homicide.[11] The socialization of new inmates into the prison subculture has been described as a process of **prisonization**,[12] through which the new prisoner learns the convict values, attitudes, roles, and even language. By the time this process is complete, new inmates have become "cons." Gresham Sykes and Sheldon Messinger recognized five elements of the prison code in 1960:[13]

prison subculture
The values and behavioral patterns characteristic of prison inmates. Prison subculture has been found to be surprisingly consistent across the country.

prisonization
The process whereby newly institutionalized offenders come to accept prison lifestyles and criminal values. Although many inmates begin their prison experience with only a few values that support criminal behavior, the socialization experience they undergo while incarcerated leads to a much wider acceptance of such values.

1. Don't interfere with the interests of other inmates. Never rat on a con.
2. Don't lose your head. Play it cool and do your own time.
3. Don't exploit inmates. Don't steal. Don't break your word. Be right.
4. Don't whine. Be a man.
5. Don't be a sucker. Don't trust the guards or staff.

Some criminologists have suggested that the prison code is simply a reflection of general criminal values. If so, these values are brought to the institution rather than created there. Either way, the power and pervasiveness of the prison code require convicts to conform to the worldview held by the majority of prisoners.

Stanton Wheeler, Ford Foundation Professor of Law and Social Sciences at the University of Washington, closely examined the concept of prisonization in an early study of the Washington State Reformatory.[14] Wheeler found that the degree of prisonization experienced by inmates tends to vary over time. He described changing levels of inmate commitment to prison norms and values by way of a U-shaped curve. When an inmate first enters prison, Wheeler said, the conventional values of outside society are of paramount importance. As time passes, inmates adopt the lifestyle of the prison. However, within the half year prior to release, most inmates begin to demonstrate a renewed appreciation for conventional values.

Different prisons share aspects of a common inmate culture.[15] Prison-wise inmates who enter a new facility far from their home will already know the ropes. **Prison argot**, or jargon, provides one example of how widespread prison subculture can be. The terms used to describe inmate roles in one institution are generally understood in others. The word *rat*, for example, is prison slang for an informer. Popularized by crime movies of the 1950s, the term is also understood today by members of the wider society. Recent research into prison language suggests that argot in prison reflects and reinforces "the organization, language, and status hierarchy of . . . prison subculture."[16] Researchers suggest that correctional administrators and staff must learn the language of prison in order to maximize staff efficiency, and to ensure the safety of staff and inmates.[17] Words common to prison argot are shown in CJ Exhibit 12–1.

prison argot
The slang that is characteristic of prison subculture and prison life.

The Evolution of Prison Subcultures

Prison subcultures change constantly. Like any other American subculture, they evolve to reflect the concerns and experiences of the wider culture, reacting to new crime-control strategies and embracing novel opportunities for crime. The AIDS epidemic of the 1970s and 1980s, for example, brought about changes in prison sexual behavior, at least for a segment of the inmate population. The emergence of a high-tech criminal group has further differentiated convict types. Because of such changes, John Irwin, as he was completing his classic study titled *The Felon* (1970), expressed worry that his book was already obsolete.[18] *The Felon*, for all its insights into prison subcultures, follows in the descriptive tradition of works by Clemmer and Reimer. Irwin recognized that by 1970, prison subcultures had begun to reflect the cultural changes sweeping across America. A decade later, other investigators of prison subcultures were able to write, "It was no longer meaningful to speak of a single inmate culture or even subculture. By the time we began our field research . . . it was clear that the unified, oppositional convict culture, found in the sociological literature on prisons, no longer existed."[19]

The Functions of Prison Subcultures

How do social scientists and criminologists explain the existence of prison subcultures? Although people around the world live in groups and create their own cultures, in few cases does the intensity of human interaction approach the level found in prisons. As we discussed in Chapter 11, many of today's prisons are densely crowded places where inmates can find no retreat from the constant demands of staff and the pressures of fellow prisoners. Prison subcultures, according to some authors, are fundamentally an adaptation to deprivation and confinement. They are a way of addressing the psychological, social, physical, and sexual needs of prisoners living within a highly controlled and regimented institutional setting.

What are some of the deprivations that prisoners experience? In *The Society of Captives*, Sykes called felt deprivations the "pains of imprisonment."[20] The pains of imprisonment—the frustrations induced by the rigors of confinement—form the nexus of a *deprivation model* of prison subculture. Sykes said that prisoners are deprived of (1) liberty, (2) goods and services, (3) heterosexual relationships, (4) autonomy, and (5) personal security. Sykes also stated that these deprivations lead to the development of subcultures intended to ameliorate the personal pains that accompany deprivation.

In contrast to the deprivation model, the *importation model* of prison subculture suggests that inmates bring with them values, roles, and behavior patterns from the outside world. Such external values (second nature to career offenders) depend substantially on the criminal worldview. When offenders are confined, these external elements shape the social world of inmates.

> Prison subcultures, according to some authors, are fundamentally an adaptation to deprivation and confinement.

Follow the author's tweets about the latest crime and justice news @schmalleger

CJ Exhibit 12-1
Prison Argot: The Language of Confinement

Writers who have studied prison life often comment on prisoners' use of a special language or slang called *prison argot*. This language generally describes the roles assigned by prison culture to types of inmates as well as to prison activities. This box lists a few of the many words and phrases identified in studies by different authors. The first group of words is characteristic of men's prisons; the last few words have been used in women's prisons.

MEN'S PRISON SLANG

Ace duce: Best friend

All day: A life sentence

Back door parole: To die in prison

Badge (bull, hack, the man, or screw): Corrections officer

Banger (burner, shank, or sticker): Knife

Billy: White man

Boneyard: Conjugal visiting area

Bug juice: Depressant drugs or intoxicants

Catch a ride: To ask a friend to get you high

Cat-J (J-cat): Prisoner in need of psychological or psychiatric therapy or medication

Cellie: Cellmate

Chester: Child molester

Chin check: Punching another inmate to test him, and to see if he'll fight back

Dancing on the blacktop: Getting stabbed

Dog: Homeboy or friend

Fag: Male inmate who is believed to be a "natural" or "born" homosexual

Featherwood: White prisoner's woman

Fish: Newly arrived inmate

Four-piece suit: A full set of restraints, including handcuffs, leg irons, and waist chains

Gorilla: Inmate who uses force to take what he wants from others

Homeboy: Prisoner from one's hometown or neighborhood

Jackrabbit parole: To escape from prison

Juice card: An inmate's influence with other prisoners or with guards

Ink: Tattoos

Kite: A contraband letter

Lemon squeezer: Inmate who masturbates frequently

Man walking: Phrase used to signal that a guard is coming

Merchant (peddler): One who sells when he should give

Peckerwood (or wood): White prisoner

Punk: Male inmate who is forced into a submissive role during homosexual relations

Rabbit: An inmate who often tries to escape

Rat (snitch): Inmate who squeals (provides information about other inmates to the prison administration)

Stainless steel ride: Death by lethal injection

Road kill: Cigarette butts picked up from the roadsides by prisoners working on a highway

Schooled: Knowledgeable in the ways of prison life

Shakedown: Search of a cell or of a work area

Teddy bear: Nonaggressive wolf

Tree jumper: Rapist

Turn out: To rape or make into a punk

Wolf: Male inmate who assumes the dominant role during homosexual relations

WOMEN'S PRISON SLANG

Cherry (cherrie): Female inmate who has not yet been introduced to lesbian activities

Fay broad: White female inmate

Femme (mommy): Female inmate who plays a submissive role during lesbian relations

Safe: Vagina (especially when used for hiding contraband)

Stud broad (daddy): Female inmate who assumes an aggressive role during lesbian relations

---

References: Gresham Sykes, Matt Soniak, "50 Prison Slang Words to Make you Sound Like a Tough Guy," October 17, 2012; http://mentalfloss.com/article/12794/50-prison-slang-words-make-you-sound-tough-guy (accessed September 12, 2018). *The Society of Captives* (Princeton, NJ: Princeton University Press, 1958); Rose Giallombardo, *Society of Women: A Study of a Woman's Prison* (New York: John Wiley, 1966); and Richard A. Cloward et al., *Theoretical Studies in Social Organization of the Prison* (New York: Social Science Research Council, 1960). For a more contemporary listing of prison slang terms, see Reinhold Aman, *Hillary Clinton's Pen Pal: A Guide to Life and Lingo in Federal Prison* (Santa Rosa, CA: Maledicta Press, 1996); Jerome Washington, *Iron House: Stories from the Yard* (Ann Arbor, MI: QED Press, 1994); Morrie Camhi, *The Prison Experience* (Boston: Charles Tuttle, 1989); and Harold Long, *Survival in Prison* (Port Townsend, WA: Loompanics, 1990).

The social structure of the prison, a concept that refers to accepted and relatively permanent social arrangements, is another element that shapes prison subculture. Clemmer's early prison study recognized nine structural dimensions of inmate society:[21]

1. Prisoner–staff dichotomy
2. Three general classes of prisoners
3. Work gangs and cell-house groups
4. Racial groups

5. Type of offense

6. Power of inmate "politicians"

7. Degree of sexual abnormality

8. Record of repeat offenses

9. Personality differences due to pre-prison socialization

Clemmer's nine structural dimensions are probably still descriptive of prison life today. When applied to individuals, they designate an inmate's position in the prison "pecking order" and create expectations of the appropriate role for that person. Prison roles serve to satisfy the needs of inmates for power, sexual performance, material possessions, individuality, and personal pleasure. They also define the status of one prisoner relative to another. For example, inmate leaders, sometimes referred to as *real men* or *toughs* by prisoners in early studies, offer protection to those who live by the rules. They also provide for a redistribution of wealth inside prison and see to it that the rules of the complex prison-derived economic system—based on barter, gambling, and sexual favors—are observed. For an intimate multimedia portrait of life behind bars, visit **http://www.radiodiaries.org/tag/prison-diaries**.

▲ Transsexual and ex-inmate Diana Acuna Talquenca (R) and prison inmate Osvaldo Martin Torres, shown on the day of their marriage at Almafuerte prison in Argentina. Homosexuality is common in both men's and women's prisons. How does it differ between the two? Why do Talquenca and Torres provide an exception to the "rule" of male prison homosexuality?

STR/AFP/Getty Images

Prison Lifestyles and Inmate Types

Prison society is strict and often unforgiving. Even so, inmates are able to express some individuality through the choice of a prison lifestyle. John Irwin viewed these lifestyles (like the subcultures of which they are a part) as adaptations to the prison environment.[22] Other writers have since elaborated on these coping mechanisms. Listed in the paragraphs that follow are some of the types of prisoners that researchers have described:

- *The mean dude.* Some inmates adjust to prison by being violent, and other inmates know that these prisoners are best left alone. The mean dude is frequently written up and spends much time in solitary confinement. This role is most common in male institutions and in maximum-security prisons. For some prisoners, the role of mean dude in prison is similar to the role they played in their life prior to being incarcerated. Certain personality types, such as the psychopath, may feel a natural attraction to this role. Plus, prison culture supports violence in two ways: (1) by the expectation that inmates should be tough and (2) through the prevalence of the idea that only the strong survive inside prison.

- *The hedonist.* Some inmates build their lives around the limited pleasures available within the confines of prison. The smuggling of contraband, homosexuality, gambling, drug running, and other officially condemned activities provide the center of interest for prison hedonists. Hedonists generally have an abbreviated view of the future, living only for the "now."

- *The opportunist.* The opportunist takes advantage of the positive experiences prison has to offer. Schooling, trade training, counseling, and other self-improvement activities are the focal points of the opportunist's life in prison. Opportunists are generally well liked by prison staff, but other prisoners shun and mistrust them because they come closest to accepting the role that the staff defines as "model prisoner."

- *The retreatist.* Prison life is rigorous and demanding. Badgering by the staff and actual or feared assaults by other inmates may cause some prisoners to attempt psychological retreat from the realities of imprisonment. Such inmates may experience neurotic or psychotic episodes, become heavily involved in drug and alcohol abuse through the illicit prison economy, or even attempt suicide. Depression and mental illness are the hallmarks of the retreatist personality in prison.

🐦 Follow the author's tweets about the latest crime and justice news @schmalleger

- *The legalist.* The legalist is the "jailhouse lawyer." Convicts facing long sentences, with little possibility for early release through the corrections system, are most likely to turn to the courts in their battle against confinement.

- *The radical.* Radical inmates view themselves as political prisoners. They see society and the successful conformists who populate it as oppressors who have forced criminality on many "good people" through the creation of a system that distributes wealth and power inequitably. The inmate who takes on the radical role is unlikely to receive much sympathy from prison staff.

- *The colonizer.* Some inmates think of prison as their home and don't look forward to leaving. They "know the ropes," have many friends inside, and may feel more comfortable institutionalized than on the streets, and they typically hold positions with power or respect among the inmate population. Once released, some colonizers commit new crimes to return to prison.

- *The religious.* Some prisoners profess a strong religious faith. They may be "born-again" Christians, committed Muslims, or even Satanists or witches. Religious inmates frequently attend services, may form prayer groups, and sometimes ask the prison administration to allocate meeting facilities or to create special diets to accommodate their claimed spiritual needs. Although it is certainly true that some inmates have a strong religious faith, staff members are apt to be suspicious of the overly religious prisoner.

- *The gangbanger.* Gangbangers are affiliated with prison gangs and depend upon the gang for defense and protection. They display gang signs, sport gang-related tattoos, and use their gang membership as a channel for the procurement of desired goods and services both inside and outside prison.

- *The realist.* The realist sees confinement as a natural consequence of criminal activity and time spent in prison as an unfortunate cost of doing business. This stoic attitude toward incarceration generally leads the realist to "pull his (or her) own time" and to make the best of it. Realists tend to know the inmate code, are able to avoid trouble, and continue in lives of crime once released.

Homosexuality and Sexual Victimization in Prison

Sexual behavior inside prisons is both constrained and encouraged by prison subculture. Sykes's early study of prison argot found many words describing sexual activity, and quite a few of them related to homosexuality. Included here are the terms *wolf*, *punk*, and *fag*. Wolves are aggressive men in homosexual relations, punks are forced into a submissive role, and fag describes a special category of men who have a natural proclivity toward homosexual activity and effeminate mannerisms. Whereas both wolves and punks are fiercely committed to their heterosexual identity and participate in homosexuality only because of prison conditions, fags generally engage in homosexual lifestyles before their entry into prison and continue to do so once incarcerated.

Prison homosexuality depends to a considerable degree on the naïveté of young inmates experiencing prison for the first time. Even when newly arrived inmates are protected from fights, older prisoners looking for homosexual liaisons may ingratiate themselves by offering cigarettes, money, drugs, food, or protection. At some future time, these "loans" will be called in, with payoffs demanded in sexual favors. Because the inmate code requires the repayment of favors, the "fish" who tries to resist may quickly find himself face-to-face with the brute force of inmate society.

Prison rape, which is generally considered to involve physical assault, represents a special category of sexual victimization behind bars. In 2003, Congress mandated the collection of statistics on prison rape as part of the Prison Rape Elimination Act (PREA).[23] PREA requires the Bureau of Justice Statistics (BJS), under the direction of the National Prison Rape Elimination Commission, to collect sexual victimization data in federal and state prisons, county and city jails, and juvenile institutions. The U.S. Census Bureau acts as the official repository for collected data.

Findings from BJS published reports on sexual victimization in correctional facilities show the following:[24]

- Around 25,000 allegations of sexual victimizations are reported in our nation's prisons annually.

- The number of allegations has risen significantly since 2005, largely due to increases in the number of people held in confinement.

- Only about 8% of reported sexual victimizatioins were substantiated (i.e., determined to have occurred upon investigation).

- About 58% of substantiated incidents of sexual victimization involved only inmates, while 42% of substantiated incidents involved staff with inmates.

- Injuries were reported in about 18% of incidents of inmate-on-inmate sexual victimization and in less than 1% of incidents of staff sexual victimizations.

- Females committed more than half of all substantiated incidents of staff sexual misconduct and a quarter of all incidents of staff sexual harassment.

- An estimated 1.8% of juveniles ages 16 to 17 held in adult prisons and jails reported being victimized by another inmate, compared to 2.0% of adults in prisons and 1.6% of adults in jails; an estimated 3.2% of juveniles ages 16 to 17 held in adult prisons and jails reported experiencing staff sexual misconduct.

- Inmates who reported their sexual orientation as gay, lesbian, bisexual, or other were among those with the highest rates of sexual victimization. Among nonheterosexual inmates, 12.2% of prisoners and 8.5% of jail inmates reported being sexually victimized by another inmate; 5.4% of prisoners and 4.3% of jail inmates reported being victimized by staff.

PREA surveys are only the first step in understanding and eliminating rape. As BJS notes, "Due to fear of reprisal from perpetrators, a code of silence among inmates, personal embarrassment, and lack of trust in staff, victims are often reluctant to report incidents to corrections authorities."[25] Learn more about the PREA and read new survey results as they become available via **https://nicic.gov/search/node/prea**.

Humbolt State University sociologist Lee H. Bowker, reviewing studies of sexual violence in prison, provides the following summary observations:[26]

- Most sexual aggressors do not consider themselves homosexuals.
- Sexual release is not the primary motivation for sexual attack.
- Many aggressors must continue to participate in gang rapes to avoid becoming victims themselves.
- The aggressors themselves have suffered much damage to their masculinity in the past.

As in cases of heterosexual rape, sexual assaults in prison are likely to leave psychological scars on the victims long after the physical event is over.[27] Victims of prison rape live in fear, may feel constantly threatened, and may turn to self-destructive activities.[28] Many victims question their masculinity and undergo a personal devaluation. Some victims of prison sexual assault become violent, attacking and sometimes killing the person who raped them. The Human Rights Watch researchers found that prisoners "fitting any part of the following description" are more likely to become rape victims: "young, small in size, physically weak, white, gay, first offender, possessing 'feminine' characteristics such as long hair or a high voice; being unassertive, unaggressive, shy, intellectual, not street-smart, or 'passive'; or having been convicted of a sexual offense against a minor." The researchers also noted that "prisoners with several overlapping characteristics are much more likely than other prisoners to be targeted for abuse." The report concluded that to reduce the incidence of prison rape, "prison officials should take considerably more care in matching cell mates, and that, as a general rule, double-celling should be avoided."

The Female Inmate's World

As Chapter 11 showed, more than 105,683 women were imprisoned in state and federal correctional institutions throughout the United States at the start of 2017, accounting for about 7% of all prison inmates.[29] Although there are still far more men imprisoned across the nation than women (approximately 15 men for every woman), the number of female inmates is rising.[30] In 1981, women made up only 4% of the nation's overall prison population, but the number of female inmates nearly tripled during the 1980s and is continuing to grow at a rate greater than that of male inmates. In fact, the rate of growth for female imprisonment has outpaced men by more than 50% between 1980 and 2016 (Figure 12–1).

Follow the author's tweets about the latest crime and justice news @schmalleger

3 Summarize the problems that female inmates face in prisons and the different ways of accommodating female prisoners.

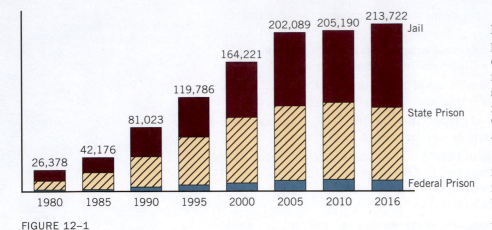

FIGURE 12–1
The Increase in Women's Incarceration

Source: Historical Corrections Statistics in the United States, 1850–1984; Prison and Jail Inmates (Washington, D.C.: Bureau of Justice Statistics, 1986); and *Prisoners in 2016* (Washington, D.C.: Bureau of Justice Statistics, 2018).

A little over 10 years ago, the National Institute of Corrections (NIC) published the results of its 3-year project on female offenders in adult correctional settings.[31] Findings from the study produced a national profile of incarcerated women that is shown in Table 12-1. Figures 12–2 and 12–3 provide additional details.

The NIC says that "women involved in the criminal justice system represent a population marginalized by race, class, and gender."[32] African-American women, for example, are overrepresented in correctional populations. White women comprise 50% of the nation's female prison population compared to 21% for black females. However, the imprisonment rate for black females (96 per 100,000) is twice the rate of white females (49 per 100,000).[33]

According to the NIC, women face life circumstances that tend to be specific to their gender, such as sexual abuse, sexual assault, and domestic violence, as well as the responsibility of being the primary caregiver for dependent children. Research shows that female offenders differ significantly from their male counterparts regarding personal histories and pathways to crime.[34] A female offender, for example, is more likely than a male offender to have been the primary caregiver of young children at the time of her arrest, more likely to have experienced physical and/or sexual abuse, and more likely to have distinctive physical and mental health needs. Women's most common pathways to crime, said the NIC, involve survival strategies that result from physical and sexual abuse, poverty, and substance abuse (Figure 12–4).

Sexual Victimization of Women Prisoners

Unfortunately, the sexual victimization of women offenders does not always end with their admission to prison. A recent U.S. Department of Justice report, for example, found "rampant sexual abuse" at Alabama's Julia Tutwiler Prison for Women. According to DOJ findings, the nearly 900 women held at the facility in the small town of Wetumpka live "in a toxic environment with repeated and open sexual behavior," and that inmates at the prison have been routinely raped, sodomized, and fondled by prison staff. Investigators

🐦 Follow the author's tweets about the latest crime and justice news @schmalleger

TABLE 12-1
National Profile of Female Offenders

A profile based on national data for female offenders reveals the following characteristics:

• Disproportionately women of color

• In their early to middle 30s

• Most likely to have been convicted of a drug-related offense

• From fragmented families that include other family members who also have been involved with the criminal justice system

• Survivors of physical and/or sexual abuse as children and adults

• Individuals with significant substance-abuse problems

• Individuals with multiple physical and mental health problems

• Unmarried mothers of minor children

• Individuals with a high school or general equivalency diploma (GED) but limited vocational training and sporadic work histories

Source: "Gender-Responsive Strategies: Research, Practice, and Guiding Principles for Women Offenders, National Institute of Corrections" by Barbara Bloom; Barbara Owen; Stephanie Covington, Bureau of Justice Statistics.

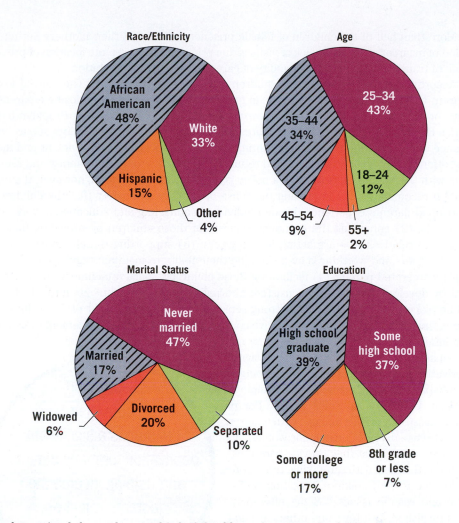

Race/Ethnicity

African American 48%
White 33%
Hispanic 15%
Other 4%

Age

25–34 43%
35–44 34%
18–24 12%
45–54 9%
55+ 2%

Marital Status

Never married 47%
Married 17%
Widowed 6%
Divorced 20%
Separated 10%

Education

High school graduate 39%
Some high school 37%
Some college or more 17%
8th grade or less 7%

FIGURE 12–2
Women State Prison Inmates: Features and Characteristics
Source: Data from Bureau of Justice Statistics.

also determined that at least a third of the 99 employees at the facility have had sex with prisoners and, in a harshly worded condemnation, concluded that "the state of Alabama violates the Eighth Amendment of the United States Constitution by failing to protect women prisoners at Tutwiler [Prison] from harm due to sexual abuse and harassment from correctional staff."

Parents in Prison

Eighty percent of women entering prison are mothers, and 85% of those women had custody of their children at the time of admission.[35] Approximately 70% of all women under correctional supervision have at least one child younger than age 18. Two-thirds of incarcerated women have minor children; about two-thirds of women in state prisons and half of women in federal prisons had lived with their young children before entering prison. One out of four women entering prison either has recently given birth or is pregnant. Pregnant inmates, many of whom are drug users, malnourished, or sick, often receive little prenatal care, a situation that risks additional complications.

More than 1.7 million American children have a parent in prison.[36] The number of mothers who are incarcerated has more than doubled in the past 15 years, from 29,500 in 1991 to over 70,000 today. Statistically speaking, 1 out of every 43 American children has a parent in prison today, and ethnic variation in the numbers is striking. Whereas only 1 out of every 111 white children has experienced the imprisonment of a parent, 1 out of every 15 black children has had that experience.

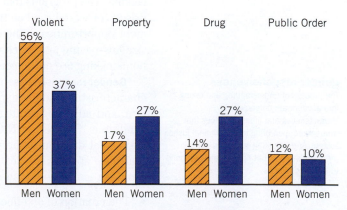

Violent — Men 56%, Women 37%
Property — Men 17%, Women 27%
Drug — Men 14%, Women 27%
Public Order — Men 12%, Women 10%

FIGURE 12–3
Offenses Committed by Men and Women in State Prisons

Source: E. Ann Carson, *Prisoners in 2016,* Bureau of Justice Statistics.

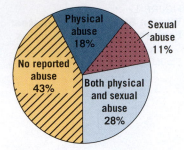

FIGURE 12–4
Women State Prison Inmates: Physical and Sexual Abuse History

Source: Lawrence A. Greenfeld and Tracy L. Snell, *Women Offenders, 2000,* Bureau of Justice Statistics.

More than half of the children of female prisoners never visit their mothers during the period of incarceration.[37] The lack of visits is due primarily to the remote location of prisons, a lack of transportation, and the inability of caregivers to arrange visitation.

According to one report on the children of incarcerated parents, "The pain of losing a parent to a prison sentence matches, in many respects, the trauma of losing a parent to death or divorce."[38] That report, *Children on the Outside,* prepared by Brooklyn-based Justice Strategies, recommends that states reduce what the report's authors see as over-reliance on incarceration as a crime-fighting strategy—especially for nonviolent and many drug offenders. Such a reduction would return many parents to the community and reunite them with their children. Until such a policy is more fully implemented, however, the organization recommends (1) improving the sense of stability and safety that the children of imprisoned parents experience through individual counseling and educational workshops in schools; (2) enhancing the economic security of those children by providing financial support to relatives who are acting as caregivers; (3) supporting the children's sense of connectedness and worthiness by facilitating their ability to maintain regular contact with their incarcerated parent; (4) facilitating those children's social attachment and ability to trust by developing stable and consistent alternative home environments into which they can be placed; and (5) fostering a strong sense of having an important place in the world among those children through supportive counseling, and prioritized placement of children with family members.

Separation from their children is a significant deprivation for many parents, and helping incarcerated parents is just as important as helping their children. Consequently, some states offer parenting classes for female inmates with children. In a national survey of prisons for women, 36 states responded that they provide parenting programs that deal with caretaking, reduction of violence toward children, visitation problems, and related issues.[39] Some offer play areas furnished with toys, and others attempt to alleviate difficulties attending mother–child visits. The typical program studied meets for 2 hours per week and lasts from 4 to 9 weeks.

> Separation from their children is a significant deprivation for many parents, and helping incarcerated parents is just as important as helping their children.

Gender-Responsiveness

Critics have long charged that female inmates face a prison system designed for male inmates and run by men. Consequently, meaningful prison programs for women are often lacking. The programs that are in place were originally based on models adapted from men's prisons or were based on traditional views of female roles that leave little room for employment opportunities in the contemporary world. Many trade-training programs still emphasize low-paying jobs, such as cook, beautician, or laundry machine operator, and classes in homemaking are not uncommon.

Gender-responsiveness means "understanding and taking account of the differences in characteristics and life experiences that women and men bring to the criminal justice system, and adjusting strategies and practices in ways that appropriately respond to those conditions."[40] A recent NIC report concluded with a call for recognition of the behavioral and social differences between female and male offenders—especially those differences that have specific implications for gender-responsive policies and practices.[41] Among the report's recommendations are the following:

- The creation of an effective system for female offenders that is structured differently from a system for male offenders

- The development of gender-responsive policies and practices targeting women's pathways to criminality in order to provide effective interventions that address the intersecting issues of substance abuse, trauma, mental health, and economic marginality

gender-responsiveness
The process of understanding and taking into account the differences in characteristics and life experiences that women and men bring to the criminal justice system, and adjusting strategies and practices in ways that appropriately respond to those conditions.

🐦 Follow the author's tweets about the latest crime and justice news @schmalleger

- The modification of criminal justice sanctions and interventions to recognize the low risk to public safety represented by the typical female offender

- The consideration of women's relationships, especially those with their children, and women's roles in the community in deciding appropriate correctional sanctions

The NIC study concluded that gender-responsive correctional practices can improve outcomes for female offenders by considering their histories, behaviors, and life circumstances. It also suggested that investments in gender-responsive policies and procedures will likely produce long-term dividends for the criminal justice system and the community as well as for female offenders and their families.

One example of gender-responsiveness can be found in a new program currently in operation at the Decatur (Illinois) Correctional Center. The program allows newborn infants to live with their mothers in a special wing called the Mom and Babies Unit, where each mother has her own room and access to large, brightly colored dayrooms decorated with painted murals. The dayrooms are equipped with toys and children's books, and lead to outdoor patios that provide additional play space for the children. The wing looks much like a typical day-care center. The Decatur program is designed to facilitate the needs of women who are likely to be released by the time their children reach 2 years of age. The success of the program, which has been in operation for a few years, can be measured in reduced recidivism. "Of the 25 offenders that have gone through this program none . . . have returned to . . . prison," says Michael Randle, director of the Illinois Department of Corrections.[42] Similarly, the Federal Bureau of Prisons operate the Mothers and Infants Together program, which allows eligible women to live in a community correctional setting with their infants for up to 18 months after giving birth.[43] Learn more about gender-responsiveness from the Center for Gender and Justice at **http://www.centerforgenderandjustice.org** and the National Resource Center on Justice Involved Women at **http://cjinvolvedwomen.org**.

▲ Colette Peters, director of Oregon's Department of Corrections. Appointed in 2012, she is the department's first female head. Do you believe that the appointment of women to higher-level positions in corrections will increase gender-responsiveness throughout the system?

Colette Peters

Institutions for Women

Most female inmates are housed in centralized state facilities that are dedicated exclusively to incarcerating female felons. Although there is not a typical women's prison, the American Correctional Association (ACA) 1990 report by the Task Force on the Female Offender found that the institutions that house female inmates could be generally described as follows:[44]

- Most prisons for women are located in towns with fewer than 25,000 inhabitants.

- A significant number of facilities were not designed to house female inmates.

- Some facilities that house female inmates also house men.

- Few facilities for women have programs especially designed for female offenders.

- Few major disturbances or escapes are reported among female inmates.

- Substance abuse among female inmates is very high.

- Few work assignments are available to female inmates.

Social Structure in Women's Prisons

"Aside from sharing the experience of being incarcerated," says Professor Marsha Clowers of the John Jay College of Criminal Justice, "female prisoners have much in common. They are likely to be black or Hispanic, poor, uneducated, abuse survivors, single parents, and in poor health."[45] Shared social characteristics may lead to similar values and behaviors. One type of behavior identified by early prison researchers as characteristic of a fair number of incarcerated women concerns the way in which female inmates construct organized pseudofamilies. Typical of such studies are D. Ward and G. Kassebaum's *Women's Prison: Sex and Social Structure*

Multiculturalism and Diversity
The Bangkok Rules on the Treatment of Female Prisoners

In December 2010, the United Nations General Assembly formally adopted the *Rules for the Treatment of Female Prisoners and Non-Custodial Measures for Women Offenders*, commonly known as the Bangkok Rules. The Rules, which were approved by the unanimous vote of all 193 member nations, address the special needs that women prisoners have, and are the first international standards to address the needs of the children of confined mothers. Many of the rules also concern women's special roles as mothers.

Although the Rules do not carry the weight of law in the United States, they reflect a world consensus concerning the treatment of incarcerated women, and any imprisonment policies or practices that are in conflict with them are likely to be challenged on the grounds that they violate human rights. The 70 rules that comprise the UN resolution are too numerous to list here in their entirety, but some of the most important are provided here in abbreviated form:

- Prior to or on admission, women with caretaking responsibilities for children shall be permitted to make arrangements for those children, including the possibility of a reasonable suspension of detention, taking into account the best interests of the children.
- Women prisoners shall be allocated, to the extent possible, to prisons close to their home or place of social rehabilitation, taking account of their caretaking responsibilities, as well as the individual woman's preference and the availability of appropriate programs and services.
- Gender-specific health-care services at least equivalent to those available in the community shall be provided to women prisoners.
- If the existence of sexual abuse or other forms of violence before or during detention is diagnosed, the woman prisoner shall be [fully] informed of her right to seek recourse from judicial authorities.
- Noncustodial sentences for pregnant women and women with dependent children shall be preferred where possible and appropriate, with custodial sentences being considered when the offence is serious or violent or the woman represents a continuing danger, and after taking into account the best interests of the child or children, while ensuring that appropriate provision has been made for the care of such children.
- Instruments of restraint shall never be used on women during labor, during birth, and immediately after birth.

- Particular efforts shall be made to provide appropriate programs for pregnant women, nursing mothers, and women with children in prison.
- Women prisoners shall not be discouraged from breastfeeding their children, unless there are specific health reasons to do so.
- Decisions to allow children to stay with their mothers in prison shall be based on the best interests of the children. Children in prison with their mothers shall never be treated as prisoners.
- Women prisoners whose children are in prison with them shall be provided with the maximum possible opportunities to spend time with their children.
- The environment provided for such children's upbringing shall be as close as possible to that of a child outside prison.
- Effective measures shall be taken to ensure that women prisoners' dignity and respect are protected during personal searches, which shall only be carried out by women staff who have been properly trained in appropriate searching methods and in accordance with established procedures.

United Nations officials note that the Bangkok Rules "do not in any way replace the Standard Minimum Rules for the Treatment of Prisoners or the Tokyo Rules and, therefore, all relevant provisions contained in those two sets of rules continue to apply to all prisoners and offenders without discrimination." The Tokyo Rules (adopted in 1990) are officially known as the United Nations Standard Minimum Rules for Non-custodial Measures, and focus on alternatives to imprisonment, including staff training, diversion, treatment, linkages with relevant agencies and the use of volunteers.

The Bangkok Rules can be read online in their entirety at **http://www.un.org/en/ecosoc/docs/2010/res%202010-16.pdf**. The United Nations Standard Minimum Rules for the Treatment of Prisoners can be found at **http://www.uncjin.org/Standards/UNRules.pdf**; and the United Nations Standard Minimum Rules for Non-Custodial Measures can be accessed at **http://www.un.org/documents/ga/res/45/a45r110.htm**.

References: Myrna Raeder, *Pregnancy- and Child-Related Legal and Policy Issues Concerning Justice-Involved Women* (Washington, D.C.: National Institute of Corrections, December 2013); United Nations General Assembly, *Rules for the Treatment of Female Prisoners and Non-Custodial Measures for Women Offenders.*

(1966),[46] Esther Heffernan's *Making It in Prison: The Square, the Cool, and the Life* (1972),[47] and Rose Giallombardo's *Society of Women: A Study of Women's Prisons* (1966).[48]

Giallombardo, for example, examined the Federal Reformatory for Women at Alderson, West Virginia, spending a year gathering data in the early 1960s. Focusing closely on the social formation of families among female inmates, she titled one of her chapters "The Homosexual Alliance as a Marriage Unit." In it, she described in great detail the sexual identities assumed by women at Alderson and the symbols they chose to communicate those roles. Hairstyle, dress, language, and mannerisms were all used to signify "maleness" or "femaleness." Giallombardo detailed "the anatomy of the marriage relationship from courtship to 'fall out,' that is, from inception to the parting of the ways, or divorce."[49] Romantic love at Alderson was of central importance to any relationship between inmates, and all homosexual relationships were described as voluntary. Through marriage, the "stud broad" became the husband and the "femme" the wife.

Studies attempting to document the extent of inmate involvement in prison "families" have produced varying results. Some have found as many as 71% of female prisoners involved in the phenomenon, whereas others have found none.[50] The kinship systems described by Giallombardo and others, however, extend beyond simple "family" ties to the formation of large, intricately related groups involving a large number of nonsexual relationships. In these groups, the roles of "children," "in-laws," "grandparents," and so on may be explicitly recognized. Even "birth order" within a family can become an issue for kinship groups.[51] Kinship groups sometimes occupy a common household, usually a prison cottage or a dormitory area. The descriptions of women's prisons provided by authors, such as Giallombardo, show a closed society in which social interactions—including expectations, normative forms of behavior, and emotional ties—are regulated by an inventive system of artificial relationships that mirror those of the outside world.

Many studies of female prisoners show that incarcerated women suffer intensely from the loss of affectional relationships once they enter prison and that they form homosexual liaisons to compensate for such losses.[52] Those liaisons then become the foundation of prison social organization.

Barbara Owen, professor of Criminology at California State University, Fresno, conducted a study of female inmates at the Central California Women's Facility (the largest prison for women in the world). Her book, *In the Mix: Struggle and Survival in a Women's Prison,*[53] describes the daily life of female inmates, with an emphasis on prison social structure. Owen found that prison culture for women is tied directly to the roles that women normally assume in free society as well as to other factors shaped by the conditions of women's lives in prison and in the free world. *In the Mix* describes the lives of women before prison and suggests that those lifestyles shape women's adaptation to prison culture. Owen found that preexisting economic marginalization, self-destructive behaviors, and personal histories of physical, sexual, and substance abuse may be important defining features of inmates' lives before they enter prison.[54] She also discovered that the sentences that women have to serve, along with their work and housing assignments, effectively pattern their daily lives and relationships. Owen described "the mix" as that aspect of prison culture that supports the rule-breaking behavior that propels women into crime and causes them to enter prison. Owen concluded that prison subcultures for women are very different from the violent and predatory structure of contemporary male prisons.[55] Like men, women experience "pains of imprisonment," but their prison culture offers them other ways to survive and adapt to these deprivations.

A study of a women's correctional facility in the southeastern United States found that female inmates who were asked about their preincarceration sexual orientation gave answers that were quite different than when they were asked about their sexual orientation while incarcerated.[56] In general, 64% of inmates interviewed reported being exclusively heterosexual, 28% said they were bisexual, and 8% said that they were lesbians before being incarcerated. In contrast, these same women reported sexual orientations while incarcerated of 55% heterosexual, 31% bisexual, and 13% lesbian. Researchers found that same-sex sexual behavior within the institution was more likely to occur in the lives of young inmates who had such experiences before entering prison. The study also found that female inmates tended to become more involved in lesbian behavior the longer they were incarcerated. However, PREA statistics, which were discussed in greater detail earlier in this chapter, show that the rate of inmate-on-inmate sexual victimization is at least three times higher for females (14%) than it is for males (4%).[57]

Finally, a significant aspect of sexual activity far more commonly found in women's prisons than in prisons for men involves sexual misconduct between staff and inmates. "Allowing male guards to oversee female prisoners is a recipe for trouble," says former California state prison inmate Laura Whitehorn.[58] Although a fair amount of such behavior is attributed to the exploitation of female inmates by male corrections officers acting from positions of power, some studies suggest that female inmates may sometimes attempt to manipulate unsuspecting male officers into illicit relationships in order to gain favors.[59]

▲ A female inmate in a segregation unit. The rate of female imprisonment has grown faster than that of men. Why?

Sirtravelalot/Shutterstock

The person of a prisoner sentenced to imprisonment in the State prison is under the protection of the law, and any injury to his person, not authorized by law, is punishable in the same manner as if he were not convicted or sentenced.

—California Penal Code, Section 2650

🐦 Follow the author's tweets about the latest crime and justice news @schmalleger

Types of Female Inmates

As in institutions for men, the subculture of women's prisons is multidimensional. Esther Heffernan, for example, found that three terms used by the female prisoners she studied—the *square*, the *cool*, and the *life*—were indicative of three styles of adaptation to prison life.[60] Square inmates had few early experiences with criminal lifestyles and tended to sympathize with the values and attitudes of conventional society. Cool prisoners were more likely to be career offenders. They tended to keep to themselves and generally supported inmate values. Women who participated in the life subculture were quite familiar with lives of crime. Many had been arrested repeatedly for prostitution, drug use, theft, and so on. They were full participants in the economic, social, and familial arrangements of the prison. Heffernan believed that the life option offered an alternative lifestyle to women who had experienced early and constant rejection by conventional society. With the life characteristics, women could establish relationships, achieve status, and find meaning in their lives. The square, the cool, and the life represented subcultures to Heffernan because individuals with similar adaptive choices tended to relate closely to one another and to support the lifestyle characteristic of that type.

The social structure of women's prisons was altered about 20 years ago by the influx of cocaine-addicted "crack kids," as they were called in prison argot. Crack kids, whose existence highlighted generational differences among female offenders, were streetwise young women with little respect for traditional prison values, for their elders, or even for their own children. They are known for frequent fights and for their lack of even simple domestic skills. Many older inmates, some of whom call the younger inmates "animalescents," quickly separate themselves from these young women.

Violence in Women's Prisons

Some authors have suggested that violence in women's prisons is less frequent than it is in institutions for men. Lee Bowker observes that "except for the behavior of a few 'guerrillas,' it appears that violence is only used in women's prisons to settle questions of dominance and subordination when other manipulative strategies fail to achieve the desired effect."[61] It appears that few lesbian liaisons are forced, perhaps representing a general aversion among women to such victimization in wider society. At least one study, however, has shown the use of sexual violence in women's prisons as a form of revenge against inmates who are overly vocal in their condemnation of lesbian practices among other prisoners.[62]

To address the problems of imprisoned women, including violence, the Task Force on the Female Offender recommended a number of changes in the administration of prisons for women:[63]

▲ A correctional officer oversees the segregation unit for violent prisoners at a California facility. The job of a corrections officer centers largely on the custody and control of inmates, but growing professionalism is enhancing both personal opportunities and job satisfaction among officers. Why is professionalism important to job satisfaction?

Marmaduke St. John/Alamy Stock Photo

- Substance-abuse programs should be available to female inmates.
- Female inmates need to acquire greater literacy skills, and literacy programs should form the basis on which other programs are built.
- offenders should be housed in buildings without male inmates.
- Institutions for women should develop programs for keeping children in the facility in order to "fortify the bond between mother and child."
- To ensure equal access to assistance, institutions should be built to accommodate programs for female offenders.

Finally, at a 2010 meeting of the United Nations General Assembly in New York City, the international body adopted the "United Nations Rules for the Treatment of Women Prisoners and Non-custodial Measures for Women Offenders"—more commonly known as "the Bangkok Rules."[64] Although the Bangkok Rules are not directly enforceable in the United

States, they reflect a world consensus concerning treatment of women prisoners and their children. Hence, any U.S. practices or policies that are in conflict with them can be challenged in the international arena on the grounds that they violate the human rights of female inmates. The rules require officials to keep in mind the best interests of dependent children, the needs of pregnant and breastfeeding mothers, personal hygiene for women prisoners, and gender-specific health-care services, gender-sensitive risk assessment and classification of prisoners. The Bangkok rules are available on the Web at **http://www.ihra. net/files/2010/11/04/english.pdf**. Their relevance to American corrections is further explained in a National Institute of Corrections publication, *Pregnancy- and Child-Related Legal and Policy Issues Concerning Justice-Involved Women*, available at **https://www. justicestudies.com/pubs/pregnancy.pdf**.

The Staff World

Facts and Figures

The flip side of inmate society can be found in the world of the prison staff, which includes many people working in various professions. Staff roles encompass those of warden, psychologist, counselor, area supervisor, program director, instructor, corrections officer, and—in some large prisons—physician and therapist.

> **4** Describe prison life from a corrections officer's point of view.

According to the federal government, approximately 785,000 people are employed in corrections, and almost half a million are correctional officers.[65] Correctional officers perform direct custodial tasks in state institutions: 61% of corrections employees work for state governments, followed by 35% at the local level and 5% at the federal level.[66] On a per capita basis, the District of Columbia has the most state and local corrections employees (53.3 per every 10,000 residents), followed by Texas (43.8).[67] Across the nation, 70% of corrections officers are Caucasian, 22% are African American, and slightly over 5% are Hispanic.[68] Women account for 20% of all corrections officers, with the proportion of female officers increasing at around 19% per year. The ACA encourages correctional agencies to "ensure that recruitment, selection, and promotion opportunities are open to women."[69]

Corrections officers, generally considered to be at the bottom of the staff hierarchy, may be divided into cell-block guards and tower guards. Others are assigned to administrative offices, where they perform clerical tasks. The ratio averages around four inmates for each corrections officer in state prisons.[70]

Like prisoners, corrections officers undergo a socialization process that helps them function by the official and unofficial rules of staff society. In a now-classic study, Lucien X. Lombardo described the process by which officers are socialized into the prison work world.[71] Lombardo interviewed 359 corrections personnel at New York's Auburn Prison and found that rookie officers quickly had to abandon preconceptions of both inmates and other staff members. According to Lombardo, new officers learn that inmates are not the "monsters" much of the public makes them out to be. On the other hand, rookies may be seriously disappointed in their experienced colleagues when they realize that the ideals of professionalism, often emphasized during early training, rarely translate into reality. The pressures of the institutional work environment, however, soon force most corrections personnel to adopt a united front when relating to inmates.

One of the leading formative influences on staff culture is the potential threat that inmates pose. Inmates far outnumber corrections personnel in every institution, and the hostility they feel for guards is only barely hidden even at the best of times. Corrections personnel know that however friendly inmates may appear, a sudden change in institutional climate—as can happen with anything from simple disturbances in the yard to full-blown riots—can quickly and violently unmask deep-rooted feelings of mistrust and hatred.

As in years past, prison staffers are still most concerned with custody and control. Society, especially under the just deserts philosophy of criminal sentencing, expects corrections staff to keep inmates in custody—the basic prerequisite of successful job performance. Custody is necessary before any other correctional activities, such as instruction or counseling, can be undertaken. Control, the other major staff concern, ensures order, and an orderly prison is thought to be safe and secure. In routine daily activities, control over almost all aspects of inmate behavior becomes paramount in the minds of most corrections officers. It is the twin interests of custody and control that lead to institutionalized procedures for ensuring security in most facilities. The enforcement of strict rules; body and cell searches; counts; unannounced shakedowns; the control of dangerous items, materials, and contraband; and the extensive use of bars, locks, fencing, cameras, and alarms all support the staff's vigilance in maintaining security.

The Professionalization of Corrections Officers

Corrections officers have generally been accorded low occupational status. Historically, the role of prison guard required minimal formal education and held few opportunities for professional growth and career advancement. The job was typically low paying, frustrating, and often boring. Growing problems in our nation's prisons, including emerging issues of legal liability, however, increasingly require a well-trained and adequately equipped force of professionals. As corrections personnel have become better trained and more proficient, the old concept of guard has been supplanted by that of corrections officer. The ACA has published a code of ethics for corrections officers that is reproduced in the Ethics and Professionalism box (American Correctional Association Code of Ethics) in this chapter.

Many states and a growing number of large-city correctional systems try to eliminate individuals with potentially harmful personality characteristics from corrections officer applicant pools. New Jersey, New York, Ohio, Pennsylvania, and Rhode Island, for example, all use some form of psychological screening when assessing candidates for prison jobs.[72]

Although only some states utilize psychological screening, all make use of training programs intended to prepare successful applicants for prison work. New York, for example, requires trainees to complete 6 weeks of classroom-based instruction, 40 hours of rifle range practice, and 6 weeks of on-the-job training. Training days begin around 5 a.m. with a mile run and conclude after dark with study halls for students who need extra help. To keep pace with rising inmate populations, the state has often had to run a number of simultaneous training academies.[73] Anyone interested in working in the field of corrections should visit the Website Discover Corrections. Funded by the Bureau of Justice Assistance, an arm of the U.S. Department of Justice, the site can be reached at **http://www.discovercorrections.com**.

Security Threat Groups and Prison Riots

In 2015, a riot broke out at the Willacy Detention Center, operated by the Bureau of Immigration and Customs Enforcement.[74] By the time the riot had ended, the facility had been destroyed. It was closed and 2,800 Bureau of Prison inmates were transferred to other facilities. The Willacy riot was followed by a smaller disturbance involving around 100 inmates at the California State Prison, Sacramento. One inmate died and another five were hospitalized with stab wounds.

| 5 | Describe the nature of security threat groups and describe riots in American prisons. |

While American prisons are relatively calm today, the 10 years between 1970 and 1980 were called the "explosive decade" of prison riots.[75] The decade began with a massive uprising at Attica Prison in New York State in September 1971, which resulted in 43 deaths and left more than 80 men wounded. The "explosive decade" ended in 1980 at Santa Fe, New Mexico. There, in a riot at the New Mexico Penitentiary, 33 inmates died, the victims of vengeful prisoners out to eliminate rats and informants. Many of the deaths involved mutilation and torture, more than 200 other inmates were beaten and sexually assaulted, and the prison was virtually destroyed.

Although the number of prison riots decreased after the 1970s, they did continue. For 11 days in 1987, the Atlanta (Georgia) Federal Penitentiary was under the control of inmates. The institution was heavily damaged, and inmates had to be temporarily relocated while it was rebuilt. The Atlanta riot followed on the heels of a similar, but less intense, disturbance at the federal detention center at Oakdale, Louisiana. Both outbreaks were attributed to the dissatisfaction of Cuban inmates, most of whom had arrived in the mass exodus known as the Mariel boat lift.[76]

Easter Sunday 1993 marked the beginning of an 11-day rebellion at the 1,800-inmate Southern Ohio Correctional Facility in Lucasville, one of the country's toughest maximum-security prisons. When the riot ended, nine inmates and one corrections officer were dead. (The officer had been hanged.) The close of the riot—involving a parade of 450 inmates—was

Ethics and Professionalism
American Correctional Association Code of Ethics

PREAMBLE

The American Correctional Association expects of its members unfailing honesty, respect for the dignity and individuality of human beings and a commitment to professional and compassionate service. To this end, we subscribe to the following principles:

- Members shall respect and protect the civil and legal rights of all individuals.
- Members shall treat every professional situation with concern for the welfare of the individuals involved and with no intent [of] personal gain.
- Members shall maintain relationships with colleagues to promote mutual respect within the profession and improve the quality of service.
- Members shall make public criticisms of their colleagues or their agencies only when warranted, verifiable, and constructive.
- Members shall respect the importance of all disciplines within the criminal justice system and work to improve cooperation with each segment.
- Members shall honor the public's right to information and share information with the public to the extent permitted by law subject to individuals' right to privacy.
- Members shall respect and protect the right of the public to be safeguarded from criminal activity.
- Members shall refrain from using their positions to secure personal privileges or advantages.
- Members shall refrain from allowing personal interest to impair objectivity in the performance of duty while acting in an official capacity.
- Members shall refrain from entering into any formal or informal activity or agreement which presents a conflict of interest or is inconsistent with the conscientious performance of duties.
- Members shall refrain from accepting any gift, service, or favor that is or appears to be improper or implies an obligation inconsistent with the free and objective exercise of professional duties.

- Members shall clearly differentiate between personal views/statements and views/statements/positions made on behalf of the agency or association.
- Members shall report to appropriate authorities any corrupt or unethical behaviors in which there is sufficient evidence to justify review.
- Members shall refrain from discriminating against any individual because of race, gender, creed, national origin, religious affiliation, age, disability, or any other type of prohibited discrimination.
- Members shall preserve the integrity of private information; they shall refrain from seeking information on individuals beyond that which is necessary to implement responsibilities and perform their duties; members shall refrain from revealing nonpublic information unless expressly authorized to do so.
- Members shall make all appointments, promotions, and dismissals in accordance with established civil service rules, applicable contract agreements, and individual merit, and not in furtherance of partisan interests.
- Members shall respect, promote, and contribute to a workplace that is safe, healthy, and free of harassment in any form.

THINKING ABOUT ETHICS

1. *How does the ACA's Code of Ethics differ from the American Jail Association's Code of Ethics found in Chapter 11? How is it similar?*

2. *Should one code of ethics cover corrections officers working in both jails and prisons? Why or why not?*

Adopted August 1975 at the 105th Congress of Correction. Revised August 1990 at the 120th Congress of Correction. Revised August 1994 at the 124th Congress of Correction.

Source: Reprinted with permission of the American Correctional Association, Alexandria, Virginia. Visit the American Correctional Association at http://www.aca.org.

◀ The Arizona State Prison Complex at Lewis, where two inmates held two corrections officers hostage in a watchtower in 2004. One officer, a female, was raped. On April 30, 2004, inmate Steven Coy was sentenced to seven consecutive life sentences for his part in the hostage crisis. How can the safety of corrections workers be improved?

Tom Hood/AP Images

televised as prisoners had demanded. Among other demands were (1) no retaliation by officials, (2) review of medical staffing and care, (3) review of mail and visitation rules, (4) review of commissary prices, and (5) better enforcement against what the inmates called "inappropriate supervision."[77]

Riots related to inmate grievances over perceived disparities in federal drug-sentencing policies and the possible loss of weight-lifting equipment occurred throughout the federal prison system in October 1995. Within a few days, the unrest led to a nationwide lockdown of 73 federal prisons. Although fires were set and a number of inmates and guards were injured, no deaths resulted. More recently, riots have occurred at Florida's Holmes Correctional Institution (where inmates damaged dormitories in 2016); Alabama's William C. Holman Correctional Facility (where inmates stabbed the warden and a correctional officer in 2016); Delaware's James T. Vaughn Correctional Center (where one correctional sergeant died in 2017);[78] and in 2018 at South Carolina's Lee Correctional Institution (where 7 inmates were killed and 17 other injured in gang-related fighting).[79]

Although riots are difficult to predict in specific institutions, some state prison systems appear ripe for disorder. The Texas prison system, for example, is home to a number of gangs, referred to by corrections personnel as **security threat groups (STGs)**, among whom turf violations can easily lead to widespread disorder. Gang membership among inmates in the Texas prison system, practically nonexistent in 1983, was estimated at more than 1,200 just 9 years later.[80] The Texas Syndicate, the Aryan Brotherhood of Texas, and the Mexican Mafia (sometimes known as *La Eme*, Spanish for the letter *M*) are probably the largest gangs functioning in the Texas prison system today. Each has around 300 members.[81] Other gangs known to operate in prisons across the country are shown in Table 12-2.

Gangs in Texas grew rapidly in part because of the power vacuum created when a court ruling ended the "building tender" system.[82] Building tenders were tough inmates who were given almost free rein by prison administrators to keep other inmates in line, especially in many of the state's worst prisons. The end of the building tender system dramatically increased demands on the Texas Department of Criminal Justice for increased abilities and professionalism among its guards and other prison staff. Today, prison gangs have developed into criminal organizations whose reach may extend far beyond prison walls. In 2013, for example, Colorado prison chief Tom Clements was gunned down by a former inmate and gang member as he answered the front door of his home. Authorities believe that the killing was ordered by imprisoned gang leaders known as *shot callers*. Similar killings of two district attorneys in 2013 may have been related to STGs in Texas prisons. Terry Pelz, a former Texas prison warden, observes that "The gangs [have gone] from protecting themselves in prison on racial lines to evolving into criminal enterprises."[83]

> Gangs are referred to by corrections personnel as security threat groups (STGs).

security threat group (STG)
An inmate group, gang, or organization whose members act together to pose a threat to the safety of corrections staff or the public, who prey on other inmates, or who threaten the secure and orderly operation of a correctional institution.

▲ Assistant Attorney General Lanny Breuer speaks to media representatives in Houston, Texas, announcing the arrest of dozens of alleged members of the white supremacist Aryan Brotherhood of Texas security threat group in 2013 on federal racketeering and other charges. The gang is suspected of involvement in the shooting deaths of Tom Clements, the head of Colorado prisons, and two Texas prosecutors.
Cody Duty/Houston Chronicle/ AP Images

Prisoners' Rights

In May 1995, Limestone Prison inmate Larry Hope was handcuffed to a hitching post after arguing with another inmate while working on a chain gang near an interstate highway in Alabama.[84] Hope was released 2 hours later, after a supervising officer determined that Hope had not instigated the altercation. During the 2 hours that he was coupled to the post, Hope was periodically offered drinking water and bathroom breaks, and his responses to those offers were recorded on an activity log. Because of the height of the hitching post, however, his arms grew tired, and it was later determined that whenever he tried moving his arms to improve his circulation, the handcuffs cut into his wrists, causing pain.

One month later, Hope was punished more severely after he had taken a nap during the morning bus ride to the chain gang's work site. When the bus arrived, he was slow in responding to an order to exit the vehicle. A shouting match soon led to a scuffle with an officer, and four other guards intervened and subdued Hope, handcuffing him and

TABLE 12-2
Ten Most Influential Security Threat Groups in American Prisons

Security threat groups, or prison gangs, are self-perpetuating criminal organizations that have significant influence beyond the penal system. Prison gangs are structured along racial or ethnic lines, and consist of a select group of inmates who participate in an organizational hierarchy and are governed by a shared code of conduct. Prison gangs vary in both organization and composition, from highly structured gangs, such as the Aryan Brotherhood and Nuestra Familia, to gangs with a less formal structure, such as the Mexican Mafia (La Eme).

	Aryan Brotherhood	Barrio Azteca	Black Guerrilla Family	Dead Man Incorporated	Texas Syndicate	NETA	Hermanos De Pistoleros Latinos	Public Enemy Number One	Mexican Mafia AKA La Eme	Nazi Low Riders	Mexikanemi AKA Texas Mexican Mafia	La Nuestra Familia
Estimated Numbers	20,000	2,000	1,000 plus associates	370 and thousands of associates	1,300 plus 10,000 associates	12,000	1,000	500	400 plus 1,000 associates	Up to 5,000 members	2,000	250 and thousands of associates
Racial Composition	White	Mexican Nationals or Mexican/ Americans	African American	White	Mexican-American Hispanic	Puerto Rican	Mexican and Mexican-American	White	Mexican-American/ Hispanic	White	Mexican nationals and Mexican-Americans	Mexican-American Hispanic
Location	Concentrated in the Western U.S.	Southwestern U.S.	California and Maryland	Maryland and Virginia	California, Texas, New Mexico, Arizona	Puerto Rico and Northeast U.S.	Texas and Southwestern U.S.	Eastern and Western U.S.	California	Pacific Coast and Southwestern U.S.	Texas and the Southwest	California

References: Michael Kelley, "America's 11 Most Powerful Prison Gangs," Business Insider Australia, http://www.businessinsider.com.au/most-dangerous-prison-gangs-in-the-us-2014-2; David Skarbek, The Social Order of the Underworld: How Prison Gangs Govern the American Penal System (Oxford Univ. Press,); "Prison in America: Protection Rackets," The Economist, August 30, 2014, http://www.economist.com/news/books-and-arts/21614090-prison-gangs-are-rational-solution-growing-problem-protection-rackets; U.S. Department of Justice, Organized Crime and Gang Section, "Prison Gangs," http://www.justice.gov/criminal/ocgs/gangs/prison.html; and Florida Department of Corrections, "Major Prison Gangs, http://www.dc.state.fl.us/pub/gangs/la.html.

6 Discuss the legal aspects of prisoners' rights, including the consequences of related, precedent-setting U.S. Supreme Court cases.

placing him in leg irons for transportation back to the prison. When he arrived at the facility, officers made him take off his shirt and again put him on the hitching post. He stood in the sun for approximately 7 hours, sustaining a sunburn; Hope was given water only once or twice during that time and was provided with no bathroom breaks. At one point, an officer taunted him about his thirst. According to Hope: "[The guard] first gave water to some dogs, then brought the water cooler closer to me, removed its lid, and kicked the cooler over, spilling the water onto the ground."

Eventually Hope filed a civil suit against three officers, claiming that he experienced "unnecessary pain" and that the "wanton infliction of pain . . . constitutes cruel and unusual punishment forbidden by the Eighth Amendment." His case eventually reached the U.S. Supreme Court, and on June 27, 2002, the Court found that Hope's treatment was "totally without penological justification" and constituted an Eighth Amendment violation. The Court ruled that "[d]espite the clear lack of emergency, respondents knowingly subjected [Hope] to a substantial risk of physical harm, unnecessary pain, unnecessary exposure to the sun, prolonged thirst and taunting, and a deprivation of bathroom breaks that created a risk of particular discomfort and humiliation."

In deciding the *Hope* case, the Court built on almost 40 years of precedent-setting decisions in the area of prisoners' rights. It may be surprising, but before the 1960s, American courts had taken a neutral approach—commonly called the **hands-off doctrine**—toward the running of prisons. Judges assumed that prison administrators were sufficiently professional in the performance of their duties to balance institutional needs with humane considerations. The hands-off doctrine rested on the belief that defendants lost most of their rights upon conviction, suffering a kind of **civil death**. Many states defined civil death through legislation that denied inmates the right to vote, to hold public office, and even to marry. Some states made incarceration for a felony a basis for uncontested divorce at the request of the noncriminal spouse. Aspects of the old notion of civil death are still a reality in a number of jurisdictions today. The Sentencing Project says that 3.9 million American citizens across the nation are barred from voting because of previous felony convictions.[85]

Although the concept of civil death has not entirely disappeared, the hands-off doctrine ended in 1970, when a federal court declared the entire Arkansas prison system to be unconstitutional after hearing arguments that it constituted a form of cruel and unusual punishment.[86] The court's decision resulted from what it judged to be pervasive overcrowding and primitive living conditions. Longtime inmates claimed that a number of other inmates had been beaten or shot to death by guards and buried over the years in unmarked graves on prison property. An investigation did unearth some skeletons in old graves, but their origin was never determined.

Detailed media coverage of the Arkansas prison system gave rise to suspicions about correctional institutions everywhere. Within a few years, federal courts intervened in the running of prisons in Florida, Louisiana, Mississippi, New York City, and Virginia.[87] In 1975, in a precedent-setting decision, U.S. District Court Judge Frank M. Johnson issued an order banning the Alabama Board of Corrections from accepting any more inmates. Citing a population that was more than double the capacity of the state's system, Judge Johnson enumerated 44 standards to be met before additional inmates could be admitted to prison. Included in the requirements were specific guidelines on living space, staff-to-inmate ratios, visiting privileges, racial makeup of staff, and food-service modifications.

The Legal Basis of Prisoners' Rights

In 1974, the U.S. Supreme Court case of *Pell* v. *Procunier*[88] established a "balancing test" that, although originally addressing only the First Amendment rights, eventually served as a general guideline for all prison operations. In *Pell*, the Court ruled that the "prison inmate retains those First Amendment rights that are not inconsistent with his status as a prisoner or with the legitimate penological objectives of the corrections system."[89] In other words, inmates have rights, much the same as people who are not incarcerated, provided that the

hands-off doctrine
A policy of nonintervention with regard to prison management that U.S. courts tended to follow until the late 1960s. For 30 years, the doctrine languished as judicial intervention in prison administration dramatically increased, although there is now evidence that a new hands-off era is beginning.

civil death
The legal status of prisoners in some jurisdictions who are denied the opportunity to vote, hold public office, marry, or enter into contracts by virtue of their status as incarcerated felons. Although civil death is primarily of historical interest, some jurisdictions still limit the contractual opportunities available to inmates.

🐦 Follow the author's tweets about the latest crime and justice news @schmalleger

legitimate needs of the prison for security, custody, and safety are not compromised. Other courts have declared that order maintenance, security, and rehabilitation are all legitimate concerns of prison administration but that financial exigency and convenience are not. As the **balancing test** makes clear, we see reflected in prisoners' rights a microcosm of the individual-rights versus public-order dilemma found in wider society.

Further enforcing the legal rights of prisoners is the Civil Rights of Institutionalized Persons Act (CRIPA) of 1980.[90] The law, which has been amended over time, applies to all adult and juvenile state and local jails, detention centers, prisons, mental hospitals, and other care facilities (such as those operated by a state, county, or city for inmates who are physically challenged or chronically ill).

Significantly, the most recent version of CRIPA states:[91]

> No action shall be brought with respect to prison conditions under section 1983 of this title, or any other Federal law, by a prisoner confined in any jail, prison, or other correctional facility until such administrative remedies as are available are exhausted.

Another federal law, the Religious Land Use and Institutionalized Persons Act (RLUIPA) of 2000, has particular relevance to prison programs and activities that are at least partially supported with federal monies. RLUIPA states:

> No government shall impose a substantial burden on the religious exercise of a person residing in or confined to an institution even if the burden results from a rule of general applicability, unless the government demonstrates that imposition of the burden on that person (1) is in furtherance of a compelling governmental interest; and (2) is the least restrictive means of furthering that compelling governmental interest.

Prisoners' rights, because they are constrained by the legitimate needs of imprisonment, can be thought of as *conditional* rights rather than *absolute* rights. The Second Amendment to the U.S. Constitution, for example, grants citizens the right to bear arms. The right to arms is, however, necessarily compromised by the need for order and security in prison, and we would not expect a court to rule that inmates have a right to weapons. Prisoners' rights must be balanced against the security, order-maintenance, and treatment needs of correctional institutions.

Conditional rights, because they are subject to the exigencies of imprisonment, bear a strong resemblance to privileges, which should not be surprising because privileges were all that inmates officially had until the modern era. The practical difference between privileges and conditional rights is that privileges exist only at the convenience of granting institutions and can be revoked at any time for any reason. The rights of prisoners, in contrast, have a basis in the Constitution and in law external to the institution. The institution may restrict such rights for legitimate correctional reasons, but those rights may not be infringed without good cause that can be demonstrated in a court of law. Mere institutional convenience does not provide a sufficient legal basis for the denial of rights.

The past few decades have seen many lawsuits brought by prisoners challenging the constitutionality of some aspect of confinement. As mentioned in Chapter 9, suits filed by prisoners with the courts are generally called writs of *habeas corpus* and formally request that the person detaining a prisoner bring him or her before a judicial officer to determine the lawfulness of the imprisonment. The ACA says that most prisoner lawsuits are based on "[1] the Eighth Amendment prohibition against cruel and unusual punishment; [2] the Fourteenth Amendment prohibition against the taking of life, liberty, or property without due process of law; and [3] the Fourteenth Amendment provision requiring equal protection of the laws."[92] Aside from appeals by inmates that question the propriety of their convictions and sentences, such constitutional challenges

balancing test
A principle, developed by the courts and applied to the corrections arena by *Pell* v. *Procunier* (1974), that attempts to weigh the rights of an individual, as guaranteed by the Constitution, against the authority of states to make laws or to otherwise restrict a person's freedom in order to protect the state's interests and its citizens.

> The Privilege of the Writ of Habeas Corpus shall not be suspended, unless when in Cases of Rebellion or Invasion the public Safety may require it.
> —Article I of the U.S. Constitution

▼ A "jailhouse lawyer" works in a prison law library. Such inmates, although they rarely have any formal legal training, help other inmates prepare legal writs and represent them in in-house disciplinary actions. Would you restrict or expand the role of jailhouse lawyers?
Sirtravelalot/Shutterstock

Freedom or Safety? You Decide
Censoring Prison Communications

While concern over the terrorist attacks of 9/11 were still high, NBC News announced that it had learned that Arab terrorists in federal maximum-security prisons had been sending letters to extremists on the outside exhorting them to attack Western interests. The terrorists included Mohammed Salameh, a follower of radical sheik Omar Abdel-Rahman. Salameh had been sentenced to more than 100 years in prison for his part in the 1993 bombing attack on New York's World Trade Center. That attack, which killed six and injured more than 1,000, blew a huge hole in the basement parking garage of one of the towers but failed to topple the buildings.

The men were being held in the federal ADMAX facility in Florence, Colorado, which is the country's most secure federal prison. While there, NBC News revealed, they sent at least 14 letters to a Spanish terror cell, praised Osama bin Laden in Arabic newspapers, and advocated additional terror attacks. In July 2002, Salameh, a Palestinian with a degree in Islamic law from a Jordanian university, sent a letter to the *Al-Quds* Arabic daily newspaper proclaiming that "Osama Bin Laden is my hero of this generation."

Andy McCarthy, a former federal prosecutor who worked to send the terrorists to prison, said that Salameh's letters were "exhorting acts of terrorism and helping recruit would-be terrorists for the *Jihad*." Michael Macko, who lost his father in the Trade Center bombing, posed this question: "If they are encouraging acts of terrorism internationally, how do we know they're not encouraging acts of terrorism right here on U.S. soil?"

Prison officials told reporters that communications involving the imprisoned bombers had not been closely censored because the men hadn't been considered very dangerous. The letters didn't contain any plans for attacks, nor did they name any specific targets. One Justice Department official said that Salameh was "a low-level guy" who was not under any special restrictions and that his letters were seen as "generic stuff" and "no cause for concern."

Rights advocates suggested that inmates should have the right to free speech—even those imprisoned for acts of terrorism—and that advocating terrorism is not the same thing as planning it or carrying it out. After all, they said, calls for a holy war, however repugnant they may be in the current international context, are merely political statements—and politics is not against the law.

YOU DECIDE

What kinds of prison communications should be monitored or restricted (letters, telephone calls, e-mail)? Do you believe that communications containing statements like those described here should be confiscated? What kinds of political statements (if any) should be permitted?

References: Lisa Myers, "Imprisoned Terrorists Still Advocating Terror," NBC Nightly News, February 28, 2005, http://www.msnbc.msn.com/id/7046691 (accessed August 28, 2005); and Lisa Myers, "Bureau of Prisons under Fire for Jihad Letters," March 1, 2005, http://www.msnbc.msn.com/id/7053165 (accessed August 28, 2010).

---

represent the bulk of legal action initiated by those who are imprisoned. However, state statutes and federal legislation, including Section 1983 of the Civil Rights Act of 1871, provide other bases for challenges to the legality of specific prison conditions and procedures. The U.S. Supreme Court has not yet spoken with finality on a number of prisoners' rights questions. Nonetheless, High Court decisions of the last few decades and a number of lower court findings can be interpreted to identify the existing conditional rights of prisoners, as shown in Table 12-3. Table 12-4 shows a number of important U.S. Supreme Court cases involving prisoners' rights claims.

Follow the author's tweets about the latest crime and justice news @schmalleger

► New Port Richey, Florida, USA—A group of inmates pray during a jailhouse bible study at the New Port Richey jail. Faith-based prison programs are sponsored by religious organizations and supplement government-sponsored training and rehabilitation programs. What special roles might such programs play?

Camille Spencer/St. Petersburg Times/ZUMA Press Inc/Alamy Stock Photo

TABLE 12-3
The Conditional Rights of Inmates[1]

Communications and Visitation

A right to receive publications directly from the publisher

A right to meet with members of the press[2]

A right to communicate with nonprisoners

Religious Freedom

A right of assembly for religious services and groups

A right to attend services of other religious groups

A right to receive visits from ministers

A right to correspond with religious leaders

A right to observe religious dietary laws

A right to wear religious insignia

Access to the Courts and Legal Assistance

A right to have access to the courts[3]

A right to visits from attorneys

A right to have mail communications with lawyers[4]

A right to communicate with legal assistance organizations

A right to consult jailhouse lawyers[5]

A right to assistance in filing legal papers, which should include one of the following:

- Access to an adequate law library
- Paid attorneys
- Paralegal personnel or law students

Medical Care

A right to sanitary and healthy conditions

A right to medical attention for serious physical problems

A right to required medications

A right to treatment in accordance with "doctor's orders"

Protection from Harm

A right to food, water, and shelter

A right to protection from foreseeable attack

A right to protection from predictable sexual abuse

A right to protection against suicide

Institutional Punishment and Discipline

An absolute right against corporal punishments (unless sentenced to such punishments)

A limited right to due process before punishment, including the following:

- A notice of charges
- A fair and impartial hearing
- An opportunity for defense
- A right to present witnesses
- A written decision

---

[1]All "rights" listed are provisional in that they may be constrained by the legitimate needs of imprisonment.

[2]But this right does not go beyond the opportunities afforded for inmates to meet with members of the general public.

[3]This right is subject to the restrictions in the Prison Litigation Reform Act of 1996.

[4]Mail communications are generally designated as privileged or nonprivileged. Privileged communications include those between inmates and their lawyers or court officials and cannot legitimately be read by prison officials. Nonprivileged communications include most other written communications.

[5]Jailhouse lawyers are inmates with experience in the law, usually gained from filing legal briefs on their own behalf or on the behalf of others. Consultation with jailhouse lawyers was ruled permissible in the Supreme Court case of *Johnson v. Avery*, 393 U.S. 483 (1968), unless inmates are provided with paid legal assistance.

TABLE 12-4
Important U.S. Supreme Court Cases Involving Prisoners' Rights Claims, by Year of Decision

Case	Year Decided	Constitutional Basis	Finding
Holt v. Hobbs	2015		The Court supported the Religious Land Use and Institutionalized Persons Act of 2000, which provides that no government shall impose a substantial burden on the religious exercise of a prisoner unless it can show that the burden "is the least restrictive means of furthering a compelling governmental interest."
Howes v. Fields	2012	Fifth Amendment	Inmates facing questioning by law enforcement officers while incarcerated need not be advised of their *Miranda* rights.
Florence v. Burlington County	2012		Officials may strip search those arrested for any offense, including minor ones, before admitting them to jail.
Brown v. Plata	2011	Fourth Amendment	Overcrowded conditions in California's prisons were so egregious that the state was unable to deliver minimal care to prisoners with serious medical and mental health problems, requiring a forced reduction in prison populations.
U.S. v. Georgia	2006	Eighth Amendment	Under the Americans with Disabilities Act, a state may be liable for rights deprivations suffered by disabled inmates held in its prisons.
Johnson v. California	2005		A California Department of Corrections and Rehabilitation's unwritten policy of racially segregating prisoners in double cells each time they enter a new correctional facility was invalidated.
Wilkinson v. Austin	2005		The Court upheld an Ohio policy allowing the most dangerous offenders to be held in "supermax" cells following several levels of review prior to transfer.
Overton v. Bazzetta	2003		The Court upheld a visitation regulation that denies most visits to prisoners who commit two substance-abuse violations while incarcerated.
Porter v. Nussle	2002	Eighth Amendment	The Prison Litigation Reform Act's "exhaustion requirement" applies to all inmate suits about prison life, whether they involve general circumstances or particular events and whether they allege excessive force or some other wrong.
Hope v. Pelzer	2002	Eighth Amendment	The Court found a constitutional violation in the case of a prisoner who was subjected to unnecessary pain, humiliation, and risk of physical harm.
Booth v. Churner	2001	Eighth Amendment	The Court upheld the Prison Litigation Reform Act's requirement that state inmates must "exhaust such administrative remedies as are available" before filing a suit over prison conditions.
Lewis v. Casey	1996		Inmates need not be given the wherewithal to file any and every type of legal claim. All that is required is "that they be provided with the tools to attack their sentences."
Sandin v. Conner	1995	Fourteenth Amendment	The Court rejected the argument that disciplining inmates is a deprivation of constitutional due-process rights.
Helling v. McKinney	1993	Eighth Amendment	Environmental conditions of prison life, including second-hand cigarette smoke, that pose a threat to inmate health have to be corrected.
Wilson v. Seiter	1991	Eighth Amendment	The Court clarified the totality of conditions concept by holding that some conditions of confinement, taken "in combination," may violate prisoners' rights when each would not do so alone.
Washington v. Harper	1990	Eighth Amendment	A mentally ill inmate who is a danger to self or others may be forcibly treated with psychoactive drugs.
Turner v. Safley	1987	First Amendment	A ban on correspondence between Missouri inmates was upheld as "reasonably related to legitimate penological interests."
O'Lone v. Estate of Shabazz	1987	First Amendment	An inmate's right to religious practice was not violated by prison officials who refused to alter his work schedule so that he could attend Friday afternoon services.

■ **TABLE 12-4**
Important U.S. Supreme Court Cases Involving Prisoners' Rights Claims, by Year of Decision (*Continued*)

Case	Year Decided	Constitutional Basis	Finding
Whitley v. *Albers*	1986	Eighth Amendment	The shooting and wounding of an inmate was not a violation of that inmate's rights, because "the shooting was part and parcel of a good-faith effort to restore prison security."
Ponte v. *Real*	1985		Inmates are entitled to certain rights in disciplinary hearings.
Hudson v. *Palmer*	1984	Fourth Amendment	A prisoner has no reasonable expectation of privacy in his prison cell and no protections against what would otherwise be "unreasonable searches."
Block v. *Rutherford*	1984	First Amendment	State regulations may prohibit meetings of inmate unions as well as the use of the mail to deliver union information within the prison; also, prisoners do not have a right to be present during cell searches.
Rhodes v. *Chapman*	1981	Eighth Amendment	Double-celling of inmates is not in itself cruel and unusual punishment.
Ruiz v. *Estelle*	1980	Eighth Amendment	Unconstitutional conditions were found to exist within the Texas prison system—including overcrowding, understaffing, brutality, and substandard medical care.
Cooper v. *Morin*	1980		Neither inconvenience nor cost is an acceptable excuse for treating female inmates differently from male inmates.
Bell v. *Wolfish*	1979	Fourth Amendment	Pretrial detainees and other prisoners may be strip searched, to include body-cavity searches, as needed, regardless of the reason for their incarceration.
Jones v. *North Carolina Prisoners' Labor Union, Inc.*	1977	First Amendment	Inmates have no inherent right to publish newspapers or newsletters for use by other inmates.
Bounds v. *Smith*	1977		This decision resulted in the creation of law libraries in many prisons.
Estelle v. *Gamble*	1976	Eighth Amendment	Prison officials have a duty to provide proper inmate medical care.
Ruiz v. *Estelle*	1975	Eighth Amendment	Conditions of confinement within the Texas prison system were found to be unconstitutional.
Wolff v. *McDonnell*	1974	Fourteenth Amendment	Sanctions cannot be levied against inmates without appropriate due process.
Procunier v. *Martinez*	1974	First Amendment	Censorship of inmate mail is acceptable only when necessary to protect legitimate governmental interests.
Pell v. *Procunier*	1974	First Amendment	Inmates retain First Amendment rights that are not inconsistent with their status as prisoners or with the legitimate penological objectives of the corrections system.
U.S. v. *Hitchcock*	1972	Fourth Amendment	A warrantless cell search is not unreasonable.
Cruz v. *Beto*	1972	First Amendment	Inmates have to be given a "reasonable opportunity" to pursue their religious faiths; also, visits can be banned if they constitute a threat to security.
Johnson v. *Avery*	1968		Inmates have a right to consult "jailhouse lawyers" when trained legal assistance is not available.
Monroe v. *Pape*	1961		Inmates have a right to bring action in federal court when deprived of their rights by state officers acting under color of state law.

Grievance Procedures

Today, all sizable prisons have established **grievance procedures** through which an inmate can file a complaint with local authorities and receive a mandated response. Grievance procedures range from the use of a hearing board composed of staff members and inmates to a single staff appointee charged with the resolution of complaints. Inmates who are

grievance procedure
A formalized arrangement, usually involving a neutral hearing board, whereby institutionalized individuals have the opportunity to register complaints about the conditions of their confinement.

dissatisfied with the handling of their grievances can generally appeal beyond the local prison.

Disciplinary actions by prison authorities may also require a formalized hearing process, especially when staff members bring charges of rule violations against inmates that might result in some form of punishment being imposed on them. In a precedent-setting decision in the case of *Wolff* v. *McDonnell* (1974),[93] the Supreme Court decided that sanctions could not be levied against inmates without appropriate due process. The *Wolff* case involved an inmate who had been deprived of previously earned good-time credits because of misbehavior. The Court established that good-time credits were a form of "state-created right(s)," which, once created, could not be "arbitrarily abrogated."[94] *Wolff* was especially significant because it began an era of court scrutiny of what came to be called *state-created liberty interests*, which were said to be based on the language used in published prison regulations and were held, in effect, to confer due-process guarantees on prisoners. Hence, if a prison regulation said that a disciplinary hearing should be held before a prisoner could be sent to solitary confinement and that the hearing should permit a discussion of the evidence for and against the prisoner, courts interpreted that regulation to mean that the prisoner had a state-created right to a hearing. Sending him or her to solitary confinement in violation of the regulation was seen as a violation of a state-created liberty interest. In later court decisions, state-created rights and privileges were called *protected liberties* and were interpreted to include any significant change in a prisoner's status.

In the interest of due process, and especially where written prison regulations governing the hearing process exist, courts have generally held that inmates going before disciplinary hearing boards are entitled to (1) a notice of the charges brought against them, (2) the chance to organize a defense, (3) an impartial hearing, and (4) the opportunity to present witnesses and evidence in their behalf. A written statement of the hearing board's conclusions should be provided to the inmate.[95] In the case of *Ponte* v. *Real* (1985),[96] the Supreme Court held that prison officials must provide an explanation to inmates who are denied the opportunity to have a desired witness at their hearing. The case of *Vitek* v. *Jones* (1980)[97] extended the requirement of due process to inmates about to be transferred from prisons to mental hospitals.

So that inmates will know what is expected of them as they enter prison, the ACA recommends that "a rulebook that contains all chargeable offenses, ranges of penalties and disciplinary procedures [be] posted in a conspicuous and accessible area; [and] a copy . . . given to each inmate and staff member."[98]

A Return to the Hands-Off Doctrine?

Many state-created rights and protected individual liberties may soon be a thing of the past in American corrections. In June 1991, an increasingly conservative U.S. Supreme Court signaled the beginning of what appears to be at least a partial return to the hands-off doctrine of earlier times. The case, *Wilson* v. *Seiter*,[99] involved a Section 1983 suit brought against Richard P. Seiter, then-director of the Ohio Department of Rehabilitation and Correction, and Carl Humphreys, warden of the Hocking Correctional Facility (HCF) in Nelsonville, Ohio. In the suit, Pearly L. Wilson, a felon incarcerated at HCF, alleged that a number of the conditions of his confinement constituted cruel and unusual punishment in violation of the Eighth and Fourteenth Amendments to the U.S. Constitution. Specifically, Wilson cited overcrowding, excessive noise, insufficient locker storage space, inadequate heating and cooling, improper ventilation, unclean and inadequate restrooms, unsanitary dining facilities and food preparation, and housing with mentally and physically ill inmates. Wilson asked for a change in prison conditions and sought $900,000 from prison officials in compensatory and punitive damages.

Both the federal district court in which Wilson first filed affidavits and the Sixth Circuit Court of Appeals held that no constitutional violations existed because the conditions cited by Wilson were not the result of malicious intent on the part of officials. The U.S. Supreme Court agreed, noting that the **deliberate indifference** standard applied in

deliberate indifference
A wanton disregard by corrections personnel for the well-being of inmates. Deliberate indifference requires both actual knowledge that a harm is occurring and disregard of the risk of harm that is occurring. A prison official may be held liable under the Eighth Amendment for acting with deliberate indifference to inmate health or safety only if he or she knows that inmates face a substantial risk of serious harm and disregards that risk by failing to take reasonable measures to abate it.

Estelle v. *Gamble* (1976)[100] to claims involving medical care is similarly applicable to other cases in which prisoners challenge the conditions of their confinement. In effect, the Court created a standard that effectively means that all future challenges to prison conditions by inmates, which are brought under the Eighth Amendment, must show deliberate indifference by the officials responsible for the existence of those conditions before the Court will hear the complaint.

The written opinion of the Court in *Wilson* v. *Seiter* is telling. Writing for the majority, Justice Antonin Scalia observed that "if a prison boiler malfunctions accidentally during a cold winter, an inmate would have no basis for an Eighth Amendment claim, even if he suffers objectively significant harm. If a guard accidentally stepped on a prisoner's toe and broke it, this would not be punishment in anything remotely like the accepted meaning of the word." At the time that the *Wilson* decision was handed down, critics voiced concerns that the decision could effectively excuse prison authorities from the need to improve living conditions within institutions on the basis of simple budgetary constraints.

In the 1995 case of *Sandin* v. *Conner*,[101] the U.S. Supreme Court took a much more definitive stance in favor of a new type of hands-off doctrine and voted 5 to 4 to reject the argument that any state action taken for a punitive reason encroaches on a prisoner's constitutional due-process right to be free from the deprivation of liberty. In *Sandin*, Demont Conner, an inmate at the Halawa Correctional Facility in Hawaii, was serving an indeterminate sentence of 30 years to life for numerous crimes, including murder, kidnapping, robbery, and burglary. In a lawsuit in federal court, Conner alleged that prison officials had deprived him of procedural due process when a hearing committee refused to allow him to present witnesses during a disciplinary hearing and then sentenced him to segregation for alleged misconduct. An appellate court agreed with Conner, concluding that an existing prison regulation that instructed the hearing committee to find guilt in cases where a misconduct charge is supported by substantial evidence meant that the committee could not impose segregation if it did not look at all the evidence available to it.

> Follow the author's tweets about the latest crime and justice news @schmalleger

The Supreme Court, however, reversed the decision of the appellate court, holding that although "such a conclusion may be entirely sensible in the ordinary task of construing a statute defining rights and remedies available to the general public, [i]t is a good deal less sensible in the case of a prison regulation primarily designed to guide corrections officials in the administration of a prison." The Court concluded that "such regulations [are] not designed to confer rights on inmates" but are meant only to provide guidelines to prison staff members.

In *Sandin*, the Court effectively set aside substantial portions of earlier decisions, such as *Wolff* v. *McDonnell* (1974)[102] and *Hewitt* v. *Helms* (1983),[103] which, wrote the justices, focused more on procedural issues than on those of "real substance." As a consequence, the majority opinion held, past cases like these have "impermissibly shifted the focus" away from the nature of a due-process deprivation to one based on the language of a particular state or prison regulation. "The *Hewitt* approach," wrote the majority in *Sandin*, "has run counter to the view expressed in several of our cases that federal courts ought to afford appropriate deference and flexibility to state officials trying to manage a volatile environment. The time has come," said the Court, "to return to those due process principles that were correctly established and applied" in earlier times. In short, *Sandin* made it much more difficult for inmates to effectively challenge the administrative regulations and procedures imposed on them by prison officials, even when stated procedures are not explicitly followed.

A more recent case whose findings support the action of federal corrections officers is that of *Ali* v. *Federal Bureau of Prisons*. The case, decided by the U.S. Supreme Court in 2008,[104] involved a federal prisoner named Abdus-Shahid M. S. Ali, who claimed that some of his personal belongings disappeared when he was transferred from one federal prison to another. The missing items, which were to have been shipped in two duffle bags belonging to Ali, included copies of the Koran, a prayer rug, and a number of religious magazines. Ali filed suit against the Bureau of Prisons (BOP) under the Federal Tort Claims Act (FTCA),[105] which authorizes "claims against the United States for money damages . . .

Freedom or Safety? You Decide
Should Prison Libraries Limit Access to Potentially Inflammatory Literature?

Prison libraries have a long history in this country. After the Civil War, as prisons filled with black Americans, prison authorities censored literature with themes of black empowerment, fearing that they would inspire riots and internal uprisings. By the late 1940s, however, a theory known as "bibliotherapy" developed as an effort to "cure" criminal behavior through reading. Censorship was a central feature of the bibliotherapy movement as it was believed that inmates could be rehabilitated only by reading carefully selected materials. The importance of libraries throughout the United States increased significantly in the 1950s and 1960s, and prison libraries, on average, grew larger. Because law-related materials were often available in such facilities, they contributed to the growth of the jailhouse lawyer phenomenon, through which inmates studied the law and filed civil rights actions with the courts. This, in turn, fed a growing prisoner's rights movement in the 1960s and 1970s.

In mid-2007, Federal Bureau of Prisons (BOP) authorities ordered the nationwide removal of potentially inflammatory religious-themed literature from the shelves of prison libraries. The move came in response to a report by the U.S. Justice Department's Office of the Inspector General, which recommended that prisons should take steps to avoid becoming recruiting grounds for militant Islamists and other radical groups.

Thousands of books were soon removed under what the BOP called the Standardized Chapel Library Project (SCLP), which it admitted was an effort to bar inmate access to literature that the BOP felt could "discriminate, disparage, advocate violence or radicalize." In identifying materials for removal, the BOP relied on the advice of experts who were asked to identify up to 150 book titles and 150 multimedia resources for each of 20 religious categories ranging from Bahaism to Yoruba. Prayer books were explicitly excluded from the list of materials targeted for removal.

Soon after the project was made public, however, members of Congress and a number of religious leaders urged the BOP to reverse its stance and return the books to chapel shelves.

In the fall of 2007, the Republican Study Committee, a group of conservative Republicans in the House of Representatives, sent a letter to BOP Director Harley G. Lappin, saying, "We must ensure that in America the federal government is not the undue arbiter of what may or may not be read by our citizens."

Representative Jeb Hensarling, then-head of the Republican Study Committee, explained that "anything that impinges upon the religious liberties of American citizens, be they incarcerated or not, is something that's going to cause . . . great concern." For its part, the BOP countered that it had a legitimate interest in screening out and removing items from inside its facilities that could incite violence.

The controversy appeared to have been partially resolved when, on September 26, 2007, a BOP spokesperson announced that "in response to concerns expressed by members of several religious communities, the Bureau of Prisons has decided to alter its planned course of action with respect to the Chapel Library Project [and] the bureau will begin immediately to return to chapel libraries materials that were removed . . . with the exception of any publications that have been found to be inappropriate, such as materials that could be radicalizing or incite violence."

The controversy appeared to have ended in 2008 with passage of the Second Chance Act (Public Law No 110–199). This federal legislation, which funded a number of reentry initiatives for people leaving prison, required the director of the BOP "to discontinue the Standardized Chapel Library project or any other project that limits prisoner access to reading and other educational material." The Second Chance Act is discussed in more detail in Chapter 10. After the act's passage, the BOP revived its plan to limit prison library books and proposed a rule that would exclude materials from chapel libraries "that could incite, promote, or otherwise suggest the commission of violence or criminal activity." The rule targeted only literature encouraging violence, but critics said that it would still result in the banning of many religious texts.

YOU DECIDE

Should prison libraries be permitted to limit access to library literature that might incite violence or endanger the safety of inmates and staff? Would it matter if that literature is religious in nature? How might the BOP meet the concerns of the Republican Study Committee, religious leaders, and authors of the Second Chance Act while still accomplishing its objective of removing literature that it believes might incite violence?

References: "What are Prison Libraries Really Like?" *The Airship,* http://airshipdaily.com/blog/06302014-prison-libraries (accessed May 18, 2018). Laurie Goodstein, "Prisons Purging Books on Faith from Libraries," *New York Times,* September 10, 2007.

Follow the author's tweets about the latest crime and justice news @schmalleger

To return to society discharged prisoners unreformed is to poison it with the worst elements possible.

—Zebulon R. Brockway
(1827–1920)[j]

for injury or loss of property . . . caused by the negligent or wrongful act or omission of any employee in the government while acting within the scope of his office or employment." In denying Ali's claim, the Court found that the law specifically provides immunity for federal law enforcement officers and determined that federal corrections personnel are "law enforcement officers" within the meaning of the law.

Similarly, in 2013, in the case of *Millbrook* v. *United States*, the Court again found that the FTCA excepts "law enforcement officers' [including correctional officers] acts or omissions that arise within the scope of their employment, regardless of whether the officers are engaged in investigative or law enforcement activity, or are executing a search, seizing evidence, or making an arrest."[106]

Finally, in two cases from 2012, the U.S. Supreme Court ruled firmly in favor of correctional officials in limiting the rights of inmates. In the first case, *Howes* v. *Fields* (2012), the Court found that inmates who face questioning by law enforcement officers while they are incarcerated need not be advised of their *Miranda* rights prior to the start of interrogation.[107] In the second case, *Florence* v. *Burlington County* (2012), the Court ruled that officials had the power to strip search persons who had been arrested prior to admission to a jail or other detention facility, even if the offense for which they were arrested was a minor one.[108] In that case, Justice Kennedy, writing for the majority, noted that "maintaining safety and order at detention centers requires the expertise of correctional officials, who must have substantial discretion to devise reasonable solutions to problems." He went on to write that "the term 'jail' is used here in a broad sense to include prisons and other detention facilities."

The Prison Litigation Reform Act of 1996

Only about 2,000 petitions per year concerning inmate problems were filed with the courts in 1961, but by 1975 the number of filings had increased to around 17,000. In 1996, prisoners filed 68,235 civil rights lawsuits in federal courts nationwide.[109] Some inmate-originated suits seemed patently ludicrous and became the subject of much media coverage in the mid-1990s. One such suit involved Robert Procup, a Florida State Prison inmate serving time for the murder of his business partner. Procup repeatedly sued Florida prison officials—once because he got only one roll with his dinner, again because he didn't get a luncheon salad, a third time because prison-provided TV dinners didn't come with a drink, and a fourth time because his cell had no television. Two other well-publicized cases involved an inmate who went to court asking to be allowed to exercise religious freedom by attending prison chapel services in the nude and an inmate who, thinking he could become pregnant via homosexual relations, sued prison doctors who wouldn't provide him with birth-control pills. An infamous example of seemingly frivolous inmate lawsuits was one brought by inmates claiming religious freedom and demanding that members of the Church of the New Song, or CONS, be provided steak and Harvey's Bristol Cream every Friday in order to celebrate communion. The CONS suit stayed in various courts for 10 years before finally being thrown out.[110]

The huge number of inmate-originated lawsuits in the mid-1990s created a backlog of cases in many federal courts and was targeted by the media and by some citizens' groups as an unnecessary waste of taxpayers' money. The National Association of Attorneys General, which supports efforts to restrict frivolous inmate lawsuits, estimated that lawsuits filed by prisoners cost states more than $81 million a year in legal fees alone.[111]

In 1996, the federal Prison Litigation Reform Act (PLRA) became law.[112] The PLRA is a clear legislative effort to restrict inmate filings to worthwhile cases and to reduce the number of suits brought by state prisoners in federal courts by the following means:

- Requiring inmates to exhaust any available administrative remedies (generally, their prison's grievance procedures) before filing a federal lawsuit challenging prison conditions
- Requiring judges to screen all inmate complaints against the federal government and to immediately dismiss those deemed frivolous or without merit
- Prohibiting prisoners from filing a lawsuit for mental or emotional injury unless they can also show there has been physical injury
- Requiring inmates to pay court filing fees (prisoners who don't have the needed funds can pay the filing fee over a period of time through deductions to their prison commissary accounts)
- Limiting the award of attorneys' fees in successful lawsuits brought by inmates
- Revoking the credits earned by federal prisoners toward early release if they file a malicious lawsuit
- Mandating that court orders affecting prison administration cannot go any further than necessary to correct a violation of a particular inmate's civil rights

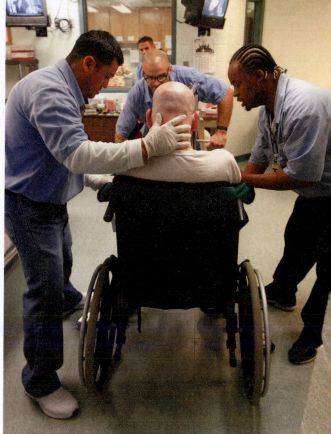

▲ Hutchinson Correctional Facility (Kansas) inmate hospice volunteers Carlos Ballesteros, left, Chad Engro, and Robert Shanklin, right, help a patient in the prison's infirmary. Court decisions over the years have established a firm set of inmate rights. Among them is the right to necessary health care. What other rights do inmates have?

Sandra J. Milburn/The Hutchinson News/AP Images

The PLRA was a legislative effort to restrict inmate filings to worthwhile cases and to reduce the number of suits brought by state prisoners in federal courts.

- Making it possible for state officials to have court orders lifted after 2 years unless there is a new finding of a continuing violation of federally guaranteed civil rights
- Mandating that any court order requiring the release of prisoners due to overcrowding be approved by a three-member court before it can become effective

The U.S. Supreme Court has upheld provisions of the PLRA on a number of occasions.[113] According to one BJS study, the PLRA has been effective in reducing the number of frivolous lawsuits filed by inmates alleging unconstitutional prison conditions.[114] The study found that the filing rate of inmates' civil rights petitions in federal courts had been cut in half four years after passage of the act.

Opponents of the PLRA fear that it is stifling the filing of meritorious suits by inmates facing real deprivations. According to the American Civil Liberties Union (ACLU), for example, "The Prison Litigation Reform Act . . . attempts to slam the courthouse door on society's most vulnerable members. It seeks to strip the federal courts of much of their power to correct even the most egregious prison conditions by altering the basic rules which have always governed prison reform litigation. The PLRA also makes it difficult to settle prison cases by consent decree, and [it] limits the life span of any court judgment."[115] The ACLU has led a nationwide effort to have many provisions of the PLRA overturned, but so far, its effort has borne little fruit.

Issues Facing Prisons Today

Prisons are society's answer to a number of social problems because they house outcasts, misfits, and some highly dangerous people. Although prisons provide a part of the answer to the question of crime control, they also face problems of their own. A few of those special problems are described here.

Geriatric Offenders

In 2013, 89-year-old Anthony Marshall, the frail and wheelchair-bound son of the late philanthropist and socialite Brooke Astor, became the oldest person ever sent to a New York prison for a nonviolent crime. Marshall, who depends on an oxygen tank to breathe, had been convicted of plundering his mother's huge fortune and was sentenced to 1 to 3 years behind bars. Although he was released on medical parole due to declining health only 2 months after he entered prison (he died in 2014 at the age of 90). Marshall's case illustrates the problems facing correctional authorities as the geriatric populations continues to expand.[116]

Crimes committed by the elderly, especially violent crimes, have recently been on the decline. Nonetheless, the significant expansion of America's retiree population has led to an increase in the number of elderly people who are behind bars. In fact, crimes of violence are what bring most older people into the correctional system. According to one early study, 52% of inmates who were over the age of 50 when they entered prison had committed violent crimes, compared with 41% of younger inmates.[117]

An ACLU survey found that there were 8,853 state and federal prisoners age 55 and older scattered throughout America's prisons in 1981.[118] Today, that number stands at 161,839, and experts project that by 2030 there will be over 400,000 such inmates. Because it is the fastest-growing segment of the inmate population, experts expect that the elderly prison population in the United States will have increased by 4,400% over this 50-year span.[119] Similarly, the per capita rate of incarceration for inmates age 55 and over now stands at 230 per 100,000 residents of like age.

Not all of today's elderly inmates were old when they entered prison. Because of harsh sentencing laws passed throughout the country in the 1990s, a small but growing number of inmates (10%) will serve 20 years or more in prison, and 5% will never be released.[120] This means that many inmates who enter prison when they are young will grow old behind bars. This "graying" of America's prison population has a number

> Unfortunately, few prisons are equipped to deal adequately with the medical needs of aging offenders.

of causes:[121] (1) the general aging of the American population, which is reflected inside prisons; (2) some new sentencing policies, such as "three strikes," "truth in sentencing," and "mandatory minimum" laws, that send more criminals to prison for longer stretches; (3) a massive prison-building boom that took place in the 1980s and 1990s and that has provided space for more inmates, reducing the need to release prisoners to alleviate overcrowding; and (4) significant changes in parole philosophies and practices.

In the recent past, state and federal authorities were phasing out or canceling parole programs, forcing the confinement of some inmates until they died. New perspectives on reentry—brought about partially by the high cost of imprisonment—have, however, caused a reassessment of such practices.

Long-termers and geriatric inmates have special needs: They tend to suffer from handicaps, physical impairments, and illnesses not generally encountered among their more youthful counterparts. Unfortunately, few prisons are equipped to deal adequately with the medical needs of aging offenders. Some large facilities have begun to set aside special sections to care for elderly inmates with "typical" disorders, such as Alzheimer's disease, cancer, or heart disease. Unfortunately, such efforts have barely kept pace with the problems that geriatric offenders present. The number of inmates requiring around-the-clock care is expected to increase dramatically during the next two decades.[122]

Incarcerating people into old age is costly and may be counterproductive. Research has consistently shown that "by age 50 most people have significantly outlived the years in which they are most likely to commit crimes."[123] Moreover, the majority of aging prisoners are not incarcerated for serious or violent offenses, and could probably be allowed to reenter the community with little danger to others. In Texas, for example, 65% of elderly prisoners are confined for nonviolent drug crimes, property crimes, and other nonviolent offenses. Because of rising medical expenses, the costs of confining a prisoner over age 50 jumps to an average of $68,270, while housing and other associated costs of keeping an inmate below that age behind bars is only $34,135.[124]

Finally, the idea of rehabilitation takes on a new meaning where geriatric offenders are concerned. What kinds of programs are most useful in providing the older inmate with the tools needed for success on the outside? Which counseling strategies hold the greatest promise for introducing socially acceptable behavior patterns into the long-established lifestyles of elderly offenders about to be released? There are few easy answers to such questions. Watch a YouTube video about the issue at **http://www.aclu.org/ criminal-law-reform/elderly-prison**, and read the report, *The Impact of an Aging Inmate Population on the Federal Bureau of Prisons*, at **https://justicestudies.com/ pubs/aging_inmates.pdf**.

▲ Salvatore LoGiudice, left, 78, is assisted by fellow inmate Dennis Galan, in the hospice section at South Woods State Prison in Bridgeton, New Jersey. Why is the proportion of geriatric inmates increasing? What special needs do they have?

Sharon Gekoski-Kimmel/KRT/ Newscom

Mentally Ill and Intellectually Disabled Inmates

In 2018, Travis Reinking, 29, was arrested after walking naked into a Waffle House near Nashville, Tennessee, at 3 a.m. and shooting eight people with an AR-15. Family members later reported that Reinking had exhibited delusional behavior for an extended time prior to the shooting, including the belief that Taylor Swift was stalking him.[125] Inmates with mental illness make up another group of special needs prisoners. Some of these inmates are neurotic or have personality problems, which increases tensions in prison. Others have serious psychological disorders that may have escaped diagnosis at trial or that did not provide a legal basis for the reduction of criminal responsibility. A fair number of offenders develop psychiatric symptoms while in prison.

Inmates suffering from significant mental illnesses account for a substantial number of those imprisoned. A 2018 study found that BOP inmates with serious mental illness were incarcerated for sex offenses, robbery, and homicide/aggravated assault at about twice the rate of inmates without serious mental illness, and were incarcerated for drug and immigration offenses at about half or less the rate of inmates without serious mental illness (Figure 12–5).[126] A second government study found that 40% of these inmates receive no treatment at all. Finally, a report by the Virginia-based Treatment Advocacy

Center found 356,268 inmates with *severe* mental illness in prisons nationally—a number 10 times greater than people being treated for similar conditions in state psychiatric hospitals.[127]

Another BJS survey of public and private state-level adult correctional facilities (excluding jails) found that 51% of such institutions provide 24-hour mental health care, and 71% provide therapy and counseling by trained mental health professionals as needed.[128] A large majority of prisons distribute psychotropic medications (when such medications are ordered by a physician), and 66% have programs to help released inmates obtain community mental health services. According to the BJS, 13% of state prisoners were receiving some type of mental health therapy at the time of the survey, and 10% were receiving psychotropic medications (including antidepressants, stimulants, sedatives, and tranquilizers).

Unfortunately, few state-run correctional institutions have any substantial capacity for the in-depth psychiatric treatment of inmates who have serious mental illnesses. Some states, however, do operate facilities that specialize in the psychiatric confinement of convicted criminals. The BJS reports that state governments throughout the nation operate 12 facilities devoted exclusively to the care of mentally ill inmates and that another 143 prisons report psychiatric confinement as one specialty among other functions that they perform. As mentioned previously, the U.S. Supreme Court has ruled that mentally ill inmates can be required to take antipsychotic drugs, even against their wishes.[129]

Inmates with intellectual disabilities constitute still another group with special needs. Some studies estimate the proportion of mentally challenged inmates at about 10%.[130] Inmates with low IQs are less likely than other inmates to complete training and rehabilitative programs successfully, and they also evidence difficulty in adjusting to the routines of prison life. As a consequence, they are likely to exceed the averages in proportion of sentence served.[131] Only seven states report special facilities or programs for inmates with intellectual disabilities.[132] Other state systems "mainstream" such inmates, making them participate in regular activities with other inmates. Read a 2018 Government Accountability Office report on mentally ill inmates in federal prisons at **https://www.justicestudies. com/pubs/mental_2018.pdf**.

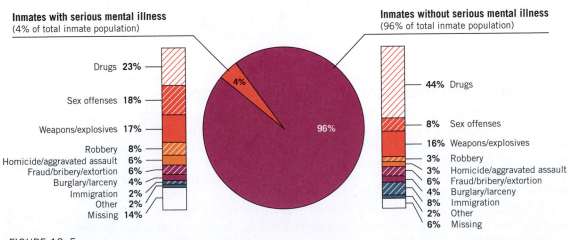

FIGURE 12–5
Federal Prisoners with and without Serious Mental Illness

Source: Government Accounting Office, *Federal Prisons: Information on Inmates with Serious Mental Illness and Strategies to Reduce Recidivism* (Washington, D.C.: GAO, 2018), p. 13.

Terrorism

Today's antiterrorism efforts have brought to light the important role that corrections personnel can play in preventing future attacks on American society and in averting crises that could arise in correctional institutions as a result of terrorist action. Some years after the attacks of 9/11, former New York City Police Commissioner Bernard B. Kerik told participants at the ACA's winter conference that corrections officers can help in the fight against terrorism through effective intelligence gathering and intelligence sharing. "Intelligence—that's the key to the success of this battle," Kerik said.[133] "You have to be part of that, because when we take the people off the streets in this country that go to jail, they communicate and they talk, they work with other criminals, organized gangs, organized units. You've got to collect that information, [and] you have to get it back to the authorities that need it."

Prison administrators must also be concerned about the potential impact of outside terrorist activity on their facility's inmate and staff populations. Of particular concern to today's prison administrators is the possibility of bioterrorism because a concentrated population like that of a prison or jail is highly susceptible to the rapid transmission of biological agents.[134]

The threat of a terrorist act being undertaken by inmates within a prison or jail can be an important consideration in facility planning and management, especially because inmates may be particularly vulnerable to recruitment by terrorist organizations. According to Chip Ellis, research and program coordinator for the National Memorial Institute for the Prevention of Terrorism, "Prisoners are a captive audience, and they usually have a diminished sense of self or a need for identity and protection. They're usually a disenchanted or disenfranchised group of people, [and] terrorists can sometimes capitalize on that situation."[135] Inmates can be radicalized in many ways, including exposure to other radical inmates, distribution of extremist literature, and anti-U.S. sermons heard during religious services.

Recently, the Institute for the Study of Violent Groups, located at Sam Houston State University, charged that the most radical form of Islam, or Wahhabism, was being spread in American prisons by clerics approved by the Islamic Society of North America, one of two organizations chosen by the BOP to select prison chaplains.[136] "Proselytizing in prisons," said an institute spokesperson, "can produce new recruits with American citizenship."

An example of one such activity can be found in the story of accused terrorist Kevin James, who, in 2009, was sentenced to 16 years in federal prison. James pleaded guilty in 2007 to conspiracy to wage war against the United States[137] and was accused of plotting terrorist attacks on Jewish and military targets throughout California. Among his targets were Los Angeles International Airport, the Israeli Consulate, and U.S. Army recruiting centers. (Read more about James and radicalism in the CJ News box Radical Islam, Terrorism, and U.S. Prisons in this chapter.)

In response to the terrorist threat, the BOP implemented a number of practices, and today it coordinates with other federal agencies to share intelligence information about suspected or known terrorists in its inmate population. The bureau closely tracks inmates with known or suspected terrorist ties and monitors their correspondence and other communications. The bureau also trains staff members to recognize terrorist-related activity and to effectively manage convicted terrorists within the correctional environment. A BOP program to counter radicalization efforts among inmates has been in place for the past 15 years.[138]

In 2018, the Program on Extremism at George Washington University released a report warning that "the U.S. lags behind many Western nations" in making in-prison anti-terror programs a priority. The report noted that as the number of jihadis in American prisons grows, "we are likely to see similar patterns" to rising European prison radicalization.[139] Learn more about prison radicalization from the FBI at **https://www.justicestudies .com/pubs/racial.pdf**; and read more about prison issues of all kinds from the Prison Policy Initiative via **http://www.prisonpolicy.org**.

🐦 Follow the author's tweets about the latest crime and justice news @schmalleger

CJ News
Radical Islam, Terrorism, and U.S. Prisons

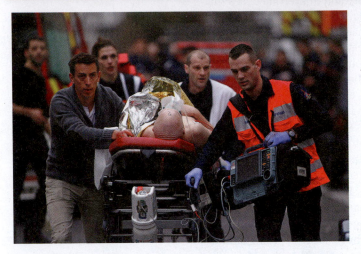

▲ A seriously wounded staffer is removed from the offices of Charlie Hebdo, the French newspaper that came under attack from Islamic militants in 2015. At least one of the two attackers had been radicalized during the 3 years he spent in a French prison. How might American correctional officers help in the national and international fight against terrorism?

Thibault Camus/AP Images

In 2015, two heavily armed terrorists, later found to be brothers, attacked the Paris offices of Charlie Hebdo, a newspaper famous for printing caricatures of the Prophet Muhammad. During the attack, the terrorists, who killed 12 of the newspaper's staff and wounded others, could be heard yelling "Allahu Akbar" (Arabic for "God is Great"), and "We have avenged the Prophet Muhammad."

Authorities later determined that at least one of the terrorist brothers, Cherif Kouachi, had become radicalized during the 3 years he spent in the French prison, Fleury-Mérogis.

Even before the attacks, a report by French police intelligence identified 95 prisoners as having become radicalized and classified them as "dangerous." Another 105 were said to "merit attention," with the report's authors noting that they could become "time bombs" once released.

American experts, however, seem to think the situation is different in this country. "The claim that U.S. prisons will generate scores of terrorists spilling out onto the streets of our cities appears to be false or, at least, much overstated," Bert Useem, PhD, a sociology professor at Purdue University, told a U.S. House panel studying the matter in June 2011. Useem noted that of 178 Muslim Americans involved in terrorism-related violence, only 12 showed any connection to radicalization behind bars.

Experts attribute this positive outcome, more than a decade after 9/11, as much to U.S. prisoners' lack of interest in Middle Eastern causes as to the steps prison authorities have taken to make sure inmates do not go down this path. The Federal BOP and state systems have improved monitoring of Muslim prisoners and reduced their access to radical Islamist literature, and authorities like the FBI have kept track of some prisoners after release.

In a country that is less than 1% Muslim, reportedly 10% of U.S. prisoners have embraced Islam. "The primary motivation I found was spiritual 'searching'—seeking religious meaning to interpret and resolve discontent," wrote Mark Hamm, PhD, a professor of criminology at Indiana State University. His 2-year study of prisoner radicalization appeared in the *National Institute of Justice Journal* in October 2008.

Although that spiritual quest is quite different from the path to Jihad, Hamm warned that "the potential for ideologically inspired criminality" still exists. He noted that a few terrorist plots had been uncovered in Florida and California prisons. In California's New Folsom Prison in 2005, several Muslim convicts led by Kevin James plotted terrorist acts against the National Guard, synagogues, and the Israeli consulate. When several members of the group were paroled, they committed a string of bank heists to finance their plan, but they were caught before they could commit it.

Middle Eastern interests have reached out to U.S. prisons. In 2003, *The Wall Street Journal* reported that Saudi Arabia "ships out hundreds of copies of the Quran each month, as well as religious pamphlets and videos, to prison chaplains and Islamic groups who then pass them along to inmates."

Many U.S. prisoners and their Islamic chaplains have embraced the Saudis' Wahhabi Salafist sect, with its Islamic-supremacist interpretation of the Quran. Warith Deen Umar, a Wahhabi Salafist who was head Muslim chaplain of the New York prisons until 2000, told *The Wall Street Journal* that prison "is the perfect recruitment and training grounds for radicalism and the Islamic religion."

The Wall Street Journal's revelations prompted a review by the Office of the Inspector General (OIG) of the use of Muslim chaplains and Islamic literature in the BOP. The OIG's 2004 report issued 16 recommendations, including requiring imams (Muslim chaplains) to work closely with security staff, closely monitoring volunteer imams, and screening prayer books. Many state prisons took up the recommendations as well.

In addition, long-standing prohibitions against using the Internet have barred prisoners' access to radical sites, although some have smuggled in smartphones. As a further precaution, the BOP in 2006 began isolating a few dozen radical Islamist prisoners in two communication management units that severely restrict visitation rights and monitor all telephone calls and mail. The CMU at the U.S. Penitentiary in Marion, Illinois, houses 18 Muslims, including Kevin James.

REFERENCES

Professor Bert Useem, "Testimony for the Committee on Homeland Security," Purdue University, June 15, 2011, http://homeland.house.gov/sites/homeland.house.gov/files/Testimony%20Useem.pdf.

Daniel J. Wakin, "Imams Reject Talk That Islam Radicalizes Inmates," *New York Times*, May 23, 2009, http://www.nytimes.com/-2009/05/24/nyregion/24convert.html?_r=1&ref=us.

Mark S. Hamm, "Prisoner Radicalization: Assessing the Threat in U.S. Correctional Institutions," *National Institute of Justice Journal*, October 2008, http://www.nij.gov/journals/261/prisoner-radicalization.htm.

Jim Yardley, "Jihadism Born in a Paris Park and Fueled in the Prison Yard, *The New York Times*, January 11, 2015, http://www.nytimes.com/2015/01/12/world/europe/jihadism-born-in-a-paris-park-and-fueled-in-the-prison-yard.html.

Summary

PRISON LIFE

- Prisons are small self-contained societies that are sometimes described as total institutions. Studies of prison life have detailed the existence of prison subcultures, or inmate worlds, replete with inmate values, social roles, and lifestyles. New inmates who are socialized into prison subcultures are said to undergo the process of prisonization. Prison subcultures are very influential, and both inmates and staff must reckon with them. Today's prisons are miniature societies, reflecting the problems and challenges that exist in the larger society of which they are a part.

- There are far more men in prison than women, with the ratio of male to female inmates being around 15 to 1. The number of female inmates is rising quickly, however. Female inmates are disproportionately victimized by both other inmates and staff in federal and state prisons, as well as local jails.

- Many female inmates have histories of physical and sexual abuse. Although they are likely to have dependent children, their parenting skills may be limited. Most female inmates are housed in centralized state facilities known as *women's prisons*, which are dedicated exclusively to incarcerating female felons. Some states, however, particularly those with small populations, continue to keep female prisoners in special wings of what are otherwise institutions for men. Few facilities for women have programs especially designed for female offenders.

- Like prisoners, corrections officers undergo a socialization process that helps them function by the official and unofficial rules of staff society. Prison staffers are most concerned with custody and control. The enforcement of strict rules; body and cell searches; counts; unannounced shakedowns; the control of dangerous items, materials, and contraband; and the extensive use of bars, locks, fencing, cameras, and alarms all support the staff's vigilance in maintaining security. Although concerns with security still command center stage, professionalism is playing an increasing role in corrections today, and today's corrections personnel are better trained and more proficient than ever before.

- Security threat groups (STGs) are prison gangs. More formally, they can be defined as inmate groups or organizations whose members act together to pose a threat to the safety of corrections staff or the public, who prey upon other inmates, or who threaten the secure and orderly operation of a correctional institution. American prisons contain a number of well-organized STGs whose influence extends between prisons and out into the general public.

- For many years, courts throughout the nation assumed a hands-off approach to prisons, rarely intervening in the day-to-day administration of prison facilities. That changed in the late 1960s when the U.S. Supreme Court began to identify inmates' rights mandated by the Constitution. Rights identified by the Court include the right to physical integrity, an absolute right to be free from unwarranted corporal punishments, certain religious rights, and procedural rights, such as those involving access to attorneys and to the courts. The conditional rights of prisoners, which have repeatedly been supported by the Court, mandate professionalism among prison administrators and require vigilance in the provision of correctional services. High Court decisions have generally established that prison inmates retain those constitutional rights that are not inconsistent with their status as prisoners or with the legitimate penological objectives of the correctional system. In other words, inmates have rights, much the same as people who are not incarcerated, provided that the legitimate needs of the prison for security, custody, and safety are not compromised. The era of prisoners' rights was sharply curtailed in 1996 with the passage of the Prison Litigation Reform Act, spurred on by a growing recognition of the legal morass resulting from unregulated access to federal courts by inmates across the nation.

- The major problems and issues facing prisons today include (1) the need to deal with a growing geriatric offender population (the result of longer sentences and the aging of the American population), (2) a sizable number of mentally ill and mentally deficient inmates, and (3) a concern over inmates with terrorist leanings and those incarcerated for terrorism-related crimes.

QUESTIONS FOR REVIEW

1. Describe early research on prison life, including the development of the concept of *total institutions*.
2. What are prison subcultures, and how do they influence prison life? How do they develop, and what purpose do they serve?
3. How do women's prisons differ from men's? Why have women's prisons been studied less often than institutions for men?
4. What are the primary concerns of prison staff? What other goals do staff members focus on?
5. What are security threat groups? What problems do they cause?
6. What are the commonly accepted rights of prisoners in the United States today? Where do these rights come from? What U.S. Supreme Court cases are especially significant in the area of prisoners' rights?
7. What are some of the major issues that prisons face today? What new issues might the future bring?

Juvenile Justice

It is with young people that prevention efforts are most needed and hold the greatest promise.

— President's Commission on
Law Enforcement and
Administration of Justice[1]

CHAPTER

13

Learning Objectives

After reading this chapter, you should be able to:

1. Describe how the juvenile justice system has evolved in the Western world. **412**

2. Describe important U.S. Supreme Court decisions relating to juvenile justice, including their impact on the handling of juveniles by the system. **415**

3. Compare juvenile and adult systems of justice. **419**

4. Briefly describe possible future directions in juvenile justice. **430**

Gregory Smith/Corbis Historical/Getty Images

Introduction

In 2010, in the case of *Graham* v. *Florida*, the U.S. Supreme Court formally recognized fundamental differences between the neurological capacity of juveniles and adults. The justices wrote that "developments in psychology and brain science continue to show fundamental differences between juvenile and adult minds." They went on to give examples, saying that "parts of the brain involved in behavior control continue to mature through late adolescence," and that "[j]uveniles are more capable of change than are adults, and their actions are less likely to be evidence of 'irretrievably depraved character' than are the actions of adults."[2] Consequently, in *Graham*, the Court abolished life imprisonment without the possibility of parole for persons who commit serious crimes (other than homicide) as teenagers.

Two years later, in 2012, the Court reinforced its view of adolescent development by holding, in the case of *Miller* v. *Alabama*, that "mandatory life without parole for a juvenile precludes consideration of his chronological age and its hallmark features—among them, immaturity, impetuosity, and failure to appreciate risks and consequences."[3] More recently, in 2016, the U.S. Supreme Court made retroactive its decision in *Miller*, opening the door for resentencing or possible parole for 2,300 people who were sentenced to mandatory life in prison as juveniles. That case, *Montgomery* v. *Louisiana*, gave those people the right to have their sentences reviewed. The *Montgomery* ruling also made clear that sentences of life without parole for crime committed by children should only be applied in rare cases of "permanent incorrigibility." While we will discuss these cases later in this chapter, the written opinions that support them provide important evidence that understandings of adolescent behavior are changing, and that those changes are now impacting the juvenile justice system in significant new ways.[4] It is important to note, however, that in 2018 the Court rejected the appeal of a man who was sentenced to 241 years in prison for a crime he committed when he was 16 years old. The lengthy prison term is equivalent to a sentence of life without parole, because the defendant involved won't be eligible for parole until he is 112 years old.[5] In short, there is disagreement among Supreme Court Justices over whether a term-of-years sentence under which a juvenile nonhomicide offender is not eligible for parole during his natural lifetime violates the Eighth Amendment.

A key finding of the Study Group on Serious and Violent Juvenile Offenders, convened by the Office of Juvenile Justice and Delinquency Prevention (OJJDP), is that most chronic juvenile offenders begin their delinquency careers before age 12, and some start as early as age 10.[6] The most recent national data show that in 2017, police arrested about 180,000 children under the age of 15.[7] These very young offenders (known as *child delinquents*) represent about 28% of the total number of **juveniles** (those up to age 18) who are arrested.

Although states vary as to the age at which a person legally enters adulthood, statistics on crime make it clear that young people are disproportionately involved in certain offenses. A recent report, for example, found that over 10% of all violent crimes and 14% of all property crimes are committed by people younger than age 18 (Figure 13–1), although this age group makes up 22.5% of the population of the United States.[8] On average, about 9% of all arrests in any year are of juveniles,[9] and people younger than age 18 have a higher likelihood of being arrested for robbery and other property crimes than do people in any other age group. Once a juvenile has been charged with an offense, he or she is sometimes referred to as a **justice-involved youth**.

The OJJDP is a primary source of information on juvenile justice in the United States. A sweeping OJJDP overview of juvenile crime and the juvenile justice system in America reveals the following:[10]

- About 700,000 thousand juveniles (under age 18) are arrested annually in America.
- Violent crime by juveniles is decreasing.
- Younger juveniles account for a substantial proportion of juvenile arrests and of the juvenile court caseload.

Follow the author's tweets about the latest crime and justice news @schmalleger

juvenile
A youth at or below the upper age of juvenile court jurisdiction in a particular state.

justice-involved youth
youth who are charged with or adjudicated for law violations.

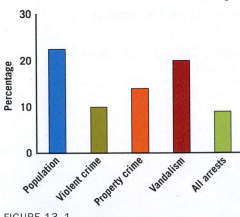

FIGURE 13–1
Juvenile Involvement in Crime versus System Totals, 2017

Note: The term *juvenile* refers to people younger than 18 years of age.
Source: Crime in the United States, 2017, Federal Bureau of Investigation.

- Relative to male delinquency, female delinquency has grown substantially.
  - Greater percentages of females than males are in placement for status offenses and assaults.
  - Both girls and boys who are in the juvenile justice system usually have problems at home and school that have put them at risk for delinquency—including maltreatment, poverty, or both—and these factors also may have a negative impact on their adjustment to young adulthood.
- Minority juveniles are greatly overrepresented in the custody population.
- Crowding is an ongoing problem in juvenile facilities.

Recent data from a 7-year collaborative, multidisciplinary project called the Pathways to Desistance Study reveal that:[11]

▲ Columbine (Colorado) High School shooters Eric Harris (*left*) and Dylan Klebold examining a sawed-off shot- gun in a still image taken from a video- tape made at a makeshift shooting range in 1999. About 6 weeks after the video was made, Harris (age 18) and Klebold (age 17) shot and killed 15 people and injured 20 more at the school. How might such disasters be averted in the future?

Jefferson County Sheriff's Department/ Hulton Archive/Getty Images

- Most youth who commit felonies greatly reduce their offending over time, regardless of the intervention or treatment they receive.
- Longer stays in juvenile institutions do not reduce recidivism.
- Community-based supervision as a component of aftercare is effective for youth who have committed serious crimes.
- Substance-abuse treatment reduces both substance use and criminal offending.

The Pathways to Desistance Study, funded by the OJJDP, followed 1,354 serious juvenile offenders ages 14 through 18 for 7 years after their conviction. The study looked at the factors that lead youth who have committed serious offenses to continue or to desist from offending, including individual maturation, life changes, and involvement with the criminal justice system. Learn more about the OJJDP via **http://www.ojjdp.gov**, and read the agency's recently launched *Journal of Juvenile Justice* at **http://www.journalofjuvjustice.org**. Additional information about the Pathways to Desistance Study can be found at **http:// www.pathwaysstudy.pitt.edu/index.html**.

This chapter has four purposes. First, we will briefly look at the history of the **juvenile justice system**, comprising government agencies involved with youth who are offenders or subjects of court oversight. The juvenile justice system has its roots in the adult system, but in the juvenile system, we find a more uniform philosophical base and a relatively clear agreement about the system's purpose. These differences may be due to the fact that the system is relatively new and that society generally agrees that young people who have gone wrong are worth salvaging. However, the philosophy that underlies the juvenile justice system in America is increasingly being questioned by "get-tough" advocates of law and order, many of whom are fed up with violent juvenile crime.

Our second purpose is to compare the juvenile and adult systems as they currently operate. The reasoning behind the juvenile justice system has led to administrative and other procedures that, in many jurisdictions, are not found in the adult system. The juvenile justice process, for example, is frequently not as open as the adult system: Hearings may be held in secret, names of offenders are not published, and records of juvenile proceedings may later be destroyed.[12]

Our third purpose is to describe the agencies, processes, and problems of the juvenile justice system itself. Although each state may have variations, a common system structure is shared by all.

Near the end of this chapter, we will turn to our fourth focus and consider some of the issues raised by critics of the current system. Although conservative attitudes brought changes in the adult criminal justice system over the past few decades, the juvenile justice system has remained relatively unchanged. Based on premises quite different from

juvenile justice system

The government agencies that function to investigate, supervise, adjudicate, care for, or confine youthful offenders and other children subject to the jurisdiction of the juvenile court.

those of the adult system, juvenile justice has long been a separate decision-making arena in which the best interests of the child have been accorded great importance. As we will see, substantial changes are now afoot.

Juvenile Justice throughout History

Earliest Times

Before the modern era (Figure 13–2), children who committed crimes in the Western world received no preferential treatment because of their youth. They were adjudicated and punished alongside adults. In fact, some recorded cases have come down through history of children as young as age six being hung or burned at the stake.[13]

In like fashion, little distinction was made between criminality and **delinquency** (misbehavior or conduct of juveniles in violation of the law) or other kinds of undesirable behavior.[14]

Early philosophy in dealing with juveniles derived from a Roman principle called *patria potestas*. Under Roman law (circa 753 B.C.), children were members of their family, but the father had absolute control over

▲ The ruins left by a disastrous fire that swept through Gatlinburg, Tennessee, in 2016. Two teenagers were later charged with aggravated arson after an investigation concluded that they threw lighted matches onto parched ground on the town's outskirts, intending to start the blaze.

Erik Schelzig/AP Images

1 Describe how the juvenile justice system has evolved in the Western world.

Colonial Period
(1636–1823)
The family was the primary means of social control of children; recalcitrant children then suffered public whipping, dunkings (partial drowning), and the stocks.

Juvenile Rights
(1967–1975)
In several court decision, the U.S. Supreme Court granted Juveniles due process rights in the juvenile justice system.

Reform Agenda
(late 1970s)
The major purpose of this agenda was to divert the handling of status offenses from a criminal to a noncriminal setting.

Juvenile Courts
(1899–1966)
Created in Cook County, Illinois, and using *parens patriae* as a legal philosophy, this court handles all illegal behaviors among juveniles.

Social Control and Juvenile Crime
(1980s)
The major thrusts were to reassess the soft-line approach to minor offenders and status offenders and to "get tough" on serious and violent juvenile crime.

Houses of Refuge
(1824–1898)
Wayward children were placed in facilities intended to reform them.

Delinquency and the Growing Fear of Crime
(1990–2010)
The "get tough" attitude toward violent juveniles led to a number of juvenile justice initiatives in the 1990s and extending to the twenty-first century that went beyond those implemented in the 1980s.

A New Understanding of Juvenile Behavior Emerges
(2010–present)
Increased understanding of juvenile behavior resulting from studies in neurobiology and developmental psychology that recognized significant differences between the minds of juveniles and adults.

| 1600 | 1700 | 1800 | 1900 | 2000 | 2020 |

FIGURE 13–2
Perspectives on Juveniles through History

Source: Based on *Juvenile Delinquency* 9e by Clemens Bartollas and Frank Schmalleger. Fig 01–03, p 12. Copyright © 2019 by Pearson Education.

🐦 Follow the author's tweets about the latest crime and justice news @schmalleger

them, and they in turn had an absolute responsibility to obey his wishes. Roman understanding of the social role of children strongly influenced English culture and eventually led to the development of the legal principle of **parens patriae** in Western law, which allowed the king (or the English state) to take the place of parents in dealing with children who broke the law.

By the end of the eighteenth century, social conditions in Europe and America had begun to change, and the Enlightenment, a highly significant intellectual and social movement, emphasized human potential. In this new age, children were recognized as the only true heirs to the future, and society became increasingly concerned about their well-being.

By the middle of the nineteenth century, large-scale immigration to America was under way. Some immigrant families became victims of the cities that drew them, settling in squalor in hastily formed ghettos. Many children, abandoned by families unable to support them, were forced into lives on the streets, where they formed tattered gangs, surviving off the refuse of the glittering cities.

An 1823 report by the Society for the Prevention of Pauperism in the city of New York called for the development of "houses of refuge" to save children from lives of crime and poverty. In 1824, the first house of refuge opened in New York City.[15] It sheltered mostly young thieves, vagrants, and runaways. Other children, especially those with more severe delinquency problems, were placed in adult prisons and jails. Houses of refuge became popular in New York, and other cities quickly copied them. It was not long, however, before overcrowding developed and living conditions deteriorated.

Not long afterward, the American child-savers movement began. Child savers espoused a philosophy of productivity and eschewed idleness and unprincipled behavior.[16] One product of the child-savers movement was the reform school—a place for delinquent juveniles that embodied the atmosphere of a wholesome family environment. By the middle of the nineteenth century, the reform-school approach to handling juveniles led to the creation of the Chicago Reform School, which opened in the 1860s. Reform schools focused primarily on predelinquent youth who showed tendencies toward more serious criminal involvement.

The Juvenile Court Era

In 1870, an expanding recognition of children's needs led the state of Massachusetts to enact legislation that required separate hearings for juveniles.[17] New York followed with a similar law in 1877,[18] which also prohibited contact between juvenile and adult offenders. Rhode Island enacted juvenile court legislation in 1898, and in 1899 the Colorado School Law became the first comprehensive legislation designed to adjudicate problem children.[19] It was, however, the 1899 codification of Illinois juvenile law that became the model for juvenile court statutes throughout the nation.

The Illinois Juvenile Court Act created a **juvenile court**, separate in form and function from adult criminal courts. To avoid the lasting stigma of criminality, the law applied the term *delinquent* rather than *criminal* to young adjudicated offenders. The act specified that juvenile court judges were to use the best interests of the child as a guide for decision making in their deliberations. In effect, judges were to serve as advocates for juveniles, guiding their development. The determination of guilt or innocence took second place to the betterment of the child. The law abandoned a strict adherence to the due-process requirements of adult prosecutions, allowing informal procedures designed to scrutinize the child's situation. By sheltering the juvenile from the punishment philosophy of the adult system, the Illinois Juvenile Court emphasized reformation in place of retribution.[20]

In 1938, the federal government passed the Juvenile Court Act, which embodied many of the features of the Illinois statute. By 1945, every state had enacted special legislation focusing on the handling of juveniles, and the juvenile court movement became well established.[21]

The juvenile court movement was based on five philosophical principles that can be summarized as follows:[22]

1. The state is the "higher or ultimate parent" of all the children within its borders.

2. Children are worth saving, and nonpunitive procedures should be used to save them.

delinquency
In the broadest usage, juvenile actions or conduct in violation of criminal law, juvenile status offenses, and other juvenile misbehavior.

parens patriae
A common law principle that allows the state to assume a parental role and to take custody of a child when he or she becomes delinquent, is abandoned, or is in need of care that the natural parents are unable or unwilling to provide.

Follow the author's tweets about the latest crime and justice news @schmalleger

juvenile court
Any court that has jurisdiction over matters involving juveniles.

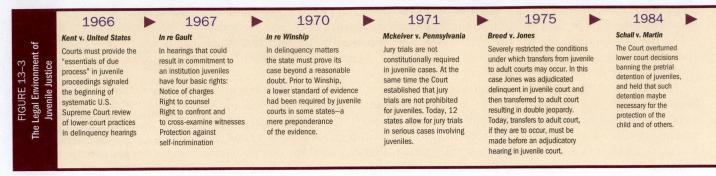

FIGURE 13-3
The Legal Environment of Juvenile Justice

1966 ▶	1967 ▶	1970 ▶	1971 ▶	1975 ▶	1984 ▶
Kent v. United States	**In re Gault**	**In re Winship**	**Mckeiver v. Pennsylvania**	**Breed v. Jones**	**Schall v. Martin**
Courts must provide the "essentials of due process" in juvenile proceedings signaled the beginning of systematic U.S. Supreme Court review of lower-court practices in delinquency hearings	In hearings that could result in commitment to an institution juveniles have four basic rights: Notice of charges Right to counsel Right to confront and to cross-examine witnesses Protection against self-incrimination	In delinquency matters the state must prove its case beyond a reasonable doubt. Prior to Winship, a lower standard of evidence had been required by juvenile courts in some states—a mere preponderance of the evidence.	Jury trials are not constitutionally required in juvenile cases. At the same time the Court established that jury trials are not prohibited for juveniles. Today, 12 states allow for jury trials in serious cases involving juveniles.	Severely restricted the conditions under which transfers from juvenile to adult courts may occur. In this case Jones was adjudicated delinquent in juvenile court and then transferred to adult court resulting in double jeopardy. Today, transfers to adult court, if they are to occur, must be made before an adjudicatory hearing in juvenile court.	The Court overturned lower court decisions banning the pretrial detention of juveniles, and held that such detention maybe necessary for the protection of the child and of others.

delinquent child
A child who has engaged in activity that would be considered a crime if the child were an adult. The term *delinquent* is used to avoid the stigma associated with the term *criminal*.

undisciplined child
A child who is beyond parental control, as evidenced by his or her refusal to obey legitimate authorities, such as school officials and teachers.

dependent child
A child who has no parents or whose parents are not available or are unable to care for him or her.

neglected child
A child who is not receiving the proper level of physical or psychological care from his or her parents or guardians or who has been placed up for adoption in violation of the law.

abused child
A child who has been physically, emotionally, or sexually abused. Most states also consider a child who is forced into delinquent activity by a parent or guardian to be abused.

status offender
A child who commits an act that is contrary to the law by virtue of the offender's status as a child. Purchasing cigarettes, buying alcohol, and being truant are examples of such behavior.

3. Children should be nurtured, and while the nurturing process is under way, they should be protected from the stigmatizing impact of formal adjudicatory procedures.

4. To accomplish the goal of reformation, justice needs to be individualized; that is, each child is different, and the needs, aspirations, living conditions, and so on of each child must be known in their individual particulars if the court is to be helpful.

5. Noncriminal procedures are necessary to give primary consideration to the needs of the child. For this reason, the denial of due process can be justified in the face of constitutional challenges because the court acts not to punish but to help.

Learn more about the history of juvenile justice and the juvenile court at **https://www .justicestudies.com/pubs/juvenile.pdf**.

Categories of Children in the Juvenile Justice System

By the time of the Great Depression, most states had expanded juvenile statutes to include the following six categories of children. These categories are still used today in most jurisdictions to describe the variety of children subject to juvenile court jurisdiction.

1. *Delinquent child.* A **delinquent child** is one who violates the criminal law. If the delinquent child were an adult, the word *criminal* would be applied instead. (As noted earlier, federal agencies recently began using the term "justice-involved youth" in place of "delinquent" in order to avoid the stigma normally associated with delinquency.)

2. *Undisciplined child.* An **undisciplined child** is said to be beyond parental control, as evidenced by his or her refusal to obey legitimate authorities, such as school officials and teachers. Such a child needs state protection.

3. *Dependent child.* A **dependent child** typically has no parents or guardians to care for him or her. The child's parents are deceased, the child was placed up for adoption, or the child was abandoned in violation of the law.

4. *Neglected child.* A **neglected child** is one who does not receive proper care from parents or guardians. Such a child may suffer from malnutrition or may not be provided with adequate shelter.

5. *Abused child.* An **abused child** is one who has been physically, emotionally, or sexually abused. Most states also consider a child who is forced into delinquent activity by a parent or guardian to be abused.

6. *Status offender.* The term **status offender** is a special category encompassing children who violate laws written only for them. In some states, status offenders are referred to as persons in need of supervision (PINS).

> Status offenses include behavior such as truancy, vagrancy, running away from home, and incorrigibility.

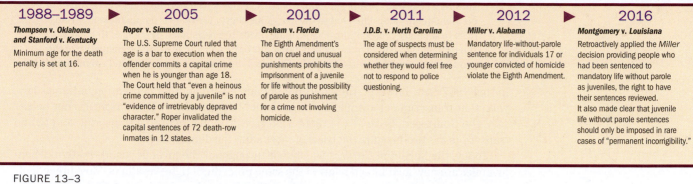

1988–1989 ►	2005 ►	2010 ►	2011 ►	2012 ►	2016
Thompson v. Oklahoma and Stanford v. Kentucky	**Roper v. Simmons**	**Graham v. Florida**	**J.D.B. v. North Carolina**	**Miller v. Alabama**	**Montgomery v. Louisiana**
Minimum age for the death penalty is set at 16.	The U.S. Supreme Court ruled that age is a bar to execution when the offender commits a capital crime when he is younger than age 18. The Court held that "even a heinous crime committed by a juvenile" is not "evidence of irretrievably depraved character." Roper invalidated the capital sentences of 72 death-row inmates in 12 states.	The Eighth Amendment's ban on cruel and unusual punishments prohibits the imprisonment of a juvenile for life without the possibility of parole as punishment for a crime not involving homicide.	The age of suspects must be considered when determining whether they would feel free not to respond to police questioning.	Mandatory life-without-parole sentence for individuals 17 or younger convicted of homicide violate the Eighth Amendment.	Retroactively applied the *Miller* decision providing people who had been sentenced to mandatory life without parole as juveniles, the right to have their sentences reviewed. It also made clear that juvenile life without parole sentences should only be imposed in rare cases of "permanent incorrigibility."

FIGURE 13–3
The Legal Environment of Juvenile Justice (continued)

Status offenses include behavior such as truancy, vagrancy, running away from home, and incorrigibility, and the youthful status of juveniles is a necessary element in such offenses. Adults, for example, may "run away from home" and not violate any law. Runaway children, however, are subject to apprehension and juvenile court processing because state laws require that they be subject to parental control.

Status offenses were a natural outgrowth of juvenile court philosophy. As a consequence, however, juveniles in need of help often faced procedural dispositions that treated them as though they were delinquent. Rather than lowering the rate of juvenile incarceration, the juvenile court movement led to its increase. Critics of the juvenile court movement quickly focused on the abandonment of due-process rights, especially in the case of status offenders, as a major source of problems. Detention and incarceration, they argued, were inappropriate options for situations in which children had not committed crimes.

status offense
An act or conduct that is declared by statute to be an offense, but only when committed by or engaged in by a juvenile, and that can be adjudicated only by a juvenile court.

The Legal Environment

2 Describe important U.S. Supreme Court decisions relating to juvenile justice, including their impact on the handling of juveniles by the system.

Throughout the first half of the twentieth century, the U.S. Supreme Court followed a hands-off approach to juvenile justice, much like its early approach to prisons (see Chapter 12). The adjudication and further processing of juveniles by the system were left mostly to specialized juvenile courts or to local appeals courts. Although one or two early Supreme Court decisions[23] dealt with issues of juvenile justice, it was not until the 1960s that the Court began close legal scrutiny of the principles underlying the system itself. Some of the most important U.S. Supreme Court cases relating to juvenile justice are shown in Figure 13–3.

In 1966, in the case of *Kent* v. *U.S.*,[24] the U.S. Supreme Court began what would become an ongoing examination of juvenile justice and the processes surrounding it. In *Kent*, the justices held that courts must provide the "essentials of due process" in juvenile proceedings. This important case signaled the beginning of systematic U.S. Supreme Court review of lower court practices in delinquency hearings.

It was followed, a year later, by *In re Gault*, in which the U.S. Supreme Court held, in part, as follows:

> [T]he Juvenile Court Judge's exercise of the power of the state as *parens patriae* [is] not unlimited. . . . Notice, to comply with due process requirements, must be given sufficiently in advance of scheduled court proceedings so that reasonable opportunity to prepare will be afforded. . . . The probation officer cannot act as counsel for the child. His role in the adjudicatory hearing, by statute and in fact, is as arresting officer and witness against the child. There is no material difference in this respect between adult and juvenile proceedings of the

It was the 1899 codification of Illinois juvenile law that became the model for juvenile court statutes throughout the nation. The act created a juvenile court, separate in form and function from adult criminal courts.

sort here involved. . . . A proceeding where the issue is whether the child will be found to be "delinquent" and subjected to the loss of his liberty for years is comparable in seriousness to a felony prosecution. The juvenile needs the assistance of counsel to cope with the problems of law, to make skilled inquiry into the facts, to insist upon regularity of the proceedings, and to ascertain whether he has a defense and to prepare and submit it.[25]

In that 1967 case, however, the Court did not agree with another contention of Gault's lawyers: that transcripts of juvenile hearings should be maintained. Transcripts are not necessary, the Court said, because (1) there is no constitutional right to a transcript, and (2) no transcripts are produced in the trials of most adult misdemeanants.

Today, the impact of *Gault* is widely felt throughout the juvenile justice system, where juveniles are now guaranteed many of the same procedural rights as adults. Most precedent-setting Supreme Court decisions that followed *Gault* further clarified the rights of juveniles, focusing primarily on those few issues of due process that it had not explicitly addressed. One of these was the 1970 case of *In re Winship*, which centered on the standard of evidence needed in juvenile hearings. Winship's attorney had argued that the guilt of a juvenile facing a hearing should have to be proved beyond a reasonable doubt—the evidentiary standard of adult criminal trials. In its ruling the Court agreed, saying:

> [T]he constitutional safeguard of proof beyond a reasonable doubt is as much required during the adjudicatory stage of a delinquency proceeding as are those constitutional guards applied in *Gault*. . . . We therefore hold . . . that where a 12 year old child is charged with an act of stealing which renders him liable to confinement for as long as six years, then, as a matter of due process . . . the case against him must be proved beyond a reasonable doubt.[26]

As a consequence of *Winship*, allegations of delinquency today must be established beyond a reasonable doubt. The Court allowed, however, the continued use of the lower evidentiary standard in adjudicating juveniles charged with status offenses. Even though both standards continue to exist, most jurisdictions have chosen to use the stricter burden-of-proof requirement for all delinquency proceedings.

🐦 Follow the author's tweets about the latest crime and justice news @schmalleger

Cases like *Gault* and *Winship* have not extended all adult procedural rights to juveniles charged with delinquency. The case of *McKeiver* v. *Pennsylvania* (1971),[27] for example, reiterated what earlier cases had established—specifically, that juveniles do not have the constitutional right to a trial by a jury of their peers. It is important to note, however, that the *McKeiver* decision did not specifically prohibit jury trials for juveniles. As a consequence, approximately 12 states today allow the option of jury trials for juveniles.

In 1975, in the case of *Breed* v. *Jones*, the Court severely restricted the conditions under which transfers from juvenile to adult courts may occur by mandating that such transfers must be made before any adjudicatory hearing in juvenile court.[28] In 1984, in the case of *Schall* v. *Martin*,[29] the U.S. Supreme Court upheld the constitutionality of a New York state statute, ruling that pretrial detention of juveniles based on "serious risk" does not violate the principle of fundamental fairness required by due process. In so holding, the Court recognized that states have a legitimate interest in preventing future delinquency by juveniles thought to be dangerous. Although the *Schall* decision upheld the practice of preventive detention, the Court seized on the opportunity provided by the case to impose procedural requirements on the detaining authority. Consequently, preventive detention today cannot be imposed without (1) prior notice, (2) an equitable detention hearing, and (3) a statement by the judge setting forth the reason(s) for detention.

In 1988, in the case of *Thompson* v. *Oklahoma*,[30] the U.S. Supreme Court determined that national standards of decency did not permit the execution of any offender who was under age 16 at the time of the crime. In 2005, in the case of *Roper* v. *Simmons*,[31] the Court set a new standard when it ruled that age *is* a bar to execution when the offender commits a capital crime when he is younger than age 18. In *Roper*, the justices stated, "[The fact] that juveniles still struggle to define their identity means it is less supportable to conclude that even a heinous crime committed by a juvenile is evidence of irretrievably depraved character." The *Roper* ruling invalidated the capital sentences of 72 death-row inmates in 12 states.[32]

In 2010, in the case of *Graham* v. *Florida*,[33] the Court interpreted the cruel and unusual punishment clause of the U.S. Constitution to mean that a juvenile offender cannot be sentenced to life in prison without parole for a crime not involving homicide. This ruling, said

CJ News
Schools Take Bullying Seriously

Bullying in schools, once thought to be just part of growing up, is now widely seen as a root cause of poor learning, school violence, and suicide—a revised view that has set off an avalanche of state anti-bullying laws and major adjustments in school policies.

Experts say anywhere from 20% to 50% of students are bullied at some point, and 10% are regularly victimized. The harmful effects have been documented in several U.S. studies. Some 160,000 children to stay home from school each day to avoid bullying, and 4.1% of victims have brought weapons to school in response. Victims are 5.6 times more likely to contemplate suicide.

But until recently, many school authorities did nothing. The National Association of School Psychologists reports that nearly 25% of teachers do not believe intervention in bullying is necessary.

In an age when students socialize online, bad behavior has moved from the stairwell and locker room to Facebook and Twitter. This so-called cyberbullying complicates the issue because it doesn't occur on school grounds, and many parents and teachers aren't involved in social media.

States began to pass anti-bullying laws after the 1999 shootings at Columbine High School in suburban Denver, which were blamed in part on bullying. Suicides of some taunted students, often outed for being gay, also prompted these laws. By May 2015, every state had an anti-bullying statute.

The laws vary widely, but in general, they include requiring schools to establish anti-bullying policies, track incidents, create training and prevention programs for teachers and students, and establish sanctions such as suspension, reassignment, or expulsion. In addition, states have amended laws to cover cyberbullying and subtler kinds of harassment, such as ostracizing.

So far, the laws have stood up in the courts. When a West Virginia high school senior was suspended from school for creating a fake Internet profile of another student, calling her a "slut who had herpes," her parents sued the school on free speech grounds, but a federal appeals court threw out their lawsuit.

Even revered high school athletics programs aren't immune from angry parents citing the new laws. A few years ago, for example, three stars of the Carmel, Indiana, high school basketball team were suspended for 5 days for bullying two freshmen team members on the bus ride home from a game.

In many cases, however, the laws are spottily enforced. In Georgia, the first state to pass an anti-bullying law in 1999, Atlanta-area schools reported more than 1,900 bullying incidents in the 2009–2010 school year, but only 30 expulsions or reassignments as a result, and a whole suburban county reported no incidents at all.

Furthermore, school policies may not deter bullying. A Massachusetts school with a suicide due to bullying had an anti-bullying policy in place.

There is a lot of bad behavior in schools, but what constitutes bullying? The test, one New York judge wrote, is whether the conduct is "sufficiently severe, persistent or pervasive that it creates a hostile environment" that "deprives a student of substantial educational opportunities." For additional information on online violence

▲ A younger boy being physically threatened and bullied by an older one. What can be done to prevent bullying in schools? In the community?

Alexandre Nunes/Shutterstock

and cyberbullying, see the Bureau of Justice Assistance publication Real Crimes in Virtual Worlds at **https://www.justicestudies .com/pubs/virtualcrimes.pdf**.

REFERENCES

Real Crimes in Virtual Worlds (Washington, D.C.: Bureau of Justice Assistance, 2013).

"Schools, parents try to keep pace with cyber-bullying tactics," *Baltimore Sun*, April 22, 2012, http://articles.baltimoresun.com/2012-04-22/ news/bs-md-ho-cyber-reader-20120422_1_cyber-bullying-anti-bullying laws-rutgers-university-freshman.

"Analysis of State Bullying Laws and Policies," U.S. Department of Education, December 2011, http://www2.ed.gov/rschstat/eval/ bullying/state-bullying-laws/state-bullying-laws.pdf.

"Law Firmer against Bullies," *Atlanta Journal-Constitution*, November 20, 2010, http://www.ajc.com/news/atlanta/law-firmer-against bullies-748057. html.

Lisa Baumann, "Gov. Bullock signs Montana anti-bullying bill into law," *Great Falls Tribune*, April 21, 2015, http://www.greatfallstribune. com/story/news/local/2015/04/21/gov-bullock-signs-montana-anti-bullying-bill-law/26145567/ (accessed January 15, 2018).

the Court, "gives the juvenile offender a chance to demonstrate maturity and reform." In 2011, *J.D.B.* v. *North Carolina*, the court held that the age of suspects must be considered when determining whether they would feel free not to respond to police questioning.

In 2012, in the case of *Miller* v. *Alabama*, the Supreme Court struck down any requirement that life without parole be the mandatory penalty for murder by a minor.[34] The Court ruled that state laws that *require* the sentencing of juveniles convicted of murder to terms of life in prison without parole are unconstitutional under the Eighth Amendment's prohibition on cruel and unusual punishment. In writing for the majority, Justice Elena Kagan concluded that mandatory life sentences prevent judges and juries from considering a juvenile's "lessened culpability." Kagan wrote: "By requiring that all children convicted of homicide receive lifetime incarceration without possibility of parole, regardless of their age and age-related characteristics and the nature of their crimes, the mandatory sentencing schemes before us violate [the] principle of proportionality, and so the Eighth Amendment's ban on cruel and unusual punishment."

Finally, in 2016, in the case of *Montgomery* v. *Louisiana*, the Court retroactively applied the *Miller* decision providing people who had been sentenced to mandatory life without parole as juveniles, the right to have their sentences reviewed. It also made clear that juvenile life without parole sentences should only be imposed in rare cases of "permanent incorrigibility."

Legislation concerning Children and Justice

In response to the rapidly increasing crime rates of the late 1960s, Congress passed the Omnibus Crime Control and Safe Streets Act of 1968, which provided money and technical assistance for states and municipalities seeking to modernize their justice systems. The Safe Streets Act also provided funding for youth services bureaus, which had been recommended by the 1967 presidential commission report *The Challenge of Crime in a Free Society*.[35] These bureaus were available to police, juvenile courts, and probation departments and acted as a centralized community resource for handling delinquents and status offenders. Youth services bureaus also handled juveniles referred by schools and young people who referred themselves. Unfortunately, within a decade after their establishment, most youth services bureaus succumbed to a lack of continued federal funding.

In 1974, recognizing the special needs of juveniles, Congress passed the Juvenile Justice and Delinquency Prevention (JJDP) Act. Employing much the same strategy as the 1968 bill, the JJDP Act provided federal grants to states and cities seeking to improve their handling and disposition of delinquents and status offenders. Nearly all the states chose to accept federal funds through the JJDP Act. Participating states had to meet two conditions within 5 years:

1. They had to agree to a "sight and sound separation mandate," under which juveniles would not be held in institutions where they might come into regular contact with adult prisoners.

2. Status offenders had to be deinstitutionalized, with most being released into the community or placed in foster homes.

🐦 Follow the author's tweets about the latest crime and justice news @schmalleger

Within a few years, institutional populations were cut by more than half, and community alternatives to juvenile institutionalization were rapidly being developed. Jailed juveniles were housed in separate wings of adult facilities or were removed from adult jails entirely.

When the JJDP Act was reauthorized for funding in 1980, the separation mandate was expanded to require that separate juvenile jails be constructed by the states. Studies supporting reauthorization of the JJDP Act in 1984 and 1988, however, found that nearly half the states had failed to come into "substantial compliance" with the new jail and lockup removal mandate. As a consequence, Congress modified the requirements of the act, continuing funding for states making "meaningful progress" toward removing juveniles from adult jails.[36] The 1988 reauthorizing legislation added a "disproportionate minority confinement" (DMC) requirement under which states seeking federal monies for their juvenile justice systems had to agree to ameliorate conditions leading to the disproportionate confinement of minority juveniles.[37]

In 1996, in the face of pressures toward punishment and away from treatment for violent juvenile offenders, the OJJDP proposed new rules for jailing juveniles. The new rules allow a justice-involved youth to be detained for up to 12 hours in an adult jail before a court appearance and make it easier for states to house juveniles in separate wings of adult jails.[38] The most recent JJDP Act reauthorization occurred in 2002.[39] It expanded the DMC concept to include all stages of the juvenile justice process. Consequently, *DMC* has come to mean "disproportionate minority contact" under today's law.[40] By 2005, 56 of 57 eligible states and U.S. territories had agreed to all of the act's requirements and were receiving federal funding under the legislation.[41]

In 2003, Congress passed child-protection legislation in what is commonly called the *AMBER Alert law*. Officially known as the PROTECT Act of 2003 (Prosecutorial Remedies and Other Tools to End the Exploitation of Children Today), the law provides federal funding to the states to ensure creation of a national AMBER (America's Missing: Broadcast Emergency Response) network to facilitate rapid law enforcement and community response to kidnapped or abducted children. The law also established the position of federal AMBER Alert coordinator and set uniform standards for the use of AMBER Alerts across our country. Another provision of the law provides for the prosecution of anyone engaged in pandering of child pornography. It also contains an extraterritorial clause that makes possible the federal prosecution of U.S. citizens who travel outside the country to engage in child sex tourism.[42] The federal government's AMBER Alert website can be accessed via **http://www.amberalert.gov**.

The Legal Rights of Juveniles

Most jurisdictions today have statutes designed to extend the *Miranda* provisions to juveniles, and many police officers routinely offer *Miranda* warnings to juveniles in their custody before questioning them. It is unclear, however, whether juveniles can legally waive their *Miranda* rights. A 1979 U.S. Supreme Court ruling held that juveniles should be accorded the opportunity for a knowing waiver when they are old enough and sufficiently educated to understand the consequences of a waiver.[43] A later High Court ruling upheld the murder conviction of a juvenile who had been advised of his rights and waived them in the presence of his mother.[44]

One important area of juvenile rights centers on investigative procedures. In 1985, for example, the U.S. Supreme Court ruled in *New Jersey* v. *T.L.O.*[45] that schoolchildren have a reasonable expectation of privacy in their personal property. The case involved a 14-year-old girl who was accused of violating school rules by smoking in a high school bathroom. A vice principal searched the girl's purse and found evidence of marijuana use. Juvenile officers were called, and the girl was eventually adjudicated in juvenile court and found delinquent.

On appeal to the New Jersey Supreme Court, the girl's lawyers were successful in having her conviction reversed on the grounds that the search of her purse, as an item of personal property, had been unreasonable. The state's appeal to the U.S. Supreme Court resulted in a ruling that prohibited school officials from engaging in unreasonable searches of students or their property. A reading of the Court's decision leads to the conclusion that a search could be considered reasonable if it (1) is based on a logical suspicion of rule-breaking actions; (2) is required to maintain order, discipline, and safety among students; and (3) does not exceed the scope of the original suspicion.

Finally, in 2011, the U.S. Supreme Court held that the age of suspects must be considered when determining whether they would feel free not to respond to police questioning. In writing for the majority in *J.D.B.* v. *North Carolina*,[46] Justice Sonia Sotomayor wrote "It is beyond dispute that children will often feel bound to submit to police questioning when an adult in the same circumstances would feel free to leave." In keeping with the Court's recent emphasis on developmental neurobiology, Sotomayor went on to say that "the law has historically reflected the same assumption that children characteristically lack the capacity to exercise mature judgment and possess only an incomplete ability to understand the world around them."[47]

Follow the author's tweets about the latest crime and justice news @schmalleger

The Juvenile Justice Process Today

Juvenile court jurisdiction rests on the offender's age and conduct. The majority of states today define a child subject to juvenile court jurisdiction as a person who has not yet turned 18 years of age. A few states set the age at 17. Figure 13–4 shows the upper ages of children subject to juvenile court jurisdiction in delinquency matters, by state. When they reach their eighteenth birthday, children in most states become subject to the jurisdiction of adult criminal courts. However, state laws continue to

3 Compare juvenile and adult systems of justice.

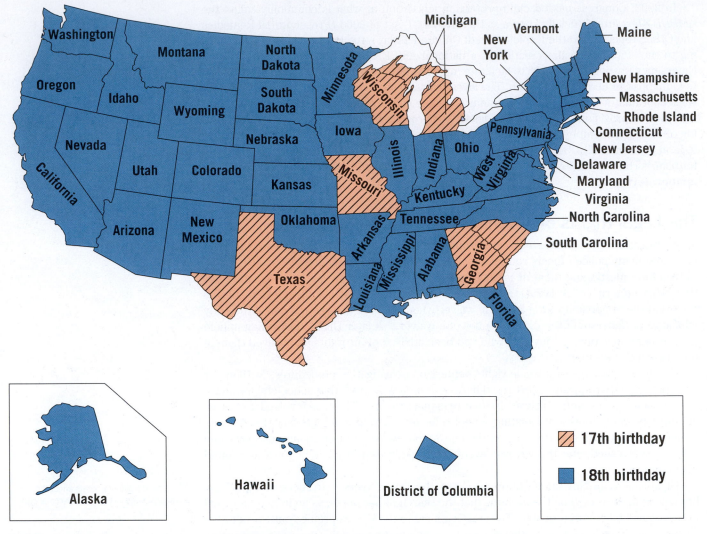

FIGURE 13–4
Maximum Age of Juvenile Court Jurisdiction over Young Offenders, by State

Note: In 2017, North Carolina raised the age of criminal responsibility to the 18th birthday for all but violent offenses.
Source: From Office of Juvenile Justice and Delinquency Prevention.

change. New York and North Carolina, the only states that had previously prosecuted all 16- and 17-year-olds as adults, recently adopted reforms so that most teenage defendants will be adjudicated in the juvenile justice system. New York raised the age of juvenile responsibility for all misdemeanors and most felony offenses to 18. North Carolina officials raised the age of juvenile jurisdiction for nonviolent crimes to 18, but still prosecute many juveniles who commit felony offenses in adult court.

In 2018, the OJJDP reported that U.S. courts with juvenile jurisdiction annually handled nearly 1 million delinquency cases.[48] Depending on the laws of the state and the behavior involved, the jurisdiction of the juvenile court may be exclusive. Exclusive jurisdiction applies when the juvenile court is the only court that has statutory authority to deal with children for specified infractions. For example, status offenses such as truancy normally fall within the exclusive jurisdiction of juvenile courts. Delinquency, which involves violation of the criminal law, however, is often not within the juvenile court's exclusive jurisdiction. All 50 states, the District of Columbia, and the federal government have provisions that allow juveniles who commit serious crimes to be bound over to criminal court. Forty-six states give juvenile court judges the power to waive jurisdiction over cases involving juveniles so that they can be transferred to criminal court.[49] Fourteen states have "direct-file" provisions that authorize the prosecutor to decide where to file certain kinds of serious cases, in either juvenile or criminal court. Juveniles who commit violent crimes or who have prior records are among the most likely to be transferred to adult courts.[50] Direct file laws permit prosecutors to effectively bypass the juvenile justice system. Consequently, in November of 2016 California voters approved Proposition 57, which ended the ability of prosecutors to "direct file" criminal cases against juveniles in adult criminal court. A number of other states are not considering similar legislation.

Where juvenile court authority is not exclusive, the jurisdiction of the court may be original or concurrent. *Original jurisdiction* means that a particular offense must originate (begin) with juvenile court authorities, and juvenile courts have original jurisdiction over most delinquency petitions and all status offenses. *Concurrent jurisdiction* exists where other courts have equal statutory authority to originate proceedings. For example, if a juvenile has committed a homicide, rape, or another serious crime, an arrest warrant may be issued by the adult court.

Some states specify that juvenile courts have no jurisdiction over certain specified offenses. Delaware, Louisiana, and Nevada, for example, allow no juvenile court jurisdiction over children charged with first-degree murder. Another 29 states have statutes that exclude certain serious, violent, or repeat offenders from the juvenile court's jurisdiction.

> Under our Constitution, the condition of being a boy does not justify a kangaroo court.
> —*In re Gault* (1967)

Adult and Juvenile Justice Compared

The court cases of relevance to the juvenile justice system that we have identified in this chapter have two common characteristics: They all turn on due-process guarantees specified by the Bill of Rights, and they all make the claim that adult due process should serve as a model for juvenile proceedings. Due-process guarantees, as interpreted by the U.S. Supreme Court, are clearly designed to ensure that juvenile proceedings are fair and that the interests of juveniles are protected. However, the Court's interpretations do not offer any pretense of providing juveniles with the same kinds of protections guaranteed to adult defendants. Although the High Court has tended to agree that juveniles are entitled to due-process protection, it has refrained from declaring that juveniles have a right to all aspects of due process afforded adult defendants. See CJ Exhibit 13–1 for a comparison of adult criminal proceedings and juvenile proceedings.

Juvenile court philosophy brings with it other differences from the adult system. Among them are (1) reduced concern with legal issues of guilt or innocence and an emphasis on the child's best interests; (2) emphasis on treatment rather than punishment; (3) privacy and protection from public scrutiny through the use of sealed records, laws against publishing the names of juvenile offenders, and so forth; (4) use of the techniques of social

Follow the author's tweets about the latest crime and justice news @schmalleger

---

CJ Exhibit 13–1
Adult Criminal Case Processing versus the Juvenile Justice System

ADULT CRIMINAL PROCEEDINGS	JUVENILE PROCEEDINGS
Focus on criminality	Focus on delinquency and a special category of "status offenses"
Comprehensive rights against unreasonable searches of person, home, and possessions	Limited rights against unreasonable searches
Right against self-incrimination	Right against self-incrimination (waivers are questionable)
Assumption of innocence until proven guilty	Guilt and innocence not the primary issues (the system focuses on the interests of the child)
Adversarial setting	Helping context
Most arrests based on arrest warrants	Apprehension based on petitions or complaints
Right to an attorney	Right to an attorney
Right to trial by jury	Closed hearing; no right to a jury trial
Right to a public trial	
System goals of punishment and reformation	System goals of protection and treatment
No right to treatment	Specific right to treatment
Possibility of bail or release on recognizance	Release into parental custody
Public record of trial and judgment	Sealed records (records may sometimes be destroyed by specified age of offender)
Possible incarceration in adult correctional facility	Separate facilities at all levels

science in dispositional decision making rather than sentences determined by a perceived need for punishment; (5) no long-term confinement, with most juveniles being released from institutions by their twenty-first birthday, regardless of offense; (6) separate facilities for juveniles; and (7) broad discretionary alternatives at all points in the process.[51] This combination of court philosophy and due-process requirements has created a unique justice system for juveniles that takes into consideration the special needs of young people while attempting to offer reasonable protection to society. The juvenile justice process is diagrammed in Figure 13–5.

How the System Works

The juvenile justice system can be viewed as a process that, when carried to completion, moves through four stages: intake, adjudication, disposition, and postadjudicatory review. Although organizationally similar to the adult criminal justice process, the juvenile system is far more likely to maximize the use of discretion and to employ diversion from further formal processing at every point in the process. Each stage is discussed in the pages that follow.

Intake and Detention Hearings

Delinquent juveniles may come to the attention of the police or juvenile court authorities either through arrest or through the filing of a **juvenile petition** by an aggrieved party. (A juvenile petition is much like a criminal complaint in that it alleges illegal behavior.) Juvenile petitions are most often filed by teachers, school administrators, neighbors, store managers, or others who have frequent contact with juveniles. Parents who are unable to control the behavior of their teenage children are the source of many other petitions. Crimes in progress bring other juveniles to the attention of the police, with three-quarters of all referrals to juvenile court coming directly from law enforcement authorities.[52]

Many police departments have juvenile officers who are specially trained in dealing with juveniles. Because of the emphasis on rehabilitation that characterizes the juvenile justice process, juvenile officers can usually choose from a number of discretionary alternatives in the form of special programs, especially in the handling of nonviolent offenders. In Delaware County, Pennsylvania, for example, police departments participate in "youth aid panels." These panels are composed of private citizens who volunteer their services to provide an alternative to the formal juvenile court process. Youngsters who are referred to a panel and agree to abide by the decision of the group are diverted from the juvenile court.

Real Justice Conferencing (RJC) is another example of a diversionary program. Started in Bethlehem, Pennsylvania, in 1995, RJC is said to be a cost-effective approach to juvenile crime, school misconduct, and violence prevention. It has served as a model for programs in other cities. It makes use of family group conferences (sometimes called *community conferences*) in lieu of school disciplinary or judicial processes or as a supplement to them. The family group conference, built around a restorative-justice model, allows young offenders to tell what they did, to hear from those they affected, and to help decide how to repair the harm their actions caused. Successful RJC participants avoid the more formal mechanisms of the juvenile justice process.

However, even youth who are eventually diverted from the system may spend some time in custody. One juvenile case in five involves detention before adjudication.[53] Unlike the adult system, where jail is seen as the primary custodial alternative for people awaiting a first appearance, secure detention for juveniles is acceptable only as a last resort. **Detention hearings** investigate whether candidates for confinement represent a "clear and immediate danger to themselves and/or to others," a judgment normally rendered within 24 hours of apprehension. Runaways, because they are often not dangerous, are especially difficult to confine. Juveniles who are not detained are generally released into the custody of their parents or guardians or into a supervised temporary shelter, such as a group home.

juvenile petition
A document filed in juvenile court alleging that a juvenile is a delinquent, a status offender, or a dependent and asking that the court assume jurisdiction over the juvenile or that an alleged delinquent be transferred to a criminal court for prosecution as an adult.

The majority of states today define a child subject to juvenile court jurisdiction as a person who has not yet turned 18.

Detention Hearing
In juvenile justice usage, a hearing by a judicial officer of a juvenile court to determine whether a juvenile is to be detained, is to continue to be detained, or is to be released while juvenile proceedings are pending.

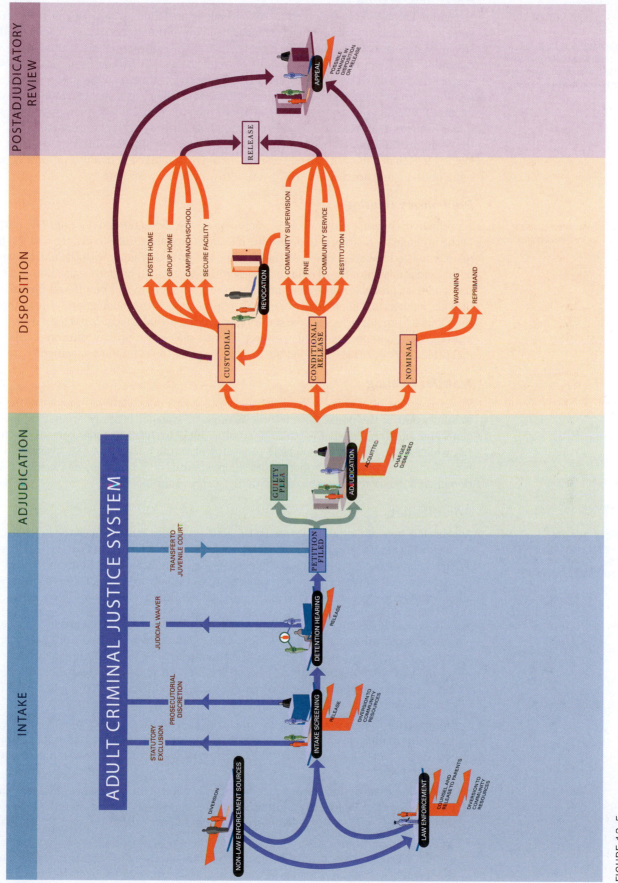

FIGURE 13–5
The Juvenile Justice System

Detention Hearing

Detention hearings are conducted by the juvenile court judge or by an officer of the court, such as a juvenile probation officer who has been given the authority to make **intake** decisions. Intake officers, like their police counterparts, have substantial discretion. Along with detention, they can choose diversion or outright dismissal of some or all of the charges against the juvenile. Diverted juveniles may be sent to job-training programs, mental health facilities, drug-treatment programs, educational counseling, or other community services agencies. When caring parents who can afford private counseling or therapy are present, intake officers may release the juvenile into their custody with the understanding that they will provide for treatment. The National Center for Juvenile Justice estimates that slightly less than half of all juvenile cases disposed of at intake are handled informally, without a petition, and are dismissed or diverted to a social services agency.[54]

Preliminary Hearing

A preliminary hearing may be held in conjunction with the detention hearing. The purpose of the preliminary hearing is to determine if there is probable cause to believe that the juvenile committed the alleged act. At the hearing, the juvenile (along with the child's parents or guardians) will be advised of his or her rights as established by state legislation and court precedent. If probable cause is established, the juvenile may still be offered diversionary options, such as an "improvement period" or "probation with adjudication." These alternatives usually provide a 1-year period during which the juvenile must avoid legal difficulties, attend school, and obey his or her parents. Charges may be dropped at the end of this informal probationary period, provided the juvenile has met the conditions specified.

Transfer Hearing

When a serious offense is involved, statutory provisions may allow for transfer of the case to adult court at the prosecuting attorney's request. Transfer hearings are held in juvenile court and focus on (1) whether transfer statutes apply to the case under consideration and (2) whether the juvenile is amenable to treatment through the resources available to the juvenile justice system. Exceptions exist where statutes mandate transfer (which, as mentioned earlier, is sometimes the case with first-degree murder).

Adjudication

Adjudicatory hearings for juveniles are fact-finding processes during which the juvenile court decides whether there is sufficient evidence of a law violation. Adjudicatory hearings are similar to adult trials, with some notable exceptions. Similarities derive from the fact that the due-process rights of children and adults are essentially the same. Differences between adjudicatory hearings and adult trials include the following:

- *Emphasis on privacy.* An important distinctive characteristic of the juvenile system is its concern with privacy. Juvenile hearings are not open to the public or to the mass media. Witnesses are permitted to be present only to offer testimony and may not stay for the rest of the hearing, and no transcript of the proceedings is created. One purpose of the emphasis on privacy is to prevent juveniles from being negatively labeled by the community.

- *Informality.* Whereas the adult criminal trial is highly structured, the juvenile hearing is more informal and less adversarial. The juvenile court judge takes an active role in the fact-finding process rather than serving as arbitrator between prosecution and defense.

- *Speed.* Informality, the lack of a jury, and the absence of an adversarial environment promote speed. Whereas the adult trial may run into weeks or even months, the juvenile hearing is normally completed in a matter of hours or days.

- *Evidentiary standard.* On completion of the hearing, the juvenile court judge must weigh the evidence. If the charge involves a status offense, the judge may adjudicate the juvenile as a status offender upon finding that a preponderance of the evidence supports this finding. (A preponderance of the evidence exists when evidence of an

intake
The first step in decision making regarding a juvenile whose behavior or alleged behavior is in violation of the law or could otherwise cause a juvenile court to assume jurisdiction.

Follow the author's tweets about the latest crime and justice news @schmalleger

adjudicatory hearing
The fact-finding process wherein the juvenile court determines whether there is sufficient evidence to sustain the allegations in a petition.

offense is more convincing than evidence offered to the contrary.) If the charge involves a criminal-type offense, the evidentiary standard rises to the level of reasonable doubt.

- *Philosophy of the court.* Even in the face of strong evidence pointing to the offender's guilt, the judge may decide that it is not in the child's best interests to be adjudicated delinquent. The judge also has the power, even after the evidence is presented, to divert the juvenile from the system. Juvenile court statistics indicate that only about 55% of all cases disposed of by juvenile courts are processed formally.[55] Formal processing involves the filing of a petition requesting an adjudicatory or transfer hearing. Informal cases, on the other hand, are handled without a petition. Among informally handled (nonpetitioned) delinquency cases, almost half are dismissed by the court, whereas 52% of petitioned cases resulted in the child being adjudicated delinquent.[56]

- *No right to trial by jury.* As referred to earlier in the U.S. Supreme Court decision in *McKeiver* v. *Pennsylvania*,[57] juveniles do not have a constitutional right to trial by jury, and most states do not provide juveniles with a statutory opportunity for a jury trial.[58]

See CJ Exhibit 13–2 for a comparison of the language used in juvenile and adult courts.

Some jurisdictions, however, allow juveniles to be tried by their peers in **teen courts**. The juvenile court in Columbus County, Georgia, for example, began experimenting with teen courts and peer juries in 1980.[59] In Georgia, peer juries are composed of youth under the age of 17 who receive special training by the court. Jurors are required to be successful in school and may not be under the supervision of the court or have juvenile petitions pending against them. Training consists of classroom exposure to the philosophy of the juvenile court system, Georgia's juvenile code, and Supreme Court decisions affecting juvenile justice.[60] The county's youthful jurors are used only in the dispositional (or sentencing) stage of the court process and only when adjudicated youth volunteer to go before the jury.

Today, hundreds of teen court programs are in operation across the country. The OJJDP notes that teen courts are "an effective intervention in many jurisdictions where enforcement of misdemeanor charges is sometimes given low priority because of heavy caseloads and the need to focus on more serious offenders."[61] Teen courts, says the OJJDP, "present communities with opportunities to teach young people valuable life and coping skills and promote positive peer influence for youth who are defendants and for volunteer youth who play a variety of roles in the teen court process." Learn more about teen courts via **https://www.justicestudies.com/pubs/teencourts.pdf**.

teen court
An alternative approach to juvenile justice in which alleged offenders are judged and/or sentenced by a jury of their peers.

Follow the author's tweets about the latest crime and justice news @schmalleger

Disposition

Once a juvenile has been found delinquent, the judge will set a **dispositional hearing**, which is similar to an adult sentencing hearing and is used to decide what action the court should take relative to the child. As in adult courts, the judge may order a presentence investigation before making a dispositional decision. This type of investigation is conducted by special court personnel, sometimes called *juvenile court counselors*, who are, in effect, juvenile probation officers. Attorneys on both sides of the issue will also have the opportunity to make recommendations concerning dispositional alternatives.

The juvenile justice system typically gives the judge a much wider range of sentencing alternatives than does the adult system. Two major classes of **juvenile disposition** exist: to confine or not to confine. Because rehabilitation is still the primary objective of the juvenile court, the judge is likely to select the least restrictive alternative that meets the needs of the juvenile while recognizing the legitimate concerns of society for protection.

dispositional hearing
The final stage in the processing of adjudicated juveniles in which a decision is made on the form of treatment or penalty that should be imposed on the child.

juvenile disposition
The decision of a juvenile court that concludes a dispositional hearing. The adjudicated juvenile might be committed to a juvenile correctional facility; be placed in a juvenile residence, shelter, or care or treatment program; be required to meet certain standards of conduct; or be released.

CJ Exhibit 13-2
Juvenile Courts versus Adult Courts

The language used in juvenile courts is less harsh than that used in adult courts. For example, juvenile courts do the following:

- Accept "petitions of delinquency" rather than criminal complaints

- Conduct "hearings," not trials
- "Adjudicate" juveniles to be "delinquent" rather than find them guilty of a crime
- Order one of a number of available "dispositions" rather than sentences

Most judges decide not to confine juveniles. Statistics indicate that in nearly two-thirds (62%) of all adjudicated delinquency cases, juveniles are placed on formal probation.[62]

Probationary disposition usually means that juveniles will be released into the custody of a parent or guardian and ordered to undergo some form of training, education, or counseling. As in the adult system, juveniles placed on probation may be ordered to pay fines or to make restitution. In 11% of adjudicated delinquency cases, courts order juveniles to pay restitution or a fine, to participate in some form of community service, or to enter a treatment or counseling program—all dispositions that require minimal continuing supervision by probation staff.[63] Because juveniles rarely have financial resources or jobs, most economic sanctions take the form of court-ordered work programs, such as refurbishing schools or cleaning school buses.

Of course, not all juveniles who are adjudicated delinquent receive probation. About one-quarter of adjudicated cases result in the youth being placed outside the home in a residential facility. In a smaller number of cases (12%), the juvenile was adjudicated delinquent, but the case was then dismissed or the youth was otherwise released.[64]

> Most juvenile complaints are handled informally, and only relatively low numbers of adjudicated delinquents are placed outside the family.

Secure Institutions for Juveniles

Juveniles who demonstrate the potential for serious new offenses may be ordered to participate in rehabilitative programs within a secure environment, such as a youth center or a training school. As of January 2016, approximately 48,043 young people were being held under custodial supervision in the United States (Figure 13–6).[65] Of these, 38% were being held for crimes against persons like murder, rape, or robbery; 22% were being held for property crimes; 6% were locked up for drug offenses; 13% were being held for public-order offenses (including weapons offenses); 15% were held for technical violations of the conditions of their release, and 5% were being held for status offenses.[66]

Most confined juveniles are held in semisecure facilities designed to look less like prisons and more like residential high school campuses. Most states, however, operate at least one secure facility for juveniles that is intended as a home for the most recalcitrant youthful offenders. There are around 80 such facilities in the country, and their locations are shown in Figure 13–7. Halfway houses, "boot camps,"[67] ranches, forestry camps, wilderness programs, group homes, and state-hired private facilities also hold some of the juveniles reported to be under confinement. Children placed in group homes continue to attend school and live in a family-like environment in the company of other adjudicated children, shepherded by "house parents." Learn more about the juvenile justice systems of each state from the Project on Juvenile Justice, Geography, Policy, Practice, and Statistics via **http://www.jjgps.org**.

The operative philosophy of custodial programs for juveniles focuses squarely on the rehabilitative ideal. Juveniles are usually committed to secure facilities for indeterminate periods of time, with the typical stay being less than 1 year. Release is often timed to coincide with the beginning or the end of the school year.

Most juvenile facilities are small, with 82% designed to hold 50 residents or fewer.[68] Many institutionalized juveniles are held in the thousand or so homelike facilities across

FIGURE 13–6
Number of Youth Held in Secure Confinement in the United States, 1997–2015

Source: Easy Access to the Census of Juveniles in Residential Placement, Office of Juvenile Justice and Delinquency Prevention.

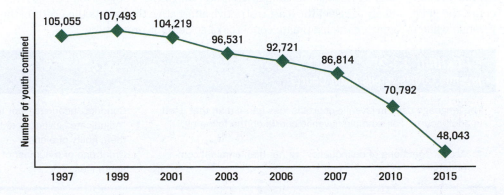

the nation that are limited to ten residents or fewer.[69] At the other end of the scale are the nation's 96 large juvenile institutions, each designed to hold more than 100 hardcore delinquents.[70] Residential facilities for juveniles are intensively staffed. One study found that staff members outnumber residents ten to nine on average in state-run institutions and by an even greater ratio in privately run facilities.[71]

Jurisdictions vary widely in their use of secure detention for juveniles. Juvenile custody populations range from a low of 21 in Vermont to a high of 3,891 in California.[72] This variance reflects population differences as well as economic realities and philosophical beliefs. Similarly, some states have more firmly embraced the reformation ideal and are more likely to use diversionary options for juveniles.

▲ Juvenile court in action. Juvenile courts are expected to act in the best interests of the children who come before them. Should that rule apply to all juveniles who come before the court, regardless of their offense? *Marmaduke St. John/Alamy Stock Photo.*

Characteristics of Juveniles in Confinement

Institutionalized juveniles are a small but special category of young people with serious problems. A recent report on institutionalized youth by the OJJDP found five striking characteristics:[73]

- 84.8% were male and 15.2% were female.
- 41.9% were black, 31.3% were white, and 21.9% were Hispanic.
- 4.8% were institutionalized for having committed a status offense, such as being truant, running away, or violating curfew.
- 59.3% were in residential facilities for a serious person or property offense.
- 1.6% were charged with homicide.

🐦 Follow the author's tweets about the latest crime and justice news @schmalleger

Overcrowding in Juvenile Facilities

As in adult prisons, overcrowding exists in a significant proportion of juvenile institutions. In one recent government survey, one in five youths were held in facilities that were at or over their standard bed capacity.[74]

A national study of the conditions of confinement in juvenile detention facilities conducted by the OJJDP found that "there are several areas in which problems in juvenile facilities are substantial and widespread—most notably living space, health care, security, and control of suicidal behavior."[75] To address these problems, the authors of the study recommended the use of alternative placement options so that only juveniles judged to be the most dangerous to their communities would be confined in secure facilities. Similarly, because it found that injuries to residents were most likely to occur within large dormitory-like settings, the OJJDP study recommended that "large dormitories be eliminated from juvenile facilities." Finally, the study recommended that "all juveniles be screened for risk of suicidal behavior immediately upon their admission to confinement" and that initial health screenings be "carried out promptly at admission." Other problems that the OJJDP found "important enough to warrant attention" included education and treatment services. Further study of both areas is needed, the OJJDP said.

Numerous states use private facilities. Surveys show that 68% of juveniles are held in public facilities, with the remaining 32% housed in private facilities.[76] In the last decade of the twentieth century, admissions to private facilities (comprising primarily halfway houses, group homes, shelters, and ranches, camps, or farms) increased

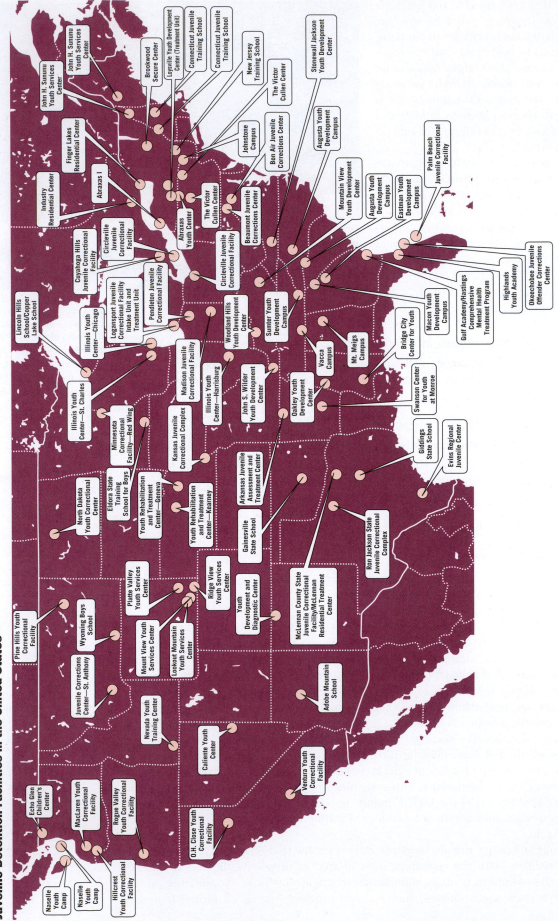

FIGURE 13-7
Juvenile Detention Facilities in the United States

CJ News
The Girls Study Group

In the 1990s, a surge of girls' arrests brought female juvenile crime to the country's attention. Girls' rates of arrest for some crimes increased faster than boys' rates of arrest. By 2004, girls accounted for 30% of all juvenile arrests, but delinquency experts did not know whether these trends reflected changes in girls' behavior or changes in arrest patterns. The juvenile justice field struggled to understand how best to respond to the needs of the girls entering the system.

Consequently, in 2004, the OJJDP convened the Girls Study Group (GSG) to establish a research-based foundation to guide the development, testing, and dissemination of strategies to reduce or prevent girls' involvement in delinquency and violence. Fiscal year 2008 saw the beginning of the OJJDP's dissemination of the GSG's findings. The study group sponsored a one-day preconference session at the March 2008 Blueprints for Violence Prevention conference in Denver, Colorado. The focus of the preconference session was to convey findings and discuss the evidence base for girls' programming and needs. In addition, GSG members presented some of the group's findings to the Coordinating Council on Juvenile Justice and Delinquency Prevention.

Soon after, the OJJDP launched a Girls' Delinquency web page and produced a series of bulletins that present the study group's findings on such issues as patterns of offending among adolescents and how they differ for girls and boys; risk and protective factors associated with delinquency, including gender differences; and the causes and correlates of girls' delinquency.

Finally, in 2012, the Georgetown Center on Poverty, Inequality and Public Policy, released a report on improving the juvenile justice system for girls. The report noted that the existing juvenile justice system was originally designed for delinquent boys, and doesn't adequately recognize the needs of girls. The Center also examined the challenges facing girls in the juvenile justice system and offered suggestions for gender-responsive reform at the local, state, and federal levels. In the words of the report:

> The typical girl in the system is a non-violent offender, who is very often low-risk, but high-need, meaning the girl poses little risk to the public but she enters the system with significant and pressing personal needs. The set of challenges that girls often face as they enter the juvenile justice system include trauma, violence, neglect, mental and physical problems, family conflict, pregnancy, residential and academic instability, and school failure. The juvenile justice system only exacerbates these problems by failing to provide girls with services at the time when they need them most.

The Center concluded its report with a number of policy recommendations that it hopes will be enacted at the federal level. They include:

- Conduct research on programs for girls, particularly regarding best practices in gender-responsive programming, and conditions of confinement for girls

▲ A female delinquent appears before a judge in juvenile court. How does the delinquency of girls differ from that of boys?
Marmaduke St. John/Alamy Stock Photo

- Mandate a comprehensive effort by the U.S. Department of Justice to improve training and technical assistance for better recognition of the unique needs of marginalized girls among judges, law enforcement, and juvenile justice staff
- Allocate federal funding and encourage states to apply for federal funding for gender-specific programming
- Close the loophole that currently allows states to detain youths for technical violations of court orders—a practice that has a disproportionate impact on girls
- Encourage the development of national standards for gender-responsive programming
- Promote policies to keep girls out of the adult criminal justice system

Today, other girls study groups include the National Girls Institute (NGI) funded by a partnership between the National Council on Crime and Delinquency (NCCD), the Office of Juvenile Justice and Delinquency Prevention (OJJDP), and the NCCD Center for Girls and Young Women. The latter provides technical assistance and training to improve outcomes for girls and young women in the juvenile justice and child welfare systems. Learn more about the Girls Study Group at **https://www .justicestudies.com/pubs/girls.pdf**.

Source: *Girls Study Group: Understanding and Responding to Girls' Delinquency* (Washington, D.C.: OJJDP, 2010); and Liz Watson and Peter Edelman, *Improving the Juvenile Justice System for Girls: Lessons from the States* (Washington, D.C.: Georgetown Center on Poverty, Inequality and Public Policy, October 2012).

▲ A young female in custody being led to a detention holding cell by a female deputy sheriff in Saline County, Nebraska. Although institutionalized juveniles are housed separately from adult offenders, juvenile institutions share many of the problems of adult facilities. What changes have recently occurred in the handling of juvenile offenders?

Mikael Karlsson/Alamy Stock Photo

4 Briefly describe possible future directions in juvenile justice.

🐦 Follow the author's tweets about the latest crime and justice news @schmalleger

by more than 100%, compared with an increase of only about 10% for public facilities (mostly detention centers and training schools).[77] The fastest-growing category of detained juveniles comprises drug and alcohol offenders. Approximately 6% of all juvenile detainees are being held because of alcohol- and drug-related offenses.[78] Reflecting widespread socioeconomic disparities, an OJJDP report found that "a juvenile held in a public facility . . . was most likely to be black, male, between 14 and 17 years of age, and held for a delinquent offense such as a property crime or a crime against a person. On the other hand, a juvenile held in custody in a private facility . . . was most likely to be white, male, 14 to 17 years of age, and held for a nondelinquent offense such as running away, truancy, or incorrigibility."[79] The report also noted that "juvenile corrections has become increasingly privatized."

Postadjudicatory Review

The detrimental effects of institutionalization on young offenders may make the opportunity for appellate review more critical for juveniles than it is for adults. However, federal court precedents have yet to establish a clear right to appeal from juvenile court, although most states do have statutory provisions that make such appeals possible.[80]

From a practical point of view, however, juvenile appeals may not be as consequential as are appeals of adult criminal convictions. Most juvenile complaints are handled informally, and only a relatively small proportion of adjudicated delinquents are placed outside the family. Moreover, because sentence lengths are short for most confined juveniles, appellate courts hardly have time to complete the review process before a juvenile is released.

Trends in Juvenile Justice

In the late twentieth century, cases of serious juvenile offending combined with extensive media coverage of violent juvenile crime across the United States to fuel public misperceptions that violence committed by teenagers had reached epidemic proportions and that no community was immune to random acts of youth violence. About the same time, the apparent "professionalization" of delinquency, the hallmark of which is the repeated and often violent criminal involvement of juveniles in drug-related gang activity, came to be viewed as a major challenge to the idealism of the juvenile justice system. Consequently, by the turn of the twenty-first century, the issue of youth violence was at or near the top of nearly every state legislature's and governor's agenda. Most states took some form of legislative or executive action to stem what was seen as an escalating level of dangerous crime by juveniles. Those actions prompted juvenile justice experts Jeffrey Butts and Ojmarrh Mitchell, members of the Program on Law and Behavior at the Urban Institute in Washington, D.C., to say that "policymakers throughout the United States have greatly dissolved the border between juvenile and criminal justice."[81] Others claimed that many states had substantially "criminalized" juvenile courts.

In an effort to better focus delinquency prevention strategies, OJJDP developed a comprehensive strategy for serious, violent, and chronic juvenile offenders. The strategy was based on five general principles. The first, which focused on the family, suggested strengthening the family "in its primary responsibility to instill moral values and provide guidance and support to children." Where no functional family exists, OJJDP said that a family surrogate must be established to fill that role. The second principle focused on supporting core institutions like schools, religious institutions, and community organizations in order to enhance their abilities to develop "capable, mature, and responsible youth." The third principle sought to promote delinquency *prevention* "as the most cost-effective approach to reducing juvenile delinquency." The fourth called for effective and immediate intervention when delinquent behavior occurs "to successfully prevent delinquent offenders from becoming chronic offenders." Finally, the fifth principle called for the identification and control of "the small group of serious, violent, and chronic juvenile offenders who have committed felony offenses," or who have "failed to respond to intervention and community-based treatment." The OJJDP strategy noted that such offenders may need to be placed "in secure

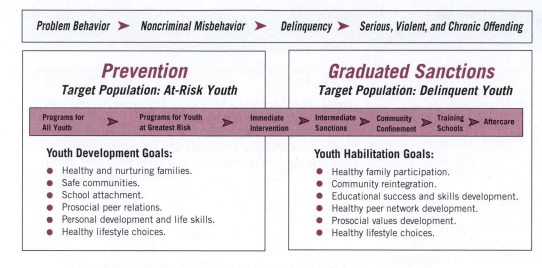

FIGURE 13–8
OJJDP's Comprehensive Strategy

Source: Guide for Implementing the Comprehensive Strategy for Serious, Violent, and Chronic Juvenile Offenders, May 1995, Office of Juvenile Justice and Delinquency Prevention.

community-based facilities, training schools and other secure juvenile facilities."[81] The strategy is illustrated in Figure 13–8.

In recent years, the pendulum has begun to swing back toward the original principles of the juvenile court. In an age of limited state budgets and lack of faith in the ability of residential placement to accomplish reformation, a number of states are moving to reestablish such principles. In 2016, for example, the Program in Criminal Justice Policy and Management at Harvard University condemned the use of large juvenile confinement facilities, saying that they were following an "inherently flawed model." According to the program: "These facilities provide too many of the elements that exacerbate the trauma that most confined youth have already experienced and reinforce poor choices and impulsive behavior."[82]

Today, the National Conference of State Legislatures (NCSL) notes that research distinguishing adolescents from adults is contributing to an important and growing trend among states to re-establish boundaries between the adult and juvenile justice systems. One of the more prominent shifts in juvenile justice policy, said the Conference, has been the focus on juveniles' developmental needs.[83] In keeping with that focus, a recent report by the National Academy of Sciences (NAS) found that "adolescents differ from adults and children in three important ways that contribute to differences in behavior."[84] NAS researchers found that, because of significant differences in developing adolescent brains, young people (1) have less capacity for self-regulation in emotionally charged contexts; (2) have a heightened sensitivity to proximal external influences, such as peer pressure and immediate incentives; and (3) show less ability than adults to make judgments and decisions that require future orientation. According to the NAS report, "the combination of these three cognitive patterns accounts for the tendency of adolescents to prefer and engage in risky behaviors that have a high probability of immediate reward but can have harmful consequences."[85] Moreover, noted the report, "Research indicates that for most youth, the period of risky experimentation does not extend beyond adolescence, ceasing as identity becomes settled with maturity. Much adolescent involvement in criminal activity is part of the normal developmental process of identity formation and most adolescents will mature out of these tendencies." The report concluded that "this knowledge of adolescent development has underscored important differences between adults and adolescents with direct bearing on the design and operation of the justice system, raising doubts about the core assumptions driving the criminalization of juvenile justice policy in the late decades of the 20th century."[86]

A few years ago, the NCSL published a report noting that: "Juvenile justice reform has become a largely bipartisan issue as lawmakers work together to develop new approaches in justice systems to align sound fiscal responsibility, community safety and better outcomes

Follow the author's tweets about the latest crime and justice news @schmalleger

> Researchers found that, because of significant differences in developing adolescent brains, young people have less capacity for self-regulation in emotionally charged contexts . . . and show less ability than adults to make judgments and decisions that require future orientation.

CJ Careers
Juvenile Justice Professional

Name: Fred Bryan

Position: Director, Juvenile Service Division, Hennepin County (Minnesota) Department of Community Corrections and Rehabilitation

Colleges attended: University of Northern Iowa

Major: Social Work

Minor: Corrections

Year hired: 1984–1990 Juvenile Correctional Officer, 1990–1991 Juvenile Corrections Supervisor, 1991–1997 Juvenile Probation (JP) Officer, 1997–2002 JP Unit Supervisor, 2002–2006 JP Administrative Manager, 2006–2007 (Acting) Superintendent of Juvenile Detention Center, 2007–2009 Asst. Superintendent of Hennepin County Home School (HCHS), 2009–2012 Superintendent of HCHS, 2012–present Director of Juvenile Services

Please give a brief description of your job: As the Area Director of Juvenile Services, I am responsible for oversight of our three juvenile services areas: our Juvenile Probation Department, our Juvenile Detention Center, and our juvenile residential treatment center (Hennepin County Home School).

What appealed to you most about the position when you applied for it? In Hennepin County we have committed ourselves to using evidenced-based juvenile services and to making decisions regarding program changes based on data collected internally and from other jurisdictions. Thus, I was at a point in my career where I wanted to be in a position that afforded me the opportunity to make policy decisions involving the implementation of evidenced-based programs that would have system-wide impacts. By being in this position I am able to work with system stakeholders and partners to implement program changes that effect how we deal with youth on a county-wide level.

How would you describe the interview process? Interviewing for a job at this level not only requires knowledge of the intricacies of the specific areas in juvenile services that are reporting to me, but also requires a knowledge and understanding of how juvenile services fit into the larger picture of our department as well as the structure of the county as a whole. During the interview process I had to articulate how I would be able to work with system partners and stakeholders such as the County Board and Administration, the Juvenile Court, the Human Services Department, and community stakeholders in such a manner that would address the needs of youth while being able to foresee how a decision in the juvenile

▲ Fred Bryan

services area may impact another aspect of our department or the community at large.

What is a typical day like? A typical day for me may require that I spend time in each area of juvenile services addressing such needs as programming, budgeting, staffing, or disciplinary issues. Each area has a manager who is responsible for the day-to-day operations, and these managers and I work closely together to ensure each area has the resources and support needed to continue to provide effective evidenced-based practices for youth. I am also part of our department's administrative team, which requires me to work with our other Area Directors and Department Directors to address department-wide issues. Additionally, on any given day I may be working with our Juvenile Judges, County Administration, Human Services Department, or community-based organizations.

What qualities/characteristics are most helpful for this job? The ability to work with a broad range of professionals who all have their own agenda is essential. Political acumen is also a highly useful skill, as often the decisions made have impact on other areas within the broader system. This job also requires the ability to assimilate a broad range of information and apply what is relevant.

What is a typical starting salary? The salary range is $95,000– $131,000 per year.

What is the salary potential as you move up into higher-level jobs? The next step in our department would be the Department Director, which has a salary range of $117,000–$176,000 per year.

What career advice would you give someone in college beginning studies in criminal justice? My advice would be to focus on what the research is saying in regard to what are the relevant and effective current practices in criminal justice. For example, in the juvenile justice field the research tells us that only high-risk juveniles should be removed from the community and placed out of their homes, that low- to moderate-risk youth are better served with a community-based approach, and that to remove these youth from their homes and communities unnecessarily will in fact make their situations worse. Additionally, spend time researching or volunteering in different areas within the criminal justice field that interest you. You will acquire a broader perspective that will aid you in determining an eventual career path.

Source: Courtesy of Fred Bryan. Reprinted with permission.

---

for youth."[87] The Conference identified recent trends to restore jurisdiction to the juvenile court. They include the following:

1. **Comprehensive Juvenile Justice Reforms**. From 2013 to 2015, legislative action in Arkansas, Georgia, Hawaii, Indiana, Kansas, Kentucky, Nebraska, New Hampshire, South Dakota, Utah, and West Virginia diverted many low risk youth from the system, and led to an investment in effective community-based programming and services.

2. **Reformation of Transfer, Waiver, and Direct-File Laws.** Recently, seven states—Arizona, Indiana, Nevada, Missouri, Ohio, Vermont, and Wisconsin—modified

CJ | ISSUES
Evidence-Based Juvenile Justice

Evidence-based research permits the identification of effective strategies through the evaluation and analysis of ongoing programs. Recently, the Committee on Assessing Juvenile Justice Reform of the National Academies of Sciences released a report on reforming juvenile justice.[a] The Committee found that "a harsh system of punishing troubled youth can make things worse, while a scientifically based juvenile justice system can make an enduring difference in the lives of many youth who most need the structure and services it can provide." The Committee recommended that the goals, design and operation of the juvenile justice system "should be informed by the growing body of knowledge about adolescent development. If designed and implemented in a developmentally informed way," the Committee said, "procedures for holding adolescents accountable for their offending, and the services provided to them, can promote positive legal socialization, reinforce a prosocial identity, and reduce reoffending." The Committee warned, however, that "if the goals, design, and operation of the juvenile justice system are not informed by this growing body of knowledge, the outcome is likely to be negative interactions between youth and justice system officials, increased disrespect for the law and legal authority, and the reinforcement of a deviant identity and social disaffection."

Two of today's best-known evidence-based initiatives in the area of juvenile justice are (1) the Blueprints for Violence Prevention program developed by the Center for the Study and Prevention of Violence (CSPV) at the University of Colorado—Boulder, and (2) the Office of Juvenile Justice and Delinquency Prevention's (OJJDP) Model Programs Guide (MPG). The Blueprints study, one of the earliest research efforts to focus on evidence-based delinquency programs, began as an effort to identify model violence prevention initiatives and implement them within the State of Colorado.[b] OJJDP soon became an active supporter of the Blueprints project and provided additional funding to CSPV to sponsor and evaluate program replications in sites across the United States. As a result, Blueprints has evolved into a large-scale prevention initiative, both identifying model programs and providing technical support to help sites choose and implement those programs that have been proved to be effective. As of mid-2018, the Blueprints study has identified 15 "model" or "model plus" programs and 65 "promising" programs that prevent violence and drug use and treat youth with problem behaviors.[c]

The MPG, also developed with support from OJJDP, is intended to assist communities in implementing evidence-based prevention and intervention programs that can make a difference in the lives of children.[d] The MPG database consists of over 200 evidence-based programs that cover the continuum of youth services from prevention through sanctions to reentry. It is used by juvenile justice practitioners, administrators, and researchers to initiate programs that have already proved their ability to enhance accountability, ensure public safety, and reduce recidivism. OJJDP offers the MPG in the form of an easy-to-use online database that address a range of issues, including substance abuse, mental health, and education programs. The MPG database contains summary information on many evidence-based delinquency programs. Programs are categorized into exemplary, effective, and promising, based on an established set of methodological criteria and the strength of the findings. View the Blueprints program at **http://www.blueprintsprograms.com**, or **https://www.colorado.edu/cspv/blueprints**.

---

[a] Richard J. Bonnie, Robert L. Johnson, Betty M. Chemers, and Julie A. Schuck, eds. *Reforming Juvenile Justice: A Developmental Approach*. Committee on Assessing Juvenile Justice Reform, Committee on Law and Justice, Division of Behavioral and Social Sciences and Education. National Research Council. (Washington, D.C.: The National Academies of Sciences Press, 2012).

[b] Sharon Mihalic, Abigail Fagan, Katherine Irwin, Diane Ballard, and Delbert Elliott, *Blueprints for Violence Prevention* (Washington, D.C.: OJJDP, July 2004).

[c] Blueprints for Healthy Youth Development, "Blueprints Programs," http://www.blueprintsprograms.com/programs (accessed June 16, 2018).

[d] OJJDP, *OJJDP Model Programs Guide*, http://www.ojjdp.gov/mpg (accessed March 10, 2018).

---

their transfer and waiver standards to enhance the choices available to juvenile court judges. Those changes resulted in far fewer transfers to the adult criminal justice system, and a reduced use of **blended sentences** for the most serious offenders.

3. **Upping the Age of Juvenile Court Jurisdiction.** In 2007, Connecticut returned 16- and 17-year-olds to the jurisdiction of the juvenile court, and in 2013 and 2014 Illinois, Massachusetts, and New Hampshire upped the age of juvenile court jurisdiction from 16 to 17 for all offenses. New York followed in 2017.

4. **The Development of Evidence-Based Prevention, Intervention, and Detention Reform.** At least 18 states currently have statutes that support a commitment to evidence-based programs. In addition, Vermont and Washington recently enacted laws to evaluate and improve research and evidence-based programs in their states. A 2014 Nebraska reform law created new evidence-based diversion programs, and Connecticut recently funded a new state family violence-mediation diversion program. Pennsylvania is in the process of implementing the Pennsylvania Juvenile Justice System Enhancement Strategy (JJ-SES), which is a statewide commitment to employ evidence-based practices, at every stage of the juvenile justice process. Similarly, Colorado's recent embrace of evidence-based programming for juveniles resulted in a statewide Evidence Based Principles and Practices committee which has developed a toolkit to help local communities in evaluating their current practices. The toolkit is available at **http://coebpp.org**.

blended sentence
A juvenile court disposition that imposes both a juvenile sanction and an adult criminal sentence on an adjudicated delinquent. The adult sentence is suspended on the condition that the juvenile offender successfully completes the term of the juvenile disposition and refrains from committing any new offense.[i]

5. **Due-Process Reforms**. Another emerging trend in juvenile justice policy has been to increase due-process protections for juvenile offenders. Much of the change occurred in the area of assessment of juvenile competency. Competency refers to a person's cognitive ability to understand and meaningfully take part in legal proceedings. A juvenile's lack of competency presents issues for both juvenile and criminal courts. As a result, in just the past 5 years, 12 states enacted legislation that expands definitions of "competence" for juveniles, and that take into account social and cognitive development. New laws in Nevada, Arkansas, California, Idaho, Louisiana, Maine, Maryland, Michigan, New Hampshire, Nevada, Ohio, Oklahoma, and South Dakota, plus the District of Columbia, bring the total to 24 states and D.C. that have revised juvenile competency laws over the past ten years.

6. **The Recognition of the Mental Health Needs of Juvenile Offenders.** A number of states are now encouraging mental health practitioners and adolescent service agencies to work together, resulting in enhanced resources needed to divert youthful offenders who have mental health issues from handling by the justice system.

7. **Addressing Racial and Ethnic Disparities.** Eighteen states have enacted laws that require enhanced training for police officers in community policing initiatives, and increase funding for community policing. Other legislative initiatives have addressed "racial profiling," and 31 states now have laws that specifically prohibit racial profiling.

8. **Improvements to Aftercare Programs.** Many states now deliver improved aftercare programs to help reintegrate juveniles back into society, and to reduce recidivism. In recent years, six states have taken steps to ensure successful reentry into the community by strengthening juvenile probation services and by measuring the effectiveness of reentry programs.

Follow the author's tweets about the latest crime and justice news @schmalleger

The Conference concludes that recent trends in juvenile justice legislation represent a significant new direction that embraces methods to deliver positive outcomes for both public safety and youthful offenders. With the availability of evidence-based techniques, the Conference notes, "policymakers are now empowered to make informed decisions based on calculated, supported research and analysis that clearly distinguishes juveniles from adults." As a result, the juvenile justice system of the mid-twenty-first century may in many respects be quite different than the one we have known.

Finally, in 2016, the Executive Session on Community Corrections at Harvard University concluded that confinement facilities for youth, no matter what they are called, are inherently flawed because they emphasize adult-style confinement and control. Such facilities, the Harvard group said, are "devoid of the essentials required for healthy adolescent development." Those essentials were identified as (1) helpful adults focused on positive youth development, (2) a peer group that models prosocial behavior, (3) opportunities for academic success, and (4) activities that contribute to developing decision-making and critical thinking skills.[88] Today, evidence-based practices in the juvenile justice arena (see the CJ Issues box in this chapter) are helping to establish a set of best practice guidelines, providing state policymakers and juvenile justice administrators insight into what works best to control juvenile crime and to rehabilitate youthful offenders.

Summary

- Under today's laws, children occupy a special status that is tied closely to cultural advances that occurred in the Western world during the past 200 years. Before the modern era, children who committed crimes received no preferential treatment and were adjudicated, punished, and imprisoned alongside adults. Beginning a few hundred years ago, England (from which we derive many of our legal traditions) adapted the principle of *parens patriae*. That principle allowed the government to take the place of parents in dealing with children who broke the law. Around the middle of the nineteenth century, the child-savers movement began in the United States. It espoused a philosophy of productivity and eschewed idleness and unprincipled behavior. Not long afterward, the 1899 codification of Illinois juvenile law became the model for juvenile court statutes throughout the United States. It created a juvenile court separate in form and function from adult criminal courts and based on the principle of *parens patriae*. To avoid the lasting stigma of criminality, the term *delinquent* (rather than *criminal*) began to be applied to young adjudicated offenders. Soon, juvenile courts across the country focused primarily on the best interests of the child as a guide in their deliberations.

- Important U.S. Supreme Court decisions of special relevance to the handling of juveniles by the justice system include (1) *Kent* v. *U.S.* (1966), which established minimal due-process standards for juvenile hearings; (2) *In re Gault* (1967), in which the Court found that a child has many of the same due-process rights as an adult; (3) *In re Winship* (1970), which held that the constitutional safeguard of proof beyond a reasonable doubt is required during the adjudicatory stage of a delinquency proceeding; (4) *McKeiver* v. *Pennsylvania* (1971), which held that jury trials were not required in delinquency cases; (5) *Breed* v. *Jones* (1975), which restricted the conditions under which transfers from juvenile to adult court may occur; (6) *Schall* v. *Martin* (1984), in which the Court held that pretrial detention of juveniles based on "serious risk" does not violate due process, although prior notice, an equitable detention hearing, and a statement by the juvenile court judge explaining the reasons for detention are required; (7) *Roper* v. *Simmons* (2005), which held that age *is* a bar to capital punishment when the offender commits a capital crime when he or she is younger than age 18; (8) *Graham* v. *Florida* (2010), in which the Court found that the Constitution does not permit a juvenile offender to be sentenced to life in prison without parole for a nonhomicide crime; (9) *J.D.B.* v. *North Carolina* (2011), which held that the age of suspects must be considered when determining whether they would feel free not to respond to police questioning; (10) *Miller* v. *Alabama* (2012), in which the Court held that *mandatory* life-without-parole sentences for individuals 17 or younger convicted of homicide violate the Eighth Amendment; and (11) *Montgomery* v. *Louisiana* (2016), which retroactively applied the *Miller* decision providing people who had been sentenced to mandatory life without parole as juveniles, the right to have their sentences reviewed.

- The juvenile justice system of today is infused with due-process guarantees designed to ensure that juvenile proceedings are fair and that the interests of juveniles are protected. Although the U.S. Supreme Court has established that juveniles are entitled to fundamental due-process protections, it has refrained from declaring that juveniles have a right to all aspects of due process afforded adult defendants. The juvenile justice system differs from the adult system in a number of ways: (1) It is less concerned with legal issues of guilt or innocence and focuses on the child's best interests; (2) it emphasizes treatment rather than punishment; (3) it ensures privacy and protection from public scrutiny through the use of sealed records and laws against publishing the names of juvenile offenders; (4) it uses the techniques of social science in dispositional decision making rather than sentences determined by a perceived need for punishment; (5) it does not order long-term confinement, with most juveniles being released from institutions by their twenty-first birthday; (6) it has separate facilities for juveniles; and (7) it allows broad discretionary alternatives at all points in the process.

- The "professionalization" of delinquency, the hallmark of which is the repeated and often violent criminal involvement of juveniles in drug-related gang activity, presented a major challenge to the idealism of the juvenile justice system in the latter part of the twentieth century. Consequently, the juvenile justice system's commitment to a philosophy of protection and restoration, expressed in the juvenile court movement of the late nineteenth and early twentieth centuries began to dissipate. However, necessitated by budgetary concerns at both the state and federal level, the tide has shifted to evidence-based models that demonstrate effectiveness in the handling of juvenile offenders. The present juvenile justice system, for the most part, continues to differ substantially from the adult system in the multitude of opportunities it provides for diversion and in the emphasis it places on rehabilitation rather than punishment. It has also been strongly influenced by neurobiological theories of human development, which have demonstrated that almost all children have the capacity for change, and that lengthy sentences of confinement can be counterproductive.

QUESTIONS FOR REVIEW

1. Describe the history and evolution of the juvenile justice system in the Western world, and list the six categories of children recognized by the laws of most states.
2. Name the important U.S. Supreme Court decisions of relevance to juvenile justice. What was the impact of each of these decisions on juvenile justice in America?
3. What are the major similarities and differences between the juvenile and adult justice systems?
4. In your opinion, should juveniles continue to receive what many regard as preferential treatment from the courts? Why or why not?

Bill of Rights The first ten amendments to the U.S. Constitution are known as the *Bill of Rights*. These amendments, ratified in 1791, have special relevance to criminal justice and are reproduced here.

Amendment I Congress shall make no law respecting an establishment of religion, or prohibiting the free exercise thereof; or abridging the freedom of speech, or of the press; or the right of the people peaceably to assemble, and to petition the Government for a redress of grievances.

Amendment II A well-regulated Militia, being necessary to the security of a free State, the right of the people to keep and bear Arms, shall not be infringed.

Amendment III No Soldier shall, in time of peace be quartered in any house, without the consent of the Owner, nor in time of war, but in a manner to be prescribed by law.

Amendment IV The right of the people to be secure in their persons, houses, papers, and effects, against unreasonable searches and seizures, shall not be violated, and no Warrants shall issue, but upon probable cause, supported by Oath or affirmation, and particularly describing the place to be searched, and the persons or things to be seized.

Amendment V No person shall be held to answer for a capital, or otherwise infamous crime, unless on a presentment or indictment of a Grand Jury, except in cases arising in the land or naval forces, or in the Militia, when in actual service in time of War or public danger; nor shall any person be subject for the same offence to be twice put in jeopardy of life or limb; nor shall be compelled in any criminal case to be a witness against himself, nor be deprived of life, liberty, or property, without due process of law; nor shall private property be taken for public use, without just compensation.

Amendment VI In all criminal prosecutions, the accused shall enjoy the right to a speedy and public trial, by an impartial jury of the State and district wherein the crime shall have been committed, which district shall have been previously ascertained by law, and to be informed of the nature and cause of the accusation; to be confronted with the witnesses against him; to have compulsory process for obtaining witnesses in his favor, and to have the Assistance of Counsel for his defense.

Amendment VII In Suits at common law, where the value in controversy shall exceed 20 dollars, the right of trial by jury shall be preserved, and no fact tried by a jury, shall be otherwise re-examined in any Court of the United States, than according to the rules of the common law.

Amendment VIII Excessive bail shall not be required, nor excessive fines imposed, nor cruel and unusual punishments inflicted.

Amendment IX The enumeration in the Constitution, of certain rights, shall not be construed to deny or disparage others retained by the people.

Amendment X The powers not delegated to the United States by the Constitution, nor prohibited by it to the States, are reserved to the States respectively, or to the people.

List of Acronyms

ABA	American Bar Association	CSC	Correctional Services Corporation
ACA	American Correctional Association	DEA	Drug Enforcement Administration
ACJS	Academy of Criminal Justice Sciences	DHS	Department of Homeland Security
ACLU	American Civil Liberties Union	DNA	deoxyribonucleic acid
ADAM	Arrestee Drug Abuse Monitoring	DOJ	U.S. Department of Justice
ADMAX	administrative maximum	DPIC	Death Penalty Information Center
AEDPA	Antiterrorism and Effective Death Penalty Act (1996)	DUI	driving under the influence (of alcohol or drugs)
AFDA	Association of Federal Defense Attorneys	DWI	driving while intoxicated
AFIS	automated fingerprint identification system	ECPA	Electronic Communications Privacy Act (1986)
AIDS	acquired immunodeficiency syndrome	EUROPOL	European Police Office
AJA	American Jail Association	FBI	Federal Bureau of Investigation
ALI	American Law Institute	FCC	federal correctional complex
AMBER	America's Missing: Broadcast Emergency Response	FCI	federal correctional institution
AOUSC	Administrative Office of the United States Courts	FLETC	Federal Law Enforcement Training Center
APPA	American Probation and Parole Association	FLIR	forward-looking infrared
ASC	American Society of Criminology	FOP	Fraternal Order of Police
ASIS	American Society for Industrial Security	FPC	federal prison camp
ASLET	American Society for Law Enforcement Training	FTCA	Federal Tort Claims Act (1946)
ATF	Bureau of Alcohol, Tobacco, Firearms and Explosives	GBMI	guilty but mentally ill
BJA	Bureau of Justice Assistance	HIV	human immunodeficiency virus
BJS	Bureau of Justice Statistics	IACP	International Association of Chiefs of Police
BOP	Bureau of Prisons	ICC	International Criminal Court
BSEBP	British Society of Evidence-Based Policing	ICE	Immigration and Customs Enforcement
CALEA	Commission on Accreditation for Law Enforcement Agencies	IDRA	Insanity Defense Reform Act (1984)
		ILC	International Law Commission (United Nations)
CAPS	Chicago's Alternative Policing Strategy	ILEA	International Law Enforcement Academy (FBI)
CAT	computer-aided transcription	INTERPOL	International Criminal Police Organization
CCA	Corrections Corporation of America	IPS	intensive probation supervision
CDA	Communications Decency Act (1996)	JJDP	Juvenile Justice and Delinquency Prevention Act (1974)
CFAA	Computer Fraud and Abuse Act (1986)	JTTF	Joint Terrorism Task Force
CIA	Central Intelligence Agency	LAPD	Los Angeles Police Department
CID	Criminal Investigative Division	LEAA	Law Enforcement Assistance Administration
CJIS	Criminal Justice Information Services (FBI)	LEMAS	Law Enforcement Management and Administrative Statistics
CLET	Certified Law Enforcement Trainer		
CODIS	Combined DNA Index System (FBI)	MCFP	medical center for federal prisoners
COPS	Community Oriented Policing Services	MDC	metropolitan detention center
CPOP	Community Police Officer Program (New York City)	MPC	Model Penal Code
CPTED	crime prevention through environmental design	NAACP	National Association for the Advancement of Colored People
CRIPA	Civil Rights of Institutionalized Persons Act (1980)		
CRIPP	Courts Regimented Intensive Probation Program	NACDL	National Association of Criminal Defense Lawyers
CSA	Controlled Substances Act (1970)	NCAVC	National Center for the Analysis of Violent Crime

NCCD	National Council on Crime and Delinquency
NCIC	National Crime Information Center (FBI)
NCISP	National Criminal Intelligence Sharing Plan
NCJRS	National Criminal Justice Reference Service
NCPC	National Crime Prevention Council
NCSC	National Center for State Courts
NCVS	National Crime Victimization Survey
NCWP	National Center for Women and Policing
NDAA	National District Attorneys Association
NDIS	National DNA Index System (FBI)
NFCA	National Fusion Center Association
NIBRS	National Incident-Based Reporting System (FBI)
NIJ	National Institute of Justice
NJC	National Judicial College
NLADA	National Legal Aid and Defender Association
NOBLE	National Organization of Black Law Enforcement Executives
NVAWS	National Violence against Women Survey
NVC	National Victims Center
NVCAP	National Victims' Constitutional Amendment Project
NW3C	National White Collar Crime Center
NYGC	National Youth Gang Center
NYPD	New York Police Department
OJJDP	Office of Juvenile Justice and Delinquency Prevention
OJP	Office of Justice Programs
ONDCP	Office of National Drug Control Policy
PCR	police–community relations
PDS	podular/direct supervision
PERF	Police Executive Research Forum
PINS	persons in need of supervision
PLRA	Prison Litigation Reform Act (1996)
POST	Peace Officer Standards and Training
PROTECT Act	Prosecutorial Remedies and Other Tools to End the Exploitation of Children Today Act (2003)
RICO	Racketeer Influenced and Corrupt Organizations (statute)
RISE	Reintegrative Shaming Experiments (Australian Institute of Criminology)
RJC	Real Justice Conferencing (Pennsylvania)
ROR	release on recognizance
RTTF	Regional Terrorism Task Force
SAMHSA	Substance Abuse and Mental Health Services Administration
SBI	State Bureau of Investigation
SCU	Street Crimes Unit (New York City)
SEARCH	National Consortium for Justice Information and Statistics
SIIA	Software and Information Industry Association
STG	security threat group
SVORI	Serious Violent Offender Reentry Initiative
SWAT	special weapons and tactics
TFJJR	Task Force on Juvenile Justice Reform
TIPS	Terrorist Information and Prevention System
TWGEDE	Technical Working Group for the Examination of Digital Evidence
UCR	Uniform Crime Reports (FBI)
UNODC	United Nations Office on Drugs and Crime
USA PATRIOT Act	Uniting and Strengthening America by Providing Appropriate Tools Required to Intercept and Obstruct Terrorism Act (2001)
U.S.C.	United States Code
USP	United States penitentiary
USSC	United States Sentencing Commission
VAWA	Violence against Women Act (1994)
VCAN	Victims' Constitutional Amendment Network
VICAP	Violent Criminal Apprehension Program (FBI)
VOCA	Victims of Crime Act (1984)
VWPA	Victim and Witness Protection Act (1982)

abused child[1] A child who has been physically, emotionally, or sexually abused. Most states also consider a child who is forced into delinquent activity by a parent or guardian to be abused.

accreditation A credentialing process which, if successful, provides recognized professional status for an organization—especially those engaged in law enforcement, public safety communications, public safety training, and the provision of campus security services.

actus reus An act in violation of the law. Also, a guilty act.

adjudicatory hearing The fact-finding process wherein the juvenile court determines whether there is sufficient evidence to sustain the allegations in a petition.

ADMAX An acronym for administrative maximum. This term is used by the federal government to denote ultra-high-security prisons.

administration of justice The performance of any of the following activities: detection, apprehension, detention, pretrial release, post-trial release, prosecution, adjudication, correctional supervision, or rehabilitation of accused persons or criminal offenders.[2]

adversarial system The two-sided structure under which American criminal trial courts operate that pits the prosecution against the defense. In theory, justice is done when the more effective adversary is able to convince the judge or jury that his or her perspective on the case is the correct one.

aggravated assault The unlawful, intentional inflicting, or attempted or threatened inflicting, of serious injury upon the person of another. Although *aggravated assault* and *simple assault* are standard terms for reporting purposes, most state penal codes use labels such as *first-degree* and *second-degree* to make such distinctions.

aggravating circumstances Circumstances relating to the commission of a crime that make it more grave than the average instance of that crime.

alibi A statement or contention by an individual charged with a crime that he or she was so distant when the crime was committed, or so engaged in other provable activities, that his or her participation in the commission of that crime was impossible.

alter ego rule In some jurisdictions, a rule of law that holds that a person can only defend a third party under circumstances and only to the degree that the third party could legally act on his or her own behalf.

alternative sentencing The use of court-ordered community service, home detention, day reporting, drug treatment, psychological counseling, victim–offender programming, or intensive supervision in lieu of other, more traditional sanctions, such as imprisonment and fines.

anticipatory warrant A search warrant issued on the basis of probable cause to believe that evidence of a crime, although not currently at the place described, will likely be there when the warrant is executed.

appeal The request that a court with appellate jurisdiction review the judgment, decision, or order of a lower court and set it aside (reverse it) or modify it.

appellate jurisdiction The lawful authority of a court to review a decision made by a lower court.

arraignment Strictly, the hearing before a court having jurisdiction in a criminal case in which the identity of the defendant is established, the defendant is informed of the charge and of his or her rights, and the defendant is required to enter a plea. Also, in some usages, any appearance in criminal court before trial.

arrest The act of taking an adult or juvenile into physical custody by authority of law for the purpose of charging the person with a criminal offense, a delinquent act, or a status offense, terminating with the recording of a specific offense.

arson (UCR/NIBRS) Any willful or malicious burning or attempt to burn, with or without intent to defraud, a dwelling house, public building, motor vehicle or aircraft, personal property of another, and so on. Some instances of arson result from malicious mischief, some involve attempts to claim insurance money, and some are committed in an effort to disguise other crimes, such as murder, burglary, or larceny.

assault (UCR/NIBRS) An unlawful attack by one person upon another. Historically, assault meant only the attempt to inflict injury on another person; a completed act constituted the separate offense of battery. Under modern statistical usage, however, attempted and completed acts are grouped together under the generic term *assault*.

attendant circumstances The facts surrounding an event.

bail The money or property pledged to the court or actually deposited with the court to effect the release of a person from legal custody.

bail bond A document guaranteeing the appearance of a defendant in court as required and recording the pledge of money or property to be paid to the court if he or she does not appear. The bail bond is signed by the person to be released and by anyone else acting in his or her behalf.

bailiff The court officer whose duties are to keep order in the courtroom, to secure witnesses, and to maintain physical custody of the jury.

balancing test A principle, developed by the courts and applied to the corrections arena by *Pell* v. *Procunier* (1974), that attempts to weigh the rights of an individual, as guaranteed by the Constitution, against the authority of any state to make laws or to otherwise restrict a person's freedom in order to protect the state's interests and its citizens.

Bill of Rights The popular name given to the first ten amendments to the U.S. Constitution, which are considered especially important in the processing of criminal defendants.

biological weapon A biological agent used to threaten human life (for example, anthrax, smallpox, or any infectious disease).[3]

***Bivens* action** A civil suit, based on the case of *Bivens* v. *Six Unknown Federal Agents*, brought against federal government officials for denying the constitutional rights of others.

blended sentence A juvenile court disposition that imposes both a juvenile sanction and an adult criminal sentence on an adjudicated delinquent. The adult sentence is suspended on the condition that the juvenile offender successfully completes the term of the juvenile disposition and refrains from committing any new offense.[4]

broken windows A model of policing based on the notion that physical decay, such as litter and abandoned buildings, can breed disorder in a community and can lead to crime by signaling that laws are not being enforced. The broken windows theory suggests that by encouraging the repair of rundown buildings and controlling disorderly behavior in public spaces, police agencies can create an environment in which serious crime cannot easily flourish.

Bureau of Justice Statistics (BJS) A U.S. Department of Justice agency responsible for the collection of criminal justice data, including the annual National Crime Victimization Survey.

burglary (UCR/NIBRS) The unlawful entry of a structure to commit a felony or a theft (excludes tents, trailers, and other mobile units used for recreational purposes). Under the UCR/NIBRS Program, the crime of burglary can be reported if (1) an unlawful entry of an unlocked structure has occurred, (2) a breaking and entering (of a secured structure) has taken place, or (3) a burglary has been attempted.

capital offense   A criminal offense punishable by death.

capital punishment   The death penalty. Capital punishment is the most extreme of all sentencing options.

case law   The body of judicial precedent, historically built on legal reasoning and past interpretations of statutory laws, that serves as a guide to decision making, especially in the courts.

caseload   The number of probation or parole clients assigned to one probation or parole officer for supervision.

chain of command   The unbroken line of authority that extends through all levels of an organization, from the highest to the lowest.

change of venue   The movement of a trial or lawsuit from one jurisdiction to another or from one location to another within the same jurisdiction. A change of venue may be made in a criminal case to ensure that the defendant receives a fair trial.

circumstantial evidence   The evidence that requires interpretation or that requires a judge or jury to reach a conclusion based on what the evidence indicates. From the close proximity of the defendant to a smoking gun, for example, the jury might conclude that he or she pulled the trigger.

civil death   The legal status of prisoners in some jurisdictions who are denied the opportunity to vote, hold public office, marry, or enter into contracts by virtue of their status as incarcerated felons. Although civil death is primarily of historical interest, some jurisdictions still limit the contractual opportunities available to inmates.

civil justice   The civil law, the law of civil procedure, and the array of procedures and activities having to do with private rights and remedies sought by civil action. Civil justice cannot be separated from social justice because the justice enacted in our nation's civil courts reflects basic American understandings of right and wrong.

civil law   The branch of modern law that governs relationships between parties.

civil liability   The potential responsibility for payment of damages or other court-ordered enforcement as a result of a ruling in a lawsuit. Civil liability is not the same as criminal liability, which means "open to punishment for a crime."[5]

classification system   A system used by prison administrators to assign inmates to custody levels based on offense history, assessed dangerousness, perceived risk of escape, and other factors.

clearance rate   A measure of investigative effectiveness that compares the number of crimes reported or discovered to the number of crimes solved through arrest or other means (such as the death of the suspect).

closing argument   An oral summation of a case presented to a judge, or to a judge and jury, by the prosecution or by the defense in a criminal trial.

common law   The body of law originating from usage and custom rather than from written statutes. The term refers to an unwritten body of judicial opinion, originally developed by English courts, that is based on nonstatutory customs, traditions, and precedents that help guide judicial decision making.

community corrections   The use of a variety of officially ordered program-based sanctions that permit convicted offenders to remain in the community under conditional supervision as an alternative to an active prison sentence.

community court   A low-level court that focuses on quality-of-life crimes that erode a neighborhood's morale, that emphasizes problem solving rather than punishment, and that builds on restorative principles such as community service and restitution.

community policing   "A philosophy that promotes organizational strategies, which support the systematic use of partnerships and problem-solving techniques, to proactively address the immediate conditions that give rise to public safety issues such as crime, social disorder, and fear of crime."[6]

community service   A sentencing alternative that requires offenders to spend at least part of their time working for a community agency.

compelling interest   A legal concept that provides a basis for suspicionless searches when public safety is at issue. In two cases, the U.S. Supreme Court held that public safety may sometimes provide a sufficiently compelling interest to justify limiting an individual's right to privacy.

competent to stand trial   A finding by a court, when the defendant's sanity at the time of trial is at issue, that the defendant has sufficient present ability to consult with his or her attorney with a reasonable degree of rational understanding and that the defendant has a rational as well as factual understanding of the proceedings against him or her.

CompStat   A crime-analysis and police-management process built on crime mapping that was developed by the New York City Police Department in the mid-1990s.

computer crime   Any crime perpetrated through the use of computer technology. Also, any violation of a federal or state computer-crime statute. Also called *cybercrime*.

computer virus   A computer program designed to secretly invade systems and either modify the way in which they operate or alter the information they store. Viruses are destructive software programs that may effectively vandalize computers of all types and sizes.

concurrence   The coexistence of (1) an act in violation of the law and (2) a culpable mental state.

concurrent sentence   One of two or more sentences imposed at the same time, after conviction for more than one offense, and served at the same time. Also, a new sentence for a new conviction imposed upon a person already under sentence for a previous offense, which is served at the same time as the previous sentence.

conditional release   The release of an inmate from prison to community supervision with a set of conditions for remaining on parole. If a condition is violated, the individual can be returned to prison or face another sanction in the community.[7]

conditions of parole (probation)   The general and special limits imposed on an offender who is released on parole (or probation). General conditions tend to be fixed by state statute, whereas special conditions are mandated by the sentencing authority (court or board) and take into consideration the background of the offender and the circumstances of the offense.

conflict model   A criminal justice perspective that assumes that the system's components function primarily to serve their own interests. According to this theoretical framework, justice is more a product of conflicts among agencies within the system than it is the result of cooperation among component agencies.

consecutive sentence   One of two or more sentences imposed at the same time, after conviction for more than one offense, and served in sequence with the other sentence. Also, a new sentence for a new conviction imposed upon a person already under sentence for a previous offense, which is added to the previous sentence, thus increasing the maximum time the offender may be confined or under supervision.

consensus model   A criminal justice perspective that assumes that the system's components work together harmoniously to achieve the social product we call *justice*.

corporate crime   A violation of a criminal statute by a corporate entity or by its executives, employees, or agents acting on behalf of and for the benefit of the corporation, partnership, or other form of business entity.[8]

corpus delicti   The facts that show that a crime has occurred. The term literally means "the body of the crime."

court of last resort   The court authorized by law to hear the final appeal on a matter.

courtroom work group   The professional courtroom actors, including judges, prosecuting attorneys, defense attorneys, public defenders, and others who earn a living serving the court.

courts of general jurisdiction Courts of law with primary jurisdiction on all issues not delegated to lower courts. Most often called major trial courts, they most often hear serious criminal or civil cases. Cases are also designated to courts of general jurisdiction based on the severity of the punishment or allegation or on the dollar value of the case.

courts of limited jurisdiction Courts of law that have jurisdiction on a restricted range of cases, primarily lesser criminal and civil matters, including misdemeanors, small claims, traffic, parking, and civil infractions. Such courts are also called inferior courts or lower courts. They can also handle the preliminary stages of felony cases in some states.

crime Conduct in violation of the criminal laws of a state, the federal government, or a local jurisdiction, for which there is no legally acceptable justification or excuse.

Crime Index A now-defunct but once-inclusive measure of the UCR Program's violent and property crime categories, or what are called *Part I offenses.* The Crime Index, long featured in the FBI's publication *Crime in the United States,* was discontinued in 2004. The index had been intended as a tool for geographic (state-to-state) and historical (year-to-year) comparisons via the use of crime rates (the number of crimes per unit of population). However, criticism that the index was misleading arose after researchers found that the largest of the index's crime categories, larceny-theft, carried undue weight and led to an underappreciation of changes in the rates of more violent and serious crimes.

crime prevention The anticipation, recognition, and appraisal of a crime risk and the initiation of action to eliminate or reduce it.

crime typology A classification of crimes along a particular dimension, such as legal category, offender motivation, victim behavior, or characteristics of individual offenders.

crime-control model A criminal justice perspective that emphasizes the efficient arrest and conviction of criminal offenders.

criminal intelligence The information compiled, analyzed, and/or disseminated in an effort to anticipate, prevent, or monitor criminal activity.[9]

criminal investigation The process of discovering, collecting, preparing, identifying, and presenting evidence to determine what happened and who is responsible when a crime occurs.[10]

criminal justice In the strictest sense, the criminal (penal) law, the law of criminal procedure, and the array of procedures and activities having to do with the enforcement of this body of law. Criminal justice cannot be separated from social justice because the justice enacted in our nation's criminal courts reflects basic American understandings of right and wrong.

criminal justice system The aggregate of all operating and administrative or technical support agencies that perform criminal justice functions. The basic divisions of the operational aspects of criminal justice are law enforcement, courts, and corrections.

criminal law The body of rules and regulations that define and specify the nature of and punishments for offenses of a public nature or for wrongs committed against the state or society. Also called *penal law.*

criminal negligence A behavior in which a person fails to reasonably perceive substantial and unjustifiable risks of dangerous consequences.

criminology The scientific study of the causes and prevention of crime and the rehabilitation and punishment of offenders.

cultural competence The ability to interact effectively with people of different cultures. Cultural competence helps to ensure that the needs of all community members are addressed.

cybercrime See *computer crime.*

cyberstalking The use of the Internet, e-mail, and other electronic communication technologies to stalk another person.[11]

cyberterrorism A form of terrorism that makes use of high technology, especially computers and the Internet, in the planning and carrying out of terrorist attacks.

danger law A law intended to prevent the pretrial release of criminal defendants judged to represent a danger to others in the community.

dangerousness The likelihood that a given individual poses a significant risk of later harm to society or to others.

dark figure of crime Crime that is not reported to the police and that remains unknown to officials.

date rape The unlawful forced sexual intercourse with a person, without his or her consent, that occurs within the context of a dating relationship. Date rape, or acquaintance rape, is a subcategory of rape that is of special concern today.

deadly force The force likely to cause death or great bodily harm. Also, "the intentional use of a firearm or other instrument resulting in a high probability of death."[12]

defense (to a criminal charge) The evidence and arguments offered by a defendant and his or her attorney to show why the defendant should not be held liable for a criminal charge.

defense counsel A licensed trial lawyer hired or appointed to conduct the legal defense of a person accused of a crime and to represent him or her before a court of law.

delayed-notification search See *"sneak and peek" search.*

deliberate indifference A wanton disregard by corrections personnel for the well-being of inmates. Deliberate indifference requires both actual knowledge that a harm is occurring and disregard of the risk of harm that is occurring. A prison official may be held liable under the Eighth Amendment for acting with deliberate indifference to inmate health or safety only if he or she knows that inmates face a substantial risk of serious harm and disregards that risk by failing to take reasonable measures to abate it.

delinquency In the broadest usage, juvenile actions or conduct in violation of criminal law, juvenile status offenses, and other juvenile misbehavior.

delinquent child A child who has engaged in activity that would be considered a crime if the child were an adult. The term *delinquent* is used to avoid the stigma associated with the term *criminal.*

dependent child A child who has no parents or whose parents are not available or are unable to care for him or her.

design capacity The number of inmates a prison was intended to hold when it was built or modified.

desistance The cessation of offending or other antisocial behavior.

detention See *investigative detention.*

detention hearing In juvenile justice usage, a hearing by a judicial officer of a juvenile court to determine whether a juvenile is to be detained, is to continue to be detained, or is to be released while juvenile proceedings are pending.

determinate sentencing A model of criminal punishment in which an offender is given a fixed term of imprisonment that may be reduced by good time or gain time. Under the model, for example, all offenders convicted of the same degree of burglary would be sentenced to the same length of time behind bars.

deterrence A goal of criminal sentencing that seeks to inhibit criminal behavior through the fear of punishment.

digital criminal forensics The lawful seizure, acquisition, analysis, reporting, and safeguarding of data from digital devices that may contain information of evidentiary value to the trier of fact in criminal events.[13]

diminished capacity A defense based on claims of a mental condition that may be insufficient to exonerate the defendant of guilt but that may be relevant to specific mental elements of certain crimes or degrees of crime.

direct evidence The evidence that, if believed, directly proves a fact. Eyewitness testimony and videotaped documentation account for the majority of all direct evidence heard in the criminal courtroom.

direct-supervision jail A temporary confinement facility that eliminates many of the traditional barriers between inmates and corrections staff. Physical barriers in direct-supervision jails are far less common than in traditional jails, allowing staff members the opportunity for greater interaction with, and control over, residents.

directed patrol A police-management strategy designed to increase the productivity of patrol officers through the scientific analysis and evaluation of patrol techniques.

discretionary release The release of an inmate from prison to supervision that is decided by a parole board or other authority.

dispositional hearing The final stage in the processing of adjudicated juveniles in which a decision is made on the form of treatment or penalty that should be imposed on the child.

dispute-resolution center An informal hearing place designed to mediate interpersonal disputes without resorting to the more formal arrangements of a criminal trial court.

diversion The official suspension of criminal or juvenile proceedings against an alleged offender at any point after a recorded justice system intake, but before the entering of a judgment, and referral of that person to a treatment or care program administered by a nonjustice or private agency. Also, a release without referral.

diversity See *social diversity*.

domestic terrorism The unlawful use of force or violence by a group or an individual who is based and operates entirely within the United States and its territories without foreign direction and whose acts are directed at elements of the U.S. government or population.[14]

double jeopardy A common law and constitutional prohibition against a second trial for the same offense.

due process A right guaranteed by the Fourth, Fifth, Sixth, and Fourteenth Amendments of the U.S. Constitution and generally understood, in legal contexts, to mean the due course of legal proceedings according to the rules and forms established for the protection of individual rights. In criminal proceedings, due process of law is generally understood to include the following basic elements: a law creating and defining the offense, an impartial tribunal having jurisdictional authority over the case, accusation in proper form, notice and opportunity to defend, a trial according to established procedure, and discharge from all restraints or obligations unless convicted.

due-process model A criminal justice perspective that emphasizes individual rights at all stages of justice-system processing.

Electronic Communications Privacy Act (ECPA) A law passed by Congress in 1986 establishing the due-process requirements that law enforcement officers must meet in order to legally intercept wire communications.

electronic evidence Information and data of investigative value that are stored in or transmitted by an electronic device.[15]

element (of a crime) In a specific crime, one of the essential features of that crime, as specified by law or statute.

emergency search A search conducted by the police without a warrant, which is justified on the basis of some immediate and overriding need, such as public safety, the likely escape of a dangerous suspect, or the removal or destruction of evidence.

entrapment An improper or illegal inducement to crime by agents of law enforcement. Also, a defense that may be raised when such inducements have occurred.

equity A sentencing principle, based on concerns with social equality, holding that similar crimes should be punished with the same degree of severity, regardless of the social or personal characteristics of the offenders.

espionage The "gathering, transmitting, or losing"[16] of information related to the national defense in such a manner that the information becomes available to enemies of the United States and may be used to their advantage.

European Police Office (Europol) The integrated police intelligence-gathering and information-disseminating arm of the member nations of the European Union.

evidence Anything useful to a judge or jury in deciding the facts of a case. Evidence may take the form of witness testimony, written documents, videotapes, magnetic media, photographs, physical objects, and so on.

evidence-based corrections (EBC) The application of social scientific techniques to the study of everyday corrections procedures for the purpose of increasing effectiveness and enhancing the efficient use of available resources.

evidence-based policing (EBP) The use of the best available research on the outcomes of police work to implement guidelines and evaluate agencies, units, and officers.[17]

evidence-based practice Crime-fighting strategies that have been scientifically tested and are based on social science research.

ex post facto Latin for "after the fact." The Constitution prohibits the enactment of *ex post facto* laws, which make acts committed before the laws in question were passed punishable as crimes.

excessive force The application of an amount or frequency of force greater than that required to compel compliance from a willing or unwilling subject.[18]

exclusionary rule The understanding, based on U.S. Supreme Court precedent, that incriminating information must be seized according to constitutional specifications of due process or it will not be allowed as evidence in a criminal trial.

exculpatory evidence Any information having a tendency to clear a person of guilt or blame.

excuse A legal defense in which the defendant claims that some personal condition or circumstance at the time of the act was such that he or she should not be held accountable under the criminal law.

exoneration The reversal of a criminal conviction by appropriate judicial authority.

expert witness A person who has special knowledge and skills recognized by the court as relevant to the determination of guilt or innocence. Unlike lay witnesses, expert witnesses may express opinions or draw conclusions in their testimony.

federal court system The three-tiered structure of federal courts, comprising U.S. district courts, U.S. courts of appeals, and the U.S. Supreme Court.

felony A criminal offense punishable by death or by incarceration in a prison facility for at least one year.

first appearance An appearance before a magistrate during which the legality of the defendant's arrest is initially assessed and the defendant is informed of the charges on which he or she is being held. At this stage in the criminal justice process, bail may be set or pretrial release arranged. Also called *initial appearance*.

fleeting-targets exception (also known as the *automobile exception*) An exception to the exclusionary rule that permits law enforcement officers to search a motor vehicle based on probable cause but without a warrant. The fleeting-targets exception is predicated on the fact that vehicles can quickly leave the jurisdiction of a law enforcement agency.

fruit of the poisonous tree doctrine A legal principle that excludes from introduction at trial any evidence later developed as a result of an illegal search or seizure.

fusion center A multiagency law enforcement facility designed to enhance cooperative efforts through a coordinated process for collecting, sharing, and analyzing information in order to develop actionable intelligence.

gain time The amount of time deducted from time to be served in prison on a given sentence as a result of participation in special projects or programs.

gender-responsiveness The process of understanding and taking into account the differences in characteristics and life experiences that women and men bring to the criminal justice system, and adjusting strategies and practices in ways that appropriately respond to those conditions.

general deterrence A goal of criminal sentencing that seeks to prevent others from committing crimes similar to the one for which a particular offender is being sentenced by making an example of the person sentenced.

good time The amount of time deducted from time to be served in prison on a given sentence as a result of good behavior.

good-faith exception An exception to the exclusionary rule. Law enforcement officers who conduct a search or who seize evidence on the basis of good faith (i.e., when they believe they are operating according to the dictates of the law) and who later discover that a mistake was made (perhaps in the format of the application for a search warrant) may still use the seized evidence in court.

grand jury A group of jurors who have been selected according to law and have been sworn to hear the evidence and to determine whether there is sufficient evidence to bring the accused person to trial, to investigate criminal activity generally, or to investigate the conduct of a public agency or official.

grievance procedure   A formalized arrangement, usually involving a neutral hearing board, whereby institutionalized individuals have the opportunity to register complaints about the conditions of their confinement.

guilty but mentally ill (GBMI)   A verdict, equivalent to a finding of "guilty," that establishes that the defendant, although mentally ill, was in sufficient possession of his or her faculties to be morally blameworthy for his or her acts.

hands-off doctrine   A policy of nonintervention with regard to prison management that U.S. courts tended to follow until the late 1960s. For 30 years, the doctrine languished as judicial intervention in prison administration dramatically increased, although there is now evidence that a new hands-off era is beginning.

hate crime (UCR/NIBRS)   A criminal offense committed against a person, property, or society that is motivated, in whole or in part, by the offender's bias against a race, religion, disability, sexual orientation, or ethnicity/national origin.

hearsay   Something that is not based on the personal knowledge of a witness. Witnesses who testify about something they have heard, for example, are offering hearsay by repeating information about a matter of which they have no direct knowledge.

hearsay rule   The long-standing precedent that hearsay cannot be used in American courtrooms. Rather than accepting testimony based on hearsay, the court will ask that the person who was the original source of the hearsay information be brought in to be questioned and cross-examined. Exceptions to the hearsay rule may occur when the person with direct knowledge is dead or is otherwise unable to testify.

home confinement   House arrest. Individuals ordered confined to their homes are sometimes monitored electronically to ensure they do not leave during the hours of confinement. Absence from the home during working hours is often permitted.

hot-spot policing   A contemporary policing strategy in which law enforcement agencies focus their resources on known areas of criminal activity.

Hudud crime   A serious violation of Islamic law that is regarded as an offense against God.

human smuggling   Illegal immigration in which an agent is paid to help a person cross a border clandestinely.

identity fraud   A crime in which an imposter obtains key pieces of information, such as Social Security and driver's license numbers, to obtain credit, merchandise, and services in the name of the victim. The victim is often left with a ruined credit history and the time-consuming and complicated task of repairing the financial damage.[19]

illegally seized evidence   Any evidence seized without regard to the principles of due process as described by the Bill of Rights. Most illegally seized evidence is the result of police searches conducted without a proper warrant or of improperly conducted interrogations.

incapacitation   The use of imprisonment or other means to reduce the likelihood that an offender will commit future offenses.

inchoate offense   An offense not yet completed. Also, an offense that consists of an action or conduct that is a step toward the intended commission of another offense.

incompetent to stand trial   In criminal proceedings, a finding by a court that as a result of mental illness, defect, or disability, a defendant is incapable of understanding the nature of the charges and proceedings against him or her, of consulting with an attorney, and of aiding in his or her own defense.

indeterminate sentencing   A model of criminal punishment that encourages rehabilitation through the use of general and relatively unspecific sentences (such as a term of imprisonment of from 1 to 10 years).

indictment   A formal written accusation submitted to the court by a grand jury alleging that a specified person has committed a specified offense, usually a felony.

individual rights   The rights guaranteed to all members of American society by the U.S. Constitution (especially those rights found in the first ten amendments to the Constitution, known as the *Bill of Rights*). These rights are particularly important to criminal defendants facing formal processing by the criminal justice system.

individual-rights advocate   One who seeks to protect personal freedoms within the process of criminal justice.

information   A formal written accusation submitted to a court by a prosecutor, alleging that a specified person has committed a specified offense.

infraction   A minor violation of state statute or local ordinance punishable by a fine or other penalty or by a specified, usually limited, term of incarceration.

inherent coercion   The tactics used by police interviewers that fall short of physical abuse but that nonetheless pressure suspects to divulge information.

initial appearance   See *first appearance.*

insanity defense   A legal defense based on claims of mental illness or mental incapacity.

intake   The first step in decision making regarding a juvenile whose behavior or alleged behavior is in violation of the law or could otherwise cause a juvenile court to assume jurisdiction.

intelligence-led policing (ILP)   The collection and analysis of information to produce an intelligence end product designed to inform police decision making at both the tactical and strategic levels.[20]

intensive probation/parole supervision (IPS)   A form of probation or parole

supervision involving frequent face-to-face contact between the correctional client and the probation/parole officer.

intermediate sanctions   The use of split sentencing, shock probation or parole, shock incarceration, mixed sentencing, community service, intensive probation supervision, or home confinement in lieu of other, more traditional sanctions, such as imprisonment and fines.

internal affairs   The branch of a police organization tasked with investigating charges of wrong-doing involving members of the department.

International Criminal Police Organization (Interpol)   An international law enforcement support organization that began operations in 1946 and today has 192 member nations.

International Justice and Public Safety Information Sharing Network (NLETS)   An important law enforcement information-sharing resource that includes state criminal histories, homeland alert messages, immigration databases, driver's records and vehicle registrations, aircraft registrations, AMBER Alerts, weather advisories, and hazardous materials (HAZMAT) notifications and regulations.

international terrorism   The unlawful use of force or violence by a group or an individual who has some connection to a foreign power or whose activities transcend national boundaries against people or property in order to intimidate or coerce a government, the civilian population, or any segment thereof in furtherance of political or social objectives.[21]

interrogation   The information-gathering activity of police officers that involves the direct questioning of suspects.

investigative detention   A temporary seizure of an individual by a police officer for investigative purposes. Also, police custody, short of arrest, that is based on reasonable suspicion. Unlike arrest, the amount of time a person may be detained depends upon how long it would reasonably take to conduct an investigation of the facts at hand or to finish police business (i.e., to issue a traffic ticket).

Islamic law   A system of laws, operative in some Arab countries, based on the Muslim religion and especially the holy book of Islam, the Koran.

jail   A confinement facility administered by an agency of local government, typically a law enforcement agency, intended for adults but sometimes also containing juveniles. Jails hold people who are being detained pending adjudication or who were committed after adjudication, usually those sentenced to a year or less.

judge   An elected or appointed public official who presides over a court of law and who is authorized to hear and sometimes to decide cases and to conduct trials.

judicial review The power of a court to review actions and decisions made by other agencies of government.

jurisdiction The territory, subject matter, or people over which a court or other justice agency may exercise lawful authority, as determined by statute or constitution.

jurisprudence The philosophy of law. Also, the science and study of the law.

juror A member of a trial or grand jury who has been selected for jury duty and is required to serve as an arbiter of the facts in a court of law. Jurors are expected to render verdicts of "guilty" or "not guilty" as to the charges brought against the accused, although they may sometimes fail to do so (as in the case of a hung jury).

jury selection The process whereby, according to law and precedent, members of a particular trial jury are chosen.

just deserts A model of criminal sentencing that holds that criminal offenders deserve the punishment they receive at the hands of the law and that punishments should be appropriate to the type and severity of the crime committed.

justice The principle of fairness; the ideal of moral equity.

justice-involved youth Youth who are charged with, or adjudicated for law violations.

justice model A contemporary model of imprisonment based on the principle of just deserts.

justice reinvestment A data-driven approach to criminal justice reform that examines and addresses justice system expenditures and population drivers in order to generate cost-saving that are then reinvested in high-performing public safety strategies.

justification A legal defense in which the defendant admits to committing the act in question but claims it was necessary in order to avoid some greater evil.

juvenile A youth at or below the upper age of juvenile court jurisdiction in a particular state.

juvenile court Any court that has jurisdiction over matters involving juveniles.

juvenile disposition The decision of a juvenile court that concludes a dispositional hearing. The adjudicated juvenile might be committed to a juvenile correctional facility; be placed in a juvenile residence, shelter, or care or treatment program; be required to meet certain standards of conduct; or be released.

juvenile justice system The government agencies that function to investigate, supervise, adjudicate, care for, or confine youthful offenders and other children subject to the jurisdiction of the juvenile court.

juvenile petition A document filed in juvenile court alleging that a juvenile is a delinquent, a status offender, or a dependent and asking that the court assume jurisdiction over the juvenile or that an alleged delinquent be transferred to a criminal court for prosecution as an adult.

Kansas City experiment The first large-scale scientific study of law enforcement practices. Sponsored by the Police Foundation, it focused on the practice of preventive patrol.

Knapp Commission A committee that investigated police corruption in New York City in the early 1970s.

landmark case A precedent-setting court decision that produces substantial changes both in the understanding of the requirements of due process and in the practical day-to-day operations of the justice system.

larceny-theft (UCR/NIBRS) The unlawful taking or attempted taking, carrying, leading, or riding away of property, from the possession or constructive possession of another. Motor vehicles are excluded. Larceny is the most common of the eight major offenses, although probably only a small percentage of all larcenies is actually reported to the police because of the small dollar amounts involved.

latent evidence Evidence of relevance to a criminal investigation that is not readily seen by the unaided eye.

law A rule of conduct, generally found enacted in the form of a statute, that proscribes or mandates certain forms of behavior.

Law Enforcement Assistance Administration (LEAA) A now-defunct federal agency established under Title I of the Omnibus Crime Control and Safe Streets Act of 1968 to funnel federal funding to state and local law enforcement agencies.

lay witness An eyewitness, character witness, or other person called on to testify who is not considered an expert. Lay witnesses must testify to facts only and may not draw conclusions or express opinions.

legal cause A legally recognizable cause. A legal cause must be demonstrated in court in order to hold an individual criminally liable for causing harm.

legalistic style A style of policing marked by a strict concern with enforcing the precise letter of the law. Legalistic departments may take a hands-off approach to disruptive or problematic behavior that does not violate the criminal law.

less-lethal weapon A weapon that is designed to disable, capture, or immobilize—but not kill—a suspect. Occasional deaths do result from the use of such weapons, however.

line operations In police organizations, the field activities or supervisory activities directly related to day-to-day police work.

malware Malicious computer programs such as viruses, worms, and Trojan horses.

mandatory release The release of an inmate from prison that is determined by statute or sentencing guidelines and is not decided by a parole board or other authority.[22]

mandatory sentencing A structured sentencing scheme that allows no leeway in the nature of the sentence imposed. Under mandatory sentencing, clearly enumerated punishments are mandated for specific offenses or for habitual offenders convicted of a series of crimes.

medical parole An early release option under which an inmate who is deemed "low risk" due to a serious physical or mental health condition is released from prison earlier than he or she might have been under normal circumstances.

mens rea The state of mind that accompanies a criminal act. Also, a guilty mind.

Miranda triggers The dual principles of custody and interrogation, both of which are necessary before an advisement of rights is required.

Miranda warnings The advisement of rights due criminal suspects by the police before questioning begins. *Miranda* warnings were first set forth by the U.S. Supreme Court in the 1966 case of *Miranda* v. *Arizona*.

misdemeanor An offense punishable by incarceration, usually in a local confinement facility, for a period whose upper limit is prescribed by statute in a given jurisdiction, typically one year or less.

mitigating circumstances Circumstances relating to the commission of a crime that may be considered to reduce the blameworthiness of the offender.

mixed sentence A sentence that requires that a convicted offender serve weekends (or other specified periods of time) in a confinement facility (usually a jail) while undergoing probationary supervision in the community.

M'Naghten rule A rule for determining insanity that asks whether the defendant knew what he or she was doing or whether the defendant knew that what he or she was doing was wrong.

motive A person's reason for committing a crime.

motor vehicle theft (UCR/NIBRS) The theft or attempted theft of a motor vehicle. *Motor vehicle* is defined as a self-propelled road vehicle that runs on land surface and not on rails. The stealing of trains, planes, boats, construction equipment, and most farm machinery is classified as larceny under the UCR/NIBRS Program, not as motor vehicle theft.

multiculturalism The existence within one society of diverse groups that maintain unique cultural identities while frequently accepting and participating in the larger society's legal and political systems.[23] *Multiculturalism* is often used in conjunction with the term *diversity* to identify many distinctions of social significance.

municipal police department A city- or town-based law enforcement agency.

murder The unlawful killing of a human being. *Murder* is a generic term that in common usage may include first- and second-degree murder, manslaughter, involuntary manslaughter, and other similar offenses.

National Crime Statistics Exchange (NCS-X) A BJS-sponsored program designed to generate nationally-representative incident-based data on crimes reported to law enforcement agencies.

National Crime Victimization Survey (NCVS)   An annual survey of selected American households conducted by the Bureau of Justice Statistics to determine the extent of criminal victimization—especially unreported victimization—in the United States.

National Incident-Based Reporting System (NIBRS)   An incident-based reporting system that collects detailed data on every single crime occurrence. NIBRS data are replacing the kinds of summary data that have traditionally been provided by the FBI's Uniform Crime Reporting Program.

neglected child   A child who is not receiving the proper level of physical or psychological care from his or her parents or guardians or who has been placed up for adoption in violation of the law.

1983 lawsuit   A civil suit brought under Title 42, Section 1983, of the U.S. Code against anyone who denies others their constitutional right to life, liberty, or property without due process of law.

NLETS   See *International Justice and Public Safety Information Sharing Network*.

nolo contendere   A plea of "no contest." A no-contest plea is used when the defendant does not wish to contest conviction. Because the plea does not admit guilt, however, it cannot provide the basis for later civil suits that might follow a criminal conviction.

nothing-works doctrine   The belief, popularized by Robert Martinson in the 1970s, that correctional treatment programs have had little success in rehabilitating offenders.

opening statement   The initial statement of the prosecution or the defense, made in a court of law to a judge, or to a judge and jury, describing the facts that he or she intends to present during trial to prove the case.

operational capacity   The number of inmates a prison can effectively accommodate based on management considerations.

organized crime   The unlawful activities of the members of a highly organized, disciplined association engaged in supplying illegal goods or services, including gambling, prostitution, loan-sharking, narcotics, and labor racketeering, and in other unlawful activities.[24]

original jurisdiction   The lawful authority of a court to hear or to act on a case from its beginning and to pass judgment on the law and the facts. The authority may be over a specific geographic area or over particular types of cases.

parens patriae   A common law principle that allows the state to assume a parental role and to take custody of a child when he or she becomes delinquent, is abandoned, or is in need of care that the natural parents are unable or unwilling to provide.

parole   A period of conditional supervised release in the community following a prison term. The term applies to parolees released through discretionary or mandatory supervised release from prison, and those released through other types of post-custody conditional supervision.

parole board   A state paroling authority. Many states have parole boards that decide when an incarcerated offender is ready for conditional release. Some boards also function as revocation hearing panels.

parole (probation) violation   An act or a failure to act by a parolee (or probationer) that does not conform to the conditions of his or her parole (or probation).

parole revocation   The administrative action of a paroling authority removing a person from parole status in response to a violation of lawfully required conditions of parole, including the prohibition against committing a new offense, and usually resulting in a return to prison.

Part I offenses   A traditional UCR/NIBRS offense group used to report murder, rape, robbery, aggravated assault, burglary, larceny-theft, motor vehicle theft, and arson, as defined under the FBI's UCR/NIBRS Program.

Part II offenses   A traditional UCR/NIBRS offense group used to report arrests for less serious offenses. Agencies are limited to reporting only arrest information for Part II offenses, with the exception of simple assault.

Peace Officer Standards and Training (POST) program   The official program of a state or legislative jurisdiction that sets standards for the training of law enforcement officers. All states set such standards, although not all use the term *POST*.

penal code   The written, organized, and compiled form of the criminal laws of a jurisdiction.

penal law   See *criminal law*.

peremptory challenge   The right to challenge a potential juror without disclosing the reason for the challenge. Prosecutors and defense attorneys routinely use peremptory challenges to eliminate from juries individuals who, although they express no obvious bias, are thought to be capable of swaying the jury in an undesirable direction.

perjury   The intentional making of a false statement as part of the testimony by a sworn witness in a judicial proceeding on a matter relevant to the case at hand.

petty crime   See *quality-of-life offense*.

plain view   A legal term describing the ready visibility of objects that might be seized as evidence during a search by police in the absence of a search warrant specifying the seizure of those objects. To lawfully seize evidence in plain view, officers must have a legal right to be in the viewing area and must have cause to believe that the evidence is somehow associated with criminal activity.

plea   In criminal proceedings, the defendant's formal answer in court to the charge contained in a complaint, information, or indictment that he or she is guilty of the offense charged, is not guilty of the offense charged, or does not contest the charge.

plea bargaining   The process of negotiating an agreement among the defendant, the prosecutor, and the court as to an appropriate plea and associated sentence in a given case. Plea bargaining circumvents the trial process and dramatically reduces the time required for the resolution of a criminal case.

police–community relations (PCR)   An area of police activity that recognizes the need for the community and the police to work together effectively and is based on the notion that the police derive their legitimacy from the community they serve. Many police agencies began to explore PCR in the 1960s and 1970s.

police corruption   The abuse of police authority for personal or organizational gain.[25]

police discretion   The opportunity of law enforcement officers to exercise choice in their daily activities.

police ethics   The special responsibility to adhere to moral duty and obligation that is inherent in police work.

police management   The administrative activities of controlling, directing, and coordinating police personnel, resources, and activities in the service of crime prevention, the apprehension of criminals, the recovery of stolen property, and the performance of a variety of regulatory and helping services.

police professionalism   The increasing formalization of police work and the accompanying rise in public acceptance of the police.

police subculture   A particular set of values, beliefs, and acceptable forms of behavior characteristic of American police with which the police profession strives to imbue new recruits. Socialization into the police subculture commences with recruit training and continues thereafter.

police use of force   The use of physical restraint by a police officer when dealing with a member of the public.[26]

police working personality   All aspects of the traditional values and patterns of behavior evidenced by police officers who have been effectively socialized into the police subculture. Characteristics of the police personality often extend to the personal lives of law enforcement personnel.

precedent   A legal principle that ensures that previous judicial decisions are authoritatively considered and incorporated into future cases.

predictive policing   A contemporary policing strategy that uses statistical techniques to analyze data in order to anticipate or predict the likelihood of crime occurrence in locations of interest.

preliminary hearing   A proceeding before a judicial officer in which three matters must be decided: (1) whether a crime was committed, (2) whether the crime occurred within the territorial jurisdiction of the court, and (3) whether there are reasonable grounds to believe that the defendant committed the crime.

presentence investigation (PSI) The examination of a convicted offender's background prior to sentencing. Presentence examinations are generally conducted by probation or parole officers and are submitted to sentencing authorities.

presumptive sentencing A model of criminal punishment that meets the following conditions: (1) The appropriate sentence for an offender convicted of a specific charge is presumed to fall within a range of sentences authorized by sentencing guidelines that are adopted by a legislatively created sentencing body, usually a sentencing commission; (2) sentencing judges are expected to sentence within the range or to provide written justification for failing to do so; and (3) there is a mechanism for review, usually appellate, of any departure from the guidelines.

pretrial release The release of an accused person from custody, for all or part of the time before or during prosecution, upon his or her promise to appear in court when required.

prison A state or federal confinement facility that has custodial authority over adults sentenced to confinement.

prison argot The slang that is characteristic of prison subculture and prison life.

prison capacity The size of the correctional population an institution can effectively hold.[27] There are three types of prison capacity: rated, operational, and design.

prison subculture The values and behavioral patterns characteristic of prison inmates. Prison subculture has been found to be surprisingly consistent across the country.

prisoner reentry See *reentry*.

prisonization The process whereby newly institutionalized offenders come to accept prison lifestyles and criminal values. Although many inmates begin their prison experience with only a few values that support criminal behavior, the socialization experience they undergo while incarcerated leads to a much wider acceptance of such values.

private prison A correctional institution operated by a private firm on behalf of a local or state government.

private protective services The independent or proprietary commercial organizations that provide protective services to employers on a contractual basis.

privatization The movement toward the wider use of private prisons.

probable cause A set of facts and circumstances that would induce a reasonably intelligent and prudent person to believe that a particular other person has committed a specific crime. Also, reasonable grounds to make or believe an accusation. Probable cause refers to the necessary level of belief that would allow for police seizures (arrests) of individuals and full searches of dwellings, vehicles, and possessions.

probation A sentence of imprisonment that is suspended. Also, a court-ordered period of correctional supervision in the community, generally as an alternative to incarceration.

probation revocation A court order taking away a convicted offender's probationary status and usually withdrawing the conditional freedom associated with that status in response to a violation of the conditions of probation.

probative value The degree to which a particular item of evidence is useful in, and relevant to, proving something important in a trial.

problem police officer A law enforcement officer who exhibits problem behavior, as indicated by high rates of citizen complaints and use-of-force incidents and by other evidence.[28]

problem-solving courts Low-level specialized courts that focus on relatively minor offenses and handles special populations or addresses special issues. Problem-solving courts are often a form of community courts.

problem-solving policing A type of policing that assumes that many crimes are caused by existing social conditions within the community and that crimes can be controlled by uncovering and effectively addressing underlying social problems. Problem-solving policing makes use of community resources, such as counseling centers, welfare programs, and job-training facilities. It also attempts to involve citizens in crime prevention through education, negotiation, and conflict management.

procedural defense A defense that claims that the defendant was in some significant way discriminated against in the justice process or that some important aspect of official procedure was not properly followed in the investigation or prosecution of the crime charged.

procedural fairness The process by which procedures that feel fair to those involved are made.

procedural justice The implementation of fair and equitable procedures in the administration of justice.

procedural law The part of the law that specifies the methods to be used in enforcing substantive law.

property bond The setting of bail in the form of land, houses, stocks, or other tangible property. In the event that the defendant absconds before trial, the bond becomes the property of the court.

property crime A UCR/NIBRS summary offense category that includes burglary, larceny-theft, motor vehicle theft, and arson.

proportionality A sentencing principle that holds that the severity of sanctions should bear a direct relationship to the seriousness of the crime committed.

prosecutor An attorney whose official duty is to conduct criminal proceedings on behalf of the state or the people against those accused of having committed criminal offenses.

prosecutorial discretion The decision-making power of prosecutors, based on the wide range of choices available to them, in the handling of criminal defendants, the scheduling of cases for trial, the acceptance of negotiated pleas, and so on. The most important form of prosecutorial discretion lies in the power to charge, or not to charge, a person with an offense.

psychological manipulation The manipulative actions by police interviewers, designed to pressure suspects to divulge information, that are based on subtle forms of intimidation and control.

public defender An attorney employed by a government agency or subagency, or by a private organization under contract to a government body, for the purpose of providing defense services to indigents, or an attorney who has volunteered such service.

public-order advocate One who believes that under certain circumstances involving a criminal threat to public safety, the interests of society should take precedence over individual rights.

quality-of-life offense A minor violation of the law (sometimes called a *petty crime*) that demoralizes community residents and businesspeople. Quality-of-life offenses involve acts that create physical disorder (for example, excessive noise and vandalism) or that reflect social decay (for example, panhandling and prostitution).

racial profiling Any police-initiated action that relies on the race, ethnicity, national origin, sexual orientation, gender or religion, rather than (1) the behavior of an individual, or (2) information that leads the police to a particular individual who has been identified as being, or having been, engaged in criminal activity.

rape (UCR/NIBRS) Unlawful sexual intercourse achieved through force and without consent. More specifically, penetration, no matter how slight, of the vagina or anus with any body part or object, or oral penetration by a sex organ of another person, without the consent of the victim. *Statutory rape* differs from other types of rape in that it generally involves nonforcible sexual intercourse with a minor. Broadly speaking, the term *rape* has been applied to a wide variety of sexual attacks and may include same-sex rape and the rape of a male by a female. Some jurisdictions refer to same-sex rape as sexual battery.

rated capacity The number of inmates a prison can handle according to the judgment of experts.

real evidence Evidence that consists of physical material or traces of physical activity.

realignment A state government initiative designed to reduce prison populations. Under initiatives like California's Public Safety Realignment program, for example, less serious offenders are sentenced to spend time in county jails rather than in state correctional facilities.

reasonable doubt   In legal proceedings, an actual and substantial doubt arising from the evidence, from the facts or circumstances shown by the evidence, or from the lack of evidence. Also, the state of a case such that, after the comparison and consideration of all the evidence, jurors cannot say they feel an abiding conviction of the truth of the charge.

reasonable doubt standard   The standard of proof necessary for conviction in criminal trials.

reasonable force   A degree of force that is appropriate in a given situation and is not excessive. Also, the minimum degree of force necessary to protect oneself, one's property, a third party, or the property of another in the face of a substantial threat.

reasonable suspicion   The level of suspicion that would justify an officer in making further inquiry or in conducting further investigation. Reasonable suspicion may permit stopping a person for questioning or for a simple pat-down search. Also, a belief, based on a consideration of the facts at hand and on reasonable inferences drawn from those facts, that would induce an ordinarily prudent and cautious person under the same circumstances to conclude that criminal activity is taking place or that criminal activity has recently occurred. Reasonable suspicion is a *general* and reasonable belief that a crime is in progress or has occurred, whereas probable cause is a reasonable belief that a *particular* person has committed a *specific* crime.

recidivism   The act of relapsing into a problem or criminal behavior during or after receiving sanctions, or while undergoing an intervention due to a previous behavior or crime. In criminal justice settings, recidivism is often measured by criminal acts that result in rearrest, reconviction, or return to prison.

recidivism rate   A measure of the rate of reoffending (usually defined by arrest) for a given population of released prisoners, or for a group of criminally sanctioned offenders, over time. Rates of recidivism are generally calculated over a 3- or a 5-year time period.

reckless behavior   An activity that increases the risk of harm.

reentry   The managed return to the community of individuals released from prison.

reentry courts   Specialized courts that help reduce recidivism and improve public safety through the use of judicial oversight to apply graduated sanctions and positive reinforcement, to marshal resources to support the prisoner's reintegration, and to promote positive behavior by the returning prisoners.[29]

regional jail   A jail that is built and run using the combined resources of a variety of local jurisdictions.

rehabilitation   The attempt to reform a criminal offender. Also, the state in which a reformed offender is said to be.

release on recognizance (ROR)   The pretrial release of a criminal defendant on his or her written promise to appear in court as required. No cash or property bond is required.

remote location monitoring   A supervision strategy that uses electronic technology to track offenders who are sentenced to house arrest or those who have been ordered to limit their movements while completing a sentence involving probation or parole.

restitution   A court requirement that a convicted offender pay money or provide services to the victim of the crime.

restoration   A goal of criminal sentencing that attempts to make the victim "whole again."

restorative justice (RJ)   A sentencing model that builds on restitution and community participation in an attempt to make the victim "whole again."

retribution   The act of taking revenge on a criminal perpetrator.

revocation hearing   A hearing held before a legally constituted hearing body (such as a parole board) to determine whether a parolee or probationer has violated the conditions and requirements of his or her parole or probation.

robbery (UCR/NIBRS)   The unlawful taking or attempted taking of property that is in the immediate possession of another by force or violence and/or by putting the victim in fear. Armed robbery differs from unarmed, or strong-arm, robbery in that it involves a weapon. Contrary to popular conceptions, highway robbery does not necessarily occur on a street—and rarely in a vehicle. The term *highway robbery* applies to any form of robbery that occurs outdoors in a public place.

rule of law   The maxim that an orderly society must be governed by established principles and known codes that are applied uniformly and fairly to all of its members.

rules of evidence   The court rules that govern the admissibility of evidence at criminal hearings and trials.

scientific jury selection   The use of correlational techniques from the social sciences to gauge the likelihood that potential jurors will vote for conviction or for acquittal.

scientific police management   The application of social sciences techniques to the study of police administration for the purpose of increasing effectiveness, reducing the frequency of citizen complaints, and enhancing the efficient use of available resources.

search incident to an arrest   A warrantless search of an arrested individual conducted to ensure the safety of the arresting officer. Because individuals placed under arrest may be in possession of weapons, courts have recognized the need for arresting officers to protect themselves by conducting an immediate search of arrestees without obtaining a warrant.

security threat group (STG)   An inmate group, gang, or organization whose members act together to pose a threat to the safety of corrections staff or the public, who prey on other inmates, or who threaten the secure and orderly operation of a correctional institution.

selective incapacitation   A policy that seeks to protect society by incarcerating individuals deemed to be the most dangerous.

self-defense   The protection of oneself or of one's property from unlawful injury or from the immediate risk of unlawful injury. Also, the justification that the person who committed an act that would otherwise constitute an offense reasonably believed that the act was necessary to protect self or property from immediate danger.

sentencing   The imposition of a criminal sanction by a judicial authority.

sentinel event   A bad outcome that no one wants repeated and that signals the existence of underlying weaknesses in the system.

sequestered jury   A jury that is isolated from the public during the course of a trial and throughout the deliberation process.

service style   A style of policing marked by a concern with helping rather than strict enforcement. Service-oriented police agencies are more likely to refer citizens to community resources, such as drug-treatment programs, than are other types of agencies.

sexual battery   The intentional and wrongful physical contact with a person, without his or her consent, that entails a sexual component or purpose.

sheriff   The elected chief officer of a county law enforcement agency. The sheriff is usually responsible for law enforcement in unincorporated areas and for the operation of the county jail.

shock incarceration   A sentencing option that makes use of "boot camp"–type prisons to impress on convicted offenders the realities of prison life.

shock probation   The practice of sentencing offenders to prison, allowing them to apply for probationary release, and enacting such release in surprise fashion. Offenders who receive shock probation may not be aware that they will be released on probation and may expect to spend a much longer time behind bars.

smart policing   A law enforcement initiative that makes use of techniques shown to work at both reducing and solving crimes.

"sneak and peek" search   A search that occurs in the suspect's absence and without his or her prior knowledge. Also known as a *delayed-notification search*.

social control   The use of sanctions and rewards within a group to influence and shape the behavior of individual members of that group. Social control is a primary concern of social groups and communities, and it is their interest in the exercise of social control that leads to the creation of both criminal and civil statutes.

social debt   A sentencing principle that holds that an offender's criminal history should objectively be taken into account in sentencing decisions.

social disorganization   A condition said to exist when a group is faced with social change, uneven development of culture, maladaptiveness, disharmony, conflict, and lack of consensus.

social diversity   Differences between individuals and groups in the same society, including differences based on culture, race, religion, ethnicity, age, gender identity, and disabilities.

social justice   An ideal that embraces all aspects of civilized life and that is linked to fundamental notions of fairness and to cultural beliefs about right and wrong.

social order   The condition of a society characterized by social integration, consensus, smooth functioning, and lack of interpersonal and institutional conflict. Also, a lack of social disorganization.

spam   Unsolicited commercial bulk e-mail whose primary purpose is the advertisement or promotion of a commercial product or service.

span of control   The number of police personnel or the number of units supervised by a particular officer.

specific deterrence   A goal of criminal sentencing that seeks to prevent a particular offender from engaging in repeat criminality.

Speedy Trial Act   A 1974 federal law requiring that proceedings against a defendant in a criminal case begin within a specified period of time, such as 70 working days after indictment. Some states also have speedy trial requirements.

split sentence   A sentence explicitly requiring the convicted offender to serve a period of confinement in a local, state, or federal facility, followed by a period of probation.

staff operations   In police organizations, activities (such as administration and training) that provide support for line operations.

stalking   Repeated harassing and threatening behavior by one individual against another, aspects of which may be planned or carried out in secret. Stalking might involve following a person, appearing at a person's home or place of business, making harassing phone calls, leaving written messages or objects, or vandalizing a person's property. Most stalking laws require that the perpetrator make a credible threat of violence against the victim or members of the victim's immediate family.

stare decisis   A legal principle that requires that in subsequent cases on similar issues of law and fact, courts be bound by their own earlier decisions and by those of higher courts having jurisdiction over them. The term literally means "standing by decided matters."

state court administrator   A coordinator who assists with case-flow management, operating funds budgeting, and court docket administration.

state court system   A state judicial structure. Most states generally have at least three court levels: trial courts, appellate courts, and a state supreme court.

status offender   A child who commits an act that is contrary to the law by virtue of the offender's status as a child. Purchasing cigarettes, buying alcohol, and being truant are examples of such behavior.

status offense   An act or conduct that is declared by statute to be an offense, but only when committed by or engaged in by a juvenile, and that can be adjudicated only by a juvenile court.

statutory law   The written or codified law; the "law on the books," as enacted by a government body or agency having the power to make laws.

strategic policing   A type of policing that retains the traditional police goal of professional crime fighting but enlarges the enforcement target to include nontraditional kinds of criminals, such as serial offenders, gangs and criminal associations, drug-distribution networks, and sophisticated white-collar and computer criminals. Strategic policing generally makes use of innovative enforcement techniques, including intelligence operations, undercover stings, electronic surveillance, and sophisticated forensic methods.

strict liability   A liability without fault or intention. Strict liability offenses do not require *mens rea.*

structured sentencing   A model of criminal punishment that includes determinate and commission-created presumptive sentencing schemes, as well as voluntary/advisory sentencing guidelines.

subpoena   A written order issued by a judicial officer or grand jury requiring an individual to appear in court and to give testimony or to bring material to be used as evidence. Some subpoenas mandate that books, papers, and other items be surrendered to the court.

substantive criminal law   The part of the law that defines crimes and specifies punishments.

supervised release   A form of reentry in the federal justice system consisting of a term of conditional community supervision, set by the court at the time of sentencing, to be served after release from prison.

suspicionless search   A search conducted by law enforcement personnel without a warrant and without suspicion. Suspicionless searches are permissible only if based on an overriding concern for public safety.

sustainable justice   Criminal laws and criminal justice institutions, policies, and practices that achieve justice in the present without compromising the ability of future generations to have the benefits of a just society.

sworn officer   A law enforcement officer who is trained and empowered to perform full police duties, such as making arrests, conducting investigations, and carrying firearms.

Tazir crime   A minor violation of Islamic law that is regarded as an offense against society, not God.

team policing   The reorganization of conventional patrol strategies into "an integrated and versatile police team assigned to a fixed district."[30]

teen court   An alternative approach to juvenile justice in which alleged offenders are judged and/or sentenced by a jury of their peers.

terrorism   A violent act or an act dangerous to human life in violation of the criminal laws of the United States or of any state, committed to intimidate or coerce a government, the civilian population, or any segment thereof in furtherance of political or social objectives.[31]

testimony   The oral evidence offered by a sworn witness on the witness stand during a criminal trial.

tort   A wrongful act, damage, or injury not involving a breach of contract. Also, a private or civil wrong or injury.

total institution   An enclosed facility separated from society both socially and physically, where the inhabitants share all aspects of their daily lives.

trafficking in persons (TIP)   The exploitation of unwilling or unwitting people through force, coercion, threat, or deception.

transnational offenses   Unlawful activity that occurs across national boundaries.

transnational organized crime   Unlawful activity undertaken and supported by organized criminal groups operating across national boundaries.

treason   A U.S. citizen's actions to help a foreign government overthrow, make war against, or seriously injure the United States.[32] Also, the attempt to overthrow the government of the society of which one is a member.

trial   In criminal proceedings, the examination in court of the issues of fact and relevant law in a case for the purpose of convicting or acquitting the defendant.

trial de novo   Literally, "new trial." The term is applied to cases that are retried on appeal, as opposed to those that are simply reviewed on the record.

truth in sentencing   A close correspondence between the sentence imposed on an offender and the time actually served in prison.[33]

undisciplined child   A child who is beyond parental control, as evidenced by his or her refusal to obey legitimate authorities, such as school officials and teachers.

Uniform Crime Reporting (UCR) Program   A statistical reporting program run by the FBI's Criminal Justice Information Services (CJIS) division. The UCR Program publishes *Crime in the United States*, which provides an annual summation of the incidence and rate of reported crimes throughout the United States.

USA PATRIOT Act   A federal law (Public Law 107–56) enacted in response to terrorist attacks on the World Trade Center and the Pentagon on September 11, 2001. The law, officially titled the Uniting and Strengthening America by Providing Appropriate Tools Required to Intercept and Obstruct Terrorism Act, substantially broadened the investigative authority of law enforcement agencies throughout America and is applicable to many crimes other than terrorism. The law was slightly revised and reauthorized by Congress in 2006.

verdict   The decision of the jury in a jury trial or of a judicial officer in a nonjury trial.

victim-impact statement   An in-court statement made by the victim or by survivors to sentencing authorities seeking to make an informed sentencing decision.

victims' assistance program   An organized program that offers services to victims of crime in the areas of crisis intervention and follow-up counseling and that helps victims secure their rights under the law.

violent crime   A UCR/NIBRS summary offense category that includes murder, rape, robbery, and aggravated assault.

voluntary/advisory sentencing guidelines   Recommended sentencing policies that are not required by law.

warehousing   An imprisonment strategy that is based on the desire to prevent recurrent crime and that has abandoned all hope of rehabilitation.

warrant   In criminal proceedings, a writ issued by a judicial officer directing a law enforcement officer to perform a specified act and affording the officer protection from damages if he or she performs it.

warrantless search   An examination by police of a person, place, or thing without a written judicial order authorizing that activity.

watchman style   A style of policing marked by a concern for order maintenance. Watchman policing is characteristic of lower-class communities where informal police intervention into the lives of residents is employed in the service of keeping the peace.

white-collar crime   Financially motivated nonviolent crime committed by business and government professionals.

workhouse   An early form of imprisonment whose purpose was to instill habits of industry in the idle.

writ of *certiorari*   A writ issued from an appellate court for the purpose of obtaining from a lower court the record of its proceedings in a particular case. In some states, this writ is the mechanism for discretionary review. A request for review is made by petitioning for a writ of *certiorari*, and the granting of review is indicated by the issuance of the writ.

writ of *habeas corpus*   A writ that directs the person detaining a prisoner to bring him or her before a judicial officer to determine the lawfulness of the imprisonment.

wrongful conviction   An unfair criminal conviction, often made on the basis of inadequate representation by counsel, inaccurate forensics analysis, eyewitness misidentification, and improper behavior by prosecutors, law enforcement officers, or jury members.

[1] All boldfaced terms are explained whenever possible using definitions provided by the Bureau of Justice Statistics under a mandate of the Justice System Improvement Act of 1979. That mandate found its most complete expression in the *Dictionary of Criminal Justice Data Terminology* (Washington, DC: Bureau of Justice Statistics, 1982), the second edition of which provides the wording for many definitions in this text.

[2] Adapted from U.S. Code, Title 28, Section 20.3 (2[d]). Title 28 of the U.S. Code defines the term *administration of criminal justice*.

[3] Technical Working Group on Crime Scene Investigation, *Crime Scene Investigation: A Guide for Law Enforcement* (Washington, DC: National Institute of Justice, 2000), p. 12.

[4] Howard N. Snyder and Melissa Sickmund, *Juvenile Offenders and Victims: 2006 National Report* (Washington, DC: Office of Juvenile Justice and Delinquency Prevention, 2006).

[5] Adapted from Gerald Hill and Kathleen Hill, *The Real Life Dictionary of the Law,* http://www.law.com (accessed June 11, 2012).

[6] Office of Community Oriented Policing Services, *Community Policing Defined* (Washington, DC: U.S. Department of Justice, 2009), p. 3.

[7] Jeremy Travis and Sarah Lawrence, *Beyond the Prison Gates: The State of Parole in America* (Washington, DC: Urban Institute Press, 2002), p. 3.

[8] Michael L. Benson, Francis T. Cullen, and William J. Maakestad, *Local Prosecutors and Corporate Crime* (Washington, DC: National Institute of Justice, 1992), p. 1.

[9] Office of Justice Programs, *The National Criminal Intelligence Sharing Plan* (Washington, DC: U.S. Department of Justice, 2005), p. 27.

[10] Wayne W. Bennett and Karen M. Hess, *Criminal Investigation*, 6th ed. (Belmont, CA: Wadsworth, 2001), p. 3.

[11] Violence against Women Office, *Stalking and Domestic Violence: Report to Congress* (Washington, DC: U.S. Department of Justice, 2001), p. 5.

[12] Sam W. Lathrop, "Reviewing Use of Force: A Systematic Approach," *FBI Law Enforcement Bulletin* (October 2000), p. 18.

[13] Adapted from Larry R. Leibrock, "Overview and Impact on 21st Century Legal Practice: Digital Forensics and Electronic Discovery," no date, http://www.courtroom21.net/FDIC.pps (accessed July 5, 2008).

[14] Federal Bureau of Investigation, *FBI Policy and Guidelines: Counterterrorism*, http://www.fbi.gov/contact/fo/jackson/cntrterr.htm (accessed August 26, 2002).

[15] Adapted from Technical Working Group on Electronic Crime Scene Investigation, *Electronic Crime Scene Investigation: A Guide for First Responders* (Washington, DC: National Institute of Justice, 2001), p. 2.

[16] Henry Campbell Black, Joseph R. Nolan, and Jacqueline M. Nolan-Haley, *Black's Law Dictionary*, 6th ed. (St. Paul, MN: West, 1990), p. 24.

[17] Lawrence W. Sherman, *Evidence-Based Policing* (Washington, DC: Police Foundation, 1998), p. 3.

[18] International Association of Chiefs of Police, *Police Use of Force in America, 2001* (Alexandria, VA: IACP, 2001), p. 1.

[19] Adapted from Identity Theft Resource Center website, http://www.idtheftcenter.org (accessed April 24, 2018).

[20] Angus Smith, ed., *Intelligence-Led Policing* (Richmond, VA: International Association of Law Enforcement Intelligence Analysts, 1997), p. 1.

[21] FBI, *Terrorism 2002–2005* (Washington, DC: FBI, 2006). Web available at http://www.fbi.gov/stats-services/publications/terrorism-2002-2005 (accessed August 14, 2012).

[22] Jeremy Travis and Sarah Lawrence, *Beyond the Prison Gates: The State of Parole in America* (Washington, DC: Urban Institute Press, 2002), p. 3.

[23] Adapted from Robert M. Shusta et al., *Multicultural Law Enforcement*, 2nd ed. (Upper Saddle River, NJ: Prentice Hall, 2002), p. 443.

[24] The Organized Crime Control Act of 1970.

[25] Carl B. Klockars et al., *The Measurement of Police Integrity*, National Institute of Justice Research in Brief (Washington, DC: NIJ, 2000), p. 1.

[26] National Institute of Justice, *Use of Force by Police: Overview of National and Local Data* (Washington, DC: NIJ, 1999).

[27] Paige M. Harrison and Allen J. Beck, *Prisoners in 2005* (Washington, DC: Bureau of Justice Statistics, 2006), p. 7.

[28] Samuel Walker, Geoffrey P. Albert, and Dennis J. Kenney, *Responding to the Problem Police Officer: A National Study of Early Warning Systems* (Washington, DC: National Institute of Justice, 2000).

[29] Christine Lindquist, Jennifer Hardison Walters, Michael Rempel, and Shannon M. Carey, *The National Institute of Justice's Evaluation of Second Chance Act Adult Reentry Courts: Program Characteristics and Preliminary Themes from Year 1* (Washington, DC: Bureau of Justice Assistance, 2013).

[30] Sam S. Souryal, *Police Administration and Management* (St. Paul, MN: West, 1977), p. 261.

[31] Federal Bureau of Investigation Counterterrorism Section, *Terrorism in the United States, 1987* (Washington, DC: FBI, December 1987).

[32] Daniel Oran, *Oran's Dictionary of the Law* (St. Paul, MN: West, 1983), p. 306.

[33] Lawrence A. Greenfeld, *Prison Sentences and Time Served for Violence*, Bureau of Justice Statistics Selected Findings, No. 4 (Washington, DC: Bureau of Justice Statistics, April 1995).

Chapter 1: What Is Criminal Justice?

i. All boldfaced terms are explained whenever possible using definitions provided by the Bureau of Justice Statistics under a mandate of the Justice System Improvement Act of 1979. That mandate found its most complete expression in the *Dictionary of Criminal Justice Data Terminology* (Washington, DC: Bureau of Justice Statistics, 1982), the second edition of which provides the wording for many definitions in this text.

ii. Adapted from U.S. Code, Title 28, Section 20.3 (2[d]). Title 28 of the U.S. Code defines the term *administration of criminal justice*.

iii. Adapted from Robert M. Shusta et al., *Multicultural Law Enforcement*, 2nd ed. (Upper Saddle River, NJ: Prentice Hall, 2002), p. 443.

1. Emily Brown, "Timeline: Michael Brown Shooting in Ferguson, Mo.," *USA Today*, December 2, 2014, https://www.usatoday.com/story/news/nation/2014/08/14/michael-brown-ferguson-missouri-timeline/14051827/ (accessed January 30, 2018).

2. J. David Goodman and Al Baker, "Wave of Protests After Grand Jury Doesn't Indict Officer in Eric Garner Chokehold Case," *The New York Times*, December 3, 2014, http://www.nytimes.com/2014/12/04/nyregion/grand-jury-said-to-bring-no-charges-in-staten-island-chokehold-death-of-eric-garner.html (accessed February 3, 2015).

3. Simon McCormack, "Cops Reportedly Say They're Not Making Arrests After Cop Killings," *The Huffington Post*, December 27, 2014, http://www.huffingtonpost.com/2014/12/30/arrests-drop-nyc_n_6397452.html (accessed February 3, 2015).

4. Matt Taibbi, "The NYPD's 'Work Stoppage' Is Surreal," *Rolling Stone*, December 31, 2014, http://www.rollingstone.com/politics/news/the-nypds-work-stoppage-is-surreal-20141231?page=2 (accessed March 4, 2015).

5. John R. Emshwiller, "Seattle Police Chafe Under New Marching Orders," *Wall Street Journal*, December 30, 2014, http://www.wsj.com/articles/seattle-police-chafe-under-new-marching-orders-1419981603 (accessed March 2, 2015).

6. Benjamin Mueller and Al Baker, "2 N.Y.P.D. Officers Killed in Brooklyn Ambush; Suspect Commits Suicide," *The New York Times*, December 20, 2014, https://www.nytimes.com/2014/12/21/nyregion/two-police-officers-shot-in-their-patrol-car-in-brooklyn.html (accessed February 28, 2018).

7. "Sniper Ambush Kills 5 Officers, Injures 7 in Dallas Following Peaceful Protest," NBC News, July 7, 2016, http://www.nbcdfw.com/news/local/Protests-in-Dallas-Over-Alton-Sterling-Death-385784431.html (accessed January 5, 2018).

8. J.J. Gallagher and Morgan Winsor, "2 Police Officers Shot, Killed in Ambush Attacks in Iowa," ABC News, November 2, 2016, http://abcnews.go.com/US/police-officers-shot-killed-ambushattack-iowa/story?id=43238960 (accessed January 17, 2018).

9. Emily Gold Lagratta and Phil Bowen, *To Be Fair: Procedural Fairness in Courts* (New York: Criminal Justice Alliance, October 2014).

10. Zusha Elinson, "Americans' Respect for Police Reaches Highest Level Since 1967, Poll Finds," *The Wall Street Journal,* October 24, 2016, http://www.wsj.com/articles/americansrespect-for-police-reaches-highest-level-since-1967-pollfinds-1477344780 (accessed January 2, 2018).

11. Ibid.

12. For a thorough discussion of immigration as it relates to crime, see Ramiro Martinez, Jr., and Matthew T. Lee, "On Immigration and Crime," in National Institute of Justice, *Criminal Justice 2000, Vol. 1: The Nature of Crime—Continuity and Change* (Washington, DC: U.S. Department of Justice, Office of Justice Programs, 2000).

13. "Inside Columbine," *Rocky Mountain News*, http://www.rockymountainnews.com/drmn/columbine (accessed July 4, 2015).

14. "Cries of Relief," *Time*, April 26, 1993, p. 18.

15. Laurence McQuillan, "Bush to Urge Jail for Execs Who Lie, *USA Today*, July 9, 2002, http://www.usatoday.com/news/washdc/2002/07/09/bush-business.htm (accessed July 9, 2006).

16. Sarbanes-Oxley Act of 2002 (officially known as the Public Company Accounting Reform and Investor Protection Act), Public Law 107–204, 116 Stat. 745 (July 30, 2002).

17. PricewaterhouseCoopers, "The Sarbanes-Oxley Act," http://www.pwcglobal.com/Extweb/NewCoAtWork.nsf/docid/D0D7F79003C6D64485256CF30074D66C (accessed July 8, 2007).

18. U.S. Department of Justice news release, January 11, 2017, https://www.justice.gov/usao-edmi/pr/volkswagen-ag-agrees-plead-guilty-and-pay-43-billion-criminal-and-civil-penalties-and (accessed March 16, 2018).

19. Richard Esposito, Eloise Harper, and Maddy Sauer, "Bernie Madoff Pleads Guilty to Ponzi Scheme, Goes Straight to Jail, Says He's 'Deeply Sorry,'" ABC News, March 12, 2009, http://abcnews.go.com/Blotter/WallStreet/Story?id=7066715&page=1 (accessed July 4, 2012).

20. Robert Lenzner, "Bernie Madoff's $50 Billion Ponzi Scheme," Forbes.com, December 12, 2008, http://www.forbes.com/2008/12/12/madoff-ponzi-hedge-pf-ii-in_rl_1212croesus_inl.html (accessed September 28, 2010).

21. Al Baker, "An 'Iceberg' of Unseen Crimes: Many Cyber Offenses Go Unreported," *The New York Times,* February 5, 2018; https://www.nytimes.com/2018/02/05/nyregion/cyber-crimes-unreported.html (accessed August 28, 2018).

22. Elliot Spagat, "Chelsea's Law Signed by Schwarzenegger, Will Give Some Sex Offenders Life in Prison," *The Huffington Post*, September 9, 2010, http://www.huffingtonpost.com/2010/09/09/chelseas-law-signed-by-sc_n_711115.html (accessed April 4, 2014).

23. Wendy Koch, "States Get Tougher with Sex Offenders," *USA Today*, May 24, 2006, p. 1A.

24. Ibid.

25. Martin Luther King, in an address to the Tenth Anniversary Convention of the Southern Christian Leadership Conference in Atlanta, Georgia, on August 16, 1967. It was abolitionist

and Unitarian minister Theodore Parker who first used a similar phrase in the mid-1800s, saying, "I do not pretend to understand the moral universe; the arc is a long one. . . . And from what I see I am sure it bends toward justice."

26. *The American Heritage Dictionary on CD-ROM* (Boston: Houghton Mifflin, 1991).

27. For a good overview of the issues involved, see Judge Harold J. Rothwax, *Guilty: The Collapse of Criminal Justice* (New York: Random House, 1996).

28. Alan Cowell, "Oscar Pistorius's Murder Sentence Is Increased to 15 Years," *The New York Times,* Nov. 24, 2017, https://www.nytimes.com/2017/11/24/world/africa/oscar-pistorius-sentence.html (accessed March 15, 2018).

29. The systems model of criminal justice is often attributed to the frequent use of the term *system* by the 1967 Presidential Commission in its report *The Challenge of Crime in a Free Society* (Washington, DC: U.S. Government Printing Office, 1967).

30. One of the first published works to use the nonsystem approach to criminal justice was the American Bar Association's *New Perspective on Urban Crime* (Washington, DC: ABA Special Committee on Crime Prevention and Control, 1972).

31. Jerome H. Skolnick, *Justice without Trial* (New York: John Wiley, 1966), p. 179.

32. "The Defendants' Rights at a Criminal Trial," http://www.mycounsel.com/content/arrests/court/rights.html (accessed February 10, 2018).

33. For a complete and now-classic analysis of the impact of decisions made by the Warren Court, see Fred P. Graham, *The Due Process Revolution: The Warren Court's Impact on Criminal Law* (New York: Hayden Press, 1970).

34. *Gideon* v. *Wainwright*, 372 U.S. 353 (1963).

35. Herbert Packer, *The Limits of the Criminal Sanction* (Stanford, CA: Stanford University Press, 1968).

36. John H. Laub, "Embracing a Culture of Science: A Message from the Director," National Institute of Justice, March 22, 2011, http://nij.ncjrs.gov/multimedia/video-laub1.htm (accessed May 12, 2012).

37. For an excellent history of policing in the United States, see Edward A. Farris, "Five Decades of American Policing, 1932–1982," *Police Chief* (November 1982), pp. 30–36.

38. Gene Edward Carte, "August Vollmer and the Origins of Police Professionalism," *Journal of Police Science and Administration*, Vol. 1, No. 1 (1973), pp. 274–281.

39. Chris Eskridge distinguishes between police *training*, which is "job specific" and is intended to teach trainees *how* to do something (like fire a weapon), and *justice education*, whose purpose is to "develop a general spirit of inquiry." See C. W. Eskridge, "Criminal Justice Education and Its Potential Impact on the Sociopolitical-Economic Climate of Central European Nations," *Journal of Criminal Justice Education*, Vol. 14, No. 1 (spring 2003), pp. 105–118; and James O. Finckenauer, "The Quest for Quality in Criminal Justice Education," *Justice Quarterly*, Vol. 22, No. 4 (December 2005), pp. 413–426.

40. "Understanding and Using Evidence-Based Practices."

41. On March 22, 1794, the U.S. Congress barred American citizens from transporting slaves from the United States to another nation or between foreign nations. On January 1, 1808, the importation of slaves into the United States became illegal, and Congress charged the U.S. Revenue Cutter Service (now known as the U.S. Coast Guard) with enforcing the law on the high seas. Although some slave ships were seized, the importation of Africans for sale as slaves apparently continued in some southern states until the early 1860s. See U.S. Coast Guard, "U.S. Coast Guard in Illegal Immigration (1794–1971)," http://www.uscg.mil/hq/g-o/g-opl/mle/amiohist.htm (accessed October 13, 2013).

42. U.S. Census Bureau website, http://www.census.gov (accessed March 22, 2010). Population statistics are estimates because race is a difficult concept to define and Census Bureau interviewers allow individuals to choose more than one race when completing census forms.

Chapter 2: The Crime Picture

i. Identity Theft Resource Center website, http://www.idtheftcenter.org (accessed April 24, 2016).

ii. Violence against Women Office, *Stalking and Domestic Violence: Report to Congress* (Washington, DC: U.S. Department of Justice, 2001), p. 5.

iii. Michael L. Benson, Francis T. Cullen, and William J. Maakestad, *Local Prosecutors and Corporate Crime* (Washington, DC: National Institute of Justice, 1992), p. 1.

iv. The Organized Crime Control Act of 1970.

v. Federal Bureau of Investigation Counterterrorism Section, *Terrorism in the United States, 1987* (Washington, DC: FBI, December 1987).

vi. Federal Bureau of Investigation, *FBI Policy and Guidelines: Counterterrorism*, http://www.fbi.gov/contact/fo/jackson/cntrterr.htm (accessed July 20, 2016).

vii. Ibid.

1. "Video: Tennessee Sheriff's Office Pays Ransom for Case Files," *Police Magazine*, November 13, 2014, http://www.policemag.com/channel/technology/news/2014/11/13/video-tennessee-sheriff-s-office-pays-ransom-for-case-files.aspx (accessed June 8, 2018).

2. Herbert Packer, *The Limits of Criminal Sanction* (Stanford: Stanford University Press, 1968), p. 364.

3. Norval Morris, "Crime, the Media, and Our Public Discourse," National Institute of Justice, Perspectives on Crime and Justice video series, recorded May 13, 1997.

4. Ibid.

5. Federal Bureau of Investigation, *Crime in the United States, 1987* (Washington, DC: U.S. Department of Justice, 1988), p. 1.

6. Federal Bureau of Investigation, "About the UCR Program," no date, http://www.fbi.gov/ucr/05cius/about/about_ucr.html (accessed May 29, 2016). The term *crime index* was originally recommended for reevaluation in 2004, but it wasn't until 2006 that use of the term was officially discontinued.

7. Statistics on state agency participation in NIBRS can be seen at Bureau of Justice Statistics, "UCR and NIBRS Participation," http://bjs.ojp.usdoj.gov/content/nibrsstatus.cfm (accessed September 4, 2015).

8. See the FBI's UCR/NIBRS website at http://www.fbi.gov/hq/cjisd/ucr.htm (accessed August 27, 2018).

9. The 1990 Crime Awareness and Campus Security Act (Public Law 101–542) required college campuses to commence publishing annual security reports beginning in September 1992.

10. National Center for Education Statistics, Digest of Education Statistics, Table 329.10, "On-campus Crimes, Arrests, and Referrals for Disciplinary Action at Degree-granting Postsecondary Institutions, by Location of Incident, Control and Level of Institution, and Type of Incident: Selected Years, 2001 Through 2015," https://nces.ed.gov/programs/digest/d17/tables/dt17_329.10.asp?current=yes (accessed October 5, 2018).

11. Katrina Baum and Patsy Klaus, *Violent Victimization of College Students, 1995–2002* (Washington, DC: Bureau of Justice Statistics, 2005).

12. Federal Bureau of Investigation, *Crime in the United States, 2017* (Washington, DC: U.S. Department of Justice, 2018).

13. President's Commission on Law Enforcement and Administration of Justice, *The Challenge of Crime in a Free Society* (Washington, DC: U.S. Government Printing Office, 1967). The commission relied on UCR data. The other crime statistics reported in this section come from Uniform Crime Reports for various years.

14. Frank Hagan, *Research Methods in Criminal Justice and Criminology* (New York: Macmillan, 1982).

15. U.S. Department of Justice, *Fiscal Years 2000–2005 Strategic Plan* (Washington, DC: U.S. Government Printing Office, 2000).

16. Jack Nicas, "Crime That No Longer Pays," *The Wall Street Journal,* February 4, 2013, professional.wsj.com/article/SB100014241278873233926104578274541161239474.html (accessed March 3, 2014).

17. Wendy Ruderman, "Crime Report Manipulation Is Common among New York Police, Study Finds," *The New York Times,* June 28, 2012, http://www.nytimes.com/2012/06/29/nyregion/new-york-police-department-manipulates-crime-reports-study-finds.html (accessed July 10, 2014).

18. Cynthia Lum and Daniel S. Nagin, "Reinventing American Policing," *Crime and Justice* (2017).

19. John J. DiIulio, Jr., "The Question of Black Crime," *Public Interest* (fall 1994), pp. 3–12.

20. Quoted in Dan Eggen, "Major Crimes in U.S. Increase," *Washington Post,* June 23, 2002, p. A1.

21. D.E. Brown, "US Murder Rate Increased Sharply in 2015," *Newswire,* September 3, 2015, http://newswire.net/newsroom/news/00090187-us-murder-rate-increase-sharply-in-2015.html (assessed February 21, 2016).

22. See Tim Johnson, "Mexico's War on Crime Now Ranks among Latin America's Bloodiest Conflicts," McClatchy Newspapers, February 21, 2013, www.mcclatchydc.com/2013/02/21/183820/mexicos-war-on-crime-now-ranks.html (accessed May 2, 2013); and Alan Taylor, "Mexico's Drug War: 50,000 Dead in Six Years," *The Atlantic,* May 17, 2012, http://www.theatlantic.com/infocus/2012/05/mexicos-drug-war-50-000-dead-in-6-years/100299/ (accessed May 2, 2113).

23. Paul Knepper, "Measuring the Threat of Global Crime: Insights from Research by the League of Nations into the Traffic in Women," *Criminology,* April 2012 doi: 10.1111/j.1745-9125.2012.00277.x.

24. For example, although crime clock data may imply that one murder occurs every half hour or so, most murders actually occur during the evening, and only a very few take place around sunrise.

25. Most offense definitions in this chapter are derived from those used by the UCR/NIBRS Program and are taken from the FBI's *Crime in the United States, 2017,* or from the Bureau of Justice Statistics, *Criminal Justice Data Terminology,* 2nd ed. (Washington, DC: BJS, 1981).

26. These and other statistics in this chapter are derived primarily from the FBI's *Crime in the United States, 2017.*

27. Bureau of Justice Statistics, *Report to the Nation on Crime and Justice*, 2nd ed. (Washington, DC: U.S. Government Printing Office, 1988), p. 4.

28. "Feds Deny Thwarting Sniper Suspect's Confession," CNN.com, October 31, 2002, http://www.cnn.com/2002/US/10/30/snipers.interrogation/index.html (accessed October 31, 2002).

29. "Sniper Malvo Given Second Life Sentence," *USA Today,* October 27, 2004, p. 3A.

30. BJS, *Report to the Nation on Crime and Justice*, p. 4.

31. Ibid.

32. For excellent coverage of serial killers, see Steven Egger, *The Killers among Us: An Examination of Serial Murder and Its Investigation* (Upper Saddle River, NJ: Prentice Hall, 1998); Steven A. Egger, *Serial Murder: An Elusive Phenomenon* (Westport, CT: Praeger, 1990); and Stephen J. Giannangelo, *The Psychopathology of Serial Murder: A Theory of Violence* (New York: Praeger, 1996).

33. *BTK* stands for "bind, torture, and kill," an acronym that Rader applied to himself in letters he sent to the media during the 1970s.

34. Several years ago, Lucas recanted all of his confessions, saying that he had never killed anyone—except possibly his mother, a killing he said he didn't remember. See "Condemned Killer Admits Lying, Denies Slayings," *Washington Post*, October 1, 1995.

35. Chikatilo was executed in 1994.

36. Public Law 108–212.

37. E-mail communication with the Criminal Justice Information Services Division of the FBI, January 6, 2012.

38. FBI, "UCR Offense Definitions," http://ucrdatatool.gov/offenses.cfm (accessed May 5, 2018).

39. "Study: Rape Vastly Underreported," *Associated Press,* April 26, 1992.

40. Ronald Barri Flowers, *Women and Criminality: The Woman as Victim, Offender, and Practitioner* (Westport, CT: Greenwood Press, 1987), p. 36.

41. A. Nichols Groth, *Men Who Rape: The Psychology of the Offender* (New York: Plenum Press, 1979).

42. Susan Brownmiller, *Against Our Will: Men, Women, and Rape* (New York: Simon and Schuster, 1975).

43. Dennis J. Stevens, "Motives of Social Rapists," *Free Inquiry in Creative Sociology*, Vol. 23, No. 2 (November 1995), pp. 117–126.

44. BJS, *Report to the Nation on Crime and Justice*, p. 5.

45. Ibid.

46. FBI, *Crime in the United States, 2017.* For UCR Program reporting purposes, *minorities* are defined as African Americans, Native Americans, Asians, Pacific Islanders, and Alaskan Natives.

47. "Easter Bunny Charged with Battery for Mall Attack," *Associated Press*, April 18, 2006.

48. This offense is sometimes called *assault with a deadly weapon with intent to kill (AWDWWITK).*

49. FBI, *Crime in the United States, 2017.*

50. BJS, *Report to the Nation on Crime and Justice*, p. 6.

51. Ibid.

52. Huffington Post, "Cheeky Thieves Are Caught on Camera Stealing Grass From a Front Lawn in Lancashire," August 22, 2014, 2014, https://www.huffingtonpost.co.uk/2014/08/22/front-lawn-grass-thief-lancashire_n_5698895.html (accessed September 12, 2018).

53. "Yale Says Student Stole His Education," *USA Today*, April 12, 1995.

54. Seena Gressin, "The Equifax Data Breach: What To Do," Federal Trade Commission, https://www.consumer.ftc.gov/blog/2017/09/equifax-data-breach-what-do (accessed August 28, 2018).

55. Al Pascual, et al., "2018 Identity Fraud: Fraud Enters New Era of Complexity," https://www.javelinstrategy.com/coverage-area/2018-identity-fraud-fraud-enters-new-era-complexity# (accessed November 1, 2018).

56. Erika Harrell, *Victims of Identity Theft, 2014* (Washington, DC: Bureau of Justice Statistics, revised November 13, 2017).

57. Ibid

58. U.S. Code, Title 18, Section 1028.

59. Public Law 108–275.

60. Much of the information in this paragraph is adapted from National White Collar Crime Center, "Identity Theft," http://www.nw3c.org/research/site_files.cfm?fileid=935cdacc-b138-483a-8d05-83e6fd3d9004&mode=w (accessed May 18, 2018).

61. FBI, *Uniform Crime Reporting Handbook, 2004,* p. 28.

62. Patsy Klaus, *Carjacking, 1993–2002* (Washington, DC: Bureau of Justice Statistics, July 2004).

63. FBI, *Crime in the United States, 2017.*

64. As indicated in the UCR definition of *arson.* See Federal Bureau of Investigation, *Crime in the United States, 2017* (Washington, DC: U.S. Department of Justice, 2018).

65. FBI, *Crime in the United States, 2017.*

66. Ibid.

67. "Trends in Crime and Victimization," *Criminal Justice Research Reports*, Vol. 2, No. 6 (July/August 2001), p. 83.

68. Bureau of Justice Statistics, *Criminal Victimization, 2016* (Washington, DC: BJS, 2018).

69. Ibid.

70. Ibid.

71. Ibid., p. 1.

72. See, for example, President's Commission on Law Enforcement and Administration of Justice, *The Challenge of Crime in a Free Society*, pp. 22–23.

73. BJS, *Report to the Nation on Crime and Justice*, p. 27.

74. FBI, Criminal Justice Information Services Division, *The Measurement of White-Collar Crime Using Uniform Crime Reporting (UCR) Data* (Washington, DC.: FBI, no date), http://www.fbi.gov/about-us/cjis/ucr/nibrs/nibrs_wcc.pdf (accessed May 2, 2018).

75. It is the national UCR Program's official position that "Computer Crime actually involves the historical common-law offenses of larceny, embezzlement, trespass, etc., which are being perpetrated through the use of a new tool, the computer." Therefore, according to the FBI, "if larcenies, embezzlements, and trespasses relating to computers were to be reported under a new classification called Computer Crime, the national UCR Program's traditional time series relating to such crimes would be distorted." To avoid such a result, NIBRS provides the capability to indicate whether a computer was the object of the crime, and/or to indicate whether the offenders used computer equipment to perpetrate a crime. The FBI says that "this ensures the continuance of the traditional crime statistics and at the same time flags incidents that involve Computer Crime." FBI, Criminal Justice Information Services Division, *National Incident-Based Reporting System, Volume 1: Data Collection Guidelines* (Washington, DC: USDOJ, 2000), pp. 19–20.

76. Hagan, *Research Methods in Criminal Justice and Criminology*, p. 89.

77. Bureau of Justice Statistics, *Criminal Victimization in the United States, 1985* (Washington, DC: U.S. Government Printing Office, 1987), p. 1.

78. FBI, *Crime in the United States, 2001*, preliminary data, http://www.fbi.gov./ucr/01prelim.pdf (accessed August 27, 2002).

79. Terance D. Miethe and Richard C. McCorkle, *Crime Profiles: The Anatomy of Dangerous Persons, Places, and Situations* (Los Angeles: Roxbury, 1998), p. 19.

80. Until recently, the definition of *rape* employed by the UCR/NIBRS Program, however, automatically excluded crimes of homosexual rape such as might occur in prisons and jails. As a consequence, the rape of males had, until recently, been excluded from the official count for crimes of rape.

81. Truman and Langton, *Criminal Victimization, 2014*, p. 7.

82. Thomas Simon et al., *Injuries from Violent Crime, 1992–98* (Washington, DC: Bureau of Justice Statistics, 2001), p. 5.

83. See, for example, Elizabeth Stanko, "When Precaution Is Normal: A Feminist Critique of Crime Prevention," in Loraine Gelsthorpe and Allison Morris, eds., *Feminist Perspectives in Criminology* (Philadelphia: Open University Press, 1990).

84. For more information, see Eve S. Buzawa and Carl G. Buzawa, *Domestic Violence: The Criminal Justice Response* (Thousand Oaks, CA: Sage, 1996).

85. "Battered Women Tell Their Stories to the Senate," *Charlotte (NC) Observer*, July 10, 1991.

86. Michele C. Black et al., *The National Intimate Partner and Sexual Violence Survey: 2010 Summary Report* (Atlanta, GA: National Center for Injury Prevention and Control, 2011).

87. VAWA 2013 was signed into law by President Obama on March 7, 2013. It is officially known as the Violence against Women Reauthorization Act of 2013.

88. Violence against Women Office, *Stalking and Domestic Violence: Report to Congress* (Washington, DC: U.S. Department of Justice, 2001).

89. U.S. Code, Title 18, Section 2261A.

90. As modified vy VAWA 2000.

91. Violence against Women Office, *Stalking and Domestic Violence*.

92. Most of the data in this section come from Bureau of Justice Statistics, *Crimes against Persons Age 65 or Older, 1993–2002* (Rockville, MD: BJS, 2005).

93. Lamar Jordan, "Law Enforcement and the Elderly: A Concern for the Twenty-First Century," *FBI Law Enforcement Bulletin*, May 2002, pp. 20–23.

94. Public Law 101–275.

95. H.R. 4797, 102d Cong. 2d Sess. (1992).

96. FBI, *Hate Crime Statistics, 2017* (Washington, DC: U.S. Dept. of Justice, 2018), http://www.fbi.gov/about-us/cjis/ucr/hate-crime/2017/topic-pages/victims/victims_final.pdf (accessed January 7, 2019).

97. "Sept. 11 Attacks Cited in Nearly 25 Percent Increase in Florida Hate Crimes," *Associated Press*, August 30, 2002.

98. Southern Poverty Law Center, "Active U.S. Hate Groups," http://www.splcenter.org/get-informed/hate-map (accessed July 11, 2012).

99. Megan Meuchel Wilson, *Hate Crime Victimization 2004–2012: Statistical Tables* (Washington, DC: BJS, 2014).

100. Richard Esposito, Eloise Harper, and Maddy Sauer, "Bernie Madoff Pleads Guilty to Ponzi Scheme, Goes Straight to Jail, Says He's 'Deeply Sorry,'" ABC News, March 12, 2009, http://abcnews.go.com/Blotter/WallStreet/Story?id=7066715&page=1 (accessed July 4, 2009).

101. Diana B. Henriques, "Madoff Is Sentenced to 150 Years for Ponzi Scheme," *The New York Times*, June 29, 2009, http://www.nytimes.com/2009/06/30/business/30madoff.html (accessed September 28, 2011).

102. Dina El-Boghdady, "Mortgage Fraud up as Credit Tightens," *Washington Post*, March 17, 2009, http://www.washington-post.com/wp-dyn/content/article/2009/03/16/AR2009031601612.html (accessed May 13, 2009).

103. Jennifer Liberto, "More Muscle Sought in Fraud Fight," CNNMoney.com, May 8, 2009, http://money.cnn.com/2009/05/08/news/economy/mortgage_fraud/index.htm (accessed May 13, 2009).

104. Federal Trade Commission, "Federal and State Agencies Crack Down on Mortgage Modification and Foreclosure Rescue Scams," http://www.ftc.gov/opa/2009/04/hud.shtm (accessed May 13, 2009).

105. *Andersen v. U.S.*, 544 U.S. 696 (2005).

106. Public Broadcasting System, "Enron: After the Collapse," http://www.pbs.org/newshour/bb/business/enron/player6.html (accessed August 27, 2005).

107. Edwin H. Sutherland, "White-Collar Criminality," *American Sociological Review* (February 1940), p. 12.

108. Public Law 107–204.

109. Quoted on the Transnational Threats Initiative home page of the Center for Strategic and International Studies (CSIS), http://www.csis.org/tnt/index.htm (accessed August 22, 2007).

110. These ideas were originally expressed by Assistant U.S. Attorney General Laurie Robinson in an address given at the Twelfth International Congress on Criminology, Seoul, Korea, August 28, 1998.

111. Caroline Wolf Harlow, *Firearm Use by Offenders* (Washington, DC: Bureau of Justice Statistics, 2001).

112. Ibid., p. 1.

113. William Lee, "Top Cop: 'Chicago is not out of Control'," http://www.chicagotribune.com/news/local/breaking/

ct-dart-johnson-city-club-crime-met-20161207-story.html, December 8, 2016 (accessed March 11, 2018).

114. *District of Columbia*, et al. v. *Dick Anthony Heller* (2008). Available at http://www.law.cornell.edu/supct/html/07-290.ZO.html (accessed August 4, 2013).

115. *McDonald* v. *Chicago,* 561 U.S. 3025 (2010).

116. Public Law 103–159.

117. U.S. Code, Title 18, Section 922(q)(1)(A).

118. Public Law 103-322, 108 Stat. 1796 (codified as amended in scattered sections of U.S. Code titles 18, 21, 28, 42, etc.).

119. Public Law 104-208, an amendment to U.S. Code, Title 18, Section 921(a). Also known as the Lautenberg Amendment.

120. Jacob R. Clark, "Police Careers May Take a Beating from Fed Domestic-Violence Law," *Law Enforcement News*, Vol. 23, No. 461 (February 14, 1997), p. 1.

121. Rick Ungar, "Here Are the 23 Executive Orders on Gun Safety Signed Today by the President," Forbes, January 16, 2013, http://www.forbes.com/sites/rickungar/2013/01/16/here-are-the-23-executive-orders-on-gun-safety-signed-today-by-the-president/ (accessed January 16, 2013).

122. Harlow, *Firearm Use by Offenders*.

123. John C. Moorhouse and Brent Wanner, "Does Gun Control Reduce Crime or Does Crime Increase Gun Control?" *CATO Journal*, Vol. 103 (2006), pp. 103–124.

124. J. Craig Anderson, "Threat of 3D-printed Guns Expected to Grow," *Portland Press Herald,* December 12, 2013, http://www.pressherald.com/news/Threat_of_3D-printed_guns_expected_to_grow_.html?pagenum=full (accessed October 2, 2018).

125. Sarah Brady, "Statement on the Sniper Shootings," October 8, 2002, http://www.bradycampaign.org/press/release.asp?Record5429 (accessed October 16, 2007); and Microstamping of Firearms Required by California Law," *Criminal Justice Newsletter*, October 2, 2007, p. 1.

126. As cited in Donna Leinwand, "Drug, Terror Rings Find New Ways to Launder Money," *USA Today*, January 12, 2006.

127. National Institute on Drug Abuse, "Opioid Overdose Crisis," February 2018; https://www.drugabuse.gov/drugs-abuse/opioids/opioid-overdose-crisis (accessed September 4, 2018).

128. Yoel Minkoff, "Cost of U.S. Opioid Epidemic Tops $500B," Seeking Alpha, November 20, 2017.

129. J. M. Chaiken and M. R. Chaiken, *Varieties of Criminal Behavior* (Santa Monica, CA: RAND Corporation, 1982).

130. D. McBride, "Trends in Drugs and Death," paper presented at the annual meeting of the American Society of Criminology, Denver, 1983.

131. National Criminal Justice Reference Service, *The Micro Domain: Behavior and Homicide,* http://www.ncjrs.org/pdffiles/167262-3.pdf (accessed February 23, 2002).

132. Bureau of Justice Statistics, *Substance Abuse and Treatment: State and Federal Prisoners* (Washington, DC: U.S. Department of Justice, January 1999).

133. Bureau of Justice Statistics, *Drug Use, Testing, and Treatment in Jails* (Washington, DC: U.S. Department of Justice, May 2000).

134. "Medical Marijuana," ProCon.org, http://medicalmarijuana.procon.org/view.resource.php?resourceID=000881 (accessed October 15, 2018).

135. U.S. Department of Justice, Press release: "Arkansas Man Sentenced to Prison for Developing and Distributing Prolific Malware," February 23, 2018; https://www.justice.gov/opa/pr/arkansas-man-sentenced-prison-developing-and-distributing-prolific-malware (accessed March 5, 2018).

136. Details for this story come from Carol Cratty, "245 Arrested in U.S.-Led Child Sex Abuse Operation," *CNN*, January 4, 2013, http://www.cnn.com/2013/01/03/us/ice-child-abuse-arrests (accessed March 14, 2018).

137. Grabosky, "Computer Crime."

138. Kevin Johnson, "Hijackers' E-Mails Sifted for Clues," *USA Today*, October 11, 2001.

139. "Invasion of the Data Snatchers!" *Time*, September 26, 1988, pp. 62–67.

140. Public Law 108–187.

141. Peter Firstbrook, "META Trend Update: The Changing Threat Landscape," Meta Group, March 24, 2005, http://www.metagroup.com/us/displayArticle.do?oid551768 (accessed July 5, 2005).

142. *MGM* v. *Grokster*, 545 U.S. 913 (2005).

143. Gregg Keizer, "Microsoft Says Phishing Bad, Offers Little New for Defense," *TechWeb News*, March 15, 2005, http://www.techweb.com/wire/159900391 (accessed July 7, 2005).

144. "Focus on Physical Security, Too," *eWeek*, January 27, 2003, p. 6a.

145. Emergency Response and Research Institute, *Summary of Emergency Response and Research Institute Terrorism Statistics: 2000 and 2001*, http://www.emergency.com/2002/terroris00-01.pdf (accessed August 22, 2002).

146. Federal Bureau of Investigation, Counterterrorism Section, *Terrorism in the United States, 1987* (Washington, DC: FBI, 1987), in which the full version of the definition offered here can be found. See also *FBI Policy and Guidelines: Counter-terrorism*, which offers a somewhat less formal definition of the term, http://www.fbi.gov/contact/fo/jackson/cntrterr.htm (accessed January 15, 2002).

147. Adapted from *FBI Policy and Guidelines*.

148. Ibid.

149. See Barry Collin, "The Future of Cyberterrorism," *Crime and Justice International* (March 1997), pp. 15–18.

150. John Arquilla and David Ronfeldt, *The Advent of Netwar* (Santa Monica, CA: RAND Corporation, 1996).

151. Mark M. Pollitt, "Cyberterrorism: Fact or Fancy?" in *Proceedings of the Twentieth National Information Systems Security Conference*, October 1997, pp. 285–289.

152. "Chief Security Officers Remind Citizens of the Dangers of Cyberattacks and Recommend Tips," *CSO Magazine*, http://www.csoonline.html/info/release.html?CID= 9065 (accessed August 28, 2016).

153. Robert S. Mueller III, executive speech at Chatham House, London, England, April 7, 2008, http://www.fbi.gov/pressrel/speeches/mueller040708.htm (accessed May 20, 2008).

154. Central Intelligence Agency, National Foreign Intelligence Council, *Global Trends, 2015: A Dialogue about the Future with Nongovernment Experts* (Washington, DC: U.S. Government Printing Office, 2000).

155. Ibid.

156. "Crime Business One of the World's 'Top 20 Economies,'" United Nations, Reuters, April 23, 2012, http://www.huffingtonpost.com/2012/04/23/crime-business-united-nations_n_1445742.html (accessed April 25, 2012).

157. For information about the latest survey, see *The 2012 United Nations Survey of Crime Trends and Operations of Criminal Justice Systems* (New York: United Nations, 2015), http://www.unodc.org/unodc/en/data-and-analysis/United-Nations-Surveys-on-Crime-Trends-and-the-Operations-of-Criminal-Justice-Systems.html (accessed August 1, 2018).

Chapter 3: Criminal Law

i. Daniel Oran, *Oran's Dictionary of the Law* (St. Paul, MN: West, 1983), p. 306.

ii. Henry Campbell Black, Joseph R. Nolan, and Jacqueline M. Nolan-Haley, *Black's Law Dictionary*, 6th ed. (St. Paul, MN: West, 1990), p. 24.

1. "California Doctor Gets 30 Years to Life for Three Patient Prescription Drug Deaths," *Associated Press*, February 5, 2015, http://www.nydailynews.com/news/crime/california-doc-30-years-life-patient-drug-deaths-article-1.2522071 (accessed March 3, 2016).

2. Ibid.

3. Henry Campbell Black, Joseph R. Nolan, and Jacqueline M. Nolan-Haley, *Black's Law Dictionary*, 6th ed. (St. Paul, MN: West, 1990), p. 884.

4. Ibid.

5. FBI press release, "Former Detroit Mayor Kwame Kilpatrick, His Father Bernard Kilpatrick, and City Contractor Bobby Ferguson Convicted on Racketeering, Extortion, Bribery, Fraud, and Tax Charges," March 11, 2013, http://www.fbi.gov/detroit/press-releases/2013/former-detroit-mayor-kwame-kilpatrick-his-father-bernard-kilpatrick-and-city-contractor-bobby-ferguson-convicted-on-racketeering-extortion-bribery-fraud-and-tax-charges.

6. Ed White, "Kwame Kilpatrick on the Hook for $4.5M Restitution," SFGate, December 10, 2012, http://www.sfgate.com/news/crime/article/Kwame-Kilpatrick-on-the-hook-for-4-5M-restitution-5050271.php (accessed January 5, 2014).

7. John F. Kennedy, *Profiles in Courage* (New York: Harper & Row, 1956).

8. Fareed Zakaria, "The Enemy Within," *The New York Times*, December 17, 2006, http://www.nytimes.com/2006/12/17/books/review/Zakaria.t.html (accessed August 28, 2008).

9. American Bar Association Section of International and Comparative Law, *The Rule of Law in the United States* (Chicago: American Bar Association, 1958).

10. Daniel Oran, *Oran's Dictionary of the Law* (St. Paul, MN: West, 1983), p. 306.

11. Black, Nolan, and Nolan-Haley, *Black's Law Dictionary*, p. 24.

12. FBI, "Former Sailor Sentenced to 30 Years in Prison for Attempted Espionage," February 10, 2014, http://www.fbi.gov/norfolk/pressreleases/2014/former-sailor-sentenced-to-30-years-in-prison-for-attempted-espionage (accessed February 3, 2016).

13. Specifically, U.S. Code, Title 21, Section 846.

14. *U.S.* v. *Shabani*, 510 U.S. 1108 (1994).

15. *Gordon* v. *State*, 52 Ala. 3008, 23 Am. Rep. 575 (1875).

16. But not for a more serious degree of homicide, since leaving a young child alone in a tub of water, even if intentional, does not necessarily mean that the person who so acts intends the child to drown.

17. O. W. Holmes, *The Common Law*, Vol. 3 (Boston: Little, Brown, 1881).

18. There is disagreement among some jurists as to whether the crime of statutory rape is a strict liability offense. Some jurisdictions treat it as such and will not accept as a defense a reasonable mistake about the victim's age. Others, however, do accept such a mistake as a defense.

19. *State* v. *Stiffler*, 763 P.2d 308 (Idaho App. 1988).

20. John S. Baker, Jr., et al., *Hall's Criminal Law*, 5th ed. (Charlottesville, VA: Michie, 1993), p. 138.

21. The same is not true for procedures within the criminal justice system, which can be modified even after a person has been sentenced and, hence, become retroactive. See, for example, the U.S. Supreme Court case of *California Department of Corrections* v. *Morales*, 514 U.S. 499 (1995), in which the Court allowed changes in the length of time between parole hearings, even though those changes applied to offenders who had already been sentenced.

22. Black, Nolan, and Nolan-Haley, *Black's Law Dictionary*, p. 127.

23. The statute also says, "A mother's breastfeeding of her baby does not under any circumstance violate this section."

24. Common law crimes, of course, are not based on statutory elements.

25. *People* v. *Hall—Final Analysis*, SkiSafety.com, http://www.skisafety.com/amicuscases-hall2.html (accessed August 28, 2012).

26. See *Maughs* v. *Commonwealth*, 181 Va. 117, 120, 23 S.E.2d 784, 786 (1943).

27. *State* v. *Stephenson*, Opinion No. 24403 (South Carolina, 1996). See also *State* v. *Blocker*, 205 S.C. 303, 31 S.E.2d 908 (1944).

28. *State* v. *Kindle*, 71 Mont. 58, 64, 227 (1924).

29. Black, Nolan, and Nolan-Haley, *Black's Law Dictionary*, p. 343.

30. Patrick L. McCloskey and Ronald L. Schoenberg, *Criminal Law Deskbook* (New York: Matthew Bender, 1988), Section 20.03[13].

31. Greg Allen, "Florida Governor Stands Firm on 'Stand Your Ground' Law," *NPR*, July 19, 2013, http://www.npr.org/2013/07/19/203594004/florida-governor-stands-firm-on-stand-your-ground-law (accessed July 19, 2013).

32. The exception, of course, is that of a trespasser who trespasses in order to commit a more serious crime.

33. Sir Edward Coke, 3 *Institute*, 162.

34. *The Crown* v. *Dudly & Stephens*, 14 Q.B.D. 273, 286, 15 Cox C. C. 624, 636 (1884).

35. "Jury Convicts Condom Rapist," *USA Today*, May 14, 1993.

36. *Nuño* v. *County of San Bernardino* (C.D. Cal. 1999) 58 F.Supp.2d 1127, 1134.

37. Black, Nolan, and Nolan-Haley, *Black's Law Dictionary*, p. 504.

38. *State of Tennessee* v. *Charles Arnold Ballinger*, No. E2000-01339-CCA-R3-CD (Tenn. Crim. App. 01/09/2000).

39. See, for example, *Montana* v. *Egelhoff*, 116 S.Ct. 2013, 135 L.Ed.2d 361 (1996).

40. Details for this story come from Brittany Green-Miller, "Man Sentenced for Shooting Neighbor He Believed Telepathically Raped Wife," Fox News, May 16, 2013, http://fox13now.com/2013/05/16/man-sentenced-for-shooting-neighbor-he-believed-telepathically-raped-wife (accessed January 7, 2014).

41. L. A. Callahan et al., "The Volume and Characteristics of Insanity Defense Pleas: An Eight-State Study," *Bulletin of the American Academy of Psychiatry and the Law*, Vol. 19, No. 4 (1991), pp. 331–338.

42. American Bar Association Standing Committee on Association Standards for Criminal Justice, *Proposed Criminal Justice Mental Health Standards* (Chicago: American Bar Association, 1984).

43. *Durham* v. *U.S.*, 214 F.2d 867, 875 (D.C. Cir. 1954).

44. American Law Institute, *Model Penal Code: Official Draft and Explanatory Notes* (Philadelphia: American Law Institute, 1985).

45. Ibid.

46. See Joan Biskupic, "Insanity Defense: Not a Right; In Montana Case, Justices Give States Option to Prohibit Claim," *Washington Post* wire service, March 29, 1994.

47. Ibid.

48. *Ford* v. *Wainwright*, 477 U.S. 399, 106 S.Ct. 2595, 91 L.Ed.2d 335 (1986).

49. U.S. Code, Title 18, Section 401.

50. *Jones* v. *U.S.*, 463 U.S. 354 (1983).

51. *Ake* v. *Oklahoma*, 470 U.S. 68, 105 S.Ct. 1087, 84 L.Ed.2d 53 (1985).

52. *Foucha* v. *Louisiana*, 504 U.S. 71 (1992).

53. U.S. Sentencing Commission, "Supplement to the 2002 Federal Sentencing Guidelines: Section 5K2.13. Diminished Capacity (Policy Statement)," April 30, 2003, http://www.ussc.gov/2002suppb/5K2_13.htm (accessed May 8, 2008). Italics added.

54. *U.S.* v. *Pohlot*, 827 F.2d 889 (1987).

55. Peter Arenella, "The Diminished Capacity and Diminished Responsibility Defenses: Two Children of a Doomed Marriage," *Columbia Law Review*, Vol. 77 (1977), p. 830.

56. *U.S.* v. *Brawner*, 471 F.2d 969 (1972).

57. Black, Nolan, and Nolan-Haley, *Black's Law Dictionary*, p. 458.

58. California Penal Code, Section 25(a).

59. Ibid., Section 28(b).

60. *Indiana* v. *Edwards*, 554 U.S. 164 (2008).

61. *U.S.* v. *Halper*, 490 U.S. 435 (1989).

62. "Robert Blake Found Liable for Wife's Death," *Associated Press*, November 18, 2005.

63. See, for example, *Hudson* v. *U.S.*, 18 S.Ct. 488 (1997); and *U.S.* v. *Ursery*, 518 U.S. 267 (1996).

64. McCloskey and Schoenberg, *Criminal Law Deskbook*, Section 20.02[4].

65. *U.S.* v. *Armstrong*, 116 S.Ct. 1480, 134 L.Ed.2d 687 (1996).

66. Speedy Trial Act, U.S. Code, Title 18, Section 3161. Significant cases involving the Speedy Trial Act are those of *U.S.* v. *Carter*, 476 U.S. 1138, 106 S.Ct. 2241, 90 L.Ed.2d 688 (1986); and *Henderson* v. *U.S.*, 476 U.S. 321, 106 S.Ct. 1871, 90 L.Ed.2d 299 (1986).

67. Peter Whoriskey, "New Orleans Justice System Besieged," *Boston Globe*, April 17, 2006, http://www.boston.com/news/nation/articles/2006/04/17/new_orleans_justice_system_besieged (accessed May 10, 2007).

68. Stephen Anderson, Ex-NYPD Cop: We Planted Evidence, Framed Innocent People to Reach Quotas," *The Huffington Post*, October 13, 2011, http://www.huffingtonpost.com/2011/10/13/ex-nypd-cop-we-planted-ev_n_1009754.html?view=print&comm_ref=false (accessed March 23, 2012).

69. Francis Fukuyama, "Extreme Paranoia about Government Abounds," *USA Today*, August 24, 1995.

Chapter 4: Policing: Purpose and Organization

i. Wayne W. Bennett and Karen M. Hess, *Criminal Investigation*, 6th ed. (Belmont, CA: Wadsworth, 2001), p. 3.

ii. Robert Kennedy, *The Pursuit of Justice*, part 3, "Eradicating Free Enterprise in Organized Crime" (New York: Harper and Row, 1964).

iii. Sam S. Souryal, *Police Administration and Management* (St. Paul, MN: West, 1977), p. 261.

iv. Office of Community Oriented Policing Services, *Community Policing Defined* (Washington, DC: U.S. Department of Justice, 2009), p. 3.

v. Lawrence W. Sherman, *Evidence-Based Policing* (Washington, DC: Police Foundation, 1998), p. 3.

1. Frank Newport, "Gallup Review: Black and White Attitudes Toward Police," *Gallup*, August 20, 2014, http://www.gallup.com/poll/175088/gallup-review-black-white-attitudes-toward-police.aspx.

2. Jeremy Ashkenas and Haeyoun Park, "The Race Gap in America's Police Departments," *The New York Times*, September 4, 2014.

3. Shaila Dewan, "Mostly White Forces in Mostly Black Towns: Police Struggle for Racial Diversity," *The New York Times*, September 9, 2014, http://nyti.ms/1tly4kU.

4. Andrew P. Sutor, *Police Operations: Tactical Approaches to Crimes in Progress* (St. Paul, MN: West, 1976), p. 68, citing Peel.

5. C. D. Hale, *Police Patrol: Operations and Management* (Englewood Cliffs, NJ: Prentice Hall, 1994).

6. Victor Kappeler et al., *The Mythology of Crime and Criminal Justice* (Prospect Heights, IL: Waveland Press, 1996).

7. Darl H. Champion and Michael K. Hooper, *Introduction to American Policing* (New York: McGraw-Hill, 2003), p. 133.

8. Details for this story come from Ted Ottley, "Bad Day Dawning," Court TV's Crime Library, http://www.crimelibrary.com/serial_killers/notorious/mcveigh/dawning_1.html (accessed June 22, 2008).

9. Ibid.

10. Wayne W. Bennett and Karen M. Hess, *Criminal Investigation*, 6th ed. (Belmont, CA: Wadsworth, 2001), p. 3.

11. This definition has been attributed to the National Crime Prevention Institute (see http://www.lvmpd.com/community/crmtip25.htm).

12. See Steven P. Lab, *Crime Prevention at a Crossroads* (Cincinnati, OH: Anderson, 1997).

13. Walter L. Perry, Brian McInnis, Carter C. Price, Susan C. Smith, and John S. Hollywood, *Predictive Policing: The Roe of Crime Forecasting in Law Enforcement Operations* (RAND, 2013).

14. Visit the Philadelphia Police Department online at http://www.phillypolice.com.

15. The term *CompStat* is sometimes interpreted to mean computer statistics, comparative statistics, or computer comparative statistics, although it is generally accorded no specific meaning.

16. Learn more about CompStat in Vincent E. Henry, *The COMPSTAT Paradigm: Management Accountability in Policing, Business, and the Public Sector* (Flushing, NY: Looseleaf Law Publications, 2002).

17. Much of the information in this section comes from the Philadelphia Police Department, "The COMPSTAT Process," http://www.ppdonline.org/ppd_compstat.htm (accessed May 28, 2009).

18. See Ned Levine, *CrimeStat: A Spatial Statistics Program for the Analysis of Crime Incident Locations*, version 2.0 (Washington, DC: National Institute of Justice, May 2002).

19. Walter L. Perry, Brian McInnis, Carter C. Price, Susan C. Smith, and John S. Hollywood, *Predictive Policing: The Role of Crime Forecasting in Law Enforcement Operations* (RAND, 2013).

20. Robert H. Langworthy and Lawrence P. Travis III, *Policing in America: A Balance of Forces*, 2nd ed. (Upper Saddle River, NJ: Prentice Hall, 1999), p. 194.

21. Adapted from Bronx County (New York) District Attorney's Office, "Quality of Life Offenses," December 24, 2002, http://www.bronxda.net/fighting_crime/quality_of_life_offenses.html (accessed June 20, 2003).

22. Other violations may be involved as well. On December 29, 2000, for example, Judge John S. Martin, Jr., of the Federal District Court in Manhattan, ruled that homeless people in New York City could be arrested for sleeping in cardboard boxes in public. Judge Martin held that a city Sanitation Department regulation barring people from abandoning cars or boxes on city streets could be applied to the homeless who were sleeping in boxes.

23. Norman Siegel, executive director of the New York Civil Liberties Union, as reported in "Quality of Life Offenses Targeted," *Western Queens Gazette*, November 22, 2000, http://www.qgazette.com/News/2000/1122/Editorial_pages/e01.html (accessed June 12, 2007).

24. The broken windows thesis was first suggested by George L. Kelling and James Q. Wilson in "Broken Windows: The Police and Neighborhood Safety," *Atlantic Monthly*, March 1982.

25. For a critique of the broken windows thesis, see Bernard E. Harcourt, *Illusion of Order: The False Promise of Broken Windows Policing* (Cambridge, MA: Harvard University Press, 2001).

26. Peter Schuler, "Law Professor Harcourt Challenges Popular Policing Method, Gun Violence Interventions," *Chicago Chronicle*, Vol. 22, No. 12 (March 20, 2003), http://chronicle.uchicago.edu/030320/harcourt.shtml (accessed August 28, 2008).

27. George L. Kelling, Catherine M. Coles, and James Q. Wilson, *Fixing Broken Windows: Restoring Order and Reducing Crime in Our Communities* (reprint, New York: Touchstone, 1998).

28. Charles R. Swanson, Leonard Territo, and Robert W. Taylor, *Police Administration: Structures, Processes, and Behavior*, 4th ed. (Upper Saddle River, NJ: Prentice Hall, 1998), p. 1.

29. Lorraine Mazerolle et al., *Managing Citizen Calls to the Police: An Assessment of Nonemergency Call Systems* (Washington, DC: National Institute of Justice, 2001), p. 1.

30. Government Accounting Office, "Federal Law Enforcement: Survey of Federal Civilian Law Enforcement Functions and Authorities," December 2006 (highlights of GAO-07-121).

31. U.S. Department of Justice, *A Proud History, a Bright Future: Careers with the FBI*, pamphlet (Washington, DC: DOJ, October 1986), p. 1.

32. Much of the information in this section comes from U.S. Department of Justice, *The FBI: The First Seventy-Five Years* (Washington, DC: U.S. Government Printing Office, 1986).

33. Some of the information in this section is adapted from Federal Bureau of Investigation, "Facts and Figures 2003," http://www.fbi.gov/priorities/priorities.htm (accessed March 25, 2006).

34. "Rising to the Occasion," FBI News Blog, October 22, 2012, http://www.fbi.gov/news/news_blog/in-new-interviews-women-agents-reflect-on-40-years (accessed February 15, 2013).

35. Telephone conversation with FBI officials, April 21, 1995.

36. FBI, "The Budapest International Law Enforcement Academy Turns Ten," May 13, 2005, http://www.fbi.gov/news/stories/2005/may/ilea051305 (accessed July 10, 2017).

37. Information in this section comes from Christopher H. Asplen, "National Commission Explores Its Future," *NIJ Journal* (January 1999), pp. 17–24.

38. The DNA Identification Act Is Section 210301 of the Violent Crime Control and Law Enforcement Act of 1994.

39. Federal Bureau of Investigation, "CODIS-NDIS Statistics," http://www.fbi.gov/about-us/lab/biometric-analysis/codis/ndis-statistics (accessed July 16, 2016).

40. Much of the information in this paragraph comes from the FBI Academy website at http://www.fbi.gov/hq/td/academy/academy.htm (accessed March 3, 2016).

41. Congressional Testimony by John S. Pistole, Deputy Director, Federal Bureau of Investigation, before the Senate Judiciary Committee, February 11, 2009, http://www.fbi.gov/congress/congress09/pistole021109.htm (accessed May 9, 2009).

42. Henry M. Wrobleski and Karen M. Hess, *Introduction to Law Enforcement and Criminal Justice*, 4th ed. (St. Paul, MN: West, 1993), p. 34.

43. Ibid., p. 35.

44. New York City Police Department website, http://www.nyc.gov/html/nypd/html/faq/faq_police.shtml (accessed July 19, 2016).

45. Brian A. Reaves, *Census of State and Local Law Enforcement Agencies, 2008* (Washington, DC: Bureau of Justice Statistics, 2011).

46. Andrea M. Burch, *Sheriffs' Offices, 2007*: Statistical Tables (Washington, DC: Bureau of Justice Statistics, 2012), p. 6.

47. Reaves, *Census of State and Local Law Enforcement Agencies, 2008*.

48. Note, however, that New York City jails may have daily populations that, on a given day, exceed those of Los Angeles County jails.

49. The Los Angeles County Sheriff's Department, http://lasd.org/public_data_sharing.html (accessed October, 2, 2018).

50. Los Angeles County Sheriff's Department, *Moving Forward: Year in Review 2016* (LASD), p. 217.

51. Ibid.

52. Andrea M. Burch, *Sheriffs' Offices, 2007*: Statistical Tables (Washington, DC: Bureau of Justice Statistics, 2012), p. 2.

53. U.S. Department of Justice Press Release, "Attorney General Sessions Delivers Remarks to the National Fusion Center Association," November 9, 2017.

54. DHS, "National Network of Fusion Centers Fact Sheet," http://www.dhs.gov/national-network-fusion-centers-fact-sheet (accessed January 9, 2014).

55. Estimates of the number of centers vary, and classifying a work group as a "fusion center" depends largely on the perspective assumed. In recent testimony before Congress, Department of Homeland Security Director Janet Napolitano put the number of active fusion centers in the nation at 72 (see https://nfcausa.org/default.aspx/MenuItemID/135/MenuGroup/Public+Home.htm).

56. Bureau of Justice Assistance, *Fusion Center Guidelines: Developing and Sharing Information in a New Era* (Washington, DC: U.S. Department of Justice, 2006), p. 2.

57. Michael C. Mines, "Statement before the House Committee on Homeland Security, Subcommittee on Intelligence, Information Sharing and Terrorism Risk Assessment," September 27, 2007.

58. *Private Security: Report of the Task Force on Private Security* (Washington, DC: U.S. Government Printing Office, 1976), p. 4.

59. "Securing the Olympic Games: $142,857 Security Cost per Athlete in Greece," *Wall Street Journal*, August 22, 2004, http://www.mindfully.org/Reform/2004/Olympic-Games-Security22aug04.htm (accessed May 17, 2007).

60. Christopher Elser, "London Olympics Doubles Spending on Security to $870 Million for Next Year," *Bloomberg*, December 5, 2011, http://www.bloomberg.com/news/2011-12-05/london-olympics-doubles-spending-on-security-to-870-million-for-next-year.html (accessed February 15, 2013).

61. John-Paul Ford Rojas, "£9 Billion Olympics 'Good Value,' Says Spending Watchdog," *The London Telegraph*, December 5, 2012 (accessed February 15, 2013).

62. Johnette Howard, "Are Olympics Too Big to Succeed? ESPN, January 25, 2014, http://www.espn.com/olympics/winter/2014/story/_/id/10334782/security-threats-expenses-making-olympics-less-attractive-bid (accessed May, 18, 2018).

63. Cunningham, Strauchs, and Van Meter, *The Hallcrest Report II*, p. 236.

64. The information and some of the wording in this paragraph come from the ASIS International website at http://www.asisonline.org (accessed August 5, 2012).

65. David H. Bayley and Clifford D. Shearing, *The New Structure of Policing: Description, Conceptualization, and Research Agenda* (Washington, DC: National Institute of Justice, 2001).

66. John Sodaro, "Move Over, Police?" *The Crime Report*, February 19, 2012, http://www.thecrimereport.org/share-post/2012-02-move-over-police (accessed March 26, 2012).

67. Bayley and Shearing, *The New Structure of Policing*, p. 15.

68. See "Interpol: Extending Law Enforcement's Reach around the World," *FBI Law Enforcement Bulletin* (December 1998), pp. 10–16.

69. Interpol, "Member Countries," http://www.interpol.int/Member-countries/World (accessed April 21, 2018).

70. "Interpol at Forty," *Criminal Justice International* (November/December 1986), pp. 1, 22.

71. Interpol General Secretariat, *Interpol at Work: 2003 Activity Report* (Lyons, France, 2004).

72. Marc Champion, Jeanne Whalen, and Jay Solomon, "Terror in London: Police Make One Arrest After Raids in North England," *Wall Street Journal*, July 12, 2005, http://online.wsj.com/article/0,SB112116092902883194,00.html?mod5djemTAR (accessed August 15, 2007).

73. Ibid.

74. ICPO-Interpol General Assembly Resolution No. AG-2001-RES-07.

75. Bureau for International Narcotics and Law Enforcement Affairs, Human Smuggling and Trafficking Center, *Distinctions between Human Smuggling and Human Trafficking* (Washington, DC: January 1, 2005).

76. Raimo Väyrynen, "Illegal Immigration, Human Trafficking, and Organized Crime," United Nations University/World Institute for Development Economics Research, Discussion Paper No. 2003/72 (October 2003), p. 16.

77. Office of the Under Secretary for Democracy and Global Affairs, *Trafficking in Persons Report* (Washington, DC: U.S. Dept. of State, June 2007).

78. Ibid.

79. Amy Farrell, Jack McDevitt, Rebecca Pfeffer, Stephanie Fahy, Colleen Owens, Meredith Dank, and William Adams, *Identifying Challenges to Improve the Investigation and Prosecution of State and Local Human Trafficking Cases: Executive Summary* (Washington, DC: National Institute of Justice, 2012), p. 3.

80. The elements of this definition draw on the now-classic work by O. W. Wilson, *Police Administration* (New York: McGraw-Hill, 1950), pp. 2–3.

81. Charles R. Swanson, Leonard Territo, and Robert W. Taylor, *Police Administration: Structures, Processes, and Behavior* (Upper Saddle River, NJ: Prentice Hall, 1998), p. 167.

82. For an organizational chart of a big-city police department, see one of the LAPD at http://assets.lapdonline.org/assets/pdf/Org_Chart_8-3-15-NEW-DP-9.pdf.

83. For more information on the first three categories, see Francis X. Hartmann, "Debating the Evolution of American Policing," *Perspectives on Policing*, No. 5 (Washington, DC: National Institute of Justice, 1988).

84. Willard M. Oliver, "The Homeland Security Juggernaut: The End of the Community Policing Era," *Crime and Justice International*, Vol. 20, No. 79 (2004), pp. 4–10. See also Willard M. Oliver, "The Era of Homeland Security: September 11, 2001 to . . ." *Crime and Justice International*, Vol. 21, No. 85 (2005), pp. 9–17.

85. Gene Stephens, "Policing the Future: Law Enforcement's New Challenges," *The Futurist*, March/April 2005, pp. 51–57.

86. As cited in Bernie G. Thompson, *A Law Enforcement Assistance and Partnership Strategy* (Washington, DC: U.S. Congress, 2008), p. 5. Congressman Thompson is a ranking member of the Democratic staff of the Committee on Homeland Security.

87. To learn more about Wilson, see http://www.nndb.com/people/796/000167295 (accessed January 5, 2018).

88. James Q. Wilson, *Varieties of Police Behavior: The Management of Law and Order in Eight Communities* (Cambridge, MA: Harvard University Press, 1968).

89. Independent Commission on the Los Angeles Police Department, *Report of the Independent Commission on the Los Angeles Police Department* (Los Angeles: The Commission, 1991).

90. Gary W. Sykes, "Street Justice: A Moral Defense of Order Maintenance Policing," *Justice Quarterly*, Vol. 3, No. 4 (December 1986), p. 505.

91. Egon Bittner, "Community Relations," in Alvin W. Cohn and Emilio C. Viano, eds., *Police Community Relations: Images, Roles, Realities* (Philadelphia: J. B. Lippincott, 1976), pp. 77–82.

92. Paul B. Weston, *Police Organization and Management* (Pacific Palisades, CA: Goodyear, 1976), p. 159.

93. Hale, *Police Patrol*.

94. Mark H. Moore and Robert C. Trojanowicz, "Corporate Strategies for Policing," *Perspectives on Policing*, No. 6 (Washington, DC: National Institute of Justice, 1998).

95. Ibid., p. 6.

96. Community Policing Consortium, *Community Policing Is Alive and Well* (Washington, DC: Community Policing Consortium, 1995), p. 1.

97. Office of Community Oriented Policing Services, *Community Policing Defined*, p. 3.

98. George L. Kelling, *The Newark Foot Patrol Experiment* (Washington, DC: Police Foundation, 1981).

99. Robert C. Trojanowicz, "An Evaluation of a Neighborhood Foot Patrol Program," *Journal of Police Science and Administration*, Vol. 11 (1983), pp. 410–419.

100. Bureau of Justice Assistance, *Understanding Community Policing: A Framework for Action* (Washington, DC: Bureau of Justice Statistics, 1994), p. 10.

101. Robert C. Trojanowicz and Bonnie Bucqueroux, *Community Policing* (Cincinnati, OH: Anderson, 1990).

102. Moore and Trojanowicz, "Corporate Strategies for Policing," p. 8.

103. S. M. Hartnett and W. G. Skogan, "Community Policing: Chicago's Experience," *National Institute of Justice Journal* (April 1999), pp. 2–11.

104. Jerome H. Skolnick and David H. Bayley, *Community Policing: Issues and Practices around the World* (Washington, DC: National Institute of Justice, 1988).

105. Ibid.

106. William L. Goodbody, "What Do We Expect New-Age Cops to Do?" *Law Enforcement News* (April 30, 1995), pp. 14, 18.

107. Sam Vincent Meddis and Desda Moss, "Many 'Fed-Up' Communities Cornering Crime," *USA Today*, May 22, 1995, p. 8A.

108. Bureau of Justice Assistance, *Neighborhood-Oriented Policing in Rural Communities: A Program Planning Guide* (Washington, DC: Bureau of Justice Statistics, 1994), p. 4.

109. U.S. Department of Justice Press Release, "Attorney General Sessions Announces $98 Million to Hire Community Policing Officers," November 20, 2017.

110. David L. Carter, *Law Enforcement Intelligence: A Guide for State, Local, and Tribal Law Enforcement Agencies* (Washington, DC: U.S. Department of Justice, 2004), p. 39.

111. Jihong Zhao, Nicholas P. Lovrich, and Quint Thurman, "The Status of Community Policing in American Cities: Facilitators and Impediments Revisited," *Policing*, Vol. 22, No. 1 (1999), p. 74.

112. For a good critique and overview of community policing, see Geoffrey P. Alpert et al., *Community Policing: Contemporary Readings* (Prospect Heights, IL: Waveland Press, 1998).

113. Jack R. Greene, "Community Policing in America: Changing the Nature, Structure, and Function of the Police," in U.S. Department of Justice, *Criminal Justice 2000*, Vol. 3 (Washington, DC: DOJ, 2000), pp. 299–370.

114. Mark E. Correla, "The Conceptual Ambiguity of Community in Community Policing: Filtering the Muddy Waters," *Policing*, Vol. 23, No. 2 (2000), pp. 218–233.

115. Adapted from Donald R. Fessler, *Facilitating Community Change: A Basic Guide* (San Diego: San Diego State University, 1976), p. 7.

116. Daniel W. Flynn, *Defining the "Community" in Community Policing* (Washington, DC: Police Executive Research Forum, 1998).

117. Robert C. Trojanowicz and Mark H. Moore, *The Meaning of Community in Community Policing* (East Lansing: Michigan State University's National Neighborhood Foot Patrol Center, 1988).

118. Robert M. Bohm, K. Michael Reynolds, and Stephen T. Holms, "Perceptions of Neighborhood Problems and Their Solutions: Implications for Community Policing," *Policing*, Vol. 23, No. 4 (2000), p. 439.

119. Ibid., p. 442.
120. Malcolm K. Sparrow, "Implementing Community Policing," *Perspectives on Policing*, No. 9 (Washington, DC: National Institute of Justice, 1988).
121. Robert Wasserman and Mark H. Moore, "Values in Policing," *Perspectives in Policing*, No. 8 (Washington, DC: National Institute of Justice, 1988), p. 7.
122. Thomas J. Deakin, "The Police Foundation: A Special Report," *FBI Law Enforcement Bulletin* (November 1986), p. 2.
123. George L. Kelling et al., *The Kansas City Patrol Experiment* (Washington, DC: Police Foundation, 1974).
124. George Kelling quoted in Kevin Krajick, "Does Patrol Prevent Crime?" *Police* (September 1978), pp. 11–13.
125. William Bieck and David Kessler, *Response Time Analysis* (Kansas City, MO: Board of Police Commissioners, 1977). See also J. Thomas McEwen et al., *Evaluation of the Differential Police Response Field Test: Executive Summary* (Alexandria, VA: Research Management Associates, 1984); and Lawrence Sherman, "Policing Communities: What Works?" in Michael Tonry and Norval Morris, eds., *Crime and Justice: An Annual Review of Research*, Vol. 8 (Chicago: University of Chicago Press, 1986), pp. 343–386.
126. Kevin Krajick, "Does Patrol Prevent Crime?" *Police Magazine* (September 1978), pp. 11–13.
127. Ibid.
128. Ibid.
129. "Evidence-Based Policing," Police Foundation press release, March 17, 1998, http://www.policefoundation.org/docs/evidence.html (accessed January 5, 2006).
130. Lawrence W. Sherman, *Evidence-Based Policing* (Washington, DC: Police Foundation, 1998), p. 3.
131. Much of the information in this section comes from Sherman, *Evidence-Based Policing.*
132. Carl J. Jensen III, "Consuming and Applying Research: Evidence-Based Policing," *Police Chief*, Vol. 73, No. 2 (February 2006), http://policechiefmagazine.org/magazine/index.cfm?fuseaction=display_arch&article_id=815&issue_id=22006 (accessed May 17, 2009).
133. Ibid.
134. University of Cambridge, "Evidence-Based Policing: Possibilities and Prospects," revised and final program announcement, June 30, 2008.
135. Bureau of Justice Assistance, "Smart Policing Initiative: Inaugural Meeting May 19–20, 2010," http://www.smartpolicinginitiative.com/sites/all/modules/modules/pubdlcnt/pubdlcnt.php?file=/sites/default/files/Smart%20Policing%20Two%20Page%20Summary.pdf&nid=11 (accessed July 20, 2012).
136. Howard Cohen, "Overstepping Police Authority," *Criminal Justice Ethics* (summer/fall 1987), pp. 52–60.
137. Kenneth Culp Davis, *Police Discretion* (St. Paul, MN: West, 1975).

Chapter 5: Policing: Legal Aspects

i. Adapted from Technical Working Group for Electronic Crime Scene Investigation, *Electronic Crime Scene Investigation: A Guide for First Responders* (Washington, DC: National Institute of Justice, 2001), p. 2.
ii. Adapted from Larry R. Leibrock, "Overview and Impact on 21st Century Legal Practice: Digital Forensics and Electronic Discovery," no date, http://www.courtroom21.net/FDIC.pps (accessed July 5, 2008).

1. Remarks of Governor Calvin Coolidge at the Worcester Police Outing, Worcester, Massachusetts (October 2, 1920).
2. Alan Blinder and Richard Perez-Pena, "6 Baltimore Police Officers Charged in Freddie Gray Death," *The New York Times*, May 1, 2015, http://www.nytimes.com/2015/05/02/us/freddie-gray-autopsy-report-given-to-baltimore-prosecutors.html.
3. "Baltimore to Pay Freddie Gray's Family $6.4 Million to Settle Civil Claims, *The Baltimore Sun*, September 8, 2015, http://www.baltimoresun.com/news/maryland/freddie-gray/bs-md-ci-boe-20150908-story.html (accessed March 16, 2016).
4. Sheryl Gay Stolberg and Jess Bidgood, "All Charges Dropped Against Baltimore Officers in Freddie Gray Case," *The New York Times*, July 27, 2016.
5. Mark Berman, Wesley Lowery, and Kimberly Kindy, "South Carolina Police Officer Charged with Murder After Shooting man during Traffic Stop," *The Washington Post*, April 7, 2015, https://www.washingtonpost.com/news/post-nation/wp/2015/04/07/south-carolina-police-officer-will-be-charged-with-murder-after-shooting.
6. Ken Murray et al., "Staten Island Man Dies After NYPD Cop Puts Him in a Chokehold," *Daily News*, July 18, 2014, http://www.nydailynews.com/new-york/staten-island-man-dies-puts-choke-hold-article-1.1871486.
7. Emily Brown, "Timeline: Michael Brown Shooting in Ferguson, Mo.," *USA Today*, August 10, 2015, http://www.usatoday.com/story/news/nation/2014/08/14/michael-brown-ferguson-missouri-timeline/14051827.
8. "Police Brutality!" Time, March 25, 1991, p. 18.
9. *Miranda* v. *Arizona*, 384 U.S. 436 (1966).
10. *Weeks* v. *U.S.*, 232 U.S. 383 (1914).
11. *Silverthorne Lumber Co.* v. *U.S.*, 251 U.S. 385 (1920).
12. *Chimel* v. *California*, 395 U.S. 752 (1969).
13. *Katz* v. *U.S.*, 389 U.S. 347, 88 S.Ct. 507 (1967).
14. *Minnesota* v. *Olson*, 110 S.Ct. 1684 (1990).
15. *Minnesota* v. *Carter*, 525 U.S. 83 (1998).
16. *Georgia* v. *Randolph*, 547 U.S. 103 (2006).
17. The ruling left open the possibility that any evidence relating to criminal activity undertaken by the consenting party might be admissible in court. In the words of the Court, refusal by a co-occupant "renders entry and search unreasonable and invalid as to him."
18. *Fernandez* v. *California*, U.S. Supreme Court, No. 12-7822 (decided February 25, 2014).
19. *Bailey* v. *U.S.*, 568 U. S. 186 (2013).
20. Nina Totenberg, "High Court Rules on Detaining Suspects, Sniffer Dogs," *NPR*, February 19, 2013, http://www.npr.org/2013/02/19/172431555/latest-supreme-court-decisions-give-police-one-victory-one-loss citing Cornell law professor Sherry Colb (accessed May 3, 2013).
21. Clemmens Bartollas, *American Criminal Justice* (New York: Macmillan, 1988), p. 186.
22. *Mapp* v. *Ohio*, 367 U.S. 643 (1961).
23. See *California* v. *Acevedo*, 500 U.S. 565 (1991); *Ornelas* v. *U.S.*, 517 U.S. 690 (1996); and others.
24. See *Edwards* v. *Balisok*, 520 U.S. 641 (1997); *Booth* v. *Churner*, 532 U.S. 731 (2001); and *Porter* v. *Nussle*, 534 U.S. 516 (2002).
25. See *Wilson* v. *Arkansas*, 115 S.Ct. 1914 (1995); and *Richards* v. *Wisconsin*, 117 S.Ct. 1416 (1997).
26. See *McCleskey* v. *Kemp*, 481 U.S. 279 (1987); *McCleskey* v. *Zant*, 499 U.S. 467, 493–494 (1991); *Coleman* v. *Thompson*, 501 U.S. 722 (1991); *Schlup* v. *Delo*, 115 S.Ct. 851, 130 L. Ed.2d 808 (1995); *Felker* v. *Turpin, Warden*, 117 S.Ct. 30, 135 L.Ed.2d 1123 (1996); *Boyde* v. *California*, 494 U.S. 370 (1990); and others.
27. See *Ewing* v. *California*, 538 U.S. 11 (2003); and *Lockyer* v. *Andrade*, 538 U.S. 63 (2003).
28. Richard Lacayo and Viveca Novak, "How Rehnquist Changed America," *Time*, June 30, 2003, pp. 20–25.

29. Erwin Chemerinsky, "The Roberts Court and Criminal Procedure at Age Five," *Texas Tech Law Review*, Vol. 43, No. 13, p. 13.
30. Ibid., p. 22.
31. *U.S.* v. *Leon*, 468 U.S. 897 (1984).
32. Judicial titles vary among jurisdictions. Many lower-level state judicial officers are called *magistrates.* Federal magistrates, however, generally have a significantly higher level of judicial authority.
33. *Massachusetts* v. *Sheppard*, 104 S.Ct. 3424 (1984).
34. *Illinois* v. *Krull*, 107 S.Ct. 1160 (1987).
35. *Maryland* v. *Garrison*, 107 S.Ct. 1013 (1987).
36. *Illinois* v. *Rodriguez*, 110 S.Ct. 2793 (1990).
37. *Arizona* v. *Evans*, 115 S.Ct. 1185, 131 L.Ed.2d 34 (1995).
38. *Herring* v. *U.S.*, 555 U.S. 135 (2009).
39. *Harris* v. *U.S.*, 390 U.S. 234 (1968).
40. The legality of plain-view seizures was also confirmed in earlier cases, including *Ker* v. *California*, 374 U.S. 23, 42–43 (1963); *U.S.* v. *Lee*, 274 U.S. 559 (1927); *U.S.* v. *Lefkowitz*, 285 U.S. 452, 465 (1932); and *Hester* v. *U.S.*, 265 U.S. 57 (1924).
41. As cited in Kimberly A. Kingston, "Look But Don't Touch: The Plain View Doctrine," *FBI Law Enforcement Bulletin* (December 1987), p. 18.
42. *Horton* v. *California*, 110 S.Ct. 2301, 47 CrL. 2135 (1990).
43. *U.S.* v. *Irizarry*, 673 F.2d 554, 556–67 (1st Cir. 1982).
44. *Arizona* v. *Hicks*, 107 S.Ct. 1149 (1987).
45. Inadvertence, as a requirement of legitimate plain-view seizures, was first cited in the U.S. Supreme Court case of *Coolidge* v. *New Hampshire*, 403 U.S. 443, 91 S.Ct. 2022 (1971).
46. *Horton* v. *California*, 110 S.Ct. 2301, 47 CrL. 2135 (1990).
47. Ibid.
48. Orin S. Kerr, "Searches and Seizures in a Digital World," *Harvard Law Review*, Vol. 119 (2005), p. 521, http://www.harvardlawreview.org/media/pdf/kerr.pdf (accessed May 1, 2013).
49. Caleb Mason, "Plain View Searches: Gen. Petraeus' Waterloo," *The Crime Report*, January 8, 2013, http://www.thecrimereport.org/viewpoints/2013-01-plain-view-searches-gen-petraeus-waterloo (accessed May 2, 2013).
50. *Brigham City* v. *Stuart*, 547 U.S. 398 (2006).
51. John Gales Sauls, "Emergency Searches of Premises," Part 1, *FBI Law Enforcement Bulletin* (March 1987), p. 23.
52. *Warden* v. *Hayden*, 387 U.S. 294 (1967).
53. Sauls, "Emergency Searches of Premises," p. 25.
54. *Maryland* v. *Buie*, 110 S.Ct. 1093 (1990).
55. *Wilson* v. *Arkansas*, 115 S.Ct. 1914 (1995).
56. For additional information, see Michael J. Bulzomi, "Knock and Announce: A Fourth Amendment Standard," *FBI Law Enforcement Bulletin* (May 1997), pp. 27–31.
57. *Richards* v. *Wisconsin*, 117 S.Ct. 1416 (1997), syllabus.
58. *Illinois* v. *McArthur*, 531 U.S. 326 (2001).
59. *U.S.* v. *Banks*, 124 S.Ct. 521 (December 2, 2003).
60. *Hudson* v. *Michigan*, 547 U.S. 586 (2006).
61. *Kentucky* v. *King*, 563 U.S. 452 (2011).
62. *U.S.* v. *Grubbs*, 547 U.S. 90 (2006).
63. *U.S.* v. *Mendenhall*, 446 U.S. 544 (1980).
64. *Stansbury* v. *California*, 511 U.S. 318 (1994).
65. *Howes* v. *Fields*, 565 U.S. 499 (2012).
66. *Yarborough* v. *Alvarado*, 541 U.S. 652 (2004).
67. *Thompson* v. *Keohane*, 516 U.S. 99, 112 (1996).
68. *Muehler* v. *Mena*, 125 S.Ct. 1465 (2005).
69. See *Michigan* v. *Summers*, 452 U.S. 692 (1981).
70. *Atwater* v. *Lago Vista*, 532 U.S. 318 (2001).
71. *Payton* v. *New York*, 445 U.S. 573 (1980).
72. In 1981, in the case of *U.S.* v. *Steagald* (451 U.S. 204), the Court ruled that a search warrant is also necessary when the planned arrest involves entry into a third party's premises.
73. *Kirk* v. *Louisiana*, 536 U.S. 635 (2002).
74. *U.S.* v. *Robinson*, 414 U.S. 218 (1973).
75. Ibid.
76. *Terry* v. *Ohio*, 392 U.S. 1 (1968).
77. *U.S.* v. *Sokolow*, 490 U.S. 1 (1989).
78. *U.S.* v. *Arvizu*, 534 U.S. 266 (2002).
79. Ibid.
80. Ibid.
81. *Minnesota* v. *Dickerson*, 508 U.S. 366 (1993).
82. *Brown* v. *Texas*, 443 U.S. 47 (1979).
83. *Hiibel* v. *Sixth Judicial District Court of Nevada*, 542 U.S. 177 (2004).
84. *Smith* v. *Ohio*, 110 S.Ct. 1288 (1990).
85. *California* v. *Hodari D.*, 111 S.Ct. 1547 (1991).
86. *Criminal Justice Newsletter*, May 1, 1991, p. 2.
87. *Illinois* v. *Wardlow*, 528 U.S. 119 (2000).
88. Ibid., syllabus, http://supct.law.cornell.edu/supct/html/98-1036.ZS.html (accessed April 1, 2010).
89. Ibid.
90. *Arkansas* v. *Sanders*, 442 U.S. 753 (1979).
91. Ibid.
92. *U.S.* v. *Borchardt*, 809 F.2d 1115 (5th Cir. 1987).
93. *FBI Law Enforcement Bulletin* (January 1988), p. 28.
94. *Carroll* v. *U.S.*, 267 U.S. 132 (1925).
95. *Preston* v. *U.S.*, 376 U.S. 364 (1964).
96. *Arizona* v. *Gant*, U.S. Supreme Court, No. 07-542 (decided April 21, 2009).
97. *South Dakota* v. *Opperman*, 428 U.S. 364 (1976).
98. *Colorado* v. *Bertine*, 479 U.S. 367, 107 S.Ct. 741 (1987).
99. *Florida* v. *Wells*, 110 S.Ct. 1632 (1990).
100. *Terry* v. *Ohio*, 392 U.S. 1 (1968).
101. *California* v. *Acevedo*, 500 U.S. 565 (1991).
102. *Ornelas* v. *U.S.*, 517 U.S. 690, 696 (1996).
103. Ibid.
104. The phrase is usually attributed to the 1991 U.S. Supreme Court case of *California* v. *Acevedo* (500 U.S. 565 [1991]). See Devallis Rutledge, "Taking an Inventory," *Police*, November 1995, pp. 8–9.
105. *Florida* v. *Jimeno*, 111 S.Ct. 1801 (1991).
106. Ibid., syllabus, http://laws.findlaw.com/us/500/248.html (accessed March 2, 2010).
107. *U.S.* v. *Ross*, 456 U.S. 798 (1982).
108. Ibid.
109. *Whren* v. *U.S.*, 517 U.S. 806 (1996).
110. See *Pennsylvania* v. *Mimms*, 434 U.S. 106 (1977).
111. *Maryland* v. *Wilson*, 117 S.Ct. 882 (1997).
112. *Brendlin* v. *California*, 551 U.S. (2007).
113. *Knowles* v. *Iowa*, 525 U.S. 113 (1998).
114. *Wyoming* v. *Houghton*, 526 U.S. 295 (1999).
115. *Thornton* v. *U.S.*, 541 U.S. 615 (2004).
116. *Illinois* v. *Caballes*, 543 U.S. 405 (2005).
117. *Davis* v. *U.S.*, U.S. Supreme Court, No. 09-11328 (decided June 16, 2011).
118. *Arizona* v. *Gant*, 556 U.S. 332 (2009).
119. *Collins* v. *Virginia*, U.S. Supreme Court, No. 16-1027 (2018).
120. *Michigan Dept. of State Police* v. *Sitz*, 110 S.Ct. 2481 (1990).
121. *U.S.* v. *Martinez-Fuerte*, 428 U.S. 543 (1976).
122. Ibid., syllabus.
123. *Illinois* v. *Lidster*, 540 U.S. 419 (2004).
124. *U.S.* v. *Villamonte-Marquez*, 462 U.S. 579 (1983).
125. *California* v. *Carney*, 471 U.S. 386, 105 S.Ct. 2066, 85 L.Ed.2d 406, 53 U.S.L.W. 4521 (1985).
126. *U.S.* v. *Hill*, 855 F.2d 664 (10th Cir. 1988).
127. *National Treasury Employees Union* v. *Von Raab*, 489 U.S. 656 (1989).

128. *Skinner* v. *Railway Labor Executives' Association*, 489 U.S. 602 (1989).

129. *Florida* v. *Bostick*, 111 S.Ct. 2382 (1991).

130. *Bond* v. *U.S.*, 529 U.S. 334 (2000).

131. *U.S.* v. *Drayton*, 122 S.Ct. 2105 (2002).

132. *U.S.* v. *Flores-Montano*, 541 U.S. 149 (2004).

133. *People* v. *Deutsch*, 96 C.D.O.S. 2827 (1996).

134. The thermal imager differs from infrared devices (such as night-vision goggles) in that infrared devices amplify the infrared spectrum of light, whereas thermal imagers register solely the portion of the infrared spectrum that we call *heat*.

135. *People* v. *Deutsch*, 96 C.D.O.S. 2827 (1996).

136. *Kyllo* v. *U.S.*, 533 U.S. 27 (2001).

137. Ibid.

138. *Aguilar* v. *Texas*, 378 U.S. 108 (1964).

139. *U.S.* v. *Harris*, 403 U.S. 573 (1971).

140. Ibid., at 584.

141. *Illinois* v. *Gates*, 426 U.S. 213 (1983).

142. *Alabama* v. *White*, 110 S.Ct. 2412 (1990).

143. Ibid., at 2417.

144. *Florida* v. *J.L.*, 529 U.S. 266 (2000).

145. *U.S. Dept. of Justice* v. *Landano*, 113 S.Ct. 2014, 124 L.Ed.2d 84 (1993).

146. Richard Willing, "Third Law First to Order Taping Murder Confessions," *USA Today*, July 18, 2003.

147. Richard A. Leo and Kimberly D. Richman, "Mandate the Electronic Recording of Police Interrogations," *Crime and Public Policy*, Vol. 6 (June 2008), http://ssrn.com/abstract= 1141335 (accessed September 8, 2010).

148. *South Dakota* v. *Neville*, 103 S.Ct. 916 (1983).

149. *Brown* v. *Mississippi*, 297 U.S. 278 (1936).

150. *Ashcraft* v. *Tennessee*, 322 U.S. 143 (1944).

151. *Chambers* v. *Florida*, 309 U.S. 227 (1940).

152. Ibid.

153. *Leyra* v. *Denno*, 347 U.S. 556 (1954).

154. *Arizona* v. *Fulminante*, 111 S.Ct. 1246 (1991).

155. *Chapman* v. *California*, 386 U.S. 18 (1967).

156. *State* v. *Fulminante*, No. CR-95-0160-AP (1999).

157. *State* v. *Henderson*, August 24, 2011.

158. *Perry* v. *New Hampshire*, U.S. Supreme Court, No. 10-8974 (decided January 11, 2012).

159. *Escobedo* v. *Illinois*, 378 U.S. 478 (1964).

160. *Edwards* v. *Arizona*, 451 U.S. 477, 101 S.Ct. 1880, 68 L.Ed.2d 378 (1981).

161. *Michigan* v. *Jackson*, 475 U.S. 625 (1986).

162. *Minnick* v. *Mississippi*, 498 U.S. 146 (1990).

163. *Arizona* v. *Roberson*, 486 U.S. 675, 108 S.Ct. 2093 (1988).

164. *Davis* v. *U.S.*, 114 S.Ct. 2350 (1994).

165. *Montejo* v. *Louisiana*, 556 U.S. 778 (2009).

166. *Maryland* v. *Shatzer*, U.S. Supreme Court, No. 08-680 (decided February 24, 2010).

167. *Miranda* v. *Arizona*, 384 U.S. 436 (1966).

168. "Immigrants Get Civil Rights," *USA Today*, June 11, 1992.

169. *U.S.* v. *Dickerson*, 166 F.3d 667 (1999).

170. *Dickerson* v. *U.S.*, 530 U.S. 428 (2000).

171. *U.S.* v. *Patane*, 542 U.S. 630 (2004).

172. *Silverthorne Lumber Co.* v. *U.S.*, 251 U.S. 385 (1920).

173. *Wong Sun* v. *U.S.*, 371 U.S. 471 (1963).

174. *Moran* v. *Burbine*, 475 U.S. 412, 421 (1986).

175. *Colorado* v. *Spring*, 479 U.S. 564, 107 S.Ct. 851 (1987).

176. *Brewer* v. *Williams*, 430 U.S. 387 (1977).

177. *Nix* v. *Williams*, 104 S.Ct. 2501 (1984).

178. *New York* v. *Quarles*, 104 S.Ct. 2626, 81 L.Ed.2d 550 (1984).

179. *Colorado* v. *Connelly*, 107 S.Ct. 515, 93 L.Ed.2d 473 (1986).

180. *Kuhlmann* v. *Wilson*, 477 U.S. 436 (1986).

181. *Illinois* v. *Perkins*, 495 U.S. 292 (1990).

182. *Rock* v. *Zimmerman*, 543 F.Supp. 179 (M.D. Pa. 1982).

183. Ibid.

184. See *Oregon* v. *Mathiason*, 429 U.S. 492, 97 S.Ct. 711 (1977).

185. *Arizona* v. *Mauro*, 107 S.Ct. 1931, 95 L.Ed.2d 458 (1987).

186. *Doyle* v. *Ohio*, 426 U.S. 610 (1976).

187. *Brecht* v. *Abrahamson*, 113 S.Ct. 1710, 123 L.Ed.2d 353 (1993).

188. Citing *Kotteakos* v. *U.S.*, 328 U.S. 750 (1946).

189. *Missouri* v. *Seibert*, 542 U.S. 600 (2004).

190. *Florida* v. *Powell*, 599 U.S. 50 (2010).

191. *Berghuis* v. *Thompkins*, 560 U.S. 370 (2010).

192. *Salinas* v. *Texas*, U.S. Supreme Court, No. 12-246 (decided June 17, 2013).

193. *Hayes* v. *Florida*, 470 U.S. 811, 105 S.Ct. 1643 (1985).

194. *Winston* v. *Lee*, 470 U.S. 753, 105 S.Ct. 1611 (1985).

195. *Schmerber* v. *California*, 384 U.S. 757 (1966).

196. "Man Coughs up Cocaine while in Custody," *Police Magazine*, March 4, 2005, http://www.policemag.com/t_newspick. cfm?rank574703 (accessed January 4, 2007).

197. *U.S.* v. *Montoya de Hernandez*, 473 U.S. 531, 105 S.Ct. 3304 (1985).

198. Ibid.

199. *Olmstead* v. *U.S.*, 277 U.S. 438 (1928).

200. *On Lee* v. *U.S.*, 343 U.S. 747 (1952).

201. *Lopez* v. *U.S.*, 373 U.S. 427 (1963).

202. *Berger* v. *New York*, 388 U.S. 41 (1967).

203. *Katz* v. *U.S.*, 389 U.S. 347 (1967).

204. *Lee* v. *Florida*, 392 U.S. 378 (1968).

205. Federal Communications Act of 1934, 47 U.S.C. Section 151.

206. *U.S.* v. *White*, 401 U.S. 745 (1971).

207. *U.S.* v. *Karo*, 468 U.S. 705 (1984).

208. *U.S.* v. *Scott*, 436 U.S. 128 (1978).

209. For more information, see *FBI Law Enforcement Bulletin* (June 1987), p. 25.

210. Electronic Communications Privacy Act of 1986, Public Law 99–508.

211. For more information on the ECPA, see Robert A. Fiatal, "The Electronic Communications Privacy Act: Addressing Today's Technology," *FBI Law Enforcement Bulletin* (April 1988), pp. 24–30.

212. Communications Assistance for Law Enforcement Act of 1994, Public Law 103–414.

213. Federal Bureau of Investigation, "Notice: Implementation of the Communications Assistance for Law Enforcement Act," February 23, 1995.

214. Administrative Office of the United States Courts, *2016 Wiretap Report*, http://www.uscourts.gov/statistics-reports/ wiretap-report-2016 (accessed July 20, 2018).

215. Telecommunications Act of 1996, Public Law 104, 110 Stat. 56.

216. Title 47, U.S.C.A., Section 223(a)(1)(B)(ii) (Supp. 1997).

217. *Reno* v. *ACLU*, 117 S.Ct. 2329 (1997).

218. 18 U.S.C. Section 1030.

219. Section 202.

220. 18 U.S.C. Section 2703(c).

221. Ibid.

222. Public Law 109–177.

223. Jim Abrams, "Patriot Act Extension Signed By Obama," *Associated Press*, May 27, 2011, https://www.huffingtonpost. com/2011/05/27/patriot-act-extension-signed-obama- autopen_n_867851.html (accessed June 13, 2018).

224. S. 754: Cybersecurity Information Sharing Act of 2015.

225. Adapted from Technical Working Group for Electronic Crime Scene Investigation, *Electronic Crime Scene Investigation: A Guide for First Responders* (Washington, DC: National Institute of Justice, 2001), from which much of the information in this section is taken.

226. Ibid., p. 2.

227. Computer Crime and Intellectual Property Section, U.S. Department of Justice, *Searching and Seizing Computers and Obtaining Electronic Evidence in Criminal Investigations*

(Washington, DC: U.S. Department of Justice, 2002), http://www.usdoj.gov/criminal/cybercrime/s&smanual2002.htm (accessed August 4, 2007).

228. Technical Working Group, *Electronic Crime Scene Investigation*, p. 2.

229. Technical Working Group for the Examination of Digital Evidence, *Forensic Examination of Digital Evidence: A Guide for Law Enforcement* (Washington, DC: National Institute of Justice, 2004).

230. *U.S.* v. *Carey*, 172 F.3d 1268 (10th Cir. 1999).

231. *U.S.* v. *Turner*, 169 F.3d 84 (1st Cir. 1999).

232. *Riley* v. *California*, U.S. Supreme Court (decided June 25, 2014).

Chapter 6: Policing: Issues and Challenges

i. Carl B. Klockars et al., "The Measurement of Police Integrity," National Institute of Justice Research in Brief (Washington, DC: NIJ, 2000), p. 1.

ii. Technical Working Group on Crime Scene Investigation, *Crime Scene Investigation: A Guide for Law Enforcement* (Washington, DC: National Institute of Justice, 2000), p. 12.

iii. Angus Smith, ed., *Intelligence-Led Policing* (Richmond, VA: International Association of Law Enforcement Intelligence Analysts, 1997), p. 1.

iv. Office of Justice Programs, *The National Criminal Intelligence Sharing Plan* (Washington, DC: U.S. Department of Justice, 2005), p. 27.

v. Adapted from Gerald Hill and Kathleen Hill, *The Real Life Dictionary of the Law*, http://www.law.com (accessed September 10, 2016).

vi. National Institute of Justice, *Use of Force by Police: Overview of National and Local Data* (Washington, DC: NIJ, 1999).

vii. International Association of Chiefs of Police, *Police Use of Force in America, 2001* (Alexandria, VA: IACP, 2001), p. 1.

viii. Samuel Walker, Geoffrey P. Albert, and Dennis J. Kenney, *Responding to the Problem Police Officer: A National Study of Early Warning Systems* (Washington, DC: National Institute of Justice, 2000).

ix. Sam W. Lathrop, "Reviewing Use of Force: A Systematic Approach," *FBI Law Enforcement Bulletin* (October 2000), p. 18.

1. Joel Leson, *Assessing and Managing the Terrorism Threat* (Washington, DC: U.S. Department of Justice, 2005).

2. "Caring and Courage: 2012 Heroes among Us Awards," *People*, December 17, 2012, p. 95.

3. Janine Rauch and Etienne Marasis, "Contextualizing the Waddington Report," http://www.wits.ac.za/csvr/papers/papwadd.html (accessed January 5, 2009).

4. Jerome H. Skolnick, *Justice without Trial: Law Enforcement in a Democratic Society* (New York: John Wiley, 1966).

5. William A. Westley, *Violence and the Police: A Sociological Study of Law, Custom, and Morality* (Cambridge, MA: MIT Press, 1970); and William A. Westley, "Violence and the Police," *American Journal of Sociology*, Vol. 49 (1953), pp. 34–41.

6. Arthur Niederhoffer, *Behind the Shield: The Police in Urban Society* (Garden City, NY: Anchor, 1967).

7. Thomas Barker and David L. Carter, *Police Deviance* (Cincinnati, OH: Anderson, 1986). See also Christopher P. Wilson, *Cop Knowledge: Police Power and Cultural Narrative in Twentieth-Century America* (Chicago: University of Chicago Press, 2000).

8. Richard Bennett and Theodore Greenstein, "The Police Personality: A Test of the Predispositional Model," *Journal of Police Science and Administration*, Vol. 3 (1975), pp. 439–445.

9. James Teevan and Bernard Dolnick, "The Values of the Police: A Reconsideration and Interpretation," *Journal of Police Science and Administration* (1973), pp. 366–369.

10. Bennett and Greenstein, "The Police Personality," pp. 439–445.

11. Jasmine R. Silver, Sean Patrick Roche, Thomas J. Bilach and Stephanie Bontrager Ryon, "Traditional Police Culture, Use of Force, and Procedural Justice: Investigating Individual, Organizational, and Contextual Factors," *Justice Quarterly,* Vol. 34, No. 7 (2017), pp. 1272–1309.

12. Jessica Lussenhop, "Who Were the Corrupt Baltimore Police Officers?" BBC News, February 13, 2018; http://www.bbc.com/news/world-us-canada-43035628 (accessed September 10, 2018).

13. Carl B. Klockars et al., "The Measurement of Police Integrity," *National Institute of Justice Research in Brief* (Washington, DC: NIJ, 2000), p. 1.

14. Michael J. Palmiotto, ed., *Police Misconduct: A Reader for the Twenty-First Century* (Upper Saddle River, NJ: Prentice Hall, 2001), preface.

15. Tim Prenzler and Peta Mackay, "Police Gratuities: What the Public Thinks," *Criminal Justice Ethics* (winter/spring 1995), pp. 15–25.

16. Thomas Barker and David L. Carter, *Police Deviance* (Cincinnati, OH: Anderson, 1986). For a detailed overview of the issues involved in police corruption, see Victor E. Kappeler, Richard D. Sluder, and Geoffrey P. Alpert, *Forces of Deviance: Understanding the Dark Side of Policing*, 2nd ed. (Prospect Heights, IL: Waveland Press, 1998); Dean J. Champion, *Police Misconduct in America: A Reference Handbook* (Santa Barbara, CA: ABC-CLIO, 2002); and Kim Michelle Lersch, ed., *Policing and Misconduct* (Upper Saddle River, NJ: Prentice Hall, 2002).

17. Frank L. Perry, "Repairing Broken Windows: Preventing Corruption within Our Ranks," *FBI Law Enforcement Bulletin* (February 2001), pp. 23–26.

18. "Nationline: NYC Cops—Excess Force Not Corruption," *USA Today*, June 16, 1995.

19. *Knapp Commission Report on Police Corruption* (New York: George Braziller, 1973).

20. U.S. Department of Justice, Civil Rights Division, *Investigation of the Baltimore City Police Department* (Washington, DC: USDOJ, 2016).

21. Sabrina Tavernise, "Victory for Officer Who Aided Corruption Inquiry," *The New York Times*, April 3, 2004.

22. Edwin H. Sutherland and Donald Cressey, *Principles of Criminology*, 8th ed. (Philadelphia: J. B. Lippincott, 1970).

23. Tim R. Jones, Compton Owens, and Melissa A. Smith, "Police Ethics Training: A Three-Tiered Approach," *FBI Law Enforcement Bulletin* (June 1995), pp. 22–26.

24. U.S. Department of Justice, *Principles for Promoting Police Integrity: Examples of Promising Police Practices* (Washington, DC: DOJ, 2001).

25. National Institute of Justice, *Enhancing Police Integrity* (Washington, DC: U.S. Department of Justice, 2005).

26. Ibid., p ii.

27. International Association of Chiefs of Police, *Employee Drug Testing* (St. Paul, MN: IACP, 1999).

28. Tom Hays, "NYPD to Start Random Steroid Testing," *Associated Press*, April 9, 2008, http://www.wtopnews.com/?sid=1383781&nid=104 (accessed July 24, 2008).

29. *Maurice Turner* v. *Fraternal Order of Police*, 500 A.2d 1005 (D.C. 1985).

30. *Philip Caruso, President of P.B.A.* v. *Benjamin Ward, Police Commissioner*, New York State Supreme Court, Pat. 37, Index no. 12632-86, 1986.

31. *National Treasury Employees Union* v. *Von Raab*, 489 U.S. 656, 659 (1989).

32. "LEO Mental Health Act Signed into Law by President Trump," Police Magazine, January 10, 2018; http://www.policemag.com/channel/patrol/news/2018/01/10/leo-mental-health-act-signed-into-law-by-president-trump.aspx (accessed May 20, 2018).

33. Hope M. Tiesman, et al., "Nonfatal Injuries to Law Enforcement Officers: A Rise in Assaults," American Journal of Preventative Medicine, Feb., 2018; http://www.ajpmonline.org/article/S0749-3797(17)30716-X/fulltext (accessed July 10, 2018).

34. Officer Down Memorial Page, https://www.odmp.org/search/year?year=2017 (accessed June 15, 2018).

35. Officer Down Memorial Page, https://www.odmp.org/search/year?year=2001 (accessed January 16, 2002).

36. Anthony J. Pinizzotto and Edward F. Davis, "Cop Killers and Their Victims," FBI Law Enforcement Bulletin (December 1992), p. 10.

37. Bureau of Justice Statistics, "Local Police Departments, 2013" (May 2015). Note that the LEMAS report only includes data from approximately 700 state and local law enforcement agencies that employ 100 or more full-time sworn personnel and that assign 50 or more of these officers to respond to calls for service. LEMAS reports finding 477,000 sworn personnel among those departments in its 2013 survey. BLS data are more comprehensive and include part-time personnel.

38. Brian A. Reaves, Federal Law Enforcement Officers, 2008 (Washington, DC: Bureau of Justice Statistics, 2012).

39. Mark Judge, "Montel Williams: 'No Civilized Society Can Tolerate Shooting at Cops'," CNS News, July 8, 2016, https://www.cnsnews.com/blog/mark-judge/montel-williams-no-civilized-society-can-tolerate-shooting-cops (accessed July 10, 2018).

40. AIDS and Our Workplace, New York City Police Department pamphlet, November 1987.

41. See Occupational Safety and Health Administration, OSHA Bloodborne Pathogens Act of 1991 (29 CFR 1910.1030).

42. National Institute of Justice Reports, No. 206 (November/December 1987).

43. "Suicides, Resignations Hit New Orleans' Thin Blue Line," USA Today, September 4, 2005, http://www.usatoday.com/news/nation/2005-09-04-neworleanspolicesuicides_x.htm (accessed April 2, 2006).

44. Ibid.

45. See "On-the-Job Stress in Policing: Reducing It, Preventing It," National Institute of Justice Journal (January 2000), pp. 18–24.

46. "Stress on the Job," Newsweek, April 25, 1988, p. 43.

47. "On-the-Job Stress in Policing," National Institute of Justice Journal, January 2000, p. 19.

48. Kevin Barrett, "Police Suicide: Is Anyone Listening?" Journal of Safe Management of Disruptive and Assaultive Behavior (spring 1997), pp. 6–9.

49. For an excellent review of coping strategies among police officers, see Robin N. Haarr and Merry Morash, "Gender, Race, and Strategies of Coping with Occupational Stress in Policing," Justice Quarterly, Vol. 16, No. 2 (June 1999), pp. 303–336.

50. Mark H. Anshel, "A Conceptual Model and Implications for Coping with Stressful Events in Police Work," Criminal Justice and Behavior, Vol. 27, No. 3 (2000), p. 375.

51. Ibid.

52. Bryan Vila, "Tired Cops: Probable Connections between Fatigue and the Performance, Health, and Safety of Patrol Officers," American Journal of Police, Vol. 15, No. 2 (1996), pp. 51–92.

53. Bryan Vila et al., Evaluating the Effects of Fatigue on Police Patrol Officers: Final Report (Washington, DC: National Institute of Justice, 2000).

54. Bryan Vila and Dennis Jay Kenney, "Tired Cops: The Prevalence and Potential Consequences of Police Fatigue," National Institute of Justice Journal, No. 248 (2002), p. 19.

55. Bryan Vila and Erik Y. Taiji, "Fatigue and Police Officer Performance," paper presented at the annual meeting of the American Society of Criminology, Chicago, 1996.

56. Police Executive Research Forum, Local Law Enforcement's Role in Preventing and Responding to Terrorism (Washington, DC: PERF, October 2, 2001), http://www.policeforum.org/terrorismfinal.doc (accessed June 1, 2003).

57. Council on Foreign Relations, "Terrorism Questions and Answers: Police Departments," http://www.terrorismanswers.com/security/police.html (accessed April 19, 2005).

58. Ibid.

59. Michael Weissenstein, "NYPD Shifts Focus to Terrorism, Long Considered the Turf of Federal Agents," Associated Press, March 21, 2003, http://www.nj.com/newsflash/national/index.ssf?/cgi-free/getstory_ssf.cgi?a0801_BC_NYPD-Counterterror&&news&newsflash-national (accessed May 25, 2003).

60. Ibid.

61. Robert J. Jordan (FBI), Congressional Statement on Information Sharing before the U.S. Senate Committee on the Judiciary, Subcommittee on Administrative Oversight and the Courts, Washington, DC, April 17, 2002, http://www.fbi.gov/congress/congress02/jordan041702.htm (accessed April 19, 2006).

62. The concept of intelligence-led policing appears to have been first fully articulated in Angus Smith, ed., Intelligence-Led Policing (Richmond, VA: International Association of Law Enforcement Intelligence Analysts, 1997).

63. David L. Carter, Law Enforcement Intelligence: A Guide for State, Local, and Tribal Law Enforcement Agencies (Washington, DC: U.S. Department of Justice, 2004), p. 7.

64. Much of the information and some of the wording in this section are taken from Carter, Law Enforcement Intelligence.

65. David L. Carter, "The Law Enforcement Intelligence Function," FBI Law Enforcement Bulletin, Vol. 74, No. 6 (June 2005), pp. 1–10.

66. Governor's Commission on Criminal Justice Innovation, Final Report (Boston: Governor's Commission, 2004), p. 57, from which much of the wording in the rest of this paragraph is taken.

67. DATA.GOV, Law Enforcement Online, https://catalog.data.gov/dataset/law-enforcement-online (accessed September 1, 2018).

68. Bernard H. Levin, "Sharing Information: Some Open Secrets and a Glimpse at the Future," Police Futurist, Vol. 14, No. 1 (winter 2006), pp. 8–9.

69. The plan was an outgrowth of the IACP Criminal Intelligence Sharing Summit held in Alexandria, Virginia, in March 2002. Results of the summit are documented in International Association of Chiefs of Police, Recommendations from the IACP Intelligence Summit, Criminal Intelligence Sharing.

70. Office of Justice Programs, The National Criminal Intelligence Sharing Plan (Washington, DC: U.S. Department of Justice, 2003).

71. Details for this story come from David Heinzmann, "Committee to Consider Settling Cop Misconduct Cases for Nearly $33 Million," Chicago Tribune, http://www.chicagotribune.com/news/local/breaking/chi-emanuel-seeks-to-settle-2-cop-misconduct-cases-for-nearly-33-million-20130114,0,4742395,full.story, January 15, 2013.

72. Charles R. Swanson, Leonard Territo, and Robert W. Taylor, Police Administration: Structures, Processes, and Behavior, 2nd ed. (New York: Macmillan, 1988).

73. Malley v. Briggs, 475 U.S. 335, 106 S.Ct. 1092 (1986).

74. Ibid., at 4246.

75. Biscoe v. Arlington County, 238 U.S. App. D.C. 206, 738 F.2d 1352, 1362 (1984). See also 738 F.2d 1352 (D.C. Cir.

1984), *cert. denied*; 469 U.S. 1159; and 105 S.Ct. 909, 83 L.E.2d 923 (1985).

76. Civil Rights Division, U.S. Dept. of Justice, *Investigation of the New Orleans Police Department*, p. xii.

77. John Hill, "High-Speed Police Pursuits: Dangers, Dynamics, and Risk Reduction," *FBI Law Enforcement Bulletin* (July 2002), pp. 14–18.

78. *City of Canton, Ohio* v. *Harris*, 489 U.S. 378 (1989).

79. Ibid., at 1204.

80. *Board of the County Commissioners of Bryan County, Oklahoma* v. *Brown*, 520 U.S. 397 (1997).

81. *County of Los Angeles* v. *Mendez*, U.S. Supreme Court, No. 16-369; decided May 30, 2017.

82. U.S. Code, Title 42, Section 1983.

83. *Bivens* v. *Six Unknown Federal Agents*, 403 U.S. 388 (1971).

84. See *F.D.I.C.* v. *Meyer*, 510 U.S. 471 (1994), in which the U.S. Supreme Court reiterated its ruling under *Bivens*, stating that only government employees and not government agencies can be sued.

85. *Wyler* v. *U.S.*, 725 F.2d 157 (2d Cir. 1983).

86. California Government Code, Section 818.

87. Federal Tort Claims Act, 28 U.S.C. 1346(b), 2671–2680.

88. *Elder* v. *Holloway*, 114 S.Ct. 1019, 127 L.Ed.2d 344 (1994).

89. Ibid.

90. *Hunter* v. *Bryant*, 112 S.Ct. 534 (1991).

91. William U. McCormack, "Supreme Court Cases: 1991–1992 Term," *FBI Law Enforcement Bulletin* (November 1992), p. 30.

92. *Saucier* v. *Katz*, 533 U.S. 194 (2001).

93. See also *Brosseau* v. *Haugen*, 543 U.S. 194 (2004).

94. *Scott* v. *Harris*, 550 U.S. 372 (2007).

95. *Mullenix* v. *Luna*, 77 U. S. ____ (2015).

96. *White* v. *Pauly*, 580 U.S. ___, ___ (2017).

97. *Idaho* v. *Horiuchi*, 253 F.3d 359 (9th Cir. 2001).

98. Police Executive Research Forum, *Civil Rights Investigations of Local Police: Lessons Learned* (Washington, DC: PERF, 2013), pp. 6–7.

99. For more information on police liability, see Daniel L. Schofield, "Legal Issues of Pursuit Driving," *FBI Law Enforcement Bulletin* (May 1988), pp. 23–29.

100. Michael S. Vaughn, Tab W. Cooper, and Rolando V. del Carmen, "Assessing Legal Liabilities in Law Enforcement: Police Chiefs' Views," *Crime and Delinquency*, Vol. 47, No. 1 (2001), p. 3.

101. PERF, *Civil Rights Investigations of Local Police*, p. 8.

102. Howard Cohen, "Overstepping Police Authority," *Criminal Justice Ethics* (summer/fall 1987), pp. 52–60.

103. Kenneth Culp Davis, *Police Discretion* (St. Paul, MN: West, 1975).

104. Adapted from Deborah Ramirez, Jack McDevitt, and Amy Farrell, *A Resource Guide on Racial Profiling Data Collection Systems: Promising Practices and Lessons Learned* (Washington, DC: U.S. Department of Justice, 2000), p. 3.

105. Ibid.

106. David Harris, *Driving while Black: Racial Profiling on Our Nation's Highways* (Washington, DC: American Civil Liberties Union, 1999).

107. "Justice Department Bars Race Profiling, with Exception for Terrorism," *Criminal Justice Newsletter* (July 15, 2003), pp. 6–7.

108. "Justice Department Issues Policy Guidance to Ban Racial Profiling," U.S. Department of Justice press release (No. 355), June 17, 2003.

109. David Cole and John Lambreth, "The Fallacy of Racial Profiling," *The New York Times* Online, May 13, 2001, http://college1.nytimes.com/buests/articles/2001/05/13/846196.xml (accessed August 28, 2004).

110. Rob Tillyer, "Opening the Black Box of Officer Decision-Making: An Examination of Race, Criminal History, and Discretionary Searches," *Justice Quarterly*, 2014.

111. Amitai Etzioni, "Another Side of Racial Profiling," *USA Today*, May 21, 2001.

112. Gallup Poll Organization, "Racial Profiling Seen as Pervasive, Unjust," July 20, 2004, http://www.gallup.com/poll/12406/Racial-Profiling-Seen-Pervasive-Unjust.aspx (accessed August 1, 2010).

113. Ramirez, McDevitt, and Farrell, *A Resource Guide on Racial Profiling Data Collection Systems*, p. 3.

114. Sid Heal, "The ABC3s," *The Tactical Edge*, Fall 2004, pp. 36-39

115. Police Executive Research Forum, *Racially Biased Policing: A Principled Response* (Washington, DC: PERF, 2001).

116. Ibid., foreword.

117. Ibid., p. 39.

118. Ibid., p. 47.

119. Sarl Horwitz, "Justice Department Launches Broad Investigation of Baltimore Police," *Washington Post*, May 8, 2015.

120. Some of the material in this section is adapted or derived from National Institute of Justice, *Use of Force by Police: Overview of National and Local Data* (Washington, DC: NIJ, 1999).

121. National Consensus Policy on Use of Force (2017). The policy resulted from a joint effort by 11 law enforcement leadership groups, including: the Association of State Criminal Investigative Agencies, the Commission on Accreditation for Law Enforcement Agencies, the Fraternal Order of Police, the Federal Law Enforcement Officers Association, the International Association of Chiefs of Police, the Hispanic American Police Command Officers Association, the International Association of Directors of Law Enforcement Standards and Training, the National Association of Police Organizations, the National Association of Women Law Enforcement Executives, the National Organization of Black Law Enforcement Executives, and the National Tactical Officers Association.

122. Ibid.

123. International Association of Chiefs of Police, *Police Use of Force in America, 2001* (Alexandria, VA: IACP, 2001), p. 1.

124. Kenneth Adams, "What We Know about Police Use of Force," in National Institute of Justice, *Use of Force by Police*, p. 4.

125. International Association of Chiefs of Police, *Police Use of Force in America, 2001*.

126. Geoffrey P. Alpert and Roger G. Dunham, *The Force Factor: Measuring Police Use of Force Relative to Suspect Resistance—A Final Report* (Washington, DC: National Institute of Justice, 2001).

127. Charlie Mesloh, Mark Henych, and Ross Wolf, "Less Lethal Weapon Effectiveness, Use of Force, and Suspect & Officer Injuries: A Five-Year Analysis," Report to the National Institute of Justice, September 2008, p. 9.

128. Samuel Walker, Geoffrey P. Alpert, and Dennis J. Kenney, *Responding to the Problem Police Officer: A National Study of Early Warning Systems* (Washington, DC: National Institute of Justice, 2000).

129. See Human Rights Watch, "The Christopher Commission Report," from which some of the wording in the paragraph is adapted, http://www.hrw.org/reports98/police/uspo73.htm (accessed March 30, 2002).

130. J. David Goodman, "Bratton Says New York Police Dept. Must Dismiss Bad Officers," *The New York Times*, October 2, 2014.

131. U.S. Department of Justice press release, "Justice Department Outlines Plan to Enable Nationwide Collection of Use of Force Data," October 13, 2016.

132. Sam W. Lathrop, "Reviewing Use of Force: A Systematic Approach," *FBI Law Enforcement Bulletin* (October 2000), p. 18.

133. *Tennessle* v. *Garner*, 471 U.S. 1 (1985).

134. *Graham* v. *Connor*, 490 U.S. 386, 396–397 (1989).

135. *Kisela* v. *Hughes*, 584 U.S. ____ (2018).

136. John C. Hall, "FBI Training on the New Federal Deadly Force Policy," *FBI Law Enforcement Bulletin* (April 1996), pp. 25–32.

137. James Fyfe, *Shots Fired: An Examination of New York City Police Firearms Discharges* (Ann Arbor, MI: University Microfilms, 1978).

138. James Fyfe, "Blind Justice? Police Shootings in Memphis," paper presented at the annual meeting of the Academy of Criminal Justice Sciences, Philadelphia, March 1981.

139. It is estimated that American police shoot at approximately 3,600 people every year. See William Geller, *Deadly Force* study guide, Crime File Series (Washington, DC: National Institute of Justice, n.d.).

140. Anne Cohen, "I've Killed That Man Ten Thousand Times," *Police Magazine* (July 1980).

141. For more information, see Joe Auten, "When Police Shoot," *North Carolina Criminal Justice Today*, Vol. 4, No. 4 (summer 1986), pp. 9–14.

142. Details for this story come from Stephanie Slater, "Suicidal Man Killed by Police Fusillade," *Palm Beach Post*, March 11, 2005, p. 1A.

143. Rebecca Stincelli, *Suicide by Cop: Victims from Both Sides of the Badge* (Folsom, CA: Interviews and Interrogations Institute, 2004).

144. Slater, "Suicidal Man Killed by Police Fusillade."

145. Anthony J. Pinizzotto, Edward F. Davis, and Charles E. Miller III, "Suicide by Cop: Defining a Devastating Dilemma," *FBI Law Enforcement Bulletin*, Vol. 74, No. 2 (February 2005), p. 15.

146. "Ten Percent of Police Shootings Found to Be 'Suicide by Cop,'" *Criminal Justice Newsletter* (September 1, 1998), pp. 1–2.

147. Robert J. Homant and Daniel B. Kennedy, "Suicide by Police: A Proposed Typology of Law Enforcement Officer–Assisted Suicide," *Policing: An International Journal of Police Strategies and Management*, Vol. 23, No. 3 (2000), pp. 339–355.

148. David Hambling, "Flash Gun," *Science News*, May 10–16, 2008, pp. 38–40.

149. David W. Hayeslip and Alan Preszler, "NIJ Initiative on Less-Than-Lethal Weapons," *NIJ Research in Brief* (Washington, DC: National Institute of Justice, 1993).

150. Ibid.

151. Thomas Farragher and David Abel, "Postgame Police Projectile Kills an Emerson Student," *Boston Globe*, October 22, 2004, http://www.boston.com/sports/baseball/redsox/articles/2004/10/22/postgame_police_projectile_kills_an_emerson_student (accessed July 25, 2005).

152. Michael Siegfried, "Notes on the Professionalization of Private Security," *Justice Professional* (spring 1989).

153. See Edward A. Farris, "Five Decades of American Policing, 1932–1982: The Path to Professionalism," *Police Chief* (November 1982), p. 34.

154. E-mail communication with Maya Mitchell, Commission on Accreditation for Law Enforcement Agencies, Dated: March 6, 2018.

155. *CALEA Update*, No. 81 (February 2003), http://www.calea.org/newweb/newsletter/No81/81index.htm (accessed May 21, 2003).

156. Brian A. Reaves, *State and Local Law Enforcement Training Academies, 2013* (Washington, DC: Bureau of Justice Statistics, 2016).

157. Information in this paragraph comes from "PTO Program," COPS Office, U.S. Department of Justice (no date), http://www.cops.usdoj.gov/print.asp?Item=461 (accessed June 3, 2007).

158. Ibid.

159. National Commission on Law Observance and Enforcement, *Report on Police* (Washington, DC: U.S. Government Printing Office, 1931).

160. President's Commission on Law Enforcement and Administration of Justice, *The Challenge of Crime in a Free Society* (Washington, DC: U.S. Government Printing Office, 1967).

161. National Advisory Commission on Criminal Justice Standards and Goals, *Report on the Police* (Washington, DC: U.S. Government Printing Office, 1973).

162. Reaves, *Law Enforcement Management and Administrative Statistics (2015)*.

163. Ibid.

164. Brian A. Reaves and Matthew J. Hickman, *Police Departments in Large Cities, 1990–2000* (Washington, DC: Bureau of Justice Statistics, 2002), p. 1.

165. "Dallas PD College Rule Gets Final OK," *Law Enforcement News* (July 7, 1986), pp. 1, 13.

166. *Davis* v. *Dallas*, 777 F.2d 205 (5th Cir. 1985).

167. David L. Carter, Allen D. Sapp, and Darrel W. Stephens, *The State of Police Education: Policy Direction for the Twenty-First Century* (Washington, DC: Police Executive Research Forum, 1989), pp. xxii–xxiii.

168. "Chicago Police Rolling Out New, Mandatory 'De-escalation' Training," *Chicago Tribune,* September 17, 2016; http://www.chicagotribune.com/news/ct-chicago-police-training-met-20160916-story.html (accessed August 28, 2018).

169. National Advisory Commission on Criminal Justice Standards and Goals, *Report on the Police*, p. 238.

170. Matthew J. Hickman and Brian A. Reaves, *Local Police Departments, 2003* (Washington, DC: Bureau of Justice Statistics, 2006), p. 5.

171. Matthew J. Hickman and Brian A. Reaves, *Local Police Departments, 2000* (Washington, DC: Bureau of Justice Statistics, 2003), p. 270.

172. August Vollmer, *The Police and Modern Society* (Berkeley: University of California Press, 1936), p. 222.

173. O. W. Wilson and Roy Clinton McLaren, *Police Administration*, 4th ed. (New York: McGraw-Hill, 1977), p. 259.

174. *Report of the National Advisory Commission on Civil Disorders* (New York: E. P. Dutton, 1968), p. 332.

175. Brian A. Reaves, *Local Police Departments, 2007.* (Washington, DC: Bureau of Justice Statistics, 2010).

176. U.S. Census Bureau, *National Population Estimates: Characteristics*, http://www.census.gov/popest/national/asrh/NC-EST2005-srh.html.

177. U.S. Department of Justice, *Advancing Diversity in Law Enforcement*, (Washington, DC: USDOJ, 2016).

178. Ibid.

179. Lynn Langston, *Women in Law Enforcement, 1987–2008* (Washington, DC: Bureau of Justice Statistics, June 2010).

180. National Center for Women and Policing, *Recruiting and Retaining Women: A Self-Assessment Guide for Law Enforcement* (Los Angeles: NCWP, 2001), p. 22.

181. Ibid.

182. Mary Dodge, "Women in Policing: Time to Forget the Differences and Focus on the Future," *Criminal Justice Research Reports* (July/August 2007), p. 82.

183. C. Lee Bennett, "Interviews with Female Police Officers in Western Massachusetts," paper presented at the annual meeting of the Academy of Criminal Justice Sciences, Nashville, TN, March 1991.

184. Ibid., p. 9.

185. Carole G. Garrison, Nancy K. Grant, and Kenneth L. J. McCormick, "Utilization of Police Women," unpublished manuscript.

186. Susan Ehrlich Martin and Nancy C. Jurik, *Doing Justice, Doing Gender: Women in Law and Criminal Justice Occupations* (Thousand Oaks, CA: Sage, 1996).

Chapter 7: The Courts

1. *The Challenge of Crime in a Free Society: Report of The President's Commission on Law Enforcement and the Administration of Justice* (Washington, DC: USGPO, 1967), p. 125.

2. Patrik Jonsson, "Forsyth County Courthouse Shooting: Dennis Marx Plotted 'Sovereign Citizen' Attack," June 7, 2014, https://

www.csmonitor.com/USA/2014/0607/Forsyth-County-Courthouse-shooting-Dennis-Marx-plotted-sovereign-citizen-attack (accessed October 11, 2018).

3. Ibid.

4. Law Enforcement Assistance Administration, *Two Hundred Years of American Criminal Justice* (Washington, DC: U.S. Government Printing Office, 1976), p. 31.

5. David B. Rottman, Carol R. Flango, and R. Shedine Lockley, *State Court Organization, 1993* (Washington, DC: Bureau of Justice Statistics, 1995), p. 11.

6. In 1957, only 13 states had permanent intermediate appellate courts. Now, all but 12 states have these courts, and North Dakota is operating one on a temporary basis to assist in handling the rising appellate caseload in that state. See Rottman, Flango, and Lockley, *State Court Organization, 1993*, p. 5.

7. *Keeney* v. *Tamayo-Reyes*, 504 U.S. 1 (1992).

8. *Herrera* v. *Collins*, 113 S.Ct. 853, 122 L.Ed.2d 203 (1993).

9. Martin Wright, *Justice for Victims and Offenders* (Bristol, PA: Open University Press, 1991), p. 56.

10. Suzanne M. Strong, Ramona R. Rantala, and Tracey Kyckelhahn, *Census of Problem-Solving Courts, 2012* (Washington, DC: BJS, 2016).

11. Greg Berman and John Feinblatt. *Good Courts* (New York: The New Press, 2005).

12. "Bridging the Gap between Communities and Courts," http://www.communityjustice.org (accessed November 22, 2018).

13. M. Somjen Frazer, *The Impact of the Community Court Model on Defendant Perceptions of Fairness: A Case Study at the Red Hook Community Justice Center* (New York: Center for Court Innovation, 2006).

14. Cynthia G. Lee, Fred L. Cheesman II, David B. Rottman, Rachel Swaner, Survi Lambson, Mike Rempel, and Ric Curtis, *A Community Court Grows in Brooklyn: A Comprehensive Evaluation of the Red Hook Community Justice Center* (Williamsburg, VA: National Center for State Courts, 2013).

15. Center for Court Innovation, "About," https://www.courtinnovation.org/about (accessed July 20, 2018).

16. Adapted from National Institute of Justice, "Specialized Courts," http://www.nij.gov/topics/courts/specialized-courts.htm (accessed July 20, 2018).

17. Rekha Mirchandani, "What's So Special About Specialized Courts? The State and Social Change in Salt Lake City's Domestic Violence Court," *Law and Society Review*, Vol. 39, No. 2 (2005), p. 379.

18. Most of the information and some of the wording in this section come from Administrative Office of the U.S. Courts, "Understanding the Federal Courts," http://www.uscourts.gov/sites/default/files/understanding-federal-courts.pdf (accessed October 11, 2018).

19. Administrative Office of the U.S. Courts, "Federal Judicial Caseload Statistics 2017," http://www.uscourts.gov/statistics-reports/federal-judicial-caseload-statistics-2017 (accessed June 11, 2018).

20. Ibid.

21. Administrative Office of the U.S. Courts, "Judicial Compensation," http://www.uscourts.gov/judges-judgeships/judicial-compensation (accessed October 20, 2018).

22. Ibid.

23. Much of the information and some of the wording in this section come from Administrative Office of the U.S. Courts, "About the Federal Courts," http://www.uscourts.gov/about-federal-courts (accessed September 10, 2018).

24. Stephen L. Wasby, *The Supreme Court in the Federal Judicial System*, 3rd ed. (Chicago: Nelson-Hall, 1988), p. 58.

25. *The Supreme Court of the United States* (Washington, DC: U.S. Government Printing Office, n.d.), p. 4.

26. *Marbury* v. *Madison*, 1 Cranch 137 (1803).

27. *Arraignment* is also a term used to describe an initial appearance, although we will reserve use of that word to describe a later court appearance following the defendant's indictment by a grand jury or the filing of an information by the prosecutor.

28. *McNabb* v. *U.S.*, 318 U.S. 332 (1943).

29. *County of Riverside* v. *McLaughlin*, 500 U.S. 44 (1991).

30. *White* v. *Maryland*, 373 U.S. 59 (1963).

31. *Rothgery* v. *Gillespie County, Texas*, 554 U.S. 191 (2008).

32. Much of the information in this section comes from Barry Mahoney et al., *Pretrial Services Programs: Responsibilities and Potential* (Washington, DC: National Institute of Justice, 2001).

33. *Taylor* v. *Taintor*, 83 U.S. 66 (1873).

34. National Advisory Commission on Criminal Justice Standards and Goals, *The Courts* (Washington, DC: U.S. Government Printing Office, 1973), p. 37.

35. C. Ares, A. Rankin, and H. Sturz, "The Manhattan Bail Project: An Interim Report on the Use of Pretrial Parole," *New York University Law Review*, Vol. 38 (January 1963), pp. 68–95.

36. H. Zeisel, "Bail Revisited," *American Bar Foundation Research Journal*, Vol. 4 (1979), pp. 769–789.

37. Ibid.

38. "Twelve Percent of Those Freed on Low Bail Fail to Appear," *The New York Times*, December 2, 1983.

39. Bureau of Justice Statistics, *Report to the Nation on Crime and Justice*, 2nd ed. (Washington, DC: U.S. Department of Justice, 1988), p. 76.

40. Tracey Kyckelhahn and Thomas H. Cohen, *Felony Defendants in Large Urban Counties, 2004* (Washington, DC: Bureau of Justice Statistics, 2008), p. 2, https://www.bjs.gov/content/pub/pdf/fdluc04.pdf (accessed June 4, 2018). See also Thomas H. Cohen and Brian A. Reaves, *Pretrial Release of Felony Defendants in State Courts* (Washington, DC: Bureau of Justice Statistics, 2007).

41. Cohen and Reaves, *Pretrial Release of Felony Defendants In State Courts*, https://www.bjs.gov/content/pub/pdf/prfdsc.pdf (accessed June 8, 2018).

42. Thomas H. Cohen, *Pretrial Release and Misconduct in Federal District Courts, 2008–2010* (Washington, DC: Bureau of Justice Statistics, 2012), p. 1, https://www.bjs.gov/content/pub/pdf/prmfdc0810.pdf (accessed June 8, 2018).

43. Donald E. Pryor and Walter F. Smith, "Significant Research Findings Concerning Pretrial Release," *Pretrial Issues*, Vol. 4, No. 1 (Washington, DC: Pretrial Services Resource Center, February 1982). See also the Pretrial Justice Institute on the Web at http://www.pretrial.org/Pages.

44. BJS, *Report to the Nation on Crime and Justice*, p. 77.

45. Mariel Alper, Matthew R. Durose, and Joshua Markham, "2018 *Update on Prisonere Recidivism: A 9-Year Follow-up Period (2005–2014)*" (U.S. Department of Justice, 2018).

46. According to Joseph B. Vaughn and Victor E. Kappeler, the first such legislation was the 1970 District of Columbia Court Reform and Criminal Procedure Act. See Vaughn and Kappeler, "The Denial of Bail: Pre-trial Preventive Detention," *Criminal Justice Research Bulletin*, Vol. 3, No. 6 (Huntsville, TX: Sam Houston State University, 1987), p. 1.

47. Ibid.

48. 18 U.S.C. 3141.

49. Bail Reform Act of 1984, 18 U.S.C. 3142(e).

50. *U.S.* v. *Montalvo-Murillo*, 495 U.S. 711 (1990).

51. Ibid., syllabus.

52. *U.S.* v. *Hazzard*, 35 CrL. 2217 (1984).

53. See, for example, *U.S.* v. *Motamedi*, 37 CrL. 2394, CA 9 (1985).

54. A few states now have laws that permit the defendant to appear before the grand jury.

55. John M. Scheb and John M. Scheb II, *American Criminal Law* (St. Paul, MN: West, 1996), p. 31.

56. Ibid.
57. The information in this paragraph is adapted from Linda Greenhouse, "Supreme Court Limits Forced Medication of Some for Trial," *The New York Times*, June 16, 2003, http://www.nytimes.com/2003/06/17/politics/17DRUG.html (accessed June 17, 2018).
58. *Sell* v. *U.S.*, 123 S.Ct. 2174 (2003).
59. Federal Rules of Criminal Procedure, Rule 5.1(a).
60. Scheb and Scheb, *American Criminal Law*, p. 32.
61. Gary Fields and John R. Emshwiller, "Federal Guilty Pleas Soar as Bargains Trump Trials," *The Wall Street Journal*, September 23, 2012, http://online.wsj.com/article/SB10000872396390443589304577637610097206808.html (accessed April 1, 2018).
62. Ibid.
63. *Kercheval* v. *U.S.*, 274 U.S. 220, 223, 47 S.Ct. 582, 583 (1927); *Boykin* v. *Alabama*, 395 U.S. 238 (1969); and *Dickerson* v. *New Banner Institute, Inc.*, 460 U.S. 103 (1983).
64. Ronald F. Wright and Paul Hofer, analysis of Bureau of Justice Statistics data from: Erica Goode, "Stronger Hand for Judges in the 'Bazaar' of Plea Deals," *The New York Times*, March 22, 2012, https://www.nytimes.com/2012/03/23/us/stronger-hand-for-judges-after-rulings-on-plea-deals.html (accessed March 23, 2018).
65. *Santobello* v. *New York*, 404 U.S. 257 (1971).
66. *Mabry* v. *Johnson*, 467 U.S. 504 (1984).
67. *U.S.* v. *Baldacchino*, 762 F.2d 170 (1st Cir. 1985); *U.S.* v. *Reardon*, 787 F.2d 512 (10th Cir. 1986); and *U.S.* v. *Donahey*, 529 F.2d 831 (11th Cir. 1976).
68. *Missouri* v. *Frye*, U.S. Supreme Court, No. 10-444 (decided March 21, 2012), and *Lafler* v. *Cooper*, U.S. Supreme Court, No. 10-209 (decided March 21, 2012).
69. For a classic discussion of such considerations, see David Sudnow, "Normal Crimes: Sociological Features of the Penal Code in a Public Defender Office," *Social Problems*, Vol. 123, No. 3 (winter 1965), p. 255.
70. Federal Rules of Criminal Procedure, No. 11.

Chapter 8: The Courtroom Work Group and the Criminal Trial

i. President's Commission on Law Enforcement and Administration of Justice, *The Challenge of Crime in a Free Society* (Washington, DC: U.S. Government Printing Office, 1967), p. 125.
ii. Quoted in Richard Willing, "Courts Try to Make Jury Duty Less of a Chore," *USA Today*, March 17, 2005.
iii. *Victor* v. *Nebraska*, 114 S.Ct. 1239, 127 L.Ed.2d 583 (1994).
iv. As found in California jury instructions.

1. D. Graham Burnett, "Anatomy of a Verdict: The View from a Juror's Chair," *New York Times Magazine*, August 26, 2001.
2. Virnelli Mercader, "Jodi Arias Prison Update: No More Contact Visit Privileges After Calling Prison Guard a Vulgar Word," *Christian Today*, February 16, 2016, http://www.christiantoday.com/article/jodi.arias.prison.update.convicted.killer.loses.contact.visit.privileges.after.calling.prison.guard.a.vulgar.word/79530.htm (accessed September 10, 2018).
3. Michelle Washington, "Five Things to Get You Up to Speed in Jodi Arias Trial," *USA Today*, May 6, 2013, https://www.usatoday.com/story/news/nation/2013/05/06/jodi-arias-trial-five-things/2138823 (accessed September 10, 2018).
4. See, for example, Jeffrey T. Ulmer, *Social Worlds of Sentencing: Court Communities under Sentencing Guidelines* (Ithaca: State University of New York Press, 1997); and Roy B. Flemming, Peter F. Nardulli, and James Eisenstein, *The Craft of Justice: Politics and Work in Criminal Court Communities* (Philadelphia: University of Pennsylvania Press, 1993).
5. See, for example, Edward J. Clynch and David W. Neubauer, "Trial Courts as Organizations," *Law and Policy Quarterly*, Vol. 3 (1981), pp. 69–94.
6. American Bar Association, *ABA Standards for Criminal Justice: Special Functions of the Trial Judge*, 3rd ed. (Chicago: ABA, 2000).
7. In 1940, Missouri became the first state to adopt a plan for the "merit selection" of judges based on periodic public review.
8. National Judicial College, "About the NJC," http://www.judges.org/about (accessed May 2, 2018).
9. See National Judicial College, "Master's and Ph.D.,", http://www.judges.org/academic/masters-and-ph-d (accessed May 22, 2018).
10. "Nonlawyer Judges and the Professionalization of Justice: Should an Endangered Species Be Preserved?" *Journal of Contemporary Criminal Justice*, No. 17 (February 2001), pp. 19–36; see also Ron Malega and Thomas H. Cohen, *State Court Organization, 2011* (Washington, DC: BJS, 2013), p. 5.
11. Town and village justices in New York State serve part-time and may or may not be lawyers; judges of all other courts must be lawyers, whether or not they serve full-time. From New York State Commission on Judicial Conduct, *2016 Annual Report*, http://www.scjc.state.ny.us/Publications/AnnualReports/nyscjc.2016annualreport.pdf (accessed May 21, 2018).
12. Ibid.
13. Bureau of Justice Statistics, *Report to the Nation on Crime and Justice: The Data* (Washington, DC: U.S. Department of Justice, 1983).
14. For a discussion of the resource limitations that district attorneys face in combating corporate crime, see Michael L. Benson et al., "District Attorneys and Corporate Crime: Surveying the Prosecutorial Gatekeepers," *Criminology*, Vol. 26, No. 3 (August 1988), pp. 505–517.
15. Carol J. DeFrances and Greg W. Steadman, *Prosecutors in State Courts, 1996* (Washington, DC: Bureau of Justice Statistics, 1998).
16. Kenneth Culp Davis, *Discretionary Justice* (Baton Rouge: Louisiana State University Press, 1969), p. 190.
17. Barbara Borland, *The Prosecution of Felony Arrests* (Washington, DC: Bureau of Justice Statistics, 1983).
18. *Brady* v. *Maryland*, 373 U.S. 83 (1963).
19. *U.S.* v. *Bagley*, 473 U.S. 667 (1985).
20. *Banks* v. *Dretke*, 540 U.S. 668 (2004).
21. *Imbler* v. *Pachtman*, 424 U.S. 409 (1976).
22. *Burns* v. *Reed*, 500 U.S. 478 (1991).
23. Ibid., complaint, p. 29.
24. *Van de Kamp* v. *Goldstein*, 129 S.Ct. 855 (2009).
25. Cassia Spohn, John Gruhl, and Susan Welch, "The Impact of the Ethnicity and Gender of Defendants on the Decision to Reject or Dismiss Felony Charges," *Criminology*, Vol. 25, No. 1 (1987), pp. 175–191.
26. Brad Heath and Kevin McCoy, "Justice Dept. Office to Punish Prosecutors' Misconduct," *USA Today*, January 19, 2011, p. 1A.
27. American Bar Association Center for Professional Responsibility, *Model Rules of Professional Conduct* (Chicago: ABA, 2003), p. 87.
28. The same is true under federal law, and in almost all of the states, of communications between defendants and members of the clergy, psychiatrists and psychologists, medical doctors, and licensed social workers in the course of psychotherapy. See, for example, *Jaffee* v. *Redmond*, 518 U.S. 1 (1996).
29. *Powell* v. *Alabama*, 287 U.S. 45 (1932).
30. *Johnson* v. *Zerbst*, 304 U.S. 458 (1938).

31. *Gideon* v. *Wainwright*, 372 U.S. 335 (1963).
32. *Argersinger* v. *Hamlin*, 407 U.S. 25 (1972).
33. *In re Gault*, 387 U.S. 1 (1967).
34. *Alabama* v. *Shelton*, 535 U.S. 654 (2002).
35. New York State Supreme Court, Appellate Division, Assigned Counsel Plan (18B), http://www.nycourts.gov/courts/ad1/Committees&Programs/18B/index.shtml (accessed June 5, 2018).
36. Erinn Herberman and Tracey Kyckelhahn, State Government Indigent Defense Expenditures, FY 2008–2012—Updated (Washington, DC: October 24, 2014).
37. Ibid.
38. National Symposium on Indigent Defense, *Improving Criminal Justice Systems through Expanded Strategies and Innovative Collaborations* (Washington, DC: Office of Justice Programs, 2000); see also Bureau of Justice Statistics, Stephen D. Owens, et. al., *Indigent Defense Services in the United States, FY 2008–2012,* revised April 21, 2015, https://www.bjs.gov/content/pub/pdf/idsus0812.pdf (accessed September 7, 2018).
39. Carol J. DeFrances, *State-Funded Indigent Defense Services* (Washington, DC: National Institute of Justice, 2001).
40. "Nationline: McVeigh's Defense Cost Taxpayers $13.8 Million," *USA Today*, July 3, 2001.
41. *Faretta* v. *California*, 422 U.S. 806 (1975).
42. S. K. Smith and C. J. DeFrances, *Indigent Defense* (Washington, DC: Bureau of Justice Statistics, 1996), pp. 2–3.
43. *Anders* v. *California*, 386 U.S. 738 (1967).
44. *People* v. *Wende*, 25 Cal.3d 436, 600 P.2d 1071 (1979).
45. *Smith* v. *Robbins*, 528 U.S. 259 (2000).
46. *Texas* v. *Cobb*, 532 U.S. 162 (2001).
47. Details for this story come from Chisun Lee, "Punishing Mmes. Stewart: The Parallel Universes of Martha and Lynne," *Village Voice*, February 15, 2005, http://www.refuseandresist.org/article-print.php?aid51757 (accessed January 5, 2006).
48. Scott Shifrel and James Fanelli, "Lynn Stewart, 70-Year-Old Radical Lawyer, Sentenced to 10 years in Prison for Aiding Bomb Plotter," *Daily News*, July 16, 2010, http://www.nydailynews.com/new-york/lynn-stewart-70-year-old-radical-lawyer-sentenced-10-years-prison-aiding-bomb-plotter-article-1.466192 (accessed July 31, 2013).
49. "Justice for Lynne Stewart," http://lynnestewart.org (accessed September 10, 2018).
50. "Lawyer Convicted of Terrorist Support," *USA Today*, February 11, 2005.
51. Mike McKee, "California State Bar to Allow Lawyers to Break Confidentiality," *The Recorder*, May 17, 2004, http://www.law.com/jsp/article.jsp?id51084316038367 (accessed August 25, 2005).
52. *Nix* v. *Whiteside*, 475 U.S. 157 (1986).
53. Ibid.
54. President's Commission on Law Enforcement and Administration of Justice, *The Challenge of Crime in a Free Society* (Washington, DC: U.S. Government Printing Office, 1967), p. 129.
55. National Advisory Commission on Criminal Justice Standards and Goals, *Courts* (Washington, DC: U.S. Government Printing Office, 1973), Standard 9.3.
56. See, for example, Joan G. Brannon, *The Judicial System in North Carolina* (Raleigh, NC: Administrative Office of the United States Courts, 1984), p. 14.
57. *Daubert* v. *Merrell Dow Pharmaceuticals, Inc.*, 509 U.S. 579 (1993).
58. *Melendez-Diaz* v. *Massachusetts*, 557 U.S. 305 (2009).
59. *Bullcoming* v. *New Mexico*, U.S. Supreme Court, No. 09-10876 (decided June 23, 2011).
60. Joseph L. Peterson, "Use of Forensic Evidence by the Police and Courts," *Research in Brief* (Washington, DC: National Institute of Justice, 1987), p. 3.
61. Ibid., p. 6.
62. *California* v. *Green*, 399 U.S. 149 (1970).
63. Patrick L. McCloskey and Ronald L. Schoenberg, *Criminal Law Deskbook* (New York: Matthew Bender, 1988), Section 17, p. 123.
64. USLEGAL.com, "Compensation And Fees For Attendance", https://witnesses.uslegal.com/compensation-and-fees-for-attendance (accessed September 7, 2018)
65. 28 U.S. Code, Section 1821 (accessed May 22, 2018).
66. Anna Johnson, "Jury with Oprah Winfrey Convicts Man of Murder," *Associated Press*, August 19, 2004.
67. *Demarest* v. *Manspeaker et al.*, 498 U.S. 184 (1991).
68. Bureau of Justice Statistics, *Report to the Nation on Crime and Justice*.
69. Johnson, "Jury with Oprah Winfrey Convicts Man of Murder."
70. *Williams* v. *Florida*, 399 U.S. 78 (1970).
71. *Smith* v. *Texas*, 311 U.S. 128 (1940). That right does not apply when the defendants are facing the possibility of a prison sentence less than six months in length or even when the potential aggregate sentence for multiple petty offenses exceeds six months (see *Lewis* v. *U.S.*, 518 U.S. 322 [1996]).
72. *Thiel* v. *Southern Pacific Co.*, 328 U.S. 217 (1945).
73. American Bar Association, *Principles for Juries and Jury Trials* (Chicago: ABA, 2005).
74. The author was himself the victim of a felony some years ago. His car was stolen in Columbus, Ohio, and recovered a year later in Cleveland. He was informed that the person who had taken it was in custody, but he never heard what happened to him, nor could he learn where or whether a trial was to be held.
75. Federal Rules of Criminal Procedure, Rule 43.
76. *Crosby* v. *U.S.*, 113 S.Ct. 748, 122 L.Ed.2d 25 (1993).
77. *Zafiro* v. *U.S.*, 113 S.Ct. 933, 122 L.Ed.2d 317 (1993).
78. *Nebraska Press Association* v. *Stuart*, 427 U.S. 539 (1976).
79. However, it is generally accepted that trial judges may issue limited gag orders aimed at trial participants.
80. *Press Enterprise Company* v. *Superior Court of California, Riverside County*, 478 U.S. 1 (1986).
81. *Caribbean International News Corporation* v. *Puerto Rico*, 508 U.S. 147 (1993).
82. *Chandler* v. *Florida*, 499 U.S. 560 (1981).
83. Rule 53 of the Federal Rules of Criminal Procedure reads, "Except as otherwise provided by a statute or these rules, the court must not permit the taking of photographs in the courtroom during judicial proceedings or the broadcasting of judicial proceedings from the courtroom."
84. Harry F. Rosenthal, "Courts-TV," *Associated Press*, September 21, 1994. See also "Judicial Conference Rejects Cameras in Federal Courts," *Criminal Justice Newsletter*, September 15, 1994, p. 6.
85. Bill Mears, "Supreme Court Secretly Recorded on Camera," CNN, https://www.cnn.com/2014/02/27/politics/supreme-court-video/index.html (accessed April 21, 2018).
86. Marc G. Gertz and Edmond J. True, "Social Scientists in the Courtroom: The Frustrations of Two Expert Witnesses," in Susette M. Talarico, ed., *Courts and Criminal Justice: Emerging Issues* (Beverly Hills, CA: Sage, 1985), pp. 81–91.
87. Dotson was the first person convicted of a crime (rape) to be exonerated by DNA evidence. Kirk Bloodsworth, whose case is discussed in a CJ News box in the next chapter, was the first death row inmate to be exonerated through the use of DNA analysis. Richard Buckland, a 17-year-old English teenager with learning disabilities, was likely the first person whose innocence was demonstrated through the use of DNA analysis. Although Buckland was a suspect in two rape

cases, he had not been convicted at the time DNA evidence proved his innocence.

88. Samuel R. Gross et al., "Exonerations in the United States, 1989 through 2003," April 4, 2004, http://www.mindfully.org/Reform/2004/Prison-Exonerations-Gross19apr04.htm (accessed May 24, 2007).

89. *Klopfer* v. *North Carolina*, 386 U.S. 213 (1967).

90. *Barker* v. *Wingo*, 407 U.S. 514 (1972).

91. *Strunk* v. *U.S.*, 412 U.S. 434 (1973).

92. Speedy Trial Act, 18 U.S.C. 3161 (1974); Public Law 93–619.

93. *U.S.* v. *Taylor*, 487 U.S. 326 (1988).

94. *Fex* v. *Michigan*, 507 U.S. 43 (1993).

95. *Doggett* v. *U.S.*, 112 S.Ct. 2686 (1992).

96. *Padilla* v. *Hanft*, No. 05-533, *cert. denied*.

97. See, for example, the U.S. Supreme Court's decision in the case of *Murphy* v. *Florida*, 410 U.S. 525 (1973).

98. *Witherspoon* v. *Illinois*, 391 U.S. 510 (1968).

99. *Mu'Min* v. *Virginia*, 500 U.S. 415 (1991).

100. Federal Rules of Criminal Procedure, Rule 24(6).

101. Learn more about shadow juries from Molly McDonough, "Me and My Shadow: Shadow Juries Are Helping Litigators Shape Their Cases during Trial," *National Law Journal* (May 17, 2001).

102. Although the words *argument* and *statement* are sometimes used interchangeably to refer to opening remarks, defense attorneys are enjoined from drawing conclusions or "arguing" to the jury at this stage in the trial. Their task, as described in the section that follows, is simply to explain to the jury how the defense will be conducted.

103. Supreme Court majority opinion in *Powers* v. *Ohio*, 499 U.S. 400 (1991), citing *Strauder* v. *West Virginia*, 100 U.S. 303 (1880).

104. *Swain* v. *Alabama*, 380 U.S. 202 (1965).

105. *Batson* v. *Kentucky*, 476 U.S. 79 (1986).

106. *Ford* v. *Georgia*, 498 U.S. 411 (1991), footnote 2.

107. *Powers* v. *Ohio*, 499 U.S. 400 (1991).

108. *Georgia* v. *McCollum*, 505 U.S. 42 (1992).

109. *J. E. B.* v. *Alabama*, 511 U.S. 127 (1994).

110. See, for example, *Davis* v. *Minnesota*, 511 U.S. 1115 (1994).

111. *Campbell* v. *Louisiana*, 523 U.S. 392 (1998).

112. *Miller-El* v. *Cockrell*, 537 U.S. 322 (2003).

113. *Miller-El* v. *Dretke*, 545 U.S. 231 (2005).

114. *Snyder* v. *Louisiana*, 552 U.S. 472 (2008).

115. *U.S.* v. *Dinitz*, 424 U.S. 600, 612 (1976).

116. *Michigan* v. *Lucas*, 500 U.S. 145 (1991).

117. *Kotteakos* v. *U.S.*, 328 U.S. 750 (1946); *Brecht* v. *Abrahamson*, 113 S.Ct. 1710, 123 L.Ed.2d 353 (1993); and *Arizona* v. *Fulminante*, 111 S.Ct. 1246 (1991).

118. The Court, citing *Kotteakos* v. *U.S.*, 328 U.S. 750 (1946), in *Brecht* v. *Abrahamson*, 507 U.S. 619 (1993).

119. *Sullivan* v. *Louisiana*, 508 U.S. 275 (1993).

120. *Griffin* v. *California*, 380 U.S. 609 (1965).

121. *Ohio* v. *Reiner*, 532 U.S. 17 (2001).

122. Leading questions may, in fact, be permitted for certain purposes, including refreshing a witness's memory, impeaching a hostile witness, introducing undisputed material, and helping a witness with impaired faculties.

123. *In re Oliver*, 333 U.S. 257 (1948).

124. *Coy* v. *Iowa*, 487 U.S. 1012 (1988).

125. *Maryland* v. *Craig*, 497 U.S. 836, 845–847 (1990).

126. *Idaho* v. *Wright*, 497 U.S. 805 (1990).

127. *White* v. *Illinois*, 503 U.S. 346 (1992).

128. *Crawford* v. *Washington*, 541 U.S. 36 (2004).

129. *Davis* v. *Washington*, 547 U.S. 813 (2006). See also *Hammon* v. *Indiana*, 547 U.S. 813 (2006).

130. *Davis* v. *Washington*, syllabus.

131. Federal Rules of Criminal Procedure, Rule 29.1.

132. See *Johnson* v. *Louisiana*, 406 U.S. 356 (1972); and *Apodaca* v. *Oregon*, 406 U.S. 404 (1972).

133. *Allen* v. *U.S.*, 164 U.S. 492 (1896).

134. Judge Harold J. Rothwax, *Guilty: The Collapse of Criminal Justice* (New York: Random House, 1996).

135. Amiram Elwork, Bruce D. Sales, and James Alfini, *Making Jury Instructions Understandable* (Charlottesville, VA: Michie, 1982).

136. "King Jury Lives in Fear from Unpopular Verdict," *Fayetteville (N.C.) Observer-Times*, May 10, 1992.

137. "Los Angeles Trials Spark Debate Over Anonymous Juries," *Criminal Justice Newsletter* (February 16, 1993), pp. 3–4.

Chapter 9: Sentencing

i. Lawrence A. Greenfeld, *Prison Sentences and Time Served for Violence, Bureau of Justice Statistics Selected Findings, No. 4* (Washington, DC: Bureau of Justice Statistics, April 1995).

ii. "Fireside chat" with U.S. Supreme Court Justices John Paul Stevens and Stephen Breyer, Fifty-third Annual Meeting of the Seventh Circuit Bar Association and Judicial Conference of the Seventh Circuit, Chicago, May 9, 2004.

iii. *Payne* v. *Tennessee*, 501 U.S. 808 (1991).

iv. *Furman* v. *Georgia*, 408 U.S. 238 (1972).

---

1. New Jersey Senate Bill 677 (January 1, 2018).

2. Matt Smith, "'Racial Justice Act' Repealed in North Carolina," CNN, June 21, 2013, http://www.cnn.com/2013/06/20/justice/north-carolina-death-penalty (accessed August 2, 2018).

3. Marc Mauer, "Racial Impact Statements: Changing Policies to Address Disparities," *Criminal Justice*, Vol. 23, No. 4 (winter 2009).

4. For a thorough discussion of the philosophy of punishment and sentencing, see David Garland, *Punishment and Modern Society: A Study in Social Theory* (Chicago: University of Chicago Press, 1990). See also Ralph D. Ellis and Carol S. Ellis, *Theories of Criminal Justice: A Critical Reappraisal* (Wolfeboro, NH: Longwood Academic, 1989); and Colin Summer, *Censure, Politics, and Criminal Justice* (Bristol, PA: Open University Press, 1990).

5. Punishment is said to be required because social order (and the laws that represent it) could not exist for long if transgressions went unsanctioned.

6. Hugo Adam Bedau, "Retributivism and the Theory of Punishment," *Journal of Philosophy*, Vol. 75 (November 1978), pp. 601–620.

7. The definitive study during this period was Douglas Lipton, Robert Martinson, and J. Woks, *The Effectiveness of Correctional Treatment: A Survey of Treatment Valuation Studies* (New York: Praeger, 1975).

8. The National Reentry Resource Center, *Reducing Recidivism: States Deliver Results (2017),* June 9, 2017; https://csgjusticecenter.org/nrrc/publications/reducing-recidivism-states-deliver-results-2017 (accessed August 28, 2018).

9. Gordon Bazemore and Mark S. Umbreit, foreword to *Balanced and Restorative Justice: Program Summary* (Washington, DC: Office of Juvenile Justice and Delinquency Prevention, 1994).

10. Shay Bilchik, *Balanced and Restorative Justice for Juveniles: A Framework for Juvenile Justice in the 21st Century* (Washington, DC: Office of Juvenile Justice and Delinquency Prevention, 1997), p. ii.

11. Ibid., p. 14.

12. Ibid.

13. U.S. Code, Title 18, Section 3563(a)(2).

14. Donna Hunzeker, "State Sentencing Systems and 'Truth in Sentencing,'" *State Legislative Report*, Vol. 20, No. 3 (Denver: National Conference of State Legislatures, 1995).

15. Paula M. Ditton and Doris James Wilson, *Truth in Sentencing in State Prisons* (Washington, DC: Bureau of Justice Statistics, 1999).

16. "Oklahoma Rapist Gets 30,000 Years," *United Press International*, southwest edition, December 23, 1994.

17. For a historical consideration of alleged disparities, see G. Kleck, "Racial Discrimination in Criminal Sentencing: A Critical Evaluation of the Evidence with Additional Evidence on the Death Penalty," *American Sociological Review*, No. 46 (1981), pp. 783–805; and G. Kleck, "Life Support for Ailing Hypotheses: Modes of Summarizing the Evidence for Racial Discrimination in Sentencing," *Law and Human Behavior*, No. 9 (1985), pp. 271–285.

18. National Council on Crime and Delinquency, *National Assessment of Structured Sentencing* (Washington, DC: Bureau of Justice Administration, 1996).

19. Kelly Lyn Mitchell, "State Sentencing Guidelines: A Garden Full of Variety," *Federal Probation*, September, 2017, pp. 28–36.

20. As discussed later in this chapter, federal sentencing guidelines did not become effective until 1987 and still had to meet many court challenges.

21. Lawrence A. Greenfeld, *Prison Sentences and Time Served for Violence* (Washington, DC: Bureau of Justice Statistics, April 1995).

22. U.S. Sentencing Commission, *Federal Sentencing Guidelines Manual* (Washington, DC: U.S. Government Printing Office, 1987), p. 2.

23. Inmates can still earn a maximum of 54 days per year of good-time credit.

24. The Parole Commission Phaseout Act of 1996 requires the attorney general to report to Congress yearly as to whether it is cost-effective for the Parole Commission to remain a separate agency or whether its functions (and personnel) should be assigned elsewhere. Under the law, if the attorney general recommends assigning the Parole Commission's functions to another component of the Department of Justice, federal parole will continue as long as necessary.

25. For an excellent review of the act and its implications, see Gregory D. Lee, "U.S. Sentencing Guidelines: Their Impact on Federal Drug Offenders," *FBI Law Enforcement Bulletin*, May 1995, pp. 17–21.

26. *Mistretta* v. *U.S.*, 488 U.S. 361, 371 (1989).

27. For an engaging overview of how mitigating factors might be applied under the guidelines, see *Koon* v. *U.S.*, 518 U.S. 81 (1996).

28. U.S. Sentencing Commission, *Federal Sentencing Guidelines Manual*, p. 207.

29. *Deal* v. *U.S.*, 589 U.S. 129 (1993).

30. U.S. Sentencing Commission, *Federal Sentencing Guidelines Manual*, p. 8.

31. National Institute of Justice, *Sentencing Commission Chairman Wilkins Answers Questions on the Guidelines*, NIJ Research in Action Series (Washington, DC: NIJ, 1987), p. 7.

32. *Melendez* v. *U.S.*, 518 U.S. 20 (1996).

33. *Apprendi* v. *New Jersey*, 530 U.S. 466 (2000).

34. See, for example, Alexandra A. E. Shapiro and Jonathan P. Bach, "Applying 'Apprendi' to Federal Sentencing Rules," *New York Law Journal*, March 23, 2001, http://www.lw.com/pubs/articles/pdf/applyingApprendi.pdf (accessed June 30, 2007); and Freya Russell, "Limiting the Use of Acquitted and Uncharged Conduct at Sentencing: *Apprendi* v. *New Jersey* and Its Effect on the Relevant Conduct Provision of the United States Sentencing Guidelines," *California Law Review*, Vol. 89 (July 2001), p. 1199.

35. *Harris* v. *U.S.*, 536 U.S. 545 (2002).

36. *U.S.* v. *O'Brien*, U.S. Supreme Court, No. 08-1569 (decided May 24, 2010).

37. *Blakely* v. *Washington*, 542 U.S. 296 (2004). Blakely was convicted in 2005 of plotting to hire hit men to kill his ex-wife and daughter from his jail cell. He was sentenced to 35 years in prison.

38. RCW 9.94A.537.

39. *Cunningham* v. *California*, 549 U.S. 270 (2007).

40. *U.S.* v. *Booker*, 543 U.S. 220 (2005).

41. Combined with *U.S.* v. *Booker* (2005).

42. Stanley E. Adelman, "Supreme Court Invalidates Federal Sentencing Guidelines . . . to an Extent," *On the Line*, newsletter of the American Correctional Association (May 2005), p. 1.

43. See *U.S.* v. *Rodriguez*, 398 F.3d 1291, 1297 (11th Cir. 2005).

44. *Kimbrough* v. *U.S.*, 552 U.S. 85 (2007), syllabus.

45. *Gall* v. *U.S.*, 552 U.S. 38 (2007).

46. *Rita* v. *U.S.*, 551 U.S. 338 (2007).

47. *Alleyne* v. *U.S.*, U.S. Supreme Court, No. 11-9335 (decided June 17, 2013).

48. The *Alleyne* case overturned the Court's earlier ruling in *Harris* v. *U.S.* (2002), which held that "judicial factfinding that increases the mandatory minimum sentence for a crime is permissible under the Sixth Amendment."

49. United States Sentencing Commission, *Report to Congress: Mandatory Minimum Penalties in the Federal Criminal Justice System*, October 2011, http://www.ussc.gov/Legislative_and_Public_Affairs/Congressional_Testimony_and_Reports/Mandatory_Minimum_Penalties/20111031_RtC_Mandatory_Minimum.cfm (accessed August 10, 2018).

50. Michael Miller, "California Gets 'Three Strikes' Anti-Crime Bill," Reuters, March 7, 1994.

51. Tamar Lewin, "Three-Strikes Law Is Overrated in California, Study Finds," *The New York Times*, August 23, 2001, http://query.nytimes.com/gst/fullpage.html?res=9505E7DB1531F930A1575BC0A9679C8B63 (accessed September 2, 2009).

52. Bruce Smith, "Crime Solutions," *Associated Press*, January 11, 1995.

53. *Ewing* v. *California*, 538 U.S. 11 (2003); and *Lockyer* v. *Andrade*, 538 U.S. 63 (2003).

54. Under California law, a person who commits petty theft can be charged with a felony if he or she has prior felony convictions. The charge is known as "petty theft with prior convictions." Andrade's actual sentence was two 25-year prison terms to be served consecutively.

55. Jill Castellano, et al., "Two Years After Prop. 47, Addicts Walk Free with Nowhere to Go," The Desert Sun, http://www.desertsun.com/story/news/crime_courts/2016/12/14/prop-47-california-addiction/94083338 (accessed January 17, 2018).

56. Much of the material in this section is derived from Dale Parent et al., *Mandatory Sentencing*, NIJ Research in Action Series (Washington, DC: NIJ, 1997).

57. In mid-1996, the California Supreme Court ruled the state's three-strikes law an undue intrusion into judges' sentencing discretion, and California judges now use their own discretion in evaluating which offenses "fit" within the meaning of the law.

58. Michael Tonry, *Sentencing Reform Impacts* (Washington, DC: National Institute of Justice, 1987).

59. D. C. McDonald and K. E. Carlson, *Sentencing in the Courts: Does Race Matter? The Transition to Sentencing Guidelines, 1986–90* (Washington, DC: Bureau of Justice Statistics, 1993).

60. U.S. Sentencing Commission, *Special Report to Congress: Cocaine and Federal Sentencing Policy* (Washington, DC: U.S. Sentencing Commission, May 2007).

61. Fair Sentencing Act of 2010, Public Law 111–22.

62. "Changes Lead to Shorter Sentences for 26,000 Drug Defendants," CBS News, http://www.cbsnews.com/news/changes-lead-to-shorter-sentences-for-26000-drug-defendants, April 14, 2016 (accessed March 31, 2018).

63. Michael Mitchell and Michael Leachman, Changing Priorities: State Criminal Justice Reforms and Investments in Education (Washington, DC: Center on Budget and Policy Priorities, 2014).

64. Richard Willing, "Thief Challenges Dose of Shame as Punishment," *USA Today*, August 18, 2004.

65. John Braithwaite, *Crime, Shame, and Reintegration* (Cambridge, England: Cambridge University Press, 1989).

66. Such evidence does, in fact, exist. See, for example, Harold G. Grasmick, Robert J. Bursik, Jr., and Bruce J. Arneklev, "Reduction in Drunk Driving as a Response to Increased Threats of Shame, Embarrassment, and Legal Sanctions," *Criminology*, Vol. 31, No. 1 (1993), pp. 41–67.

67. Council of State Governments, *Lessons from the States, Reducing Recidivism and Curbing Corrections Costs through Justice Reinvestment* (Council of State Governments, 2013).

68. Nicole D. Porter, *The State of Sentencing 2012* (Washington, DC:The Sentencing Project, 2013).

69. Council of State Governments, *Lessons from the States: Reducing Recidivism and Curbing Corrections Costs through Justice Reinvestment* (New York: Council of State Governments, 2013).

70. Communities United, "The $3.4 Trillion Mistake: The Cost of Mass Incarceration and Criminalization, and How Justice Reinvestment Can Build a Better Future for All," http://www.reinvest4justice.org/report (accessed March 31, 2018).

71. Joan Petersilia, *House Arrest*, National Institute of Justice Crime File Study Guide (Washington, DC: NIJ, 1988).

72. Privacy Act of 1974, 5 U.S.C.A. 522a, 88 Statute 1897, Public Law 93–579, December 31, 1974.

73. Freedom of Information Act, 5 U.S.C. 522, and amendments. The status of presentence investigative reports has not yet been clarified under this act to the satisfaction of all legal scholars, although state and federal courts are generally thought to be exempt from the provisions of the act.

74. City of New York, Citywide Accountability Program, S.T.A.R.S. (Statistical Tracking, Analysis, and Reporting System), http://www.nyc.gov/html/prob/pdf/stars_92005.pdf (accessed May 12, 2008).

75. For a good review of the issues involved, see Robert C. Davis, Arthur J. Lurigio, and Wesley G. Skogan, *Victims of Crime*, 2nd ed. (Thousand Oaks, CA: Sage, 1997); and Leslie Sebba, *Third Parties: Victims and the Criminal Justice System* (Columbus: Ohio State University Press, 1996).

76. President's Task Force on Victims of Crime, *Final Report* (Washington, DC: U.S. Government Printing Office, 1982).

77. Peter Finn and Beverly N. W. Lee, *Establishing and Expanding Victim-Witness Assistance Programs* (Washington, DC: National Institute of Justice, 1988).

78. Senate Joint Resolution (SJR) 65 is a major revision of an initial proposal, SJR 52, which Senators Kyl and Feinstein introduced on April 22, 1996. Representative Henry Hyde introduced House Joint Resolution (HJR) 174, a companion to SJR 52, and a similar proposal, HJR 173, on April 22, 1996.

79. Senate Joint Resolution 44, 105th Congress.

80. See the National Center for Victims of Crime's critique of the 1998 amendment at http://www.ncvc.org/law/Ncvca.htm (accessed January 10, 2009).

81. National Victims' Constitutional Amendment Passage, "States Victim Rights Amendments," http://www.nvcap.org/stvras.htm (accessed August 28, 2006).

82. National Victims' Constitutional Amendment Project, http://www.nvcap.org (accessed June 9, 2009).

83. CalVCB, "2016 Legislation," https://victims.ca.gov/law/legislation/2016.aspx (accessed August 28, 2018).

84. USA PATRIOT Act of 2001, Section 624.

85. Office for Victims of Crime, *Report to the Nation, 2003* (Washington, DC: OVC, 2003).

86. Crime Victims' Rights Act, 18 U.S.C. 3771.

87. U.S. Senate, Republican Policy Committee, Legislative Notice No. 63, April 22, 2004.

88. Proposition 8, California's Victims' Bill of Rights.

89. National Victim Center, Mothers against Drunk Driving, and American Prosecutors Research Institute, *Impact Statements: A Victim's Right to Speak; A Nation's Responsibility to Listen* (Washington, DC: Office for Victims of Crime, July 1994).

90. *Kelly* v. *California*, 555 U.S. 1020 (2008).

91. Robert C. Davis and Barbara E. Smith, "The Effects of Victim Impact Statements on Sentencing Decisions: A Test in an Urban Setting," *Justice Quarterly*, Vol. 11, No. 3 (September 1994), pp. 453–469.

92. "CA Murder Raises Pretrial Risk Assessment Issues," *Crime and Justice News*, August 19, 2017; https://thecrimereport.org/2017/08/19/ca-murder-raises-pretrial-risk-assessment-issues (accessed August 28, 2018).

93. Bureau of Justice Statistics, *Report to the Nation on Crime and Justice*, 2nd ed. (Washington, DC: U.S. Government Printing Office, 1988), p. 90.

94. Sean Rosenmerkel, Matthew Durose, and Donald Farole, Jr., *Felony Sentences in State Courts, 2006—Statistical Tables* (Washington, DC: Bureau of Justice Statistics, December, 2009). Data for 1990 come from Matthew R. Durose, David J. Levin, and Patrick A. Langan, *Felony Sentences in State Courts, 1998* (Washington, DC: Bureau of Justice Statistics, 2001).

95. Ibid., p. 2.

96. Sally T. Hillsman, Joyce L. Sichel, and Barry Mahoney, *Fines in Sentencing* (New York: Vera Institute of Justice, 1983).

97. Ibid., p. 2.

98. Ibid., p. 4.

99. Ibid.

100. "Swiss Speeder Fined a Record $290,000," *USA Today*, January 7, 2010, http://content.usatoday.com/communities/ondeadline/post/2010/01/swiss-speeder-fined-a-record-290000/1 (accessed July 5, 2010).

101. James S. Tyree and Tony Thornton, "Judge Sentences Underwood to Die," *Oklahoman*, April 3, 2008, http://newsok.com/article/3224954/1207252268 (accessed May 28, 2008).

102. Capital Punishment Research Project, University of Alabama Law School.

103. Death Penalty Information Center, "Fact Sheet: Executions by Year," http://deathpenaltyinfo.org/executions-year (accessed October 2, 2018).

104. Some states no longer permit new death sentences, but continue to maintain death rows housing previously convicted capital offenders. See also Death Penalty Information Center, "Facts about the Death Penalty,", 2018, http://www.deathpenaltyinfo.org/documents/FactSheet.pdf (accessed July 20, 2018).

105. "Proposition 66: California Voters Approve Faster Death Penalty Process," CBS Sacramento, November 22, 2016, http://sacramento.cbslocal.com/2016/11/22/proposition-66-california-voters-approve-faster-death-penalty-process/ (accessed September 7, 2018).

106. Emma Lake, "Died by the Sword," *The Sun*, December 1, 2017; https://www.thesun.co.uk/news/5034878/saudi-arabi-beheaded-130-prisoners-dangled-corpses-helicopter (accessed August 29, 2018).

107. Amnesty International, "Death Sentences and Executions 2017," https://www.amnesty.org/en/latest/news/2018/04/death-penalty-sentences-and-executions-2017 (accessed April 23, 2018).

108. Richard Willing, "Expansion of Death Penalty to Nonmurders Faces Challenges," *USA Today*, May 14, 1997.

109. *Kennedy* v. *Louisiana*, 554 U.S. 407 (2008).

110. Death Penalty Information Center, "Facts About the Death Penalty," http://www.deathpenaltyinfo.org/documents/FactSheet.pdf (accessed September 5, 2018).

111. Ibid.

112. In 2004, Utah repealed the use of a firing squad as a method of execution for all persons sentenced to death on or after May 3, 2004 (Utah Code Ann. section 77-18-5.5). The law allows for use of a firing squad for those sentenced prior

to that date or in the event that lethal injection is found to be unconstitutional.

113. Death Penalty Information Center, "Time on Death Row," https://deathpenaltyinfo.org/time-death-row (accessed March 31, 2018).

114. Murderpedia, http://murderpedia.org/male.S/s/schad-edward.htm (accessed March 31, 2018).

115. Details for this story come from Jenifer Warren and Maura Dolan, "Tookie Williams Is Executed," *Los Angeles Times*, December 13, 2005, http://www.latimes.com/news/local/la-me-execution13dec13,0,799154.story?coll=la-home-headlines (accessed May 20, 2006).

116. "Warden: Williams Frustrated at End," CNN.com, December 13, 2005, http://www.cnn.com/2005/LAW/12/13/williams.execution (accessed July 2, 2006).

117. "Chief Justice Calls for Limits on Death Row *Habeas* Appeals," *Criminal Justice Newsletter* (February 15, 1989), pp. 6–7.

118. *McCleskey* v. *Zant*, 499 U.S. 467, 493–494 (1991).

119. *Coleman* v. *Thompson*, 501 U.S. 722 (1991).

120. *Schlup* v. *Delo*, 513 U.S. 298 (1995).

121. Public Law 104–132.

122. *Felker* v. *Turpin*, 518 U.S. 1051 (1996).

123. *Elledge* v. *Florida*, No. 98-5410 (1998).

124. Murderpedia, http://murderpedia.org/male.E/e/elledge-william.htm (accessed March 31, 2018).

125. Michelle Locke, "Victim Forgives," *Associated Press*, May 19, 1996.

126. Ibid.

127. Arthur Koestler, *Reflections on Hanging* (New York: Macmillan, 1957), p. xii.

128. "Longest Incarcerations before Exoneration: Richard Phillips," *The National Registry of Exonerations*, http://www.law.umich.edu/special/exoneration/pages/casedetail.aspx?caseid=5298 (accessed July 3, 2018).

129. Death Penalty Information Center, "Innocence: List of Those Freed from Death Row," http://www.deathpenaltyinfo.org/innocence-list-those-freed-death-row (accessed October 11, 2018).

130. The National Registry of Exonerations, "Exonerations by Year: DNA and Non-DNA," https://www.law.umich.edu/special/exoneration/Pages/Exoneration-by-Year.aspx (assessed September 30, 2018).

131. Barry Scheck and Peter Neufeld, "DNA and Innocence Scholarship," in Saundra D. Westervelt and John A. Humphrey, eds., *Wrongly Convicted: Perspectives on Failed Justice* (New Brunswick, NJ: Rutgers University Press, 2001), pp. 248–249.

132. Ibid., p. 246.

133. James S. Liebman, Jeffrey Fagan, and Simon H. Rifkind, *A Broken System: Error Rates in Capital Cases, 1973–1995* (New York: Columbia University School of Law, 2000), http://justice.policy.net/jpreport/finrep.PDF (accessed March 3, 2004).

134. Jon B. Gould, Julia Carrano, Richard Leo, and Joseph Young, "Predicting Erroneous Convictions: A Social Science Approach to Miscarriages of Justice—Final Report to the National Institute of Justice, February 2013," https://www.ncjrs.gov/pdffiles1/nij/grants/241389.pdf (accessed August 21, 2018).

135. See, for example, Jim Yardley, "Texas Retooling Criminal Justice in Wake of Furor on Death Penalty," *The New York Times*, June 1, 2001.

136. In a sad footnote to the Illinois proclamation, former Governor Ryan, who drew international praise for his stance against the death penalty and who had been nominated for the Nobel Prize, was found guilty in 2006 of racketeering and fraud in a corruption scandal that ended his political career.

137. "New Jersey Suspends Death Penalty Pending a Task Force Review," *Criminal Justice Newsletter* (January 17, 2006), p. 8.

138. Title IV of the Justice for All Act of 2004.

139. At the time the legislation was enacted, Congress estimated that 300,000 rape kits remained unanalyzed in police department evidence lockers across the country.

140. The act also provides funding for the DNA Sexual Assault Justice Act (Title III of the Justice for All Act of 2004) and the Rape Kits and DNA Evidence Backlog Elimination Act of 2000 (42 U.S.C. 14135), authorizing more than $500 million for programs to improve the capacity of crime labs to conduct DNA analysis, reduce non-DNA backlogs, train evidence examiners, support sexual assault forensic examiner programs, and promote the use of DNA to identify missing persons.

141. In those states that accept federal monies under the legislation.

142. See N.C. G.S. section 15A-1460-75.

143. See: The Innocence Project, "Criminal Justice Reform Commissions: Case Studies," https://www.innocenceproject.org/criminal-justice-reform-commissions-case-studies (accessed August 28, 2018).

144. Samuel R. Gross, Barbara O'Brien, Chen Hu, and Edward H. Kennedy, "Rate of False Conviction of Criminal Defendants Who Are Sentenced to Death," Proceedings of the National Academy of Sciences, Vol. 111., No. 20 (March 25, 2014) http://www.pnas.org/content/111/20/7230 (accessed May 4, 2018).

145. Laura Bauer, "DNA Tests on Inmates Sometimes Proved They Were Guilty," *Kansas City Star*, April 7, 2009.

146. *District Attorney's Office* v. *Osborne*, 129 S.Ct. 2308 (2009).

147. Studies include S. Decker and C. Kohfeld, "A Deterrence Study of the Death Penalty in Illinois: 1933–1980," *Journal of Criminal Justice*, Vol. 12, No. 4 (1984), pp. 367–379; and S. Decker and C. Kohfeld, "An Empirical Analysis of the Effect of the Death Penalty in Missouri," *Journal of Crime and Justice*, Vol. 10, No. 1 (1987), pp. 23–46.

148. See, especially, W. C. Bailey, "Deterrence and the Death Penalty for Murders in Utah: A Time Series Analysis," *Journal of Contemporary Law*, Vol. 5, No. 1 (1978), pp. 1–20; and W. C. Bailey, "An Analysis of the Deterrent Effect of the Death Penalty for Murder in California," *Southern California Law Review*, Vol. 52, No. 3 (1979), pp. 743–764.

149. B. E. Forst, "The Deterrent Effect of Capital Punishment: A Cross-State Analysis of the 1960's," *Minnesota Law Review*, Vol. 61, No. 5 (1977), pp. 743–767.

150. Hashem Dezhbakhsh, Paul Rubin, and Joanna Mehlhop Shepherd, "Does Capital Punishment Have a Deterrent Effect? New Evidence from Post-Moratorium Panel Data," Emory University, January 2001, http://userwww.service.emory.edu/cozden/Dezhbakhsh_01_01_paper.pdf (accessed November 13, 2006).

151. Ibid., abstract.

152. Ibid., p. 19.

153. As some of the evidence presented before the Supreme Court in *Furman* v. *Georgia*, 408 U.S. 238 (1972), suggested.

154. *USA Today*, April 27, 1989.

155. Thomas J. Keil and Gennaro F. Vito, "Race and the Death Penalty in Kentucky Murder Trials: 1976–1991," *American Journal of Criminal Justice*, Vol. 20, No. 1 (1995), pp. 17–36 (published December 1996).

156. *McCleskey* v. *Kemp*, 481 U.S. 279 (1987).

157. *The Federal Death Penalty System: Supplementary Data, Analysis and Revised Protocols for Capital Case Review* (Washington, DC: Department of Justice, 2001).

158. David Stout, "Attorney General Says Report Shows No Racial Bias in Federal Death Sentences," *The New York Times*, June 7, 2001, http://nytimes.com/2001/06/07/politics/07DEAT.html (accessed September 19, 2010).

159. "Expanded Study Shows No Bias in Death Penalty, Ashcroft Says," *Criminal Justice Newsletter*, Vol. 31, No. 13 (June 18, 2001), p. 4.

160. Mary P. Gallagher, "Race Found to Have No Effect on Capital Sentencing in New Jersey," *New Jersey Law Journal* (August 21, 2001), p. 1.

161. "Nebraska Death Penalty System Given Mixed Review in a State Study," *Criminal Justice Newsletter*, Vol. 31, No. 16 (August 2001), pp. 4–5.

162. Details for this story come from Michael Graczyk, "Killer of Pregnant 10-Year-Old Set to Die Tonight," *Associated Press*, February 10, 2004; and Texas Execution Information Center, "Edward Lagrone," http://www.txexeutions.org/reports/318.asp (accessed May 15, 2004).

163. Justice Potter Stewart, as quoted in *USA Today*, April 27, 1989.

164. Arthur Koestler, *Reflections on Hanging* (New York: Macmillan, 1957), pp. 147–148; and Gennaro F. Vito and Deborah G. Wilson, "Back from the Dead: Tracking the Progress of Kentucky's *Furman*-Commuted Death Row Population," *Justice Quarterly*, Vol. 5, No. 1 (1988), pp. 101–111.

165. *Wilkerson* v. *Utah*, 99 U.S. 130 (1878).

166. *In re Kemmler*, 136 U.S. 436 (1890).

167. Ibid., p. 447.

168. *Louisiana ex rel. Francis* v. *Resweber*, 329 U.S. 459 (1947).

169. *Furman* v. *Georgia*, 408 U.S. 238 (1972).

170. A position first adopted in *Trop* v. *Dulles*, 356 U.S. 86 (1958).

171. *Gregg* v. *Georgia*, 428 U.S. 153 (1976).

172. *Ring* v. *Arizona*, 536 U.S. 584 (2002).

173. "Dozens of Death Sentences Overturned," *Associated Press*, June 24, 2002.

174. The ruling could also affect Florida, Alabama, Indiana, and Delaware, where juries recommend sentences in capital cases but judges have the final say.

175. *Hurst* v. *Florida*, U.S. Supreme Court, No. 14-7505 (decided 2016).

176. *Poyner* v. *Murray*, 508 U.S. 931 (1993).

177. *Campbell* v. *Wood*, 511 U.S. 1119 (1994).

178. *Director Gomez, et al.* v. *Fierro and Ruiz*, 117 S.Ct. 285 (1996).

179. The court issued its decision after reviewing two cases: *Dawson* v. *State* and *Moore* v. *State*.

180. Death Penalty Information Center "Methods of Execution", https://deathpenaltyinfo.org/methods-execution?scid=8&did=245 (accessed May 31, 2018).

181. Sasha Goldstein, "Friend of Victim Have Zero Sympathy for Clayton Lockett," *New York Daily News*, http://www.nydailynews.com/news/crime/friends-victim-zero-sympathy-clayton-lockett-inmate-botched-okla-execution-article-1.1777463 (accessed March 31, 2018).

182. Adam Liptak, "Judges Set Hurdles for Lethal Injection," *The New York Times*, April 12, 2006.

183. "North Carolina, Using Medical Monitoring Device, Executes Killer," *Associated Press*, April 22, 2006.

184. *Hall* v. *Florida*, 572 U.S. ___ (2014).

185. *Baze* v. *Rees*, 553 U.S. 35 (2008).

186. James D. Unnever and Francis T. Cullen, "Executing the Innocent and Support for Capital Punishment," *Criminology and Public Policy*, Vol. 4, No. 1 (2005), p. 3.

Chapter 10: Probation, Parole, and Reentry

i. Jeremy Travis and Sarah Lawrence, *Beyond the Prison Gates: The State of Parole in America* (Washington, DC: Urban Institute Press, 2002), p. 3.

ii. Christine Lindquist, Jennifer Hardison Walters, Michael Rempel, and Shannon M. Carey, *The National Institute of Justice's Evaluation of Second Chance Act Adult Reentry Courts: Program Characteristics and Preliminary Themes from Year 1* (Washington, DC: Bureau of Justice Assistance, 2013).

1. Council of State Governments Justice Center, *The Impact of Probation and Parole Populations on Arrests in Four California Cities* (Lexington, KY: CSG 2013), p. 1.

2. Amy Brittain, "He Says He Robbed 100 People in D.C. Could He Have Been Stopped Before He Killed?", *The Washington Post*, December 21, 2016.

3. Ibid.

4. "Desistance" is defined later in this chapter.

5. James M. Byrne, *Probation*, National Institute of Justice Crime File Series Study Guide (Washington, DC: U.S. Department of Justice, 1988), p. 1.

6. Alexander B. Smith and Louis Berlin, Introduction to Probation and Parole (St. Paul, MN: West, 1976), p. 75.

7. John Augustus, First Probation Officer: John Augustus' Original Report on His Labors—1852 (Montclair, NJ: Patterson-Smith, 1972).

8. Smith and Berlin, Introduction to Probation and Parole, p. 77.

9. Ibid., p. 80.

10. George C. Killinger, Hazel B. Kerper, and Paul F. Cromwell, Jr., *Probation and Parole in the Criminal Justice System* (St. Paul, MN: West, 1976), p. 25.

11. Danielle Kaeble, *Probation and Parole in the United States, 2016* (Washington, DC: BJS, 2018).

12. Sean Rosenmerkel, Matthew Durose and Donald Farole, *Felony Sentences in State Courts, 2006* (Washington, DC: Bureau of Justice Statistics, 2009), Table 1.2.

13. "Woman Gets Probation for Shooting Fiancé," *Associated Press*, April 16, 1992.

14. "On Deadline: Getting Away with Murder in Dallas," *USA Today*, November 14, 2007.

15. Kaeble, *Probation and Parole in the United States, 2016*.

16. Ibid.

17. This section owes much to Sanford Bates, "The Establishment and Early Years of the Federal Probation System," *Federal Probation* (June 1987), pp. 4–9.

18. *Ex parte United States*, 242 U.S. 27 (1916).

19. Bates, "The Establishment and Early Years of the Federal Probation System," p. 6.

20. U.S. Probation and Pretrial Services System, *Year-in-Review Report: Fiscal Year 2004* (Washington, DC: U.S. Probation and Pretrial Services System, 2005).

21. See Brian A. Reaves and Timothy C. Hart, *Federal Law Enforcement Officers, 2000* (Washington, DC: Bureau of Justice Statistics, 2002), p. 4, from which some of the wording in this paragraph has been adapted.

22. John M. Hughes, "We're Back on Track: Preparing for the Next 50 Years," *Federal Probation*, Vol. 75, No. 2 (September 2011), http://www.uscourts.gov/uscourts/FederalCourts/PPS/Fedprob/2011-09/back_on_track.html (accessed August 28, 2013).

23. Adapted from Timothy A. Hughes, Doris James Wilson, and Allen J. Beck, *Trends in State Parole, 1990–2000* (Washington, DC: Bureau of Justice Statistics, 2001), p. 1.

24. *How to Safely Reduce Prison Populations and Support People Returning to their Communities* (Washington, DC: Justice Policy Institute, 2010), p. 4.

25. Ibid.

26. California Penal Code Section 3450, Postrelease Community Supervision Act of 2011.

27. Those ineligible for participation under the California Post-release Community Supervision Act of 2011 have committed crimes described under California Penal Code Section 1192.7(c)1, which include murder, mayhem, rape, sodomy by force, and other specified violent offenses.

28. Office of Research, California Department of Corrections and Rehabilitation, *Realignment Report: An Examination of Offenders Released from State Prison in the First Year of Public Safety Realignment* (Sacramento, CA: December 2013).

29. "State Prisons Relying More on Parole," Report of the Arkansas Senate, May 3, 2012, http://www.arkansas.gov/senate/newsroom/index.php?do:newsDetail=1&news_id=340 (accessed January 19, 2014).

30. Ibid.

31. Danielle Kaeble, *Probation and Parole in the United States, 2016.*

32. Ibid.

33. "The Effectiveness of Felony Probation: Results from an Eastern State," *Justice Quarterly* (December 1991), pp. 525–543.

34. Danielle Kaeble, *Probation and Parole in the United States, 2016.*

35. United States Parole Commission, *2019 Performance Budget,* (Washington, DC: USPC, January 2018). https://www.justice.gov/file/1034131/download).

36. State of Georgia, Board of Pardons and Paroles, *Annual Report Fiscal Year 2017,* https://pap.georgia.gov/sites/pap.georgia.gov/files/Annual_Reports/PAP_AnnualReport-Final_WEB.pdf (accessed March 28, 2018).

37. See Andrew von Hirsch and Kathleen J. Hanrahan, *Abolish Parole?* (Washington, DC: Law Enforcement Assistance Administration, 1978).

38. *Griffin* v. *Wisconsin*, 483 U.S. 868, 107 S.Ct. 3164 (1987).

39. *Pennsylvania Board of Probation and Parole* v. *Scott*, 524 U.S. 357 (1998).

40. Kaeble, *Probation and Parole in the United States, 2016.*

41. Robyn. L. Cohen, *Probation and Parole Violators in State Prison, 1991* (Washington, DC: Bureau of Justice Statistics, 1995).

42. California Department of Corrections and Rehabilitation, Division of Adult Parole Operations, "Non-Revocable Parole," http://www.cdcr.ca.gov/Parole/Non_Revocable_Parole/index.html (accessed April 28, 2018).

43. *Harlow* v. *Clatterbuick*, 30 CrL. 2364 (Va. S.Ct. 1986); *Santangelo* v. *State*, 426 N.Y.S.2d 931 (1980); *Welch* v. *State*, 424 N.Y.S.2d 774 (1980); and *Thompson* v. *County of Alameda*, 614 P.2d 728 (1980).

44. *Tarter* v. *State of New York*, 38 CrL. 2364 (N.Y. Sup. Ct. 1986); *Grimm* v. *Arizona Board of Pardons and Paroles*, 115 Ariz. 260, 564 P.2d 1227 (1977); and *Payton* v. *U.S.*, 636 F.2d 132 (5th Cir. 1981).

45. Rolando V. del Carmen, *Potential Liabilities of Probation and Parole Officers* (Cincinnati, OH: Anderson, 1986), p. 89.

46. See, for example, *Semler* v. *Psychiatric Institute*, 538 F.2d 121 (4th Cir. 1976).

47. *Minnesota* v. *Murphy*, 465 U.S. 420 (1984).

48. National Advisory Commission on Criminal Justice Standards and Goals, *Task Force Report: Corrections* (Washington, DC: U.S. Government Printing Office, 1973).

49. Council of State Governments Justice Center, *The Impact of Probation and Parole Populations on Arrests in Four California Cities* (New York, 2013).

50. National Institute of Justice, *Stress among Probation and Parole Officers and What Can Be Done about It* (Washington, DC: NIJ, 2005).

51. Ibid., p. 1.

52. Ibid., p. ii.

53. From the introduction to James Austin, Michael Jones, and Melissa Bolyard, *The Growing Use of Jail Boot Camps: The Current State of the Art* (Washington, DC: National Institute of Justice, 1993), p. 1.

54. Michael McCarthy and Jodi Upton, "Athletes Lightly Punished after Their Day in Court," *USA Today*, May 4, 2006.

55. Sentencing Project, *Changing the Terms of Sentencing: Defense Counsel and Alternative Sentencing Services* (Washington, DC: Sentencing Project, n.d.).

56. Joan Petersilia, *Expanding Options for Criminal Sentencing* (Santa Monica, CA: RAND Corporation, 1987).

57. Ohio Revised Code, Section 2946.06.1 (July 1965).

58. Lawrence Greenfield, *Probation and Parole, 1984* (Washington, DC: U.S. Government Printing Office, 1986).

59. For a good overview of such programs, especially as they apply to juvenile corrections, see Doris Layton MacKenzie et al., *A National Study Comparing the Environments of Boot Camps with Traditional Facilities for Juvenile Offenders* (Washington, DC: National Institute of Justice, 2001).

60. Doris Layton MacKenzie and Deanna Bellew Ballow, "Shock Incarceration Programs in State Correctional Jurisdictions—An Update," *NIJ Reports* (May/June 1989), pp. 9–10.

61. "Shock Incarceration Marks a Decade of Expansion," *Corrections Compendium* (September 1996), pp. 10–28.

62. National Institute of Justice, *Multisite Evaluation of Shock Incarceration* (Washington, DC: NIJ, 1995).

63. "Ninth Circuit Upholds BOP Boot Camp Termination," *Prison Legal News*, August 15, 2013; https://www.prisonlegalnews.org/news/2013/aug/15/ninth-circuit-upholds-bop-boot-camp-termination (accessed March 28, 2018).

64. See, Nevada Department of Corrections, "Three Lakes Valley Boot Camp," http://doc.nv.gov/Facilities/Home (accessed March 28, 2018).

65. Wyoming Department of Corrections, "Youthful Offender Program (Wyoming Boot Camp), http://corrections.wyo.gov/home/institutions/whcc (accessed March 28, 2018).

66. Douglas C. McDonald, *Restitution and Community Service*, National Institute of Justice Crime File Series Study Guide (Washington, DC: U.S. Department of Justice, 1988).

67. Richard J. Maher and Henry E. Dufour, "Experimenting with Community Service: A Punitive Alternative to Imprisonment," *Federal Probation* (September 1987), pp. 22–27.

68. James P. Levine, Michael C. Musheno, and Dennis J. Palumbo, *Criminal Justice in America: Law in Action* (New York: John Wiley, 1986), p. 549.

69. Billie S. Erwin and Lawrence A. Bennett, "New Dimensions in Probation: Georgia's Experience with Intensive Probation Supervision," *Research in Brief* (Washington, DC: National Institute of Justice, 1987).

70. State of Colorado, Department of Public Safety, *Colorado Community Corrections: FY13 and FY14 Annual Report*, https://cdpsdocs.state.co.us/occ/Reports/FY13FY14AnnualReportAsPublished.pdf (accessed April 5, 2018).

71. Texas Department of Criminal Justice, "Contact Information - Electronic Monitoring," https://www.tdcj.state.tx.us/divisions/pd/contracts_em.html (accessed September 1, 2018).

72. Crystal A. Garcia, "Using Palmer's Global Approach to Evaluate Intensive Supervision Programs: Implications for Practice," *Corrections Management Quarterly*, Vol. 4, No. 4 (2000), pp. 60–69.

73. Joan Petersilia, *House Arrest*, National Institute of Justice Crime File Series Study Guide (Washington, DC: U.S. Department of Justice, 1988).

74. Darren Gowen, "Remote Location Monitoring: A Supervision Strategy to Enhance Risk Control," *Federal Probation*, Vol. 65, No. 2 (2001), p. 39.

75. Kristen De Groot and Michael R. Sisak, "Bill Cosby, Fitted with Ankle Bracelet, to be Prisoner Inside Home," *SFGate*, April 28, 2018, https://www.sfgate.com/nation/article/Bill-Cosby-fitted-with-ankle-bracelet-to-be-12872170.php (accessed August 28, 2018).

76. Marc Renzema and David T. Skelton, *The Use of Electronic Monitoring by Criminal Justice Agencies, 1989* (Washington, DC: National Institute of Justice, 1990).

77. U.S. Probation and Pretrial Services, *Court and Community* (Washington, DC: Administrative Office of the U.S. Courts, 2000).

78. The PEW Charitable Trusts, *Use of Electronic Offender-Tracking Devices Expands Sharply, 2016;* http://www.pewtrusts.org/en/research-and-analysis/issue-briefs/2016/09/use-of-electronic-offender-tracking-devices-expands-sharply (accessed May 19, 2018).

79. U.S. Probation and Pretrial Services, "Home Confinement," http://www.nhp.uscourts.gov/sites/default/files/pdf/cchome.pdf (accessed March 22, 2018).

80. State of Georgia Board of Pardons and Paroles, "Adult Offender Sanction Costs for Fiscal Year 2001," http://www.pap.state.ga.us/otisweb/corrcost.html (accessed September 20, 2005).

81. Construction costs are for cells classified as "medium security."

82. *BI Home Escort: Electronic Monitoring System*, advertising brochure (Boulder, CO: BI Inc., n.d.).

83. William Bales, et al., *A Quantitative and Qualitative Assessment of Electronic Monitoring* (Washington, DC: National Institute of Justice, U.S. Department of Justice), May 2010, http://www.ncjrs.gov/pdffiles1/nij/grants/230530.pdf (accessed May 20, 2013).

84. Stephen V. Gies, et al., *Monitoring High-Risk Sex Offenders With GPS Technology: An Evaluation of the California Supervision Program, Final Report* (Washington, DC: National Institute of Justice, 2012).

85. James A. Inciardi, *Criminal Justice*, 2nd ed. (New York: Harcourt Brace Jovanovich, 1987), p. 664.

86. E. Ann Carson, *Prisoners in 2016* (Washington, DC: Bureau of Justice Statistics, 2018.

87. Jeremy Travis, Ronald Davis and Sarah Lawrence, "New Perspectives in Policing: Exploring the Role of the Police in Prisoner Reentry," https://www.ncjrs.gov/pdffiles1/nij/238337.pdf (accessed March 28, 2018).

88. Bureau of Justice Statistics, "Forty-Two Percent of State Parole Discharges Were Successful," October 3, 2001, http://www.ojp.usdoj.gov/newsroom/2001/bjs01181.html (accessed July 3, 2007).

89. Council of States Government Justice Center, *The Impact of Probation and Parole Populations on Arrests in Four California Cities* (Lexington, KY: CSG, 2013).

90. Urban Institute and RTI International, *National Portrait of SVORI* (Washington, DC: Urban Institute Press, 2004).

91. Abby Sewell, "L.A. County Seeing High-Risk Offenders Entering Its Probation System," *Los Angeles Times*, November 30, 2012, http://articles.latimes.com/2012/nov/30/local/la-me-realignment-20121130 (accessed March 28, 2018).

92. American Probation and Parole Association and the Association of Paroling Authorities International, *Abolishing Parole: Why the Emperor Has No Clothes* (Lexington, KY: APPA, 1995).

93. Much of this information is taken from Reentry Policy Council, *Report of the Reentry Policy Council: Charting the Safe and Successful Return of Prisoners to the Community—Executive Summary* (New York: Council of State Governments, 2005).

94. Langan and Levin, *National Recidivism Study of Released Prisoners;* and *Does Parole Work? Analyzing the Impact of Postprison Supervision on Rearrest Outcomes* (Washington, DC: Urban Institute Press, 2005).

95. Esther Griswold, Jessica Pearson, and Lanae Davis, *Testing a Modification Process for Incarcerated Parents* (Denver: Center for Policy Research), pp. 11–12.

96. Ibid.

97. See Pamela K. Lattimore, "Reentry, Reintegration, Rehabilitation, Recidivism, and Redemption," *Criminologist*, Vol. 31, No. 3 (May/June 2006), pp. 1, 3–6.

98. Urban Institute and RTI International, *National Portrait of SVORI*, from which some of the wording in this section is taken.

99. See Laura Winterfield and Susan Brumbaugh, *The Multi-site Evaluation of the Serious and Violent Offender Reentry Initiative* (Washington, DC: Urban Institute Press, 2005).

100. Wording in this paragraph is adapted from Debbie Dawes, *The National Institute of Justice's Evaluation of Second Chance Act Adult Reentry Courts: Program Characteristics and Preliminary Themes from Year 1* (Washington, DC: Bureau of Justice Assistance, 2013).

101. Lane County (Oregon) Circuit Court, "Drug Court," http://www.ojd.state.or.us/lan/drugcrt/index.htm (accessed May 29, 2009).

102. See, for example, Jeremy Travis, *But They All Come Back: Facing the Challenges of Prisoner Reentry* (Washington, DC: Urban Institute Press, 2005).

103. Bureau of Justice Assistance, *Second Chance Act State, Local, and Tribal Reentry Courts FY2010 Competitive Grant Announcement* (Washington, DC: U.S. Department of Justice, Office of Justice Programs, 2010), http://www.ojp.usdoj.gov/BJA/grant/10SecondChanceCourtsSol.pdf (accessed May 3, 2013).

104. Public Law 110–199.

105. Congressional Budget Office Cost Estimate, "Second Chance Act of 2007," https://www.cbo.gov/publication/18570 (accessed March 29, 2018).

106. Department of Justice Press Release, "Department of Justice Announces New Reforms to Strengthen the Federal Bureau of Prisons," April 25, 2016, https://www.justice.gov/opa/pr/department-justice-announces-new-reforms-strengthen-federal-bureau-prisons (accessed May 18, 2018).

107. Shannon M. Carey, et. al., "Reentry Court Research: Overview of Findings from the National Institute of Justice's Evaluation of Second Chance Act Adult Reentry Courts," Bureau of Justice Assistance, 2018.

108. Christine Lindquist, et al., "The National Institute of Justice's Evaluation of Second Chance Act Adult Reentry Courts: Lessons Learned about Reentry Court Program Implementation and Sustainability," Bureau of Justice Assistance, 2018.

109. Administrative Office of the United States Courts, "Post-Conviction Supervision: Judicial Business 2015," http://www.uscourts.gov/statistics-reports/post-conviction-supervision-judicial-business-2015 (accessed March 10, 2018).

110. National Institute of Corrections, *Evidence-Based Policy, Practice, and Decisionmaking: Implications for Paroling Authorities* (Washington, DC: U.S. Department of Justice, 2011).

111. Kevin McEvoy, "Hope: A Swift and Certain Process for Probationers," *National Institute of Justice Journal*, No. 269 (March 2012), pp. 16–17, from which some of the wording in the next two paragraphs is taken.

112. Francis T. Cullen and Travis C. Pratt, "It's Hopeless: Beyond Zero-Tolerance Supervision," *Criminology and Public Policy*, Vol. 15, No. 4 (2016), p. 1215–1227.

113. Nancy Ritter, "New Tool Will Manage Community Corrections . . . and Beyond," National institute of Justice, 2013, p. 1.

Chapter 11: Prisons and Jails

i. Zebulon R. Brockway, *The Ideal of a True Prison System for a State* (1865), reprinted in *Journal of Correctional Education*, Vol. 46, No. 2 (June 1995), pp. 68–74.

ii. Paige M. Harrison and Allen J. Beck, *Prisoners in 2005* (Washington, DC: Bureau of Justice Statistics, 2006), p. 7.

1. Myrna Raeder *The State of Criminal Justice 2010* (Chicago, IL: American Bar Association, 2010), p. 12.

2. "Steven Martinez, Quadriplegic Rapist, Will Be Freed from California Prison," *The Huffington Post*, http://www.huffington-

post.com/2012/11/16/steven-martinez-quadriplegic-rapist-n2145339.html (accessed October 15, 2013).

3. Rob Quinn, "Quadriplegic Rapist Denied Parole," Newser, May 25, 2011, http://www.newser.com/story/119382/quadriplegic-rapist-denied-parole.html (accessed June 1, 2011).

4. Lauren Steussy and Chris Chan, "Quadriplegic Rapist to Be Released from Prison," NBC San Diego, http://www.nbcsandiego.com/news/local/Quadriplegic-Rapist-to-be-Released-from-Prison-179722421.html (accessed March 3, 2018).

5. David G. Savage and Patrick McGreevy, "U.S. Supreme Court Orders Massive Inmate Release to Relieve California's Crowded Prisons," *Los Angeles Times*, May 24, 2011, http://articles.latimes.com/2011/may/24/local/la-me-court-prisons-20110524 (accessed June 1, 2011).

6. *Brown* v. *Plata*, 563 U.S. 493 (2011).

7. *Plata* v. *Brown*, U.S. Court of Appeals for the Ninth Circuit, No. 13-15466 (decided May 28, 2014).

8. Arthur Evans Wood and John Barker Waite, *Crime and Its Treatment: Social and Legal Aspects of Criminology* (New York: American Book Company, 1941), p. 488.

9. John Howard, *State of Prisons* (London, 1777; reprint, New York: E. P. Dutton, 1929).

10. Harry Elmer Barnes and Negley K. Teeters, *New Horizons in Criminology*, 3rd ed. (Upper Saddle River, NJ: Prentice Hall, 1959), p. 428.

11. For a description of the community-based format in its heyday, see Andrew T. Scull, *Decarceration: Community Treatment and the Deviant—A Radical View* (Upper Saddle River, NJ: Prentice Hall, 1977).

12. Ibid., p. 51.

13. National Advisory Commission on Criminal Justice Standards and Goals, Standard 2.17, Part 2c.

14. Recidivism can be defined in various ways according to the purpose the term is intended to serve in a particular study or report. Recidivism is usually defined as rearrest (versus reconviction) and generally includes a time span of five years, although some Bureau of Justice Statistics studies have used six years, and other studies one or two years, as definitional criteria.

15. U.S. Department of Justice, *Office of Justice Programs Fiscal Year 2000 Program Plan: Resources for the Field* (Washington, DC: Office of Juvenile Justice and Delinquency Prevention, 1999).

16. Timothy A. Hughes, Doris James Wilson, and Allen J. Beck, *Trends in State Parole, 1990–2000* (Washington, DC: Bureau of Justice Statistics, 2001).

17. E. Ann Carson, *Prisoners in 2013* (Washington, DC: Bureau of Justice Statistics, 2014).

18. Allen J. Beck and Paige M. Harrison, *Prisoners in 2004* (Washington, DC: Bureau of Justice Statistics, 2005).

19. While both state and federal drug arrests rates increased dramatically, most of the increase was at the federal level. See President's Council of Economic Advisers, *Economic Perspectives on Incarceration and the Criminal Justice System* (Washington, DC: The White House, 2016), p. 3.

20. The state of Washington is generally credited with having been the first state to pass a three-strikes law by voter initiative (in 1993).

21. Roy Walmsley, *World Prison Population List* (Essex, England: International Center for Prison Studies, 2013).

22. Peter Wagner and Bernadette Robuy, "Mass Incarceration: The Whole Pie 2017," Prison Policy Initiative; https://www.prisonpolicy.org/reports/pie2017.html (accessed March 28, 2018).

23. Carson, *Prisoners in 2016*. (Washington, DC: Bureau of Justice Statistics, 2018), p. 1. All other statistics in this section refer to inmates sentenced to a year or more in prison.

24. Ibid.

25. Ibid.

26. Public Safety Performance Project of the Pew Charitable Trusts, *One in 100: Behind Bars in America, 2008* (Philadelphia: Pew, 2008), p. 5.

27. Federal Bureau of Investigation, *Crime in the United States, 2017*, and other years.

28. Carson, *Prisoners in 2016*.

29. Ibid.

30. Robert M. Carter, Richard A. McGee, and E. Kim Nelson, *Corrections in America* (Philadelphia: J. B. Lippincott, 1975), pp. 122–123.

31. Federal Bureau of Prisons, "Federal Prison System Per Capita Costs - FY 2015," https://www.bop.gov/foia/fy15_per_capita_costs.pdf (accessed October 19, 2018).

32. Tracey Kyckelhahn, *Justice Expenditures and Employment Extracts Program 2010* (Washington, DC: Bureau of Justice Statistics, July 2014).

33. Carson, *Prisoners in 2016*.

34. Federal Bureau of Prisons, "Statistics: Inmate Statistics," https://www.bop.gov/about/statistics/statistics_inmate_offenses.jsp (accessed March 27, 2018); and National Corrections Reporting Program, 1998 (Ann Arbor, MI: Interuniversity Consortium for Political and Social Research, 2001).

35. Federal Bureau of Prisons, "Quick Facts About the Bureau of Prisons," January 27, 2018, http://www.bop.gov/news/quick.jsp#4 (accessed March 27, 2018).

36. Carson, *Prisoners in 2016*.

37. Bonczar, *Prevalence of Imprisonment in the U.S. Population, 1974–2001*, p. 1.

38. Ibid., p. 8.

39. Carson, *Prisoners in 2016*. Much of the decline in state prison populations, however, can be accounted for the way in which incarcerated felons are counted—especially in the state of California, where a strategy of realignment has shifted state prisoners to county jails.

40. Ibid.

41. "Governing: State Prison Capacity, Overcrowded Prisons Data," http://www.governing.com/gov-data/safety-justice/state-prison-capacity-overcrowding-data.html (accessed March 27, 2018).

42. *Rhodes* v. *Chapman*, 452 U.S. 337 (1981).

43. D. Greenberg, "The Incapacitative Effect of Imprisonment, Some Estimates," *Law and Society Review*, Vol. 9 (1975), pp. 541–580. See also Jacqueline Cohen, "Incapacitating Criminals: Recent Research Findings," National Institute of Justice *Research in Brief* (December 1983).

44. For information on identifying dangerous repeat offenders, see M. Chaiken and J. Chaiken, *Selecting Career Criminals for Priority Prosecution*, final report (Cambridge, MA: Abt Associates, 1987).

45. J. Monahan, *Predicting Violent Behavior: An Assessment of Clinical Techniques* (Beverly Hills, CA: Sage, 1981).

46. S. Van Dine, J. P. Conrad, and S. Dinitz, *Restraining the Wicked: The Incapacitation of the Dangerous Offender* (Lexington, MA: Lexington Books, 1979).

47. Paul Gendreau, Tracy Little, and Claire Goggin, "A Meta-Analysis of the Predictors of Adult Offender Recidivism: What Works!" *Criminology*, Vol. 34, No. 4 (November 1996), pp. 575–607.

48. Nicole D. Porter, *On the Chopping Block 2012: State Prison Closings* (Washington, DC: The Sentencing Project, December 2012).

49. California Department of Corrections and Rehabilitation, *The Future of California Corrections* (Sacramento, CA: California Department of Corrections and Rehabilitation, 2012), http://www.cdcr.ca.gov/2012plan/docs/plan/complete.pdf (accessed March 3, 2018).

50. Jon Lender, "Prisoner Release Bill Wins Final Approval," *The Hartford Courant*, May 31, 2001, http://articles.courant.com/2011-05-31/news/hc-house-prisoners-program-0601-20110531_1_violent-crimes-prison-inmates-senate-democrats (accessed March 27, 2018).

51. George Camp and Camille Camp, "Stopping Escapes: Perimeter Security," *Prison Construction Bulletin* (Washington, DC: National Institute of Justice, 1987).

52. Adapted from G. A. Grizzle and A. D. Witte, "Efficiency in Collections Agencies," in Gordon P. Whitaker and Charles D. Phillips, *Evaluating the Performance of Criminal Justice Agencies* (Washington, DC: NIJ, 1983).

53. Patricia L. Hardyman et al., *Internal Prison Classification Systems: Case Studies in Their Development and Implementation* (Washington, DC: National Institutions of Corrections, 2002), from which some of the wording in this section is taken.

54. Ibid.

55. *Johnson* v. *California*, 543 U.S. 499 (2005).

56. Federal Bureau of Prisons, *Staff Ethnicity/Race*, http://www.bop.gov/about/statistics/statistics_staff_ethnicity_race.jsp (accessed March 29, 2018).

57. Most of the information in this section comes from telephone conversations with and faxed information from the Federal Bureau of Prisons, August 25, 1995.

58. For additional information, see Dennis Cauchon, "The Alcatraz of the Rockies," *USA Today*, November 16, 1994.

59. "Congress OKs Inmate Fees to Offset Costs of Prison," *Criminal Justice Newsletter*, October 15, 1992, p. 6.

60. Federal Bureau of Prisons, "Federal Prison System Per Capita Costs - FY 2015," https://www.bop.gov/foia/fy15_per_capita_costs.pdf (accessed October 19, 2018).

61. Federal Bureau of Prisons, "Statistics", January 16, 2014, http://www.bop.gov/about/statistics/population_statistics.jsp (accessed September 11, 2016).

62. Carson, Prisoners in 2016.

63. Kamala Malli-Kane, Barbara Parthasarathy, and William Adams, *Examining Growth in the Federal Prison Population, 1998 to 2010* (Washington, DC: Urban Institute, 2012), p. 3.

64. National Institute of Corrections, https://nicic.gov (accessed March 2, 2018).

65. Ibid.

66. Bureau of Justice Statistics, Census of Jails, http://bjs.ojp.usdoj.gov/index.cfm?ty=dcdetail&iid=254 (accessed March 28, 2018).

67. Zhen Zeng, *Jail Inmates in 2016* (Washington, DC: Bureau of Justice Statistics, 2018).

68. Ibid.

69. Ibid.

70. James Stephan, *Census of Jail Facilities* (Washington, DC: Bureau of Justice Statistics, 2011), p. 22.

71. Ibid.

72. *Zeng, Jail Inmates in 2016.*

73. Ibid.

74. James, *Profile of Jail Inmates, 2002.*

75. Stephan, *Census of Jails, 1999.*

76. "5 Largest U.S. Jails," CNN; https://www.cnn.com/2016/09/22/us/lisa-ling-this-is-life-la-county-jail-by-the-numbers/index.html (accessed March 31, 2018).

77. See Dale Stockton, "Cook County Illinois Sheriff's Office," *Police* (October 1996), pp. 40–43. The Cook County Department of Correction operates ten separate jails, which house approximately 9,000 inmates. The department employs more than 2,800 correctional officers.

78. *Zeng, Jail Inmates in 2016* (Washington, DC: Bureau of Justice Statistics, 2018).

79. Ibid.

80. Ibid.

81. Ibid.

82. Ibid., p. 21.

83. Ibid.

84. Ibid., p. 55.

85. American Correctional Association, *Vital Statistics in Corrections* (Laurel, MD: ACA, 2000).

86. Mills and Barrett, "Meeting the Special Challenge," p. 55.

87. Ibid.

88. Linda L. Zupan, "Women Corrections Officers in the Nation's Largest Jails," *American Jails* (January/February 1991), pp. 59–62.

89. Ibid.

90. Linda L. Zupan, "Women Corrections Officers in Local Jails," paper presented at the annual meeting of the Academy of Criminal Justice Sciences, Nashville, TN, March 1991.

91. Ibid., p. 6.

92. "Jail Overcrowding in Houston Results in Release of Inmates," *Criminal Justice Newsletter*, October 15, 1990, p. 5.

93. Bureau of Justice Statistics, *Census of Local Jails, 1988* (Washington, DC: BJS, 1991), p. 31.

94. Kathleen Maguire and Ann L. Pastore, *Sourcebook of Criminal Justice Statistics, 1994* (Washington, DC: U.S. Government Printing Office, 1995).

95. Zeng, *Jail Inmates at Midyear in 2016.*

96. Carson, *Prisoners in 2016.*

97. Christopher J. Mumola, *Suicide and Homicide in State Prisons and Local Jails* (Washington, DC: Bureau of Justice Statistics, 2005), p. 1.

98. George P. Wilson and Harvey L. McMurray, "System Assessment of Jail Overcrowding Assumptions," paper presented at the annual meeting of the Academy of Criminal Justice Sciences, Nashville, TN, March 1991.

99. Andy Hall, *Systemwide Strategies to Alleviate Jail Crowding* (Washington, DC: National Institute of Justice, 1987).

100. Ibid.

101. Linda L. Zupan and Ben A. Menke, "The New Generation Jail: An Overview," in Joel A. Thompson and G. Larry Mays, eds., *American Jails: Public Policy Issues* (Chicago: Nelson-Hall, 1991), p. 180.

102. Ibid.

103. Herbert R. Sigurdson, Billy Wayson, and Gail Funke, "Empowering Middle Managers of Direct Supervision Jails," *American Jails* (winter 1990), p. 52.

104. Byron Johnson, "Exploring Direct Supervision: A Research Note," *American Jails* (March/April 1994), pp. 63–64.

105. H. Sigurdson, *The Manhattan House of Detention: A Study of Podular Direct Supervision* (Washington, DC: National Institute of Corrections, 1985). For similar conclusions, see Robert Conroy, Wantland J. Smith, and Linda L. Zupan, "Officer Stress in the Direct Supervision Jail: A Preliminary Case Study," *American Jails* (November/December 1991), p. 36.

106. For a good overview of the future of American jails, see Ron Carroll, "Jails and the Criminal Justice System in the Twenty-First Century," *American Jails* (March/April 1997), pp. 26–31.

107. Robert L. May II, Roger H. Peters, and William D. Kearns, "The Extent of Drug Treatment Programs in Jails: A Summary Report," *American Jails* (September/October 1990), pp. 32–34.

108. See, for example, John W. Dietler, "Jail Industries: The Best Thing That Can Happen to a Sheriff," *American Jails* (July/August 1990), pp. 80–83.

109. Robert Osborne, "Los Angeles County Sheriff Opens New Inmate Answering Service," *American Jails* (July/August 1990), pp. 61–62.

110. See J. R. Dewan, "Regional Jail—The New Kid on the Block," *American Jails* (May/June 1995), pp. 70–72.

111. Tom Rosazza, "Jail Standards: Focus on Change," *American Jails* (November/December 1990), pp. 84–87.

112. American Correctional Association, *Manual of Standards for Adult Local Detention Facilities*, 3rd ed. (College Park, MD: ACA, 1991).

113. Ken Kerle, "National Sheriff's Association Jail Audit Review," *American Jails* (spring 1987), pp. 13–21.

114. Norimitsu Onishi, "In California, County Jails Face Bigger Loads," *The New York Times*, August 5, 2012, http://www.

nytimes.com/2012/08/06/us/in-california-prison-overhaul-county-jails-face-bigger-load.html (accessed March 20, 2018).

115. Ibid.

116. Allen J. Beck and Paige M. Harrison, *Prisoners in 2000* (Washington, DC: Bureau of Justice Statistics, 2001), p. 7.

117. Carson, *Prisoners in 2016*.

118. Eric Bates, "Private Prisons: Over the Next Five Years Analysts Expect the Private Share of the Prison 'Market' to More Than Double," *The Nation*, Vol. 266, No. 1 (1998), pp. 11–18.

119. Gary Fields, "Privatized Prisons Pose Problems," *USA Today*, November 11, 1996.

120. Dale K. Sechrest and David Shichor, "Private Jails: Locking Down the Issues," *American Jails* (March/April 1997), pp. 9–18.

121. U.S. General Accounting Office, *Private and Public Prisons: Studies Comparing Operational Costs and/or Quality of Service* (Washington, DC: U.S. Government Printing Office, 1996).

122. Sechrest and Shichor, "Private Jails," p. 10.

123. James Austin and Garry Coventry, *Emerging Issues on Privatized Prisons* (Washington, DC: Bureau of Justice Statistics, 2001), p. ix.

124. For a more detailed discussion of this issue, see Austin and Coventry, *Emerging Issues on Privatized Prisons.*

125. *Richardson* v. *McKnight*, 521 U.S. 399 (1997).

126. *Minneci* v. *Pollard*, 565 U.S. 118 (2012).

127. *Correctional Services Corporation* v. *Malesko*, 534 U.S. 61 (2001).

128. Ibid.

129. Quoted in Bates, "Private Prisons."

Chapter 12: Prison Life

i. Zebulon R. Brockway, *The Ideal of a True Prison System for a State* (1865); Reprinted in the *Journal of Correctional Education*, Vol. 46, No. 2 (1995), pp. 68–74.

1. "Miss Wisconsin Makes Father's Prison Time a Miss America Platform," CBS News, January 15, 2012, https://www.cbsnews.com/news/miss-wisconsin-makes-fathers-prison-time-a-miss-america-platform/ (accessed March 19, 2018).

2. Hans Reimer, "Socialization in the Prison Community," *Proceedings of the American Prison Association, 1937* (New York: American Prison Association, 1937), pp. 151–155.

3. Donald Clemmer, *The Prison Community* (Boston: Holt, Rinehart and Winston, 1940).

4. Gresham M. Sykes, *The Society of Captives: A Study of a Maximum Security Prison* (Princeton, NJ: Princeton University Press, 1958).

5. Richard A. Cloward et al., *Theoretical Studies in Social Organization of the Prison* (New York: Social Science Research Council, 1960).

6. Donald R. Cressey, ed., *The Prison: Studies in Institutional Organization and Change* (New York: Holt, Rinehart and Winston, 1961).

7. Lawrence Hazelrigg, ed., *Prison within Society: A Reader in Penology* (Garden City, NY: Anchor, 1969), preface.

8. Charles Stastny and Gabrielle Tyrnauer, *Who Rules the Joint? The Changing Political Culture of Maximum-Security Prisons in America* (Lexington, MA: Lexington Books, 1982), p. 131.

9. Erving Goffman, *Asylums: Essays on the Social Situation of Mental Patients and Other Inmates* (Garden City, NY: Anchor, 1961).

10. For a firsthand account of the prison experience, see Victor Hassine, *Life without Parole: Living in Prison Today* (Los Angeles: Roxbury, 1996); and W. Rideau and R. Wikberg, *Life Sentences: Rage and Survival behind Prison Bars* (New York: Times Books, 1992).

11. Gresham M. Sykes and Sheldon L. Messinger, "The Inmate Social System," in Richard A. Cloward et al., eds., *Theoretical Studies in Social Organization of the Prison* (New York: Social Science Research Council, 1960), pp. 5–19.

12. The concept of prisonization is generally attributed to Clemmer, *The Prison Community*, although Quaker penologists of the late eighteenth century were actively concerned with preventing "contamination" (the spread of criminal values) among prisoners.

13. Sykes and Messinger, "The Inmate Social System," p. 5.

14. Stanton Wheeler, "Socialization in Correctional Communities," *American Sociological Review*, Vol. 26 (October 1961), pp. 697–712.

15. Sykes, *The Society of Captives*, p. xiii.

16. Christopher Hensley, Jeremy Wright, Richard Tewksbury, and Tammy Castle, "The Evolving Nature of Prison Argot and Sexual Hierarchies," *The Prison Journal*, Vol. 83 (2003), pp. 289–300.

17. Ibid., p. 298.

18. As cited in Stastny and Tyrnauer, *Who Rules the Joint?* p. 135.

19. Ibid.

20. Sykes, *The Society of Captives*.

21. Clemmer, *The Prison Community*, pp. 294–296.

22. John Irwin, *The Felon* (Englewood Cliffs, NJ: Prentice Hall, 1970).

23. Public Law 108–79.

24. Bureau of Justice Statistics, *Sexual Victimization Reported by Adult Correctional Authorities, 2012–2015* (Washington, DC: BJS, 2018)

25. Dee Halley, "The Prison Rape Elimination Act of 2003: Addressing Sexual Assault in Correctional Settings," *Corrections Today* (June 2005), p. 2.

26. Lee H. Bowker, *Prison Victimization* (New York: Elsevier, 1980), p. 42.

27. Ibid., p. 1.

28. Hans Toch, *Living in Prison: The Ecology of Survival* (New York: Free Press, 1977), p. 151.

29. E. Ann Carson, *Prisoners in 2016* (Washington, DC: USDOJ, 2018).

30. Some of the information in this section comes from the American Correctional Association, Task Force on the Female Offender, *The Female Offender: What Does the Future Hold?* (Washington, DC: St. Mary's Press, 1990); and "The View from behind Bars," *Time* (fall 1990, special issue), pp. 20–22.

31. Much of the information and some of the wording in this section come from Barbara Bloom, Barbara Owen, and Stephanie Covington, *Gender-Responsive Strategies: Research, Practice, and Guiding Principles for Women Offenders* (Washington, DC: National Institute of Corrections, 2003).

32. Barbara Bloom, "Triple Jeopardy: Race, Class and Gender as Factors in Women's Imprisonment," paper presented at the annual meeting of the American Society of Criminology, 1997.

33. *Prisoners in 2016.*

34. Joanne Belknap, *The Invisible Woman: Gender, Crime, and Justice* (Belmont, CA: Wadsworth, 2001).

35. Barbara Bloom, Barbara Owen, and Stephanie Covington, *Gender-Responsive Strategies: Research, Practice, and Guiding Principles for Women Offenders* (Washington, DC: National Institute of Corrections, 2003).

36. Data in this paragraph come from L. E. Glaze and L. M. Maruschak, *Parents in Prison and Their Minor Children* (Washington, DC: Bureau of Justice Statistics, 2008).

37. B. Bloom and D. Steinhart, *Why Punish the Children? A Reappraisal of the Children of Incarcerated Mothers in America* (San Francisco: National Council on Crime and Delinquency, 1993).

38. Patricia Allard and Judith Greene, *Children on the Outside: Voicing the Pain and Human Costs of Parental Incarceration* (New York: Justice Strategies, 2011), pp. 4–5

39. Mary Jeanette Clement, "National Survey of Programs for Incarcerated Women," paper presented at the annual meeting of the Academy of Criminal Justice Sciences, Nashville, TN, March 1991, pp. 8–9.

40. Bloom, Owen, and Covington, *Gender-Responsive Strategies: Research, Practice, and Guiding Principles for Women Offender.*

41. Barbara Bloom and Stephanie Covington, "Gendered Justice: Programming for Women in Correctional Settings," paper presented at the annual meeting of the American Society of Criminology, San Francisco, November 2000, p. 11.

42. Huey Freeman, "Illinois Program Guides New Mothers," *Pantagraph*, April 12, 2010, http://www.pantagraph.com/news/state-and-regional/illinois/article_ab1d5106-4631-11df-97d4-001cc4c002e0.html (accessed June 7, 2011).

43. Myrna Raeder, *Pregnancy- and Child-Related Legal and Policy Issues Concerning Justice-Involved Women* (Washington, DC: National Institute of Corrections: December 2013).

44. ACA, *The Female Offender.*

45. Marsha Clowers, "Dykes, Gangs, and Danger: Debunking Popular Myths about Maximum Security Life," *Journal of Criminal Justice and Popular Culture*, Vol. 9, No. 1 (2001), pp. 22–30.

46. D. Ward and G. Kassebaum, *Women's Prison: Sex and Social Structure* (London: Weidenfeld and Nicolson, 1966).

47. Esther Heffernan, *Making It in Prison: The Square, the Cool, and the Life* (London: Wiley-Interscience, 1972).

48. Rose Giallombardo, *Society of Women: A Study of Women's Prisons* (New York: John Wiley, 1966).

49. Ibid., p. 136.

50. For a summary of such studies (including some previously unpublished), see Lee H. Bowker, *Prisoner Subcultures* (Lexington, MA: Lexington Books, 1977), p. 86.

51. Giallombardo, *Society of Women*, p. 162.

52. David Ward and Gene Kassebaum, *Women's Prison: Sex and Social Structure* (Piscataway, NJ: Aldine Transaction, 2008).

53. Barbara Owen, *"In the Mix": Struggle and Survival in a Women's Prison* (Albany: State University of New York Press, 1998).

54. Barbara Owen, "Prisons: Prisons for Women—Prison Subcultures," available online at http://law.jrank.org/pages/1802/Prisons-Prisons-Women-Prison-subcultures.html.

55. See Joanne Belknap, book review of Barbara Owen, "'In the Mix': Struggle and Survival in a Women's Prison," in *Western Criminology Review* (1999), http://wcr.sonoma.edu/v1n2/belknap.html (accessed April 11, 2009).

56. Mary Koscheski and Christopher Hensley, "Inmate Homosexual Behavior in a Southern Female Correctional Facility," *American Journal of Criminal Justice*, Vol. 25, No. 2 (2001), pp. 269–277.

57. "PREA Data Collection Activities, 2012," https://www.bjs.gov/content/pub/pdf/pdca12.pdf (accessed June 17, 2018).

58. Eleanor J. Bader, "Women Prisoners Endure Rampant Sexual Violence; Current Laws Not Sufficient," http://www.truth-out.org/news/item/13280-women-prisoners-endure-rampant-sexual-violence-current-laws-not-sufficient (accessed June 17, 2018).

59. See, for example, Margie J. Phelps, "Sexual Misconduct between Staff and Inmates," *Corrections Technology and Management*, Vol. 12 (1999).

60. Heffernan, *Making It in Prison.*

61. Bowker, *Prison Victimization*, p. 53.

62. Giallombardo, *Society of Women.*

63. ACA, *The Female Offender*, p. 39.

64. United Nations General Assembly, *United Nations Rules for the Treatment of Women Prisoners and Non-custodial Measures for Women Offender* (New York: UN, 2010).

65. Tracey Kyckelhahn, *Justice Expenditure and Employment Extracts, 2012 – Preliminary*, http://www.bjs.gov/index.cfm?ty=pbdetail&iid=5239 (accessed September 11, 2018).

66. Ibid. Note: numbers do not total to 100% due to rounding.

67. Hughes, *Justice Expenditure and Employment in the United States, 2003*, data table 5: "Justice System Employment and Percent Distribution of Full-Time Equivalent Employment, by State and Types of Government."

68. American Correctional Association, "Correctional Officers in Adult Systems," in *Vital Statistics in Corrections* (Laurel, MD: ACA, 2000). "Other" minorities round out the percentages to a total of 100%.

69. Ibid.

70. Ibid.

71. Lucien X. Lombardo, *Guards Imprisoned: Correctional Officers at Work* (New York: Elsevier, 1981), pp. 22–36.

72. Leonard Morgenbesser, "NY State Law Prescribes Psychological Screening for CO Job Applicants," *Correctional Training* (winter 1983), p. 1.

73. "A Sophisticated Approach to Training Prison Guards," *Newsday*, August 12, 1982.

74. Kenneth Rosen, "Inmates to Be Transferred After Riot at Texas Prison," *New York Times*, February 21, 2015.

75. Stastny and Tyrnauer, *Who Rules the Joint?* p. 1.

76. See Frederick Talbott, "Reporting from behind the Walls: Do It before the Siren Wails," *The Quill* (February 1988), pp. 16–21.

77. "Ohio Prison Rebellion Is Ended," *USA Today*, April 22, 1993.

78. "Officials: 1 Hostage Dead After Inmates Take Over Prison," Associated Press, February 2, 2017, https://apnews.com/e714740299554c4894fb7238871bc99c/Delaware-inmates-release-2,-still-hold-2-hostages-at-prison (accessed April 30, 2018).

79. Teddy Kulmala, "7 Inmates Killed in 'Mass Casualty Incident' at SC Prison," The State, April 16, 2018, http://www.thestate.com/news/local/crime/article208982794.html (accessed October 30, 2018).

80. Robert S. Fong, Ronald E. Vogel, and S. Buentello, "Prison Gang Dynamics: A Look Inside the Texas Department of Corrections," in A. V. Merlo and P. Menekos, eds., *Dilemmas and Directions in Corrections* (Cincinnati, OH: Anderson, 1992).

81. Ibid.

82. *Ruiz* v. *Estelle*, 503 F. Supp. 1265 (S.D. Texas, 1980).

83. Alan Greenblatt, "Experts: Prison Gang Reach Increasingly Extends into Streets," *NPR*, April 5, 2013, http://www.npr.org/2013/04/02/176035798/experts-prison-gang-reach-increasingly-extends-into-streets (accessed April 10, 2018).

84. The facts in this story are taken from *Hope* v. *Pelzer*, 536 U.S. 730 (2002).

85. "Convictions Bar 3.9 Million from Voting," *Associated Press*, September 22, 2000.

86. *Holt* v. *Sarver*, 309 F. Supp. 362 (E.D. Ark. 1970).

87. Vergil L. Williams, *Dictionary of American Penology: An Introduction* (Westport, CT: Greenwood Press, 1979), pp. 6–7.

88. *Pell* v. *Procunier*, 417 U.S. 817, 822 (1974).

89. Ibid.

90. Title 42 U.S.C.A. 1997, Public Law 104–150.

91. Civil Rights of Institutionalized Persons Act, Section 1997e.

92. American Correctional Association, *Legal Responsibility and Authority of Correctional Officers: A Handbook on Courts, Judicial Decisions and Constitutional Requirements* (College Park, MD: ACA, 1987), p. 8.

93. *Wolff* v. *McDonnell*, 418 U.S. 539 (1974).

94. Ibid.

95. Ibid.

96. *Ponte* v. *Real*, 471 U.S. 491 (1985).

97. *Vitek* v. *Jones*, 445 U.S. 480 (1980).

98. American Correctional Association, Standard 2–4346. See ACA, *Legal Responsibility and Authority of Correctional Officers*, p. 49.

99. *Wilson* v. *Seiter*, 501 U.S. 294 (1991).

100. *Estelle* v. *Gamble*, 429 U.S. 97, 106 (1976).

101. *Sandin* v. *Conner*, 63 U.S.L.W. 4601 (1995).

102. *Wolff* v. *McDonnell*, 418 U.S. 539 (1974).

103. *Hewitt* v. *Helms*, 459 U.S. 460 (1983).

104. *Ali* v. *Federal Bureau of Prisons*, 552 U.S. 214 (2008).

105. 28 U.S.C. Section 1346(b)(1).

106. *Milbrook* v. *U.S.*, U.S. Supreme Court (decided March 27, 2013).

107. *Howes* v. *Fields*, 566 U.S. 499 (2012).

108. *Florence* v. *Burlington County*, 566 U.S. 318 (2012).

109. Laurie Asseo, "Inmate Lawsuits," *Associated Press*, May 24, 1996; and Bureau of Justice Statistics, "State and Federal Prisoners Filed 68,235 Petitions in U.S. Courts in 1996," press release, October 29, 1997.

110. Ibid.

111. Asseo, "Inmate Lawsuits."

112. 42 U.S.C. Section 1997e(a). Public Law 104–134. Although the PLRA was signed into law on April 26, 1996, and is frequently referred to as the Prison Litigation Reform Act of 1996, the official name of the act is the Prison Litigation Reform Act of 1995.

113. See *Edwards* v. *Balisok*, 520 U.S. 641 (1997); *Booth* v. *Churner*, 532 U.S. 731 (2001); *Porter* v. *Nussle*, 534 U.S. 516 (2002); and *Woodford* v. *Ngo*, 548 U.S. 81 (2006).

114. John Scalia, *Prisoner Petitions Filed in U.S. District Courts, 2000, with Trends 1980–2000* (Washington, DC: Bureau of Justice Statistics, 2002).

115. American Civil Liberties Union, *Prisoners' Rights*, http://www. aclu.org/prisoners-rights (accessed March 23, 2018).

116. Shayna Jacobs and Corinne Lestch, "Astor Swindler Anthony Marshall Released from Prison After Only 2 Months due to Medical Condition," *New York Daily News*, August 22, 2013, http://www.nydailynews.com/new-york/astor-swindler-anthony-marshall-released-prison-2-months-due-medical-condition-article-1.1434322 (accessed February 4, 2018).

117. Lincoln J. Fry, "The Older Prison Inmate: A Profile," *Justice Professional*, Vol. 2, No. 1 (spring 1987), pp. 1–12.

118. American Civil Liberties Union, *The Mass Incarceration of the Elderly* (New York: ACLU, June 2012).

119. Office of Inspector General, *The Impact of Aging Inmate Population on the Federal Bureau of Prisons* (Washington, DC: U.S. Dept. of Justice, 2015).

120. "The Nation's Prison Population Grew by 60,000 Inmates Last Year," Bureau of Justice Statistics, press release, August 15, 1999.

121. Jim Krane, "Demographic Revolution Rocks U.S. Prisons," APB Online, April 12, 1999, http://www.apbonline.com/safestreets/oldprisoners/mainpris0412.html (accessed January 5, 2006).

122. Ronald Wikbert and Burk Foster, "The Longtermers: Louisiana's Longest Serving Inmates and Why They've Stayed So Long," paper presented at the annual meeting of the Academy of Criminal Justice Sciences, Washington, DC, 1989, p. 51.

123. American Civil Liberties Union, *The Mass Incarceration of the Elderly*, p. vi.

124. Ibid., p. vii.

125. Alan Blinder, "Waffle House Shooting: Police Say Suspect Is in Custody," *New York Times*, April 23, 2018, https://www.nytimes.com/2018/04/23/us/waffle-house-shooting-nashville.html?hp&action=click&pgtype=Homepage&clickSource=story-heading&module=first-column-region&region=top-news&WT.nav=top-news (accessed April 23, 2018).

126. Government Accounting Office, *Federal Prisons: Information on Inmates with Serious Mental Illness and Strategies to Reduce Recidivism* (Washington, DC: GAO, 2018), p. 13.

127. Stephanie Mencimer, "There Are 10 Times More Mentally Ill People Behind Bars Than in State Hospitals," *Mother Jones*, April 8, 2014.

128. Allen J. Beck and Laura M. Maruschak, *Mental Health Treatment in State Prisons, 2000*, BJS Special Report (Washington, DC: Bureau of Justice Statistics, 2001), p. 1, from which most of the information in this paragraph and the next is derived.

129. *Washington* v. *Harper*, 494 U.S. 210 (1990).

130. Robert O. Lampert, "The Mentally Retarded Offender in Prison," *Justice Professional*, Vol. 2, No. 1 (spring 1987), p. 61.

131. Ibid., p. 64.

132. George C. Denkowski and Kathryn M. Denkowski, "The Mentally Retarded Offender in the State Prison System: Identification, Prevalence, Adjustment, and Rehabilitation," *Criminal Justice and Behavior*, Vol. 12 (1985), pp. 55–75.

133. "Opening Session: Kerik Emphasizes the Importance of Corrections' Protective Role for the Country," http://www. aca.org/conferences/Winter05/updates05.asp (accessed July 20, 2012).

134. Keith Martin, *Corrections Prepares for Terrorism*, Corrections Connection News Network, January 21, 2002, http://www. corrections.com (accessed June 15, 2016).

135. Quoted in Meghan Mandeville, "Information Sharing Becomes Crucial to Battling Terrorism behind Bars," Corrections.com, December 8, 2003, http://database.corrections.com/news/results2.asp?ID_8988 (accessed July 11, 2016).

136. Institute for the Study of Violent Groups, "Land of Wahhabism," *Crime and Justice International* (March/April 2005), p. 43.

137. *International Herald Tribune*, "Man behind U.S. Terrorism Plot Gets 16 Years," March 6, 2009, http://www.iht.com/articles/ap/2009/03/06/america/NA-US-Terrorism-Probe.php (accessed March 27, 2016).

138. Federal Bureau of Prisons, *State of the Bureau, 2004* (Washington, DC: BOP, 2005).

139. Alexander Meleagrou-Hitchens, Seamus Hughes and Bennett Clifford, *The Travelers: American Jihadists in Sybria and Iraq*, Feb. 2018, https://extremism.gwu.edu/sites/g/files/zaxdzs2191/f/TravelersAmericanJihadistsinSyriaandIraq.pdf (accessed July 10, 2018).

Chapter 13: Juvenile Justice

i. Howard N. Snyder and Melissa Sickmund, *Juvenile Offenders and Victims: 2006 National Report* (Washington, DC: Office of Juvenile Justice and Delinquency Prevention, 2006).

1. President's Commission on Law Enforcement and Administration of Justice, *The Challenge of Crime in a Free Society* (Washington, DC: 1967, USGPO), p. 58.

2. *Graham* v. *Florida*, 560 U.S. 48 (2010).

3. *Miller* v. *Alabama*, 132 S.Ct. 2455 (2012).

4. Greg Miller, "Brain Science a Factor in Supreme Court Decision on Juvenile Crimes," *Science Magazine*, May 2010, http://www.sciencemag.org/news/2010/05/brain-science-factor-supreme-court-decision-juvenile-crimes (accessed September 11, 2016).

5. *Bostic* v. *Pash*, certiorari denied, U.S. Supreme Court (2018).

6. Office of Juvenile Justice and Delinquency Prevention, *OJJDP Research, 2000* (Washington, DC: OJJDP, 2001).

7. Federal Bureau of Investigation, *Crime in the United States, 2017* (Washington, DC: FBI, 2018) from which many of the statistics in this section are taken. https://ucr.fbi.gov/crime-in-the-u.s/2016/crime-in-the-u.s.-2016/tables/table-20

8. U.S. Census Bureau, "Resident Population for The United States and Puerto Rico, July 1, 2017" https://tinyurl.com/y9h5x78l

9. The term *juvenile* refers to people under 18 years of age.

10. OJJDP, *Statistical Briefing Book*; https://www.ojjdp.gov/ojstatbb/crime/qa05101.asp?qaDate=2016 (accessed March 28, 2018).

11. Edward P. Mulvey, *Highlights from Pathways to Desistance: A Longitudinal Study of Serious Adolescent Offenders* (Washington, DC: OJJDP, 2011).

12. A reform movement, now under way, may soon lead to changes in the way juvenile records are handled.

13. For an excellent review of the handling of juveniles throughout history, see Wiley B. Sanders, ed., *Juvenile Offenders for a Thousand Years* (Chapel Hill: University of North Carolina Press, 1970).

14. Robert M. Mennel, *Thorns and Thistles: Juvenile Delinquents in the United States, 1925–1940* (Hanover, NH: University Press of New England, 1973).

15. See Sanford Fox, "Juvenile Justice Reform: An Historical Perspective," in Sanford Fox, ed., *Modern Juvenile Justice: Cases and Materials* (St. Paul, MN: West, 1972), pp. 15–48.

16. Anthony Platt, *The Child Savers: The Invention of Delinquency*, 2nd ed. (Chicago: University of Chicago Press, 1977).

17. Thomas A. Johnson, *Introduction to the Juvenile Justice System* (St. Paul, MN: West, 1975), p. 3.

18. Ibid.

19. Ibid.

20. Fox, "Juvenile Justice Reform," p. 47.

21. Ibid., p. 5.

22. Principles adapted from Robert G. Caldwell, "The Juvenile Court: Its Development and Some Major Problems," in Rose Giallombardo, ed., *Juvenile Delinquency: A Book of Readings* (New York: John Wiley, 1966), p. 358.

23. See, for example, *Haley* v. *Ohio*, 332 U.S. 596 (1948).

24. *Kent* v. *U.S.*, 383 U.S. 541 (1966).

25. *In re Gault*, 387 U.S. 1 (1967).

26. *In re Winship*, 397 U.S. 358 (1970).

27. *McKeiver* v. *Pennsylvania*, 403 U.S. 528 (1971).

28. *Breed* v. *Jones*, 421 U.S. 519 (1975).

29. *Schall* v. *Martin*, 467 U.S. 253 (1984).

30. *Thompson* v. *Oklahoma*, 487 U.S. 815, 818–838 (1988).

31. *Roper* v. *Simmons*, 543 U.S. 551 (2005).

32. Death Penalty Information Center, "Juvenile Offenders Currently on Death Row, or Executed, by State," http://www.deathpenaltyinfo.org/article.php?scid527&did5882 (accessed September 10, 2007).

33. *Graham* v. *Florida*, 130 S.Ct. 2011 (2010).

34. *Miller* v. *Alabama*, 132 S.Ct. 2455 (2012).

35. President's Commission on Law Enforcement and Administration of Justice, *The Challenge of Crime in a Free Society* (Washington, DC: U.S. Government Printing Office, 1967).

36. "Drug Bill Includes Extension of OJJDP, with Many Changes," *Criminal Justice Newsletter*, Vol. 19, No. 22 (November 15, 1988), p. 4.

37. The Formula Grants Program supports state and local delinquency prevention and intervention efforts and juvenile justice system improvements. Through this program, the OJJDP provides funds directly to states, territories, and the District of Columbia to help them implement comprehensive state juvenile justice plans based on detailed studies of needs in their jurisdictions. The Formula Grants Program is authorized under the JJDP Act of 2002 (42 U.S.C. 5601 *et seq.*).

38. See "OJJDP Eases Rules on Juvenile Confinement," *Corrections Compendium* (November 1996), p. 25.

39. Juvenile Justice and Delinquency Prevention Act of 2002 (Public Law 107–273).

40. Melissa Sickmund and Charles Puzzancherea, *Juvenile Offenders and Victims: 2014 National Report* (Washington, DC: Office of Juvenile Justice and Delinquency Prevention, 2014).

41. Ibid., p. 97.

42. See, for example, *U.S.* v. *Williams*, 553 U.S. 285 (2008), which upheld the law's provision criminalizing the possession and distribution of material pandered as child pornography; and U.S. Department of State, *Trafficking in Persons Report* (Washington, DC: U.S. Department of State, June 2007), p. 72.

43. *Fare* v. *Michael C.*, 442 U.S. 707 (1979).

44. *California* v. *Prysock*, 453 U.S. 355 (1981).

45. *New Jersey* v. *T.L.O.*, 469 U.S. 325 (1985).

46. *J.D.B.* v. *North Carolina*, 131 S.Ct. 2394 (2011).

47. Ibid.

48. Office of Juvenile Justice and Delinquency Prevention, "Juveniles in Court," *Statistical Briefing Book*, https://www.ojjdp.gov/ojstatbb/court/overview.html (accessed August 12, 2018).

49. National Center for Juvenile Justice, *State Juvenile Justice Profiles*, http://www.ncjj.org/stateprofiles (accessed March 18, 2018).

50. Charles M. Puzzanchera, *Delinquency Cases Waived to Criminal Court, 2011* (Washington, DC: Office of Juvenile Justice and Delinquency Prevention, 2014). In November, 2016, however, California voters approved Proposition 57 which, among other things, eliminated prosecutors' ability to direct file criminal cases against juveniles in adult court. Utah and Vermont have moved in a similar direction, but "direct file" still exists in those states for certain criminal law violations.

51. Adapted from Peter Greenwood, *Juvenile Offenders: A Crime File Study Guide* (Washington, DC: National Institute of Justice, n.d.).

52. Bureau of Justice Statistics, *Report to the Nation on Crime and Justice*, 2nd ed. (Washington, DC: U.S. Government Printing Office, 1988), p. 78.

53. Ibid.

54. Sarah Hockenberry and Charles Puzzanchera, *Juvenile Court Statistics 2016* (Pittsburgh, PA: National Center for Juvenile Justice, 2018).

55. Ibid.

56. Ibid, p. 46

57. *McKeiver* v. *Pennsylvania*, 403 U.S. 528 (1971).

58. Some states, such as West Virginia, do provide juveniles with a statutory right to trial.

59. Other early peer juries in juvenile courts began operating in Denver, Colorado; Duluth, Minnesota; Deerfield, Illinois; Thompkins County, New York; and Spanish Fork City, Utah, at about the same time. See Philip Reichel and Carole Seyfrit, "A Peer Jury in the Juvenile Court," *Crime and Delinquency*, Vol. 30, No. 3 (July 1984), pp. 423–438.

60. Ibid.

61. Tracy M. Godwin, *A Guide for Implementing Teen Court Programs* (Washington, DC: Office of Juvenile Justice and Delinquency Prevention, 1996).

62. Hockenberry and Puzzanchera, *Juvenile Court Statistics 2016*.

63. Ibid.

64. Ibid.

65. Office of Juvenile Justice and Delinquency Prevention, "Detailed Offense Profile by Placement Status for United States," https://www.ojjdp.gov/ojstatbb/ezacjrp/asp/Offense_Adj.asp (accessed May 23, 2018).

66. Ibid.

67. See, for example, Blair B. Bourque et al., "Boot Camps for Juvenile Offenders: An Implementation Evaluation of Three Demonstration Programs," *NIJ Research in Brief* (Washington, DC: National Institute of Justice, 1996).

68. OJJDP, Statistical Briefing Book, https://www.ojjdp.gov/ojstatbb/jrfcdb/asp/display_profile.asp (accessed May 23, 2018).

69. Ibid.

70. Ibid.

71. Ibid.

72. OJJDP, *Easy Access to the Census of Juveniles in Residential Placement*: https://www.ojjdp.gov/ojstatbb/ezacjrp/asp/state_adj.asp (accessed May 25, 2018).

73. Ibid.

74. Sarah Hockenberry, Andrew Wachter, and Anthony Sladky, *Juvenile Residential Facility Census, 2014* (Washington, DC: OJJDP, 2016), https://www.ojjdp.gov/pubs/250123.pdf (accessed March 23, 2018).

75. Dale G. Parent et al., *Conditions of Confinement: Juvenile Detention and Corrections Facilities* (Washington, DC: Office of Juvenile Justice and Delinquency Prevention, 1994).

76. OJJDP, "Juveniles in Residential Placement," https://www.ojjdp.gov/ojstatbb/snapshots/DataSnapshot_CJRP2015.pdf (accessed May 28, 2018).

77. Corrections Compendium (December 1993), p. 14.

78. Sickmund et al., "Easy Access to the Census of Juveniles in Residential Placement," http://www.ojjdp.gov/ojstatbb/ezacjrp/ (accessed April 27, 2018).

79. Office of Juvenile Justice and Delinquency Prevention, *National Juvenile Custody Trends, 1978–1989* (Washington, DC: U.S. Department of Justice, 1992), p. 2.

80. Section 59 of the Uniform Juvenile Court Act recommends the granting of a right to appeal for juveniles (National Conference of Commissioners on Uniform State Laws, Uniform Juvenile Court Act, 1968).

81. Jeffrey A. Butts and Ojmarrh Mitchell, "Brick by Brick: Dismantling the Border between Juvenile and Adult Justice," in Phyllis McDonald and Janice Munsterman, eds., *Criminal Justice 2000, Vol. 2: Boundary Changes in Criminal Justice Organizations* (Washington, DC: National Institute of Justice, 2000), p. 207.

82. Patrick McCarthy, Vincent Schiraldi, and Miriam Shark, "The Future of Youth Justice: A Community-Based Alternative to the Youth Prison Model," The Harvard Kennedy School, October 2016; https://www.ncjrs.gov/pdffiles1/nij/250142.pdf (accessed September 2, 2018).

83. Sarah Alice Brown, *Trends in Juvenile Justice State Legislation: 2001–2011* (Washington, DC: National Conference of State Legislatures, 2012).

84. Richard J. Bonnie, et al, *Reforming Juvenile Justice: A Developmental Approach* (Washington, DC: National Academies Press, 2012).

85. Ibid.

86. Richard J. Bonnie, et al, "Abstract: Reforming Juvenile Justice: A Developmental Approach," http://www.nap.edu/catalog.php?record_id=14685 (accessed September 11, 2016).

87. National Conference on State Legislatures, *Trends in Juvenile Justice State Legislation 2011–2015* (Washington, DC: NCSL, 2015).

88. Patrick McCarthy, Vincent Shiraldi, and Miriam Shark, *The Future of Youth Justice: A Community-Based Alternative to the Youth Prison Model* (Cambridge, MA: Harvard Program in Criminal Justice Policy and Management, 2016).

Name Index

Case Index

Subject Index

G

V